Literature and Its Times

Supplement 1

PART 1

Ancient Times to the
Harlem Renaissance
(Beginnings-1920s)

Literature and Its Times
Supplement 1

Profiles of Notable Literary Works and the
Historical Events That Influenced Them

Joyce Moss

MAGNIFICAT HIGH SCHOOL
RESOURCE CENTER
ROCKY RIVER, OH 44116-3397

GALE

THOMSON
GALE

Detroit • New York • San Diego • San Francisco • Cleveland • New Haven, Conn. • Waterville, Maine • London • Munich

Literature and Its Times

Supplement 1
Part 1: Ancient Times to the
Harlem Renaissance
(Beginnings —1920s)

JOYCE MOSS

STAFF

Project Editor—David Galens

Editorial—Sara Constantakis, Elizabeth Cranston, Kristen Dorsch, Anne Marie Hacht, Michael L. LaBlanc, Ira Mark Milne, Pamela Revitzer, Kathy Sauer, Tim Sisler, Jennifer Smith, Carol Ullmann, Maikue Vang

Research—Barbara McNeil

Permissions—Kim Davis, Lori Hines

Imaging and Multimedia—Dean Dauphinais, Robert Duncan, Leitha Etheridge-Sims, Mary K. Grimes, Lezlie Light, Dan Newell, David G. Oblender, Christine O'Bryan, Kelly A. Quin, Luke Rademacher

Product Design—Michael Logusz

Manufacturing—Stacy L. Melson

© 2003 by Gale. Gale is an imprint of The Gale Group, Inc., a division of Thomson Learning Inc.
Gale and Design™ and Thomson Learning™ are trademarks used herein under license.

For more information, contact
The Gale Group, Inc.
27500 Drake Rd.
Farmington Hills, MI 48331-3535
Or you can visit our Internet site at
http://www.gale.com

ALL RIGHTS RESERVED
No part of this work covered by the copyright hereon may be reproduced or used in any form or by any means—graphic, electronic, or mechanical, including photocopying, recording, taping, Web distribution, or information storage retrieval systems—without the written permission of the publisher.

For permission to use material from this product, submit your request via Web at http://www.gale-edit.com/permissions, or you may download our Permissions Request form and submit your request by fax or mail to:
Permissions Department
The Gale Group, Inc.
27500 Drake Rd.
Farmington Hills, MI 48331-3535
Permissions Hotline:
248-699-8006 or 800-877-4253, ext. 8006
Fax: 248-699-8074 or 800-762-4058

While every effort has been made to ensure the reliability of the information presented in this publication, The Gale Group, Inc. does not guarantee the accuracy of the data contained herein. The Gale Group, Inc. accepts no payment for listing; and inclusion in the publication of any organization, agency, institution, publication, service, or individual does not imply endorsement of the editors or publisher. Errors brought to the attention of the publisher and verified to the satisfaction of the publisher will be corrected in future editions.

ISBN 0-7876-6551-7

Library of Congress Control Number: 2002152062
Printed in the United States of America

10 9 8 7 6 5 4 3 2 1

Contents

Preface. . . . . *vii*
Acknowledgments . . . . *xi*
Introduction. . . . . *xv*
Chronology of Relevant Events . . . . *xix*
Contents by Title. . . . . *xxxv*
Contents by Author . . . . *xxxvii*
Photo Credits. . . . . *xxxix*
Entries *1*
Index. *503*

General Preface

"Even a great writer can be bound by the prejudices of his time . . . we cannot place Shakespeare in a sealed container. He belonged to his time," notes Alexander Leggatt in his essay "*The Merchant of Venice*: A Modern Perspective" (William Shakespeare, *The Merchant of Venice* [New York: Washington Square Press, 1992], 217). This reasoning, applicable to any work and its author, explains why *Literature and Its Times* fixes a wide range of novels, short stories, biographies, speeches, poems, and plays in the context of their particular historical periods.

In the process, the relationship between fact and fantasy or invention becomes increasingly clear. The function of literature is not necessarily to represent history accurately. Many writers aim rather to spin a satisfying tale or perhaps to convey a certain vision or message. Nevertheless, the images created by a powerful literary work—be it the Greek poem *Iliad*, the Spanish novel *The Adventures of Don Quixote*, or the American play *The Crucible*—leave impressions that are commonly taken to be historical. This is true from works that depict earlier eras to ones that portray more modern occurrences, such as World War II or postwar race relations. The fourteenth-century poem *Inferno* from the *Divine Comedy* by Dante Alighieri is probably the most powerful example. So vividly does *Inferno* describe Hell that for more than two centuries people took its description as fact, going so far as to map Hell according to the details of the poem.

In taking literature as fact, one risks acquiring a mistaken or an unverified notion of history, as the foregoing example suggests. Yet, by the same token, history can be very well informed by literary works. An author may portray events in a way that for the first time aptly captures the fears and challenges of a period, enabling readers to better understand it and their own place in the historical continuum. This is easily illustrated by tracing novels that feature women's issues, from Nathaniel Hawthorne's *The Scarlet Letter* (1640s setting), to Leo Tolstoy's *Anna Karenina* (1870s), to Alice Walker's *The Color Purple* (1920s-40s) and Amy Tan's *The Joy Luck Club* (1940s-80s).

Placing a given work in historical context involves pinpointing conditions in the society in which it was written as well as set. Stephen Crane's *Red Badge of Courage* is set in the early 1860s. Published three decades later, it was written in a different social context and as part of a literary trend in Crane's own era. Only by gaining insight into this later era along with the one in which it takes place can a work be fully appreciated; *Literature and Its Times* therefore addresses the author's time frame too.

The task of reconstructing the historical contexts of a work can be problematic. There are stories—the tales of England's King Arthur, for example—that defy any attempt to fit them neatly into a particular time. Living in a later era, their authors, consciously or not, have mixed together events that belong to two or more different periods. In some cases, this is an innocent mistake by

Preface

a writer who did not have the benefit of accurate sources. In other cases, fidelity to the actual events of the time is of little concern to the writer; his or her main interest is the fictional world to be portrayed. In still other cases, the mixture of times is intentional. Happily, present-day knowledge makes it possible for this series to begin unweaving the historical mixture in such works.

Literature and Its Times relates history to literature on a case-by-case basis, intending to help readers respond fully to a work and to assist them in distinguishing fact from invention in the work. The series engages in this mission with a warm appreciation for the beauty of literature independent of historical facts, but also in the belief that ultimate regard is shown for a work and its author by positioning it in the context of pertinent events.

Selection of Literary Works

Literature and Its Times includes novels, short stories, plays, poems, biographies, essays, speeches, and documents. The works chosen for inclusion have been carefully selected on the basis of how frequently they are studied and how closely they are tied to pivotal historical events. Reflected in the selection are works written not only by classic and still widely read authors but also by noteworthy ethnic and female authors of the past and present. To finalize the selection, a panel of librarians, secondary teachers, and college professors reviewed the complete list of titles. Please see "Acknowledgments" for a specific listing of these reviewers.

Format and Arrangement of Entries

The five volumes of *Literature and Its Times* and the two volumes of *Literature and Its Times Supplement 1* are arranged chronologically from ancient to future times. The set of entries within each volume is arranged alphabetically by title. As the series progresses, the range of years covered in each successive volume grows narrower due to the increasing number of works published in more recent times.

Each entry is organized according to the following sections.

1. **Introduction**—identifying information in three parts:

    The literary work—describes the genre, the time and place of the work, and the year(s) it was first performed or published;
    Synopsis—summarizes the storyline or contents;
    Introductory paragraph—introduces the literary work in relation to the author's life.

2. **Events in History at the Time the Literary Work Takes Place**—describes social and political events that relate to the plot or contents of the literary work and that occurred during the period the story takes place. Subsections vary depending on the literary work. The section takes a deductive approach, starting with events in history and telescoping inward to events in the literary work.

3. **The Literary Work in Focus**—describes the plot or contents of the work. Following this summary comes a second subsection that focuses on one or more elements in the work to demonstrate how it illuminates real events or attitudes of the period. This subsection takes an inductive approach, starting with the literary work and broadening outward to events in history. It is followed by a third subsection detailing the sources used by the author to create the work. In addition to sources, *Literature and Its Times Supplement 1* discusses the work's literary context, or relation to other works.

4. **Events in History at the Time the Literary Work Was Written**—describes social, political, and/or literary events in the author's lifetime that relate to the plot or contents of the work. When relevant, the section includes events in the author's life. Also discussed in this section are the initial reviews and reception accorded to the literary work.

5. **For More Information**—provides a list of all sources that have been cited in the entry as well as sources for further reading about the different issues or personalities featured in the entry.

If a literary work is set and written in the same time period, sections 2 and 4 of the entry ("Events in History at the Time the Literary Work Takes Place" and "Events in History at the Time the Literary Work Was Written") are combined into a single section, "Events in History at the Time of the Literary Work."

Additional Features

Whenever possible, primary source material is provided through quotations in the text and material in sidebars. There are also sidebars with historical details that amplify issues raised in the main text and with anecdotes that give readers a fuller understanding of the temporal context. Timelines appear in various entries to summarize intricate periods of history. To enrich and further clarify information, historically noteworthy illustrations have been included in the series. Maps as well as photographs provide visual images of potentially unfamiliar settings.

Comments and Suggestions

Your comments on this series and suggestions for future editions are welcome. Please write: Project Editor, *Literature and Its Times*, Gale, 27500 Drake Road, Farmington Hills, Michigan 48331-3535.

Acknowledgments

Literature and Its Times Supplement 1 is a collaborative effort that evolved through several stages of development, each of which was monitored by a team of experts in literature and history. For their incisive participation in selecting the literary works to cover in *Supplement 1*, the editors extend deep appreciation to the following professors, teachers, and librarians:

Robert Aguirre, Wayne State University, Department of English

Roger Beck, Eastern Illinois University, Department of History

Julia Brown, Boston University, Department of English

Barri J. Gold, Muhlenberg College, Department of English

Carol Jago, Santa Monica High School, English Department

Emmanuel Obiechina, Harvard University, Department of Afro-American Studies

Robert Sumpter, Mira Costa High School, History Department

Hilda K. Weisburg, Morristown High School, Library

The following professors, teachers, and librarians carefully reviewed the entries to insure accuracy and completeness of information. Sincere gratitude is extended to these reviewers:

Robert Aguirre, Wayne State University, Department of English

Ehrhard Bahr, University of California at Los Angeles, Department of Germanic Languages

Roger Beck, Eastern Illinois University, Department of History

Michael Bourdaghs, University of California at Los Angeles, Department of Comparative Literature

Matthew Brosamer, Mount St. Mary's College, Los Angeles, Department of English

Julia Brown, Boston University, Department of English

Howard Eiland, Massachusetts Institute of Technology, Department of English

Ana Paula Ferreira, University of California at Irvine, Chair, Department of Spanish and Portuguese

David William Foster, Arizona State University, Department of Languages and Literatures

Eric Gans, University of California at Los Angeles, Department of French and Francophone Studies

Benjamin Hudson, Pennsylvania State University, Department of History

Carol Jago, Santa Monica Public High School, Department of English

Randal Johnson, University of California at Los Angeles, Department of Spanish and Portuguese

Acknowledgments

James Kincaid, University of Southern California, Department of English

Kathryn King, University of California at Los Angeles, Department of Comparative Literature

Efraín Kristal, University of California at Los Angeles, Department of Spanish and Portuguese; Department of Comparative Literature

Kenneth Lincoln, University of California at Los Angeles, Department of English

Eleanor Kay MacDonald, Beverly Hills Public Library

Edwin McCann, University of Southern California, Department of Philosophy

David McCully, St. John's Child and Family Development Center

Michael McGaha, Pomona College, Department of Romance Languages and Literatures, Spanish Section

John McLeod, Leeds University, Department of English

Peter Manning, State University of New York at Stony Brook, Chair, Department of English

Gloria Montebruno, Ph.D. candidate, University of Southern California, Department of East Asian Languages and Cultures

Barbara Moss, Clark Atlanta University, Department of History

Kenneth Moss, Ph.D. candidate, Stanford University, Department of History

Emmanuel Obiechina, Harvard University, Department of Afro-American Studies

Kenneth Orona, University of Colorado, Ethnic Studies

Rafael Pérez-Torres, University of California at Los Angeles, Department of English

Indira Peterson, Mount Holyoke College, Department of Asian Studies

Josna Rege, Dartmouth College, Department of English

Karen Rowe, University of California at Los Angeles, Department of English

Ross Shideler, University of California at Los Angeles, Department of Comparative Literature

Min Song, Boston College, Department of English

Robert Sumpter, Mira Costa High School, Department of History

Hilda K. Weisburg, Morristown High School, Library

Raymond Williams, University of California at Riverside, Department of Hispanic Studies

Olga Yokoyama, University of California at Los Angeles, Slavic Languages and Literature

Steven Young, Pomona College, Department of English

For their painstaking research and composition, the editors thank the writers whose names appear at the close of the entries that they have contributed. A complete listing follows:

Adeleke Adeeko, Associate Professor, University of Colorado, Boulder

Robert Aguirre, Assistant Professor, Wayne State University

Anne Brannen, Associate Professor, Duquesne University

Luke Bresky, Ph.D., University of California at Los Angeles

Lilian P. Carswell, Ph.D. candidate, Columbia University

Francesca Coppa, Assistant Professor, Muhlenberg College

Ruth Feingold, Assistant Professor, St. Mary's College of Maryland

David Frier, Senior Lecturer, University of Leeds

Barri J. Gold, Assistant Professor, Muhlenberg College, Department of English

Martin Griffin, Ph.D. candidate, University of California at Los Angeles

Elisabeth Rose Gruner, Associate Professor, University of Richmond

Ingrid Gunby, Ph.D. candidate, University of Leeds

David K. Herzberger, Professor, Department Head, University of Connecticut

Megan Isaac, Ph.D., University of California at Los Angeles

Lynn Itagaki, Ph.D. candidate, University of California at Los Angeles

Despina Korovessis, Ph.D. candidate, Boston College

Albert Labriola, Professor, Duquesne University

Gail Low, Lecturer, University of Dundee

Pamela S. Loy, Ph.D., University of California at Santa Barbara

Christopher J. Mitchell, Assistant Professor, Eastern Illinois University

Acknowledgments

Jeff Morris, Assistant Professor, Carroll College

Keidra Morris, Ph.D. candidate, University of California at Los Angeles

Joyce Moss, M.Ed., University Southern California

Christopher M. Mott, Lecturer, University of California at Los Angeles

Danielle Price, Ph.D., University of California at Los Angeles

Diane Renée, B.A., University of California at Los Angeles

Catharine C. Riggs, Ph.D., University of California at Los Angeles

Diane Riggs, Ph.D. candidate, University of California at Los Angeles

Traci Roberts, Ph.D. candidate, University of California at Riverside

David Rosen, Visiting Assistant Professor, Wesleyan University

Susan Staves, Professor, Brandeis University

Erika M. Sutherland, Assistant Professor, Muhlenberg College

Susan Elizabeth Sweeney, Associate Professor, College of the Holy Cross

Erin Templeton, Ph.D. candidate, University of California at Los Angeles

Rachel Trousdale, Assistant Professor, Department of English, Agnes Scott College

Carolyn Turgeon, M.A., University of California at Los Angeles

Amy M. Ware, Ph.D. candidate, University of Texas at Austin

Colin Wells, M.A., Oxford University

Michael Wenthe, Teaching Fellow, Ph.D. candidate, Yale University

Margaret Wong, Assistant Professor, Quinsigamond Community College

Deep appreciation is extended to Michael L. LaBlanc of The Gale Group for his role as production editor. Anne Leach indexed the two volumes of *Literature and Its Times Supplement 1* with great sensitivity to readers and subject matter. Lastly the editors thank Danielle Price for her deft developmental editing, Monica Riordan for her skillful copyediting, and Lisa Blai for her proficient proofreading, word processing, and organizational management.

Introduction

"History repeats itself," or so the adage goes. On February 15, 1894, a terrorist died trying to blow up a landmark scientific edifice, the Greenwich Observatory in London, England, taking, it seems, only himself with him. On September 11, 2001, terrorists died crashing explosive, fuel-laden planes into the World Trade Center and into a landmark military edifice, the Pentagon, in the United States, taking with them close to 3,000 lives. The modus operandi, carnage and destruction, was the same for both sets of terrorists. But the circumstances—time, place, and motivation—diverged radically. So in one sense, history repeated itself; in another, it took on new substance. *The Secret Agent*, a novel by Joseph Conrad, memorializes the first incident, fictionalizing it in ways that document the anarchism of Conrad's generation, along with other currents of late-nineteenth-century human activity. The still-recent second incident will no doubt be memorialized by literary works yet to come, along with other early-twenty-first-century currents of human activity. Understanding the connections between such currents—be they political, social, economic, artistic, or scientific—and the literary works that memorialize them is the central aim of *Literature and Its Times*.

Extending from ancient Greece, through medieval Japan, to Renaissance Europe and revolutionary America, to post-apartheid South Africa, *Literature and Its Times Supplement 1, Parts 1* and *2* continues the foundational *Literature and Its Times* series. Like the original volumes, the *Supplement* covers novels, short stories, essays, drama, and poetry, bringing to the fore nuances of history through works that give voice to perspectives long left out of standard histories. A survey of the works covered shows a resurfacing of issues set forth very early in the *Supplement*'s historical span. Sophocles' *Oedipus the King*, for example, struggles with questions of fate, an issue that reappears 23 centuries later in Samuel Beckett's *Waiting for Godot*. Much has changed in the interim. Oedipus is a king who wrestles with fate as foretold through prophecy in a play that was written during an era of religious controversy. Partly a product of Beckett's experience in the French underground during World War II, his play features two hobos who grapple with fate and despair in an era that gave rise to existential philosophy. In the 23 centuries, the focus has shifted from aristocracy to commoners, the intellectual preoccupation from the validity of prophecy to an existential outlook on the human condition as expressed by the ordinary man.

Additional titles reveal other issues that recur across the ages and take on nuances tied to their own times and places:

Justice
Plato's *Apology* (399 B.C.E. Athens); *Crime and Punishment* (1865 Russia); *The Trial* (early 1900s Prague); *The Fixer* (1910s Russia); *A Lesson Before Dying* (late 1940s Louisiana)

Introduction

Individual's relationship to society
I, Claudius (41 B.C.E. Rome); *Candide* (1700s world); *A Christmas Carol* (1843 England); *The Stranger* (late 1930s Algeria)

Slavery and social class
Great Expectations (early 1800s England); *Kindred* (early 1800s Maryland); *"MASTER HAROLD"... and the boys* (1950 South Africa)

Prejudice and racism
The Little Gipsy Girl (early 1600s Spain); "Rothschild's Fiddle" (1890s Russia); *Passing* (1927 New York); "Letter from Birmingham Jail" (1963 Alabama); *The God of Small Things* (late 1900s India)

Minority identity—ethnic and gender experience
Fools Crow (1860s Montana); *Sense and Sensibility* (1790s-1810s England); *Annie John* (1950s-85 Antigua); *Woman Hollering Creek and Other Stories* (1900s Mexico and American Southwest); *Native Speaker* (1990s New York)

Family and generational relations
Twelfth Night (1601 England); *Mill on the Floss* (1800 England); *Fathers and Sons* (1859 Russia); *Dinner at the Homesick Restaurant* (1930-80 Maryland); *Parrot in the Oven: Mi Vida* (1970s California)

Colonial and postcolonial societies
A House for Mr. Biswas (early-to-mid 1900s Trinidad); *Midnight's Children* (1914-77 India); *Anthills of the Savannah* (1960s Nigeria); *Krik? Krak!* (1980s Haiti)

Love and marriage
The Tale of Genji (900s Japan); "My Last Duchess" (1500s Italy); *Emma* (early 1800s England); *The Age of Innocence* (1870s New York); *Blood Wedding* (early 1900s Spain); *The Glass Menagerie* (1930s St. Louis)

Dictatorship, socialism, and the power of the state
The Communist Manifesto (mid-1800s Europe), *Major Barbara* (1906 England); *In the Time of the Butterflies* (1948-60 Dominican Republic); *A Dry White Season* (late 1970s South Africa)

Rise of science, psychology, and the unconscious
On the Origin of Species (mid-1800s England); *Dracula* (1890s Balkans and England); *On Dreams* (1901 Austria); *The Sound and the Fury* (1928 Mississippi)

Ethics and the struggle between good and evil
The Lord of the Rings (a distant time in Middle Earth); *Faust* (1500s Germany); *The Misanthrope* (1600s France); *Blindness* (1900s)

War and power
Richard III (1483-85 England); *The English Patient* (1945 northern Italy); *The Things They Carried* (Vietnam 1969-70; United States 1990); *Martian Chronicles* (near future on Mars)

Of course, new as well as recurring issues emerge with the passage of time, and the new issues also surface in literature. The plight of off-reservation, urban American Indians, a relatively recent subgroup, to take one example, finds expression in novels such as Louise Erdrich's *The Antelope Wife*. Innovation has furthermore affected style as well as content in works of the last hundred years, beginning with stream-of-consciousness writing, related to developments in early-twentieth-century psychology (see, for example, Virginia Woolf's *To the Lighthouse*).

A survey of titles in the original *Literature and Its Times* and in *Literature and Its Times Supplement 1* reveals a dialogue in which later works address much earlier or slightly earlier works in the world literary canon. The interchange joins an even longer-standing dialogue between literature and history. This older, historical-literary dialogue is readily apparent in fiction, poetry, and drama, all of which have invested real-life figures with thoughts and emotions that are mostly unverifiable. William Shakespeare's *Richard III*, about the last king in an English dynasty, is one example. Closer to this day and age, *The Milagro Beanfield War*, about a conflict between Anglos and Hispanics in New Mexico, is another. In such cases, the two parts of *Supplement 1* follow the lead of the earlier volumes in *Literature and Its Times*, laying out the known facts to facilitate distinctions between reality and invention and presenting cutting-edge research that sheds new light on historical periods and peoples (see Bernard Malamud's *The Fixer* or Kyoko Mori's *Shizuko's Daughter*, for example). Going even further, the *Supplement* brings into play another interchange, a type of literary-literary dialogue, which occurs between related works. Featured in this second dialogue are titles that respond to preceding works, which are covered in the original series:

- Anton Chekhov's "The Lady with the Dog" (A response to Leo Tolstoy's *Anna Karenina*)

- Jean Rhys's *Wide Sargasso Sea*
  (A response to Charlotte Brontë's *Jane Eyre*)
- Tom Stoppard's *Rosencrantz and Guildenstern Are Dead*
  (A response to Shakespeare's *Hamlet*)
- John Gardner's *Grendel*
  (A response to the epic *Beowulf*)

Building on and diverging from the originals, writing, in some cases, from the viewpoints of villains and minor characters, the later authors produce works that in effect communicate with the earlier works, as if they were living entities, a characterization well deserved by virtue of the enduring popularity of the earlier works. Certainly the universal qualities of these earlier works have helped them endure, yet they too are a reflection of their times and places, as are the later literary responses to them.

The works in *Literature and Its Times Supplement 1* take on another, more general vitality too, related to their role in promoting self-scrutiny and understanding. This vital attribute is perhaps best illustrated by recent African American literature. From African American drama to fiction, work after late-twentieth-century work features children of the migration North reclaiming their roots in the American South and even in the Caribbean (see Toni Morrison's *Song of Solomon*, Paule Marshall's *Praisesong for the Widow*, and August Wilson's *The Piano Lesson*). In the loftiest tradition of literature, such works both reflect and advance the strivings of their readers to orient themselves in today's world. "The poet's voice," said William Faulkner in his Nobel acceptance speech, "need not merely be the record of man, it can be one of the props, the pillars to help him endure and prevail" (Lewis Copeland, Lawrence W. Lamm, and Stephen J. McKenna, eds., *The World's Great Speeches*, [Mineola, N.Y.: Dover, 1999], 638). From the Greeks to the present day, from the essay to poetry, drama, the short story, and the novel, the works in *Literature and Its Times* and its two-part *Supplement* help people endure and prevail.

Chronology of Relevant Events

CHRONOLOGY OF RELEVANT EVENTS

Note: The following chronology correlates historical events to the literary works covered in *Literature and Its Times Supplement 1* only. For events beside which there is no literary work, please see volume timelines in the original *Literature and Its Times* volumes.

FROM THE ANCIENT WORLD TO CLASSICAL CIVILIZATIONS

Originating in Crete and the Greek mainland, respectively, the Minoan and Mycenaean cultures were considered the first advanced cultures to develop in Europe. Both gave rise to the classical civilizations of Greece and, later, Rome. While Rome dominated the Italian peninsula for several centuries and spread its influence as far as what would become Great Britain, its far-flung Empire ultimately declined, but not before embracing the new faith of Christianity that was to spread throughout the world.

Date	Historical Events	Related Literary Works (date indicates period in which the work is set)
c. 3000–1400 B.C.E.	Minoan civilization is established on Crete, flourishes for several centuries	
c. 2000–1600 B.C.E.	Mycenae, on the Greek mainland, becomes center of another powerful civilization	
1200s B.C.E.	Thebes is the dominant city in central Greece, rivals Mycenae as main city in all Greece	1200s B.C.E. *Oedipus the King* by Sophocles
c. 1200 B.C.E.	Approximate date of the Trojan War; legendary survivor of the Trojan War, Aeneas, is said to have landed in Italy	
c. 1100 B.C.E.	Disappearance of Mycenaean civilization	
c. 974–443 B.C.E.	Greek colonies are founded in Sicily and southern Italy	

Date	Historical Events	Related Literary Works
c. 850–700 B.C.E.	Homer composes epic poems the *Iliad* and *Odyssey*	
c. 800–701 B.C.E.	Celts move into England	
776 B.C.E.	Traditional date of the first Olympic Games	
753 B.C.E.	Date ascribed to the mythical founding of Rome by the legendary Romulus	
509 B.C.E.	Establishment of Roman Republic	
479–31 B.C.E.	Golden age of Greece: under the leadership of Pericles, Athens enjoys a democratic period rich in intellectual and artistic creativity	
431–04 B.C.E.	Peloponnesian War—Sparta and other commercial rivals strip Athens of much of its maritime power, prestige, and wealth.	
399 B.C.E.	Athenians place the philosopher Socrates on trial, then condemn him to death for corrupting the youth of Athens and not believing in the city's gods.	399 B.C.E *Apology* by Plato
334–23 B.C.E.	Greece's Alexander the Great conquers Egypt, Persian Empire, and most of India—cultures merge to form Hellenistic Age	
c. 300 B.C.E.	Greeks introduce Stoic ideals, maintaining that humans should resign themselves to fate and subordinate passion to reason	
264–146 B.C.E.	Punic Wars—Rome, now the dominant power on the Italian peninsula, conquers Sicily, Greece, and Carthage	
60 B.C.E.	Pompey, Crassus, and Julius Caesar rule Rome in the first triumvirate	
58–51 B.C.E.	Caesar conquers Gauls, invades Britain	
49–44 B.C.E.	Caesar rules Rome as dictator until his assassination	
27 B.C.E.	Augustus Caesar declares Rome an empire	41 B.C.E.–41 C.E. *I, Claudius* by Robert Graves
c. 30 C.E.	Crucifixion of Jesus Christ	
43	Roman emperor Claudius conquers southeast England; Celtic tribes eventually surrender to Rome	
142	Construction of Antonine Wall marks northern boundary of Roman Empire in Britain	143–180 C.E. *The Mark of the Horse Lord* by Rosemary Sutcliff
180–211	Caledonian tribes of area now known as Scotland fight Romans	
c. 200	Christianity is introduced into Britain	
313	Roman emperor Constantine issues Edict of Milan, allowing free practice of Christianity	
395	Roman Empire separates into eastern and western divisions	
476	End of Roman Empire in the West	

THE MIDDLE AGES

In the wake of Rome's decline and fall, Germanic kingdoms sprang up throughout Europe. Of these dominions, only two endured: the Anglo-Saxons in Britain and the Franks in Gaul. The former were themselves conquered by the Normans in 1066. In the centuries that followed, Norman kings established a centralized government in England, which held fast despite bitter, bloody conflicts over royal succession that ensued for centuries. Meanwhile, the founding of the Plantagenet royal

Date	Historical Events	Related Literary Works
	dynasty produced a line of kings that brought England memorable triumphs and humiliating defeats. The last Plantagenet king, Richard III, was killed at Bosworth Field by Henry Tudor, Earl of Richmond, who founded a new royal dynasty. In Europe as a whole, the Catholic Church reached the height of its powers during the Central Middle Ages, as Christians across the continent embarked upon military campaigns—Crusades—to subdue the Muslims and recover the Holy Land. During the fourteenth century, Europe also reeled under the "Black Death," the bubonic plague, which, after killing half of Europe in the years immediately following 1347, continued to crop up and kill widely every few years for the rest of the Middle Ages.	
c. 450	Anglo-Saxons invade England, conquer native Britons	
500–1000	Early Middle Ages, sometimes called the Dark Ages	500s *Grendel* by John Gardner
794–1185	Heian period in imperial Japan; Fujiwara clan comes to power, dominating court society	905–75 *The Tale of Genji* by Murasaki Shikibu
800	Charlemagne of France is crowned "Emperor of the Romans"	
800s	Vikings invade Europe; establish large settlements on the continent	
871–99	Reign of Alfred the Great—first king of England—who defeats Vikings	
962	Holy Roman Empire begins with German emperor Otto I	
c. 1000s	Composition of earliest surviving manuscript of the English epic *Beowulf*, whose hero performs legendary feats in sixth-century Scandinavia	
1000–1350	Central Middle Ages	
1017–35	Cnut of Denmark reigns as uncontested king over England, Denmark, and Norway	
1066	William of Normandy defeats Anglo-Saxon forces at Battle of Hastings, becomes king of England	
1095	First Crusade begins as Christians embark on military expedition to recover the Holy Land from the Muslims	
1138–49	Bitter civil war in England between rival heirs to the throne—Mathilda of Anjou and Stephen of Blois	
1147	Second Crusade begins	
1154–89	Reign of Henry II of England, who founds Plantagenet royal dynasty; Archbishop Thomas Becket is assassinated	1170 *Murder in the Cathedral* by T. S. Eliot
1189	Third Crusade begins; King Richard the Lionhearted of England becomes principal Christian leader	
1199–1216	Reign of John I of England, who loses Normandy to France	
1215	King John signs the Magna Carta—a decree to protect feudal rights against royal abuse	
1290	Jews are expelled from England	
1300s–1500s	Late Middle Ages; Dante Alighieri writes *Divine Comedy* in Italian vernacular in early 1300s	
1337–1453	Hundred Years' War—Edward III of England lays claim to the French throne; a century of strife ends with the English being expelled from most of France	

Date	Historical Events	Related Literary Works
1347–51	The "Black Death"—bubonic plague—ravages Europe	
1381	Peasants' Revolt occurs in England but is suppressed and its leader, Wat Tyler, killed by the Lord Mayor of London	
1399	Henry Bolingbroke usurps English throne from King Richard II, becoming King Henry IV	
1415–20	Henry V of England defeats French at Battle of Agincourt; after signing the Treaty of Troyes, he becomes the next designated king of France	
1422	Death of Henry V of England; his infant son Henry VI succeeds him	
1429–31	Joan of Arc leads French troops to victory, has French Dauphin crowned as Charles VII; she is later caught, sold to the English, tried as a witch, and burned at the stake	
1455–85	Wars of the Roses—a civil war erupts between the houses of York and Lancaster in England; the most intense fighting takes place between 1460–61	
1461–83	Edward of York defeats Lancastrians, rules England as Edward IV	
1477–91	William Caxton produces first books in England with printing press	
1483–85	Reign of Richard III, who deposes his nephew Edward V, then is killed by Henry Tudor at the Battle of Bosworth Field	1483–85 *Richard III* by William Shakespeare
1485	Henry Tudor accedes to English throne as Henry VII, marries Elizabeth of York, founds the Tudor dynasty	

FROM THE RENAISSANCE TO THE ENLIGHTENMENT

The political, intellectual, and cultural flowering known as the Renaissance first blossomed in Italy in the fourteenth century. Powerful and influential families dominated Italian society, many of them supporting the arts and sciences. Later similar developments occurred elsewhere in Europe as the Renaissance spread to England, France, the Netherlands, Spain, and other countries. New ideas were introduced not only into intellectual and political life but into religious life as well. Beginning around 1517, theological disputes gave rise to a new division of Christianity into the two branches of Protestantism and Catholicism, and to changes within the existing Catholic Church. Meanwhile, the rulers of many European nations became increasingly interested in establishing their dominance on the world stage, financing expeditions that led to the discovery of the Americas and the establishment of colonies on continents across the globe. Over time, these colonies developed their own societies and sought to establish their own identities. Back in Europe, succeeding centuries witnessed popular revolts, civil wars, and the start of the Enlightenment, a philosophical movement placing a high value on the ability of people to govern themselves and to reason independently of divine revelation.

Date	Historical Events	Related Literary Works
1330s–40s	Italian writer Petrarch begins humanism movement	
1434	Rise of Medici family in Florence	
c. 1450	Development of printing press	
1450–1535	Sforza family rules Milan	

Date	Historical Events	Related Literary Works
1469–92	Florentine culture flourishes under Lorenzo de Medici	
1480	Catholic Church begins Inquisition, persecuting Jewish and Muslim converts suspected of heresy	
1490s–1520s	High Renaissance in Italy	1500s "My Last Duchess" and Other Poems by Robert Browning
1492	Under the Catholic monarchs Ferdinand and Isabella, Spain expels Jews, conquers Muslim kingdom of Granada, begins era of world dominance	
1492–1504	Christopher Columbus completes four voyages of discovery to the Americas	
1494	French troops invade Italy	
1494–1559	Italian Wars—foreign powers, invited into Italy to support factions, stay and dominate; France and Spain struggle for power in Italy	
1495	Jews are expelled from Portugal	
1497	John Cabot claims North America for the English	
1498	Leonardo da Vinci completes fresco of *The Last Supper*	
1508–12	Michelangelo paints frescoes on the ceiling of the Sistine Chapel	
1516	English humanist Thomas More writes *Utopia*	
1517	Protestant Reformation begins when Martin Luther openly opposes papal authority	1500s *Faust* by Johann Wolfgang von Goethe
1529	NiccolÚ Machiavelli publishes *The Prince*	
1534	King Henry VIII of England breaks with Catholic Church of Rome in Act of Supremacy, establishes Church of England with himself as head	
1535	Sir Thomas More is tried and executed for treason in England	
1550–1650	Golden Age of Spain—period of Spanish dominance in New and Old Worlds	1613 *The Little Gypsy Girl* by Miguel de Cervantes
1558–1603	Reign of Elizabeth I of England—sectarian disputes are quelled; Shakespeare writes *Hamlet* and other landmark plays	(date unspecified) *Twelfth Night* by William Shakespeare; c. 1601 *Rosencrantz and Guildenstern Are Dead* by Tom Stoppard
1588	Defeat of the Spanish Armada by the English navy	
1600s–1700s	Enlightenment Movement flourishes, places high value on people's ability to reason and on the doctrine of natural rights of humans	
1607	First permanent English colony is founded at Jamestown, Virginia	
1613	British East India Company establishes its first trading station	
1618–48	Thirty Years' War in Europe	
1620	French nobles revolt against King Louis XIII but Richelieu makes peace; Plymouth colony is founded in Massachusetts by the Pilgrims	
1627	Uprising of French Protestants, or Huguenots	
1630–43	Great Migration of Puritans from England to Massachusetts	
1639	Catholic-dominated France enters the Thirty Years' War on Protestant side	
1640	New England merchants enter the slave trade	
1642–46	Puritans and Parliamentarians defeat Royalists in English civil war	

Date	Historical Events	Related Literary Works
1649–60	After executing King Charles I of England, Parliament dissolves the monarchy and declares England a commonwealth, which Oliver Cromwell rules	
1643–1715	Reign of Louis XIV in France marks high point of absolute monarchy; his court becomes hub of French society	mid-1600s *The Misanthrope* by Molière
1660	Restoration of the monarchy in England; Charles II returns from exile to assume the throne; English Parliament passes first Navigation Act to create a monopoly over shipping and trade in its colonies	
1665–66	Plague claims 70,000 lives in London; Great Fire consumes most of London	
1666	Cardinal Richelieu founds French Academie Royale des Sciences	
1667	John Milton publishes his religious epic *Paradise Lost*	
1688–89	Glorious Revolution in England—James II is deposed; William and Mary are invited to take the throne on condition that they sign Bill of Rights, signifying the primacy of parliament over the monarchy	
1692–93	Witchcraft trials in Salem, Massachusetts	
1707–1815	European commercial penetration into India	
1729	Ireland suffers third year of famine due to lack of corn	
1733	England passes Molasses Act to stop trade between its American colonies and the French West Indies	
1754	Anglo-French war, known in America as the French and Indian War, erupts in British colonies in North America	
1755	Lisbon, the capital of Portugal, suffers a devastating earthquake in which thousands are killed	1750s *Candide* by Voltaire
1756	Nawab of Bengal imprisons British soldiers in Black Hole of Calcutta; British retaliate with punitive expedition led by Robert Clive	
1756–63	Seven Years' War between England and France; France loses territories in India, Canada, and all areas east of Mississippi River, except for New Orleans, which France cedes to Spain, effective 1764	1750s *Candide* by Voltaire
1772–1885	British extend their rule over most of India	

ROMANTICISM, REVOLUTION, AND REFORM

The mid- to late-eighteenth century saw a twofold reaction to the Enlightenment: an espousal of its ideas—specifically, the individual's right to life, liberty, and the pursuit of happiness—and, in some circles, a rejection of its aesthetics. Starting with the American War for Independence, a series of uprisings and revolutions erupted over the next century and a half. Even more spectacularly than the American colonies, France threw off the yoke of its oppressors: the landed aristocrats who had ruled French society for generations. The noble, democratic ideals of the French Revolution soon gave way to bloodthirsty vengeance. France's King Louis XVI was executed, helping precipitate a war between France and England that was to last the better part of 25 years. Other European nations feared that they would be the next to suffer through so tumultuous an uprising, their fears resulting in the passage of repressive laws and the suspension of certain political freedoms for the lower classes. An associated, literary response to the Enlightenment was the development

Date	Historical Events	Related Literary Works

of Romanticism—best illustrated by William Wordsworth and Samuel Taylor Coleridge's *Lyrical Ballads*—which elevated nature and emotional spontaneity above reason and neoclassical art. While revolutions and Romanticism dominated the early nineteenth century, the 1830s saw the implementation of important reforms, including the passage of a Parliamentary Reform Bill in England and the ending of slavery in the British Empire.

Date	Historical Events	Related Literary Works
1760s–1830s	Industrial Revolution transforms England from agrarian, handcraft-based economy into urban, machine-driven economy; factories and mill towns grow, steam replaces water power in many industries	c. 1800 *The Mill on the Floss* by George Eliot; c. 1800–50 *Great Expectations* by Charles Dickens
1763–74	England attempts to control American colonies through a series of restrictive acts, culminating in the Coercive Acts (called Intolerable Acts by the American colonists)	
1770s–1800s	Abolitionist movement in Britain gains momentum; Britain extends its rule over most of India	late 1700s *Songs of Innocence and of Experience* by William Blake
1775–83	American colonies fight War of Independence to free themselves from England	1775 *April Morning* by Howard Fast
1776	Thomas Paine publishes *Common Sense*; Thomas Jefferson composes the *Declaration of Independence*	
1789	The French Revolution begins, spreading republican fervor and reactionary fears throughout Europe	
1792–93	The Reign of Terror begins in France as revolutionaries execute those they suspect of opposing the new regime	
1793–1815	Louis XVI of France is executed; England and France go to war for the next 25 years	
1797	Series of mutinies break out in British navy	
1798	The Romantic movement begins in England; inspired by the French Revolution, the United Irishmen stage a revolt that ends in failure and the execution of its leaders	late 1700s *Lyrical Ballads* by William Wordsworth and Samuel Taylor Coleridge
1799	Napoleon Bonaparte, a Corsican general in the French army, seizes control of the French government by coup d'état	
1801–03	Toussaint L'Ouverture seizes control of Hispaniola in the French West Indies; must later surrender to French; dies in prison.	
1802–03	The Treaty of Amiens establishes a brief peace between England and France; war resumes 14 months later	
1803	Robert Emmet leads a poorly planned rebellion in Ireland, which ends in failure; decimated by yellow fever, French forces surrender to blacks in French West Indies	
1804	Napoleon becomes emperor of France; Napoleonic Code becomes basis of French law; Jean-Jacques Dessalines proclaims the birth of a new nation, Haiti—formerly the French colony of Saint Domingue	
1805	Napoleon defeats Austrian and Russian troops at Austerlitz; Admiral Horatio Nelson of England defeats Franco-Spanish fleet at Trafalgar	
1807	French forces invade Portugal; Portuguese royal family flees to Brazil	
1808	Spanish colonies in Americas begin independence movements	

Date	Historical Events	Related Literary Works
1808–14	Peninsular War begins after Napoleon deposes Spanish king and replaces him with his own brother, Joseph Bonaparte	
1811	Luddite rebellions in England—textile workers protest new machinery, smashing looms	
1811–20	The Regency period begins in England after George III suffers incurable attack of madness and his eldest son, the Prince of Wales, rules in the king's stead	1790s–1810s *Sense and Sensibility* by Jane Austen; early 1800s *Emma* by Jane Austen
1812	Napoleon invades Russia, retreats in disarray	
1814	Spain, England, and Prussia attack France, dismantling its army; Napoleon abdicates and is exiled to Elba; Congress of Vienna meets and restores most of the deposed monarchs to power	
1815	Napoleon escapes from Elba and returns to France, is defeated conclusively by British and Prussian forces at Waterloo and then exiled to St. Helena; Corn Laws are passed in England to protect agricultural interests	
1816	Divorce, available since 1792, is outlawed in France	
1819	British militia violently suppresses gathering of millworkers, killing 11 and injuring hundreds in "Peterloo" massacre	
1820s	Paris acquires the first professional municipal police force—the *gendarmerie*	c. 1840 "The Murders in the Rue Morgue" by Edgar Allan Poe
1821	Revolution breaks out in Greece	
1825	Tsar Nicholas I suppresses December Revolution in Russia	
1826	Sir Robert Peel reforms penal code in England	
1829	Metropolitan Police Act of 1829 establishes the London Metropolitan Police, called Scotland Yard	
1830	Charles X of France abolishes freedom of the press, dissolves lower house of French Parliament, and reduces the electorate drastically; Louis Philippe, Duke of Orleans, replaces him as "citizen king"	
1832	Passage of Parliamentary Reform Bill in England; Republicans try to dethrone King Louis Philippe in France; cholera epidemic kills 20,000 in Paris	
1833–38	Bill abolishing slavery in British empire substitutes apprenticeship for bondage for seven years; apprenticeship system proves unfeasible, ending on August 1, 1838	1838–50s *Wide Sargasso Sea* by Jean Rhys
1834	New Poor Law in England cuts off aid to outdoor workers	
1834–39	Spanish Civil War	

FROM THE REIGN OF QUEEN VICTORIA TO THE FIRST WORLD WAR

The long reign (1837–1901) of England's Queen Victoria coincided with a century of change, conflict, and colonial expansion. Major European powers—including Germany, Great Britain, France, Russia, and the Netherlands—sought to expand their territories, carving out empires in Africa and Asia. Competition over these spheres of influence was ferocious, sometimes resulting in open conflict between colonizing nations. Then, as the century waned, new and more dangerous tensions escalated, most notably between Great Britain and the increasingly militaristic Germany. When Archduke Franz Ferdinand of Austria-Hungary was assassinated by Serbs in 1914 and Germany entered the conflict on the side of Austria-Hungary, war, a development many felt was inevitable, finally broke into armed conflict. The

Date	Historical Events	Related Literary Works
	conflict—World War I—was to prove more momentous and terrible than any of the nations had anticipated. It would introduce the machinery of modern warfare and cost millions of lives before an armistice was declared on November 11, 1918.	
1837–1901	Reign of Queen Victoria of England	
1839	Opium War breaks out between England and China	
1840s	The Hungry '40s—Britain suffers severe economic depression, resulting in widespread unemployment, starvation, disease and death; riots and uprisings plague many European nations;	1843 *A Christmas Carol* by Charles Dickens
1840s–50s	In Russia, liberal and radical factions emerge; while differing about the nature of solutions to their nation's ills, both groups are driven by concern for the common man	1859 *Fathers and Sons* by Ivan Turgenev
1842	England forms its first detective force; China loses Hong Kong to Great Britain in Treaty of Nanking	
1845–48	Britain annexes the Punjab in India	
1846–51	Repeal of Corn Laws in Britain (1846); potato famine in Ireland leads to disease, death, large-scale emigration	
1848	More than 50 separate revolutions break out in European countries, including Ireland, France, Spain, Denmark, Prussia, Hungry, and Germany	mid-1800s *Communist Manifesto* by Karl Marx and Friedrich Engels
1850s–60s	Establishment of Pre-Raphaelite "fleshy school of poetry" in Britain—specializing in the erotic and sensual	c. 1862 "Goblin Market" by Christina Rossetti
1850s–1910s	Upsurge of Czech nationalism and dominance of German culture in Prague leaves Jews there increasingly isolated	early 1900s *The Trial* by Franz Kafka
1852	Louis Napoleon becomes emperor of France, ruling as Napoleon III	
1853–56	Crimean War is fought between Russia and Turkey	
1855	Tsar Alexander II assumes power in Russia	
1857	Sepoy Mutiny occurs in India	
1859	Charles Darwin posits the theory of natural selection as the means by which species develop; War of Italian Liberation erupts	mid-1800s *On the Origin of Species* by Charles Darwin
1860s	New radical faction known as nihilists develops in Russia, claim that the masses contribute little of value to society	c. 1865 *Crime and Punishment* by Fyodor Dostoyevsky
1861	Serfdom is abolished in Russia; peasants begin to seek new jobs in Russian cities	
1863	London's subway opens; Polish insurrection against Russia occurs	
1864	Russian legal system undergoes several sweeping judicial reforms, including the establishment of a permanent judgeship, a judiciary independent of other ministries, and equality of all citizens before the law.	1850s–82 *The Death of Ivan Ilyich* by Leo Tolstoy
1868	Japan enters the modern age as the Meiji Restoration leads to social reforms and increased contact with the west	
1870	French eliminate the monarchy, establish Third Republic; Franco-Prussian War breaks out	
1870s–1913	Norwegian women begin to assert themselves, demanding increased legal rights and the voting franchise; they are granted universal suffrage in 1913	late 1800s *Hedda Gabler* by Henrik Ibsen

Date	Historical Events	Related Literary Works
1871	Germany first emerges as a unified nation	
1871–1914	Uneasy balance of power exists between six major European nations: Britain, France, Russia, Italy, Germany, and Austria-Hungary	1886 *The Secret Agent* by Joseph Conrad
1875	Irish independence movement intensifies	
1875–90s	Theosophical Society—an influential group interested in occultism—is founded in England; interest in the supernatural rises in response to Victorian rationalism	late 1890s *Dracula* by Bram Stoker
1876	Queen Victoria is proclaimed "Empress of India"	
1877	Russo-Turkish War is fought	
1878	The Salvation Army is founded by William Booth to help London's poor	
1880s	Fenian (Irish) terrorists set off explosions at several well-known sites in London	1886 *The Secret Agent* by Joseph Conrad
1880s–90s	French acquire colonies in North Africa and Asia	
1880s–1920s	Irish Cultural Revival begins, tries to re-establish Irish language and celebrate Irish literature, arts, and history	
1881	Tsar Alexander II of Russia is assassinated	
1881–94	Reign of Tsar Alexander III is marked by pogroms against Russian Jews and their expulsion from designated areas	1890s "Rothschild's Fiddle" and "The Lady with the Dog" by Anton Chekhov
1884–1902	British Empire acquires 2.5 million square miles of new territory.	
1890s	Aesthetic and decadent movements spread through Europe, acquire following in London society	1890s *The Importance of Being Earnest* by Oscar Wilde
1890s–1910s	European upper and middle classes enjoy period of peace and prosperity; tensions build between militaristic Germany and other European nations, especially Britain.	1911 *Death in Venice* by Thomas Mann
1890s–1930s	Period of political turmoil in Spain; opposing factions pit Spanish traditionalism against Spanish republicanism	early 1900s *Blood Wedding* by Federico García Lorca
1894–1917	Reign of Tsar Nicholas II of Russia	1910s *The Fixer* by Bernard Malamud
1900–01	Viennese psychologist Sigmund Freud publishes groundbreaking studies on dreams, laying the foundation for his later development of psychoanalytic theory	c. 1901 *On Dreams* by Sigmund Freud
1901	Death of Queen Victoria; Britain claims Nigeria, forming a protectorate	
1902–05	Joseph Chamberlain offers persecuted Jewish populations in Russia and Poland 5,000 acres of land in British East Africa, an offer they ultimately decline	
1903	Pogrom against Russian Jews	
1904	Russia and Japan go to war; Japanese victories shake European power structure and lead to uprisings in Russia	
1905	Great Britain appoints Royal Commission to study problem of British poor and unemployed; Sinn Fein movement is founded by Irish nationalists; Russia becomes constitutional monarchy; new wave of pogroms against Russian Jews	1906 *Major Barbara* by George Bernard Shaw
1910	The Mexican Revolution begins	1889–1959 *The Death of Artemio Cruz* by Carlos Fuentes
1911–13	A Russian Jew, Mendel Beilis, is framed in a case of the murder of a Christian boy	1910s *The Fixer* by Bernard Malamud
1914	Archduke Franz Ferdinand of Austria-Hungary is assassinated by Serbian revolutionaries; World War I begins, pits Germany and Austria-Hungary against the Allies (Great Britain, France, Russia, and in 1917 the United States)	

Date	Historical Events	Related Literary Works
1914–18	World War I introduces modern (trench) warfare; Allies win, demand harsh reparations from Germany	early 1900s *To the Lighthouse* by Virginia Woolf
1916	Sinn Féin political party—prepared to use violence in the cause of Irish independence—mounts Easter Rebellion in Dublin	
1917	Russian Revolution topples Tsar Nicholas II; Balfour declaration suggests Palestine as a homeland for European Jews	
1918	Armistice ends World War I in the west on November 11	

FROM THE ANTEBELLUM ERA TO THE ROARING TWENTIES—THE UNITED STATES

The nineteenth century proved momentous in terms of both survival and expansion for the United States. In the early decades of the century, the new country was mainly concerned with proving itself a force to be reckoned with, buying the Louisiana territory from Napoleon Bonaparte, mounting an expedition to explore its new purchase, and fighting the British in the War of 1812, which is sometimes described as a second war of independence. Internally, an ongoing conflict over slavery would split the United States into Northern (urban) and Southern (rural) factions; tensions culminated in 1860, after Abraham Lincoln was elected president and South Carolina seceded from the Union. Other Southern states followed suit and the nation was soon embroiled in a bloody civil war, whose scars lingered long after Union forces prevailed, slavery ended, and peace was declared in 1865. After Lincoln's assassination, the process of Reconstruction was carried out under the leadership of radical Republicans in Congress. Although the Fourteenth Amendment gave African Americans citizenship and legal status equal to that of a white American, in the South their rights dissolved once Reconstruction ended and federal troops left. In the late nineteenth and early twentieth centuries, southern blacks suffered a pervasive segregation that was officially sanctioned by local laws. Seeking better opportunities, large numbers of African Americans moved into the urban North, especially in the early twentieth century. A thriving black community established itself in Harlem, New York City, and for a time attracted national attention through the Harlem Renaissance, a movement that brought black writers, artists, and thinkers to prominence. Meanwhile, the country as a whole continued to develop, implementing new technology, including railroads and telegraph lines, and acquiring and settling new territories. The United States continued also to emerge as a world power. When World War I erupted in 1914, President Woodrow Wilson declared the country neutral. But in 1917, provoked by Germany's actions, America entered the war on the side of the Allies. In 1918 they emerged victorious, and in the 1920s the United States experienced a decade of prosperity.

Date	Historical Events	
1800	The national capital is transferred to Washington, D.C.	
1803	United States makes Louisiana Purchase from France for about $15 million	
1804	Underground Railroad begins helping slaves escape to the North	
1804–06	U.S. Government mounts Lewis and Clark Expedition to explore Louisiana Purchase	

Date	Historical Events	Related Literary Works
1812–15	War of 1812 between Great Britain and the United States	
1814	The British burn Washington, D.C.; Francis Scott Key writes "Star Spangled Banner"; Treaty of Ghent restores peace, without either side emerging as victor	
1820	Missouri Compromise admits Maine as a free state, lets Missouri continue without restricting slavery but prohibits it in the rest of the Louisiana Purchase north of 36°30; U.S. is world's largest cotton producer	
1823	Monroe Doctrine proclaims the Americas off-limits to European colonization	
1827–38	First great wave of Irish and German immigrants arrive in the United States	
1830	Colombia becomes an independent South American republic; Indian Removal Act to resettle American Indians from eastern U.S. to Oklahoma Territory	
1830s	Hudson River School, the first school of American landscape painting, is founded	
1831	William Lloyd Garrison and Isaac Knapp establish antislavery newspaper *The Liberator*; Nat Turner stages antislavery uprising	early 1800s *Kindred* by Octavia Butler
1833	American Anti-Slavery Society is founded	
1835–36	Texas War of Independence succeeds	
1837–1910s	New England society (especially Bostonian society) adopts the values and rituals of Victorian and Edwardian society in England	1910s "The Love Song of J. Alfred Prufrock" by T. S. Eliot
1846	Smithsonian Institute opens in Washington D.C.	
1846–48	War with Mexico; U.S. wins present-day California, Nevada, Utah, Arizona, New Mexico, and parts of Colorado, and claims over Texas. In return U.S. gives Mexico $15 million; Mexicans in ceded lands get U.S. citizenship and promise to recognize their land rights	
1847	The Mormons reach Utah	
1848	First women's rights meeting at Seneca Falls, New York; wave of Chinese arrive in California; gold rush to California begins	
1850	Fugitive Slave Law mandates forcible return of runaway slaves to the South, raises accomplices penalties to $1,000 for criminal damages and $1,000 for civil damages; the Gold Rush drives enough people to California for it to qualify for statehood	
1850s–1900s	New waves of immigrants to America from Germany, Scandinavia, and southern and eastern Europe; many settle in farming states like Wisconsin, Iowa, and Nebraska	1880s *My Ántonia* by Willa Cather
1851	First printing of the *New York Times*	
1852	Publication of *Uncle Tom's Cabin*, which protests Fugitive Slave law; polarizes nation; helps spark Civil War	
1854	Kansas Nebraska Act lets slavery in Kansas and Nebraska be decided by the territories themselves; Republican Party is formed	
1857	Dred Scott decision rules that a slave is not a citizen and cannot sue in the courts	
1858	Debates between Stephen Douglas and Abraham Lincoln in contest for Illinois senatorial seat	

Date	Historical Events	Related Literary Works
1859	John Brown leads raid on Harper's Ferry	
1860	Lincoln is elected President; South Carolina secedes from Union	
1861–65	Civil War—Southern states secede from the Union and form Confederacy, are ultimately defeated by the North	
1862	Homestead Act decrees that any American citizen or citizen-in-training can obtain 160 acres of land free of charge, if the claim is occupied and farmed for five years.	
1863	Lincoln issues Emancipation Proclamation: after January 1, 1863, declares all slaves in Confederate states to be free; Lincoln delivers Gettysburg Address	
1865	Confederate General Robert E. Lee surrenders to Ulysses S. Grant at Appomattox; President Abraham Lincoln is assassinated; Thirteenth Amendment completes the abolition of slavery in the United States	
1865–77	Post–Civil War Reconstruction of the South; under supervision of federal troops, Southern states are compelled to ratify the Thirteenth Amendment (abolishes slavery) before reentering the Union	
1866	Ku Klux Klan is organized in Tennessee	
1867	Peace Commission to convince Indians to move onto reservations receives a mandate to use volunteer troops if necessary; U.S. buys Alaska from Russia for $7.2 million	1860s *The Antelope Wife* by Louise Erdrich
1868	Fourteenth Amendment grants citizenship to African Americans; President Andrew Johnson impeached and acquitted; Ulysses S. Grant becomes president.	
1870	White soldiers massacre 173 Blackfeet Indians (of the Pikuni tribe); Fifteenth Amendment prohibits discrimination in voting because of "race, color, or previous condition of servitude"; New York's first elevated train line opens; John D. Rockefeller founds Standard Oil	late 1860s *Fool's Crow* by James Welch
1870s	Former Confederates return to power in the South; with the withdrawal of federal troops from the region, blacks lose rights gained during Reconstruction; a strict system of segregation is set up throughout the South	
1870s–80s	Nouveau riche families infiltrate society of Old New York, previously dominated by old monied families	1870s *The Age of Innocence* by Edith Wharton
1873	Jay Cooke bank collapses; financial panic ensues throughout nation	
1875–76	Sioux War; U.S. Colonel George A. Custer and his men are wiped out at Little Bighorn	
1876	Alexander Graham Bell invents the telephone	
1878	Thomas A. Edison patents the phonograph	
1879	Edison perfects the first practical incandescent lamp	
1880	First gold strike in Alaska; U.S. surpasses Great Britain in steel production; Salvation Army is founded	
1880s	70,000 miles of railroad are built in America; 164,000 miles in operation by 1894	
1881	Booker T. Washington and Olivia Davidson found vocational school for African Americans—Tuskegee Institute; President James A. Garfield is assassinated	
1882	U.S. Congress prohibits immigration of Chinese to the United States	

Date	Historical Events	Related Literary Works
1886	African Americans found exclusively black town of Eatonville, Florida; Geronimo's capture marks end of organized Indian resistance to U.S. government	
1887	First electric trolley line begins service in Richmond, Virginia	
1890	U.S. Cavalry massacres Sioux Indians at Wounded Knee Creek; passage of Sherman Antitrust Act	
1890s	State and local laws ("Jim Crow" laws) legalize segregation in public facilities in the South; African Americans from rural South move to industrial cities in the North	
1892	Rudolf Diesel patents internal combustion engine; General Electric is founded; Ida B. Wells-Barnett begins anti-lynching crusade	
1893	Financial crash and depression	
1894	Pullman strike pits workers against bosses and government	
1894–1910s	Boll weevil destroys Southern cotton crop, forcing the South to diversify its economic base; industrialization of Southern cotton industry begins	
1895	Booker T. Washington delivers "Atlanta Compromise" speech, advising blacks to learn useful skills in the belief that economic advancement will lead to political and social equality; Guglielmo Marconi invents wireless telegraph	
1896	*Plessy v. Ferguson*: Supreme Court upholds "separate but equal" doctrine, legalizing segregation; Henry Ford constructs first automobile	
1897	First American subway opens in Boston.	
1897–98	Gold rush in the Klondike	
1898	Spanish-American War: Spain cedes Puerto Rico, Guam, and the Philippines to U.S. for $20 million	
1900s	About 1,000 mining companies are established in Mexico, 85 percent owned or run by Americans	1889–1959 *The Death of Artemio Cruz* by Carlos Fuentes; early 1900s "Spunk" and "Sweat" by Zora Neale Hurston
1901	Theodore Roosevelt becomes President after William McKinley is assassinated; Socialist Party of America is founded	
1903	Orville and Wilbur Wright take first successful airplane flight; Women's Trade Union League is formed. Ford Motor Company is founded	
1904–14	Construction of Panama Canal	
1905–06	Robert M. LaFollette's Wisconsin reforms set pattern for U.S. Progressivism	
1906	Upton Sinclair's novel *The Jungle* inspires Meat Inspection Act and Pure Food and Drug Act	
1907	U.S. restricts number of Japanese immigrants	
1908	Ford's Model T is first produced; child labor laws are introduced	
1909	Black scholar and political activist W. E. B. Du Bois (1868–1963) helps found National Organization for the Advancement of Colored People (NAACP)—first national organization to advocate the cause of African Americans	
1910	Formerly categorized separately, mulattos are classed as Negroes in U.S. census	
1910–30	700,000 Mexicans immigrate legally to American Southwest	

Date	Historical Events	Related Literary Works
1912	Federal workers begin eight-hour workday; Industrial Workers of the World (IWW) strike in Lawrence, Massachusetts; "Bull Moose" Progressive Party is founded	
1913	First assembly line is set up by Henry Ford; Sixteenth Amendment gives Congress power to collect income tax	
1914–18	World War I	
1915	German sinkings of *Lusitania* and *Arabic* enflame U.S. public against Germany; NAACP wins Supreme Court case against "grandfather clause," which limits voting to citizens whose grandfathers were registered voters January 1, 1867 (used in Southern states to prevent blacks from voting)	
1915–34	U.S. dispatches troops to Haiti to protect American interests	
1916	Railroad workers begin eight-hour workday	
1916–30	Great Migration—1.5 million African Americans migrate to the North, mostly from the rural South	
1917–18	U.S. enters the war against Germany, fights until armistice is declared November 11, 1918	
1917	Race riots in East St. Louis, Illinois, kill 39 African Americans	
1919	"Red Summer"—20 race riots in U.S. cities, including Chicago and Washington, D.C.; Marcus Garvey begins Black Star Shipping to facilitate travel and trade between Africans and African Americans; Eighteenth Amendment forbids manufacture, sale, and distribution of alcohol in America; will be repealed by Twenty-First Amendment in 1933	
1920s	Americans in urban areas enjoy economic prosperity while farmers suffer agricultural depression; radio and silent movies flourish as mediums of mass communication; Harlem Renaissance—black writers, artists, and thinkers gain national prominence	
1920	Nineteenth Amendment gives American women the right to vote; image of flapper, female who defies convention, proliferates; trial of anarchists Nicola Sacco and Bartolomeo Vanzetti (both of whom will be executed in 1927)	
1921	In post–World War world, American expatriates relocate to Europe, especially to Paris; this "lost generation" founds a creative community of writers and artists	1925 *The Sun Also Rises* by Ernest Hemingway
1924	Ku Klux Klan membership reaches 4.5 million; Congress passes National Origins Quota Act, restricts immigration from southern and eastern Europe and practically bars immigration from Asia	
1928	Herbert Hoover is elected President of the United States; Chicago's black community sends Oscar DePriest to Washington as congressman	
1929	*Pittsburgh Courier* reports that as many as 20,000 blacks are passing as whites; Harlem Renaissance fades with onset of Great Depression	1927 *Passing* by Nella Larsen

Contents by Title

Age of Innocence, The
    Edith Wharton. 1

April Morning
    Howard Fast 11

Candide
    Voltaire, François Marie Arouet de 21

Christmas Carol, A
    Charles Dickens. 31

Communist Manifesto, The
    Marx, Karl, and Friedrich Engels 41

Crime and Punishment
    Fyodor Dostoyevsky. 51

Death in Venice
    Thomas Mann 61

Death of Ivan Ilyich, The
    Leo Tolstoy 71

Dracula
    Bram Stoker. 79

Emma
    Jane Austen 89

Fathers and Sons
    Ivan Turgenev 99

Faust
    Johann Wolfgang von Goethe. 107

Fixer, The
    Bernard Malamud. 117

Fools Crow
    James Welch 129

"*Goblin Market, The*"
    Christina Rossetti 139

Great Expectations
    Charles Dickens 149

Hedda Gabler
    Henrik Ibsen 159

I, Claudius
    Robert Graves 169

Importance of Being Earnest, The
    Oscar Wilde. 179

Little Gipsy Girl, The
    Miguel de Cervantes Saavedra 189

"*Love Song of J. Alfred Prufrock, The*"
    T. S. Eliot 199

Lyrical Ballads
    William Wordsworth and Samuel
    Taylor Coleridge. 207

Major Barbara
    George Bernard Shaw 219

Mark of the Horse Lord, The
    Rosemary Sutcliff 229

Mill on the Floss, The
    George Eliot. 239

Contents by Title

Misanthrope, The
    Jean-Baptiste Poquelin de Molière 249

Murder in the Cathedral
    T. S. Eliot 259

"Murders in the Rue Morgue, The"
    Edgar Allan Poe 271

My Ántonia
    Willa Cather 281

"My Last Duchess" and Other Poems
    Robert Browning 291

Oedipus the King
    Sophocles 301

On Dreams
    Sigmund Freud 313

On the Origin of Species
    Charles Darwin 323

Passing
    Nella Larsen. 333

Plato's *Apology*
    Plato 343

Richard III
    William Shakespeare. 355

"Rothschild's Fiddle" and "The Lady with the Dog"
    Anton Chekhov 367

Secret Agent, The
    Joseph Conrad 377

Sense and Sensibility
    Jane Austen 387

"Shooting an Elephant"
    George Orwell 399

Songs of Innocence and of Experience
    William Blake 407

Sound and the Fury, The
    William Faulkner 417

"Spunk" and "Sweat"
    Zora Neale Hurston 429

Sun Also Rises, The
    Ernest Hemingway 439

Tale of Genji, The
    Murasaki Shikibu 449

To the Lighthouse
    Virginia Woolf 463

Trial, The
    Franz Kafka 473

Twelfth Night, Or, What You Will
    William Shakespeare 483

Wide Sargasso Sea
    Jean Ryhs 493

Contents by Author

Austen, Jane
    Emma 89
    Sense and Sensibility 387

Blake, William
    Songs of Innocence and of Experience 407

Browning, Robert
    "My Last Duchess" and Other Poems . . 291

Cather, Willa
    My Ántonia 281

Cervantes Saavedra, Miguel de
    The Little Gipsy Girl 189

Chekhov, Anton
    "Rothschild's Fiddle" and "The Lady
    with the Dog" 367

Conrad, Joseph
    The Secret Agent 377

Darwin, Charles
    On the Origin of Species 323

Dickens, Charles
    A Christmas Carol 31
    Great Expectations 149

Dostoyevsky, Fyodor
    Crime and Punishment 51

Eliot, George
    The Mill on the Floss 239

Eliot, T. S.
    "The Love Song of J. Alfred Prufrock" . . 199
    Murder in the Cathedral 259

Fast, Howard
    April Morning 11

Faulkner, William
    The Sound and the Fury 417

Freud, Sigmund
    On Dreams 313

Goethe, Johann Wolfgang von
    Faust 107

Graves, Robert
    I, Claudius 169

Hemingway, Ernest
    The Sun Also Rises 439

Hurston, Zora Neale
    "Spunk" and "Sweat" 429

Ibsen, Henrik
    Hedda Gabler 159

Kafka, Franz
    The Trial 473

Larsen, Nella
    Passing 333

Malamud, Bernard
    The Fixer 117

Contents by Author

Mann, Thomas
   Death in Venice 61

Marx, Karl, and Friedrich Engels
   The Communist Manifesto 41

Molière, Jean-Baptiste Poquelin de
   The Misanthrope 249

Murasaki Shikibu
   The Tale of Genji 449

Orwell, George
   "Shooting an Elephant" 399

Plato
   Plato's *Apology* 343

Poe, Edgar Allan
   "The Murders in the Rue Morgue" 271

Rhys, Jean
   Wide Sargasso Sea 493

Rossetti, Christina
   "The Goblin Market" 139

Shakespeare, William
   Richard III 355
   Twelfth Night, Or, What You Will 483

Shaw, George Bernard
   Major Barbara 219

Sophocles
   Oedipus the King 301

Stoker, Bram
   Dracula 79

Sutcliff, Rosemary
   The Mark of the Horse Lord 229

Tolstoy, Leo
   The Death of Ivan Ilyich 71

Turgenev, Ivan
   Fathers and Sons 99

Voltaire, François Marie Arouet de
   Candide 21

Welch, James
   Fools Crow 129

Wharton, Edith
   The Age of Innocence 1

Wilde, Oscar
   The Importance of Being Earnest 179

Woolf, Virginia
   To the Lighthouse 463

Wordsworth, William, and Samuel Taylor Coleridge
   Lyrical Ballads 207

Photo Credits

Wharton, Edith, seated at desk, photograph. —Pfeiffer, Michelle, and Daniel Day-Lewis, in the film *The Age of Innocence*, 1993, photograph by Phillip Caruso. The Kobal Collection. Reproduced by permission. —Howard Fast: Photograph. AP/Wide World Photos. Reproduced by permission. —Lithograph of the Battle of Lexington. Corbis. Reproduced by permission. —Voltaire, engraving. —Leibniz, Gottfried Wilhelm von, print. The Library of Congress. —*Earthquake at Lisbon*, 1755, engraving by Pearson. Corbis/Bettmann. Reproduced by permission. —Dickens, Charles, photograph. Hesketh Pearson. Reproduced by permission. —Rackham, Arthur, illustrator. From an illustration in *The Annotated Christmas Carol: A Christmas Carol*, by Charles Dickens. Clarkson N. Potter, Inc., 1976. —Marx, Karl, engraving. The Library of Congress. —Title page from *Manifesto der kommunistischen Partei*, or *Manifesto of the Communist Party*, commonly known as *The Communist Manifesto*, published by J. C., Burghard, London, 1848, photograph. Hulton Archive/Getty Images. Reproduced by permission. —Dostoevsky, Fyodor, photograph. Archive Photos. Reproduced by permission. —Lorre, Peter, in the film *Crime and Punishment*, photograph. Archive Photos. Reproduced by permission. —Napoleon, illustration. Source unknown. —Mann, Thomas, Erlenbach, Switzerland, 1955, photograph. AP/Wide World Photos. Reproduced by permission. —Andresen, Bjorn (forefront) as Tadzio and Dirk Bogarde as Gustav von Aschenbach (gazing after the boy) in the 1971 film based on the novella *Death in Venice* by Thomas Man, photograph. The Kobal Collection / Alfa. Reproduced by permission. —Tolstoy, Leo, 1897, photograph. The Library of Congress. —General Headquarters, across square from the Winter Palace, Alexander Column of red granite surmounted by an angel, sculpture by R. de Montferrand, 1834, St. Petersburg (Leningrad), Russia, c. 1985-1995, photograph. © Michael Nicholson/Corbis. Reproduced —Stoker, Bram, 1906, photograph. AP/Wide World Photos. Reproduced by permission. —Lugosi, Bela, in the film *Dracula*, 1930, photograph. AP/Wide World Photos, Inc. Reproduced by permission. —Austen, Jane, print. Reproduced by permission. —Gwyneth Paltrow as Emma, in the film *Emma*, movie still. The Kobal Collection. Reproduced by permission. —Turgenev, Ivan, photograph. The Library of Congress. —Chernyshevsky, Nioklay, drawing. The Library of Congress. —Goethe, Johann, painting. Archive Photos, Inc. Reproduced by permission. —Ekman, Gosta as Faust and Emil Jannings as Mephisto in the 1926 film version of *Faust* by Goethe, photograph. The Kobal Collection. Reproduced by permission. —Title page from *Faust*, written by Johann Wolfgang von Goethe. Special Collections Library, University of Michigan. Reproduced by permission. —Malamud, Bernard, photograph. The Library of Congress. —Hartman, Elizabeth, as Zinaida and Hugh Griffith as Lebedev in the 1968 film version of the novel *The Fixer* by Bernard Malamud, photograph. MGM/Kobal Collection. Reproduced

Photo Credits

by permission. —Blackfoot Indians hunting buffalo, photograph by John M. Stanley. National Archives and Records Administration. —Blackfoot Indian, 1833-34, painting by Karl Bodmer. National Archives and Records Administration. —Rossetti, Christina, portrait by James Collinson. —Rossetti, Dante Gabriel. From line shot in *"The Goblin Market" and Other Poems* by Christine Rossetti. Second edition. Macmillan, 1865. —Dickens, Charles, photograph. Viking Press. —Wager, Anthony, as Magwich, grabbing Pip, in the film *Great Expectations*, 1946, photograph. Springer/Corbis-Bettmann. Reproduced by permission. —Ibsen, Henrik, photograph. AP/Wide World Photos. Reproduced by permission. —York, Susannah, as Hedda Gabler, in the theatrical production *Hedda Gabler*, 1981, photograph. AP/Wide World Photos. Reproduced by permission. —Graves, Robert, photograph. AP/Wide World Photos, Inc. Reproduced by permission. —Wilde, Oscar, photograph. The Library of Congress. —Illustration of "The Closing Scene at the Old Bailey: Trial of Oscar Wilde," which appeared in *The Illustrated Police News*. —Saavedra de Cervantes, Miguel, photograph. —*Gypsies Rest by Their Caravan*, book illustration by Francis Donkin Bedford, 18th century. © Historical Picture Archive/Corbis. Reproduced by permission. —Eliot, T. S., photograph. The Library of Congress. — *The Mermaid*, print after a painting by Edward Burne-Jones, photograph. © Bettmann/Corbis. Reproduced by permission. —From an illustration for Samuel Taylor Coleridge's "The Rime of the Ancient Mariner, illustrated by Gustave Dore. Dover Publications, 1970. Copyright © 1970 by Dover Publications, Inc. All rights reserved. Reproduced by permission of the publisher. —Tintern Abbey, illustration. Archive Photos, Inc. Reproduced by permission. —Shaw, George Bernard, photograph. The Library of Congress. —An actor beats his bass drum playing the part of a Salvation Army worker in a stage production of *Major Barbara* by George Bernard Shaw, photograph. Hulton-Deutsch Collection/Corbis. Reproduced by permission. —Sutcliff, Rosemary, photograph by Mark Gerson. Reproduced by permission of Mark Gerson. —Scottish Picts, lithograph. Hulton Archive/Getty Images. Reproduced by permission. —Eliot, George, drawing. The Library of Congress. —Geraldine Fitzgerald, being consoled by Griffith Jones, in a scene from the film version of George Eliot's novel, *The Mill on the Floss*, directed by Tim Whelan. The Kobal Collection. Reproduced by permission. —Molière, engraving. The Library of Congress. —Pennington, Michael, and Elaine Page, in a scene from Molière's play *The Misanthrope*, photograph. © Robbie Jack/Corbis. Reproduced by permission. —Eliot, T. S., London, England, 1956, photograph. AP/Wide World Photos. Reproduced by permission. —*Murder in the Cathedral*, by T. S. Eliot, with John Westbrook as Thomas Becket being murdered at Canterbury Cathedral, performed September 23, 1970, photograph. Hulton-Deutsch Collection/Corbis. Reproduced by permission. —Poe, Edgar Allen, photograph. —Robards, Jason, in the 1971 film *Murders in the Rue Morgue*, based on the short story by Edgar Allen Poe, photograph. The Kobal Collection. Reproduced by permission. —Cather, Willa, photograph. AP/Wide World Photos. Reproduced by permission. —Woman walking in wind, illustration by W. T. Benda. From *My Ántonia*, by Willa Cather. Source unknown. —Browning, Robert, photograph. —Azulejo tile portrait of King Alfonso II of Portugal, photograph by Tony Arruza. Corbis. Reproduced by permission. —Sophocles, photograph of an illustration. Archive Photos, Inc. Reproduced by permission. —Oedipus, nude, painting. © Louvre, Paris, France/The Bridgeman Art Library. Reproduced by permission. —Greek Sphinx, stone sculpture, photograph. © Vanni Archive/Corbis. Reproduced by permission. —Freud, Sigmund, painting. The Library of Congress. —General Hospital in Vienna, Austria, photograph. © Austrian Archives/Corbis. Reproduced by permission. —Darwin, Charles, photograph. Photo Researchers. Reproduced by permission. —1890 illustration of the H.M.S. *Beagle* carrying Charles Darwin's expedition in the Straits of Magellan. © Bettmann/Corbis. Reproduced by permission. —Larsen, Nella, photograph. UPI/Corbis-Bettmann. Reproduced by permission. —Men and women of Harlem high society listening to a concert by W.C. Handy at an art gallery, two men in white tie and tails leaning against wall in background, Harlem, New York, 1936, photograph. © Lucien Aigner/Corbis. Reproduced by permission. —Plato (bust), photograph. The Library of Congress. —Socrates drinking hemlock, engraving. —Shakespeare, William, drawing. The Library of Congress. —The royal children and their murderers, in *Richard III*, engraving. —Chekov, Anton, photograph. International Portrait Gallery/Library of Congress. —View of Moscow, Summer 1912, photograph by Thomas H. Hartshorne. Archive Photos, Inc. Reproduced by permission. —Conrad, Joseph, photograph. The Library of Congress. —Royal Greenwich Observatory, southeast London, founded by King Charles II in 1675, illustration/engraving, c. 1850, photograph. Hulton Archive/Getty Images. Reproduced by permission. —Kate Winslett far left, Emma Thompson (far right), two unidentified actresses, from the movie version of Sense and Sensibility written by Jane Austen. The Kobal Collection. Reproduced by permission. —Wedding banquet, photograph. Leonard de Selva/CORBIS. Reproduced by permission. —Orwell, George, photograph. Archive Photos, Inc. Reproduced by permission. —Man sitting on the back of an elephant in Burma, photograph. © Michael Maslan Historic Photographs/Corbis. Reproduced by permission. —The Chimney Sweep, by Jonathan Eastman Johnson. Christies Images/CORBIS. Reproduced by permission. —Blake, William, illustrator. From an illustration in William Blake at the Huntington, by Robert N. Essick. Harry N. Abrams Inc., Publishers, and The Henry E. Huntington Library and Art Gallery, 1994. —Faulkner, William, photograph. Getty Images. Reproduced by permission. —Mississippi Confederate soldier monument and courthouse entrance behind, clock tower above Neoclassical porch with pediment and four columns, Oxford, Mississippi, August 12, 1996, photograph. © Kevin Fleming/Corbis. Reproduced by permission. —Hurston, Zora Neale, photograph. AP/Wide World Photos. Reproduced by permission. —Boas, Dr. Franz, photograph. The Library of Congress. —Hurston, Zora Neale singing, playing drum and holding gourd rattle, dressed as a voodoo dancer; after graduating in 1928 she worked as an apprentice anthropologist studying Caribbean voodoo, 1937, photograph. The Library of Congress. —Hemingway, Ernest, photograph. AP/Wide World Photos. Reproduced by permission. —Spanish bullfighter Juan Belmonte, son of matador Juan Belmonte, during a bullfight in Seville, Spain, June 29, 1946, photograph. Hulton Archive/Getty Images. Reproduced by permission. —Ishiyama Moon, Lady Musrasaki inspired to write The Tale of Genji, Japanese, Meiji Period, woodcut. Asian Art & Archaeology, Inc./Corbis. Reproduced by permission. —Scene from the Tale of Genji, photograph. © Archivo Iconografico, S.A./CORBIS. Reproduced by permission. —Woolf, Virginia, photograph. AP/Wide World Photos. Reproduced by permission. —Lighthouse in the distance on an island in the Inner Hebrides, Scotland, large expanse of sky and lighted clouds above, c. 1985-1995, photograph. © Buddy Mays/Corbis. Reproduced by permission. —Kafka, Franz, photograph. AP/Wide World Photos. Reproduced by permission. —Perkins, Anthony as Josef K in the film version of The Trial, based on the novel by Franz Kafka, photograph. The Kobal Collection. Reproduced by permission. —Shakespeare, William, illustration. AP/Wide World Photos. Reproduced by permission. —Olivia, Maria, and Malvolio at Olivia's house, in Twelfth Night, engraving, Act 3, Scene 4. —Rhys, Jean, photograph by Jerry Bauer. © Jerry Bauer. Reproduced by permission. —West Indian slaves celebrating their emancipation, white planter in background reading proclamation, engraving. © Corbis. Reproduced by permission.

The Age of Innocence

by
Edith Wharton

> **THE LITERARY WORK**
>
> A novel set in New York City in the 1870s; published in 1920.
>
> **SYNOPSIS**
>
> Newland Archer, a lawyer and member of the elite, falls in love with his fiancée's cousin and the cultured, permissive sensibility she represents, then struggles between his passion for her and the demands of upper-class New York.

Edith Wharton was born January 24, 1862, into a family known as one of the pillars of New York society. Her parents, George Frederic Jones and Lucretia Stevens Rhinelander Jones, descended from prosperous English and Dutch businessmen, which meant they belonged to New York's elite "old money." Such a position did not necessarily indicate that they had vast wealth; in fact, the family spent much of Wharton's childhood in Europe, where her parents went to economize. Wharton would continue this bi-continental lifestyle as she grew older, until she settled permanently in Paris in the early 1900s. Although her mother discouraged Wharton's academic pursuits, a beloved nanny and several governesses schooled Wharton privately at home, fostering her astounding intellect. She spoke several languages before the age of 10 and read voraciously in her father's library. As an author she also showed great promise, writing a novel and a self-published book of poetry by the age of 16 (*Verses,* 1878). Writing, however, was not an acceptable occupation for young women of Wharton's social class—only a proper marriage would suffice. At the age of 23, Wharton married the highly acceptable, somewhat older Edward (Teddy) Wharton from Boston's elite. Never a particularly happy marriage, the match ended in divorce in 1913 after Teddy became mentally unstable. Wharton first attracted notice as a writer with her short-story collection *The Greater Inclination* (1899); a half dozen years later *The House of Mirth* (also in *Literature and Its Times*) catapulted her to fame. From then until her death, Wharton wrote prolifically, producing nonfiction prose, poetry, translations, short stories, and 16 novels. Her eleventh novel, *The Age of Innocence* is a critical yet loving depiction of the New York she knew. More than any type of character, it features an upper-class code of conduct that embodied laudable standards of loyalty, fidelity, and honesty, but could also demand tremendous personal sacrifice.

Events in History at the Time the Novel Takes Place

Old money greets new. Old wealth, that is, wealth earned by merchants such as the Astor, Roosevelt, and Dodge families, still dominated New York upper-class society at the beginning of the 1870s. However, the newly wealthy, the families of bankers and manufacturers, were rapidly

Age of Innocence

Edith Wharton

gaining ground. The 1870s and 1880s would in fact prove to be pivotal decades in this regard. Three events signaled the relaxation of boundaries set up by old wealth to let in the new. In 1874 railroad and steamship magnate Cornelius Vanderbilt, one of the newly wealthy, organized a ball at Delmonicos in New York, inviting members of old wealth, who for the first conspicuous time crossed boundaries by attending the event. The other two events occurred early in the 1880s. Refused a box at the opera at the time, staged at the New York Academy of Music, another Vanderbilt, railroad magnate William H. Vanderbilt, joined with other newly wealthy families (the Goulds, Morgans, Rockefellers) to establish the grander Metropolitan Opera House Company with which the Academy of Music could not compete. It therefore closed its doors in 1885, forcing the old merchant families to join the new industrialist and banking families to attend the opera. Finally, Alva Vanderbilt, William's wife, repeating the strategy employed a decade earlier, invited 750 guests to a housewarming party after completing her $3 million mansion on Fifth Avenue in New York in 1883. She invited members of the old elite to the party, including Caroline Astor, who then reciprocated by adding the Vanderbilts to her exclusive list of invitees.

The penetration that had begun in the 1870s quickened as the 1880s progressed. Merchant families, on the one hand, and industrial and banking families, on the other, forged marriage alliances between them. In 1887 the industrialist Andrew Carnegie married Louise Whitfield, daughter of a New York City merchant. In 1860 banker J. Pierpont Morgan married Amelia Sturges, also the daughter of a merchant. Meanwhile, the bankers and manufacturers joined elite, previously merchant-dominated social clubs in the city (the Union Club, the Union League Club, the St. Nicholas Society). As the years rolled by, the penetration would continue, with the old monied families retaining a strong position in upper-class society. As late as 1892, two of three millionaires had inherited their wealth from their parents or grandparents.

Historians would refer to the several decades from 1880-1910 as "The Gilded Age." Ostentatious displays of wealth and consumption typified these years, among which the most lavish was the Bradley Martin ball of 1897. A costume ball featuring historic characters, its guests dressed in the gem-studded attire of kings, queens, and courtiers. They arrived at the Waldorf-Astoria hotel to dance in a room decorated to resemble the great hall in France's Palace of Versailles. Fearing retribution from other segments of New York, who were suffering from a severe economic depression, the hotel managers sealed the windows shut and stationed police officers around the premises to protect the partygoers.

Edith Wharton belonged to a segment of society that frowned on public display but participated nonetheless in such balls. She described herself as a child of the well-to-do, the set of interconnected families who lived on investments of inherited money and tried to resist the encroachment of the newly wealthy. Her set tried also to resist ostentation. As her biographer writes: "It was a closed world where nobody engaged in retail trade, where nobody, for that matter, engaged in very much of anything" (Auchincloss, p. 19). While Wharton criticized the fear of innovation among her family's circle, she defended certain standards and forms they upheld: "Their value lay in upholding two standards of importance in any community, that of education and good manners, and of scrupulous probity in business and private affairs" (Wharton, *A Backward Glance,* p. 799). *The Age of Innocence* shows what happens when the circle's scrupulously proper standards are threatened. One of its members comes perilously close to transgressing the bounds of marital fidelity, and fierce group loyalty swings into action to protect the fabric of social convention.

TENEMENTS AND SKYSCRAPERS

Wharton's focus in the novel is on such an exclusive and insular group that the reader might scarcely guess any other part of New York City existed. In fact, the 1870s were a time of tremendous change in the city. America's annual number of immigrants approached 150,000, nearly a quarter of whom entered through New York City and stayed. The population became more ethnically mixed, in part because of immigration from southern and eastern Europe, in part because of the migration to the North of ex-slaves. The migrants and immigrants swelled the ranks of the poor and working classes, increasing the demand for basic housing. In response, tenements appeared, their areas quickly degenerating into crowded, unhealthy slums with little access to clean air, water, or light. There was a clear need for public works to manage the mounting filth, to provide sanitation services, and to procure pure drinking water. To make matters worse, an economic downturn plagued most of the decade (1873-79), introducing the phenomenon of widespread unemployment into America's most populous city.

Meanwhile, the city's architectural environment changed dramatically. American businesses like J. D. Rockefeller's Standard Oil and Carnegie Steel moved their headquarters to New York, and the first buildings to rise more than several stories were erected. The introduction of elevated trains expanded the city's public transportation system, joining the familiar horse-drawn streetcars. Forming the grid design that would come to characterize Manhattan, miles of road, sewer, and water lines were laid, and construction of the Brooklyn Bridge began. Cultural venues appeared too. The novel's Newland and Ellen meet in the little frequented art museum that in 1880 would be organized into the Metropolitan Museum of Art and relocated in Central Park. Including another landmark, the novel opens at the opera in the Academy of Music, which, thankfully from the point of view of the old monied families, had only 18 theater boxes and so could not accommodate upstart newcomers. It would not be displaced by the larger Metropolitan Opera House—which boasted 122 boxes—until 1883, which is shortly after the novel takes place.

As indicated, the days of a New York elite that included only old monied families were numbered. It would ultimately be infiltrated by the *nouveaux riches*, the newly wealthy, who amassed fabulous fortunes in the post Civil War decades, ushering in unprecedented opulence in the United States. Wharton situates her novel at the precise moment these new fortunes are attempting to enter New York "high society," which, as shown, remained impenetrable for only a short while. Two characters, the newly wealthy Julius Beaufort and Mrs. Struthers, signal this change: Beaufort's extravagant entertainments set the style for the near future, while Struthers hosts Sunday evenings for guests who quickly cease caring about the mercantile taint to her fortune.

Social conventions. Complex conventions of behavior and manners characterized late-nineteenth-century upper-class society in New York. Inhabiting a democratic country without a hereditary aristocracy, the group guarded class distinctions perhaps more carefully and strictly than in Europe. Central to its survival were marriage connections. A round of balls and visits brought together the sons and daughters of well-to-do families in close quarters. Although love played a part, marriage was, above all, an economic arrangement. Families made matches with the social standing, wealth, and even business of the two partners in mind. Once married, the wife took on the responsibility of solidifying the union of the two families by inviting relatives to family affairs or visiting them. She, and the elite in general, paid careful attention to forging and maintaining a kin network, that is a network of family connections, which figured prominently in the financial health of her family.

Age of Innocence

As increasing numbers of the newly wealthy moved into New York and sought inclusion in the upper echelons of society, the display of manners and taste when visiting and on other occasions became a litmus test for acceptance. Again, the women served as arbiters and enforcers of convention. Numerous etiquette books counseled the initiated and the uninitiated in the correct procedures for managing the business of social interaction. One manual advised that, "A true lady in the street, as in the parlor or *salon* is modest, discreet, kind and obliging. . . . The truly well-educated, well-born and well-bred *never* betray vanity, conceit, superciliousness or hauteur [arrogance]. Set this down as an invariable law, and male or female, let it guide all of your actions" (*Beadles Dime Book of Etiquette*, p. 45).

One activity governed by strict rules of etiquette was the practice of call paying and card leaving. Society matrons established regular days and hours when they would be "at home" (available to receive visitors) or "not at home" (unavailable to all visitors, or to certain visitors). If a hostess was not receiving, a visitor might anyway leave a card, indicating that the social rite had been observed even though a call had not been made. Calling cards themselves adhered to strict rules of convention; for example, a young woman who had made her debut into society but was not yet married ought to have her name placed on her mother's calling card. In addition, calls and cards were to be reciprocated according to a prescribed arrangement. A woman of high social standing might initiate friendly contact with a newcomer or a woman lower in the hierarchy, but not the reverse. If a higher-status contact made a call or left a card, the initiate was expected to respond in kind within a given amount of time, after which it was up to the first lady to decide whether relations between them would continue.

Even the hours of social visits followed a structure: "Ceremonial calls [paid to offer thanks for entertainment or gifts] were expected between about three and four in the afternoon; semi-ceremonial calls [as perhaps are May and Newland's visits to various family members on the occasion of their engagement in *The Age of Innocence*] between four and five; intimate visits from close friends occurred between five and six" (Preston, p. 4). The later the hour, the greater the degree of intimacy between individuals. When Ellen Olenska asks Newland to call on her later in the evening, Newland understands this to imply a visit of some intimacy; thus, we understand his surprise and annoyance at finding Julius Beaufort there at the same hour, whose relation to Countess Olenska ought not to be as intimate as his.

The Novel in Focus

The plot. The novel opens at the opera, where Newland Archer surveys members of New York society in an array of theater boxes. He converses with other inhabitants of the club box (the set of seats reserved for members of his gentleman's club), stopping only for a few select arias when everyone pays attention to the opera. From across the theater, Newland admires his fiancée, the lovely, well-bred May Welland, daughter of one of the most powerful society families, the Mingotts. May is joined by her cousin, the Countess Ellen Olenska, recently returned from Europe after fleeing an unhappy marriage with a profligate Polish count. Gossip in the club box turns to the Countess Olenska, to the whiff of scandal trailing her, and to the audacity of the Mingott family in including her in this public display. Newland and May decide to announce their engagement later that evening at a ball given by the Beauforts. (Julius Beaufort has penetrated New York society by marrying the well-connected Regina Dallas and providing lavish entertainments with his fortune.) By making their announcement earlier and more publicly than desired, Newland and May aim to deflect attention from Ellen Olenska.

Newland joins in the efforts of May's family to incorporate Ellen into New York society, which is unwilling to open its doors to her. When invitations to a welcoming dinner for the countess are universally and icily declined, members of the family plead for the intercession of the ultimate arbiters of convention and taste, the van der Luydens, who then host a dinner no one dares decline. Society proceeds to subject Ellen to its strict rules. When she plans to divorce her profligate husband, the head of Newland's law firm asks him to dissuade her. He must make her understand that New York society will not countenance divorce for any reason.

Newland develops a friendship with Ellen as he helps educate her about the social mores of upper-crust New York. At the same time, Ellen opens his eyes to the ways in which his world is stifling and dull. The relationship is a liberating one for Newland; he feels unbridled and refreshed in the company of Ellen's worldliness and unconventionality. Approaching her house on

Daniel Day-Lewis (left) as Newland Archer and Michelle Pfeiffer as Countess Ellen Olenska in the 1993 film version of *The Age of Innocence*.

one of his early visits, Newland becomes aware of "the curious way in which she reversed his values, and of the need of thinking himself into conditions incredibly different from any that he knew" (Wharton, *The Age of Innocence*, p. 103). Fearing his growing attraction to Ellen, Newland urges May to move up their wedding date. Immediately after Newland realizes that he is in love with Ellen, he receives a telegram announcing that May and her mother have agreed to a wedding date only a month away.

Newland marries May, and the two honeymoon in Europe for several months. Instead of opening her eyes to the glories of Old World culture and literature, the trip shows May to be such a product of her upbringing, in Newland's view, as to be incapable of this sort of appreciation. Pushing thoughts of Ellen to the back of his mind, Newland settles down to the familiar social routines of winter in New York and summer in Newport, Rhode Island. Ellen has meanwhile moved to Washington, D.C.

Ellen's husband sends an emissary to retrieve her. Her family urges Ellen to go back to her husband, but Newland refuses to share the family's opinion. When she goes to Boston to meet the emissary, Newland follows her and they openly acknowledge their love for each other. Ellen agrees to remain in America as long as Newland loves her; they part with the understanding that they will carry on their love from afar without seeing each other.

If their love is less than proper, according to upper-crust standards, so are Julius Beaufort's business dealings. When his shady business dealings become public and threaten financial ruin, his wife asks Mrs. Mingott to back him and thus save him from social ruin as well. The effrontery of this request causes Ellen and May's grandmother to have a stroke. Ellen is summoned to Granny Mingott's side. Newland picks her up from the train station, and they talk in the carriage about the impossibility of their love. While Newland is prepared to leave his comfortable life and escape somewhere with Ellen, he recoils from the idea of making Ellen his mistress. Eventually he accepts Ellen's suggestion that she spend one night with him and then return to Europe.

A few days later Newland learns that Ellen has announced her imminent return to Europe. May hosts a goodbye dinner, and Newland realizes that everyone suspects he and Ellen of being lovers. The professed purpose of the dinner is a sham; the ceremony actually signifies Ellen's expulsion from the family. Ellen offers no explanation to Newland for not following through with their arrangement to spend a night together. Only after the guests leave does May tell Newland she is pregnant. Earlier May had told Ellen about the pregnancy. When Newland learns that May already told Ellen about the pregnancy, he understands her sudden departure.

The final chapter of the book takes place 26 years later. May has died and the oldest of their three children, Dallas, is engaged to the illegitimate daughter of Julius Beaufort, a fact that no longer raises eyebrows in New York. Traveling to Paris with Dallas, Newland gets as far as Ellen's apartment building. He sits looking up at her window for some time, but declines to go inside with Dallas. Instead the unrequited lover simply walks away.

A room full of books. In the final chapter of *The Age of Innocence*, Newland Archer sits in his library reflecting on his life. The library "was the room in which most of the real things of his life had happened" (*The Age of Innocence,* p. 344). When younger, Newland had anticipated with pleasure arranging the library in his future home, of filling it with the "'sincere' Eastlake furniture, and the plain new bookcases without glass doors" (*The Age of Innocence,* p. 71). His emphasis on sincerity and plainness shows his intent to preserve the library as an honest space, one that will feed his mind. His books will be for reading, not decoration; the furniture will accommodate the reader. Newland prides himself on being widely read, if conventionally so. He even daringly rejects dinner invitations in order to read works newly arrived from his London bookseller. His reading habits show his degree of nonconformity to his elite society.

Likewise, Ellen Olenska's reading habits show her degree of nonconformity to the New York elite. Books left about her drawing room are a clear signal that she does not conform to their notions of proper domestic décor, nor of the place of literature in a woman's life. New York's social conventions dictated that women ought to confine their reading to light novels or poetry and that they should not conduct their reading in rooms where they receive visitors, as one would in one's drawing room. The titles of Ellen's books indicate her failure to limit herself to light reading and her acquaintance with contemporary European artists and scientists. Not as conventional as the others, Newland is charmed by the books in Ellen's drawing room. During the moments he spends alone there (without other visitors because of her unconventional observance of calling times), he is introduced to new authors and works. The novel mentions the real-life writer Paul Bourget (1852-1935), who examined the upper classes through the lens of social anthropology. One wonders if Ellen had read Bourget's *Outre Mer*, a book that attempted to explain American culture by categorizing its social groups, including the elite of Newport, Rhode Island. In such a drawing room, thinks Newland, he could openly enjoy the kind of stimulating conversation he then engaged in only covertly, in unfashionable venues with Bohemian acquaintances, social rebels such as the novel's Ned Winsett or Monsieur Rivière.

The final chapter reveals that Newland's son Dallas has "done over" the library, the only vestige of Newland's original vision for that room being the "old Eastlake writing table" (*The Age of Innocence*, p. 347). In the end, the space Newland hoped to retain for intellectual freedom was surrendered to domestic convention; when he says that most of the real things of his life had happened there, he is referring to family affairs—christenings, engagements, conversations about the children—not to books. In essence, what has happened to Newland's library mirrors on a small scale his capitulation to convention in romance, which has cost him "the flower of life" (*The Age of Innocence*, p. 347).

Sources and literary context. In *A Backward Glance* Wharton expresses annoyance at having her novels read as if they are items in the society gossip column:

> All novelists who describe (whether from without or within) what is called "society life," are pursued by the exasperating accusation of putting flesh-and-blood people into their books. Any one gifted with the least creative faculty knows the absurdity of such a charge. "Real people" transported into a work of the imagination would instantly cease to be real; only those born of the creator's brain can give the least illusion of reality.
> (Wharton, *A Backward Glance*, p. 942)

Nevertheless, several characters in *The Age of Innocence* do have "flesh-and-blood" counterparts, most recognizably August Belmont as Julius Beaufort. Belmont was a newly monied young Wall Street financier of vast fortune. He had married into an established family, and was famous for lavish entertaining. Upon the death of his first wife, he married an opera singer, who became a patroness of the arts in New York, particularly the Metropolitan Opera House.

Wharton enlisted the help of her sister-in-law Minnie Jones in researching some of the details and in reading the finished product. Minnie recognized people from their youth. She shared the effect with her sister, referring to sources of inspiration for characters, identifying Mary Mason Jones, for example, as the model for the novel's Mrs. Mingott.

> You bring back that time as if it were last week. I wonder how many people will recognize old Aunt Mary, and August Belmont—and I do remember your mother's saying that when she was a girl one knew all the carriages in town.
> (Jones in Dwight, p. 225)

Wharton's *Age of Innocence* has sometimes been described as a novel of manners reflective of her own times and comparable in some ways to those of Henry James (see *Daisy Miller* and *The Turn of the Screw*, also in *Literature and Its Times*). This was the era of vigorous research and development in anthropology, from which novelists of the times borrowed concepts and vocabulary. "Both James and Wharton are able to imagine drawing rooms as sites of modern sacrifice" (Bentley, p. 77). Wharton is said to have devoured studies of manners published in her own times, from vast works like James Frazer's *The Golden Bough* (first published in 1890, then republished in 12 volumes, 1911-15), which surveys the religious beliefs of cultures around the world, to the *History of Primitive Marriage* by E. A. Westermarck, to groundbeaking books on tribal life by Bronislaw Malinowski, who examined beliefs, customs, and ritual and sexual taboos.

Events in History at the Time the Novel Was Written

Anthropology. When Newland and May announced their engagement they went by carriage "from one tribal doorstep to another, and Archer, when the afternoon's round was over, parted from his betrothed with the feeling that he had been shown off like a wild animal cunningly trapped" (*The Age of Innocence*, p. 67). Newland reflects that his "readings in anthropology" must have caused him to apply such terms to what is only a "natural" family function—natural, that is, in the sense that it is customary for the New York elite.

By the middle of the nineteenth century, anthropology had begun to emerge as distinct from history, philosophy, and other disciplines. As expanding European empires came into greater contact with non-European cultures, a method for studying and decoding those cultures developed into a science. The notion of culture came to encompass the beliefs and practices of a given group in a given environment.

The latter half of the nineteenth century saw several important strains of thought emerge in anthropology. Early ethnography (the branch of anthropology concerned with describing human culture) sought to gather information about native peoples as a way of better understanding how to educate and control them, or as an effort at preserving information about certain groups before they became assimilated into Western culture or died out. As the idea of evolution—or development of a being into ever-higher stages of life—gained acceptance, the notion of cultural evolutionism emerged. The suggestion was that all societies and cultures developed along similar lines and through a series of predictable stages. So-called "primitive" cultures were seen to reflect the earlier stages of Western culture (meaning Europe and America), which were regarded as the apex of cultural development. In 1892 Franz Boas challenged this idea, arguing that cultures could not be understood in terms of just one evolutionary scheme. Instead, a person had to regard each culture as a distinct group with a unique history of development and with a unique set of standards, customs, and habits. Around this same time, anthropology adopted a new technique—the study of a culture based on a reconstruction of events before that culture was influenced by outsiders. Anthropologists continued using the technique up through the year *Age of Innocence* was written. Wharton takes the technique and applies it not to another culture but to a strata of her own society, re-evoking old upper-crust New York before its members assimilated with the nouveau riche. Her plot hinges on a taboo of this strata, a taboo the love-struck pair is not prepared to break—he is married to her cousin and must not violate the kinship bond. It is to keep this bond intact that Ellen is expelled from the tribe.

In using terms such as "tribe," "rite," "clan," and "instinct," Wharton makes clear that she is treating old New York as a separate (and in this case vanished) culture, whose rituals and beliefs no longer survive. In one of the most famous lines in the novel, Wharton refers to this society as "a hieroglyphic world, where the real thing was never said or done or even thought, but only represented by a set of arbitrary signs" (*The Age of Innocence*, p. 44). Wharton's project is to decode those hieroglyphics, to demonstrate that those arbitrary signs had meaning and value. They amounted to a group of traits, in keeping with an approach taken by American anthropologists of the early twentieth century:

Age of Innocence

> Of late years the most distinctive American contribution to ethnological method and theory is the . . . culture-area concept. This was the outcome of the detailed study of a large number of tribes in North America which seemed to show that their cultures could be grouped around certain centers. Concentrated in each of these centers was found a specific group of traits. As we move away from each center, these specific traits diminish in number and new ones appear . . . until another center of concentration is reached. Regions characterized by possessing such a grouping of specific traits are called culture-areas.
>
> (Radin, p. 9)

THE PULITZER PRIZE

The Age of Innocence first appeared in serial form during 1920 in *Pictorial Review*. Tremendously successful in the magazine, it became a bestseller when released in book form the following year. Edith Wharton won the Pulitzer Prize for the novel in 1921, the third time the award had been made. The honor was diminished by the news that her novel served as a substitute for Sinclair Lewis's *Main Street*, which had actually received the first vote but was considered too offensive to certain Midwesterners.

A vanished world. In a *Harper's* article published near the end of her life, Wharton writes, "Everything that used to form the fabric of our daily life has been torn in shreds, trampled on, destroyed; and hundreds of little incidents, habits, traditions which, when I began to record my past, seemed too insignificant to set down, have acquired the historical importance of fragments of dress and furniture dug up in a Babylonian tomb" (Wharton in Goodwyn, p. 132). Indeed the New York of Wharton's childhood would have been unrecognizable to a New Yorker of the 1920s. The principles, or mores, of established old New York families gave way to the pressure of the newly wealthy in the last decades of the nineteenth century, and the exclusive enclave of old families disappeared through intermarriage with the rising nouveau riche. The disintegration of "old New York" is evident even within the novel. From an old New York family, Dallas Archer is engaged to Fanny Beaufort, the daughter of the self-made Julius Beaufort and the actress for whom he abandoned his wife after his financial downfall. Julius's acceptance by the upper crust was precarious to begin with, won only through his alliance with his wife's family; 30 years later his illegitimate daughter is accepted into society without question. More central to the novel is Newland Archer's socially unacceptable love for the married Countess Olenska. Star-crossed, the two lovers had no thoughts of divorce.

The difference in attitudes toward divorce between Wharton's subjects and her audience is striking. Nineteenth-century life invented the doctrine of separate spheres for men and women, with women confined to the domestic and discouraged from public life. Given this separation, women felt intense pressure to marry as a means of providing for themselves economically; by the end of the nineteenth century 90 percent of American women married. The cost was high. Economic security came at the price of relinquishing to one's husband all rights to property, money, and custody of one's children, and made women vulnerable to physical and sexual abuse. Nevertheless, divorce was mostly a male prerogative and involved tremendous social stigma for a woman. Her divorce violated the domestic ideal that taught women to tend the home and protect cultural values by providing comfort for their husbands and guidance for their children.

Early feminist leaders, including Elizabeth Cady Stanton and Susan B. Anthony, argued that the foundation of all reforms for women had to be the question of a woman's rights within marriage. Married women slowly gained legal status, as laws granted women some rights to property, earnings, and her children. Nevertheless, the definition of a wife's duty remained entrenched and a married woman was always subordinate to her husband. Women objected, agitating for autonomy and equality, including equal access to divorce.

Wharton herself divorced her husband only after years of hesitation and at the insistence of friends both in America and abroad. She and Teddy had been separated for a number of years while Teddy slipped further and further into dissolution. In a reversal of the usual roles, Edith helped support him and made many generous gestures toward reconciliation, not out of love but from wifely duty. Biographer R. W. B. Lewis describes her divorce as the most painful decision of her life: "She knew perfectly well that divorce had become common, even casual, among the younger American generation of the best society . . . but her own fifty-one-year-old character had been shaped by the conventions and pieties of a much older and narrower New York" (Lewis, p. 333).

Reviews. Like Wharton's other most famous novel, *The House of Mirth, The Age of Innocence* was an immediate popular and critical success. The *New York Times Book Review* crowed, "the appearance of such a book as *The Age of Innocence* by an American is a matter for public rejoicing" (*New York Times Book Review* in Tuttleton, p. 286). Critics universally applauded Wharton's seamless prose and uncanny attention to detail in rendering a bygone era. But several were uncomfortable with the author's expatriate status, uncertain they wanted to hail the novel as a great work of American literature when its author herself had resoundingly abandoned America. The *New York Evening Post* skirted the issue by declaring the book "a credit to American literature—for if its author is cosmopolitan, her novel, as much as **Ethan Frome** [also in *Literature and Its Times*], is a fruit of our soil" (Tuttleton, p. 289). But Vernon Parrington in *Pacific Review* felt, "there is more hope for our literature in the honest crudities of the young naturalists, than in her classic irony; they at least are trying to understand America as it is" (Tuttleton, p. 295). While conceding that Wharton was particularly skilled at rendering the social world of her youth, he charged that she was incapable of portraying anything else: "Why waste such skill upon such insignificant material? There were vibrant realities in the New York of the seventies, Commodore Vanderbilt, for example, or even Jay Gould or Jim Fiske. If Mrs. Wharton had only chosen to throw such figures upon her canvas, brutal, cynical, dominating, what a document of American history—but the suggestion is foolish. Mrs. Wharton could not do it. Her distinction is her limitation" (Tuttleton, p. 294). Wharton's champions would argue, as would she, that the world she depicted on her canvas was also an important document of American history. Moreover, the critics among them would praise the effect of her particular rendering: "Mrs. Wharton's triumph is that she has described these rites and surfaces and burdens as familiarly as if she loved them and as lucidly as if she hated them" (Van Doren in Tuttleton, p. 287).

—Catharine Riggs

For More Information

Auchincloss, Louis. *Edith Wharton: A Woman in Her Time*. New York: Viking, 1971.

Beadles Dime Book of Etiquette. New York: Irwin P. Beadle and Co., 1861, and Adams, 1864.

Beckert, Sven. *The Monied Metropolis: New York City and the Consolidation of the American Bourgeoisie, 1850-1896*. Cambridge: Cambridge University Press, 2001.

Bentley, Nancy. *The Ethnography of Manners*. Cambridge: Cambridge University Press, 1995.

Dwight, Eleanor. *Edith Wharton: An Extraordinary Life*. New York: Harry N. Abrams, 1994.

Goodwyn, Janet. *Edith Wharton: Traveller in the Land of Letters*. New York: St. Martin's Press, 1990.

Lewis, R. W. B. *Edith Wharton: A Biography*. New York: Harper and Row, 1975.

Montgomery, Maureen E. *Displaying Women: Spectacles of Leisure in Edith Wharton's New York*. New York: Routledge, 1998.

Preston, Claire. *Edith Wharton's Social Register*. New York: St. Martin's Press, 2000.

Radin, Paul. *Social Anthropology*. New York: McGraw-Hill, 1932.

Tuttleton, James W., et al, Eds. *Edith Wharton: The Contemporary Reviews*. Cambridge: Cambridge University Press, 1992.

Wharton, Edith. *The Age of Innocence*. New York: Macmillan, 1987.

———. *A Backward Glance*. In *Edith Wharton: Novellas and Other Writings*. New York: The Library of America, 1990.

April Morning

by
Howard Fast

Born in New York City in 1914, Howard Melvin Fast was the son of immigrant parents: his father was from the Ukraine; his mother from Lithuania. Educated at George Washington High School and the National Academy of Design, Fast dropped out of the latter after a year, when he sold a story to a science-fiction magazine. In 1933 Fast published his first novel *Two Valleys*, which was favorably received; his second novel, *Strange Yesterday* (1934) was less successful. After a brief slump, Fast's literary career regained momentum with the 1937 printing of his short story "The Children" in *Story* magazine. A string of successful novels followed—*Conceived in Liberty* (1939), *The Last Frontier* (1941), *The Unvanquished* (1942), and *Citizen Tom Paine* (1944). During the Second World War, Fast served first on the overseas staff of the U.S. Office of War Information (1942-44), then worked as a war correspondent in the China-Burma-India theater (1944-45). Fast also joined the Communist Party in 1944, devoting several years to the left-wing cause. His political views resulted in his being brought before the House Un-American Activities Committee (HUAC) and then jailed briefly on contempt charges in 1950. Fast's time in prison, inspired a hugely popular historical novel, *Spartacus* (1951), which he was obliged to publish at his own expense because interference from the FBI (Federal Bureau of Investigation) prevented him from finding a publisher. Russian leader Nikita Krushchev's revelations about the atrocities of his country's earlier Stalin regime prompted Fast to

> **THE LITERARY WORK**
> A novel set in colonial New England around April 19, 1775; published in 1961.
>
> **SYNOPSIS**
> A boy is forced to become a man after taking part in the Battle of Lexington.

resign from the Communist Party in 1956. His subsequent works, including *April Morning* (1961) and *The Hessian* (1972), were subsequently published by mainstream publishing houses. While Fast's political sympathies changed throughout his career, his interest in history—especially American history—and the historical novel remained constant. *April Morning* has been widely praised for its painstaking depiction of the events surrounding the Battle of Lexington, during which a boy and a nation are forced to come of age.

Events in History at the Time the Novel Takes Place

Lexington and Concord. *April Morning* covers a span of perhaps 36 crucial hours in the life of Adam Cooper, a 15-year-old boy who, along with his family, is caught up in the drama surrounding the Battle of Lexington. The novel describes not only the battle itself but also the chain of events immediately leading up to it, creating

April Morning

Howard Fast

a mood of mounting tension. A description of the battle according to historical records follows.

British troops, under the command of General Thomas Gage, British Military Governor of Massachusetts, had long been stationed in Boston. But while the city of Boston was itself under military rule, the British did not have the authority to enforce the king's law in the surrounding countryside. As British and colonial relations worsened during the 1760s and 1770s, rebel militias began to form in rural towns and villages. Eventually, the British declared the Colony of Massachusetts to be in a state of rebellion against the mother country and attempted to stamp out colonial resistance to British rule.

The breaking point came on April 15, 1775, when Gage received orders to take decisive action against the colonists. He decided to send an expedition to destroy the rebels' military supplies that were being stockpiled at Concord. Gage assembled his British troops, drawing on the "flank companies"—consisting of grenadiers and light infantry—of eight regiments for this mission; Lieutenant Colonel Francis Smith and Marine Major John Pitcairn were put in charge. Gage also composed a relief column under the command of Lord Hugh Percy that was scheduled to leave six hours after the main column departed. Although Gage attempted to keep the mission a secret by not telling his officers of his plan until the very last minute, the colonists had been watching every move the British made and were quick to report any suspicious troop activity.

By the evening of April 18, 1775, the residents of Boston knew of the British plan to march on Concord. Around midnight, British forces—numbering from 600 to 900 troops—crossed the Charles River but were followed closely by the American alarm rider Paul Revere. With the help of fellow riders William Dawes and Samuel Prescott, Revere spread the word of the British advance throughout the Massachusetts countryside, including Lexington, Concord, and Watertown. Rebel militia was quickly deployed to meet the enemy.

Arriving in Lexington around dawn (5:00 A.M.), British troops under the command of Major Pitcairn were confronted by a group of about 70 colonial militia, armed and in formation on the village green. Both British and colonial forces had apparently agreed among themselves not to shoot unless fired upon. Pitcairn ordered the rebels, led by Lexington militia captain John Parker, to lay down their arms. In response, Parker ordered his men to disperse; reluctantly, they started to obey. Then a single shot, followed by two or three more, rang out. It remains unclear to this day who fired those shots, but on hearing them, the British fired upon the militia, killing eight and wounding ten. Among the dead were Parker's cousin, Jonas, who was bayoneted as well as wounded, and another soldier, Jonathan Harrington, who crawled home to die on his own doorstep. The remaining militia fled into the woods to avoid capture.

Victorious, the British troops advanced to Concord, but the colonists were ready for them. At Concord's North Bridge, a group of armed militia routed the British who were forced to retreat. Meanwhile, militia from surrounding towns had also advanced towards Concord. As the British marched back along Menotomy road towards Lexington and Boston, they were promptly attacked by Americans shooting at them from behind trees, walls, and other hiding places. The battle continued for most of the day; British morale crumbled beneath the onslaught—so different from their own way of fighting—and the troops broke ranks while retreating to Lexington. Instead of meeting the enemy in direct confrontation, the Americans fired at the British from behind the cover. The relief efforts of Lord Percy, who used his two cannons to disperse the rebels and then led the retreat back to Boston, saved the British from total defeat. Nonetheless, British forces suffered significant casualties: out of 1,800 men, 73 were reported killed, 147 wounded, and 26 missing (Nolan, p. 170). By contrast, colonial casualties consisted of 49 dead, 39 wounded, and 5 missing (Birnbaum, p. 191). The events of Lexington and Concord marked the true beginning of the American Revolution. In *April Morning*, Adam undergoes a bloody rite of passage when he sees his father killed at Lexington, then participates in the roadside attacks on the British as they retreat from Concord. Although Fast ends his novel with the close of day, it is implied that Adam, now the man of the family, will eventually join the fight against the British on a full-time basis.

Colonial committees. Repeatedly in *April Morning*, Adam Cooper refers to "Committees" that have been established throughout the colonies but provides little clarification regarding their function and purpose. Secret colonial societies did in fact spring up in the colonies, beginning around the passage of the Stamp Act in 1765. During the American Revolution and the years preceding it, these societies went by many names—Sons of Liberty, Committees of Correspondence, Committees of Safety—but all included radicals who favored rebellion against Britain.

Certain differences existed between Committees of Correspondence and Committees of Safety. The former were created in 1772, for the purpose of coordinating the activities of colonial agitators and organizing public opinion against the British ministry. The first of these was established in Boston at the urging of Samuel Adams, and consisted of 21 members who were empowered to communicate with other Massachusetts towns, which soon followed suit by creating committees of their own. Thomas Jefferson and Patrick Henry successfully urged their native Virginia to establish one, and soon Committees of Correspondence spread throughout the colonies. News, pamphlets, and the political writings of Committee members were carried from town to town by riders on horseback. Among them was Paul Revere, a Boston silversmith who became one of the Committees' busiest couriers.

By contrast, Committees of Safety followed a more military agenda. Created by the Massachusetts Provincial Congress in 1774, its Committee of Safety had the authority to mobilize and train the local militia, issue orders, purchase equipment, and seize military stores. Members included such figures as Dr. Joseph Warren (elected committee president), the merchant John Hancock, and Artemas Ward. As with Committees of Correspondence, other colonies quickly established their own Committees of Safety, which, until the adoption of new state constitutions in 1776, essentially functioned as state governments, maintaining order and furnishing men and supplies to the Continental Army.

THE MINUTEMEN

Intriguingly, April Morning never uses the term "minutemen," the name most often associated with the colonial militia of Massachusetts at the time of the American Revolution. Almost since the start of their history, the American colonies had maintained local companies of militia, which consisted of able-bodied men, commanded by officers who were commissioned by the royal governors. These militia companies marched in parade once or twice a year; drilled frequently with such weapons as muskets, fowling pieces, and squirrel guns; and could be called out by the governor to participate in certain conflicts. For example, the militia of New England and Virginia fought in the French and Indian Wars of the 1750s and 1760s; one young Virginian, George Washington, distinguished himself in that campaign. During the 1770s, however, relations between Britain and the American colonies deteriorated. To eliminate Tories—pro-British colonists—from the old militia organization, three regiments in Worcester, Massachusetts called for the resignation of all officers in September 1774. These regiments were broken up to form seven new regiments, under the command of new officers. It was the task of these new officers to elect one-third of each new regiment to be ready to assemble at a minute's notice in the event of an emergency: hence the name "minutemen" (first used in the town of Brookfield in 1774). While this new system was not adopted in every colony, Massachusetts maintained a dual system of militia and minutemen companies and regiments. The minutemen were those who assembled on the green on April 19, 1775, and later led the attack on Concord bridge.

In *April Morning*, Adam's father Moses Cooper and many of his neighbors serve as "Committeemen," meeting to discuss everything from military stores to the establishment of a newspaper. Initially, they seem mostly concerned with the

April Morning

writing and circulation of political statements—the main agenda of Committees of Correspondence—but all are ready to mobilize at a moment's notice when they receive news of British troops approaching Lexington.

British and colonial relations. During the 1760s and 1770s, relations between the American colonies and Britain, their "mother" country became increasingly strained. Much of this hostility could be attributed to the more stringent colonial policy Britain adopted after the conclusion of the French and Indian War (1756-63), waged by France and Britain for dominance in the New World. Although Britain had emerged victorious, it faced a heavy national debt and the difficult task of administering vast territorial holdings in its empire.

During the war, American colonies had profited by continued trade with the French West Indies and had begun to feel less dependent upon Britain. Therefore, attempts by Britain to bring the colonies more firmly under control of the British king and Parliament met with growing resistance. From 1763 the British ministry implemented several unpopular parliamentary measures that worsened British-colonial relations: the Currency Act (1764), which forbade the issuance of legal tender paper money by the colonial assemblies; the Sugar Act (1764) which levied a three-penny-per-gallon duty upon molasses imported from the West Indies; the Quartering Act (1765), which required colonists to supply quarter and supplies to British troops stationed in settled areas of the colonies.

A crisis erupted after the passage of the Stamp Act (1765), which required colonists to purchase stamps for newspapers, playing cards, marriage licenses, and other legal documents. Colonists from all professions and walks of life were affected by this tax and angrily demanded its repeal on the grounds of unconstitutionality, asserting that they could be taxed only by their elected representatives. Stamp distributors were harassed, even attacked, and pressured to resign. Ultimately no stamps at all were being sold in the colonies. Meanwhile, Americans successfully boycotted British goods, prompting British merchants and manufacturers to likewise call for the repeal of the Stamp Act. Although the Stamp Act was indeed repealed in 1766, the British Parliament rejected the colonists' cry of "no taxation without representation" and asserted through the Declaratory Act that its Parliamentary authority extended over the colonies in all cases.

Matters continued to deteriorate with the passage of the Townshend Acts (1767), which levied import duties on lead, tea, painter's colors, and paper. A colonial boycott led to the 1770 repeal of these duties as well, except for the tax on tea. The repeal did not, however, usher in any wholehearted loosening of the reins on the part of Britain. Several British regiments had occupied Boston from 1768, and they continued to do so, to the great dismay of the city's inhabitants. Violence erupted between the soldiers and civilians on March 5, 1770, when British troops fired upon an angry mob outside the Customs House, killing five and wounding several others. Colonial outrage over the incident led to the withdrawal of British troops from Boston; in 1774, however, British forces again occupied the city after several Bostonians, disguised as Indians, dumped three shiploads of tea into the harbor to protest the continuing tax on tea. The Coercive Acts of 1774 closed the port of Boston until the town compensated the wronged party (the British East Indian Company) for dumping its tea. They also increased royal control over Massachusetts, reducing it to a crown colony—one in which the government in London exercises some control over lawmaking and appoints the governor.

Meanwhile, mutual animosity continued to grow. If the colonists regarded the British as tyrannical and arrogant, the British looked down upon the colonists as ignorant, ungrateful upstarts. British disdain for the colonial militia was especially pronounced. In a letter to his family, one British soldier wrote, "As to what you hear of their taking arms to resist the force of England, it is mere bullying, and will go no further than words; whenever it comes to blows, he that can run fastest will think himself best off . . . they are a mere mob, without order or discipline and very awkward in handling their arms" (Anonymous in Birnbaum, p. 86).

In *April Morning*, despite his youth and relative innocence, Adam becomes aware of the deteriorating relations between Britain and the colonies, mainly through listening to the complaints made by his father and other committeemen. After the Battle of Lexington and the death of his father, Adam receives a sobering lecture from Solomon Chandler, a veteran of the French and Indian War, about the depth of the hostilities on both sides. Encouraging the boy to take a long hard look at the enemy, Chandler explains, "They have a great contempt for us, and they call us peasants and louts, but not one in ten of them can read or write his letters. A good half of them are convicts, cutthroats and footpads, serving out their time in His Majesty's colors instead of in jail. The rest of them are poor, ignorant devils, with a religion as cloudy as their minds" (Fast, *April Morning*, p. 120).

Rural life in colonial New England. In *April Morning*, the close-knit rural community of Lexington is almost a character in its own right. The Coopers and their neighbors, most of whom are descended from the seventeenth-century Puritans who first settled in the Massachusetts colony, are bound to each other by ties of faith and kinship. Historians Oscar and Lilian Handlin write, "From the start, the Church had been important in the life of this region. A yearning for purified forms of worship had been one motive for the original migration. . . . Throughout New England, faith linked the minister to society and impinged upon government, economic attitudes, and family relations" (Handlin and Handlin, p. 9).

If the Church was the source of spiritual and intellectual development in rural communities, the farm was the source of economic livelihood. Harsh winters, rocky soil, short growing seasons, and unpredictable weather meant that New England farmers had to work constantly in order to prosper or even survive. Children as well as adults were expected to participate in the maintenance of the farm, and people showed scant patience for laziness or indolence. Quality of life was determined by how much effort a person was willing to expend cultivating his or her property. "The unending struggle shaped Yankee character. The lesson that life was a battle against uncongenial elements, learned early in life, trained people to strive lest they go under" (Handlin and Handlin, p. 11). Traits such as industry, determination, and obstinacy—especially in the face of adversity—became identified with the New England farmer.

Fast's novel depicts the Coopers as a typical Yankee family of the colonial era: hardworking, stubborn, and independent. Stern, outspoken Moses Cooper manages the family farm; sons Adam and Levi perform chores—and receive scoldings when they do not perform them with sufficient promptness; and the Cooper women are likewise preoccupied with necessities. They sew, they quilt, they cook. Granny Cooper speaks with some pride of the family's industry and accomplishments: "Coopers have been teachers and pastors and free yeomen farmers and ship captains and merchants for a hundred and fifty years on this soil, and I don't recall one who couldn't write a sermon and deliver it too, if the need ever arose" (*April Morning*, pp. 10-11). The Coopers' strength and determination, nurtured by their rigorous way of life, help them survive and adjust.

RELIGIOUS ATTITUDES IN COLONIAL AMERICA

Although the events of the Battle of Lexington form the crux of the novel's plot, Fast nonetheless emphasizes the role religion plays in the daily life of a New England family. The Coopers, who appear to be descended from Puritan stock, say grace before meals and attend church regularly. Like his Puritan ancestors, Mr. Cooper has little tolerance for the more pompous religious practices of the Anglican Church; Adam observes, "The Church of England was one of the things—one of the very few things, I should say—that he couldn't argue about. Not that he wasn't willing; but ten words after he began, his face flushed, his neck thickened, and he became near apoplectic" (*April Morning*, p. 51). Curiously, Mr. Cooper shows more open-mindedness about other faiths, visiting a synagogue while in Rhode Island: "Father said that apart from the fact that they kept their hats on in church and read from the Bible in Hebrew—something he had always aspired to—they didn't seem any different from Presbyterians" (*April Morning*, p. 52). Indeed, religious minorities—including Jews, Moravians, and Catholics—who were discriminated against in Europe found a relative haven in the American colonies: in most regions, they were free to worship as they pleased. Historians Oscar and Lucinda Handlin write, "In New England the descendants of the Puritans had accepted the presence of the Church of England and then of various deviant groups, Congregationalists and Anglicans dominated Bristol, Rhode Island; across the bay in East Greenwich most families were Baptists and Quakers" (Handlin and Handlin, p. 161).

The Novel in Focus

The plot. The novel begins on an ordinary afternoon at the home of the Coopers, a farming family in Lexington, Massachusetts. Fifteen-year-old Adam, the eldest son and narrator of the novel, goes through his daily routine—performing his chores, quarreling with his younger brother Levi, bantering with his mother and grandmother, and wondering if he can ever please his stern, undemonstrative father, Moses. That evening at supper, the Coopers are visited by Joseph Simmons, a cousin and the town blacksmith. In the course of the conversation, it is revealed that Mr. Simmons and Mr. Cooper both belong to a local Committee, which meets regularly at church to discuss possible solutions to the deteriorating relations between Britain and her colonies. Appointed to write a statement on the rights of man, which would then be posted in Boston, Mr. Simmons wishes to show his draft to Mr. Cooper, known in the community for his oratorical skills.

After a lengthy discussion, the two men depart for that evening's Committee meeting. Adam asks to attend the meeting but his father refuses to bring him, citing Adam's youth and immaturity. Adam's mother and grandmother try to comfort the boy but he remains disconsolate. Seeking additional sympathy, Adam visits Mr. Simmons's daughter, Ruth, whom he has known since childhood. During an evening walk, Adam complains to Rachel about his father, argues with her about politics and religion, then startles them both by suddenly kissing her.

Later, at home, Adam eavesdrops on his father's report to the Cooper women on what happened at the meeting. Members had discussed the village weapons count, the possibility of drilling, or training with their weapons, the viability of a local newspaper to connect the Committees with the people, and finally, the issue of whether minutes from the meetings should be kept. Adam's father, Mr. Cooper, had spoken out strongly in favor of keeping minutes and so had prevailed. Afterwards, the Cooper women bring up the subject of Adam. Mr. Cooper is astonished and dismayed to learn that his son thinks he does not care for him. Adam falls asleep feeling better about his relationship with his father.

That night, a rider from Boston rouses the community with the news that a British army is marching towards Lexington and Concord. The men of Lexington argue about what should be done next; some dismiss the rider's report as nonsense. Others call for an immediate muster of the militia. Still others, including Adam's father, believe a Committee meeting should be convened to discuss the matter more reasonably. Finally the reverend suggests that nothing be done until more details are known, especially since the local militia are likely to be outnumbered and easily defeated by British troops. The reverend's last claim, however, causes the outspoken Mr. Cooper to side with those eager to muster the militia, the position that finally prevails.

The boys of the community are excited to learn that the muster book is being signed. Determined to participate in whatever action occurs, Adam hurries over to the common, or village green, to sign up. Mr. Cooper consents to his son placing his name in the muster book, after which father and son return home to collect their guns and take leave of their family. The two share a rare moment of closeness as the elder Cooper advises his son how to load and prepare his gun for battle before they gather on the common with the rest of the militia.

Waiting before dawn, the men discuss what may happen. Although some are eager to fight, most hope that reason will triumph and war will be avoided. In the morning, the British troops finally reach Lexington and confront the Massachusetts militia on the village green. The reverend attempts to speak to Major Pitcairn, the British officer in charge, but the effort is disregarded. After the militia refuses the order to disperse, the redcoats (British soldiers) fire upon them. Mr. Cooper and several others are killed in the first volley; panicked, the rest of the militia scatters. Sickened and frightened by what he has just experienced, Adam manages to escape the British and hides in a neighbor's smokehouse.

Eventually Adam regains his composure, forcing himself to accept his father's death and acknowledge the militia's foolhardiness in confronting the more numerous British troops. Later, Adam's brother Levi finds him in his hiding place and fills him in on the terrible details of what happened to some of their neighbors in the battle. Mr. Cooper's body has been retrieved by the women of Lexington and brought home. Levi also informs Adam that he cannot come home yet because redcoats are patrolling the area and that Granny Cooper advises he hide in the woods until nightfall. Realizing that he is now the man of the family, Adam comforts Levi, then sends him back to the farm, assuring the boy that he can take care of himself.

Leaving the smokehouse, Adam is nearly captured by redcoats but manages to outrun them in the woods. He encounters an ally—the 61-year-old Solomon Chandler, a veteran of the French and Indian wars. Together, they travel through the woods, finally reaching Lincoln, where the Dovers—Adam's cousins—live. Adam tells the Dovers what happened at Lexington that morning, then the men proceed to an assembly held at a local pasture. More men—committee members from other towns—have gathered there, including some of the survivors from Lexington; Adam is reunited with the Reverend and Cousin Simmons.

Discovering that the British are returning to Lexington from Concord, the assembly, led by Solomon Chandler, vow revenge on their enemy. From vantage points behind walls and trees, the militia shoot at British troops as they march along the road, killing or wounding several redcoats. After this skirmish, the men decide to divide into small groups and lead separate attacks on the British. Cousin Simmons takes Adam with him; they encounter and fire upon British soldiers. Sickened by all he has seen that day, Adam longs for an end to the fighting. Simmons, however, insists that a war is upon them and the fighting has only just begun.

Arriving at a friendly farm, Adam and Cousin Simmons join a party of men hoping to trap the British on the road between Lexington and Menotomy and keep them there until more committee men arrive. En route, the militia surprise a British cavalry patrol, wounding and capturing one of the officers, a boy of about 20. Continuing on, Adam and Simmons discuss the likelihood of war; Adam complains that he has "had a bellyful of war and killing," but Simmons maintains that the colonists cannot stop fighting until the British depart and leave them in peace (*April Morning*, p. 159).

Hearing a report that Lexington is burning, Adam grows even more worried about his family. He marches on with the rest of the militia to Menotomy, however, and takes his place among the fighters. While the campaign does not go entirely as planned (the British are not successfully contained between Metonomy and Lexington), both sides continue to fire at each other. Realizing that his fowling piece is useless at this distance, Adam stops shooting and falls asleep, exhausted by all that has occurred that day. On awakening, he discovers that the fighting has apparently stopped; he also overhears the reverend and Cousin Simmons discussing him as though he has been killed and hastens to reassure them of his survival. Both men are happy to see him alive and astonished that he slept during part of the battle.

As the day draws to a close, Adam, Simmons, and the reverend head back to Lexington, where they discover to their relief that only three houses have been burned, rather than the whole village. Adam continues on alone to the Cooper farm, where he has an emotional reunion with his family.

The Battle of Lexington, April 19, 1775.

Over the next several hours, Adam tries to cope with his new responsibilities as the man of the house—comforting his grieving relatives, filling them in on the details of the day's battle, and helping with the arrangements for his father's burial. Later, Cousin Simmons again broaches the subject of war to Adam, remarking that both of them must soon decide whether they will fight in it. Feeling painfully suspended between childhood and manhood, Adam wishes he could return to the former and not have to make such decisions.

At home, Adam encounters Ruth Simmons and they achieve an understanding about their relationship, agreeing to marry when they are old enough. When the neighbors have left the Cooper farm, Adam tries again to console his mother and grandmother. The latter wants to know if Adam means to sign the muster book for the siege of Boston, now circulating through the town. Adam reluctantly admits that he probably will, but does not wish to talk about that tonight. Retiring to his bed, Adam thanks God that this day is finally over and bids "farewell to a childhood, a world, a secure and sun-warmed existence and past that was over and done with and gone away for all time" (*April Morning*, p. 202).

Rite of passage. In *April Morning*, the Battle of Lexington serves as a catalyst on several levels. Just as the American colonies take their first

April Morning

painful step towards nationhood, so does Adam Cooper take his first painful step towards manhood. The opening shots of the American Revolution provide a backdrop against which to view a boy's rapid maturation in the space of less than 36 hours.

Throughout the novel, Adam's character is mainly defined through his problematic relationship with his father, the stern, outspoken Moses Cooper. In the first half of the story, Adam is described as being almost as tall and strong as a grown man; emotionally and intellectually, however, he is still a child, dawdling over performing his chores, fretting over his father's frequent reprimands, quarreling with his younger brother, and receiving comfort and sweets from the Cooper women, who dote upon him. Like a child, Adam sulks when his father refuses to take him to a committee meeting and runs off to a neighbor's house in hopes of receiving sympathy there.

Learning of the British troops' projected arrival and preparing for the impending confrontation alters Adam's perception of his entire world, including his father. Moses Cooper's insistence on discipline and occasional harshness are revealed as a sincere attempt to guide his son towards manhood and thus improve his chances of survival. Armed with this new understanding, Adam willingly heeds his father's instructions on how to load and prepare his gun before facing the British.

> "Load it up. I want to watch you."
> I nodded and took my powder bottle and measured out the cap measure for the muzzle.
> "It's not enough," Father said harshly.
> "It's the hunting measure."
> "You're not hunting."
> My mouth was dry. "How much?" I asked.
> "Three times."
> . . .
> "How many pellets?" he demanded
> "Twenty."
> "Do you count them?" he asked scornfully.
> "Yes, sir—I count them."
> "You'll stop to count pellets tomorrow? Is that it?"
> "No, sir. I wasn't thinking."
> "Then think!" he shouted. "Think! Use your head! Put your hand in the shot pouch and pull out a handful. Feel it in your hand . . . remember what it feels like. . . ."
> (*April Morning*, pp. 76-77)

Adam's first experience of battle and his father's death further propel him towards maturity. Despite his grief, the youth quickly realizes that he is now the head of the Cooper family and responsible for the well-being of his mother, brother, and grandmother. This realization is reinforced by the attitudes of neighbors, who, after witnessing Mr. Cooper's death at Lexington, afford Adam a man's place in their company as they march off to engage the British once more. Although daunted by his new responsibilities and the knowledge that he has "parted with childhood and boyhood forever," Adam attempts to adjust to his new role (*April Morning*, p. 182). Returning home, he consoles his bereaved family and tries to help Levi accept the same harsh realities he has had to face: "Now listen to me, Levi. Father's dead. That's all there is to it, and you might as well be a man enough to face it. You can't break into tears every time anyone mentions his name. We have very large responsibilities, you and me" (*April Morning*, p. 176).

The difficult, often contentious interaction between Moses and Adam Cooper accurately reflects parent-child relationships in colonial New England communities. Indeed, as strict as the Cooper parents, especially Mr. Cooper, may appear to modern readers, they actually demonstrate the more lenient parenting style that developed during the 1700s. A century earlier, Puritan families—from whom people such as the Coopers were most likely descended—exercised a much greater and sterner degree of control over their children. Historians Steven Mintz and Susan Kellogg write, "Seventeenth-century Puritans cared deeply for their children and invested an enormous amount of time and energy in them, but they were also intent on repressing what they perceived as manifestations of original sin through harsh physical and psychological measures" (Mintz and Kellogg, p. 2). The authority of Puritan patriarchs in their own homes was absolute and unquestioned: "Law and church doctrine made it the duty of wives, children, and servants to submit to the father's authority" (Mintz and Kellogg, p. 9).

By the time of the American Revolution, however, significant changes had occurred in parenting practices. Colonial development weakened paternal authority by providing economic opportunities that could render adult children less dependent on their parents for their future provision; new philosophies, like those espoused by French intellectual Jean Jacques Rousseau, posited that children were not inherently sinful beings but "innocent and malleable creatures whose characters could be molded into any shape" (Mintz and Kellogg, p. 17). The emotional climate within the family unit thus began to change; relations between all members became warmer, more openly affectionate. In *April Morning*, Adam and Levi are occasionally indulged, even spoiled, by the women in the family; Moses Cooper, himself the product of a stricter upbringing, is astonished and dismayed to hear that Adam doubts his love, protesting to his wife, "[W]hy, how could any man love a son any more than I love that boy? . . . I was somewhat sharp with him at the table, but boys get over that kind of thing. I'm old enough and wise enough now to thank the good God that my own father never spared the rod and spoiled the child" (*April Morning*, p. 45).

Sources and literary context. The plot of *April Morning* revolves mainly around the events surrounding the Battle of Lexington and the battle itself, both of which are well-documented. Fast probably drew from a variety of historical sources to provide the details he needed. Several real-life figures are mentioned in the novel, including John Hancock and Samuel Adams; others appear as characters—Jonas Harper and Caleb Harrington, for example, are killed at Lexington. But not all of the real-life figures are specifically named, like Paul Revere who brings the news to Lexington of the British troops' impending arrival. The Coopers, however, are Fast's own invention, a device that allows the author to explore momentous events through the eyes of an ordinary New England family.

April Morning fits squarely into the category of historical fiction, a genre that held a lingering appeal for Fast. Several of his early works, including his first novel *Two Valleys*, were set during the American Revolution. Throughout his literary career, Fast returned continually to that time period, writing about such figures as George Washington (in *The Unvanquished*) and focusing upon such themes as the fight for freedom. His filtering of the events of Lexington and Concord, through the eyes of a 15-year-old boy, renders the novel as much a coming-of-age story as a historical recreation. Fast's painstaking depiction of Adam Cooper's particular thoughts and fears have led several critics to compare *April Morning* favorably to Stephen Crane's *The Red Badge of Courage*, which also features a boy's first experience of battle and subsequent growth to manhood (also in *Literature and Its Times*).

Events in History at the Time the Novel was Written

Youth activism and the New Frontier. While *April Morning* painstakingly recreates colonial New England in the days before the American Revolution, the novel also reflects the spirit of activism that pervaded 1960s America. Activists of the 1960s staged demonstrations, sit-ins, and protest marches in a struggle for causes such as civil rights, women's rights, and the Vietnam War. And often America's youth—high school and college students—stood in the forefront of the struggle.

Teenage youth had begun to emerge as a subculture in the United States in the 1950s, becoming more conspicuous than in any previous generation. A distinct set of teenage habits gained currency, tied to preferences in music, clothing, and cars. Slowly youth became politically engaged. The 1950s gave rise to some major civil rights victories—the Supreme Court ruling of *Brown v. Board of Education* (which outlawed segregation in American schools) and the Montgomery bus boycott (ended segregation on Montgomery, Alabama, buses). Encouraged by these victories, African American students numbered among the earliest activists in the 1960s.

On February 1, 1960, four students from the North Carolina Agricultural and Technical College, a black college in Greensboro, North Carolina, staged the first sit-in at the all-white lunch counter of a local department store. Refused service because they were black, the students sat at the counter until the store closed that day, then returned the next day, and the next. Soon, a wave of sit-ins swept the country—mainly in the South but also in some areas of the North. Together black students and white students occupied white libraries, white beaches, and the lobbies of hotels that catered to whites, in protest against policies of discrimination and segregation. Youth involvement was not confined to protest movements either.

This wave of youthful activism coincided with the campaign of Democratic presidential hopeful John F. Kennedy. Ambitious, dynamic, energetic, and the youngest candidate yet, Kennedy exhorted America to meet the challenges of the "New Frontier"—to tackle "uncharted areas of science and space, unsolved problems of peace and war, unconquered pockets of ignorance and prejudice, [and] unanswered questions of poverty and surplus"—if it truly aspired to become the world's greatest nation (Kennedy in Nash, p. 960). Elected in 1960, he expanded upon this theme in his inaugural address, evoking the nation's past as well as its promise for the future, emphasizing the need to work together, appealing especially to the young: "The torch has

April Morning

been passed to a new generation of Americans—born in this century, tempered by war, disciplined by a hard and bitter peace, proud of our ancient heritage. . . . And so, my fellow Americans: Ask not what your country can do for you—ask what you can do for your country" (Kennedy in Nash, pp. 960-961).

This "new generation" eagerly answered his call. Many young people joined a volunteer organization created by President Kennedy on March 1, 1961. Called the Peace Corps, the organization sent members to work in impoverished countries for two years, promoting world peace and friendship. A type of revolutionary fervor spread, filling at least some young people with the conviction that they could and should do something to make a difference in the world. By the end of 1961, an estimated 500 volunteers had completed their training and had taken up their new responsibilities in various African, Asian, and Caribbean countries.

While it is unclear how much of an influence any of this ferment had on Fast's writing of *April Morning*, a parallel can be drawn between the young people of the Revolutionary and modern eras. Like the fictional Adam Cooper and his real-life peers, the youthful activists of the 1960s shouldered adult roles and responsibilities. Both eras gave rise to young people who set out to shape their future in ways that would give reality to lofty ideals.

Reviews. On its publication in 1961, *April Morning* received mostly positive reviews. Critics praised Fast's attention to detail and recreation of an exciting period in American history. The reviewer for the *Times Literary Supplement* thought that the story slowed down once Fast began describing the battles and M. C. Scoggin of *Horn Book* felt that "[s]ome of the ideas expressed by the characters sound anachronistic," but these were minor complaints in what most critics felt to be an excellent historical novel (Scoggin in Davison, p. 419).

Fast's meticulous depiction of everyday colonial life on the eve of the American Revolution garnered particular praise. Kenneth Fearing, in the *New York Times Book Review*, observed, "A veteran of this sort of historical recreation, Howard Fast has admirably recaptured the sights and sounds, the religious and political idioms, the simple military tactics and strategies of that day—maneuvers that foreshadow the painful development of a professional army" (Fearing in Hunter, p. 54). Dorothy Nyren wrote in *Library Journal*, "There is nothing grandiose, nothing inflated, nothing chauvinistic about this book, but the rugged virtues, the simple uprightness of the Coopers and their neighbors are presented with conviction and grace" (Nyren in Davison, p. 419).

Other critics commended Fast's decision to portray the war through its impact on a single New England family and community. R. H. Glauber, of the *New York Herald Tribune Lively Arts*, wrote, "It is a fine book which catches not only the tremendous excitement of this famous encounter that started the Revolutionary War, but also its inevitably more personal aspects" (Glauber in Davison, p. 419). Calling *April Morning* the author's "best to date," Curt Gentry of the *San Francisco Chronicle*, declared, "Here Fast has achieved a rare thing—he has caught with remarkable simplicity that long moment when all men entering their first battle are as Adam, newborn, afraid, astonished that war is really as it is" (Gentry in Davison, p. 419).

—Pamela S. Loy

For More Information

Birnbaum, Louis. *Red Dawn at Lexington*. Boston: Houghton Mifflin, 1986.

Boatner, Mark M. *Encyclopedia of the American Revolution*. New York: David McKay, 1976.

Countryman, Edward. *The American Revolution*. New York: Hill and Wang, 1985.

Davison, Dorothy, ed. *Book Review Digest*. New York: H. W. Wilson, 1962.

Fast, Howard. *April Morning*. New York: Bantam, 1961.

Handlin, Oscar and Lilian. *A Restless People*. Garden City: Anchor Press, 1982.

Hunter, Jeffrey W., ed. *Contemporary Literary Criticism*. Vol. 131. Detroit: Gale Group, 2000.

Macdonald, Andrew. *Howard Fast: A Critical Companion*. Westport: Greenwood Press, 1996.

Martine, James L., ed. *Dictionary of Literary Biography*. Vol. 9. Detroit: Gale Research, 1981.

Mintz, Steven, and Susan Kellogg. *Domestic Revolutions*. New York: Collier Macmillan, 1988.

Nash, Gary B., ed. *The American People*. Vol. 2. New York: Harper & Row, 1990.

Nolan, Jeannette Covert. *The Shot Heard Round the World*. New York: Julian Messner, 1963.

Wright, Louis B. *Life in Colonial America*. New York: Capricorn, 1971.

Candide

by
François Marie Arouet de Voltaire

François Marie Arouet was born in Paris, France, in 1694, the youngest child of a cultured middle-class family. Educated by the Jesuits at the College Louis-Le-Grand, Arouet abandoned the study of law for a literary career. His first work (*Imitation de l'ode du R.P. Lejay sur Sainte Germaine*) was published in 1710. Arouet soon discovered his gift for satire, which would land him in trouble over and over again. In 1717 Arouet was imprisoned in the Bastille for 11 months on the suspicion of having written "J'ai vu" (I have seen), a poem defaming the regent. The true author was eventually revealed, prompting Arouet's release; he left prison with a manuscript for what would be a successful play, *Oedipus* (1718), and a new name, Voltaire, by which he was thereafter known. Over the years, Voltaire experienced literary successes and failures, financial prosperity, another stint of imprisonment in the Bastille, and a period of voluntary exile in England, where he met such literary figures as Jonathan Swift and Alexander Pope. Returning to France in 1728, Voltaire again became the center of controversy when his *Lettres Philosophiques* (1734) were condemned and burned by the parliament of Paris. Fleeing Paris, Voltaire set up residence with his mistress, Madam de Chatelet, first in her home at Cirey, France, later in Belgium. A correspondence with King Frederick the Great of Prussia led to a place at the Prussian court; the friendship ultimately soured, however, and Voltaire left in 1753. After a period of wandering, Voltaire settled with his niece and mistress, Madame Denis, in Switzerland

THE LITERARY WORK

A satiric novel, set in various Old and New World countries during the mid-eighteenth century; published in French (as *Candide, ou l'Optimisme*) in 1759, in English in 1759.

SYNOPSIS

An innocent young man travels the world in search of love and fortune, losing his illusions as he encounters vice in all its forms.

in 1755 (Madame de Chatelet had died in 1749). While living in Switzerland, he was shaken by the news of the earthquake in Lisbon, Portugal, in which thousands were killed. The disaster profoundly affected Voltaire's philosophical and religious views and became an important plot point in his masterpiece, *Candide* (1759). Set during the eighteenth century, *Candide* nonetheless possesses a timeless appeal. Not only does the novel explore the breakdown of established systems; using scathing satire and wit, it also exposes the flaws of optimism—the belief that all happens for the best in this best of all possible worlds.

Events in History at the Time of the Novel

Leibnizian optimism. Although Voltaire satirizes religion, politics, the military, and human vice and folly, his primary target in *Candide* is

François Marie Arouet de Voltaire

the philosophy of optimism, especially as formulated by the German intellectual, Gottfried Wilhelm von Leibniz (1646-1716) and later circulated—in somewhat distorted form—by Leibniz's disciple, Christian Wolff (1679-1754). An accomplished scientist and mathematician, Leibniz was a physicist, a co-discoverer—along with Sir Isaac Newton—of differential calculus, and a student of the great philosophers of the past.

There was a popular philosophy in Leibniz's day called "mechanism," which held that all natural phenomena could be explained by concrete causes and mechanical principles in the material world. Attempting to reconcile a mechanistic interpretation of the universe with belief in a just and benevolent God, Leibniz developed a system of metaphysics—the branch of philosophy concerned with the ultimate nature of reality. In his *Essais de Theodicee* (1710), Leibniz responded to the age-old question "What is the nature of divine Providence and how can one reconcile it with the presence of evil in the world?" By way of response, Leibniz proposed the Principle of Sufficient Reason (there must be some logical reason why anything is as it is), along with two main assumptions: 1) God is good; 2) of all the possible worlds God could have created, he must have chosen the best when he created this one. Since God is perfection, anything he created apart from himself must be imperfect, including the world; yet in his goodness, God would still have created the best of all possible worlds. This positive view explains the name attached to Leibniz's system of thought—optimism. Optimism acknowledges the existence here of evil in the world, recognizing the inevitability of evil occurrences but maintaining that these occurrences have moral value in the greater scheme of things. As a corollary to his system, Leibniz posited that matter was made up of monads, spiritual units rising in gradations from the lowest to highest, with God being the highest monad of all. His belief was that these monads functioned according to a divine, pre-established harmony with the material universe.

Although Voltaire apparently respected Leibniz's breadth of intellect, he rejected out of hand the German thinker's metaphysical system, as he had many others. In a 1737 letter to Frederick the Great of Prussia, Voltaire declared, "All metaphysics contains two things: first, all that which men of good sense know; second, that which they will never know" (Voltaire in Foster, p. 75). News of natural disasters, such as the Lisbon earthquake in 1755, further increased Voltaire's doubts about whether optimism was a valid philosophy of life. *Candide* exposes the ineffectiveness of such thinking, as its hero faces a string of random disastrous events, which no amount of philosophizing ameliorates. During a shipwreck, Candide wishes to save his drowning benefactor Jacques the Anabaptist but "Pangloss the philosopher prevented him, arguing that the Lisbon harbour had been created expressly so that the Anabaptist would be drowned in it. While he was proving this a priori, the ship foundered and everyone perished" (Voltaire, *Candide*, p. 11).

The Lisbon earthquake. Among the historical occurrences that inspired Voltaire's writing of *Candide*, the earthquake in Lisbon, Portugal, on November 1, 1755, was arguably the most important. The earthquake, which modern seismologists estimate as being 8.6 in magnitude, struck between nine and ten in the morning on All Saints' Day, while most of Lisbon's population was in church. Three shocks were apparently felt; the second was especially severe, toppling buildings and contributing to many of the 40,000 or so deaths, half of which occurred in Lisbon alone.

In the wake of the initial disaster, severe aftershocks further rattled the population, then fires and tidal waves ravaged the city. Fire raged through Lisbon for three days after the earthquake, while the huge waves crashed over the quays, causing widespread damage and drown-

Candide

This is indeed a cruel piece of natural philosophy! We shall find it difficult to discover how the laws of movement operate in such fearful disasters *in the best of all possible worlds*—where a hundred thousand ants, our neighbours [the Portuguese], are crushed in a second on our ant-heaps, half dying undoubtedly in inexpressible agonies, beneath débris from which it was impossible to extricate them. . . . What a game of chance human life is! What will the preachers say—especially if the Palace of the Inquisition is left standing! [The reference here is to the tribunal to suppress deviation from the teachings of the Roman Catholic Church; in effect in Portugal from 1536-1820, the Inquistion exiled and even burned offenders at the stake.] I flatter myself that those reverend fathers, the Inquisitors, will have been crushed just like other people. That ought to teach men not to persecute men: for, while a few sanctimonious humbugs are burning a few fanatics, the earth opens and swallows up all alike.

(Voltaire, *Letters*, p. 155)

Gottfried Wilhelm von Leibniz, a German mathematician, philosopher, and statesman. In *Candide*, Voltaire criticizes Leibniz's philosophy of optimism.

ing thousands of people. Three-quarters of Lisbon was leveled, with lasting repercussions for the survivors. A bitter conflict sprang up between the Marques de Pombal, the chief minister of Portugal, and religious orders, specifically the Society of Jesus (also known as the Jesuits), over the cause of the earthquake. Pombal chose to regard the earthquake as a natural disaster and advocated a practical solution to the devastation—namely, burying the dead and feeding the living. The Jesuits, however, preached that the earthquake was God's punishment on the Lisboners for their sins. Displeased, Pombal worked to undermine the Jesuits' preachings about the earthquake and encouraged the rapid rebuilding of the city. Later, he successfully attempted to remove the Jesuits' influence over the government, spearheading their eventual expulsion from Portugal in 1759, the same year *Candide* was published.

The Lisbon earthquake horrified people across Europe. Many thinkers and philosophers reevaluated their positions in the wake of the catastrophe. Voltaire, living in Geneva, Switzerland, at the time, was especially effected; his faith in God was shaken and he found himself questioning the optimistic belief that everything happens for the best. A few weeks after the earthquake, Voltaire wrote to M. Tronchin of Lyons:

PARTIAL EVIL, UNIVERSAL GOOD

The philosophy of optimism was not preached only by Leibniz. He had a disciple, Christian Wolff, who preached it as well, albeit in a form that deviated from Leibniz's own. Voltaire's mistress, Madame du Chatelet, warmed to the philosophy too. Above all, though, the philosophy was touted by Leibniz and by the English poet Alexander Pope, who expressed remarkably similar views in his *Essay on Man* (1733-34):

> All nature is but art, unknown to thee;
> All chance, direction which thou canst not see;
> All discord, harmony not understood;
> All partial evil, universal good:
> And, spite of pride, in erring reason's spite,
> One truth is clear, Whatever is, is right.
>
> (Pope, pp. 2270-71)

Voltaire, who met Pope when visiting England, admired the Englishman's work. Yet *Candide* refuses to subscribe to the notion that "Whatever is, is right," and to this extent can be viewed as a refutation of Pope's views.

Soon after the earthquake, Voltaire wrote his *"Poème sur le désastre de Lisbonne"* (Poem on the disaster of Lisbon), which was published in 1756 and expressed the changes in his philosophy about the nature of good and evil in the world. Translator Roger Pearson notes that "the poem

Candide

begins by asking, first, how such carnage can be in accordance with the eternal laws of a good and free God, and, second, how it can be a punishment from God" (Pearson in Voltaire, *Candide*, p. xix). Unable to find ready answers to his questions, Voltaire concludes his poem in skepticism, slightly leavened with hope.

In *Candide*, the Lisbon earthquake is revisited. The novel's hero and his companion, Dr. Pangloss, find themselves in the city as disaster strikes: "Whirlwinds of flame and ash covered the streets and public squares: houses disintegrated, roofs were upended upon foundations, and foundations crumbled. Thirty thousand inhabitants of both sexes and all ages were crushed beneath the ruins" (*Candide*, p. 12). Candide is injured by falling debris while the ineffectual Pangloss speculates endlessly about the cause of the earthquake. Afterwards, both men are caught up in the Inquisitors' need to punish somebody for the quake, reflecting the real-life dispute between Pombal and the Jesuits.

The Jesuit influence. Organized religion in general takes a beating in *Candide*, but the Jesuits, whose influence extended across continents, bear the brunt of Voltaire's attacks. Founded by Saint Ignatius of Loyola in 1540, the Society of Jesus—a Roman Catholic male religious order—was formed to promote the salvation of all men and women and to foster the spiritual growth of the Jesuits themselves. The order grew rapidly, spreading throughout Catholic Europe in the form of schools and colleges during the sixteenth and seventeenth centuries. Jesuit missionaries also introduced Catholicism to other parts of the world, including Asia, Africa, and Latin America. During their years of dominance, Jesuits made substantial scholarly contributions to philosophy, language studies, and theology; they also served as royal confessors and papal legates.

The Jesuits' involvement in various governments antagonized Protestants as well as political leaders who wished to increase the state's power over the church. Moreover, during the seventeenth century, Jesuit moral theology was frequently attacked by its enemies as lax, unethical, self-serving, and manipulative. The Jesuits became associated with the qualities of craftiness and duplicity; they were accused of allowing the end to justify the means, even though their moral theology strictly forbade this teaching.

By the time of Voltaire, the Jesuits had established colleges attended by the nobility and middle class of Catholic Europe. Voltaire himself was a pupil of the Jesuits; he studied classical languages and literature, philosophy, and theology at the College Louis-Le-Grand, although later in life he would become an implacable foe of the Jesuits. Jesuit missionaries achieved considerable success among native peoples in the Philippines and Latin America, too. However, by the mid-eighteenth century, the Jesuit influence had begun to wane in Europe. Intellectuals and philosophers found Jesuit teachings contrary to their own. As members of the Englightenment era, the intellectuals stressed the power of reason and knowledge gained by empirical experience of the world, while the Jesuits stressed the power of faith and held that God was the source of all knowledge. Kings and ministers likewise found the Jesuits' presence in government a hindrance to the state's increasing control over the church. During the 1750s and 1760s, the rulers of Portugal, Spain, France, and Naples worked successively to suppress the Jesuits on both a national and colonial scale, finally pressuring Pope Clement XIV into stamping out the order worldwide in 1773. Only in Prussia and Russia did the Jesuits continue to work, since neither Frederick the Great nor Catherine the Great had agreed to promulgate the suppression.

In *Candide*, Voltaire casts a jaundiced eye over the Jesuits' accomplishments at home and abroad, depicting them as ultimately self-serving, greedy, and exploitative. In Latin America, Candide's servant, Cacambo, a former servant at the Jesuit College of the Assumption, remarks to his new master: "It's a wonderful way of governing [the Jesuits] have. Their kingdom is already more than three hundred leagues wide, and it's been divided into thirty provinces. Los Padres own everything in it, and the people nothing—a masterpiece of reason and justice" (*Candide*, p. 32).

The Seven Years' War. Voltaire's writing of *Candide* coincided with a bloody international struggle for dominance in the world. Known as the Seven Years' War (1756-63), this conflict was fought in Europe, North America, and India. On one side were France, Austria, Russia, the Germanic state of Saxony, Sweden, and (after 1762) Spain; on the other side, Great Britain and the Germanic states of Prussia and Hanover.

The Seven Years' War stemmed mainly from two conflicts: 1) the colonial rivalry between France and England and 2) the struggle for supremacy in Germany between the house of Austria and the rising kingdom of Prussia. In 1755, after hostilities broke out in North America (the French and Indian War), King George II of England, elector of Hanover, negotiated the Treaty of Westminster with King Frederick II of Prussia, guaranteeing the neutrality of Hanover. In response, France and Austria formed an alliance in 1756 in which they were later joined by Sweden and Russia. The main European phase of the war began in 1757, after Frederick II invaded Saxony and Bohemia.

Early in the war, Prussia's Frederick II enjoyed several victories, although the Austrians defeated him at Kolin and he was forced to withdraw from Bohemia. Meanwhile, Britain and France faced off in several locations, the latter losing many of its overseas possessions, including Louisburg in America and Quebec in Canada. In 1757 the French enjoyed a rare victory at sea over the British by taking Port Mahón in Minorca, Spain, an event that had shocking repercussions in Britain. Admiral John Byng, who had commanded a fleet sent to support the British forces in Minorca, retired to Gibraltar after an indecisive engagement with the French. On his return to England, Byng was arrested and tried by court-martial for cowardice; hostile public opinion and bitterly divisive politics contributed to a verdict of "guilty" and a sentence of execution. Byng was executed by firing squad on the quarter-deck of his own ship, HMS *Monarch*.

After protracted negotiations between the war-weary participants, peace was re-established by two treaties in 1763. The Treaty of Hubertusberg settled hostilities between Prussia, Austria, and Saxony by restoring the pre-war status quo, except in the case of Prussia. It gained status, emerging as a dominant European power. Similarly, the Treaty of Paris—between Britain, France, and Spain—elevated Britain to the status of world's chief colonial empire.

The Seven Years' War provided Voltaire, a Frenchman and a former guest at the Prussian court, with plenty of fodder for a satire. In *Candide*, Voltaire depicts the senselessness of war in general, through the bloody and essentially pointless struggle between the king of the Bulgars and the king of the Abars, whose armies are responsible for equal amounts of carnage. Voltaire also satirized the Byng incident, in which he had been more personally involved, having met the admiral while in England. Distressed to hear of Byng's court-martial, Voltaire interceded with a letter written by his friend the Duc de Richelieu; the letter praised Byng's conduct and character and Voltaire had it sent to the admiral himself in hopes of gaining clemency for him. But the effort failed and Byng was executed. All Voltaire could do was immortalize the incident, as he did in *Candide* with the scathing remark, "[I]n this country it is considered a good thing to kill an admiral from time to time to encourage the others" (*Candide*, p. 68).

A RAW DEAL

In self-defense, Byng explained at his trial reasons for his behavior at Minorca. "Every person there concluded the place lost, and all relief impracticable.... But why (it may be asked) was not Minorca at this time relieved? I answer, because I was not sent in time enough to prevent the enemy's landing, and that when I was sent, I was not strong enough to beat the enemy's fleet.... Had I been defeated, what refuge would have been left for the shattered fleet, what security for Gibraltar [at the time a British colony in southern Spain"] (Byng in Tunstall, pp. 233-34). Further confirmation of his good character could be found in the letter about him that Voltaire received from the Duc de Richelieu: "Whatever I have seen or heard of him does him honour. He ought not to be attacked in this manner when he has been defeated after doing all that could be expected of him.... All Admiral Byng's manoeuvres were excellent, the two fleets being equal... but [ours, the French] better equipped.... Had the English persisted in the engagement, they would have lost their entire fleet" (Richelieu in Tunstall, p. 251). Before being executed, Byng handed over a note to the marshal, declaring his innocence, identifying himself as a scapegoat for the military loss. At 12:00 P.M., Byng was shot to death on the quarterdeck of the *Monarque*. In front of his remains, which were buried in the family vault, is an inscription:

To the Perpetual Disgrace
Of Publick Justice,
The Honourable John Byng, Esq.,
Admiral of the Blue,
Fell a Martyr to Political Persecution,
May 14 in the Year MDCCLVII [1757]
When Bravery and Loyalty
Were Insufficient Securities
For the Life and Honour
Of a Naval Officer

[Byng family in Tunstall, p. 286)

The Novel in Focus

The plot. The novel, which purports to be translated from the writings—in German—of the late Dr. Ralph, begins by relating the youth of Candide, an innocent young man rumored to be

Engraving depicting the Lisbon earthquake of 1755, one of the events portrayed in *Candide*.

the illegitimate nephew of Baron Thunder-ten-tronckh of Westphalia, a province in Germany. Reared in the Baron's household, Candide grows up with the Baron's own children and studies with the family tutor, Dr. Pangloss, a disciple of Leibniz, who teaches him the satirically named discipline of metaphysico-theological-cosmocodology. Pangloss asserts, and Candide believes, that all things happen for the best in this best of all possible worlds.

This dictum is put to the test when Candide falls in love with the baron's daughter, Cunégonde. Observing the young people kissing behind a screen, the baron expels Candide from his estate. Penniless and hungry, Candide is conscripted into the king of the Bulgars' army and forced to become a soldier, after which he suffers severe birchings (floggings) for failed maneuvers and perceived disobedience. After a horrendous battle between the king of Bulgaria and the king of Abares, Candide deserts and spends some time as a beggar. He is eventually taken in by Jacques, a kindly Anabaptist (Protestant radical advocating baptism and church membership for adult believers only). The next day, Candide again meets Dr. Pangloss, now a beggar himself and suffering from the pox. Pangloss informs Candide of the sack of Baron Thunder-ten-tronckh's castle during the war and the brutal deaths of the entire family, including Cunégonde, at the hands of Bulgar soldiers. Jacques takes Pangloss into his household as well and sees to his being cured of his disease.

Traveling to Lisbon on business, Jacques, Candide, and Pangloss are shipwrecked just off the coast of Portugal. Jacques drowns, but Candide and Pangloss are among the wreck's few survivors. The two reach Lisbon just as a great earthquake devastates the city, killing 30,000 people. The Inquisition in Portugal decides to punish sinners whose wickedness may have brought about the earthquake by holding an auto-da-fé (public execution for their penalties). Candide and Pangloss are among those accused; the former is flogged, the latter hanged, while other victims are burned to death at the stake.

An old woman tends to Candide's injuries, and conveys him to a country house, where he is reunited with Cunégonde who, contrary to Pangloss's report, survived the Bulgar attack. Presently she is the kept woman of two men (an Inquisitor and a Jew), although she has denied both her sexual favors. Cunégonde is overjoyed to see Candide. Her two men arrive, interrupting the reunion, and Candide kills them both. Candide, Cunégonde, and the old woman flee to Cadiz, Spain, but find themselves robbed of the gold and jewels Cunégonde had brought with her. The trio sail for Paraguay in Latin America, where Candide hopes to join the Spanish army, now engaged in fighting the Jesuits. During the voyage, the old woman tells her story, revealing that she was Pope Urban X's daughter and the Princess of Palestrina (in Italy), but had suffered many misfortunes—being captured by pirates, sold into slavery, and raped and mutilated by various captors before becoming Cunégonde's servant.

The trio arrive in Buenos Aires, where the governor falls in love with Cunégonde. Scheming to win her for himself, he arranges to have Candide accused of several crimes, including robbery and murder. Candide, accompanied by his faithful servant Cacambo, is obliged to flee, leaving Cunégonde and the old woman behind. Candide and Cacambo reach Paraguay and decide to fight *for* the Jesuits, recognizing this as the more practical and profitable alternative. At a border post, they meet the Jesuit commander, who turns out to be Cunégonde's brother. The new baron had also miraculously survived the attack on the palace, thanks to the ministrations of the Jesuits, who educated him for their order. At first pleased to see each other, Candide and the baron quarrel after the latter learns Candide wishes to marry Cunégonde; they come to blows and Candide, fearing he has killed the baron, again flees with Cacambo.

Master and servant have several adventures together. Captured by the Oreillons, a savage tribe of cannibalistic natives, they are released once they prove they are not Jesuits. Candide and Cacambo then find their way to Eldorado, a legendary land where gold and jewels have no monetary value, faith in the deity does not require organized religion, and the inhabitants all live in peace and harmony. Love for Cunégonde and the desire for worldly success eventually impel Candide to leave Eldorado; at Candide's request, the king of Eldorado gives him 100 sheep, which the young man loads with gold and jewels. On the arduous journey back to the world, Candide and Cacambo experience more misfortunes, eventually losing all but two of their sheep and the wealth they carried. Reaching Surinam, Candide is so distraught by the sight of a black slave, maimed by labor in a sugar mill and a failed escape attempt, that he vows to renounce Pangloss's philosophy of optimism.

While trying to book passage to Buenos Aires, Candide is further devastated by the news that Cunégonde has become the governor's mistress. He dispatches Cacambo to Buenos Aires with jewels to bribe the governor into giving up Cunégonde. Candide plans to wait for his servant's return in Venice and arranges passage there for himself and his two sheep. An unscrupulous Dutch captain steals the sheep and sails away with them, leaving Candide stranded. Unable to gain redress from the law, an embittered Candide sails for Bordeaux, France; during the voyage he acquires a new companion, Martin the scholar, chosen on the basis of his own misfortunes and disgust with life.

Together, Candide and Martin embark upon a new sequence of adventures. Candide's optimism is somewhat restored by the recovery of one of his Eldorado sheep, rescued when the Dutch captain's ship is sunk during a fierce sea battle. On arriving in France, Candide samples Parisian high society, including the theater and gambling houses. France likewise proves full of rogues, and they trick Candide out of more of his wealth. Resuming his travels with Martin, Candide sails on a Dutch ship to Portsmouth, England, where he witnesses the execution of an English admiral by his own countrymen. Horrified by the sight, Candide refuses to go ashore and negotiates with the ship's master to convey him to Venice at the earliest opportunity.

In Venice, Candide finds no sign of Cacambo or Cunégonde, although he sees still more examples of human vice and folly. He does meet Paquette, Cunégonde's maid from Westphalia, who is now the mistress of a monk named Brother Giroflee; both are unhappy with their situation and Candide gives them some money in hopes of improving their lot. Finally, Candide again encounters Cacambo. On the way to Venice, he and Cunégonde were captured and enslaved by Turks. Cunégonde, who by now has lost her looks, is working as the Prince of Transylvania's dishwasher in Constantinople. Candide buys Cacambo's freedom and, with his companions, boards a Venetian galley to Constantinople. Among the galley slaves, the astonished Candide finds Pangloss and Baron Thunder-ten-trockh; the former had escaped death in Lisbon because of an incompetent hangman, the latter had survived the wound Candide had inflicted. Candide buys the freedom of Pangloss and the baron as well, and, after the ship docks, the entire company hurries to ransom Cunégonde and the old woman from the Turks.

Reunited with his sweetheart, Candide loyally resolves to marry her, although she has lost her beauty and he no longer desires her. The baron continues to oppose the marriage on the grounds of social inequality, whereupon Candide has him taken back to the galleys. After his marriage,

Candide and his companions, later joined by Paquette and Brother Giroflee, settle down, but not happily, on a small farm; boredom makes everybody quarrelsome and discontented. Seeking solutions to their problems, Candide, Pangloss, and Martin call upon a neighbor, a dervish reputed to be a great philosopher, but he refuses to discuss the nature of good and evil with them and slams the door in their faces. On their way back to the farm, the trio meets a contented Turkish orange-grower who recommends work as a panacea for "three great evils: boredom, vice, and need" (*Candide*, p. 92). Taking this lesson to heart, Candide and his companions decide to develop their particular talents for the good of their little household. The farm begins to thrive, as each member does his or her best to be useful, and Candide decides that the best thing one can do is to cultivate one's own garden.

The limits of philosophy. Much has been written about the nature of Candide's quest and the timeless examples of human vice and folly he encounters. The physical terrain Candide travels parallels his mental journey; the idealistic hero learns more with each country he visits, experiencing countless hardships before formulating a philosophy that allows him to make peace with an imperfect world.

Candide (from the Latin *candidus*, meaning "white") begins as a sheltered innocent, absorbing even the most absurd teachings of Dr. Pangloss without question:

> Pangloss taught metaphysico-theological-cosmocodology. He could prove wonderfully that there is no effect without cause that, in this best of all possible worlds, His Lordship the Baron's castle was the most beautiful of castles and Madam the best of all possible baronesses. . . . Candide would listen attentively, and innocently he would believe.
> (*Candide*, p. 2)

Candide's innocence dissipates quickly enough, however. As shown, the young man's expulsion from the castle after his love for Cunégonde is discovered, initiates a hazardous, global adventure during which Candide experiences or witnesses various atrocities and disasters, including murder, rape, religious persecution, storms, shipwrecks, earthquakes, disease, and slavery. There is no fair or logical reason underlying any of these occurrences, yet Pangloss, who accompanies Candide on the early phases of his journey, continues to parrot the same metaphysical declarations about "the best of all possible worlds." Although Pangloss himself suffers numerous cruelties, including a brush with death at the hands of the Inquisition, he refuses to recant or reevaluate his optimistic stance even at the novel's end:

> I still feel now as I did at the outset . . . I am a philosopher after all. It wouldn't do for me to go back on what I said before, what with Leibniz not being able to be wrong, and pre-established harmony being the finest thing in the world.
> (*Candide*, p. 87)

But if Pangloss's adherence to optimism, in the face of injustice and misery, becomes increasingly absurd, the pessimistic, even nihilistic, philosophy of Martin, another of Candide's companions, proves just as limited in outlook. A self-professed Manichean—one who believes, like the Persian sage Mani, that the universe is governed by two equal forces of Good and Evil—Martin initially seems to have a surer grasp on the way the world works than Candide or Pangloss. When Candide wistfully asks if men have always been "feeble, fickle, envious, gluttonous, drunken, avaricious, ambitious, bloodthirsty, slanderous, debauched, fanatical, hypocritical, and stupid," Martin inquires why Candide should suppose men to have changed their character, when animals, such as hawks, have not changed theirs (*Candide*, p. 47). As the pair travel through Europe, Martin's cynicism about the human race continues to prove justified. However, Martin is proved wrong in one very significant instance, after he predicts that Candide's servant Cacambo, entrusted with wealth and the task of bringing Cunégonde to Venice, will abscond with Candide's jewels and mistress himself. Cacambo instead remains true to his master, his return to Candide's side delayed not because of greed and self-interest but because of his capture and enslavement by pirates.

Ultimately, as Voltaire sees it, neither Leibnizian optimism nor Manichean pessimism adequately explains how humankind and the universe work. In fact, metaphysical philosophy in general fails to provide Candide and his companions with answers once they settle down in a state of peevish discontent after their wanderings. A learned philosopher in the neighborhood refuses to discourse with them about the nature of Good and Evil; instead, a kindly orange-grower directs the squabbling travelers towards the practical plan of developing their individual talents for the benefit of their community and impresses them with the necessity of cultivating their garden. Even gloomy Martin acquiesces in this plan, remarking, "Let's get down to work and stop all this philosophizing. . . . It's the only way to make life bearable" (*Candide*, p. 92).

While thwarted love and other misfortune initially spur Candide on his journey, he ultimately continues to travel as much to educate himself in the ways of the world. The emphasis on education in *Candide* reflects the philosophical, scientific, and political changes sweeping through Europe during the seventeenth and eighteenth centuries. These changes were all part of the larger intellectual movement often referred to as the Enlightenment. Rather than accepting established tenets of thought without question, scholars and thinkers began to reevaluate politics and, especially, religion in the light of individual freedoms as well as knowledge gained through experience. Such works as Isaac Newton's *Principia* (1687) posited the idea of the natural world as an orderly place governed by universal mathematical principles. By the time of *Candide*'s composition, European intellectual society had become associated with such qualities as good sense, a belief in reason and moderation, and empirical knowledge. It is to common sense and empiricism that Voltaire seems to appeal in *Candide*, even as he rejects the more exotic metaphysical systems and abstruse reasonings that were another end product of the Enlightenment. Pearson writes, "It is education, then, the process of enlightenment, which gives shape to experience, and not only for Candide" but for his companions, and by extension, the novel's readers as well (*Candide*, p. xxii).

Sources and literary context. Voltaire's disillusionment with Leibnizian optimism was the primary impetus behind *Candide*. One character, Dr. Pangloss, exemplifies all the shortcomings of that philosophy as he attempts to explain away all injustice, misery, and wretchedness in the world as part of some grand metaphysical plan. Other characters meanwhile seem based on recognizable types in romantic or picaresque literature: an innocent, questing hero; a high-born beloved; arrogant enemies; and faithful companions. Voltaire was probably inspired by the writings of his British contemporaries Jonathan Swift (see **Gulliver's Travels** and **A Modest Proposal**, also in *Literature and Its Times*) and by Alexander Pope, whom he met while living abroad in England. Parallels to Samuel Johnson's *Rasselas*, also published in 1759, may be detected too. Other possible influences are the writings of Rabelais, Boccaccio, and Cervantes (see **Don Quixote** and **The Little Gypsy Girl** also in *Literature and Its Times*).

Candide satirizes elements of various types of writing, including romances, travel narratives, and picaresque novels. As for the work itself, *Candide* probably fits best in the genre of *conte philosophique*, or philosophical tales, since it blends a brief fictional narrative with searing commentary on the nature of philosophy. The philosophical tale, says translator Roger Pearson, was a perfect vehicle for such a skeptical author, who relied on experience rather than theory. "Deeply suspicious of metaphysics and 'systems', [Voltaire] was constantly appealing to the facts: fiction, paradoxically, allowed him to show the ways in which the muddle and miseries of life could not be reduced to neat, abstract theories" (Pearson in Voltaire, *Candide,* pp. viii-ix).

Publication and reception. The publication of *Candide* is a fascinating story in itself. On the 15th and 16th of January 1759, unbound copies were quietly sent from Geneva to various cities: Paris received 1,000 copies, while Amsterdam, London, and Brussels also received sizable shipments. The manuscripts were bound at their respective destinations and published on a previously agreed-upon date. The intent was to circulate as many copies as possible throughout Europe, before either pirated, corrupted editions could appear or the authorities could suppress Voltaire's subversive work. The plan succeeded. Although the Vatican placed *Candide* on its index of forbidden books on May 24, 1762, the tale had been in wide circulation for over three years by then. Owing to the inflammatory nature of the ideas in *Candide*, Voltaire himself maintained a discreet silence about the work during its composition. He did not even mention it in correspondence until after its publication and, for a time, denied authorship. His silence may have helped him evade unpleasant legal consequences—the authorities in Paris and Geneva attempted to suppress the distribution of *Candide* but took no action against Voltaire himself.

Contemporary opinions were sharply divided on *Candide*. Conservatives roundly condemned it; Genevan pastors termed it "full of dangerous principles concerning religion and tending to moral deprivation" (Mason, p. 14). Other detractors complained that, despite its wit and insight, *Candide*'s vision was ultimately too despairing. France's Madame de Stael observed that *Candide* appears to be written "by a being of a different order from ourselves, insensible to our condition, well pleased with our sufferings, and laughing like a demon or an ape at the miseries of that human species with which he has nothing in common" (de Stael in Foster, p. 91). One of the harshest criticisms of both work and author may have come from the English Romantic poet William Wordsworth, who termed *Candide* "this dull product of a scoffer's pen, / Impure conceits discharging from a heart / Hardened by impious pride!" (Wordsworth in Foster, p. 92).

The reading public disagreed. In France and other countries, people devoured the book, which went through over 17 editions in its first year of publication. The duc de la Vallière informed Voltaire, "Never perhaps has a book sold so briskly" (de la Vallière in Mason, p. 14). Voltaire's friend, Nicholas Claude Thierot, was similarly enthusiastic, writing to the author, "Oh most cherished *Candide*, most excellent author and inventor of quips and jests! Your book is snatched from hand to hand. It so delights the heart that those who usually laugh with tight lips are forced to laugh with open mouths" (Thierot in Foster, p. 89). England's critic James Boswell declared that *Candide*'s attempt to "refute the system of Optimism" was "accomplished with brilliant success" (Boswell in Foster, p. 91). The success of *Candide* continued well into the nineteenth century; William Hazlitt, the British critic, wrote, "*Candide* is a masterpiece of wit. . . . It is in the most perfect keeping, and without any appearance of effort. Every sentence tells, and the whole reads like one sentence" (Hazlitt in Foster, pp. 92-93).

—Pamela S. Loy

For More Information

Ayer, A. J. *Voltaire*. New York: Random House, 1986.

Foster, Milton P., ed. *Voltaire's Candide and the Critics*. Belmont: Wadsworth, 1962.

Knapp, Bettina L. *Voltaire Revisited*. New York: Twayne, 2000.

Manceron, Claude. *Twilight of the Old Order*. Trans. Patricia Wolf. New York: Alfred A. Knopf, 1977.

Mason, Haydn. *Candide: Optimism Demolished*. New York: Twayne, 1992.

Pearson, Roger. *The Fables of Reason: A Study of Voltaire's Contes Philosophiques*. Oxford: Clarendon Press, 1993.

Pope, Alexander. "Essay on Man." In *The Norton Anthology of English Literature*. Vol. 1. Ed. M. H. Abrams. New York: W. W. Norton, 1986.

Roche, Daniel. *France in the Enlightenment*. Cambridge: Harvard University Press, 1998.

Tunstall, Brian. *Admiral Byng and the Loss of Minorca*. London: Philip Allan, 1928.

Voltaire. *Candide and Other Stories*. Trans. Roger Pearson. New York: Alfred A. Knopf, 1990.

———. *Voltaire in His Letters*. Trans. S. G. Tallentyre. New York: G. P. Putnam's Sons, 1919.

Walsh, Thomas, ed. *Readings on Candide*. San Diego: Greenhaven, 2001.

A Christmas Carol

by
Charles Dickens

Charles Dickens was born in 1812, in Portsea, England, as the second child of John Dickens, a middle-class naval clerk. At 11, Dickens had his formal education interrupted; his father was too debt-ridden to afford it. At 12, Dickens went to work in a shoe-blacking warehouse. Soon after, John Dickens's debt landed him in Marshalsea prison. Though his father was in prison for only three months, and Dickens returned to school shortly after, the experience proved formative: Dickens, isolated and ashamed during this time, resolved to make a success of himself. In quick order, he went from office boy, to parliamentary reporter, to a writer of short stories or "sketches" under his long-lasting pseudonym "Boz." *Sketches by Boz*, published when Dickens was just 24, heralded the arrival of a new talent. This was followed by the *Posthumous Papers of the Pickwick Club* (1836-37), which made "Boz" and his characters famous. The novel established the combination of comedy and social critique that would emerge in Dickens's next stories, up to and including *A Christmas Carol*.

Events in History at the Time the Story Takes Place

The "Hungry '40s." *A Christmas Carol* occurs during the "Hungry Forties," a time of economic depression, high unemployment, failed crops, starvation, and disease. During the period from 1815 to 1842, the standard of living for the middle classes had improved dramatically and the rich had held their own, while the working

> **THE LITERARY WORK**
>
> A ghost story set in London during the Christmas season of 1843; published in 1843.
>
> **SYNOPSIS**
>
> Four ghosts transform Ebenezer Scrooge from a hard-hearted Victorian businessperson into a charitable man who knows how to keep the spirit of Christmas.

classes saw their standard of living at best hold steady—perhaps decline. In 1842 public charities assisted 15 percent of the population, and private ones supported a great many more. According to Richard D. Altick, the first decade of Queen Victoria's reign (1837-47) was "the most harrowing and dangerous of the entire century" (Altick, p. 89). Despair and disenfranchisement (the working classes could not vote) fueled a growing radicalism called "chartism," its name derived from a "People's Charter" presented to Parliament. Chartism led to strikes and riots in 1839, 1842, and 1848, after which it weakened. On the whole, Dickens sympathized with the chartists, who advocated the following six points in their "People's Charter":

1. Annual meetings of Parliament
2. The right to vote for all men
3. Removal of property qualifications for men running for the House of Commons
4. Secret ballots

A Christmas Carol

Charles Dickens

5. Equally divided electoral districts
6. Salaries for members of Parliament

An underlying social belief in unfettered market forces prevented the government from putting any brakes on them to ease the miseries of the poor. Utilitarianism, a complex philosophy emphasizing the good of society rather than the individual, promoted laissez-faire economics. Ebenezer Scrooge's comment that "It's enough for a man to understand his own business, and not to interfere with other people's" is in tune with this philosophy (Dickens, *A Christmas Carol*, p. 51). Compounding the ill effects of utilitarianism was a fear that the poor were reproducing too quickly. Thomas Malthus (1766-1834) had warned of the dangers of overpopulation in his *Essay on the Principles of Population* (1803). *A Christmas Carol*'s Scrooge makes the Malthusian remark that if the poor would rather die than enter a state institution, "they had better do it, and decrease the surplus population" (*A Christmas Carol*, p. 51).

The New Poor Law. Paradoxically the laws that purported to help the poor increased their miseries. Dickens was a vigorous critic of the "New Poor Law," instituted in 1834, a law founded on utilitarian principles. His second novel, **Oliver Twist** (1837-39; also in *Literature and Its Times*), opens in a poorhouse, or "workhouse," and attacks the system that supports it. In *A Christmas Carol*, when a gentleman soliciting charity says to Ebenezer Scrooge, "Many thousands are in want of common necessaries; hundreds of thousands are in want of common comforts," Scrooge delivers his ironic reply for managing the poor: "Are there no prisons? . . . Are they [the workhouses] still in operation? . . . The Treadmill and the Poor Law are in full vigour then?" (*A Christmas Carol*, pp. 50-51). The Poor Law Amendment reorganized aid for the poor by providing support for the old and handicapped in their own homes, while requiring everyone else to enter a workhouse. The workhouse meant severe privation: jobs were monotonous, food scanty, and families divided. As Edgar Johnson comments on the new Poor Law, "In theory . . . [it] distinguished between the helpless and the man or woman who could work but wouldn't. In practice, however, it mingled the idler, tramp, drunkard, and prostitute in the same workhouse with the aged, ill, and infirm, and with the foundling children. The children suffered worst of all" (Johnson, p. 275).

Poor children: "ragged schools" and child labor. Dickens was keenly sensitive to the plight of poor children, and his awareness was heightened by two important events that preceded the writing of *A Christmas Carol*. In September 1843, Dickens visited a "ragged school," a charity school for the poorest children. While grateful that the school existed, Dickens was shocked by the "dire neglect of soul and body exhibited among these children," and convinced by the sight that "in the prodigious misery and ignorance of the swarming masses of mankind in England, the seeds of its certain ruin are sown" (Dickens in Johnson, p. 461).

That same year the Children's Employment Commission reported on the situation of children in manufacturing and the trades. Children worked in dangerous factories and cottage industries with few breaks for play, education, or even sleep. Earlier the Commission had reported that children as young as five worked up to 14 hours a day in the mines, with children from the workhouse receiving the worst jobs. Many Victorians were shocked. Dickens responded with fury, and described himself as "stricken down" (Dickens, *The Letters*, Vol. 3, p. 459). He pledged to react with the force of a "sledge hammer" (Dickens, *The Letters*, Vol. 3, p. 461). *A Christmas Carol* may be that hammer. In his story, Dickens depicts "Ignorance" and "Want" as two small and ragged children, hiding under the gown of Christmas Present. He also designates the crippled child, Tiny Tim, as an agent of redemption. Tiny Tim, who is, as his father states, "as good as gold," thaws Scrooge's icy heart, and draws the miser into a paternal relationship with the boy and his family (*A Christmas Carol*, p. 94).

Report on Child Labor, 1843

The Commission made the following comments on the state of laboring children. *On the age of child workers*: "That instances occur in which Children begin to work as early as three or four years of age; not infrequently at five, and between five and six; while, in general, regular employment commences between seven and eight; the great majority of the Children having begun to work before they are nine." *On the hours of work*: "in some few instances the regular hours of work do not exceed ten, exclusive of the time allowed for meals; sometimes they are eleven, but more commonly twelve; and in great numbers of instances the employment is continued for fifteen, sixteen, and even eighteen hours consecutively." *On the injuriousness of the work*: "from the early ages at which the great majority commence work, from their long hours of work, and from the insufficiency of their food and clothing, their 'bodily health' is seriously and generally injured; they are for the most part stunted in growth, their aspect being pale, delicate, and sickly, and they present altogether the appearance of a race which has suffered general physical deterioration."

(*Second Report* in Mitchell, pp. 43-44)

The Novel in Focus

The plot. "A Christmas Carol" opens on Christmas Eve, when Ebenezer Scrooge is visited by the ghost of his dead business partner, Jacob Marley. The restless ghost tells Scrooge that unless he changes his ways, he too will be condemned to wander the earth, tormented by human misery, fettered by a chain of his own making. Scrooge must learn what Jacob Marley learnt too late; that his business is not money-making, but "mankind" (*A Christmas Carol*, p. 62). As Marley's ghost states, "Mankind was my business. The common welfare was my business; charity, mercy, forbearance, and benevolence, were, all, my business" (*A Christmas Carol*, p. 62). Scrooge's chance to avoid Marley's fate will come through the visits of three ghosts.

The Ghost of Christmas Past makes Scrooge revisit the Christmases of his youth. In a schoolroom, young Scrooge sits forlorn during the Christmas holidays, entertained only by books and his imagination. At a later Christmas, in the same schoolroom, Scrooge's loneliness is interrupted by the arrival of his young sister, who comes to bring him home. The ghost prompts Scrooge to remember that this adored sister, now dead, has a living nephew (whom Scrooge has ignored). The ghost then shows Scrooge his past employer making merry with his family and clerks at Christmas time; this sight leads Scrooge to consider his own, mistreated, clerk. The next memory is of Scrooge's young fiancée, breaking her engagement to him, because he has become mesmerized by money: "I have seen your nobler aspirations fall off one by one, until the master-passion, Gain, engrosses you" (*A Christmas Carol*, p. 79). Finally the ghost shows Scrooge this same woman, happily married and surrounded by her children on the very night, seven years ago, that Jacob Marley died and that Scrooge spent alone in his office.

The Ghost of Christmas Present shows Scrooge various Christmas festivities, beginning with those

UTILITARIANISM

Jeremy Bentham (1748-1832), the father of utilitarianism, believed that policy should be determined by a "felicific calculus," which measured the greatest happiness for the greatest number of people. He and his disciples, who included John Stuart Mill (1806-1873) in his early career, advocated a hands-off approach to the economy, but a guiding hand in areas of social policy. Utilitarianism was characterized by a reliance on rational thought, and a corresponding disdain for the abstract and imaginative. Though utilitarianism was a bedrock Victorian philosophy, it attracted notable critics, including John Stuart Mill himself and Charles Dickens. Dickens's lengthiest critique is his novel *Hard Times* (1854), in which he attacks what he saw as the excess rationality of utilitarianism. As Dickens wrote, "My satire is against those who see figures and averages, and nothing else—the representatives of the wickedest and most enormous vice of this time—the men who, through long years to come, will do more to damage the real useful truths of political economy than I could do (if I tried) in my whole life" (Dickens, *Hard Times*, p. 277). In contrast to people so fixated on "figures and averages," Dickens takes pains in *A Christmas Carol* to separate the term *profit* in its business sense from its more general meaning. Scrooge's nephew articulates the difference: "There are many things from which I might have derived good, by which I have not profited . . . Christmas among the rest" (*A Christmas Carol*, pp. 48-49).

A Christmas Carol

at his clerk's house. The large Cratchit family enjoy simple holiday pleasures. Dressed in their best clothes, happy to be together, they share a scanty feast of goose and pudding. One child, Tiny Tim, walks with a crutch and an iron frame supporting his limbs. Scrooge asks the ghost whether Tiny Tim will live; the ghost says that if nothing changes, he will not. When Scrooge asks that Tiny Tim be spared, the ghost repeats Scrooge's own words to him: "If he be like to die, he had better do it, and decrease the surplus population" (*A Christmas Carol*, p. 97). The ghost then comments: "It may be, that in the sight of Heaven, you are more worthless and less fit to live than millions like this poor man's child" (*A Christmas Carol*, p. 97). The ghost whisks Scrooge past many who are poor, yet merry. At Scrooge's nephew's house, Scrooge hears a companionable group discussing his refusal to come for Christmas dinner. When the party amuses itself with music and games, Scrooge becomes engrossed, even if some of the fun is at his expense. The ghost, intent on showing Scrooge the joy the arrival of Christmas can bring to all people, takes him again on a pilgrimage: "In almshouse, hospital, and jail, in misery's every refuge, where vain man in his little brief authority had not made fast the door, and barred the Spirit out, he left his blessing, and taught Scrooge his precepts" (*A Christmas Carol*, p. 107). Finally, the ghost reveals to Scrooge a horrible sight. Hiding under the Spirit's robes are two dejected and degraded children:

> "They are Man's," said the Spirit.... "And they cling to me, appealing from their fathers. This boy is Ignorance. This girl is Want. Beware them both, and all of their degree, but most of all beware this boy, for on his brow I see that written which is Doom, unless the writing be erased."
>
> (*A Christmas Carol*, p. 108)

BOB CRATCHIT'S WAGES

Bob Cratchit earns 15 shillings a week as Scrooge's clerk. The Cratchits' Christmas dinner would take almost all of a week's salary (Hearn, p. 118). Though Bob Cratchit's job places him in the lower middle class, his income is below that of most members of the working classes, who, according to Gertrude Himmelfarb, would have made between 18 and 24 shillings per week (Himmelfarb, p. 463). The Victorians referred to people like the Cratchits—industrious and happy—as the "deserving poor" (Himmelfarb p. 465).

The Ghost of Christmas Yet to Come gestures rather than speaks. He shows Scrooge the reactions of people to the death of an unidentified man, reactions ranging from indifference, to greed, to pleasure. When Scrooge begs to be shown tenderness in relation to death, the ghost takes him to the house of the Cratchits, who are mourning Tiny Tim. Bob Cratchit is consoled by the example his son set while alive: "I know, my dears, that when we recollect how patient and how mild he was; although he was a little, little child; we shall not quarrel easily among ourselves, and forget poor Tiny Tim in doing it" (*A Christmas Carol*, p. 123). At last, the specter brings Ebenezer Scrooge to the grave of the unidentified man. There Scrooge reads his own name, and promises to change: "I will honour Christmas in my heart, and try to keep it all the year. I will live in the Past, the Present, and the Future. The Spirits of all Three shall strive within me" (*A Christmas Carol*, p. 126).

Christmas Day finds Scrooge a changed man, full of giddiness and good intentions. He begins his new life by sending an anonymous gift—the largest turkey around—to the Cratchits. Then he promises a charitable donation to a gentleman he had previously rebuffed. For Christmas dinner, Scrooge accepts an invitation, previously declined, to his nephew's house. The day after Christmas, Scrooge starts on a new footing with his clerk, pledging to assist him and his family. All these promises Scrooge keeps, becoming "as good a friend, as good a master, and as good a man, as the good old city knew," and to Tiny Tim, who lives, a "second father" (*A Christmas Carol*, p. 133).

A Christmas revival. The Ghost of Christmas Present, described and illustrated as dressed in a green robe with a holly wreath on its head, appears jovial and magnanimous, a source of plenty. The spirit transforms Scrooge's room:

> The walls and ceiling were so hung with living green, that it looked like a perfect grove, from every part of which, bright gleaming berries glistened. The crisp leaves of holly, mistletoe, and ivy reflected back the light.... Heaped up on the floor... were turkeys, geese, game, poultry, brawn, great joints of meat, suckling-pigs, long wreaths of sausages, mince-pies, plum-puddings, barrels of oysters, red-hot chestnuts, cherry-cheeked apples, juicy oranges, luscious pears, immense twelfth-cakes, and seething bowls of punch.
>
> (*A Christmas Carol*, p. 86)

Scrooge, who is used to dining on meager fare alone, will learn that food and festivity are an intrinsic part of the Christmas season.

For Victorian reviewers and readers, the most important section of *A Christmas Carol* was its treatment of Christmas Present, its depiction of their own world and times (Davis, p. 41). In this book, published specifically for the Christmas season of 1843, Dickens was not merely descriptive but prescriptive as well—showing people how to celebrate Christmas in traditional ways that had mostly vanished by the nineteenth century.

December 25th began as a Christian feast day in celebration of the birth of Jesus Christ at the beginning of the fourth century. Christmas evolved from a mixture of pagan holidays occurring around the winter solstice and the new year, including the Roman Saturnalia (a period of feasting and license that included the exchange of presents) and the Saxon Yule (a feast honoring the sun—hence the yule logs—burned at Christmas—in which evergreens were used for decoration). Greenery sacred to the ancient priestly Druids, such as holly and mistletoe, were incorporated into the new feast day, and given Christian meaning. Holly, for example, alive in the midst of winter with its green leaves and red berries in sets of three, became variously a symbol of hope, the Christ child himself, and the Holy Trinity.

Over the centuries, Christmas grew from a feast day to the twelve days of Christmas, culminating with the Epiphany on January 6, a day commemorating the revelation of Christ to the Magi, the wise men from the East who came to Bethlehem to pay their respects to the baby Jesus. During this festival, plays were performed and Christmas carols sung. With the Puritan ascendancy in England (1649-60), however, came the death of the medieval Christmas. Oliver Cromwell and the Puritans forbade the celebration of Christmas, charging that it reeked of paganism. Even the restoration of the monarchy in 1660 did not fully restore the old Christmas. By the nineteenth-century Victorian era, many of the ancient rites were no longer remembered or followed, though some survived in the countryside.

The Victorians, however, were intent on resurrecting Christmas traditions, and in doing so they were aided by some of their favorite writers, including the British writer Sir Walter Scott (1771-1832) and the American writer Washington Irving (1783-1859). Scott's *Marmion* (1808) and Irving's *Sketch Book* (1819-20) both con-

Illustration by Arthur Rackham from a 1915 edition of *A Christmas Carol*.

tained memorable scenes of a rural Christmas. It is Dickens's *A Christmas Carol*, though, which is "the most significant Christmas text of the nineteenth century" (Marling, p. 27). The Spirit of Christmas Present, a "jolly Giant," is Father

WHAT AILS TINY TIM?

Various critics have proposed that Tiny Tim was afflicted with tuberculosis. At the time of *A Christmas Carol*, the death rate from this disease had climbed to one in 100 in England. Some 50 percent of the population is said to have been affected by the disease, which was then the scourge of all Europe (Callahan, p. 214). In "Tiny Tim: The Child with a Crippling Fatal Illness," Charles W. Callahan Jr. makes the case that Tiny Tim's symptoms were consistent with those of tuberculosis, which could lead to infections in the bones and joints. Pott's disease, or tuberculosis of the spine, could cause paralysis in the legs. Callahan also points out that Tiny Tim's death could be averted by better care—a stay at a sanitarium, for example, which would have placed the disease in remission (Callahan, p. 215).

A Christmas Carol

Christmas himself, a figure heralding secular good cheer, accompanied by his usual yule log, Christmas punch, holly, and mistletoe (*A Christmas Carol*, p. 86). The ghost reveals to Scrooge the basic components of a festive Christmas: feasting on goose and Christmas pudding, singing Christmas songs, and playing games. Scrooge's nephew articulates Dickens's philosophy of the season:

> I have always thought of Christmas time, when it has come round—apart from the veneration due to its sacred name and origin, if anything belonging to it can be apart from that—as a good time: a kind, forgiving, charitable, pleasant time: the only time I know of, in the long calendar of the year, when men and women seem by one consent to open their shut-up hearts freely, and to think of people below them as if they really were fellow-passengers to the grave, and not another race of creatures bound on other journeys.
> (*A Christmas Carol*, p. 49)

Even the organization and title of *A Christmas Carol* reinforce an old Christmas tradition: the medieval practice of carol singing. Just ten years before *A Christmas Carol* appeared, William Sandys published his *Selection of Christmas Carols, Ancient and Modern*, to preserve the old songs. In writing his prose Christmas carol, Dickens called the chapters of his story "staves," or verses. In Stave One, Scrooge frightens off a young caroler who sings "God bless you merry gentleman! / May nothing you dismay!" (*A Christmas Carol*, p. 53)—a version of the actual carol "God Rest You Merry, Gentlemen." The change Dickens makes is significant, however; for the invocation of God's blessing appears as a refrain in *A Christmas Carol*. Tiny Tim's statement at his family's dinner, and the last words of the story are "God bless us everyone!" (*A Christmas Carol*, p. 97).

Dickens's depiction of Christmas resonated with the secular life of the times, not only with an interest in the past. His version of Christmas celebrated family gatherings and community in an urban setting, which appealed to the values of the English middle classes. The fact that the first Christmas card was sent in the same year that *A Christmas Carol* was published testifies to the growing popularity of the holiday. As Edgar Johnson writes of Dickens, "It should not be imagined that Christmas has for Dickens more than the very smallest connection with Christian dogma or theology. For Dickens Christmas is primarily a human not a supernatural feast" (Johnson, p. 484). This is the case even though one brand of religious conservatism—the Oxford Movement, or the Anglo-Catholic strain within the Church of England—favored the return of a more ritualistic Christmas.

Dickens kept Christmas in the way that he advocated. As he wrote in a letter to a friend, "Such dinings, such dancings, such conjurings, such blindmans-buffings [sic], such theatre-goings, such kissings-out of old years and kissings-in of new ones, never took place in these parts before." (Dickens, *The Letters*, Vol. 4, pp. 2-3). In fact, the association between Dickens and Christmas became so fixed in his own time that Dickens was seen as Father Christmas himself, and it is reported that on his death, a poor working girl asked "Dickens dead? Then will Father Christmas die too?" (Davis, p. 53).

Sources and literary context. Dickens was inspired to write *A Christmas Carol* as a response to problems both social and personal. Parliamentary reports on child labor as well as his visit to the ragged school fired his social conscience. Meanwhile, the serial novel that he was in the process of writing, *Martin Chuzzlewit*, was not bringing in the amount of money Dickens wanted, and he felt dismayed with his publishers. Thus, Dickens undertook to publish *A Christ-*

SUNDAY OBSERVANCE BILL

From the early moments of his writing career, Dickens was critical of people misusing religion to control the lives of others, especially the poor. When Scrooge accuses the Ghost of Christmas Present of seeking to close bakeshops on Sundays, in observation of the Sabbath, he is revisiting an issue about which Dickens had strong partisan feelings. Between 1832 and 1837, Sir Andrew Agnew had repeatedly attempted to pass a Sunday Observance Bill, which would have closed pubs, bakeries, shops, and other public places on the Sabbath. An infuriated Dickens published a pamphlet, signed with a pseudonym, entitled *Sunday Under Three Heads: As it is; As Sabbath Bills would make it; As it might be made*. Dickens believed that these bills would hurt the working classes most of all, depriving them of innocent enjoyments on their only day free of labor. Sunday should, Dickens thought, be a time for working people to enjoy life with their families. The Ghost of Christmas Present tells Scrooge to place blame where it lies, on human beings, not the gods they invoke.

mas Carol in a different way: he would take on all expenses and reap most of the profits. Unfortunately, Dickens underestimated the cost of printing the book in the format that he wanted, with colored pages and plates, and he made a profit of only 230 pounds on his first 6,000 copies, when he had expected to clear four times that amount (Johnson, p. 495).

A Christmas Carol was not Dickens's first attempt at a Christmas story, though it was his most sustained. *Sketches by Boz* contains a brief descriptive piece entitled "A Christmas Dinner," which emphasizes the renewal of family ties during this holiday season. The negative portrait of the opening lines foreshadows the detailed portrayal of Scrooge as misanthrope and miser: "Christmas time! That man must be a misanthrope indeed, in whose breast something like a jovial feeling is not roused—in whose mind some pleasant associations are not awakened—by the recurrence of Christmas" (Dickens, "A Christmas Dinner," p. 220). A more significant source for *A Christmas Carol* is Dickens's first novel, *The Posthumous Papers of the Pickwick Club*. The main characters make a detour to Dingley Dell for Christmas, where they partake in an abundance of dancing and feasting and game playing and under-the-mistletoe kissing. The manor owner tells a Christmas Eve story that has often been cited as a precursor to *A Christmas Carol*. In "The Story of the Goblins Who Stole a Sexton," Gabriel Grub, a moody and miserable grave digger who hates Christmas, is captured by goblins and forced to watch scenes of human resolve and contentment. He learns that

> Men like himself, who snarled at the mirth and cheerfulness of others, were the foulest weeds on the fair surface of the earth; and setting all the good of the world against the evil, he came to the conclusion that it was a very decent and respectable sort of world after all.
> (Dickens, *The Posthumous Papers of the Pickwick Club*, p. 489)

Thus, Gabriel Grub is a prototype of Ebenezer Scrooge, and Dingley Dell the rural predecessor of the festive London Christmases in *A Christmas Carol*.

Several of *A Christmas Carol*'s characters were probably based on real people. Dickens's lame nephew, Harry Burnett, who would die of tuberculosis, may have been the model for Tiny Tim, though the original working name for the character, Little Fred, also points to Dickens's younger brother Frederick. Scrooge's nephew was taken by a nineteenth-century writer to be a portrait of Dickens himself, especially in this opening scene: "He had so heated himself with rapid walking in the fog and frost . . . that he was all in a glow; his face was ruddy and handsome; his eyes sparkled, and his breath smoked again" (*A Christmas Carol*, p. 48; Hearn, p. 61). Dickens's biographer Peter Ackroyd sees a more diffused influence on the story:

> In Scrooge's infancy . . . the familiar elements of Dickens's own past are dispersed. The blacking factory and Gad's Hill Place [a house that Dickens coveted and eventually owned] are wonderfully knit together in an image of a decaying building which is made of red brick and has a weathercock on the top of it: it is here that Scrooge sees . . . the heroes of his boyhood reading just as Dickens had once done. . . . The Cratchit family live in a small terraced house which is clearly an evocation of that house in Bayham Street where the Dickens family had moved after their arrival in London, and their crippled infant had first been christened not Tiny Tim but "Tiny Fred"—the name of his own brother who was two years old at the time of their journey to the capital. . . . Much of its [*A Christmas Carol*'s] power derives from the buried recollections which animate it.
> (Ackroyd, p. 410)

Dickens's story became the originator of the holiday book (Hearn, p. 19). *A Christmas Carol* was the first (and most successful) of five Christmas books published for each of the Christmas seasons from 1843 to 1847. The others are *The Chimes* (1844), *The Cricket on the Hearth* (1845), *The Battle of Life* (1846), and *The Haunted Man* (1847). In them Dickens usually mingled the realistic with the supernatural (*A Christmas Carol* is subtitled "*A Ghost Story of Christmas*"); in fact, he is one of the writers who defined the immensely popular Victorian genre of the ghost story.

Reception. Dickens wrote of himself and his success to a professor at Harvard University in a letter that accompanied a copy of *A Christmas Carol*:

> Over which Christmas Carol, Charles Dickens wept, and laughed, and wept again, and excited himself in a most extraordinary manner, in the composition; and thinking whereof, he walked about the black streets of London, fifteen and twenty miles, many a night when all the sober folks had gone to bed. . . . Its success is most prodigious. And by every post, all manner of strangers write all manner of letters to him about their homes and hearths, and how this same Carol is read aloud there, and kept on a very little shelf by itself. Indeed it is the great-

A Christmas Carol

est success as I am told, that this Ruffian and Rascal has ever achieved.

(Dickens, *The Letters*, vol. 4, p. 2)

Indeed, Dickens was right. *A Christmas Carol* became his greatest success; as Edgar Johnson states, it was "the most widely known and best beloved of all his stories" (Johnson, p. 483). Reviewers almost unanimously praised it for the good it would do. Thackeray famously wrote that *A Christmas Carol* is a "national benefit and to every man and woman who reads it a personal kindness"; apparently Dickens's cantankerous contemporary, Thomas Carlyle, was so moved by the spirit of the story that he was "seized with a perfect *convulsion* of hospitality" (Thackery in Dickens; Jane Carlyle in Dickens, *A Christmas Carol*, pp. 36, 35).

A CHRISTMAS CAROL'S ILLUSTRATIONS

Charles Dickens chose John Leech (1817-64) to illustrate *A Christmas Carol*. In doing so, he picked a man like himself: young and very talented. In 1841, Leech began an immensely successful career as a caricaturist for *Punch* magazine. Dickens requested four hand-colored plates (to be set off from the text) and four vignettes (in-text pictures) for *A Christmas Carol*. The scenes that Leech illustrated most likely were chosen by Dickens himself. The colored plates included "Mr. Fezziwig's Ball," "Marley's Ghost," "Scrooge's Third Visitor" (the Ghost of Christmas Present), and "The Last of the Spirits." The vignettes included "The Phantoms" (the spirits attempting but failing to allay suffering), "The End of the First Spirit" (Scrooge extinguishing the light of the Ghost of Christmas Past), "Ignorance and Want," and "The Christmas Bowl" (a reformed Scrooge sharing punch with Bob Cratchit). As Michael Patrick Hearn points out, Leech did not illustrate what almost every illustrator since has: Bob Cratchit with Tiny Tim on his shoulder (Hearn, p. 19).

A Christmas Carol became, above all his works, the story most closely connected with Dickens himself because of the starring role it played in his public readings. In fact, *A Christmas Carol* was the first public reading he gave, in 1853. It was also the centerpiece of the readings he gave just before his death in 1870. Dickens adapted his own work, eventually trimming it to an hour and a half; he took on all the roles and captivated his audiences. These oral performances allowed him to reach the large illiterate population, and he always insisted that there be cheap seats, so that the poor could attend. Dickens's listeners described the experience as "sacramental"; it was "like hearing the very sound of the Christmas bells" (Davis, pp. 57-58).

A Christmas Carol appeared in other (mostly pirated) versions almost immediately following its publication, and has continued to appear in various forms up to this day. As Paul Davis states, *A Christmas Carol* "has been adapted, revised, condensed, retold, reoriginated and modernized more than any other work of English literature" (Davis, p. 4). Dickens's little Christmas story has appeared as a play, a silent film, a musical, a piano suite, black-and-white as well as color motion pictures, animated films, radio dramas, a ballet, and an opera. It is a tale that has been retold many times, with many artists following in the path of *A Christmas Carol*'s original illustrator, John Leech.

Furthermore, the English language has claimed "Scrooge" as a synonym for miser, and in Scrooge as well as Tiny Tim, Bob Crachit, and the Ghosts of Christmas Past, Present, and Future, *A Christmas Carol* has left its mark on the popular imagination.

—Danielle Price

For More Information

Ackroyd, Peter. *Dickens*. New York: HarperCollins, 1990.

Altick, Richard D. *Victorian People and Ideas*. New York: Norton, 1973.

Callahan, Charles W. Jr. "Tiny Tim: The Child with a Crippling Fatal Illness." *The Dickensian* 89, no. 431 (winter 1993): 214-17.

Davis, Paul. *The Lives and Times of Ebenezer Scrooge*. New Haven, Conn.: Yale University Press, 1990.

Dickens, Charles. *A Christmas Carol. The Christmas Books*. Vol. 1. Ed. Michael Slater. Harmondsworth, U.K.: Penguin, 1971.

———. "A Christmas Dinner." In *Sketches By Boz*. London: Oxford University Press, 1957.

———. *Hard Times*. Norton Critical Edition. Eds. George Ford and Sylvère Monod. New York: Norton, 1966.

———. *The Letters of Charles Dickens*. Vol. 3. Eds. Madeline House, Graham Storey, and Kathleen Tillotson. London: Oxford University Press, 1974.

———. *The Letters of Charles Dickens*. Vol. 4. Ed. Kathleen Tillotson. London: Oxford University Press, 1977.

———. *The Posthumous Papers of The Pickwick Club*.

Ed. Robert L. Patten. Harmondsworth, U.K.: Penguin, 1986.

Hearn, Michael Patrick, ed. *The Annotated Christmas Carol*, by Charles Dickens. New York: Clarkson N. Potter, 1976.

Himmelfarb, Gertrude. *The Idea of Poverty: England in the Early Industrial Age*. New York: Alfred A. Knopf, 1984.

Johnson, Edgar. *Charles Dickens: His Tragedy and Triumph*. Vols. 1 and 2. Boston: Little, Brown, 1952.

Marling, Karal Ann. *Merry Christmas! Celebrating America's Greatest Holiday*. Cambridge, Mass.: Harvard University Press, 2000.

Mitchell, Sally. *Daily Life in Victorian England*. Westport, Conn.: Greenwood, 1996.

The Communist Manifesto

by
Karl Marx and Friedrich Engels

Widely considered to be the nineteenth century's most influential revolutionary thinker, Karl Marx (1818-83) laid the theoretical foundations of modern socialism and communism. Born in Trier, Prussia (now part of Germany), Marx was educated primarily there and at the University of Berlin, receiving his doctorate in philosophy in 1841. Shortly afterward he met Friedrich Engels (1820-95), who belonged to the same circle of radical young Germans that Marx had joined as a student. Their friendship would ripen into one of history's most fruitful intellectual collaborations, with Marx's strong theoretical abilities complemented by Engels's practical knowledge and organizational skills. Though living and working mainly in Britain after 1848, they wrote in their native German. Their masterpiece would be the monumental *Das Kapital* ("Capital," 1867-94). Like *The Communist Manifesto*, *Das Capital* was written largely by Marx but drew on theories that he and Engels had developed together, and two of its three volumes were edited by Engels for publication after Marx's death. Virtually all of the major ideas elaborated in *Das Capital* were first set forth in much shorter form in *The Communist Manifesto*. Their first major published work, it remains the most concise statement of an ideology that would ultimately change the course of history and hold sway over billions of lives.

Events in History at the Time of the Pamphlet

Industrial revolutions. Over the first half of the nineteenth century, European civilization began

> **THE LITERARY WORK**
>
> A political pamphlet first distributed in mid-nineteenth-century Europe; published in London in 1848 (as *Manifest der Kommunistischen Partei*), in English in 1850.
>
> **SYNOPSIS**
>
> Proclaiming that conflict between economic classes has been the driving force of history, the authors outline the growth of socialist movements in Europe and predict the imminent collapse of capitalism.

struggling to deal with the social and political upheavals unleashed by the Industrial Revolution. All European nations would eventually be swept up in the profound changes that accompanied the transformation from predominantly agrarian to modern industrial economies, but those changes came earlier to some than to others. The leader was Britain, where many of the technological innovations that spurred industrialization were first developed starting in the mid-eighteenth century. By the early decades of the nineteenth century, Belgium had become the first industrializing nation on the European continent, with France following more slowly by the mid-nineteenth century. Along with the United States, which began industrial growth soon after Britain, these three countries were the earliest to begin the shift over to modern industrial economies.

The Communist Manifesto

Karl Marx

Originating among British textiles (cloth) manufacturers in the 1770s, a new method of manufacturing—the factory system—lay at the heart of the Industrial Revolution. Because factories ran on coal and required large amounts of iron and other metals, the spread of factories vastly accelerated mining operations. Factories, mines, and other aspects of industrial production brought greater economic productivity and higher overall prosperity to the countries that developed them. Yet, as critics began pointing out almost immediately, such benefits came at a high cost: industrialization also created serious social problems and, in many cases, great human misery. As the earliest to experience the benefits of the industrial age, Britain was also the first to suffer its ills. The prevailing economic theory of laissez-faire (French for "allow to do") capitalism dictated that employers should be free from restrictive regulations. It was believed that this hands-off approach would promote general prosperity and thus would ultimately be best for everyone. However, in reality the ideal of laissez-faire capitalism was not evenly applied. For while employers were unrestricted, workers were not—with the result that employers enjoyed special protections under the law as compared with workers. For example, British workers were forbidden by law from forming unions, or from going on strike for better wages, shorter hours, or safer working conditions. By the 1840s the exploitation of workers had begun drawing sympathy from a wide range of writers and social critics in Britain.

Particularly brutal was the plight of child laborers in coal mines and factories, where they commonly worked 16-hour days in the most grueling conditions. Exposed by a British Government investigation in 1843, such exploitation was publicized that same year by Elizabeth Barrett Browning's widely quoted poem "The Cry of the Children":

> "For oh," say the children, "we are weary,
> And we cannot run or leap;
> If we cared any for meadows, it were merely
> To drop down in them and sleep. . . .
> For, all day, we drag our burden tiring
> Through the coal-dark, underground;
> Or, all day, we drive the wheels of iron
> In the factories, round and round."
> (Browning in Abrams, p. 1,091)

For many observers, the worst that industrialism had to offer could be seen in the slums of Manchester, the northern English industrial city that was the center of British textiles manufacturing. In 1848, the year that *The Communist Manifesto* appeared, English author Elizabeth Gaskell published *Mary Barton*, an influential novel that graphically described the filthy, overcrowded living conditions of Manchester factory workers and their families.

By that time, owing to his own family's background, Friedrich Engels was already well acquainted with Manchester. Engels's father, a wealthy German textiles manufacturer, was part owner of a Manchester textiles factory. In the early 1840s, Engels had spent nearly two years living mostly in Manchester, recording workers' conditions there as well as in other British industrial cities. He published his observations in his book *The Condition of the English Working Class* (1845). "The area is full of ruined or half-ruined buildings," Engels wrote of one working-class Manchester neighborhood:

> Everywhere one sees heaps of refuse, garbage, and filth. There are stagnant pools instead of gutters and the stench alone is so overpowering that no human being, even partially civilized, would find it bearable to live in such a district.
> (Engels in Abrams, pp. 1,644-45)

Engels's firsthand knowledge of British working-class conditions would provide a firm empirical basis for the theories that he and Marx would articulate a few years later in *The Communist Manifesto*.

> ### FROM "HOME MADE" TO "FACTORY MADE"
>
> Before the Industrial Revolution, production of material goods had typically occurred in three ways:
>
> - Household production, in which the occupants of a household (including servants) manufactured items for use within the household.
> - Handicraft or artisan production, in which a few skilled workers, laboring in small shops, turned out specialized goods.
> - Domestic or cottage industry, in which employers owned raw materials that they sent out to a number of craft workers, who in turn made the finished products themselves, in their own homes or small shops.
>
> During the Industrial Revolution, factories greatly increased the amount of goods that could be produced, transforming not just the means but also the scale of production. The factory system combined four major innovations:
>
> - Large concentrations of workers in sizeable buildings or building complexes (the factories themselves) devoted exclusively to production.
> - Heavy reliance on machines. Throughout the nineteenth century, factory machines were powered by steam, which was created by burning fuel (most often coal) to heat water.
> - Highly coordinated production, with workers specializing in particular stages of the process rather than creating the finished product from the beginning. Workers were also now closely monitored and disciplined by supervisors.
> - The rise of a class of wealthy owners of industrial enterprises like factories. Because such enterprises require large capital expenditures to get started, those who could afford to set up (and thus to profit from) large industrial operations have been called "capitalists." The economic system of free enterprise in which they flourish, called capitalism, is the major target of Marx and Engels's critique in *The Communist Manifesto*.

As industrialization proceeded, so did the growth of an urban working class needed to perform industrial labor. Hand-in-hand with the poverty of this growing working class came its lack of a political voice in early-nineteenth-century Britain, as in most other European countries. Discontented workers contributed significantly to a wave of revolutions that swept Europe from the 1820s through the 1840s, although other forces also played a part in the turbulent events of these decades. In Britain, a series of reforms staved off the outright revolts that other countries suffered. However, the reforms came only after riots and violent uprisings, starting with the Peterloo Massacre (1819) in Manchester, when armed troops killed 11 people while crushing a workers' protest. At least 571 others were injured in the incident. Thereafter a major piece of British legislation, the Reform Bill of 1832, extended voting rights from upper-class men to middle-class men. But property qualifications continued to deny British working-class men the right to vote (no women could vote until 1918).

Between 1832 and 1848, the strongest calls for continued reform in Britain came from the working-class Chartist Movement, which Marx and Engels refer to in *The Communist Manifesto*. The Chartists took their name from their so-called People's Charter, drafted in 1838, in which they presented six demands for Parliamentary reform. The demands included the abolition of property qualifications for election to Parliament, as well as for voting in the elections themselves. The Chartists presented petitions to Parliament in 1839, 1842 (when they garnered 3 million signatures), and 1848, but the British legislative body rejected each of the petitions. Engels knew many of the Chartists' leaders, several of whom he introduced to Marx during the latter's visits to London in the 1840s.

The Communist Manifesto

Early socialist movements. By the mid-nineteenth century, observers of all political stripes were struggling to formulate solutions to the ills of the industrial age. The Scottish-born historian and social critic Thomas Carlyle (1795-1881) was one of the most influential shapers of nineteenth-century British culture. Essentially conservative, this engaging but often contradictory writer exalted the principle of work, but decried the way that mechanized industry reduced it to a virtueless cash horde. In books such as *Past and Present* (1843), Carlyle opposed laissez-faire capitalism. Instead, he expressed nostalgia for the feudal relationships of the medieval world, in which (as he saw it) the powerful were protective patrons and the less powerful were loyal clients. In contrast with Carlyle, the equally influential British historian and political leader Thomas Babington Macaulay (1800-59) viewed the problems of industrialism as temporary and surmountable. Whereas Carlyle distrusted democracy, the liberal Macaulay argued for further extending the vote. He championed the industrial age as a shining example of progress, trumpeting its achievements and innovations as proof of humanity's ultimate perfectibility.

Carlyle was not alone in focusing on the ways that industrialization had altered the relationship between employers and workers. Already the extraordinary British industrialist-turned-reformer Robert Owen (1771-1858) had engaged in a series of startlingly successful social experiments, starting with the creation in the 1810s of a progressive community around a textile factory in New Lanark, Scotland. Owen stressed education above all and argued that humans were entirely the product of social forces. By controlling these social forces, Owen and his followers believed, society could positively influence the shaping of individuals. Owen helped in early attempts to organize labor unions, which the British government treated as criminal conspiracies. The word "socialist" first appeared in print in 1827 in the Owenite periodical *Co-operative Magazine*, describing Owen's followers and their beliefs.

The word "socialism" appeared soon after, in 1832—but in a French newspaper, where it was applied to the views of another reformer, the French social theorist Henri de Saint-Simon (1760-1825). Saint-Simon, whose ideas strongly influenced those of Carlyle and later British socialists, called for voluntary cooperation between workers and employers. Arguing that together this industrial class should overthrow Europe's older aristocratic elites, Saint-Simon envisioned a harmonious society founded on rational, scientific principles and mutual cooperation. By the 1830s in Britain and France, the words "socialism" and "socialist" were being commonly applied not only to the Owenites and Saint-Simonians, but also to a wide range of competing but broadly similar movements. The followers of another French reformer named Charles Fourier (1772-1837) also began calling themselves socialists in the 1830s, for example. Like Owen, but unlike Saint-Simon, Fourier stressed the building of small communities, and had little interest in larger political issues.

While differing in some important respects, these early socialist movements did have several key elements in common. They agreed that the exploitation of workers should be ended, and they agreed as well that society should enact some sort of limitation on property rights in order to curtail the power of the wealthy. They argued that society, not individuals, should own factories and other industrial facilities. But they also agreed that in general terms the ultimate target of such measures was (as Saint-Simon stressed) the old aristocratic elites. It was against this traditional oppressor of the common people, rather than against the emerging class of capitalist employers, that the early socialists directed

---

THE UNRULY 1840S

Social unrest combined with agricultural catastrophes to create an atmosphere of seething revolt throughout Europe in the 1840s. In 1845 and 1846, potato and grain crops failed in Britain, Ireland, and other countries, leading to higher food prices across Europe. Peasants agitated for the abolition of the feudal system, middle-class professionals such as doctors and lawyers demanded greater political rights, and industrial workers too called for a political voice. As *The Communist Manifesto* predicted, these pressures would result in widespread revolutions in Europe in 1848, but—contrary to Marx and Engels's predictions—those revolutions were not communist in character. Nor, as it turned out, were they successful. They seem, however, to have had an effect on later history. Harsh oppression followed the crushing of these revolutions in most countries, yet despite this oppression, many of the democratic reforms that the rebels sought were enacted during the second half of the nineteenth century.

their strongest efforts. These thinkers also envisioned utopias, or idealistic and cooperative societies, and their proposed changes were based on reform, not revolution. For these reasons, *The Communist Manifesto* dismisses the movements of these thinkers as helpful and well-intentioned but ultimately misguided.

Communism. There were attacks on the wealth of the capitalists too, most notably by the followers of the French radical Gracchus Babeuf (1760-97). Babeuf had been a relatively unimportant figure in the French Revolution of 1789. Later he was executed for hatching a conspiracy to overthrow the revolutionary government and install what he termed a dictatorship of the people. A key element in Babeuf's plan was the elimination of all private property, and it is this point that has led later historians to see him as a forerunner of communism. The idea would be taken up by France's Pierre Joseph Proudhon, whose book *What Is Property?* (French; 1840) answered that question with the famous aphorism "property is theft." Followers of Babeuf, a number of zealous but disorganized French radicals, called themselves *babouvistes*. They rose up especially during the July Revolution of 1830 in France, when French industrial workers—themselves inspired by socialist ideas—took to the streets to demand greater political rights, including the right to vote. The July Revolution overthrew the conservative King Charles X and installed Louis Phillipe on the French throne, to the relief of the middle class and of business interests in France.

In France, as in the rest of Europe, the aftermath of the July Revolution was marked by continuing social and political unrest. Revolution was still in the air, and secret societies flourished. It was in Paris during the 1830s that some of these clandestine political groups started calling their beliefs "communism." The word first came into wide use in the 1840s, to describe the ideas of the French social theorist Étienne Cabet, whose utopian doctrines had been influenced by Owenite socialism. But it also continued to be used by underground radical groups of the far left, often made up of exiles, who found "socialism" too soft to describe their militant views. For example, a number of young German exiles gathered with others in Paris, Brussels, and London, after their views had caused them to be banished by the conservative German government. Calling themselves the League of the Just, the more radical members also referred to themselves as communists. Among that faction were Marx and Engels, who met in Paris in 1844 when Engels,

then working on *The Condition of the English Working Class*, visited France.

Engels had joined the League's London group after moving to Britain in 1842. Marx himself, exiled from Germany for his activities, had joined the Paris group until he was expelled from France in 1845. Moving to Brussels, from 1845 to 1848 Marx then took over leadership of the Brussels group. Though Marx lived in Brussels and Engels in Britain, the two of them worked together closely after 1845, when Marx briefly visited Engels in London. In 1847, at their instigation, the League of the Just became the Communist League, and Marx was given the task of composing its manifesto, or statement of beliefs.

SOCIALISM, COMMUNISM, AND MARXISM

Socialism generally refers to political systems in which the state owns the means of production, along with important services, such as transportation and communications.

Communism can be defined as a socialist system in which all property is theoretically owned in common, and a single (communist) party monopolizes political power in the name of the workers or the people.

Marxism can be seen as socialism or communism organized along the lines proposed by Marx in *The Communist Manifesto* and other writings.

The Pamphlet in Focus

The contents. *The Communist Manifesto* runs to fewer than 50 pages in most editions, and it is divided into four sections. A brief preamble begins, "A spectre is haunting Europe—the spectre of communism" (Marx and Engels, *The Communist Manifesto*, p. 130). The preamble then asserts that because this spectre has struck fear into governments across Europe, mystery and misunderstandings have clouded any true understanding of the communists' actual aims. Communists, therefore, should now openly publish their views and goals.

Part 1, entitled "Bourgeois and Proletarians," opens with the statement that "The history of all hitherto existing society is the history of class struggles" (*The Communist Manifesto*, p. 131). All societies, in other words, have been divided into social ranks, and the struggles between these ranks is what has driven historical change.

The Communist Manifesto

Adopting terminology used by some earlier socialist writers, Marx and Engels assert that in the industrial age the class struggle ultimately comes down to a conflict between two groups: capitalists, whom they call bourgeois or the bourgeoisie, and workers, whom they call proletarians or the proletariat. The bourgeoisie evolved out of the serfs of the Middle Ages, some of whom became merchants and grew more and more powerful as exploration opened up the world to European commercial domination. With the rise of industry, leadership of the bourgeoisie fell to the capitalist owners of industrial production. "Each step in the development of the bourgeoisie was accompanied by a corresponding political advance of that class," as it gradually overthrew the power of the feudal aristocracy that had ruled in the Middle Ages (*The Communist Manifesto*, p. 134).

With its restless energy, the bourgeoisie has created all of the urban expansion and technological progress of the modern industrial world. But in doing so, the bourgeoisie has also "called into existence" the very class that will "bring death to itself": the proletariat, or modern working class (*The Communist Manifesto*, p. 140). The proletariat "is recruited from all classes of the population," as those classes are whittled away by the power of the bourgeoisie. At the beginning, the proletariat fights against "the enemies of its enemies," that is, against the remnants of the once dominant aristocracy. Thus, it helps consolidate the power of the bourgeoisie. Only after growing in strength and number can the mature proletariat finally face and vanquish its true enemy, the bourgeoisie. This victory allows the proletariat to replace the bourgeoisie as the "revolutionary class, the class that holds the future in its hands" (*The Communist Manifesto*, p. 145).

Part 2, "Proletarians and Communists," begins by asserting that the interests of the communists are identical to "those of the proletariat as a whole" (*The Communist Manifesto*, p. 149). The communists, however, serve at the forefront of the proletariat's struggle against the bourgeoisie. Their ideas are not based on the theories of "this or that would-be universal reformer," but reflect "actual relations springing from an existing class struggle, from a historical movement going on under our very eyes" (*The Communist Manifesto*, p. 150). In the context of this struggle, "the abolition of existing property relations is not at all a distinctive feature of communism," declare Marx and Engels (*The Communist Manifesto*, p. 150). Other revolutionary movements overturn these property relations too; in this regard, communism is not alone.

> All property relations have in the past continually been subject to historical change . . . The French Revolution, for example, abolished feudal property in favor of bourgeois property. The distinguishing feature of communism is not the abolition of property generally, but the abolition of bourgeois property.
> (*The Communist Manifesto*, pp. 150-51)

All other property besides that of the bourgeois, Marx and Engels argue, has already either been destroyed or is in the process of being destroyed by the power of the bourgeoisie.

Similarly, the communists are accused of wanting to do away with the family—but it is only the bourgeois family that they wish to abolish, since the bourgeois have already destroyed the family structure of the other classes:

> The bourgeois claptrap about family and education, about the hallowed correlation of parent and child, becomes all the more disgusting, the more, by the action of modern industry, all family ties among the proletarians are torn asunder, and their children transformed into simple articles of commerce and instruments of labour.
> (*The Communist Manifesto*, p. 156)

Likewise, the *Manifesto* counters another common bourgeois charge against the communists—that they wish to "abolish countries and nationality" (*The Communist Manifesto*, p. 157). In their oppression by the bourgeoisie, "working men have no country" in the first place, meaning the same sort of oppression resurfaces in country after country; communists are not out to abolish nationality or country. That would be impossible since they "cannot take from them what they have not got" (*The Communist Manifesto*, p. 157). It is only bourgeois nationality that the communists will abolish.

The last section of Part 2 sketches the steps by which the proletariat will fulfill its historic mission:

> The first step in the revolution by the working class is to raise the proletariat to the position of ruling class to win the battle of democracy. The proletariat will use its political supremacy to wrest, by degrees, all capital from the bourgeoisie, to centralize all instruments of production in the hands of the state, i.e. of the proletariat organized as the ruling class.
> (*The Communist Manifesto*, p. 160)

Different countries will implement communist revolutions differently, Marx and Engels suggest, but they list a number of measures that might occur under a communist government:

- Takeover of all land by the state
- Imposition of a heavy graduated income tax
- Abolition of inheritance
- Consolidation of banking into one state bank
- State control of all communication and transportation
- State ownership of all industry
- Obligation of all to work
- Free education for all children

In Part 3, "Socialist and Communist Literature," Marx and Engels address the ideas of earlier socialists and communists. They divide these ideas into three categories: reactionary socialism, conservative or bourgeois socialism, and critical-utopian socialism. Reactionary socialism includes early aristocratic and petty-bourgeois responses to bourgeois ascendancy (Marx and Engels use the term "petty-bourgeois" to mean shopkeepers, small farmers, and other members of the lower bourgeois class). It also includes some of the Germans who imported socialist ideas into Germany in the 1830s. These socialists are called "reactionary" because they ultimately act in favor of the old feudal social structure. Conservative or bourgeois socialism comprises those bourgeois "economists, philanthropists, humanitarians, improvers of the condition of the working class, organisers of charity," and others who concern themselves with "redressing social grievances" only in order to preserve the bourgeoisie itself (*The Communist Manifesto*, p. 171). Finally, the last category, critical-utopian socialism, reflects the utopian ideas of Saint-Simon, Owen, Fourier and others. While praising their works as valuable beginnings, Marx and Engels state that these socialists reflect the "early, undeveloped period" of the class struggle mentioned in Part 1, when the proletariat unwittingly opposes not its true enemy, the bourgeoisie, but the old aristocratic elite (*The Communist Manifesto*, p. 173).

Part 4, "Position of the Communists in Relation to the Various Existing Opposition Parties," takes up only a few pages. Communists, write Marx and Engels, are willing to ally themselves with any political party that sides with the working class. In countries such as Britain, which have organized working-class political parties like the Chartists, communists clearly side with those parties. But in countries such as Germany, where no true working class yet exists, they fight alongside the bourgeoisie "whenever it acts in a revolutionary way, against the absolute monarchy, the feudal squirearchy, and the petty-bourgeoisie"

(*The Communist Manifesto*, p. 178). Indeed, communists focus their attention on Germany. It is there that the bourgeoisie is about to carry out a revolution under "more advanced conditions" than the already completed bourgeois revolutions in Britain and France; yet "the bourgeois revolution in Germany will be but the prelude to an immediately following proletarian revolution" (*The Communist Manifesto*, p. 178).

Thus communists support revolutionary movements everywhere, while always seeking to promote the interests of the working class within those movements. "Let the ruling classes tremble at a communist revolution," the *Manifesto* concludes: "The proletarians have nothing to lose but their chains. They have a world to win. Working men of all countries, unite!" (*The Communist Manifesto*, p. 179).

DIALECTICAL MATERIALISM

Marx's materialistic conception of history is combined in Marxist theory with the "dialectical" ideas of the German philosopher W. F. Hegel, who suggested that history moves forward by the clash of one idea, which he called the thesis, with its opposite, the antithesis. The two ideas then combine to form a new, higher idea, the synthesis. This in turn becomes the thesis for a new "dialectical" conflict. For Hegel, these conflicts were abstract collisions that occurred only in the world of ideas. Marx took this view of historical progress and rooted it firmly in the material world, where he believed all history originated. Hence, the Marxist view of how history progresses is called "dialectical materialism." For Marx, history will end when the final synthesis, that of a classless society, emerges from the revolution of the proletariat against the bourgeoisie. *The Communist Manifesto* predicts that such a revolution is about to occur.

Marx's view of history. With their famous opening statement that "the history of all hitherto existing society is the history of class struggles," Marx and Engels suggested a new and compelling interpretation of history. In Marxist terms, human history began with the production of material goods—clothes, food, shelter—that people needed for survival. Classes arose, Marx believed, when some people began appropriating the goods produced by others. The class struggles that Marx describes as governing history in *The Communist Manifesto* represent the ongoing

The Communist Manifesto

Original title page from *Manifest der Kommunistischen Partei,* or *Manifesto of the Communist Party.*

battle between such opposing groups throughout history. (In the industrial age, according to this view, capitalists appropriate the goods produced by workers.) Because the class struggles that determine history are conducted over material goods, Marx's idea of history has been called historical materialism.

In some ways, historical materialism turned earlier ideas of history upside down. For example, in the English-speaking world, one school of nineteenth-century historians tended to view history as "the biography of great men," to use Thomas Carlyle's well-known phrase (Carlyle in Carr, p. 61). This view emphasized the roles of outstanding individuals in shaping events. Another common nineteenth-century view characterized history as an inspiring tale of human progress towards liberty and enlightenment. This was Thomas Macaulay's view, and because Macaulay was a prominent political leader in the Whig party, it was known as the Whig interpretation. The Whig interpretation became the dominant view of history in nineteenth-century Britain, and it continued to influence British historical writing well into the twentieth century. Historians in both centuries have criticized historical materialism as ignoring the impact on history of individuals and of ideas such as liberty.

Such critics argue that Marx (and the many historians whom he influenced) improperly elevated what the poet T. S. Eliot called "vast impersonal forces," such as economics, over human beings and ideas (Eliot in Carr, p. 54). Because it is the classes' differing economic power—their wealth or their poverty, as measured in material goods—that separates them and constitutes the means over which they struggle, economic factors do indeed shape Marx's view of history. Yet in emphasizing economic forces, Marx did not claim that either individuals or ideas are unimportant. As Marx himself wrote:

> *History* does nothing, it possesses no immense wealth, fights no battles. It is rather *man,* real living *man* who does everything, who possesses and fights.
> (Marx in Carr, p. 61; emphasis original)

In his influential book *What Is History?* (1961, from which the above quotations are taken), Edward Hallett Carr observes that all historical interpretations are shaped by the historian's own circumstances and values. Marx's interpretation of history was an economic one, because above all Marx was reacting to the economic exploitation of real people—both in his own age and in other ages as well.

Sources. In building on the ideas of the early socialists that have been outlined above, Marx and Engels also drew heavily on the work of other thinkers, especially in the areas of economics and philosophy. In economics, the most important influence on Marxist theory was Adam Smith (1723-90), the Scottish economist whose book *The Wealth of Nations* (1776) provided the classic exposition and defense of laissez-faire capitalism. Hence, in terms of economic theory, it was largely against Smith that Marx and Engels were reacting, both in *The Communist Manifesto* and in later works such as *Capital*. Smith's ideas had been refined by English economist David Ricardo (1772-1823), whose emphasis on the inherent conflicts between economic classes—especially capitalist employers and industrial workers—contributed significantly to the class struggle outlined in *The Communist Manifesto*. In addition, Ricardo theorized that the value of goods could be expressed as a function of the labor required to produce them. This so-called "labor theory of value" also played an important part in shaping Marx's thought.

Marx's most profound intellectual debt, however, was to the German philosopher Wilhelm Friedrich Hegel (1770-1831). As students, Marx and Engels had both belonged to the Young Hegelians, a group dedicated to exploring and promoting Hegel's concept of the dialectic.

Publication and impact. Published in late February 1848, at first *The Communist Manifesto* was almost completely ignored outside of the Communist League, which disbanded shortly afterward. The pamphlet's predictions of imminent victory for the working class seemed permanently dashed by the failure of the revolutions that broke out all over Europe in 1848. In particular, it was clear that Marx had seriously misjudged the readiness of Germany for the revolution predicted so confidently at the end of *The Communist Manifesto*. In 1864 a London gathering of workers, later called the First International, took place under Marx's leadership, and a few years later the first volume of *Das Capital* (1867) appeared. Marx by that point was the undisputed leader of the international socialist movement, and his followers now took up *The Communist Manifesto* as the boldest and most accessible expression of his ideas. Over the coming years, Marx and Engels oversaw translations of *The Communist Manifesto* into German, English, Danish, Russian, Polish, and many other languages.

The influence of Marx's thought has been incalculable, but was most apparent in the establishment of communist governments in Soviet Russia (1917), China (1949), and numerous other countries during the twentieth century. Many of these regimes collapsed in the 1990s, after the end of the Cold War—the long competition for world leadership between the Soviet Union (with its communist allies) and the United States (with its allied capitalist democracies). Indeed, in the eyes of many, they had been discredited years before they fell. The document that helped give rise to these regimes remains vital, nonetheless. As it was for Russian, Chinese, and other communists, *The Communist Manifesto* has remained an inspiration for revolutionary movements around the world.

—Colin Wells

For More Information

Abrams, M. H., ed. *The Norton Anthology of English Literature*. 4th ed. Vol. 2. New York: Norton, 1979.

Berlin, Isaiah. *The Power of Ideas*. Princeton: Princeton University Press, 2000.

Carr, Edward Hallett. *What Is History?* New York: Vintage, 1961.

Cole, G. D. H. *Socialist Thought: The Forerunners 1789-1850*. New York: Macmillan, 1955.

Kolakowski, Leszek. *Main Currents of Marxism: Its Rise, Growth, and Dissolution: The Founders*. Vol. 1. Trans. P. S. Falla. Oxford: Oxford University Press, 1978.

Marx, Karl, and Friedrich Engels. "The Communist Manifesto," in *Harold J. Laski on The Communist Manifesto*. New York: Pantheon, 1967.

Mayo, Henry B. *Introduction to Marxist Theory*. New York: Oxford University Press, 1960.

Crime and Punishment

by
Fyodor Dostoyevsky

The son of an army doctor, Fyodor Dostoyevsky (1821-81) was educated to be a military engineer, but he rejected a career in the army for literature, publishing *Poor Folk* in 1846. Though this first novel was hailed by critics, several subsequent works were less well received. In 1849 the Russian authorities arrested Dostoyevsky for subversive activity. After spending ten years in exile in Siberia, he returned to Saint Petersburg and began writing again, beginning a major phase of his career a few years later with the novella *Notes from the Underground* (1864). Important works such as *The Idiot* (1868-69) and *The Possessed* (1872) came between two long masterpieces: Dostoyevsky's first great novel, *Crime and Punishment*, and his last, *The Brothers Karamazov* (1879-80). Both focus on murder, guilt, and faith, but in different ways. While *The Brothers Karamazov* represents a more mature development of Dostoyevsky's ideas, *Crime and Punishment* is generally considered to put those ideas in a more dramatic and gripping form. It also grounds them firmly in their immediate historical context, sweeping the reader into the dark mind of a murderer as it links his motivations directly to Russia's intellectual climate in the mid-1860s.

Events in History at the Time of the Novel

Reform and reaction in nineteenth-century Russia. The specific concerns that spurred Dostoyevsky to write *Crime and Punishment* grew out

THE LITERARY WORK
A novel set in Saint Petersburg, Russia, around 1865; published in Russian (as *Prestupleniye i Nakazaniye*) in 1866, in English in 1886.

SYNOPSIS
Raskolnikov, a young Russian intellectual, theorizes that superior men are justified in committing certain crimes. He proceeds to commit a brutal double murder, but the pressures of pursuit and conscience force him to confess.

of a larger pattern of reform and reaction that dominated Russian history throughout the nineteenth century. This pattern, in turn, stemmed from increased exposure to Western European ideas by the Russian upper class. Unlike Western Europe, Russian society continued to consist largely of peasants and lords, with a small, economically weak middle class. Dostoyevsky was alone among Russia's major nineteenth-century novelists in belonging to that middle class, for the others all came from the small but powerful ruling class, or nobility. (Dostoyevsky's contemporary Leo Tolstoy, for example, was a count.) Amounting to about one percent of the population, the nobility included large landowners whose estates subsumed entire villages, and who controlled vast numbers of serfs, the laboring peasants whose position resembled that of the slaves in the southern United States. Though

Crime and Punishment

Fyodor Mikhaylovich Dostoyevsky

nominally free, the serf was in fact bound to the land and the service of a lord. In *Crime and Punishment* the character of Svidrigaïlov (svih drih gaiˊ luhf), a landowner and serial child rapist who beats and sexually abuses his serfs, represents this system's worst abuses. Serfdom remained the leading issue for Russian intellectuals until its abolition in 1861, but even afterwards Russian leaders continued the pattern of alternation between reforms aimed at modernizing on the European model, and harsh, oppressive reactions against those attempted reforms.

The pattern began with Tsar (Emperor) Alexander I, who came to the Russian throne in 1801 as an idealistic young man with intentions of reforming the nation's backward institutions. Alexander met up with institutional inertia, the tsar's conservative advisors, and the invasion of Russia by Napoleon in 1812, all of which combined to overwhelm his early reforming impulses. By the end of the Napoleonic Wars in 1815, the now-seasoned Tsar had turned authoritarian and repressive. Meanwhile, the wars had exposed a younger generation of the nobility to Western ideas, leaving them frustrated with Alexander's abandonment of reform. Alexander died childless in December 1825, and progressive army officers (called the Decembrists) revolted to support Alexander's brother Constantine—a liberal whom Alexander had excluded from the succession—against his younger and more conservative brother Nicholas, the designated heir.

Constantine, however, refused the throne, and the new Tsar Nicholas I easily defeated the Decembrists, but the experience hardened him further against reform and put him on guard against activity the government deemed subversive. Dostoyevsky was a boy of five when Nicholas I came to power. By the late 1830s and 1840s, when Dostoyevsky was a student and a young man, Nicholas I's regime had settled into promoting "Russian" values such as absolute loyalty to the tsar and Orthodox Christianity, while his secret police monitored individuals and organizations that did not adhere to those values. By that time, too, intellectuals had split into two groups: Westernizers, who embraced new ideas coming from Europe, and Slavophiles, who endorsed the traditional "Russian" values espoused by Nicholas I.

Dostoyevsky, who at the time held mildly liberal views, fell into the Westernizing camp. Like many young Russians, he hated serfdom and was attracted by the idealism of European Romantic authors such as the German poet Friedrich Schiller (1759-1805) and the British novelist Sir Walter Scott (1771-1832; see *Ivanhoe*, also in *Literature and Its Times*). In 1849 Dostoyevsky and several other members of the so-called Petrashevsky circle, a discussion group of intellectuals interested in a newly fashionable French ideology known as utopian socialism, were ar-

---

NAPOLEON'S LONG SHADOW

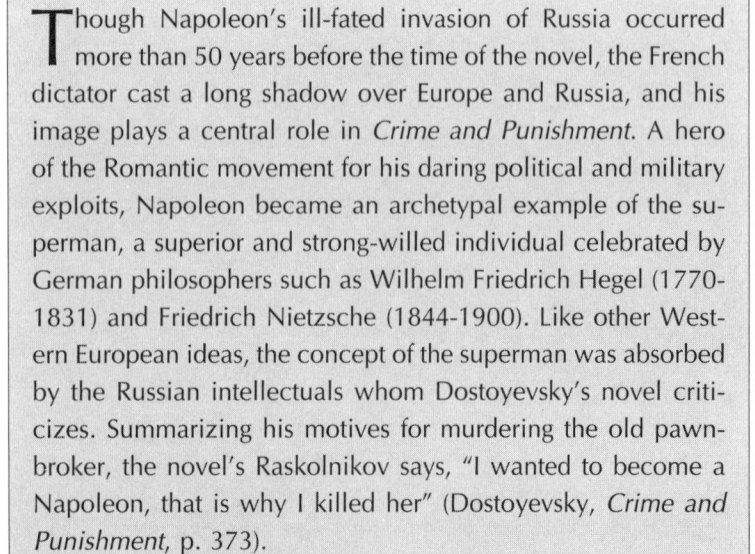

Though Napoleon's ill-fated invasion of Russia occurred more than 50 years before the time of the novel, the French dictator cast a long shadow over Europe and Russia, and his image plays a central role in *Crime and Punishment*. A hero of the Romantic movement for his daring political and military exploits, Napoleon became an archetypal example of the superman, a superior and strong-willed individual celebrated by German philosophers such as Wilhelm Friedrich Hegel (1770-1831) and Friedrich Nietzsche (1844-1900). Like other Western European ideas, the concept of the superman was absorbed by the Russian intellectuals whom Dostoyevsky's novel criticizes. Summarizing his motives for murdering the old pawnbroker, the novel's Raskolnikov says, "I wanted to become a Napoleon, that is why I killed her" (Dostoyevsky, *Crime and Punishment*, p. 373).

> ## SAINT PETERSBURG
>
> Tsar Peter the Great founded Saint Petersburg in 1703, intending to replace Moscow as Russia's imperial capital. Anxious to introduce Western European culture into Russia, Peter chose a site on the Gulf of Finland that would be easier to reach from Western Europe than remote Moscow. The city would do justice to Peter's intention. It has always been celebrated for its European feel, as well as its great beauty. By the time of the novel, the city's population stood at 550,000, and its thriving literary culture included most of Russia's leading journals and newspapers. With its Western flavor and its large university (founded in 1839), Saint Petersburg attracted many of the leading figures of Russia's intelligentsia (progressive intellectuals). It would continue to be a hotbed of revolutionary activity up to the Russian Revolution, which broke out there in 1917.
>
> Emancipation of the serfs (1861) led large numbers of peasants to seek new lives and jobs in Saint Petersburg, and the city's population was growing rapidly at the time of the novel (it would triple by 1900). Like impoverished gentry also drawn to try their luck in the city, many of these peasants lived in the squalid slum conditions that Dostoyevsky describes in the novel. While working on *Crime and Punishment*, Dostoyevsky himself lived in the poor neighborhood of the Hay Market, where he sets much of the action. He follows the literary fashion of his day in referring to many specific locations by only an initial, but scholars have been able to retrace Raskolnikov's travels and to identify the locations of many episodes in the novel. Its opening sentence, for example, describes Raskolnikov as walking from his apartment on S. Place towards K. Bridge (near the pawnbroker's); these have been identified as Stolyarny Place, near Hay Market Square, and Kokushkin Bridge, which crosses Ekaterinsky Canal several blocks to the west (*Crime and Punishment*, p. 1). A good discussion of the correspondences can be found in Gary Cox's *Crime and Punishment: A Mind to Murder* (see p. 35).

rested. Told that they were to be executed, they were led blindfolded to what they believed was a firing squad. Only at the last second did a messenger arrive with news that the tsar had spared their lives, commuting the sentences to imprisonment and lesser penalties. Alarmed by the revolutions of 1848 that had recently rocked much of Europe, Nicholas I himself had staged the incident in order to terrify the group and set an example to others. One of the men was driven insane by the cruel hoax.

As part of his sentence, Dostoyevsky spent four years in a Siberian prison camp and six more years in Siberia as a private in the Russian army. After his return to Saint Petersburg in 1859, he based a novel, *The House of the Dead* (1861-62), on his prison camp experiences, and they would continue to inspire episodes and characters in much of his subsequent writing. In fact, a fellow prisoner of Dostoyevsky's in Siberia, an unscrupulous and depraved noble named Aristov, served as the real-life model for *Crime and Punishment*'s Svidrigaïlov, whom Dostoyevsky calls Aristov in early notes for the novel.

Nicholas I died in 1855, while Dostoyevsky was still in Siberia, and his reformist son Alexander II acceded to the throne. Even before coming to power Alexander II had made clear his intention to free the serfs, and, though the nobility mounted great resistance, his regime announced the abolition of serfdom in 1861, to go into effect in 1863. In the novel the lively and clear-headed Razumihin, Raskolnikov's friend and former fellow student, recalls the recent emancipation of the serfs, calling it "the great hour" (*Crime and Punishment*, p. 137). Yet the end of serfdom did not mean the end of Russia's troubles; already by the early 1860s new battle lines were being drawn.

The new radicals of the 1860s. In addition to providing rich material for his writing, Dostoyevsky's Siberian exile profoundly altered his

Crime and Punishment

political and philosophical outlook. Rejecting the Westernizing liberalism of his youth, he now moved towards his own personal brand of Slavophile conservatism. Dostoyevsky scorned the lofty social engineering (planning of society through, for example, state housing) of the progressive intellectuals. As a group, these intellectuals had come to be known by the Russian word *intelligentsia* (the group would grow to include educated professionals, such as doctors and lawyers). Proclaiming the native Russian dignity of the common folk as contrasted with the pretensions of the Westernizing intelligentsia, Dostoyevsky embraced traditional Orthodox Christianity, which he saw as the natural expression of the Russian people's spirituality. Above all, he stressed the importance of freedom and the worth of the individual, declaring that our need for freedom is what makes each of us truly human.

While Dostoyevsky's ideas had begun to change before he left Siberia, developments on the intellectual scene soon after his return strengthened his new convictions. His own movement towards conservatism came just as other Russian writers were also moving away from the old radicalism of the 1840s—but these writers were moving in the opposite direction, not towards conservatism but towards a new and more extreme radicalism. Whereas the old radicals, influenced by socialist ideas, had shared Dostoyevsky's esteem for the common people, the new radicals, known as nihilists, elevated the intellectuals over the masses. They were led by the writer Dimitry Pisarev, who claimed that art was useless except to manipulate public opinion, and who trumpeted the right of the superior man to ignore the life and death of individual lesser beings in a scientifically inspired quest to improve society as a whole. (These Russian nihilists of the 1860s should not be confused with the later Western European nihilist school of existentialist philosophy.)

Pisarev and the other Russian nihilists were heavily influenced by the utilitarian doctrine of philosophers such as Britain's John Stuart Mill, whose 1863 book *Utilitarianism* argued that actions should be judged not by any abstract moral standard, but by their consequences for society's overall welfare. Pisarev extended (or perverted) Mill's ideas to claim that the ultimate value of a person lies in his or her usefulness to society, and that because the masses generally contribute nothing of value, their existence has little meaning. Dostoyevsky implicitly criticizes the views of both the old and new radicals in *Crime and Punishment*. However, because he insisted on the individual worth of every human, however lowly, he found the new radicals particularly dangerous. Their ideas play a central role in the novel, by providing Raskolnikov with a theoretical rationalization for murdering the "useless" old woman Alyona Ivanovna, a greedy pawnbroker whom Dostoyevsky clearly wishes to portray as serving no good purpose in society (*Crime and Punishment*, p. 60).

MAJOR CHARACTERS IN *CRIME AND PUNISHMENT*

Russians use a first name and patronymic (middle name derived from the father's first name) when addressing each other in familiar conversation. The patronymic has both masculine (*–ovitch*) and feminine (*–ovna*) endings. Also reflecting common usage, most characters in the novel have several nicknames (listed here in parentheses).

Name

Rodion Romanovitch Raskolnikov (Rodya, Rodenka, Rodka)
A poverty-stricken writer and former student in Saint Petersburg. The word *raskol* means "split" or "schism." The name reveals Raskolnikov's conflicting dual natures (good and evil); also, a *raskolnik* was a religious dissenter.

Avdotya Romanova Romanovna (Dounia)
Raskolnikov's sister.

Pulcheria Alexandrovna Raskolnikov
Raskolnikov's mother.

Semyon Zaharovitch Marmeladov
An alcoholic former clerk.

Katerina Ivanovna Marmeladov
Marmeladov's wife.

Sofya Semyonovna Marmeladov (Sonia)
Marmeladov's daughter by a previous marriage. The name *Sofya* comes from the Greek word for "wisdom," a quality associated with holiness in Orthodox Christian tradition.

Dmitry Prokovitch Razumihin
Raskolnikov's friend, a student. *Razum* means "reason," reflecting Razumihin's role as a rational counselor.

Pyotr Petrovitch Luzhin
Dounia's fiancé.

Arkady Ivanovitch Svidrigaïlov
Dounia's corrupt former employer.

Porfiry Petrovitch
A police investigator.

Peter Lorre as Roderick Raskolnikov in the 1935 film version of *Crime and Punishment*.

The Novel in Focus

The plot. Presented in six parts, *Crime and Punishment* is told in the third person, but the storytelling voice often temporarily shifts to follow the thoughts of major characters in a form that resembles first-person narrative. Usually it is the thoughts of the central character, Raskolnikov, that the reader follows in this way. Part 1 opens as Raskolnikov, a writer and penniless student whose poverty has forced him to leave the university, walks through the streets of Saint Petersburg on his way to pawn some items with the old pawnbroker Alyona Ivanovna. Isolated and confused, he seems to be in a daze, and his business at the pawnbroker's leaves him feeling humiliated. His nervous attempts to note the details of the pawnbroker's flat make it clear that he is forming some plan involving the malignant old woman.

Leaving the pawnshop, Raskolnikov stops at a tavern, where he meets a down-and-out alcoholic, Semyon Marmeladov, who tells Raskolnikov his troubles. Marmeladov is married to Katerina Ivanovna, a woman of higher social rank, a widow with three young children. He himself has an older daughter from a previous marriage named Sonia. His ill fortune has become hers. After Marmeladov lost his respectable job as a government clerk because of his drinking, Sonia was forced to turn to prostitution to help feed the family. Marmeladov recently won the job back, but he went on a five-day drinking spree and now fears he has lost his job and ruined his last hope of supporting his family. Accompanying Marmeladov home, Raskolnikov sees the family's dire living conditions and quietly leaves them some money.

The next morning Raskolnikov sleeps late, awaking only when his landlady's servant, a friendly peasant girl named Nastasya, brings him morning tea. She tells him that the landlady is going to complain to the police because Raskolnikov has failed to pay the rent for the tiny, dreary attic room he inhabits. Nastasya also gives him a letter from his mother, Pulcheria Alexandrovna. The letter informs him that his sister Dounia has become engaged to a prosperous lawyer named Luzhin, and that mother and daughter will be visiting Saint Petersburg together so that Dounia can join Luzhin there. Raskolnikov's mother also writes that Dounia, a governess, met Luzhin through her employers, the Svidrigaïlovs. Svidrigaïlov had attempted to seduce the beautiful Dounia, and his wife Marfa Petrovna had at first tried to bring the girl into disgrace by spreading vicious rumors about her through the town where they live. In the end, however, Marfa Petrovna publicly acknowledged

Crime and Punishment

Dounia's blamelessness in the matter and introduced Dounia to Luzhin, a relative of hers.

Disturbed, Raskolnikov concludes that Dounia is sacrificing herself by entering a loveless marriage so that she can help support him financially. As he walks the streets pondering the situation, he sees an adolescent girl staggering around with an older man following her. The man has given her alcohol in hopes of seducing her, and Raskolnikov tries to have him arrested. After offering the girl money for a cab, Raskolnikov suddenly decides it is none of his business and moves on, planning to visit his one friend from the university, Razumihin. He changes his mind, however, and impulsively enters a tavern, ordering a glass of vodka. Making his way to a park, he falls asleep on the ground and dreams that he is again a young boy, walking with his father, and that they witness a drunken peasant angrily beating an old mare to death. In the dream, the tearful boy hugs the dying mare and kisses it. Awakening, Raskolnikov sees the dream as relating to a scheme to kill the pawnbroker, which the reader now learns he has conceived. Agonizing over his violent thoughts, he asks himself how he could ever take an axe to the old woman, for such is his particular plan. By chance, however, as he walks around the poor neighborhood of the Hay Market, he learns that the pawnbroker's sister, a pious and simple-minded woman named Lizaveta who acts as her servant, will be absent from the pawnbroker's the next evening at seven, and the old woman will be alone.

Raskolnikov remembers how, the previous winter, he had learned about the pawnbroker from a student he knew. Then, about six weeks ago, he had overheard a conversation about the woman between two young army officers, who agreed that it would be no loss to society if the woman were killed. Their words shocked Raskolnikov—because he was already thinking exactly the same thing.

Awaking late again the next day, Raskolnikov prepares himself by making a noose for the axe, which he will hang along his arm under his coat, and tightly tying up a parcel that he will pretend he wants to pawn. He will strike while the woman tries to untie the knot. Delayed by these preparations, he arrives at the old woman's flat at seven-thirty. After he rings many times, she finally lets him in and takes the package, turning her back to him as she works on the knot. Raskolnikov smashes the axe into her head twice, killing her, but as he ransacks her apartment Lizaveta appears and he is forced to kill her as well. When he tries to make his escape with a few valuables he has found, he is held up at the building's front door by the arrival of two pawn customers, and briefly hides in the newly painted flat below the pawnbroker's. Making his way back to his own little room, he collapses in a daze before falling into a deep slumber.

The next day a policeman arrives with a summons that terrifies Raskolnikov, but at the police office he learns that the summons was instigated by his landlady. Then he hears the police discussing the murder and passes out. After he comes to, he fears the police will now suspect him and hides the few valuables from the pawnbroker's under a stone in a park. After a brief visit to his university friend, Razumihin, the still agitated Raskolnikov is nearly run down by a coach on the street. Returning home sick, he falls into a nightmare-ridden sleep and remains ill and weak for several days, during which Razumihin cares for him. When he begins to recover, Raskolnikov learns that his mother has sent him 35 roubles, enough money to live on for several months. He also becomes aware that the police visited while he was ill and that he made delirious statements that aroused their suspicion. While a doctor checks on the convalescent Raskolnikov, the lawyer Luzhin, his sister's fiancé, arrives and introduces himself. Luzhin leaves angrily when Raskolnikov treats him with contempt.

Later, while reading newspaper accounts of the pawnbroker's murder in a restaurant, Raskolnikov encounters a policeman and again makes suspicious statements. After witnessing a woman's attempted suicide and revisiting the pawnbroker's flat, Raskolnikov decides to turn himself in. On his way to do so, however, he witnesses an accident in which Marmeladov, the drunk he met earlier in the tavern, stumbles under a carriage and is horrifically injured by the wheels and the horses' hooves. He helps Marmeladov home in time to watch the man die in front of his grief-stricken family, and gives Marmeladov's widow, Katerina Ivanovna, the money that remains from the 35 roubles his mother sent. Deciding that his life is not yet over after all, he changes his mind about confessing. He visits Razumihin, who accompanies him home, where they find Raskolnikov's mother and sister waiting.

Uncomfortable with their presence, Raskolnikov asks Razumihin—who is immediately captivated by Dounia—to escort them both to the rooms that Luzhin has arranged for them. When the family meets again the next day, Raskolnikov quarrels with Dounia about her engagement.

Marmeladov's daughter Sonia, still a prostitute, arrives to invite Raskolnikov to the meal following her father's funeral, and although she is embarrassed, he honors her by asking her to sit next to his sister. Later, he and Razumihin meet the subtle police investigator Porfiry Petrovitch, an uncle of Razumihin's. Raskolnikov is shocked to hear Porfiry describe perfectly an article Raskolnikov published some time earlier entitled "On Crime":

> In his article all men are divided into "ordinary" and "extraordinary." Ordinary men have to live in submission, have no right to transgress the law, because, don't you see, they are ordinary. But extraordinary men have a right to commit any crime and to transgress the law in any way, just because they are extraordinary. That was your idea, if I'm not mistaken?
> (*Crime and Punishment*, p. 234)

Raskolnikov haltingly attempts to clarify his theory by offering further details, but he is forced to concede that Porfiry has accurately summed it up. He leaves convinced that Porfiry knows his secret and is merely playing with him.

That night, Raskolnikov awakens from a nightmare to see a figure in his doorway. The man introduces himself as Svidrigaïlov, Dounia's former employer, and asks Raskolnikov to persuade Dounia to see him. Svidrigaïlov openly boasts about how he beat his wife, Marfa Petrovna, who (it was earlier revealed) has recently died. Despite Raskolnikov's refusal to let him see Dounia, he reveals that in her will, his wife left Dounia 3,000 roubles—a small fortune. Svidrigaïlov himself offers to give Dounia a present of 10,000 roubles as atonement, he says, for the pain he has caused her. Later that day, in a meeting between the Raskolnikov family and Luzhin, Raskolnikov makes a fool of Luzhin and Dounia proceeds to break her engagement to him, to Razumihin's great pleasure. Razumihin suggests they all open a small publishing firm with the money Dounia has inherited from Marfa Petrovna, but Raskolnikov interrupts and suddenly declares that he needs to be alone. He says farewell to his mother and sister, explaining just enough to Razumihin to let his friend know that he is somehow involved in the pawnbroker's murder and asking Razumihin to look after his family.

Raskolnikov goes to Sonia, and together they read passages from the Bible. He promises to tell her who committed the murder the next day, but his sister's erstwhile employer, Svidrigaïlov, eavesdrops from nearby. The next day Porfiry Petrovitch officially interviews Raskolnikov at the police office, and again Raskolnikov feels exposed by the investigator's insistent probing. Meanwhile, Luzhin plots revenge by attempting to frame Sonia for theft. Raskolnikov has been his biggest detractor to Dounia, and Luzhin believes that if he can discredit Raskolnikov, who has defended the prostitute's character to Dounia, Dounia will take her old fiancé back. The plot backfires when Luzhin's attempt to frame Sonia is exposed in front of everyone at Marmeladov's funeral lunch. Afterward, Raskolnikov and Sonia meet in her room, and there he confesses his crime to her. She urges him to turn himself in, for he must suffer the punishment in order to atone for his crime: "Suffer and expiate your sin by it, that's what you must do" (*Crime and Punishment*, p. 378). She tells him she loves him and promises to visit him while he is in prison. Shortly afterward, her stepmother, Katerina Ivanovna, becomes mentally unbalanced, forcing her children to beg on the streets. Wracked by tuberculosis, the stepmother dies, declaring that God will let her into heaven because she has suffered so much.

Raskolnikov is not ready to confess, but Svidrigaïlov has again eavesdropped and confronts Raskolnikov with knowledge of his guilt, adding to his growing panic. Svidrigaïlov also reveals many of his own crimes of lust and violence, including the seduction and rape of several adolescent girls and hinting that he had murdered Marfa Ivanovna after marrying her for her money. Yet he professes true love for Dounia. Porfiry Petrovitch comes to Raskolnikov's room and tells him outright that he knows Raskolnikov committed the murder. He refuses to arrest him, however, because he believes in Raskolnikov's greatness and in his potential to serve Russian society. Porfiry wants Raskolnikov to turn himself in on his own, thereby improving his chances of a lighter sentence and ultimate rehabilitation. Yet Raskolnikov still refuses to confess. Telling Dounia of her brother's guilt, Svidrigaïlov attempts to blackmail her into marrying him, and when she refuses, he kills himself in despair.

Finally, supported by his family and by Sonia's love, Raskolnikov confesses to the police, and after a trial he receives the light prison sentence of eight years in Siberia. Dounia and Razumihin marry and establish a small publishing house, and Sonia follows Raskolnikov to Siberia. There the compassion and piety she shows on her visits to the prison make her popular with the other prisoners, who call her "our dear good little mother" (*Crime and Punishment*, p. 488). Raskolnikov undergoes a period of continued

Crime and Punishment

Napoleon, shown here, inspires Raskolnikov's behavior in *Crime and Punishment*.

religious skepticism and deep despair during his first year in prison, but Sonia's faith and love ultimately lead him to embrace God and the future. Only then does Raskolnikov begin "his gradual regeneration" (*Crime and Punishment*, p. 492).

Extraordinary men: from Napoleon to Stalin. The motive for Raskolnikov's crime has been the subject of much critical debate, since the novel's artistic and psychological complexity presents the reader with a constantly shifting range of possibilities. Raskolnikov himself shows confusion about what drove him to kill. At first he dwells on money, suggesting that the murder will allow him to escape poverty and help his family, although in fact he never really tries to profit financially from the crime. After confessing to Sonia, he repeats the utilitarian rationale already familiar to the reader from his thoughts: he intended to benefit mankind by removing "a useless, loathsome, harmful creature" (*Crime and Punishment*, p. 374). Just a few minutes later, however, he puts forward a more egotistical but still flattering purpose: "I only wanted to have the daring, Sonia! That was the whole cause of it" (*Crime and Punishment*, p. 376). Significantly, Raskolnikov virtually ignores his second murder, the slaying of Lizaveta, which can only be attributed to an unflattering and selfish desire to escape detection.

One overarching consideration, however, connects each of these disparate impulses: Raskolnikov's extraordinary-man theory, which is most concisely reflected in his desire "to become a Napoleon" (*Crime and Punishment*, p. 373). Regarding the financial motive, for example, Raskolnikov tells Sonia that, had Napoleon been faced with Raskolnikov's poverty, he would not have hesitated to murder "some ridiculous old hag" in order to "get money from her trunk (for his career, you understand)" (*Crime and Punishment*, p. 373). Then, too, only a Napoleon would possess the drive and the daring to take the drastic step of killing for the benefit of society. Though he never attempts to do so, Raskolnikov could conceivably use this same theory to cover even Lizaveta's murder, arguing that it would ultimately benefit society if a Napoleon could cover his tracks and therefore remain free to continue his historic mission.

The pattern of reform and reaction that characterized Russian history after Napoleon did not end with the accession of the reformist Alexander II in 1855, nor with the end of serfdom and the rise of the new radicalism in the 1860s. Indeed, despite his reforms, Alexander II would die at the hands of radicals in 1881 (the same year Dostoyevsky died), and his assassination would spark another round of repression by his successor, Alexander III. This round would, in turn, set the stage for one of history's momentous events, the Russian Revolution of 1917, bringing to power the Soviet communist dictatorship of Vladimir Lenin, followed by that of Joseph Stalin.

Observers have noted the remarkable relevance of *Crime and Punishment* to this cycle of events. The Italian novelist Alberto Moravia, for example, has pointed out that the murderous commissars (officials) of Soviet Russia relied on the same arguments that provide Raskolnikov with his rationalization for murder. Along these same lines, the leading Dostoyevsky scholar Joseph Frank has suggested more recently that Raskolnikov represents Dostoyevsky's prediction "of how such a human type eventually would come to be born and of what its arrival on the historical scene might presage for Russia" (Frank, *Through the Russian Prism*, pp. 122-23). That the novel appeared almost exactly midway in time between Napoleon and the Russian Revolution is but one indication of Dostoyevsky's acute historical intuition.

Sources and literary context. Despite its unusual insights into the grand sweep of history, *Crime and Punishment* remains grounded in its own times, literally and philosophically. The Soviet commissars who insisted that the ends justify the means used arguments first made in Russia by the new radicals of the 1860s; as Joseph Frank observes, the novel's ultimate origins lie in how Dostoyevsky's outlook changed after his Siberian exile and how that changed outlook shaped his response to these radical arguments.

On a more literal level, in seeking inspiration for specific episodes and characters in the novel, Dostoyevsky found abundant contemporary source material both in the public record and in his own private life. For example, in the novel the investigator Porfiry Petrovitch holds the office of examining magistrate, a new law enforcement position created in 1860 to give investigators greater independence. Similarly, Dostoyevsky's letters from the period mention recent news stories of murders committed by coldly calculating university students, which he writes persuaded him that his basic idea of a student murderer was believable. Dostoyevsky, who with his brother published two magazines in the early 1860s, had himself written news stories about a cultured French murderer named Pierre-Francois Lacenaire. Dostoyevsky attributed to Lacenaire some of the same qualities (such as fear of poverty combined with massive vanity) that he confers on the fictional Raskolnikov. Pavel Aristov, Dostoyevsky's aristocratic but morally corrupt fellow prisoner in Siberia, inspired not only Svidrigaïlov but also a part of Raskolnikov as well, for Svidrigaïlov represents the dark side of what critics have seen as Raskolnikov's dual character. (Sonia represents Raskolnikov's positive side.) That his main character had two sides reflects Dostoyevsky's particular attraction to the motif of the split personality, which is the subject of his earlier novel *The Double* (1846).

Other major characters based on real-life models include the combative and long-suffering Katerina Ivanovna, fictional wife to Marmeladov, considered a portrait of Dostoyevsky's first wife, Marya Dimitrievna. Like Katerina, the real-life Marya was a vivacious woman, "a knight in female clothing," said Dostoyevsky (Frank, *Dostoevsky*, p. 65); she died of tuberculosis in 1864. Marmeladov is thought to have been based on Marya Dimitrievna's previous husband Alexander Isaev, to whom she was married when Dostoyevsky met her. Like Marmeladov, Isaev was a government official who lost his job because of alcoholism, throwing his family into poverty. Despite Isaev's addiction, Dostoyevsky saw kindness, intelligence, and nobility in the man, characteristics he gives Marmeladov. As part of the intelligentsia's rising social consciousness, the causes and social consequences of alcoholism were being widely discussed in literary journals and newspapers of the 1860s; Dostoyevsky's notebooks refer to many such articles on drunkenness. In fact, the Marmeladov subplot in *Crime and Punishment* originally formed the basis for a separate novel that Dostoyevsky planned to call *The Drunkard*.

Crime and Punishment was released in the middle of the Russian novel's golden age, a period commonly held to have started with the publication of Ivan Turgenev's *Rudin* in 1856 and to have ended with Dostoyevsky's *The Brothers Karamazov* in 1879-80. At work also were such masters as Leo Tolstoy, whose novel *War and Peace* (1865-69) was serialized concurrently with *Crime and Punishment* in the same journal, *The Russian Messenger*. Novels of the period rang with urgent social messages and theories, and critics have seen *Crime and Punishment* partly as a reply to an earlier novel, *What Is To Be Done?* (1863), by the radical author N. G. Chernyshevsky, who espoused an ideology called "rational egoism," which combined elements of socialism and utilitarianism. In *Crime and Punishment* these ideas are put into the mouth of a minor character named Lebeziatnikov, a naïve but well-meaning friend of Luzhin's. Chernyshevsky's book itself is seen as a reply to Ivan Turgenev's **Fathers and Sons** (1862; also in *Literature and Its Times*), which dramatizes the conflict between the old radicals of the 1840s and the new radicals of the 1860s.

Reception. *Crime and Punishment* was well received in Russia both by contemporary critics and by the reading public, becoming Dostoyevsky's first widely selling novel. Early critics praised its exploration of the contemporary issues that preoccupied Russians so urgently, applauding Dostoyevsky's skill in weaving those issues into an artistically compelling tale. The critic N. Strakhov, for one, praised Dostoyevsky's sensitive characterization of a nihilist central character. Unlike previous attempts of this kind, Strakhov observed, Raskolnikov "is not a phrase-monger devoid of blood and nerves; he is a real man. . . . For the first time, an unhappy nihilist, a nihilist suffering in a deeply human way, is depicted before us" (Strakhov, p. 485).

Despite both critical esteem and popularity during his lifetime, however, Dostoyevsky's literary reputation suffered somewhat in the decades after his death. In particular, Soviet critics of the

Crime and Punishment

twentieth century condemned his conservatism and religiosity, which conflicted with the socialist atheism of Soviet doctrine.

More recent criticism has restored Dostoyevsky to the first rank of the nineteenth century's great novelists. His fiction has been identified as a major inspiration for leading twentieth-century authors such as James Joyce and William Faulker, with *Crime and Punishment*'s influence extending to genres as diverse as suspense fiction (of which it has been called an early example) and existential novels such as Albert Camus's **The Stranger** (1942; also in *Literature and Its Times*). Modern critics have particularly acclaimed *Crime and Punishment* for its subtle artistic complexity and psychological insight. Sigmund Freud (see **On Dreams**, also in *Literature and Its Times*) credited Dostoyevsky for foreshadowing his revolutionary psychological theories, and scholar Gary Cox writes that the novel "has probably inspired more psychoanalytic criticism than any other work of literature, except perhaps **Hamlet** or **Oedipus Rex** (Cox, pp. 20-21; both also in *Literature and Its Times*).

—Colin Wells

For More Information

Conradi, Peter. *Fyodor Dostoyevsky*. New York: St. Martin's, 1988.

Cox, Gary. *Crime and Punishment: A Mind to Murder*. Boston: Twayne, 1990.

Crankshaw, Edward. *The Shadow of the Winter Palace: Russia's Drift Toward Revolution 1825-1917*. New York: Viking, 1976.

Dostoyevsky, Fyodor. *Crime and Punishment*. New York: Modern Library, 1950.

———. *The Notebooks for Crime and Punishment*. Ed. and trans. Edward Wasiolek. Chicago: University of Chicago Press, 1967.

Frank, Joseph. *Dostoevsky: The Miraculous Years 1865-1871*. Princeton: Princeton University Press, 1995.

———. *Through the Russian Prism: Essays on Russian Literature and Culture*. Princeton: Princeton University Press, 1990.

Hingley, Ronald. *Russian Writers and Society 1825-1904*. New York: McGraw-Hill, 1967.

Strakhov, N. "The Nihilists and Raskolnikov's New Idea." in *Crime and Punishment*, by Fyodor Dostoyevsky. Ed. George Gibian. New York: Norton, 1989.

Wasiolek, Edward. *Crime and Punishment and the Critics*. San Francisco: Wadsworth, 1961.

Death in Venice

by
Thomas Mann

Thomas Mann (1875-1955) was born in the North German city of Lübeck. His father was a wealthy businessman and municipal leader. His mother was half-Portuguese; the daughter of a German trader, she had spent her childhood in Brazil. When Mann's father died in 1891, the family moved south to Munich. Showing little interest in business, both Thomas and his older brother Heinrich decided to pursue writing careers. Heinrich Mann gained global renown for his novel *Professor Unrat* (1905), made world-famous by the film version *The Blue Angel*, with actress Marlene Dietrich in her first starring role. At 25 Thomas Mann garnered substantial praise, and enjoyed high sales, for his first novel *Buddenbrooks* (1900), a story about three generations of a merchant family. He went on to write a series of popular and critically respected novels and novellas, including *Tonio Kröger* (1903), *Death in Venice* (1912), *The Magic Mountain* (1924), and *Joseph and His Brothers* (1933). In the midst of the series, in 1929, he won the Nobel Prize for Literature. Mann meanwhile became disaffected from Germany. Although a patriot and a passionate believer in German culture, he grew more liberal in his politics after World War I. In 1933, when the Nazis completed their takeover of Germany, Mann went into exile, and during the Second World War, he became a U.S. citizen. He completed what is probably his most complex novel, *Doctor Faustus*, in 1947. Mann spent the last years of his life in Switzerland, as one of the two great German-language novelists of the century, the other being the Czech Franz

> **THE LITERARY WORK**
>
> A novella, set in Munich, Germany, and Venice, Italy, in 1911; published in German (as *Der Tod in Venedig*) in 1912; in English in 1925.
>
> **SYNOPSIS**
>
> Gustav von Aschenbach, a middle-aged writer, vacations in Venice, where an epidemic and his obsession with a young boy bring Aschenbach's previously well-ordered existence into turmoil.

Kafka. Throughout his life, Mann was fascinated by the workings of imagination as it transforms experience. His *Death in Venice* explores the nature of the creative mind and the relationship between the conscious artist and his or her unconscious drives, focusing in particular on a member of the German upper middle class.

Events in History at the Time of the Novella

Golden age of the upper middle class. The action of Thomas Mann's *Death in Venice* takes place a few years before World War I broke out in August 1914. At the time, as far as most of Europe was concerned, there had been a century of peace, more or less. No major conflict involving all the European powers had taken place since the

Death in Venice

Thomas Mann

Napoleonic Wars at the beginning of the previous century. The Congress of Vienna in 1815 had closed those wars with a set of political and diplomatic arrangements that were designed to stabilize international relations on a long-term basis. When hostilities did occur, they were usually elsewhere in the world, as the European imperial powers sought to secure territory, raw materials, or influence in Asia, Africa, or Latin America. Conflict had not, however, disappeared from Europe completely: Britain and Russia had gone to war over the Crimea in the 1850s; France and Prussia had clashed in 1870-71; and from the middle of the nineteenth century, the rise of nationalism had resulted in new tensions as anticolonial rebellions took place in countries like Hungary and Ireland. Internally, the labor movements in various countries had often turned militant in their battles for workers' rights, and near the end of the century there were anarchist movements that planned and carried out assassinations of heads of state. U.S. President William McKinley, for example, was shot by a young anarchist in 1903. Yet, despite all these worrisome events, the end of the nineteenth and beginning of the twentieth century was the golden age of the European upper middle class. Whether in France, Britain, Sweden, or Germany, this upper middle class, the bourgeoisie—including industrialists, bankers, lawyers, doctors—could look around and see a world set up in its own image. Probably the most visible aspect of this image was the growth of industrial centers.

Industrialization had gradually shifted power from the landed aristocracy to the bourgeoisie, and over the course of the nineteenth century this cycle of change became locked into place in the advanced European nations, including Germany. But the economic ascendancy of the bourgeoisie did not always lead to a change in political rule. Rather, in the major European countries, the aristocracy and the monarchy came to an unspoken but mutually profitable arrangement with the bourgeoisie. The upper middle class would have commercial, professional and educational power in society, but it would not challenge the authority of the monarch, or military and diplomatic policy. Indeed, in Germany, the industrial Ruhr region, with its huge Krupp and Thyssen steel and armaments plants, made possible Germany's bid for international power and influence in the years leading up to World War I. For its part, the aristocracy would accept the best talents of the upper middle class into its ranks. The sons of businessmen could become army officers; the daughters of surgeons married into the landed gentry. This was true elsewhere in Europe too. Obviously there were differences in the different countries, but the basic shift in the social and economic balance was the same.

Germany and national culture. In Germany, a *cultural* nation (manifested in language, folklore, literature, and drama) existed for centuries before a unified *political* nation. Throughout the nineteenth century, the bourgeoisie had often been the most passionate supporters of a unified Germany; they were convinced that the old collection of dukedoms, kingdoms, and independent cities had been preventing Germany's transformation into a fully modern nation. In 1848, as revolutions broke out within countries all over Europe, tensions between the urban, industrialized bourgeoisie and the more provincial aristocracy exploded into armed conflict in Germany and nearby Austria. Ultimately the aristocratic, conservative forces won, but to maintain peace, they were forced to bring the middle classes more and more into the center of political power. In Germany, authority became concentrated in the capital city of Berlin; limited voting rights went to members of the upper middle class (generally only to adult males with fixed assets), and access eased to positions in public office and the civil service. Despite this new state of affairs in the various post-1848 German lands, more than 20 years would pass before Germany became a unified nation. It first emerged as a nation in 1871 after the Franco-Prussian War, under the rule of the King of Prussia. Prussian government would provide the model on which the new nation of Germany was founded. Based on a social ethic of loyalty and obedience, and administered by the aristocracy and a streamlined, military-style civil service, nineteenth-century Prussia, in contrast to France or the United States, was relatively unconcerned with the ideals of political freedom. Instead, duty and authority were considered important factors for national survival, not only to Prussians but to Germans in general, including artists, many of whom were deeply invested in the new nation (as Mann himself was for the first half of his life).

German intellectuals, such as the poet Johann Wolfgang von Goethe (see *Faust*, also in *Literature and Its Times*), had achieved renown before 1871, proving their land to be the cultural equal of the leading European countries. After national unification in 1871, however, the humanistic and universal aspects of German works were often downplayed in favor of a narrower cultural nationalism. German writers were caught between their loyalty to the universal values of their art and the expectation that they must support, and not criticize, the German Empire. In Germany, the idea of the artist as a natural outsider and renegade, no matter how true in certain individual cases, remained a somewhat foreign concept. German writers and intellectuals often felt torn between their duty as patriotic citizens and as critics. They tended to experience, perhaps a lot more keenly than other European peoples, a deep divide between the dutiful, social self and the "real" inner self. In his own career, Thomas Mann felt the pull of opposing forces. He had nationalist feelings about Germany and German prestige, but was also willing to look at society with a critical gaze. The son of a successful Lübeck businessman, he was used to a high standard of living, yet drawn to work that called for sacrificing the security of a respectable professional career for the literary life.

The role of the artist at the turn of the century. Belief in education and intellectual freedom is the great cultural legacy from the European bourgeois tradition to the rest of the world. But latent within this tradition was a cultural crisis: a conflict between the increasingly rational, organized, and industrial nature of society on the one hand, and the need to recognize the non-rational, local, and emotional forces that make up a person on the other. While the bourgeoisie transformed society with revolutionary movements in economics, government, and art, they also brought various forms of restraint into this transformed society: order, respectability, and a functional attitude to the world. Artists in particular balked at this restraint. In protest to it came the late-eighteenth and early-nineteenth-century Romantic movement, which showed high regard for nature, emotion, spontaneous behavior of the individual, and, late in the movement, national culture.

MANN AND THE NAZIS

The conflict between artistic values and national feeling that Thomas Mann experienced would become deeply problematic for German writers after World War I. When younger, Mann saw a positive side to German Romanticism and rejected modern democracy and technocratic civilization, but in the 1920s he became hostile to the violent, anti-Semitic nationalism that permeated Germany. Mann began to see himself as a socialist (although not a supporter of Soviet Communism) and grew increasingly pessimistic regarding the German people as a whole. Convinced that they could not be diverted from the road to war and destruction down which the Nazi Party was taking them, he went into exile. He proceeded to adopt American citizenship and engage in anti-Nazi propaganda work. When Mann returned to Germany for a brief visit in 1948, he found himself in the middle of the ideological struggle between the Federal Republic of Germany (West Germany, allied with the U.S.) and the German Democratic Republic (East Germany, a Soviet satellite state). Both Germanies wanted to claim Mann, the century's leading German novelist, as their own. Throughout his life, Mann remained deeply involved with German ideas and German culture, even though he never returned on a permanent basis after 1933. His 1947 novel, *Doctor Faustus*, is among other things an attempt to understand how a whole culture, as if of a single mind, can travel without blinking toward national self-destruction.

The Romantic movement dwindled as the nineteenth century progressed, but a vestige of it remained, a legacy of opposition to bourgeois conventions on the part of an art that never fully died out. The radical tendency grew toward the end of the nineteenth century. In the 1880s the

Death in Venice

idea emerged that art was a separate, independent creative activity. As though compelled to be at loggerheads with the surrounding society, artists felt they had no duty to nation or society, but only to art. A whole movement revolved around this concept, the so-called Aesthetic Movement, taking root in countries across Europe. Under the banner of "art for art's sake," the movement exalted the status of the artist as a superior, indeed a heroic individual. "Art for art's sake" declared that middle-class society's notion of what was important in life (prosperity, education, stability, good behavior, and so on) could be overturned by a completely different hierarchy of values, one that placed artistic creativity at the forefront. Life itself, went the theory, should be approached as a work of art: it was either beautiful or ugly; no other criterion was relevant. Even nature was subordinate; no longer was it a source of joy or a reflection of the divine order, as under the Romantic movement. Nature now ranked beneath art. The painting of a sunset, for example, was superior in every way to the experience of a real sunset.

The idea of "art for art's sake" had its glory days in the 1890s and faded in the early years of the twentieth century. But this movement too left a legacy; it too influenced future writers. From the Aesthetic movement came an enduring belief that the artist must resist bourgeois society's pressures and assumptions. While the new writings of the early 1900s (D. H. Lawrence in Britain, Marcel Proust in France, James Joyce in Ireland, Thomas Mann in Germany) were not as removed from society, they showed a more assertive belief in artistic independence than was previously the case among novelists and more preoccupation with the very process of writing. At the same time, despite their belief in creative independence, these new writers produced works tied to their own cultures. Lawrence brings England into his fiction, as does Joyce with Ireland (see Lawrence's **Sons and Lovers**, and Joyce's **Dubliners**, also in *Literature and Its Times*). In *Death in Venice*, Mann portrays within one human being the very German tension between the "artist" and the "citizen." The protagonist, Aschenbach, struggles with a number of ungovernable conflicts revolving around his craft, his community, and his social position. He is a German who aims as a writer to enhance the stature of Germany, but he also is an artist with an individual creative imagination. He enjoys the bourgeois lifestyle and the social prestige that his work has brought him, but he also harbors suppressed unconscious desires that threaten this lifestyle. And ultimately, his seemingly secure social personality will disintegrate under the force of these unconscious desires.

The Novella in Focus

The plot. *Death in Venice* opens as the protagonist, the writer Gustav von Aschenbach, leaves his Munich apartment to take a long stroll. Aschenbach has recently (on his fiftieth birthday) been granted the right to use the aristocratic honorific "von" with his name as a reward for his services to the nation. He is clearly a man who has earned his position in life. The books he has written over the previous 25 years (beginning with a popular biography of Frederick the Great of Prussia), have earned him his upper-middle-class status and financial security, as well as his national reputation as a writer. He is a disciplined, almost obsessive worker, sitting at his desk every morning of his adult life, summoning his willpower to overcome his tendency toward indolence. Despite his social position, however, Aschenbach's life is not going well. The accumulated strain of several months' work, as well as the fact that his current project is not advancing, has begun to oppress him. He decides to get out in the early May weather and shake off his writer's block.

Wandering near Munich's North Cemetery, Aschenbach waits at a tram stop. He notices a figure in the doorway of the mortuary chapel: a strange, red-haired man in odd clothes who stares at him in a challenging way. Slightly disturbed by the incident, Aschenbach finds himself longing for a real vacation, something that will break up his routine. He needs to escape the rigid routine he has imposed on himself for so many years. Neither his status in life nor his reputation as a writer satisfies him any more.

Next comes a biographical account of Gustav von Aschenbach. Born in Silesia (a region of east-central Europe), he is the son of a proper middle-rank Prussian civil servant and a mother who is less emotionally restrained. Like Mann himself, Aschenbach grows up under the double influence of his parents, his disciplined father and his artistic, spontaneous mother. "The marriage," as the narrator says, "of sober, official punctiliousness with darker, more fiery impulses brought forth an artist" (Mann, *Death in Venice and Other Tales*, p. 293). Aschenbach has grown up in a solitary way, without knowing "the carefree heedlessness of youth" (*Death in Venice*, p. 294). The loneliness has enabled the writer's talent to emerge—but at a price. The narrator reveals with a surgical accuracy the nature of Aschenbach's literary talent. The writer incorporates a youthful passion into a formal structure that over the years increases in elegance and purity. He can write stories with strange and grotesque elements that nonetheless seem to have a message of moral rectitude and propriety. He is gifted, but his success seems to have involved as much loss as gain. "At an early age," says the narrator, "he married a girl from an academic family, but she passed away after a short period of bliss. He had been left with a daughter, who was now married. He had never had a son" (*Death in Venice*, p. 300).

Returning to the present, Aschenbach takes his badly needed trip. On the steam ferry heading for the city of Venice in Italy, he observes a group of young people and an older man who seems to be in their company. Aschenbach is surprised and disgusted when he sees that the elderly man is trying to create the illusion of a youthful appearance with makeup and inappropriate dress. He feels that the man is humiliating himself and others with his shoddy display of fraudulent youth and energy. Watching the man and his group, Aschenbach, who suffers from lack of sleep, feels "as if a dream-like alienation were spreading out, a bizarre warping of the world" (*Death in Venice*, p. 303). He is not certain how much of his feeling is due to his physical condition and how much to the scene he is looking at; this same uncertainty will recur throughout the novella. Arriving in Venice, Aschenbach feels disappointed in the gray and dreary city. He hires a gondola to take him from the port into the city, and is disturbed by the gondolier, who keeps answering his queries in a way that seems arrogant and sarcastic. The gondolier's appearance is odd, with one or two vaguely diabolical physical traits similar to those of the man that Aschenbach had seen briefly as he waited for the streetcar in Munich. Aschenbach does not seem to notice this resemblance, although he is becoming generally unsettled by the strain of the journey and all his various experiences.

Among the guests in Aschenbach's hotel is a Polish family that includes a boy of about 14 who attracts the writer's attention. He is good-looking but delicate, pale, and graceful. Aschenbach becomes fascinated with the boy, "astonished, indeed, alarmed by the truly godlike beauty of this mortal" (*Death in Venice*, p. 316). He follows the family on their daily outing to the beach, and spends the time trying to watch the boy as he plays with his friends. He cannot fully make out the name that the boy's friends are calling him (it sounds like "Adgio") until he dredges up some memory of his childhood in the German-Polish province of Silesia and realizes the name is Tadeusz, Tadzio for short.

GERMANY AND ITALY

For many years, Italy had represented for Germans and other northern Europeans a world apart—a world of sensual, exotic life and an authentically pre-industrial culture. For the traveler from Munich or Frankfurt or Berlin, the Italian cities and towns were old, mysterious places, full of artistic treasures and dimly lit churches. The Italian countryside was replete with olive trees and sunshine, cheap food and wine, and amusing characters. Thomas Mann uses this standard image for a number of his early novellas, including *Death in Venice*. "Aschenbach," writes one literary historian, "travels to Italy, since by means of its colorful, spirited animation he promises himself deliverance from his previous isolation and self-discipline" (Jonas, p. 35). The relationship between Germany and Italy was complicated. Germans enjoyed the country of Italy but often looked down on Italians as emotional and backward; on the other hand, the growth of Italian fascism preceded the German variety, though the Italian brand lacked the fierce anti-Semitism that marked the German variety from its beginnings. The two countries, both of which came late to political unity, have tended to regard each other with a mixture of fascination, affection, and reserve.

Aschenbach decides to leave Venice the following day, suspecting that the city and its humid atmosphere are gnawing away at his physical and psychological well-being. He has his luggage sent on from the hotel to the railway station, but when he hires a gondola to catch his train he finds himself increasingly divided in his wishes. He wants to go, but is desperate to stay. Almost as if the victim of a savage practical joke, he discovers that his luggage has already been dispatched—to the wrong destination. Feigning annoyance but secretly delighted, Aschenbach returns to the hotel and takes up once more his observation of Tadzio who, he realizes, was the real reason he could not leave the city.

Aschenbach's obsession with Tadzio grows. At the same time, he discovers that he can finally

Death in Venice

Björn Andrésen (left) as Tadzio and Dirk Bogarde as Gustav von Aschenbach in the 1971 film version of *Death in Venice*.

relax his self-discipline in Venice. For the first time in his life, Aschenbach can let go, sit back, and watch the world go by. The central organizing principle of his life—his devotion to his writing and the prestige and respectability that were his reward for that devotion—begins to give way to indolence and sensuality. He spends hours sitting in a deck chair on the beach, watching the boy interacting with his family and playing with friends. His perception of Tadzio seems to swing between a half-platonic, half-sexual attraction and a vision of the boy as a kind of work of art:

> His honey-colored curls snuggled against his temples and his neck, the sun illuminated the down on his upper spine, the fine lineation of the ribs, the symmetry of the chest emerged through the sheer skin on his torso. . . . What breeding, what precision of thought were expressed in this elongated and youthfully perfect body!
> (*Death in Venice*, p. 332)

To the writer, Tadzio is a classical Greek statue come to life.

Aschenbach is dimly aware that he can no longer control his thinking. He realizes that he might be seen stalking Tadzio, but is rapidly ceasing to care. What he gains by the infatuation is another life: "Long-lost feelings, early and precious sufferings of his heart, all of them having died in the severe servitude of his life, now returned, strangely transformed" (*Death in Venice*, p. 338). For one unexpected, captivating moment, Tadzio smiles at Aschenbach as they pass each other on the hotel terrace; the writer is shaken and retreats to the park behind the hotel where, standing alone, he confesses his love for the boy.

After that chance meeting, the pace of the novella quickens and events begin to spiral to a conclusion. It is now four weeks since Aschenbach has arrived in Venice, and he notices that the hotel is losing guests and the city becoming emptier. He questions the hotel barber but receives an evasive answer. From reading the local and foreign papers he realizes that some kind of public health crisis is taking place, but facts are few and far between. That evening, as Aschenbach sits on the hotel terrace after dinner, a group of itinerant musicians performs for the guests. The singer is an aggressive and rather frightening character who, like the gondolier in the earlier passage, seems to bear an eerie resemblance to the man in the Munich cemetery. Again Aschenbach does not notice the resemblance. What he has noticed, however, is that Tadzio's family are trying to keep the boy from approaching him.

The next day, when he talks to an English travel agent, he is informed that a cholera epidemic has broken out in Venice and that the authorities are trying to keep it quiet. Aschenbach realizes that he could resolve a number of situations simply by telling the Polish family that the city is infested and that, for the safety of the whole family, they should leave immediately. But he fails to do so, realizing that he has long since left normal judgment and behavior behind. His keeping quiet about the epidemic becomes analogous to nurturing his secret desires for Tadzio.

That night, Aschenbach has an "appalling dream" in which he is a participant in some ancient and violent rite involving animal sacrifice and sexual excess (*Death in Venice*, p. 357). He feels as if an alien force, suppressed all his life, is finally breaking out from his own soul. The next morning he has himself cosmetically treated, with hair-coloring and rouge, to make himself look younger and more attractive, apparently not realizing that he is doing exactly what he found so objectionable about the old dandy on the ferry. Aschenbach begins to feel physically ill, consumed with dizzy spells and a raging thirst. A few days later, he finds out that the Polish family is planning to leave Venice. He goes to the beach as usual, and watches Tadzio. Perspiring and delirious, the writer is clearly suffering from cholera. The final vision of the boy marching into the waves is obviously too much for his health and sanity, and Aschenbach dies in the deck chair.

Dreams and the unconscious. In *Death in Venice*, Gustav von Aschenbach has a frightening dream after his discovery of the cholera threat. He is in Greece 2,500 years ago, on a hillside in the middle of a primitive rite. Men and women dressed in animal skins dance in the darkness to the pounding cymbals; unearthly howling from the dancers matches the hypnotic flute music. Goats are there, ready for sacrifice to Dionysis, god of wine and of an orgiastic cult bent on celebrating the fertility of nature. The phrase "the alien god" comes to him in the dream. Filled with fear and disgust, he nevertheless wants to join the dance.

> With foaming mouths, they stormed, egged one another on with lewd gestures and lecherous hands, laughing and groaning, thrust the prickle-prod goads into one another's flesh and licked the blood from their limbs. But now the dreamer was with them, one of them, and belonged to the alien god. Yes, they were he himself . . . and on the churned-up mossy ground the promiscuous mating began—a sacrifice to the god. And his soul tasted the frenzy and fornication of doom.
> (*Death in Venice*, p. 359)

In this dream, Aschenbach's intellectual discipline, his belief in a literature of balance and composure, his services to German culture, the solid bourgeois respectability he has maintained—all are crumbling. An absurd infatuation with a young boy in a hotel in Italy over a couple of weeks is enough, as the dream orgy shows, to bring back years of repressed sexual desire and wild sensuality. What he thought he wanted—bourgeois respectability and prestige—he does not care to have; what he really desires and has suppressed now demands to be heard. As he discovers the secret that there is a cholera epidemic, he discovers the secret of himself: his psychic landscape of unconstrained and self-destructive desire.

CHOLERA

Mann and his family did not experience a cholera epidemic directly during the trip they made to northern Italy in 1911. There was a small epidemic at that time, but it was much further south, in the Sicilian capital of Palermo. Mann's use of the disease as a metaphor for a destructive force probably mirrors the fear that the sickness triggered before sanitation and drainage improvements removed the context for the bacterial growth (water infected with human and animal waste is the best environment for the bacterium *Vibrio cholerae*).

Cholera terrified the public imagination during the nineteenth and early twentieth centuries, as a result of major epidemics that hit Asia, Africa, and Europe at various times. Two of the worst epidemics ravaged Russia in the 1890s and India in the early 1900s. Fatalities ran in the hundreds of thousands on each occasion, with the fear of cholera affecting immigration procedures in the United States. In *Death in Venice*, Aschenbach's sudden physical collapse reflects cholera's effect on otherwise healthy individuals. Key to survival are rapid detection and treatment. For victims who do not realize they have been infected, or who cannot quickly replace bodily fluids that have been lost through vomiting and diarrhea, the illness can often be fatal.

Thomas Mann wrote *Death in Venice* before he had read Sigmund Freud's *The Interpretation of Dreams*, or any other of Freud's works. Mann's novella, nonetheless, resembles Freud's investigations of the hidden, powerful, psychic processes that determine human life and the decisions we make (or the decisions we think "we" are making). His description of Aschenbach's dream matches almost precisely the map of repressed desires making themselves felt in dreams that Freud describes in his work:

> A form of expression for impulses which are hampered by resistance by day, but are able to draw reinforcements from deep sources of excitation by night. . . . The respect ancient peoples paid to dreams is a tribute, based on a true psychological intimation, to the untamed, indestructible elements in the human soul, the *daemonic* powers that produce the dream-wish.
> (Freud, p. 406)

Aschenbach has subjected everything in life to control, but his dream shows that what he believed he banished, or successfully suppressed is still present, still an insistent part of him.

Over 20 years after *Death in Venice* was published, Thomas Mann gave a lecture in Vienna in honor of Sigmund Freud's eightieth birthday. In this 1936 lecture, published as "Freud and the Future," Mann expresses his respect and admiration for Freud and his work on dreams, the unconscious, and psychoanalysis (Mann, *Essays of Three Decades*, pp. 411-28). Mann explains also that he came late in life to Freud's work—he first read it in the 1920s—but that Freud's key texts clarified some concerns he had been wrestling with in his own writing. He suggests that authors and philosophers over the ages had always sensed the presence of unconscious forces, but had never approached them with the scientific detachment of Freud and his colleagues. Thus, psychoanalysts like Freud and writers like Mann himself were at the cutting edge of a scientific and creative movement that sought, at the beginning of the twentieth century, to shed light on the inner workings of the mind, and strove to give humanity new ways of thinking about itself.

Sources and literary context. In his novella *Tonio Kröger* (1903), Thomas Mann created a young, sensitive artist who eventually finds his self-confidence and comes to terms with his separation from the social mainstream (this sense of separation involves, among other things, a shifting sexual orientation). Readers had responded positively to *Tonio Kröger*, so the publication, nine years later, of *Death in Venice* took a risk by showing the same kind of artist-protagonist in a much more negative light: middle-aged, with a fragile grip on his life and an obsession for a young boy. The issue of homoerotic attraction is a key element of both works, and his biographers have suggested that Mann's own divided sexual feelings were being explored in the two novellas.

In part, the motive for the later novella appears to have been a desire on Mann's part to write a darker, more serious and mature version of *Tonio Kröger*. According to one critic, in the later novella he was "passing a ruthless judgment on himself" (Lukacs, p. 24).

Tonio Kröger and *Death in Venice*, although more ambitious than similar efforts from that period, were also part of a wider literary fashion. The so-called *Künstlerroman*, a novel with an artist as the central character, became exceptionally popular in Germany around the turn of the century. It was a national variant of a wider European genre (see, for example, James Joyce's **A Portrait of the Artist as a Young Man,** also in *Literature and Its Times*). The German variety seemed to capture a specifically German phenomenon. In the wider European sense, the artist is usually a withdrawn, passive figure, committed to art but guilt ridden: "effete, sexually impotent, crippled with doubts . . . unproductive in contrast with the robust society that has no place for him" (Gray, p. 31). But in German stories (like Hermann Hesse's *Rosshalde* [1914] and Jakob Wassermann's *Das Gänsemännchen* [1931, The Goose Man]), the ideology of the social mainstream always seems to have the upper hand. There seemed to be little space in German culture for the more critical stance toward middle-class society reflected in novels like Joyce's *Portrait of the Artist as a Young Man*.

As in the work of other novelists over the first couple of decades of the twentieth century, Mann's writing is often concerned with the artist and his ability (or inability) to transform his experience into something new. In *Death in Venice*, Mann created a composite portrait of a German artist and intellectual. One of the specific figures that he drew on for his character Aschenbach was the composer Gustav Mahler. Mahler died while the Mann family was on their Italian trip in 1911, and Mann decided to use the composer's first name in *Death in Venice* as a memorial gesture. Mann drew also on German philosophers, among them Friedrich Nietzsche, who wrote *Beyond Good and Evil* (1886), Nietzsche criticized Christian morality and optimistic theories of historical progress. Along with other nineteenth-century philosophers, he saw morality as a relatively recent development in human history, one that was many-leveled and self-lacerating.

Reception. *Death in Venice* went into its second printing within weeks of its 1912 publication. Although reviews were generally enthusiastic, there was some negative response—primarily from Mann's own colleagues. Both older German writers, who objected to Mann's themes, and younger writers, who regarded his commitment to realism as limiting and dull, found fault with *Death in Venice*. The poet Rainer Maria Rilke (1875-1926), for one, felt the second half sloshed "all over the place like a spilt bottle of ink" (Rilke in Schröter, p. 80). Writer Stefan Zweig (1881-1942) condemned what he saw as an obsession with bourgeois experience.

The initial American response to *Death in Venice* was generally positive, although the theme of the story caused some consternation. The *New York Times* commented that "it should in fairness be added that it is written with exquisite tact and delicacy and that its implications will only be misunderstood by the coarse and literal mind" (*New York Times* in Knight and James, p. 450). The *Literary Review* spoke of the novella's dealing "with more or less abnormal twistings of natural instincts" in a way that "leaves you with a sense of immaculate purity" (*Literary Review* in Knight and James, p. 450).

A second translation that appeared in the collection entitled *Stories from Three Decades* (1936) garnered reviews that suggest a distinct increase in Mann's reputation. Cyril Connolly in the London *New Statesman and Nation* commented that "this book presents, in the most readable way possible, the picture of a fine writer and his time"; with less reserve, Louis Gannet in the *New York Herald Tribune* wrote: "No writer in the present-day world has faced his age with a more profound pessimism; none has left his readers so little depressed" (*New Statesman and Nation* and *New York Herald Tribune* in James and Brown, pp. 644-45).

—Martin Griffin

For More Information

Brose, Eric Dorn. *German History 1789-1871*. Providence, R.I.: Berghahn Books, 1997.

Freud, Sigmund. *The Interpretation of Dreams*. Trans. Joyce Crick. New York: Oxford University Press, 1999.

Gray, Ronald. *The German Tradition in Literature*. New York and London: Cambridge University Press, 1965.

James, Mertice M., and Dorothy Brown, eds. *The Book Review Digest*. 32nd Annual Cumulation. New York: H. W. Wilson, 1937.

Jonas, Ilsedore B. *Thomas Mann and Italy*. Trans. Betty Crouse. Tuscaloosa: The University of Alabama Press, 1979.

Knight, Marion A., and Mertice M. James, eds. *The Book Review Digest*. 21st Annual Cumulation. New York: H. W. Wilson, 1926.

Lukacs, Georg. *Essays on Thomas Mann*. Trans. Stanley Mitchell. London: Merlin, 1965.

Mann, Thomas. *Death in Venice and Other Tales*. Trans. Joachim Neugroschel. New York: Viking, 1998.

———. "Freud and the Future." In *Essays of Three Decades*. Trans. H. T. Lowe-Porter. New York: Alfred A. Knopf, 1948.

Prater, Donald. *Thomas Mann: A Life*. New York: Oxford University Press, 1995.

Schröter, Klaus. *Thomas Mann, mit Selbstzeugnissen und Bilddokumenten*. Reinbek, Germany: Rowohlt, 1964.

The Death of Ivan Ilyich

by
Leo Tolstoy

Leo Tolstoy had reason enough to lead a happy life. Born into an aristocratic and wealthy family in 1828, his material needs were easily met. His greatest novels, *War and Peace* and **Anna Karenina** (also in *Literature and Its Times*) brought him the adulation of his contemporaries and enduring fame as one of the world's greatest writers. Yet, despite his successes, he suffered great emotional torment. He longed for the mother who died in his infancy, and he lost his father and other important family members during his childhood. The fear of his own death haunted him, sometimes propelling him toward religious orthodoxy, at other times creating nearly psychotic levels of anxiety. The subject of death surfaces frequently in his writings, but is treated most fully and with the greatest emotional depth in *The Death of Ivan Ilyich*.

Events in History at the Time of the Novella

Bureaucracy in nineteenth-century Russia. Throughout the nineteenth century, czars and ministers attempted repeatedly to reorganize Russia's burgeoning administration to keep pace with changes confronting the nation. They needed an administrative system that, among other things, would support imperial expansion, guide the emancipation of serfs, regularize the government of the provinces, and modernize the nation's laws and their enforcement. While Russia obtained a measure of success with each of these objectives, the bureaucracy remained inefficient. Corruption

THE LITERARY WORK

A novella set in St. Petersburg and in the provinces of Russia from the 1850s to 1882; published in Russian (as *Smert Ivana Ilycha*) in 1886, in English in 1887.

SYNOPSIS

A magistrate in Russia's legal bureaucracy, Ivan Ilyich preoccupied himself with promotions, prestige, and the quest for ever higher standards of living. These preoccupations, however, dissolve after a minor accident in his home leads to a mysterious illness that slowly takes his life.

was commonplace. Payment for empty, upper-level jobs that demanded little work was expected. Many departments and offices were redundant, while some appeared to have no use at all. Yet despite its inefficiencies and continued attempts at reform, the system remained largely intact until the Russian Revolution.

The difficulty in reforming the Russian bureaucracy was related to its design in the previous century, when Peter the Great (1682-1725) revised the government to imitate administrative bodies in Western Europe. Following the Swedish model of government, he instituted "colleges," or ministries, for branches such as finance, justice, commerce, and foreign affairs. Rather than having a single chief minister, each ministry was governed by a board of 12 individuals. The

The Death of Ivan Ilyich

Leo Tolstoy

colleges were responsible to the Senate, which did not have independent deliberative power but served as a council to do the bidding of the czar, who was the undisputed center of political control. Over this whole apparatus Peter the Great devised the office of the procurator-general—a particularly Russian position, which was given wide powers of surveillance to make sure that the Senate and other ministries were enacting the czar's will. Another important practice modeled on those of Western Europe was the structure for placement and promotion within the ministries. In 1722 Peter developed the Table of Ranks, which consisted of 14 grades and indicated one's rank in the civil service, the military, and at court (one could hold different ranks in each area of service). Somewhat democratic, the system required that gentry and non-gentry alike all begin at the bottom rank, and that the non-gentry, upon attaining the eighth grade of service, receive the hereditary rights of the nobility. Although this system of ranking and promotion was revised slightly over the years, it remained intact until 1917.

Neither the administrative system of colleges nor the Table of Ranks provided the machinelike precision that its founders had sought. In theory, the college structure, with its 12-person leadership, would ensure that collective wisdom prevailed in policy decisions. In practice, it led to frequent stalemates and a lack of personal responsibility. Early in the nineteenth century, Czar Alexander I replaced the colleges with ministries headed up by one minister, though some structures of the college system lingered on. In general, the leadership structure and the number of ministries changed, or rather continued to change throughout the nineteenth century, while the rank and file in the civil service experienced little reform, living and dying by a system of rankings that promoted abuse, bitterness, and stagnation. The nobility monopolized the upper-level positions. The many nobles already occupying the higher ranks tended to select other nobles for promotions. Some nobles even jumped ahead several ranks because they had been registered for civil service at birth, and they received regular promotions when they were still children. Practices such as these created resentment, especially among those in the lower ranks who did the bulk of the work, and, as a revenge tactic, learned to do it as inefficiently as possible.

Throughout the nineteenth century, corruption, an emphasis on surveillance, and over-centralization plagued government administration. Especially in the provinces, away from Moscow and St. Petersburg, citizens suffered bribery and extortion at the hands of government officials who ostensibly were being paid to serve them. Each czar instituted increasingly powerful agencies of surveillance that not only tried to suppress political and religious dissent, but also kept an eye on other policing agencies. The climate of paranoia and officiousness gave the people the urge to document everything, which increased the load of paperwork to be scrutinized and acted upon. Such a climate also made them less inclined to take responsibility for their decisions, which led to an increasingly centralized bureaucracy, involving the highest levels of the ministry and even the czar himself in the trivial details of government. Rather than collapse under its own weight, however, it took a revolution to undo the system. As Vladimir Lenin predicted, the proletariat would "break up the bureaucratic apparatus . . . shatter it to its very foundations, until not one stone is left upon another" (Lenin in M. N. Pokrovskii, p. 68).

Reforms in the ministry of justice. Despite the systematic intransigence of Russia's bureaucracy, the 1860s witnessed the "Great Reforms," which included the emancipation of the serfs, the establishment of elected assemblies at the provincial and county levels (called *zemstvos*), and changes in the military. But perhaps the most striking of all the reforms was the thorough revision of the nation's legal system. In a few short years, Russia's judiciary system was transformed from one of the worst in Europe to, arguably, one of the finest.

Indeed, in the first half of the nineteenth century, the word "system" hardly applied to the chaotic assemblage of courts and procedures in charge of enforcing the equally chaotic law of the land. Throughout the nation, there was little consistency in the powers and jurisdictions of the various courts, and the procedures for trials in one court might not apply in another. Appeals could delay a case for years, and the slowness of the procedure often ruined the fortunes of the litigants before their affairs were settled. Juries were nonexistent. The fate of the litigants rested in the hands of judges who were often appointed because of their political connections, not for their knowledge of law. Ignorant and prone to corruption, many judges succumbed to political influence, since they could easily be replaced if their decisions were unpopular with the officials on whom the courts depended.

In the decades before the 1860s, there was much talk of legal reform but very little action. In 1833, Count Michael Speransky provided a much needed codification of Russian law, but the legal system itself remained unaffected. By 1862, S. I. Zarudny and K. N. Zamiatnin had formulated a set of "Basic Principles" for a restructured judiciary, and these principles met with the approval of learned jurists, university authorities, and Czar Alexander II as well as his Council of State. Statutes were formulated in accordance with these principles, and in 1864, they were enacted first in Moscow and St. Petersburg, and then throughout the country.

These judicial reforms of 1864 gave Russia a legal system modeled on those found in Western Europe, particularly in France. It created a permanent judgeship and a judiciary independent of other ministries. Procedural matters became regularized, juries were instituted, and equality of all citizens before the law was somewhat accepted. Consistency and order began to characterize the system of courts as well. In the provinces, justices of the peace heard cases that involved reprimands, fines under 300 rubles, or jail sentences from three months to a year. More significant cases would be handled by regional courts headed by judges who were appointed by the czar at the recommendation of the judicial ministry, which ensured a more learned and competent judgeship. The appeal process was also improved by the establishment of separate courts for civil and criminal actions while the Senate, acting as the Supreme Court, remained the final appellate body. Finally the statutes established an official bar for lawyers, which brought standards of education and discipline to professional litigants.

> **FRUSTRATIONS WITH BUREAUCRACY**
>
> In his memoirs, Baron Korf recounts the dismay felt by an official who temporarily headed up the secretariat of Czar Nicholas I:
>
> In the midst of matters of first-rate importance, on which the sovereign's attention should be concentrated, they loaded him with an innumerable multitude of trivial affairs, and yet how simple and convenient it would have been to lighten the emperor's labours at least by half, without doing any harm to the business of government.
>
> (Korf in Seton-Watson, p. 210)

Despite these sweeping changes, some limitations remained. Military and ecclesiastical courts still had a great deal of power in that they decided a wide range of issues, from criminal cases to divorce proceedings. Moreover, the notion of equality before the law did not take root thoroughly. Czars, ministers, reactionaries, and revolutionaries regarded themselves as above the law when it suited their political aims. At the other end of the spectrum came groups deemed "beneath" the law, that is, not deserving of its benefits. By the 1880s, some of the legal reforms had been rolled back, particularly those dealing with emancipated serfs, and curbs had been put on the privilege to exile "undesirables." Nevertheless, the changes enacted in 1864 acquired great political importance, making the courts a center of public interest where participants enjoyed greater freedom of expression than anywhere else in Russian society. Of all the Great Reforms, the ones overhauling the judicial system were widely considered the most successful.

The Novella in Focus

The plot. While at recess during a trial, four members of the law courts in St. Petersburg are discussing another, more famous case. One of the

The Death of Ivan Ilyich

four glances through a recently delivered newspaper and announces that their colleague, Ivan Ilyich Golovin, has died. The news causes them to express sadness outwardly; inwardly they consider how his death might lead to promotions or new positions for themselves. One of the four, Pyotr Ivanovich, had studied law with Ivan Illyich and was his oldest friend. Yet even he seems inconvenienced by the death, irritated that he must now pay his last respects rather than go to dinner and play cards with his friends.

While paying his respects, he meets Ivan Ilyich's wife, who wants to have a word with him in private. Clearly uncomfortable, Pyotr Ivanovich makes a few sympathetic remarks, which interests the wife much less than how she might receive a larger pension from the government than it had already offered upon her husband's death. When it becomes clear that she knows more about these affairs than Pyotr Ivanovich, they politely yet awkwardly end the interview. During the memorial service that follows their discussion, Pyotr Ivanovich recognizes other members of the Golovin household: the daughter, who appears to resent the inconvenience of these proceedings; her fiancée, who looks equally annoyed; and the son, whose red-rimmed eyes reveal his grief. Upon leaving the household, Pyotr Ivanovich again struggles to find a socially acceptable remark to make about Ivan Ilych's death to the peasant boy Gerasim, who cared for Ivan Ilyich during his final weeks. While helping Pyotr Ivanovich into his carriage, Gerasim serenely replies that Ivan Ilyich's death is God's will and that we all have to die sometime. Pyoty Ivanovich proceeds to focus on the moment. Having escaped the atmosphere of death and realizing the evening is still young, he joins his friends for a game of cards.

Now that it has shown us a wide range of social reactions to the death of Ivan Ilyich, the novella turns to the man himself, revealing how he lived and the terror with which he confronted his own mortality. He was the son of a bureaucrat who had received a sinecure (paid position that demanded little work) in one of the many useless ministries in the Russian government. Like his father, Ivan Ilyich became a civil servant. He attended law school, established a reputation for being likeable and good-natured, and followed the trends and manners of those with high social standing. He graduated from law school with a degree that allowed him a position in the tenth rank of the civil service, and his father gave him money for his uniform and found him a position in an unnamed province (as an assistant to the governor). In his work he cultivated an efficient and at times severe manner, but in society he was pleasant and affable, ever seeking what was most fashionable and most proper, always taking his cues from the upper ranks of society. In both his work and his social life, Ivan Ilyich steered a firm course, guided by self-interested pleasure on the one side and social propriety on the other.

Thus lived Ivan Ilyich for about five years, after which he was promoted during the sweeping reforms of the justice system in 1864. He had a reputation for being the sort of "new man" the government needed to foster order and reason in the reformed court system, so he was assigned to a judicial post in a new province. As before, he pursued efficiency, a good reputation, and, most of all, the feeling of power that his work gave him. He prided himself on being above corruption and on reducing his cases to their absolute essentials, leaving no trace of his personal judgments or sympathies in them. He acclimated just as quickly to a new social circle, where he met Praskovya Fyodorovna. She fell in love with him, and though he had not intended to marry, he proposed nevertheless. After all, Praskovya Fyodorovna was attractive, came from a good family, and had a little money—a good match, Ivan thought, if not the dazzling one he would have hoped for had marriage been his intention.

Ivan Ilyich planned to conduct his marriage by the same values of pleasure and propriety that had served him so well to this point. But he soon learned that his marriage, however proper, was not going to be pleasant. He was dismayed by his wife's unfounded jealousies and demands, her criticisms and her outbursts, all of which grew worse with the birth of each child. Alienated from his wife and children, he took refuge in his work; from his home life he sought only the expected conveniences of good food, a well-managed dwelling, and sexual pleasure.

Three years after his marriage, he was promoted to assistant public prosecutor, and later was promoted again to public prosecutor for a new province. Despite his higher salary, his household was always short of money. His wife despised the new town, and the raising of their children was a constant source of conflict. He endured these unpleasantries for many years, during which he became increasingly obsessed with promotions and salaries and refused many positions offered to him in hopes of a more prestigious post. In 1880 he hoped to receive a

The General Staff Headquarters, one of the centers of bureaucracy in St. Petersburg.

position as the presiding judge in a university town, but was passed over in favor of a close associate. Incensed, Ivan Ilyich argued with this associate and with superiors, creating a great deal of resentment toward himself. Seeing that any further promotion might be denied him, he began looking for any position that would provide a salary of 5,000 rubles.

He met with surprisingly quick success. On a job-prospecting visit to St. Petersburg, he landed a position in the Ministry of Justice that put him two ranks above his colleagues in the provinces, provided a 5,000-ruble salary, and an additional 3,000 rubles for relocating. Triumphant, Ivan Ilyich related the news to his overjoyed family, and he began to hope that he might yet obtain the pleasant and proper life that he believed was owed him. He rented an apartment and undertook all the arrangements for furnishing and decorating their new home. One day, while showing an upholsterer exactly how he wanted some draperies hung, he slipped off a stepladder. He avoided serious injury, but received a bruise on his side. The pain quickly receded, however, and Ivan Ilyich did not give the incident another thought, other than to joke about it with his family. For a time, his happiness was greater than it had ever been. His home was impeccable, his family circulated in the best social circles, and his work life was easy and orderly.

Ivan Ilyich's injury, however, turned out to be no joke. He began to notice a strange taste in his mouth and felt a pressure in his side that, while not painful, caused discomfort. Gradually discomfort grew into a dull, constant ache, and he became irritable and distracted. His perplexed wife persuaded him to visit a famous physician, and the visit went as he had expected. The doctor was as brisk and indifferent in the examining room as Ivan Ilyich was in the courtroom, yet for all the confidence he exuded, he could not identify Ivan Ilyich's illness. When the magistrate asked if his condition was serious, the doctor regarded the question as irrelevant and whisked the frightened magistrate out of his office.

His condition worsened. Ivan Ilyich's breath became decidedly foul. His appetite failed him, and he was losing strength. He sought the opinion of another celebrated physician, who provided no more clarity or hope than the first. More doctors followed, but to no avail. Ivan Ilyich came to understand that his illness was fatal, that a life of pleasure and propriety—the only thing that mattered to him—was coming to an end. The prospect of his death became a constant terror, and he experienced an absolute break between himself and the living. He felt no connection even with his family, who could not accept his imminent death. In fact, Ivan Ilyich developed contempt for the living because they were happily unaware of their own mortality. Only Gerasim, one of the peasant servants in the household, became a source of consolation. The boy changed Ivan Ilyich's bedding, administered medicines, and patiently allowed the invalid to put his legs on the boy's shoulders to relieve the pain. Of all who spoke with Ivan Ilyich, only Gerasim saw no shame in dying, and no need to ignore the fact of death.

In his final days, Ivan Ilyich experienced an emotional and spiritual suffering that rivaled his physical pain, but he also achieved awareness of salvation. As his illness progressed he recognized that his life, guided by propriety and pleasure, was not really life at all, but delusion. The agony of these perceptions climaxed one evening when his wife persuaded him to take communion. Afterwards, when she asked if he felt better, he first said "yes," but later, realizing that the answer was untrue, screamed "no" and continued screaming for three straight days. On the third day, however, his son reached out to hold his hand, and this gesture helped Ivan Ilyich realize that he could still have a true life by doing something for others, even if all he had left to do was to die. At this realization, a light penetrated his spiritual darkness. Beyond speech, he tried to ask his family to forgive him, and though he failed to communicate with them, he realized God had heard him. And with that realization, he died.

Changes in the Russian family. In the final moments of his life, Ivan Ilyich feels a new kind of grief—not for himself this time, but for his wife and his son who watch him die. Seeing their tears, he realizes that by hanging on to life he causes them great pain, and that his dying would free them to seek a better life. This last-minute empathy for his own family is not separate from the spiritual breakthrough that gives him the courage to let go of life, but rather lies at the very core of his transformation. In doing something for his family—even dying—he overturns his deep-seated convictions that the family centers on him, existing for his convenience and requiring his presence for its sustenance. These convictions were far from unique to Ivan Ilyich, but belonged to a whole set of assumptions and practices about the family that were undergoing gradual change throughout the nineteenth century. The traditional Russian family included a married couple, their children, and unmarried adult relatives, and often more than one married couple lived in a household. The typical family was father-centered—or, more exactly, it was patriarchal, hierarchical, and authoritarian, with the oldest father holding sway over the other men. The men ranked higher than the women in a household, and both ranked higher than the children. Throughout most of the nineteenth century, Russian law supported this family arrangement, vesting all legal powers in the male head of the family, providing virtually no legal standing to women, and promoting strict obedience from children through bodily punishment. While a family strove for the collective good of the whole, it was the father who dictated how the family would work toward that good. Increasing modernization and urbanization, however, reshaped both the size of the traditional family, and the relationships within it. The demands of urban labor and work in the civil service promoted what we recognize today as the modern nuclear family—a married couple, their children, and occasionally an unmarried relative. Compared to the traditional family, which has its roots in the largely agrarian Russian society, these more modern families could better respond to transfers in work assignments or other sudden shifts in the job market. These smaller, more mobile families retained many of the patriarchal and authoritarian assumptions of the traditional family, but the roles became less rigidly distinct. Gradually the authority of the father weakened throughout the nineteenth century. Wives became more active in managing the business affairs of the household and enjoyed more protection from the law after wife beating became a criminal offense in 1845. Children could still be disciplined physically, but in general the relationship between father and offspring was dominated less by strict obedience and more by affection. In *The Death of Ivan Ilyich*, Tolstoy provides his thoroughly modern man with a thoroughly modern family, one that, with the exception of servants, differs little from the nuclear family that has become the norm in developed countries throughout the world. Ivan Ilyich and his wife, Praskovya Fyodorovna, have two children, a daughter and a son, and they live a somewhat rootless existence, following Ivan Ilyich on his various governmental appointments. Their contact with an extended family is minimal. To cut down on expenses one summer, the wife and children stay with Ivan Ilyich's brother-in-law and sister-in-law, who receive them tepidly and are glad to see them go. Within the family itself, Ivan Ilyich's experience as a father and a husband reflects the decreased stature of these roles. His wife is openly critical of him and constantly questions their finances. The daughter also has a lot of freedom. She seems to visit her fiancé with minimal supervision, and she is clearly eager to cast off her affiliation with her parents and brother. The son remains very undeveloped as a character, but it is clear that his relationship to his father is shaped more by affection than obedience. In general, the family of Ivan Ilyich reflects a modern ideal that Tolstoy acknowledges, but, being deeply traditional in this regard, does not endorse. He himself idealized the older model, still evident in the lifestyles of Russia's rural peasants; Tolstoy strove to model his own family after theirs.

Tolstoy's sources. As with many of his other fictional works, Tolstoy synthesized a wide range of events, personal experiences, and convictions into *The Death of Ivan Ilyich*. The premise of the novella came from the death in 1881 of Ivan Ilich Mechnikov, who was a judge in the court at Tula, a provincial town near Tolstoy's estate. Tolstoy had learned of the death from Mechnikov's brother, and from this news Tolstoy developed the idea for a story called *The Death of a Judge*. Tolstoy's first idea was to tell the story through the judge's diary, which, using the first person, would reveal the man's struggles with his own mortality. Ultimately, however, Tolstoy chose to write the narrative in the third person, giving more scope to the social reactions to his character's impending death and providing a wider view of his conventional, materialistic life. Tolstoy may have had a separate interest in Mechnikov's occupation, as his original title for the story suggests. Here was a judge who had to render judgment on himself and stand before the highest judge of all. Considering Tolstoy's life, his own activities support his having such an interest. The year Mechnikov died, Tolstoy frequently visited prisoners in the jail at Tula, sometimes accompanying them to the train platform as they were deported to Siberia. In his diary, he marvels at the arbitrariness of the deportations, finding that although some deportees were indeed corrupt, others received the same fate for trivial offenses or no offenses at all.

While the occasion for the story came from the death of a provincial judge, Tolstoy drew amply from his own life to give Ivan Ilyich the contours of his character, particularly in the face of death. Many years before the composition of *The Death of Ivan Ilyich*, Tolstoy had had a terrifying encounter with his own mortality that surfaced recurrently the rest of his days. On the evening of September 3, 1869, Tolstoy was far from home on a business venture when he suddenly became unsettled, losing any sense of purpose in his trip. He and the servant boy with whom he traveled stopped for the night in the village of Arzamas. Tolstoy's anxiety grew, and he became unsettled by the very room in which he was to stay—its dimensions, its white walls, its dark red furniture. When he later awoke in the dark, not knowing where he was or what he was doing there, he became entirely gripped by the fear of death. He felt not only its inevitability but also its presence in every moment of life. The terror of this night stayed with Tolstoy the rest of his days. Five years before beginning *The Death of Ivan Ilyich*, Tolstoy tried to shape the terror of Arzamas into a story. He never finished the tale, but the terror of death, along with the devastating awareness of wasted life, endured in Tolstoy's mind until it became the thematic core of his successful novella.

Other incidental details also appear to derive from Tolstoy's life. The perpetual enmity between Ivan Ilyich and his wife parallels the struggle between Leo and Sonya Tolstoy, particularly in the years leading up to *The Death of Ivan Ilyich*. During this time, Tolstoy's interest in philosophy and his vocal criticisms of Russian Orthodoxy alienated him from his own family, which, to him, seemed concerned only with material wealth and pleasure. Conversely Tolstoy's abandonment of a literary career and his desire to live alongside the peasants dismayed his wife, who was left alone to manage the estate and to raise the children. Their differences caused frequent and perhaps even violent arguments. Lastly, the circumstances surrounding Ivan Ilyich's injury are drawn loosely from the author's own experiences. His wife yearned for city life, and his older children needed to pursue advanced education in the city as well, so, in one of his few capitulations to his family, he helped them move to Moscow in 1881. The following year, Tolstoy put himself in charge of buying a house in the city and became absorbed in all the details of renovation—the wallpaper, the carpentry, and the furnishings. Here too we see Tolstoy using the details of his own life to decorate the world of his hapless judge.

Reception. Tolstoy's novella was an immediate success. It was the first piece of substantial fiction that Tolstoy had published since the dazzling triumph of *Anna Karenina* ten years earlier, and it has come to be regarded as one of the finest novellas of all time. What it lacks in the expansive scope of Tolstoy's novels, it gains in intense focus and compression. After reading the novella, the Russian composer Peter Ilich Tchaikovsky remarked in his diary that "more than ever, I am convinced that the greatest author-painter who ever lived is Leo Tolstoy" (Tchaikovsky in Troyat, p. 462). In a similar vein, the Russian critic Vladimir Stasov wrote to Tolstoy, claiming "no nation anywhere in the world has a work as great as this. Everything is little and petty in comparison with these seventy pages" (Stasov in Troyat, p. 462). The world at large was inclined to agree. The French writer Romain Rolland, one of Tolstoy's first biographers, said the novella had a remarkable impact even among the normally staid, unshakable French bourgeoisie. Of those who responded less than favorably, perhaps the most noteworthy was the brother of the judge upon whom Tolstoy based his story. Although he did not like careerists like his brother, the other Mechnikov claimed that the judge's enlightenment was far greater than even a master like Tolstoy could render it.

Most of the literary world, however, has been satisfied with Tolstoy's achievement. The premise of Tolstoy's novella, along with the delicate treatment he afforded its main character, has influenced the works of subsequent authors, from Arthur Miller's **Death of a Salesman** (also in *Literature and Its Times*) to Alexander Solzhenitsyn's *Cancer Ward*. In these and many other works, authors owe a debt to Tolstoy's rendering of the death of an average man, one who makes no great stir in the world, but whose suffering and salvation reveal his humanity and his dignity.

—Jeff Morris

For More Information

Blythe, Ronald. "Introduction." *The Death of Ivan Ilyich*. New York: Bantam, 1981.

Charques, R. D. *A Short History of Russia*. New York: Dutton, 1956.

Florinsky, Michael T. *Russia: A Short History*. New York: Macmillan, 1964.

Mironov, Boris N., with Ben Eklof. *The Social History of Imperial Russia*. Vol. 1. Boulder, Colo.: Westview, 2000.

Pokrovskii, M. N. *Russia in World History: Selected Essays*. Ed. Roman Szporluk. Ann Arbor: University of Michigan Press, 1970.

Riasanovsky, Nicholas V. *A History of Russia*. 5th ed. Oxford: Oxford University Press, 1993.

Seton-Watson, Hugh. *The Russian Empire: 1801-1917*. Oxford: Clarendon, 1967.

Tolstoy, Leo. *The Death of Ivan Ilyich*. New York: Bantam, 1981.

Troyat, Henri. *Tolstoy*. New York: Doubleday, 1967.

Dracula

by
Bram Stoker

Anglo-Irish author Bram Stoker (1847-1912) was born in Dublin, Ireland, where he spent a decade as a civil servant before moving to London in 1878. The move was prompted by Stoker's becoming the business manager of the era's best known actor, Henry Irving (1838-1905), who had just taken over London's Lyceum Theater. For the next 27 years, until Irving's death, Stoker helped run the theater, managing and promoting Irving's career, writing letters in his name, and accompanying the actor on tours to various parts of the world (including the United States, which Stoker avidly admired). Stoker began a supplementary career as a novelist when he published *The Snake's Pass* in 1890; his later novels include *The Mystery of the Sea* (1902), *The Jewel of Seven Stars* (1903), *The Lady of the Shroud* (1909), and *The Lair of the White Worm* (1911). Like *Dracula*, these works combine elements of Gothic horror and often grotesque fantasy. None, however, has enjoyed *Dracula*'s lasting success. Written in a period of national anxiety in Britain, the novel reflects a society that fears its own vitality may somehow be draining away.

Events in History at the Time of the Novel

Certainty and doubt in late Victorian Britain. The late Victorian period (c. 1875-1901) was an age of contrasting certainties and doubts for the British. On one hand, national confidence was high as Britain's worldwide empire expanded

> **THE LITERARY WORK**
>
> A novel set in the Balkans and England in the late 1890s; first published in London in 1897.
>
> **SYNOPSIS**
>
> From his home in the Balkans the vampire Count Dracula journeys to England, where he uses supernatural powers to enthrall his victims, who become vampires themselves after he sucks their blood. Led by the Dutch scientist Dr. Abraham Van Helsing, a group of young friends combats Dracula.

rapidly in the last quarter of the nineteenth century. By 1897, when the nation marked Queen Victoria's sixtieth year of rule with an exuberant public celebration called the Diamond Jubilee, Britain held sway over about a fourth of the world's population and landmass. Of that territory, 2.5 million square miles—an area the size of the entire Roman Empire at its peak—had come under British rule in the previous twelve years alone, from 1884 to 1896. From Ireland to India, from the Americas to Asia and Africa, Britain seemed destined to rule.

Yet even as British world power reached its apogee, some believed they saw signs of vulnerability, portents of a feared and inevitable decline. Subject peoples in Ireland, India, Africa, and elsewhere had resisted British rule, at times violently. In addition, other Western nations, particularly Germany and the United States,

Dracula

Bram Stoker

seemed to possess energy and ambition that threatened to undo Britain's global leadership should the British grow soft or degenerate. Such apprehensions, while pushed into the background in the grandly imperial 1890s, nonetheless reflected nagging concerns about Britain's future.

Much more overtly worrisome to most cultural observers at the time was a deep religious crisis that was seen as undermining society's very foundations. Fueled by the impersonal harshness of an industrial revolution that resulted in urban poverty, and by scientific developments such as Charles Darwin's *On the Origin of Species* (1859; also *Literature and Its Times*), religious skepticism flourished on an unprecedented scale in the later decades of the nineteenth century. Though this crisis of faith had its best known expression in Alfred, Lord Tennyson's Poem *In Memoriam* (1850), a number of novelists addressed the issue too toward the end of the century. One of them, a then- popular but now forgotten writer named Hall Caine (1853-1931), sold 50,000 copies of his novel *The Christian* in the first month of publication. Published (like *Dracula*) in 1897, the book tells the story of a clergyman, torn between his faith and his love for a woman, who revolts against organized religion and devotes himself to aiding the poor in crowded cities. Caine was a good friend of Stoker's, and *Dracula* is dedicated to him (under the nickname "Hommy-Beg"). While it does not invoke Caine's type of realism, *Dracula* does portray its protagonist as planning to prey on London's "teeming millions" (Stoker, *Dracula*, p. 51).

By the end of the nineteenth century, science and industrialization had combined to produce a newly secular outlook in contrast to the long-standing religious one. This new outlook was "conducive to demystification," not an altogether welcome development (Harrison, p. 130). Many Victorians felt the loss of mystery keenly, and the void it left created an often ambivalent reaction to the new secularism. Stoker's novel reflects this ambivalence clearly. For example, the band of friends that opposes Dracula includes two scientists and enthusiastically relies on rational, modern scientific methods to demystify the alien threat represented by the vampire Count. In the end, however, they are forced to fall back on religious symbols as well, such as the crucifix and the Host (communion wafer). One of them, Jonathan Harker, a British lawyer imprisoned in Dracula's castle in the novel's early pages, acknowledges fearfully in his "up-to-date" shorthand diary that "the old centuries . . . have powers of their own that mere 'modernity' cannot kill" (*Dracula*, p. 36).

Modern technology and "the New Woman." Along with shorthand (which had actually been around for some two centuries but was coming into wider business and personal use), the modern weapons in the vampire hunters' arsenal include such high-tech communications and information processing tools as the telegraph, the phonograph, and the typewriter. (The telephone had been invented and would come into commercial use just a few years after the novel is set.) Dr. Seward, one of the vampire hunters in the novel, keeps his journal on an early phonograph that records his voice on wax cylinders. The typewriter had been invented in the 1860s by American Christopher Sholes, who contracted with the arms manufacturer Remington and Sons to mass produce the machines in the 1870s. Remington opened a British dealership in 1886, and by the 1890s typewriters had come into widespread use in British businesses. In *Dracula*, Mina Murray (who marries Jonathan Harker midway through the novel) plays a key role in the hunt for Dracula by efficiently collecting and transcribing relevant but scattered documents on her typewriter, including various telegrams, her husband's shorthand diary, and Dr. Seward's phonograph journal.

As Mina's central part in the story suggests, the advent of the typewriter and other technologies created a revolutionary new role for women in British society. Suddenly, women were offered avenues of employment far different from any available to them before. One Englishman, returning to England in 1904 after a 30-year absence, was shocked to find women pursuing jobs that had either been reserved for men or had not even existed when he left:

> So far as I remember in days gone by the only lines of employment open to girls or women were: teaching, assisting in a shop, dressmaking, or bar-keeping. In these days there is hardly an occupation . . . into which a girl may not aspire to enter. Type-writing provides a living for many thousands, perhaps hundreds of thousands. There are women newspaper reporters almost as numerous as men. Accountants and book-keepers crowd the trains morning and evening . . . while many branches of postal, telegraph and telephone work are entirely managed by women.
>
> (Harrison, p.168)

The typewriter led the way in this revolution in the 1890s, as girls and young women skilled in shorthand and typing found work as secretaries in otherwise all-male offices. Wages, however, were too low for such employees to live independently, and they were expected to leave when they married. If they did not leave by their mid-twenties, they were generally replaced by younger, newly trained girls or women. Those women who did work nevertheless had a significant impact on late Victorian society; their jobs gave them a degree of financial independence, which contributed greatly to the formation of an assertive female identity.

Limited independence was more than women had enjoyed before, and in 1894 feminist novelist Sarah Grand coined the phrase "the New Woman" to describe the phenomenon. The New Woman was neither a prostitute nor a confirmed homebody; in fact, she did not consider the home her exclusive sphere. While Grand introduced the phrase "the New Woman," the writer Ouida (pen name for Marie Louise de la Ramée) popularized it. She replied to Grand that this variety of female was a bore, and controversy ensued. Novelists meanwhile helped define the image. Middle-class and educated, as portrayed in popular novels by Grant Allen, Thomas Hardy, George Gissing, and others, the typical New Woman sought greater sexual freedom, smoked cigarettes, and drank in public. She also supported the growing women's suffrage movement, which aimed to secure the vote for British women (a goal that would not be achieved until 1918 for women over the age of 30, until 1929 for women 21 and older, and until 1969 for those 18 and older). As Sally Ledger notes, the New Woman was an invented persona too, a characterization in reaction to this growing movement.

> The New Woman of the fin de siècle had a multiple identity. She was, variously, a feminist activist, a social reformer, a popular novelist, a suffragette playwright, a woman poet; she was also often a fictional construct, a discursive response to the activities of the late nineteenth-century women's movement.
>
> (Ledger, p. 1)

In *Dracula,* Mina, an assistant schoolmistress at a girls' school, rejects the New Woman's radical values but seems to appreciate her abilities, having acquired typing and other secretarial skills in order to assist her husband's career as a lawyer. Mina's ambivalence regarding the New Woman reflects a genuine widespread cultural anxiety of the day. Many feared that new opportunities would lead women to neglect their civic responsibility to become mothers. The New Woman was perceived as an internal threat to national strength and security—a threat every bit as grave as the threat of colonial resistance. There was also a fear that if other nations did a better job of reproducing than Britain, they would grow stronger and the two threats would combine to dislodge the preeminence of the British. In view of this fear, what happens to Mina in the novel is doubly reassuring. She bears a British baby and is also prevented from helping to reproduce threatening outsiders, in this case, vampires.

Occultism and psychology. The late Victorians' questioning of previous scientific, religious, and social certainties may help explain a surge of interest in the occult as the century drew to a close. Certainly many of the same people doing the questioning were drawn to the occult, which perhaps served to restore a sense of mystery to lives increasingly illuminated by the glaring spotlight of Victorian rationalism. Séances, clairvoyance, mesmerism (hypnosis), astrology, palmistry, crystal-gazing, faith healing, alchemy, witchcraft, astral projection—these and other mysterious practices and entertainments flourished, both in public spaces such as theaters and in private homes. Clubs and societies pursued occult ideas with avid curiosity, their members often sport-

> ## THE "CRIMINAL TYPE"
>
> One discipline that blended science and the occult was phrenology, which held that character traits and mental qualities can be discerned by the shape of the head or the dimensions of the brow. The discipline, now thoroughly discredited, played a part in late Victorian criminology. Society boasted "scientific" criminologists, men who based their study of criminals on dissection and anatomy, as well as on observation of the head. In *Dracula,* Mina Harker names one such criminologist, Cesare Lombroso (1835-1909), when she describes Count Dracula as "a criminal type," and elsewhere the novel echoes very closely Lombroso's description of the typical criminal when it describes Count Dracula (*Dracula,* p. 342):
>
> **Stoker Describes Dracula**
>
> - "[Count Dracula's] face was . . . aquiline, with high bridge of the thin nose and peculiarly arched nostrils."
> - "His eyebrows were very massive, almost meeting over the nose."
> - "His ears were pale and at the tops extremely pointed. . . ."
>
> **Lombroso Describes the Criminal Type**
>
> - "[The criminal's] nose . . . is often aquiline, like the beak of a bird of prey."
> - "The eyebrows are bushy and tend to meet across the nose."
> - "A relic of the pointed ear. . . ."
>
> (Adapted from Wolf, p. 300)

ing an attitude of scientific detachment. Many believed that occult phenomena could be scientifically explained.

For example, the Society for Psychical Research attempted to inquire scientifically into curiosities such as thought reading and haunted houses. The society also hosted a talk that Stoker may have attended on the groundbreaking work of Sigmund Freud, the Viennese doctor who was laying the foundations of modern psychology. Stoker incorporates contemporary ideas about mental illness into Dracula, citing Jean Martin Charcot, a French neurologist who worked with Freud in Paris in 1885 and who demonstrated the usefulness of hypnosis in treating mental illness. In the novel Dr. Seward runs a "lunatic asylum" (institution for the mentally ill) in which one of the patients, Renfield, is depicted as being psychically linked with Count Dracula, though Renfield is never properly bitten. Like Dracula's female victims, Renfield is controlled through his psychic link with the vampire, who possesses supernaturally hypnotic powers of mind control.

The most influential of the many occult groups was the Theosophical Society, founded in 1875 by the eccentric Russian immigrant Helena Petrova Blavatsky (1831-91), who is also credited with popularizing the term "occultism." Madame Blavatsky (as she was known) promoted both mysticism and science as paths toward enlightenment, and the Theosophical Society attracted a wide range of Victorian nonconformists, including feminists, socialists, and vegetarians. Though not a "Theosophist" himself, Stoker belonged to a social set that included Theosophical Society members. One was Constance Wilde, wife of the celebrated writer and wit Oscar Wilde, a friend, fellow-Dubliner, and one-time rival of Stoker's. (Before marrying Constance, Wilde had unsuccessfully wooed Florence Balcombe, who became Stoker's wife in 1878.)

Oscar Wilde's own occult novel, *The Picture of Dorian Gray,* published in 1890, features a sexually ambiguous central character who (like Dracula) acquires eternal youth from the powers of darkness.

The Novel in Focus

Plot summary. The story is told through the journal entries, letters, newspaper articles, notes, and telegrams that Mina Harker assembles and transcribes during the course of the developing campaign against the vampire. The longest continuous narrative is the first, from the journal of Jonathan Harker. The young British lawyer has traveled to the Balkans at the request of his firm's client, a certain Count Dracula, who wishes to purchase a house in London. Jonathan writes the first entry as he arrives in Transylvania (today the center and northwest of Romania), the region of the Balkans where the Count lives in his castle. As he awaits a coach that will take him closer to Castle Dracula, he is perturbed when an innkeeper's wife implores him not to go and then gives him a crucifix, which she says will protect him. The coach is met later by another, smaller coach, driven by a tall man who hides his features but who has eyes that seem to gleam red in the lamplight. Dogs howl as the coach passes farms along the way, and, as it approaches the castle, wolves join in, forming a chorus of howling animals.

At the castle Jonathan is welcomed by Dracula, "a tall old man, clean-shaven save for a long white moustache, and clad in black from head to foot, without a single speck of colour about him anywhere" (*Dracula*, p. 15). At first, Dracula's friendly welcome allays Jonathan's growing sense of foreboding, but after a few days his nervousness returns. Several strange incidents add to his fears: the Count does not seem to cast a reflection in mirrors, for example, and reacts violently to the sight of blood when Jonathan cuts himself. Then from a window one night he sees the Count crawling headfirst, like a lizard, down the outside of the castle wall. Furthermore, Dracula only seems to be around at night; Jonathan never sees him during the day, when the castle doors are all locked. Gradually Jonathan realizes that he is a prisoner in the castle.

Against his host's orders Jonathan explores the castle. In one of the rooms he experiences what seems to be a nightmare: he is menaced by three voluptuous women who excite in him a "deadly fear" yet also "a wicked burning desire" to be kissed with their red lips (*Dracula*, p. 37). One of the women is about to touch her sharp teeth to his neck when Dracula suddenly appears. His eyes glowing red with rage, the Count pushes them away with a furious warning: "This man belongs to me!" (*Dracula*, p. 39). The women seem to vanish, and Jonathan awakens in his room. Yet he feels certain the experience was real and dreads that the women still wish to suck his blood. He also sees and hears evidence that Dracula and the women are preying on young children. Another time, while exploring in the basement, he discovers 50 large wooden crates of earth, in one of which rests the Count himself, seemingly dead. In growing panic Jonathan decides to flee the castle, and his last entry is written as he plans to climb down the steep outer stone wall. Better, he resolves, to die in the attempt than to suffer whatever fate the Count and the ghoulish women have in store for him.

Bela Lugosi in the 1931 classic film version of *Dracula*.

The next documents in the narrative are letters between Mina Murray and her upper-class friend Lucy Westenra, a beautiful and stylish young woman. Mina looks forward to her fiancé Jonathan Harker's return, and Lucy has recently received three proposals of marriage: one from the aristocratic Arthur Holmwood, Lord Godalming, and two others from his friends Dr. Jack Seward and Quincey Morris from Texas in the United States. She agrees to wed Arthur Holmwood, and the rejected suitors gallantly pledge their friendship and best wishes. Mina and Lucy have planned to meet in Whitby, a small coastal resort town in the northern English county of Yorkshire. By the time they do so, Mina has grown anxious about Jonathan, from whom she has not heard in over a month. Meanwhile, entries from Dr. Seward's journal reveal that (despite sadness at Lucy's rejection) he has grown interested in what he calls a "zoophagous" (life-eating) patient in his lunatic asylum (*Dracula*, p.

70). The man, whose name is Renfield, catches flies in his cell, first eating them, but then feeding them to spiders and eating the spiders; he soon progresses to feeding the spiders to sparrows and eating the birds himself. Renfield has asked for a kitten.

Entries from Mina's journal reflect her growing concern about Jonathan, who still has not been heard from; Mina also mentions that Lucy has begun walking in her sleep. A newspaper cutting relates that a violent and sudden storm at sea off Whitby has resulted in the shipwreck of the Russian sailing vessel *Demeter*, driven aground in Whitby harbor. Oddly, the cargo vessel was empty except for a huge dog that leaped off as the vessel came to rest, and the dead captain, who had lashed himself to the wheel. The captain's log tells how the crew disappeared at night one by one during the voyage until only the captain was left; terrified, the man lashed himself to the wheel, and was found with a crucifix and rosary beads around his bound wrists. The vessel's cargo includes 50 large boxes of earth, which are sent on to their destination.

As Mina records, Lucy's sleepwalking worsens. Mina follows her friend one night to the ruins of a local abbey, where she seems to see a figure with gleaming red eyes bending over Lucy. When Mina approaches, the figure is gone, and Lucy is unconscious. She has two small pinpricks in her throat. Two nights later, Mina finds Lucy sitting up in bed, asleep, pointing to her bedroom window, around which Mina sees a large bat flying. Lucy grows languid and exhausted during the daytime, and she starts talking in her sleep. Instead of healing, the two wounds in her throat get larger. A document records the shipping of 50 crates to Carfax, the ruined manor house next to Dr. Seward's asylum in London that Jonathan's firm arranged for Dracula to purchase.

Mina finally receives word of Jonathan, who has been ill in a hospital in the Hungarian city of Budapest for some six weeks. She journeys to Budapest, where she and the now recovering Jonathan are married. Dr. Seward makes entries in his phonograph journal that chart the strange behavior of Renfield, who babbles excitedly about awaiting the commands of his approaching master. Holmwood, worried about Lucy, asks Dr. Seward to examine her. Seward can find nothing wrong, but writes to his old teacher, the renowned Dutch scientist Professor Abraham Van Helsing. Arriving from Amsterdam, Van Helsing transfuses blood from Holmwood to Lucy, then repeats the operation with blood from himself, Seward, and Quincey Morris at intervals of several days, as Lucy somehow keeps losing blood and growing paler and weaker. Despite Van Helsing's efforts, Lucy dies; she is entombed in her family's crypt in Hampstead, close to London.

Mina and Jonathan, who have returned to England, are in London where Jonathan, aghast, sees the Count on the street one day. Dracula has somehow grown younger, with black hair instead of gray. Meanwhile, newspaper cuttings report that several young children, missing after playing on Hampstead Heath, have returned with tales of a "bloofer lady" (beautiful lady) who lures them away (*Dracula*, p. 177). The children also came home with unexplained wounds on their throats. Mina, having read Jonathan's journal, prepares herself for the struggle she senses coming against "that fearful Count" by typing up her husband's record of his days as Dracula's prisoner (*Dracula*, p. 179). The Dutch scientist Van Helsing contacts her to ask for Lucy's diary, which Mina has also typed out; she gives him both documents. Van Helsing alarms Seward with talk of hypnotism and thought-reading, insisting that Seward keep an open mind while declaring that it was Lucy who attacked the children on Hampstead Heath. That night they go to the crypt, entering the cold dark chamber to find

---

BLOODTHIRSTY TYRANTS, VAMPIRE LEGENDS

The clearest historical model for Count Dracula was a notoriously bloodthirsty Balkan nobleman called Vlad Tepes or Vlad the Impaler, after his preferred method of executing his enemies. The ruler of the Balkan principality of Wallachia from 1456 to 1462, he was also known as Vlad Dracula. Dracula means "Devil" or "Dragon" in Wallachian; Stoker makes clear in the novel that Dracula's powers originate with the Devil, and hints that he may be the Devil himself. Another Central European historical figure, the sixteenth-century Hungarian countess Elizabeth Bathory, was infamous for killing young girls and bathing in their blood in order to rejuvenate herself. While vampires have been a staple of folklore in many cultures since ancient times, such behavior may have helped give rise to an epidemic of vampire sightings in the early eighteenth century in Central Europe.

that Lucy's coffin is empty. The next day, however, they find her again in the coffin.

Van Helsing tells the disbelieving Seward that Lucy has become a vampire, one of the "Un-Dead," and that they must kill her by driving a stake through her heart and cutting off her head (*Dracula*, p. 201). They must do the same, he says, to Dracula, "the great Un-Dead," who has made Lucy into a vampire by sucking her blood (*Dracula*, p. 203). After the vampire Lucy attacks them on a subsequent visit, Holmwood, Morris, and Seward believe Van Helsing. The night following the attack they return with him to the crypt, where Lucy's fiancé, Holmwood, hammers a stake through her heart and Van Helsing and Seward cut off her head. Van Helsing says that only after this can her soul rest in peace.

Mina comes to Dr. Seward's asylum, where she transcribes the doctor's phonograph journal and gives him typescripts of her and Jonathan's diaries to read. Seward realizes that Renfield's odd behavior, alternately violent and peaceful, has been "a sort of index to the coming and going of the Count" (*Dracula*, p. 225). Van Helsing's occult research has taught him that Dracula's powers are at their lowest by day, when the vampire must rest, and he can only do so on his native soil. They must find the boxes of earth and "sterilize" them by placing pieces of the Host (sanctified communion wafer) in them (*Dracula*, p. 242). Once they have done so, the vampire will be unable to rest. They can then find and attack him during his weakest hours, between noon and sunset.

While the men begin tracking the boxes, some of which Dracula has removed to other houses he has purchased, Dracula goes on the offensive against his hunters. Taking the form of mist, he enters Mina's bedroom at night and begins to suck her blood as he sucked Lucy's. Soon afterward, Renfield is found beaten in his cell; his back broken, he dies after revealing that Dracula, his assailant, has targeted Mina. Van Helsing and the others hurry to Mina's room, where they find Jonathan in a trance-like stupor as Dracula, having drunk Mina's blood, forces her to drink his own in turn. This, the vampire has told her, will place her mind under his command from any distance. Some hours later, as the men locate and sterilize the last of the boxes except for one, Dracula attacks them, but they drive him back with a crucifix, and he flees.

Mina suggests that Van Helsing hypnotize her. As she hopes, under hypnosis her mind-link with the vampire provides a vital clue to his whereabouts. She hears water lapping and sails creaking: Van Helsing assumes that Dracula has fled England in the remaining box and is returning to Transylvania. But the struggle is not over, for Van Helsing says they must pursue him—both for Mina's sake, since she will remain under the vampire's influence, and also "for the sake of humanity," since he is immortal and will continue to make new vampires unless stopped (*Dracula*, p. 319). They travel to the Black Sea port of Varna, where they await Dracula's arrival. Overcoming a number of obstacles, they finally intercept the band of gypsies that is transporting Dracula's box from the ship to the castle. Just as the sun is about to set, the men fight their way through the gypsies to the box, where the mortally injured Quincy Morris plunges his bowie knife through Dracula's heart as Jonathan Harker simultaneously cuts Dracula's throat. The vampire's body immediately crumbles into dust.

Evolution and degeneration. Throughout *Dracula* Stoker portrays the Texan Quincey Morris as a man of action who outshines his British fellow vampire hunters in resourcefulness, initiative, and strength. At one point in the novel, Renfield flatters Morris by predicting that America will become a world power: he foresees a day when "the Pole and the Tropics may hold allegiance to the Stars and Stripes" (*Dracula*, p. 244). Dr. Seward, the Victorian man of science, puts this potential in terms of breeding: "If America can go on breeding men like that, she will be a power in the world indeed" (*Dracula*, p. 173). In other words, imperial success results from breeding. And breeding, the Victorians had realized, is closely linked to the process of evolution.

The publication of Charles Darwin's *On the Origin of Species* in 1859 had made evolution the most influential idea of the later nineteenth century. Whereas Darwin had limited himself to the area of biology, by the 1870s British thinkers such as Herbert Spencer had applied Darwin's ideas, popularly summed up in the phrase "survival of the fittest," to the social realm. In contrast to Darwin's explanation of biological success, however, this "social Darwinism" was invoked not merely to explain but also to justify social or political success. Politically powerful nations and individuals, the argument went, were inherently superior to less powerful ones, and therefore justified in expanding their power. The imperial Victorians viewed evolution as a ladder of progress, a ladder at the top of which they themselves stood. From the top of a ladder, however, one can easily go down. Progress thus also entails an implicit threat, the danger of its opposite, degeneration, which was (like evolution) a widely discussed idea at the time of the novel.

This often unconscious recognition lay behind the vague fears of the imperial 1890s. Like other nineteenth-century Europeans, the Victorians viewed blood and bloodlines as closely linked to the idea of racial vitality, and saw both as subject to degeneration. Degeneration could come through moral laxness or indulgence, vices they believed had caused the earlier downfall of the Roman Empire, with which the Victorians were fond of comparing their own. Or degeneration could come simply with age. In *Dracula*, these imperial fears are symbolized by the foreign vampire's draining of British blood in the very process through which he breeds vampires. Recounting medieval battles in his homeland, Dracula describes himself as belonging to "a conquering race" but one whose "blood" is old and needs to be revived (*Dracula*, p. 29). Drinking blood from his British victims physically rejuvenates him as it enervates them. The vampire thus demonstrates that a degenerate, parasitical fate potentially awaits those whose conquests lie in the past—as many feared was the case with Britain and her empire by the 1890s.

HOMOEROTIC UNDERTONES

In a sensational trial in 1895, two years before *Dracula* was published, Stoker's friend Oscar Wilde was sentenced to prison for his part in a homosexual love affair. In general, Victorian society viewed homosexuality as an evil perversion. Stoker, who as a young man had idolized the homosexual American poet Walt Whitman, adopted an attitude of similar hero-worship toward his employer, the actor Henry Irving. Discerning homoerotic undertones in *Dracula*, modern critics have speculated about Stoker's own sexual orientation. Stoker depicts the seductive and commanding Dracula as physically resembling Irving, and he attempted in vain to interest the actor in playing the vampire in a stage version. Some critics have therefore argued that Stoker's novel cloaks an attraction toward Irving that the author felt unable to show openly. Regardless of the truth, the dangers of such impulses in Victorian society were clearly demonstrated by the fate of Oscar Wilde, who emerged from prison a broken man in May 1897, the very month of *Dracula*'s publication.

Sources and literary context. Aside from Central European vampire legends and the historical figures of Vlad the Impaler and Elizabeth Bathory, Stoker also drew on an already existing body of vampire tales in English. Like Mary Shelley's ***Frankenstein*** (1817; also in *Literature and Its Times*), they originated in the Romantic movement, which was dominated by such poets as Percy Bysshe Shelley (Mary's husband) and Lord Byron. Some of these Dracula predecessors include:

- Lord Byron's "The Giaour" (1813), an occult narrative poem that mentions a vampire emerging from its tomb to suck the blood of humans.
- Dr. John Polidori's *The Vampyre* (1819), featuring a seductive and aristocratic vampire modeled on Lord Byron himself. Polidori was Byron's physician, and he was present when Byron and the Shelleys held a horror story contest one stormy night in June 1816. Polidori based *The Vampyre* on an idea Byron himself had that night; Mary Shelley's contribution would become *Frankenstein*.
- James Malcolm Rymer's *Varney the Vampire* (1847), a long (nearly 900 pages) and turgidly written potboiler that introduces features Stoker would borrow for *Dracula*: Central European origins; long, fanglike canine teeth; a black cloak; the abilities to climb down sheer castle walls and put female victims in a trancelike state; arriving in Britain in a shipwrecked vessel.
- Sheridan Le Fanu's *Carmilla* (1872), in which a sensuous female vampire preys on female victims.

Reception. Published on May 26, 1897, *Dracula* received mixed reviews and enjoyed only moderate sales during Stoker's lifetime. Seeing the novel as a straightforward Gothic adventure story in which good triumphs over evil, Victorian readers and reviewers alike ignored the sexual elements that have proven so alluring for modern literary critics.

In addition to the novel's sexual aspects, critics have found the figure of Count Dracula himself a strikingly rich source of symbolism, most of which plays off taboos or alienation of one kind or another. As one critic writes in the introduction to a recent edition, Dracula has been seen as standing for "perversion, menstruation, venereal disease, female sexuality, male homosexuality, feudal aristocracy, monopoly capitalism, the proletariat, the Jew, the primal father, the Antichrist, and the typewriter" (Ellmann in *Dracula*, p. xxviii). Along with being perennially fashionable among literary critics, Dracula has proven immensely popular on both stage and screen, where (beginning with Bela Lugosi's classic 1931 film portrayal) he has found his widest exposure in popular culture.

—Colin Wells

For More Information

Belford, Barbara. *Bram Stoker: A Biography of the Man Who Wrote Dracula.* New York: Knopf, 1996.

Glover, David. *Vampires, Mummies, and Liberals: Bram Stoker and the Politics of Popular Fiction.* Durham, N.C.: Duke University Press, 1996.

Harrison, J. F. C. *Late Victorian Britain 1875-1901.* London: Routledge, 1991.

Hughes, William, and Andrew Smith, eds. *Bram Stoker: History, Psychoanalysis and the Gothic.* London: Macmillan, 1998.

Jarret, Derek. *The Sleep of Reason: Fantasy and Reality from the Victorian Age to the First World War.* London: Weidenfield and Nicolson, 1988.

Jenner, Michael. *Victorian Britain.* London: Weidenfield and Nicolson, 1999.

Leatherdale, Clive. *The Origins of Dracula.* London: William Kimber, 1987.

Ledger, Sally. *The New Woman: Fiction and Feminism at the Fin de Siècle.* New York: St. Martin's, 1997.

Mitchell, Sally. *Daily Life in Victorian England.* Westport, Conn.: Greenwood, 1996.

Rosenbach Museum. *Bram Stoker's Dracula: A Centennial Exhibition at the Rosenbach Museum and Library.* Philadelphia: Rosenbach Museum, 1997.

Stoker, Bram. *Dracula.* Ed. Maud Ellmann. Oxford World's Classics Series. Oxford: Oxford University Press, 1996.

Wolf, Leonard. *The Annotated Dracula.* New York: Clarkson N. Potter, 1975.

Emma

by
Jane Austen

> **THE LITERARY WORK**
>
> A novel set in Highbury, a fictional village about 16 miles from London, during the early nineteenth century; published in London in 1816.
>
> **SYNOPSIS**
>
> Emma Woodhouse, "handsome, clever, and rich," has a penchant for matchmaking. But she avoids matrimony for herself until, after a series of errors in which she learns to criticize her own conduct, she comes to know her own heart.

Born on Dec. 16, 1775, to Cassandra Leigh and George Austen, Jane Austen was the seventh of eight children. Educated at Oxford, her father was rector of Steventon, the small Hampshire village where Jane lived until 1801, when the family moved to Bath. Jane and her only sister, Cassandra, had several years of schooling away from home, but most of their education came from the family library (which held some 500 volumes, making the Austens a very bookish nineteenth-century family indeed). Though courted on a number of occasions, Jane remained unmarried. Her closest relationship was with Cassandra; the two sisters maintained an extensive correspondence and deep intimacy despite circumstances that pulled them apart (after their father died, the sisters often circulated among their brothers' households). In 1808, both sisters moved with their mother to a cottage on the property of their brother Edward in Chawton, Hampshire. It was then that Jane Austen embarked on her most prolific period of writing and publishing. She would receive most of her acclaim after her death. In 1811 Austen published *Sense and Sensibility*, followed by *Pride and Prejudice* in 1813, and Mansfield Park in 1814. Two years later she published *Emma*, dedicating it to the Prince Regent, convinced she had created "a heroine whom no one but myself will much like" (Austen, *Emma*, p. viii). Austen could hardly have been more wrong.

Events in History at the Time of the Novel

Revolutions and wars abroad. From initial sympathy, English public opinion regarding the French Revolution (1789) moved rapidly to ambivalence and fear. While the overthrow of the French monarchy inspired some Englishmen to press for reform in their own country, the horrors of revolutionary France soon turned sympathy into anxiety. If the lower classes in France could protest so violently, what was to stop the English lower classes from doing the same? The line between reform and revolution seemed altogether too thin while the guillotine lurked over the horizon (or just across the channel), and the British government started to come down hard on potential reformers. New legislation prevented unsanctioned public meetings, made trade unions illegal, and expanded definitions of treason to include writing and speaking as well as acting against the government. This new era

Emma

Jane Austen

of conservatism in England would last for more than a quarter century. The squelching of nearly all opposition to the government continued from 1793-1815, during which time England (along with most of Europe) battled with little respite the French Republican army, eventually led by Napoleon Bonaparte, who rose to virtual dictatorship in France and sought to conquer all of Europe.

The defeat of Napoleon by England's Duke of Wellington at the decisive Battle of Waterloo, fought near Brussels on June 18, 1815, ended Napoleon's career and ushered in an era of peace and internal reform in England. This period also witnessed the dissolution of the Irish Parliament—for which the Irish were compensated with seats in the British parliament, but not with the promised Catholic emancipation (the abandonment of policy that excluded Catholics from holding senior government offices, being judges, and so forth). On the other hand, Parliament did abolish the slave trade in 1807 (slavery itself would not be abolished in the British Empire until 1833). At first glance, these events seem to have little impact on the novels of Austen (who preferred to write from her own experience). Upon closer examination, however, their effects surface, not only in the shortage of eligible men at home and the presence (or absence) of soldiers, but also in the characters' anxieties over class mobility and even class conflict.

Monarchs, morals, and manners. Though Americans know King George III as the monarch who taxed the colonies into revolt, the English, by the early nineteenth century, were more concerned with the fact that he was prone to bouts of insanity. When it became clear that he could not rule, his son was made Prince Regent to rule in his stead, and England entered the *Regency* period. The Prince Regent (called "Prinnie") was known for his opulent and immoral lifestyle, much flash, and multiple mistresses. As a lasting monument to the excesses of his reign, the Royal Pavilion—built for the Regent in conspicuous oriental style by renowned architect John Nash—still stands at Brighton, a town that the Regent made a popular seaside resort (one of many to which the genteel might repair for health and recreation). General prosperity enabled the very upper crust to indulge in a level of promiscuity and display worthy of such a regent—expanding houses into castles, employing unprecedented numbers of servants, and blithely scattering illegitimate "love" children.

Emma is dedicated to the Prince Regent shortly after his—or more accurately, Wellington's—triumph at Waterloo, but the novel's implicit critique of the morals of the Regent and his set suggest that the dedication may have been grudging—even satirical. Among the gentry (the class below the aristocracy) in Austen's novels, one begins to see a reaction to the decadence of Prinnie's crowd. Indeed, such behavior started to smack too much of the French for England's gentry. Traditionally, French fashion had been quite influential in England. Clothes, manners, even the method of serving food *à la française* (i.e., in just a few "removes," or what we might call "spreads"), were all copied from the French. But such style became increasingly suspect during the long wars with Napoleon. Decadent behavior had long been associated with the French by the English so they grew especially intolerant of such behavior at this time. A new emphasis on morality spread among the genteel and was supported by an evangelical trend in religion, which caught hold among the propertied classes, especially those merging with the professional classes. While evangelism sought to reform both lax and corrupt church practices, the trend also had a broader, social aspect that emerges in Austen's novels. Led by such social conservatives as William Wilberforce, with his rallying cry of "reform or ruin," upper-class evangelism moralized about behaving properly and setting a good example to inferiors (Grey, p. 205). It did so, at least in part, to help maintain the existing social hierarchy.

The gentry in Austen's novels display carefully structured manners that show how pervasive these "reform or ruin" concerns were. They suffused social custom. In subtle ways, Austen's characters maintain distinctions of rank and behave in ways that appease the potentially feisty lower orders. When, for example, Emma offends Miss Bates (a character far lower in rank and wealth), Emma is chastised by Mr. Knightley, a landowning gentleman. His reprimand aims not only to protect Miss Bates's feelings; it also indicates the importance of considerate treatment of the lower orders in maintaining social stability.

Changing social order and the limits of economic prosperity. *Emma* is a novel extremely sensitive to the many, increasingly subtle, gradations of rank among the English gentry and professional classes. (Members of other classes—the poor, workers and servants, aristocrats—do not put in much of an appearance in the novel.) Simple distinctions between upper and lower "orders" do not begin to describe the complex class structure. Among the gentry, for example, those whose income derived from the land, ranked higher than those whose wealth derived from investments. Even within families, one finds important distinctions: under the system of *primogeniture*, all of the family land and much, if not all of the wealth, devolved upon the firstborn son, in an effort to keep the estate itself intact through successive generations, rather than split it into ever smaller parcels. A gentleman's younger son, who had to earn his living, entered the professional classes, though only a few professions were acceptable for the younger sons of the gentry: the clergy, the military, and the law.

These carefully maintained distinctions were in flux by the late eighteenth and early nineteenth centuries. In England, upper-class status was not legally defined (as it had been in France). One had always to work to preserve social standing—to earn money and maintain social connections (through land, profession, or marriage). As the nation grew in wealth through the changes wrought by the industrial revolution (improved agricultural techniques, greater circulation of goods, and the economic stimulus of war), it became increasingly possible to move into and out of the higher orders. Social standing itself became an object of consumerism; one could not only be born or marry into the higher classes but also buy one's way up the social ladder, as those in industry or trade bought property. There were no strict rules about how to achieve this—a social climber might step into a higher class by buying land or succeeding in industry and acting sufficiently genteel. *New money* carried a stigma, but one that wore off as the nouveau riche socialized with and married their offspring into the established gentry. Class mobility was also facilitated by the possibility of military advancement—more likely in times of war, such as the Napoleonic strife that plagued Europe in Austen's day. In short, one could increase one's social distinction through military achievement, advantageous marriage, or purchase. As Austen's novels suggest, the opportunity for social climbing was open to the deserving and undeserving alike.

Meanwhile, as some grew richer, others grew poorer. *Emma* provides glimpses of the so-called "lower orders" in the fear that Emma's father, Mr. Woodhouse, has of poachers and in a run-in that another character, Harriet Smith, has with gypsies. These examples bespeak a larger social problem that mystified economic observers at the time: as the country grew more prosperous, the situation of the poor worsened. Yes, the industrial revolution helped the British finally win the war against the French, but it also sparked an economic upheaval that, along with a long period of conservatism, left the poor in dire straits. British commerce expanded, factories could produce more because of advances in machinery, but traditional workers lost their jobs and the crackdown on reform around the turn of the nineteenth century meant the usual avenues for agitation were closed. In the depression of 1811-13, the poor textile workers staged the so-called Luddite riots, destroying the machines they blamed for the loss of their jobs. At the same time, more and more land used by the public was enclosed, that is, made into private property. Between 1761 and 1801, some 3 million acres were surveyed and distributed among the wealthy landowning class, which dominated Parliament. Given improved farming methods and the high price of corn (by which the British meant grains such as wheat, barley, and oats) during the war years, landlords and independent farmers grew richer; the gentleman farmer emerged as a common fixture of the landscape. But at the same time industrialization and enclosures produced a population of dislocated people. Out of jobs and no longer able to avail themselves of land, these people shifted increasingly to the cities, where, instead of finding a solution, many of the rural poor adopted the problems of the urban poor.

Emma

Marriage . . . a happy ending? Though Emma's position seems in many ways enviable, most women in nineteenth-century England enjoyed considerably less power and privilege. Emma's wealth spares her many privations, but law and custom were not kind to women of any class. A female's education was extremely limited, even among the upper classes. Women could not enter the professions, nor could they vote. They could, of course, marry, but contrary to popular belief, marriage made the situation in many ways worse, not better.

By marrying, a woman avoided the stigma of being an old maid or a spinster and could secure her financial security by one of the only routes open to her. But the cost was considerable. The marriage might elevate her social status, but her legal status simply vanished. Legally, a husband and wife were considered one person, and that person was he. This meant that a married woman could not enter into a contract or write a will without her husband's consent—or, for that matter, commit a crime (he was held responsible on the logic that she must, after all, be acting under his influence). Nor could a married woman own property. Anything she had inherited or earned was automatically his for the duration of the marriage, or during what was called her coverture (because the wife was considered covered by her husband). This would remain the case until the 1870s and 1880s, when the Married Women's Property Acts eventually gave married women the same rights over their property that unmarried women had. Before then, only a few measures could ensure a woman ever regaining her former property. Her husband could leave it, or give it back to her in his will. Or the groom (and his family) could enter into a premarital agreement with the bride (and her family) called a settlement. This was a legal document; usually it specified that some or all of the property that the wife brought to the marriage would revert to her or her children after the husband's demise, though this did not mean that she had control over any of this property during his lifetime.

Divorces were extremely difficult to obtain. Until 1857 secular divorce could be acquired only by an act of Parliament, a method that was both costly and extremely rare. Otherwise, divorce remained under the purview of the Church of England, whose officials granted it only in extreme cases of violence, adultery, sodomy, or marriage to a close relative. If a couple separated or divorced, custody of the children automatically went to the man until the 1839 Custody of Infants Act, which allowed a woman of "unblemished character" to ask for custody of young children.

All these disadvantages suggest that the single state was not without its attractions. Never married, Harriet Martineau (1802-76), also a writer, celebrated her own choice to remain unmarried: "The older I have grown, the more serious and irremediable have seemed to me the evils and disadvantages of married life, as it exists among us at this time" (Martineau in Hellerstein, Hume, and Offen, p. 155). It is true that since the eighteenth century the situation for married women had been improving somewhat; as preachers and others spoke of the need for companionship in marriage, the expectations that a wife should always be subordinate and obedient began to fade. Yet, although more and more lip service was paid to love and companionship, marriage remained serious business for men and women alike among the gentry of Austen's England. For a man, marriage could mean the acquisition of property, for whatever is hers became legally his. For a genteel woman without property of her own, marriage might well be the one respectable—or palatable—career move available. Few women wanted to risk the stigma or privations of spinsterhood, and there were few like Emma who could easily afford to do so.

The Novel in Focus

The plot. When her companion and former governess marries, Emma Woodhouse is left at loose ends. Not only has her companion, Miss Taylor (now Mrs. Weston) left; her sister Isabella has married Mr. John Knightley and moved to London. Now Emma, a clever and imaginative 21-year-old, has only her sickly and not very bright father for company, and he can do little to alleviate the boredom and isolation. He is part of the gentry of Highbury. Owner of the Hartfield estate, Mr. Woodhouse opposes matrimony on principle, since it precipitates change, which, for him, necessarily implies discomfort. Unable to see that others might view their own marriages in a different light, he always refers to both Isabella and Miss Taylor with the epithet "poor" as he bemoans the cruelty of fate in taking each of them away from Hartfield.

Emma's well-wishers, including her sister and Mr. Knightley (George, elder brother to John) agree that Jane Fairfax—elegant, talented, and the same age—would make a delightful companion for Emma. Jane, an orphan, has been raised in the family of her late father's friend, Colonel Campbell, whose own daughter has recently married a Mr. Dixon. When the Campbells travel to Ireland, Jane returns to Highbury to stay with her aunt, Miss Bates, and her grandmother, Mrs. Bates, who have fallen on hard times. This visit is to be the last prior to Jane seeking a post as a governess. Emma imagines that Jane has returned to Highbury because she has fallen in love with the recently married Mr. Dixon, a suspicion Emma does not keep entirely to herself.

But for all of Jane's elegance and education, Emma prefers the company of the adoring and naive Harriet Smith to the superior company of Jane Fairfax. Harriet's lovely face convinces Emma that Harriet must, in fact, be more genteel than the undisclosed circumstances of her birth seem to warrant. Crediting herself with having made the match between the Westons, Emma shortly begins a campaign to marry Harriet well. She settles first on the parson, Mr. Elton, whose attentions to the two women convince Emma of his interest in Harriet. When he proposes to Emma herself, her error—indeed, a whole series of errors—becomes clear, including her mistake in having dissuaded Harriet from marrying the respectable (but not genteel) farmer, Mr. Robert Martin. Mr. Elton marries shortly thereafter. Since he and his wife cannot afford to snub the prominent Miss Woodhouse, they snub her friend Harriet at a ball instead. At this point, Mr. Knightley comes to the rescue by asking Harriet to dance.

Meanwhile, Highbury has finally been graced with a visit from the much-talked-of Frank Churchill. Though he is Mr. Weston's son, Frank has been adopted by his wealthy uncle and aunt, and does not come to Highbury to pay his respects to his father's new bride until long after he is expected. It is clear that both of the Westons would like Frank and Emma to make a match of it, and Emma, flattered by the attentions Frank shows her, imagines herself first in and then out of love with him. Yet she never makes plans to marry him. She does, however, start making plans for Harriet again, deciding that Frank would make a good match for the young woman. When he rescues Harriet from a band of rowdy gypsies, this fortuitous circumstance seems, to Emma, to seal the match.

Frank, however, has other plans. Unbeknownst to the villagers of Highbury, he has long been secretly engaged to Jane Fairfax. As soon as his domineering aunt dies, Frank seeks his uncle's approval for the match. He thereby prevents Jane from taking up a post that has been arranged for her (against her wishes) by the interfering and self-aggrandizing Mrs. Elton. The Westons worry that Emma will be hurt by the news, but she is not. Emma worries that Harriet will be hurt by the news, but she is not. In fact, it is when Emma shares the story of Frank Churchill's engagement that Harriet discloses the true object of her current affections: Mr. Knightley. Shocked by the disclosure, Emma finally recognizes not only her own mistakes, but also her own feelings: "It darted through her, with the speed of an arrow, that Mr. Knightley must marry no one but herself!"

> ### WHAT MAY I CALL YOU?
>
> The proper form of address is a delicate matter among Austen's gentry. A name, when properly used, indicates much about a person's rank and family position. The privilege of bearing the family name falls to the eldest son or unmarried daughter; thus in *Emma*, the title "Mr. Knightley" belongs only to George, the older brother, who will inherit the property as well. His younger brother goes by the name of Mr. John Knightley. Isabella, as the eldest sister, would have been "Miss Woodhouse" until she married. She then becomes Mrs. John Knightley, and Emma (formerly, Miss Emma Woodhouse) assumes the title "Miss Woodhouse."
>
> To dispense with formal address without permission is to reveal one's own lack of breeding. It would be considered extremely presumptuous to address someone by their first or "Christian" name unless one were a relation or an intimate friend (of the same sex). In Austen's novel, only Mrs. Elton is vulgar enough to routinely dispense with proper address. It is presumptuous indeed that she should refer to Mr. Knightley as "Knightley" (in striking contrast to Emma, who still calls him "Mr. Knightley" though she has known him all his life). Nor is it surprising that Frank Churchill writes (in righteous indignation that Mrs. Elton should dare to address his fiancée by her first name), "'Jane,' indeed!–You will observe that I have not yet indulged myself in calling her by that name" (*Emma*, p. 290). That the book itself should refer to Emma by her first name—even in the title—attests to how intimately the narration follows the thoughts, perceptions, and growth of its heroine.

After a short time—though long enough for introspection and remorse—Emma is visited by Mr. Knightley who, believing her to be attached to Frank Churchill, hopes to comfort her for the

Emma

Gwyneth Paltrow as Emma in the 1996 film version of *Emma*.

behavior of that "abominable scoundrel" (*Emma*, p. 279). So relieved is Mr. Knightley to find that Emma's affections have not been engaged, that he confesses his own feelings for her. Uncharacteristically reticent, he explains his silence: "If I loved you less, I might be able to talk about it more" (*Emma*, p. 282). The sentiment is promptly—though somewhat inaudibly—returned, and only Harriet's happiness and that of Emma's father remain uncertain. Harriet's is secured when, on a trip to London, she transfers her volatile affection once more, from Mr. Knightley to Mr. Robert Martin. Mr. Woodhouse is reconciled to Emma's marriage by design (Mr. Knightley suggests that he move in to Hartfield rather than upset Emma's father) and by chance (a raid on Mrs. Weston's poultry house makes Mr. Woodhouse eager for his son-in-law's in-house protection). The story ends with Emma and Mr. Knightley's wedding. And in spite of Mrs. Elton's jealous comment about there being hardly any white lace at the wedding, we are assured that the union between Emma and Mr. Knightley is a happy one.

Courtship plotting. The structure of *Emma* is what is known as a *marriage plot*, or perhaps more accurately, a *courtship plot*, for marriage is the end (meaning "the finale" and "the goal") of both the courtship and the plot. We see little of what goes on within marriages; we see much of what goes into making matches. Thus the novel focuses on a finely delimited period of a woman's life, during which she is marriageable but unmarried—the period of courtship. This period, moreover, endows a woman (socially, imaginatively, legally) with the most power she has ever had or ever will have. By the custom—or at least the rhetoric—of courtship, hers is the power to choose, the power to refuse, the power to be pleased or displeased. As Mr. Elton's conundrum suggests, during courtship, "Man's boasted power and freedom, all are flown . . . And woman, lovely woman, reigns alone" (*Emma*, p. 46). Of course, this power effects its own removal. The successful courtship ends in marriage, at which time, a woman in Austen's England ceases to reign in any sense; she yields her power, her property, and her independent existence under the law. *Emma* stages this loss as well. Putting on airs, Mrs. Elton repeatedly refers to her husband as "my lord and master," a refrain that, although affected in her case, is nevertheless all too accurate. Mr. Knightley confirms the state of affairs when he observes that Mrs. Weston's former position as governess was good training "on the very material matrimonial point of submitting your own will, and doing as you were bid" (*Emma*, p. 23). Frank Churchill's aunt is the exception who proves the rule—and is, significantly, despised for it. Another character calls Mrs. Churchill, who rules at Enscombe [the Churchill's home] "a very odd-tempered woman"; in less gentle language, we learn at her death that she has been "disliked at least twenty-five years" (*Emma*, pp. 79, 254).

What the courtship plot does is focus on the heightened significance and power of a woman during courtship. Meanwhile, it ignores much of the downside of marriage, writing it off, or at least writing it offstage, as others have noted (Poovey in Austen, p. 396). In this regard, the marriage plot can be said to serve social stability, for such a plot entices readers, especially women, into socially acceptable roles. Thus, Austen's novels have come under considerable criticism for their conservatism—for Austen's tacit acceptance of women's social and legal position.

On the other hand, in Emma's case, the courtship plot can be said to create a space for female power. Emma is the most powerful of all of Austen's heroines—thanks to her money, her class, her position. She does not need to get married to secure her position or her future. So Emma stands poised at the intersection of social distinction and gender subordination: her class gives her power; her gender takes it away. She herself introduces a critique of the current status of married women: "I believe few married women are half as much mistress of their husband's house, as I am of Hartfield; and never, never could I expect to be so truly beloved and important, so always first and always right in any man's eyes as I am in my father's" (*Emma*, p. 55). On the one hand, her comment can be compared to that of a small child who wants to remain with a father she can wrap around her finger. On the other hand, it can be taken seriously, as a rational, critical assessment of the married state, which has nothing to offer a woman who is already financially and thereby socially secure.

Taking Emma seriously raises the issue of her eventual marriage to Mr. Knightley. His position as her future husband is reinforced by their age disparity, and by his brotherly/fatherly solicitude and corrective manner toward her. At the same time, the two of them spar verbally in the novel—more or less as equals. Also Mr. Knightley shows an unusual willingness to move to her home. This willingness to postpone indefinitely what he says "a man would always wish [for]," that is, "to give a woman a better home than the one he takes her from," suggests that perhaps this marriage, and Austen's views, are based on compensation and compromise (*Emma*, p. 281).

Sources and literary context. The literary context of *Emma* is indicative of the position of the gentlewoman as well as the position of the novel in the late eighteenth and early nineteenth century. Austen herself had little or no contact with the literary world. As a woman, she did not have the classical education her brothers would have received at school. But she read extensively, consuming the works of Shakespeare, Alexander Pope, Dr. Samuel Johnson, and the poetry of her contemporaries: Lord Byron, Sir Walter Scott, Robert Burns, and especially William Cowper. She routinely heard the Bible read and, of course, read the Book of Common Prayer. Indeed, the style of the latter is in many ways like her own. She had, moreover, what might have been considered a "low" taste for verse riddles and conundrums as well as for novels—a much more controversial form of writing in her day than in ours (Grey, p. 356). Austen would read (often aloud with her family) even a mediocre novel multiple times as she gradually formed her thoughts on it.

Though Austen is far too subtle to engage in the conspicuous performance of erudition by quoting classical authors at every turn, which was popular at the time, she speaks to the literary movements that immediately preceded her and were evolving around her. Her novels draw on comic tradition, on the satire as well as on the courtship plot, made big in the eighteenth century by writers like Henry Fielding and especially Samuel Richardson. Despite her use of the courtship plot, Austen disclaims any wish or ability to write a romance—a term that at the time referred to a highly unrealistic adventure story with sharply delineated heroes and villains. She preferred, as she said, to "go on in my own Way," in the satire of people and manners (*Emma*, p. 350).

NOT ASHAMED OF READING NOVELS

Though it is perhaps not surprising to her readers now, Austen's predilection for novels would have been mildly scandalous in her day. As she put it, her family were "great Novel-readers & not ashamed of being so" (Austen in Grey, p. 357). This comment is significant and gives us a hint of the problematic status of novels at the time. They were often frowned upon as too fanciful, insufficiently instructive, and even too feminine in the sense that they were too tied in with women's fantasies. One novel that quite obviously influenced Austen's work is Charlotte Lennox's *The Female Quixote,* which Austen read many times and admired. Isolated because of her father's preferences, the heroine Arabella (who is wealthy and beautiful, of course) takes her idea of life from fantastic romances of her day (mostly French ones); she sees love, abduction, mystery, and adventure in every mundane occurrence. The novel is a satire that shows concern for how detrimental reading fiction can be, an eighteenth-century worry, and shows sympathy for Arabella's wish to create a world in which she is much more powerful and important than a woman (even a wealthy one) can ever be in her era. Another novel of Austen's, *Northanger Abbey,* traces the re-education of a similarly mislead heroine. *Emma* too takes up this satire, but in far more subtle ways. It uses the language of heroic romances ironically, applying it to everyday problems: "The real *evils* indeed of Emma's situation were the power of having rather too much her own way," although the "danger" at the start of the novel goes unperceived (*Emma*, p. 1, emphasis added). The irony resides in the existence of a danger that threatens to harm neither life nor limb, but only to diminish slightly Emma's many enjoyments.

Emma

Though *Emma* displays elements of romances such as Regina Maria Roche's *The Children of the Abbey* (1798) and Fanny Burney's *Cecilia* (1782), it is clearly not Austen's intent to reproduce these texts. *Emma* instead reorganizes traditional tropes, relegating a superior woman (like Jane Fairfax, someone beautiful and talented who might have been the persecuted heroine of another novel) to the sidelines, and exploring the complex motivations of a flawed heroine. As she does so, Austen establishes herself as an innovator in the novel of ordinary life. She also reveals her complex relation to the shifting literary trends of her day, especially the Romantic poets, whose verse often stressed intuition and emotion over reason. Prevalent in Romantic poetry is the belief that the road to truth is through the self, through one's imagination and insight, rather than through "any irritable reaching after fact & reason" (Keats, p. 193). On the one hand, *Emma* is fully aware of the pleasures and uses of imagination. On the other hand, the novel finds fault not only with the excessive imagination associated with the prose romances that preceded Austen's novels but also with the spontaneous overflow of feelings that defined poetry for Romantics like William Wordsworth. In *Emma*, too much of one's own desire, unchecked by rational thought, distorts truth. Such emphasis on rationality has led scholars to class Austen as a daughter of the earlier Enlightenment movement, which gave higher priority to reason than emotion, but (like Romantic writers of her time) Austen diverges from her Enlightenment predecessors in important ways. Her fiction demonstrates a distaste for the didactic or preachy, an emphasis on particulars rather than abstractions, and a belief that human nature is neither fixed nor universal. Thus, *Emma* suggests a happy balance between Enlightenment sense and Romantic sensibility, a blend wherein the pleasures of imagination (and undoubtedly, much of Emma's charm comes from her warm and lively imagination) must always be tempered by rationality and social responsibility.

Publication and reviews. Austen's moment was a strange one for women writers. On the one hand, there were more opportunities for women to publish than ever before, and many women were publishing—Ann Radcliffe, Frances Burney, and Maria Edgeworth are only the most visible among the large numbers of women writers. On the other hand, authorship seemed too public for the genteel (modest, retiring, emphatically private) woman, and indeed women were attacked for writing without adequate education. Many women, including Austen, published their first novels anonymously. And many women apologized for having the temerity to write for profit—prefacing their work with descriptions of the desperate financial need (usually in support of family members).

It is perhaps, no wonder then, that Austen's brother Henry paints a picture of Jane Austen as genteel amateur, writing predominantly for the amusement of her family. Certainly her family, especially her sister Cassandra, were her first readers, though Austen's letters show us another side. She was clearly gratified by the limited success of her novels and evinced a real pleasure in earning money from them. Publishing mostly "on commission," a method wherein the author was responsible for all the costs if sales fell short, Austen was both financially and personally invested in the sales of her novels. Due to a still small novel-reading public, considerable risk was involved, and the 2,000 copies of *Emma* published in 1816 (the largest known edition of an Austen novel) failed to sell out. After four years, only 1,437 copies had been sold and the rest were remaindered.

Contemporary reviewers could be rather condescending and formulaic. Sir Walter Scott's respectful and in many ways positive 1815 review is an exception that reflects his interest in a then-new type of novel—the novel of ordinary life. As raves go, however, Scott's review is more than understated; he asserts that *Emma*—a novel "we peruse with pleasure, if not with deep interest"—"has even less story than either of the preceding novels" and describes Emma herself as "vainly engaged in forging wedlock-fetters for others" (Scott in Austen, pp. 357-58). To Victorian reviewers, however, *Emma* becomes the test of the reader's acuity; George Henry Lewes observes in 1852 that "only cultivated minds fairly appreciate the exquisite art of Miss Austen" (Lewes in Austen, p. 360). So popular was Austen by mid-century that Lewes claimed only to be "echoing a universal note of praise in speaking thus highly of her works" (Lewes in Austen, p. 360). Lewes goes on to admire what he considered the special touch of the female writer in the novel. Charlotte Brontë disagreed. While acknowledging the "fidelity" and "delicacy" of *Emma*, Brontë bemoaned Austen's lack of passion, a complaint echoed by Victorian poet Elizabeth Barrett Browning, who observed that Austen's characters lacked "souls" (Grey, p. 98).

Austen's fame grew mostly after she died. Numerous editions have been published in the two centuries since she wrote. Modern readers are often ambivalent about the novel: on the one hand, they wish that Austen would take her heroines out of their traditional, constricted roles; on the other, they can't help admiring her portrayal of women's lives. Many authors have attempted to pick up where she left off or to tell the story from another point of view, as does Naomi Royd Smith's *Jane Fairfax* (1940). Still others have tried to adopt Austen's style or setting or both, giving rise to a subtype of literature—Regency Romances.

Emma has also been repeatedly transformed for the screen, by, among others, Amy Heckerling, whose *Clueless* updates the story to a contemporary California setting and has a high-school "Emma" fix up two teachers whose wedding closes the film. Rivaled only by **Pride and Prejudice** (also in *Literature and Its Times*), *Emma* is considered by many to be the best of Austen's novels. Scholars, Hollywood, and successive generations of readers make it clear: far from being the heroine that, as Austen predicted, "no one but myself will much like," Emma is the heroine whom (like Mr. Knightley) everyone loves—flaws and all (Austen, p. viii).

—Barri J. Gold

For More Information

Austen, Jane. *Emma*. Norton Critical Edition. Ed. Stephen M. Parrish. New York: W. W. Norton, 2000.

Copeland, Edward, and Juliet McMaster, eds. *The Cambridge Companion to Jane Austen*. Cambridge: Cambridge University Press, 1997.

Grey, J. David, et. al. *The Jane Austen Companion*. New York: MacMillan, 1986.

Hellerstein, Erna Olafson, Leslie Parker Hume, and Karen M. Offen, eds. *Victorian Women: A Documentary Account of Women's Lives in Nineteenth-Century England, France, and the United States*. Stanford, Calif.: Stanford University Press, 1981.

Keats, John. *The Letters of John Keats*. Ed. Hyder Edward Rollins. Cambridge, Mass.: Harvard University Press, 1958.

Pool, Daniel. *What Jane Austen Ate and Charles Dickens Knew: From Fox Hunting to Whist—the Facts of Daily Life in 19th-Century England*. New York: Simon and Schuster, 1993.

Stone, Lawrence. *The Family, Sex and Marriage in England 1500-1800*. New York: Harper Torchbooks, 1979.

Fathers and Sons

by
Ivan Turgenev

Born to a wealthy and aristocratic family in the Russian province of Orel, Ivan Sergeyevich Turgenev (1818-83) was educated in Moscow and Saint Petersburg, Russia, before going on to study philosophy at the University of Berlin in Germany. He established his literary reputation with a series of brief portraits of Russian village life published from 1847 to 1852 and collected as *A Sportsman's Sketches* in 1852. After 1856 Turgenev lived primarily in Western Europe. His writings continued to focus on Russian country life, depicting the concerns of Russian nobility and peasants within their rural environment, but his outlook continued to be strongly influenced by Western European ideas. In fact, Turgenev stands out as the most Westernized of Russia's great nineteenth-century writers. His novels typically feature a young Russian who presents new, Western ideas to a more conservative audience, often in the setting of a country estate. Turgenev's first major novel, *Rudin* (1855), follows this basic formula, as do (with some variation) later works such as *On the Eve* (1860) and *Virgin Soil* (1876). Conforming to but also going beyond this pattern is *Fathers and Sons*. Regarded as Turgenev's most artistically successful work, it dramatizes the social and ideological conflict between two generations of Westernized Russians: the older liberals of the 1830s and 1840s, and the younger radicals of the 1850s and 1860s.

Events in History at the Time of the Novel

The fathers: Russian liberals of the 1840s. Russia in the first half of the nineteenth century

> **THE LITERARY WORK**
> A novel set largely in several Russian country homes in the summer of 1859; published in Russian (as *Otsi i dyeti*) in 1862, in English in 1867.
>
> **SYNOPSIS**
> Family ties and romantic entanglements strain the friendship between two young Russian intellectuals, as well as the radical ideas on which their friendship is based.

was just beginning to loosen the grip on a system of serf and peasant labor similar to ones that Western Europe had shaken off centuries earlier. Under the autocratic rule of the Russian tsar, or emperor, nearly all of the land was owned either by the state or by a small proportion of nobles and gentry. Amounting to about 1 percent of the population, the landowning upper class controlled slavelike serfs who lived on its land, peasants bound to an estate and its lord. Serfs made up about two-thirds of the population, the remainder of which consisted mostly of other peasants, who held a non-serf status. Russia's middle class—primarily doctors, lawyers, and government officials—remained small; politically and economically, it was far less powerful than Western Europe's. Limited reforms occurred during the eighteenth century, under Westernizing tsars such as Peter the Great (1682-1725) and Cather-

Fathers and Sons

Ivan Turgenev

ine the Great (1762-96), but by and large Russian society's comparative isolation and stagnation continued until the beginning of the nineteenth century.

ONCE A SERF, ALWAYS A SERF

At the time of the novel, the population of the Russian empire stood at an estimated 75 million. Of that number, perhaps 50 million were serfs, with about half the serfs on land owned by nobles and about half on land owned by the state (so-called state serfs). Most of the rest of the population were peasants of non-serf status. Like Bazarov's father in the novel, a former army surgeon, some peasants might work their way up to professional status and eventually own a small estate with a few serfs of their own. Yet they would still be looked down upon by members of the nobility, even by lesser gentry such as the Kirsanovs. In *Fathers and Sons* Nikolai Kirsanov's servants Peter and Dunyasha make the best life they can for themselves in their situation. They become house-serfs, performing domestic duties in the master's abode. Owing to class distinctions, only rarely could a peasant woman like the novel's Fenichka hope to marry a widowed or unmarried master who was a noble, even if he was liberal and even if—as was more common—she bore his child.

The majority of the population, the Russian peasants, lived in rural villages (there were few isolated farms) that actually formed part of the larger estates. Food was often scarce and conditions were harsh in the villages, with streets blanketed by deep snow in winter and with thick mud in summer. Turgenev's family estate, a large one located about halfway between Moscow and Kiev, contained some 30 villages and 5,000 "souls," as the common expression went. While serfs were nominally free, and different gradations of serfdom existed, the populations of the towns and villages were for all practical purposes considered the property of a landowner. Like many liberal landowners, the novel's Nikolai Kirsanov has recently improved conditions for his serfs by changing to the quit-rent system, under which a peasant paid a regular sum, the quit-rent (*obrok*), to the landowner, in place of indentured service (*barshchina*). Since landowners who switched to this system gave their peasants plots of land as well, it allowed the peasants more opportunity to grow their own food.

Russia's isolation began to erode because of a single momentous event and its aftermath: the invasion of Russia in 1812 by the French emperor Napoleon. Russia successfully repulsed the French invaders. More than merely a military victory, the event proved to be a far-reaching catalyst for social transformation, which originated among Russian army officers who commanded troops occupying France after Napoleon's defeat in 1815. In an age of cultural and political ferment throughout Europe, these young, educated aristocrats hungrily soaked up the ideas of French, German, and other European writers. Among the major influences on the young Russians were the German Romantic poets Johann Wolfgang von Goethe (1749-1832) and Friedrich Schiller (1759-1805), and especially the German idealist philosopher Wilhelm Friedrich Hegel (1770-1830). (For a sample of one of their works, see Goethe's *Faust,* also in *Literature and Its Times.*) These and other intellectuals imparted to the Russians concepts central to their writings, such as the notions of national identity and historical progress.

By the time a decade had passed, the young Russian officers had returned to Russia and achieved influential positions in the army. In December 1825, after the death of Tsar Alexander I, a small group of Westernized officers revolted against the planned accession of Alexander's designated successor, Nicholas I, who was known to oppose Western-style reforms. The officers wished not to overthrow the tsarist system, but to reform it. They hoped to install on the throne Nicholas's liberal older brother Constantine, known to support reforms, and they called for the creation of a constitutional monarchy, in which a legislative assembly of nobles (like Britain's House of Lords) would limit the power of the tsar. Nicholas I (ruled 1825-55) easily quashed this so-called Decembrist Revolt, but as he persisted in oppressive and autocratic policies, growing numbers of young nobles came to favor reforms, inspired by Western political and social ideas. By the 1830s and 1840s, these young Westernizing Russians had begun defining themselves as liberals.

In *Fathers and Sons*, this generation—the "fathers" of the title—is represented by the aristocratic and cultivated brothers Pavel and Nikolai Kirsanov. Significantly, both are described as having served in the army as young men. Since the novel portrays them as aged in their sixties, their stint in the army would have occurred around the time of the Decembrist Revolt. Both also revere their generation's Western literary idols, mentioning Goethe, Schiller, and Hegel by name. Calling himself "a man of liberal ideas," Pavel Kirsanov particularly admires the British political system of limited constitutional monarchy based on a historically strong aristocracy: "the aristocracy has given freedom to England, and supports it for her," he tells the novel's main character, the young radical Evgeny Bazarov (Turgenev, *Fathers and Sons*, p. 37).

The sons: the new radicals of the 1850s. In the early 1850s, as the oppressive Nicholas I aged, Russians awaited the accession of Alexander II, whom the public knew as a reform-minded liberal, and who duly came to power after the death of Nicholas I in 1855. While other issues (for example, the Crimean War, 1853-56) demanded Alexander's immediate attention, none was as pressing as the emancipation of the serfs, and the redistribution of the land on which they lived. Solid liberals were a minority among the nobles; most of the politically powerful landowning families resisted giving up their land and the peasants who came with it. Even after they realized that reform was inevitable, they angled for the best deal possible; consequently the pace of reform was slow, intolerably slow for at least one camp. By the mid-1850s, the slow pace of reform had already prompted an attack on the liberals' ideals by younger, more extreme intellectuals. *Fathers and Sons* gives voice to this new generation of radicals in the character of Evgeny Bazarov and his disciple Arkady Kirsanov, Nikolai Kirsanov's son. These are the "sons" of the novel's title (in Russian, the word *dyeti* in the title literally means "children," but most translators have found that the English "sons" captures Turgenev's meaning more accurately).

THE FLOWERING OF RUSSIAN LITERATURE

The Western ideas introduced into Russia in the 1820s to 1840s instigated the nation's first real flowering of literary creativity and political thought. Taking their cue from European Romanticism, Russian Romantic poets such as Aleksandr Pushkin (1799-1837) and Mikhail Lermontov (1814-41) led the way in the 1820s and 1830s, a period known as the golden age of Russian poetry. Both Pushkin and Lermontov then turned largely to prose, Pushkin in the 1830s and Lermontov in the 1840s. They were succeeded by such prose masters as the Ukraine-born comic novelist Nikolai Gogol (1809-52), founder of the school later known as Russian Realism. Russian literary criticism began with Vissarion Belinsky (1811-48), a mentor to Turgenev and many other young writers (Turgenev dedicated *Fathers and Sons* to his memory). Like other Westernizing writers including Turgenev, Belinsky, who brought Western cultural and political values to bear in his reviews of Russian literary works, found himself persecuted by Nicholas I's authoritarian regime (1825-55). Russia's emerging liberal political thinkers fell subject to government persecution too, including Turgenev's friends Mikhail Bakunin (1814-76) and Aleksandr Herzen (1812-70), both of whom moved, like Turgenev, to Western Europe. Herzen settled in England in 1852, where, in his Russian-language newspaper *The Bell* (to which Turgenev frequently contributed, and which was widely read in Russia), he called for liberal political reforms in his home country—above all for the abolition of serfdom, which had become Russia's leading political issue.

Emancipation of the serfs involved complex negotiations over land and compensation that took several years. The final result, enacted in February 1861, was a compromise. Approximately 20 million serfs were freed from servitude and allowed to purchase allotments of land, but the land was often poor in quality and the allotments were small. The government paid landowners for the land, and the new peasant owners were to reimburse the government through so-called redemption payments.

Fathers and Sons

> ## DIFFERENCES BETWEEN TWO GENERATIONS
>
> A number of major differences distinguished the radical "sons" of the 1850s from the liberal "fathers" of the 1830s and 1840s:
>
> - **Class differences** Whereas the liberals nearly all came from the landowning nobility, the radicals came from a new class, the *raznochintsy*, a mixed group of priests, civil servants, merchants, and descendents of foreigners, among others. The term denoted those from lower-class backgrounds who had broken free of traditional class restraints. In the novel, the radical Bazarov is a *raznochinyets* (the singular form). The *raznochintsy* reflect a gradual loosening of class divisions that began in the 1820s.
> - **Revolution vs. reform** The liberals had generally wished merely to reform the tsarist system, while the radicals called for its outright overthrow, by violence if necessary. They wished to remake Russian society completely, calling for an end to the class system with its aristocratic privileges.
> - **Aesthetic values** Unlike the cultivated liberals, the hard-headed radicals had little use for literature or art. In the novel, for example, the older Nikolai Kirsanov enjoys quoting Pushkin—the most beloved of Russian poets—but Bazarov derisively asserts that "A good chemist is twenty times as useful as a poet" (*Fathers and Sons*, p. 19).
> - **Science and reason vs. intuition and passion** As Bazarov's declaration suggests, the radicals exalted science and reason above all, denigrating the intuition and passion favored by Romantic writers and their liberal heirs.
> - **Attitudes towards nature** The novel's Nikolai Kirsanov exemplifies the liberal Romantics' worship of nature, which Bazarov disparages: "Nature's not a temple," Bazarov affirms, "but a workshop, and man's the workman in it" (*Fathers and Sons*, p. 33).
> - **Religion** While the liberals considered themselves progressive and enlightened, many continued to observe traditional Russian Orthodox Christianity. In contrast, the radicals scorned religion as outmoded and superstitious.
> - **The peasants** Liberals like Nikolai Kirsanov struck a paternal and protective attitude towards the peasants, but the radicals often contemptuously dismissed the peasants in their writings. In the novel Bazarov characterizes most peasants as ignorant, drunken and crooked.

The radicals' movement arose in the atmosphere of tense public discussion over these issues in the middle and late 1850s. At the head of the movement stood three writers: Nikolai Chernyshevsky (1828-89), Nikolai Dobrolyubov (1836-61), and Dmitri Pisarev (1840-68). Like the liberals, these younger thinkers were influenced by cultural currents from Western Europe. Liberalism had been dealt a severe blow there in 1848, a tumultuous year in which Europe was wracked by failed liberal revolutions, which drove many liberals towards more radical positions (such as Turgenev's friend and fellow Russian Mikhail Bakunin, who became the father of anarchism). Also Western advances in science drove Chernyshevsky and his fellow thinkers to champion a scientific and rational approach to social problems. Another important influence was the utilitarian doctrine of British philosopher John Stuart Mill (1806-73), who questioned the idea of inherent moral value, suggesting that qualities like right and wrong derive not from an action itself, but only from its consequences.

Turgenev lived in Paris during most of this period but followed events in Russia closely. He felt ambivalent about the radicals: his own generation had failed to effect significant change, he believed, and perhaps its romantic idealism was to blame. The radicals seemed to take a more realistic view of things. Yet while he endorsed their overall goal of social change, Turgenev disapproved of their calls for violent revolution. Fascinated by this ambivalence, he completed the outline of *Fathers and Sons* in August of 1860, six months before emancipation, finishing the book the following August, six months after emancipation was enacted.

The Novel in Focus

The plot. The action of *Fathers and Sons* takes place from late May to August 1859. The novel opens as Arkady Kirsanov, a young university student who has just graduated, comes home to Marino, the modest country estate of his widowed father Nikolai. Arkady's older friend and mentor Evgeny Bazarov, a doctor in his mid-twenties on his way to visit his own parents, accompanies Arkady on the open-ended visit. Among those already living at Marino are Nikolai's older brother, Pavel, a dandified former army officer; Nikolai's servants Peter and Dunyasha; and Fenichka, a young peasant woman with whom Nikolai has recently fathered a child.

Arkady has been away from home for some time. Embarrassed, his father, Nikolai, hesitates in acknowledging his relationship with Fenichka. Arkady, however, approves his father's happiness, assuring Nikolai proudly that he and Bazarov disdain all conventional class distinctions. Bazarov and Pavel, meanwhile, dislike each other on sight. The young doctor's seemingly deliberate lack of manners irritates the older man, who interrogates Arkady about his friend. Bazarov, Arkady tells his uncle, is a "nihilist," which he defines as someone "who does not bow down before any authority, who does not take any principle on faith, whatever reverence that principle may be enshrined in" (*Fathers and Sons*, p. 17).

Pavel observes ironically that he will stick with his "old-fashioned" belief in principles. Shifting his attention directly to Bazarov, who admires the work of German physicists and other scientists, Pavel tries to get him to admit that he accepts them as authorities. Bazarov, however, insists that he believes in nothing and accepts no authorities: "But why should I accept them? And what is there to believe in? They talk sense, I agree, that's all" (*Fathers and Sons*, p. 19). Bazarov learns that the course of Pavel's life was changed years ago by an unhappy love affair, after which he left his promising army career and withdrew from life to his current stagnant existence in the remote countryside. He scorns Pavel as weak, dismissing the idea of love as nothing more than "romanticism, nonsense, rot, artiness" (*Fathers and Sons*, p. 25).

Bazarov also scoffs at Nikolai's laxness in dealing with his serfs, telling Arkady sarcastically, "the good peasants are taking your father in for sure" (*Fathers and Sons*, p. 33). Arguing with Pavel over politics, Bazarov rejects all liberal values and denies even that emancipation will do any good, because the serfs will be too lazy and drunken to make anything of it. Bazarov and Arkady boast that nihilism's value lies in pure destructive force, in tearing down all aspects of society in order to start over, but Pavel fumes at such barbarism.

After a few weeks, during which Bazarov passes the time dissecting frogs, Arkady and Bazarov leave Marino to visit a large town nearby, the capital of the province (the novel, following common literary practice of the day, does not name the town or the province). There an influ-

Fathers and Sons

Turgenev endorsed the general good of the "new radicals" of 1850s Russia, including writer Nikolai Gavrilovich Chernyshevsky, seen here.

ential cousin of Nikolai's gets them invited to a ball to be given in two days by the provincial governor, and they run into an acquaintance of Bazarov's, a would-be radical and self-serving flatterer named Sitnikov. Sitnikov will also be attending the ball. Presently he introduces them to his friend Evdoksya Kukshin, "an advanced woman" who smokes cigars, drinks champagne, and spouts the latest intellectually fashionable ideas (*Fathers and Sons*, p. 50). Bazarov shows little interest in the homely Kukshin or her trendy talk, but he does perk up when she mentions an attractive friend of hers, Anna Odintsov. At the ball Arkady dances with Odintsov, a striking and aristocratic young widow, whose wealthy husband left her a large estate with a substantial income.

The next day, Bazarov—who saw Arkady dance with the attractive, dark-haired Odintsov—insists that they call upon her at her hotel. Bazarov and Arkady are both attracted to her, and the three strike up a friendship. When Odintsov invites them to visit her at Nikolskoe, her estate, Bazarov insists that they accept, telling Arkady that it is on the way to his parents' house. Odintsov welcomes them, and during their two-week stay as guests at the well-run estate, both Bazarov and Arkady fall in love with her. Bazarov is disgusted with himself: "In his conversations . . . he expressed more than ever his calm contempt for everything romantic; but when he was alone, with indignation he recognized the romantic in himself" (*Fathers and Sons*, p. 73). While Bazarov monopolizes her time, Arkady spends much of his with Odintsov's serious and rather quiet younger sister, Katya, who lives there as well, along with their maiden aunt (their parents are both deceased). Bazarov decides to leave, and when Odinstov presses him in a friendly way to stay, he awkwardly proclaims his love and attempts to embrace her. She reacts with discomfort, even fright, at his sudden advances. She likes and admires him, but makes it clear that although they have much in common, she would never marry a poor man of such low social rank.

Humiliated, Bazarov persuades Arkady to leave with him, and after returning to Marino to pick up Bazarov's luggage, they go visit Bazarov's parents. His devoted parents are overjoyed at his arrival, fussing so much over him that Bazarov feels suffocated. He again persuades Arkady to leave with him, and after only a couple of days the two return to Marino. So distraught are Bazarov's parents that he promises to return for a longer visit soon. Back at Marino, Bazarov distracts himself from his bitter thoughts of Odintsov by befriending Fenichka, the pretty young peasant woman who has born Nikolai's child. He sets her at ease with his casual manner and reassures her by offering medical care to her baby son. Pavel, however, suspects that Bazarov is up to no good, and then catches Bazarov in the act. When Bazarov tries to kiss the shocked girl in the garden one day, Pavel sees the incident. He challenges Bazarov to a duel, and Bazarov—intrigued, he says, by the very pointlessness of such an outmoded ritual—accepts. The two men meet secretly at dawn with pistols, Pavel is slightly wounded, and Bazarov gives him medical attention. Recovering from what he claims was an accident with his gun, Pavel tells Nikolai that he must marry Fenichka. Nikolai happily admits he would have done so long ago, but feared Pavel would snobbishly object.

Unbeknownst to Bazarov, Arkady had returned to Nikolskoe before the duel. There he had realized that his feelings for Odintsov were mere infatuation. Instead he and her sister fell in love and got engaged, as Bazarov learns when he arrives. Odintsov is happy to see Bazarov, and apologizes if she led him on in any way earlier. However, she realizes, to her discomfort, that he still loves her. Without anger, Bazarov informs Arkady that their friendship must now end, because if Arkady plans to marry, he will lack the inner fire necessary to be a nihilist. Bazarov returns home, to his parents' great joy, but is aimless and unhappy. He helps his father tend to the medical needs of the nearby peasants, but contracts typhus conducting an autopsy on a peasant who had died of the fatal disease. On his deathbed he calls for Odintsov, who visits him shortly before he breathes his last breath. In the years that follow, his poor old parents find comfort in visiting their son's silent grave.

The liberals' dilemma. Disturbed by Bazarov's arguments with Pavel, the liberal Nikolai Kirsanov wonders to himself what gives the radicals' position its strange attractiveness:

> I do think . . . that they are further from the truth than we are, though at the same time I feel there is something behind them we have not got, some superiority over us. . . . Doesn't their superiority consist in there being fewer traces of the slave owner in them than in us? . . . But to renounce poetry? . . . to have no feeling for art, for nature.
>
> (*Fathers and Sons*, p. 44)

The radicals' extremism seems both purer and yet somehow less human than his own liberalism. Hence Nikolai at once feels marginalized and repelled.

The radicals co-opted the liberals' goals, and then took those goals to their logical extreme, the radicals in effect reduced any objections on the liberals' part to mere hand-wringing over methods. At the same time, they made the liberals appear to themselves as less than wholeheartedly committed, thus turning their moderation into a fatal weakness. In an influential essay on *Fathers and Sons*, Isaiah Berlin—often called the twentieth century's leading liberal historian—argues that the novel's depiction of this process pinpoints what has since proved to be liberalism's classic dilemma when faced by radicalism. The same quandary had perplexed French liberals, Berlin observes, after radicals took over the French Revolution of the late eighteenth century. It appeared in Russia for the first time with the radical generation of the 1850s and 1860s. There, in Berlin's words, the liberals' dilemma, highlighted by the novel, "became a chronic condition—a long unceasing malaise of the entire enlightened section of society" that ultimately set the stage for the Russian Revolution of 1917 (Berlin, p. 298).

Sources and literary context. As the most popular Russian writer in the 1850s, Turgenev knew Russia's leading liberals and radicals, and he drew on this personal knowledge for both the ideas in the novel and the portraits of the characters who expound them. The major sources for Bazarov's ideas were the writings of radical leaders such as Chernyshevsky and Dobrolyubov. For example, Bazarov's assertion in the novel that nature is not a temple but a workshop closely paraphrases a passage from Chernyshevsky's book *The Aesthetic Relation of Art to Reality* (1855). In this influential work, Chernyshevsky argues that art is no more than a pale imitation of reality, and that therefore reality always has more value. As part of his presentation of the radicals, Turgenev also weaves into his story references to Western works upon which the radicals based their approach: a leading example is a book of materialist philosophy called *Force and Matter* (German; 1855) by Ludwig Büchner, which Arkady gives to his father to read instead of the "useless" Pushkin (*Fathers and Sons*, p. 35). (Referring to Büchner by name, Turgenev mistakenly calls the book *Matter and Force*.) Scholars also speculate that Bazarov's deliberate rudeness was partly based on Dobrolyubov, who disliked the amiable Turgenev and repeatedly snubbed him socially.

Much of the novel's literary context stems from the intellectual journals in which these writers carried on their dialogues over Russia's future. Some famous encounters between Turgenev and Dobrolyubov, for example, took place during Turgenev's visits to the offices of the leading radical journal *The Contemporary*. Chernyshevsky, Dobrolyubov, and Pisarev participated heavily in the production of this journal, which published several pieces by Turgenev in the 1850s. However, *The Contemporary* grew steadily more radical, so Turgenev found another outlet. He wrote instead for the journal *Russian Herald*, published by the more conservative intellectual Mikhail Katkov.

NIHILISTS AND SUPERFLUOUS MEN

For the radical Russian literary critics, one of an author's most important functions was to illustrate and define emerging social types as society produced them. Turgenev had done precisely that for his own generation in his 1850 story "The Diary of a Superfluous Man," which portrays just such a type: the educated, aristocratic liberal who finds no outlet for his energies in the oppressive society of tsarist Russia. In *Fathers and Sons*, the character of Pavel Kirsanov can be considered a "superfluous man." While this sort of character had appeared in earlier literary works (for example, Pushkin's verse novel *Eugene Onegin*), Turgenev's popular story brought the term "superfluous man" itself into wide use. *Fathers and Sons* would do the same for the radicals, by bringing the term "nihilist" into common usage. An unhappy philosophy, nihilism holds that all values are worthless and that humanity knows nothing. While Turgenev was not the first to use the term, the novel's controversial reception forever fixed "nihilist" as the label for the Russian radical generation of the 1850s and 1860s. It came specifically to stand for the movement to effect radical change through terrorism and assassination in view of the belief that one must destroy the current system to improve it.

Reception. Katkov's *Russian Herald* published *Fathers and Sons* in the spring of 1862 to immediate and unprecedented controversy. *Fathers and Sons,* says Isiah Berlin, "caused the greatest storm among its Russian readers of any novel before, or indeed, since" (Berlin, p. 280). The fiery debate centered around Turgenev's depiction of the radical Bazarov, and brought attacks upon the author from all points of the political spectrum, ranging from Bazarov's real-life radical counterparts on the far left, to Turgenev's fellow liberals in the center, to conservatives on the far right. Many conservatives—including *Russian Herald* publisher Katkov himself—objected that the portrait of Bazarov was too positive and sympathetic, while liberals such as Turgenev's friend Aleksandr Herzen complained that the novel's Pavel and Nikolai Kirsanov made liberals appear weak and irrelevant. The strongest outcry, however, came from the radicals, many of whom condemned Bazarov as a gross distortion, a boorish woman-chaser who mouthed half-digested arguments without grasping their true meaning. Chernyshevsky took Turgenev on; in direct response to *Fathers and Sons*, Chernyshevsky penned a different picture of a radical hero in his novel *What Is To Be Done?* (1863), which became perhaps the most influential Russian political novel of all time.

Not all reaction was negative, however. The influential conservative critic Nikolai Strakhov praised Bazarov as a grandly conceived hero whose depiction rises above ideological arguments of the day to explore the sorts of conflicts that will always arise between one generation and the next. And from a very different viewpoint, the radical author Dmitri Pisarev endorsed Bazarov as an entirely fair and accurate portrait. Calling Turgenev "one of the best men of the last generation," Pisarev praises the novel's "artistic beauty" in terms echoed by many later critics:

> The author himself is not clearly aware of his feelings; he does not subject them to analysis, nor does he assume a critical attitude toward them. This circumstance gives us the opportunity to see these feelings in all their unspoiled spontaneity.
>
> (Pisarev in Turgenev, p. 195)

—Colin Wells

For More Information

Berlin, Isaiah. *Russian Thinkers*. Harmondsworth: Penguin, 1978.

Crankshaw, Edward. *The Shadow of the Winter Palace: Russia's Drift To Revolution 1825-1917*. New York: Viking, 1978.

Hingley, Ronald. *Russian Writers and Society 1825-1904*. New York: McGraw-Hill, 1967.

Knowles, A. V. *Ivan Turgenev*. Boston: Twayne, 1988.

Pritchett, V. S. *The Gentle Barbarian: The Life and Work of Turgenev*. New York: Random House, 1977.

Turgenev, Ivan. *Fathers and Sons*. New York: Norton, 1966.

Wasiolek, Edward. *Fathers and Sons: Russia at the Cross-Roads*. New York: Twayne, 1993.

Faust

by
Johann Wolfgang von Goethe

By common consent, Johann Wolfgang von Goethe (1749-1832) is the foremost writer Germany has produced. Constantly experimenting with new styles and subjects, the prolific Goethe (pronounced GUR-tuh) continually reinvented his own authorial persona and seldom repeated himself. The widely imitated Goethe established whole new genres with a single work before moving on to something equally original with his next achievement. Aside from *Faust*, considered his masterpiece, Goethe is best known today for novels such as *The Sorrows of Young Werther* (1774) and for his lyric poetry. *Faust*, written over 60 years of Goethe's life, reflects the poet's versatility both in its wide-ranging themes and in its dazzling array of different poetic styles. Goethe adapts the medieval legend of Dr. Faustus, a scholar who sells his soul to the Devil for knowledge and magical powers. Goethe's treatment of this old story—updated for the late eighteenth and early nineteenth centuries—offered readers fresh insights into the central problems of their own turbulent age.

Events in History at the Time the Play Takes Place

Renaissance and Reformation. During the sixteenth century two connected movements transformed the largely German-speaking lands of northern Europe. First, from its origins in fourteenth-century Italy, the Renaissance brought a new perception of humanity's place in the world. No longer did the best minds call for slav-

> **THE LITERARY WORK**
>
> A long poetic drama loosely set in the idealized past, primarily in sixteenth-century Germany and ancient Greece; published in two parts in German (as *Faust: Der Tragödie erster Teil* [1808] and *Faust: Der Tragödie zweiter Teil* [1832]), in English in 1838.
>
> **SYNOPSIS**
>
> A jaded scholar makes a wager with the Devil. The scholar, Faust, will give up his eternal soul if the Devil can offer him a single moment that he would wish to prolong.

ish obedience to religious authorities and acceptance of Church dogma. Instead a group of Renaissance thinkers celebrated the individual and the power of human reason. The thinkers, who called themselves humanists, rediscovered many classical literary and scientific works, making this rediscovery the mainspring of their movement. Greek texts especially had, for the most part, been ignored during the preceding centuries, a period that humanists labeled the Middle Ages. Through its emphasis on the power of reason, Renaissance humanism became associated as well with the scientific revolution inaugurated by Polish astronomer Nicolas Copernicus (1473-1543) and others. Often magic and other occult practices were pursued along with science by the same scholarly practitioners.

Faust

Johann Wolfgang von Goethe

As Renaissance ideals spread northward, the second transformative movement emerged. A religious revolt known as the Protestant Reformation erupted in 1517 when a German priest named Martin Luther openly opposed the pope's authority. Denying that the Church or priests must mediate between God and humanity (a necessity according to the central tenets of the Catholic Church), Luther's followers insisted that all individuals could commune directly with God. From its origins in the German Holy Roman Empire, the Reformation spread rapidly throughout much of northern Europe, shattering the unity of the Catholic Church.

It is true that many humanists rejected Protestantism, just as many Protestants ignored humanism. Equally, both Protestantism and humanism represented a wide variety of viewpoints and embraced various and at times conflicting beliefs. Yet these two broad movements shared a common fundamental attitude. Both reflected a deep and widespread need to question traditional authority, especially that of the Church, and to challenge old assumptions about the nature of humanity. In the character of Faust, the turbulent sixteenth century found a hero who reflected this attitude perfectly: a humanistic scholar who seeks knowledge and power through magical means, uses them to make a fool of the Catholic pope, and then suffers eternal damnation.

The legend of Faust. A few historical sources record the existence of one Georg Faust, a wandering scholar and trickster who lived in Germany between about 1480 and 1540. Apparently he died while staging an exhibition of his flying ability. This historical Faust claimed to have magical powers and to enjoy the friendship of the Devil. Yet despite his shady reputation, this historical Faust was respected for his humanistic learning by a number of Protestant leaders. Popular folk stories embellished these bare bones after his death, magnifying him into Dr. Johannes Faust or Faustus (the Latin form of the name means "happy" or "fortunate"), a proud and ambitious scholar who makes a bet with the Devil in exchange for secret magical knowledge, conjures up spirits from the ancient Greek past such as Helen of Troy, and plays magical tricks on the emperor and the pope. In accordance with the pact, after 24 years he is torn to pieces by demons and carried off to the eternal torments of hell.

The folktales spread as the century progressed, their popularity suggesting that Germans were both excited and fearful about the momentous changes taking place. On the one hand, advances in science and learning held great promise of liberating the human intellect from the Church's rule, just as the Reformation allowed Germans a greater measure of freedom in worshipping as they chose. Yet like the old, the new knowledge was held by only a few, who remained figures of mystery to the common people. A residual fear persisted that perhaps the old authorities were correct after all, and that those who challenged them risked eternal damnation. The Faust tales, dramatizing the challenges to authority but ending in the punishment of the challenger, offered satisfaction in both directions, appealing to the spirit of innovation as well as conservatism.

Eventually the tales were collected and printed in chapbooks or pamphlets, of which the oldest surviving example dates from 1587. One of these chapbooks, translated into English, provided the basis for English playwright Christopher Marlowe's drama *The Tragical History of Doctor Faustus*, acted on the Elizabethan stage in the 1590s and first published in 1604. Immensely influential, this version soon found its way back into the cycle of Faust tales in Germany, where simplified adaptations were widely produced for popular puppet theaters. Like the English characters Punch and Judy, Faust became a stock character in common puppet shows, continuing to please crowds in German towns and cities into the eighteenth century. By then these formulaic presentations were little more than the colorful but fossilized remnants of a once vital folk myth. It was through such puppet shows that Goethe first encountered the Faust legend as a boy in Frankfurt in the 1760s.

The Play in Focus

The plot. Although written in the form of a play, because of its great length Goethe's *Faust* is virtually never performed uncut. Goethe himself, who ran a theater for almost three decades, shortened it significantly for performance (he himself never directed this play). Of the two parts, Part 1 is the more commonly read and performed, and even when staged alone, it is almost always heavily cut. The two parts differ greatly in structure, theme, and subject matter. Part 1, shorter and more cohesive, focuses on a single storyline—Faust's pact with the Devil and his subsequent seduction of the innocent woman Gretchen. This single storyline unfolds in a series of consecutive scenes without act divisions. By contrast, the almost double-sized Part 2 unfolds in five separate acts that range widely in subject matter as well as in space and time.

Part 1. Part 1 begins with three brief prefatory sections: a Dedication, in which the author looks back on the dimly remembered times when he began the work; a Prelude on the Stage, in which three theatrical characters (Director, Poet, and Clown) discuss their distinctive contributions to the audience's experience; and the Prologue in Heaven, featuring the Lord, the Archangels of heaven, and the Devil, called Mephistopheles (pronounced meh fis stah' fuh leez). Mephistopheles and the Lord argue over human nature, Mephistopheles suggesting that by giving humans the power of reason the Lord has only made them miserable. To settle the issue, they pick the case of Faust, a restless scholar who is always striving for new knowledge but is never satisfied. Mephistopheles believes he can easily win Faust over, but the Lord is confident that in the end "man in his dark impulse always knows the right road from the wrong" (Goethe, *Faust*, p. 760). The Lord gives Mephistopheles complete freedom to tempt Faust, and they wager on the outcome.

The first scene opens as Dr. Heinrich Faust sits late at his desk in his cramped and narrow study, surrounded by books and scientific instruments. It is the night before Easter. Faust has lost all joy in life. A university teacher, he has mastered every academic discipline but all he has learned is that no one can really know anything useful. In frustration, he experiments with magic, hoping to find out what "holds the world together" (*Faust*, p. 761). Faust conjures a magical Earth-Spirit, which terrifies him briefly and expresses contempt for him before disappearing. Wagner, Faust's learned but pedantic and unimaginative assistant, completely fails to grasp Faust's frustration. Faust contemplates suicide, but he rejects the option when he hears church bells and a choir celebrating Easter, with its message of resurrection and eternal life. On the morrow, Faust and Wagner mingle with happy townsfolk enjoying the spring Easter Day. They are followed home by a mysterious black poodle in which Faust senses some occult presence. That evening Faust uses magic to make the poodle reveal its true form, and Mephistopheles appears, dressed as a wandering scholar. Mephistopheles reveals his identity but then lulls Faust to sleep, so he later wonders whether he dreamed the episode.

The next day, however, Mephistopheles returns (this time disguised as a nobleman) and tempts Faust with unlimited wealth and pleasure. When Faust declines the offer, Mephistopheles volunteers to be Faust's servant for life if Faust will be Mephistopheles' servant after death. Instead, Faust counters with an offer to become the Devil's servant if Mephistopheles can ever present the unsatisfied scholar with a single moment that he would wish to prolong:

> If you can delude me into feeling pleased with myself, if your good things ever get the better of me, then may that day be my last day. This is my wager.... If ever the passing moment is such that I wish it not to pass and I say to it "You are beautiful, stay a while," then let that be the finish. The clock can stop. You can put me in chains and ring the death-bell.
> (*Faust*, p. 787)

Mephistopheles agrees, and they seal this wager in blood. The rest of the drama follows the resulting lifelong contest, as the ironic, cynical, and inventive Mephistopheles seeks to satiate the earnest, driven, and ever-restless Faust.

As soon as he signs the wager, Faust is eager to begin. "I'm sick of learning," he declares, "have been for ages. Let us spend our passions, hot in sensual deeps" (*Faust*, p. 788). He exits to prepare for "a whirl of dissipation" that he anticipates will bring him to "the peak of humanity" (*Faust*, p. 799). A freshman student arrives hoping to meet the famous scholar, and Mephistopheles,

Gösta Ekman (left) as Faust and Emil Jannings as Mephisto in the 1926 silent-film version of *Faust*.

putting on Faust's academic gown, pretends to be Faust. His sarcastic attack on academic learning and pedantry thoroughly confuses the naïve student.

The first stage of Faust's "whirl of dissipation" takes place in Auerbach's Tavern, a drinking establishment frequented by university students, where Mephistopheles hopes to tempt Faust with the pleasures of tavern life. Mephistopheles plays magical tricks on four drunken customers, but Faust is merely disgusted. Next Mephistopheles takes Faust to the Witch's Kitchen, where an apelike witch gives Faust a potion that magically rejuvenates him. Then, in a brief street scene, Faust catches sight of the beautiful Margaret, or Gretchen (the German nickname). Aroused by her beauty and innocence, Faust is overwhelmed with lust. The next scene shows Gretchen in her tiny room. She braids her hair and muses about the attractive gentleman she saw on the street, then exits, whereupon Faust and Mephistopheles enter quietly. Mephistopheles gives Faust some jewels to leave in the girl's cupboard; alone again in the room, Gretchen spots them and puts them on wonderingly.

When the girl's suspicious mother turns the jewels over to a priest, sensing something wrong with them, Mephistopheles replaces them. This time Gretchen keeps the treasure secret from her mother, though she too senses something amiss. With Mephistopheles' help, Faust spends time with Gretchen. His lust deepens into a love that she returns. Still wracked by lust for her, he is now also torn by guilt over his dishonorable intentions. After seeking solitude in a woodland cavern, he reappears to seduce Gretchen. The next scene shows Gretchen at her spinning wheel, singing a lyrical song about her love for Faust and her fears that once she has been seduced by him, he will abandon her. When they meet in her neighbor's garden, she asks Faust why he never goes to church. Faust answers that he despises conventional religion but worships the "eternally mysterious" forces that work through nature: "call it what you like: happiness, heart, love, God. I have no words for it. Feeling is everything" (*Faust*, p. 837). Gretchen expresses her instinctive revulsion at the sight of Mephistopheles, whom she has met in Faust's company. She also agrees to let Faust into her room that night.

In the next scene Gretchen chats with a friend as they draw water from a well. The two gossip about a woman who has been made pregnant and then abandoned by her lover to face disgrace. Alone, Gretchen reveals that now she understands what such women go through, for she is in the same state. Several months go by, and in a brief scene the deserted and pregnant Gretchen prays to the Virgin Mary, Mother of Sorrows, for salvation. One night her brother Valentin, a soldier, waits outside her door planning to ambush the man who has ruined her. Faust arrives and in the resulting fight he kills Valentin with Mephistopheles help.

The climactic scene of Part 1 takes place some months later, when Mephistopheles and Faust attend the fantastic and fiendish celebration of Walpurgis Night (the annual date witches and devils are thought to hold orgies). As he dances among the dark twisting shapes in the bizarre rite, Faust has a disturbing vision of Gretchen in chains. He has now reached the depths of moral degradation. After a brief interlude in which he and Mephistopheles watch a short fantastical play, Faust learns that Gretchen is indeed in chains and is sentenced to die. Ashamed at having been mercilessly cast out by society, she killed their child, then was thrown into prison, where she awaits execution for infanticide. With Mephistopheles' magical help, Faust visits Gretchen in her cell. Her tragic fate has driven her insane, but she recovers her senses on seeing Faust. Despite her joy at his return, she refuses his offer of escape with Mephistopheles's assistance. Recognizing Mephistopheles as the Devil, Gretchen rejects him and gives herself over to the mercy of God. As Faust and Mephistopheles depart, a voice from above proclaims that she is saved. Part 1 closes to the sound of her own fading voice crying Faust's name.

Part 2. Whereas Part 1 concentrates on the intimate world of the two lovers, Part 2 moves out into the wider world of sweeping historical, cultural, and political forces. At the same time, the primarily German storyline of Part 1 largely gives way to classical Greek preoccupations. Divided into five acts, Part 2's contents are more diffuse than Part 1's. As the narrative unfolds, events are filled out by complex allegorical descriptions and philosophical digressions.

- **Act 1.** Faust rests in a pleasant meadow, where airy spirits sing to him. Disguised as a jester, Mephistopheles appears at the Emperor's court and advises him that mining gold and printing paper money will solve the empire's economic woes. In a carnival pageant Faust appears dressed as Plutus, the Greek God of Wealth. He impresses the Emperor with magic tricks and rides in a chariot driven by a Boy Charioteer (who allegorically represents the spirit of poetry). The Emperor asks Faust to conjure the spirits of Helen of Troy and her lover, Paris, for his courtiers. After overcoming many obstacles, with Mephistopheles's help, Faust succeeds. The onlookers are unimpressed, but Faust falls in love with Helen's legendary beauty. When he tries to seize her, he is struck by a thunderclap, and Mephistopheles carries him off unconscious.

- **Act 2.** Mephistopheles bears the still unconscious Faust back to his study, and calls Nicodemus, Faust's new assistant (Wagner, the old assistant, has replaced Faust at the university). Mephistopheles encounters the same student, now an arrogant graduate, whom he harassed at the beginning of Part 1. Despite the pride he takes in his intellect, the graduate still fails to recognize Mephistopheles as the Devil. Wagner creates a tiny human being, a Homunculus, in a test tube. Without physical form but visible as a small flamelike ray of light, Homunculus reads Faust's dreams and suggests that rather than awaken Faust at home, they take him to Greece to participate in the Classical Walpurgis Night. Homunculus explains that classical spirits are superior to northern German ones and have their own version of the Witch's Sabbath. In the lengthy and complex Classical Walpurgis Night scene that follows, Faust remains obsessed with Helen of Troy and Homunculus seeks to gain human form. Mephistopheles meanwhile engages in sexual escapades and seeks to assume the shape of a figure in Greek mythology.

- **Act 3.** Act 3 opens in the palace of Helen's husband, Menelaus, King of Sparta and leader of the Greeks in the Trojan War. Troy has fallen to the Greeks, and Helen (whose flight with her Trojan lover Paris started the war) is being returned, along with her handmaids. Disguised as Phorkyas, a hideous old woman, Mephistopheles warns the women that Menelaus plans to execute them all, including Helen, and offers to rescue them. He magically takes them across space and time to a medieval German castle, where Faust appears as a knight. After defeating the attacking Menelaus's army, Faust and Helen go to the mythical Greek paradise Arcadia, where they have a son, Euphorion. However, the exuberant Euphorion (symbolizing Faust's restlessness) falls to his death while climbing a high cliff. The loss drives a wedge between Faust and Helen.

- **Act 4.** The action returns to the imperial court, where the Emperor—who has made the economic situation worse by following Mephistopheles's advice—now faces a rival Counter-Emperor. With the aid of Faust (backed by Mephistopheles's magic), the Emperor defeats his rival in battle. As a reward, Faust asks for and gets a large strip of underwater land along the coast.

- **Act 5.** Faust, now over 100 years old, has nearly finished a massive project of reclaiming the underwater land in the name of progress. A small coastal plot occupied by an old couple, Philemon and Baucis, is all that stands in the way of his ambitious plans to own all the land in the area, but they refuse to sell. At Faust's urging, Mephistopheles burns down the tiny cottage where the couple have lived happily all their lives, and they perish in the flames. The remorseful Faust is visited by four hags: Want, Debt, Distress, and Care. Care blinds Faust and warns him that her brother, Death, is coming. Faust orders Mephistopheles to make sure that work on the reclamation project continues, but in his blindness he doesn't realize that the shovels he hears are really digging his own grave. Although deceived, Faust finally appears content. He dies happy, and Mephistopheles attempts to claim him according to the terms of the wager. However, heavenly spirits intervene, and Faust, blessed by a penitent spirit identified as the former Gretchen, is carried to heaven amid a chorus of angels.

The uses of dissatisfaction. "Striving and straying, you can't have one without the other," the Lord tells Mephistopheles as they make their wager in the Prologue (*Faust*, p. 759). This idea—that endeavor and error are two sides of the same coin—lies at the heart of Goethe's *Faust*. On one hand, the play suggests that striving is necessarily accompanied by error or even evil, which helps explain the Lord's willingness to forgive Faust because error is inevitable. On the other hand, the inevitability of error does not absolve the striving individual of responsibility for this error. The individual, having fallen, needs to be redeemed, but in Goethe's universe, man cannot redeem himself. Redemption requires divine love or grace.

Mephistopheles strives too, defeating his own aims when good issues forth from his attempts to incite evil. He functions as the Lord's servant in the drama, even as his gadfly, but not as pure evil. This explains the Lord's indulgent attitude towards him. "You act as a stimulant," the Lord tells Mephistopheles, "and so serve a positive purpose in spite of yourself" (*Faust*, p. 760). Mephistopheles himself recognizes this duality: when he first meets Faust, he identifies himself as "a part of the force that always tries to do evil and always does good" (*Faust*, p. 780).

Against the restless striving of Faust and Mephistopheles, Goethe poses two ideals of placid perfection: the humbly passive Gretchen in Part 1, and the spirit of classical antiquity in Part 2. In both parts, Faust's deepest desires are aroused by these ideals, but he repeatedly destroys the things that he so ardently desires. His physical lust for Gretchen ruins the very innocence that spurred it, just as Faust's own restless spirit (symbolized by Euphorion) shatters the harmony of his visit to Arcadia with Helen. Similarly, at the end of the poem, Philemon and Baucis (the old couple whose Greek names suggest that they too represent the classical spirit) are consumed in the flames of what one critic has called "Faust's ruthless vitality" (Atkins, p. 3).

Alienated, skeptical, true only to himself, Faust is defined by dissatisfaction, which drives him to destroy but also to create. Critics have taken Gretchen to represent the unquestioning faith of the Middle Ages, and have likewise suggested that Arcadia and the other Greek motifs symbolize an ideal of classical balance and restraint. By contrast, Faust stands for the modern age, with its probing curiosity and secular outlook. These two qualities have traditionally been seen as originating in ancient Greek thought (which first attempted to explain nature without recourse to the divine), as reappearing during the Renaissance, and finally as being fully expressed in the eighteenth-century intellectual movement called the Enlightenment. Goethe's drama can be understood as a reaction to the Enlightenment, one that expresses the idea that "striving" has spiritual costs as well as material and intellectual benefits. The play itself can be viewed as a response to the newly secular outlook, the message being threefold: go ahead and strive; striving entails mistakes so you will err; in the final analysis, divine love will redeem you. It was a message that addressed humanity at a crossroads. Indeed Goethe's life—and the poem's long composition—spanned a time that historians point to as the very dawn of the modern age. Faust has thus been described as the first truly modern hero in world literature. In this respect, the play's attitude towards "striving and straying" not only comments on Goethe's age, but also predicts our own, which grew out of it.

Sources and literary context. Aside from the Faust legends of the sixteenth century, many literary influences and one real-life event contributed to the making of Goethe's play. The Lord's allowing Mephistopheles to tempt Faust in the Prologue, for example, is modeled on the biblical Book of Job, in which God allows Satan to tempt the pious Job. In contrast, the doomed love affair with Gretchen, which takes up most of Part 1, draws on a real-life event. Gretchen's fate, scholars suggest, was likely based on the well-publicized case of Susanna Brandt, a German woman executed in 1772 for murdering her illegitimate child.

Just as the Faust storyline draws on older Faust legends, the Gretchen storyline shares elements with another European folktale, the legend of Don Juan, which was first put in literary form by the Spanish playwright Tirso de Molina in his play *The Trickster of Seville* (1630). The play features the handsome rake Don Juan, who, among other misdeeds, seduces a beautiful young girl and kills her father, whose ghost drags an unrepentant Don Juan off to hell. Like Faust, Don Juan entered into common European lore and inspired numerous treatments in various literary forms. Also like Faust, this originally medieval folktale enjoyed a resurgence in popularity at the hands of numerous authors during Goethe's own age. For example, Austrian composer Wolfgang Mozart created one of the best-known versions of the tale in his highly successful opera *Don Giovanni*, which opened in Vienna in 1787 as Goethe was working on Part 1 of *Faust*.

Because Goethe worked on the poem over most of his long career and because that career was so immensely influential in European literary history, parallels can be drawn between elements in *Faust* and the literary movements with which Goethe has been associated:

- **Storm and Stress** (*Sturm und Drang*). The young Goethe helped to found this movement with his play *Götz of Berlichingen* (1773; *Goetz of Berlichingen with the Iron Hand*) and his novel *The Sorrows of Young Werther* (1774). Lasting from the early 1770s to the early 1780s, the time in which Goethe conceived and began work on *Faust*, the Storm and Stress movement rebelled against the Enlightenment ideal of rationalism and the imitation of French literature. It celebrated nature and the instinctive and emotional spirit as the source of literature, giving rise to passionate, action-oriented works. Examples of Storm and Stress themes in *Faust* include the ceaseless striving of the individual, the rejection of reason as the path to truth, and a mystical worship of nature in place of orthodox religion. Other major Storm and Stress authors included Goethe's friends Johann Gottfried von Herder (1744-1803) and Friedrich Schiller (1759-1805).

- **Neoclassicism.** By the early 1780s, Goethe, Herder, Schiller and others had begun to formulate a more balanced approach, in keeping with virtues ascribed to classical art. Their work now tempered the antirational, egoistic, and rebellious passion of Storm and Stress with other influences, many of which derived from a resurgence of interest in classical Greek and Latin literature. This balance is reflected in Part 2 (especially Act 3), where Goethe depicts Faust as striving for a synthesis of German energy and passion with Greek moderation and restraint.

- **Romanticism.** Storm and Stress and German Neoclassicism both foreshadowed the rise of the Romantic movement in European literature, which started in the 1790s and extended well into the nineteenth century. While Goethe is often considered a Romantic author, he himself looked down on what he saw as a lack of form and polish in the work of some Romantics. Still, Romantic currents such as the presence of the supernatural and the exaltation of the individual, especially the rebel, figure clearly in *Faust*.

Events in History at the Time the Play Was Written

Questioning the Enlightenment. By the beginning of the eighteenth century, European thinkers and scientists had consolidated the new learning of the Renaissance. A scientific revolution, first suggested by Copernicus in the sixteenth century, had been boldly supported and built upon by scientists and philosophers such as Sir Francis Bacon (English, 1561-1626), Galileo Galilei (Italian, 1564-1642), René Descartes (French, 1596-1650), John Locke

Faust

(English, 1632-1704), Sir Isaac Newton (English, 1642-1727), and Gottfried Wilhelm von Leibniz (German, 1646-1716). At the same time, violent and persistent religious wars had followed the Reformation, pitting Catholics against Protestants throughout much of northern Europe. Consequently the eighteenth century saw many thinkers turn away from traditional religion altogether.

> ### MAKING A PLACE FOR GERMANY IN EUROPEAN LETTERS
>
> "From the flowering of German literature in the twelfth century," writes critic Jane K. Brown, "until the eighteenth century, no writer in German is thought of today as a great European writer or was even especially influential outside Germany in his own day" (Brown, p. 30). Before the late eighteenth century, Brown goes on to observe, German literature consisted primarily of translations or adaptations of French, Italian, or Spanish works. The puppet shows on Faust that Goethe saw as a boy constituted the closest thing that Germany had to an indigenous literary tradition. As they began searching for German themes in the mid-eighteenth century, talented German writers naturally gravitated toward the Faust legend. Gotthold Lessing, for example, published a sketch of a Faust play in 1759, Act 1 of which was published posthumously in 1784. Lessing, an Enlightenment rationalist who celebrated Faust as a hero of reason, was the first to depict Faust as being saved rather than damned at the end of the story. With the publication of *The Sorrows of Young Werther* in 1774, the German public immediately anointed the young Goethe as Germany's greatest writer, and his *Faust* was eagerly awaited by German readers, who even before publication anticipated it as *the* great work of German literature. Focusing on *Faust*'s complex literary allusiveness, Brown argues that Goethe aimed not so much to establish a German literature as to ground that new literature firmly within the larger European literary context.

The eighteenth-century European intellectual movement known as the Enlightenment (*Aufklärung* in German) took the humanist reliance on reason to a new level. Whereas Renaissance humanists had given reason a place alongside religion, some atheistic Enlightenment thinkers such as Denis Diderot (French, 1713-84) and the Marquise de Condorcet (French, 1743-94) attempted to enshrine reason in place of religion. Others, such as Voltaire (French, 1694-1778), David Hume (British, 1711-76), and Immanuel Kant (German, 1724-1804) emphasized reason but stopped short of rejecting religious faith out of hand.

By the end of the eighteenth century, in turn, a reaction against Enlightenment rationalism had set in, which contributed to the passionate spiritualism of the Storm and Stress period and the rising Romantic outlook. In *Faust* generally, Faust's restlessness with academic learning represents Goethe's sense that Enlightenment rationalism lacked a human or spiritual dimension. In particular, Goethe satirizes the dryness of Enlightenment learning in the character of Wagner, Faust's shallow pedantic assistant, who knows much but understands little.

The French Revolution and the Napoleonic Wars. The central event in Europe during Goethe's lifetime was the French Revolution of 1789 and its aftermath—the long set of international wars that ended in France's final defeat by Britain and its European allies in 1815. Historians view these years of disturbing and bloody upheaval as ushering in the modern age. First, by overthrowing and executing the French King Louis XVI, along with much of France's hereditary aristocracy, the revolutionaries ended the medieval system of monarchy in France and created Europe's first modern state. Then, after hostile action from their monarchical neighbors—especially the Austrian Holy Roman Empire—the French rebels sought to export their revolution through a violent and determined campaign of conquest. The resulting wars extended from Spain in the west to Poland and Russia in the east, and from Britain in the north to Egypt in the south.

The second phase of France's campaign of conquest is known as the Napoleonic Wars (1803-15), after the French general Napoleon Bonaparte, who assumed dictatorial power in 1799 and proclaimed himself Emperor Napoleon I of France. Napoleon admired Goethe and requested a meeting with the famous author after occupying German lands in 1806. Shortly thereafter, Napoleon dissolved the Holy Roman Empire, forcing the Emperor Francis I to abdicate. Upon Napoleon's final defeat in 1815, the emperor was restored as Francis I of Austria, but his empire itself remained dissolved, its German lands instead reconstituted as the German Federation. In *Faust*, this turbulent sequence of events supplies the background for the struggles between the Emperor and Counter-Emperor in Part 2. "What madness is abroad in these disordered days," comments the Emperor's Minister of War: "There isn't anyone that isn't either killing or being killed" (*Faust*, p. 877).

Goethe wrote much of Part 2 more than a decade after the end of the Napoleonic Wars. By then, Europe was entering a new age of commercial expansion, which was backed by the Industrial Revolution, the emergence of modern European states in the wake of the war, and a growing middle class. In Faust's callous treatment of the old couple displaced by his reclamation project, Goethe questions the values of that new age. Chief among those values was the ideal of progress. Goethe was very interested in projects like the Suez Canal and the Panama Canal, which were first discussed in the early nineteenth century. Yet this final episode of Faust's life implies that Goethe himself felt ambivalent about progress: while it has positive aspects, the play seems to suggest, progress can too easily be pursued at the expense of humanity.

Publication and impact. Goethe composed most of *Faust* in four main periods:

c. 1770-75 Goethe conceives *Faust*, beginning work on what would become Part 1. A manuscript of an early version in Goethe's hand survives. Scholars call it the *Urfaust* (original Faust), but Goethe never intended it for publication.

c. 1787-90 Goethe resumes work on a section of what would become Part 1, publishing it in 1790 as *Faust: A Fragment*.

1797-1801 Goethe again resumes work on *Faust*, deciding to divide it into two parts and nearly completing Part 1. In 1805 he decides to publish Part 1 and does so in 1808 (after further work).

1825-32 Goethe writes nearly all of Part 2 in the last seven years of his life. Goethe dies in March 1832, within a few weeks of completing the work, which is published later that year.

The two parts of *Faust* enjoyed significantly different receptions. Part 1, eagerly awaited by Goethe's avid readership, was immediately acclaimed as the great work of literature that by then the German public was fully expecting. Indeed, on the basis of the 1790 fragment alone the German critic Friedrich Schelling had already described the work as Germany's greatest poem. The influential Swiss cultural critic Madame de Staël, a major voice in spreading German Romanticism to the rest of Europe, wrote in 1814 that Goethe's "astonishing" poem "cannot be exceeded in boldness of conception," and she particularly praised its "potency of sorcery, a poetry . . . that makes us shudder, laugh, and cry, in a breath" (de Staël in Hamlin, p. 441). Schelling and de Staël were among the first to observe that the character of Faust can be taken as representing humanity itself. By contrast, Part 2 was less popular, even among German readers. In general it caused less of a stir, occasioning little comment abroad.

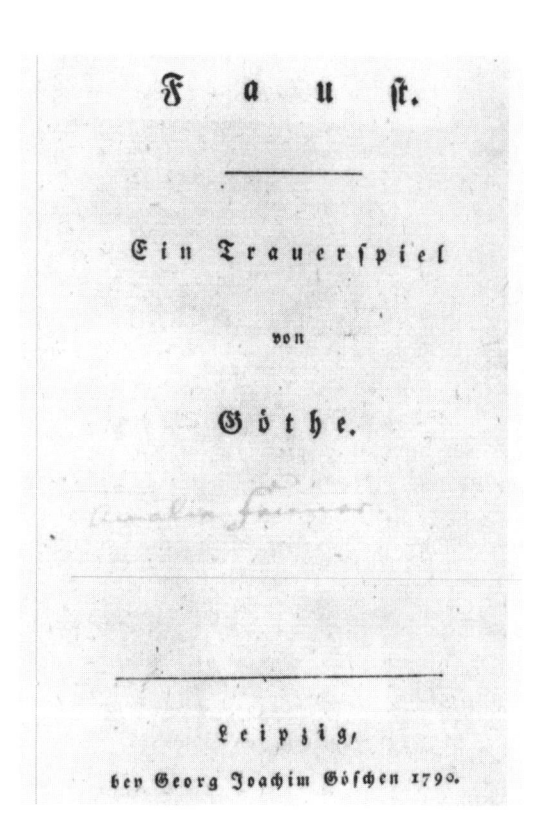

Title page from a 1790 edition of *Faust*.

While interpretations of Faust vary widely, later criticism has been most conspicuously and sharply divided on questions of structure. One school of critics argues that the work stands as a unified whole. Against these so-called "unitarians" are critics who, owing to thematic differences and gaps in composition, maintain that the two parts should be read as two separate works. Goethe himself weighed in on the issue shortly after completing Part 2. In his last letter, written less than a week before his death, he wrote of conceiving the work as a unified whole from the earliest stage:

For more than sixty years the conception of *Faust* has lain here before my mind with the clearness of youth, though the sequence with less fulness. I have let the idea go quietly along with me through life and have only worked out the scenes that interested me most from time to time.

(Goethe in Hamlin, p. 431)

It was only during the latter half of the twentieth century that the aspects of modernism in *Faust Part 2* were discovered. The second part of *Faust* is now highly appreciated and performances are no longer a rare occasion. In 1999 at the World's Fair in Hanover, the German director Peter Stein staged a 30-hour production of *Faust Part 1* and *Part 2* with the text uncut. This production traveled throughout German-speaking countries in 2000 and 2001.

—Colin Wells

For More Information

Atkins, Stuart. *Goethe's Faust: A Literary Analysis*. Cambridge, Mass.: Harvard University Press, 1958.

Boyle, Nicholas. *Goethe: The Poet and the Age*. 2 vols. Oxford: Oxford University Press, 1991-99.

Brown, Jane K. *Goethe's Faust: The German Tragedy*. Ithaca: Cornell University Press, 1986.

Gillies, Alexander. *Goethe's Faust: An Interpretation*. Oxford: Blackwell, 1957.

Goethe, Johann Wolfgang von. *Faust*. Trans. Barker Fairley. In *Selected Works*. New York: Alfred A. Knopf, 2000.

Hamlin, Cyrus, ed. *Faust*. Trans. Walter Arndt. New York: Norton, 1976.

Mason, Eudo. *Goethe's Faust: Its Genesis and Purport*. Berkeley: University of California Press, 1967.

Stawell, F. Melian, and G. Lowes Dickinson. *Goethe and Faust: An Interpretation*. New York: Dial Press, 1929.

The Fixer

by
Bernard Malamud

> **THE LITERARY WORK**
>
> A novel set in Russia under tsarist rule, shortly before the revolution of 1917; published in 1966.
>
> **SYNOPSIS**
>
> Anti-Semitic officials arrest Yakov Bok, a Jew, on charges of the ritual murder of a Christian child and spend nearly two years trying to force a confession out of him.

Bernard Malamud was born April 26, 1914, in Brooklyn, New York, and died March 18, 1986, in New York City. His parents were Russian Jews who immigrated to the United States as part of a wave of more than 2 million newcomers. Malamud attended City College of New York and Columbia University, then taught at various high schools as well as Oregon State University and Bennington College in Vermont. Despite a heavy teaching schedule, Malamud wrote three novels and award-winning short stories before producing *The Fixer*. His first novel, **The Natural** (1952; also in *Literature and Its Times*), draws on Arthurian legend to spin a modern fable about a baseball hero. His next novel, the critically acclaimed *The Assistant* (1957), features Frank Alpine, a young non-Jewish hoodlum who learns about suffering and salvation from an old Jewish grocer. Asked why he writes about Jews, Malamud said, "I know them. But more important . . . Jews are absolutely the very *stuff* of drama" (Malamud in Unger, p. 431). Affirming this point to the extreme, *The Fixer* fictionalizes the real-life case of Mendel Beilis, a victim of anti-Semitism in early 1900s Russia.

Events in History at the Time the Novel Takes Place

Russia and the Jews before 1881. When the Romanov dynasty came to power in Russia in the seventeenth century, it inherited a tradition of religious intolerance toward Jews. For hundreds of years, the Jews in Russian lands had suffered official pressure to convert to Christianity or leave Russian territory. Seen as morally and ethnically inferior, they were subjected to violence at the hands of both the Russian army and the Russian people. In 1727 this haphazard, unofficial persecution coalesced into an official policy of exclusion, or formal banishment of the Jews. That the policy was not strictly enforced is evident in a subsequent *ukase* (order) issued by Tsarina Elizabeth in 1742:

> All Jews, male and female, of whatever occupation or standing shall, at the promulgation of this Our ukase, be immediately deported, together with all their property, from Our whole Empire, both from the Great Russian and the Little Russian cities, villages and hamlets. They shall henceforth not be admitted to our Empire under any pretext and for any purpose, unless they be willing to adopt Christianity of the Greek persuasion.
>
> (Baron, p. 11)

The Fixer

Bernard Malamud

Still Russia remained home to some Jews; while no formal census was taken then, they were but a fraction of the numbers to come.

The Jewish population escalated precipitously after Russia acquired a large swath of Polish lands in 1772, 1793, and 1795. After the first partition, Russia outlined the area in which its Jewish inhabitants could live, extending the boundaries beyond the former Polish terrain but restricting Jews from moving inland to, for example, Moscow. There emerged on the western rim of Russia's empire the so-called "Pale of Jewish Settlement," which would endure until 1917. The label itself did not exist in the 1790s. If it had, it would have suggested that the tsarina attached an importance to the Jews that the group did not then have, given the far more pressing problems that faced her and her successors. As one historian explains, the Jews "were but a minor and marginal constellation" in the scheme of imperial life (Stanislawski, p. 264). They would remain so for most of the nineteenth century.

On the other hand, Russia did inherit a huge Jewish population with the Polish partitions. Around one million Jews joined a land that previously had a relative handful. Slowly, as the 1800s progressed, the tsars developed policies in relation to the Jews, but the policies were fitful and contradictory. They entailed discrimination, as did government policies to other minorities. The authorities tried to suppress the use of Jewish languages (Yiddish and Hebrew), to reform education (replacing study of traditional religious texts with modern subjects), to wipe out Jewish-style clothing and occupations (peddling and petty trade), and to modernize and convert Jews to Christianity through service in the army. All these measures figured into an effort to make the Jews more beneficial to Russia and, as the tsars saw it, less potentially harmful to its peasants. At times the tsars tried to prevent the Jews from living and trading in peasant villages, but local officials protested, arguing that the loss had a harmful effect on their rural economy, so a loophole sprang into being. Jews could register permanently in towns and cities while officially living as temporary residents of the villages (when in fact they were permanent). Over the years Jews still suffered periodic expulsions from rural areas. Every so often a tsar would evacuate the Jews from the countryside, then enthusiasm for banishment would diminish, and the old ways resume.

From the 1840s forward, the Russian government to some extent allied itself with that faction of Russian Jewry that sought to modernize its own people. Under Alexander II (1855-81), the Russian Jews themselves took an increasing interest in adopting progressive ways. A growing number flocked to Russian-speaking secular schools; some 12 percent of all Russian Jewish secondary students attended Russian gymnasia, or high schools, by 1880 (Stanislawski, p. 275). Their attendance dovetailed with a larger drive on the part of the tsar to Russify Jews and non-Jews alike; he outlawed books in the Lithuanian language and the performance of plays in the Ukranian language as part of this same drive.

The Jewish population grew (to 5.2 million by 1897). Only a tiny minority (medical personnel, university graduates), whose talents stood the Russians in good stead, were allowed beyond the Pale, where there was ample opportunity to prosper. Perhaps 94 percent lived inside the Pale, forming about 12 percent of the region's total population. The Jews lived in a mix of large cities (e.g., Odessa, Kiev, Kishinev, Minsk, Warsaw) and smaller towns (known as "shtetls" or "shtetlekh"). Increasingly they moved to the larger urban centers, this migration quickening from the 1880s forward. The blending of Russian Jews into the larger population progressed. A minority—doctors, lawyers, and businessmen—moved upward through the social ranks. But the majority experienced an economic decline; struggling to survive, they labored as wage earners in city industries or in one or another of the old fading occupations (small trader, storekeeper, peddler) of the shtetlekh.

A few Jews became farmers, and a few earned their livelihoods as day laborers or private servants. A large fraction of the Jews in a community were unbound to any occupation—they seemed to survive by their wits, latching on to any opportunity to earn a living. Known as *luftmentshn*—"people of the air"—the fraction could climb as high as 40 percent of a town's working population. In their daily labors, men often wandered from place to place to sell items at a slight profit. They frequently left home for the entire work week or even for months at a time. Such conditions help position *The Fixer*'s Bok as someone justifiably frustrated at working hard but not earning a living. They also help explain his frustration at glimpsing advantages denied him because he is a Jew, such as the right to live and work in non-Jewish Kiev.

Post-1881 anti-Semitism. Whereas Jews were largely considered just another minority before 1881, afterward the attitude shifted. The Jews suffered officially sanctioned anti-Semitism under the next-to-last and the last tsars of Russia—Alexander III (1881-1894) and Nicholas II (1895-1917). Earlier tsars had practiced an on-again, off-again policy of trying to integrate Russia's Jews into the country's larger social order, but both of these wanted only to rid Russia of what they considered the menacing Jews. The two tsars harbored an intense religious hatred of the Jews and subscribed as well to a pan-European fallacy that the Jews were conspiring to dominate the world and that they infected others with dangerous ideas, prompting them to doubt traditional authority figures. Neither Alexander nor Nicholas stemmed the growing tendency of Russia's Jews to assimilate or merge with the larger population, but both tsars instituted various policies to contain them, or limit their presence in society at large. In 1882 Russia's military medical academy established the first Jewish educational quota (5 percent of all students). Other quotas followed, leading up to the famous *numerus clausus* (quota system) of 1887, which limited Jewish students to 10 percent of the population at schools inside the Pale, 5 percent outside the Pale, and only 3 percent in Moscow and St. Petersburg. This official policy coincided with currents of virulent anti-Semitism among the general populace; three such currents erupted before the era of *The Fixer*. Fellow Russians mounted pogroms, or wholesale persecutions of Jewish communities, in 1881-82, 1903, and 1905-06. The attackers raped; they plundered; they murdered.

The pogroms of 1881-82 were vicious attacks against both property and person. Mobs looted Jewish homes, beat Jewish men, and raped Jewish women. How many the mobs killed remains debatable, perhaps under 100, certainly fewer than in subsequent pogroms. Along with other newspapers, Russia's *Novoye Vremya* promoted the violence, agitating readers with misinformation about the Jews, and accusations that they had killed Alexander II. In fact, his demise was a disaster from their point of view. Alexander II had encouraged their assimilation, raising hopes for a rosier future in many Jews, but after his assassination, the disheartened lot of them was pushed back into the "ghetto from which they had begun to emerge" (Gitelman, p. 10). Pogroms recurred under Nicolas II, in 1903, and especially in 1905, after Nicholas, under duress, issued the October Manifesto, introducing constitutional government into Russia. The Manifesto prompted a severe round of at least 300 pogroms, in which mobs parroted anti-Semitic accusations, which they themselves deeply believed and which Tsar Nicolas endorsed. Rioters blamed the Jews for undermining the tsar's authority and promoting anarchy (a force, in their minds, associated with democracy). "Hurrah beat the Zhyds [Yids]!" they shouted. "The Zhyds are eager for liberty. They go against our Tzar to put a Zhyd in his place" (Gitelman, p. 23). Again mobs raped, injured, and pillaged, and this time they killed Jews in high numbers. In Odessa alone, more than 300 Jews perished in the violence.

Fortunately for the Jews, the anti-Semitism that characterized both Alexander II and Nicholas II was less of a driving force than their intense fear of social unrest, and their commitment to maintaining order and their own authority. Given these priorities, neither tsar issued orders for violence against the Jews; they seem even to have tried to restrain such violence. Indirectly, however, Nicholas II encouraged the anti-Semitic attacks by routinely pardoning army officers who committed the crime of sacking a Jewish village. Indeed, this type of pardon became so common that the ministry of justice initiated a "clemency form" for such cases—officials needed only to fill in the name of the culprit to free him from charges. Exactly this sort of miscarriage of justice is at work in *The Fixer*, whose Russian officials do everything short of issuing a pardon to the guilty party in order to focus public attention on a Jew.

The Fixer

The Beilis case. In the small village of Dubossary, near Kishinev, during the Passover/Easter season of 1903, police received a report that a young boy had been murdered, his body laced with 24 stab wounds. The local paper claimed that the boy was killed by Jews as part of a "blood ritual"; the Jews, said the paper, had again killed a Christian child to obtain his blood for use in Jewish rites. The specific claim was that Jews used Christian blood to make the unleavened bread (matzos) eaten during the Passover holiday. On Easter Sunday, a crowd entered the Jewish district and began throwing rocks at Jewish shop windows. Over the next two days the assailants murdered 47 Jews, wounded 424, burned 700 houses, and looted 600 shops, touching off a string of subsequent pogroms. Eight years later a similar horror threatened.

ANTI-SEMITIC VIOLENCE—1880s-1910s

1881-82 Pogroms claim several hundred lives, cause great material and psychological damage.
1903 Pogrom erupts in Kishniev—45 Jews are killed, 86 wounded, and several hundred injured. Assailants attack 1,500 shops and houses.
1905-06 Tsar issues October Manifesto; *Protocols of Elders of Zion* is published—written by one of the tsar's police agents, it warns of a Jewish conspiracy to dominate the world; pogroms erupt in at least 300 cities—the killing of Jews increases, producing 600 orphans.
1911 In February a proposal to abolish the Pale of Settlement is introduced in the Russian parliament; a month later Mendel Beilis is arrested on charges of committing a ritual murder.
1913 In October, the jury in the Beilis case unanimously declares him not guilty but deems that a ritual murder has been committed.

On March 19, 1911, the body of Andrei Yutchinsky, a 12-year-old Christian boy, was found in a cave outside Kiev. The body was badly mutilated; the boy had been stabbed 47 times. Andrei's funeral drew a massive crowd, including members of the anti-Semitic Black Hundreds, more formally known as the Union of the Russian People (URP). The group was a weak bunch, but its members found willing listeners among the authorities in Kiev. Especially receptive to their message was a member of the tsar's team, the minister of justice, I. G. Shcheglovitov.

The Black Hundreds distributed pamphlets accusing Jews of the murder, claiming that the number of wounds and loss of blood indicated the boy had been killed as part of a Jewish rite. Full of false accusations, the mimeographed pamphlets read:

> ORTHODOX CHRISTIANS!
> The Yids have tortured Andryusha Yushchinsky to death! Every year, before their Passover, they torture to death several dozens of Christian children in order to get their blood to mix with their *matzos*. They do this in commemoration of our Saviour, whom they tortured to death on the cross. The official doctors found that before the Yids tortured Yushchinsky they stripped him naked and tied him up, stabbing him in the principal veins so as to get as much blood as possible. They pierced him in fifty places. Russians! If your children are dear to you, beat up the Yids! Beat them up until there is not a single Yid left in Russia. Have pity on your children! Avenge the unhappy martyr! It is time! It is time!
> (Black Hundreds in Samuel, p. 17)

This time the anti-Semitic propaganda did not lead to a rash of violence in Kiev or anywhere else. Jews had been mounting a campaign in their own defense. To correct all the misinformation being filtered to the public, they organized, among other efforts, the Society for the Dissemination of True Knowledge on the Jews and Judaism. Also, rabbis from all over the region sent protest letters declaring that there was no such thing as a blood ritual in Judaism—and to good effect. In 1911 many Russians were showing disgust for the raids against Jewish homes and businesses. Russian writers, scholars, and politicians published a joint declaration condemning anti-Semitism. To some degree, all this was a reaction to the unfavorable worldwide attention that the earlier spates of pogroms had attracted. In any case, this time there was no support for unbridled, anti-Semitic violence. Reactionaries and extreme nationalists still dominated government, to be sure, and they were determined to put a stop to Jewish demands for equality and to deal a decisive blow to all liberal tendencies in Russia, but the extremists refrained from overt acts of racial hatred. Instead they pursued a more subtle form of persecution. They manufactured a blood ritual case against a single Jew, the hope being that average Russians would see him as symbolic of all Jews. In reaching for Beilis as a scapegoat, the Kiev officials deferred to the slandering lies of the Black Hundreds, and Russia's minister of justice, Shcheglovitov, worked along with the Kiev officials to obtain a conviction. Years later, after the Bolshevik Revolution had toppled tsarism, archives of the case were opened and it was revealed that the authorities knew all along that Beilis was innocent. Why did they frame him? To some degree, the answer lies in intense anti-Semitism. Shcheglovitov, along with Tsar Nicholas himself, saw Jews as a sullied race, born with criminal intentions and angling to overtake the world. To some degree too, the answer lies in the government's effort to divert criticism from its own failings and unite a discontented, divided populace by offering up a common foe. *The Fixer* captures this scapegoating aspect in the name of its protagonist: Yakov Bok. *Bok* is Yiddish for "goat."

Investigators were pressured to produce a Jewish murderer in the Andrei Yutchinsky case. Those who refused to cooperate were dismissed from the case, demoted, and threatened with punishment. In fact, most of the officials realized that the boy, a lookout for a gang of thieves, had been killed by the gang because they thought he betrayed them to the police. A preponderance of evidence piled up against the slain boy's Christian neighbor, Vera Cheberyak. Involved with the gang of thieves, she ran a fencing operation from her home (which was spattered with evidence of wild parties and debauchery). Cheberyak had intimidated her neighbors to the point where one family moved to Moscow, and she poisoned her own children to keep them from talking. Although the authorities recognized her as the most likely culprit, they set out to bribe material witnesses, to produce their own "expert" witnesses, and to manufacture evidence to convict a Jew. The nearly two years spent in prison by Beilis (and *The Fixer*'s Bok) were not only an attempt to torture a confession from a scapegoat; they were also a tactical delay in the hope that some evidence could be manufactured to incriminate him. Beilis was arrested in 1911 and tried before a Kiev jury in 1913, which found him innocent. The victory was not total, however, for the jury declared that a ritual murder, by an unknown party, had been committed.

No fewer than three investigating magistrates worked on the Beilis case because the first two refused to limit their investigation to finding or fabricating evidence that pointed exclusively to a Jewish murderer. Some doctors not only refused to testify against Beilis, they signed petitions condemning the so-called medical evidence that had been gathered against him. These physicians took great risks; the Kharkov Medical Society was forced to disband and several members were threatened with revocation of their licenses and even prison for signing protest petitions. Lawyers suffered too. In 1914 as many as 25 attorneys were put on trial for their protests in the Beilis case. Given the radically unstable political atmosphere in which the tsar governed, he and his allies interpreted every protest as a threat.

The Dreyfus Case. The Beilis case echoed a slightly earlier case—the 1894 indictment of Alfred Dreyfus, a Jewish officer in the French army. Dreyfus's is probably the most infamous example of the legal persecution of a Jew by a national government. The case occurred in France, whose government was considered one of the most enlightened in the world at the time. French Jews held high positions in politics, the French military, and business. In fact, France was the first European country to award Jews full civil equality. Indeed the Dreyfus Affair is puzzling: how could a modern, progressive nation harbor such reactionary anti-Semitism?

France had suffered a great depression in 1893, and it was still smarting from a costly military defeat in the Franco-Prussian war of the 1870s. Popular sentiment seemed poised to find a scapegoat for the nation's economic and military setbacks. And the opportunity to light on such a scapegoat beckoned when French military intelligence determined that secrets were being sold to the German embassy. A fragment of a note suggested that the spy's name began with *D*. The French Minister of War jumped to conclusions and publicly proclaimed Dreyfus's guilt at the same time that a virulent anti-Semite, the editor of a scandal rag called *La Libre Parole*, Eduoard Drumont, ran a series of anti-Jewish articles. The articles accused Jews of a conspiracy to achieve global domination by infiltrating and destroying national economies and militaries, beginning with France's.

On his arrest, Dreyfus was offered a pistol and the honorable way out (suicide). All over France, rioters turned violently on Jewish shops and synagogues, and attacked Jews themselves, in circumstances that historian Albert Lindemann describes as being "right out of Russia" (Lindemann, p. 116). Dreyfus faced four separate trials, but only after a full judicial review in 1906 was he exonerated of all charges, reintegrated into the military with a promotion, and awarded the Legion of Honor.

In France, as in Russia, reactionary agents employed a case against a Jew in an effort to halt social progress. Drumont, along with some countrymen, showed nostalgia for France's old monarchy and a hatred not only for the Jews but also for the 1789 French Revolution. In Russia, Beilis was to some extent viewed as an instrument of

The Fixer

the tsar's attempt to roll back recent progress, including the establishment of the Duma, the Russian parliament. As Nicholas saw it, Jewish causes of the day, from giving the Jews seats in the Duma to liberating them from the Pale, were bound up with movements that threatened the very structure of the Russian monarchy. In *The Fixer*, Yakov Bok learns that he has become part of an inexorable shift in the world from monarchy to democracy, from tyranny to liberty. His allies, the investigating magistrate B. D. Bibikov and the attorney Julius Ostrovsky, try to educate him about the larger picture into which his life is being painted.

AN INTRAFAITH REVOLUTION

Russian Jewry itself was in the midst of its own tumultuous shift when *The Fixer* takes place. The previous century had brought into Russia the Jewish Enlightenment (Haskalah) movement, which sought to modernize Jews by increasing their contact with outside society and introducing them to the benefits of European culture. Though the majority of Russian Jews remained rooted in tradition, a substantial minority began mixing modern ways with the traditional ones. Some adopted the new secular philosophy of socialism, a few converted to Christianity. Others heeded the Zionist call to immigrate to Palestine, a suggestion the fixer's father-in-law makes in the novel. Still others agitated for fuller, more equitable immersion into Russian society. They work for emancipation—to be free and equal members of the society. In short, the scrutiny of faith and ideas by the novel's fixer reflects a genuine soul searching in Russian Jewish society at the time.

The Novel in Focus

The plot. Yakov Bok, a fixer or handyman, begins to worry when he sees Russians running past the brickyard where he works illegally. He reads in the paper the next day that a 12-year-old Christian boy, Zhenia Golov, has been murdered; his body, bearing multiple stab wounds, was discovered in a cave. After Zhenia's funeral, the Black Hundreds, an anti-Semitic organization, circulates leaflets accusing Jews of the murder. Yakov worries because the district in which he lives and works is forbidden to Jews; he is there under a false name without identification papers. Also he fears the onset of a pogrom like the earlier three-day raid on his village, which left his father slaughtered, along with dozens of other Jews.

Five months earlier, Yakov had shared a final glass of tea with his father-in-law, Shmuel, before departing the shtetl for Kiev. Shmuel brought his skeletal horse to Yakov, the only transportation available, trading it and a wagon for Yakov's cow. There was nothing to keep his son-in-law here. Raisl, Shmuel's daughter, has left Yakov after several years of a childless marriage. Feeling no compassion for his wife or the villagers, Yakov leaves on the Sabbath, heading for the city of Kiev. When Shmuel gives him some phylacteries (Jewish prayer articles), admonishing him not to "forget [his] God," Yakov angrily replies, "Who forgets who?" (Malamud, *The Fixer*, p. 13). While crossing the river to Kiev, he drops the phylacteries in the river.

One night, after settling in the Jewish section of Kiev, Yakov finds a fat, well-dressed man lying face down in the snow. On turning him over, Yakov smells his drunken breath and sees the emblem of the Black Hundreds pinned to his lapel. Nonetheless, Yakov begins to drag him out of the street when a startling cry issues from the man's grown, crippled daughter, Zina. Together they carry Nikolai Maximovitch Lebedev home. The next day Yakov returns to receive a promised reward but does not identify himself by his own name. Instead he assumes a Gentile or non-Jewish name.

Nikolai offers to pay Yakov generously for painting and wallpapering some rooms. Yakov rationalizes working for an anti-Semite, telling himself, "It's only a job, I'm not selling my soul" (*Fixer*, p. 35). Pleased that Yakov is "not a political person," Nikolai offers him the position of overseer at a brick factory (*Fixer*, p. 40). Insisting on honesty in accounting, Yakov soon alienates the brickyard foreman, Proshko. His other relationships are less than ideal too. Yakov feels anxious about misrepresenting himself to Lebedev, who has not asked to see his identity papers. Also Yakov alienates Zina, declining her offer of sexual involvement. Isolated by the brickyard workers, he devotes his spare time and money to books, mostly about Russian history and the life of the Dutch philosopher Baruch Spinoza. One evening two schoolboys disturb Yakov by throwing rocks at the kilns. He chases them away. Weeks later Yakov happens upon several boys attacking a Hasidic Jew, part of a movement of very observant followers who subscribe to Jewish mysticism. Yakov takes the old man back to his apartment at the brickyard and tends to the Hasid's wounds. After refusing

> ## SPINOZA
>
> Benedict (Baruch) Spinoza, who was born in Amsterdam, Holland, in 1632, provides the biographical and philosophical basis for many of Yakov Bok's ideas, characteristics, and experiences. Spinoza's family immigrated to Holland to avoid persecution in Portugal. In Holland, they could raise Spinoza openly as a Jew. His thoughts, however, drifted from orthodox teachings—he abandoned Judaism, as Bok does in the novel.
>
> Spinoza took up the life of a lens grinder and wrote philosophical tracts in his spare time, refusing a university position to keep his thoughts free from influence. He resolved to search for a good that would so fill the mind that all uncertainty and dependence on contingent circumstances would end. Spinoza defined the state of bondage as someone's being moved by causes of which that person is unaware. In his view, freedom began with realizing the conditions that shape one's life. He advocated taking action against governments and other institutions that imposed their ideas on individuals because, he suggested, they fostered inadequate thinking about true causes. In 1672 Spinoza nearly lost his life for this idea when he tried to protest the political assassination of Jan De Witt, a Dutch statesman. Only the intervention of a friend, who locked Spinoza in a room, saved the philosopher's life.
>
> According to Spinoza, people are conditioned by nature to pursue their own advantage. They will restrict some of their natural desires if doing so enables them to realize more satisfying advantages. A person can finally attain freedom only by escaping the bondage of his or her desires. For this to happen, people have to develop adequate thoughts that will allow them to understand and transcend their desires. The state should refrain from imposing ideas and conditions on individuals so that they can develop such thoughts. Like Spinoza, the novel's Yakov Bok abandons Judaism. But he shares a deeper connection with Spinoza than this. Bok finds liberation in thought (as he believes Spinoza did) and comes to see himself as part of the flow of history.

Yakov's offer of bread and tea, the Hasid draws some matzos from his caftan pocket and rattles off a prayer before eating. Yakov is surprised to realize that it is Passover, the holiday commemorating the Jews' exodus from ancient Egypt. After sneaking the old man out of the brickyard, Yakov returns to find the foreman, Proshko, in high spirits. Yakov notices that his apartment has been searched.

The next day Yakov reads about the murder of a 12-year-old boy, Zhenia Golov, whose body has been found in a cave, drained of blood. At Zhenia's funeral, the Black Hundreds distribute pamphlets accusing Jews of murdering Golov to obtain blood for a religious ritual. Early the next morning Yakov packs to escape possible trouble, but the authorities arrest him for Zhenia's murder before he can make his way out the door. Yakov confesses to being a Jew: "Otherwise he was innocent" (*Fixer*, p. 61).

B. D. Bibikov, Investigating Magistrate for Cases of Extraordinary Importance, interrogates Yakov. In response to Bibikov's questions, Yakov blames Raisl for his predicament. Bibikov invites Yakov to discuss Spinoza, the magistrate's favorite author. Ending the interrogation, Bibikov suggests that Yakov read and reflect more. He advises the prisoner to have fortitude—the law will protect him. The following day Bibikov confronts Yakov with Lebedev's deposition, which accuses Yakov of deceiving the factory owner with a false, Gentile name. Yakov again admits the deception but insists that he is not a religious man. The empire considers him a Jew nevertheless, says Bibikov. But he is willing to listen to Yakov's story and appears to pursue an objective investigation. In contrast, Colonel Bodyansky and Prosecuting Attorney Grubeshov are convinced that Yakov is guilty and that blood rituals are common Jewish practice. Bibikov tells Yakov that he will recommend that the fixer be prosecuted for living in a district forbidden to Jews. Grubeshov angles for murder, producing a bloody rag and part of a matzo, then asks if Yakov remembers chasing children around the brickyard.

When the police escort Yakov back to the brickyard, Proshko informs on the Jew, describing him as someone who consorts with Hasids and prays to the Jewish God. The dead boy's mother reports that she warned her son not to approach Yakov, in whose room he once spotted a bottle of blood. Next Father Anastasy, an Orthodox priest, accompanies a group to the cave where the boy's body was found. Anastasy regales the group with anti-Semitic cant: "many innocent Christian children . . . tortured to death by Christ-hating Jews," who used the young blood in "sorcery and witches rituals" (*Fixer*, pp. 117-18). The "Bible," insists Yakov, "forbids us to eat blood," yet he is urged to confess (*Fixer*, p. 120).

After three months in prison, Yakov concludes that the authorities have a "plot against a Jew, any Jew" and that it is his bad luck to be that Jew (*Fixer*, p. 137). He reasons, "being born a Jew meant being vulnerable to history, including its worst errors." Still he wonders, "Who will help me?" (*Fixer*, p. 138). Almost in answer to his question, a new prisoner, Gregor Gronfein, a Jewish counterfeiter, enters the cell. Gronfein shares some food and goods he receives, winning Yakov's confidence. At Gronfein's urging, Yakov writes two letters, one to his father-in-law and one to his best friend in the shtetl, asking him to rally Jewish support. Within 15 minutes of Gronfein's departure, Yakov is escorted to the warden's office. He sees his letters in the warden's hands and Gronfein in a shadowy corner. Yakov is given solitary confinement for trying to contact someone on the outside.

In the middle of summer, Bibikov visits the fixer to let him know that he is not friendless. The investigating magistrate, who knows Yakov is falsely accused, says he is pushing to drop the murder charge. Bibikov reveals his theory of the crime. Marfa's boyfriend committed the murder and, along with Marfa, hatched the anti-Semitic accusation to cover their crime. To bolster Yakov's spirits, Bibikov reminds him of Russian decrees and papal interdictions forbidding blood libel against Jews. He is going to all this trouble, says Bibikov, not just for the fixer, but for Russia: "If the law does not protect you, it will not, in the end, protect me" (*Fixer*, p. 156). Later a new prisoner, locked into the cell next to Yakov's, attempts to communicate with him by pounding the wall with his shoes, but Yakov can decipher no message. After some time Yakov is troubled by the silence from the other cell. When a drunken guard leaves his own cell unlocked, Yakov steals a glance next door. He sees Bibikov's body dangling by his belt.

Without warning, Yakov's food rations improve: he receives more and meatier portions. In a week or two, however, Yakov starts feeling nauseous and his hair falls out. He dreams of a pogrom and of Bibikov, then wakes with a brass taste in his mouth and the realization that the authorities are poisoning him. Yakov fasts until they meet his demand to eat from the common pot.

One morning, Yakov returns from breakfast to find a prayer shawl and phylacteries in his cell. He uses the shawl for warmth and ignores the phylacteries. With nothing to read, Yakov recalls by memory his study of Spinoza, then biology, then the psalms. He also ruminates on his life with Raisl; remembering that he cursed her when she first left, he now admits that she "tied herself to the wrong future" (*Fixer*, p. 191).

After nine months in prison, Yakov is taken to Grubeshov. The prosecuting attorney tells him that the tsar himself believes that the fixer is guilty. Grubeshov gives Yakov another chance to confess. Later Yakov imagines himself wrestling the tsar. When a guard brings him the *New Testament*, Yakov reads sympathetically about the persecution of Christ. Soon a priest urges Yakov to convert to Christianity. In response, he stands motionless, garbed in the prayer shawl and holding the phylacteries. As punishment, Yakov's trips to the common pot stop, and the *New Testament* is confiscated. The guards do not talk to him. He is utterly isolated and alone.

Yakov is visited by Shmuel. His father-in-law informs Yakov that he has not been forgotten; Jews all over Russia know of his plight. Once again Shmuel advises Yakov to remember God. Yakov replies that he is a freethinker, someone who rejects religious teachings in favor of rational thought and speculation. Chained to the wall by day and in stocks at night, Yakov considers suicide. At this point he dreams that Shmuel is dead. "Live, Shmuel, live," sighs Yakov. "Let me die for you" (*Fixer*, 247). Yakov resolves to live, to suffer "for something," for Shmuel (*Fixer*, p. 248).

After nearly two years in prison, Yakov receives a visit from Raisl. She asks him to sign paternity papers claiming that he fathered a son whom she has conceived with another man. Seeing Raisl's tears, Yakov says he has learned something about tears, about suffering. With a sigh,

Elizabeth Hartman (left) as Zinaida and Hugh Griffith as Lebedev in the 1968 film version of *The Fixer*.

he agrees to claim Raisl's son, Chaim (the child's name is also the Hebrew word for "life").

Yakov receives a visit from the prosecutor, Grubeshov, too. After imprisoning him for close to two years, the authorities finally issue an indictment; it is filled with anti-Semitic myths about Jewish blood rituals. Grubeshov's visit is a last attempt to get Yakov to confess. The fixer's confession, says Ghrubeshov, will save Jews from pogroms, a certainty if Yakov goes to trial. Grubeshov reveals the government's true fears when he warns Yakov that such a pogrom will not "stimulate active subversion among Socialist revolutionaries"; that is, it will not stimulate the socialists to overthrow the tsar (*Fixer*, p. 275). He alludes here to his belief in a connection between the socialists and the Jews.

Soon after Grubeshov's visit, a Jewish lawyer, Julius Ostrovsky, visits Yakov. Like Shmuel, the lawyer reminds the fixer that he is not alone in this fight. Many Jews and some Gentiles are working for him to receive a fair and just trial. "You suffer for us all," the lawyer tells Yakov (*Fixer*, p. 278). The lawyer says Yakov is in a better position than Dreyfus, the French army officer accused of treason, remarking wryly that Jews are "persecuted in the most civilized languages" (*Fixer*, p. 279). Ostrovsky describes the historical conditions leading up to Yakov's case, including the pogroms of 1905-06, perpetrated by right-wing groups because 12 Jews were included in the Duma, the Russian parliament. Debates in the Duma had progressed to the point of abolishing the Pale of Jewish Settlement, which drove the Black Hundreds frantic with fear. At this moment, a Christian boy was found dead in a cave and into the picture came Yakov Bok.

The night before his trial, Yakov envisions the tsar offering him poisoned milk. He also imagines Bibikov's telling him to sleep without fear; remember, says Bibikov, that the "purpose of freedom is to create it for others" (*Fixer*, p. 291). The next morning, given food, a warm shower, and civilian clothes, Yakov prepares to leave for his trial. The deputy warden brings him back to his cell for another search and when Yakov resists, draws his pistol. At this point, Kogin, Yakov's longtime guard, interferes, shooting his gun in the air. Cossack guards come running, but they arrive too late for Kogin. The deputy warden has shot him.

YAKOV BOK AND MENDEL BEILIS: A COMPARISON

Unlike Yakov Bok, Mendel Beilis was a family man who enjoyed a long marriage to his wife and raised five children. Beilis also had a permit to live and work in a restricted area of Kiev. A popular man, Beilis won the heart of the local priest by giving him a price break on bricks for the local parochial school and by allowing him to lead funeral processions through the brickyard on the way to the cemetery. This was unusual treatment for a Jew at the time. Curiously the fictional Yakov Bok represents the more common treatment of Jews than the real Mendel Beilis. Jews living and working in Kiev around the time of the novel often experienced harassment from fellow workers, supervisors, and the police, who would check work permits and identity papers.

On the way, Yakov's carriage is rocked by a bomb, and one of his Cossack escorts loses a foot in the explosion. The procession continues with Yakov in the damaged carriage, imagining a final confrontation in which he shoots Tsar Nicholas II in the heart. It is impossible, Yakov decides, for a man to be unpolitical, especially a Jewish man. One cannot just sit still and let oneself be destroyed. As the carriage rolls off, Yakov spots Jews among the crowd of onlookers. Some shout his name.

Protest novels—about the universal or the particular? At a key moment in the story, Bibikov tells Yakov that if the law will not protect the fixer, it will surely not protect the investigating magistrate either. Bibikov's subsequent arrest and suicide reveal the novel's critique of the corrupt Russian legal system and reflects also the attempt to make a larger statement about persecution and moral behavior that transcends this moment in Russian history. On the larger scale, *The Fixer* features a protagonist at the mercy of an intractable bureaucratic force, a prospect all the more frightening for being based on reality. As scholars note, "The [Beilis] case was one of the early [twentieth century] instances of the use by a government of the big lie, through which a powerful bureaucracy . . . 'makes its assertions with brazen disregard for what is known'" (Samuel in Alter, p. 38). The lie would resurface on a far grander scale later in the century, during the Holocaust, Hitler's brazen attempt to destroy European Jewry. *The Fixer*, as scholar Robert Alter notes, "holds within it the core of the cultural sickness around which the Nazi madness grew," resting, as it does, on the "conception of the Jew as a satanic enemy to Christ and mankind" (Alter, p. 38).

Ironically the novel's bid to protest the persecution of Jews and of individuals in general situates it squarely in a particular historical moment and genre: the American protest novel of the 1950s and 1960s. Novelists in this genre struggled with the conflict between fighting for civil rights by portraying wrongs suffered by specific ethnic groups at specific historical moments and by showing that these wrongs could happen to anyone at any time in ways that appealed to everyone's moral sensibility.

Built into *The Fixer* is an unresolved tension of other novels in its day, a tension born of the drive to both represent the particulars of an ethnic experience and appeal to a wider audience by generalizing ethnic history. In Alter's view, *The Fixer* is one of the finest novels of its day because it negotiates this conflict so successfully. Yakov Bok appears to be "a Jew in all the distinctive qualities of his mental and physical being," but he has also been conceived "as an extreme . . . instance of all men's inevitable exposure to the caprice of circumstance and the insidious snarl of history"—as an "Everyman" (Alter, p. 42).

Sources and literary context. Malamud drew inspiration for *The Fixer* from events that span a half-century. The most direct source, the real-life Beilis case, was described to him by his father, an immigrant from tsarist Russia. Other influences include the Dreyfus case (1894-1906); the Sacco-Vanzetti case, involving two Italians in

Massachusetts (1920s); events in Nazi Germany (1930s-40s); and the American civil rights movement (1950s-60s).

Novels by Jewish American authors flourished after World War II, appearing on bestseller lists and garnering literary prizes. These writers, and their readers, were greatly influenced by the war, especially by the devastation of the Holocaust and subsequent attempts to found the Jewish state of Israel. In postwar America, writers laid claim to their Jewish identities and the public showed a new receptiveness to their work, a willingness to look beyond previous stereotypes to see Jews as individuals.

Though Malamud became one of the best-known Jewish American writers of his generation, he was not the first, nor the most celebrated. For inspiration and ideas about the shtetl and the Eastern European Jewish experience in general, Malamud could call upon the Yiddish literature of I. L. Peretz (c.1851-1915) and Sholem Aleichem (1859-1916), both of whom produced stories with characters and situations similar to Yakov Bok's struggles in and beyond the Pale. A more immediate precursor was Isaac Bashevis Singer (1904-91), who wrote in Yiddish, but lived in the United States beginning in 1935.

Malamud's contemporaries have dealt with issues similar to his own in their writings. Saul Bellow (1915-) published *The Victim* in 1947. In the novel, the protagonist suffers an anti-Semitic act and meditates on who is the greater victim of the hateful incident, he himself or the bigot. A less well-known contemporary was Edward Lewis Wallant (1926-62), whose novel *The Pawnbroker* appeared in 1961. Wallace's main character, a withdrawn Holocaust survivor, adopts the only position the world seems to afford him and becomes a pawnbroker; overcoming the stereotype of greedy Jew, he begins to connect with others through the personal belongings they bring him. Finally, around the same time that *The Fixer* first appeared, so did a detailed nonfiction account of the Beilis case—*Blood Accusation* by Maurice Samuel.

Events in History at the Time the Novel Was Written

The American civil rights movement. According to historian Cornel West, the American civil rights struggle of the 1960s "began as a black response to white violent attacks" (West, p. 49). Specifically West cites a series of murders that occurred in Mississippi: Reverend George W. Lee in May 1955, Lamar Smith in August 1955, and 14-year-old Emmett L. Till in late August 1955. All three black males were aligned with the struggle to secure civil rights for African Americans. In the following decade violence erupted in conjunction with a series of "Freedom Rides." In May 1961 seven blacks and six whites left on an interstate bus from Washington, D.C., to promote integration in the South. They met with attack after attack at cities in Alabama. In May 1963, Martin Luther King, Jr., led a march against segregation and unfair employment in Birmingham, Alabama. During the march, police commissioner Bull Connor unleashed dogs and high-pressure water hoses on the protestors. The following month civil rights leader Medgar Evers was killed in Jackson, Mississippi. Two years later the black leader Malcolm X was killed in New York City and later in 1965 the local police clubbed demonstrators in Selma, Alabama. In 1966, the year *The Fixer* was published, Stokely Carmichael launched the Black Power Movement, urging civil rights activists to carry weapons for self-defense, a development that brings to mind the fixer's militancy at the end of the novel. There were successes along the way, culminating in the Civil Rights Act of 1964, which outlawed segregation in public facilities, and the Voting Rights Act of 1965, which guaranteed the vote to African Americans, but as shown by the acts of violence listed above, these advances met with backlashes, just as the advances in Russia had.

Malamud, writing his novel in 1966, was heavily influenced by the civil rights movement. He was angling "for an idea in the direction of injustice on the American scene, partly for obvious reasons—this was a time of revolutionary advances in Negro rights" (Malamud in Hicks, p. 37). When he considered the plight of agitators for civil rights, he thought of a story his father had told him—the story of Mendel Beilis. In an interview, Malamud clarified the relation of his novel to civil rights issues:

> One of the things I think of now is the Negro, the Negroes who live lives of second-class citizens. Their story is one leading up to a situation that is revolutionary—call it Black Power if you wish. Our country is lucky if this slow bloodletting, these riots that come and then disappear, are all we have to pay for what has happened to the Negro. If the Negroes' story today is revolutionary, Yakov's is pre-revolutionary.
> (Malamud in Frankel, p. 39)

Jews in 1960s Russia. Not in the United States alone was the 1960s a volatile racial decade. From

The Fixer

1957-64 Soviet premier Nikita Khruschev mounted a general antireligious campaign against the Jews as well as members of other faiths. Over 300 articles attacking Judaism surfaced in the Soviet press from 1960-64 and more than 50 synagogues were closed down (mostly in the Slavic republics). Russians published anti-Semitic books, such as Trofim Kichko's *Judaizm bez prikras* (Judaism without embellishment), featuring ribald caricatures of Jews. Soon heated protest from abroad prompted the Soviet government to rescind some of its tactics. It, for example, rethought an early 1960s edict that outlawed the baking of matzos for Passover by Jews; by 1964 Soviet authorities had renewed permission for Jews in several major cities to bake the ritual bread.

Reviews. Granville Hicks proclaimed *The Fixer* "one of the finest novels of the postwar period" (Hicks, p. 37). Hicks's comment reflects a consensus among most reviewers. *The Fixer* received praise from nearly all major critics, won the National Book Award and a Pulitzer Prize, and firmly established Malamud's place among the most respected authors in the United States. Indeed it is somewhat ironic that Malamud's first novel to focus exclusively on a Jewish protagonist and Jewish issues, lifted him onto a general plateau from a specialty category of Jewish American writer. Keying into the feat of creating a character that embodies both the particular and universal, *The Nation*'s review also acknowledges the novel's impact on its author's new status. "The main success of the novel," concludes this review, "lies in the creation of Bok, free of any false pathos or any false grandeur . . . a kind of Jewish Everyman. . . . In *The Fixer*, Malamud has . . . staked a claim in the territory of the great 'classical' novelists" (Fanger, p. 389).

—Christopher M. Mott

For More Information

Alter, Robert. "Jewishness as Metaphor." In *Bernard Malamud and the Critics*. Ed. Leslie A. Field and Joyce W. Field. New York: New York University Press, 1970.

Baron, Salo W. *The Russian Jew Under the Tsars and the Soviets*. New York: MacMillan, 1976.

Fanger, Donald. Review of *The Fixer*, by Bernard Malamud. *The Nation* 203 (17 October 1966): 389.

Frankel, Haskel. "Bernard Malamud." *Saturday Review*, 10 September 1966, 39.

Gitelman, Zvi. *A Century of Ambivalence: The Jews of Russia and the Soviet Union, 1881 to the Present*. Bloomington: Indiana University Press, 2001.

Hicks, Granville. "One Man to Stand for Six Million." *Saturday Review*, 10 (September 1966): 37-38.

Lindemann, Albert S. *The Jew Accused: Three Anti-Semitic Affairs (Dreyfus, Beilis, Frank) 1894-1915*. New York: Cambridge University Press, 1991.

Malamud, Bernard. *The Fixer*. New York: Washington Square, 1976.

Rogger, Hans. *Jewish Policies and Right-Wing Politics in Imperial Russia*. London: Macmillan, 1986.

Samuel, Maurice. *Blood Accusation: The Strange History of the Beilis Case*. New York: Alfred A. Knopf, 1966.

Stanislawski, Michael. "Russian Jewry, the Russian State, and the Dynamics of Jewish Emancipation." In *Paths of Emancipation*. Ed. Pierre Birnbaum and Ira Katznelson. Princeton, N.J.: Princeton University Press, 1995.

Unger, Leonard, ed. *American Writers: A Collection of Literary Biographies*. Supplement 1, Part 2. New York: Scribners, 1979.

West, Cornel. "The Paradox of the Afro-American Rebellion." In *The 60s without Apology*. Ed. Sohnya Sayres. Minneapolis, Minn.: University of Minnesota Press, 1984.

Fools Crow

by
James Welch

Of mixed Blackfeet and Gros Ventre ancestry, James Welch was born in 1940 in Browning, Montana, the tribal headquarters of the Blackfeet Indian Nation. Educated at the University of Minnesota, Northern Montana College, and the University of Montana, Welch published his first novel, *Winter in the Blood*, to critical acclaim in 1974. Like *Winter in the Blood* (and like his 1971 book of poems *Riding the Earthboy 40*), several of Welch's subsequent novels focused on problems of achieving cultural identity for Blackfeet living in modern Montana (e.g., *The Death of Jim Loney* [1979] and *The Indian Lawyer* [1990]). His most recent novel, *The Heartsong of Charging Elk* (2000), leaves the Blackfeet and Montana to follow a Lakota Sioux main character named Charging Elk, who witnesses the Battle of Little Bighorn as a child and subsequently travels to Europe with Buffalo Bill's Wild West Show; the novel is loosely based on the life of an actual Lakota, Black Elk, whose story is told in John Neihardt's *Black Elk Speaks* (1932; also in *Literature and Its Times*). Welch has also written nonfiction about the West and its history, notably (with Paul Stekler) *Killing Custer: the Battle of Little Bighorn and the Fate of the Plains Indians* (1994). In coauthoring this nonfiction work, Welch incorporated research that he himself had earlier conducted for *Fools Crow*, a novel that blends historical events and people with fictional ones to recount a pivotal period during the subjugation of the Blackfeet.

> **THE LITERARY WORK**
>
> A novel set in western Montana in the late 1860s; published in New York in 1986.
>
> **SYNOPSIS**
>
> Fools Crow, a young man who belongs to the Blackfeet Indian nation, struggles to help his people respond to the threat of encroaching white civilization.

Events in History at the Time the Novel Takes Place

A band of Blackfeet. By the 1860s the Blackfeet Indians had enjoyed about a century in which they were the dominant power of the northern plains. Blackfeet lands stretched from southern Alberta and Saskatchewan in Canada south into the uplands of western Montana, where some of these nomadic buffalo hunters made their winter camps in the sheltered valleys along the Marias, Teton, and Sun rivers. The Blackfeet were divided into three tribes:

- The Siksika or Northern Blackfeet (also called the Blackfeet proper), located in Canada
- The Kainah or Bloods, living south of the Siksika Blackfeet and ranging on both sides of the U.S.-Canada border
- The Pikuni or Piegan Blackfeet, living mostly in Montana but also ranging on both sides of the border

Fools Crow

The three Blackfeet tribes were politically independent, although they shared a common culture and a tongue derived from the Algonkian family of Native American languages. Within each tribe were further subdivisions into numerous bands, consisting of between about 150 and 250 people each, though they fluctuated both in size and number. Each band had both a band chief and a war chief charged with leading its warriors in battle; the most respected of the band chiefs became the leader chosen as head chief of the whole tribe.

> **BUFFALO: THE "STAFF OF LIFE"**
>
> A white observer in the middle of the nineteenth century called the buffalo "staff of life" for the Plains Indians because the large animals provided so many aspects of their subsistence (Vaughan in Ewers, p. 73). From flavorful meat to durable skins used in clothing and tipis and sinew for bowstrings, virtually every part of the animal filled a practical need in Blackfeet camp life. Hunting the buffalo was made more efficient by the arrival of the horse, but Plains Indians continued to favor bows and arrows over guns in hunting by horseback, finding them easier to aim and reload during the chase. By the middle of the nineteenth century, dressed buffalo skins had begun to replace beaver pelts as highly sought trade items by eastern whites, who used them as coats. Besides bringing them food, clothing, shelter, and durable goods, trade in buffalo skins also gave the Blackfeet and other Plains peoples access to luxury items such as kettles and axes. Once vast herds had filled the plains—in 1700 there were 15 million buffalo. But with the help of the U.S. government, white hunters would nearly extinguish them by the 1880s. From 1881-83, the government hired marksmen to kill the remaining 2.5 million buffalo, bringing to an end traditional life for the Blackfeet and other Plains Indians. Thus, at the time of *Fool's Crow*, the demise of buffalo hunting was fast approaching.

In the late 1860s the Blackfeet population stood at an estimated 6,000. The largest tribe was the Pikuni, with at least 15 bands; the Siksika and Kainah comprised about 10 bands each. *Fools Crow* follows one particular band of Pikuni Blackfeet, the Lone Eaters, who make their winter camp near where the Marias River flows east out of the Rocky Mountains in western Montana, before it joins the Missouri River north of Fort Benton. The Lone Eaters were a historical band of the Pikuni, but because the bands were either wiped out or broken up in the years following the white conquest, the Lone Eaters' exact geographical setting in the novel, while plausible, remains speculative. Little is known of them beyond their name and their membership in the Pikuni tribe.

Fire and horse power. The Blackfeet rose to their position of strength by exploiting two novelties introduced into their world in the eighteenth century: the horse and the gun. Long extinct in North America, horses first came to the Plains Indians by way of the Spanish colonizers in Mexico and the American Southwest and then by way of the English colonizers of the United States. Guns were introduced to the Plains Tribes mostly by French trappers and traders who ventured into the continent from Canada. Isolated in the continent's interior, the Blackfeet obtained both horses and guns after their neighbors. As the later recollections of Pikuni elders went, it was sometime around the 1730s that the Pikuni were dealt a severe defeat by their great enemies to the south, the Shoshoni (or as the Blackfeet called them, the Snakes). The Shoshoni warriors were mounted on huge, strange animals "on which they rode swift as a deer" to strike at the Pikuni (Ewers, p. 21). When the Pikuni turned for help to allies among the Cree and Assiniboine Indians to their northeast, they received assistance not just in the form of warriors, but also in muskets and ammunition. Instructed by their allies, they mastered the new weapons, using them to great effect against the bows and arrows of the Shoshoni.

By the middle of the nineteenth century, the Pikuni's relentless attacks had pushed the Shoshoni across the Rockies, expanding the territory of the Pikuni Blackfeet to the south and west. From time to time, Blackfeet raiding parties crossed the Rockies to harry the Shoshoni or their neighbors the Flatheads and Nez Perce. The Blackfeet also conducted frequent raids against their enemies to the southeast, the Crow Indians, and even against their former allies among the Cree and Assiniboine Indians. In all directions, the only tribes safe from attacks by the powerful Blackfeet were their subordinate allies, the Sarsi and the Gros Ventre Indians. Like similar raids made by their enemies, the Blackfeet raids were executed primarily in order to seize the foes' horses and often their scalps as well. Both horse-seizing and scalping brought honor to the warrior who performed these deeds, and

Blackfeet Indians hunting for buffalo on the plains of Montana 1835–55. Artwork by John M. Stanley.

young Blackfeet males eagerly sought to prove themselves in these ways on raiding parties. Occasionally a band or tribe mounted a larger, more concerted raid, usually to take revenge for an outstanding offense by the other group. *Fools Crow* prominently features both a horse-seizing raid and a larger revenge raid, the first mounted by the Lone Eaters and the second by warriors from all the Pikuni bands acting in concert.

Arrival of the Napikwan. Through the eighteenth and much of the nineteenth centuries, the Blackfeet encountered only handfuls of whites, whom they called Napikwan, or Old Man People, because the whites' pale skin color was like an old man's snowy hair. The first whites the Blackfeet met were French traders, who took beaver pelts in exchange for guns, ammunition, and other useful metal goods, such as kettles and axes. When Canada fell to British control after the French and Indian War of the 1760s, British traders replaced the French ones. In 1803 the United States vastly extended its western territory by transacting the Louisiana Purchase, which included Blackfeet lands up to the Canadian border. Shortly afterward, President Thomas Jefferson charged the Lewis and Clark expedition (1804-06) with the task of exploring the West and seeking a water route to the Pacific. On its way to the Pacific, the expedition passed through Pikuni lands, naming the Marias River (which the Pikuni called the Bear) for Lewis's cousin Maria Wood. American trappers began arriving in Blackfeet territory soon thereafter, in competition with the British, who still ventured in from eastern Canada.

In contrast with the French and British, who mostly traded for pelts acquired by the Blackfeet, the Americans preferred to trap their own animals. The Blackfeet, angered by the trespassing and direct trapping, responded by killing American trappers whenever they could, which earned them a reputation as a warlike and bloodthirsty tribe. So wary of these Indians were the whites that when settlers began pouring west along the Oregon Trail in the 1840s, they chose a path well to the south of Blackfeet territory, even though a more logical route would have been to follow the Missouri River through Pikuni lands before crossing the Rockies.

Owing to their warlike reputation and their remoteness, the Blackfeet were the last of the Plains Indians below the Canadian border with whom the U.S. government negotiated a treaty. Not until 1853, a half century after the Louisiana Purchase, did the U.S. open talks with the Blackfeet, the most distant inhabitants of that huge ceded region. In 1855 the government signed a treaty with the Blackfeet. The treaty declared perpetual peace between the Blackfeet and the United States, and confirmed that the lands of

Fools Crow

the "Blackfeet Nation" in the United States consisted essentially of north-central Montana above the Musselshell and Missouri rivers, from the Rocky Mountains in the west to the confluence of the Milk and Missouri rivers in the east. As with other tribes, the government appointed an agent to manage its relations with the Blackfeet, and the Blackfeet were told to go to this agent, who would be headquartered at the major trading post of Fort Benton, if they had "any trouble" (Ewers, p. 226).

Despite the good feelings generated by the treaty, relations between the Blackfeet and the Napikwan deteriorated steadily during the 1860s. In the first years of that decade, the Civil War (1860-63) monopolized the attention of the U.S. government. For the most part, the office of agent was either left unfilled or was occupied by inept or inexperienced men. In 1862, at the height of this neglect, gold was discovered at Bannock, in Blackfeet hunting grounds along the eastern base of the Rockies in Montana. Responding to the ever attractive call of gold, would-be prospectors now began streaming through Blackfeet lands, a rush that was accelerated by the end of the Civil War in 1863. Only a few years earlier the Blackfeet had been skeptical about whether the Napikwan even existed in large numbers. Now more and more Napikwan miners, traders, missionaries, soldiers, woodcutters, and finally settlers seemed suddenly to materialize on Blackfeet territory. The Blackfeet grew increasingly anxious about retaining their ancestral lands, an anxiety that is echoed by Pikuni characters in the opening chapters of *Fools Crow*.

THE SCOURGE OF SMALLPOX

Brought to North America by Europeans, smallpox kills nearly half of those it infects. Over the centuries, the disease played a central role in decimating American Indians, who lacked immunity to the virus. The Blackfeet suffered thousands of deaths in two major smallpox epidemics during 1781 and 1837. Some 6,000, almost two-thirds of the Blackfeet population, died in the 1837 epidemic. After each outbreak, it took decades for the population to recover. Fools Crow portrays the historical epidemic of 1869-70, the third and last major epidemic of the so-called "white-scabs disease" to strike the Blackfeet.

Massacre on the Marias. Fueled by illegal whisky traders who plied their low-grade liquor to the Indians around Fort Benton, violent incidents between the Blackfeet and the Napikwan mounted in the late 1860s. Typically, small groups of Blackfeet would be killed by whites as they visited Fort Benton, while small parties of whites would be killed by the Indians after venturing away from the security of the fort. In 1865 a new treaty ceded Blackfeet lands south of the Teton River, which white settlers wished to occupy, in exchange for yearly payments of cash. Although the settlers arrived, the yearly payments promised the Blackfeet did not, since Congress never ratified the treaty.

The sporadic but ongoing violence began to reach a peak in the fall of 1869, when whites at Fort Benton gunned down the brother of Mountain Chief, the new head chief of the Pikuni. Enraged Pikuni warriors reacted by attacking and killing a well-known settler, Malcolm Clark, despite Clark's being married to a Pikuni woman. On January 1, 1870, General Alfred Sully, the new Blackfeet agent, met several Pikuni chiefs to discuss the rising tensions. As part of the climax of *Fools Crow*, James Welch fictionally recreates Clark's murder and the chiefs' meeting with Sully, as well as the tragic events that followed. Sully ordered the chiefs to find Clark's murderers and turn them over to him, dead or alive, or face open war with the U.S. Army. Among the chiefs was a friendly Pikuni band chief named Heavy Runner, and the lot of them agreed to try. Giving the chiefs two weeks, but knowing that they might not have the power to comply, Sully prepared an attack on Mountain Chief's band, to be led by Colonel E. M. Baker.

On the bitterly cold day of January 23, 1870, after the two-week period expired, Baker attacked the winter camp not of Mountain Chief's band, but of the friendly Heavy Runner's, which he came across first. Already decimated by smallpox, and with many of its younger men away hunting, the demoralized camp on the Marias River consisted mostly of women, children, and old men. According to a later Army investigation, of the 173 Pikuni killed in the resulting massacre, 90 were women and 50 were children under 12. Evoking a public outcry among Americans further east, the massacre on the Marias also marked the abrupt end of Blackfeet resistance to whites. With the people ravaged by disease and deeply demoralized, the Blackfeet leaders—led by Mountain Chief—decided that they had no chance against the great numbers and power of the Napikwan, and that their very survival depended on peaceful cooperation. The events leading up to the massacre on the Marias, and the massacre itself, thus form the pivotal episode in modern Blackfeet history. They also constitute the historical core and the climax of *Fools Crow*. Reconstructing these events in fictional form, the novel recounts their unfolding as the Pikuni may have perceived it.

The Novel in Focus

The plot. Throughout *Fools Crow* the omniscient narrator uses language in a way that most readers will at first find unfamiliar, but that has the effect of immersing them in the Blackfeet world from the novel's opening lines:

> Now that the weather had changed, the moon of the falling leaves turned white in the blackening sky and White Man's Dog was restless. He chewed the stick of dry meat and watched Cold Maker gather his forces.
> (Welch, *Fools Crow*, p. 3)

The narrative focus stays primarily on White Man's Dog, an 18-year-old Pikuni warrior, whose father, Rides-at-the-door, is war chief of the Lone Eater band. A respected leader, Rides-at-the-door has three wives and many horses. His son habitually follows an older man called Victory Robe White Man around the camp like a dog; only later will readers learn that White Man's Dog's name comes from this childhood habit. By this point, nearly halfway through the novel, White Man's Dog has become Fools Crow, taking his new name from an exploit during a raid on a Crow village in which he is thought to have tricked an enemy Crow by playing dead.

When the novel opens White Man's Dog has a reputation for bad luck among the Lone Eaters. His accomplished friend Fast Horse ridicules him for his awkwardness with girls, and his younger brother Running Fisher seems to hold more promise of becoming a successful warrior and thus securing an enviable position within the band. However, when Fast Horse and White Man's Dog join a raiding party against a Crow village, the boastful Fast Horse arrogantly lets out a war cry that alerts the Crow Indians and results in the capture and maiming of the party's leader, an experienced warrior named Yellow Kidney. White Man's Dog, by contrast, quietly but competently carries out the tasks that Yellow Kidney has assigned him, and his status is enhanced by his killing of a Crow warrior. The raiding party marks the beginning of White Man's Dog's rise within the band. It also leads to Fast Horse's eventual alienation from the Lone Eaters, as he takes up with the renegade Pikuni Owl Child, whose roving band of warriors carries out bloody attacks against the encroaching whites, or Napikwan.

Another outcome of the raiding party is that White Man's Dog starts hunting to help Yellow Kidney's family, supplying them with food after Yellow Kidney's maiming at the hands of the Crow. White Man's Dog's personal wealth has been established by the horses he won during the raiding party. He is thus ready to marry, and chooses Yellow Kidney's young daughter, Red Paint, who becomes pregnant soon after they wed. At the same time, White Man's Dog begins having visions that lead to his initiation into the spirit world of the powerful old healer, Mik-api. Under Mik-api's supervision, and with a talking raven as his guide, White Man's Dog is led to a wolverine or skunk-bear that has been caught in a Napikwan trap. After White Man's Dog frees the wolverine, the raven tells him, "Of all the two-leggeds, you alone will possess the magic of Skunk-Bear" (*Fools Crow*, p. 58). In Blackfeet religious terms, the wolverine thus becomes White Man's Dog's animal helper.

White Man's Dog successfully undergoes painful ritual torture at the Sun Dance, the yearly ceremony at which the Pikuni bands gather together to honor their leading deity, the sun or Sun Chief. Afterward White Man's Dog falls asleep, and the wolverine appears to him in a dream, giving him a slender white stone and a song to sing for power in battle. The wolverine

MEDICINE BUNDLES

Traditionally, a Blackfeet warrior would find an animal helper during dreams in which the animal appeared to him and instructed him in assembling a medicine bundle. This collection of personal articles was imbued with power and symbolized the assistance that the animal helper gave the warrior, often in the form of prowess in battle and hunting. Medicine bundles could be passed on or sold from one owner to another. The novel's Boss Ribs, Fast Horse's father, hopes to pass his powerful beaver bundle on to Fast Horse. Beaver bundles—those assembled with the assistance of a beaver helper—were the most potent medicine bundles for the Blackfeet. In the late nineteenth century there were several beaver bundles famous among the Blackfeet for their power.

Fools Crow

departs, and White Man's Dog sees his father's youngest wife, Kills-close-to-the-lake, who is his own age, and with whom he has felt a mutual attraction. They make love in the dream, and after he wakes up White Man's Dog realizes that this dream act has purged him of the shameful desire he had felt for his father's wife in waking life. As he awakes, he finds the slender white stone in his sleeping robe. Later Kills-close-to-the-lake tells him that she has had a dream that echoes the details of White Man's Dog's. In an important subplot, it is White Man's Dog's younger brother Running Fisher, disgruntled at his brother's success, who later risks dishonoring the whole family by seducing Kills-close-to-the-lake.

The Pikunis decide to mount a large revenge raid on the Crow village where Yellow Kidney was maimed, and if possible to kill the Crow chief, Bull Shield, who maimed the Pikuni warrior. In the heat of battle, White Man's Dog prepares to attack Bull Shield, but is shot in the side and falls. Losing consciousness, he regains it just in time to see the Crow chief advancing on him, and he manages to fire his own rifle three times, killing Bull Shield. Urged on by his father, Rides-at-the-door, White Man's Dog (who is not seriously wounded) takes the fallen chief's scalp. "My fine son, this day you are a brave!" Rides-at-the-door declares (*Fools Crow*, p. 147). It is this exploit, magnified into a deliberate stratagem in the reports of the other warriors, that gives White Man's Dog his new name, Fools Crow. He is now firmly established as a rising leader in the band, "a man of much medicine" (*Fools Crow*, p. 151).

Shortly after Fools Crow receives his new name, the Lone Eaters' camp is visited by a column of blue-uniformed seizers, as the Blackfeet call the Napikwan soldiers. The seizers are guided by a half-breed scout and trader named Joe Kipp, who acts as a translator. Their commanding officer announces the murder of a nearby white settler, Malcolm Clark, and says that Clark's children have identified Owl Child and his band of renegades as the killers. The seizers are pursuing Owl Child, known to be a member of Mountain Chief's band. As a result, the whole band, including Mountain Chief, leader of the Pikuni tribe, has to flee the seizers. Later Fools Crow reflects that war between the Pikuni and the increasingly aggressive Napikwans seems inevitable.

That winter, after further bloodshed, in which Owl Child and Fast Horse are implicated, the seizers propose a meeting between their chiefs and the Blackfeet chiefs. Mountain Chief—still on the run—does not attend, and in the end only a few chiefs make their way to meet the Napikwan. Among them are the well-respected pair Rides-at-the-door and a Kainah band chief named Sun Calf. Three more Pakuni band chiefs accompany them—Heavy Runner (whom Rides-at-the-door privately finds too conciliatory to the whites), Big Lake, and Little Wolf, all of whom carry little weight with the younger braves. They meet with the new Blackfeet agent, General Sully, who presents a warrant for the arrest of Owl Child and several of his men and demands that the Blackfeet turn them over, dead or alive. The chiefs agree to do their best. Before leaving, Heavy Runner and then the other chiefs request written statements from Sully that they and their bands are at peace with the whites. Sully signs the statements, which are dated January 1, 1870.

THE SUN DANCE

The summer ceremony of the Sun Dance, during which the tribe's various bands assembled together at a large encampment, was the major religious festival of many Plains Indian tribes, including the Blackfeet. In the Blackfeet version the leading role in the ceremony was played by a woman whose virtue was unquestioned, and who assumed the responsibility by making a sacred vow to take this role at a time of personal crisis during the previous year. A successful outcome to the crisis—the recovery of a loved one from illness, or the safe return of a husband or son from a dangerous raid, for example—meant that the sun had answered her prayers. Her band then sent out word of her vow to the rest of the tribe in preparation for the coming test. During the ceremony itself, she took responsibility for the correct performance of the complex rituals; if anything went wrong, it reflected badly on her virtue. In *Fools Crow*, Heavy Shield Woman, the wife of the maimed warrior Yellow Kidney, makes such a vow in exchange for Yellow Kidney's safe return from the novel's raiding party on the Crow.

Likewise, White Man's Dog makes a vow to the sun in connection with the raiding party. It is in fulfillment of this vow that he undergoes ritual torture in the novel's Sun Dance. Such vows were made with deadly seriousness, since neglect of a vow resulted in sure misfortune. In the novel, the ostracized warrior Fast Horse's troubles are presented as stemming from his failure to fulfill a vow to Cold Maker, the bringer of wintry weather.

A Blackfeet Indian riding a horse and carrying a rifle: two innovations that allowed the Blackfeet to become one of the most powerful Native American tribes.

Some time later at their winter camp, the Lone Eaters get word that several Pikuni encampments further down the Marias River have been stricken with white-scabs disease. Many Pikuni are dying. Furthermore, at a full tribal council Rides-at-the-door has failed to persuade the other Pikuni chiefs to accept Sully's demands. Even Mountain Chief, forced by the younger braves' intransigence, refuses to turn Owl Child over. In an extended series of mystical experiences, Fools Crow meets So-at-sa-ki, or Feather Woman, a mythological figure. In Blackfeet legend she lives between heaven and earth, outcast by her husband, Morning Star. Feather Woman imparts to Fools Crow several visions of his people's future, including "the end of the blackhorns [buffalo] and the starvation of the Pikunis," along with the sight of a forlorn handful of Pikuni children amid happy white youngsters in a Napikwan school (*Fools Crow*, p. 358).

Soon afterward smallpox strikes the winter camp of the Lone Eaters, spreading rapidly. In two weeks, when nearly 40 of the band have perished, Fools Crow and the others spot a small, ragged group of Pikuni approaching the camp on foot. They are the stunned remnant of Heavy Runner's band, whose camp further down the Marias has been attacked by a large group of seizers. Heavy Runner is dead, shot down while waving his signed paper at the approaching soldiers, and the camp has been virtually wiped out.

The narrative jumps forward in time to that spring, when the healer Mik-api leads the remaining Lone Eaters in the Thunder Pipe ceremony, which celebrates the season's arrival. Fools Crow thinks of Feather Woman and the visions she gave him, and he knows that his people will at least survive. After describing the feasting and children's' games in camp that evening, the novel closes as spring rains glisten on the buffalo that stand humpbacked and dark on the prairies around the camp: "The blackhorns had returned and, all around, it was as it should be" (*Fools Crow*, p. 319).

Rationalizing defeat and conquest. In its fictional depiction of historical events, *Fools Crow* suggests that a major stumbling block to mutual understanding between the Pikuni and the Napikwan lay in the different conceptions of power and authority of the two cultures. In political terms, the Blackfeet's loose, consensus-based power structure, based on personal influence, contrasts sharply with the whites' tighter, more hierarchical power structure, in which authority is vested in political office or military rank. In the case of the Owl Child, for example, the white officers hold Mountain Chief accountable for the young brave as they themselves would be responsible for a soldier under their command. This expectation baffles the Pikuni:

> It angered them that the seizers thought he [Mountain Chief] could control Owl Child, as one hobbles a horse that has a tendency to wander. Now the seizers were determined to make Mountain Chief pay for the crimes of Owl Child. That was like shooting one gopher because another gopher had bitten a child's finger.
> (*Fools Crow*, p. 159)

As with authority, the Pikunis' approach to religion is diffuse rather than hierarchical. In the Pikuni world, any dream carries religious import, regardless of the dreamer's status. Also, unlike a priest, the medicine man Mik-api does not practice in a different realm from his fellow Pikunis. He simply has greater skills in a realm with which they too are familiar.

Yet both cultures share a need to link worldly power with religious devotion and to rationalize political outcomes in religious terms. After the massacre of Heavy Runner's band, Fools Crow remembers the visions of his people's future that Feather Woman has given him. He realizes:

> that his father had been right all along—the Pikunis were no match for the seizers and their weapons. That the camps were laid low with the white-scabs disease did not even matter. The disease, this massacre—Sun Chief favored the Napikwans. The Pikunis would never possess the power to make them cry.
> (*Fools Crow*, p. 383)

Elsewhere the Pikunis wonder if their sacrifices to the Sun Chief have been inadequate in some way, since their deity has seen fit to bestow greater power on the whites. As in other cultures, they reach for religious explanations for defeat.

Fools Crow portrays a proud people struggling to come to terms with defeat. It thus offers a mirror image of white Americans in the nineteenth century, who saw their rising fortunes as the "manifest destiny" of a godly people to expand across the continent and, by logical extension, to impose their superior culture on savage Indians along the way. Some early Christian missions among the Blackfeet are mentioned in passing in *Fools Crow*. The novel also briefly touches on their secular equivalents, the whites' largely unsuccessful attempts to induce the as-yet unconquered Pikuni to adopt white farming techniques and attend white schools. Fools Crow's visions clearly foresee the next step, which will be the fast-approaching U.S. government campaign to force the Blackfeet to abandon their traditional culture. By ending the story where he does, James Welch recreates in fictional form the last historical moment before his people had the biting suspicion of cultural inferiority pressed upon them by their more numerous Napikwan conquerors.

Sources. Welch relied on published accounts of Blackfeet life as well as on his own family's oral tradition in constructing the fictional version of historical events in *Fools Crow*. James Willard Schultz (1859-1947), a white man who lived for many years with the Blackfeet and married a Pikuni woman, wrote a number of colorful magazine articles about Blackfeet life, social customs, and legends. Collections of Schultz's articles include *My Life as an Indian* (1907) and, more recently, *Why Gone Those Times?* (1974). Another source Welch used, *Blackfeet Lodge Tales* (1962), was compiled from Schultz's work by George Bird Grinnell, the magazine editor who published much of Schultz's material originally. Welch also read John Ewers's authoritative account, *The Blackfeet: Raiders on the Northwestern Plains* (1958), which drew on the memories of Blackfeet informants who lived during the 1850s and 1860s.

Additionally, as Welch relates in an interview, his great grandmother was alive at the time of the novel, and she herself actually lived through the massacre on the Marias:

HISTORICAL BLACKFEET

Historical Figures	Names Used Fictionally	Fictional Characters
• Heavy Runner, a Pikuni band chief killed in the massacre on the Marias.	• Owl Child, in the novel a renegade, but in real life a well-known Blackfeet farmer in the 1880s and 1890s.	• Fools Crow
• Mountain Chief, chief of the Pikuni.		• Red Paint
• Malcolm Clark, white settler (and ancestor of James Welch) killed by Blackfeet in 1869.	• Rides-at-the-door, an actual Pikuni warrior's name.	• Kills-close-to-the-lake
	• Mik-api, or "Red Old Man," the novel's medicine man, is the name of a great chief from Blackfeet mythology mentioned in *Blackfeet Lodge Tales*.	• Yellow Kidney
• General Alfred Sully, Blackfeet agent.		• Fast Horse
• Joe Kipp, a mixed-blood (Indian-white) trader and scout.		

She and a small group of people managed to sneak up the river. . . . That's how they escaped. She is one of the survivors Fools Crow comes upon. She told my dad many stories of life during that time. He told those stories to me. A lot of them form the basis for parts of the book.
(Welch, "Interview")

Welch portrays some genuine historical figures in the novel, using their real-life names. For other characters, he appropriates genuine names from Blackfeet history and applies them to fictional figures, and some characters he invents completely:

Events in History at the Time the Novel Was Written

The Blackfeet in the 1980s. In 1874 the government established the Blackfeet on a large reservation occupying the area north of the Marias River and of its tributary to the west, Birch Creek. By the 1880s the buffalo had nearly vanished from the plains. Many Blackfeet faced starvation and disease, while those who survived struggled to make their way as farmers. In 1888 and 1896 the Blackfeet further ceded the bulk of that territory north of the Marias and Missouri Rivers, so that today's smaller Blackfeet reservation lies north of Birch Creek in Montana.

Like other Indians in late nineteenth- and early twentieth-century America, the Blackfeet were expected to give up their traditional culture and adopt the ways of the dominant white majority. Blackfeet children were taught exclusively European and American subjects in school, and were punished if they spoke a native language. This repressive policy began shifting in the 1940s, as white authorities began gradually to acknowledge that Indian culture and history possessed a rightful place in their lives and classrooms. But many Blackfeet have felt dispossessed and uprooted in modern America. Reservation life has presented difficult challenges and often bleak prospects in a world far from conducive to the age-old Indian sense of tribal life.

> To Indians tribe means family, not just bloodlines but extended family, clan, community, ceremonial exchanges with nature, and an animate regard for all creation as sensible and powerful. Tribe means an earth sense of self, housed in an earth body, with regional ties. . . .
> (Lincoln, p. 8)

In the 1980s about 6,000 Blackfeet, most of them Pikuni but many of mixed descent, lived on the Montana reservation, while some 9,000 Pikuni, Kainah, and Siksika lived on similar reservations in Canada.

Native American Renaissance. Around 1960, there began a resurgence of American Indian culture and identity that scholars have called the Native American Renaissance. This revival has economic, political, artistic, and academic dimensions. Its literary side is commonly viewed as beginning with Native American author N. Scott Momaday's Pulitzer Prize-winning novel, ***House Made of Dawn*** (1969; also in *Literature and Its Times*). James Welch's first novel, *Winter in the Blood* (1974) is often cited as the movement's second landmark. Since then a profusion of American Indian authors has burst on the U.S. literary scene, many of them women, such as poet and novelist Leslie Marmon Silko and Louise Erdrich (see Silko's *Ceremony* [1978] and Erdrich's **Love Medicine** [1984] and **Antelope Wife** [1998], also in *Literature and Its Times*). Together they have developed "a written renewal of oral traditions translated into Western literary forms" (Lincoln, p. 8). The literary works themselves span a wide range of themes and settings. Like *Fools Crow*, a number of the works incorporate supernatural elements as part of the daily lives of their Native American characters. Critics have suggested that these fictional depictions of the supernatural represent a vital component of recent Native American literature, in that they imaginatively attempt to recreate traditional ways of experiencing the world. As with *Fools Crow*, such portrayals may combine anthropological research with the author's own background and experience to achieve a feel of authenticity. At issue in the Native American Renaissance has been the use of the white man's language to portray Indian life. Some have objected to Indians' employing English to explore native identities and concerns, even though only a few people are able to read native languages. Others have celebrated the racially mixed audiences that these writers have attracted by doing so.

Reception. While not accorded the critical and scholarly attention given to Welch's earlier two novels, *Fools Crow* enjoyed fine sales and received positive reviews, winning the 1987 *Los Angeles Times* Book Prize for fiction. Writing for *The Los Angeles Times Book Review*, scholar Louis Owens called *Fools Crow* "a painful, stunning act of recovery" that "marks an important step . . . toward a maturation of both style and vision" in the American Indian literary movement (Owens, Review, p. 1). Critic Peter Wild has objected that Welch's attempts to recapture the phrasing of the Blackfeet language in English come off as stilted and unconvincing. (Welch himself knew the Blackfeet language as a young child but no longer speaks it.) Others, however, have seen Welch's unusual style in *Fools Crow* as a strength, a feature that adds both beauty and a vivid sense of reality to the story. In his discussion of American Indian novels, Louis Owens echoes these sentiments. He argues further that "Welch, more fully than any other Native American novelist, explicitly seizes control of the language of the Blackfeet's oppressors," thus subtly using language to subvert the very conquest that the novel describes (Owens, *Other Destinies*, p. 157).

—Colin Wells

For More Information

Ewers, John C. *The Blackfeet: Raiders on the Northwestern Plains*. Norman: University of Oklahoma Press, 1958.

Grinnell, George Bird. *Blackfoot Lodge Tales: The Story of a Prairie People*. Lincoln: University of Nebraska Press, 1962.

Lincoln, Kenneth. *Native American Renaissance*. Berkeley: University of California Press, 1983.

Owens, Louis. Review of *Fools Crow*. *The Los Angeles Times Book Review*, 14 December 1986, 1.

———. *Other Destinies: Understanding the American Indian Novel*. Norman: University of Oklahoma Press, 1992.

Schultz, James Willard. *Why Gone These Times? Blackfoot Tales*. Norman: University of Oklahoma Press, 1974.

Trigger, Bruce G., and Wilcomb E. Washburn. *The Cambridge History of the Native Peoples of the Americas*. Vol. 1, *North America*. Cambridge: Cambridge University Press, 1996.

Welch, James. *Fools Crow*. New York: Penguin, 1987.

Welch, James, and Kenn Robbins. "An Interview with James Welch." *South Dakota Review*. 1990. *Literature Resource Center*. http://galenet.galegroup.com (27 May 2002).

"The Goblin Market"

by
Christina Rossetti

The youngest of four children in a family of scholars and artists, Christina Georgina Rossetti was born in 1830. Her mother, Frances Polidori, was a staunch Anglican of English and Italian descent, who had earlier worked as a governess and made two unsuccessful attempts to run a day school. Her father, Gabriele, was a political refugee from Italy and a scholar in the writings of Dante Alighieri (1265-1321). Rossetti's two brothers, Dante Gabriel and William Michael, helped found the prominent group of artists known as the pre-Raphaelite brotherhood. A pre-Raphaelite quality of lush, even sensuous detail graces Christina Rossetti's writing, as does a strong religious and moral sense; the mix made her particularly appealing to her contemporaries. Like her mother, Rossetti was a devout High Anglican, much influenced by a religious movement known as Tractarianism. Apparently for religious reasons, she twice declined offers of marriage. Rossetti spent most of her adulthood living in relative seclusion in London, where she cared for invalid relations, did charity work (particularly at the St. Mary Magdalene Home for Fallen Women), and pursued her writing. While she also wrote prose, she specialized in poetry, writing over 900 poems in English and 60 more in Italian. In 1847 Rossetti's grandfather Gaetano Polidori printed her first volume *Verses* on his private press. She began more formal publication of her work by submitting poems to the pre-Raphaelite journal, *The Germ*. During her lifetime, she achieved her greatest acclaim with her 1881 volume *A Pageant and Other Poems*, a work that would elevate Rossetti's name into the circle of the most well-known female poets. Her best-known work is "The Goblin Market," which treats the most provocative of adult issues—race, class, sex, drugs, disease, infertility, spirituality, and commercialism—in the singsong tones of a children's poem.

THE LITERARY WORK
A poem set in a fairy-tale countryside at an unspecified time; published in London in 1862.

SYNOPSIS
Encountering a group of goblin men, Laura trades a lock of her hair for some goblin fruit. The goblins vanish, leaving her pining for more fruit and wasting away until her sister Lizzie comes to the rescue.

Events in History at the Time of the Poem

Evolution, race, and empire. Published just three years after Charles Darwin's landmark essay ***On the Origin of Species*** (also in *Literature and Its Times*), "The Goblin Market" resonates with concerns raised by evolutionary theory. Though the *Origin of Species* does not directly address the evolution of humans from animals (Darwin would not address this directly until his 1871 *The Descent of Man*), the essay fostered a

"The Goblin Market"

Christina Rossetti

widespread anxiety regarding the nearness of humans to other species. Positing a mechanism called "Natural Selection," whereby new species could evolve from old, the *Origin* implied that the apparently stable (some even said, a divinely ordained) natural order, which set humanity clearly apart from and above other species, was neither so stable nor so clear-cut. The lines between species were, it now seemed, impossible to draw for they were perpetually in flux. The essay thus destabilized certain comforting views of a permanent natural order for many Victorians. But at the same time it was used to reinforce beliefs that served the dominant Victorian culture. The social application of Darwinian theory, known as "Social Darwinism" began immediately upon (perhaps even before) the publication of the *Origin of Species*. Though biologists today insist that evolution has no particular direction, a number of Victorians interpreted evolution as progressing to increasingly perfect forms; older or more primitive forms, they reasoned, were less perfect. In this way, they translated the mechanism of natural selection into a hierarchy—a model of the world that understands some "species" as better or higher than others. (A number of Victorians also conflated the terms "species" and "race," often treating them more nearly as synonyms than we currently do.) Applying hierarchical versions of an evolutionary ladder to the various races (and classes, for that matter) of people, these Victorians went on to reason that some races were more evolved, or less primitive, than others. The idea emerged that Europeans stood higher on the evolutionary scale than Asians, who, in turn, stood higher than Africans; there were even some scientific textbooks of the era that implied this was the case.

The goblin men in Rossetti's poem embody all of these concerns. Their recurring animal traits—"One had a cat's face, / One whisked a tail"—blur the distinction between human beings and animals (Rossetti, "The Goblin Market," p. 2). Their portrayal also raises a question regarding their origins and overlays this concern with implications regarding the animality of foreigners. The dangers that the goblin men pose relate to an increasingly visible anxiety of otherness (fears of all kinds of difference, including gender, race, nation, sexuality, and species) that laced the Victorian discourse of empire more and more as the century progressed. The expansion of British empire during Victoria's reign, to its greatest size and influence in the 1880s, brought with it not only riches and power, but anxiety and guilt. In numerous ways, Victorians indicated their fear that the empire would indeed strike back. Real rebellions such as the "Indian Mutiny" of 1857-58 gave rise to fears of out-and-out invasions, as fictionalized in novels such as *The Moonstone,* **Dracula,** and **The War of the Worlds** (also in *Literature and Its Times*). Such fears manifested themselves on a personal as well as a societal level, in the representations of interracial rape that British women might suffer if they went abroad. It was alleged that they had been violated in this way during the "Indian Mutiny," raising a fear that tourism promoters worked to dispel by promising safe spaces for Britains abroad. There was, moreover, a fairly common sense that rebellion and "reverse colonization" (in which colonized people make their presence felt back in England) were not entirely unwarranted, and that they were payback for the highly questionable treatment of colonial peoples by the British.

Class, commerce, and dangerous imports. The anxieties about foreignness, or otherness, which "The Goblin Market" conveys, cannot be separated from the mobile nature of society produced by the changing economy of nineteenth-century England. The industrial revolution contributed much to the emergence of an increasingly powerful middle class. "The Goblin Market" seems to take place in rural England, but the buying and selling that defines the "goblin merchant men" suggests a specific concern with the commercialism stimulated not only by industrialism but also by the expansion of the British empire. British ships sailed all over the world, distributing products and passengers, and importing exotics in the form of goods and even of people. Some of these imports seemed as innocuous as fruit, including the staple that became so consummately English that we forget it was an import of the empire: tea. Other imports were more troubling. Opium, imported from China, was in common medicinal use alongside morphine and cocaine. Like these substances, opium was highly addictive. It figured as a centerpiece of Victorian drug culture, pervading the slums of London's East End and in common use among many late-Victorian artists and intellectuals.

Nineteenth-century commercialism also brought with it a new mobility. The British toured the world, guided by the services of Thomas Cook (who, starting in 1841, organized the first package tours) and by such helpful publications as Karl Baedeker's travel guides. Also, traveling salesmen toured the country, buying, selling, and earning commissions. Many people gained considerable wealth "in trade"—a phrase used to indicate that they earned their fortunes through commerce rather than inheritance and still laced with the disdainful tone of the upper for the lower classes. Indeed Americans are often confused by the complications of social class introduced by the possibilities of wealth due to commercialism and industrialization, since in Victorian England, class was not just about wealth but also about where that wealth came from. It was entirely possible to be decidedly middle class, if one's income came from trade or industry, and to have a whole lot more money than many of the upper class, whose income and position derived from land ownership, established in an earlier, agrarian economy. As often as society saw middle-class wealth on the rise, moreover, it saw this upper class in decline, a phenomenon that led to the practice of marrying new money to save an old name.

Marriage, prostitution, and disease. On the surface a children's poem, "Goblin Market" can be viewed as a commentary on issues crucial to women's options and limitations in mid-Victorian society. By the 1840s and 1850s, traditional views of women's roles were coming under fire. The middle-class insistence that women must marry was harder and harder to sustain under evidence from the 1851 census that said women outnumbered men in the population, men tended to marry younger women, and almost half of all women over 20 had no spouse to support them. The unmarried women were called "redundant" or "odd," and there were few respectable ways in which they could support themselves, since the middle classes still frowned upon a woman's working outside the home. (Of course, most working-class women, which is to say most women, did work outside the home at the time.) Such work went against the idea that men and women should occupy "separate spheres"—his public, hers private. This put the middle-class woman in a difficult position, which was further sustained by certain ideologies of womanhood that praised the female for her "moral greatness" as well as for her asexuality, building a myth that had its most popular expression in the phrase "The Angel in the House" (originally the title of a poem by Coventry Patmore, which sold about a quarter million copies in the second half of the century). A physician, William Acton, is known for his observation that "the majority of women . . . are not much troubled with sexual feelings of any kind" as well as for his 1857 book on prostitution, which argued for sympathy and humane treatment of prostitutes, who should be viewed as victims rather than seducers (Acton in Tucker, p. 126).

Though Acton's views on women's asexuality were by no means universal, his book showed a preoccupation with prostitution as a social concern that increased throughout the late century. At the same time that Victorian commentators celebrated the virtues of self-control and marital fidelity, prostitution became a more and more visible feature of middle-class life. Middle-class men, with an ambition to rise in the world, postponed marriage until they were well-established, often seeking out prostitutes in the meantime. Aside from the full-time professionals, some, mostly working-class women, struggling to make ends meet on notoriously low wages, sought to supplement their incomes with the occasional exchange of sex for pay. Prostitution, among the Victorians, was not necessarily the full-time occupation we currently imagine it to be, though Victorian legislation played a part in this shift of attitudes. With the Contagious Diseases Acts of 1864, 1869, and 1870, prostitution came under state regulation and the women involved in sex for money began to be considered prostitutes, *per se*. These acts mandated compulsory genital inspection of women suspected of being prostitutes; they were screened for venereal disease

"The Goblin Market"

(syphilis, in particular, was extremely common), and those women who were infected were detained in lock hospitals, or hospitals containing venereal wards. This legislation itself was largely motivated by concerns for the spread of such diseases among enlisted men in naval ports and army garrison towns. But these men were never inspected or detained (after all, that would have been humiliating to the soldiers and might lower morale), and by 1870, the inequity of this treatment became the focus of feminist protest. The campaign against these acts brought to light many of the inequities as well as the errors of the Victorian sexual double standard, although the language of protest often drew on traditional views of middle-class femininity. Protesters argued, for example, that not only prostitutes but married women were the innocent victims of male promiscuity, as men (much like goblin men) brought diseases such as syphilis from the ports and into the home. The acts were repealed in 1886.

Victorian sexualities. Though often read to children, "The Goblin Market" was written also for adults and can be read for its complex portrayal of Victorian sexual concerns. While people today associate Victorianism with not only a sexual double standard but also a pervasive prudishness, Victorian views on sexuality were in fact far more diverse and open than is often assumed. The work of avant-garde poets and artists of the 1850s and '60s—Robert Browning, Algernon Charles Swinburne, Dante Gabriel Rossetti—is full of erotic content, enough to have given rise to the so-called "fleshly school of poetry" (Tucker, p. 131). Mid-to-late Victorian medicine is fascinated with sex and sexuality in a wide variety of forms. "Deviant" sexual preferences and practices, especially masturbation and inversion (similar to what would come to be called homosexuality), were favorite topics. William Acton's views on women's asexuality (see above) were by no means generally held; indeed, many felt that sexual desire in women remained latent until awakened, at which point it became insatiable, and others seem to have supported views that many would consider enlightened, even today. Female orgasm was also a subject of considerable medical attention, not least because some people of the era believed that it was necessary in order for a woman to conceive. Among the general population, limiting conception was a common concern, and contraception seems to have been in wide use by the 1860s, to judge from the shrinking size of England's middle-class families. On the other hand, the nineteenth century saw the beginnings of the use of artificial insemination on humans; 1884 marks the first recorded artificial insemination using donor (not the husband's) semen, a practice that became visible enough by 1897 for the Pope to ban it as adulterous.

The nineteenth century also saw the invention of the concept of the homosexual. Sex between men, which had been around forever, was reconstrued. Formerly understood as a behavior or series of acts, it became, by the end of the century, a defining category closely associated with political identity. One no longer merely happened to have sex with men; one *was* an invert or a homosexual. The term "heterosexual" followed. But lesbianism, as we think of it, would not be visible until even later. This invisibility stemmed in part from a common inability or unwillingness to imagine sex as sex without the presence of male genitalia. Nonetheless, erotic connections between women were probably common—facilitated, in fact, by some of the more traditional sexual ideology of the Victorian era. The myth of women's asexuality served to mask women's erotic lives. And the doctrine of separate spheres so effectively divided middle-class men from women that each could readily form intimate relationships within one's own sex. This is not to say that there weren't also plenty of close and highly sexual marriages between men and women, in the middle and other classes. Nonetheless, there had been a long tradition of "romantic friendship" among women in the eighteenth and nineteenth centuries, and when we look at the letters and diaries of Victorian women, many of them read with the intensity and passion of love letters. This does not indicate differences in modes of expression alone. It points also to intense emotional commitments, and the existence of bodily erotic practices.

The Poem in Focus

The contents. Like all the other maidens, as they go about their daily work, sisters Laura and Lizzie routinely hear the cry of the goblin merchant men hawking their forbidden fruits. Evincing a wide range of animal characteristics—a cat's face, a rat's pace, a cooing like doves—the goblin men entice young women to buy their fruit, after which they vanish from the sight and hearing of those who succumb. The sisters know that they are not supposed to look at the goblin men or buy their fruits, and though Laura is the first to voice this injunction, she is already peeping as she does so. From peeping, she moves to looking in earnest as Lizzie warns her not to.

Lizzie recounts the story of Jeannie, who ate the goblin fruit, "who for joys brides hope to have / Fell sick and died" ("Goblin Market," p. 9). And such is the effect of the goblin fruit that even Jeannie's grave proves infertile, barren of grass, and unable to support the daisies that Lizzie plants. But it is too late. Laura has already sought the fruit. Having no silver currency and no gold but what is on the land in the form of yellow flowers on the shrub and her golden hair, she trades a lock of hair, drops a tear, and secures the fruit.

After tasting the goblin fruit, Laura wants more. Her mouth waters as she begins to pine. But though other maidens, including Lizzie, can still hear the goblins cry, Laura hears nothing. She tries to grow her own from the "kernel-stone" or pit that she had saved. She even waters it with her own tears, but nothing grows from it. Laura's health gets progressively worse, and her interest in domestic duties flags. She refuses to eat.

Lizzie, unable to sit by and watch her sister's decline, and mindful of Jeannie's fate, sets out to look for the goblin men. Cautious, she brings a silver penny in her purse to purchase the fruit. But when she finds them, the goblin men refuse her offer of currency, inviting her to sit and eat with them instead. She refuses, and they grow violent. They start by calling her names, but their aggression escalates until they have "tor[n] her gown and soiled her stocking" ("Goblin Market," p. 11). They try to force her to eat, coaxing, bullying, pinching, kicking, mauling, and mocking to no avail; Lizzie "Would not open lip from lip / Lest they should cram a mouthful in" ("Goblin Market," p. 12).

Frustrated, the goblins eventually scatter, and Lizzie triumphs. She departs in possession of the "juice that syrupped all her face" as well as of her penny, jingling in her purse ("Goblin Market," p. 12). Inviting Laura to "Hug me, kiss me, suck my juices" Lizzie reveals that she has braved the goblin men for the sake of her sister ("Goblin Market," p. 13). And the antidote—the juice—works. After a fiery struggle, Laura recovers and is back to her old self.

Years later, when both are wives and mothers (though husbands are conspicuously absent), it is Laura who recounts to their children (all daughters, it would seem) the tale of the goblin men, and impresses on them that "there is no friend like a sister" ("Goblin Market," p. 16).

Illustration by Rossetti's brother, Dante Gabriel Rossetti, from an 1865 edition of "The Goblin Market."

Dangerous desire. Manifestly a story of forbidden fruit, "The Goblin Market" is one of the juiciest poems—literally and figuratively—to grace the pages of Victorian literature. The poem can easily be understood to be dealing with the extramarital sexual seduction of adolescent girls. A cautionary tale from this angle, it establishes clearly that dangerous men will love you and leave you. Beyond this, "The Goblin Market" suggests that the penalties for promiscuous sexuality may be even more severe. With it come the threats of disease, infertility, and even death. The poem recounts the destiny of Jeannie, who ate the goblin fruit and then "for joys brides hope to have / Fell sick and died," which can be taken to mean that she forfeited her virginity with fatal consequences ("Goblin Market," p. 9).

Moreover, the danger in the animalized goblin men relates not only to their masculinity but also to their strangeness. It is clear when Laura first utters an injunction against looking at goblin men that they embody a wide range of Victorian fears of otherness:

> We must not look at goblin men,
> We must not buy their fruits,
> Who knows upon what soil they fed
> Their hungry thirsty roots?
> ("Goblin Market," p. 2)

"The Goblin Market"

Whether "they" refers to the goblin men themselves, or to their sexualized fruits (an image which evokes the sexual temptation the men represent, or even their private parts), is extremely ambiguous, and may imply any number of other questions: Upon what "soil" have they fed? Where do they come from? Are they English or foreign? What are their "roots?" Upper class or lower? Or alternately, Where have they been? Who have they been with? In what "soil" have they planted their phallic, penetrative, "hungry, thirsty roots?" And what "soil"—what dirt, contamination, disease—have they brought with them?

One set of anxieties that the poem evokes is the possibility of mixed (race or class) coupling, as the lily white sisters, landed though cashless, mix with the decidedly foreign goblin men. Another anxiety is the ever-too-easy slippage into prostitution, as Laura trades a piece of herself ("Buy from us with a golden curl," the goblins suggest for the fruit she so desires ("Goblin Market," p. 4). As Laura pines away, her attempts to grow her own fruit can be seen as an attempt to regain fertility lost through contracting a vaguely specified sexually transmitted disease. But Jeannie's fate suggests the hopelessness of Laura's efforts; Jeannie's infertility persists even in her death: "While to this day no grass will grow / Where she lies low; I planted daisies there a year ago / That never blow" ("Goblin Market," p. 5).

Another Victorian anxiety surfaces in connection with what Laura's encounter may imply about female sexuality and desire. In the poem, even the most well-trained of Victorian girls (for it is Laura who first voices the prohibition against goblin men) cannot resist the lure of the fruit. And Laura's previously latent desire, once awakened, becomes insatiable: "I ate and ate my fill, / Yet my mouth waters still" ("Goblin Market," p. 5).

Other kinds of female desire suffuse the poem as well—including a desire to enter the marketplace, not as an object but as a subject performing the exchange, not as goods or currency but as a buyer or seller. That is to say, the poem contrasts the woman who is positioned as the desired object, for whom a prospective husband (in marriage) or a client (in prostitution) might barter, and the woman who wishes to go out into the world with money or goods to buy or sell. The poem can be seen as one that expresses considerable anxiety and ambivalence about the woman's making this move into the public sphere, which leads to a continual threat to violate the woman who tries. When Lizzie enters, armed with currency and ready to buy, the goblin men refuse to sell to her in ways that suggest the escalation of sexual harassment from flirtation ("Nay take a seat with us, / Honour and eat with us"), to bullying ("One called her proud, / Cross-grained, uncivil"), to physical assault and even rape ("Goblin Market," p. 11):

> They trod and hustled her,
> Elbowed and jostled her,
> Clawed with their nails,
> Barking, mewing, hissing, mocking,
> Tore her gown and soiled her stocking . . .
> ("Goblin Market," p. 11)

But Lizzie preserves at once her silence and her virginity, as she "Would not open lip from lip" ("Goblin Market," p. 12). Through Lizzie's silence, the poem may also be articulating the female writer's ambivalence about entering the public sphere, as suggested by the words used to describe the pain involved when the goblins "pinched her black as ink" ("Goblin Market," p. 12). But, though silenced, Lizzie manages to reverse the usual double standard, as she absconds with the juice of the goblin fruit and still in possession of her money (why buy the fruit when you can have the juice for free?). Her penny—representing at once her sexual self-possession and her financial independence—still jingles in her purse. Not only does the poem thus protest women's objectification in the marketplace, it also posits an alternative model of female love and community.

When one reads the poem as commentary on female desire, that desire takes a new form at this point, as Lizzie's love of her sister is represented as deeply passionate and manifestly erotic:

> "Did you miss me?
> Come and kiss me.
> Never mind my bruises,
> Hug me, kiss me, suck my juices . . . .
> Eat me, drink me, love me;
> Laura, make much of me. . . ."
> ("Goblin Market," p. 13)

Through the depiction of this highly eroticized sisterly love, Rossetti promotes salvation for women through sisterhood (a term that we can read more broadly to imply identification with other women). In doing so, she evokes her own work with fallen women and at the same time suggests that fallen women are not a category apart from so-called honest women, as the dominant culture would have it. Instead, these categories prove temporary and incidental. Neither sister is ruined; neither is even unmarriageable

> ### A NEW SPIN ON FORBIDDEN FRUIT
>
> Most readers familiar with the biblical story of the Garden of Eden will see echoes of the story in Christina Rossetti's "The Goblin Market." In the biblical tale, a serpent tempts Eve with the forbidden fruit, and she, in turn, tempts Adam. Both then realize that they are naked, become embarrassed, and cover themselves up. God, angry that they have disobeyed him, expels them from the Garden of Eden. This story has frequently been used in Western, Christian-dominated cultures to justify unequal treatment of women, who (along with Eve) are held responsible for the fall of man. Undoubtedly, Rossetti's fruit-bearing goblin men have animalistic (if not precisely serpentine) characteristics, and function as dangerous tempters of women. As in the Garden of Eden story, the fruit can represent sexual temptation, and Laura experiences an awakening to sexual knowledge not unlike Adam and Eve's. But Rossetti refuses to adopt the dominant interpretations of women as temptresses of men. She rewrites the story in such a way that Laura is never responsible for anyone's fall but her own, and even then, she is posited very much as an innocent victim. Rossetti, moreover, rethinks religiously based concepts of fallen-ness (as applied to women), purity, and the possibilities for salvation. Resisting irreversible categories such as the fallen woman (a concept based on the religiously driven idea that once a woman has sex, especially extramarital sex, she can never go back, never regain her lost virginity), Rossetti insists that so-called fallen women can be saved. Purity, the poem suggests, is less about virginity and more about one's personal integrity, goodness, and capacity to love. As Lizzie helps to restore her sister, Rossetti speaks not only to the Old Testament, but also to the New Testament, in which Jesus is said to sacrifice himself to save all of mankind from its original fall from grace in the Garden of Eden. By creating a female Christ-figure, Rossetti not only refuses to blame women for the fallen state of mankind, she also suggests that salvation (traditionally seen in Christianity as the province of man, and only one man at that) is something that women can do for each other. In this way, she feminizes the idea of salvation itself, even as she suggests that it is something that can occur any or every day.

or for that matter, infertile; the poem brings us to a moment "Afterwards, when both were wives / With children of their own" ("Goblin Market," p. 15). The end of the poem, when one reads it as commentary on female desire, seriously rethinks what constitutes a family as well. The anxieties of infertility, the stealing of the goblin juice followed fast by the proliferation of children, gesture ever so subtly to the possibilities of artificial insemination. That all the children seem to be sisters further suggests a fantasy of predominantly female community, wherein the implicit presence of husbands serves merely to lend social sanction to Rossetti's alternative version of the happy ending. Unlike so many other fairy tales, which end with the union of man and woman, it is a new generation of girls who are now joined "hands to little hands" as Laura bids them "cling together, / For there is no friend like a sister ("Goblin Market," p. 16).

Sources and literary context. Though largely intended for an adult audience, "The Goblin Market" reads like a children's poem in its rhythm and rhyme as well as in its strong moral tone. By the end of the nineteenth-century, it had found its way into Victorian school anthologies, a surface reading of it fitting nicely with moralistic writings that encouraged children to be good, stay within boundaries, and avoid talking to strangers. Rossetti's poem combines the concerns of earlier religious tracts for children, which focused on what children must do to achieve salvation, with the concerns of Victorian children's fiction, which tended to locate the source of the

"The Goblin Market"

child's problems in the errors of the surrounding adult population. Since raising children was considered the particular province of women, few would object to a woman writing children's stories. In fact, women were welcomed to this genre because of traditional gender roles, and they shrewdly took advantage of the freedom they had in it. It was quite common among Victorian women writers to subtly question, even subvert, traditional female roles through their stories. In its creation, Christina Rossetti joins many Victorian women writers who found the children's story a safe, even tactful medium through which to wrestle with a number of highly vexed social, sexual, and religious issues.

The religious character of the poem is manifest, though what it has to say about religion is quite subtle. Perhaps the most obvious literary source for "The Goblin Market" is the biblical story of the Garden of Eden. Explicitly a tale of the "fruit forbidden," the poem takes up the biblical themes of temptation and salvation with its undercurrents of sexual knowledge. The animalistic goblins are readily compared to the serpent, and Laura, to Eve. But "The Goblin Market" is no simple allegory, and further one-to-one correspondences to biblical characters and events begin to elude the reader: Where is Adam? Is Lizzie another Eve? Jesus? In this way, Rossetti builds on a tradition of poetic biblical revision. A perhaps inescapable source of religious literary material in the Rossetti family was Dante, though "The Goblin Market" is more directly a response to the writings of Milton, specifically his ***Paradise Lost*** (1667; also in *Literature and Its Times*), as well as his *Comus* (1634). Drawing on such influences, Rossetti rewrites the biblical story of the savior with a female Christ figure (Lizzie); salvation now comes through sisterhood.

Other literary sources came to Rossetti through members of her family. The first of these is the more subtle: her connection to sensation fiction and more particularly, the vampire story. Rossetti's uncle, John Polidori wrote *The Vampyre* (1819), one of the founding texts of the subgenre of vampire fiction that would climax in the nineteenth century with the 1897 publication of Bram Stoker's *Dracula*. Like Polidori's vampire Ruthven, Rossetti's not-quite-human goblin men inspire both fear and desire in their female victims. But just as Rossetti introduces important changes to her religious sources, so too does she revise her vampire source. In *The Vampyre*, Ruthven's female victims fall by the wayside—beyond the point of salvation, they are no longer of interest to the text. In contrast, the pair of females victimized by the goblins in Rossetti's poem save themselves and each other and emerge as the heroines. No longer divided into the innocent and corrupt, women in "The Goblin Market" are grouped together in the more general category of sisters, among whom such distinctions as pure versus fallen women are only superficial. Rossetti's depiction of the sisters as desiring and as sexual subjects, moreover, places her poem in the realm of the 1860s sensation novels, such as *Lady Audley's Secret* (by Elizabeth Braddon), whose heroines possess a disturbingly seductive sexual autonomy.

Another literary source from Rossetti's family life is that of the pre-Raphaelite brotherhood, among whose founders were both of her brothers. The pre-Raphaelites sought to resist what they saw as the materialism, artificiality, and formality of mid-Victorian painting. To do so, they looked to the past—especially to the medieval period, which they viewed as a simpler and less repressed time—for inspiration on new ideas of value, behavior, and aesthetics. Devoutly religious (in contrast to the many pre-Raphaelites

---

A REPUTATION ON THE RISE

Upon her death, Rossetti's work enjoyed a surge of popularity and eulogistic praise. At last, she vied for critical popularity with the most prominent female poet of the Victorian era, Elizabeth Barrett Browning. By the early twentieth century, Rossetti's popularity seemed to exceed Browning's; her treatment of troubled love (as compared to Browning's many depictions of happy and fulfilled love) appear to have come into vogue. In the early twentieth century, critics turned more of their attention to the biographical elements of Rossetti's work, as well as to the figure of Rossetti as a distinctly *female* writer. These concerns led to their understanding the line "there is no friend like a sister," for example, to be a reference to Christina's elder sister Maria, who helped save so-called sullied women and joined the Anglican order of the All Saints Sisterhood. Increasingly at this time, Rossetti's work was placed in the company of the great male religious voices. And in ***A Room of One's Own*** (1929; also in *Literature and Its Times*), Virginia Woolf identifies Rossetti as the female counterpart to the celebrated poet Alfred Lord Tennyson. Now, with the growing body of feminist scholarship, earlier images of Christina Rossetti as only a minor female poet or merely the younger sister of her famous brother have been almost entirely dispelled.

who claimed to be without religion at all), Christina Rossetti at once draws on and resists the movement's elaborate sensuality. "The Goblin Market" exhibits many of the characteristics associated with pre-Raphaelite art, including its lush imagery, its preoccupation with love, its association of the visible and natural world with the unseen and even sacred, right down to the sensuous implications of a woman's hair. Also, like the pre-Raphaelites, Rossetti counted among her favorite poets John Keats. "The Goblin Market" has echoes of Keats's "La Belle Dame Sans Merci," which also depicts wasting away, following an encounter with a magical other being.

Reception and impact. Always a well-received poet, Christina Rossetti's work seems to have risen steadily in popularity and critical interest from her day to our own. And though, until very recently, her work seemed to be overshadowed by that of her famous pre-Raphaelite brother, the painter and writer Dante Gabriel Rossetti, some contemporaries felt that Christina enjoyed a wider reputation as a poet and larger readership in their day. During her lifetime, Rossetti's greatest recognition came with the publication of *A Pageant and Other Poems* (1881). "The Goblin Market," though widely read and commented on after its publication in 1862, received mixed reviews. The fact that the devotional poems published with it received unanimous praise suggests that not all readers were equally pleased with this poem's considerable sensuality, its revisionist treatment of religious subject matter, or its fusing of the real and the unreal. Though conservative critics objected to the elements of fantasy in her work—finding something "grotesque and disproportionate in it," something that makes the two girls seem "inhuman and unreal"—fans found it to be a poem of "singular sweetness" (Charles, pp. 31, 32). Contemporaries compared the depiction of the goblin fruit with the vivid colors of her brother Dante Gabriel's painting. And, they debated the religious character of Rossetti's heroine Lizzie: Was she a saint, a savior, or merely a "little girl struggling to prevent the little goblin-men from pressing their fatal fruit into her mouth" (Charles, p. 61). The possibilities would continue to entrance readers from Rossetti's era to our own, continuing all the while to elicit admiration for this, her best-known poem, still considered a work "of fantastic subtlety, of airy grace, of remote and curious charm" (Charles, p. 35).

—Barri J. Gold

For More Information

Bristow, Joseph. "No Friend Like a Sister"?: Christina Rossetti's Female Kin." *Victorian Poetry* 33, no. 2 (summer 1995): 257–82.

Charles, Edna Kotin. *Christina Rossetti: Critical Perspectives, 1862-1982*. Selinsgrove, Pa.: Susquehanna University Press; London: Associated University Presses, 1985.

Gilbert, Sandra M., and Susan Gubar. *The Madwoman in the Attic: The Woman Writer and the Nineteenth-Century Literary Imagination*. New Haven: Yale University Press, 1979.

Harrison, Anthony H. *Christina Rossetti in Context*. Chapel Hill: University of North Carolina Press, 1988.

Morrison, Ronald D. "'Their Fruits Like Honey in the Throat / But Poison in the Blood': Christina Rossetti and *The Vampyre*." *Weber Studies* 14, no. 2 (1997): 86-96.

Rossetti, Christina. "The Goblin Market." In *The Goblin Market and Other Poems*. Mineola, N.Y.: Dover, 1994.

Tucker, Herbert F., ed. *A Companion to Victorian Literature*. Malden, Mass.: Blackwell, 1999.

Great Expectations

Charles Dickens

THE LITERARY WORK

A novel set in England in the first half of the nineteenth century; published in 1860-61.

SYNOPSIS

The orphan Pip, a blacksmith's apprentice, harbors aspirations to gentility that are inspired by his love for the disdainful Estella and that are mysteriously supported by an anonymous benefactor.

Great Expectations was the penultimate novel completed by the most popular novelist of Victorian England, Charles Dickens. Born in Kent, England, in 1812 to a family of modest means but great pretensions, Dickens's early life was marked by both humiliation and ambition. Dickens never forgot the period of financial crisis during his childhood, when following his father's bankruptcy, he was taken out of school and forced to work in a shoe-polish warehouse. While the episode was relatively brief, it marked Dickens's later life in many ways: in the development of his own ambitions, in his sympathy for the poor and especially children, and in his outrage at social injustice and bureaucratic heartlessness. *Great Expectations*, written when Dickens was at the height of his popularity and success, demonstrates all these concerns. His thirteenth novel, it was not overtly autobiographical, as his earlier *David Copperfield* (1850) had been, but in writing it Dickens employed a first-person narrative that elicits mixed sympathy and judgement for the protagonist Pip, an orphan raised by an abusive elder sister and her saintly husband, a blacksmith. Pip's story invokes an assortment of real-life issues of Victorian England, ranging from its relationship to its colonies, to its imperfect educational system, to its overarching concern with social mobility and status.

Events in History at the Time the Novel Takes Place

Economic anxiety and social mobility. Dickens set the substance of *Great Expectations* at roughly the time of his own childhood; the action of the novel begins in 1812, the year Dickens was born, when Pip is seven. This was a time of great economic anxiety in England; the American Revolution, Napoleonic wars, and the War of 1812 had caused a drain on the national economy, and industrial developments were putting agricultural as well as other manual laborers out of work. The development of the threshing machine in farming (patented 1788; in widespread use by 1830) and mechanized looms in clothmaking (patented 1786; in widespread use 1815-1840) were two significant changes in labor practice; both inventions increased production, which led to greater economic security for their owners and managers, but also reduced the need for unskilled laborers, which created unemployment at the lower ends of the economic scale. Manual labor, always a marker of lower social status, was giving way to industrialized forms of doing business, and the new industrial elite was

Great Expectations

Charles Dickens

reshaping the English class system. Alongside the old class system, which was based on land and status, a new economy arose, based on industry, information, and capitalist investment. While these changes generated anxiety, especially among the landed aristocracy, they at the same time augmented opportunity and excited hopes among the lower orders. If hard work could earn money, perhaps it could also earn higher social standing.

Education, always a marker of class standing, was beginning to be a means to social mobility as well. In an era before compulsory or standardized education (attendance at elementary school would not be made mandatory until 1880), a "gentleman's" education in classics, mathematics, and literature conveyed a social standing that more technical or skill-based education did not. At the beginning of the nineteenth century, there was no national educational system in England. Wealthy children were usually educated at home, and middle-class children attended private schools. The options for poor and working-class children were limited to unregulated, unprofessional schools like "dame schools," often run by poorly trained women who supervised children in cottage industries (such as plaiting straw or lacemaking) while they performed a perfunctory instruction in reading. In the novel Biddy improves on her dame-school education and uses it as a means of self-support and social improvement.

Poor or laboring-class children, and even some middle-class youths, might also serve an apprenticeship as their education into a trade. In the apprentice system, a child or youth was legally "bound" for seven years to a master who would, in return for a premium paid at the beginning of the contract and free labor throughout its term, teach him the trade. After seven years an apprentice could become a "journeyman," free to hire himself out for daily wages. Blacksmithing, shoemaking, and millinery—as well as law and surgery—were taught through the apprenticeship system, which varied widely in efficacy and professionalism.

As the century progressed, a variety of educational organizations were formed to provide free or inexpensive education for the poorer classes; both religious and secular educations were provided through these philanthropic organizations. Basic literacy and arithmetic skills could and did increase one's economic viability in the new economy, as they opened up white-collar professions such as clerk, accountant, or trader.

But economic improvement did not always translate into social mobility. England at the beginning of the nineteenth century was still a very hierarchical, socially stratified society. Social status depended on blood and birth, land and leisure. While money could not buy blood or birth, or lineage, (except through a socially advantageous marriage), fresh sources of wealth such as factory-owning and overseas trade meant that land and leisure could now occasionally be purchased by a new social strata, the middle-class professional. A gentleman's status was derived primarily from his leisure: a gentleman lived off investments (or land) and hired servants. While most of the newly rich were not themselves considered "gentlemen," having derived their wealth through hard work, their children might possibly aspire to that status, with an education to polish off the rough edges and servants to maintain their households. Pip's education with Mr. Pocket is concerned with giving him the appearance of gentility, while his legacy provides him leisure. Ironically, in *Great Expectations*, when Pip is given both the financial means and the education to become a gentleman, a role he has aspired to only for Estella's sake, he is given them by an escaped convict who also turns out to be her father. Social status, the novel suggests, is both ephemeral and implicated in the very crimes it condemns.

Crime and punishment. *Great Expectations* begins and ends with the pursuit and apprehension of an escaped convict, and crime and punishment figure largely in the plot of the novel. The criminal justice system was changing in England at the turn of the nineteenth century; in 1800, there were over 200 crimes for which capital punishment could be imposed, while by 1841 only eight remained (Philips, p. 156). Dickens had treated the failures of the criminal justice system directly in his early novel *Oliver Twist* (1838), in which his young thieves are threatened with the death penalty for stealing silk handkerchiefs. His outrage at the injustice of the death penalty for relatively minor crimes against property was widely shared, and contributed to the changing climate of criminal justice in the early part of the nineteenth century.

"Transportation," or forced resettlement in one of England's colonies (first America and, after American independence, Australia) offered an alternative to capital punishment, which was felt to be far more humane, and indeed some former prisoners prospered in the colonies. Convicts working under government supervision were allowed some hours a day to work for themselves; others, however, labored under "private assignment" to non-government employers, who might maintain them in virtual slavery. Their terms and conditions varied widely, as did the entire administration of criminal justice before the various reforms of the nineteenth century.

By 1830 about 58,000 convicts had come to Australia; this marked the high point of transportation, after which the practice began a gradual decline because anti-slavery feeling came to influence the convict system as well. Private assignment of transported criminals was abolished in 1840, the sentence of transportation was abolished in 1858, and the practice of transportation in lieu of execution gradually decreased after that time. Like Magwitch in the novel, most transported criminals were career criminals and thieves, though some were political prisoners as well. Transported criminals were barred, under penalty of their original death sentences, from ever returning to England, even after their terms of labor (usually between seven and fourteen years) had expired.

The crimes in *Great Expectations* include both the "white collar" crimes of forgery and fraud, and more violent attacks on persons and property. Of course the class system infected the criminal justice system; the lower-class Magwitch is condemned far more harshly for his part in the forgery and swindling scheme than his more genteel partner Compeyson. Access to legal representation could make the difference between life and death for the accused prisoner, and in the absence of a public defense system, many accused criminals were unable to defend themselves. Prisoners did not speak in their own defense, nor did they speak directly to the lawyers who would represent them in court. Legal cases were prepared by an attorney or solicitor, such as the novel's Mr. Wemmick, who would then usually turn over the actual arguing of the case to a "barrister," a lawyer licensed to appear in court, such as Mr. Jaggers. The system set up barriers between the lower-class accused and the upper-class legal community that often resulted in the former's being only seen, not heard.

Criminal justice in the early nineteenth century was as swift as it was severe. In London, criminals awaited trial only briefly (although in some rural areas criminal trials were held only once a year), and sentencing and punishment followed rapidly upon conviction. Prisons were for the most part mere holding cells, often operated by private individuals for profit. The concept of the prison as a locus of either reform or punishment was still relatively new in the nineteenth century; convicted criminals were either executed or served hard labor, either on the "Hulks"—prison ships that also provided lodging for prisoners awaiting transportation—or in Australia.

England and its colonies. England had been a colonial power for over two centuries by the era depicted in *Great Expectations*; the nineteenth century was, however, a time of great expansion and re-evaluation of England's colonial presence. England began to settle Australia in 1788 as a penal colony. Having lost the American colonies in the Revolution, England maintained its presence in Canada and Australia, and began expanding its political and economic presence in Asia and Africa as well. By the end of the Napoleonic Wars in 1815, England had expanded its holdings in the Indian subcontinent to include Afghanistan and Burma, and had acquired Holland's former colonial holdings in South Africa as well. Both commerce and conviction underlay England's imperial development; what novelist Rudyard Kipling would later call "the white man's burden" to spread Christianity and, more generally, "Englishness" throughout Asia and Africa co-existed, more or less comfortably, with capitalist expansion of trade throughout the world. Among the colonial

Great Expectations

reaches of the empire, India and Africa, in particular, provided a combination of missionary and capitalist opportunities for the younger sons of the gentry and for the hard-working sons of modest families, who could become rich and respected through trade or government service. In *Great Expectations*, empire is the source of wealth, even redemption, for convict and respectable citizen alike.

The Novel in Focus

Plot summary. The action of the novel takes place between 1812 and 1829, and is narrated by its main character, Pip (Philip Pirrip) from the vantage point of adulthood, sometime in the late 1850s or early 1860s. His story begins on Christmas Eve, when Pip is in his seventh year; an orphan being raised by his sister, known always as Mrs. Joe, and her husband Joe, a blacksmith, Pip is visiting his parents' and brothers' gravesites when he is accosted by a convict. The convict threatens to kill him if he does not bring food the next day; this Pip does, stealing the food out of his sister's pantry. On his way to deliver the food, he encounters another, younger, escaped convict, but eludes him to deliver the food. On Christmas Day, during a family party, soldiers arrive at the blacksmith's house—not to arrest Pip for pilfering the food, as he at first believes, but to enlist the blacksmith's help in mending some handcuffs. Pip and Joe join the soldiers in their search for the escaped convicts. Both are apprehended, and Pip sees "his" convict take responsibility for the stolen food before being taken away in chains.

Months pass. Pip endures his sister's abuses and the difficulties of life in the forge, as well as a growing sense of guilt at his still unacknowledged theft. An eccentric wealthy woman living in the town, Miss Havisham, requests Pip's presence at her manor house (Satis House). There, Pip meets a proud and beautiful girl, Estella, who is Miss Havisham's ward. Miss Havisham lives with her in almost complete isolation and decay, surrounded by the appurtenances of a wedding that never occurred. Miss Havisham asks to have Pip visit often, and amuse her by playing cards with Estella. During one of these visits, Pip meets relatives of Miss Havisham's who resent him for his assumed closeness to her; among them is a boy of his own age who challenges him to fight. Pip does so reluctantly; he beats the boy, and for the first time Estella seems pleased with him. After eight or ten months, Miss Havisham ends the arrangement when she pays the requisite premium to have Pip apprenticed to Joe. The visits with Estella cease, but Pip continues to call upon Miss Havisham once a year, on his birthday.

During this early time, Pip attends a local school, run by an incompetent old woman and her great niece, Biddy. Pip confesses to Biddy that he wants to become a "gentleman" to impress Estella, though he laments openly not having chosen a more attainable object, like herself. Biddy teaches Pip as much as she can, and lets him know that she is bothered by the attentions of the blacksmith's journeyman, a worker named Orlick. Orlick resents the fact that Pip's relationship with Joe makes him "superior," and after Pip is apprenticed, his resentment only increases. One evening, while both Pip and Joe are out of the house, Mrs. Joe is attacked and left for dead; Pip suspects Orlick, but cannot prove his suspicions. In the aftermath of the attack, Biddy moves to the forge to help care for Mrs. Joe.

Pip feels ashamed of Joe and the forge because of his attachment to the heartless and snobbish Estella. Thus, he is delighted when, after he has served four years of his apprenticeship, Miss Havisham's lawyer, Mr. Jaggers, announces that Pip has come into "great expectations," and that he is to be released from his apprenticeship and educated in London to be a gentleman. The only two conditions attached to his new status are that he will not attempt to identify his benefactor and that he will retain the name Pip. While Pip assumes that Miss Havisham is his benefactor, Mr. Jaggers will not confirm his suspicions.

Pip moves to London, where he lodges with a distant relative of Miss Havisham's, Herbert Pocket (the young boy who had challenged him to fight at Satis House) and is educated by Herbert's father, Matthew. Herbert tells him Miss Havisham's story: the daughter of a brewer, she was engaged to be married when her fiancé jilted her on the morning of the wedding. The fiancé, now revealed as a forger and swindler, was in league with a half-brother of Miss Havisham's. Her heart broken, Miss Havisham laid waste to her house and stopped all the clocks at the moment she learned of her failed engagement (twenty minutes past nine). Estella, he learns, was adopted by Miss Havisham when a child, and has been brought up to wreak Miss Havisham's revenge on the male sex.

Befriended by Jaggers's clerk, Mr. Wemmick, Pip also learns more about Mr. Jaggers's criminal practice. Wemmick is a businesslike man who maintains a tiny "castle," complete with

In a scene from the 1946 film version of *Great Expectations*, Anthony Wager, as Magwich, grabs Pip when he encounters him in the graveyard.

drawbridge, turrets, and cannon, in Walworth, a suburb of London, where Pip visits him and meets his father, known as the "Aged Parent." At Walworth, Wemmick becomes a friend and confidant to Pip, but he adopts an air of businesslike unapproachability in the office, maintaining a strict separation of private and public life. Another curious character enters the picture, Mr. Jaggers's housekeeper, a former client whom Mr. Jaggers claims to have "tamed" (Dickens, *Great Expectations*, p. 195). The housekeeper, it is said, had murdered a younger woman whom she perceived as a rival; Jaggers has engineered her acquittal and with it her continuing service to him.

Estella moves to Richmond, another suburb of London, and Pip sees her frequently. Suspecting that Miss Havisham intends Estella for him, he does not speak to her of his attachment, but suffers when she seems to flirt with other men.

Pip and Herbert fall greatly into debt, not being educated for any profession, yet having great expectations of themselves. Mrs. Joe dies, and Pip makes a rare return to the forge to attend her funeral. Since coming into his "expectations" he has distanced himself from Joe and the forge even further than when he was visiting Miss Havisham. When Pip turns 21, he is given an annual income but does not learn any further details about his benefactor. He resolves, however, to use part of his income to endow a position for Herbert at a shipping and trading company, Clarriker's, without Herbert's knowledge, and Herbert begins to succeed in the business, learning all about England's trade with its Asian colonies.

Estella becomes engaged to a former student of Matthew Pocket's, a well-to-do man named Bentley Drummle (nicknamed the "Spider" by Mr. Jaggers for his sneaky, brutal appearance). Drummle is brutal and cruel, and Pip remonstrates with Estella about her choice, but she claims that, since she has been brought up without a heart, she cannot bestow it on anyone. Even Miss Havisham is shocked at her cruelty, but Estella reminds her that she is Miss Havisham's creation and cannot be expected to act otherwise.

Pip is 23 when he learns the true identity of his benefactor: it is not Miss Havisham, but the convict he had fed on the marshes that long-ago Christmas Eve, a man named Abel Magwitch. Magwitch had been transported to Australia for his crimes (as yet unnamed) and in returning to England, he risks the death penalty. He has prospered as a sheep-farmer in Australia, and devoted all his income (via Jaggers, who had been his

Great Expectations

attorney) to Pip's education and transformation into a "gentleman." Ashamed of his benefactor, Pip endeavors to hide him, and soon learns that the other convict, a man named Compeyson, is aware of Magwitch's return. Through Herbert Pocket, Pip also discovers that Compeyson is the man who jilted Miss Havisham. Details in Magwitch's story convince Pip that Estella is his daughter and that Jaggers's "tamed" housekeeper is her mother. Jaggers is the surprising link between all these disparate characters; his legal profession connects him across class boundaries to virtually everyone in the novel.

After learning the truth about his benefactor, Pip returns to Satis House to confront Miss Havisham. She admits that she has used him and his expectations to confound her own relatives (by letting them believe he, not they, might inherit her substantial wealth) but has otherwise had nothing to do with his legacy. Pip forgives Miss Havisham and as he is leaving, a fire breaks out and he saves her from the conflagration, at some cost to himself. Injured, he returns to London. Miss Havisham survives the fire but dies soon thereafter.

Pip resolves to leave England with Magwitch, whom he has learned to love and respect. He sequesters him in a boarding house near the Thames River and plans to depart with him on a freighter to Europe as soon as Wemmick suggests that it is safe. Just before the planned departure, Pip receives a mysterious message inviting him to a limekiln near the old forge; he complies, and is met by Joe's former journeyman Orlick who, now mysteriously in league with Compeyson, has resolved to kill Pip. Mystified by Orlick's malevolence, Pip learns that the journeyman's resentment motivated the attack on Mrs. Joe as well as this final attack. Saved by Herbert Pocket, who has followed him, Pip returns to London and tries to carry out the escape plan, but Orlick has warned Compeyson, and their boat is met before Magwitch can escape. Magwitch and Compeyson struggle, and Compeyson is drowned. Magwitch is condemned to death, his wealth a forfeit to the crown. But before he can be executed, Magwitch dies of injuries sustained in the struggle with Compeyson. As he lies dying, Pip reveals to Magwitch that he knows and loves Magwitch's daughter.

Pip falls ill, and is nursed back to health by Joe, who also pays his debts. When he is fully recovered, Pip returns to the forge, intending to discard his expectations and propose to Biddy. However, she and Joe have just been married, and Pip wisely says nothing of his plan. Chastened, he joins Herbert Pocket at Clarriker's and rises from clerkship to partnership; he lives in Cairo in charge of the Eastern Branch of the business.

Eleven years pass. Pip returns to England, where he sees that Joe and Biddy have a child named for him. Visiting Satis House for a final time, he meets Estella there. Bentley Drummle, who mistreated her, has died in a fall from a horse. Estella and Pip are reconciled in the ashes of Satis House, and as the novel ends they leave the house together, hand in hand.

Gender and violence. *Great Expectations* depicts male-female relationships as violent and destructive in all but a few rare cases. Mrs. Joe beats both her husband and Pip; Joe is himself a vic-

---

VICTORIAN PHILANTHROPY

The Victorian period was a great age of philanthropy. The rise of evangelical Christianity in the late eighteenth and early nineteenth centuries awakened the consciences of many, and indeed it is impossible to contemplate Victorian society without being aware of the great social injustices which divided it. While in earlier times private charity or church-based charity had been common, the large-scale social change of the Victorian period rendered such solutions impotent, and many philanthropic organizations sprang up to fill the void. Organizations such as the Royal Society for the Prevention of Cruelty to Animals (founded 1824), the National Society for the Prevention of Cruelty to Children (founded 1884), the National Society for Promoting the Education of the Poor in the Principles of the Church of England (1811), the British and Foreign Schools Society (1808), and many others, were motivated to a great extent by the energetic women who found in philanthropy a socially acceptable outlet for their skills and talents. Dickens was ambivalent about such efforts. In *Bleak House* he satirizes the philanthropic women who tirelessly raise money for evangelizing Africa but ignore their own children, in characters like Mrs. Jellyby. Yet he was himself involved in a small-scale effort, spearheaded by his friend Angela Burdett-Couts, to train former prostitutes in useful skills and help them to emigrate. Dickens seems to have preferred such private generosity as Magwitch's and Pip's, which was based on personal connection rather than self-aggrandizement or a desire for structural reform.

tim and witness of domestic violence. As he informs Pip, Joe's father, also a blacksmith, "were given to drink, and when he were overtook with drink, he hammered away at my mother, most onmerciful. It were a'most the only hammering he did, indeed, 'xcepting at myself" (*Great Expectations*, p. 61). Miss Havisham inflicts her own violence on herself at the failure of her intended marriage, and Estella is, we learn after the fact, "used with great cruelty" by her husband, Bentley Drummle (*Great Expectations*, p. 437). Although Wemmick and Herbert Pocket both marry, presumably happily, in the course of the novel, as do Biddy and Joe, their peaceful relationships are anomalous in this novel. Orlick evidently beats and leaves Mrs. Joe for dead, and Estella's mother has killed a woman out of sexual jealousy. Pip himself seems to understand his relationship with Estella in violent terms; he claims, for example, that he has "suffered every kind and degree of torture that Estella could cause [him]" (*Great Expectations*, p. 280).

The novel's emphasis on the violence seemingly inherent in sexual relations comes at a time when issues of gender were hotly debated. Although England was ruled by a queen, women in general had few if any legal rights at the beginning of Victoria's reign; throughout the century, what came to be called "The Woman Question" grew ever more urgent, as women (and some men) pressed for female emancipation in marriage, in property rights, in child custody, and in social and professional relations. In 1839 the Infant Custody Act was passed, allowing women to petition for custody of their infant children in the rare case of divorce or separation; this was the first instance in English legal history of legislation specifically concerning women's rights. The act was followed by decades of debate about, and the eventual passage of, the Matrimonial Causes Act (1857) and the Married Woman's Property Acts (1870, 1882), the first of which legislated more liberal divorce laws and the second of which allowed women to retain some control of their property in marriage. A corollary to the Matrimonial Causes Act was a right gained by magistrates in 1878 to grant separation to wives if their husbands were convicted of aggravated assault. Although women would not be granted the vote in England until 1928, the foundation of a woman's movement was laid in the nineteenth century even in politics: John Stuart Mill introduced the first bill for woman suffrage in 1867, during his brief career as a member of Parliament.

The debates about custody, married women's property, and divorce made public the private operations of the Victorian home. They revealed the ugly and often violent realities of gendered power relations that lay behind the public ideology of domesticity. Put baldly, they demonstrated that domestic bliss was frequently an illusion based on the often-violent suppression of one human being's rights, most often the wife.

THE TWO ENDINGS OF *GREAT EXPECTATIONS*

Great Expectations was completed in June 1861, with the final episode scheduled for publication in August. During that year, Dickens had been in constant contact with the novelist Edward Bulwer-Lytton, whose novel *A Strange Story* was scheduled to follow the serial publication of *Great Expectations* in the magazine *All the Year Round*. The two novelists had read and critiqued each other's work throughout the year, and when Bulwer-Lytton read the conclusion to *Great Expectations* in proof, he advised Dickens to change it. Dickens had originally written a briefer, more somber conclusion in which Pip and Estella—who had remarried after Bentley Drummle's death—meet only briefly on the street and are parted forever. Bulwer-Lytton objected to the sadness of this ending, and Dickens's revised version, with the meeting between Estella and Pip at Satis House, was published in its place. Dickens continued to edit the final words of the novel; in manuscript and in proof, he wrote, "I saw the shadow of no parting from her but one." However, at the proof stage he dropped the last two words, and the sentence appeared in *All the Year Round* as "I saw the shadow of no parting from her." Finally, in the 1862 one-volume edition, the line appears as, "I saw no shadow of another parting from her" (*Great Expectations*, pp. 440-41). This is the version quoted above, as it is the standard printed version. While the differences between these latter versions may seem minor—especially compared to the major difference wrought between the proof and published versions—they indicate Dickens's continued wrestling with the question of Pip and Estella's future even after the novel was published.

Dickens's depictions of gendered violence likewise operate to reveal the failures of domesticity and its disconnection from romantic love. His violent women, often brutally tamed by even more violent men, are aberrations, women who have seized power and often masculine identity

Great Expectations

and are then punished for it. Mrs. Joe is the most striking example of a woman who is masculinized by her dominance in the household, and who is tamed by Orlick, an even more brutal force than herself.

Conversely, both Wemmick and Herbert Pocket find brides for themselves who support their desire for a quiet domesticity; like Biddy, Wemmick's Miss Skiffins and Herbert's Clara are quiet, efficient, and long-suffering women who willingly enter a secluded domesticity based on mutual concern, companionship, and care, rather than property or status. Pip's fruitless attachment to Estella, and his inability to recognize until too late the love and care that someone like Biddy could offer him, are symptomatic of the failure of his romantic ideals, which had—as so many nineteenth-century novels do—linked love and status, here with disastrous results. It is significant in this regard that Pip's ultimate union with Estella is accomplished only after she has been ill-treated by her first husband, Bentley Drummle; like Mrs. Joe, perhaps, she is brutally "tamed" into domesticity.

Sources and literary context. Dickens was the most popular novelist in England at the time he was writing *Great Expectations*. The realistic novel had become the dominant literary form by then, due in large part to Dickens's and other writers' development of it in the earlier part of the century. The novel's most direct antecedent, though, is not another novel but the Renaissance sonnet cycle by Sir Philip Sidney, *Astrophil and Stella*. In that cycle, the helpless lover (Astrophil, or "star-lover," a stand-in for the author), pines for his beloved, Stella (or "star"). The cycle is written in the traditional Petrarchan mode, in which the beloved becomes the metaphoric light by which the lover steers, but is also the source of all his frustration and anxiety. By taking the names (Philip/Pip; Stella/Estella) and the basic relationship from the sonnet cycle and turning them into a realistic novel, Dickens explores the destructiveness as well as the power of romantic love.

Estella is the one character in the novel for whom biographers and critics have consistently sought a real-life counterpart. Dickens's personal life at the time he was writing *Great Expectations* was itself public knowledge, even public scandal: he had separated from his wife, Catherine (née Hogarth) in 1858, and was living with her sister Georgina and nine of his children while Catherine stayed in London with their eldest son Charley. In a strikingly open admission of the failure of his domestic ideal, Dickens published a statement in his magazine *Household Words* soon after the split, recognizing the separation but claiming that all parties involved were guiltless. Georgina's position in the household was officially that of housekeeper and substitute mother, and Dickens was widely believed to be involved at the time with an actress, Ellen Ternan, who retired in 1859. Dickens's financial responsibilities in 1860, then, were legion: he sup-

---

DICKENS AS PUBLISHER

Dickens's first novel, *The Pickwick Papers*, which began appearing in 1836, marked the beginning of a revolution in publishing. Dickens had first come to public attention with *Sketches by Boz* earlier that same year; these were a series of illustrations accompanied by Dickens's text, originally meant simply to illuminate the image, but used by Dickens to develop longer and more complex characters and incidents. Dickens turned the sketch, a popular eighteenth-century form, into something larger, a novel, in his *Pickwick Papers*, with the text now dominating in the illustrations. Both the *Sketches* and *Pickwick Papers* were published in monthly "numbers," paperbound booklets containing a single episode. Often working only hours ahead of a printer's deadline, Dickens continued to publish his subsequent novels serially. Readers eagerly anticipated the next installment of their favorite novel, passing the current issue from reader to reader while they awaited further development of their hero's life.

Already popular beyond imagination, Dickens took control of the publishing process for his novels in the 1850s. As editor of the magazines *Household Words* and later *All the Year Round*, Dickens serialized his own and other authors' novels. *Great Expectations* was originally designed for monthly publication, but Dickens decided to issue it in weekly parts in *All the Year Round* when sales for another novel by Charles Lever proved disappointing. Sales of the magazine increased dramatically when Dickens's novel replaced Lever's, thus suggesting—along with the number of other venues in which the novel appeared—its immediate popularity. The novel appeared in *Harper's Weekly* in the United States while it was running in *All the Year Round* in England; Harper's subsequently published it in a two-volume book form, while Dickens's English publishers, Chapman & Hall, issued it in a three-volume version for libraries, and at least four other editions appeared in England and the United States in the next three years.

ported his wife and one child in one home, himself, his sister-in-law, and nine children in another, his mother, her daughter-in-law, and five children in yet a third, and Ellen Ternan and, at times, her mother and two sisters in a fourth. If Ternan was not the cold and contemptuous Estella, she may have served that function in Dickens's imagination, as she was certainly a financial and emotional drain on him (Carlisle, "Introduction," p. 15).

Another potential model for Estella is Maria Beadnell, Dickens's first serious love, whom he courted in the early 1830s. Seductive, witty, and both older and better educated than he was, Maria seems never to have taken Dickens's suit seriously, and she wounded him desperately by calling him a "boy" at his coming-of-age party; Estella is similarly contemptuous of Pip (Kaplan, p. 53). Whether Estella's original is Maria Beadnell, Ellen Ternan, or Sir Philip Sidney's "Stella," however, she remains the motivating force of the novel and entirely Dickens's own creation as well.

Finally, *Great Expectations* is a realistic novel. Realism, the dominant literary form of the middle nineteenth century, is a set of literary conventions that equate the "real" with material life in society; works that take for their subject the daily lives of relatively ordinary people, in a believable setting, are thus classed as "realistic." While events in the novel may strain credulity at times, Dickens's emphasis on the economic and social struggles of a single character, and the relationships he makes and breaks during those struggles, mark it as realistic in a solidly Victorian sense. Dickens emphasizes the conditions of Pip's life and Pip's own concerns with social status and hierarchy throughout the novel. Realism took many forms in the Victorian period, from the broad social satire of William Makepeace Thackeray (in, for example, his novel *Vanity Fair*) to the working-class fictions of Elizabeth Gaskell (in, for example, *Mary Barton*). Dickens's *Great Expectations* shares significant elements with works at both ends of the spectrum.

Events in History at the Time the Novel Was Written

England and India. In the beginning of the nineteenth century, England's presence in India was controlled by a single private enterprise, the British East India company. In 1857, however, the Sepoy Rebellion (also known as the Indian Mutiny) demonstrated to the English at home that all was not well in their distant colony. The thrust of the rebellion by Indian soldiers (known as sepoys) who served the East India Company lasted from May to December 1857, and marked the beginning of widespread Indian resistance to British rule. The British reaction was to transfer control of India from the East India Company directly to the English government. Victory for the British was hard-won, with traces of armed resistance erupting until the spring of 1859. Meanwhile, the popular press in England published accounts of the rebellion that captured the English imagination, which led to India and things Indian becoming extremely popular. From perceptions of it as a rather distant colony, India became central to England's conception of itself; popular imperialism took hold and was consolidated when England's Queen Victoria crowned herself Empress of India in 1877. In *Great Expectations* the fictional firm Clarriker profits from the India trade, and the shift in the novel from Australia as a place of punishment to India as a

---

DICKENS AND COMEDY

A brief summary cannot convey the tone or quality of the comic writing for which Dickens was so justly famous. *Great Expectations*, to some reviewers' minds, marked Dickens's welcome return to his earlier, comic style, after the publication of "darker" masterpieces such as *Dombey and Son* and *Bleak House*. While the emphasis on crime and punishment, violence and degradation may not seem funny to contemporary readers, Dickens's genius lay in his ability to move freely between tragedy, melodrama, and comedy, sometimes even in one scene. In *Great Expectations* much of the comedy derives from the persistent social climbing of a variety of characters, from Mrs. Joe's "Uncle Pumblechook" to the church clerk, Mr. Wopsle, to Miss Havisham's obsequious and fawning relatives. Mr. Wopsle's abandonment of the church for the stage is the occasion of a famously comic scene in which Herbert and Pip attend an extremely unskilled production of *Hamlet*, which features a ghost who has a cough and a Hamlet who is badly overplayed by the foolish Wopsle. Pip himself does not escape the satirist's eye; his desperate attempts at gentility are often foiled by his own excesses, as when he hires a servant (whom he refers to as the "Avenger") and then has nothing for him to do.

source of wealth parallels the larger shift in England's imperial ambitions during the period.

Criminal justice. Although there were over 200 capital offenses on the books in the beginning of the nineteenth century, by the time Dickens was writing *Great Expectations* the death penalty was rarely invoked. Also by 1860, the hulks had been demolished and the sentence of transportation had been abolished. The middle nineteenth century saw the increasing professionalization of criminal justice, with the development of a professional police force, sentencing reforms, and the introduction of parole. Our sympathy for the convict Magwitch is thus consonant with the tenor of the times; an increasing emphasis on repentance and reform had replaced the earlier, more punitive system of criminal justice.

Reception. Early reviews of *Great Expectations* were somewhat mixed. While the critic in *Saturday Review* found it "new, original, powerful, and very entertaining," the novelist Margaret Oliphant, writing in *Blackwood's Edinburgh Magazine*, claimed that it "occupie[d] itself with incidents all but impossible, and in themselves strange, dangerous, and exciting . . . " (Oliphant in Rosenberg, pp. 617, 625). Writers such as George Gissing, G. B. Shaw, and George Orwell all praised *Great Expectations* for its realistic depiction of childhood, its use of the first-person narrator, and—as Shaw said—its "consistent truthful[ness]" (Shaw in Rosenberg, pp. 627, 633, 641). Edward Whipple, reviewing the novel in *Atlantic Monthly* in 1861, particularly praised Dickens's achievement in the character of Magwitch, and voiced the opinion which still stands today:

> The character [of Magwitch] is not only powerful in itself, but it furnishes pregnant and original hints to all philosophical investigators into the phenomenon of crime. In this wonderful creation Dickens follows the maxim of the great master of characterization and seeks "the soul of goodness in things evil." . . .

> Altogether we take great joy in recording our opinion that *Great Expectations* is a masterpiece.
> (Whipple in Tredell, p. 23)

—Elisabeth Rose Gruner

For More Information

Carlisle, Janice. "Introduction." *Great Expectations*. Boston: Bedford, 1996.

Cody, David. "British Empire." *The Victorian Web*. 1988. http://landow.stg.brown.edu/victorian/history/empire/Empire.html (12 Oct. 2000).

Dickens, Charles. *Great Expectations*. Ed. Janice Carlisle. Boston: Bedford, 1996.

Everett, Glenn. "Political and Economic History of Great Britain." *The Victorian Web*. 1987. http://landow.stg.brown.edu/victorian/history/empire/Empire.html (12 Oct. 2000).

Gilmour, Robin. *The Idea of the Gentleman in the Victorian Novel*. London: Allen & Unwin, 1981.

Kaplan, Fred. *Dickens: A Biography*. New York: William Morrow, 1988.

Mitchell, Sally, ed. *Victorian Britain: An Encyclopedia*. New York: Garland, 1998.

Patten, Robert L. *Charles Dickens and his Publishers*. Oxford: Oxford University Press, 1978.

Philips, David. "'A New Engine of Power and Authority': The Institutionalization of Law-Enforcement in England 1780-1830." *Crime and the Law: The Social History of Crime in Western Europe since 1500*. Ed. V. A. C. Gatrell, et al. London: Europa, 1980.

Pool, Daniel. *What Jane Austen Ate and Charles Dickens Knew: From Fox-Hunting to Whist—the Facts of Daily Life in 19th-Century England*. New York: Simon & Schuster, 1993.

Rosenberg, Edgar, ed. *Great Expectations: A Norton Critical Edition*, by Charles Dickens. New York: Norton, 1999.

Tredell, Nicholas, ed. *Charles Dickens: Great Expectations*. New York: Columbia University Press, 1998.

Walder, Dennis. "Reading *Great Expectations*." *Approaching Literature: The Realist Novel*. Ed. Dennis Walder. London: Routledge in association with The Open University, 1995.

Hedda Gabler

by
Henrik Ibsen

Born at Skien, Norway, in 1828, Henrik Ibsen was the son of a merchant family that for a few years of his life remained well-to-do. In 1836, however, Ibsen's father went bankrupt and the now poverty-stricken family was forced to move to an isolated farm. Intending to become a doctor, the 15-year-old Ibsen was apprenticed to an apothecary at Grimstad where he lived until 1850. During that period, Ibsen fathered an illegitimate child, to whose financial support he contributed for 15 years. He also published his first play *Catiline* (1850). After failing his university entrance examinations for medicine, Ibsen turned to literature as a full-time pursuit and became artistic director of the struggling Christiana Norwegian Theater. In 1864, frustrated by the theater's failure and other professional tribulations, Ibsen, now married with a son, left Norway for a lengthy, self-imposed exile. He spent 27 years abroad, during which Ibsen composed many of his best-known plays: *Brand* (1866), *Peer Gynt* (1867), The *Pillars of Society* (1877), *A Dolls' House* (1879), and *Ghosts* (1881). The 1870s saw a maturing Ibsen move away from the romantic, phantasmagoric plays of his youth to the realistic, socially oriented works on which his modern reputation mainly rests. One of Ibsen's mature plays, *Hedda Gabler* (1890) is a dark domestic drama. By turns, its protagonist fascinates, repels, and bewilders with behavior rooted in an upbringing at odds with the role prescribed for middle-class Norwegian women in her day.

> **THE LITERARY WORK**
>
> A play set in Norway during the late nineteenth century; first performed in 1891, published in 1890.
>
> **SYNOPSIS**
>
> Frustrated by her lack of purpose, a bored wife attempts to manipulate the lives of others, with disastrous consequences.

Events in History at the Time of the Play

Norwegian society in the nineteenth century. The nineteenth century saw Norway undergo some transformative political developments. In 1814, following a brief struggle with Denmark, Sweden won control of Norway, then went on to rule both nations through the time of Ibsen's play until the union was dissolved in 1905. At the outset, Norway adopted its own constitution (established in 1814 at Eidsvoll) and assembled its own parliament, undergoing a vigorous period of political change that prompted social and economic changes as the century progressed. These changes, reflected in *Hedda Gabler*, bespoke greater power for formally disenfranchised groups.

- Farmers and labor groups became a political power in Norway.
- The country granted its citizenry full religious freedom.
- Parliament revised Norway's Poor Laws several times over.

Hedda Gabler

Henrik Ibsen

- Criminal laws and punishments grew increasingly humane.
- Primary education law decreed seven years of compulsory schooling for all.
- New labor commission started to investigate working conditions.
- Norwegian women's suffrage movement began in earnest.

> **FROM *THE DISTRICT GOVERNOR'S DAUGHTERS***
>
> "I was told in straight-forward, clear-cut words what I had fearfully suspected: *it almost never falls to a woman's lot to marry the man she loves; and yet it is her destiny to marry someone,* because the unmarried state is the saddest of all. 'In this respect, you are all princesses,' Mother said.... To be married off without inclination ... without love! And then, suppose you loved someone else?... Oh God ... Let me escape my fate! I want to live alone...."
>
> (Collett, p. 108)

Not until the 1870s did Norwegian women begin to agitate for the vote in earnest. Consciences were stirred by the spread of British writer John Stuart Mill's *Subjection of Women*, which argued persuasively to various Scandinavians that "the legal subordination of one sex to the other" was "one of the chief hindrances to human improvement" (Mill, p. 196). In truth, agitation for the vote involved only a minority of women in this early stage. On the other hand, it cloaked a less obvious but far more pervasive discontent that Norwegian women, or at least one groundbreaking Norwegian woman, had expressed decades earlier. Recognized as a direct influence on Ibsen and the first to seriously discuss women's rights in Norway, Camilla Collett ignited dialogue on the subject by publishing *The District Governor's Daughters* (1854-55). "The long-repressed scream of my life" was how she described the novel, generalizing the plight of the heroines, describing it as not only her saga but also the fate to which most women of the Norwegian upper classes were confined (Collett in Garton, p. 35).

Featured in *The District Governor's Daughters* are four sisters—Marie, Louise, Amalie, and Sofie. The first marries a religious, middle-aged pedant, then dwindles away in the short space of a few years, the stifling marriage robbing her of her will to live. Though she does not love him, the second daughter marries a promising enough prospect, a tutor who turns alcoholic, after which she drones away her days, taking up weaving in order to pay for her son being raised away from his father. Just as dishearteningly, Amalie ensnares herself in a tedious, humdrum marriage. At the heart of the novel is Sofie, who becomes smitten with her father's private secretary and with his help escapes marrying another disreputable man, only to end up, through a mix of unhappy coincidences and social conditioning, in a plainly loveless match.

The publication of *The District Governor's Daughters* generated a storm of debate, not because the novel agitated for anything as overt as votes for women. Rather the plot lobbied for an attitudinal change, in contrast to all the moralizing texts of the era, which counseled women to take up their dutiful roles as wives and mothers with nary a murmur. Collett's novel challenged this age-old cant, aiming to effect an inner liberation from the sexist, still-pervasive socialization of the day. In her view, a wife's feelings deserved to be privileged on par with her husband's. She too deserved happiness. Through this and later writings, Collett sparked nothing short of a revolution, one that Ibsen would do much to advance.

More social developments energized the century, including the opening of new railways and banks and the successful development of commerce between nations and within Norway itself. Lands formerly belonging to the Crown became available to everyone by public sale, while laws governing monetary loans were liberalized. Generally, Norway's social system became less aristocratic than in the past. An increasingly populous, upwardly mobile middle class emerged. Yet even in the 1890s, Norwegians adhered to a rigid, albeit weakening, social hierarchy, a reality that undergirds relationships in Ibsen's *Hedda Gabler*.

> Aristocrats, officials of the state, officers of the army, and large landowners constituted the leisure class. Next in importance were the professional classes: doctors, professors, lawyers, and important merchants, who operated the large and growing merchant marine. Below them in prestige were the middle classes, including burghers, small business men, artisans, ships' captains and officers, small landowners, and minor district officials who had privileges dating from the middle ages. At the bottom of the social scale came the laborers and landless farmers . . . upon whom fell the maintenance of the state.
> (Kildahl in Trudeau, p. 337)

As the daughter of General Gabler, Hedda occupies the highest social rank in the play. But if her superior social status makes her envied and desired by others, it becomes a source of increasing frustration for Hedda herself. Her father's death leaves the play's protagonist in a fine fix: she is a 29-year-old spinster without the financial means to support the lifestyle to which she is accustomed. Seeing no other recourse, Hedda steps down a social notch to marry the plodding but dependable Tesman—a middle-class academic. Long before their wedding trip is over, Hedda comes to despise him. But despite her contempt, she is too much the aristocrat and too afraid of scandal ever to contemplate leaving him.

On learning that her former schoolmate Thea Elvstead has dared to abandon a loveless marriage to follow Eilert Løvborg to town, a shocked Hedda exclaims, "But what do you think people will say about you, Thea?" (Ibsen, *Hedda Gabler*, p. 240).

By contrast, the lower-middle-class Thea, a governess who became her employer's second wife, expresses indifference to society's opinion: "God knows they'll say what they please. I only did what I had to do" (*Hedda Gabler*, p. 240). While the mousy Thea manages to adapt, change, and survive, the bolder Hedda remains trapped by the tenets of her class and upbringing.

Marriage among the upper classes. In nineteenth-century Europe, romantic love became an increasingly important factor in courtship and marriage, especially among the middle and upper classes. Women and men sought emotional as well as economic fulfillment from their prospective spouses; courting couples were often openly affectionate towards each other, walking arm in arm and embracing in public.

NINETEENTH-CENTURY SEXUAL REVOLUTION

The writings of Camilla Collett have been identified as a source of the current of feminism that runs through Ibsen's plays. The current runs strongly through his *A Doll's House* and, to an extent, through *Hedda Gabler*. Neither Nora in the first play nor Hedda in the second are reared to consider any other future but a secure and respectable marriage to a man of their own class. In this respect, Collett herself is like them. The condition of marriage, points out one scholar, is what Collett strives to change. "Neither here nor anywhere else in her writings does Camilla Collett dispute the fact that marriage is a woman's ideal state" (Garton, p. 36). Some forty years later, Ibsen takes a next step. To be sure, all his heroines have not evolved to this point yet, a reflection of a range of attitudes in a transformative era. In *A Doll's House*, Nora has the courage to break free from an inhibiting marriage, to venture forth in search of the wisdom and experience she feels she lacks. But Hedda, hampered by her aristocratic upbringing and fear of scandal, remains imprisoned in her marriage, meddling in the lives of others to alleviate her frustrations.

Despite the new emphasis on mutual affection and tenderness, economic and social considerations remained very much a part of matchmaking. Among the Scandinavian bourgeoisie, men seldom married or were accepted as suitors unless they had the financial means to provide a comfortable home and to support a wife, children, and at least one household servant in a manner befitting their social status. Not every man could meet this criteria for eligibility, with the result that the frequency of marriage among the middle-to-upper classes dropped sharply toward the end of the nineteenth century. Cultural anthropologists Jonas Frykman and Orvar Löfgren note that "it was the daughters of the bourgeoisie who were hardest hit by this development. The unmarried woman had few opportunities to pursue her own career and acquire her own home" (Frykman and Löfgren, p. 101).

Generally, it was expected that men would be firmly established in their careers and public life before they married. In many situations, that meant that the husband was often several years older than his wife, who usually married straight from her parents' home or from finishing school. She thus knew little of the world, except what her father and, later, her husband chose to share with her. "Marriage was based upon the two being united into one—the one being the man" (Frykman and Löfgren, p. 101). The dynamics of power within such marriages had the potential to become more complex, however. If wives depended on their husbands economically, in time the husbands became emotionally dependant on their wives, expecting to receive "womanly" care and affection after returning home from daily toil in the public sphere. The house was to be a haven, with wife as guardian of a husband's private life and future mother of the husband's children.

Throughout his work, Ibsen explores the issues associated with upper-class marriages. In Isben's play *A Doll's House* (also in *Literature and Its Times*), Nora's realization that her upbringing has left her woefully ignorant of the world prompts her to leave her overprotective husband and educate herself to become a fit wife and mother. In *Hedda Gabler*, the title figure, well past her youth, marries for financial security, only to discover that she despises her doting but mediocre husband and fiercely resents the constricting world of middle-class respectability to which he belongs and to which she has committed herself. Hedda rejects nearly everything about her new role as Tesman's wife, dismissing *love* as "that syrupy word" and refusing to entertain the possibility that she is pregnant with her husband's child (*Hedda Gabler*, p. 250).

Bourgeoisie versus bohemianism. Early in the play, the recently married Hedda Gabler Tesman complains to a friend about "this tight little world I've stumbled into"—referring to the bourgeois existence she now faces as George Tesman's wife (*Hedda Gabler*, p. 256). Secretly she yearns after the reckless bohemian lifestyle led by her former flame, Eilert Løvborg. In nineteenth-century Europe, the terms *bourgeois* and *bohemian*, both notoriously difficult to define, took on greater meaning and significance. *Bourgeois*, derived from the Old French *borjois*, became associated, not always flatteringly, with middle-class materialism and respectability. To disdainful bohemians, "the bourgeois was the person enjoying a secure income and no debts, who passed through life comfortably with warm feet, cotton in his ears, and a walking-stick in his hand. This was the bourgeois existence to which every small shopkeeper aspired" (Seigel, p. 6).

By contrast, the term *bohemian*—derived from the French *bohemien* meaning "vagabond" or "gypsy"—was generally used to describe the rootless lifestyle of a community of artists, writers, and intellectuals. While the bohemian movement may have originated in France during the 1840s and 1850s, it spread throughout much of nineteenth-century Europe, including Russia, England, and Scandinavia. Distinguishing characteristics included artistic aspirations, financial instability, romanticism, and, in some circumstances, criminal connections to the underworld. Sexual freedom, political radicalism, excessive drinking, and drug-taking were also often associated with—but by no means exclusive to—bohemianism.

Historian Jerrold Seigel writes that bohemianism developed largely out of opposition to respectable bourgeois life. Bohemia, he asserts "was not a realm outside bourgeois life but the expression of a conflict that arose at its very heart"; in his words, "it was a space within which newly liberated energies were continually thrown up against the barriers being erected to contain them, where social margins and frontiers were probed and tested" (Seigel, pp. 10-11).

In *Hedda Gabler*, Ibsen confines most of the play's action to the solid, respectable bourgeois world—of devoted maiden aunts, embroidered bedroom slippers, and scholars angling for professorships—a world his protagonist finds stifling. However, he continually hints at a darker, more dangerous world existing alongside it. Hedda, Thea, and Judge Brack each allude to the red-headed Mademoiselle Diana, an opera-singer and prostitute, who is Løvborg's former mistress. Moreover, Hedda reveals to Løvborg that his bohemian lifestyle had been part of what attracted her to him, that, as a young girl, she desired "some glimpse of a world that . . . [she was] forbidden to know anything about" (*Hedda Gabler*, p. 265). On learning that Løvborg has reformed his wild lifestyle through the influence of Thea Elvstead, Hedda does what she can to manipulate him into backsliding. Lacking the courage to free herself from the constraints of respectability, she conspires to sample the bohemian life vicariously through Løvborg, whom she pictures presiding over a society party "with vine leaves in his hair" (*Hedda Gabler*, p. 272).

The Play in Focus

The plot. The play begins as Miss Juliana Tesman, an elderly spinster living with her invalid sister, visits the home of her orphaned nephew, George Tesman, recently married and just returned from an extended wedding trip. Nephew and aunt greet each other fondly. During the course of their conversation, it is revealed that George has married Hedda Gabler, the beautiful, aristocratic 29-year-old daughter of the late General Gabler; that the newlyweds are living somewhat beyond their means in a recently built townhouse that George has bought to please his bride; and that George, a rising young scholar, has prospects of gaining a university professorship that would solve their economic difficulties. Miss Tesman offers financial assistance, which George gratefully accepts, and assures her nephew that he will surely gain the professorship, owing to the absence of any serious competition for the position. The most likely rival would have been George's old classmate, Eilert Løvborg, who has recently published a much-praised book but whose dissipated habits have continually undermined his professional success.

When Hedda enters, Miss Tesman greets her effusively but Hedda remains aloof. She becomes vexed, however, when George hints to his aunt that a child may be on the way, and denies that she is expecting. After Miss Tesman departs, Hedda receives another visitor, Thea Elvsted, whom she knew as a girl at school and with whom, years before, George had been briefly involved. Thea informs the Tesmans that Eilert Løvborg, her stepchildren's former tutor, has returned to town, and she asks them to treat him kindly. Tesman soon leaves to write Løvborg a friendly letter. Alone with her one-time schoolmate, Hedda manages to discover that Thea was unhappily married to a much older man, whom she has now left, and that Thea's devotion to the erratic Løvborg had inspired him to reform and try to reclaim his reputation as a serious scholar. Thea fears, however, that Løvborg still loves a woman from his past, who supposedly threatened to shoot him with a pistol after the romance ended. Hedda suggests that the woman in question may have been a red-headed opera singer who is also one of the town's foremost courtesans.

Judge Brack, a sophisticated man of the world, is the next visitor to call on the Tesmans. The judge brings disturbing news: Løvborg's new book and reformation may make him a serious contender for the university professorship. Consequently the Tesmans might have to forego the luxuries Hedda was counting on enjoying, like a butler and a riding horse. Displeased by the prospect of straitened circumstances, Hedda leaves to practice with her father's pistols, one of the few amusements she has left.

Later, calling upon Hedda, Brack finds her alone with her pistols. Hedda confides to the judge that she is bored already in her marriage to a plodding scholar and that she only accepted George's proposal because her father's death left her without money or prospects. Clearly her discontent stems from more than her disdain for

> ### ILLICIT PASSIONS
>
> The sexual double standard is portrayed as alive and well at the time in which *Hedda Gabler* takes place. Among the Scandinavian upper classes, chastity and propriety were expected from young unmarried women; however, it was not considered unusual or even undesirable for young men to acquire extramarital sexual experience with women of the lower classes (servants and tradeswomen) or prostitutes. In some cases, the charms of respectable—and therefore inaccessible—women were even blamed for young men's sexual indulgences. It is this very line of reasoning that surfaces in a parliamentary debate against prostitution in Stockholm, Sweden, towards the end of the nineteenth century: "Would that the educated and wealthy Stockholm woman could learn to dress for festive occasions in such a way that her attire would not arouse emotions and passions in young men, driving them, after they leave the party, to go to places where they can satisfy their lust before they go home!" (Frykman and Löfgren, p. 103). In Ibsen's play, *Hedda Gabler*, as a general's daughter, led a fairly sheltered life but thrilled to hear of Eilert Løvborg's illicit pursuits, which no doubt included liaisons with prostitutes. But however titillating Hedda might find Løvborg's accounts of his amorous adventures, she shrinks from indulging in any herself, rejecting Løvborg as a sexual partner and committing suicide rather than becoming Judge Brack's mistress.

George and his family, however; Hedda feels her entire life lacks purpose. Like Tesman, Brack hints at the possibility of Hedda's becoming a mother but again she hotly denies the likelihood. Brack also insinuates the he desires a more intimate relationship with Hedda, whereupon she asserts her intention to remain faithful to George, despite her contempt for him.

As Thea predicted, Eilert Løvborg calls upon the Tesmans that day. Løvborg reassures George that he is not contending for the professorship.

Hedda Gabler

Susannah York as Hedda in a 1981 Off-Broadway production of *Hedda Gabler*.

He does, however, wish to rebuild his reputation as a scholar and, to this end, has written the manuscript for a sequel—which he believes is superior—to his recently published book. Løvborg shows the manuscript to the Tesmans and Brack, who are suitably impressed. The men try to persuade Løvborg to join them at a party Brack is giving that evening but he refuses: Hedda invites Løvborg to take afternoon tea with her and Thea instead. During a private conversation between Hedda and Løvborg, it is revealed that they were once strongly attracted to each other and that Løvborg had at the time tried in vain to persuade Hedda to become his lover. Even now they experience the old attraction; Løvborg reproaches Hedda for having thrown herself away on the mediocre George; Hedda meanwhile resents Thea's influence over her former suitor.

At the tea table, Hedda seats herself between Thea and Løvborg, becoming increasingly jealous of their connection. Intending to sow dissension, Hedda betrays Thea's earlier confidence that Thea is worried about Løvborg's resuming his old habits while in town. This revelation makes Løvborg perversely determined to prove Thea wrong. Encouraged by Hedda, he agrees to accompany Brack and Tesman to the party, promising to return to the house at ten o'clock. While Thea worries, Hedda exults in her ability to manipulate Løvborg and predicts his triumphant return from the party "with vine leaves in his hair—fiery and bold" (*Hedda Gabler*, p. 271).

Løvborg does not return at the appointed hour, but George comes home the next morning with a sad tale of how Løvborg gave in to his vices, drank too much, and, while inebriated, dropped his precious manuscript, which George retrieved. Admitting the brilliance of Løvborg's projected sequel and his own envy, George nonetheless resolves to return the manuscript—Løvborg's only copy—to his rival. But when news of his invalid aunt's impending death distracts him, Hedda seizes and hides the manuscript.

George leaves to visit his dying aunt, whereupon Brack arrives at the Tesmans' and informs Hedda that a drunken Løvborg ultimately ended up at the police station after an altercation at the establishment of a former mistress, Mademoiselle Diana. Brack further remarks that Løvborg's conduct has made him a social outcast. Brack, for one, would be displeased to see Løvborg as the Tesmans' frequent guest.

Soon after Brack's departure, a distraught Løvborg shows up at the Tesmans' house. Thea, who has spent the night there, greets him eagerly but is shattered by his confession that he has resumed his old lifestyle, destroyed the manuscript on which they labored together, and concluded that they have no future together. Comparing Løvborg destroying the manuscript to killing a child, Thea breaks with him. Alone, Løvborg confesses to Hedda that he had actually lost the manuscript but could not bring himself to confess his irresponsibility to Thea. His life in ruins, Løvborg only wants to end it all. Hedda gives him one of her father's pistols and urges him to arrange his suicide "beautifully" (*Hedda Gabler*, p. 288). Løvborg sadly bids her farewell and leaves. Hedda then destroys Løvborg's manuscript in earnest by burning it in the stove.

Returning home after his aunt's death, George asks Hedda about the manuscript and is horrified to learn that she destroyed it. Hedda claims that she did it for George's sake, to prevent anyone from eclipsing him. George believes her and even feels flattered that his wife would take such risks to protect him. The destruction of Løvborg's masterpiece still distresses him, however. Just then, Thea arrives at the Tesmans', upset over rumors she has heard in town about Løvborg's being hospitalized. Judge Brack arrives to confirm those rumors, reporting that Løvborg is dying of a gunshot wound. George is astounded, Thea distraught, but Hedda rejoices that Løvborg "had the courage to do what—had to be done," a reaction not lost on Brack (*Hedda Gabler*, p. 296). The judge's suspicions are further roused by Thea's artless confession that Løvborg destroyed the manuscript. George again regrets the loss of his rival's masterpiece, but Thea reveals that she still has Løvborg's notes. To Hedda's chagrin, George immediately resolves to put aside his own work and dedicate his life to the reconstruction of Løvborg's manuscript. Thea eagerly volunteers to help him in this pursuit.

Meanwhile, Brack draws Hedda aside and disillusions her about the nature of Løvborg's death. Far from arranging a beautiful suicide, Løvborg was found mortally wounded in the stomach at Mademoiselle Diana's and died in the hospital without regaining consciousness. Moreover, Brack recognized the pistol Løvborg was carrying, which is now in police custody, as belonging to the late General Gabler. It is only a matter of time before Hedda will be implicated in Løvborg's sordid death and face a terrible scandal—unless she buys Brack's silence by agreeing to become his mistress, as the judge has long desired. Refusing to accept his power over her, Hedda retires to an inner room and commits suicide by shooting herself in the temple with her father's other pistol, to the incredulity of George, Thea, and Brack.

An unwomanly woman. The enigmatic figure of Hedda Gabler has come to dominate much of the criticism and commentary about Ibsen's play. In an 1890 essay, the Irish-born dramatist George Bernard Shaw declared:

> Hedda Gabler has no ethical ideals at all, only romantic ones. She is a typical nineteenth-century figure, falling into the abyss between the ideals which do not impose on her and the realities she has not yet discovered. The result is that though she has imagination and an intense appetite for beauty, she has no conscience, no conviction: with plenty of cleverness, energy, and personal fascination she remains mean, envious, insolent, cruel in protest against others' happiness, fiendish in her dislike of inartistic people and things, a bully in reaction from her own cowardice.
>
> (Shaw in Trudeau, p. 334)

Many of Shaw's contemporaries shared his view, considering Hedda to be a monster, a destroyer, or a likely inmate for an insane asylum. Repellent though her character was, most scholars conceded that she held their attention.

In a letter to his French translator, Ibsen himself provided important additional insights into the anti-heroine: "Hedda as a personality is to be considered rather as her father's daughter than as her husband's wife" (Ibsen in Trudeau, p. 337). Indeed, the play's stage directions place a portrait of the late General Gabler in a prominent location in the Tesmans' drawing room; several references are also made to the general's influence in his daughter's life—specifically, how they rode together and how he taught her to shoot his pistols. One might argue that Hedda was reared almost more as a son than a daughter, which accounts at least partly for her poisonous discontent and rejection of traditional feminine roles.

Thea Elvstead and Miss Tesman serve as foils to Hedda in that they *do* accept those roles. Thea has audacity that Hedda lacks—the former schoolmate leaves a loveless marriage. Subsequently Thea transforms herself into a helpmate, or more exactly an amanuensis, for Eilert Løvborg and, later, for George Tesman. His aunt, Miss Tesman, the lone spinster in the trio, is likewise willing to sacrifice herself for others: loaning money to her newly married nephew, tending to her invalid sister, and eagerly anticipating the birth of Hedda and George's children, to whom she may further devote herself. By contrast, Hedda presently has little use for the life of the mind, although she is jealous of Thea's influence over Løvborg, and even less use for living vicariously through others. Money and respectability interest her. But she refuses to trouble herself over whether Tesman lands his "wretched professorship," and she recoils in disgust at the prospect of motherhood, declaring "You'll never see me like that! . . . I won't have responsibilities!" (*Hedda Gabler*, p. 256). Caught in a vise, Hedda chafes at the limitations society places on her but lacks the moral courage to defy them. Ultimately, her intense self-absorption costs her even her influence over the husband she battles, who turns from his devotion to her to his reconstruction of Løvborg's manuscript, with Thea by his side. To his wife's query of "Is there nothing the two of you can use me for?" the oblivious Tesman responds, "No, nothing in the world," an exchange that underscores Hedda's increased isolation (*Hedda Gabler*, p. 303). In the final moments of the play, Hedda also rejects the role of mistress—which Judge Brack offers as the price for his suppressing her complicity in Løvborg's sordid death. Instead she opts for the romantic "solution" she had aspired for Løvberg. She commits suicide.

Hedda can be viewed as a woman caught betwixt and between. Her inability to find or make a niche for herself in the society in which she lives coincides with the dramatic transformations that women in Norway were beginning to experience. Emancipation, a gradual process, had in fact started as early as 1854, when Norwegian women acquired the same inheritance rights as men. This, it will be remembered, was the same year Collett first published *The District Governor's Daughters*, exposing the unhappiness of many middle-to-upper-class wives. This emotional reality began with the help of this novel to dawn on more and more Norwegians; meanwhile, the country's women gained an ever-growing number of rights. In 1863 the government declared women over 25 to be legally competent. Further developments in the women's movement included the right to take university entrance examinations (1882) and to earn a university degree (1884), as well as the founding of the Norwegian Association for the Rights of Women (1884), and the more specific Association of Women's Suffrage (*Stemmerettes foreeninger*; 1889). Barely a decade later Norway became the first European nation to grant suffrage to women, who received the vote in municipal elections in 1901 and universal suffrage in 1913. Ibsen's play found its way onto the stage in the midst of all this flux. As noted, the suffragettes of his day were a minority; nevertheless, the social and political changes inspired by actual Norwegian women of the era provide an ironic counterpoint to the plight of the fictional Hedda Gabler Tesman, chafing at her restraints but lacking the courage to break free of them in a constructive manner.

Sources and literary context. Scholars have often debated whether Ibsen based Hedda Gabler on anyone he knew in real life. If such a person existed, then the most likely candidate is 18-year-old Emilie Bardach, fashioned more diabolically in the drama. Ibsen met Bardach in the summer of 1889, while vacationing with his wife in Gossensass, a small town in the mountainous Austrian Tyrol. The only daughter of wealthy Viennese Jews, Bardach led the typically sheltered, ornamental life of a young woman in upper-class society, calling upon her peers, attending balls and concerts, and making the acquaintance of eligible men, although, ultimately, Bardach was never to marry. Ibsen and Bardach met in early August and spent much time together before her return to Vienna in September. Although they never saw each other again afterwards, they exchanged letters for several months, until Ibsen essentially curtailed the correspondence in February 1890. Bardach, however, kept a diary of that Gossensass summer and had Ibsen's letters to her published after the playwright's death in 1906. The printing of the letters caused a scandal, but Bardach maintained that her relationship with Ibsen was entirely innocent. Nonetheless, Ibsen apparently harbored affectionate, even romantic feelings towards Bardach, referring to her as an "enigmatical princess" and later declaring, "The summer in Gossensass was the happiest, most beautiful of my whole life. I scarcely dare to think about it, And yet I must, always. Always!" (Ibsen in Templeton, pp. 238, 241).

How was this woman like the fictional Hedda? In February 1891 Ibsen described the character of a woman he had met in the Tyrol to his friend the scholar Julius Elias, who thus recorded the conversation:

> What fascinated and delighted her was to steal other women's husbands. She was a demonic little wrecker; she often seemed like a little beast of prey who would have liked to include [Ibsen] in her booty. He had studied her up close. But she had no luck with him. "She did not get me, but I got her—for a play. I imagine (here he chortled again) that afterwards she consoled herself with another man." In matters of love, she could only experience morbid fantasies.
> (Elias in Templeton, pp. 244-45)

Several Ibsen scholars point out that Hedda's grasping, predatory personality is impossible to reconcile with that of the young woman to whom Ibsen wrote so fondly after their summer idyll. It has been suggested that the unflattering portrait may have represented his attempt to exorcise any lingering romantic feelings for Bardach by transforming her into a seductress and himself into her victim.

Models for Hedda Gabler were perhaps drawn from other sources, however. At least one critic has suggested that Ibsen may have reworked the Norse legend of Brynhild, the Valkyrie (supernatural handmaiden) who is rescued from an enchantment by the hero Sigurd but, in a case of mistaken identity, marries not him but his passive friend Gunnar. Tragedy results when Brynhild discovers her error. Ibsen's earlier play, *The Vikings of Helgeland* (1858), was a more straightforward adaptation of the legend, in which Hjordis (the Brynhild figure) slays the conflicted Sigurd, cherishing the pagan hope of being reunited with him in death, only to discover that his wife has converted him to Christianity. At this point in Ibsen's play a furious, despairing Hjordis throws herself into the sea. The tragedy in the play focuses not so much on the fall of the great but on the destruction wrought by human deceit and falsehood. In *Hedda Gabler*, the protagonist marries not the fiery Løvborg, whose bohemian lifestyle excites her, but the dull, plodding academic Tesman, whom she soon comes to despise. Jealous of Løvborg's intimacy with another woman, Hedda practices deceit, setting in motion a chain of events that culminates not in glorious liberation but in sordid scandal, sexual blackmail, and her own suicide.

Hedda Gabler tends to be classed among Ibsen's realistic plays, most of which were written between the 1870s and 1890s. Like *The Pillars of Society*, *A Doll's House*, and *Ghosts*, the play concerns itself with domestic, social, and psychological drama. In Ibsen's words, the intent is "to describe human beings, human emotions and human destinies on the basis of certain prevailing social conditions and views" (Ibsen in Beyer, p. 157).

Reviews. The month was December 1890. A few weeks before *Hedda Gabler* premiered onstage, Ibsen published his play to some of the harshest reviews in his career. Most critics—whether in Scandinavia, England, or the United States—were astonished and horrified by the complex and often-unsympathetic protagonist. The literary critic of *Morgenbladet* in Oslo called the character of Hedda Gabler "a monster created by the author in the form of a woman who has no counterpart in the real world" (*Morgenbladet* in Templeton, p. 204). The reviewer for *Aftenposten* similarly declared, "We neither understand nor believe in Hedda Gabler. She is not related to any one we know" (*Aftenposten* in Templeton, p. 204). Of the work as a whole, Georg Gothe in *Nordsik Tridskrift* wrote, "The whole characterization of the play is obscure . . . [The characters] are alive, but only to a degree; deep inside them there is something abstract, cold, dead" (Gothe in Lyons, p. 17).

Early productions of *Hedda Gabler* in performance were likewise poorly received. Its premiere at the Residenztheater in Munich, Germany, on January 31, 1891, failed to yield accolades. Seven more productions within the year—in Germany, France, and Scandinavia—also fared poorly with audiences and critics. In April 1891, however, a London production—starring Elizabeth Robins, a talented American actress—played to full houses and attracted considerable attention, both positive and negative. Nearly all the critics conceded the strengths of the cast, even if they expressed ambivalence towards the play itself. A reviewer for *The Times* wrote, "[Ibsen] is really admirable in the dissection of character. The subjects that he operates on and whose vitals he lays bare for our inspection are the reverse of heroic. They are all poor creatures at bottom, with selfishness for their mainspring of action, but they are undeniably human, and to that extent interesting, if repulsive" (Egan, p. 219). Justin McCarthy of *Black and White* was more enthusiastic, calling *Hedda Gabler* "Ibsen's greatest play" and the title figure "the most interesting woman that Ibsen has ever created. Not Nora, nor Ellida, nor Hedvig, nor Svanhild approach her for intensity of interest, for complexity of character" (McCarthy in Egan, p. 221). Finally, a critic writing for the *Pall Mall Gazette* acknowledged the play's dark tone and the disturbing nature of its protagonist but argued that the play nonetheless cast a formidable and seductive spell:

> *Hedda Gabler*, though tragic enough in all conscience, is brilliant and powerful throughout. . . . There is no question that the play caught hold of the audience. Some who went to curse, not inaudibly blessed; and to many who went willing to bless it was a dramatic revelation. Critics who feel it is expected of them may pretend that they were shocked or that they were bored. But they certainly followed the play for three good hours with every outward sign of lively interest.
> (*Pall Mall Gazette* in Egan, p. 220)

—Pamela S. Loy

For More Information

Beyer, Edward. *Ibsen: The Man and His Work*. Trans. Marie Wells. New York: Taplinger, 1978.

Collett, Camilla. *The District Governor's Daughters*. Trans. Kirsten Seaver. Norwich, England: Norvik Press, 1991.

Egan, Michael, ed. *Ibsen: The Critical Heritage*. London: Routledge and Kegan Paul, 1972.

Frykman, Jonas, and Orvar Löfgren. *Culture Builders: A Historical Anthropology of Middle-Class Life*. New Brunswick: Rutgers University Press, 1987.

Garton, Janet. *Norwegian Women's Writing 1850-1990*. London: Athlone, 1993.

Ibsen, Henrik. *Hedda Gabler*. In *Four Plays*. Trans. Rolf Fjelde. New York: Signet Classic, 1992.

Lyons, Charles R. *Hedda Gabler: Gender, Role, and World*. Boston: Twayne, 1991.

Mill, John Stuart. "The Subjection of Women." In *The Feminist Papers*. Ed. Alice S. Rossi. New York: Bantam, 1973.

Hedda Gabler

Popperwell, Ronald G. *Norway*. New York: Praeger, 1972.

Seigel, Jerrold. *Bohemian Paris: Culture, Politics, and the Boundaries of Bourgeois Life, 1830-1930*. New York: Elizabeth Sifton Books, 1986.

Shideler, Ross. *Questioning the Father: From Darwin to Zola, Ibsen, Strindberg, and Hardy*. Stanford: Stanford University Press, 1999.

Templeton, Joan. *Ibsen's Women*. Cambridge: Cambridge University Press, 1997.

Trudeau, Lawrence J., ed. *Drama Criticism*. Vol. 2. Detroit: Gale Research, 1995.

I, Claudius

by
Robert Graves

Born in Wimbledon, England, in 1895, Robert Graves was the son of a schoolmaster who was also a poet and songwriter. Graves attended Charterhouse, a British public school (the equivalent of an American private school). He grew, in his school years, increasingly committed to becoming a poet. When World War I broke out (1914), Graves joined the Royal Welsh Fusiliers; seriously wounded in 1916, he was initially left for dead. That same year saw the publication of his first book of poems, *Over the Brazier*. After a lengthy recovery, during which Graves, like many of his comrades, suffered nightmares and shattered nerves, he returned to garrison duty in Wales until the last year of the war, 1918. Grave subsequently studied at St. John's College, Oxford, meanwhile continuing to write poetry. In 1926 he met the American poet, Laura Riding, with whom he founded the Seizin Press; in 1929 Graves left his wife of 11 years and four children for Riding. The two settled in Majorca, Spain, where they lived through the time *I, Claudius* was published until the outbreak of the Spanish Civil War in 1936. Graves had by then achieved some financial success with *Good-bye to All That* (1929), a bitter autobiography describing his own wartime experiences. He would achieve still more with *I, Claudius*. His first historical novel, it purports to be the ancient Roman emperor's lost autobiography. Graves aimed to compensate for traditional historical accounts that in his view failed to do Claudius justice in a tale that fleshes out not only the man but also his ancient Roman society.

> **THE LITERARY WORK**
>
> A historical novel set in the Roman Empire between 41 B.C.E. and 41 C.E.; published in 1934.
>
> **SYNOPSIS**
>
> The despised weakling in the Roman imperial family survives the deaths and misfortunes of his more famous relatives, ultimately becoming emperor of Rome.

Events in History at the Time the Novel Takes Place

Republicanism. While *I, Claudius* provides detailed accounts of three imperial reigns (those of Augustus, Tiberius, and Caligula), it also depicts the ongoing political tension between Romans who accepted the monarchy and those who longed for a return to the republic. Although the empire had been established for about 70 years at the time of Claudius's accession in 41 C.E., "The Roman aristocracy [still] resented the rule of a Single Person. For centuries no title was more deeply hated than 'king'" (Massie in Graves, *I, Claudius*, p. ix).

Legend has it that this antipathy dates back to around 510 B.C.E., when the Romans overthrew and expelled a line of monarchs in their region—the Etruscan kings who for roughly a century had dominated the Latium area, a plain south of the Tiber River. The Roman nobility

I, Claudius

Robert Graves

then devised a constitution, designed to prevent any danger of the return of the monarchy, and established a republic to be governed by two elected officials (called consuls), an advisory body known as the Senate, and a popular collection of adult male citizens called the Assembly. The Assembly approved or rejected whatever laws were proposed, and elected magistrates—officials with a mix of judicial, administrative, and priestly duties. The two chief magistrates, called consuls, commanded the army and fulfilled all sacred and sacrificial functions, often serving as judges and generals. In ascending order, lesser magistrates were the quaestors, aediles, and praetors. Quaestors had mainly financial duties; aediles were in charge of public works and festivities; praetors were usually judges. Another branch of magistracy, outside the pyramid, was the tribunate; elected by the commoners to protect their rights, tribunes were magistrates without administrative duties. Like all magistrates, they could propose laws to the Assembly. Unique to the tribune was the right to interpose a veto on any legislation.

By virtue of their office, all magistrates except for the tribunes were members of the Senate. Magistrates could propose and debate legal measures among themselves in the Senate, which had little power at first but then gained in authority and dominance, becoming more powerful than the Assembly of the People. As the years passed, the republic turned into more of an oligarchy, with control increasingly in the hands of wealthy, aristocratic landowners. Known as *patricians*—from the term, "patres" (fathers)—this coterie of citizens gained command of the Senate, the Assembly, and the consulships. For many years, the plebeians (common people) had to struggle for the redistribution of lands won in war, the granting of social and economic rights, and representation in government. Around 400 B.C.E., the plebeians won a significant victory by forcing the Senate to integrate the previously unwritten criminal code and laws of debt and property into the Law of the Twelve Tablets, which served as Rome's basic legal code for nearly a thousand years.

But the Roman republic soon faced problems beyond internal class struggles. As Rome acquired more territories and wealth through conquest, establishing itself as the dominant power throughout the Mediterranean, the republican system as devised proved inadequate to manage the needs of the expanding empire. Other problems surfaced. Within Rome itself, tributes from new colonies made the ruling classes richer, and a new middle class arose and prospered; meanwhile, the poor grew poorer. Ominous developments mounted abroad too: magistrates appointed to govern the foreign provinces established independent power bases, aided by the military forces assigned to support their authority. So appealing was this independence that ambitious office seekers worked to acquire rich provincial commands more assiduously than to establish power bases within Rome itself. The challenges Rome faced on the frontiers of its growing empire led to the emergence of Lucius Cornelius Sulla, Pompeius Magnus (Pompey), and Julius Caesar, each of whom sought to consolidate his power in the developing empire. Changes in the army also strained republicanism; conscripted citizens were replaced by professional soldiers whose first loyalty was to their individual commander rather than the state.

Despite the virtual collapse of the republic during Julius Caesar's rise to power c. the 40s B.C.E., many Romans continued to distrust and fear a single person ruling the state. This ongoing fear contributed to Caesar's assassination, shortly after he was elected dictator for life, in 44 B.C.E.; not even the successful reign of Augustus, who became Rome's first emperor in 27 B.C.E. entirely dispelled that fear. Some yearned for the return of the republic, despite its shortcomings. In *I, Claudius*, several characters, including Drusus, Claudius's father, and Claudius himself, remain staunchly republican in their sympathies, especially as they witness the unscrupulous, even murderous, dealings of their own family to gain power within the imperial regime.

Accession and reign of Augustus. The years following Caesar's assassination were marked by further political turmoil. Octavian, Caesar's grandnephew, was posthumously adopted as his uncle's son and heir; the young man hastened to Rome to claim his inheritance, gathering followers as he advanced. Seeking to avenge Caesar's murder, Octavian allied himself, somewhat uneasily, with Marcus Antonius (Mark Antony), who had been Caesar's principal supporter, and ultimately defeated the two main assassins, Brutus and Cassius, at Philippi in 42 B.C.E.

Octavian spent most of the next decade fighting for control of the empire against Antony. For much of this time, Antony was situated in the East, where he had become involved with the Egyptian queen Cleopatra. The tug of war ended with Antony's defeat at the Battle of Actium (31 B.C.E.) and the suicides of Antony and Cleopatra (30 B.C.E.). With his rival quashed, Octavian Caesar emerged as undisputed and unchallenged leader of the Roman Empire.

In 27 B.C.E., after serving as consul for several consecutive terms, Octavian proposed to resign all his offices and restore the republic. The senators protested. Rome, they said, could not survive without his efforts. Octavian agreed to serve as proconsul, or provincial governor, in Gaul, Spain, Syria, and Egypt. Octavian retained his position as commander-in-chief of the Roman Army, along with the rights to declare war and negotiate treaties. At this time, he took the name Augustus, by which he was thereafter known. Over the next few years Augustus's powers and privileges increased; his proconsular authority exceeded that of other provincial governors and he was granted the power of a tribune, which enabled him to summon the Senate. By 23 B.C.E. Augustus had become emperor or "princeps" of Rome in all but name, a position he would hold until his death in 14 C.E.

Augustus's imperial accession introduced a long era of peace and prosperity for Rome, known as the Pax Romana (Roman peace, a peace maintained by Rome crushing any military threat). During his four-decade reign (31 B.C.E.-14 C.E.), Augustus reorganized the army, created a permanent navy, and extended his empire northward to the Rhine and Danube rivers in Germany. He also built temples, libraries, theaters, and roads to link his far-flung empire, which stretched from the Mediterranean to much of western Europe, including northern Britain. Finally, Augustus provided a centralized administration and a uniform system of law and justice within that empire. In *I, Claudius*, all of Augustus's achievements are noted, although some critics complain that Graves's portrayal of the emperor as a rather boyish figure manipulated by his conniving wife, Livia, does Augustus less than proper justice.

Tiberius and Caligula. Emperor Augustus faced a series of disappointments when trying to groom an heir to the throne. Lacking a son of his own, he chose, in turn, his nephew Marcellus, his son-in-law Agrippa, and, finally, his grandsons Gaius

I, Claudius

LIVIA: PARAGON OR POISONER?

In *I, Claudius*, the mysterious deaths by poisoning of various claimants to the imperial throne are all attributed to Livia. The historical Livia, however, is not drawn so blackly. Born in 58 B.C.E., Livia Drusilla was a member of a powerful Roman family, the Claudians; when she was 15 or 16, she married her cousin Tiberius Claudius Nero and bore him two sons, Tiberius and Drusus. Livia divorced her husband in 39 B.C.E. and married Octavian, later Augustus, Caesar. Though she bore no children in this second marriage, the relationship endured for more than 50 years, until Augustus's death in 14 C.E. During his long reign, Livia had been influentially involved in nearly all the emperor's major decisions. Augustus trusted her to the extent that he allowed her to use his personal seal when he traveled abroad. Contemporary historians lauded Livia for her virtues and her grandson Claudius deified her as a goddess after her death. Graves's more sinister portrait of Livia is not wholly without foundation, however. The empress did become deeply estranged from her elder son, Tiberius, who succeeded his stepfather as emperor and seems to have found his mother difficult and domineering. On several occasions, he sternly ordered her not to meddle in affairs of state. Some slightly later historians, including Plutarch, suggested that Livia's influence on Augustus was malign—that she deliberately conspired against his chosen heirs to the throne to promote the interests of her own sons, especially Tiberius. The truth probably lies somewhere in the middle, making the real Livia less diabolical than later portrayals suggest.

and Lucius. Sadly, all of them predeceased Augustus, who was left with no other choice but to fall back on his stepson, Tiberius Claudius Nero, whom he did not especially like but whose abilities as a general and service to the empire he could not ignore.

Tiberius acceded to the throne in 14 C.E., when he was 55. Generally he ruled with prudence, following many of Augustus's precedents. He adopted a defensive foreign policy and strengthened the frontiers of the empire, meanwhile practicing a frugality that enabled him to leave the empire very wealthy at his death in 37 C.E. However, Tiberius was not a popular emperor; violent conflicts within his own family and growing distrust between him and the senatorial aristocracy undermined his reputation. For the last 11 years of his life, he estranged himself even further by moving from Rome to the isle of Capri and governing from there. Worst of all, Tiberius fell prey to an ambitious adviser, Sejanus, who encouraged the emperor's suspicious, even paranoid, tendencies while plotting his own rise to the throne. Sejanus was executed for his betrayal in 31 C.E.; Tiberius retaliated brutally, eliminating Sejanus's adherents as well as his relatives.

Like Augustus, Tiberius was plagued by the need to find a successor. His heir and nephew Germanicus, a popular figure in the empire, had died mysteriously in 19 C.E. Tiberius's own son Drusus was poisoned, apparently by his wife and her lover, Sejanus. Ultimately Tiberius chose Germanicus's youngest son, Gaius (called Caligula), to succeed him. The reign of Caligula, who acceded in 37 C.E., began auspiciously enough. He recalled and pardoned many prisoners persecuted under Tiberius, reduced some taxes, distributed largesse, and held lavish games and public spectacles. But after a grave illness in 38 C.E., Caligula exhibited increasingly irrational behavior. He became convinced he was a living god and demanded to be worshipped as such; he turned against the Senate and enraged the empire's Jewish subjects by insisting that his statue be displayed in synagogues. He also spent lavishly, dabbled in several unsuccessful military campaigns, and revived treason trials, attempting to eliminate whomever he perceived as a threat. With no other recourse to check the powers of an absolute ruler, several senators and members of the Praetorian guard assassinated Caligula in 41 C.E., ending his brief chaotic reign.

Marriage and divorce in imperial Rome. Throughout *I, Claudius*, marriages are negotiated, contracted, and dissolved with an ease modern readers might find disconcerting. In fact, the novel's depiction of marriage and divorce in imperial Rome, especially among the upper classes, is historically accurate.

Theoretically, marriages could take place when both parties were little more than children.

> Most Roman women entered a first marriage at ages some five, ten, or more years earlier than did a man, with virtually all women married by their early twenties. If marrying for the first time, brides from elite and propertied families were sometimes as young as ten to thirteen years.
>
> (Hanson in Potter and Mattingly, p. 31)

When a Roman girl married, she became a part of her husband's family; her spouse legally acquired control and jurisdiction over her from her father, who had previously held this control. It was expected that the married couple's bond would be strengthened by the growth of mutual respect and affection and the birth of legitimate children, the main purpose of marriage.

A wife was expected to bear her children by the age of about 20. Then her duty was to instill proper Roman values in them and to promote their political, social, and economic careers. In sons, a mother instilled manliness and loyalty; in daughters, the importance of fertility, beauty, and faithfulness. Parents expended great effort on advancing a son in society, be it through military forays, high public office, marriage, or a mix of these means. For a daughter, they worked to arrange a beneficial marriage. Although women were not just wives and mothers in Rome, society did regard these two functions as a woman's primary roles. A wife who could not bear children, preferably sons, might easily find herself discarded. Her husband might cast her out for a potentially more fertile bride.

Divorce became more common in imperial Rome from the first century B.C.E. onward. A century earlier, only a few reasons—infertility, infidelity, and drunkenness—justified a man divorcing his wife (women, unsurprisingly, could not repudiate their husbands). The rampant power-seeking that developed as a result of Rome's expanding empire, however, increased the frequency of divorce for personal and family advancement. In divorce, as in marriage, the husband retained the greater power; the children of a dissolved union, even those still in their mother's womb, were acknowledged as his. Often he kept the children, sending her away without them. He could also retain a portion of his former wife's dowry.

In *I, Claudius*, the imperial family marries and divorces for solely political reasons. Claudius's scheming grandmother, Livia, marries Augustus, future emperor of Rome, after her first husband divorces her for infidelity. Conversely, Livia's elder son, Tiberius, is compelled by Augustus himself to divorce his beloved wife Vipsania and marry Augustus's daughter Julia instead. Claudius too is manipulated into several marriages, either by his domineering family or unscrupulous acquaintances.

Imperial deification. Roman religion encompassed the worship of countless deities. Many Roman gods were inherited from the Greeks (whom the Romans conquered during the second century B.C.E.) and given new names. For example, the Greek supreme god Zeus became the Roman god Jupiter, his wife Hera became Juno, and Ares, the god of war, reappeared as Mars. The Roman religious pantheon developed beyond this too, expanding over time.

> In the Roman view, there was an enormous number of gods, and it was possible for a new god to be born at any time; the gods of classical antiquity had active sex lives, and most Romans felt that if one god could beget another god in the distant past, there was no reason why a god could not have a divine child in the present.
> (Potter in Potter and Mattingly, p. 114)

The pantheon could also be enlarged by the apotheosis of mortal heroes and kings, a practice that likewise originated with the Greeks. The practice of this belief gained momentum during Julius Caesar's career. From 46 B.C.E. on, Caesar became the recipient of divine honors, and after his assassination, this deification continued, promoted by a bright comet's appearing in the sky around the time his body was cremated. In 42 B.C.E. Caesar was officially designated a god of the Roman state, and the month of Quintilis was renamed Julius (July) in his honor.

Caesar's heir, Augustus, was similarly exalted. The poets Virgil and Horace both spoke of Augustus as a god. Intellectuals of the day did not take his elevation to this status seriously. Still, in 8 B.C.E. the month of August was named in Augustus's honor and, after his death in 14 C.E., he was deified. In *I, Claudius*, the idea of conferring godhood on mortals resurfaces in relation not only to Augustus but also to Livia, his scheming empress. Having poisoned or discredited various claimants to the imperial throne, an aging, apprehensive Livia makes Claudius promise to ensure her being named as a goddess so that she may escape punishment for her crimes after death.

The Novel in Focus

The plot. Long ridiculed as a weak, stammering cripple, the now-elderly Tiberius Claudius Drusus Nero Germanicus, commonly known as "Claudius," begins writing his autobiography. Although he has already written literary and historical works during his life, Claudius sets particular value on this effort, inspired by the prophecy of a sibyl (prophetess) he visited ten years before. In addition to predicting the course of his life over the next decade, the sibyl had asserted that, one day some 1,900 years later, the stammering Claudius would finally speak clearly. Mindful of the prophecy, Claudius realizes that his story must be addressed to a far-distant posterity.

The first part of Claudius's autobiography concerns itself with events that transpire before his birth. Livia, Claudius's ambitious, power-hungry grandmother, secures a divorce from her first husband (Claudius's grandfather) and marries Augustus Caesar, although the marriage is never sexually consummated. Augustus becomes emperor of Rome, whereupon Livia grows determined that Tiberius, her eldest son by her first husband, should succeed his stepfather. To this end, she spends many years eliminating other claimants to the throne by poison or trickery. These rivals include Augustus's friend General Agrippa and even Augustus's grandchildren by his only daughter, Julia, who had been married to Agrippa. Tiberius also becomes a pawn in his mother's schemes; he is forced to divorce his beloved wife, Vipsania, to marry Julia, who becomes violently infatuated with him. Meanwhile, full of distrust for his mother, Livia's younger son, Drusus, nurses the hope that Rome would someday become a republic again.

Drusus marries Antonia, one of Mark Antony's daughters, by whom he has three children: Germanicus, Livilla, and Claudius. When Claudius is a year old, Drusus, a successful general currently fighting in Germany, falls from his horse and dies of a gangrened leg. The widowed Antonia returns to Rome with her children. Unlike his siblings, Claudius has a sickly constitution: he limps, stammers, and gives the impression of being feeble-minded. Most of the family despises and ignores Claudius; his only friends are his brother Germanicus, Julia, and Agrippa's youngest son, Postumus. One day a flock of fight-

I, Claudius

ing eagles drops an injured wolf cub into young Claudius's arms. An old diviner who is visiting suggests privately to Antonia that sometime in the future Rome will be wounded and need Claudius's protection.

Unable to train as a soldier, Claudius devotes himself to his studies. In the course of his education, he meets several notable Roman scholars, orators, and historians, one of whom advises him to exaggerate his infirmities to ensure his own survival. While still a boy, Claudius falls in love with the sweet-natured Medullina Camilla, who is mysteriously poisoned on the day of their betrothal. Livia arranges another marriage for Claudius to the granddaughter of Urgulania, one of her few confidantes. The bride, a sullen, oversized girl named Urgulanilla, is no fonder of Claudius than he is of her; they have one child together but essentially lead separate lives. In time, Claudius's scholarship earns him some approval from Augustus and Livia, who make him a priest of Mars, but for the most part they pay him little attention. After Claudius faints during a brutal public sword fight held to commemorate the exploits of his late father, Livia declares her grandson unfit to appear in public.

Over the years, Livia continues to scheme for the advancement of Tiberius, who does not always appreciate her efforts. The marriage between Julia and Tiberius sours, owing to his indifference and her promiscuity; both are exiled from Rome, to separate islands. After the mysterious deaths of Julia's two eldest sons, Tiberius is recalled to Rome and restored to the good graces of Augustus, who eventually adopts him as his own son. Livia frequently disparages Julia's youngest son, Postumus, to Augustus, then conspires with Claudius's sister, Livilla, to frame Postumus for attempted rape. The young man is exiled to a desert island but not before telling Claudius what has truly happened. Claudius advises Postumus to wait for the right opportunity and promises to pass along the truth to Claudius's brother Germanicus as well.

Tiberius and Germanicus are meanwhile fighting the Germans in a long, costly war that ends in Roman victory. Germanicus, in particular, earns the troops' love, which Tiberius has never managed to do. After Germanicus returns from the war, Claudius tells him about Postumus's being framed; Germanicus, in turn, informs Augustus, who resolves to restore his grandson to favor and reward Claudius for his loyalty to his friend. But one month later Augustus suffers stomach disorders and dies. Livia's plan materializes. Tiberius accedes to the throne, despite his lack of popularity with the Senate. Shortly thereafter, on Tiberius's orders, Postumus is secretly captured, tortured, and killed.

Accompanied by his devoted wife, Agrippina, and their children, Germanicus resumes his military campaigns against the Germans, winning many victories for Rome. The army comes to regard Germanicus as the empire's bright new hope and adopts his youngest son, Gaius, as an army mascot, nicknaming the boy "Caligula" (little boots). Though Germanicus makes much of his loyalty to Emperor Tiberius, the emperor grows increasingly jealous of his nephew's popularity. He recalls Germanicus to Rome in 17 C.E. Claudius does not witness his brother's triumphant return, for Livia, suspecting the brothers of conspiring against Tiberius, has sent him to Carthage to dedicate a temple to Augustus, now deified as a god. The following year, Germanicus is sent to command the Roman armies in the East; his wife and her two youngest children, Caligula and Lesbia, accompany him. Back in Rome, Tiberius nurses fears of his nephew's success, inflamed by Livia and Sejanus, his ambitious new commander of the guard.

In Syria, Germanicus falls ill and suspects poisoning. His tentative recovery is undermined by the discovery of ghastly objects in the house—decaying corpses of babies and animals, bloody cocks' feathers, lead tablets inscribed with his name. Then Germanicus's name appears upside-down on the wall, every day shortened by a letter. After his good-luck charm vanishes, the superstitious Germanicus weakens and dies. His family returns to Rome, whose citizens are plunged into grief over Germanicus's death. While Claudius offers what protection he can to his late brother's family, Tiberius eliminates Germanicus's Roman friends on one pretext or another.

During his later years as emperor, Tiberius sinks deeper into sexual depravity, holding orgies and pursuing women and young boys. He breaks with Livia, whose maternal influence over him has waned. As Caligula matures, he becomes one of Tiberius's boon companions, luring the emperor into even worse excesses. Meanwhile, Sejanus attempts to acquire more power by marrying his relatives into the imperial family. A betrothal between Claudius's son and Sejanus's daughter is thwarted by the former's mysterious death, but Sejanus succeeds in getting Claudius to divorce Urgulanilla and contract a marriage of convenience to Sejanus's sister Aelia. Sejanus himself becomes the lover of Livilla, Claudius's depraved sister, and together, they poison her husband, Castor. After a soothsayer warns him of his impending death, Tiberius moves to Capri and leaves Sejanus to look after Rome.

At this point, Livia takes increased interest in Claudius. One night, she invites her formerly despised grandson to dinner, and they declare a wary truce. The aging empress informs Claudius of what the fates have in store for them: his dissolute nephew Caligula will be the next emperor, Claudius will avenge Caligula's murder, and she herself will die in three years. Claudius agrees to use whatever influence he wields to have Livia declared a goddess after her death; in return, Livia confesses to instigating various murders—including that of Augustus. Always, she claims, she acted for the good of the state. She adamantly denies poisoning Germanicus but hints to Claudius that he himself may one day discover the culprit.

After Livia's death, Tiberius behaves more cruelly than ever; he banishes Germanicus's wife and her eldest son to desert islands, where they die, imprisons her second son in an attic of the palace, where he too dies, and eliminates adherents of his mother's faction. Meanwhile, Sejanus and Livilla secretly conspire to seize power for themselves. The plot leaks out, whereupon Tiberius executes Sejanus and several members of his family, including his children. As for the equally culpable Livilla, her mother locks the culprit in her room and starves her to death for disgracing the family.

Five years later, Tiberius himself lies dying. Caligula loses no time in announcing his own imperial accession, only to be brought up short by a servant's report that Tiberius still breathes. Caligula and Macro, commander of the guards, silence the servant and, on finding Tiberius attempting to rise from his bed, quickly smother him.

As he is Germanicus's son, Caligula initially enjoys great popularity, and in the first months of his reign, he makes several magnanimous gestures, such as recalling all the banished and releasing all political prisoners. Privately, Caligula continues to have incestuous relations with his sisters and schemes to eliminate his young cousin Gemellus, whom Tiberius has named joint-heir to the throne. Struck down with brain fever for a month, Caligula emerges from his illness more dangerous than ever—believing that he has been transformed into a god. While informing a stunned Claudius of this metamorphosis, Caligula identifies himself as the one who frightened Germanicus to death. Caligula planted those grisly objects in the house and stole his father's protective charm.

Once his divinity is acknowledged by his subjects, Caligula sets about destroying those he considers a threat, including his own sister, Drusilla. His grandmother Antonia commits suicide because of her grandson's monstrous deeds. Even Caligula's old ally, Macro, is arrested and forced to kill himself. Meanwhile, Caligula turns the palace into a brothel and squanders the money in the imperial treasury. The emperor's depravities and extravagances finally turn the populace against him. Seeking to raise money and gain prestige, Caligula leads military expeditions into France and Germany, but accomplishes little; indeed his behavior during the campaign testifies to his increased mental instability. Returning to Rome, Caligula capriciously arranges a marriage between Claudius and Messalina, a distant cousin only 15 years old. Despite his better judgment, Claudius falls in love with his young bride.

Sickened by the emperor's excesses, Caligula's surviving enemies plot his assassination. The murder is to take place during a grand festival in honor of Augustus. As Caligula leaves the theater at noon to return to the palace, the conspirators surround him in a passage and stab him to death. Conflicting reports about what has transpired cause mass confusion among the crowd assembled for the festival. Some of the conspirators escape into the palace, where they kill Caligula's wife, Caesonia, and their child. A handful of soldiers find Claudius hiding behind a curtain and drag him out. Recognizing him as Germanicus's harmless scholar brother, the guards spare Claudius's life, then change it forever by proclaiming him the next emperor. Claudius, a proponent of republicanism, is horrified by the prospect, but Messalina persuades him to comply. A dazed Claudius is carried out to the Great Court on the shoulders of his supporters, while crowd members hasten to prostrate themselves before their new ruler.

The real Claudius. As early as 1929, after completing *Good-bye to All That*, Graves became intrigued by the figure of Emperor Claudius, writing in his journal:

> It is not long since a complete historical romance or interpretative biography occurred to me—"The Emperor Pumpkin." I had been reading Suetonius and Tacitus. It was about Claudius, the emperor came between Caligula and Nero.... Claudius has always been a puz-

zle to the historians, as indeed he was to his contemporaries.

(Graves, *Robert Graves*, p. 187)

Graves was especially intrigued by the paradox of how Claudius, whom many considered a feeble-minded buffoon (Seneca satirized him in *The Pumpkinification of Claudius*), emerged as, for the most part, a capable administrator who carried out valuable public works once he became emperor. In *I, Claudius*, Graves persuasively resolves that paradox by presenting Claudius as a secret Republican, idealistic, scholarly, and shrewder than even his own family realizes. Part of this shrewdness lies in his ability to use his physical infirmities as a disguise so he can escape notice and assassination. In the novel, Pollio, an elderly historian, advises young Claudius to "exaggerate your limp, stammer deliberately, sham sickness frequently, let your wits wander, jerk your head, and twitch with your hands on all public or semi-public occasions. If you could see as much as I can see you would know that this was your only hope of safety and eventual glory" (Graves, *I, Claudius*, p. 92).

Claudius's ruse proves successful; he is continually overlooked and underestimated by unscrupulous power-seekers, attaining late middle age, while many of his relatives are murdered or disgraced. Some of the more perceptive members of the imperial family, however, recognize Claudius's foolishness as a mask. His brother Germanicus and his friend Postumus appreciate Claudius's worth from the start; shortly before his death, Augustus too commends Claudius's loyalty to Rome, his friends, and the truth. Even Livia recognizes that her neglected grandson is not the fool she initially took him for. Given Graves's sympathetic and persuasive character portrayal, Claudius's accession to the imperial throne, after surviving the murderous reigns of Tiberius and Caligula, seems almost farcical: the despised idiot takes the prize, although it is the very last thing he desires. Claudius painted himself one way—as a fool; Graves another way—as a serious person behind this façade. So the question left to posterity is, What was the real Claudius like?

Modern historians recognize Claudius as a competent ruler who introduced numerous social reforms, including an administrative bureaucracy structured around his freedmen (former slaves granted their liberty). He built aqueducts in Rome, roads in the provinces, and a great harbor at Ostia, at the mouth of the Tiber River. His foreign policy also succeeded: the empire won Mauretania and Thrace, then conquered Britain, which became a Roman province. Claudius's personal relations were less successful; his connection with the senatorial aristocracy was uneasy, even hostile, and his choice of wives proved disastrous. His much-younger third wife, Messalina, had numerous sexual affairs and was finally executed after she publicly married her lover, Gaius Silius, during Claudius's absence from Rome and tried to make her new "husband" emperor. Claudius's fourth wife, his niece Agrippina the Younger, successfully schemed to make her son Lucius Domitius Ahenobarbus (Nero) the imperial heir over Claudius's own son, Brittanicus. In 54 C.E. Agrippina murdered Claudius by feeding him a dish of poisoned mushrooms. After his death, Claudius was deified by the Senate, which grudgingly recognized that he had been a better ruler than Tiberius or Caligula.

Sources and literary context. Graves, a good amateur classical scholar, consulted many sources while writing *I, Claudius*. Primary among these sources were the writings of Roman historians Tacitus and Suetonius, to whom Graves adhered faithfully with regard to events, going on to develop his own interpretations of the personalities involved. There has been much speculation about how significantly Graves's own life influenced his portrayal of the more extreme characters.

In particular, Livia, Claudius's ruthless, power-hungry grandmother, evokes comparisons with Laura Riding, the American poet for whom Graves abandoned his wife and family in 1929, following a scandal as lurid as any recorded in Roman history. For a time, Graves and his wife, Nancy Nicholson, were involved with Riding in an apparent *ménage à trois*, which became a quartet with the addition of Geoffrey Phipps, who was first Laura's, then Nancy's, lover. The situation deteriorated when Riding attempted suicide by jumping from a fourth-story window, and Graves leaped after her from the floor below. Both survived, and, after Riding—the more seriously injured of the two—recovered, the couple left England for Majorca, Spain. They were still living together during the composition of *I, Claudius*. Riding herself was considered by many to be a demanding, domineering woman, who expected complete devotion and obedience from the men in her life. Some years previously, her sexual relationship with Graves had ceased—at her insistence—a circumstance that may be reflected in Augustus and Livia's unconsummated marriage. Although Graves devoted himself to Riding until they parted company in the 1940s, it has been suggested that he may have resented her domination of him at times, using fiction as the means to exorcise these darker feelings.

Several authors had explored the fictional possibilities of ancient Rome before *I, Claudius* appeared in print. In her novel *The Conquered* (1924), Naomi Mitchison told the story of Caesar's Gallic Wars from the point of view of the Gauls. In 1933 James Leslie Mitchell, writing as Lewis Grassic Gibbon, published *Spartacus*, the story of a great slave rebellion. The noted historical novelist Allan Massie sums up *I, Claudius*'s contribution to such fictionalizations. The novel brought to the fore the fact that ancient Rome "was peopled by real human beings, not abstractions"; Graves had "animated the dry bones of its history," reminding readers that "events now in the past were once in the future, their outcomes uncertain, hoped for, or dreaded" (Massie in Graves, *I, Claudius*, p. xi).

Events in History at the Time the Novel Was Written

Fascism and the Roman Empire. Graves's writing of *I, Claudius* coincided with the rise of *fascism* (a term for any totalitarian, right-wing regime) in 1930s Europe. After World War I, fascism established itself in Italy and Spain, which had a great impact on Graves's sense of the parallels between the Roman dictatorships and the fascist dictatorships. The Italian term *fascio* ("bundle") was in fact derived from the Latin *fasces*, meaning a bundle of elm or birch rods containing an axe—an insignia of authority in Claudius's day.

Common features of Italian and Spanish fascism included the primacy of the state, complete obedience to its leader, and the celebration of martial virtues and prowess. On the basis of absolutism and the glorification of war and conquest, striking parallels can be drawn between fascist Italy under Benito Mussolini and imperial Rome under the Caesars. Indeed, fascist rhetoric commonly expressed the belief in a glorious destiny for the state and its people. Perhaps envisioning himself as a latter-day Caesar, Mussolini even went so far as to prophesy a rebirth of the ancient Roman Empire under his leadership.

Certainly Mussolini's actions in assuming power recall some of the worst political excesses of imperial Rome. On October 28, 1922, Mussolini and his black-shirted followers marched into Rome, threatening to seize the government unless he was appointed prime minister. The king acceded to their demands and, the next day, invited Mussolini to form a government. Fascist gangs targeted leftist parties, terrorizing their headquarters, assaulting and killing their members. In January 1920, Mussolini outlawed all political parties but the Fascist Party and transformed Italy into a totalitarian state. As in the imperial reigns of Tiberius and Caligula, Mussolini's regime was constantly on the watch for threats from within—opposition parties were prohibited while critics of the regime suffered imprisonment or exile.

Though Graves wrote his novel for profit and to correct the injustice done to Claudius in history, he was certainly aware of the rise of fascism on the modern-day grounds of what had once been ancient Rome. Meanwhile, Spain, where Graves lived during the final writing of *I, Claudius*, was undergoing a power struggle remarkably similar to that in ancient Rome—a tussle between republicanism and dictatorship. The late nineteenth century had seen the abdication of the monarchy and the brief heyday of the First Spanish Republic (1873-74), after which a monarchy was restored. Champions of the republic survived, however, much as in ancient Rome. On April 14, 1931, they realized their dream, when King Alfonso XIII abdicated and authorities proclaimed the Second Spanish Republic. But again the republic was short-lived. The first two years saw the new regime backed by a coalition of factions from conservative republicans to socialists and anarchists. There was infighting among them and attempts to unseat the lot of them by anti-republican monarchists and their allies—priests, soldiers, wealthy individuals. At the end of 1933 came elections that brought some of these anti-republicans to power. One of their leaders, the monarchist Antonio Goioechea, met with Italy's dictator Mussolini, who promised to help topple Spain's republic. Did the anti-republicans need weapons? The Italians gave them 20,000 rifles, 20,000 grenades, and 200 submachine guns to overthrow the republic and restore the monarchy. Back in Spain, republicans agitated. Workers struck, universities turned into shooting ranges, and Spain's troops were called in from part of its old empire (Spanish Morocco) to quell a 1934 revolt (the October Revolution). Atrocities proliferated, with republicans and anti-republicans killing each other in cold blood. "A tremendous regression occurred, a simplification, a return to a sort of

I, Claudius

coarseness, to the least intelligent and most fanatical approaches to things . . . all sorts of manipulations became possible" (Marías, p. 390). Mayhem reigned, worthy again of ancient Rome's worst excesses. In Spain, as in Italy, history repeated itself the year *I, Claudius* was published.

Reviews. After its initial release, *I, Claudius* quickly went through six editions, an indication of its popular reception. Critically, the novel received mostly positive reviews in Britain as well as the United States. Some reviewers complained that the pacing was slow and the novel stopped at its most interesting point—when Claudius acceded to the imperial throne—but overall, most commended *I, Claudius* for its thoroughness, attention to detail, and sharpness of character delineation:

> • The whole reads like a genuine human document. It gives an elaborate picture of Roman life in its brilliance and decadence . . . reconstructed with the resources of scholarship and . . . seen through shrewd and generous eyes.
> (*Times Literary Supplement* in Knight, p. 381)

> • Mr. Graves has presented the small things of Roman life as well as the big things, and it is all vital, living, human drama.
> (*Springfield Republican* in Knight, p. 381)

> • Mr. Graves has put into the mouth of the unfortunate emperor an autobiography of such learning, spirit, and perspicacity that long-dead Claudius ought surely to live again.
> (McCarthy for the *Nation* in Knight, p. 380)

In sum, said *New York Times* reviewer P. M. Jack, "The general reader may safely throw his Roman history out of the window and rely on the knowledge and intuition of Graves. . . . 'I, Claudius' is one of the really remarkable books of our day, a novel of learning and imagination, fortunately conceived and brilliantly executed" (Jack for *New York Times* in Knight, p. 380).

—Pamela S. Loy

For More Information

Alfoldy, Geza. *The Social History of Rome*. Trans. David Braund and Frank Pollock. Totowa: Barnes & Noble, 1985.

Canary, Robert H. *Robert Graves*. Boston: Twayne, 1980.

Carcopino, Jerome. *Daily Life in Ancient Rome*. Trans. E. O. Lorimer. New Haven: Yale University Press, 1940.

Grant, Michael. *The Roman Emperors*. London: Weidenfeld and Nicolson, 1985.

Graves, Richard Perceval. *Robert Graves: The Years with Laura 1926-1940*. New York: Viking Penguin, 1990.

Graves, Robert. *I, Claudius*. London: The Folio Society, 1994.

Kersnowski, Frank L., ed. *Conversations with Robert Graves*. Jackson: University Press of Mississippi, 1989.

Knight, Marion A., Mertice M. James, and Dorothy Brown, eds. *Book Review Digest*. New York: H. W. Wilson, 1935.

Marías, Julián. *Understanding Spain*. Ann Arbor: The University of Michigan Press, 1990.

Potter, D.S., and D. J. Mattingly, eds. *Life, Death, and Entertainment in the Roman Empire*. Ann Arbor: University of Michigan Press, 1999.

Rostovzeff, Michael Ivanovitch. *Greece*. Trans. J. D. Duff. London: Oxford University Press, 1963.

Suetonius, Tranquilius. *The Lives of the Twelve Caesars*. Trans. Philemon Holland. New York: The Heritage Press, 1965.

Tacitus. *The Annals of Tacitus*. Trans. Alfred John Church and William Jackson Brodribb. Franklin Center: The Franklin Library, 1982.

The Importance of Being Earnest

by
Oscar Wilde

Born in Dublin in 1854, Oscar Wilde was the son of the distinguished surgeon Sir William Wilde and of Jane Francesca Elgee, a feminist and ardent proponent of Irish nationalism. After studying classics at Trinity College, Dublin, Wilde won a scholarship to Oxford University, where he earned a reputation as a brilliant scholar. After his graduation in 1878, Wilde took up residence in London, where he soon established himself as a writer and leader of a new aesthetic movement that championed "art for art's sake" and promoted the works of contemporary French poets and critics. Witty, outspoken, and flamboyant, Wilde enjoyed great success as a spokesman for aestheticism in both England and America; he also attracted considerable notoriety—in 1881, Sir William Schwenk Gilbert and Sir Arthur Sullivan poked fun at Wilde and aestheticism in their comic opera, *Patience*. That same year, Wilde's novel *The Picture of Dorian Gray*, in which a handsome young man's moral corruption is reflected in the increasing ugliness of his portrait, caused a sensation among the English reading public. Outside the novel, Wilde was a successful poet and essayist too, but he achieved his greatest triumphs as a writer of social comedies for the stage—*Lady Windermere's Fan* (1892), *A Woman of No Importance* (1893), *An Ideal Husband* (1895). Best-known is his masterpiece *The Importance of Being Earnest* (1895). Although the play purports to deal with trivialities (Wilde actually subtitled the play "A trivial comedy for serious people"), it deftly satirizes institutions and characteristics of the era—from social class, marriage, and morality, to hypocrisy, social conformity, and the desire for respectability.

THE LITERARY WORK

A play set in London and Hertfordshire, during the 1890s; first performed in 1895; published in 1899.

SYNOPSIS

Comic mishaps ensue when two gentlemen court two ladies who have a fondness for the name Ernest.

Events in History at the Time of the Play

The importance of earnestness. Above all, Wilde's play satirizes "earnestness," a peculiarly Victorian quality usually associated with sober behavior and a serious turn of mind. The concept of "earnestness" had its origins in several nineteenth-century phenomena: the outbreak of revolutions in Europe; the subsequent reevaluation of political and social attitudes; the growing reaction of the rising middle class to the selfish hedonism of the aristocracy; and the Evangelical Movement of the Anglican Church, which had advocated worthy causes (such as the abolition of slavery), had favored the observance of a strict code of morality, and had rigorously censured worldliness in others. "Earnestness" also carried multiple meanings:

The Importance of Being Earnest

Oscar Wilde

> To be in earnest meant *intellectually* is to have or to seek to have genuine beliefs about the most fundamental questions in life, and on no account merely to repeat customary and conventional notions insincerely. . . . To be in earnest *morally* is to recognize that human existence is . . . a spiritual pilgrimage from here to eternity in which [one] is called upon to struggle with all his power against the forces of evil, in his own soul and in society. . . . The prophets of earnestness were attacking a casual, easygoing, superficial, or frivolous attitude, whether in intellectual or moral life; and demanding that men should think and men should live with a high and serious purpose.
> (Houghton, pp. 220-22)

In *The Importance of Being Earnest*, the comedic conflict between "earnestness" and frivolity manifests itself in a number of ways: from the pun in the title, to the squabbles between serious Jack Worthing and the more lighthearted Algernon Moncrieff, to the irresistible fascination the name "Ernest" holds for the play's two heroines. Jack's intended, Gwendolen Fairfax, ardently declares that "[Ernest] is a divine name. It has music of its own. It produces vibrations" (Wilde, *The Importance of Being Earnest*, p. 13). Similarly, Cecily Cardew confesses to a smitten Algernon that "it has always been a girlish dream of mine to love someone whose name was Ernest. There is something in that name that seems to inspire absolute confidence. I pity any poor married woman whose husband is not called Ernest" (*Importance of Being Earnest*, p. 41). Even Algernon demonstrates his awareness of the Victorian passion for "earnestness" when he reacts to Jack's revelation of his true name: "You answer to the name of Ernest. You look like an Ernest. You are the most earnest-looking person I ever saw in my life. It is perfectly absurd your saying that your name isn't Ernest" (*Importance of Being Earnest*, p. 6).

Ironically, the term "earnestness" had yet another, more exotic, meaning:

> Homosexual members of [Wilde's] audience probably grasped the pun's other significance in the subculture of the nineties, for Uranian "love in earnest" was the love of the same sex. The term *Uranian* was derived from the name of the Greek God Uranus ("Heaven"), whose genitals were severed by his son, Chronus, and cast into the sea, the bubbling foam around them generating the birth of Aphrodite. The focus in the myth is on the male's creative capacity without the female. In fin-de-siècle London, a Uranian . . . was a male homosexual.
> (Beckson, *London in the 1890s*, p. 186)

As a practicing homosexual, Wilde would almost certainly have been aware of the additional implications of the term "earnestness." He may even have taken a secret pleasure in perpetrating this esoteric pun on a largely unsuspecting Victorian audience, which would have perceived nothing untoward in the plot of *The Importance of Being Earnest*, ending as it does with two heterosexual marriages.

Courtship, marriage, and social class. Throughout the nineteenth century, courtship and marriage were conducted according to certain rules, especially among the upper classes. For the wealthy and well-established, courtship revolved around the "London Season," a three-month-whirligig of social occasions, ranging from parties and balls to sporting events and artistic exhibitions. The Season began after Easter, coinciding with the opening of Parliament, and ended around late July, after Parliament declared a recess, at which point the aristocrats retired to their country estates.

The Season's main objective was far more serious than the calendar of events suggests, the goal being suitable marriage matches. For 17- or 18-year-old young women, this meant matches to men of equal or superior wealth and status. The population of debutantes grew more mixed in the latter half of the century; the season "in Oscar Wilde's London" took on an extra dimension, providing "the social link between the old landed gentry and the new industrial wealth" (Von Eckhardt, Gilman, and Chamberlin, p. 116). Featured, along with aristocrats' daughters, were the daughters of successful businessmen and bankers, who showed an eagerness to marry into "good families" and a willingness to spend thousands of pounds to do so. Wealthy young American women entered the mix too, finding the often impoverished English lord receptive; apparently their money was not too "new" for these lords, the way it was for upper-class families in New York. England's aristocrats were encumbered at the time not only by their everyday expenses but also by the imposition on their estates of heavy taxes or "duties," to be paid during their lives and even after their deaths. In the play, Lady Bracknell demonstrates her awareness of this circumstance when she declares, "What between the duties expected of one during one's lifetime; and the duties exacted from one after one's death, land has ceased to be either a profit or a pleasure. It gives one position, and prevents one from keeping it up" (*Importance of Being Earnest*, p. 16).

In many respects, steps in courtship and marriage were the same as earlier in the century. Men and women still chose prospective partners with care. The man especially looked upon marriage as a career move since the woman's property became his after the wedding, although the Married Women's Property Acts of 1870 and 1882, respectively, gave the wife some control over bequests and over property that she managed to acquire on her own. After a man proposed and a woman accepted, he was expected to inform her parents of his intentions and acquaint them with his financial circumstances. Her parents, in turn, acquainted him with the amount of their daughter's fortune. Then lawyers for the bride and groom negotiated a marriage settlement, resolving such concerns as the wife's spending or "pin" money, the "portions" that would go to any children of the marriage, and the "jointure"—in the form of money or property—that would be bequeathed to the wife should her husband predecease her. In *The Importance of Being Earnest*, Wilde satirizes the mercenary and businesslike aspects of Victorian courtship in his depiction of a grueling interview between Lady Bracknell and Jack after Jack has proposed to her daughter, Gwendolen. Producing a pencil and notebook, Lady Bracknell interrogates the suitor on every particular from his income—between 7,000 and 8,000 pounds a year—to the address of his London townhouse:

LADY BRACKNELL: What number in Belgrave Square?
JACK: 149.
LADY BRACKNELL: (*shaking her head*) The unfashionable side. I thought there was something. However, that could easily be altered.
JACK. Do you mean the fashion, or the side?
LADY BRACKNELL: (*sternly*) Both, if necessary, I presume.
(*Importance of Being Earnest*, p. 17)

A fly in the ointment—marriage and the "New Woman." In Wilde's time, the rituals of courtship and marriage were complicated by a social phenomenon: the rise of the "New Woman." The term was mostly applied to a vanguard of middle- to upper-class women of the 1880s and 1890s who increasingly forsook the traditional female role of self-effacing wife and mother and sought lives beyond the domestic sphere. In her most extreme form, the New Woman sought to claim the same freedoms of thought, speech, and dress that men had possessed for generations. Many in the mainstream regarded her with alarm and disdain—in the popular press, she was derided, ridiculed, and exhorted to return to hearth and home. "There is a New Woman" quipped *Punch* magazine on May 26, 1894, "and what do you think? / She lives upon nothing but Foolscap and Ink! / But though Foolscap and Ink are the whole of her diet, / This nagging New Woman can never be quiet!" (*Punch* in Marks, p. 11). From the vantage point of the mainstream press, she was a wild woman, a social insurgent, a manly woman. She threatened to take the initiative, reverse gender roles, and confuse society altogether. Certainly she confounded the etiquette of courtship.

From a *Punch* Cartoon, September 26, 1896

"Two Sides to a Question"

"Oh, Flora, let us be man and wife. You at least understand me—the only woman who ever did!"
"Oh yes, I understand *you* well enough, Sir Algernon. But how about your ever being able to understand *me*?"
(*Punch* in Marks, p. 35)

Marriage-minded masculine contemporaries wondered how to court this more assertive female. How dominant was she going to be? They worried about being "emasculated by feminine aggressiveness" (Marks, p. 38). In *The Importance of Being Earnest,* Wilde examines the more comic aspects of this potential situation. Gwendolen and Cecily are not representative of the New Woman—both grew up in sheltered upper-class households with the expectation of marrying. Nonetheless, they are more aggressive and forthright than their suitors. Gwendolen criticizes Jack for taking so long to propose and notes his lack of polish when he at last makes her an offer of marriage. Cecily meanwhile informs an astonished Algernon, masquerading as Jack's brother Ernest, that in her imagination she has carried out an entire romance—complete with courtship, engagement, and separation—with his alter ego.

Aesthetes, decadents, and dandies. During the latter half of the nineteenth century, many artists and intellectuals were caught up in the aesthetic movement that had spread throughout Europe. The movement had its roots in a German theory proposed by philosopher Immanuel Kant that a pure aesthetic experience resulted from disinterested contemplation of an object, without reference to reality or consideration of the object's utility or morality. French intellectuals further developed the doctrine, declaring that works of art were self-sufficient and had no purpose beyond existing and being beautiful. French aestheticism adopted as its slogan *L'art pour l'art* or "art for art's sake," a rallying cry taken up by converts to the movement, who included Charles Baudelaire and, later, Oscar Wilde.

Some aesthetes, notably Baudelaire, also became involved in another movement, called the decadence, which admired the artistic qualities of ancient, even decaying, cultures such as those of the late Roman Empire and Byzantine Greece. The Decadent writer usually adopted a highly artificial style and bizarre subject matter, seeking to shock, enthrall, or even to appall the audience. In its most extreme forms, Decadence "emerged as the dark side of Romanticism in its flaunting of forbidden experiences, and it insisted on the superiority of artifice to nature" (Beckson, *London in the 1890s,* p. 33).

The Decadent movement, in its turn, helped to revive and redefine the concept of the "dandy," a term that, at the beginning of the nineteenth century, was usually applied to foppish men of fashion largely concerned with fine clothes and polished manners. In his essay "Le Dandy" (1863), however, Baudelaire argued that the dandy's taste for satorial elegance was only "a symbol of the aristocratic superiority of his mind" (Baudelaire in Beckson, *London in the 1890s,* p. 35). The new dandyism of the late Victorian Age shared several characteristics with Decadence, including "worship of the town, and the artificial; grace, elegance, the art of the pose; sophistication and the mask. The wit of epigram and paradox was called upon to confound the bourgeois" (Baudelaire in Beckson, *London in the 1890s,* p. 35).

In *The Importance of Being Earnest,* the characters reflect the aesthetic, decadent, and dandified attitudes of Wilde himself, albeit in exaggerated form. Artifice, not nature, rules the play's drawing-room milieu. Jack exhibits the dandy's preference for London when he remarks to Algernon: "When one is in the town one amuses oneself. When one is in the country one amuses other people. It is excessively boring" (*Importance of Being Earnest,* p. 2). The young women in the play also express their preference for the artificial and beautiful over the natural and genuine. When Cecily praises the "wonderful beauty" of Algernon's explanation for his deceit, Gwendolen concurs, declaring, "In matters of grave importance, style, not sincerity is the vital thing" (*Importance of Being Earnest,* p. 55).

The play itself, on the other hand, goes beyond art for art's sake, its dialogue constituting satiric social commentary on earnestness, courtship, and other aspects of late Victorian life. Farce was a popular genre in Wilde's era and *The Importance of Being Earnest* invokes many ingredients of the average Victorian farce—the vacation resort, the imaginary identity, competing claims to the same name, and the figure of the foundling or homeless child (see **Great Expectations** and **Jane Eyre**, also in *Literature and Its Times*). There was an iconoclastic bent to other farce too; the forward female was a common type of character, for instance. But in other farce of Wilde's time, the iconoclasm remains beneath the surface; after getting laughs, characters apologize for their transgressions "as a violation of the good order and just standards of society" (Powell, p. 120). In contrast, Wilde's dialogue shows open irreverence for those standards, and without apology or retraction.

> JACK: If you don't take care, your friend Bunbury will get you into a serious scrape some day.
> ALGERNON: I love scrapes. They are the only things that are never serious.
> JACK: Oh, that's nonsense, Algy. You never talk anything but nonsense.
> ALGERNON: Nobody ever does.
> (*Importance of Being Earnest,* pp. 23-24)

The Play in Focus

Plot summary. The play opens with Algernon Moncrieff, a young dandy, preparing to entertain his formidable aunt, Lady Bracknell, and her daughter, Gwendolen Fairfax, for afternoon tea. As his butler, Lane, sees to the refreshments, Algernon receives a visit from his friend, Ernest Worthing, newly returned to London after a short stay in the country. Ernest is delighted to hear that Gwendolen, whom he hopes to wed, will be coming to tea. Algernon, however, demands that his friend explain the meaning of the inscription on a cigarette case he left behind at Algernon's: "From little Cecily, with her fondest love to her dear Uncle Jack." After several futile attempts at prevarication, Ernest finally admits that he has a young ward, Cecily Cardew; that his real name is "Jack"; and that he has invented "Ernest"—a profligate younger brother—to serve as a scapegoat for his own adventures in town. Amused by these disclosures, Algernon reveals that to escape boring social obligations in London, such as his aunt's dinner parties, he resorts to a similar ruse—he has invented an imaginary invalid friend, "Bunbury," who frequently requires Algernon's companionship and assistance in the country.

Lady Bracknell and Gwendolen arrive for tea; Jack contrives to be alone with Gwendolen so he can propose marriage. Gwendolen delightedly accepts, telling Jack that it has long been her fondest dream to wed a man named Ernest. Dismayed by Gwendolen's aversion to his real name, Jack inwardly resolves to be christened "Ernest" as soon as possible. Meanwhile, he and Gwendolen break the news of their engagement to a displeased Lady Bracknell, who subjects Jack to an interrogation regarding his finances and family history. Although Jack can reassure Lady Bracknell that he is wealthy enough to support a wife, he is ultimately forced to admit he knows nothing of his family history: as an infant, he was found in a leather handbag in the cloakroom of the Victoria Railway Station by one Mr. Thomas Cardew. Cardew named him and raised him. Shocked, Lady Bracknell refuses to consider a marriage between her daughter and a foundling. Despite her opposition, Jack and Gwendolen vow eternal devotion and resolve to remain in contact. Unknown to Jack, Algernon secretly writes his friend's country address on his shirt cuff and plans a "Bunburying" expedition to Hertfordshire to meet the mysterious Cecily.

Living in quiet seclusion with Miss Prism, her governess, Cecily is thrilled to receive a visit from her uncle Jack's so-called younger brother "Ernest"—in reality, a disguised Algernon—about whom she has woven several romantic fantasies. Algernon, for his part, falls instantly in love with Cecily and begins to court her; he also learns that, like Gwendolen, Cecily is enamored of the name "Ernest." The lovers' idyll is interrupted by the arrival of Jack who, on his own, has decided to "kill off" his troublesome younger brother and is displeased to see Algernon impersonating "Ernest" and wooing Cecily. The two friends quarrel vehemently, especially after they learn that each has approached Dr. Chasuble, the local clergyman, about being rechristened "Ernest" to please his respective sweetheart.

Meanwhile, Gwendolen arrives at Jack's country house and makes Cecily's acquaintance; for a time, both ladies mistakenly believe they are rivals for the same man, leading to an exchange of insults over the tea table. The appearances of Jack and Algernon clear up this confusion but the ladies accuse their suitors of wooing them under false pretenses and retire to the house in high dudgeon. Alone, Jack and Algernon argue over who has the superior claim to the name of "Ernest"—and who gets to eat the last muffin on the tea table.

Gwendolen and Cecily decide to forgive their suitors but remain firm in their resolve only to wed men named Ernest. Jack and Algernon quickly reassure the ladies that they plan to be christened that very afternoon. The couples' reconciliations, however, are interrupted by the arrival of Lady Bracknell, who has come in search of her missing daughter. Discovering Gwendolen with Jack, Lady Bracknell again forbids their engagement. She is doubly astonished to hear that Algernon has affianced himself to Cecily and subjects the girl to the same cross-examination she earlier suffered Jack to undergo. On learning that Cecily has a fortune of 130,000 pounds, Lady Bracknell quickly withdraws her objections to the match. Jack, however, informs Lady Bracknell that Cecily cannot wed without his consent until she is 35 years old and coldly voices his own opposition to the marriage, citing Algernon's lack of moral character. But Jack offers to give his consent to Algernon and Cecily's marriage if Lady Bracknell will consent to his and Gwendolen's. Lady Bracknell indignantly refuses his terms.

Matters seem at an impasse until Lady Bracknell recognizes Miss Prism as a former nurse who had worked in Lord Bracknell's household. Many

The Importance of Being Earnest

years ago, Miss Prism had taken one of the children—a male infant—out in his pram one day, only to disappear with him completely. Lady Bracknell demands to know what became of the baby. A shamefaced Miss Prism admits that she had gotten the baby mixed up with a manuscript for a three-volume novel she had written. The manuscript was left in the pram, and the baby was placed in a leather handbag that she deposited in a cloakroom at the Victoria Railway Station. Stunned, Jack produces that handbag, which Miss Prism verifies as her own. Believing Miss Prism to be his long-lost mother, Jack attempts to embrace her, but Lady Bracknell sets the record straight, informing Jack that he is the son of her sister, Mrs. Moncrieff, making him Al-

---

WILDEAN WIT

One trademark of Wilde's wit is his use of the epigram, a short, polished, often paradoxical verbal statement intended to surprise and amuse its audience. *The Importance of Being Earnest* contains many memorable examples of Wildean epigrams:

> Divorces are made in Heaven.
> The truth is rarely pure and never simple. Modern life would be very tedious if it were either, and modern literature a complete impossibility.
> [I]n married life three is company and two is none.
> All women become like their mothers. That is their tragedy. No man does. That's his.
> (*Importance of Being Earnest*, pp. 3, 7, 9, 20)

---

gernon's older brother. Jack embraces Algernon as his brother, then quickly searches through army lists for the name of his true father, for whom he himself was named. Finally locating the correct list, Jack discovers to his astonishment that his Christian name really is "Ernest John." The last obstacles to his happiness are removed and the two couples (plus Miss Prism and Dr. Chasuble) joyously unite, while Jack assures the still-censorious Lady Bracknell that he has at last realized "the vital Importance of Being Earnest" (*Importance of Being Earnest*, p. 17).

Double lives. Much of the comedy of Wilde's play hinges upon the elaborate double lives led by the two dandy-heroes, Algernon and Jack. Both have created an imaginary person who serves as a "blind" for their activities, but while Algernon's invalid friend, Bunbury, merely functions as his excuse to avoid boring social responsibilities, Jack's scapegrace brother "Ernest" is actually a facet of Jack himself, a facet that he wishes to conceal from his young ward, Cecily. Exhibiting the typically Victorian concern for propriety and respectability, Jack explains to Algernon:

> When one is placed in the position of guardian, one has to adopt a very high moral tone on all subjects. It's one's duty to do so. And as a high moral tone can hardly be said to conduce very much to either one's health or one's happiness, in order to get up to town I have always pretended to have a younger brother of the name of Ernest, who lives in the Albany, and gets into the most dreadful scrapes.
> (*Importance of Being Earnest*, p. 7)

The whole concept of leading a double life was by no means unheard of among Victorians. Indeed, Victorian life seemed to incline naturally towards duality, with public and private spheres making up the separate halves of existence. For men, life in the public sphere involved duty, service, and pursuit of a profession. The private sphere, usually presided over by women, provided men with a domestic haven, a retreat from public duties, in the form of a peaceful home and, ideally, a loving marriage. The separation between public and private life could take on sinister implications, however—especially for men, who possessed more freedom and autonomy than their wives. It was entirely possible for an otherwise respectable middle-class husband to lead a life of promiscuity and depravity, of which his wife might be kept completely unaware. Indeed, during the 1880s, an anonymous Victorian gentleman published *My Secret Life*, an 11-volume series of memoirs chronicling his many sexual encounters with servants, prostitutes, courtesans, and women of his own class. The author marries twice, once unhappily—which he cites as a partial justification for his promiscuity—and once happily, yet he continues with his secret life despite having found domestic bliss:

> For fifteen months, I have been contented with one woman. I love her devotedly. I would die to make her happy. Yet such is my sensuous temperament, such my love of women, that much as I strive against it, I find it impossible to keep faithful to her, to keep to her alone . . . . My life is almost unbearable from unsatisfied lust. It is constantly on me, depresses me, and I must yield.
> (Marcus, p. 96).

In 1886 Robert Louis Stevenson also explored the hazards of a double life, though in a more fantastic form. In his novel *The Strange Case of Dr. Jekyll and Mr. Hyde*, (also in *Literature and Its Times*), the upright physician Henry Jekyll divides himself in two by becoming the sensualist Edward Hyde, who pursues diabolical pleasures that Jekyll denies himself. Both identities perish, however, when a guilt-ridden Jekyll commits suicide.

While Jekyll's carnal excesses remained confined to the pages of Stevenson's novel, there were, as revealed in *My Secret Life*, Victorians in real life who had illicit sexual and other experiences while wearing an outward mantle of respectability. Wilde's play alludes to this deception when Cecily tells Algernon, "If you are not [wicked], then you have certainly been deceiving us all in a very inexcusable manner. I hope you have not been leading a double life, pretending to be wicked and being really good all the time. That would be hypocrisy" (*Importance of Being Earnest*, p. 29).

For some, including Wilde himself, homosexuality represented perhaps the most extreme example of a double life, as noted by literary scholar Elaine Showalter:

> By the 1880s . . . the Victorian homosexual world had evolved into a secret but active subculture, with its own language, styles, practices, and meeting places. For most middle-class inhabitants of this world, homosexuality represented a double life, in which a respectable daytime world often involving marriage and family, existed alongside a night world of homoeroticism.
>
> (Showalter, p. 106).

The consequences of being caught in homosexual acts were severe. From the time of Henry VIII, the crime of "buggery," or sodomy, had carried the death penalty, although history does not record anyone ever being executed for the crime. The law was not officially changed until 1861, with the passage of the Offenses against the Person Act of 1861, which imposed prison sentences ranging from 10 years to life on those caught committing anal intercourse or sexually exploiting people under the legal age of 21. In 1885, the Criminal Law Amendment Act, which had been passed to protect women and girls by suppressing brothels, was revised to include an amendment making "any act of gross indecency" between males an offense punishable by a year—later two years—in prison, with or without hard labor. The law considered males who were intimate with each other criminals, whether the two males were in a committed relationship or not. In 1889, several male aristocrats narrowly escaped prosecution when the police discovered a male prostitution ring in London's West End. Sir Arthur Somerset, a frequent customer at the brothel and superintendent of the Prince of Wales's stables, was permitted to escape to the Continent, where he would remain until his death in 1926. To protect the royal family from publicity, other clients were likewise saved from exposure; the British press provided virtually no coverage of the scandal.

Wilde himself was less fortunate. A decade after its passage, the conditions of the Criminal Law Amendment Act imposed a sentence of two years' imprisonment with hard labor on the playwright: his own double life was over. Wilde's prison sentence began in 1895, after the debut that same year of *The Importance of Being Earnest*. In the play, Jack becomes indignant and offended when Algernon, drawing a parallel between their similar ruses, refers to Jack as "one of the most advanced Bunburyists I know" and offers to explain to Jack how the pretense can be maintained after marriage (*Importance of Being Earnest*, p. 5).

From *The Illustrated Police News* of May 4, 1895, depicting Wilde's fall from the height of fashionable grace to the depth of public contempt.

The Importance of Being Earnest

"I am not a Bunburyist at all," Jack retorts. "If Gwendolen accepts me, I am going to kill my brother. . . . And I strongly advise you to do the same with Mr. . . . with your invalid friend who has the absurd name" (*Importance of Being Earnest*, p. 8). Jack's reluctance even to utter the name Bunbury may be significant if, as one recent critic argues, the play was using the name as a "private joke" because it was a term that Wilde used for a homosexual pickup (Beckson, *London in the 1890s*, p. 187). There is, however, no evidence that the term was used in this way *before* Wilde's play opened, though "bunburying" did acquire homosexual implications soon *after* the play's performance and Wilde's trial for homosexuality.

Sources and literary context. While *The Importance of Being Earnest* is justly celebrated for its originality, Wilde did in fact draw on his own life and history for some particulars, especially names and personalities he had known. Wilde's biographer Richard Ellmann speculates that the original for Lady Bracknell may have been Wilde's maternal aunt, Emily Thomazine Warren, who was several years older than Wilde's mother, married to an officer in the British army, and disapproving of her sister's Irish nationalist activities. Other acquaintances lent only their names—for example, Henry St. Bunbury, a classmate of Wilde's at Trinity, whose surname became the term used to describe Algernon's elaborate ruse in the play. As a student, Wilde stayed with the Cardews at their country house, promising to name the heroine of his next play Cecily Cardew after one of the family. Similarly, names of real places, such as Worthing and Bracknell, became surnames for characters.

While the preposterous workings-out of the plot were Wilde's own invention, the playwright had recourse to the tried-and-true devices of Victorian stage melodrama and, as noted, farce: secret engagements, tyrannical parents, hidden family scandals, missing heirs, and foundling babies.

Wilde may have owed a debt to a particular play if he saw *The Foundling*, a three-act farce by W. Lestocq and E. M. Robson, performed at Terry's Theatre in the autumn of 1894. Dick Pennell, the hero of the play, is a foundling who, after various misadventures, discovers that his mother was a woman of rank, lawfully married, and his father pursued a career in India, discoveries likewise made by Jack Worthing, himself a foundling, in *The Importance of Being Earnest*. But if Wilde drew some inspiration from this farce, his sources were multiple; he drew also upon his own classical scholarship: his use of the device of the misplaced baby was taken from the works of Menander, a dramatist of ancient Greece. Moreover, *The Foundling* was a conventional farce, emphasizing fast-paced action, more than the quick-witted turn of a phrase. The ordinary farce stressed the physical over the verbal; Wilde's comedy, on the other hand, featured clever epigrams and elegant phrases. It used language to subvert ordinary farce, creating a "new sensation" and heightening the comic effect of such fare (Powell, p. 119). "Such playing with language . . . was for Wilde one of the . . . secrets of his art, of absurdly reversing the ten-

---

FALL FROM GRACE

Wilde's triumph with *The Importance of Being Earnest* was short-lived. In the spring of 1895, Wilde was accused of homosexuality—then considered a serious criminal offense—by the Marquis of Queensberry, the irascible father of Lord Alfred Douglas, with whom Wilde had established a relationship several years earlier. At Lord Alfred's urging, Wilde sued the marquis for libel. Although Wilde's friends advised him to withdraw the suit, the playwright pursued the case, only to find the tables turned on him when Queensberry produced male prostitutes who testified as to Wilde's sexual preferences. Wilde was subsequently arrested, convicted of sodomy, and sentenced to two years of hard labor in prison. He served most of his imprisonment at Reading Gaol. During his incarceration, Wilde wrote *De Profundis*, a confessional letter addressed to Lord Alfred Douglas, in which he dissected the self-destructive impulses that had led to his fall from grace. After being released from jail in 1897, his reputation in tatters, his health seriously undermined, Wilde emigrated to France, where he lived for the rest of his life, mainly on the financial support of his friends. Estranged from his wife, Constance, who had visited him in prison and sent him money from her own dowry, Wilde was denied access to their two sons. The notoriety and grief of Wilde's conviction probably contributed to Constance's early death in 1898. Wilde himself was prompted by the hardships and indignities he suffered in jail to compose *The Ballad of Reading Gaol* (1898) and to advocate prison reform in Britain. He died of cerebral meningitis in 1900 in Paris, where he was buried.

dencies of language in *The Foundling* specifically, in Victorian farce generally" to produce a play that became a "stage classic while almost all other farces of the day vanished" (Powell, p. 120).

The wit, wordplay, and worldliness of *The Importance of Being Earnest* is not, however, unprecedented; it recalls some of the more lighthearted comedies of the seventeenth and eighteenth centuries, such as William Congreve's *Way of the World* and Oliver Goldsmith's *She Stoops to Conquer*. Like these predecessors, *The Importance of Being Earnest* shuns sentimentality: its potentially maudlin moments are invariably interrupted by squabbles between the characters and by frequent pauses for food and drink.

Reviews. *The Importance of Being Earnest* first opened on February 14, 1895, to great critical and popular acclaim. In a distinct minority, fellow playwright and Irishman George Bernard Shaw was unenthusiastic. Shaw wrote of his displeasure in *The Saturday Review*: "I cannot say that I greatly cared for *The Importance of Being Earnest*. It amused me, of course; but unless comedy touches me as well as amuses me, it leaves me with a sense of having wasted my evening" (Shaw in Beckson, *Wilde: The Critical Heritage*, p. 195).

Other critics, however, were dazzled by Wilde's display of wit and absurdity, even those who found fault with his earlier plays. H. G. Wells, who had not liked Wilde's previous play *An Ideal Husband*, offered the author warm congratulations in the *Pall Mall Gazette* for his "delightful revival of theatrical satire" (Wells in Beckson, *Wilde: The Critical Heritage*, p. 188). Similarly, William Archer, writing for the *World*, called *The Importance of Being Earnest* "an absolutely wilful expression of an irrepressibly witty personality" (Archer in Beckson, *Wilde: The Critical Heritage*, p. 190) A. B. Walkley, reviewer for the *Speaker*, hailed Wilde as "an artist in sheer nonsense" and said of his new play that "better nonsense, I think our stage has not seen" (Walkley in Beckson, *Wilde: The Critical Heritage*, p. 196). Finally, Hamilton Fyfe, the London correspondent for the *New York Times*, cabled America with the news that the opening night audience responded to *The Importance of Being Earnest* with "unrestrained, incessant laughter from all parts of the theatre" (Fyfe in Beckson, *Wilde: The Critical Heritage*, p. 189). The knowledge that Wilde had created a masterpiece was not lost on the actors either. Allan Aynesworth, who originated the role of Algernon Moncrieff, later recalled, "In my fifty-three years of acting, I never remember a greater triumph than the first night of *The Importance of Being Earnest*. The audience rose in their seats and cheered and cheered" (Aynesworth in Beckson, "Oscar Wilde," p. 214).

—Pamela S. Loy

For More Information

Beckson, Karl. *London in the 1890s: A Cultural History*. New York: Norton, 1992.

———, ed. *Oscar Wilde: The Critical Heritage*. London: Routledge & Kegan Paul, 1970.

Ellmann, Richard. *Oscar Wilde*. New York: Vintage, 1987.

Houghton, Walter E. *The Victorian Frame of Mind, 1830-1870*. New Haven: Yale University Press, 1957.

Marcus, Steven. *The Other Victorians: A Study of Sexuality and Pornography in Mid-Nineteenth Century England*. New York: Basic, 1964.

Marks, Patricia. *Bicycles, Bangs, and Bloomers: The New Woman in the Popular Press*. Lexington: University of Kentucky Press, 1990.

Pool, Daniel. *What Jane Austen Ate and Charles Dickens Knew: From Fox-Hunting to Whist—the Facts of Daily Life in 19th-Century England*. New York: Touchstone, 1993.

Powell, Kerry. *Wilde and the Theatre of the 1890s*. Cambridge: Cambridge University Press, 1990.

Sammells, Neil. *Wilde Style: The Plays and Prose of Oscar Wilde*. Harlow: Pearson Education, 2000.

Showalter, Elaine. *Sexual Anarchy: Gender and Culture at the Fin de Siècle*. New York: Viking Penguin, 1990.

Von Eckhardt, Wolf, Sander L. Gilman, and J. Edward Chamberlin. *Oscar Wilde's London: A Scrapbook of Vices and Virtues 1880-1900*. New York: Anchor Press, 1987.

Wilde, Oscar. *The Importance of Being Earnest*. Essex: Longman, 1983.

The Little Gipsy Girl

by
Miguel de Cervantes Saavedra

Miguel de Cervantes Saavedra, considered by many the originator of the modern novel, was born in 1547 in Alcalá de Henares in central Spain. He died in 1616, on April 23, the same day William Shakespeare (1564-1616) died. Unable to afford a university education, Cervantes joined the military, served overseas, and upon his return found a job as a tax collector. At the age of 58, after a lifetime of poverty and failure, his writing career began to soar when he published Part 1 of his masterpiece **The Adventures of Don Quixote** (1605; also in *Literature and Its Times*). Cervantes went on to write numerous poems, plays, and fictional works, most notably the *Exemplary Tales* (including *The Little Gipsy Girl*) in 1613 and Part 2 of *Don Quixote* in 1615. Writing in a time of imperial glory and tumultuous change, he incorporated into his works the ironies and surprises of contemporary life. *The Little Gipsy Girl*, published between the two parts of *The Adventures of Don Quixote*, encapsulates all the social possibilities and tensions of Golden Age Spain. Much of the story's power comes from its focus on one of the most reviled groups in Spanish society then and later.

Events in History at the Time of the Novella

A nation defines itself: Spain's Golden Age. In many ways the year 1492 was an *annus mirabilis* (miraculous year) for Spain. With a great portion of its present-day geography united by the marriage of the so-called Catholic Monarchs, Isabella of Castile and Ferdinand of Aragon, the task that remained was to create some sense of national cohesion and unity in the subjects of their previously individual realms. On the first day of 1492, Ferdinand and Isabella entered Granada to accept the capitulation of the last Muslim kingdom in Spain. This final consolidation of Spain's territories was followed by events destined to bring about greater religious, nationalistic, and even linguistic unity: Jews were given the option of expulsion or conversion to Christianity, a decree that prompted the mass exodus of much of Spain's important Jewish community; Christopher Columbus encountered and claimed the Americas for the Spanish crown, expanding Spain's sphere of influence and opportunity; and Antonio de Nebrija published his *Manual of Castilian Grammar*, the first grammar of any modern language, which would facilitate the

THE LITERARY WORK

A novella set in Spain, from the central city of Madrid to the southern city of Murcia, about 1613; published in Spanish (as *La gitanilla*) in 1613, in English in 1630.

SYNOPSIS

When a beautiful young Gypsy (also spelled *Gipsy*) requires that her noble suitor become a Gypsy too, a series of adventures, misadventures, and surprising discoveries ensue.

The Little Gipsy Girl

Miguel de Cervantes Saavedra

standardization and spread of Castilian Spanish throughout the new empire. Over the next hundred years, through the reigns of Charles V, Phillip II, Phillip III, and beyond, Spain would struggle to define and redefine itself amidst a constantly changing set of internal and international factors.

The unity of Spain was not simply a matter of geography: the kingdoms brought together at the close of the fifteenth century retained considerable independence. Local laws, languages, and traditions were preserved by royal agreements. In the kingdoms that formerly made up Ferdinand's territory of Aragon, "the allegiance of subjects was conditional on the king's part of the bargain: the defense of their customs and liberties" (Fernández-Armesto, pp. 121-22). Preaching "peace among Christians and war on infidels," the monarchs sought to impose uniformity in religion. Although the Moors who remained in Granada were initially allowed to practice Islam, Carlos V mandated a strict campaign of Christian baptism in 1526. These forced conversions were of dubious worth, the suspicion being that the converts were not earnest Christians but were only going through the motions. This skepticism is reflected in ongoing fears that the Moriscos, Spain's christianized Moors, would aid the Turks in the event of an invasion. To stave off this risk and respond to the popular revolts of 1568-70, Philip II decreed the dispersal of the Moriscos throughout Castile. They were ultimately considered too dangerous to remain and, on the advice of the count of Lerma and archbishop of Valencia, Philip III expelled the Moriscos in 1609. Nearly 300,000 Moriscos were shipped across the border, leading to the unsurprising result of labor shortages, unpaid loans, and a deflated economy. In Valencia, Aragon, and Murcia, where Moriscos had formed as much as a third of the population, the economies were devastated (Kamen, *Spain 1469-1714*, pp. 220-221).

As brutal as they were dramatic, the progressive measures against Spaniards of Muslim descent echoed earlier laws against Jews and Conversos (Christianized Jews). When the edict of expulsion was proclaimed in the spring of 1492, Spain's Jewish population was estimated at between 80,000 and 100,000 (Kamen, *Spanish Inquisition*, p. 23, Suárez Fernández, p. 50). Though many chose expulsion, perhaps half opted to remain in Spain as converts (Kamen, *Spanish Inquisition*, p. 24). The Conversos would be subject to constant vigilance and increasing restrictions. They could not hold positions in the Church or become nobles.

Perhaps the most dramatic repression came in the form of the Inquisition, a tribunal set up to suppress deviation from the teachings of the Roman Catholic Church. The tribunal was "clearly directed at the Conversos on the grounds that they remained secret Judaizers after conversion to Christianity" (Peters, p. 88). Founded in the twelfth century, the Inquisition began to flex its muscle when it became affiliated with the Crown of Castile in 1478. It was known officially as the Council of the Supreme and General Inquisition, and its first leader in this period was, ironically, a Converso—Tomás de Torquemada (1420-98).

Though its terrifying legacy appears to be more myth than substantiated reality, the Inquisition was certainly an entity to be avoided. Charges and evidence were presented in strict anonymity and the accused were generally imprisoned with their assets frozen while awaiting their hearing. The Inquisitors, contrary to popular belief, did not employ torture on a regular basis, but they did occasionally employ the methods that follow:

- **The garrocha**: The prisoner was raised and repeatedly dropped while suspended by the wrists from a pulley on the ceiling, with heavy weights attached to his feet

- **The toca**, or water torture: A cloth was inserted into the prisoner's mouth and water poured in; when the prisoner swallowed the cloth and neared death by choking, it was pulled out.
- **The potro**, or rack: The prisoner was tied to a rack with cords; as the rack was tightened, the cords bit into the prisoner's body, cutting deeper with each turn of the rack.

"In all these tortures it was the rule to strip the accused first" (Kamen, *Spanish Inquisition*, p. 190). Guilty verdicts were common and they generally resulted in an *auto de fe*, a public display of guilt and penitence, which sometimes concluded in execution by the secular authorities, who worked alongside the Inquisition.

As noted, the Inquisition originated to handle charges of heresy and Judaizing, but during the second half of the sixteenth century other issues—notably bigamy and fornication—led the list of causes for trials. The tribunal became, as one historian has observed, "a social safety valve for the complaints of the poor and unsophisticated, who could never indict their neighbors or challenge their social superiors in ordinary courts" (Fernández-Armesto, p. 133). Without money or power, Spain's poorer classes often did have something of value: a lineage completely free of Jewish or Muslim blood, a "purity" that the bourgeoisie and nobles could not always claim. In short, the minorities of Spain—converted Jews and Muslims, as well as Gypsies—became marginalized even among the poor. Spain was a nation on the move at the time, one that seemed united geographically, spiritually, and even linguistically. But its unity was more gilt than gold, more apparent than real. Forced conformity and intolerance were actually the order of the day. For the Gypsies, it was a time of repression, suspicion, and outright danger. For Cervantes the writer, it was a time to reassess the values of a nation.

The Gypsies of Spain. Noted for their extraordinary appearance and mysterious ways, Gypsies travel in caravans, introducing a sense of the exotic into the towns and fairs where they ply their skills and wares (e.g., dancing, palm reading, livestock trading). Like the biblical wandering Jew, they are "pilgrims in the original sense of the word: travelers and strangers [who] travel and only ever pass through" (Leblon, p. 17; trans. E. Sutherland). Originating in India, the first group of Gypsies arrived in Spain around 1425 professing to be victims of Muslim persecution. The word *Gypsy* (*gitano*, in Spanish), comes from Egypt, the homeland often described by the Gypsy travelers who doubtless passed through Egypt on their way to Spain. (Today's Gypsies generally prefer other names, in particular *Rom* or *Romany*, both derived from the word for *man*.)

Armed with papal letters of safe conduct, the Gypsies were received by Spain's monarch as they had been by other pious kings across Europe, who saw in these Christians a personification of the ancient wandering Jew. As Christians, their wandering was considered a sort of pilgrimage to unspecified holy sites. Alfonso V, king of Aragon, welcomed the first group of Gypsies warmly, calling their leader "our beloved and devout" Juan of Egypt Minor and granting them protection (Albaicín, p. 109; trans. E. Sutherland). Before long, however, it became apparent that their pilgrimages were without end and that the age-old association between the Gypsies and the Jews was dangerous (Albaicín, p. 113).

By the close of the fifteenth century the Gypsies were no longer welcome in Spain. Its larger society had begun to see them as vagrants rather than pilgrims and to take legal steps to oust them. The Catholic Monarchs signed the first *pragmática* (edict or law) in 1499, ordering the removal or forced settlement and employment of the Gypsies. They were given 60 days to choose between exile, mutilation, forced labor (as galley oarsmen in military or privately owned commercial vessels), on the one hand, and cultural death through settlement, on the other hand. Additional anti-Gypsy *pragmáticas* were issued at regular intervals throughout the sixteenth century, by both the Crown and the Church, culminating in a 1609 order of six years in the galleys for any Gypsy laboring at anything other than farming (Leblon, p. 117). Still another expulsion of the Gypsies was ordered in 1611, but that this edict, like others, went unfulfilled is evidenced by subsequent laws restricting Gypsy work, travel, dress, and language (which would not be abolished until after the Francisco Franco dictatorship [1939-75]—only with Article 14 of the Constitution of 1977 were the anti-Gypsy provisions erased).

The Gypsies' gifts as dancers, acrobats, musicians, tinkers, and livestock traders were equaled by their skill in storytelling and allegedly in palm reading. Alternately called witchcraft and deceit, these last skills in particular attracted both popular awe and official distrust of the Gypsies. As early as 1525, the Cortes (parliament) of Toledo requested that "the Egyptians" stay away "since they steal from the fields

The Little Gipsy Girl

> **GYPSIES AND THE INQUISITION**
>
> "Black sheep or perhaps scapegoats bearing Spain's and even all of Europe's sins" is the way one historian describes the Gypsies (Leblon, p. 39; trans. E. Sutherland). Though from such a characterization, one would expect a history of conflict between Gypsies and the Inquisition, the reality was somewhat different. In some ways, the Inquisition highlights how marginalized the Gypsies were, even from their Jewish and Muslim counterparts. As Rom historian Joaquín Albaicín points out, his ancestors had more fearsome persecutors than the Inquisition in Spain: "poor and therefore arousing less envy, the Gypsy was more likely to be persecuted by the *Santa Hermandad*—the police—than by the Inquisition" (Albaicín; trans. E. Sutherland, p. 112). Of some 30 cases brought before the Inquisition in Madrid, Cuenca, and Valencia, about two-thirds of the charges brought against Gypsies were for witchcraft, including such diverse spells as money-making schemes, herbal healing, and love potions. The tribunals determined that most of the charges were accurate, but their sentences varied wildly. One case featured a woman described as little more than a vain enchantress, sentenced to the extraordinarily harsh punishment of torture followed by an *auto de fe*, 200 lashes, and eight years exile from Madrid (Leblon, p. 155). This extreme case was not typical. Another Gypsy was brought up on charges of "an explicit pact with the devil, lethal powders, lies, tricks, fortune telling, use of holy words and the mysteries of the faith for illicit and dishonest ends, demonic invocations, loitering, [and] perjury" (Leblon, p. 155; trans. E. Sutherland). For this string of punishable offenses, he received just a warning. Such charges, concludes another Rom historian, are based more on ignorance than on malice, an ignorance likely born of the profound segregation in which the Gypsies lived (Leblon, p. 165).

and destroy orchards and deceive people" (Kamen, *Spain 1469-1714*, p. 109). This early petition combines the notions of trickery with theft, a charge that will be leveled against the Gypsies more than any other. Another common charge was kidnapping children to sell them. Notable in early reports of cases involving Gypsies was the men's ability to keep silent when questioned and to avoid arrest by seeking refuge in churches or simply disappearing from the caravan until the police left. In rural areas, where friendships were more common among Gypsies and non-Gypsies, this sort of evasion was facilitated through shared interests with local authorities. In cities, where Gypsies were less likely to establish relationships, well-placed bribes were doubtless useful investments.

Of the marginal subpopulations in Spain, the Gypsies have been perhaps the most marginal of all. The Cortes of Castile decreed in 1594 that the group be forbidden to speak its language, live together, or marry among itself so that "the memory and name of the Gypsies be lost . . . and that no one in these kingdoms be called a Gypsy" (Leblon, p. 33; trans. E. Sutherland). Others called into question the very existence of the Gypsies as an ethnic group. For example, in 1631, Juan de Quiñones argued that the group's exotic dress, dark skin, and foreign tongue were all ruses to facilitate trickery (Leblon, p. 33).

Nobility and social classes. One of the defining characteristics of Spain's Golden Age (primarily 1550-1650) was a new social mobility. By the end of the 1500s, Spain's noble classes comprised some 10 percent of the overall population (Kamen, *Spain 1469-1714*, p. 103). Noble status conferred, among other benefits, freedom from taxes, extraordinary leeway in issues of law, and the right to self-defense in case of danger or insult. A person's nobility could be based on hereditary factors dating hundreds of years back or might be awarded to those serving in politics, excelling in exploration and commerce or performing special favors—including making loans—for the Crown. In the early years of the Golden Age,

"America and the Seville trade [commerce in goods to and from the New World, which passed through the river port of Seville] were the most striking cause of social advance," swelling the ranks of the nobility (Kamen, *Spain 1469-1714*, p. 104). As the number of tax-exempt nobles grew, so did the financial burden on the rest of the population.

When Phillip II fixed the Spanish capital in Madrid (1561), the court and would-be courtiers flocked there. For the first time, large numbers of nobles with inherited land grants found themselves in direct contact—and competition—with more newly appointed nobles and even with those seeking titles of nobility, all of them angling for royal attention and favors. Because nobility in itself was no longer a guarantee of long-inherited privilege, blood purity—proof of neither Jewish nor Muslim ancestry—took on a new significance. This new concept of blood purity succeeded in barring social advancement to the Conversos, creating conflicts within the elite. The concern for blood purity furthermore added a racial sense to the view of honor in Spanish society. It "supported the claims of nobles to be an exclusive hereditary caste" of not only Christian but also untainted—preferably Iberian—blood (Kamen, *Spain 1469-1714*, p. 106).

The riches from the mines of Mexico and Peru paid off loans and other expenses, and what was left found its way into the hands of only a small minority of Spaniards. Yet most of the population suffered the consequences in the form of rampant inflation, which saw the cost of goods go up for everyone without a parallel increase in the average income. When mine production fell off towards the end of the sixteenth century, economic disaster set in. The logical result was a general social instability affecting virtually every social class. Thousands migrated, voyaging to cities like Madrid and Seville or to other parts of the Empire, leaving in their wake large sections of rural Spain seriously underpopulated. Poverty pervaded in both formerly self-sufficient farm villages that no longer had enough laborers and in cities too swollen to accommodate new migrants. As a resentful Sancho de Moncada observed in his 1619 *Discourse Against the Gypsies*, a new class of people was pushed to the margins: "hordes of vagrants and atheists without law or religion, Spaniards who have joined this Gypsy life or sect and who welcome other lazy and washed-up people from all over Spain" (Moncada in Leblon, p. 36; trans. E. Sutherland). At the other end of the social scale, money also grew scarce. As the Venetian ambassador to Spain wrote in 1681, "There is hardly a noble who . . . in the absence of royal pensions, could keep himself on his own income" (cited in Fernández-Armesto, p. 150). In 1607 Philip III was forced to declare bankruptcy: Spain was, much like the magistrate and his wife in *The Little Gipsy Girl*, without a single *cuarto*, without a single coin (Cervantes, *The Little Gipsy Girl*, p. 22).

AT THE MARGINS OF SOCIETY, AT THE CENTER OF THE ARTS

The figure of the rogue or *pícaro* captured the imagination of Spain and soon all of Europe in the sixteenth and seventeenth centuries. The paintings of José de Ribera (1591-1652), Diego de Velázquez (1599-1660) and Bartolomé Murillo (1617-1682) abound in marginal figures, with sympathetic portraits of street urchins and vendors, drunks, beggars, and even dancing girls. Readers devoured picaresque literature, tales that featured the adventures of a pícaro, or "popularised and romanticised the delinquency of the urban poor" (Kamen, *Spain 1469-1714*, p. 251). Two examples, *Lazarillo de Tormes* (1554), and Mateo Alemán's *Guzmán de Alfarache* (1598), provide rich views into the daily life of an era even as they offer scathing social commentary on that era. That this critical view surfaces again and again in Golden Age literature is strong proof of at least the writers' awareness of the contrast between social status and the honorable nature of individual behavior.

The Novella in Focus

The plot. Raised by an old Gypsy woman as her granddaughter, Preciosa is a lovely and talented Gypsy girl whose sterling qualities stand out that much more sharply against her harsh surroundings.

> [Her environment] only served to reveal that she had been born of better stock than a line of gipsies, for she was exceedingly polite and well-spoken. And yet, in spite of this, she was somewhat brazen, but not to the extent that it gave way to any impropriety. On the contrary, although she was quick-witted, she was so virtuous that in her presence no female gipsy, whether young or old, dared to sing lascivious songs or use indecent language.
>
> (*Gipsy*, p. 7)

The Little Gipsy Girl

Preciosa's wit and self-assurance are highlighted in this first section through a series of songs. When her songs attract a crowd of admirers, a local magistrate passing by approaches to see what is happening. "Since the young gipsy girl had made a particularly good impression on him," he orders the Gypsies to sing that evening for his wife (*Gipsy*, p. 14). On her way to Doña Clara's house, Preciosa is accosted by a suspiciously well-dressed poet-page. He offers her gold and a lovesick ballad to sing (*Gipsy*, p. 15). Curiously the magistrate's lavish household lacks any coin at all for the Gypsy who has come to entertain its lady. Obliged to tell Doña Clara's fortune with a borrowed silver thimble, Preciosa sings the woman's fortune with lyrics that subtly cast aspersions on the woman's character. She leaves the house with some irritation, saying she will return if required and adding, "I'll take it for granted that you won't give me anything and so save myself the bother of expecting something" (*Gipsy*, p. 22).

Returning to Madrid another day, the Gypsy women encounter an elegant young man who offers his gold and his love to Preciosa. Don Juan de Cárcamo agrees to renounce his wealth and position and join her Gypsy caravan for two years, accepting as well the new name of Andrés Caballero. When the caravan leaves Madrid, Andrés is initiated into the customs and traditions of the Gypsies and soon distinguishes himself as a talented athlete and charming companion. He also determines "as was to be expected from someone of his genteel breeding" that, unlike the other Gypsies, he would only pretend to steal (*Gipsy*, p. 44). This is an important distinction to Cervantes's readers, who saw petty thieving as the Gypsies' main occupation: "we work by day and we steal by night or, more precisely, we warn people not to be careless about where they leave their property" (*Gipsy*, p. 40). In a period whose popular image of Gypsies was very much one of vagrants, thieves, and liars, Cervantes appears to have at least partly shared this image, though his tale also questions the standard view.

One circumstance clouds the growing love of this special pair: Andrés is unable to overcome his jealousy at the impassioned verses the poet-page sends Preciosa, even fainting when he first hears them. Preciosa rejects this jealousy, reviving him with a stern rebuke: "That's a fine gipsy spirit you're showing there. Andrés, how will you ever endure the water torture if you can't cope with the paper test?" (*Gipsy*, p. 35). When the poet-page reappears among the Gypsies, now camped out in Extremadura, Andrés assumes the worst. Alonso Hurtado, the poet-page, puts all such fears to rest, though. He confides that he is fleeing a scandal in Madrid, and the Gypsies welcome him into their troupe, renaming him Clemente (*Gipsy*, p. 50). Like Preciosa and Andrés, Clemente soon distinguishes himself as a talented athlete and charming companion. But he will disappear as soon as trouble rears its head.

The carefree existence of the pretend Gypsies continues until they arrive in Murcia, where the handsome Andrés catches the eye of a lusty young woman "more forward than she was beautiful" (*Gipsy*, p. 58). Juana Carducha propositions him directly: "I like the look of you; and if you want to marry me, it's up to you. Give me an answer quickly" (*Gipsy*, p. 58). When Andrés declines the offer, she feels "embarrassed, wretched, and hell-bent on revenge" (*Gipsy*, p. 59). "[W]ith the cunning, subtlety, and secrecy engendered by her evil intent," she plants some jewelry in his bags and denounces him as a thief (*Gipsy*, p. 59). The situation worsens when a "swaggering soldier, the mayor's nephew" insults and strikes Andrés hard. So hard was the blow that "it shook him out of his abstraction and reminded him that he was not Andrés Caballero but don Juan and a gentleman. He rushed at the soldier, deftly unsheathed his sword, and furiously plunged it into his body, leaving him dead on the ground" (*Gipsy*, p. 60). Don Juan, alias Andrés, is imprisoned.

With her beloved facing certain death, and the other Gypsies arrested or in hiding, Preciosa is devastated. Hearing that "Preciosa's beauty was so radiant that no one could look at her without blessing her," the Chief Magistrate's wife asks to see her and is instantly charmed by her looks (*Gipsy*, p. 61). As the Gypsy girl weeps and begs to delay the hearing so that Juan's father could intervene, her presumptive grandmother reveals an important secret. Years earlier she had stolen the girl from the very same chief magistrate, writing the child's name and date of the kidnapping on a piece of paper. The jewelry belonging to the infant doña Costanza de Azevedo, a mark on the girl's breast, and two conjoined toes provide irrefutable proof of the truth of Preciosa's identity. It is then Preciosa's turn to reveal the truth about Andrés and his crime, explaining that the soldier had "tried to dishonour him, and he could do no less than act according to his true nature and kill him" (*Gipsy*, p. 65). When he discovers that Andrés is really the son of a noble knight, and that Preciosa loves him, the magistrate agrees to their

Gypsies Rest By Their Caravan, 1899 painting by Francis Donkin Bedford.

marriage. The murder charges are quickly dropped with the promise of two thousand gold ducats to the dead man's uncle in exchange for his pardon of don Juan (*Gipsy*, p. 69). The social order reestablished, all ends well with a joyous marriage between the two lovers now confirmed to be as noble in birth as they are in character.

A literary challenge to established stereotypes. The novella opens with a sharp denunciation of the Gypsies as a race of thieves, a ploy almost certainly calculated to attract readers fascinated by tales of the pícaros. "In such a people the desire to steal and the act of stealing are inseparable instincts which remain with them until they die," the reader is told (*Gipsy*, p. 7). The negative image of the Gypsies is reinforced through a series of details. At the center of the plot is the kidnapping of the infant doña Costanza de Azevedo, later known to her Gypsy kidnapper as Preciosa. Seeing that the girl's talent and beauty "were bound to be powerful attractions and enticements with which to accrue her fortune," Preciosa's "crafty grandmother" first fosters her charms and abilities and later scolds her for hesitating to take some coins (*Gipsy*, p. 7). When Andrés learns the Gypsy ways, his first lessons are on the art of thieving. Classes are imparted with humor and the promise that "you'll like it so much that your fingers will be itching to get on with it" (*Gipsy*, p. 42).

In the story, the Gypsies take great pride in their talents as thieves. But this dark portrait of the Gypsies is not as straightforward as these examples suggest. Throughout the novella, Cervantes alternates "between the acknowledgement of popular stereotypes about Gypsies and his own questioning of these attitudes by showing that Gypsies can be as good as any non-Gypsy" (Ricapito, p. 23). Gypsies are shown to be fiercely independent, aware of and prepared to pay the cost of their free existence. The Gypsies facilitate dealings with corrupt judges with pieces of gold and insure good relations with the local authorities by "handing over some cups and other items of silver" (*Gipsy*, p. 58). When Andrés observes that Gypsies are often whipped, he receives a philosophical response from an older Gypsy:

> Everything in this life's subject to its own dangers, and in his actions a thief risks such consequences as lashes, the galleys, or the gallows. But just because one ship ends up in a storm or sinks doesn't mean that no other ship should sail.... Especially since any man among us who has been lashed by the law wears an insignia on his back that looks far more impressive than the finest one he could wear across his chest.
>
> (*Gipsy*, p. 42)

The Little Gipsy Girl

The joking tone of the older Gypsy belies the seriousness of this point of pride: to be a Gypsy is to survive harsh trials with a strength of character not easily understood, even by Andrés.

Preciosa is first distinguished from the Gypsies, notable among the Gypsy girls not only for her beauty but also for her cleanliness and good manners, proof positive "that she had been born of a better stock than a line of gipsies" (*Gipsy*, p. 7). Her virtue is praised, but on closer reading the other Gypsy girls are virtuous as well. They refuse, out of fear, to venture into a room filled with gentlemen. Gypsy women, explain the elders, are always careful about their virtue—any one guilty or even suspected of adultery is subject to judgment and execution by her peers.

Like Preciosa, the noble don Juan stands out among the real Gypsies. He outshines them at every athletic event and either fakes or pays for the thefts he commits. Petty thieving is indeed portrayed as their stock in trade, served when necessary by lies—"between 'yes' and 'no' we make no distinction when it suits our purpose," observes an older Gypsy (*Gipsy*, p. 39). But the Gypsy men are shown to have extraordinary character as well. They welcome newcomers into their midst without hesitation and offer assistance to the injured poet-page without asking for anything in return. As "lords of the pastures, of the ploughed fields, of the woods and hills, of the springs and rivers," their nearly idyllic lifestyle is based on a profound connection with nature (*Gipsy*, p. 39). This connection is apparent in their love for animals (the thought of killing Andrés's mule, an "innocent" and "blameless creature," is repugnant to them [*Gipsy*, p. 38]) and in their embrace of their surroundings, as the old Gypsy explains:

> We cherish these huts and camps of ours as if they were sumptuous palaces with gilded roofs; we have our own Flemish scenes and landscapes in the lofty crags and snow-covered peaks, in the wide meadows and dense woodlands which surround us every step of the way.
> (*Gipsy*, p. 40)

So detailed a portrayal of basic virtues suggests that they at least partly compensate for the more negative traits presented.

The behavior of the couple bespeaks a class division, relegating Preciosa and Andrés, who are not really Gypsies, to a seemingly higher, more ethical status. This class division is problematic however, once the story shows some crude suppositions about "typical" Gypsy behavior to be untrue, or rather true of everyone. For example, another Gypsy girl, Christina, is moved to jealousy by the celebration welcoming Andrés as Preciosa's suitor, an emotion the narrator is quick to describe as natural, "[f]or envy inhabits barbarian camps and shepherds' huts as well as the palaces of princes, and it is annoying to see your neighbour, who seems no more deserving than yourself, exalted in such a way" (*Gipsy*, p. 43). Here the sin of envy is shown to be universal, as is robbery elsewhere, though this sin is also shown as particular to the Gypsies, keeping with the stereotypes of Cervantes's time.

A large share of the non-Gypsy population is shown to be corrupt. Madrid, "where everything is bought and sold," is home to indolent gentlemen passing the day at cards and magistrates quick to order Preciosa and her colleagues to entertain them (*Gipsy*, pp. 8, 15, and 14). The song Preciosa sings for the magistrate's wife includes wittily veiled slurs on the lady's virtue (suggesting that she has had other husbands and will go on to have many more) and origins (in saying her son the canon will not work in Toledo, the song suggests he is of Converso ancestry) (*Gipsy*, pp. 20-22). The mysterious poet-page Alonso Hurtado seeks Preciosa's love with his sudden, public declarations of passion; his insincerity becomes clear when he explains why he has fled the capital. Almost surprised that Andrés would suggest it, he declares that he has not sought out the Gypsies because of Preciosa: "Madrid has beauties of its own who can and do steal hearts and subjugate souls as well as, and even better than, the loveliest gipsies" (*Gipsy*, p. 50). Instead, Hurtado has fled the capital—with plans to leave the country—following a street fight over a woman in which two men are killed. The seediness of this crime, his vague explanations, and even his name (*hurtado* is Spanish for "stolen") all suggest a more profound and general slipperiness of character.

That the pure love of Andrés and Preciosa develops within the Gypsy camp, not the standard world of class and honor, suggests that there is something of profound value among Gypsies lacking in outside society, which is shown in the story to be highly flawed.

In the prologue to the collection of his 12 exemplary stories, or *novelas ejemplares*, Cervantes explains that he calls the tales exemplary because "on close examination you will see that there is not one from which you cannot extract some profitable example" (Cervantes, p. 4). As the lead story, the importance of the example set forth in *The Little Gipsy Girl* is underscored. Challenging

> ### PRECIOSA AS AN EXEMPLARY LADY
>
> Clever, beautiful, and self-confident, Preciosa appears to the modern reader to be an ideal role model. Within her Golden Age context, however, the Little Gypsy Girl is "the antithesis of a virtuous woman" (Márquez-Raffetto, p. 57). Her Gypsy ties make her morality automatically suspect: at least one 1619 critic denounced Gypsy women as "public whores, common (as they say) to all Gypsy men, who with their lewd dances, gestures, words, and songs do grave damage to the souls of Your Majesty's subjects" (Moncada in Leblon, p. 37; trans. E. Sutherland). Preciosa, who insists on maintaining both her virginity and a level of decency in the songs she sings, clearly shows this racist image to be false. However, her public performances and directness indicate that she is no lady. Golden Age educators had a clear view of what a lady should know and do. A woman's discretion was all-important: in 1524 Juan Luis de Vives advised young women to "be retiring and to take care to not go out much; [a young woman] should know that it reflects poorly on her honor to be known to many and to have her name spoken publicly" (Vives in Márquez-Raffetto p. 57; trans. E. Sutherland). Inside or out, young ladies were counseled to remain silent, as Fray Luis de León advises in his 1583 *La perfecta casada* (*The Perfect Wife*):
>
>> It is right that women take pride in their silence, both those who do well to hide their little wisdom and those who could reveal what they know without shame; because silence and only the least bit of talking are not only a pleasant condition but a necessary virtue in all women.
>>
>> (Léon in Márquez-Raffetto; trans. E. Sutherland, p. 56)
>
> The moment she discovers her true identity, Preciosa becomes an exemplary lady, confessing her love for Andrés with a sigh and murmuring "[w]ith her eyes fixed bashfully on the ground" that "she had only the desire her parents wanted her to have" (*Gipsy*, p. 67). In losing her voice, Preciosa becomes an exemplar according to the social norms of her day. However, there is a careful bit of juggling here in the portrayal of Preciosa's character. Her immense appeal as a Gypsy girl and her willing conformity to the expectations of a lady at the end can be seen as more evidence of Cervantes's desire to challenge contemporary assumptions—this time in relation to women.

stereotypes, the novella thwarts expectations among readers of Cervantes's day, prompting them to question longstanding assumptions and to identify, at least in some ways, with a disparaged ethnic group. "Cervantes makes a very strong statement about cruelty, narrowness of vision, closure of mind, and the place for compassion and understanding toward individuals whose lives are different from that of the average Spaniard" (Ricapito, p. 37). At the same time, the stories promote self-scrutiny on the part of readers. The Gypsy world, segregated from mainstream Spanish society, serves not as a model but as a mirror in which readers can consider the strengths and weaknesses of their own culture and character.

Sources. The choice to feature a Gypsy troupe in this story is both calculated and natural: calculated in that readers of Cervantes's day would be attracted to a picaresque tale about a group as familiar as it was exotic, and natural in that the story of Preciosa and even the anecdote of Juana Carducha are drawn from folklore (Avalle-Arce, pp. 15-16). Cervantes may have drawn his inspiration from versions of these folktales included in a late fifteenth-century comic play (Juan del Encina's *Égloga de requiebro de amor*) and the fourteenth-century miracle tale of Santo

Domingo de la Calzada, respectively. Cervantes had family connections to Gypsies as well: his cousin Martina was the product of his aunt and a half-Gypsy, and it has been speculated that the family had Jewish ancestors as well (Durán, pp. 29-30). Such autobiographical connections are perhaps less important than Cervantes's well-known life of travels and poverty. True to his family history, Miguel de Cervantes spent his life largely on the road. Following a decade overseas, in Italy and later as a prisoner of the Turks in Algiers (1575-80), he would return to Spain to spend 15 years traveling through Andalusia during his stint as a tax collector. Not only was Cervantes familiar with the wandering lifestyle of his time but also with the prisons. (Andrés is imprisoned toward the end of *The Gipsy Girl*.) Imprisoned for debts and other offenses, Cervantes learned firsthand the power a person of rank could wield to effect an early release. His vivid portrait of Gypsy life is clearly a reflection of Cervantes's own complex biography: "he was at the same time *inside* and *outside* the mainstream of Spanish life" (Durán, p. 28).

Reception. The *Exemplary Novels* received no critical attention at the time of their publication, a fact that is not unsurprising given the era. But the censor's seal of approval, required of all publications under the Inquisition, offers a glimpse of how contemporary readers saw them:

> Given as the angelic doctor St. Thomas states that *eutropelia*, or honest entertainment, is a virtue, I judge that true *eutropelia* is in these *Novels*, because they entertain with their originality, they teach with their examples to flee vice and follow virtue, and because the author is true to his intent, thereby giving honor to our Castilian tongue.
>
> (Juan Bautista, p. 248; trans. E. Sutherland)

This blend of entertainment and education evidently appealed to the limited population of seventeenth-century readers, for popular reaction to the *Exemplary Novels* was immediate. They were enormously successful, as indicated by the production of as many as 23 editions within the century. Early critical reaction focused on the exemplary quality of the stories and appeared primarily in other works. One of these reactions came from the still unidentified person who wrote under the pseudonym of Alonso Fernández de Avellaneda and in 1614 produced an imitation of Cervantes's *Don Quixote*. This contemporary found the *Novels* "more satirical than exemplary" but thought them quite clever (Fernández de Avellaneda in Amezúa y Mayo, trans. E. Sutherland, p. 608). Another contemporary was more pointed in his critique, accusing the stories of doing harm, saying that the "lascivious foolishness" of these stories "combats the virtue of married women, the chastity of maidens, and the precious honesty of widows, who often end up seduced by their reasoning" (Cristóbal Suárez de Figueroa in Amezúa y Mayo, trans. E. Sutherland, pp. 609-10). Despite such reactions, the *Novels* spawned multiple imitations in Spain as well as translations and imitations abroad. The first recorded English translation appears to have been in 1630, with dramatic versions appearing as early as 1653 (Amezúa, p. 589). Other translations have been published at regular intervals to the present.

—Erika M. Sutherland

For More Information

Albaicín, Joaquín. *En pos del sol. Los gitanos en la historia, el mito y la leyenda*. Barcelona: Ediciones Obelisco, 1997.

Amezúa y Mayo, Agustín de. *Cervantes, creador de la novela corta española*. Vol. 1. Madrid: Consejo Superior de Investigaciones Científicas, 1982.

Avalle-Arce, Juan Bautista. "La gitanilla." *Cervantes: Bulletin of the Cervantes Society* 1 (1981): 9-17.

Cervantes, Miguel de. *The Little Gipsy Girl*. In *Exemplary Stories*. Trans. Lesley Lipson. New York: Oxford University Press, 1998.

Durán, Manuel. *Cervantes*. New York: Twayne, 1974.

Fernández-Armesto, Felipe. "The Improbable Empire." In *Spain. A History*. Ed. Raymond Carr. New York: Oxford University Press, 2000.

Juan Bautista, Fr. "Aprobación." In *Novelas ejemplares. La ilustre fregona. El casamiento engañoso. Coloquio de los perros*. By Miguel de Cervantes. Madrid: Castalia didáctica, 1997.

Kamen, Henry. *Spain 1469-1714: A Society of Conflict*. New York: Longman, 1983.

———. *The Spanish Inquisition: A Historical Revision*. New Haven: Yale University Press, 1997.

Leblon, Bernard. *Los gitanos de España. El precio y el valor de la diferencia*. Trans. Irene Agoff. Barcelona: Editorial Gedisa, 1993.

Márquez-Raffetto, Tamara. "Inverting the Paradigm: Preciosa's Problematic Exemplarity." *Mester* 25 (1996): 49-78.

Peters, Edward. *Inquisition*. New York: The Free Press, 1988.

Ricapito, Joseph V. *Cervantes's* Novelas ejemplares. *Between History and Creativity*. West Lafayette, Ind.: Purdue University Press, 1992.

Suárez Fernández, Luis. "La población judía en vísperas de 1492. Causas y mecanismos de la expulsión." *Los judíos de España. Historia de una diáspora*. Ed. Henry Méchoulan. Madrid: Ediciones Trotta, 1993.

"The Love Song of J. Alfred Prufrock"

by
T. S. Eliot

Born in St. Louis, Missouri in 1888, Thomas Stearns Eliot attended Milton Academy in Massachusetts, then went on to Harvard University in 1906. As an undergraduate, Eliot developed numerous academic interests, especially in Elizabethan and Jacobean literature, English idealist philosophy, and Indian mystical philosophy. Graduating in 1910, Eliot spent a year abroad, studying literature in France and Germany before returning to Harvard to pursue graduate studies in philosophy. In 1914, shortly after the outbreak of World War I, Eliot moved to England, where he studied Greek philosophy at Merton College, Oxford. Around this time, he also began a close association with poet Ezra Pound, whose help and sponsorship eventually led to the publication of Eliot's early work and to several reviewing, writing, and editing assignments. In 1915 Eliot married Vivien Haigh-Wood, an English writer, and the pair embarked on what was to be an often-troubled marriage. That same year marked the first publication of Eliot's work—"The Love Song of J. Alfred Prufrock" was printed in *Poetry* magazine—as well as the beginning of what was to be a successful career as a poet, critic, and dramatist. Although more notable successes were to follow, such as the landmark publication of *The Waste Land* (1922), Eliot's "The Love Song of J. Alfred Prufrock" remains one of his most frequently studied poems. Evocative, lyrical, and fragmented, it poignantly explores the divided self and the tragedy of inaction.

> **THE LITERARY WORK**
> A dramatic monologue set during the 1910s; published in 1915.
>
> **SYNOPSIS**
> A middle-aged man tries to summon the courage to ask a question that might change his life, but ultimately fails to act.

Events in History at the Time of the Poem

The unconscious mind. The enigmatic opening line of Eliot's poem—"Let us go then, you and I"—has generated much speculation on the part of critics and biographers. Like many dramatic monologues, "The Love Song of J. Alfred Prufrock" addresses an unseen listener; "Prufrock," however, is unusual in that the listener remains not only unseen but unidentified throughout.

Eliot's own remarks on the relations between the mysterious "you and I" have been subject to change over the years. In 1949 Eliot wrote to critic Kristian Smidt:

> As for THE LOVE SONG OF J. ALFRED PRUFROCK anything I say now must be somewhat conjectural, as it was written so long ago that my memory may deceive me; but I am prepared to assert that the "you" in THE LOVE SONG is merely some friend or companion, presumably of the male sex, whom the speaker is at that moment addressing . . .
>
> (Eliot in Headings, p. 24)

"The Love Song of J. Alfred Prufrock"

T. S. Eliot

In an interview in 1962, however, Eliot gave a very different explanation, saying that Prufrock was in part a man of about 40 and in part Eliot himself. Eliot also said that he was using the notion of the split personality, first studied and popularized in his youth.

While it is unclear which interpretation is closer to the truth, Eliot's writing of "Prufrock" did coincide with major developments in behavioral science. During the late nineteenth century, the study of human behavior and human consciousness became more widespread. Experiments were conducted and observations made by a new generation of physicians and scientists, including the Austrian physician Sigmund Freud (1856-1939), giving rise to what would become modern psychology.

The 1900s and 1910s witnessed the publication of groundbreaking works like Freud's *The Interpretation of Dreams* (1900) and Carl Jung's *The Psychology of the Unconscious* (1912), which further explored the workings of the human mind (see Freud's **On Dreams,** also in *Literature and Its Times*). In the first work, Freud maintained that dreams have meaning that can be interpreted on at least two levels—a dream's surface details (what he calls its "manifest content") and its hidden thoughts (its "latent content"). Freud also argued that dreams had their origin in the same unconscious impulses that could, when unbalanced, result in mental illnesses, including phobias and obsessions. In the second work, Jung—a former disciple of Freud's—advanced the theory that the mind consisted of three levels: the conscious, the personal unconscious, and the collective unconscious. The conscious, represented by the ego (a person's conception of himself), consisted of perceptions and memories, serving as the conduit between the person and external reality. By contrast, the personal unconscious, an entity unto itself, consisted of impulses, wishes, and all experiences that had been suppressed or forgotten. Finally, the collective unconscious, located below the personal unconscious, contained—in a form accessible to the individual only indirectly (e.g., through dreams)—latent traces of all the memories inherited from past generations, including primitive ancestors.

"Split personalities." Scientific theories regarding so-called split or multiple personalities were less well known during the early 1900s. However, in 1911, Swiss psychiatrist Eugen Bleuler introduced the term "schizophrenia" (literally, "split mind") to denote a condition characterized by disorganized thought processes and incoherent expressions of ideas and emotion. Schizophrenic patients also exhibited a turning inward, a splitting off from reality. Bleuler's use of the term "split" applied to a split between the intellect and emotion rather than between personalities, although followers and laymen often failed to make that distinction.

It is not known whether Eliot was familiar with the works of Freud, Jung, or Bleuler during the period when "Prufrock" was composed. Nonetheless, lack of certainty has not deterred Eliot scholars and critics from analyzing "Prufrock" according to the tenets of modern psychology, of speculating whether the "you and I" referred to unconscious and conscious mind, respectively. A case could be made for Prufrock's mind appearing to function on several levels, one preoccupied with the stifling social minutiae of tea parties and polite conversation, another teeming with sensual yearnings and erotic fantasies of "sea-girls wreathed with sea-weed red and brown" (Eliot, "The Love Song of Alfred J. Prufrock," line 130).

Bostonian upper-class society. The dreamy, suggestive quality of Eliot's poem makes the setting of "Prufrock" difficult to identify. However, several Eliot scholars have argued persuasively that the landscape of the poem—with its "saw-

"The Love Song of J. Alfred Prufrock"

> ### THE LOVE SONG OF THOMAS STEARNS ELIOT?
>
> In 1915, the same year "Prufrock" was first published, Eliot met Vivienne Haigh-Wood, a dancer and aspiring poet, who was the daughter of English painter Charles Haigh-Wood. After a two-month courtship—whose brevity would probably have astounded the timid, fictional "Prufrock"—Eliot and Vivienne wed, without even informing Eliot's own family. Critic Lyndall Gordon writes, "Eliot, silent and shy, was touched by [Vivienne's] free manner, her lavish temperament, and her downright opinions, frank to the point of what was then thought vulgar—but still charming. . . . He admired her daring, her lightness, her acute sensitivity, and her gift for speech" (Gordon, p. 73). Vivienne, for her part, saw similar potential in Eliot: "He was good-looking, and shared her own quick-wittedness, [he was] a foreigner who might extricate her from the world of Edwardian respectability, and a poet for whom friends like Scofield Thayer predicted a great future" (Ackroyd, p. 63). Despite the initial attraction on both sides, the marriage was not successful, partly because of their unfamiliarity with each other's characters, partly because of her uncertain physical and mental health. For some years Vivienne had been prone to nervous complaints, including migraine headaches and mood swings; shortly after the wedding, she suffered a nervous collapse and was prostrate for months. Eliot himself occasionally suffered from acute nervousness, a tendency aggravated by the necessity of caring for Vivienne, whose life eventually formed a pattern of illnesses, recoveries, and relapses. In 1933 Eliot left Vivienne, who was ultimately committed to a sanitorium, where she died in 1947.

dust restaurants with oyster shells" ("Prufrock," line 7)—mirrors that of late Victorian or Edwardian Boston. As an undergraduate at Harvard University, Eliot had the opportunity to experience the ways of upper-class New England society. Certainly, New England furnished the setting for many of Eliot's early poems, including "Cousin Nancy" and "The Boston Evening Transcript," the latter referring to a now-defunct newspaper noted for its exhaustive coverage of prominent Bostonians' activities and its lengthy obituaries.

Even more than British society, whose customs proper Bostonians were swift to adopt as their own, Boston society had acquired a longstanding reputation over the centuries for excessive formality, propriety, and insularity. Upper-class social life was dominated by the customs and rituals of the "First Families," clans that rose to prominence through successful industrial enterprises or advantageous marriages during Boston's infancy as a town. One famous Bostonian, the writer and doctor Oliver Wendell Holmes described "a man of Family" in Boston as numbering among his ancestors "[f]our or five generations of gentlemen and gentlewomen; among them a member of his Majesty's Council for the Provinces, a Governor or so, one or two Doctors of Divinity, a member of Congress, not later than the time of long boots with tassels" (Holmes in Amory, p. 17). Of necessity, the cream of Boston society was quite small; writer Cleveland Amory noted in 1947 that while Boston itself consisted of about 2.35 million people, Boston Society, according to the *Boston Social Register*, consisted of only 8,000 people (Amory, p. 12).

During the Victorian era (1837-1901), Bostonians evinced a deep interest in manners, publishing numerous books on etiquette. These books addressed a variety of concerns, ranging from how one should conduct oneself at a formal dinner party (quietly and decorously) to how a gentleman should propose to a lady (always under her own roof and never without asking her father's permission first). By the time of Eliot's Harvard career, however, manners—at least in terms of maintaining an openly pleasant and courteous demeanor—had become less important to Bostonians than rigid adherence to social forms and customs. Eliot himself later described Boston society as "quite uncivilized—

"The Love Song of J. Alfred Prufrock"

but refined beyond the point of civilization" (Eliot in Amory, p. 229).

As stultifying as Eliot found turn-of-the-century Boston, he nonetheless drew creative inspiration from it. Literary scholar Lyndall Gordon writes, "To some extent, [Eliot] mastered Boston by understanding it; he felt aversion for it, but aversion did not mean he was immune. He took upon himself, perhaps involuntarily, the character of late nineteenth-century Boston . . . its rigid manners, its loss of vigour, its estrangement from so many areas of life, its painful self-consciousness" (Gordon, p. 18). Many of the aforementioned qualities associated with genteel Bostonian life can be detected in "The Love Song of J. Alfred Prufrock"—the sterile round of tea parties and formal calls, the brittle, artificial conversation considered proper at such social functions, and the "painful self-consciousness" of Prufrock himself who does not know how to break out of his circumscribed surroundings and declare himself to the nameless lady he desires: "Should I, after tea and cakes and ices, / Have the strength to force the moment to its crisis?" ("Prufrock," lines 79-80).

Modernism and symbolism. The modernist movement, which dominated literature during the first half of the twentieth century, featured, among other characteristics, textual experimentation, an emphasis on subjective experience, and a radical break with traditional forms of Western culture. Modernist writers continually questioned the certainties of established institutions of religion, morality, and self-definition, often concluding that there were no ready answers or solutions to whatever problems they perceived.

Although modernism in literature gathered momentum in the years after World War I, many literary historians contend that the seeds for the movement were sown back in the 1890s. The Aesthetic movement in England, which espoused the cause of "art for art's sake," widened the gap between the expectations of the largely middle-class public and the aspirations of the artist, fostering a sense of alienation in the latter. This phenomenon was not exclusive to England. Aestheticism in England was an offshoot of a kindred movement in France, whose roots went back to the 1830s. Similarly English modernism was influenced in large part by a movement in France, namely by the French Symbolist Movement, which included such writers as Charles Baudelaire, Arthur Rimbaud, Paul Verlaine, Stéphane Mallarmé, and Jules Laforgue. Baudelaire, often regarded as the father of the Symbolist movement, based the symbolic mode of his poetry "on the ancient belief in correspondences—the doctrine that there exist inherent and systematic analogies between the human mind and the outer world, and also between the natural and the spiritual world" (Abrams, *Glossary,* p. 209). The writings of French Symbolists tended to be atmospheric and suggestive rather than direct and explicit. Conventional expectations about life and art, along with the ordinary society that fostered those expectations, were to be rejected by the artist in favor of a more untrammeled lifestyle and aesthetics.

The ideas formulated by the Aesthetes and Symbolists found a receptive audience in the generation that followed. Although many British poets in the years before World War I wrote in traditional lyrical modes, celebrating nature, love, and England, others poets experimented with form, imagery, and tone. The same could be said of poets in America. Eliot himself fell under the spell of the French Symbolists during his time at Harvard. After reading Arthur Symons's *The Symbolist Movement in Literature* (1909), he went on to acquaint himself with the works of Baudelaire and Laforgue. In later years, Eliot praised Baudelaire for revealing to him the poetic possibility of "the more sordid aspects of the modern metropolis, of the possibility of fusion between the sordidly realistic and the phantasmagoric, the possibility of the juxtaposition of the matter-of-fact and the fantastic" (Eliot in Headings, p. 10). From Baudelaire, Eliot learned that the sort of material that he had experienced as an adolescent in an industrial city of America could be turned into poetry, that "the business of the poet was to make poetry out of the unexplored resources of the unpoetical" (Eliot in Headings, p. 10). The Symbolist influences can be readily detected in "The Love Song of J. Alfred Prufrock," no less in the details of the poem's setting—the "one-night cheap hotels" and dingy "yellow fog that rubs its back upon the windowpanes"—than in the resoundingly unpoetical name of the speaker, preoccupied with the mundane realities of his thinning hair and spindly physique ("Prufrock," lines 6, 15).

The Poem in Focus

The plot. "The Love-Song of J. Alfred Prufrock" is prefaced by a passage from Dante's ***Inferno*** (also in *Literature and Its Times*). Spoken by Guido da Montefeltro, imprisoned in a flame as punishment for being a false counselor in his life, the lines can

"The Love Song of J. Alfred Prufrock"

The narrator of T.S. Eliot's *The Love Song of J. Alfred Prufrock* finds solace in the sensual symbolism of the mermaid. Shown here, a painting by Sir Edward Burne-Jones (1833–98), who made mermaids a common subject of his works in the 1880s.

be translated as, "If I thought that my reply would be to one who would ever return to the world, this flame would stay without further movement; but since none has ever returned alive from this depth, if what I hear is true, I may answer you without fear of infamy" (Eliot in Abrams, *Norton Anthology* p. 2140 n. 2). Montefeltro will speak to Dante of his shameful life only if he can be sure that Dante will never return to earth to repeat the tale. The passage proves relevant—and prophetic—to Eliot's fearful narrator, who likewise can only express himself in a void.

The poem itself begins as the middle-aged J. Alfred Prufrock remarks to an unseen listener, "Let us go then, you and I, / When the evening is spread out against the sky / Like a patient etherized upon a table" ("Prufrock," lines 1-3). This startling comparison sets the stage for an equally startling journey, as Prufrock and his unidentified companion travel through "certain half-deserted streets" towards a destination where "an overwhelming question" may be asked (lines 4, 10). Prufrock himself shies away from discussing the nature of the question: "Oh, do not ask, 'What is it?' / Let us go and make our visit" ("Prufrock," lines 11-12).

Although random details of the physical landscape through which he travels impinge on Prufrock's consciousness, he remains preoccupied by thoughts of this visit—to a tea party where elegant women discuss art, literature, and other genteel topics. The middle-aged Prufrock feels daunted by whatever question he intends to ask. Sensual musings on women's arms

"The Love Song of J. Alfred Prufrock"

"braceleted and white and bare" and women's perfumed dresses are continually undercut by Prufrock's own feelings of inadequacy as a potential suitor—thin, advanced in age, and balding, despite his fine clothes and manners ("Prufrock," line 63). Remarking with a certain self-contempt "I have measured out my life with coffee spoons," Prufrock wonders how he could break out of the polite, artificial society, in which he himself has lived so long, to make a declaration to one of the ladies who is attending the party: "And should I then presume? / And how should I begin?" ("Prufrock," lines 51, 68-69).

The poem undergoes a sudden break as Prufrock tries to frame a beginning to his question, "Shall I say, I have gone at dusk through narrow streets / And watched the smoke that rises from the pipes / Of lonely men in shirt-sleeves, leaning out of windows?" ("Prufrock," lines 70-71). The question chokes to a stop, leaving Prufrock to conclude pessimistically that he "should have been a pair of ragged claws / Scuttling across the floors of silent seas" ("Prufrock," lines 73-74).

An indefinite number of hours seem to have elapsed between the earlier and later sections of the poem. On resuming his monologue, Prufrock speaks of the tea party and the "overwhelming question" as events that have already taken place. Although nothing is explicit, it is implied that the evening has passed, and so has Prufrock's opportunity to declare himself. As Prufrock muses over what did or, rather, did *not* take place at the party, all his insecurities resurface—fear of exposure, ridicule, aging, and even death, which Prufrock inevitably views in social terms: "I have seen the moment of my greatness flicker, / And I have seen the eternal Footman hold my coat, and snicker, / And in short, I was afraid" ("Prufrock," lines 84-86). Prufrock's fears of loneliness and death, however, are superseded by his fear of rejection. He wonders continually, "Would it have been worth while" to have asked that question, "If one, settling a pillow or throwing off a shawl, / And turning towards the window, should say: 'That is not it at all, / That is not what I meant, at all'" ("Prufrock," lines 106, 107-110).

Defeated by his own timidity, Prufrock again deflates himself as a romantic figure—in the play of life, he is "not Prince Hamlet" but only "an attendant lord . . . / Deferential, glad to be of use, / Politic, cautious, and meticulous" ("Prufrock," lines 111, 112, 115-116). Contemplating the empty years before him, Prufrock indulges briefly in a whimsical fantasy of himself as an eccentric elderly beachcomber in white flannel trousers. But his melancholy returns as he imagines the mermaids of legend, whom he does not think will ever sing to him. Prufrock's sensual yearnings and fantasies are destined to be fulfilled only in his imagination. The poem ends with Prufrock and his still-unidentified companion seeking solace in one such fantasy: "We have lingered in the chambers of the sea / By sea-girls wreathed with seaweed red and brown / Till human voices wake us, and we drown" ("Prufrock," lines 129-131).

A modern voice. Eliot's emphasis on negativity and impersonality in his poetry has been the focus of many scholarly studies. In his 1919 essay "Tradition and the Individual Talent," Eliot rejected the idea that the poet's own personality should in any way impose upon the poem:

> Poetry is not a turning loose of emotions, but an escape from emotion; it is not the expression of personality, but an escape from personality. But, of course, only those who have personality and emotions know what it means to want to escape from those things. . . . The emotion of art is impersonal. And the poet cannot reach this impersonality without surrendering himself wholly to the work to be done.
> (Eliot in Abrams, *Norton Anthology* pp. 2175-76)

In his early poems, Eliot often experimented with the concept of impersonality through the creation of a separate persona. This technique was common practice in the dramatic monologue, a revelatory lyric poem uttered by a speaker distinct from the poet, in a specific situation at a critical moment. In the nineteenth century, several Victorian poets had popularized the dramatic monologue through such poems as Alfred Tennyson's "Ulysses" and Robert Browning's "My Last Duchess." Like Tennyson and Browning, Eliot sets his monologue "The Love Song of J. Alfred Prufrock" during a crucial moment in the speaker's life, allowing the speaker to reveal his true temperament and character in the course of the poem.

While Tennyson and Browning chose mythological or historical figures as their narrators, Eliot chooses a contemporary persona—a timid, middle-aged man, painfully self-conscious about his thinning hair and his emotional and physical limitations as a romantic suitor. Much of Prufrock's personality and his journey are described in negative terms. Literary scholar Eloise

Knapp Hay points out that "Prufrock summons us to go a certain way with him and then takes us nowhere" (Hay, p. 1). The visit that is to culminate in the asking of "an overwhelming question" ends in silence and a retreat, on Prufrock's part, into romantic fantasies. Similarly, Prufrock tends to define himself mainly by what he is not—not young, not handsome, not a prophet or a prince—rather than by what he is or what he has to offer. The poem's "last words lead to total self-effacement. The 'crisis' is ended when Prufrock resorts to the seashore and mythical dreams to escape his treacherous society. . . . in the last strophe he attains the refuge of total immersion in dream," through which the speaker achieves a virtual self-sacrifice (Hay, pp. 19-20).

Between the 1910s and 1920s, artistic restlessness, a sense of alienation from the general public, and a cataclysmic world war all contributed to a desire on the part of poets to reinvigorate and revolutionize their craft. Eliot's own experiments with verse, character, and tone became part of what would be called the modernist movement in literature. Several qualities of "Prufrock" mark it as a modern poem: its irregular free verse rhythms, its fragmentary structure (consisting of loosely connected sections), and its self-centered narrator. Some critics have even chosen to read "Prufrock" as the confessional of a "modern" man, sensitive, cultured, but incapable of action and doomed to futility.

Sources and literary context. Eliot drew from a variety of sources, both mundane and romantic, to write "The Love Song of J. Alfred Prufrock." The speaker's prosaic surname, which appears only in the poem's title, was the name of a firm of furniture wholesalers in Eliot's home town of St. Louis, during the 1900s. The poem itself, however, contains numerous allusions to Dante, Shakespeare, and the Bible. Like the Dantean speaker in the poem's epigraph, Prufrock is unwilling to tell his story to any listener who might reveal it to the world. Unlike the Shakespearean Hamlet and the biblical Lazarus, Prufrock—in his own eyes—cuts an insignificant and unromantic figure; he is neither a dashing prince nor someone resurrected from the dead.

Other influences include contemporary authors and literary movements, specifically, the French symbolist poets Rimbaud, Baudelaire, and Laforgue. Likewise, Eliot's work owes something to the Imagism movement. Popular in both England and the United States, Imagism called for a poetry that abandoned conventional subjects and traditional versification in favor of freer choices of subject and metrical patterns, common speech, and sharp, clear images.

As previously discussed, Eliot also drew upon the works of the past for "Prufrock," specifically the dramatic monologues of the Victorian poets Tennyson and Browning. One literary critic writes that "Like Tennyson and Browning, Eliot uses the dramatic monologue to explore man's imprisonment within his own consciousness" (Christ, p. 46). There is, notes the critic, a resemblance especially between Eliot's monologues and Tennyson's, with certain comparative advances in the later poet's verse.

> The Modernist techniques that separate Eliot from Tennyson in fact allow him to intensify the effects that Tennyson also sought to achieve. Readers have frequently noted the vagueness in the definition of setting and audience in Tennyson's dramatic monologues. Eliot quite brilliantly transforms what is sometimes a confusion of address in Tennyson's poems to a deliberately manipulated dissonance that confirms the speaker's isolation.
> (Christ, p. 48)

Reviews. "The Love Song of J. Alfred Prufrock" appeared first in *Poetry* magazine in 1915, then was published two years later in the 1917 volume *Prufrock and Other Observations*. The book received mixed reviews. Detractors, such as the reviewer for the *Times Literary Supplement*, complained, "Mr. Eliot's notion of poetry . . . seems to be a purely analytical treatment verging sometimes on the catalogue, of personal relations and environments, uninspired by any glimpse beyond them and untouched by any genuine rush of feeling" (Anonymous in Grant, p. 73). The reviewer for *Literary World* was likewise unimpressed, calling Eliot "one of those clever young men who find it amusing to pull the leg of a sober reviewer" and dismissing "The Love Song of J. Alfred Prufrock" as "neither witty nor amusing" (Anonymous in Grant, p. 74).

Eliot had his admirers, however. In an essay of 1917, Ezra Pound defended his protégé, declaring, "I should like the reader to note how complete is Mr. Eliot's depiction of our contemporary condition. He has not confined himself to genre nor to society portraiture" (Pound in Grant, p. 76). Comparing Eliot's dramatic monologues favorably to those of Victorian poet Robert Browning, Pound added, "Mr. Eliot's work interests me more than that of any other poet now writing in English"

"The Love Song of J. Alfred Prufrock"

(Pound in Grant, p. 77). Eliot's contemporary and fellow poet Conrad Aiken wrote in *Dial* magazine, "For the two semi-narrative psychological portraits which form the greater and better part of his book, 'The Love Song of J. Alfred Prufrock' and the 'Portrait of a Lady,' one can have little but praise. . . . Mr. Eliot writes pungently and sharply, with an eye for unexpected and vivid details" (Aiken in Grant, p. 81). The English novelist May Sinclair, writing for *Little Review*, predicted a great future for Eliot and singled out several poems, including "The Love Song of J. Alfred Prufrock," for special praise.

> Mr. Eliot . . . knows what he is after. Reality, stripped naked of all rhetoric, of all ornament, of all confusing and obscuring association. . . . Mr. Eliot is careful to present his street and his drawing-room as they are, and Prufrock's thoughts as they are; live thoughts, kicking, running about and jumping, nervily, in a live brain.
> (Sinclair in Grant, pp. 86-87)

—Pamela S. Loy

For More Information

Abrams, M. H. *A Glossary of Literary Terms*. Fort Worth: Harcourt Brace Jovanovich, 1993.

———. *The Norton Anthology of English Literature*. Vol. 2. New York: W. W. Norton, 1993.

Ackroyd, Peter. *T. S. Eliot: A Life*. New York: Simon and Schuster, 1984.

Amory, Cleveland. *The Proper Bostonians*. New York: E. P. Dutton & Co., 1947.

Bergonzi, Bernard. *T. S. Eliot*. New York: Macmillan Company, 1972.

Bush, Ronald. *T. S. Eliot: A Study in Character and Style*. New York: Oxford University Press, 1983.

Christ, Carol T. *Victorian and Modern Poetics*. Chicago: University of Chicago Press, 1984.

Eliot, T. S. "The Love Song of J. Alfred Prufrock." In *The Norton Anthology of English Literature*. Vol. 2. Ed. M. H. Abrams. New York: W. W. Norton, 1993.

Gordon, Lyndall. *Eliot's Early Years*. Oxford: Oxford University Press, 1977.

Grant, Michael, Ed. *T. S. Eliot: The Critical Heritage*. London: Routledge & Kegan Paul, 1982.

Hay, Eloise Knapp. *T. S. Eliot's Negative Way*. Cambridge: Harvard University Press, 1982.

Headings, Philip R. *T. S. Eliot*. Boston: Twayne Publishers, 1982.

Kirk, Russell. *Eliot and His Age*. New York: Random House, 1972.

Lyrical Ballads

by
William Wordsworth and Samuel Taylor Coleridge

Born in West Cumberland, England, in 1770, William Wordsworth was educated at a local school in Hawkshead in the heart of the English Lake District, and later at St. John's College, Cambridge. In 1791 he traveled to France, where he became an ardent advocate of the French Revolution, then in its earliest and most idealistic stages. He also became romantically involved with a Frenchwoman, Annette Vallon, who bore him an illegitimate daughter. They planned to wed, but lack of money forced Wordsworth to return to England in December 1792. Guilt over the separation and disillusionment with the direction that the Revolution had taken drove Wordsworth to the brink of an emotional breakdown. Turning to poetry as an escape, he published *Descriptive Sketches* (1793), which recounts his tour of the Swiss Alps. In 1795 Wordsworth received a legacy from a friend that enabled him to pursue a career as a poet; he also met Samuel Taylor Coleridge. Born in Devonshire in 1772, Coleridge attended Jesus College, Cambridge. He was a voracious reader, devouring libraries of books, and was more a philosopher than a poet. Oppressed by debt and despondent over a brother's death, he dropped out of Cambridge in his third year of college, served briefly in a cavalry regiment, and then met Wordsworth. He also became politically active, advocating Utopian schemes and promoting a sort of nonviolent revolution to eradicate social and political barriers in England. His radicalism was channeled into poetry as the 1790s progressed. In 1798 Coleridge and Wordsworth published—anonymously—a small volume of their work, *Lyrical Ballads, with a Few Other Poems*, which launched a revolutionary movement in poetry.

THE LITERARY WORK

A collection of 23 poems set in rural England during the late eighteenth century; first published anonymously in 1798.

SYNOPSIS

Conveyed through the poems are emotional responses to the natural and supernatural in conversational verse. The initial poem, Coleridge's "The Rime of the Ancient Mariner," concerns a supernatural curse; the final one, Wordsworth's "Lines Composed a Few Miles Above Tintern Abbey," features a changing relationship to the natural world.

Events in History at the Time of the Poems

From Neoclassicism to Romanticism. From 1660 to the 1789 outbreak of the French Revolution, the type of literature dominating England was Neoclassicism; the term stems from the intense admiration that seventeenth- and eighteenth-century authors held for the "classical" writers of ancient Greece and Rome, who were considered models to imitate. Neoclassic poets shared:

Lyrical Ballads

1) A reverence for tradition, often paired with a distrust of innovation
2) The conception of literature as an art that could be perfected only by study and practice
3) The belief that poetry should hold a mirror up to nature and should provide instruction as well as aesthetic pleasure
4) An emphasis on shared human experiences
5) The acceptance of man as a limited being who must resign himself to his place in the natural hierarchy and submit to God's superior wisdom and authority

A shift away from Neoclassicism became noticeable toward the end of the eighteenth century, after William Blake and Robert Burns published poems in a very different style than that employed by earlier eighteenth-century poets, such as Alexander Pope, and found a significant following among contemporary readers (see Blake's *Songs of Innocence and of Experience*, also in *Literature and Its Times*). Other poets soon followed Blake's lead, breaking new literary ground.

In contrast to the Neoclassic poets, the "Romantics" developed a new school of writing with its own set of shared characteristics:

1) A preference for poetic innovation over adherence to tradition
2) The belief that the composition of poetry should be spontaneous and natural
3) An emphasis on landscape and nature, especially as they affect the poet's perceptions
4) The choice of the self or social outcasts as poetic subjects
5) The conception of man as a being of limitless potential and aspirations whose failures could be considered as glorious as his successes

Many of these Romantic characteristics can be observed in the poems in *Lyrical Ballads*; Coleridge's "The Rime of the Ancient Mariner" and Wordsworth's "The Mad Mother" both feature outcasts as their protagonists, while Wordsworth's "Lines Composed a Few Miles Above Tintern Abbey" explores the emotional and spiritual effects that revisiting a well-loved landscape has upon the mind of the poet.

Politically, the Romantic movement has been linked to the outbreak of the French Revolution in 1789. At first English liberals and radicals supported the popular revolution. A new age of "liberty, equality, and fraternity" seemed about to dawn and many young Englishmen, including William Wordsworth, eagerly lent their efforts to the cause. But the carnage of France's 1792-94 Reign of Terror (in which the revolutionaries guillotined tens of thousands of alleged opponents) and the ascent of Napoleon Bonaparte as emperor diminished hopes of social equality in Wordsworth and his contemporaries. Still, the dream of fresh beginnings persisted, leading to a new literary tradition that would dominate the next three decades. This tradition was part and parcel of the revolutionary spirit in an age during which old idols were toppled, new ideas and doctrines introduced, and bold experiments performed.

The "Great Chain of Being." The Neoclassic poets and their eighteenth-century contemporaries subscribed to the theological concept of the Great Chain of Being, which stipulated that the universe held every possible kind and variety of life, that each species differed from the next by the least possible degree, and that all of creation was arranged in a hierarchy, extending from the least to the greatest species, all the way up to God Himself. According to this model, humans occupied a middle position, above the animals but below the angels: all creatures—especially humanity—were expected to accept their divinely allotted place in God's scheme and not attempt to reach beyond their position with vain aspirations.

In *Lyrical Ballads*, these tenets are subtly but continually challenged, most notably in "The Rime of the Ancient Mariner." The Mariner's thoughtless and wanton shooting of the albatross results in as rigorous a punishment—for him and his shipmates—as if the bird were indeed the "Christian soul" to which the sailors have compared it (Coleridge, "Rime," line 65). Moreover, the Mariner's redemption does not begin until he learns to reverence what he has formerly despised—the "thousand thousand slimy things" of the deep, which are nonetheless God's creatures, too ("Rime," line 238). In his final injunction to his captive listener, the Mariner implicitly dismisses the belief that one form of life is superior to another, in the lines, "He prayeth well, who loveth well / Both man and bird and beast" ("Rime," lines 611-12).

Religious temper of the times. During the 1740s, a new religious movement developed in opposition to the Anglican Church. Called the Methodist movement, it was led by John Wesley, an English theologian educated at Oxford, and it emphasized the importance of faith over good works as the road to salvation. Although Anglican clerics and members of the upper classes were often repelled by the emotionalism and zeal aroused by Methodist preachers, the new religious awakening flourished, reinvigorating both the Anglican Church and some of the Dissenters' sects, which diverged from it. During the 1780s and 1790s, Methodism was growing among university students, especially at Cambridge.

Many of these students objected to the Test Acts, which stipulated that scholars who wished to receive a university degree had to subscribe to the Thirty-nine Articles of the Anglican faith. Rejection of Anglican doctrines contributed to a resurgence of Unitarianism around this time, a creed that emphasized the role of reason in religion and presented an increasingly scientific view of the universe. Main tenets of eighteenth-century Unitarianism stressed the oneness or unipersonality of God, the humanity—rather than divinity—of Jesus, and the importance of man's rational faculty.

Many young intellectuals embraced Unitarianism, including Coleridge early in his university career. To be a Unitarian at the time implied certain other traits pertaining to the follower, namely that one sympathized with the French Revolution and opposed aristocracy. "Radicalism in politics and rationalism in religion went hand in hand" (Willey, p. 16). In 1794 Coleridge made a full conversion to Unitarianism, enthusiastically supporting—even propagandizing—its agenda. For a time, he and the poet Robert Southey planned to found a democratic community based on Unitarian ideals in the United States. The scheme fell through, but not before Coleridge had committed himself to marrying Sara Fricker, the sister of Southey's own fiancée. The marriage later foundered, as did Coleridge's belief in Unitarianism, but at the time that *Lyrical Ballads* was being composed, Coleridge's faith was still intact.

In general, Coleridge developed a concept of nature as an entity comprised "of living intelligent forces, seen sometimes as parts of a divine mind which transcend[s] them and sometimes as agents of that mind, but always as working to fulfill divine purpose" (Piper, pp. 86-87). Scholars trace this concept to his Unitarianism. In "The Rime of the Ancient Mariner," even the spirits of the polar region are presented as thinking beings with clearly defined purposes, a view that the Mariner, despite his delirium, acknowledges and understands: "Under the keel nine fathom deep / From the land of mist and snow / The spirit slid: and it was he / That made the ship to go" ("Rime," lines 377-80).

An illustration by Gustave Doré of the line "It ate the food it ne'er had eat," from Coleridge's "The Rime of the Ancient Mariner."

Rural and industrial England. *Lyrical Ballads* struck a chord with contemporary readers for several reasons, in part because it evoked the natural world and a rural way of life that was rapidly vanishing. Since the mid-eighteenth century, the Industrial Revolution had been ushering in dramatic economic and social changes. James Watt's invention of the steam engine in 1765 introduced a power source that would replace wind and water. In the textile and other industries, machines began to replace manual labor. Mill towns and factories arose in northern and central England, where a new laboring population gathered in search of work, inhabiting slums and tenements that sprang up to shelter the newly arrived workers.

The advance of technology, as well as other changes, impinged on the lives of many rural dwellers. New machines led to the end of home and cottage industries. Meanwhile, enclosures of open-field and communally worked lands, creating new private holdings, drove many small farmers out of rural areas. Such enclosures had been taking place for centuries, unofficially, but

Lyrical Ballads

the pace quickened from 1761 to 1801. Parliament passed 1,1479 acts that legislated the enclosure of some 2.4 million acres, threatening to wipe out small farmers and rural laborers in the designated areas (Mahoney, p. 67). As stone walls and hedges partitioned off lands that had once been cultivated by communities, many rural dwellers were left with two choices: to migrate to the industrial towns or to eke out a living as farm workers on subsistence wages.

Meanwhile, the war between England and France—which had begun in 1793—helped drive up the cost of living. "Between 1790 and 1795 the price of oats rose 75 percent, that of a loaf of bread doubled in the country and tripled in London, and that of a pound of potatoes quadrupled.... These economic factors... were catastrophic for the rural poor" (Johnston, p. 478). At the time, Wordsworth was setting up a household with his sister Dorothy in the rural town of Racedown. "The country people here," he told his friend William Mathews, "are wretchedly poor" (Wordsworth in Johnston, p. 478). Perhaps because of their wretched poverty, the "country people" of Racedown and, later, Somersetshire attained a powerful hold on Wordsworth's imagination, as manifested in *Lyrical Ballads*. "Simon Lee" tells of an old huntsman and his wife who have fallen on hard times since the death of his master:

> A scrap of land they have, but they
> Are poorest of the poor.
> This scrap of land he from the heath
> Enclosed when he was stronger;
> But what avails the land to them,
> When they can till no longer?
> (Wordsworth, "Simon Lee," lines 59-64).

The Poems in Focus

Contents summary. *Lyrical Ballads* is prefaced with an "Advertisement" that identifies the collected poems as experiments: "They were written chiefly with a view to ascertain how far the language of conversation in the middle and lower classes of society is adapted to the purposes of poetic pleasure" (Wordsworth and Coleridge, *Lyrical Ballads*, p. 7). The poems themselves concentrate on humble subjects and rustic settings, although a few explore the mythical and supernatural. Of the total 23 poems, Coleridge contributed only four. Framing the initial 1798 edition are Coleridge's "The Rime of the Ancient Mariner" and Wordsworth's "Lines Composed a Few Miles Above Tintern Abbey."

"The Rime of the Ancient Mariner." The poem begins as an ancient mariner approaches a guest at a wedding and begins to tell him a tale. Although the wedding guest tries to fend the mariner off, he mesmerizes the guest into submission: "He holds him with his glittering eye— / The Wedding Guest stood still / And listens like a three year's child; / The Mariner hath his will" ("Rime," lines 17-20).

The mariner continues with his tale, relating how his ship sailed to the equator, then was driven toward the South Pole by a storm, where it drifted through freezing mists, past arctic wastelands. An albatross flies toward the ship, and the crew, taking the bird's appearance as a good omen, receives it hospitably. When the ice breaks, allowing the ship to pass through and resume a northward course, the albatross follows. The mariner shoots the bird with his crossbow.

Fearing an ill omen, the crew initially cries out against the mariner's killing of the albatross, but when the wind holds and the sun rises, they agree that the killing was justified, making themselves complicit in the deed. As they near the equator, the wind dies down and the ship is becalmed. Parched with thirst and convinced that they are being pursued by a vengeful spirit, the angry crew hangs the body of the albatross around the mariner's neck, as a sign of his guilt.

Sometime later, the mariner spies a shape approaching them and manages to call out to his shipmates. Hoping for rescue, all are horrified when they behold a ghostly ship drawing near, with only two spectral inhabitants on board—a man who looks like Death himself and an even more terrifying woman: "Her skin was white as leprosy, / The Night-Mare LIFE-IN-DEATH was she, / Who thicks man's blood with gold" ("Rime," lines 192-94). Death and Life-in-Death throw dice for the ship's crew, the latter winning the mariner. The ghost-ship vanishes at sunset and as the moon rises, the mariner's shipmates drop dead, leaving him the sole survivor: "And every soul, it passed me by, / Like the whizz of my crossbow!" ("Rime," lines 222-23).

In the present, the wedding guest fears he is being held captive by a spirit, but the mariner reassuringly affirms that he is a living man and continues his story. On board ship, surrounded by the corpses of his comrades, the mariner experiences agonies of loneliness and self-loathing: "The many men, so beautiful! / And they all dead did lie: / And a thousand, thousand slimy things / Lived on; and so did I" ("Rime," lines 236-39). Desolate, the mariner tries in vain to pray and yearns for death, but to no avail. After seven days and nights, he sees two water snakes swimming in the deep and is struck by their beauty:

> A spring of love gushed from my heart,
> And I blessed them unaware . . .
> The self-same moment I could pray;
> And from my neck so free
> The Albatross fell off, and sank
> Like lead into the sea.
> ("Rime," lines 284-85, 288-91)

Exhausted, the mariner sinks into a healing slumber, awakening to find himself drenched in rain: the drought has ended. Suddenly, the ship's sails fill and the ship, so long becalmed, begins to move. To the mariner's astonishment, the bodies of his shipmates arise and begin to pilot the vessel. The mariner realizes that spirits have inhabited the corpses of the dead crew. The ship sails smoothly on until it reaches the equator, then stops abruptly; the mariner swoons, falling to the deck. Returning gradually to consciousness, he hears "two voices in the air" discussing his situation and learns that he has been given a long, heavy penance by the Spirit of the South Pole for shooting the albatross, and his punishment is not yet over ("Rime," line 397).

Meanwhile, the ship has sped northward while the mariner lay unconscious; the speed slackens when he regains his senses, but the mariner can nonetheless see that the ship is approaching his own land and safe harbor and is overjoyed. Just as the ship nears the bay, the mariner sees that his shipmates' bodies have again collapsed on the deck, but "[a] man all light, a seraph man / On every corse [corpse] there stood" ("Rime," lines 490-91). The sound of oars breaks the silence; the mariner sees a boat carrying a pilot, the pilot's boy, and the local hermit, who lives in the wood by the sea. When the ship suddenly sinks, casting the mariner into the water, the pilot comes to the rescue, pulling him into the boat. The mariner's presence, however, disturbs his rescuers, sending the pilot into a fit and the pilot's boy into a mad frenzy. Once on land, the mariner pleads with the hermit to shrive his soul. Compelled by a "woeful agony" to relate his tale of misfortune to the hermit, the mariner at last finds himself free, but only for the present: "Since then, at an uncertain hour, / That agony returns: / And till my ghastly tale is told / This heart within me burns" ("Rime," lines 582-85).

The mariner informs the wedding guest that he always knows the person to whom he must tell his tale and, before taking his leave, urges him to love and honor all God's creatures: "He prayeth best, who loveth best / All things both great and small; / For the dear God who loveth us, / He made and loveth all" ("Rime," lines 614-17).

Alone and much shaken by what he has heard, the wedding guest leaves the festivities: "He went like one that hath been stunned, / And is of sense forlorn: / A sadder and a wiser man, / He rose the morrow morn" ("Rime," lines 622-25).

"Lines Composed a Few Miles Above Tintern Abbey." The poem begins as Wordsworth revisits—after a 5-year absence—one of his favorite places, the banks of the Wye River, a few miles above the ruins of Tintern Abbey:

> Once again
> Do I behold these steep and lofty cliffs
> Which on a wild secluded scene impress
> Thoughts of a more deep seclusion: and connect
> The landscape with the quiet of the sky.
> (Wordsworth, "Tintern Abbey," lines 4-8)

Traces of civilization intrude on the serene scene, not all of them happy.

> These hedge-rows; hardly hedge-rows, little lines
> Of sportive wood runs wild; these pastoral farms
> Green to the very door; and wreathes of smoke
> Sent up, in silence, from among the trees,
> With some uncertain notice, as might seem,
> Of vagrant dwellers in the houseless woods,
> Or of some hermit's cave, where by his fire
> The hermit sits alone.
> ("Tintern Abbey," lines 18-23)

The scene stimulates Wordsworth's memory. Recalling his recent sojourns "in lonely rooms, and mid the din / Of towns and cities," he reflects on how his memories of nature brought him "sensations sweet, / Felt in the blood and felt along the heart" ("Tintern Abbey," lines 25-26, 27-28).

Returning to the present, Wordsworth gazes on the scene before him, storing up memories for the future. He thinks back to the time when he first visited this spot as a boy and "bounded o'er the mountains, by the sides / Of the deep rivers, and the lonely streams, / Wherever nature led . . . / I cannot paint / What then I was" ("Tintern Abbey," lines 68-70, 75-76). Despite having outgrown the "aching joys" and "dizzy raptures" of boyhood, the adult Wordsworth nonetheless believes that he has received "abundant recom-

Wordsworth composed his poem a few miles above Tintern Abbey, seen here.

pense" through a more mature appreciation of what nature has to offer:

> For I have learned
> To look on nature, not as in the hour
> Of thoughtless youth, but hearing oftentimes
> The still, sad music of humanity,
> Not harsh nor grating, though of ample power
> To chasten and subdue.
> ("Tintern Abbey," lines 88-93)

THE BALLAD STANZA

The publication of Bishop Thomas Percy's *Reliques of Ancient Poetry* (1765) revived the ballad as a poetic genre and inspired countless modern imitators, including Wordsworth and Coleridge. Popular ballads were generally written in quatrains in alternating four- and three-stress iambic (an unstressed syllable preceding a stressed syllable) lines. Generally, the second and fourth lines—and occasionally, the first and third—rhymed. While not all of the *Lyrical Ballads* use the ballad stanza, the form can be seen in Wordsworth's "We Are Seven" and Coleridge's "The Rime of the Ancient Mariner": "Alóne, alóne, all, áll alóne, / Alóne on a wíde wide séa! / And néver a sáint took píty ón / My sóul in ágony!" ("Rime," lines 232-35)

Grateful for this heightened understanding, Wordsworth hails nature as "the anchor of my purest thoughts, the nurse, / The guide, the guardian of my heart, and soul / Of all my moral being" ("Tintern Abbey," lines 109-11).

Moreover, Wordsworth contends, he can experience vicariously the childlike joy his companion and younger sister, Dorothy, still feels: "In thy voice I catch / The language of my former heart, and read / My former pleasures in the shooting lights / Of thy wild eyes" ("Tintern Abbey," lines 116-19). Wordsworth enjoins Nature to bestow upon his sister the same blessings and teachings he has received, then maintains that not even his death can sunder him and Dorothy, who are connected through their love of nature as well as blood. He concludes his address to her by stating that "these steep woods and lofty cliffs, / And this green pastoral landscape, were to me / More dear, both for themselves, and for thy sake" ("Tintern Abbey," lines 157-59).

Beginning with the "Ancient Mariner" and ending with "Tintern Abbey" infused the 1798 *Lyrical Ballads* with a progression. Haunted by his experience, the mariner endures alienation from society (the wedding party) that he imposes on his listener, the wedding guest, who is rendered "sadder" but "wiser" by this encounter. The collection builds from this alienation to "Tintern Abbey," in which the speaker, who, since the first edition was anonymous, might easily be presumed to be the same for both poems, finds consolation and joy in nature and in his satisfying intimacy with his sister.

Nature and the supernatural. Several years after the publication of *Lyrical Ballads*, Coleridge described in his *Biographia Literaria* the creative decisions that he and Wordsworth made while compiling their project:

> It was agreed that my endeavours should be directed to persons and characters supernatural. . . . Mr. Wordsworth, on the other hand, was to propose to himself as his object to give the charm of novelty to things of every day.
> (Coleridge in Abrams, II, p. 388)

Despite this seemingly polarized division of labor, the natural and the supernatural continually intertwine in the poems of both Wordsworth and Coleridge. While "The Rime of the Ancient Mariner" is undeniably a tale of imagination and the supernatural, Coleridge nonetheless maintains a connection to the everyday world and its wonders. Before the mariner's adventure takes on its nightmarish cast after his shooting of the albatross, for example, he witnesses nature's stark beauty while voyaging through the polar seas: "And now there came both mist and snow, / And it grew wondrous cold: / And ice, mast-high, came floating by, / As green as emerald" ("Rime," lines 51-54).

While Coleridge provides a wealth of sensory details in mapping out a supernatural landscape, Wordsworth uses a minimum of detail to convey an overall impression of peace and tranquility; his description of the natural landscape is as serene as Coleridge's is restless. However, Wordsworth too reveals a sense of the interconnection of nature and the supernatural. "Tintern Abbey" may lack the ghostly apparitions of "Rime," but Wordsworth imbues nature itself with a living spirit that has the power to teach and inspire:

> And I have felt
> A presence that disturbs me with the joy
> Of elevated thoughts; a sense sublime
> Of something far more deeply interfused,
> Whose dwelling is the light of setting suns,
> And the round ocean and the living air,
> And the blue sky, and in the mind of man:
> A motion and a spirit, that impels
> All thinking things, all objects of all thought,
> And rolls through all things.
> ("Tintern Abbey," lines 93-102)

Although the terms "Romantic poet" and "nature poet" seem to be synonymous, Wordsworth and Coleridge were indebted to such pre-Romantic poets as William Cowper (1731-1800), Oliver Goldsmith (1730-74), Thomas Gray (1716-71), and James Thomson (1700-48). Often called the "poets of sensibility" for their intense responsiveness to extremes of beauty and ugliness, these writers set the trend of eighteenth-century nature poetry. Thomson, who grew up in the Scottish countryside and did not see London until he was 25, was considered the first and most popular nature poet of his time. His poem "The Seasons" became an emulated model: "Generations of readers learned to look at the external world through Thomson's eyes and with the

---

WREATHES OF SMOKE AND VAGRANT DWELLERS

An atmosphere of tranquil solitude hangs over the Tintern Abbey of Wordsworth's poem. But the air harbors disturbing traces of contemporary history, too. Adversity prompts beggars and the miserable poor—the vagrants of Wordsworth's poem—to take respite in the abbey's ruins. Intruding also on the peace are wreathes of smoke, traces of an encroaching industrialization. Wordsworth lamented the intrusion of factories, railroads, and the like into rural areas such as his Lake District. As for the poem's reference to beggars, when read in conjunction with the other *Lyrical Ballads*—points out Peter Manning—one perceives the sense of "social injustice" that the vagrant brings to "Wordsworth's meditative landscape" (Manning, p. 24). England was witness to many social injustices connected to events of the time, from the French Revolution, to the enclosure acts, to the American Revolution. As a result of this last revolution, poor rural dwellers, such as the husband of the "Female Vagrant" (in the *Lyrical Ballads* poem of that name), were conscripted into the British army to put down the rebellion. Wordsworth's and Coleridge's feelings about contemporary events found their way into *Lyrical Ballads*, under less-than-ideal conditions. In 1797, the British government feared a naval invasion by the French. Coleridge, who had published political pamphlets and preached in Unitarian pulpits, became known for his republican and socially liberal sympathies, and the government jumped to conclusions. It assumed, mistakenly, that Coleridge and his friends were helping France to plan such an invasion, and so "dispatched its own spy to keep track of their doings." (Fry, p. 6)

emotions which he had taught them to feel. The *eye* dominates the *literature* of external nature during the eighteenth century as the imagination was to do in the poetry of Wordsworth" (Abrams, I, p. 2471).

> ### "MY DEAR, DEAR SISTER!"
>
> Dorothy Wordsworth (1771-1855), the only girl among the five Wordsworth children, was born 21 months after William, to whom she was devoted. The Wordsworths' mother died when Dorothy was seven, and the children were separated, the boys attending boarding school while Dorothy lived with various relatives, seeing her brothers only during their summer vacations. After William received a bequest from his friend Raisley Calvert in 1795, the 24-year-old Dorothy set up housekeeping with her brother. They soon became fast friends with Coleridge, forming a familiar threesome. Dorothy herself had writing talent. For several years, she kept journals, one at Alfoxden in 1798—the year *Lyrical Ballads* was published. Modern scholars consider her journals invaluable for various reasons, including their record of natural scenes that would later be immortalized in her brother's poetry and the intimate details they provide of his daily life.

From "Autumn" by James Thomson, a Poet of Sensibility

Now black and deep the night begins to fall,
A shade immense! sunk in the quenching
   gloom,
Magnificent and vast, are heaven and earth.
Order confounded lies, all beauty void,
Distinction lost, and gay variety
One universal blot. . . .
Drear is the state of the benighted wretch
Who then bewildered wanders through the
   dark. . . .
   (Thomson in Abrams, *Autumn,* lines 1138-46)

From "The Thorn" by William Wordsworth, a Romantic Poet

There is a thorn; it looks so old,
In truth you'd find it hard to say,
How it could ever have been young,
It looks so old and grey.
   . . .
Now would you see this aged thorn . . .
You must take care and chuse your time . . .
. . . for oft there sits . . .
A woman in a scarlet cloak,
And to herself she cries,
"Oh misery! oh misery!
"Oh woe is me! oh misery!"
   (Wordsworth, "The Thorn," lines 1-4, 57-69)

While the nature poetry of Thomson and his contemporaries concentrated on accurately conveying the beauties of the external world, that of Wordsworth and Coleridge dealt more with the poet's *response* to the external world: "Romantic 'nature poems' are in fact meditative poems, in which the presented scene usually serves to raise an emotional problem or personal crisis. . . . In addition, Romantic poems habitually imbue the landscape with human life, passion, and expressiveness" (Abrams, II, p. 8). Wordsworth and Coleridge's achievement was to transform the poetry of natural description by turning the eye, previously trained upon the external world, *inward* upon the soul. By connecting the natural world to human responses to it, nature became an extension of the poet's own imagination or, as Wordsworth was later to describe it, "that *inward* eye / Which is the bliss of solitude" (Wordsworth in Abrams, II, p. 207).

Literary partnership. While history does not record the exact details of the first meeting between Wordsworth and Coleridge, after making each other's acquaintance in 1795, the two men quickly became indispensable to each other. Their personalities and temperaments were complementary:

> Coleridge, with his enormous reading, his scholarship, his religious enthusiasm, his knowledge of classical and European literatures, his scientific interests, his emotional approach to politics, was a man of speculation, restless enquiry and self-questioning. While Wordsworth, with his passionate response to the natural world, was a man of physical experience and steadily accumulating moral certainties by which ideas might be judged and settled.
>   (Holmes, p. 151)

Coleridge's wide-ranging intellectual interests at first made him the dominant partner in the relationship with Wordsworth, although their positions would eventually reverse themselves. Both, however, had an unerring sense of what the other needed most. Coleridge supplied Wordsworth with unfailing admiration for his writing, and helped shape its direction, while Wordsworth provided emotional support by validating Coleridge's sense of himself and his own genius.

In the three years between their first meeting and the publication of *Lyrical Ballads*, Wordsworth and Coleridge spent much of their time together. Often accompanied by Wordsworth's sister, Dorothy, the two men took long walks through the countryside, picnicked, read poetry aloud, and avidly discussed their own potential contribution to literature. Coleridge believed Wordsworth to be the premier poet of the era, though Coleridge himself was more prolific in 1797 "and his conversational style of writing influenced Wordsworth rather than the other way around" (Fry, p. 5).

> With the fervor of high-minded youth, they talked of making the world better through their poetry. They hoped in that time of national crisis and pessimism to bring to men, disillusioned by the French Revolutionary idea, the secret they had discovered of the principle of joy in the universe. They would preach no political or social reform; and, in order to reach men, they would cast out of their writing all poetic diction and return to directness, sincerity, and basic human emotions.
> (Noyes, p. 23)

Although they shared similar goals, Wordsworth and Coleridge soon discovered they were incapable of collaborating on a single poem. At first, Wordsworth suggested the killing of the albatross and even penned a few lines of "The Rime of the Ancient Mariner," but he quickly sensed that Coleridge had his own ideas of how the poem ought to develop and so dropped out of the project. Nonetheless, the two poets continued to rely on each other's feedback and suggestions. By the summer of 1798, most of the poems that comprise *Lyrical Ballads* had been completed and offered to Joseph Cottle of Bristol for publication. Wordsworth's "Lines Composed a Few Miles Above Tintern Abbey," however, was an exception, a last-minute contribution, added just as the other poems were going to press. Neither poet suspected that their poorly received literary experiment would ultimately lay the foundation for much of modern poetry.

Ironically, *Lyrical Ballads* marked both the beginning and the end of the poets' literary partnership. Wordsworth, the more driven of the pair, even came to dislike "The Rime of the Ancient Mariner," blaming it for the hostile reviews *Lyrical Ballads* received after its initial publication. He moved the poem to next-to-last in the 1800 edition and also convinced Coleridge to modernize its diction, then continued to do so himself for later editions. (Sometime after 1805, Coleridge wrote explanatory glosses for the poem, included in most editions today.) In 1810 the two quarreled bitterly over the married Coleridge's doomed infatuation with Sara Hutchinson—Wordsworth's sister-in-law—and Coleridge's growing addiction to opium, which interfered with his productivity as a poet; the breach was not mended until nearly 20 years later.

Sources and literary context. Wordsworth rarely attempted to disguise the autobiographical nature of his poems. Many of his contributions to *Lyrical Ballads* were based on real-life encounters; Wordsworth's meetings with an old man who had been the huntsman to the squires of Alfoxden and a young girl living in the Wye Valley provided the inspiration for "Simon Lee" and "We Are Seven," respectively. Of the deeply personal "Lines Composed a Few Miles Above Tintern Abbey," Wordsworth wrote:

> No poem of mine was composed under circumstances more pleasant for me to remember than this. I began it upon leaving Tintern, after crossing the Wye, and concluded it just as I was entering Bristol in the evening after a ramble of 4 or 5 days, with my sister. Not a line of it was altered, and not any part of it written down till I reached Bristol.
> (Wordsworth in Abrams, II, p. 151)

TINTERN ABBEY

Visiting architectural ruins was a favorite pastime of nineteenth-century British travelers. Tintern Abbey, to which Wordsworth refers in the title of his poem, was founded in 1131 by Walter de Clare for Cistercian monks who had emigrated from France. Like many small monasteries, the abbey was dissolved under Henry VIII in 1537, after England broke from the Roman Catholic Church. By Wordsworth's time, the roofless, fourteenth-century church was all that remained of the original edifice. The building's graceful proportions and attractive natural setting (Tintern Abbey was located south of Monmouth on the west bank of the Wye River) endeared it to Wordsworth. Although the poet never mentions the abbey itself in his poem, his title and praise of the surrounding region—the "steep woods and lofty cliffs" and "green pastoral landscape"—contributed to the ruin's popularity as a tourist attraction. ("Tintern Abbey," lines 158-59)

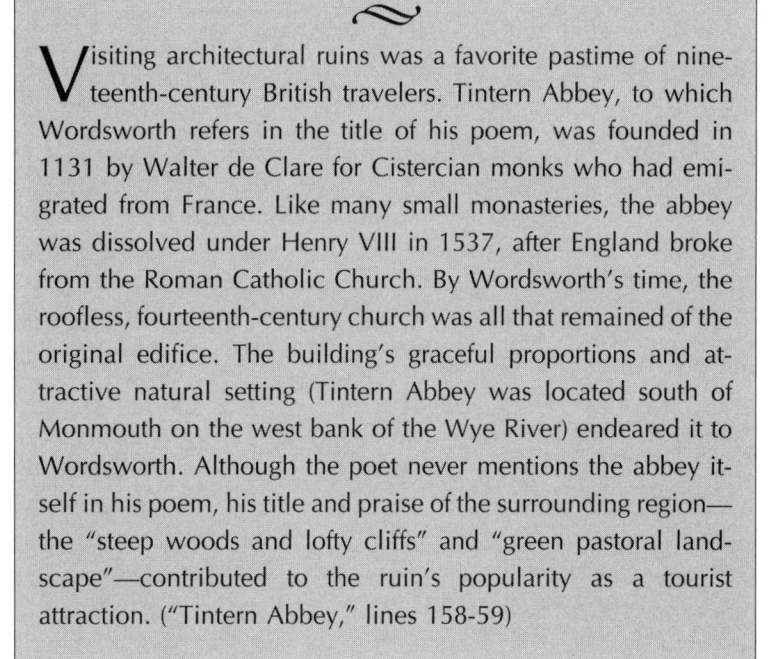

Lyrical Ballads

By contrast, Coleridge's poems in *Lyrical Ballads* were based more on his own imaginings. While "The Nightingale" was similar in tone and subject to Wordsworth's poems, "The Foster-Mother's Tale" and "The Dungeon" were both taken from the unfinished play *Osorio*, on which Coleridge was working. "The Rime of the Ancient Mariner" can be tied to several influences: John Cruikshank, a friend and neighbor of Coleridge's, had told him of a dream he once had about "a skeleton ship, with figures on it" (Cruikshank in Bate, p. 51). Coleridge himself had meanwhile been thinking of outcast figures in literature, such as the Wandering Jew. Finally, Wordsworth had been reading Captain George Shelvocke's *Voyage Round the World by the way of the Great South Sea* (1726), which mentioned that a man who killed an albatross—a bird of good omen—could incur the vengeance of the spirits who inhabited the Antarctic region. Also from Wordsworth came the idea of resurrecting the dead bodies to sail the ship.

LITERARY MILESTONE

"The 1798 *Lyrical Ballads* . . . is considered one of the most important turning points in English literary history. It was a challenge to conventional tastes both in politics and literature: the focus on rustic persons and themes, together with the implicit attack on the artificial poetic diction of most eighteenth-century poetry . . . presented the reading public with fare that seemed starkly new." (Fry, p. 11)

Although the foundation for a new poetic tradition had been tentatively laid by the poets of sensibility mentioned above, Wordsworth and Coleridge were the ones to propel poetry in a new direction for the next 30 years. Rejecting ancient Greek and Roman models, they turned instead to rustic ballads—such as those found in Bishop Thomas Percy's *Reliques* and the Scots dialect poems of Robert Burns—and to their own subjective experience for inspiration. In this, they were greatly influenced by John Locke's *An Essay Concerning Human Understanding,* which described sensation as the basis of knowledge, and by Addison and Steele's periodical *The Spectator,* which popularized Locke's notions about how the imagination interacts with the world to shape one's experience of it. All these influences led to the project, whose aims Wordsworth would clarify in his famous "Preface to *Lyrical Ballads*" of 1800. "All good poetry," says the Preface, "is the spontaneous overflow of powerful feelings" and the poet himself "is a man speaking to men" (Wordsworth in Abrams, II, pp. 160, 164).

Reviews. In retrospect, *Lyrical Ballads* is a literary milestone, but the majority of critics hardly recognized this at the time. On its first appearance in print, the collection received some scathing reviews. Noting that Wordworth's "Advertisement" for *Lyrical Ballads* revealed that the poems were intended as experiments, Robert Southey curtly declared in *The Critical Review,* "The 'experiment,' we think, has failed, not because the language of conversation is little adapted to 'the purposes of poetic pleasure,' but because it has been tried on uninteresting subjects" (Southey in Jones and Tydeman, p. 54). Southey singled out individual poems for blame or praise, remarking of Wordsworth's "The Idiot Boy," "No tale less deserved the labour that appears to have been bestowed upon this" (Southey in Jones and Tydeman, p. 53). He was similarly unenthusiastic about Coleridge's "The Rime of the Ancient Mariner": "Many of the stanzas are laboriously beautiful; but in connection they are absurd or unintelligible. . . . Genius has here been employed in producing a poem of little merit" (Southey in Jones and Tydeman, p. 53). Southey did admire what he saw as the "superior powers" of Wordsworth's "Tintern Abbey": "On reading this production, it is possible not to lament that he should have condescended to write such pieces as 'The Last of the Flock,' 'The Convict,' and most of the ballads" (Southey in Jones and Tydeman, p. 54). Finally, in the *Edinburgh Review,* Southey tied the ballads to the historical moment, reprovingly, it seems: "They are filled with horror and compassion at the sight of poor men spending their blood in the quarrels of princes, and brutifying their sublime capabilities in the drudgery of unremitting labour. . . . The present vicious constitution of society alone is responsible for all these enormities" (Southey in Manning, p. 24).

Charles Burney, writing for *The Monthly Review,* had somewhat warmer praise for *Lyrical Ballads,* noting of the authors' use of the ballad form, "The style and versification are those of our ancient ditties but much polished, and more constantly excellent" (Burney in Jones and Tydeman, p. 56). While Burney expressed views similar to

Southey's on "The Rime of the Ancient Mariner," calling it "the strangest story of a cock and a bull that we ever saw on paper," he nonetheless conceded that "there are in it poetical touches of an exquisite kind" (Burney in Jones and Tydeman, p. 55). Burney also called "Lines Composed a Few Miles Above Tintern Abbey" the "reflections of no common mind; poetical, beautiful, and philosophical" (Burney in Jones and Tydeman, p. 57). Despite reservations about the authors' choice of subjects—the rural poor, mad, and dispossessed—and the collection's melancholy tone, Burney concluded, "So much genius and originality are discovered in this publication, that we wish to see another from the same hand, written on more elevated subjects and in a more cheerful disposition" (Burney in Jones and Tydeman, p. 57).

Significantly, neither Southey nor Burney perceived the appeal *Lyrical Ballads* would hold for readers, nor did they foresee the new direction that poetry would take as a result of this poetic experiment. But William Hazlitt, who would become one of the most influential critics of the Romantic period, recorded his own reaction to some of the poems in *Lyrical Ballads* after meeting Wordsworth at Alfoxden in 1798:

> I was not critically or skeptically inclined. I saw touches of truth and nature, and took the rest for granted . . . [but] the sense of a new style and a new spirit in poetry came over me. It had to me something of the effect that arises from the turning up of the fresh soil, or of the first welcome breath of Spring. (Hazlitt in Noyes, p. 46)

—Pamela S. Loy

For More Information

Abrams, M. H., ed. *The Norton Anthology of English Literature*. 2 vols. 5th ed. New York: W. W. Norton, 1986.

Bate, Walter Jackson. *Coleridge*. New York: Macmillan, 1968.

Fry, Paul H., ed. *The Rime of the Ancient Mariner*, by Samuel Taylor Coleridge. Boston: Bedford/St. Martin's, 1999.

Holmes, Richard. *Coleridge: Early Visions*. New York: Viking, 1989.

Johnston, Kenneth R. *The Hidden Wordsworth: Poet, Lover, Rebel, Spy*. New York: W. W. Norton, 1998.

Jones, Alun R., and William Tydeman, eds. *Lyrical Ballads: A Casebook*. London: Macmillan, 1979.

Mahoney, John L. *William Wordsworth: A Poetic Life*. New York: Fordham University Press, 1997.

Manning, Peter J. "Troubling the Borders: *Lyrical Ballads* 1798 and 1998." *The Wordsworth Circle* 30, no. 1 (winter 1999): 22-27.

Noyes, Russell. *William Wordsworth*. Boston: Twayne, 1991.

Piper, H. W. *The Active Universe: Pantheism and the Concept of Imagination in the English Romantic Poets*. London: Athlone, 1962.

Willey, Basil. *Samuel Taylor Coleridge*. New York: W. W. Norton, 1972.

Wordsworth, William, and Samuel Taylor Coleridge. *Lyrical Ballads*. 1798. Reprint, London: Methuen, 1968.

Major Barbara

by
George Bernard Shaw

George Bernard Shaw, (usually referred to either as "Bernard Shaw" or "G.B.S.", as he hated and never used the name George) was born in Dublin, Ireland, on July 26, 1856 and died in Hertfordshire, England, on November 2, 1950. In the intervening 94 years, Shaw wrote five novels, three volumes of music criticism, three volumes of theater reviews, and more than 50 plays. He was also a famous speaker for socialist politics and a founding member of the Fabian Society. The Fabian Society is a socialist organization that had a significant impact on British social and political policy. What makes Shaw practically unique among dramatists is his combination of wit and serious political purpose; most plays that are as political as Shaw's are not as funny. To describe a play as a "socialist comedy" may seem a contradiction in terms, but Shaw's works are among the very few for which the label is apt. Only Shaw would have the temerity to subtitle his play *Man and Superman* (1905): "A Comedy and A Philosophy," and indeed, it is both. Other famous works include *Pygmalion* (1912, later turned into the popular musical *My Fair Lady*), *Heartbreak House* (1920), and *Saint Joan* (1923). For his great literary achievements, Shaw was recognized with the Nobel Prize for Literature in 1925. Ironically, Alfred Nobel himself was one of the models for Shaw's character Andrew Undershaft in *Major Barbara*; Nobel invented dynamite before becoming a famous philanthropist. Shaw echoes this double-edged impact in *Major Barbara*, in which appearances prove deceptive and Undershaft too has a mixed effect on society at large.

> **THE LITERARY WORK**
>
> A play set in England in January 1906; first performed in 1905.
>
> **SYNOPSIS**
>
> Weapons manufacturer Andrew Undershaft returns home to entice his evangelical daughter Barbara and her philosopher-fiancé, Adolphus Cusins, into running Undershaft's arms factory.

Events in History at the Time of the Play

A note about the play's setting and time. *Major Barbara* was written during the summer of 1905 and first produced in December of that year. But the 1905 program clearly states that the play's time is January 1906—or one month into the future! Shaw has therefore made the unusual choice of setting his story in the near-future. It is worth considering the implications of this: given conditions in the present, can or should the future be changed?

Poverty and the workhouse. In 1905 England was the wealthiest and most powerful nation in the world, controlling an Empire that spanned the globe. Yet one person in 36 was a pauper, and in the city of London, the number was one person in 31. While Britain had never been richer, many of her citizens were destitute.

Nearly a million people in England received Poor Law relief. The Poor Laws of 1834 pro-

Major Barbara

George Bernard Shaw

vided help only to those who would consent to live in a workhouse. Conditions in these workhouses were intentionally horrible; the reasoning went that anyone willing to live in such a grim, prison-like barrack must indeed need help. Poor, orphaned, and disabled inmates worked in exchange for beds to sleep on in the workhouse and food to eat there, managing in this way to survive. But once in such a house, it became difficult to get out again. How, if they earned no salary, could they possibly save anything? Recognizing how dismal and inescapable life there was, many poor people would endure nearly anything rather than go into the workhouse.

It is important to remember that there were almost no special benefits for the poor, elderly, children, or the disabled at this time—no unemployment stipends, no disability insurance, no welfare system, no social security or old-age pensions. Many workers labored simply for the food they ate and nothing else. If a factory worker lost an arm in an accident, that was the worker's bad luck; an injured party was not entitled to any sort of compensation. Those who were unable to work or too old or unsuccessful at finding a job had little choice. Going into the workhouse was one of their only options. Perhaps the jobless could turn for help to a charity such as the Salvation Army, but there were few such organizations.

In December 1905, the same year and month as the first production of Shaw's *Major Barbara*, a Royal Commission on the Poor Law and the Unemployed was appointed:

> To inquire: (1) Into the working of the laws relating to the relief of poor persons in the United Kingdom; (2) Into the various means which have been adopted outside of the Poor Laws for meeting distress arising from want of employment, particularly during periods of severe industrial depression; and to consider and report whether any, and if so what, modification of the Poor Laws or changes in their administration or fresh legislation for dealing with distress are advisable.
>
> (Higginbotham)

Shaw's friend Beatrice Webb, one of the inspirations for the dramatic character of Barbara and a member of the Fabian Society, was a member of this committee. Like many people at the time, she felt that society had to stop seeing poverty as a moral failing and instead understand it as part of modern economics. Capitalism, as these people viewed it, requires that a certain portion of the population be unemployed, so that employers have a ready pool of applicants for new jobs; however, society must then help people cope with the effects of unemployment and help those who are, for one reason or another, unemployable. The Royal Commission, an official panel appointed to investigate and advise, studied the problem of poverty for four years and made recommendations but no immediate action was taken. It would be 1927 before the Poor Laws would be amended. The workhouses were not abolished until after 1930.

The Salvation Army. In 1878 William Booth founded an organization to help the body and souls of poor people living in the East End of London. The Salvation Army, as its name implies, is based in evangelical Christian faith and organized on a military model. From the beginning, because of the work of Catherine Booth, William's wife, women were a full part of the organization and could hold high-ranking positions of power. They enjoyed no such opportunity elsewhere in religious or military life at this time.

Booth famously said that one person in ten lived "below the standard of the London cab-horse," meaning that the horses that pulled the cabs in London were better fed, housed, and treated than many of London's own citizens. Salvation Army missions offered food, housing, and other services to some of the poor, but also tried to convert them to Christianity by holding worship services that consisted of singing, music, hand-clapping, prayers, personal testimony, and an invitation for sinners to repent. In *Major Barbara*, Shaw paints a complicated portrait of the Army; on the one hand, the play supports their goals and genuinely good intentions, but it also shows concern that poor people are being blackmailed into spirituality, and that the Army itself is in danger of being enslaved to corporate interests.

Shaw, a noted freethinker, attended a Salvation Army meeting at the invitation of General Booth during the writing of *Major Barbara*. Relishing the service, he sang hymns along with the rest, and later joked that his conversion would "be announced in *The Times* tomorrow." (Shaw in Holroyd, vol. 2, p. 108). The Salvation Army would continue to be headquartered in London, though today it has divisions in more than 80 countries and operates more than 3,000 shelters, hospitals, schools, and social agencies worldwide.

The Fabian Society and the British Labor Party. The Fabian Society was a socialist political organization founded in the early 1880s. Shaw was one of its first members. In 1889 he edited a collection of essays that articulated the society's goals of social, economic, and political equality. Unlike many Marxist groups, which advocated revolution, the Fabians believed in gradual change from within the system. (Their very name "Fabian" refers to the Roman commander Fabius Maximus, whose surname, Cunctator, means "delayer": Fabius was famous for his patience in war.)

By holding meetings, staging lectures, and organizing discussion groups and conferences, the Fabians hoped to introduce socialist ideas into the Liberal and Conservative parties in Britain. But in the years preceding *Major Barbara*, many Fabians grew disenchanted with this goal. They came to believe that the major parties were not going to listen to them. Consequently, Fabians helped found the Labour Representation Committee, which was officially renamed the British Labour Party in 1906.

During the early years of its existence, the Labour Party struggled for membership. But after the First World War, Fabian leaders Sidney and Beatrice Webb drafted a new statement of the Labour Party's program and called for radical new changes such as a minimum wage, a maximum workweek, progressive taxation, the expansion of public services, and public ownership of industry.

By 1922 the Labour Party would become one of the two leading political parties in Britain. In 1924 its candidate James Ramsay MacDonald won the office of Prime Minister, the first from the party, which would go on within the next five years to become the largest in Parliament. At the time of the play, though, the Labour Party was just finding its footing as a new voice in the political arena.

Arms manufacturing and dealing. In 1905, the year of Shaw's *Major Barbara*, the three largest weapons manufacturers in England were Armstrong, Vickers, and the Nobel Dynamite Trust. Armstrong was the second-largest arms manufacturer worldwide; the first was the German company Krupp, run by Friedrich Alfred Krupp, "the Cannon King," one of the real-life inspirations for the play's Andrew Undershaft. (Like the character Major Barbara, Krupp's daughter Bertha took over her father's company. A heavy gun used in World War I, the "Big Bertha" is named for her. Like the character Adolphus Cusins, who took the name Undershaft when he assumed control of the cannon-works, Bertha's husband, Gustav, also took the family name of Krupp). By 1902 the Krupp firm employed more than 40,000 people in model factories: Krupp's workers had sick-pay, a free hospital, new schools for their children, pension plans, and retirement homes. (Unfortunately, the First World War and the subsequent German depression eroded Krupp's progressive labor policies. Worse yet, Gustav and Bertha's son, Alfried, was a high ranking member of the Nazi party. Under his control, the Krupp factories became forced labor camps during the Second World War, and the

---

THE RUSSO-JAPANESE WAR—JAPAN'S NOT-SO-SECRET WEAPONS

"*Major Barbara* was written the year of the Russo-Japanese war, in which the Imperial Russian fleet was sunk by armaments supplied [to Japan] by the British firm, Vickers: a tangible demonstration of a small nation defeating a colossus through modern weaponry." (Innes, p. 39)

Major Barbara

workers there suffered horribly in concentration-camp-like conditions. Alfried Krupp was convicted as a war criminal at the Nuremberg trials in 1950, though he was later granted amnesty and had his property returned to him. This perhaps supports *Major Barbara*'s point that men such as Krupp and Undershaft are beyond the law, even international law.)

Arms manufacturers were among the most powerful men in the world, and sold their goods internationally with very little discrimination or regard for patriotism. As Sir Basil Zharoff, chief salesman for Vickers's noted: "I sold armaments to anyone who would buy them. I was a Russian in Russia, a Greek in Greece, a Frenchman in Paris. I made wars so that I could sell arms to both sides" (Vickers in Holroyd, vol. 2, p. 105).

Many arms manufacturers hoped that the proliferation of dangerous weapons would ultimately prevent wars, because the price of war in terms of damage and human life would simply become too high. An overly optimistic Alfred Nobel believed that, "The day two army corps can destroy each other in one second, all civilised nations will recoil from war and disband their armies" (Nobel in Holroyd, vol. 2, p. 105). History would certainly not prove this to be the case.

Instead, the late nineteenth and early twentieth centuries saw a massive, international arms buildup that culminated in the outbreak of World War I in 1914. As Peter Lewis notes, "The weapons which were turned on the German, British, and French armies had often been made by their fellow-countrymen. Krupp's guns were fired on the Germans by the Russians, British guns were fired by the Turks at the Dardanelles" (Lewis, program). Even the devastation of the First World War would not end the arms race; although arms trading would pass primarily into the hands of governments, nations would continue to make huge profits by selling weaponry, often secretly, to foreign powers. Shaw, however, always saw arms as having good possibilities as well as bad ones; in the right hands, weapons could be tools of liberation, even as in the wrong hands, they were tools of oppression.

BEATRICE WEBB: THE REAL MAJOR BARBARA?

Beatrice Potter was born on January 2, 1868, the eighth daughter of rich parents. Unlike most women of her generation and class, Potter had little interest in getting married; she even thought about becoming a nun. Instead, at the age of 25, she joined the Charity Organization Society in order to help the poor. But Potter soon realized that charity was not enough. Determined to investigate the causes of poverty and solve the problem at its root, she studied the statistics and went to work among the poor and downtrodden. All this research led to her writing some important articles on the lives of dock workers and "sweated laborers," laborers who worked often 12 or more hours a day for little pay in unsanitary conditions (many sweated laborers were women and children). Her writings led to Potter meeting Stanley Webb, a writer like herself and a Fabian Socialist. "One grasp of the hand," she said, "and we were soon in a warm discussion of Economics" (Potter in Holroyd, vol. 1, p. 264). The warm discussion grew into more than either must have anticipated. Potter fell in love with Webb and married him in 1892. Together, Beatrice and Stanley Webb became one of the most famous intellectual couples of the age, writing books, helping to formulate policy, and helping to establish what would ultimately become the British Labour Party.

The Play in Focus

The plot—Act 1. The play opens in Lady Britomart Undershaft's house on the upscale street of Wilton Crescent in West London. She sends for her son Stephen to discuss their family affairs. Recently, her two daughters, Barbara and Sarah, have both gotten engaged and Lady Britomart believes that they will need more money than their fiancés can provide to establish their married households. To get a hold of the money, she will have to contact their father, the arms dealer Andrew Undershaft, from whom they are all estranged. Lady Britomart explains to Stephen that her husband runs a weapons factory and she separated from him because he would not let Stephen inherit the factory. The Undershaft Armory runs by a particular set of rules: Andrew Undershaft was a foundling who was adopted by the previous Andrew Undershaft, who himself was adopted by the Andrew Undershaft before that, all the way back to Shakespeare's time. The current Andrew Undershaft is determined to keep the tradition of passing the factory to yet another foundling rather than bequeathing it to his son in the more traditional fashion. Stephen, upset by this news and by his father's profession, wants nothing to do with him. But, holding firm, Lady Britomart informs her son that she has invited her husband to the house that very evening.

Lady Britomart then calls for Barbara and Sarah, and their respective husbands-to-be, Adolphus Cusins and Charles Lomax. Barbara is dressed in full uniform; she is a major in the Salvation Army, much to her mother's distress. Cusins is described as a "spectacled student"; he is a professor of Greek. Sarah and Charles are conventional and rather dim young people whose inherited incomes aren't quite enough to support them. Lady Britomart announces that their father is coming to visit this evening: though the news distresses Sarah and Charles, it leaves Barbara cheerful. Her father, notes Barbara, "has a soul to be saved like anybody else." (Shaw, *Major Barbara*, p. 9)

When Andrew Undershaft arrives, he does not recognize his children, as he has not seen them since they were babies. In fact, he mistakes first Charles and then Cusins for his son. The matter is soon cleared up, and Undershaft and Barbara end up discussing her work in the Salvation Army. Undershaft notes that the Army's motto—"Blood and Fire"—might be his own, which shocks everyone except Barbara. Surely a man like Undershaft, whose business is making weapons of destruction, has no interest in religion? Charles is even tactless enough to say to Undershaft, "Getting into heaven is not exactly in your line, is it?" (*Major Barbara*, p. 14)

In fact, the character of Charles establishes the position the play aims to subvert—that arms manufacturing is simply "wrong," and that religion, as represented by the Salvation Army, is "right." Undershaft explains that his religion has a place for cannons and torpedoes in it. Barbara offers to try to save his soul, and her father makes a counteroffer:

> UNDERSHAFT: If I go to see you tomorrow in your Salvation Shelter, will you come the day after to see me in my cannon works?
> BARBARA: Take care. It may end in your giving up the cannons for the sake of the Salvation Army.
> UNDERSHAFT: Are you sure it will not end in your giving up the Salvation Army for the sake of the cannons?
>
> (*Major Barbara*, p. 15)

The bargain is made, and all the characters except Stephen exit to the drawing room.

Act 2. The second act takes place in the cold yard of the Salvation Army shelter in West Ham, a neighborhood in the poor East End of London. Rummy (a poor woman) and Price (a poor man) are finishing a lunch of bread and milk. They speak to each other, as many characters in this

A Salvation Army worker beats his bass drum in a production of *Major Barbara*.

act do, in a working-class dialect that Shaw represents phonetically. While difficult on the eyes, these speeches generally make sense to the ear, and are best read aloud: "Yus, you dessay!" equals "Yes, you dare say!" and so forth.

It turns out that Price and Rummy are both good, hardworking people—Price is an out-of-work painter, and Rummy is a respectable married woman—but they're both pretending to be morally worse than they are because: "Them Salvation lasses is dear good girls; but the better you are, the worse they likes to think you were before they rescued you. Why shouldnt they av a [have a] bit o [of] credit, poor loves?" Price agrees: "I know wot [what] they like. I'll tell em how I blasphemed and gambled and wopped my poor old mother" (*Major Barbara*, p. 19). The first part of the act is a portrait of London poverty; we hear the stories of a few men, including Peter Shirley, who explains that he's "worked ten to twelve hours a day since I was thirteen, and paid my way all through; and now am I to be thrown into the gutter . . . because I've black hair that goes white?" (*Major Barbara*, p. 20).

They are all being fed by a young Salvation Army worker, Jenny Hill. Upon being physically slapped by a man named Bill Walker who has come there looking for his girlfriend, Jenny calls for someone to get Major Barbara, quick! Barbara, calm and businesslike, comes out, and embarrasses Bill by describing him in her log book as, "the man who—struck—poor little Jenny Hill—in the mouth." (*Major Barbara*, p. 25) She informs him that his former girlfriend has fallen in love with another of the Army's converts, who is a boxer. Bill, feeling afraid and somewhat guilty now, sits down and shuts up.

Undershaft arrives and asks to watch Barbara work, whereupon Barbara explains to Bill that the devil is making him unhappy and he should let God help him. Cusins arrives, banging a big drum, and Barbara introduces him to Bill, who says, nervously, "Gowin to merry im? . . . Gawd elp im!" [You're going to marry him? God help him!](*Major Barbara*, p. 29) Cusins goes to talk to Undershaft while Barbara continues her work. Undershaft wonders if Cusins is interested in the Salvation Army or just in Barbara; Cusins replies that he is a collector of religions, and he believes in all of them. Undershaft then explains his own religion to Cusins: in his view, the two things necessary for salvation are money and gunpowder.

> CUSINS: Excuse me: is there any place in your religion for honor, justice, truth, love, mercy and so forth?
> UNDERSHAFT: Yes: they are the graces and luxuries of a rich, strong, and safe life.
> (*Major Barbara*, p. 31)

Cusins predicts that Barbara won't care for this philosophy; Undershaft replies that Barbara also won't care for the fact that Cusins is more interested in Greek gods than Christian ones. The two men quite like each other. Undershaft explains to Cusins that he wants Barbara to preach his gospel of money and gunpowder; he wants Barbara to put her enthusiasm to work at his arms factory. Shocked, Cusins thinks that Undershaft is crazy. Undershaft suggests that the three of them are crazy, each in their own way: "I am a millionaire; you are a poet; Barbara is a savior of souls. What have we three to do with the common mob of slaves and idolaters?" (*Major Barbara*, p. 34) Cusins tells Undershaft that he'll never convince Barbara, but Undershaft replies that he doesn't have to convince her; he can buy the Salvation Army. "All religious organizations," Undershaft explains, "exist by selling themselves to the rich" (*Major Barbara*, p. 34).

Barbara returns, happy that someone has just donated four shillings, and Undershaft offers to donate a couple of pennies as well, or more if she wants it. But Barbara refuses his money because he made it by selling cannons and hand grenades; the Salvation Army, she says, can't be bought. Still, though, Barbara is worried about money; the shelter needs it to survive, and she needs money to save souls: "I can't talk religion to a man with bodily hunger in his eyes" (*Major Barbara*, p. 36).

Bill Walker offers to donate a pound to make up for his past bad behavior, but Barbara doesn't want his money; she wants his soul for salvation. At that point, Mrs. Baines, a Salvation Army Commissioner, arrives and announces that their money problems are solved: Lord Saxmundham will donate five thousand pounds if five other men will donate a thousand pounds each. Barbara has never heard of Lord Saxmundham, but Undershaft has: he used to be Sir Horace Bodger, of Bodger's Whiskey. Mrs. Baines asks Undershaft to donate, and Undershaft agrees to give her five thousand pounds. Bill meanly whispers to Barbara, who will not take his money: "Wot prawce selvytion nah?" [What price salvation now?] (*Major Barbara*, p. 41).

Barbara is shocked that Mrs. Baines is going to take her father's money. She points out that Undershaft makes weapons and that Bodger's whiskey is responsible for alcoholism among the poor. But Mrs. Baines argues that the money will help the Army put Bodger and Undershaft out of business—they are, after all, for peace and against drinking! Cusins orchestrates a parade, handing Jenny a tambourine and Undershaft a trombone. But Barbara's heart is breaking and she won't go with them. Instead, she takes her Army badge off and pins it on her father's chest. "Drunkenness and Murder!" Barbara exclaims. "My God: why hast thou forsaken me?" Echoing the words of Jesus Christ during his crucifixion, the exclamation shows the profound depth of Barbara's anguish and suffering at that moment.

Act 3. This act opens back in Lady Britomart's house, with Barbara now dressed in normal clothes. Undershaft arrives to take everyone to the cannon factory. Next Lady Britomart asks him to give Barbara and Sarah more money once they are married, and Undershaft agrees. Lady Britomart asks Undershaft to let Stephen inherit the arms factory, but Undershaft refuses to do so. He explains that the sons of rich men don't understand business and don't have the drive for success that foundlings do. Unfortunately, though, a good foundling is hard to find nowadays; Undershaft has been looking for a suitable successor but hasn't yet located one.

Stephen tells Undershaft that he doesn't want to take over the factory anyway. In fact, he repudiates the cannon business altogether. Undershaft, who is relieved, asks Stephen what he does want to do: art, philosophy, law? Stephen has no interest in any of these fields; he wants to go into politics. Undershaft laughs at him: "He knows nothing and thinks he knows everything. That points clearly to a political career" (*Major Barbara*, p. 52). Stephen is insulted on behalf of the government, but Undershaft explains that he and men like him rule the country, not politicians:

> [Y]ou will do what pays us. You will make war when it suits us, and keep peace when it doesn't. You will find out that trade requires certain measures when we have decided on those measures. When I want anything to keep my dividends up, you will discover that my want is a national need. When other people want something to keep my dividends down, you will call out the police and the military. And in return you shall have the support and applause of my newspapers, and the delight of imagining that you are a great statesman. Government of your country! Be off with you, my boy . . .
> (*Major Barbara*, p. 53)

The second scene of this act takes place in Perivale St. Andrews, a beautiful hillside town where the workers in Undershaft's factory live. The cannon works are nearby, in small, separate buildings in case any one of them blows up by accident. As the other characters eagerly approach her, Barbara looks over the town. It is a heavenly place—clean! There are libraries and schools. It has a nursing home and pension plan for the workers! Immensely profitable, the factory provides a wonderful quality of life for everyone associated with it, even old Peter Shirley from Act 2, who now has a job here. Everyone is impressed; even Stephen apologizes to his father. Lady Britomart loves the town and the factory and suggests that if Undershaft can't give it to Stephen, then why not give it to Cusins? That way Barbara can have it when she marries him. Undershaft objects that Cusins isn't a foundling, but Cusins makes a sudden confession: while his parents are legally married in Australia, their union would not be legal in England, because his father married his sister-in-law after the death of his first wife, which is prohibited in England. (This, by the way, would literally make Cusins his own "cousin" because his father is both his father and his uncle.) Undershaft agrees that Cusins is eligible. But will Cusins take the job? Undershaft offers him a salary, but Cusins argues that he should get three times as much; they eventually haggle a price. Cusins then wants to discuss the morality of the job: can he sell weapons only to the good guys? No, Undershaft says, the job of an armorer is to sell weapons to anyone who can pay without making moral judgments. It's up to people to decide what they're willing to fight for: "If you good people prefer preaching and shirking to buying my weapons and fighting the rascals, dont [sic] blame me. I can make cannons: I cannot make courage and convictions" (*Major Barbara*, p. 64). Undershaft then turns to Barbara, who knows all about courage and convictions. She begs him to justify the work of the factory: "Shew [sic] me some light through the darkness of this dreadful place, with its beautifully clean workshops, and respectable workmen, and model homes"; Undershaft replies that "Cleanliness and respectability do not need justification" (*Major Barbara*, p. 65). In fact, the quality of life Undershaft provides actually saves souls, because poverty is the worst of crimes. "Poverty blights whole cities; spreads horrible pestilences; strikes dead the very souls of all who come within sight, sound, or smell of it" (*Major Barbara*, p. 65). Only when a person is healthy and well fed, argues Undershaft, can he be truly open to spirituality. Laying down a challenge, he urges Barbara to bring religion to his men: "Their souls are hungry because their bodies are full" (*Major Barbara*, p. 66). Undershaft then quotes Plato to Cusins: "Society cannot be saved until either the Professors of Greek take to making gunpowder, or else the makers of gunpowder become Professors of Greek" (from Plato's **Republic,** also in *Literature and Its Times*).

"Cunning tempter!" Cusins moans (*Major Barbara*, p. 69). Cusins and Barbara are left alone to talk, but Cusins immediately tells her that he's going to accept Undershaft's offer. He wants to make weapons for the world, wants to give common people the tools to fight oppression. Barbara agrees, and tells him that if he didn't accept her father's offer, she would marry the man who did: she's attracted to "all the human souls to be saved: not weak souls in starved bodies, sobbing with gratitude for a scrap of bread and treacle, but fullfed, quarrelsome, snobbish, uppish creatures" (*Major Barbara*, p. 72). Joyfully, Barbara runs to her mother and asks her to help them to pick a house to live in, while Undershaft turns to Cusins and tells him to report for work the next morning.

Andrew Undershaft's profession. Shaw had originally considered another title for *Major Barbara*: *Andrew Undershaft's Profession*. Already Shaw had written two other works with such a title: a novel, *Cashel Byron's Profession* (1882),

Major Barbara

and a play, *Mrs. Warren's Profession* (performed 1902). Cashel Byron's profession is boxing and Mrs. Warren's profession is prostitution; in neither case would the Victorian audience have dignified the occupation with the name of "profession." But, as Michael Holroyd points out in his biography of Shaw, Shaw often took "a profession which society officially repudiates as a metaphor for the way in which that larger society is really conducted." (Holroyd, vol. 1, p. 290). In *Major Barbara*, the unpleasant profession is arms-making, and the point is that those who have money and guns are the truly powerful in any society.

Shaw took interest in how economics was related to society and its values, and, of course, there are good economic reasons that young men in the East End of London turned to boxing and women turned to prostitution. Then, as now, sports was a way for the otherwise underprivileged to rise up in the economic world, and the sex industry was the only one in which women routinely earned more money than men did.

Major Barbara, like these other works, shows Shaw examining a society through its economics. This time, Shaw's subject is arms making. While the characters all initially assume manufacturing weapons to be a bad profession, the play argues that the profits from arms result in a greater quality of life for the workers in a factory such as Undershaft's. Furthermore, Shaw shows that it is through the donations of men like Undershaft and Sir Horace Bodger, the whiskey maker, that religious and charitable organizations like the Salvation Army can exist. The name Bodger is probably a pun on the name Dewar, a real-life manufacturer of scotch whiskey. "Dewar" sounds like "do-er," but Shaw's "Bodger" is a "botcher," someone who botches or messes up what he does. Dewar and Sons had moved part of their business from Scotland to England in 1885, and by 1892 they were well on their way to becoming an international brand. Tommy and John A. Dewar, two of the sons, became Members of Parliament in 1900, one in the Conservative Party, the other in the Liberal Party, supporting Shaw's theory that men like Undershaft are, in fact, the government. In fact, *Major Barbara* was prophetic regarding the Dewars: John A. Dewar became a baronet in 1907, where Shaw's fictional Bodger was already a baronet.

Major Barbara was prophetic in other ways, as well; the tradition of philanthropy by great men of industry was only just beginning in 1905. Alfred Nobel had already founded the Nobel prizes, but in the next two decades, U.S. tycoons took similar steps. Many other captains of industry founded charitable organizations: steel magnate Andrew Carnegie formed the Carnegie Corporation, John D. Rockerfeller started the Rockerfeller Foundation, and auto maker Henry Ford established the Ford Foundation, which today makes grants of more than 100 million a year for education, social welfare, the arts and free speech, and conservation of natural resources. The Ford Foundation also provides direct aid to poor foreign countries, which suggests that Shaw's play may well have been right to show that more good comes from Bodger's Whiskey than from the Salvation Army.

Sources and literary context. In the author's statement that opens the 1944 film version of *Major Barbara*, Shaw notes that, "Some of the people in it are real people, whom I have met and talked to. One of the others may be YOU" (Shaw in Innes, p. 20). Many of the play's characters were, in fact, based on real people. Barbara Undershaft was modeled physically on the actress Eleanor Robson (though Robson was never able to play the part) and intellectually on Shaw's friend and fellow Fabian Socialist Beatrice Webb. A rich young woman, Webb devoted her life to preaching social justice in the East End of London.

The character of Adolphus Cusins was largely based on the real-life classics professor Gilbert Murray, who provided the play's translations of Greek dialogue by Euripides. Harley Granville Barker, who first performed the role, even wore a pair of Murray's glasses on stage. Cusins first name, Adolphus, is a reference to Gustavus Adolphus, the King of Sweden, "a brilliant linguist who subsequently mastered the art of war" (Holroyd, vol. 2, p. 207).

There are many candidates who might have inspired the role of arms-dealer Andrew Undershaft. These include Prussian cannon maker Friedrich Alfred Krupp, who established model factories for his workers in Essen and whose son-in-law, like Cusins, changed his name to Krupp and took over the family business. Other candidates are Basil Zahroff, a salesman with the British arms maker Vickers who boasted that he made war so that he could sell arms to both sides, and even American auto manufacturer Henry Ford. But the most likely model is Alfred Nobel, who both invented dynamite and created the Nobel Peace Prize. At the time of his death in 1896, Nobel had 93 dynamite factories, which he always hoped would avert wars and not cause them. (The first round of Nobel Prizes—in chemistry, medicine, physics, literature, and peace—were awarded in 1901, four years before the play debuted. Shaw himself won the Nobel Prize for Literature in 1925, two decades after the first performance of *Major Barbara*.)

Reception. In his preface to the published version of *Major Barbara*, Shaw wrote, "When *Major Barbara* was produced in London, the second act was reported in an important northern newspaper as a withering attack on the Salvation Army, and the despairing ejaculation of Barbara deplored by a London daily as a tasteless blasphemy.... Indeed, nothing could be more ironically curious than the confrontation *Major Barbara* effected of the theater enthusiasts with the religious enthusiasts" (Shaw, *Prefaces*, p. 123). Barbara's despairing quotation of the words of the crucified Christ was considered blasphemy at worst and bad taste at best, marking *Major Barbara* as a controversial play. G. K. Chesterton, disappointed that the religious element in the play was so badly defeated, wrote, "I must frankly say that Bernard Shaw always seems to me to use the word God not only without any idea of what it means, but without one moment's thought about what it could possibly mean" (Chesterton, p. 357). Interestingly, the Salvation Army itself didn't seem to mind the play, though Shaw reports that, "[T]hey questioned the verisimilitude of the play, not because Mrs. Baines took the money, but because Barbara refused it" (Shaw, *Prefaces*, p. 124). Some later critics, viewing the play with the hindsight of humanity's having endured two World Wars, criticized the dramatic portrayal of the arms race, calling it naive, foolish, dangerous, and even evil. And yet, many people still share Shaw's belief that technology itself is neutral; that weapons can be used for good or evil purposes, and that humanity must choose to put power to moral uses.

—Francesca Coppa

For More Information

Bloom, Harold, Ed. *George Bernard Shaw's* Major Barbara. New York: Chelsea House, 1988.

Chesterton, G. K. "A 1909 View of *Major Barbara*." In *Bernard Shaw's Plays*. Ed. Warren Sylvester Smith. New York: W.W. Norton, 1970.

Higginbotham, Peter. "The Poor Laws." *The History Of The Workhouse*. 15 October 2000. http://www.workhouses.org.uk/ (8 June 2002).

Holroyd, Michael. *Bernard Shaw*. 4 vols. London: Chatto & Windus, 1988-92.

Innes, Christopher, ed. *The Cambridge Companion to George Bernard Shaw*. Cambridge: Cambridge University Press, 1998.

Lewis, Peter. "George Bernard Shaw and the World of *Major Barbara*." Program of Peter Gill's National Theater Production of *Major Barbara*, 1982.

Rogers, Kevin E. "The Machiavellian Tendencies of Adolphus Cusins." *Shaw: The Annual of Bernard Shaw Studies* 12 (1992): 261-70.

Shaw, George Bernard. *Bernard Shaw's Plays: Major Barbara, Heartbreak House, Saint Joan, Too True To Be Good*. Ed. Warren Sylvester Smith. New York: W.W. Norton, 1970.

———. *Prefaces by Bernard Shaw*. London: Constable, 1934.

Zimbardo, Rose. *Twentieth Century Interpretations of Major Barbara: A Collection of Critical Essays*. Englewood Cliffs, N.J.: Prentice-Hall, 1970.

The Mark of the Horse Lord

by
Rosemary Sutcliff

> **THE LITERARY WORK**
>
> A historical novel set in the area now known as Scotland, sometime between 143 and 180 C.E.; published in 1965.
>
> **SYNOPSIS**
>
> After winning his freedom, the enslaved gladiator Phaedrus is aimless and alone. He accepts the challenge of impersonating Midir, the lost prince of the Dalriads, and in the midst of new battles and adventures discovers the true meaning of freedom.

Rosemary Sutcliff (1920-92) is generally considered one of the finest authors of historical fiction for young people; many critics view her as the undisputed master of the genre. The details of her early life would have a major impact on her novels. She contracted Still's Disease, a form of rheumatoid arthritis, at the age of two, and suffered through hospitalizations, painful operations, and frustrating physical limitations throughout her life. Not surprisingly, many of her characters struggle and succeed at overcoming handicaps and the stereotypes that often accompany them. Born in Surrey, England, Sutcliff developed a love of the countryside as a child and spent most of her adult life in the South Downs, the area directly south of London extending roughly from Winchester to Eastbourne. A strong sense of place and the relationship between people and their physical setting pervades Sutcliff's writings, as shown in *Warrior Scarlet* (1958) and her Carnegie Medal winning novel *The Lantern Bearers* (1959) among many others. Her father, an officer in England's Royal Navy, bore a devotion to duty and country that may have strongly influenced her. The dangers of battle as well as the virtues of courage, loyalty, and integrity appear again and again in her fiction. The settings of Sutcliff's British historical novels range from the Bronze Age, to the period of Roman colonization of Britain, through its settlement by Normans, to the seventeenth-century British Civil War. Often discussed as her finest but most demanding novel, *The Mark of the Horse Lord* showcases the best of Sutcliff's talents. Along with a compelling, fast-paced plot and a strong, sympathetic protagonist, it explores the relationship between freedom and responsibility in ways that transcend its historical setting.

Events in History at the Time the Novel Takes Place

The Dalriads and the Caledones. Much of Sutcliff's second-century novel is set in the northern region of Great Britain in what would eventually become Scotland. During the period of *The Mark of the Horse Lord*, this land was inhabited by at least two different Celtic peoples. The Caledones belonged to a larger group known as the Picts—meaning "the painted people"—a term describing their tattoos or their practice of decorating themselves with woad, a blue dye. The Dalriads

The Mark of the Horse Lord

Rosemary Sutcliff

HADRIAN'S AND THE ANTONINE WALLS

Hadrian's Wall, erected between 122 and 128 C.E., was named for the Emperor at whose behest it was built. At 77 miles in length, it was an amazing fortification with both offensive and defensive functions. More than half of the wall was built of stone, about 10 feet thick and 15 feet high. The eastern end was built, initially, of turf, though later rebuilt with stone. Every mile of the wall was marked with a small fort called a milecastle and a gate to provide access through the wall. Two watch turrets were built between every milecastle. Sixteen different larger forts were built at regular intervals along the length of the wall. Behind the wall, a ditch, approximately 20 feet wide and 10 feet deep, completed the fortifications.

Finished about 142 C.E., The Antonine Wall, named for Antonius Pius who ordered its construction, was 37 miles long and built completely of turf on top of a stone foundation. This wall included 19 forts spaced at two-mile intervals. Like Hadrian's Wall, it also included a deep ditch in front. The Romans abandoned the Antonine Wall in either 162 or 180 C.E. Hadrian's Wall was overrun by the Celts during several different uprisings, but was not finally abandoned by the Romans until between 383 and 388 C.E. Remains of both walls are still visible today.

(known also as the Dal Riatans) were an Irish group who immigrated to Britain during the Roman era. The northern tip of Ireland and the southern shores of Scotland are at the narrowest juncture no more than 25 miles apart. So, it is no surprise that some settlers continued to move back and forth between these two regions. These people became the Dalriads. During the time of the novel, the expansion of the Dalriads into Scotland was probably not hostile. Most likely the Picts saw the Dalriads as a neighboring people rather than an invading force. Several centuries later, the Dalriads would arrive in much larger numbers. In the middle of the ninth century, the Picts would be absorbed into one nation with the Dalriads, who came to be called the Scots. As Sutcliff explains in the historical note that begins her novel, the Caledones and the Dalriads are simply more precise names for the peoples commonly known as the Picts and the Scots. In fact, the main difference between the two groups was language. The Scots spoke the ancestor of a language now called Gaelic—Scots is one of its main variations. The Pictish language quickly disappeared.

Very little is known about these two groups during the second century before they converted to Christianity. Sutcliff has built her story on the bones of what little anthropological and documentary evidence exists. For example, the early scholar Bede (circa 673-735 C.E.) records that the Pictish kingdoms, which would include the Caledonians, sometimes traced their kingship through the female line (Laing, p. 58). Sutcliff has used this possibility to frame one of the central conflicts of the novel—the question of whether the Caledonian Queen Liadhan or the Dalriad Prince Midir should be the next ruler of the Dalriads.

Roman Britain. The Roman occupation of Britain began in August of 55 B.C.E. when Julius Caesar crossed the British Channel with about 10,000 men to claim the island for the Empire. His visit was brief, and although he returned again with a larger force the next year, this first set of invasions had almost no impact on the Celtic kingdoms of the island. Not until the reign of the Emperor Claudius (41-54 C.E.), nearly one hundred years later, did Rome truly turn its attention to Britain. Gradually the Celtic tribes of the south and east were conquered or surrendered to Rome, but the northern tribes proved more of a problem for the invaders.

Under Gnaeus Julius Agricola, who governed Britain from 78 to 84 C.E., the Romans established their northern frontier in Britain at the Forth-Clyde line near the site of the modern city of Edinburgh, Scotland and constructed a series of forts. These forts were used as staging grounds for further advancements into the north, and they enabled Agricola to win a decisive victory over the Caledonians who resisted this invasion. The Caledonians, who fought with long swords, were unprepared for the more complicated and flexible battle techniques of the Roman army.

About 50 years later, in 142 C.E., the Antonine Wall was built along this frontier to mark the northern boundary of the Roman Empire in Britain. The Antonine Wall had a stone foundation that was piled high with turf. A wide ditch in front of it provided further protection. The wall extended for 40 miles with small forts spaced along its length. From approximately 180 to 211 C.E., the Caledonians crossed the wall and attacked the Romans many times. Sometimes the Roman soldiers subdued their attackers through warfare and sometimes by paying them to keep the peace. Eventually the Romans were forced to abandon their hopes of conquering the North and retreated south to the much larger fortification of Hadrian's Wall, running west to east from the modern cities of Carlisle to Newcastle, England.

The Mark of the Horse Lord is set during the brief period when the Antonine Wall was successfully held by the Romans—before the Caledonians caused the Roman troops any significant problems. In the novel, the Caledonians and the Dalriads are preoccupied with battles among themselves. In fact, the Romans preferred it when local tribes engaged in civil conflict. The military leaders from Rome realized that when the various tribes that came to be referred to as the Picts and the Scots united forces to attack the Romans, the wall fortifications were likely to be overrun. In *The Mark of the Horse Lord,* the Roman Commander's decision to protect Queen Liadhan, and even to provide her with a secure sea passage to safety in the south, accurately represents this Roman preference for sustaining conflict among the northern Celtic tribes. Later, in the fourth century, the Romans would set up more stable regions in this part of their empire, organizing what is now southern Scotland into the Northern Treaty States.

Gladiators. The origin of gladiatorial contests is not entirely clear, but some of the earliest facts we know about gladiators come from their participation in funeral ceremonies in Etruria, a region of Italy that later fell under the control of

An early idealized image of the Picts.

Rome, during the sixth century B.C.E. The gladiators probably served to provide armed soldiers or attendants for the dead. The practice of pitting men against each other enhanced the reputation of the dead man and of his family. The Romans borrowed the practice and eventually politicians began sponsoring gladiatorial contests to win favor with the citizens. The first known exhibition of Roman gladiators was in 264 B.C.E., and over the next several hundred years they grew in popularity. One Roman emperor kept 10,000 gladiators for his entertainment. The men who became gladiators can be divided into two groups. The first group consists of prisoners of war, slaves, and condemned criminals who could all be forced to become gladiators. The second group is composed of the many free men who chose to join the profession. These free men hoped to win enough money to support their families or to better their position in society, but this was a very risky trade, and few survived very long.

Gladiators were trained in schools—at least the lucky ones were. Some men were forced into the arena with no combat experience at all. Students in the schools were trained first with wooden, and then with real weapons. As they gained more skill and experience, the gladiators also gained more prestige. Gladiator schools rented out their students for a fee and received

The Mark of the Horse Lord

a set price for any who were killed. Some combats were duels to the death. Other combats were left to the will of the audience. When a gladiator fell, his opponent would look to the emperor or other official for a signal. If the spectators approved of the fallen gladiator's fighting skill and courage, they would yell their support. The emperor would raise his thumb upward and the gladiator would be spared. If, as usually happened, the blood-thirsty crowd indicated disapproval, the emperor would give a thumb down signal, and the successful gladiator would finish off his opponent. Many other gladiators were killed by wild animals that were also imported to different parts of the Roman Empire to be sacrificed in the arena.

Eventually the cruelty of gladiator contests was recognized, and in 325 C.E. the emperor Constantine attempted, unsuccessfully, to ban them. Slowly, over the next hundred years or more, they faded from favor.

Rome was the center of gladiator contests, but ruins of arenas, the performance spaces used for gladiator fights and other sports, have been found throughout the area ruled by the Roman Empire. No records of gladiator contests from the area now known as Great Britain survive, but it is possible that such contests were held. Artifacts depicting gladiator contests have been excavated in several parts of the country. These may represent local contests, or they may represent the nostalgia of someone posted to the far frontiers of the Empire.

Religions of the era. Although Christianity had been introduced into the Roman Empire by the second century C.E., it was not yet the dominant religion. In Britain the Caledones, Dalriads, and Romans worshipped different pagan gods.

The Caledonians, as they are recreated by Sutcliff, worship Cailleach, a goddess who is sometimes referred to as the "Mother of All." Worship of Cailleach was common throughout Ireland and parts of Scotland. Legends surrounding her include stories of rocks that dropped from her apron creating cairns, small islands, and mountains. She lived so long that one after another of her husbands would grow old and die, forcing her to choose a new one. Cailleach is simultaneously indispensable and terrible to her people. Creator of the land and an important harvest deity, she is also sometimes represented as an old hag with the teeth of a wild bear and the tusks of a boar. In ancient Irish, her name, Cailleach, can mean either "hag" or "goddess." From this dual identity comes an age-old tale about an old woman who transforms into a young girl in the course of an evening. This ambiguity in her myths reflects both the power the Celts invested in her and the awe they felt for her fertility, and their fear of a woman who seemed, at least symbolically, to consume men. Their youth and energy waned, but her powers only grew as her children and grandchildren multiplied. Sutcliff embodies the power and danger of such a goddess in the character of Queen Liadhan, who serves as Cailleach's representative among the Caledones. The Dalriads who are temporarily forced to acknowledge her rule describe Queen Liadhan as "a woman like a she-wolf in a famine winter" (Sutcliff, *The Mark of the Horse Lord*, p. 41). She leads her people with strength, but also with a bloodthirsty cruelty. As described in the novel, Queen Liadhan takes a new consort as her king every seven years. But when the king's term is up, he is killed by the queen's newly chosen consort. Consequently, queens can grow old and cunning like Cailleach. For tribes who worship this goddess, male strength becomes the material that sustains female leadership, and women, rather than men, direct the long-term destiny of the people.

The Dalriads desire freedom from the Caledones in part so that they can return to their own religious practices. They long ago left the worship of Cailleach in favor of the Celtic god Lugh.

TYPES OF GLADIATORS

The most common gladiators were, like Phaedrus in *The Mark of the Horse Lord*, Samnites, who fought with an oblong shield, plumed helmet, and a short sword. Other important kinds of gladiators were:

Thraces Men armed with a round buckler and a curved dagger.
Mirmillones Men armed with a sword, shield, and a helmet crested with a fish design.
Retiarius Men armed with a net and a trident who faced secutors.
Secutors Fully armed men who faced the retiarius.
Andabatae Men who fought on horseback with their visors closed (making them nearly blind).
Dimachaeri Men armed with a short sword in each hand.
Essedarii Men who fought from chariots.
Hoplomachi Men who fought in complete suits of armor.
Laquearii Men who used lassos to capture their opponents.

Lugh is the lord of every art, craft, and skill, but he is often titled "Lugh the Long Arm" because of his proficiency with his great spear and sling. Like Cailleach, Lugh oversees the harvest festival, but is associated with the sun and generally lacks the monstrous attributes of Cailleach. Most importantly, Lugh is male, and so unlike the Caledones, tribes who worship Lugh look to men for leadership and pass the kingship of the tribe from father to son instead of from mother to daughter. Sutcliff emphasizes the Dalriads' relationship with Lugh the Long Arm in the novel by imagining them as particularly brave and resourceful fighters, even when they are outnumbered.

The last religion of *The Mark of the Horse Lord* is only alluded to in the novel. The Roman Commander, who plays a small role in the book, swears by the name of Mithras when he is frustrated. The worship of Mithras was very popular among Roman soldiers, who adapted the practice from an earlier Persian faith and brought it with them to various countries as the Roman Empire expanded. Mithras was a hero who killed a great bull. From the body of this bull sprang wheat, wine, animals, and many other good things, but also evil on earth. During this period Mithraism was a serious rival to the still developing Christian religion. Soldiers who joined the cult of Mithras worked their way through a series of seven initiations and ranks that included the Raven, Bridegroom, Soldier, Lion, Persian, Courier of the Sun, and Father.

The Novel in Focus

The plot. Phaedrus's early years as a Roman slave seemed ideal in retrospect. His owner, who was also his unacknowledged father, made certain Phaedrus was educated, but died before he could make good on his promise to free Phaedrus and his mother. Unwilling to face the difficulties of life with a new master, Phaedrus's mother killed herself. For two years, Phaedrus was shunted from master to master learning a bit about swordplay and a bit about driving a chariot, but ultimately, at age 16, he was sold to the Gladiator's School in Corstopitum, a small Roman town in the north of Britain. The novel opens with Phaedrus recalling his childhood as a way to distract himself before entering the gladiatorial ring for a particularly disturbing fight.

The life of a gladiator provides Phaedrus with unexpected freedoms—from worries about money, or consequences, or the future. After four years of combat, he has little to show for his difficult and deadly work except for his friendship with Vortimax, who was trained with Phaedrus and like him has survived longer than most. When Phaedrus must perform a fight to the death with Vortimax for the pleasure of the new Governor, both the prospect of dying and of killing Vortimax are unthinkable.

The battle nearly kills both of them, but luck favors Phaedrus, and as a reward for his fine fight and for four years of service, he is unexpectedly given a wooden sword, the prize reserved for those few gladiators who are freed from service. Quickly his wounds heal, but his understanding of what freedom means comes more slowly. Although Phaedrus can, at long last, call his life his own, he does not know what to do. Wandering about Corstopitum, he falls into drunkenness, street brawls, and eventually prison.

A week after Phaedrus is imprisoned, he finds himself being hustled out onto the street and whisked away to the back room of a local alehouse by an unknown benefactor. Sinnoch the Merchant introduces himself to Phaedrus and explains how the guards were bribed to release him, but Phaedrus is more interested in learning why anyone would come to his aid. The proposition that meets his question astounds him. Seven years earlier, the King of the Dalriads, a northern Celtic tribe beyond the territory occupied and ruled by Rome, was murdered, and his teenage son, Midir, disappeared. Everyone has long presumed that he died too. Sinnoch, one of the few northern men who travel between the Celtic kingdoms and the outposts of Rome, had noted, however, a stunning resemblance between Phaedrus and the missing Midir. Thus Sinnoch proposes, with the support of several of the tribe's leaders, that Phaedrus should assume the identity of Midir of the Dalriads and return with Sinnoch to the north to reclaim the kingdom.

Phaedrus replies with a variety of protests. Why now, after seven years have passed? What if the real prince returns? The answers to his questions fascinate Phaedrus. The Dalriads are sun worshipers who trace their kingship through the male line. The Caledones, a different Celtic tribe, who conquered the Dalriads, worship a goddess and trace the tribe's leadership through the queen. Every seven years the queen chooses a new young man to challenge the Old King to the Death Fight. The virility of the new king and the sacrifice of the Old King's blood keep the land and the tribe healthy. Liadhan, the queen, has chosen one of the Dalriads, Conory, as her

The Mark of the Horse Lord

new consort. Conory scorns her choice and the conquered men of the Dalriads want to exploit this rare moment that occurs only once every seven years to upset the balance, break the cycle of inheritance, and regain their own independent kingdom.

Phaedrus, half-regretfully, turns Sinnoch down. Only when Midir, the missing prince himself, steps from behind a curtained doorway, is Phaedrus convinced to accept a part in this ruse. Midir is blind. Seven years earlier Queen Liadhan, fearing to kill him outright, maimed Midir, rendering him, by the laws of his people, unfit to rule. The cruelty of the act and Midir's own role in the plot to place an imposter on the throne at last convince Phaedrus to accept the challenge. And with this new decision Phaedrus exchanges his unfettered and unsettling new freedom for a chance to fight, for a sense of belonging, and for "a lost flavour to be caught back into life" (*The Mark of the Horse Lord*, p. 44).

Over the next few months Phaedrus studies with Midir, learning intimate details of his childhood, the ways he recognizes people, and the deep personal vengeance Midir feels for the woman who robbed him of his throne and his sight. Phaedrus also receives a special tattoo on his forehead called the mark of the horse lord, which identifies him as the heir to the kingdom of the Dalriads and provides Sutcliff with the title for the novel. Phaedrus then travels north to meet with the six men of the Dalriad council who must approve the ruse and his performance. He struggles to master simple skills like balancing in a small boat and more complex ones, like driving a mountain chariot, that Midir, even as a boy, would have been at ease performing.

Finally, the night approaches for the ceremony of the Death Fight, the night the Dalriads have chosen to rise against the Caledones. Outnumbered, the Dalriads must rely on surprise for their attack to succeed, but a twist of fate exposes them a few seconds too soon when Phaedrus falls and his special tattoo is revealed. While they succeed in driving the Caledones out of Dun Moniath, the sacred and ceremonial gathering space of the Dalriads, Queen Liadhan escapes. The Dalriads make the best of their partial victory. They introduce Phaedrus as the lost Midir and arrange a marriage between him and Queen Liadhan's daughter Murna.

At first Phaedrus is unhappy in his new role as king. His bride would rather kill him than be seen with him and Conory, Midir's best friend, suspects he is an imposter. Phaedrus decides to tell Conory the truth, and to his surprise, they become fast friends. Murna is harder to win over; Phaedrus cannot tell whether she hates him because he is Midir or because she too suspects that he is not.

Soon Queen Liadhan arranges for an army of Caledones to support her return to the leadership of the kingdom, and the Dalriads are forced to go to war. Throughout the summer battles rage. Even though he is proficient at fighting, Phaedrus learns new tactics. The marvelous horsemanship of the mountain charioteers impresses him, and once he has become accustomed to the strange idea, the fighting prowess of the Dalriad women, including Murna, gains his respect. Slowly, Phaedrus learns to trust Murna. Murna, for her part, begins to realize that her new husband has changed immensely from the thoughtless lad she knew Midir to be seven years ago. By the end of the summer Murna is pregnant and must leave the battlegrounds to prepare for the child's birth.

The Dalriads may be the more determined fighters, but the Caledones have the strength of greater numbers. The Dalriad war effort teeters ominously. Cunning proves more important than strength, however, and the Dalriads trap and burn a valley filled with their enemies to gain the upper hand at last. To Phaedrus and Conory's immense frustration, Queen Liadhan again escapes. This time she flees south to a Roman fortress on the border between the Roman territory and the Celtic kingdoms.

With a small band of Dalriads, Phaedrus rides to the Roman fort and demands the return of Queen Liadhan, but the soldiers refuse. Aware that his war weary tribe cannot successfully attack a Roman stronghold, Phaedrus retreats in disappointment. But, unexpectedly, he receives a late night visitor, Midir. The true prince of the Dalriads has made his way north to await news of his people and of the ploy to place Phaedrus on his throne. Working in the Roman fort he has learned the commander's plans to have Queen Liadhan removed by boat and conveyed to a safer haven in the south the next day. The two men devise a bold plan to assassinate the Queen even under the very noses of her Roman guards.

Crouched in waiting for the moment he can throw his knife and remove the final threat to his newly won kingship, Phaedrus is betrayed. His conference with Midir was overheard and reported. Midir has already been captured. Queen Liadhan comes out to gloat over Phaedrus as she awaits her ship, but her pride finally proves her undoing. Taking advantage of the fact that the soldiers underestimate a blind man, Midir escapes from his cell and makes a suicidal lunge that carries both him and Queen Liadhan over a seawall to their deaths.

The next morning the Roman commander, embarrassed by his loss of Queen Liadhan and determined to make the best of the situation, offers Phaedrus a bitter choice. Either Phaedrus can order one thousand of the Dalriad warriors to accept service as Roman auxiliaries and be posted overseas to fight foreign wars, or Phaedrus will be held as a hostage king, perhaps even crucified, as an example to other tribesmen.

There is no choice to be made. The loss of so many warriors would mean the end of the Dalriads. The Caledones would overrun them again immediately. Phaedrus realizes that true kingship also means sacrifice. Standing atop the battlements of the fort, Phaedrus announces his decision to a war band of Dalriads, and before the Roman guards can stop him, he stabs himself with his cloak pin and leaps to his death. In giving his own life to preserve the well-being of the tribe, Phaedrus becomes in truth the king whose identity he had only aspired to imitate.

Beyond the arena. Once Phaedrus wins his wooden sword and is released from the gladiatorial school, he feels stunned by his new freedom. Real Roman gladiators probably felt much the same way. Although surely most gladiators dreamed of earning their release from combat, all of them knew that violent death was by far the most common fate for men in their profession. Death rates are hard to calculate, but one scholar theorizes that in the first century about 20 percent of gladiators died in each fight (which means a gladiator was unlikely to survive more than ten battles). As time went on the death rate increased to 50 percent or more in most contests, making extended survival less and less likely in the later years of the Roman Empire (Kyle, p. 86).

Phaedrus spends his first day as a free man wondering what to do with himself. The options available to released gladiators were quite limited. First, he considers seeking work as a soldier with the Roman legions, though he fears his former status as a slave and gladiator will invite the Romans to treat him with disdain rather than the respect that his fierce and finely tuned battle skills are due, and his suspicions are justified. The Roman Empire maintained a strictly hierarchical society, and gladiators were counted among the lowest classes—their origins as slaves, prisoners of war, or criminals tainted their reputations no matter how bravely and honorably they conducted themselves in the arena. Like prostitutes and other members of the most shameful professions, gladiators were labeled *infamis* and deprived of personal dignity and social standing. Most commanders would not respect a former gladiator enough to let him join the military ranks of Rome, even in the farthest outposts in places like Britain where recruitment standards were more lax.

Yet at the same time that they were treated with such disdain, gladiators were also glorified by the audiences who loved to watch them perform. The courage of gladiators who so skillfully fought against great odds and the honor that accrued for those who risked violent death without flinching appealed tremendously to the citizens of Rome. They associated the fights with "Roman" qualities such as courage, loyalty, and discipline; relished the excitement provided by man-to-man combat; and enjoyed cheering for their favorite fighters. But these same citizens of Rome feared gladiators. Their violent skills made the combatants threatening; their familiarity with cruelty and death made them uncivilized. Romans admired gladiators from a distance but did not want freed gladiators as their "neighbors, magistrates, or in-laws" (Kyle, p. 80). When a gladiator died, his corpse was not even permitted honorable burial unless some relative, friend, or special burial society came forward to claim it.

Some historical records include complaints about former gladiators and their children bettering themselves in society. These writers resented that men with a tainted past, besmirched by their time in the arena, should receive any respect at all in society. Slaves or prisoners of war who were forced to become gladiators, like Phaedrus in the novel, would not even have had families or homes to return to when they were freed. Unless they had won especially rich prizes through their fighting skills or become the favorite of a wealthy patron who might set them up in a respectable business, freed gladiators like Phaedrus, were apt to turn around and take jobs as overseers and instructors in the gladiatorial schools or even return to the arena again simply to avoid starvation. Unlike regular gladiators, freed gladiators could control the terms and length of their contracts when they re-enlisted. They could, within certain limits, negotiate their pay, the types of combat in which they would engage, and the length of time they wanted to continue employment. However, once con-

The Mark of the Horse Lord

tracted, freed gladiators were bound to the same oath of loyalty and subject to the same harsh dangers as other gladiators.

In *The Mark of the Horse Lord*, Sinnoch the Merchant's proposition gives Phaedrus a second chance at life outside the gladiatorial world, though, of course, the opportunity to impersonate a king would not have been a path open to real Roman gladiators. The idea, however, of an affiliation between kings and gladiators does have some historical accuracy. A number of Roman emperors are reputed to have dabbled in the arena as amateur gladiators. The most famous of these is the Emperor Commodus (161-92 C.E.), son of Marcus Aurelius. According to Dio Cassus, a writer of the era, Commodus devoted much of his life to fighting wild beasts and men in the arena. He claimed to have fought more than 1,000 bouts and to have bested more than 12,000 opponents. By virtue of his position, he, of course, had advantages other gladiators did not. No one dared to defeat Commodus in the arena, and the prizes he awarded himself for each day's work as a gladiator were astronomically higher than any opponent would receive. Despite his success in the arena, Commodus died a violent death; he was assassinated at age 31. The novel's Phaedrus too faces violent death as a king, but it is different from Commodus's, or, for that matter, from the kind either of them would have experienced as gladiators. Phaedrus at least knows he is sacrificing his life for a cause much more meaningful than the mere entertainment of a Roman crowd.

Sources and literary context. Sutcliff emphasizes in her introduction to *The Mark of the Horse Lord* that the individual characters and most of the specific settings in her novel grew from her imaginative reconstruction of Celtic and Roman life in early Britain rather than from any historical records. Some of the characters, like Midir, may, however, have modern inspirations; it is possible to see echoes of Sutcliff herself in the figure of the blind and disenfranchised prince. Like Midir, Sutcliff experienced disabilities that separated her from most of her peers. Despite many surgeries and treatments, she could never walk well and most physical games and sports were impossible for her. She was also acutely aware of how stereotypes about the disabled limited the imaginations of many healthy individuals. In her autobiography, Sutcliff remarks that especially in her youth it had not "begun to dawn on the able-bodied world that it is possible to combine an unsatisfactory body with a perfectly satisfactory brain, and a personality at any rate as satisfactory as most other people's" (Sutcliff, *Blue Remembered Hills*, pp. 128-29).

In *The Mark of the Horse Lord,* Midir demonstrates a resourcefulness and independence that few would expect to find in a blind man. After he leaves the Dalriads, he educates himself as a leather worker, travels about the north by himself, and uses his well-honed hearing to lead him to Queen Liadhan in one of the book's climaxes. Instead of making him timid or helpless, Midir's disability helps him develop exactly the kind of courage and determination necessary to dislodge a usurper from his throne. Like Sutcliff's, Midir's apparent limitations are only barriers in other people's perception of him, but never in his own thoughts or deeds.

Events in History at the Time the Novel Was Written

The Irish question. During Sutcliff's lifetime and for centuries preceding it, England's relationship with its neighbor and subject country Ireland was fraught with conflicts. One of the most emotionally laden of these conflicts had to do with religion. Ireland began its conversion to Christianity in 432 C.E. and eventually England too began the transition from varied pagan practices to the unifying practice of Christianity. During the sixteenth century, however, for both political and spiritual reasons, England broke with the established Roman Catholic church, the primary form of Christianity, and became a Protestant Christian nation. Ireland, unmoved by the religious turmoil of the century, remained Catholic. This difference became more and more important as English landowners in Ireland asserted their authority over the Irish and set up laws and practices that assured the continuing poverty and disadvantage of the Irish people. During the early years of the twentieth century the dissatisfaction of the Irish became impossible for the English to ignore. Civil uprisings and armed conflicts escalated as some Irish leaders tried to force England to permit home rule—to permit Ireland to govern itself. For these Irish patriots, the idea of freedom was worth almost any price, in some cases, even their lives. The Dalriads, who also struggled to maintain their political and religious independence when the Roman Empire expanded to Britain would certainly have sympathized with the struggles of the Irish.

In 1921 the Anglo-Irish treaty proposed that Ireland should become like many of the other parts of the crumbling British Empire and have its own parliament and executive leader, but the treaty was accepted only in the southern 26 counties of Ireland. The six northern counties chose to remain part of Great Britain, largely because many Protestant English had settled in this area, and they failed to see themselves as having enough in common with the Irish Catholics of the southern counties. Consequently, the compromise proved only a limited success at solving the problems between Ireland and England.

Conflict continued, and in 1949 the Republic of Ireland Act ended the pretense that Ireland was a member of the British Commonwealth. The 26 southern counties were recognized as an independent nation by England. Once again, the Parliament of Northern Ireland refused to consent to the cessation, and so problems continued.

During the 1950s and 1960s the Irish Republican Army (IRA) led attacks on British outposts in the six northern counties of Ireland in an attempt to drive the English out of the country altogether. Hostilities between the two parts of Ireland and between the independent Irish and England grew ever more intense and bloody. Much of this anger and antagonism was expressed as a near religious war between the Catholics and the Protestants of Ireland.

Whether Sutcliff consciously realized the parallels between the historical Roman attempts to colonize and control the Dalriads and the Caledones and the English attempts during her own lifetime to continue the colonial control of the Irish, the two situations have many similarities. The importance of religious practice as a means of generating cultural identity and of causing civil strife only reinforces the resemblances between the circumstances of the northern Celtic tribes and the people of Ireland. During Roman times, the conquerors claimed that the peace and order (the *pax romana*) brought by Rome was worth the price the Celts had to pay in taxes, conscripts, and lost territory, but the Celts disagreed. For them the freedom to live under their own rule was by far the greater good, one worth fighting for and dying to preserve. For many years, the British made similar arguments in regard to Ireland. They claimed Ireland was more productive and better managed under British care, but to the Irish such help was not only an unwelcome interference, but a damper on their ability to prosper. Like the Dalriads, many Irish ultimately chose to give up their lives rather than their freedom.

Whose island is it? The island recognized today as Great Britain has been peopled, conquered, colonized, and repeopled many times during the course of history. The various Celtic cultures were invaded by the Romans, whose fortifications were over run by the Angles and the Saxons, whose communities were attacked by the Norman French. Each new wave of immigration added new facets to the cultures of the island. Yet these waves of change are not simply a part of history—they continue to reshape the country today. At the beginning of the twentieth century the British Empire stretched across the globe from Australia to Canada to India and many points in between. Only the Roman Empire nearly twenty centuries earlier could compare in scope and influence. In 1914 a law was passed in England that demonstrated the broad view of what it meant to be a citizen of the British Commonwealth. Nearly anyone born in any part of the Empire was considered a citizen and was theoretically free to move, work, or live in any part of the Commonwealth. Though the law did restrict entry into Britain for those outside the Empire, like the Eastern European Jews who had been immigrating to England, in many ways the British Nationality and Aliens Act of 1914 sought to include rather than exclude people. In 1948 the British Nationality Act reaffirmed the right of all Commonwealth citizens to enter and work in Britain. Manpower shortages following World War II made the idea of immigration into England seem appealing to the government. Enticed by the economic opportunities being offered to them, many Commonwealth citizens from the Caribbean, Guyana, India and other areas accepted the invitation. Unfortunately the rising number of racially diverse immigrants led to unease in Britain. This discomfort was expressed in restrictive government measures, like the Commonwealth Immigrants Act of 1962. This act enforced a system of employment vouchers for Commonwealth immigrants that effectively shifted their status from that of citizens to alien contract laborers. Under this new law only people whose parents or grandparents had been born in the United Kingdom or a self-governing Commonwealth country would have the full privileges of citizenship. Whereas the migration of citizens to Britain was formerly seen as beneficial, it was now seen as socially costly and disruptive of the national character. In short, many people feared the changes that new people, especially people of color, would bring—just as the Celts, or the Romans, or the Angles and Saxons

The Mark of the Horse Lord

before them had feared the costs of sharing their territory with other people. And just as earlier people resorted to violence to protect themselves, the modern British also resorted at times to vicious discrimination and even violent riots in an attempt to drive out the newcomers, but unlike previous waves of immigrants, these newcomers had been invited. Sensitized to the realities of discrimination by her own physical disabilities, Sutcliff may have been more aware than many of her peers in the 1960s of the difficulties outsiders face when joining an unwelcoming community. *The Mark of the Horse Lord* never deals explicitly with racial issues, but it does explore the clash of cultures. Just as the novel was being written in the mid 1960s, so too were laws in England regarding discrimination. The 1965 Race Relations Act attempted, with only very modest success, to address the racism directed against many of the new Commonwealth immigrants by making it unlawful to discriminate on the grounds of race, color, or ethnic origin in public places. Over the next decade stronger laws and various boards and committees charged with hearing and settling discrimination complaints took greater steps in working toward a more equitable England.

Although it would have taxed the imaginations of Sutcliff's Dalriads and Caledones to envision it, within several centuries these two warring tribes would come to share a national identity as Scots. Similarly, the turmoil caused in Britain by the immigration of citizens from distant parts of the Commonwealth is leading toward a new cultural identity in Britain, and not, as history makes clear, for the first time.

Reviews. All the reviewers of *The Mark of the Horse Lord* recognized the compelling power of Sutcliff's novel as soon as it was published. Virginia Kirkus credited Sutcliff with writing the best historical novel available for either children or adults (Block and Riley, p. 188). Others praised the power of her language, exciting plotting, and authentic detail, including one critic who predicted that "the debt which children's literature owes to Miss Sutcliff has yet to be assessed," and concluded that *The Mark of the Horse Lord* was "a thundering good story from a complete artist" (Hedblad, p. 159). Even critics who found grounds for grumbling, like Marcus Crouch, who complained that the novel was "grossly over-written," also acknowledged that it was grimly compelling and her finest work (Block and Riley, p. 189).

At least as important as the reception at its publication in 1965, however, is the novel's continuing ability to attract readers. The rough imagery and grim events of *The Mark of the Horse Lord* never sensationalize violence, but they do acknowledge it with an unflinching accuracy. Some modern critics may be surprised at the demanding balance that Sutcliff exacts between sacrifice and freedom in her novel for children, but having lived through war herself and having seen its effects on citizens of all ages, she writes novels that effectively put a human face on the darker parts of history, as well as the more joyous ones, without putting a mask over it. In tribute to Sutcliff's undiminished appeal, in 1985 *The Mark of the Horse Lord* was awarded the first Phoenix Award, an honor extended to a novel for young people published at least 20 years earlier that did not receive a significant literary prize at publication but which has proved its durability, popularity, and quality.

—Megan Isaac

For More Information

Anwar, Muhammad. *Race and Politics*. London: Tavistock, 1986.

Block, Anne, and Carolyn Riley, eds. *Children's Literature Review*. Vol. 1. New York: Gale Research, 1976.

Davies, Norman. *The Isles: A History*. Oxford: Oxford University Press, 1999.

Grant, Michael. *Gladiators*. Middlesex, U.K.: Penguin, 1971.

Hedblad, Alan, ed. *Children's Literature Review*. Vol. 37. New York: Gale Research, 1996.

Kyle, Donald G. *Spectacles of Death in Ancient Rome*. New York: Routledge. 1998.

Laing, Lloyd and Jenny. *The Picts and the Scots*. Phoenix Mill, U.K.: Sutton, 1998.

Meek, Margaret. *Rosemary Sutcliff*. London: The Bodley Head, 1962.

Scullard, H. H. *Roman Britain: Outpost of the Empire*. London: Thames and Hudson, 1979.

Sutcliff, Rosemary. *Blue Remembered Hills*. William Morrow, 1984.

———. *The Mark of the Horse Lord*. Oxford: Oxford University Press, 1965.

Talcroft, Barbara L. *Death of the Corn King: King and Goddess in Rosemary Sutcliff's Historical Fiction for Young Adults*. Metuchen, N.J.: The Scarecrow Press, 1995.

The Mill on the Floss

by
George Eliot (Marian Evans)

The Mill on the Floss was the second novel Marian Evans published under the pseudonym George Eliot. Born in 1819 to a prosperous estate manager, Marian Evans spent her youth much as her heroine did, in reading and outdoor activities. In 1850 Evans moved to London where she worked as a translator and editor, and fell in love with the writer and editor George Henry Lewes, a married man. Contemporary marriage law prevented Lewes from obtaining a divorce from his adulterous wife; the law held that, having condoned the adultery previously, he now had no grounds for divorce. Knowing this, Evans and Lewes pursued their relationship anyway. The two eloped to the Continent in 1854, then lived together as husband and wife until Lewes's death in 1878. During her life with Lewes, Evans suffered the disapproval of her older brother Isaac, who cut off all contact with her. His rejection of her remained one of the great sadnesses of her life until their reconciliation upon her marriage in 1880 to John Walter Cross, an investment banker who had been Evans's financial advisor. Evans's scandalous personal history led her to publish under the male pseudonym George Eliot when she began writing fiction in the late 1850s. She followed the success of her first book, *Scenes From Clerical Life* (1858) with two novels—*Adam Bede* (1859) and *The Mill on the Floss* (1860) in rapid succession. Altogether George Eliot published seven novels as well as short stories, essays, and poetry. *The Mill on the Floss* remained her most autobiographical and most tragic novel—the

> **THE LITERARY WORK**
>
> A novel set in the English Midlands around the turn of the nineteenth century; published in 1860.
>
> **SYNOPSIS**
>
> Maggie and Tom Tulliver are siblings bound to each other by love and duty; but Tom's provincial prejudices oppress Maggie's imaginative nature, with tragic results for both.

freedoms that Marian Evans was beginning to enjoy as a writer in mid-Victorian England would be forever denied her heroine, a woman oppressed by the narrowness of her family and the provincial community of her pre-Victorian childhood.

Events in History at the Time of the Novel

Catholic emancipation. *The Mill on the Floss* opens in 1829, at the time of the great debates over Catholic emancipation. Three centuries earlier, at the time of the Reformation, the birth of Protestantism led, in turn, to the birth of the Church of England and consequent changes in English politics, which restricted voting and posts in Parliament to Anglicans, members of the Church of England, or Anglican Church. Since 80 percent of the Irish population belonged to

Mill on the Floss

George Eliot

the Roman Catholic Church, the Irish were effectively disenfranchised by this legislation. Opponents mounted efforts to remedy the situation with new legislation that would extend the franchise to Catholics, an issue that became more public in the early 1820s. In 1828 a leader of the Catholic Emancipation movement, Daniel O'Connell, stood for and won election to Parliament from County Clare. (A loophole in the legislation allowed him to run for office, though he could not in fact take office as a Roman Catholic.) He won in a landslide, and the British prime minister Wellington (Arthur Wellesley, first duke of Wellington, famous for his victories against Napoleon) faced a constitutional crisis. Wellington's ministry had to either pass Catholic Emancipation legislation and allow the election to stand or void the election and face the possibility of violence, even civil war. In 1829 Wellington's ministry passed Catholic Emancipation (giving Catholics the right to hold office in Parliament and elsewhere) and civil war was averted. The Anglican Church's hegemony in civil and cultural affairs had begun to crumble.

Agriculture and industry. George Eliot set *The Mill on the Floss* in the English Midlands of her childhood, a prosperous agricultural community. The "mill" of the title is a water-powered flour mill, not a factory—though it had become a common meaning for the term by the time the novel was published. Industrialization had been penetrating England's north first and increasingly affecting the rest of the country as well. By the end of the novel, Tom Tulliver suggests applying steam to the mill in order to modernize it. The English economy is in great flux, putting the mill itself in jeopardy; water-powered mills will ultimately give way to more modern means of production.

The shift from water to steam power represents a larger shift from agricultural production to industrial trade as the dominant sector of England's economy. England, an island nation, has always had a trading economy. By the early part of the nineteenth century, industrial production and international trade had almost replaced land ownership as a means to wealth. As George Eliot's biographer Frederick Karl notes, the author was born into a traditional society. Karl describes it as "one of the most historically fixed societies possible, where rules established almost as far back as Henry VIII [300 years] dominated" (Karl, p. 7). This traditionalism began to erode with Catholic Emancipation, but such legislation was perhaps less significant than industrial development in reshaping English society. During the period of the novel, rigid class distinctions were slowly but surely beginning to fade as new fortunes were made in trade and industry. In *The Mill on the Floss*, the patriarch Mr. Tulliver has a bare inkling of this possibility when he plans for his son's education. He wants to prepare his son for "one o' them smartish businesses as are all profits and no outlay" (Eliot, *The Mill on the Floss*, p. 9). Tom eventually makes a living in the import-export business, a type of trade his father, firmly tied to the land and the mill, can barely imagine.

The growth of industry and trade created a new class in England, a middle class positioned between the land-owning aristocracy and the laboring poor. Educated and prosperous, middle-class men and women began to reshape England's economy, its politics, and its social structure during the nineteenth century. While the "professions" of law, medicine, and the church had always occupied a middle ground between upper and lower social classes, the new wealth and power of industrialists and investors reshaped the middle class into the powerful social and economic force it remains today.

The changing family. The English family before the nineteenth century could be a rather loose affiliation of blood relatives, friends, servants, and others. Adoption was informal. Church rather than state courts controlled marriage, and economics as much as kinship determined who made up a family. To a great extent, the family was an economic unit even more than a unit bound by affection or blood. As industrial capitalism came increasingly to supplant the farm and other small family businesses in the English economy, the family itself underwent change, growing more nuclear. While society channeled middle-class men primarily into the public world of business, it limited these women to the "sphere" of the family, which was increasingly not the extended family of agricultural England but rather the smaller, nuclear family. Although historians disagree about when and even to what extent the actual make-up of the family shifted, it seems undeniable that between the mid-eighteenth century and the mid-nineteenth century the concept of the family changed. Instead of seeing it as a loose affiliation of kin and friends, most people saw family as a biologically based nuclear unit consisting first of parents and children and, more remotely, of cousins, grandparents, and other blood relatives as well. A conflict between the two ways of thinking about the family emerges in *The Mill on the Floss*. While Mrs. Tulliver insists on calling a family council to consult with her sisters before any major family decision, Mr. Tulliver insists that decisions regarding his family are his and his alone. Mrs. Tulliver's sisters, the Dodsons, participate in the older family model, in economic as well as other ways, preserving their own fruits and vegetables, making wine, and selling eggs and butter at market. While these pursuits are of little economic consequence, they still evoke the older model of family that is slowly fading away.

The position of women in Victorian society. The rise of the middle class and the increasing nuclearization of the family greatly affected the position of women in English society. Those who had been economic participants when agriculture was dominant became more confined to the home in the new economy and, at least in the middle classes, more concerned with consumption than production. Women had long lacked legal standing in England: at the turn of the nineteenth century, they could not vote, own property, testify in court, or maintain custody of their children in the (rare) event of divorce or separation. They did not, however, take their inequality without creating a stir, although it was still faint at the time in which the novel takes place. Modern historians often date the nineteenth-century women's movement from Mary Wollstonecraft's *A Vindication of the Rights of Woman* (also in *Literature and Its Times*), published in 1792. Wollstonecraft's essay is largely concerned with the equal education of girls and women rather than with their political enfranchisement, but her emphasis on education would inspire mid-century feminists to political action around the time that Eliot wrote the novel. At the time the novel takes place, however, individual women found their lives radically constrained by social custom and propriety. (This would in fact be true later in the century too, despite the slow achievement of political and educational victories.) Victorian etiquette kept middle-class women from mixing freely with men outside their own families. Girls and boys were educated separately, and after completing their education women were expected to remain at home caring for family members until they could be married to a suitable husband. While upper-class couples might meet at balls and dances, social opportunities were more limited for middle-class women, especially outside the cities in the provinces. The charity bazaar and other socially sanctioned philanthropic events were among the few means of encountering members of the opposite sex on relatively informal terms. Provincial society such as that depicted in *The Mill on the Floss* was especially limited and hierarchical, making gender relations even more difficult.

The Novel in Focus

The plot. *The Mill on the Floss* begins with an extended reverie by an unnamed narrator who sets the action in the recent past and recalls the events of the story. The narrator reappears occasionally throughout the novel with more extended reveries that do not advance the plot but are an important counterpoint to it.

The novel proper begins with Mr. Tulliver, a seemingly prosperous miller, deciding where to send his son Tom, aged 12, to school. After a year at the local "academy," Tom is not progressing as his father wishes. His hope for Tom, that he will surpass his father's position in life, can only be met by a "gentleman's education." Encouraged by his friend, the surveyor Mr. Riley, Tulliver determines to place his son in the home of the Reverend Stelling, a local clergyman who is taking in students. Mrs. Tulliver—her maiden name was Dodson—calls in her three sisters for a family consultation on Tom's education. Her husband, who has already made up his mind, adopts an attitude that alienates one of the

Mill on the Floss

> ## NINETEENTH-CENTURY EDUCATION
>
> There was no compulsory public education in England until 1880; the 1870 Education Act established universal education at the primary level, but it was not compulsory. Poor children were often apprenticed to a craftsperson at a very early age; their education, if any, was provided by philanthropic institutions known as "ragged schools," which initially emphasized religious over secular education. The ragged schools increasingly provided basic education in reading and writing as the nineteenth century progressed, but their quality varied greatly. At a slightly higher level were "training schools," which educated poor and working-class children with a fairly steady diet of facts. A teacher would train older teenagers to be "monitors," who then taught younger children. Often there was only one trained teacher for up to 500 children.
>
> Education for the middle classes was equally haphazard, though with a very different emphasis. Aside from the elite "public schools"—boys' boarding schools (for example, Eton, Harrow, Westminster, and Rugby), most schooling was a local and private affair. The so-called public schools did not operate at a profit, but they were actually private. People considered them "public" because they provided an alternative to private tutoring, and had initially been founded as schools for the deserving poor, meaning those who worked. Many of these boarding schools had some affiliation with the Church of England, preparing boys for universities whose business it was to educate men for the clergy.
>
> The various academies, boarding schools, and informal educational arrangements in *The Mill on the Floss* reflect the state of middle-class education in early-nineteenth-century England. Early education was provided in the home, with mothers (usually) teaching their children to read and write and perhaps to do simple arithmetic. More prosperous middle-class children might then attend a boarding school, as George Eliot did at age 5, and as the novel's Maggie Tulliver does at 9 or 10. For girls, education focused on "accomplishments"—sewing, painting, and music—with perhaps some modern languages (French or German) but little academic rigor. Boys generally received a "classical" education, emphasizing Latin, Euclidean geometry, and the like. In *The Mill on the Floss,* Tom will find Latin and geometry to be only a hindrance in his post-school life. Indeed, some historians have argued that the heavy emphasis on the classics in private and "public" schools of the time produced an anti-technological elite, ill-equipped for the Industrial Revolution and its aftermath.

three Dodson sisters, now named Mrs. Glegg, who threatens to call in a loan she has made to him. Tom is sent to Stelling's despite the Dodsons' disapproval; Mr. Tulliver repays his loan to the sister by borrowing money from Mr. Wakem, a lawyer who has opposed Tulliver in an earlier legal battle over water rights. Tulliver's entanglement with Wakem and estrangement from Mrs. Tulliver's family will have repercussions throughout the novel.

Tom's nine-year-old sister Maggie is disappointed by Tom's departure. Tom is both her idol and her bully. Far more than her father, Tom disciplines Maggie, reprimanding her for her absent-minded dreaminess. Maggie's intelligence is a source of both pride and dismay to her father, who enjoys her imagination but fears it is wasted on a girl. In one early episode, Maggie—in disgrace for fighting with her brother and cousin—runs off to the Gypsies, hoping they will accord her more respect and freedom than her family. Disappointed by the harsh realities of Gypsy life, she is returned safely to her father, who welcomes her warmly, saying, "I couldn't afford to lose the little wench" (*The Mill on the Floss*, p. 97). While her escapade goes unpunished, its psychological effects linger: Maggie never again overtly defies her family.

Tom's education progresses poorly. Latin and geometry are difficult for him and, he suspects, irrelevant to his future. Complicating his life even further, the son of his father's enemy, the hunchback Philip Wakem, joins him as a fellow student at Mr. Stelling's and succeeds while Tom struggles. Maggie, who visits Tom at school, enchants Philip with her dark eyes and active imagination. Though she finds Tom's schoolwork more captivating than he does, her interest is discouraged by Mr. Stelling, who dismisses girls as "quick and shallow" (*The Mill on the Floss*, p. 126).

Several years pass during which Mr. Tulliver is engaged in a lawsuit over water rights for the mill. In the meantime Maggie has been placed in a boarding school with her cousin, Lucy Deane. Both Maggie and Tom are called home from school when their father loses his lawsuit and suffers a stroke. Paralyzed and not fully cognizant of his surroundings, he loses his property—including Maggie's treasured books—at an auctioneer's sale to pay off his debts. He suffers a final indignity when Wakem, who buys the mill, hires Tulliver to run it as a manager. Despite his hatred for Wakem, Tulliver accepts the humiliating demotion for the sake of his family. At this point, Tulliver instructs his son to write into the family Bible his undying hatred of Wakem and his refusal to forgive him. These words haunt Tom throughout the rest of the novel.

Tom finds a job working for his uncle, Mr. Deane (cousin Lucy's father, who is married to one of the Dodson sisters), who runs an import-export business in St Ogg's, the town nearest the mill. All the education Tom received proves of little use in this commercial business, but he takes accounting lessons and rises rapidly in the firm. Assisted by a childhood acquaintance, Bob Jakin, Tom begins to "speculate" in small shipments of cargo with money borrowed from one of his aunts. The income he earns over the next three years enables him to pay off his father's debts.

While Tom is working hard to restore his family's credit, Maggie suffers from the loss of the family's books and status almost as intensely. She strives for the self-denying peace of Thomas à Kempis (author of *Imitation of Christ*, 1470). In this mystical work Maggie reads: "Forsake thyself, resign thyself, and thou shalt enjoy much inward peace," a doctrine of self-denial that she finds difficult to follow (*The Mill on the Floss*, p. 237). But her brother's former schoolmate, Philip Wakem, tempts her to indulge her taste for reading and art. Meeting Philip secretly—knowing her father and brother would disapprove—she continues to read and study, meanwhile taking in sewing to assist with the family's finances. Philip surprises Maggie by confessing his love for her; she agrees to a secret engagement but suspects that she feels gratitude for his friendship rather than true love.

"LIKE A GYPSY AND 'HALF WILD'"

Maggie's appearance is almost always at issue in *The Mill on the Floss*. Her mother laments that her brown skin and brown hair make her look "like a mulatter [mulatto]" (*The Mill on the Floss,* p. 12). Breeding is at issue again when Maggie is told that she is "like a gypsy and 'half wild'" (*The Mill on the Floss*, p. 88). Though a commonly disparaged group, Gypsies filled an important need in rural England at the turn of the nineteenth century, providing goods and services to remote areas, increasingly, in light of the industrial revolution, manufactured goods. Camps of traveling Gypsies sold inexpensive wares, repaired household goods, worked as seasonal farmhands, and served as temporary entertainers. Rumors abounded about their depravity. Considered outsiders, not English, they were relegated to the margins of society and associated with shady practices. But actually they were only one of a wide range of England's wandering groups at the time, from tramps to temporary laborers, to tinkers, horse-dealers, and fairground people. A few do-gooders attempted to reform the Gypsies in early- to mid-nineteenth-century England, by educating and converting them to Christianity. Generally these attempts failed, since they called for abandoning Gypsy ways.

Just before Tom earns enough money to pay off the debts, he discovers Maggie's meetings with Philip and, in an angry scene, forbids them to meet again. Maggie reluctantly agrees to end the relationship to avoid upsetting her father, who has never fully recovered from his stroke. She promises Tom that she will not see Philip again without his knowledge. Several weeks later Tom restores his father's credit in a public ceremony at which all his debts are paid. The celebration is short-lived, however. On his way home, Mr. Tulliver encounters Mr. Wakem and, in the triumph of the moment, acts out his hatred of Wakem and horsewhips him, then collapses in another paralytic stroke. This time, Tulliver dies.

Now fatherless, Maggie takes a position as governess, and Tom continues to rise in the firm

Mill on the Floss

1937 film version of *The Mill on the Floss,* with Griffith Jones as Stephen Guest and Geraldine Fitzgerald as Maggie Tulliver.

of Deane & Guest. After the death of Mrs. Deane, Mrs. Tulliver comes to keep house for cousin Lucy and her father, and Maggie returns to St Ogg's for a visit. Lucy's fiancé, Stephen Guest (the son of her father's senior partner), brings Philip Wakem to call on Lucy. Maggie both reconnects with Philip and inadvertently interests Stephen Guest. Unable to commit to Philip because of her promise to her brother, she unconsciously encourages Stephen, whose attentions flatter and confuse her. Lucy tries to make peace between Tom and Philip by encouraging her father to buy the mill from Wakem and install Tom as manager. Wakem reluctantly agrees to his son's engagement to Maggie, but she insists on leaving to take up a new governess position rather than re-engaging herself to Philip. Just before her scheduled departure, she agrees to a boat ride with Stephen Guest, who allows the boat to be carried further downriver than planned, hoping she will agree to elope with him rather than return home to St Ogg's. Although she knows her reputation will be ruined—they are gone overnight—Maggie chooses to reject Stephen rather than break her ties to the past, that is, to Lucy, Philip, and her brother. She returns to St Ogg's in disgrace. When Tom turns her out of the house, Maggie takes lodgings with the family's old friend Bob Jakins. The community rejects her too, though Philip and Lucy forgive her indiscretion. Stephen meanwhile continues to tempt her, writing to her with a repeated proposal. Just as she finally decides to leave town for a new governess position, the river floods.

She sets out by boat from the Jakins house, determined to rescue her brother, who is at the mill. Successful in her search, she hands over the oars to Tom, who seems finally reconciled to his wayward and passionate sister. But the reconciliation is a brief one, cut short by their death by drowning when parts of the mill machinery strike the boat. On their tombstone sits a phrase of small comfort: "In their death they were not divided."

Brothers and sisters. *The Mill on the Floss*'s most striking feature is the strength of the brother-sister bond. George Eliot even considered titling the novel *Sister Maggie*, though she feared such a title would make it sound too much like "a child's story" (Haight, p. xv). Maggie's attachment to her brother motivates her throughout the novel, and she repeatedly characterizes her connection to Philip Wakem in sibling terms as well, wishing to be "brother and sister in secret" and realizing "what a dear, good brother [he] would have been" (*The Mill on the Floss*, pp. 273, 267). Mr. Tulliver himself has strong ties to a sister, Gritty Moss. In fact, rather than call in money owed him by her and her husband, he borrows from Wakem to repay his own debts, which leads to his losing the mill and all his property to this hated enemy. Tulliver worries about Maggie, thinking that "the little wench [would] be poorly off, and Tom rather hard upon her" if Tulliver set an example of acting harshly to his own sister (*The Mill on the Floss*, p. 69). Sadly his worries come true. While Maggie values the sibling relationship as a source of love and fond memory, Tom thinks only in terms of duty and obligation; he resembles his mother's side of the family in this regard. In part because she is so invested in the sibling bond, Maggie, on the other hand, does not reject her family's narrow judgments or move away (as Eliot herself did), despite her relatively free and passionate spirit.

Historians suggest that several aspects of Victorian culture may have together elevated the sibling bond in the Victorian period. First was a tendency towards late marriage, which kept many young women like Maggie living at home with their fathers and brothers well into their twenties. Combined with a cultural emphasis on domestic purity, this tendency meant that for most young women the brother was the only man, or one of only a few men, with whom she related on terms of intimacy and relative freedom. Some Victorian commentators even encouraged thinking of sibling relationships as quasi-marriages: "a young man of kind and social feelings," advised a writer of the day, "is often glad to find in his sister, a substitute for what he afterwards ensures more permanently in his wife"—domestic management, affection, and the creation of a loving home environment (Ellis, p. 171). The Victorian ideology of separate spheres granted women little access to the public realm other than what they could gain vicariously through their male relations. Maggie looks to Tom, and later Philip Wakem (as a pseudo-sibling), for instruction and connection to the outside world from which she is barred. In their early childhood, Tom brings her stories from school; in later years, Philip provides her with novels and poetry to which she would otherwise not have access. It is in her brief visit to Tom's school, moreover, that Maggie's intellectual curiosity and promise become obvious, a promise destined sadly to remain unfulfilled.

Sources and literary context. George Eliot's emphasis on the importance of childhood memory has been tied to the writings of turn-of-the-nineteenth-century poet William Wordsworth. More recently the novel's emphasis on the brother-sister bond has been tied to Wordsworth himself, who shared a precious connection with his own sister Dorothy. In Wordsworth's case, the younger sister becomes a willing student of the older, more experienced brother. In *The Mill on the Floss*, Maggie fails to play the same role with Tom (or is it Tom who fails Maggie?). Eliot read and admired Wordsworth's work, and took the brother-sister relationship so seriously that she published a sonnet sequence, "Brother and Sister," in 1874, which recasts some of the material of Maggie and Tom's childhood in *The Mill on the Floss*. The sonnets have a distinctly Wordsworthian cast to them, in their elevation of childhood memory and in their emphasis on the children's relationship to the natural world. Sonnet Nine of the sequence, for example, reads:

> We had the self-same world enlarged for each
> By loving difference of girl and boy:
> The fruit that hung on high beyond my reach
> He plucked for me, and oft he must employ
>
> A measuring glance to guide my tiny shoe
> Where lay firm stepping-stones, or call to mind
> 'This thing I like my sister may not do,
> For she is little, and I must be kind.'
>
> Thus boyish Will the nobler mastery learned
> Where inward vision over impulse reigns,
> Widening its life with separate life discerned,
> A Like unlike, a Self that self restrains.
>   His years with others must the sweeter be
>   For those brief days he spent in loving me.
>   (Eliot, "Brother and Sister," p. 431)

The Mill on the Floss frequently refers to other novels, particularly the novels of Sir Walter Scott, popular in George Eliot's childhood and therefore in the time the novel is set. Maggie reads *The Pirate*, *Waverley*, and **Ivanhoe** (also in *Literature and Its Time*), identifying in every case with "the dark unhappy ones," the anti-heroines of novels in which "blond-haired women carry away all the happiness" (*The Mill on the Floss*, p. 270). Maggie's friend and suitor Philip Wakem teasingly suggests that Maggie herself might "avenge the dark-haired women in [her] own person" by ensnaring a suitor of her cousin Lucy Deane, a prediction that comes to pass when Maggie encounters Lucy's unacknowledged fiancé Stephen Guest (*The Mill on the Floss*, p. 270). While Maggie rejects Philip's playful suggestion angrily, clearly George Eliot toys with the romantic conventions of the Scott novel in setting Lucy and Maggie up as an opposing pair.

A third possible source is Elizabeth Gaskell's novella *The Moorland Cottage* (1850). While it cannot be positively established that George Eliot read the novella, she certainly read many of Gaskell's works, and the similarities between it and *The Mill on the Floss* are at least superficially striking: both stories concern a brother and sister whose father dies when they are still children. In *The Moorland Cottage,* the brother, Edward tyrannizes the sister, Maggie. Unlike Tom Tulliver, Edward is a domestic tyrant, a cheat and a liar, even a thief. Maggie Browne is freed from her brother's tyranny when he dies by drowning; unlike Maggie Tulliver, however, Gaskell's dark heroine is saved from the same wreck and lives to marry her suitor. Both stories emphasize the potentially destructive power of the sibling bond, choosing remarkably similar ways of ending it through a watery death.

Finally, of course, the novel has many antecedents in George Eliot's own life. Biographers have frequently found in Maggie's ambivalent relationship with her brother reflections of George Eliot's own vexed relationship with her brother, Isaac Evans. Indeed, John Cross (George Eliot's husband and first biographer) draws on *The Mill on the Floss* in his depiction of his wife's childhood:

> The child turns over the book with pictures that she wishes her father to explain to her—or that perhaps she prefers explaining to him. Her rebellious hair is all over her eyes, much vexing the pale, energetic mother who sits on the opposite side of the fire . . . the brother . . . keeps assuring himself by perpetual search that none of his favorite means of amusement are escaping from his pockets.
>
> (Cross, p. 9)

The emphasis on reading, the notion of "rebellious hair," and even the brother's pockets all surface in the first part of *The Mill on the Floss*.

As noted, Eliot and her brother had been close as children. Isaac had frequently acted the disciplinarian with his younger sister, and after learning of her relationship with G. H. Lewes, he cut off all contact with her. Thus, the disapproving older brother who acts as a surrogate for a loving but distant father seems linked to the author's own life. Eliot claimed that "her own experience . . . was worse," that the narrow-mindedness of her relatives had indeed hampered her development. But ultimately Marian Evans was able to transform herself into George Eliot; Maggie Tulliver, on the other hand, stagnates in her provincial setting and is released only by death. (Letter from Emily Davies to Jane Crow, in Eliot, *The Mill on the Floss*, p. 433).

Events in History at the Time the Novel Was Written

Challenges to religious orthodoxy. *The Mill on the Floss* was published in 1860, just one year after the publication of Darwin's **On the Origin of Species** (also in *Literature and Its Times*). While George Eliot may not have read Darwin, in part or in his entirety before finishing her novel, certainly the theory of evolution was widely discussed and in a novel so obsessed with kinship and breeding it would be surprising not to find some connections. Most obvious are Mr. Tulliver's speculations about "the crossing o' breeds" (*The Mill on the Floss*, p. 11). He marvels that on choosing a certain kind of wife, he was nonetheless unable to control the kinds of offspring they might jointly produce.

The publication of *Origin of Species* marked a watershed in English intellectual life. While George Eliot and others had privately entertained doubts as to the historical accuracy of the Bible before 1859, Darwin's publication made those doubts part of public debate. Challenges to historical Christianity were not new—for example, in the 1830s, Lyell's *Principles of Geology* had already suggested that the earth was much older than a biblical account would suggest. George Eliot and other intellectuals were also familiar with the so-called German Higher Criticism of the Bible. An eighteenth and early-nineteenth-century movement, it subjected scripture to critical analysis out of which came qualifications and even denials of the orthodox belief that all scripture was divinely inspired truth.

Origin of Species was simply the most public, most widely-read, of the theological and scientific challenges. Its account of evolution directly contradicted the account of creation in the biblical book of Genesis. Since England was an officially Christian country, challenges to religious orthodoxy were also challenges to national pride and, indeed, the national character at the time. George Eliot was an author who wrestled with the challenge. In *The Mill on the Floss* as well as her other novels, Eliot attempted to work out a secular ethics, a creed of human relationships that, while it might be based on Christian principles, did not require a literal belief in the Christian Bible for its validity. Maggie's experimentation with the doctrine of self-renunciation she finds in the work of Thomas à Kempis fails, but it closely resembles some of Eliot's own efforts to find a satisfying spiritual path after the loss of her orthodox Christian faith.

Women's issues. The early- to mid-nineteenth century saw a changing political and social climate in England—Catholics gained rights under the Catholic Emancipation Act of 1829, middle-class Englishmen gained the vote under the Great Reform Bill of 1832 and slavery was abolished throughout the British Empire in 1834. All this reform inspired the beginnings of a women's movement. First came political efforts to change the marriage, custody, and property statutes that put women at a disadvantage. They scored major advances with the Child Custody Act of 1839 (which not only allowed women to petition for the right to maintain custody of their children but was the first parliamentary act to treat women as legal agents), the Matrimonial Causes Act of 1857 (which made divorce far more possible than it had been), and the Married Women's Property Act of 1870 (which allowed some married women to control their own earnings, savings, and inheritances). But perhaps most pertinent to *Mill on the Floss* is the educational victory. In 1870 the Education Act provided for the country's first tax-supported schools, including a provision that allowed women to serve on school boards, their first entrance into the public forum. Not until 1880, close to a century after the novel is set and two decades after it is written, would attendance at elementary school be compulsory for both males and females. Debates about all these issues raged on in English society, though, from the 1830s through the time Eliot wrote her novel. Nine years before it was published, Harriet Taylor released a pamphlet arguing for the right for women to become more involved in politics, up to and including being able to vote. Taylor's famous husband, the philosopher John Stuart Mill, would argue the same, nine years after the release of *The Mill on the Floss*. His essay *The Subjection of Women*, a landmark work in the history of women's rights, argues for women's entitlement to equal rights as men. Eliot's novel straddles the two works, appearing at midpoint between the wife's pamphlet and the husband's expansion of this point of view.

George Eliot herself refused many invitations to join feminist causes, believing that the scandal about her private life might make her support less than desirable. She was also skeptical throughout most of her life about public "causes." Nonetheless Maggie's fate is deeply entwined with the issues raised by nineteenth-century feminists: her exclusion from "masculine" education, a double standard regarding sexuality, and the control of women by the men of their family are all at issue in Maggie's life. Women had few legal rights in nineteenth-century England. Excluded from the vote, property owning, and post-secondary education, most women were relegated to marriage and family as their only calling. Unusual women like George Eliot herself found ways to circumvent legal restrictions—she read widely, availed herself of all educational opportunities, and established herself as a leading intellectual even before she was a novelist. Yet even George Eliot paid a heavy price for her rejection of Victorian sexual mores, rarely visiting friends and losing almost all contact with her family after her elopement with Lewes. While a man might engage in extra-marital sexual affairs (prostitution was rampant in the Victorian period) as long as he remained discreet, a woman's reputation was ruined by even the implication of illicit sexuality. Thus Maggie's disappearance with Stephen Guest marks her as "fallen" in much the same way that Marian Evans's more serious liaison with George Henry Lewes had done.

Reception. *The Mill on the Floss* was George Eliot's first novel after the uncovering of her pseudonym, a fact that concerned her. Her concern seems to have been at least partly well founded. The discovery that the novel was written by a woman allowed one reviewer to applaud her as "a third female novelist not inferior to Miss Austen and Miss Brontë" (*Saturday Review* in *The*

Mill on the Floss, p, 444). But other reviewers found fault with the writer's allegedly feminine concern for propriety: "A man writing such a story would have made Maggie transgressing but loveable, would not have taken such care to be yet on the right side of rules declaimed against" (*Westminster Review* in Carroll, p. 140).

Apart from comments on the gender of the novelist, early reviews were largely positive. The author, declared one critic, "is attempting not merely to amuse us as a novelist, but, as a preacher, to make us think and feel. The riddle of life as it is here expounded is more like a Greek tragedy than a modern novel" (Dallas in *The Mill on the Floss*, p. 455). There was some objection to the novel's pace; one critic observed that the early "longing and suspense . . . is too forcibly contrasted with the rapid movement of the conclusion" (*Westminster Review* in Carroll, p. 139). But quibbles were merely that. More sweeping were judgements like the one pronounced by the popular author Dinah Mulock, who pronounced *Mill on the Floss* "a work of art . . . as perfect as the novel can well be made" (Mulock in Carroll, p. 154).

For More Information

Carroll, David. *George Eliot: The Critical Heritage*. New York: Barnes & Noble, 1971.

Cross, John Walter. *Life of George Eliot as Related in her Letters and Journals*. New York: Thomas Crowell, 1884.

Eliot, George. "Brother and Sister." *Selected Essays, Poems, and Other Writings*. Ed. A. S. Byatt and Nicholas Warren. London: Penguin, 1990.

———. *The Mill on the Floss: An Authoritative Text, Backgrounds and Contemporary Reactions, Criticism*. Ed. Carol T. Christ. New York: W. W. Norton, 1994.

Ellis, Sarah Stickney. *The Women of England: Their Social Duties, and Domestic Habits*. New York: 1839.

Gaskell, Elizabeth. *The Moorland Cottage and Other Stories*. Oxford: Oxford University Press, 1995.

Haight, Gordon. "Introduction." In *The Mill on the Floss*, by George Eliot. Oxford: Clarendon Press, 1980.

Homans, Margaret. "Eliot, Wordsworth, and the Scenes of the Sister's Instruction." *Critical Inquiry* 8:2 (winter 1981): 223-41.

Karl, Frederick. *George Eliot, Voice of a Century: A Biography*. New York: W. W. Norton, 1995.

Landow, George. "A Critical View of British Public Schools." *The Victorian Web*. 2002. http://65.107.211.206/history/eh4.html (5 March 2002).

Semmel, Bernard. *George Eliot and the Politics of National Inheritance*. New York: Oxford University Press, 1994.

Stone, Lawrence. *The Family, Sex and Marriage in England 1500-1800*. New York: Harper Torchbooks, 1979.

The Misanthrope

by
Jean-Baptiste Poquelin de Molière

> **THE LITERARY WORK**
>
> A comic play set in Paris, France, during the seventeenth century; published in French (as *Le Misanthrope*) in 1666; in English in 1714.
>
> **SYNOPSIS**
>
> A rigorous idealist antagonizes others through his relentless honesty and inability to compromise, bringing on his own emotional isolation.

Born in 1622 in Paris, France, Jean-Baptiste Poquelin was the eldest child of Jean Poquelin, an upholsterer who was attached to the royal household as a valet de chambre (gentleman of the bed chamber). Educated at the Jesuit College de Clermont, Jean-Baptiste was later sent to Orléans to complete legal studies; ultimately, he was expected to follow the family trade. In 1642 Jean-Baptiste represented his father in his tour of duty as upholsterer to the king. The following year, he sold his right of succession to the family upholstery business and chose the stage for his livelihood instead, taking the name *Molière* when he joined an acting company called L'Illustre Théâtre. In time, Molière became head of this troupe, which toured southern France for several years before settling in Lyons in 1653. Molière had his sights on Paris, however; in 1658, with the patronage of the duke d'Orléans, brother of Louis XIV, the company performed Corneille's tragedy *Nicomède* before an audience that included the king and his court. While Molière's performance in the tragedy was not considered especially impressive, the king was charmed by Molière's farce *Le Docteur amoureux* (The Lovelorn Doctor), which concluded the entertainment. On the strength of that piece, Molière received royal authorization to install his company at the theater of the Petit-Bourbon, near the Louvre in Paris. Although Molière continued to act, he soon discovered that his greatest talent lay in writing comedies and farces. His first comedy of manners, *Les Précieuses ridicules* (The Ridiculous Bluestockings) opened in November 1659 and made his fortune. A string of successes followed, including *L'École des maris* (The School for Husbands, 1661), *L'École des femmes* (The School for Wives, 1662), *Le Tartuffe ou l'Hypocrite* (Tartuffe, or the Hypocrite, 1664), and *Le Misanthrope ou L'Atrabilaire amoureux* (The Misanthrope, or The Irritable Lover, 1666). While darker in tone than some of Molière's earlier comedies, *The Misanthrope* is often considered Molière's masterpiece, satirizing not merely the uncompromising rigidity of the title figure but the shallowness and artificiality of Parisian high society.

Events in History at the Time of the Play

The court of Louis XIV. During the sixteenth century, the fortunes of the French nobility had undergone a sharp decline. The influx of gold and silver from New World mines produced a

The Misanthrope

Molière

monetary revolution throughout Europe. Prices rose sharply, sometimes by as much as 400 percent (Lough, p. 61). Landed French aristocrats who relied on rents from their tenants to support lavish lifestyles suddenly found themselves struggling financially. Many had to mortgage their great estates to wealthy bourgeoisie, while some lost those properties altogether to their creditors. No longer the powerful autonomous force they had been during the Middle Ages, the nobility gravitated towards the royal court, in hopes of gaining honors and favors from the king himself. Eventually Parisian high society, which provided both the subject and audience for Molière's play, came to revolve around the court, especially after Louis XIV acceded to the throne. He would rule for 72 years (1638-1715), earning the nickname "The Sun King" because of the magnificence of his reign.

Louis XIV first acceded to the throne as a child-ruler in 1643; his mother, Anne of Austria, as the regent, nominally ruled in his stead, but Cardinal Guilio Mazarin essentially governed France as prime minister. After Mazarin's death in 1661 and the achievement of his own majority, Louis quickly seized the reins of government himself. One of his most startling decisions was to abolish the office of prime minister completely, declaring that "there is nothing more shameful than the sight of all the practical authority on the one side and nothing but the title of king on the other" (Louis XIV in Goubert, p. 65). Determined to rule as an absolute monarch, Louis also dismissed nearly all the members of the King's Council, including his own mother, and retained only three men, of humble birth and proven loyalty.

In the early years of his reign, Louis XIV worked to establish his court as the center of power and influence in France. High-born potential rivals were shrewdly thwarted by royal hospitality. Historian John Lough explains the box into which the king cornered them:

> To keep the nobles out of any mischief the King insisted on their coming to court. And the nobles came, not only because the life at court suited their tastes for luxury and amusement but because it was the only way of obtaining all the favours which the king had at his disposal. They knew that if they did not come to court, they had no chance of obtaining any assistance from the King.
>
> (Lough, p. 146)

Aristocrats struggling with debts, mortgages, and other economic burdens eagerly accepted the king's invitation. In hopes of restoring their fortunes, the aristocrats angled to acquire a position, preferably in the royal household. Pensions might also be conferred upon courtiers whose service pleased Louis. Among the nobility of the time, to be summoned to court was the greatest honor, whereas to be dismissed from court to rusticate on some country estate was the greatest disgrace and an end to all hope for betterment. An invitation to the court meant being able to mingle with the highest society. Those invited usually found lodging in or near the palace. The most ambitious hoped never to leave, but sometimes personal necessity or the king's disfavor forced them to do so.

Along with the attention he paid to the nobility, Louis XIV also patronized the arts, encouraging the talents of playwrights, poets, and men of letters. His lavish palace at Versailles, to the north of Paris, became more and more the hub of political and social life in France. The king also expended huge sums on developing the grounds and buildings of Versailles, creating gardens and even an entirely artificial town. Like its setting, the court society of Louis XIV was sumptuous, brilliant, and artificial, its magnificence partly masking the unglamorous jockeying by the nobles for royal favor and position.

In *The Misanthrope*, Molière makes no direct reference to the king, nor does he set any of the

> **DEVELOPMENT OF THE PROFESSIONAL THEATER**
>
> Amateur theater had long existed in France, most often in the form of traveling troupes and student productions. Professional theater had its embryonic beginnings in the 1550s, when Henri II and his queen, Catherine di Medici, imported Italian comedians to perform at the royal court. An era of domestic harmony and unity during the reign of Henri IV (1589-1610) and the ascent of the powerful Cardinal Richelieu, Louis XIII's prime minister, who worked to consolidate power under a central government, fostered an encouraging atmosphere for professional theater. Over time the French monarchy assumed command of all aspects of government and culture in France; Richelieu was among the first to perceive the role public theater might play in shaping the thoughts, opinions, and tastes of the people. He favored the idea of the king's overseeing cultural activities, and he himself was an enthusiastic patron of the arts. In this regard, Richelieu had company. Royalty and nobles alike quickly realized the political and personal advantages to be gained by encouraging the arts. The atmosphere proved profitable for struggling writers. Playwrights like Alexandre Hardy, Tristan L'Hermite, Théophile de Viau, and Thomas and Pierre Corneille received support from wealthy, influential patrons. By the 1620s both amateur and professional theaters were flourishing—and competing fiercely for space in which to perform. Creative output was also high; some 414 plays survive from the period 1589 to 1634. In 1641 the acting profession was declared beneficial to the state and theaters were legitimized, just as the young Molière was embarking upon his theatrical career.

play's scenes at court. Nonetheless, the attractions of court society and its possible rewards are continually alluded to by various characters. The prudish Arsinoé offers to use her own connections at court to benefit the main character, Alceste, professionally. Meanwhile, the flirtatious Célimène revels in high society and reacts with dismay when Alceste demands that she renounce it in favor of a quiet life with him.

Marriage and widowhood. In Molière's play, Alceste alienates himself from the rest of society. This willful self-alienation stems at least partly from his complicated dealings with Célimène, a flirtatious young widow whom he hopes both to marry and reform. While little is revealed about Célimène's marriage or her late husband, the overall conditions of marriage and widowhood in seventeenth-century France may explain her somewhat fickle behavior.

During the 1600s, marriage, especially among the middle and upper classes, was considered and conducted as a business arrangement. Of paramount importance was the union to be made among titles, estates, and fortunes. Often the bride and groom were virtual strangers. She was educated in a convent until her mid-to-late teens; he was older and already established in life. A third party would negotiate and contract the marriage, primarily for purposes of procreation. Love and personal compatibility were seldom, if ever, considered. Indeed it was common practice among upper-class husbands to seek love and passion outside marriage. Wives, by contrast, were expected to remain faithful, or at least discreet.

Marriage brought husbands total control over their wives and whatever properties their wives owned. A wife could not sell or exchange her property without her husband's authorization. Also she had to have his official permission to sign contracts, appear before a court of law, accept a donation or legacy, or enter into a legal agreement on someone else's behalf. Such a one-sided and inflexible framework tended to foster antagonism between spouses. As one historian points out, the effect was quite antithetical to the whole idea of marriage.

> Legal discrimination, religious taboos and social pressures, by undermining the status of women and debasing conjugal love, all contributed to put asunder those whom God had joined together. The seventeenth-century hus-

band was conditioned to regard his nominal co-partner as an inferior whose physical and mental weakness justified his almost complete control over her property and person.
(Gibson, pp. 68-69)

By contrast, widowhood—especially after a marriage devoid of affection or esteem—proved liberating for women, at least in some respects. After their husbands' deaths, widows retained their social prestige and achieved a greater measure of independence than they had as wives. If their late husbands' businesses and household affairs had been handled properly during their lifetimes, widows usually found themselves with considerable financial assets to invest as they chose. Widows were expected to mourn at least a full year, the first 40 days of which were spent in seclusion in black-draped rooms where condolence visits were held. Rigid moralists and the Church might thereafter encourage widows to live retired lives, devote themselves to their late husband's memories, and perform good works, but overall, widows were not strictly forbidden to reenter society once the one year of mourning had elapsed. Nor was remarriage impossible, if the widow was young and attractive enough to inspire proposals from likely suitors, although widows who married before a year of widowhood was over often became the butts of scorn, ridicule, and public harassment.

In *The Misanthrope*, Célimène, who frequently boasts that she is only 20 years old, clearly enjoys the greater freedom her widow's status has granted her. Her youth and good looks attract many high-born suitors. When Alceste demands that Célimène choose the one she loves from among her admirers, Célimène balks and, up until the end, refuses. Perhaps she prefers the existence of a much-courted widow to that of a wife once again under a husband's control.

Salons. Prominent in upper-class French social life was the salon, a periodic gathering of notable persons held at the home of a distinguished citizen, usually a woman. Many a salon hostess did not wield overwhelming influence at the royal court. Instead she created her own private little court, to which she invited those acquaintances whose company and conversation she enjoyed.

Salon entertainments varied according to the hostess's tastes and inclinations. Some salons engaged or were suspected of engaging in subversive political activities; such a salon ran the very real risk of becoming the object of government surveillance. Others served as a forum where aspiring men of letters had the opportunity to try out their writings on an audience before publication. In general, however, guests attended salons for the opportunity of meeting other socially prominent persons and conversing with them in pleasant surroundings. It was common practice for aspiring writers and scholars to make the rounds at many salons. The hope was to increase one's circle of acquaintances and one's chance of finding patrons.

Salon talk could run the gamut from the highly philosophical to the slightly prurient, or dirty. Gibson writes, "Three topics provided focal points for conversation and pastimes: love, literature and philosophy. . . . Love, in the form of studied gallantry, was a major preoccupation of worldly ruelles [salons]. Rechristened with poetic pseudonyms . . . ladies and gentlemen assembled as in the fabled 'Courts of Love' of medieval times to pose ticklish 'love-questions'" (Gibson, pp. 176-77). In many salons, discussion was far less noble; talk about love merely afforded guests an opportunity to engage in gossip.

In *The Misanthrope*, coy Célimène frequently entertains callers at her home in a salonlike setting. Indeed, the entire action of the play takes place at her house. But while aspiring poets and various noblemen attend, Célimène's gatherings serve less as a venue for intellectual or philosophical discussion than as opportunities for the hostess to display her wit and charms before her many admirers. The disgruntled Alceste complains, "You're always ready to receive a call, / And you can't bear for ten ticks of the clock, / Not to keep open house for all who knock" (Molière, *The Misanthrope*, p. 55).

Lawsuits and litigation. As depicted in *The Misanthrope*, another curious pastime among the French upper-class appears to have been suing each other for various offenses; both Célimène and Alceste are involved in lawsuits. Alceste's appears to be the more serious of the two, perhaps another cause of his simmering discontent at the start of the play and certainly a contributing factor to his misanthropy when he ultimately loses the suit. Although Molière provides no particulars about Alceste's case, it seems likely to have been a civil suit; for his unknown offense, Alceste receives not a prison sentence but a fine of 20,000 francs.

Civil procedure in seventeenth-century France was a complicated, lengthy, and expensive process, guaranteed to sour tempers and erode patience. Prior to coming before the judges, a case required numerous arrangements to be made—summons had to be issued, procurers established, and documents registered at the court and exchanged between litigants. The process was far from smooth:

> Proceedings were often delayed while defendants challenged the jurisdiction of the court or a prospective judge or questioned the validity of a claimant's evidence. When the case came before the magistrate(s), litigants had to secure the services of an advocate. Each of these steps was expensive because numerous documents had to be filed and because the fees of the many lesser officials involved in litigation—procureurs, greffiers [notaries], and advocates—were high and often unregulated.
> (Hamscher, pp. 160-61)

The judicial process might be further delayed even after those preliminaries were settled. Judges might take additional time to consider how a case would be heard—orally and summarily or, as often happened, through additional written procedures, which cost the litigants still more time and money. Nor did the legal problems necessarily end after trial and sentencing; if the judicial verdict was subject to appeal, the entire process could start all over again in a higher court. In The Misanthrope, however, Alceste, who has the option of appealing his sentence, proclaims his intent to let it stand as a testament to injustice and treachery, further declaring that his defeat has given him additional reason "to storm and rage at human evil / And send the race of mankind to the devil" (The Misanthrope, p. 132).

The Play in Focus

The plot. The play begins at the house of Célimène, a fashionable woman of society. Two friends, the self-proclaimed honest man Alceste and the more diplomatic Philinte, are quarreling over the latter's warm greeting of a chance acquaintance. As the two gentlemen attempt to settle their differences, Alceste rails against what he sees as the hypocrisy and artificiality of their society and roundly condemns people who conform to its social standards. Philinte does not disagree with Alceste's complaints but maintains that some measure of civility and courtesy must be observed or one risks alienating everybody. He points out that Alceste is facing a lawsuit and would do well to adopt a more moderate attitude if he wished the court to rule in his favor. Alceste, however, refuses to consider the suggestion.

The conversation turns from litigation to love as Philinte wonders why Alceste, who purports to despise artifice and shallowness, should be enamored of the coquettish Célimène, who embodies the flaws of high society. Philinte mentions several other women whom he feels would be better suited to his friend—Célimène's cousin Eliante and the prudish Arsinoé. Alceste admits he is aware of Célimène's faults but cannot help desiring her. He hopes somehow to reform her. The friends' conversation is interrupted by the arrival of Oronte, another of Célimène's suitors. An amateur poet, Oronte wishes Alceste, whose intelligence is held in high regard by all, to hear and critique his latest sonnet. The amateur poet proceeds to read the sonnet aloud. Philinte responds to it with fulsome praise, but Alceste refuses to do likewise, ultimately condemning the verses as affected and artificial. Having insisted on hearing his opinion, Oronte now takes offense and quarrels with Alceste. Philinte prevents the altercation from growing even worse. Oronte departs and Alceste sulks, refusing to speak to Philinte.

Alone, Alceste encounters Célimène, whom he upbraids for her frivolity and encouragement of other suitors. Célimène, in her turn, rebukes Alceste for his rudeness and incivility. Alceste's displeasure grows when Célimène receives more callers, including the marquesses Acaste and Clitandre, who are high-born romantic rivals. The company, which includes Philinte and the widow's cousin Eliante, settles down to a long conversation. The marquesses bring up the names of mutual acquaintances. Eliante and Philinte try to makes some complimentary remarks about the acquaintances, but to the delight of the two marquesses, Célimène makes malicious witticisms about each person mentioned. Alceste is more censorious than ever towards Célimène and her friends. The three rivals for Célimène's affections vow to outstay each other and be the last to leave her house that day. Alceste's plan is foiled, however, by the arrival of a guard summoning him before a tribunal to settle his recent quarrel with Oronte. Still vowing never to praise Oronte's mediocre poetry, Alceste is led away.

Back at Célimène's house, the two marquesses complacently discuss their attractions as rival suitors. Each agrees to step aside if Célimène favors the other. Arsinoé, an older woman with a reputation for strict propriety, calls upon Célimène and the two exchange barbed comments that reveal their mutual dislike. Arsinoé

The Misanthrope

Michael Pennington and Elaine Page in the 1998 production of *The Misanthrope*.

criticizes Célimène's coquetry and malicious tongue, while Célimène mocks Arsinoé's sanctimony and lack of suitors. Alceste returns from the tribunal during this encounter and Célimène airily leaves the proper Arsinoé alone with him. Displaying her fondness for Alceste, Arsinoé offers to use her influence at court to advance him professionally, and to show him proof of Célimène's inconstancy to him. Alceste politely declines the former but ultimately succumbs to Arsinoé's claim to having ocular proof of Célimène's betrayal.

Philinte and Eliante discuss Alceste's fierce honesty and his regrettable inability to compromise. Philinte asks whether Célimène truly loves Alceste; in response, Eliante suspects her cousin is unsure of her own feelings. Eliante herself would be happy to accept Alceste's attentions if Célimène refused him. Philinte then confesses his own affections for Eliante, hoping she would entertain his suit if Alceste and Célimène married. At this point, Alceste storms in, furious over having discovered a love letter Célimène wrote to Oronte. Wishing to avenge himself on his faithless beloved, Alceste proposes to Eliante; she gently suggests that his anger with Célimène will pass and urges him not to do anything rash.

When Célimène enters, Alceste melodramatically confronts her with the letter. Unruffled, she dismisses the accusation of treachery and calmly suggests that the letter was written to a woman. Having never considered this possibility, Alceste is disarmed. Célimène goes on to mock and rebuke him for his jealousy and lack of trust, intimating that she still cares for him and has not made a final choice among her suitors. In a complete reversal of attitude, Alceste wishes Célimène were destitute and friendless so he could prove his love (and power over her) by coming to her rescue.

Alceste's legal troubles escalate; he loses his lawsuit and must pay 20,000 francs in damages. Also another case threatens. Alceste faces an accusation of having written and circulated a scandalous book, a charge springing from the malice of an unnamed enemy. What's more, Oronte, the "mediocre" poet, still seeks revenge for their earlier quarrel. Despite Philinte's reassurances that nobody truly believes him guilty of the scandalous-book charge, Alceste refuses to seek redress and insists that he will retire from society to live the life of a hermit. Again Philinte tries to persuade his friend to adopt a more moderate, tolerant view of humanity, but Alceste will not heed his advice.

Determined to discover the nature of Célimène's love, Alceste demands that she choose between him and Oronte, who is also visiting her house and makes the same condition. Resenting the position in which they have placed her, Célimène refuses to state her preference. Eliante and Philinte witness the last part of this encounter but will not be drawn into the argument. Just then, the two marquesses and Arsinoé converge upon Célimène's house. They are agitated. The two marquesses have compared letters written to them by Célimène and discovered that she ridiculed one to the other along with the rest of her suitors. The two marquesses read Alceste and Oronte the unflattering passages about themselves. Offended, Célimène's suitors storm from the house, vowing to transfer their affections elsewhere. Only Alceste remains; he silences Arsinoé's attempt to defend him by stating that he is not in the least interested in *her*. Equally incensed, Arsinoé departs, haughtily denying that she ever wanted Alceste for herself.

Touched by Alceste's apparent fidelity and exposed in her game of slanderous wit, an uncharacteristically meek Célimène admits her faults and acknowledges that he has the right to upbraid her. Alceste proposes marriage and Célimène almost accepts—until she learns of Alceste's plan to retire from society and live in solitude. She starts to suggest a compromise but Alceste rejects it and her, declaring he no longer loves her because she won't give up the world for him. Alceste offers sincere praise to Eliante for her virtue but fears he is not intended for the married state. Eliante assures him that she and Philinte will likely make a good match of it. Wishing them both happiness, Alceste reiterates his intention to retire into seclusion, but Philinte and Eliante are determined to persuade him otherwise.

A man alone. The contradictions inherent in Alceste, the title figure in *The Misanthrope*, have become the basis for many scholarly studies. Is he a tragic or comic figure? A fair and honest man or a hypocritical poseur, who affects an attitude just to impress others? Audiences have also been divided on this issue. A nobleman who erroneously believed himself to be the model for Alceste was flattered when he saw *The Misanthrope* in performance, considering the character to be a worthy gentleman. Similarly the eighteenth-century writer and philosopher Jean-Jacques Rousseau sympathized with Alceste and complained about how the character was made a subject of ridicule by the playwright. Rousseau spoke to the standard portrayal. In Molière's own time, the performance normally presented Alceste in a comic light, emphasizing the excessiveness and inconsistencies of his relentless honesty.

Certainly the play does not always present Alceste as being in the wrong. As Molière depicts it, the society against which his protagonist rails so indiscriminately merits many of those complaints. Members of high society greet each other effusively in public and rip each other to shreds in private; litigants flatter and bribe judges in hopes of winning lawsuits; aspiring poets demand honest opinions of their work and turn nasty when they receive them. It is not difficult to sympathize with Alceste's views on the subject even if his proposed solution appears extreme:

> I fall into deep gloom and melancholy
> When I survey the scene of human folly,
> Finding on every hand base flattery,
> Injustice, fraud, self-interest, treachery....
> Ah, it's too much; mankind has grown so base,
> I mean to break with the whole human race.
> (*The Misanthrope*, p. 20)

Philinte, Alceste's best friend, provides a necessary corrective to those absolute views: "Yes, man's a beastly creature; but must we then / Abandon the society of men? / Here in the world, each human frailty / Provides occasion for philosophy, / And that is virtue's noblest exercise" (*The Misanthrope*, p. 132). To live in the world, among other people, one must learn to compromise, a practice Alceste cannot or, more likely, will not master.

Alceste's inability to compromise, however, is not his only flaw. Like many comic characters, he is blind to the contradictions in his own nature. Translator Richard Wilbur writes, "If Alceste has a rage for the genuine and he truly has, it is unfortunately compromised and exploited by his vast, unconscious egotism.... Like many humorless and indignant people, he is hard on everybody but himself, and does not perceive it when he fails his own ideal" (Wilbur in Molière, p. 7). A jealous friend and lover, Alceste flies into a passion when Philinte greets a chance acquaintance warmly and when Célimène dares to entertain other men besides himself in her home. Unaware of his own selfishness, he wishes aloud that Célimène were "wretchedly poor, / Unloved, uncherished, utterly obscure" so that he might raise her from the dust "and proudly prove / The purity and vastness of my love" (*The Misanthrope*, pp. 119-20).

To possess this most-desired of women, Alceste is even willing to sacrifice his commitment to honesty if she will just deny writing an affectionate letter to one of his rivals: "Defend this let-

The Misanthrope

ter and your innocence, / And I, poor fool, will aid in your defense. / Pretend, pretend, that you are just and true, / And I shall make myself believe in you" (*The Misanthrope*, p. 117). Finally, after Célimène is spurned by her other suitors, Alceste has the opportunity to prove his devotion but he too rejects her when she expresses reluctance to withdraw from society as he desires: "Ah, if you really loved me as you ought, / You wouldn't give the world a moment's thought; / Must you have me, and all the world beside?" (*The Misanthrope*, p. 150). Certainly it is to Alceste's credit that he yearns after an ideal of honesty and good faith, that he does not wish to be considered as trivial and insincere as most of his peers are. But at the same time it is to his detriment that he is not honest enough with himself to perceive that his own vanity and rigidity hinder him from ever achieving the ideal.

> ### MOLIÈRE'S FORMULA?
>
> Literary critic Gertrud Mander sees Molière's farces and comedies as all tending to follow a similar pattern:
>
> One character becomes the victim of an intrigue because his specific weaknesses hinder a group of characters—who are dependent upon or in some way involved with him—from pursuing their own natural interests. The victim never learns from experience: ridiculous characters are incapable of learning in this manner, for one of their weaknesses is always unreasonableness, lack of insight, and unresponsiveness in the face of attempts to persuade them of their folly. Thus every "ridiculous" character really becomes the victim of his own weakness or presumption. The victim becomes isolated, confused, and finally rendered harmless.
>
> (Mander, pp. 32-33)

In the abstract, the quality of unsparing honesty was considered a virtue, prized by the early Romans and Spartans and by some in the playwright's own day. Pierre Corneille (1606-84), Molière's contemporary and the author of numerous historical tragedies, tended to depict heroes who possessed that trait, along with other sterner, more martial virtues. However, the moral temper of seventeenth-century Paris was closer in sympathy to the views expressed by Philinte early in *The Misanthrope*. Attempting to persuade Alceste to adopt a more moderate stance on humanity, Philinte argues, "The rigid virtues of the ancient days / Are not for us; they jar with all our ways / And ask of us too lofty a perfection. / Wise men accept their times without objection" (*The Misanthrope*, p. 23). Of course, the complacency of this view is no less subject to ridicule in the play.

Sources and literary context. Although the characters in *The Misanthrope* would have been recognizable types to Molière's audience, speculation regarding their models and sources of inspiration is perhaps inevitable. Molière himself played Alceste, the title figure in *The Misanthrope*. While it was not uncommon for the head of an acting-company to take the leading role in a play, some scholars have wondered whether Molière saw similarities between himself and Alceste—unsparingly idealistic, critical of the fashionable world, and unhappily enamoured of a flighty young beauty. It may be significant that Molière was himself married to the much-younger actress Armande Béjart—she was half his age when they wed in 1662—and the union was marred by frequent quarrels and separations. Like Alceste with Célimène in his play, Molière was infatuated with a pretty, flirtatious young woman, whose nature was different from his and whose various habits made him unhappy. It was therefore fitting that he chose Armande to play Célimène to his Alceste. Several of Molière's contemporaries, however, spread the rumor that the model for Alceste was not Molière but the duc de Montausier, tutor to the dauphin (crown prince). On hearing the rumor, an enraged Montausier threatened to thrash Molière with his cane when they next met. But after seeing the play, Montausier pronounced himself quite flattered to have served as the model for so noble a man as Alceste and embraced Molière warmly, to the astonishment of the playwright who had never thought of him at all while creating the character.

Although Moliére had studied the classical plays of ancient Greece and Rome and the later Italian school of commedia dell'arte, he did not copy either source to any great extent. Earlier in his career, Molière had been criticized by contemporary scholars for disregarding dramatic rules, such as observing the three unities of time, place, and action. He also incurred censure for daring to mingle sophisticated comedy with farce, rather than maintaining purity of genre. As a practical man of the theater, however, Molière did not consider himself inextricably bound to comply with those rules. In such satirical works as *The Critique of the School for Wives* (1663) and *The Versailles Impromptu* (1663), Molière defended his particular aesthetics, maintaining that the foremost purpose of comedy was to please its audience, whether that audience was noble, bourgeois, or common, while attempting to improve morals. Moreover, the task of the comic playwright was to portray faithfully the people of his age, to be true to his own time.

The Misanthrope, and Molière's work in general, is most often categorized as a comedy of manners, which deals with the relations and intrigues among members of sophisticated upper-class society. Much of the comedy stems from the characters' witty repartee, the quick give-and-take of conversation. Molière's comic plots often revolve around a particular foible or ridiculous quality of the protagonist—avarice in *The Miser* (1669), hypocrisy in *Tartuffe* (1669), and the inability to compromise in *The Misanthrope*—a foible that leads the main character into a serious but usually soluble predicament.

Although happy endings tend to prevail in Molière's comedies, they are often brought about by intervention from the outside, the deus ex machina, the person or thing introduced suddenly as a contrived solution to a problem. However, in the case of some plays, Molière provided deliberately inconclusive endings. At the end of *The Misanthrope,* the idealistic Alceste remains determined to retire from society and live as a hermit, while his more emotionally balanced friends Philinte and Eliante remain equally determined to persuade him otherwise.

Reception. First performed on June 4, 1666, *The Misanthrope* appeared to be well-received in literary and court circles. "All the contemporary references to the play were favourable. The Court rhymsters [sic], echoing the general verdict of Versailles, celebrated it as a masterpiece, and exclaimed that Molière had surpassed himself" (Palmer, p. 392). Yet the play did not enjoy the widespread popular success of some of Molière's earlier works, although it fared well enough when teamed with one of the dramatist's farcical pieces *Le Medicin Malgré Lui* (The Doctor in Spite of Himself) later in the year. One of the highest compliments paid to *The Misanthrope* and its author may have come from the playwright Jean Racine, with whom Molière was actually engaged in a bitter professional feud. An acquaintance of Racine's reportedly attended the opening of *The Misanthrope* and gloatingly described the play as a failure. Racine, who had not yet seen the play himself, retorted, "I don't believe you. Molière could not write a bad play. Go and see it again" (Racine in Bulgakov, p. 183).

—Pamela S. Loy

For More Information

Bulgakov, Mikhail. *The Life of Monsieur de Molière.* Trans. Mira Ginsburg. New York: New Directions Book, 1986.

Gibson, Wendy. *Women in Seventeenth-Century France.* London: Macmillan, 1989.

Goubert, Pierre. *Louis XIV and Twenty Million Frenchmen.* Trans. Anne Carter. New York: Vintage Books, 1970.

Hamscher, Albert N. *The Parlement of Paris after the Fronde, 1653-1673.* Pittsburgh: University of Pittsburgh Press, 1976.

Lough, John. *An Introduction to Seventeenth Century France.* London: Longmans, Green, 1954.

Mander, Gertrud. *Molière.* Trans. Diana Stone Peters. New York: Frederick Ungar, 1973.

Molière, Jean Baptiste Poquelin de. *The Misanthrope and Tartuffe.* Trans. Richard Wilbur. San Diego: Harcourt Brace Jovanovich, 1965.

Palmer, John. *Molière.* New York: Brewer and Warren, 1930.

Treasure, G. R. R. *Seventeenth Century France.* New York: Barnes & Noble, 1966.

Walker, Hallam. *Molière.* Boston: Twayne, 1990.

Murder in the Cathedral

by
T. S. Eliot

Although T. S. Eliot (Thomas Sternes Eliot) was born in 1888 in St. Louis, Missouri, he moved to England in 1914 and officially became a British subject in 1927. The choice to leave America for England was one of many that reflect a conservative frame of mind. In 1929, Eliot described himself as an Anglo-Catholic in religion, a classicist in literature, and a royalist in politics; all three look back to traditional forms of belief, literature, and government. Yet Eliot's literary work was simultaneously revolutionary and conservative; he caught the spirit of his age by marrying modern language and classical allusion in his poetry. Eliot's first major published poem, "**The Love Song of J. Alfred Prufrock**" (1915), captured the spiritual paralysis of a world suddenly and radically changed by the First World War. In his later and perhaps most famous poem, "**The Waste Land**" (both also in *Literature and Its Times*), Eliot juxtaposed historical and literary allusions with the common speech of everyday people. When Eliot turned his attention to drama, he maintained his commitment to marrying the new to the old; for instance, he championed the writing of drama in verse, as Shakespeare and the ancient Greeks had done. Eliot's first drama was *The Rock* (1934), a pageant play. Then came *Murder in the Cathedral* (1935), followed by plays such as *The Family Reunion* (1939) and *The Cocktail Party* (1950). Eliot was also the editor of the publishing house Faber & Faber, and a major literary critic whose essays shaped two generations of scholars. By turning

THE LITERARY WORK
A play set in Canterbury Cathedral in 1170; first performed in Canterbury, England, in June 1935.

SYNOPSIS
Archbishop Thomas Becket returns from exile abroad to face martyrdom—he must resist the temptations of King Henry II's agents and come to terms with his impending death.

to the past in his poetry, drama, and criticism, Eliot defined the literary taste of the twentieth century. In *Murder in the Cathedral*, Eliot tells a story from the past in a style of the past to illuminate the brutality of his own 1930s world.

Events in History at the Time of the Play

Henry II vs. Becket: A historical overview. *Murder in the Cathedral* is a play based on the real-life historical conflict between King Henry II of England and Archbishop Thomas Becket. Becket had risen from lowly origins to become King Henry's close friend, loyal servant, advisor and ambassador. In 1154 Henry appointed Becket to the post of chancellor, arguably the most powerful secular post in England. King Henry (reigned 1154-89) was trying to consolidate England into a nation at the time, which involved his regaining control over its Catholic Church. But the Church had obligations to the

Murder in the Cathedral

T. S. Eliot

Pope in Rome, and these obligations could conflict with loyalty to king and state. Henry decided to appoint his good friend and right-hand man, Thomas Becket, to the post of archbishop of Canterbury so that he would have an insider in the Church. But to everyone's surprise, once Becket had been consecrated archbishop his attitudes changed entirely; he became a devout Catholic entirely devoted to Rome, which infuriated Henry. Further enraging the king, Becket began to excommunicate Henry's supporters, to expel them from the Church, inflicting a very serious punishment on them for prioritizing the king's will over what he saw as God's will. The relationship between the former friends deteriorated rapidly, and in 1164, Becket was summoned to trial. Instead, he fled to France.

There were many attempts to reconcile Henry and Becket, but all of them failed. Henry seized Becket's property and exiled his relatives from England; Becket continued to excommunicate the king's supporters. The dispute came to a head in 1170 when Henry had his eldest son crowned as co-king by the archbishop of York. By the existing protocol, Henry had overstepped his authority: the right to crown kings was exclusive to the archbishop of Canterbury. Becket, supported by the Pope, thus excommunicated everyone involved. Henry, fearing papal wrath, allowed Becket to return to England. The archbishop reentered England, returning to Canterbury December 2, 1171, the date on which the first part of *Murder in the Cathedral* takes place. But though reinstated, Becket refused to compromise on any issue; which allegedly prompted Henry to muse aloud, "Will no one rid me of this troublesome priest?"

Four leading knights seem to have taken Henry at his word. They went to Canterbury on December 29th, 1171, the date on which the second part of *Murder in the Cathedral* takes place. When Becket refused to reinstate Henry's excommunicated supporters, the Knights followed him into the Cathedral and tried to drag him out. The situation turned violent and the knights killed him with their swords. The entire murder was eyewitnessed and recorded by a man named Edward Grim, whose account Eliot uses as a basis for his play.

Within days, Becket's tomb became a destination for pilgrims. Henry was instantly labeled a murderer. Now at a disadvantage, he gave Pope Alexander an opportunity to forge peace with England to the benefit of the Church. A year later, Henry would perform an act of public penance and renounce many of his plans for bringing the Church under state control. Two years later the martyred Becket would be canonized as a saint.

The aim of Church reform. Gregorian Reform is a term coined in the twentieth century (by historian Augustin Fliche) for a series of spiritual and intellectual reforms that were set in motion by Pope Gregory VII (reigned 1073-85). In particular, Pope Gregory was interested in stopping simony (obtaining church blessings or high positions in unethical ways, by, for example, buying them or offering them for political gain). In the *Libri tres adversus simoniacos* (1057-58; "Three Books Against the Simoniacs"), Humbert of Silva Candida argued that all sacraments performed by priests who were simoniacs or who had been ordained by simoniacs were invalid. This issue arises implicitly in *Murder in the Cathedral* when Becket refuses to undo the excommunications of the priests who crowned Henry II's son. Those priests went beyond their authority since the archbishop of Canterbury alone had the right to crown the English king in order to oblige a king's political wish to see his son crowned.

Another important issue for the eleventh and twelfth century was enforcing celibacy for priests. At this time, many lower-level priests were married, despite the fact that marriage for priests had been forbidden by the Council of Nicaea in 325 c.e. Various popes during these years repeatedly ordered priests to give up their wives and barred the sons of priests from inheriting their father's church positions and church property, but the orders were widely ignored across Europe. Furious that papal orders were being disobeyed, Pope Gregory VII insisted upon complete obedience to papal legislation. This had the unfortunate side effect of sowing discontent between the Church and the emerging European nation-states, whose leaders wanted allegiance from their priests. Gregory's insistence left kings with the uneasy concern that the clergy's loyalties were divided between their own secular authority and that of Rome.

The issue of church-state conflict was also seen in the "investiture controversy." This controversy revolved around whether or not lay rulers could appoint bishops, abbots, or even popes. Because clergymen generally had political as well as religious influence across Europe at this time, functioning as local politicians as well as spiritual leaders, kings and emperors were understandably interested in controlling who was appointed to what post. Gregory VII prohibited secular rulers from making such appointments in November 1078 at the Lateran Palace Council in Rome. The later Concordat of Worms (1122) tried to settle matters further by distinguishing between a clergyman's state and religious roles.

The larger goal of many of these reforms was to make clergy accountable to Rome rather than to the king or state, thereby reducing Church corruption and restoring its purity of aims. In the following century, the Church sought to have free elections to clerical posts, complete protection for Church property, and clerical submission to Church law rather than local tribunals or courts. This last goal became a particular bone of contention, as it exempted priests from being accountable to secular, national laws.

The aim of royal reform. The Constitutions of Clarendon (1164) were 16 articles issued by Henry II of England in an attempt to reassert control over the Church in the wake of the Gregorian Reforms. Under these articles, clergymen (including archbishops, bishops, and priests) had to ask the king's permission before leaving the country, and they had to assure the king that they were not planning any treasonous acts while abroad. The Church was restricted in its powers of excommunication and forbidden to take action against laymen on the strength of secret information. The king also was to have control over any vacant church offices.

The most controversial articles stated that members of the clergy were now accountable to state courts. Previously, "criminous clerks"—members of the clergy who were accused of a crime—could be tried in the much more lenient Church or ecclesiastical courts. Now they would have to answer to the king if they committed a crime. Furthermore, clergymen used to be able to appeal directly to Rome for justice; the Constitution of Clarendon prohibited such appeals without royal permission. Finally, if there was a conflict between a layman and Church member, the king's court was to have clear jurisdiction.

Church leaders in England, including Thomas Becket, reluctantly agreed to the provisions. But when Pope Alexander condemned the Constitutions, Becket reversed his position, infuriating his former friend, King Henry. The issue of whether or not clergy were accountable to the state was, as noted, an especially sore point between Church officials and state authorities; it was perhaps the primary bone of contention between Henry and Thomas Becket. After Becket's martyrdom, Henry was forced to relent on the issue, though he never did specifically repudiate the Constitutions. In the next century, clerics would be tried in Church courts for their first offense, but if they committed a second crime, they were remanded to secular court.

Henry II and the legal system. Henry II became king of an England that had been wracked by feudal wars and civil disorder. Over the course of his reign, Henry, who would prove to be one of England's ablest rulers, reorganized the nation as well as its justice system. He managed in the process to give the King's law nationwide authority through a series of reforms. It is in the context of these reforms that we must understand Henry's actions against Thomas Becket in *Murder in the Cathedral*.

With the help of the Constitutions of Clarendon, Henry attempted to make clergy accountable to state law rather than to have cases in his realm decided in two separate (and unequal) systems of justice. But this was only part of a much larger reworking of legal processes. Before Henry, the most common way of ascertaining justice was "trial by ordeal," in which an accused person would have to endure some form of torture, such as carrying a red-hot iron bar or putting his or her hands in boiling water. If the person was, by some miracle, not wounded by the torture, or if the injuries healed quickly, the response was taken as a sign from God, and the person was declared "not guilty."

Murder in the Cathedral

Henry replaced this barbaric system with something much more like our contemporary legal system. His reforms (dictated by the Assize of Clarendon [1166]) called for accusations against a person to be supported by a 12-man grand jury. Only if the grand jury was convinced that a crime had been committed was further legal action taken. Additionally four law-abiding men had to testify under oath before that grand jury as to the accused person's guilt or innocence. Henry also built prisons to house those awaiting justice, which meant that there were fewer hasty and impassioned verdicts. Putting an accused person into prison allowed time for criminal investigation and cooled the tempers of those involved. As a result of Henry's reforms, the judge and jury system eventually supplanted "trial by ordeal" in England.

The life and death of St. Thomas Becket. Thomas Becket (1118-70) was born in Normandy to a well-off merchant family. After being educated in Merton, England, and Paris, France, Becket joined the household of Theobold, who was then the archbishop of Canterbury. In 1154 Theobold introduced Becket to Henry II, and the two men took an instant liking to each other. Some contemporaries described them as more like brothers than friends. It was soon after their meeting that Henry named Becket his chancellor, and as chancellor, Becket helped the king enlarge the power of the monarchy. By all accounts Becket appeared to take pleasure from living the high-life of a top official; he enjoyed luxurious goods, lavish clothes and furniture, sumptuous meals, and riding and other sport. He seemed to relish the rise in status from upper-middle-class merchant's son to consort of royalty.

All this would change when Henry decided to make Becket archbishop of Canterbury. Ironically Becket warned Henry that the appointment could affect their friendship, but Henry was convinced that having his friend in England's highest church position would bring further unity to the nation. He could not have been more wrong. Thomas Becket was made a priest, then a bishop, and then archbishop of Canterbury in the space of two days, undergoing a personal transformation in the process. His lifestyle changed entirely upon the assumption of his new religious role. Becket set aside his lavish clothes and took to wearing the simple robes of a cleric, often with a coarse hair shirt underneath for penance. He stopped endorsing Henry II's state policies and strictly followed the dictates of Rome. The year was 1162, so Becket was in his forties at the time. His transformation would puzzle historians, who have had a difficult time explaining how the worldly, fun-loving courtier became a devout priest almost overnight. Becket, on the other hand, retained the strength of character and iron will that he had shown in his tenure as chancellor; these same qualities would be evident in Becket-the-Archbishop-and-future-saint.

Henry was incensed at what he saw as a betrayal by a friend, and after a series of clashes, Becket fled to France for seven years, where he lived under the protection of King Louis VII. Henry confiscated the property of Becket and his supporters. There followed many failed attempts to reconcile the former friends before Henry finally met Becket at Freteval on July 22, 1170. A truce was negotiated, which allowed Becket to return to Canterbury on December 2. Twenty-seven days later, Becket was murdered by agents of the king; it is the time between these two events that is the subject of Eliot's *Murder in the Cathedral*.

The Play in Focus

The plot—Part 1. (In the Archbishop's hall, December 2, 1170). Members of the Chorus of the Poor Women of Canterbury set the scene for the audience, explaining that they have been drawn to the cathedral to bear witness to the coming events. They explain that the Archbishop (Thomas Becket) has been gone for seven years, and while they miss him, they fear his return because they know that there will be conflict between him and the King. "King rules or barons rule," they tell us. "We have suffered various oppressions / But mostly we are left to our own devices / And we are content if we are left alone" (Eliot, *Murder in the Cathedral*, p. 12). Unfortunately all they can do is wait and bear witness.

Three Priests then take up the narrative, informing the audience that the Archbishop, the Pope, and the kings of England and France have been involved in conflicts, intrigues, and negotiations. The Priests argue that the goal of secular government is only to take power and stay in power. They wonder if everyone has forgotten "their father in God" (*Murder*, p. 14).

A messenger arrives to announce that the Archbishop is coming, whereupon the Three Priests wonder, "Is our Lord Archbishop / Reunited with the King?" (*Murder*, p. 15). The messenger explains that Becket is coming home to a great fanfare and outpouring of love from the people, but that while he is "at one with the Pope, and with the King of France," he still has not been united to the English King (*Murder*, p. 16). The women of the Chorus worry about Becket's return, feeling that it will disrupt local life and hurt "the small folk drawn into the pattern of fate" (*Murder*, p. 20). They also fear for Thomas Becket's life and wish he would stay away. The Priests rebuke them, calling them "foolish, immodest, and babbling women" (*Murder*, p. 21). But when Becket arrives, he supports the women's position, "They speak better than they know, and beyond your understanding," because they know suffering (*Murder*, p. 21). Becket further explains that "action is suffering" and implies that the actions to come are painful but are also the will of God (*Murder*, p. 21). The Priests welcome Becket and bid him rest, but he says he is surrounded by enemies and spies who will attack when they are ready.

At this point, Becket is approached by Four Tempters. The First Tempter tries to seduce him with memories of his old life as a rich and favored courtier. Becket resists him easily; he is no longer interested in worldly pleasures. The Second Tempter tells Becket he could do more good for the world by working within the king's system than by opposing it, and suggests that Becket resume his career in politics. "Real power / Is purchased at a price of a certain submission. / Your spiritual power is earthly perdition" (*Murder*, p. 28). But Becket rejects the idea. He is the servant of God and the Pope; shall he "descend to desire a punier power?" (*Murder*, p. 30). The Third Tempter tells Becket that he will never be reconciled to King Henry, so he should join the forces that wish to overthrow the King. But Becket is horrified by the suggestion: "No one shall say I betrayed a king" (*Murder*, p. 34).

A Fourth Tempter arrives—to Becket's surprise, since he expected only three. The Fourth Tempter is hardest for Becket to overcome because this one suggests that Becket succumb to the lure of the power he can exert from beyond the grave—he will have glory after death and tremendous influence as a saint. "Saint and Martyr rule from beyond the grave," he tells Becket, asking him to picture his dismayed enemies, the lines of pilgrims to his tomb, his glittering jeweled shrine (*Murder*, p. 38). Becket admits that he has thought of these things. The Tempter insists that he take the way of saintly martyrdom—he will achieve the glory of God while his persecutors live in torment. But this would be doing the right thing for the wrong reasons; it is wrong to desire sainthood for one's own personal glory and to triumph over one's enemies. Becket despairs: "Is there no way, in my soul's sickness, / Does not lead to damnation in pride?" (*Murder*, p. 40).

At this low point, everyone comes together to haunt him—the Women of Canterbury wail about their suffering, the Priests caution him not to fight an unwinnable fight, the Tempters tell him that "life is a cheat and a disappointment (*Murder*, p. 41). Finally the Women caution him, "Destroy yourself and we are destroyed." (*Murder*, p, 44). But Becket suddenly sees that he must submit himself to martyrdom for this is the will of God, though it may seem to everyone else to be the "Senseless self-slaughter of a lunatic / Arrogant passion of a fanatic" (*Murder*, p. 45). History, Becket realizes, will have to draw its own conclusions as to his motives.

Interlude. (In the cathedral on Christmas morning, 1170). The two parts of the play are separated by Becket's Christmas morning sermon, which is preached directly to the audience as if they were the congregation of Canterbury Cathedral. The text on which he preaches is the fourteenth verse of the second chapter of the Gospel according to Saint Luke: "Glory to God in the highest, and on earth peace to men of good will" (Luke 2:14). Becket explains that mourning and rejoicing coexist in Christianity, particularly on Christmas Day where both Christ's birth and death are celebrated in the mass. He asks the congregation, "Does it seem strange to you that angels should have announced Peace when ceaselessly the world has been stricken with War and the fear of War?" (*Murder*, p. 48). God does give peace, he assures the congregation, but not necessarily worldly peace. Becket goes on to note that the day after Christmas is St. Stephen's day, celebrating the first martyr; just as the churchgoers simultaneously celebrate the birth and death of Christ, so they should both rejoice and mourn martyrs like Stephen. "A Christian martyrdom," says Becket, "is never an accident, for Saints are not made by accident . . . a martyrdom is always the design of God" (*Murder*, p. 49). He concludes his sermon by telling the assembled people: "I do not think I shall ever preach to you again; and because it is possible that in a short time you may have yet another martyr, and that one perhaps not the last." (*Murder*, p. 50).

Part 2, Scene 1. (In the Archbishop's hall, December 29, 1170). The Chorus of the Poor Women of Canterbury opens the scene; the women are still wondering about what the future

Murder in the Cathedral

holds, what consequences it will bring for them in the spring. The time is four days after Christmas, as shown by the entrance of the Three Priests. Each carries a banner: The First Priest carries the banner of Saint Stephen (St. Stephen's Day, December 26); the Second Priest carries the banner of St. John The Apostle (December 27); the Third Priest carries a banner of the Holy Innocents (December 28). That makes the current date December 29th.

Four Knights arrive and announce themselves as servants of the King who have urgent business with the Archbishop. Becket grants them audience, and they explain to him that he is in revolt against his monarch. He has "cheated, swindled, lied; broke his oath and betrayed his King" (*Murder*, p. 60). Becket denies this and claims to be a loyal subject. When the Knights attack him, he is saved by a number of priests and attendants who interpose themselves between the Knights and the Archbishop. The Knights then lay out the specific charges against Becket: he fled England to stir up trouble against King Henry with the King of France and the Pope, and he "suspended those who crowned the young prince," (he cast a number of Henry's followers out of the Church.) The Knights ask Becket to absolve these followers and reinstate them in the Church. Becket says they should petition the Pope for this, not him. The Knights then ask Becket to leave England again, but Becket refuses; he has already been away from Canterbury and his people for seven years. He further tells the Knights that he is not their enemy; their problem is that they have broken Church laws. At this point the Knights threaten him: "Priest, you have spoken in peril of your life," and exit the stage (*Murder*, p. 65).

The Chorus bursts out in a long poetic speech; they are having visions of death and waste. Becket reassures them, saying they will soon forget these horrors. The Priests arrive and tell Thomas to hide from his attackers in the Church. Becket refuses; he is ready for his death when and if it should come. But the Priests forcibly drag him away.

Part 2, Scene 2. (In the cathedral, December 29, 1170). The Chorus of Women pray to God that suffering should not be in vain. Inside the Cathedral, the Priests are barring the door against the Knights, but Becket demands they open the doors: "I will not have the house of prayer . . . turned into a fortress" (*Murder*, p. 73). The Priests argue that the Knights are not men but beasts—and surely Becket would secure the cathedral against beasts? But Becket insists that the church doors remain open to all men, even enemies. The doors are opened, and the Knights enter, apparently drunk, demanding to see Becket. One last time they lay down conditions: "Absolve all those you have excommunicated. Resign the powers you have arrogated. Restore to the King the money you appropriated. Renew the obedience you have violated" (*Murder*, p. 75). Becket replies that he is ready to die, and with cries of "Traitor!" they kill him while the Chorus of Women give voice to their poetry of woe: "The land is foul, the water is foul, our beasts and ourselves defiled with blood" (*Murder*, p. 76).

FROM EDWARD GRIM'S EYEWITNESS ACCOUNT OF BECKET'S MURDER

The murderers followed him; "Absolve," they cried, "and restore to communion those whom you have excommunicated, and restore their powers to those whom you have suspended."

He answered, "There has been no satisfaction, and I will not absolve them."

"Then you shall die," they cried, "and receive what you deserve."

"I am ready," he replied, "to die for my Lord, that in my blood the Church may obtain liberty and peace. But in the name of Almighty God, I forbid you to hurt my people whether clerk or lay". . . .

At the third blow he fell on his knees and elbows, offering himself a living victim, and saying in a low voice, "For the Name of Jesus and the protection of the Church I am ready to embrace death."

Then the third knight inflicted a terrible wound as he lay, by which the sword was broken against the pavement, and the crown which was large was separated from the head. The fourth knight prevented any from interfering so that the others might freely perpetrate the murder.

As to the fifth, no knight but that clerk who had entered with the knights, that a fifth blow might not be wanting to the martyr who was in other things like to Christ, he put his foot on the neck of the holy priest and precious martyr, and, horrible to say, scattered his brain and blood over the pavement, calling out to the others, "Let us away, knights; he will rise no more."

(Grim)

Murder in the Cathedral

The murder of Thomas Becket dramatized in the 1970 production of *Murder in the Cathedral*

At this point, the play takes a radical turn. Up until now, the narrative had unfolded almost entirely in poetry; now the Knights step up and address the audiences in the colloquial speech of the 1930s. The first Knight, Reginald Fiz Urse, says he and his companions know that they look like the villains of the play:

> You are Englishmen, and therefore you believe in fair play: and when you see one man being set upon by four, then your sympathies are all with the underdog. . . . Nevertheless, I appeal to your sense of honor. You are Englishmen, and therefore you will not judge anybody without hearing both sides of the case.
> (*Murder*, p. 78)

He then asks each of the other Knights to introduce themselves and present their justifications for Becket's murder to the audience.

The Third Knight introduces himself as Baron William de Traci. He tells the audience that their actions have been perfectly disinterested; they are just putting their country first. He explains that they had to get drunk to get up their courage: "When you come to the point, it does go against the grain to kill an Archbishop," he confesses (*Murder*, p. 79). He further says that it was their duty to perform this horrible act, even though they know that the King will have to publicly repudiate and exile them.

The Second Knight, Sir Hugh de Morville, explains that Becket is not really the underdog and asks the crowd to weigh King Henry's aims against Becket's. King Henry is trying to unite a kingdom, to curb the excessive powers of local government, to reform the English legal system. Becket, on the other hand, puts God before the King, confusing Church and State and placing them at odds with each other. Morville says that the audience should remember that if the Church in modern days is subservient to the state, it was the Knights who began to make that possible.

The Fourth Knight, Richard Brito, asks the audience, "Who killed the Archbishop?" (*Murder*, p. 83). Brito claims that Becket sought his own death; clearly he wanted to be a martyr. "Even at the last, he could have given us reason; you have seen how he evaded our questions . . . he could still have easily escaped" (*Murder*, p. 83). Instead, he insisted that the doors be opened and let the Knights in while they were still in a murderous rage.

The First Knight then dismisses the audience in a tone of authority worthy of a police state: "I suggest that you now disperse quietly to your homes. Please be careful not to loiter in groups at street corners, and do nothing that might provoke any public outburst" (*Murder*, p. 84).

The Knights exit and the Priests rush onstage. The First Priest worries that "the heathen shall

Murder in the Cathedral

build on the ruins / Their world without God," but he is assured by the other priests that the Church will be stronger as a result of today (*Murder*, p. 84). They join in with the Chorus to give thanks to God, to acknowledge their human weakness in fearing worldly leaders more than the justice of God, and to ask God for His mercy.

The role of the audience: Witness, judge, criminal—or hero? Late in the second act, right after their killing of Thomas Becket, the murderous Knights address the audience in the colloquial speech of the 1930s: "We beg you to give us your attention for a few moments. We know that you may be disposed to judge unfavorably of our action" (*Murder*, p. 78). This is not the first time that the audience has been given an explicit role in the play; in the opening lines, the Chorus, whose members function as representatives of the audience, notes that they have been called to the cathedral to bear witness. But the witnesses are abruptly recast as judges at the end of the second act: "You are Englishmen, and therefore will not judge anybody without hearing both side of the case" (*Murder*, p. 78).

A GENUINE MARTYR?

Even today, historical opinion on Thomas Becket is deeply divided. He was canonized a saint three years after his death, and many people view Becket as a martyr who heroically withstood the demands of a tyrannical king; this is Eliot's view. Others have been less impressed with Becket. King Henry VIII (1491-1547) destroyed his shrine, burned his bones, and had Becket's name removed from religious missals, and the historian Thomas Carlyle (1795-1881) called Becket, "a noisy egotist and hypocrite" (Carlyle in Tydeman, p. 44). In *Murder in the Cathedral*, Becket asks history to judge him, but there may never be one final verdict.

From that point on, the Knights try to win the audience's support for their murder of Becket, and the arguments they make are eerily persuasive. Of course a modern-day audience supports the subordination of church to state, doesn't it? Of course such an audience recognizes that violence is necessary for maintaining the social order. Of course, the audience is patriotic and wishes to have a strong and powerful nation. "At another time," the Second Knight says, "you would condemn an Archbishop by a vote of Parliament and execute him formally as a traitor, and no one would have to bear the burden of being called murderer" (*Murder*, p. 82).

By appealing directly to the audience in this fashion, the Knights illustrate that its members are not mere witnesses, but are actually complicit in the murder of Becket and men like him. "You" would condemn an archbishop in another time, the Knights say; Eliot is implicitly challenging the audience to repudiate this assertion, thereby bringing the story of Becket into the 1930s, the "other" time to which the Knights allude. There were certain parallels, to be sure. In his sermon, Becket talks to an audience "stricken with War and the fear of War," a reality also true in the post-World War I and pre-World War II 1930s (*Murder*, p. 48). Also the 1930s were years when state power was being consolidated by monarch-like dictators such as Adolf Hitler in Germany. Eliot's play does not put King Henry II onstage as a character, which makes the state power that Becket is opposing faceless and vague, and invites the audience to draw a comparison with its own time. Like the nation-building monarchs of the twelfth century, the dictators of Eliot's era promoted national loyalty over religious faith and individual conscience. It is important to note that these dictators had not yet committed most of the heinous crimes for which their names have since become infamous. However, the Knights in Eliot's play, prophetically, justify Becket's murder with an excuse that is now sadly familiar: they were only following orders.

Eliot's play therefore lays down a challenge to the audience: it invites theatergoers of his day to resist both "reason" and "the law" when it comes to opposing tyranny and state-mandated violence. The audience is encouraged not to think of the play as dealing with a particular historical moment, but to realize that Becket's choice to put his conscience before his country is one that they themselves may be called upon to make.

Sources and literary context. Eliot wrote *Murder in the Cathedral* to fulfill a commission from the sponsors of the 1935 Canterbury Festival for a Christian-themed play. The fact that the play was to be performed in Canterbury Cathedral clearly inspired Eliot to try his hand at the historical tale. Initially the play's sponsors were disappointed with Eliot's choice, since the Becket story is such an obvious theme for Canterbury. In fact, a previous Becket play by Lord Alfred Tennyson had been written in 1879 and revived for the 1932 and 1933 Canterbury

> ### THE GOLDEN AGE OF DETECTIVE FICTION
>
> The original title of Eliot's play was "Fear in the Way," a biblical quote from the book of Ecclesiast. According to William Tydeman, it was the director's wife, Henzie Raeburn, who suggested that Eliot coin a title more suggestive of a murder mystery. The 1920s and '30s were considered to be the "Golden Age" of the English murder mystery, featuring writers such as Agatha Christie (*Murder on the Orient Express,* 1934), John Dickson Carr (*The White Priory Murders,* 1934), and Dorothy Sayers, (*Murder Must Advertise,* 1933). Raeburn hoped that a more contemporary-sounding title would draw people to Eliot's play. From just the few titles listed, one can easily see that *Murder in the Cathedral* sounds like a typical example of the genre. But certainly, Eliot's play is not a typical "whodunit." The murder mystery was nicknamed a "whodunit" because it challenged readers to figure out who committed the crime, but in *Murder in the Cathedral,* Becket's murder happens right in front of the audience. So there is no mystery as to who really killed Thomas Becket—or is there? It is worth considering to what extent Eliot's title—so evocative of a murder mystery—invites the audience to play detective and examine what they see and know. Yes, the four Knights killed Becket, but were they the only ones? Doesn't Henry II bear some responsibility, since the Knights were acting on his command, and what about the people who let it happen—the Priests, the citizens, all those who failed to stand up, as Becket did, to tyranny? How does one apportion responsibility in a situation like this?

Festivals, so it is understandable that the sponsors' first reaction to Eliot's idea was dismay.

However, Eliot's version is very different from Tennyson's. Eliot went back to primary source material, and his play relies heavily on Edward Grim's eyewitness account of the killing. Tennyson, like most people who have retold the tale, focused directly on the quarrel between Becket and his one-time friend, Henry II. But King Henry doesn't even appear as a character in *Murder in the Cathedral.* Resisting the obvious drama to be found in the onstage clash of two powerful men, Eliot focuses instead on Becket's internal conflict as he prepares himself for martyrdom, even going so far as to structure the play like a Catholic mass. There are two sections (a mass is divided into "The Liturgy of the Word" and "The Liturgy of the Eucharist") divided by a sermon, all leading up to the climax of Becket's redeeming death (which mirrors Christ's crucifixion). By drawing upon history and ritual, Eliot was able to construct an entirely new Becket play.

Events in History at the Time the Play Was Written

The rise of dictators. "I wanted to bring home to the audience the contemporary relevance of the situation," Eliot wrote of *Murder in the Cathedral*. "The style therefore had to be neutral, committed neither to the present nor the past" (Eliot, *Poetry and Poets*, p. 80). As noted, the story of how one man resisted the pressure of his King to ignore his obligations to the Church was highly relevant for Europe in the 1930s, when many nations were falling under increasingly tyrannical regimes. Adolph Hitler ruled Germany, Benito Mussolini ruled Italy, Joseph Stalin had total control of Russia, Englebert Dollfuss ruled Austria, and Turkey continued along under the more benevolent dictatorship of Mustafa Kemal Ataturk. It was an era in which state power was being solidified and wielded to an extreme degree.

In Germany, Hitler's Nazi Party won power in 1933; these elections would be the last until after the Second World War. The following year gave rise to the Night of the Long Knives, in which Hitler arranged for the murder of his enemies within the Nazi party. There was little protest from organized religion during these early years of Hitler's regime; in fact, quite the contrary. At first the regime won the support of the Protestant Church. A group of "Deutsche Christen," or "German Christians," not only accepted the Nazi Party but attempted to have it

Murder in the Cathedral

officially sanctified. On November 20, 1933, an agreement was signed between the Deutsche Christen and the Hitler Youth Movement, uniting the 800,000 members of Christian youth groups with the Hitler Youth. From then on, anyone who did not belong to the Hitler Youth could not participate in church youth activities.

The Deutschen Christen understood that this meant a new relationship between church and state:

> But it is clear that . . . we must find a new form of collaboration between State and Church. The State is interested in seeing order prevail in the internal working of the Church, and that is also the Führer's will and desire. We implicitly trust the Führer to find the proper contemporary form of State/Church collaboration.
>
> (Reichsbischof in Lyons)

TWO SAINTS OF THE HOLOCAUST

Saint Maximilian Kolbe (1894-1941) was a Polish priest who helped hundreds of Jews escape the terror of the Nazis and later offered his life in place of a fellow prisoner's at Auschwitz. He was canonized in 1982.

Saint Edith Stein (1891-1942), feminist, scholar, and theologian, was born Jewish in Germany. She converted to Catholicism in 1922, and became a nun in 1933, taking the religious name Teresa, Benedicta a Cruce (Teresa, Blessed of the Cross). She died in the Auschwitz gas chamber on August 9, 1942, when she refused to deny her Jewish heritage. A witness to her arrest by the Nazis says that she took her sister Rosa's hand and said, "Come Rosa. We're going for our people."

Meanwhile, Germany's Catholic Church did little to stem the rising tide of Hitler's murderous regime during these early years, partly because the Nazis were at that time enemies of the overtly atheistic Soviet Communists, whom the Church feared even more. But while Hitler had yet to commit the horrendous mass murders that would make his name infamous, there were already those who felt that the Church should be taking more of a stand. In 1935, the same year that *Murder in the Cathedral* debuted, theologian Karl Barth wrote:

> The story of the Confessing Church [i.e. the Catholic Church] in the Nationalist Socialist Germany of these years is no glorious chronicle for its participants, no heroic or saintly story. . . . We can and must reproach this Confessing Church for not recognizing the enemy early on in its real dangerousness and for not unambiguously and forcefully opposing to him early on. . . . She [the Church] has . . . remained silent on the action against the Jews, on the amazing treatment of political opponents, on the suppression of the freedom of political opponents, on the suppression of the freedom of the press in the new Germany and on so much else against which the Old Testament prophets would certainly have spoken out.
>
> (Barth, p. 45)

Barth here reproaches the German Catholic Church for remaining silent in the face of so many political injustices; even today, historians debate to what extent Catholics bear responsibility for not sufficiently opposing the will of Nazi and Fascist regimes. To be fair, many Catholics did eventually resist the orders of Hitler and the other dictators, often at the risk of their own lives. By 1941, at least 700 priests had been killed in Poland alone, and 3,000 more were in prisons or concentration camps. Many priests and nuns hid persecuted Jews in their homes, rectories, convents or monasteries. Some historians believe that between 700,000 and 860,000 Jewish lives were saved by the intervention of the Church.

But in 1935, Karl Barth was regretting that there was as yet no heroic or saintly story to be told. The age had not yet produced its Thomas Beckets, though, unhappily, a decade of murderous tyranny would soon produce countless martyrs.

Poetic drama. Theater in Eliot's day was dominated by a style known as "realism," which attempted to portray how people really live and speak. But theater had not always been realist; in fact, historically, drama had been created in verse—whether written by ancient Greek dramatists like Sophocles and Euripides or by Shakespeare. Drama was actually a subvariety of poetry. In the 1930s, T. S. Eliot, then the world's most-famous poet, attempted to bring poetic drama back to the stage.

Murder in the Cathedral is a play largely written in verse. Its lines qualify as poetry by the broadest definition: words chosen for their sound and rhythm as well as their sense. Eliot's poem uses a range of poetic devices:

Rhyme

You see, my Lord, I do not wait upon
 ceremony:
Here I have come, forgetting all acrimony,
Hoping that your present gravity
Will find excuse for my humble levity.
                                    (*Murder*, p. 23)

Alliteration (note the repetition of beginning letters and sounds—for example, *m* in the first line; *w* and *f* in the second):

Yes! men must maneuver. Monarchs also,
Waging war abroad, need fast friends at
 home.
Private policy is public profit;
Dignity still shall be dressed with decorum.
                                    (*Murder*, p. 29)

Repetition (of whole phrases and of individual words; note how the word "good" appears four times in the four lines below):

For good or ill, let the wheel turn.
The wheel has been still, these seven years,
 and no good.
For good or ill, let the wheel turn.
For who knows the end of good and evil?
                                    (*Murder*, p. 18)

Metaphor and imagery (consider Becket's comparison of his encroaching enemies to hawks):

For a little time the hungry hawk
Will only soar and hover, circling lower,
Waiting excuse, pretense, opportunity.
End will be simple, sudden, God-given.
                                    (*Murder*, p. 23)

Eliot also adopts a number of devices from the history of poetic drama and from Christian liturgy. The Chorus of the Poor Women of Canterbury recalls the choruses of Greek drama, which in the classics often commented on the action. Christian liturgy uses a rhythmic repetition of phrases in prayer—as in the Christian chant, "Lord Have Mercy. Christ Have Mercy. Lord Have Mercy"— and Eliot's play includes similarly structured lines such as "A doom on the house, a doom on yourself, a doom on the world" (*Murder*, p. 19).

Eliot and other verse dramatists such as W. B. Yeats and Christopher Fry were considered a miniature movement in the 1930s and 1940s; as modernist poets, they were interested in combining past and present through art by updating older forms. But poetic drama has yet to recapture the imagination of the mainstream theater-going public.

Reception. Eliot joked, in a lecture, that he had "an advantage" as a beginning playwright. "It [*Murder in the Cathedral*] was a religious play, and people who go deliberately to a religious play at a religious festival expect to be patiently bored and to satisfy themselves with the feeling that they have done something meritorious" (Eliot, *Poetry and Poets*, p. 79). If the audiences who saw *Murder in the Cathedral* were expecting boredom, they were disappointed; the play was a great success in its initial eight-day run and soon moved south to the secular London stage.

> ### A MODERN BECKET?
>
> The situation in Russia in 1934 was no better than that of Germany; this year saw the beginning of "the Great Terror" (1934-38), during which Joseph Stalin purged the state of his enemies by the use of secret police, rigged trials, deportations, and speedy executions. Catholic priests were accused of destroying bridges, railways, and factories, and of spying. The regime put them on trial, as it had in the previous decade for practicing religion when the Soviets had officially rejected it. From the trials of Archbishop John Cieplak and various Roman Catholic clergy in Stalinist Russia, as witnessed by Father Walsh in 1923. N. V. Krylenko was the prosecutor.
>
> "Will you stop teaching the Christian religion?" "We cannot," came the uniform reply. "It is the law of God." "That law does not exist on Soviet Territory," replied Krylenko. "You must choose. . . . As for your religion, I spit on it, as I spit on all religions."
>
>   (Walsh, p. 13)

While favorably reviewed by most critics, *Murder in the Cathedral* was always the focus of critical arguments. Reviewers faulted the play for a lack of action on the stage. Eliot's own director, Martin Browne, admitted that Eliot "has no experience of the actor's art" (Browne in Tydeman, p. 67). Christopher Innes summarizes much of the critical opinion when he states that the play "denies any suspense: 'A man comes home foreseeing that he will be killed, and he is killed'" (Innes, pp. 392-93). There was also controversy over the play's being in verse: theater critic Kenneth Tynan argued that despite Eliot's defense of poetry as the natural medium for the stage, the best parts of *Murder in the Cathedral* are the knight's self-justifying speeches and Becket's sermon—all written in prose. Still, many critics continue to be awed by the beauty of the play's language and spirit, deeming it remarkable for its portrayal of an individual "mind and spirit together at war with the innermost temptations that can beset the human soul" (Morrah, p. 9).

—Francesca Coppa

For More Information

Barth, Karl. *The German Church Conflict*. Richmond: John Knox Press, 1965.

Bloom, Harold, ed. *T. S. Eliot's Murder in the Cathedral*. New York: Chelsea, 1998.

Eliot, T. S. *Murder in the Cathedral*. New York: Harcourt, Brace, 1935.

———. *On Poetry and Poets*. London: Faber & Faber, 1957.

Grim, Edward. "The Murder of Thomas Becket, 1170." *EyeWitness—History through the Eyes of Those Who Lived It*. 1997. www.ibiscom.com (11 Aug. 1997).

Innes, Christopher. "T.S. Eliot: the Drama of Conversion." In *Modern British Drama 1890-1990*. Cambridge: Cambridge University Press, 1992.

Lyons, James R. "Idolatry: The Impact of National Socialism on the Churches of Nazi Europe." *The Ecumenical Institute for Jewish-Christian Studies*. 1999. http://www.j-cinstitute.org/Articles/Lyons_Idolatry.htm (1 Aug. 2002).

McGill, William J. "Voices in the Cathedral: The Chorus in Eliot's *Murder in the Cathedral*." *Modern Drama* 23 (1980): 292-96.

Morrah, Dermot. Review of *Murder in the Cathedral*. *The Times*, 2 November 1935, 9.

Tydeman, William. *Murder in the Cathedral and The Cocktail Party: Text and Performance*. London: Macmillan Education, 1988.

Walsh, Edmund A. "The Catholic Church in Present Day Russia." Report delivered before the American Catholic Historical Association, Minneapolis 29 December 1931.

"The Murders in the Rue Morgue"

by
Edgar Allan Poe

Edgar Allan Poe (1809-49) was born in Baltimore, where in the 1830s he began an unsettled career in magazine editing and writing. Over the next two decades, heavy drinking and frequent quarrels with his employers lost him a number of jobs. Poe meanwhile lived in Richmond, New York, Philadelphia, New York again, then Richmond again, and finally Baltimore, where he died at age 40. Despite his stormy relations with magazine publishers, he produced a steady output of widely read poems, stories, and critical reviews that often brought success to the magazines where he worked. Among Poe's best known poems are "Lenore" (1843), "The Raven" (1845), "Annabel Lee" (1848), and "The Bells" (1849); his short stories include "The Fall of the House of Usher" (1839), "The Tell-Tale Heart" (1843), and **"The Cask of Amontillado"** (1846; also in *Literature and its Times*). Like such works, "The Murders in the Rue Morgue" conveys an atmosphere of mystery, gloom, and foreboding, and dramatizes death, loss, and grotesque violence. Unlike them, however, it is credited with introducing an entirely new figure into world literature: the investigator whose powers of detection can be used to combat—or at least illuminate—those dark forces. Considered the world's first detective story, "The Murders in the Rue Morgue" would give rise to a literary genre rooted in and characteristic of the modern age.

> **THE LITERARY WORK**
>
> An American short story set in Paris around 1840; first published in Philadelphia in 1841.
>
> **SYNOPSIS**
>
> The brilliant, eccentric French aristocrat C. Auguste Dupin uses his uncanny reasoning power to solve a brutal double murder.

Events in History at the Time of the Short Story

Growing cities and urban violence. The decade of the 1830s brought the beginning of a surge in the United States population that would continue throughout the rest of the nineteenth century. Fed by high birthrates and especially by a sharp rise in immigration from Europe, America's growing population not only spurred the nation's rapid westward expansion, but also created new challenges for the older and increasingly crowded cities of the East. While an estimated 250,000 immigrants had arrived in America between 1800 and 1830, more than 10 times that many—over 2.5 million—came in the next two decades, attracted partly by the labor demands of the emerging industrial revolution. America's largest city, New York, would see its population increase from about 200,000 in 1830 to nearly 500,000 in 1850, and other major cities such as Philadelphia, Baltimore, and Boston experienced similar growth.

"The Murders in the Rue Morgue"

Edgar Allan Poe

Excluding Boston, these were the cities in which Edgar Allan Poe lived and wrote, and their urban environments shaped his work profoundly. While "The Murders in the Rue Morgue" is ostensibly set in Paris, it is almost certain that Poe never actually visited France. Critics have instead seen the Paris of the story's setting as a thinly disguised amalgam of the various American cities that Poe himself knew intimately. This conclusion is supported by the sequel to "The Murders in the Rue Morgue," in which Poe's detective C. Auguste Dupin solves his second literary case. The sequel, entitled "The Mystery of Marie Roget" (1841), was based on the real life murder of a woman named Mary Rogers that occurred in New York just a few months after "The Murders in the Rue Morgue" was published. Describing a crime closely similar to Mary Rogers's murder but altering the victim's name to sound French, Poe simply transferred his second detective tale to the same fictionalized Parisian setting as the first.

The wide publicity accorded Mary Rogers's murder in the American press has been cited as the first time a brutal crime caused a media sensation among the American public. But the Mary Rogers case did have some less sensational precedents, for as cities grew in the 1830s so did public concern about the crime and violence perceived as growing with them. Accurate data on violent personal crimes such as robberies or murders are unavailable, leading some historians to suggest that the public perception of an increase in such crimes did not accurately reflect reality. More historically certain is the rising incidence of violent urban riots in the early nineteenth century. In 1834, for example, 16 violent riots occurred in American cities, and the number multiplied the following year, to 37 riots in which 61 people were killed. A major catalyst was economic hardship and related labor unrest (aggravated by a severe depression from the late 1830s to the early 1840s). Other factors included tensions between established groups and recent immigrants, and the abolition movement, whose working-class opponents feared that freed blacks would take their jobs.

Early police forces. A public's growing concern with crime was not unique to American society in the early nineteenth century. Europeans too experienced a mounting fear of crime. In response to this fear, they founded the earliest modern police forces in Paris and London, which then inspired similar organizations in American cities such as New York. Paris boasted the first professional municipal police force; called the *gendarmerie*, it arose in the 1820s out of earlier state security forces. London soon followed the Parisian example, when Britain's Metropolitan Police Act of 1829 established the London Metropolitan Police, called Scotland Yard after its London address.

DETECTING THE DETECTIVES

Like the Parisian gendarmerie, Scotland Yard's 3,200 constables—known as "peelers" after their founder, Sir Robert Peel—could be easily distinguished by their blue uniforms. Peel's first name gave rise to the later nickname "bobbies," still used today for Britain's uniformed constables. Although these early police forces were founded in the 1820s to prevent and control crime, not until the 1840s did they begin methodical detective work. In fact, the word detective did not exist when Poe wrote "The Murders in the Rue Morgue." The term was first used in print in 1843, two years after the story and one year after Scotland Yard established a genuine Detective Department, whose officers dressed in plain clothes. The expression "Scotland Yard" has since been used to refer to the larger London Metropolitan Police Force as well as to the detective force operating out of it.

THE NEW YORK *SUN*—FIRST PENNY PAPER

In 1833, when the *Sun* began circulation, New York City boasted 11 newspapers, each at six cents a copy. The *Sun*, a 4-page paper with a first page that offered some catchy slice of fiction or history, sold for 1 cent. By 1835, the *Sun* had become the world's largest circulating daily, selling roughly 19,000 copies in contrast to the 17,000 sold by the London *Times*. The writer who took the *Sun* to this height was Richard Adams Locke, whom Poe credits with establishing the penny paper in America and setting a stellar example with topnotch writing. "His face is strongly pitted by the smallpox," but his eyes shine, and his forehead "is truly beautiful in its intellectuality. . . . His prose style is noticeable for its concision, luminosity, completeness. . . . Everything he writes is a model . . . serving just the purposes intended and nothing to spare" (Poe in O'Brien, p. 38). Locke published some sensational reports about a huge telescope that gave earth its first clear view of the moon, news that took not just America but Europe by storm. His story was a hoax, but, observed Poe, a grand hoax, "the greatest hit in the way of sensation . . . ever made by any similar fiction either in America or Europe"; with it, the *Sun* "established the 'penny system' through America, "one of the most important steps ever yet taken in the pathway of human progress" (Poe in O'Brien, pp. 56-57).

Murder stories peppered the penny papers at the time too. Later in 1835, Locke wrote another set of articles, this time grounded in fact, about one Manuel Fernandez, alias Richard C. Jackson, who killed John Roberts for his attentions to Fernandez's mistress, Harriet Schultz, at whose rooming house the two men boarded. Jackson shot Roberts in cold blood, through the head with a brass pistol, a deed reported not only by the *Sun* but also by its only successful one-penny rival, the New York *Herald*. The *Herald*, a paper inspired by the good fortune of the *Sun*, was not without descriptive flair of its own. The alleged killer Jackson, it reported, appeared at court in a blue jacket, white trousers, some boots, a black silk neckerchief, and a high shirt collar.

> He is rather a small slim man with a dark complexion, heavy shaggy eye brows, protuding [sic] thick lips. . . . Jackson perpetrated the act in the coolest manner possible. He fired the pistol with a segar in his mouth. After the deed was done there was no attempt made by him to escape. 'Roberts destroyed my happiness' said he, 'and I killed him.' . . . That same evening, he attempted to commit suicide by hanging himself up by a handkerchief. He was cut down in almost the agonies of death.
>
> (*Herald*, September 23, 1835, p. 2)

The next year, 1836, both papers reported on the infamous murder of Helen Jewett at a house of ill repute. She was allegedly killed by a man whom the courts acquitted but the *Sun* condemned: "Our opinion, calmly and dispassionately formed from the evidence, is that Richard P. Robinson is guilty. . . . Any good-looking young man, possessing . . . fifteen hundred dollars to retain . . . counsel, might murder any person he chose with perfect impunity" (*Sun* in O'Brien, p. 69). In sum, penny dailies offered no shortage of real murders in the 1830s to inspire short fiction.

"The Murders in the Rue Morgue"

"The Murders in the Rue Morgue"

The gendarmerie were well publicized in America, and were likely part of Poe's reason for setting "The Murders in the Rue Morgue" in Paris. In the story the amateur detective C. Auguste Dupin gains access to the crime scene because he knows the Prefect of Police, the gendarmerie's chief officer, whom he then outwits in solving the crime.

The rise of the periodical. Whether or not the public was justified in its growing fear of violent crimes, those fears were amply fed by a proliferation during the 1830s of cheap, mass-produced newspapers, many of which specialized in sensational stories of violent urban crime. Before the Mary Rogers murder other similar cases reached New York's hungry reading public through "penny" newspapers such as the New York *Sun* and the New York *Morning Post*, both founded in 1833 and both capitalizing on lurid, allegedly true accounts of murder and mayhem. One literary historian describes the earlier "trickle" of such penny newspapers as "swelling into a broad river in the 1830s and into a virtual flood in the 1840s" (Reynolds, p. 175). In an 1846 essay, Poe himself declared that by deluging the public with cheap, plentiful and sensationalized information, the penny papers were changing American culture in a way that was "probably beyond all calculation" (Poe, *Essays and Reviews*, p. 1214).

Newspapers play a central role in "The Murders in the Rue Morgue," which contains a number of newspaper articles; embedded whole within the narrative, they provide Dupin's most important clues to solving the mystery. The fictional articles recount the circumstances of the story's "most extraordinary and frightful affair" in the sensational style of the penny papers, alternating between graphic descriptions of the mutilated corpses and polite expressions of horror:

> A search was made of the chimney, and (horrible to relate!) the corpse of the daughter was dragged therefrom. . . . Upon the face were many severe scratches, and, upon the throat, dark bruises, and deep indentations of finger nails, as if the deceased had been throttled to death.
> (Poe, "The Murders in the Rue Morgue," p. 481)

The technological advances and associated drop in printing costs that allowed the penny newspapers to flourish allowed a greater number of less sensational periodicals to appear as well. By 1840 the rapid expansion of magazines and serious newspapers led the *New-York Mirror* to declare, "This is the golden age of periodicals!" (Mott, p. 341). Many weekly or monthly magazines published fiction, serializing novels or presenting the relatively new publishing phenomenon of the short story, which now took its place as a distinctively American literary form. Many of the stories written by Washington Irving, Nathaniel Hawthorne, Herman Melville, and other American writers of the period first appeared in magazines. Unlike those authors, Poe wrote many of his stories for magazines that he himself edited. Only later did he secure his stories' publication in book form.

Despite his success in publishing, Poe long remained impoverished. In 1835 and 1836, for example, when he edited *The Southern Literary Messenger* on the small salary of about $15 a week, Poe boosted its circulation from 500 to 3,500, earning a modest fortune of $10,000 for the magazine's owner. As the popularity of stories like "The Murders in the Rue Morgue" suggests, Poe appealed to the public's appetite for mystery, crime, and horror while striving for literary quality.

A gathering scientific revolution. Like the growth of cities, the related urban tensions, and the rise of mass media, advances in science also accompanied the industrial revolution in the early 1800s. By the end of the century the scientific discoveries would amount to a revolution of their own; already in Poe's time the outlines of the emerging scientific outlook were perceptible. The most influential scientific event of the nineteenth century would be the publication of Charles Darwin's ***On the Origin of Species*** (also in *Literature and Its Times*), in which the British biologist argues that life evolves and proposed a theory called natural selection to explain that evolution. Though Darwin published the work in 1859, he had formulated his theory by 1840, the year in which Poe's short story takes place. As later scholars have observed, Darwin delayed publication for some two decades out of fear that people would not accept it. So Darwin was not a direct influence on Poe, but their creative ideas emerged from the same intellectual and scientific context, a milieu in which evolution was an increasingly discussed concept. Darwin based his ideas partly on the work of earlier scientists, such as British geologist Charles Lyell (1797-1875), who perceived that natural forces can work gradually over immensely long periods of time, and French paleontologist Georges Cuvier (1769-1832), who was the first to use fossils in classifying extinct species. Evolution, in fact, had already been suggested by Cuvier's colleague and contemporary Jean-Baptiste Lamarcke (1744-1829), and the idea was supported by a few other scientists (such as Darwin's own grandfather, Erasmus), though Cuvier himself steadfastly opposed it.

As with many later detective stories, scientific knowledge comprises an essential element of the background to "The Murders in the Rue Morgue." Although history would prove him wrong about evolution, at the time of the story Cuvier was still remembered as France's greatest scientist, a highly skilled anatomist, famed for his baffling ability to look at a single tiny bone and recognize the animal it came from. Like his literary descendent the detective Sherlock Holmes (who mentions Cuvier as an inspiration for his own methods), Poe's detective C. Auguste Dupin also relies on Cuvier. Near the end of the story, he consults Cuvier's scientific writings to confirm the identity of the killer—a creature of which (in the narrator's words) "the gigantic stature, the prodigious strength and activity, the wild ferocity, and the imitative propensities . . . are sufficiently known to all" ("Rue Morgue," p. 498).

The Short Story in Focus

The plot. The story is narrated by an unnamed American living in Paris, who prefaces his "somewhat peculiar narrative" with an extended discussion of what he calls "the mental features discoursed of as the analytical" ("Rue Morgue," p. 473). To illustrate his ideas he brings up a number of games, suggesting, for example, that to the truly analytical mind, chess is less profound than either draughts (checkers) or the card game whist. This is because chess forces players to focus on the moves themselves; the other games have simpler moves, allowing a master of analysis to focus on seemingly trivial details and get to "the true state of affairs" ("Rue Morgue," p. 475).

Declaring that what he is about to relate will offer a "commentary upon the propositions just advanced," he then introduces the reader to his friend C. Auguste Dupin, a young French aristocrat who has lost his money owing to undisclosed misfortunes, and who has relinquished "the energy of his character" along with his fortune ("Rue Morgue," p. 476). The narrator and Dupin live together, sharing "a time-eaten and grotesque mansion, long deserted through superstitions into which we did not inquire, and tottering to its fall in a retired and desolate portion" of the city ("Rue Morgue," p. 476). There they live in isolation, "within ourselves alone," reading, writing, or talking in darkened rooms during the day, and only venturing out at night, when they stroll the Paris streets "seeking, amid the wild lights and shadows of the populous city, that infinity of mental excitement which quiet observation can afford" ("Rue Morgue," p. 476).

From their observations of the city's street life, the narrator has noticed "a peculiar analytic ability in Dupin" ("Rue Morgue," p. 476). As an example, the narrator relates how, during one of their walks, Dupin breaks a long silence with a surprising statement that seems to read the narrator's thoughts. The narrator listens in amazement as Dupin accurately retraces the narrator's train of thought, step by step, from fifteen minutes earlier, beginning when the narrator was jostled on the street by a fruit seller.

GAMES AND PUZZLES IN "THE MURDERS IN THE RUE MORGUE"

Poe often played cards with his male friends, and likely enjoyed whist, a popular card game, similar to bridge, that he mentions along with other games in "The Murders in the Rue Morgue." Poe uses these descriptions to illustrate various aspects of mental superiority. Most prominently, however, he describes the superior "analyst" in the story's first paragraph as "fond of enigmas, conundrums, hieroglyphics; exhibiting in his solutions of each a degree of *acumen* which appears to the ordinary apprehension praeternatural" ("Rue Morgue," p. 473). Poe himself loved riddles and especially relished cryptography. As a magazine editor, he challenged his readers to send in codes and ciphers, against which he tested his wits—succeeding every time. Modern critics have highlighted the role of cryptography in many of Poe's stories. Hieroglyphics was another fashionable intellectual topic of his day. The ancient Egyptian pictograms (pictorial writing) had only recently been deciphered, owing to the discovery in 1799 of the famous Rosetta Stone, a block of basalt (now in the British Museum) with the same text inscribed in both Greek and hieroglyphic characters. Since Greek was well understood, the Greek text offered a key to the hieroglyphic text. Using that foothold, other hieroglyphic texts were then painstakingly deciphered by the French scholar Jean-Francois Champollion (whose dictionary of hieroglyphics was published in 1841-43).

"The Murders in the Rue Morgue"

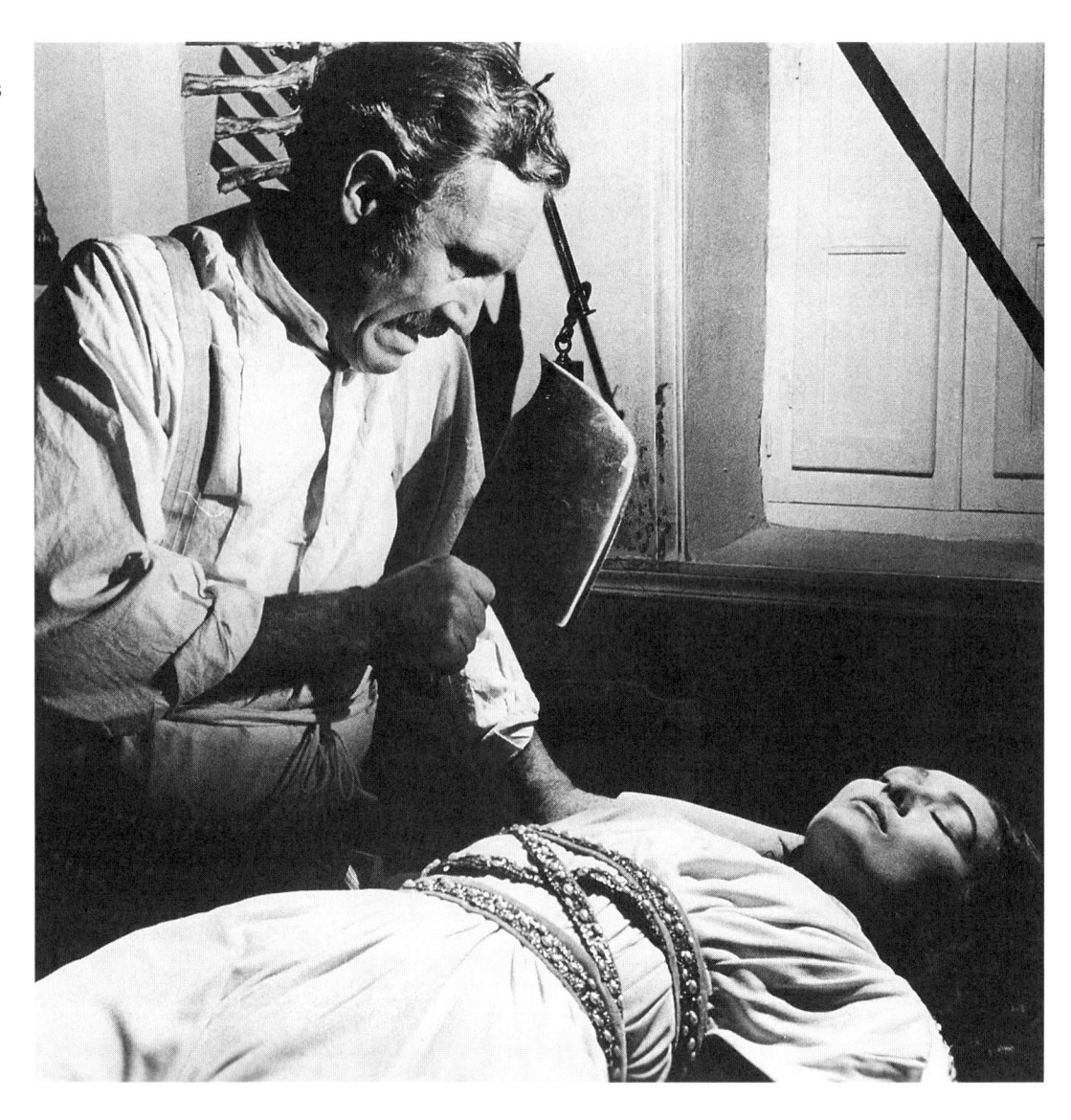

1971 film rendition of *Murders in the Rue Morgue,* with Jason Robards.

Soon after that incident, the two read in the newspaper about the gruesome double murder of two women, Madame L'Espanaye and her daughter, who lived together in a Paris apartment on the Rue Morgue (Morgue Street). At around three o'clock that morning, the neighborhood was awakened by loud shrieks coming from the women's fourth-floor dwelling. After the shrieks stopped, a crowd of onlookers forced its way into the locked apartment, which was in a shambles and appeared empty. Shortly thereafter, Madame L'Espanaye was found on the street outside, beaten and decapitated with a straight razor. A subsequent search of the apartment located her daughter, who had been strangled and stuffed, feet first, up the chimney. A safe was open, and a large pile of cash lay on the floor. The case is especially baffling because the door and windows of the apartment were all locked from the inside. The following day another newspaper article gives the accounts of a number of witnesses, several of whom overheard a loud, angry conversation after the shrieks stopped between a Frenchman and what sounded like another person speaking a foreign language. None of the witnesses, who are of various nationalities, can agree on what language the other person was speaking, but agree in describing the voice as harsh. A third article states that one of the witnesses, a bank clerk named Adolphe Le Bon, has been arrested for the crime.

Expressing skepticism about the *gendarmerie*'s ability to solve the mystery, Dupin takes an interest in it and obtains permission from his friend, the Prefect of Police, to visit the scene. There, as the narrator watches, Dupin carries out a detailed examination of the entire neighborhood as well as the apartment itself. On the way home, he stops briefly at a newspaper office.

The next day Dupin shocks the narrator by announcing that he has solved the crime. Moreover, he says that he expects a visit momentarily from, if not the murderer, someone who at least played a role in the murders. He and the narrator wait and prepare to detain the visitor, pistols at the ready. As they wait, Dupin explains that the key lies in the accounts of the loud overheard conversation, in which each witness was certain that the second person was speaking a different language—one that the witness himself or herself did not speak. Thus, for example, the English witness is certain the second person was speaking German, but he himself does not know German, while an Italian thinks it was Russian, but speaks no Russian. As for the murderer's escape from the locked apartment, Dupin's examination revealed that, while the chimney was too narrow for anyone to fit through, a nail used to secure one of the windows was broken, allowing the window to appear nailed shut when it could actually be opened. It was just possible for an extraordinarily athletic person to have climbed down the building from the window.

Dupin had also found a small tuft of hair, and had measured the strangulation marks on the daughter's throat. Neither the hair nor the handprints on the throat seemed human, and consulting the work of the anatomist Cuvier revealed that the handprints on the throat matched those of an orangutan. A small piece of ribbon found at the scene was the sort manufactured on the Mediterranean island of Malta. Dupin now reveals that, when he stopped by the newspaper office after observing the crime scene, he placed an advertisement claiming to have found an orangutan that was believed to have been lost by a sailor from a Maltese vessel, and saying that the animal could be recovered at Dupin's address. It is that sailor that Dupin now expects to arrive.

As Dupin finishes his explanation, the sailor does indeed arrive. He confirms Dupin's deductions, saying that he brought the orangutan from the South Seas to sell in Paris, but that it escaped. Tracking it, he was horrified to see the disoriented animal attack the two women through the apartment window, and he angrily tried to summon it to the ground. The orangutan's agitated vocalizations were the harsh voice overheard by the witnesses. In conclusion the narrator relates that the sailor subsequently recovers the orangutan, and that after Dupin explains what occurred to the Prefect of Police, the innocent bank clerk Le Bon is released.

Reading the grotesque. The word *grotesque* shows up repeatedly in "Murders in the Rue Morgue." Near the end, for example, Dupin calls the double murder "a *grotesquerie* in horror" (*Collected Stories*, p. 497). The word, meaning "bizarre or outlandishly distorted" hails from the Greek *cryptos* or "hidden"—as in cryptography, or hidden writing, the deciphering of which was one of Poe's favorite pastimes. Given Poe's longstanding interest in codes and how to read them, one better understands a key phrase in the story. Dupin had an "expectation of reading the entire riddle" a choice of words that is quite deliberate in that Dupin's most important clues literally come from reading—reading the newspaper, that is, and decoding the contradictory accounts of the uncomprehending witnesses. ("Rue Morgue," p. 489).

Writing at the dawn of a great expansion in print media, an age when penny newspapers glutted the reading public with their own *grotesqueries*, Poe offered his readers contrasting approaches to reading itself. On one hand, the narrator—an unnamed, faceless man who feels conventional bafflement and alarm on reading about the shocking crime—provides insight into the experience of the penny newspapers' average reader. Indeed, only in the mid-nineteenth century did an average reader emerge in America, as literacy rates rose for the first time to include a majority of the population.

In contrast with the everyman represented by the narrator, Dupin embodies an ideal reader whose "praeternatural" abilities go far beyond those of others ("Rue Morgue," p. 473). A hero for a newly literate general public—a public faced with potentially overwhelming and often grotesquely sensationalized printed matter—Dupin is skilled above all (as he repeatedly boasts) at sifting significant nuggets from an accumulation of seemingly trivial information. He is the consummate literary detective, emerged from a background shaped by scientific progress and by the industrial revolution's new mass-printing techniques. In command of skills to match his age, Dupin's abilities allow him to master the resulting flood of information, which also helps to explain the detective story's ongoing resonance for modern readers.

"The Murders in the Rue Morgue"

Sources and literary context. Murder and riddles have been staples of vivid storytelling going back to the Bible (the story of Cain and Abel; the riddle of Samson) and the ancient Greeks (for example, Sophocles's *Oedipus the King* [also in *Literature and Its Times*] features both murder and a riddle). Detection, too, has some literary precedent; scholars point to one of the tales from the *Arabian Nights* as an early example. In it three traveling princes are asked if they have seen a stolen camel. Inquiring if the animal was blind in one eye, missing a tooth, and lame in one leg, they are immediately arrested for seemingly guilty knowledge, since the stolen camel was indeed as they described. They explain that along the road they had been traveling, grass had been grazed on one side only, though it grew better on the other side; clumps of grass the size of a camel's tooth had been left standing; and marks had been made in the dust that indicated a dragging foot.

VIDOCQ: THE FIRST DETECTIVE

For the figure of the detective, Poe found his major source in the real-life French investigator Eugène François Vidocq (1775-1857), a thief-turned-detective whose spectacular career and widely read *Mémoires* (1828-29) made him an international celebrity. In 1810 Vidocq became the first professional detective when he founded the national French police force called the *Sûreté*, an important model for the Parisian *gendarmerie*. Fired in 1832 for allegedly engineering a theft, Vidocq went on to found the first private detective agency, which the government soon disbanded. His colorful life is thought to have inspired the character of the criminal mastermind Vautrin, who appears in several novels by French author Honoré de Balzac, including *Father Goriot* (1835), *Lost Illusions* (1837-43), and *A Harlot High and Low* (1843-47). In "The Murders in the Rue Morgue," Dupin refers to Vidocq by name, disparaging the famous investigator as "a good guesser" but one whose methods lack "educated thought" ("Rue Morgue," p. 487). More than any other individual, Vidocq points to the French role in the development of policing and the emergence of the professional detective. Along with the strong tradition of French interest in rationalism and science, these associations made the story's Paris setting seem both believable and appropriate to its American audience—despite Poe's lack of firsthand knowledge about the French capital.

In general Poe's short fiction was heavily influenced by the Gothic tradition of European literature, and Gothic features abound in "The Murders in the Rue Morgue" (two such features are a socially isolated, aristocratic hero and the gloomy mansion or castle he occupies). For the puzzle of the murder victim found in a locked room (an especially popular scenario for later detective stories), Poe may have drawn on a short story entitled "Passage in the Secret History of an Irish Countess" (1838), by the young Irish author J. Sheridan Le Fanu, subsequently known for his Gothic mystery novels. In Le Fanu's story, however, the solution of the locked-room mystery is discovered by accident, not through the deductive abilities of an investigator. Poe's "murderer" may have been inspired by an incident reported in the *Shrewsbury* (England) *Chronicle* in the summer of 1834. The newspaper recorded that, on entering her second-floor bedroom, a lady had been attacked by a baboon, which her husband then chased out the window. It was thought that the baboon, owned by performers in a traveling show, had been specially trained to burgle bedrooms by climbing up the outside wall and entering through the window, and that the lady had interrupted it during such a burglary. Poe may have been led to make the animal in his story into an orangutan by the display of a captive orangutan in Philadelphia in July 1839, which caused a sensation in that city at a time when Poe was living there.

Publication and impact. "The Murders in the Rue Morgue" first appeared in the April 1841 issue of *Graham's Magazine*, a monthly Philadelphia periodical that Poe edited from February 1841 to April 1842. The story was the first of several Poe stories that *Graham's* published, including "A Descent into the Maëlstrom" (May 1841) and "The Masque of the Red Death" (May 1842). Poe's stories helped make *Graham's* into the nation's leading monthly magazine during his tenure as editor, when its circulation soared from 5,000 to 40,000. Poe himself was becoming one of the nation's most popular authors by the early 1840s.

Included in a collection of stories published serially in 1843 under the title *Prose Romances*, "The Murders in the Rue Morgue" was singled out by a review in the *Pennsylvania Inquirer*. Praising Poe's originality, the anonymous reviewer wrote that the story "proves Mr Poe to be a man of genius. The inventive power exhibited is truly wonderful. At every step it whets the curiosity of the reader . . . with an inventive power and skill, of which we know no parallel" (*Pennsylvania Inquirer*, p. 2).

Poe followed up "The Murders in the Rue Morgue" with two more Dupin tales, "The Mystery of Marie Roget (1842) and "The Purloined Letter" (1845). But despite Dupin's popularity, the detective gave rise to no similar characters in literature until the 1850s, when the English novelist Charles Dickens published *Bleak House*, featuring the famous Inspector Bucket. In the 1860s, the French writer Emile Gaboriau created another literary detective, Monsieur Lecoq, in *L'Affaire Lerouge* (1866; *The Widow Lerouge*). A few decades later, England's Arthur Conan Doyle released the **Adventures of Sherlock Holmes** (1891-92; also in *Literature and Its Times*), which boosted the character of the detective to preeminence in the literary marketplace. A key to Sherlock Holmes's wide success was his affable and slower-witted companion Dr. Watson, who narrates the tales—a device inspired by the unnamed narrator in "The Murders in the Rue Morgue" and one copied by many later practitioners of the genre.

—Colin Wells

For More Information

Brand, Dana. *The Spectator and the City in Nineteenth-Century American Literature*. Cambridge: Cambridge University Press, 1991.

Emsley, Clive. *Policing and Its Context 1750-1870*. New York: Schocken, 1983.

Irwin, John. *The Mystery to a Solution: Poe, Borges, and the Analytic Detective Story*. Baltimore: Johns Hopkins University Press, 1994.

May, Charles E. *Edgar Allan Poe: A Study of the Short Fiction*. Boston: Twayne, 1991.

Mott, Frank Luther. *A History of American Magazines, 1885-1905*. Vol. 1. Cambridge, Mass.: Harvard University Press, 1957.

New York Herald. "Trial of Jackson for Murder." *Herald*, 23 September 1835, 2.

O'Brien, Frank M. *The Story of the Sun*. New York: D. Appleton, 1928.

Poe, Edgar Allan. "The Murders in the Rue Morgue." In *The Complete Stories*. New York: Knopf, 1992.

———. *Essays and Reviews*. New York: Library of America, 1984.

Price, Kenneth M., and Susan Belasco Smith, eds. *Periodical Literature in Nineteenth-Century America*. Charlottesville: University of Virginia Press, 1995.

Review of "The Murders in the Rue Morgue," by Edgar Allan Poe. *Pennsylvania Inquirer*, 26 July 1843, 2.

Reynolds, David S. *Beneath the American Renaissance: The Subversive Imagination in the Age of Emerson and Melville*. New York: Knopf, 1988.

My Ántonia

by
Willa Cather

> **THE LITERARY WORK**
>
> A novel set in Nebraska during the 1880s; published in 1918.
>
> **SYNOPSIS**
>
> The narrator, Jim Burden, recalls growing up on the Nebraska prairie through his memories of a Bohemian immigrant girl, Ántonia, who symbolizes for him the country, conditions, and adventure of his childhood years.

Willa Cather was born in 1873 and raised in Virginia, where her ancestors had farmed since the late eighteenth century. At the age of nine, she moved with her family to Red Cloud, Nebraska, to join her grandparents and uncle. At first shocked and disoriented by the change in environment, Cather soon grew to love the prairie landscape. She later recalled becoming particularly attached to many of her immigrant neighbors: "I liked them from the first and they made up for what I missed in the country. I particularly liked the old women, they understood my homesickness and were kind to me" (Cather in Bohlke, p. 10). Much of *My Ántonia* stems from Cather's childhood memories, a source she drew on only after becoming an established writer. Graduating from the University of Nebraska in 1895, Cather went to work in magazine publishing, then left it in 1912 to write three novels, including *O Pioneers!* (also in *Literature and Its Times*), which won her renown as a first-rate novelist. *My Ántonia* is Cather's fourth and, for many readers, her most successful work. Later Cather's novel *One of Ours* (1922) would win a Pulitzer Prize, and the novelist would continue turning out new titles until 1940. *My Ántonia* is considered her ultimate achievement, a novel that captures the essence of life on the Nebraska frontier.

Events in History at the Time the Novel Takes Place

The Homestead Act. Nebraska belonged to what was once known as The Great American Desert, which encompassed much of the land between the Missouri River and the Rocky Mountains. Early pioneers either settled in the fertile regions west of the Appalachian Mountains, or followed the Oregon Trail to the West Coast, bypassing the flat, arid, treeless center of the country. As the fertile regions and Far West became more thickly settled, pressure to open the treeless center to settlement mounted. The building of the transcontinental railroad (a cause championed from c. 1848 to its completion in 1869) fomented interest in settling the interior of the country. To this end, the Kansas-Nebraska Act of 1854 established the territories of Kansas and Nebraska; but the bill left unresolved the issue of extending slavery into these territories, a hotly debated question that would help propel the country into fighting a civil war.

Encouraging settlement, the Homestead Act of 1862 determined how public lands would be distributed. Any American citizen or citizen-in-

My Ántonia

Willa Cather

training could obtain 160 acres of land free of charge, if the claim was occupied and farmed for five years. Along with the Homestead Act, the construction of new railroads led to a boom in migration to Nebraska, particularly in the 1870s. Recognizing that their own success depended on vigorous agricultural production and a large rural population, railroad companies advertised Nebraska as a land of prosperity and abundance to future settlers in both the United States and abroad. The railroads themselves acted as land agents, selling portions of their enormous federal land grants at something of a premium because of the grants' proximity to a railroad. In fact, many settlers arrived to take up a claim under the Homestead Act only to find that the best lands were already owned by the railroads. Developed by railroad land companies, towns sat along railroad lines, well positioned in relation to the tracks and stations.

The promise of free land, combined with the active recruitment of the railroads, spurred immigration to the area, raising hopes but proving to be the undoing of many settlers who arrived in an inhospitable environment without farming skills or equipment. In the early years, there were no towns to draw on for provisions and no close neighbors to turn to for companionship or support. The way the land was measured off only added obstacles; it was surveyed in a square grid, without consideration for access to water or suitability of the soil for farming; all claims were the same size but not equally able to sustain an agricultural enterprise. So the 1870s saw first an explosive growth in population, then the financial ruin of many settlers. Several years of severe drought coupled with devastating swarms of grasshoppers destroyed multiple lives and livelihoods. Yet land speculators and railroad advertisers still promoted the region as a potential paradise. Future prosperity, said the experts, was assured. Increased rains showered the region in the late 1870s, part of a natural cycle following a drought—but Professor Samuel Aughey of the University of Nebraska did not attribute the increased rains to nature. Instead he formulated a theory that said the increased rainfall of the late 1870s was the result of new land being brought under cultivation. Wild prairie land, said the professor, shed water into creeks and rivers but cultivated land absorbed and stored rainwater, thereby increasing evaporation and precipitation over the region. It followed that more farms would lead to more rain and greater prosperity for all farmers. Embracing the theory, eager settlers occupied nearly every available fertile area in the 1880s. They flocked to the region with high hopes, hearkening to the promise of successful farming. The cycle of drought and disaster would repeat in the 1890s, but during the 1880s, when *My Ántonia* takes place, Nebraska enjoyed a period of confident prosperity and growth.

Immigrants to Nebraska. In *My Ántonia*, the town of Black Hawk is populated by many European immigrants: Swedes, Norwegians, Germans, the Russians Peter and Pavel, the Danish

---

U.S. CENSUS OF 1910—WHERE THE CZECHS LIVED

Of close to 540,000 Czechs in the United States, the largest populations lived in the following few states:

Illinois	124,225
Nebraska	50,680
Ohio	50,004
New York	47,400
Wisconsin	45,336

As the chart indicates, in moving to Nebraska the novel's Shimerda family were likely eventually to encounter at least some immigrants who came from the same home country.

laundry girls, the three Marys from Bohemia, and most importantly the Bohemian Shimerda family. This mix of backgrounds and cultures typifies Nebraskan towns in the 1870s and 1880s. The federal census for 1880 estimated that over half of Nebraska residents were foreign-born or had at least one foreign-born parent. Lured by the free land and promise of prosperity and driven from Europe by significant changes in its economy, an enormous influx of European immigrants entered America in the mid-to-late 1800s. Industrialization in Europe had led to the spread of large commercial farms and the decline of the small family farm, on top of which rises in population and life expectancy added pressure to already limited land resources. So people of modest means or no hope of land inheritance looked to the United States for opportunities. Those from Bohemia and Moravia were counted together as Czech immigrants. Mostly farmers at home, they set themselves up as homesteaders in Wisconsin, Iowa, Nebraska, and Texas, and settled in cities too, especially in Chicago, Illinois. (By the time the novel was written, Nebraska would be second only to Illinois in the number of Czechs living in the state.)

Most Czech immigrants were farmers back in Europe, but, like other European immigrants, the majority had never owned land. Certainly they did not have any experience that prepared them for farming on an unbroken prairie, where equipment, soils, climate, and viable crops were all unfamiliar. Establishing a prosperous farm took years of back- and heart-breaking labor, performed by various family members in an assortment of ways. The presence of "hired girls" and "Danish laundry girls" in *My Ántonia* indicates a demand for unskilled labor in the burgeoning United States, and for several sources of income on the part of immigrant families.

Settling the treeless plains. Pioneering met with a whole new set of obstacles when it moved beyond the wooded Ohio Valley to the treeless plains of the Midwest. While the very first settlers found some timber along rivers, the supply was quickly depleted. The majority of families faced building a home without trees for lumber or fuel. An alternative building material (used extensively in Nebraska) was the prairie itself, rectangular pieces of sod cut from the prairie and stacked like bricks. A special plow cut sections of sod 3 feet long and 1.5 feet wide, which, when stacked, resulted in extremely thick walls that kept "soddies" cool in the summer and warm in the winter. Some sod houses were extensions built outward from a hollowed out hill or creek bank; others were freestanding structures. When manufactured doors and windows became available, they could be installed in the walls, but the sod brick settled unevenly, making such an investment precarious. Invariably small, sod houses were also dark, dirty, and infested with insects and other vermin. Whitewashing the interior and hanging a cloth ceiling could alleviate the discomfort, but rather than settle for such improvements, most frontierspeople rushed to build log cabins or frame houses as soon as finances allowed.

> **BOHEMIA**
>
> The novel's Shimerda family hails from the present-day Czech Republic, which once included the ancient kingdom of Bohemia. Part of the Austrian Empire for 400 years and oppressed in terms of culture and religion, the region joined the revolutions sweeping Europe during the nineteenth century. At first the Czech National Revival movement agitated for just a reintroduction of Czech language and culture, but eventually the movement sought political independence from the Austrian Empire as well. Success would come at the end of World War I, with the triumphant declaration of an independent state of Czechs and Slovaks. *My Ántonia* ends in this year of triumph for the family's homeland, after which would come a turnaround in the country's fortune. Following a brief era of stability, Czech lands were occupied by the German Nazi regime (1939-45), then fell to Soviet control (1945-89). Only after the overthrow of the Soviet regime would the region regain independence, whereupon it divided into the Czech and Slovak Republics.

When the Shimerda family of *My Ántonia* arrives in Black Hawk, they live in the most primitive of sod dwellings, truly no more than a crude dugout. The fact that their house is the exception and their nearest neighbors live in a fairly large frame house indicates how well-established the town of Black Hawk has become by the 1880s. The Shimerdas begin life in Nebraska as early pioneers while most of their neighbors have had at least a generation to develop their homes and land. When Jim visits Ántonia at the end of the novel, her substantial frame farmhouse, surrounded by outbuildings, fields, and an orchard, testifies to how well she has closed the gap and prospered.

My Ántonia

Because of the lack of timber, settlers constantly had to seek alternative sources of fuel not only for construction but also for heat and cooking. Coal could be used in railroad towns, but most settlers found it prohibitively expensive. Buffalo or cow chips—dried dung—provided an expedient and effective fuel but an unpleasant one to handle. To make use of the most abundant material around, the settlers turned to various innovations in burning prairie hay, but hay burns too quickly and the heat it emits is too intense to make it a viable alternative. On the other hand, local produce—specifically, corncobs, cornstalks, and, when the prices were low, whole ears of corn—made a reasonable substitute for wood; even sunflowers were grown as a fuel source.

THE ORIGINS OF ARBOR DAY

Now a worldwide celebration to honor trees, Arbor Day began in the nearly treeless state of Nebraska. When Julius Sterling Morton and his wife Caroline moved from densely wooded Michigan onto the Nebraska prairie, they quickly realized the need for trees and shrubs. They therefore did an extensive planting of trees on their own property (now Arbor Lodge State Historical Park in Nebraska City), and Morton used his position as editor of the local newspaper to encourage his neighbors to do likewise. As a member of the state board of agriculture, he furthermore proposed that a special day be dedicated to the importance of trees. On the first Arbor Day, April 10, 1872, more than a million trees were planted. A second Arbor Day was celebrated in 1884, and in 1885 Nebraska set the day on April 22 (Morton's birthday), making it an annual state holiday. From Nebraska, Arbor Day spread to neighboring states, then nationwide, and eventually to other countries.

Women in the West. The Homesteading era marks a unique phase in the collective life of American women. Many pioneer women were hesitant partners in the project of homesteading, loyally following their husbands at great emotional peril to themselves. Setting up a home in a difficult, unfamiliar environment required not only grueling labor but also tremendous ingenuity. For some women, the challenges of housekeeping on the plains and prairie called out skills and creativity that never would have found expression in their former "civilized" lives (Myres, p. 146).

The West also offered unique financial and civil opportunities to women. In most states, women could and often did file for their own homesteads, with or without the partnership of a husband. Divorce laws were quite liberal and recognized as grounds for divorce adultery, prolonged absence, drunkenness, and cruelty. More women than men availed themselves of this legal liberality. Moreover, women in the West most often retained custody of their children and property, rights almost inevitably forfeited by women in the East who sought divorce. It was not uncommon to find single or unmarried women on the frontier for assorted reasons—widowhood, abandonment, or divorce.

Unlike their eastern counterparts, western women to a great extent were responsible for establishing community and civic connections. Resisting lonely isolation, women often turned the chores of housekeeping into occasions for social interaction, joining with other women to wash, sew, iron, or cook. Informal visiting and entertainment was common. Dances became a particularly important social outlet; generally they included all the members of a family and a community.

Children growing up on the frontier often found themselves pulled in opposite directions by their parents' wishes versus their own inclination. Many frontierspeople, particularly mothers, did not want their children to continue pioneering as adults, particularly not their daughters; they hoped to provide well enough for the children so that they could return "home" to the East. The need to procure education and instill culture in their offspring was a source of tremendous anxiety for parents. Meanwhile, the children, who were often put to work at an early age, enjoyed a sense of independence and precocious adulthood. "Children grew up pulled between two sets of influences, their identification with the land about them and their parents' dogged efforts to instill . . . traditions from another world" (West, p. 260). This dichotomy is illustrated in the character of Ántonia; both Jim and her cultured father fear that her work on the land will make her coarse, while Ántonia prides herself on being able to shoulder as much labor as her grown brother.

The Novel in Focus

The plot. The novel opens with a brief framing section in which the unnamed "author," traveling on a train, meets a friend from childhood,

Jim Burden, and reminisces with him about their growing up. The two agree that more than anything or anyone else, a Bohemian girl they both knew, "seemed to mean to us the country, the conditions, the whole adventure of our childhood" (Willa Cather, *My Ántonia*, p. xii). The author encourages Jim to write about this girl, Ántonia, and a few months later Jim appears with a manuscript in hand. The novel that follows is purportedly Jim's manuscript, which he says hasn't any form but is just a collection of memories.

Orphaned at ten, Jim Burden travels by train from his home in Virginia to live with his grandparents on their farm outside Black Hawk, Nebraska. Arriving on the same train is a Bohemian family, the Shimerdas, who turn out to be the Burdens' nearest neighbors. The eldest daughter, Ántonia, becomes Jim's good friend and also his student when Ántonia's father asks Jim to teach her English. The Shimerdas are destitute, having been bilked by a countryman, the unsavory Krajiek. They live in a small sod dugout and face the prospect of enormous labor ahead to establish a farm. Convinced that her son, Ambrosch, will find riches here, Mrs. Shimerda has harried her husband into immigrating. He seems hopelessly homesick and disheartened by the conditions of life in the new land.

Ántonia, on the other hand, blossoms on the prairie. She finds beauty in the land, and it brings her happiness. At their first meeting Ántonia enlists Jim to help her name the world around her in a new language: "While we snuggled down there out of the wind, she learned a score of words. She was quick, and very eager. We were so deep in the grass that we could see nothing but the blue sky over and the gold tree in front of us" (*My Ántonia*, p. 19). She and Jim spend a great deal of time together, exploring what is for both of them a new and adventure-filled environment. When they visit a prairie-dog town (a large area inhabited by a colony of prairie dogs), Jim kills a large rattlesnake; this event marks a turn in his relationship with Ántonia, who suddenly regards him with more respect. While visiting Mr. Shimerda's friends, the Russians Peter and Pavel, the children hear the chilling story of why Peter and Pavel were forced to flee Russia: driving a bride and groom home through the winter woods, they sacrificed the pair to a pack of pursuing wolves in order to save their own lives.

Among Jim's other close friends are farm hands hired by his grandfather, Otto and Jake. At Christmastime they bring an evergreen tree (a

Sketch by W. T. Benda, illustrating a scene from *My Ántonia*.

rarity in Nebraska) home as a special treat for Jim. On Christmas Day Mr. Shimerda pays a visit to thank Jim Burden's family for their help and kindness. He remains in the warm kitchen all afternoon. Jim feels a rush of empathy for this lonely, cultured man: "When his deep-seeing eyes rested on me, I felt as if he were looking far ahead into the future for me, down the road I would have to travel" (*My Ántonia*, p. 57). New Year's Day starts with the horrifying news that Mr. Shimerda has killed himself. With the Burdens' help, he is buried at a corner of the Shimerda property that will eventually become a crossroads, with the roads built around the grave in respect for its occupant.

Her father's death forces Ántonia to take on a tremendous share of the farm work. She no longer has time for English lessons or play. Jim worries that in working like a man, the education and appreciation for higher culture instilled in Ántonia by her father will be lost on her. But Ántonia prides herself on being able to work as hard as her brother and help provide for her family.

Jim's grandparents decide that they have grown too old to continue working their farm so they move into the town of Black Hawk. In town, Jim becomes great friends with the family next door, the Harlings. At Mrs. Burden's suggestion, Mrs. Harling hires Ántonia as the family's cook. The position allows her to escape the harsh and grasping control of her brother and mother, and become part of a nurturing environment. Ántonia becomes a beloved member of the Harling family. Of course, Jim is glad to have her close by once more. "Every morning before I was up, I could hear Tony [Ántonia] singing in the garden rows. After the apple and cherry trees broke into bloom, we ran about under them, hunting for new nests, throwing clods at each other, and playing hide-and seek" (*My Ántonia*, p. 124).

The domestic situation remains happy until the Vannis's dancing tent comes to town for the summer. Many of the "hired girls" like Ántonia go regularly to the dancing tent to socialize with the boys in town. Their behavior is considered promiscuous and dangerous. Jim likes to go dancing too, but when he learns that his presence at the tent worries his grandmother, he promises to stay away. Mrs. Harling forbids Ántonia to go to the dances because of the reputation she is gaining in town. Angered and unwilling to give up her freedom, Ántonia quits. Still a hired girl, she goes to work in the home of Wick Cutter, an underhanded moneylender, and his wife.

Jim graduates from high school with high honors, and Ántonia feels very proud for her friend. Together with two other hired girls, Tiny Soderball and Lena Lingard, Jim and Ántonia go on a celebratory picnic on the prairie. As the sun sets, its light catches and magnifies spectacularly the image of a plow on the horizon.

Ántonia suspects that Wick Cutter may have dishonorable designs on her when he and his wife leave on a trip and insist that Ántonia stay in the house alone. To forestall trouble, Jim's mother suggests that her son stay there in Ántonia's place. On Jim's third night at the Cutter house, Wick comes home unexpectedly, apparently intending to rape Ántonia. Finding Jim in her bed, Cutter beats him up. Ántonia leaves the Cutters' home, but her friendship with Jim suffers. He blames her for involving him in the sordid business and resolves to avoid her thereafter.

In the fall Jim leaves for Lincoln, the main city in Nebraska, to attend the university. He studies classics under his tutor, Gaston Cleric, who inspires Jim to pursue an advanced degree. Lena Lingard, who has established a successful dressmaking business in Lincoln, visits Jim at school. They begin a relationship. Gaston Cleric worries that Jim will be distracted from his studies and unwilling to follow Cleric to Harvard University in Massachusetts, so he warns Jim to stay away from Lena. Accompanying Cleric, Jim enters Harvard Law School.

Later Jim learns of Ántonia's life while he has been at school. Engaged to a railroad worker named Larry Donovan, she followed him to Denver. He abandoned her there, whereupon she returned to Black Hawk pregnant and shamed. Unsympathetic, Jim feels disappointed in Ántonia for having let herself be tricked by Donovan and then becoming an object of pity in the town. One of the other hired girls, Tiny Soderball, has had a more successful career, learns Jim. She went out west and became wealthy catering to mining camps in Alaska. To find out more about Ántonia, Jim visits the Widow Steavens, who has nothing but empathy for the girl. Her account of Ántonia's joy in her baby softens Jim's heart, and the next day he visits the Shimerdas. Jim and Ántonia rekindle their friendship. He thinks of her often, says Jim, more than of anyone else in Black Hawk. They will always be important in each other's lives, she replies. He promises to visit her.

Twenty years pass before Jim makes good on that promise. A lawyer for a railroad company, he lives in New York and is unhappily married to a woman who shares none of his sensibilities. On a trip in San Francisco, Jim sees Tiny Soderball and Lena Lingard. Jim takes Lena up on her suggestion that he go see Ántonia, who is now married to Anton Cuzak and has many children. His visit to the Cuzak farm is a poignant one. A fulfilled woman, Ántonia is the mother of a large, loving family, the wife of a good man, and the proud proprietress of a beautiful farm. Jim leaves over the road that he and Ántonia first took into Black Hawk, feeling saddened by the changes he notices in the town. But he takes heart from the sight of the prairie and from his bond with Ántonia: "Whatever we had missed, we possessed together the precious, the incommunicable past" (*My Ántonia*, p. 360).

Moving east to understand the West. The structure of *My Ántonia* shows narrator Jim Burden taking progressively further steps away from his childhood Nebraska home and meanwhile becoming emotionally more attached to his childhood memories of the place. With his physical removal away from the Midwest come advances in his education, sophistication, and culture; the East, in comparison to the newly settled West, offers him contact with art and literature and European culture in general. However, Jim credits his western upbringing with giving him the capacity to appreciate culture.

Jim's double-edged progression—physical removal east and emotional attachment to his western home—parallels the real-life development of

Willa Cather. Like Jim, she first attended the university in Lincoln, Nebraska, where she was exposed to elements of culture, then moved east, traveled in Europe, and settled in New York City. Like him too, Cather felt a lifelong spiritual pull from the frontier, a need to preserve her experience there. For both Jim, Cather, and *My Ántonia* stands as the expression of that impulse; while she has authored the novel, he authors the manuscript referred to in the frame story, which in fact forms the heart of the novel. Interestingly, as the nineteenth century progressed, the nation as a whole began to feel a similar impulse to interpret and preserve the pioneer epoch in America's history. Painters rushed to create grandiose canvasses depicting the monumental scenery of the West, ethnographers sought to codify Indian languages and folkways, and the new technology of photography was employed to fix a permanent record of an era as it passed.

Before leaving Black Hawk for the university, Jim feels increasingly disgruntled by the town's narrowness: "On starlight nights I used to pace up and down those long, cold streets, scowling at the little, sleeping houses on either side.... The life that went on in them seemed to me made up of evasions and negations; shifts to save cooking, to save washing and cleaning, devices to propitiate the tongue of gossip. This guarded mode of existence was like living under a tyranny" (*My Ántonia*, p. 212). At the university he experiences an intellectual awakening in studying Greek and Latin. There is an intriguing juxtaposition of old and new (in Jim's new life, he reads old texts; in his old life, he lived in a new settlement).

Jim is surprised to find that in reading the most ancient cultural antecedents, his experience of the world's newest frontier culture helps his understanding: "When one first enters that world [of ideas] everything else fades for a time, and all that went before is as if it had not been. Yet I found curious survivals; some of the figures of my old life seemed to be waiting for me in the new" (*My Ántonia*, p. 250). While studying Virgil Jim thinks of the hired girls in Black Hawk and realizes, "if there were no girls like them in the world, there would be no poetry. I understood that clearly, for the first time" (*My Ántonia*, p. 173). The reverse is true as well—the new life enlightens the old. In reading *Georgics* by the ancient Virgil, Jim discovers a vocabulary that expresses his own attachment to the landscape of his childhood when a professor explains that *patria* means "not a nation or even a province, but the little rural neighborhood on the Mincio where the poet was born" (*My Ántonia*, p. 256).

In fact, the responses of various characters in the novel and of Cather herself to the disappearing frontier typify various responses in the United States as a whole at the time. Jim Burden's attachment becomes an increasingly nostalgic longing for his past. He is disappointed in returning to Black Hawk to find strangers occupying his familiar haunts; only when he walks out onto the prairie can he regain his love for it, looking not to the present or future, but taking comfort in having shared a precious past here with Ántonia. Ántonia herself demonstrates a second response. Joyously connected to the land in her childhood, she remains firmly rooted in place, and, unlike Jim, is clearly happier and more comfortable in her adult life than in her childhood. She belongs to the land in the present, not just in memory. Cather shares something with both characters. Like Jim, she is now an outsider, but she remains connected to the land in the present as well. The novel itself is perhaps the strongest testament to her sense of *patria*.

This concept of allegiance to and love for the landscape of one's childhood influenced certain tenets to which Cather adhered in writing fiction. On her mind was advice from an important literary mentor, Sarah Orne Jewett: "one must know the world *so well* before one can know the parish" (*My Ántonia*, p. xv). Cather heeded this advice, gaining education and experience of the world in preparation for giving voice to her native materials. "When a writer once begins to work with his own material," Cather would later write, "he finds that he need have little to do with literary devices. He comes to depend on something else—the thing by which our feet find the road home on a dark night, accounting of themselves for roots and stones which we had never noticed by day" (Cather in Robinson, p. 214). Her regular trips back to Nebraska were not only a direct source of material for her writing, but also a more general source of inspiration and renewal. "I do get freshened up by coming out here. I like to go back to my home town, Red Cloud, and get out among the folk who like me for myself, who don't know and don't care a thing about my books" (Cather in Bennett, p. 77). *My Ántonia*, which she and many of her readers felt was her best work, attests to Cather's sense of *patria* and its impact on her art.

Sources. Cather drew richly and heavily on her own life for *My Ántonia*. Nearly every character in the novel has a real-life counterpart in Cather's childhood. Convinced that writers had the

My Ántonia

materials for their work gathered in them by the age of 15, Cather pinpointed the source of hers: "The ideas for all my novels have come from things that happened around Red Cloud when I was a child" (Cather in Bennett, p. 60). For *My Ántonia*, Cather perhaps drew more immediate inspiration from her contact with Red Cloud than for some of her other novels. In 1917 Cather made several visits back to Nebraska, first to receive an honorary doctorate from the University of Nebraska and then for an extended stay because of her mother's long illness. Cather kept house and cared for a family of eight during this time: "On the whole . . . she rather enjoyed it. She thought she'd got the secret of good pastry at last and, one thing was certain, she'd never be intimidated by a kitchen range again" (Robinson, p. 210). This was the year Cather became reacquainted with her childhood friend, Annie Sadilek, a Bohemian immigrant girl. Just as Jim Burden visited Ántonia, Cather visited Annie on her lovely farm full of contented children and rejoiced in her happiness. "Annie became for her . . . the embodiment of all her feelings about the early years and the immigrants she had known on the prairie" (Robinson, p. 212).

While Cather acknowledged the origins of her inspiration, she insisted that in all of her books only one character was meant to be drawn as a portrait; all else was drawn from the emotions evoked by her childhood contacts. The one character was Mrs. Harling, a tribute to the real-life Mrs. Miner, Cather's next door neighbor in Red Cloud. Upon hearing of her death "the resolve came over me that I would put her into that book as nearly drawn from life as I could do it" (Cather in Bennett, p. 60). The Miner daughters, to whom Cather dedicated the novel, recognized and loved its portrayal of their mother. As for other hometown folk, Cather worried about how the book would be received in Red Cloud. She did not want her readers to seek out real-life counterparts for her characters and decide whether she had gotten them right; she wanted them to understand "that a story was not made out of legs and arms and faces of an author's friends and acquaintances, but out of an emotion or an excitement" (Robinson, p. 213).

Events in History at the Time the Novel Was Written

Thirty years later—the frontier vanishes. Over the course of the nineteenth century a staggering amount of United States territory was explored, settled, and frequently exploited or devastated. From the very first settlers, Americans had exuberantly embraced the idea that the wilderness must be subdued, and settlement means progress. As the years passed, advances in transportation along with greater wealth and leisure time led to more and more Americans traveling within their own country. People suddenly saw both the wonders of progress and the devastation it wrought. From the 1840s, they had considered it their manifest destiny (the idea that the continued expansion of the United States was inevitable) to "civilize" America from "sea to shining sea," but now they began to question the cost of that project, and to experience the first impulses toward preservation. Many readers celebrated Cather's books as preserving a pioneer past that had already vanished by the time she wrote the novel.

In documenting the nineteenth-century response to dwindling wilderness, Lee Clark Mitchell writes, "America had been imagined from the beginning . . . as a vacant land awaiting the starter's gun of history" (Mitchell, p. 6). As it became clear that vacant land was not a limitless resource, Americans became anxious to understand its meaning in the country's development. In 1893 few years after Cather's novel takes place, historian Fredrick Jackson Turner argued that "the existence of an area of free land, its continuous recession, and the advance of American settlement westward, explain American development" (Turner, p. 1). At the same time, Turner declared that the 1890 census showed that the frontier no longer existed. If all that was essentially American came from the frontier, the closing of the frontier was cause for concern. Certainly it was cause for recording and interpreting the pioneer past, an endeavor in which Americans took increasing interest. The belief was that the effort would enable them to maintain contact with the nation's origins. Not surprisingly, the interest came almost exclusively from Easterners long settled in their part of America, the region furthest removed from its past.

Nebraska and Red Cloud 30 years later. In the year that Cather and her family arrived in Red Cloud, the *Lincoln State Journal* predicted great things for the town's future: "Red Cloud is destined to be one of the foremost cities in Nebraska . . . and in years not distant will be the leading town along the southern border of the state" (Bennett, p. 94). This prediction was not borne out because, at the beginning of the twentieth century, the railroad company that built the town (in 1878) shifted its main line 40 miles north to Hastings. The population steadily dwindled; even now the town is smaller than when Cather lived there. Famous because of her, it boasts as its main attractions the historical sites relating to Cather. Its development did not, fortunately for Cather, keep pace with that in much of the United States, so when she returned on her regular visits, she found the town remarkably unchanged from the Red Cloud she knew as a child.

The same could not be said about the Midwest in general. Cather published *My Ántonia* within a few years of Sinclair Lewis's scathing satires of the provinciality and mediocrity of midwestern life (see ***Babbitt***, also in *Literature and Its Times*). The two writers knew each other and admired each other's work (when Lewis won the Nobel Prize for Literature in 1930, he said publicly that Willa Cather should have won). Not uncritical of the region, Cather shared many of Lewis's feelings about the contemporary Midwest. In a 1921 address to the Fine Arts Society in Omaha, Nebraska, she vented her dissatisfaction:

> At present in the west there seems to be an idea that we all must be like somebody else, as much as if we had all been cast in the same mold. We wear exactly similar clothes, drive the same make of car, live in the same part of town, in the same style of house. It's deadly! . . . New things are always ugly. . . . An old house built in miserable taste is more beautiful than a new house built and furnished in correct taste. The beauty lies in the associations that cluster around it, the way in which the house has fitted itself to the people.
> (Cather in Bennett, p. 147)

Cather and modernism. Willa Cather never aligned herself with any particular literary movement or school of thought, and her works are not easily classifiable. Nevertheless, Cather's work was almost certainly affected and informed by the literary movements of the first several decades of the twentieth century, most importantly modernism and primitivism. Modernism is characterized by experimentation with voice, structure, and form. Modernist works often express a sense of disillusionment with modern society, the fragmentation and mechanization of which can lead to a feeling of pessimism or despair. While modernism reached its fullest flowering in the post-World War I years, the stirrings of dissatisfaction and striving to break with traditional forms began earlier. Cather might not have called herself a modernist, but she certainly intended to be an innovator in narrative structure and voice. The framing device, inconsistent chronology, and plotting of *My Ántonia* all break with novelistic convention. She herself described the novel's structure as "just the other side of the rug, the pattern that is supposed not to count in a story. In it there is no love affair, no courtship, no marriage, no broken heart, no struggle for success. I knew I'd ruin my material if I put it in the usual fictional pattern. I just used it the way I thought absolutely true" (Cather in Bennett, p. 210).

One form of modernist criticism of contemporary society was primitivism, a belief that pre-industrialized societies still in close contact with nature were more innocent and fostered higher human values than modern corrupt societies. Many artists became fascinated with depicting primitive cultures or idealizing the cultural past. If, as Turner determined, the frontier had indeed vanished by 1890, then it no longer existed by the time Cather wrote her novel. However, one cannot necessarily number Cather among those who idealized the American frontier; her novel espouses the values of independence, hard work, family loyalty, and an attachment to nature that she herself saw fostered there. The radically different life paths she creates for the dual protagonists of *My Ántonia* does, however, indicate her allegiance to frontier ideals: Ántonia's life culminates in happiness on a prosperous farm and in the embrace of a devoted family, while Jim ends up in a childless and loveless marriage, his greatest passion and mode of expression being his preoccupation with his own past.

Reviews. Like literary creation, literary criticism experienced a split between an established order and agitation for a new set of standards around the time *My Ántonia* was published. The old order still appreciated traditional forms and well-crafted plots, while younger critics and writers hungered for innovation, fresh voices, and authentically American material. Not surprisingly Cather's novel was overlooked, misunderstood, or only blandly praised in many of the mainstream publications. The Chicago *Daily News* told its readers "if you want to brush away stiff-jointed literary puppets and live for a while with real people, you will read and give thanks for *My Ántonia*" (Robinson, p. 213). However, a few critics (Randolph Bourne, H. L. Mencken, and Carl Van Doren) deemed *My Ántonia* an unqualified success. H. L. Mencken wrote in the *Smart Set* that Cather "has got such a grip upon her materials—upon the people she sets before us and the background she displays behind them—-that they both take on an extraordinary reality. I know of no novel that makes the remote folk of the western prairies more real than *My Ántonia* makes them, and I know of none that makes them seem better worth knowing" (Mencken in Schroeter, p. 9). First in the *Nation* and later in the book *Contemporary American Novelists*, Carl van Doren celebrates the qualities that set Cather's work apart from local colorists or regionalists: "Narrow as Miss Cather's scene may be, she fills it with a spaciousness and candor of personality that quite transcends the gnarled eccentricity and timid inhibitions of the local colorists. Passion blows through her chosen characters like a free, wholesome, if often devastating wind" (Van Doren in Schroeter, p. 14). Perhaps Cather herself best understood the import of the novel in preserving not only a slice of an earlier era but also a quintessential response to its passing; 20 years after publication, she reflected, "The best thing I've done is *My Ántonia*. I feel I've made a contribution to American letters with that book" (Cather in Bennett, p. 203).

—Catharine C. Riggs

For More Information

Bennett, Mildred R. *The World of Willa Cather*. New York: Dodd, Mead, 1951.

Bohlke, L. Brent. *Willa Cather in Person: Interviews, Speeches*, and Letters. Lincoln: University of Nebraska Press, 1986.

Cather, Willa. *My Ántonia*. Lincoln: University of Nebraska Press, 1994.

Luebke, Frederick C. *Nebraska: An Illustrated History*. Lincoln: University of Nebraska Press, 1995.

Mitchell, Lee Clark. *Witnesses to a Vanishing America*. Princeton, N.J.: Princeton University Press, 1981.

Myres, Sandra L. *Westering Women and the Frontier Experience 1800-1915*. Albuquerque: University of New Mexico Press, 1982.

Olson, James C., and Ronald C. Naugle. *History of Nebraska*. Lincoln: University of Nebraska Press, 1997.

Riley, Glenda. *The Female Frontier: A Comparative View of Women on the Prairie and the Plains*. Lawrence: University of Kansas Press, 1988.

Robinson, Phyllis C. *Willa: The Life of Willa Cather*. New York: Doubleday, 1983.

Schroeter, James, ed. *Willa Cather and Her Critics*. Ithaca, New York: Cornell University Press, 1967.

Turner, Frederick Jackson. *The Frontier in American History*. Tucson: The University of Arizona Press, 1986.

West, Elliot. *Growing Up with the Country: Childhood on the Far Western Frontier*. Albuquerque: University of New Mexico Press, 1989.

"My Last Duchess" and Other Poems

by
Robert Browning

Born in Camberwell, London, in 1812, Robert Browning was the son of a bank clerk, a learned man who kept an extensive library. Browning attended a boarding school near Camberwell as a boy, and later attended the University of London for a time. However, he preferred to pursue his education at home. Aside from being tutored in subjects such as foreign languages, music, boxing, and riding, Browning read widely. His diverse interests provided him with a store of knowledge from which he drew when composing his poems. In 1833 Browning published his first poem, *Pauline*, anonymously: the work failed to sell and went virtually unnoticed by critics. Browning took trips to Russia in 1834 and Italy in 1837, from which he would draw for future poems. *Pauline* was followed by *Paracelsus* (1835); published at Browning's father's expense, it too was ignored, and *Sordello* (1840) was a critical failure that actually impeded Browning's poetic reputation. Browning briefly experimented with writing plays, but soon abandoned the stage, though his fascination with the dramatic monologue appears to date from that time. Between 1841 and 1846, Browning produced an eight-volume series of poetic pamphlets, *Bells and Pomegranates*. In the series was a collection of monologues that included "My Last Duchess"; also in the series was *Dramatic Romances and Lyrics* (1845), which contained the companion poems "Meeting at Night" and "Parting at Morning." Browning undertook a correspondence with the poet Elizabeth Barrett, whom he married a year later. The couple

> **THE LITERARY WORK**
>
> Four poems—one set in sixteenth-century Italy, three set in an unspecified time and place; published in 1842, in 1846, and one in 1864 (the middle two originally published together as one poem, "Night and Morning").
>
> **SYNOPSIS**
>
> In "My Last Duchess," an Italian duke relates the history of his previous marriage to an emissary; in "Meeting at Night" and "Parting at Morning," a man trysts with his lover by night and leaves her in the morning; in "Prospice," a male speaker envisions his death and the afterlife.

afterwards emigrated from England to Italy, where Browning sets "My Last Duchess."

Events in History at the Time of the Poems

Victorians and the past. The Victorian interest in the past found its most dramatic expression in the growing fascination with medievalism, which can be traced back to the late 1700s. Scholars, antiquarians, and artists of the Romantic period fell increasingly under the spell of the Middle Ages, taking its artifacts, architecture, legends, and values to heart. As early as the eighteenth century, medieval people came to be re-

"My Last Duchess"

Robert Browning

garded by some artists and intellectuals as more vital, uncorrupted, and closer to nature than their modern counterparts, a belief that persisted well into the nineteenth century and the onset of the Victorian Age. As rapidly advancing technology transformed England from a primarily agricultural nation into a major industrial power, many Victorians turned nostalgically to contemplation of the medieval world for a sense of harmony and stability that eluded them in the present. The literature of the times often reflected authors' sympathy with the medieval period, from the historical novels of Sir Walter Scott to the Arthurian poems of Lord Tennyson and William Morris. Ever an original, Robert Browning was *not* among the poets who became enamored of medieval subjects and legends. One literary scholar observes that, "In an age when the poets were mostly interested in escaping to the past . . . , Browning almost alone wrote of contemporary ideas and contemporary life, often in colloquial and contemporary phrase" (DeVane, p. 282). Another scholar argues that Browning did a brilliant job of evoking earlier periods than his own, but for him, the qualities of vigor, variety, sweeping change, and unfettered imagination "belong[ed] primarily to the Renaissance and later periods"; moreover, Browning's poems set in the past evinced an interest in "a world of history more than a world of myth or literary legend" (Taylor in Peterson, pp. 58, 61). His duke in "My Last Duchess" seems representative of a particular Renaissance type, with values peculiar to that specific time period and society, rather than as a hero of timeless legend. He also bears a striking resemblance to a particular duke.

The real duke of Ferrara. Although Browning's arrogant, autocratic duke in "My Last Duchess" is an original creation in many respects, the poet drew at least in part on his knowledge of the powerful Este family, who ruled Ferrara, a duchy in northern Italy. Browning did not actually visit Ferrara when he traveled through Italy in June 1838, but he had read extensively on its history while composing his poem, *Sordello*. At the same time, Browning was engaged in reviewing R. H. Wilde's *Conjectures and Researches concerning the Love Madness and Imprisonment of Torquato Tasso*; Browning's research into the life of Tasso—an Italian poet—uncovered the figure of Alfonso II, fifth and last duke of Ferrara, who was Tasso's patron and the one who consigned him to a mental hospital after the poet experienced delusions and exhibited violent behavior.

Alfonso II (1533-1597) was the son of Ercole II and Renee of France. As the scion of a noble family and the heir to a dukedom, Alfonso received an extensive literary and social education, mastering such languages as Latin and French and devoting himself to courtly pursuits like hunting, fighting in tourneys, and attending plays and festivals. Owing to his French ancestry, Alfonso was sympathetic to France as a nation. He defied his father—who wanted his duchy Ferrara to remain neutral—by fighting beside his French cousin, Henry II, in a war against Charles V, emperor of the Holy Roman Empire. With the help of Cosimo I de Medici, Duke of Tuscany, the father, Ercole II managed to negotiate a peace with the emperor that included restoration of confiscated Ferrara lands. To strengthen the alliance between the Este and the de Medici families, Alfonso, then 25 years old, entered into an arranged marriage with Cosimo's 14-year-old daughter, Lucrezia de Medici, in 1558. Three days after the wedding, Alfonso returned to France, where he continued to fight in Henry II's wars.

After the death of Ercole II in 1559, Alfonso returned to Ferrara to assume his responsibilities as duke. In February 1560, Alfonso II sent for his wife—described as a serious, devout girl of not much education—to join him. Extensive details of their marriage are not known but Lucrezia, then 17, died on April 21, 1561. There were suspicions—which remained unproven—that she had been poisoned. Soon after Lucrezia's death, Alfonso began negotiating with Ferdinand, Count of Tyrol and son of Emperor Ferdinand I of Austria, for the hand of the emperor's daughter, Barbara. Ferdinand used an envoy—Nikolaus Madriz of Innsbruk—to negotiate the match to its successful conclusion. The marriage between Alfonso II and Barbara of Austria took place in 1565. Like her predecessor, Barbara died young—in 1572—and, like the duke's first marriage, his second was without issue. Alfonso then married Margherita Gonzaga in 1579 but she too bore him no children. Although Alfonso tried to have his illegitimate cousin Cesare named as his successor, his efforts were ultimately unsuccessful, in large part because of a papal bull (decree) in 1567 that prevented the investiture of illegitimate heirs with church lands. With the death of Alfonso II, the male line of the House of Este in Ferrara became extinct and the duchy reverted to the possession of the Church. The court of Ferrara—among the most brilliant in Italy for 200 years—fell into eclipse.

Browning did not name the duke and duchess in the first published version of his poem—it was not until 1849 that he added the subtitled "Ferrara" to "My Last Duchess." But the situation of the speaker negotiating for a new bride through a count's envoy encourages identification with the story of Alphonso II and Lucrezia de Medici. Literary scholar William Clyde DeVane observes, "In almost every respect Alfonso II meets the requirements of Browning's Duke. He was a typical Renaissance grandee: he came of the proud Este family, rulers in Italy for hundreds of years, not merchants and upstarts like the Medici; he was cold and egotistical, vengeful and extremely possessive; and a patron of the arts, painting, music, and literature" (DeVane, p. 108). While it is unclear how closely Browning's duchess resembles Lucrezia de Medici, the circumstances surrounding both women's deaths remain mysterious. Asked about his duchess's fate, Browning refused to commit himself to a definitive explanation. The poem's lines in which the duke "gave commands; / Then all smiles stopped together" prompted a question to Browning about what happened to her (Browning, *Poetry*, "My Last Duchess," line 46). In response, the poet first said that "the commands were that she should be put to death," then almost immediately added, "or he might have had her shut up in a convent" (Browning in DeVane, p. 109).

Public vs. private life. Despite their brevity, Browning's companion poems "Meeting at Night" and "Parting at Morning"—originally published together in 1845 as one poem "Night and Morning"—comment on the middle-class Victorian drive toward separate public and private lives.

ART AND PATRONAGE

Renaissance princes were often patrons of the arts and the Estes of Ferrara were no exception, their collection of adornments in an already splendid court benefitting from their generous support of talented painters and poets. Alfonso I, third duke of Ferrara and grandfather to Alfonso II, was a patron to several painters, including Dosso Dossi, Giovanni Bellini, Titian, and Raphael. In the last case, the relationship between patron and artist did not always run smoothly. At one point, Raphael promised to paint a picture for Alfonso I (*A Triumph of the Bacchus in India*), but Raphael already had so many commissions in Rome that he never even started it. Three years later, the angry duke wrote to the Ferrara ambassador in Rome:

> We wish you to find him and tell him . . . that it is now three years since he has given us only words; and that this is not the way to treat men of our rank; and that, if he does not fulfill his promise toward us, we shall make him know that he has not done well to deceive us. And then, as though from yourself, you can tell him that he had better take care not to provoke our hatred, instead of the love we bear him; for as, if he keeps his promise, he can hope for our support, so on the contrary, if he does not, he can expect one day to get what he will not like.
> (Alfonso I in Prescott, p. 236)

In Browning's poem, the duke of Ferrara is a patron to two artists: monastic painter Fra Pandolf, who paints the portrait of the last duchess, and the sculptor Claus of Innsbruck, who crafted a statue of Neptune taming a seahorse. Both artists are imaginary, although a painter named Giovanni Antonio Pandolfi was employed by the Este family to paint a portrait of Alfonso II's sister in 1570, and classical subjects in sculpture—such as Neptune taming a sea horse—were typical of the period.

They are indeed something of a parody of this desire. In general, the middle class created a mythology of individual spheres of existence consisting of the world of work, duty, and service—dominated by men—and the world of home and domestic concerns (and love), tradi-

"My Last Duchess"

tionally the province of women. In a famous 1865 lecture, the Victorian intellectual John Ruskin described, albeit from a very conservative point of view, gender roles prescribed for middle-class couples:

> The man's power is active, progressive, defensive. He is eminently the doer, the creator, the discoverer, the defender. His intellect is for speculation and invention; his energy for adventure, for war, and for conquest whenever war is just, whenever conquest is necessary. But the woman's power is for rule, not for battle—and her intellect is not for invention or creation, but for sweet ordering, arrangement, and decision. . . . The man, in his rough work in the open world, must encounter all peril and trial. . . . But he guards the woman from all this, within his house, as ruled by her, unless she herself has sought it, need enter no danger, no temptation, no cause of error or offence. This is the true nature of home—it is the place of Peace; the shelter, not only from all injury, but from all terror, doubt, and division.
> (Ruskin in Mitchell, p. 266)

According to this broadly painted conception, middle-class men were considered the breadwinners and warriors of public life, and women were often designated the guardians of private life. How far these myths extended into actual lives or even into a general belief system is unclear, but one feminine ideal of the mid-nineteenth century was the Angel in the House, a term derived from the title of a popular Victorian poem by Coventry Patmore. According to the poem (as often parodied as it was honored), this self-sacrificing domestic saint devoted herself entirely to the affairs of her household, tended to the needs of her husband and children, and provided through her own pure morals an example of Christian virtues in action. This Angel in the House never questioned her position nor attempted to prevent the men in her family from assuming their own places in the outside world. Some moralists of the day, such as Baldwin Brown, praised "women whose hearts are an unfailing fountain of courage and inspiration to the hard-pressed man . . . and who send forth husband or brother each morning with new strength for his conflict, armed, as the lady armed her knight of old, with a shield which he may not stain in any unseemly conflicts, and a sword which he dares only use against the enemies of truth, righteousness, and God" (Baldwin in Houghton, pp. 351-352). The Angel in the House also respected the boundary between public and private life: she kept the softer emotions, especially love, confined to the home so that the man in the family could perform his work in the world without distractions. Of course, this figure was in large part a projection of somewhat sappy wishful thinking, and many Victorians, Browning included, recognized the menacing patriarchal power lurking behind the adoration.

In Browning's companion poems, the heady bliss of a private romantic encounter—as two lovers tryst in a farmhouse, their "two hearts beating each to each!" (Browning, *Poetry*, "Meeting at Night," line 12)—gives way to a presumably inevitable separation as the sun rises and the male lover recalls "the need of a world of men for me" (Browning, *Poetry*, "Parting at Morning," line 4). Many years after these poems appeared in print, Browning was asked if the speaker was a woman lamenting the departure of her lover or else the loss of her purity. Browning replied, "Neither: it is *his* confession of how fleeting is the belief (implied in the first part) that such raptures are self-sufficient and enduring—as for the time they appear" (Browning in DeVane, p. 178). Browning thus casts these poems as existential laments, resisting the comfortable gender politics by which they often were (and are) read.

FROM "THE ANGEL IN THE HOUSE" BY COVENTRY PATMORE

Becoming one of the best-selling poems in Victorian England, "The Angel in the House" (1854-56) concerns a husband's intense love for his wife, describing their courtship and marriage. The poem reveals little about the nature of Victorian home life but fully expresses the feminine ideal of woman being queen of the domestic sphere, a separate world in which she "exercise[d] power in secret and subtle ways" (Hellerstein, et al, p. 134).

> Why, having won her, do I woo? . . .
>   Because, although in act and word
> As lowly as a wife can be,
>   Her manners, when they call me lord,
>   Remind me 'tis by courtesy . . .
> Because, though free of the outer court
>   I am, this Temple keeps its shrine
> Sacred to Heaven; because, in short,
>   She's not and never can be mine.
> (Patmore in Hellerstein, pp. 139-40)

Religious doubt and certainty. At the start of the Victorian Age, many Dissenting Christians in England, that is, many of those who dissented from the mainstream Anglican Church, tended towards a literal reading of the Bible. They considered the Scriptures infallible and free of error; challenging this belief at the time was geological evidence and linguistic criticism, developed especially in Germany, which traced changes and inconsistencies in key texts. Meanwhile, scholars were conducting their own investigations, comparing biblical events with historical records and exploring, from an archaeological standpoint, the lifestyles in ancient cultures, like those of Egypt and Palestine.

Religious certainties were further undermined by sectarian conflicts, several of which originated in the earliest decades of the nineteenth century. One such conflict involved Utilitarianism—a philosophy founded by Jeremy Bentham (1772-1832)—which held that all institutions of society should be examined in the light of reason to discern whether they were "useful," that is, contributed to the greatest happiness of the greatest numbers. Benthamite Utilitarians tended to agree that established religion was not useful, but rather an outmoded superstition. This viewpoint, in turn, was challenged by religious conservatives, like John Henry Newman, who insisted that a powerful, dogmatic, and traditional religious institution was the best defense against mechanistic and secular Benthamitism. Other scholars and intellectuals—including Thomas Carlyle—abandoned institutional Christianity but held that people needed some kind of religious faith to sustain them.

As a result of these ongoing religious debates, coupled with the emergence of scientific theories such as Charles Darwin's theory of human evolution, many Victorians suffered crises of faith. "Doubt arose . . . because of evangelical religion's emphasis on progress and reform. Was it really possible to accept the idea of hell, everlasting punishment, and a jealous deity who demanded obedience? The struggles to reconcile conflicting beliefs gave religion its active presence in many lives—and often, when faith failed, the struggle to live well by works of reform grew even stronger" (Mitchell, p. 247). Doubtless some Victorians came to believe that their reward, their claim to immortality, would rest on their accomplishments in the earthly world, rather than whatever they were granted in a possibly nonexistent heaven. The scholar Walter E. Houghton cogently sums up this position: "There may be a God—and maybe not. And if there is, is there a life after death? in a heaven? or a hell? Let us forget the insoluble questions and plunge into some useful career" (Houghton, p. 258).

Despite this resolve, questions about the nature of God, the afterlife, and immortality continued to vex and trouble Victorian thinkers and writers, including Alfred Tennyson and Robert Browning. Both poets explored the nature of spiritual crises in their works—Tennyson, most notably, in his famous elegy *In Memoriam*. Browning was to return time and again to the subject of faith in such poems as "Cleon," "Karshish," and "Saul." After facing his own religious doubts in his younger years, the mature Browning explored many positions, ranging from satiric nihilism (in his poem "Caliban Upon Setebos") to a kind of stoicism, close to belief. In "Prospice," composed soon after the death of Browning's wife, the speaker, imagining his own death, envisions an afterlife in which love somehow survives.

The Poems in Focus

The contents. "My Last Duchess" begins as the Duke of Ferrara points out to his listener the lifelike portrait of his late wife. Inviting the listener to "sit and look at her," Ferrara mentions the artist, Fra Pandolf, and remarks on how strangers who beheld the portrait seemed mesmerized by "the depth and passion of [the duchess's] earnest glance" and curious about how she came to wear such an expression ("My Last Duchess," lines 5, 8). Ferrara reveals that the flush on the duchess's cheek might have been evoked not only by her husband's presence but by Fra Pandolf's compliments.

Warming to his theme, Ferrara describes his late wife as having "a heart—how shall I say?—too soon made glad, / Too easily impressed; she liked whate'er / She looked on, and her looks went everywhere" ("My Last Duchess," lines 22-24). The duke goes on to list the many things that pleased the duchess, ranging from wearing her husband's favour, to sunsets, boughs of cherries, and white mules. He recalls how his wife seemed to thank men as though their gifts to her were all of the same value, including the duke's own gift of "a nine-hundred-years-old name" ("My Last Duchess," line 32). Ferrara wonders aloud how a man in his exalted position could criticize this habit of the duchess without somehow lowering or embarrassing himself in the

"My Last Duchess"

process: "E'en then would be some stooping; and I choose / Never to stoop" ("My Last Duchess," lines 42-43).

After noticing how the duchess's smiles seem bestowed on everyone she encounters, Ferrara reveals that he "gave commands; / Then all smiles stopped together. There she stands / As if alive" ("My Last Duchess," lines 45-47). Immediately after that disclosure, the duke addresses his visitor—now identified as an envoy of a count, whose daughter Ferrara wishes to wed if she comes with the desired dowry. He invites the envoy to rise and go with him to meet the rest of the company downstairs. As Ferrara insists that he and the envoy go together, he points out to him a final masterpiece in his art collection: "Notice Neptune, though, / Taming a sea-horse, thought a rarity, / Which Claus of Innsbruck cast in bronze for me!" ("My Last Duchess," lines 54-56).

"Meeting At Night" begins as a man sails eagerly by moonlight towards a distant cove. Leaving his boat on the sands, he hurries across "a mile of warm, sea-scented beach" and three fields to reach a farm. He taps at the pane to be let in, a match is quickly struck, and his lover welcomes him with equal fervor. However, as the companion poem "Parting at Morning" reveals, when the sun rises, the male lover prepares for his inevitable departure and the resumption of his worldly duties: "And the sun looked over the mountain's rim: / And straight was a path of gold for him, / and the need of a world of men for me" ("Parting at Morning," lines 14-16).

"Prospice"—meaning "look forward"—opens with the question "Fear death?" and segues into the speaker's vision of what he might experience after death: "The power of the night, the press of the storm, / The post of the foe; / "Where he stands, the Arch Fear in a visible form, / Yet the strong man must go" (Browning, *Poetry*, "Prospice," lines 5-8). The speaker senses that "a battle's to fight ere the guerdon be gained"; he welcomes the impending conflict, "I was ever a fighter, so—one fight more, / The best and the last" ("Prospice," lines 13-15). Determined to face death bravely, like "the heroes of old," the speaker imagines the darkness and pain yielding ultimately to joy and a reunion with his lost love:

> And the elements' rage, the fiend-voices that rave,
> Shall dwindle, shall blend,
> Shall change, shall become first a peace out of pain,
> Then a light, then thy breast,
> O thou soul of my soul! I shall clasp thee again,
> And with God be the rest!
> ("Prospice," lines 23-28)

Victorian love. Overall, Victorians of the vocal but still small middle class tended to speak of love in highly idealized terms. As opposed to lust and sensuality, love—which presumably led to marriage and children—purified and strengthened the (male) lover against sin and temptation. Love represented "not only the supreme experience of life but its end and object—the very means by which the soul is saved" (Houghton, p. 373). Lovers' lives were defined by the moment in which each met and recognized the other as

> the one person in the wide world who was made for him or her, made to be loved forever, here and hereafter. After finding one's affinity, to draw back . . . out of timidity or apathy or any consideration of 'the world's honours,' is failure in life. Success is to seize the predestined moment and love on, even if love is unrequited . . . even if the beloved is dead—always to be faithful until, in heaven, the perfect union is achieved or renewed.
> (Houghton, pp. 373-74)

The literature of love, as written in the 1840s and 1850s, often seems to reflect (or mock) what might be called the official line on love: "Love is not something carnal and evil to be ashamed of but something pure and beautiful; it is not a temptation to be struggled against but a great ethical force which can protect men from lust and even strengthen and purify the mortal will" (Houghton, p. 375).

Much of Browning's verse falls within the purview of love poetry and engages these notions in many ways, usually playfully or ironically. While the exact nature of the lovers' relationship in "Meeting at Night" is never specified, the headlong ecstasy of the man to reach his beloved is, at least on one level, presented sympathetically, even exultantly, and with imagery that slyly suggests a consummation even before the reunion: "And the startled little waves that leap / In fiery ringlets from their sleep, / As I gain the cove with pushing prow, / And quench its speed i' the slushy sand" ("Meeting at Night," line 3-6). Meanwhile, "Prospice" captures the Victorian ideal of the perfect love that transcends death itself when the speaker reunites with his beloved—"thou soul of my soul!" ("Prospice," line 27)—at the poem's conclusion.

Even a resoundingly unromantic poem like "My Last Duchess" can be explored in the context of Victorian love. The duke, however oddly sympathetic, is the exact antithesis of the ideal Victorian lover, a man who has in fact failed in his life because he cared too much for "the world's honors," specifically, his "gift of a nine-hundred years' old name" ("My Last Duchess," line 33). "Browning, observes one literary historian, could not have created the complex ironies of 'My Last Duchess' (1842)—in which the Duke complains about the inadequacy of his first wife while negotiating the dowry for his second—if he had not been able to set the Victorian reader's presumed expectations about marital relations against the duke's renaissance views" (Tucker, p. 89). Ferrara and his first wife seem emotionally and spiritually incompatible. Possessive and arrogant, the duke cannot tolerate, understand, or love a duchess who prizes sunsets, white mules, and cherry-boughs at the same worth as his own offerings, nor one who smiles upon all whom she beholds. Having rid himself of her, the duke chooses to concentrate instead upon his art collection, including the portrait of the duchess, which he can control as he never could the living woman. Even the bride he now courts is to become another piece in his collection, as he assures the envoy that "[the Count's] fair daughter's self, as I avowed / At starting, is my object" ("My Last Duchess," lines 52-53).

Sources and literary context. While researching the historical background of his poem *Sordello*, Browning discovered the Este family of Ferrara, particularly the figure of Alfonso II, the real-life model for the duke in "My Last Duchess." His sources most likely included *Biographie universelle* (1822)—a reference text Browning had consulted on several previous occasions—and Muratori's *Della Antichita Estensi*, both of which Browning had also used for *Sordello*. R. H. Wilde's *Conjectures and Researches concerning the Love Madness and Imprisonment of Torquato Tasso*, of which Browning was writing a review in spring of 1842, may have provided further details on Alfonso II, who was Torquato Tasso's patron.

The companion poems "Meeting at Night" and "Parting at Morning" do not appear to be rooted in any historical situation. "Prospice," by contrast, shows definite autobiographical influences: it was written shortly after the death of Elizabeth Barrett Browning in 1861 and was interpreted as an expression of Browning's own ideas about love and immortality transcending death. Well aware of his wife's failing health, Browning nursed her patiently and devotedly through her final illness: she died in his arms. Writing to inform his father and sister of Elizabeth's death, Browning told them not to worry about him and asserted that his own life was to be devoted to the upbringing of his son, and that something of Elizabeth's spirit still sustained him, "I have some of her strength, really, added to mine"; in a postscript, Browning reflected on his last sight of his wife, "How beautiful she looks now—how perfectly beautiful!" (Browning in Markus, pp. 333, 334). Even Browning, however, could not remain stoic forever; some weeks later, he broke down in front of Isa Blagden, a female friend, gasping in uncontrollable grief, "I want her, I want her" (Browning in Markus, p. 332). The prospect of being reunited with Elizabeth after death may indeed have been in his mind.

THE ROMANCE OF THE CENTURY?

During the mid-1840s, Robert Browning became less famous for his poetry than for the role he played in what has been considered one of the most famous love stories in the Victorian Age. In January 1845, Browning wrote his first letter to the poetess Elizabeth Barrett, six years his senior and a semi-invalid living in her father's house. The letter was in response to a compliment she had paid his verse in one of her own poems ("Lady Geraldine's Courtship"). Praising Barrett's own work, Browning boldly declared, "I do, as I say, love these verses with all my heart—and I love you too" (Browning in Markus, p. 3). Startled by the young man's audacity, yet intrigued as well, Barrett continued to correspond with him by letter. They at last met face to face in May 1845, and, soon after, Browning initiated a clandestine courtship, clandestine because Elizabeth's father was a domestic tyrant who had forbidden any of his eleven children to marry. In 1846, the two poets were secretly married; a few days later, they eloped to Italy, for which Mr. Barrett never forgave his daughter. The Brownings nevertheless lived happily in Florence for the next 15 years, writing poetry, raising a son, Robert Weidemann Barrett Browning, and, in Elizabeth's case, becoming involved in local politics. After her death in 1861, Browning and his son returned to England; he never remarried.

"My Last Duchess"

Alfonso II, the fifth duke of Ferrara, Italy, served as a real-life model for the duke in "My Last Duchess."

"Meeting at Night," "Parting at Morning," and "Prospice" fall within the category of lyric poetry, brief pieces which convey the mood or state of mind of a single speaker. "My Last Duchess," however, is a dramatic monologue, a form that Browning helped make famous. The dramatic monologue as executed by Browning and others was characterized by a single character—clearly not the poet himself—who delivers his speech in a specific temporal and situational context while interacting with one or more silent auditors. Browning's taste for the theatrical often led him to choose particularly dramatic situations for his characters: thus, the avaricious bishop in "The Bishop Orders his Tomb at St. Praxed's Church" is on his deathbed, the rebellious monk in "Fra Lippo Lippi" has just been apprehended in the red-light district by the night watchman, and the duke of "My Last Duchess" is on the brink of remarrying. Fittingly, "My Last Duchess" marked what was to be a rewarding new direction in Browning's poetry. Literary scholar William Clyde DeVane observed, "The poem far surpasses its source in subtlety and suggestiveness. In the character of the Duke, Browning makes his first brilliant study of the culture and morality of the Italian Renaissance . . . 'My Last Duchess,' though one of the earliest of Browning's dramatic monologues, has always been considered one of his greatest" (DeVane, p. 109).

Reception. For much of Browning's youth, critical and popular success as a poet eluded him. Many critics complained of his rough, unmusical style and eclectic choice of subject matter, which some tended to find either obscure or disturbing. In 1846, an anonymous reviewer of his eight-pamphlet series *Bells and Pomegranates* made the following pronouncement in *The Eclectic Review*:

> Mr. Browning would be a poet of high order, if he could free himself from his affectations, and set before himself a great aim in poetry . . . besides muddiness of style, Mr. Browning has also much muddiness of matter to get rid of. There is a sensual trait about his writings which will bring him one day a bitterness that no amount of reputation will be found an antidote for. Let him purify his style and his spirit, and we shall hope to meet him again on a future day in a far higher and nobler position.
> (Litzinger and Smalley, p. 113)

The *Athenauem* reviewer of Browning's *Dramatic Lyrics* (1842)—in which "My Last Duchess" first appeared—expressed similar reservations about his style, declaring "that what Mr. Browning may, perhaps, consider as an evidence of his strength is a sign of weakness—what he may regard as a portion of his wealth, is a witness of its limitation. The inaptitude for giving intelligible expression to his meanings . . . is a defect, lessening the value, in any available sense of the meanings themselves" (Litzinger and Smalley, p. 84).

While these are harsh evaluations, the young Browning had his defenders as well. John Forster, writing for *The Examiner*, declared that "in the simple but manly strain of some of these *Dramatic Lyrics*, we find proof of the firmer march and steadier control. Mr. Browning will win his laurel" (Forster in Litzinger and Smalley, p. 82). Forster also singled out "My Last Duchess"—then titled "Italy"—and other monologues in the 1842 volume as "full of the quick turns of feeling, the local truth, and the picturesque force of expression, which the stage so much delights in" (Forster in Litzinger and Smalley, p. 83). After the publication of *Dramatic Romances and Lyrics* (1845)—which included "Meeting at Night" and "Parting at Morning"—an increasing number of reviewers found favorable things to say about Browning's poetry. One critic, writing for *The Examiner*, noted,

> His writing has always the stamp and freshness of originality. It is in no respective imitative or commonplace. Whatever the verse may be, the

man is in it: the music of it echoing to his mood. When he succeeds, there have been few so successful in the melodious transitions of his rhythm. In all its most poetical and most musical varieties, he is a master; and to us it expresses, in a rare and exquisite degree, the delicacy and truth of his genius.
(Litzinger and Smalley, p. 104)

A reviewer for *The Oxford and Cambridge Review and University Magazine* concurred,

Mr. Browning has many faults which, were we disposed to be severe, might be mentioned with proper censure; but his beauties are exceedingly more numerous, and on these we are better pleased to enlarge.
(Litzinger and Smalley, p. 107)

After the publication of his epic, *The Ring and the Book* (1868-69), Browning acquired a large following, which lionized him for the very things he had been criticized for in his youth. Much of his earlier work was reevaluated in light of his new fame. "Meeting at Night" and "Parting at Morning" were praised by *Athenaeum* reviewer Walter Theodore Watts for their lyricism and for the way in which the "'still, sad music of humanity' floats over all the passion" (Watts in Litzinger and Smalley, p. 447). And "My Last Duchess" came to be regarded as one of Browning's best dramatic monologues. *The Saturday Review* described the poem as "a page long since placed near Mr. Tennyson's "Ulysses" by the admirers of exquisite poetical characterization" (Litzinger and Smalley, p. 264), while Richard Henry Stoddard, writing for *Appleton's Journal*, contended that "[Browning] excels Shakespeare, I think, in the art—if it be art—with which he makes his characters betray what they really are. They may deceive themselves, but they cannot deceive us. 'My Last Duchess' is a fine instance of this art" (Stoddard in Litzinger and Smalley, p. 372).

—Pamela S. Loy

For More Information

Browning, Robert. *Robert Browning's Poetry*. ed. James F. Loucks. New York: Norton, 1980.

DeVane, William Clyde. *A Browning Handbook*. New York: Appleton-Century-Crofts, 1955.

Erickson, Lee. *Robert Browning: His Poetry and His Audiences*. Ithaca: Cornell University Press, 1984.

Hair, Donald S. *Robert Browning's Language*. Toronto: University of Toronto Press, 1999.

Hellerstein, Erna Olafson, Leslie Parker Hume, and Karen M. Offen. *Victory Women: A Documentary Account of Women's Lives in Nineteenth-Century England, France, and the United States*. Stanford, Calif.: Stanford University Press, 1981.

Houghton, Walter E. *The Victorian Frame of Mind, 1830-1870*. New Haven: Yale University Press, 1957.

Litzinger, Boyd, and Donald Smalley, eds. *Browning: The Critical Heritage*. London: Routledge & Kegan Paul, 1970.

Markus, Julia. *Dared and Done: The Marriage of Elizabeth Barrett and Robert Browning*. New York: Alfred A. Knopf, 1995.

Mitchell, Sally. *Daily Life in Victorian England*. Westport: Greenwood Press, 1996.

Peterson, William S. ed. *Browning Institute Studies*. Vol. 8. New York: The Browning Institute, 1980.

Prescott, Orville. *Princes of the Renaissance*. New York: Random House, 1969.

Ryals, Clyde de L. *The Life of Robert Browning: A Critical Biography*. Cambridge, Mass.: Blackwell, 1993.

Tucker, Herbert F., Jr. *Browning's Beginnings: The Art of Disclosure*. Minneapolis: University of Minnesota Press, 1980.

Oedipus the King

by
Sophocles

Sophocles was born at Colonus, just a mile outside Athens, in the year 496 B.C.E. The son of a wealthy family, he was raised with every possible educational and social advantage. At age 16 he made his debut in the theater by performing in a chorus that celebrated an Athenian victory (at Salamis), and soon afterward he began composing original poems and songs. Sophocles entered his first dramatic competition at the age of 28, where he took the top prize over Aeschylus, who was then considered the reigning master of tragedy. Apart from his dramatic interests, Sophocles was quite civic minded; he held a variety of political and military offices in his lifetime, including appointments to embassies, a position as an official of a religious organization, and two generalships, one under Pericles and once under Nicias. Sophocles' long life of 90 years spanned the Peloponnesian War and Athens's corresponding rise and fall as a great empire. He meanwhile is credited with the writing of 123 plays, only seven of which have survived intact. These plays are widely considered perfectly structured dramatic masterpieces. His tragedies (including *Antigone*, also in *Literature and Its Times*) question inexorable forces of fate that frustrate humanity's best laid plans, and the justness of a cosmos that allows individuals and cities to experience undeserved reversals of fortune. While it too deals with such universal issues, *Oedipus the King* is simultaneously a response to exceptional changes experienced by Athens during Sophocles' lifetime.

> **THE LITERARY WORK**
>
> A play set in Thebes during the thirteenth century B.C.E.; first performed between 429 and 425 B.C.E.
>
> **SYNOPSIS**
>
> In fulfillment of a divine prophecy, Oedipus, the ruler of Thebes, falls from the height of success and power to a position of staggering misfortune and misery.

Events in History at the Time the Play Takes Place

The ancient city of Thebes. The myth of the House of Oedipus, upon which Sophocles' play is based, takes place in Thebes in the thirteenth century B.C.E. Thebes was the dominant city of Boeotia (central Greece), located in that region's eastern part. The city had its own acropolis, or fortress, which stood on a plateau overlooking the lower city, with portions of the rivers Dirce and Ismenus on either side.

Thebes had an especially rich mythology. It was said to have been founded by Cadmus, who arrived there from Phoenicia. According to the myth, he used dragon's teeth to sow a harvest of splendid warriors, several of which were said to be the ancestors of the Theban aristocracy. The play takes place during the Bronze Age, at which time Thebes rivaled Mycenae as the dominant city in all of Greece. Thebes's success during this

Oedipus the King

Sophocles

period is attributed to the richness of its soil, and its geographic location, which gave it access to a variety of routes between Attica and central Greece. Archaeological evidence indicates, however, that by the end of the Bronze Age, the center of the city had been "sacked, burned, and abandoned," and Thebes never regained its former glory (Grant, p. 643). Sophocles may have intended the setting to have particular resonance for his audience, who probably saw fifth-century Thebes, a frequent military enemy of Athens, merely as a city in decline. His audience would be reminded by the play's setting that Thebes too, had had a "Golden Age," and that the fortunes not just of individuals, but also of cities, often rise and fall very quickly.

The Play in Focus

The plot. The play opens with Oedipus, King of Thebes, at the center of attention. He is talking to a priest who represents a group of Theban citizens begging for relief from a terrible plague. As Oedipus tries to console them, he speaks of having already dispatched his brother-in-law, Creon, to ask the Oracle at Delphi how the city might be saved. Creon returns with the oracle's pronouncement, which is that Thebes is suffering because the murderer of its former king, Laius, lives within its walls unpunished. Oedipus curses the killer and vows to save the city by searching out this murderer and bringing him to justice. As Oedipus turns to go into the palace, the chorus begins to chant a prayer for Thebes and its recovery, but ominously worries about the repercussions of this investigation into the past. Oedipus is advised to send for Tiresius, the blind prophet, since "anyone searching for the truth, my king, might learn it from the prophet, clear as day" (Sophocles, *Oedipus the King*, p. 174). Under questioning, Tiresias refuses to say much. He hints that he knows some awful truth, but keeps insisting that it is better for everyone if he does not reveal it. His reticence proves too much for Oedipus to bear, and the king explodes in fury, accusing Tiresias of conspiring with Creon in a plot to overthrow him. After being pushed to the limits of his patience by Oedipus, Tiresias finally foretells a very dark prophecy for Oedipus indeed:

> Blind who now has eyes, beggar who now is rich, he will grope his way toward a foreign soil, a stick tapping before him step by step. Revealed at last, brother and father both to the children he embraces, to his mother son and husband both—he sowed the loins his father sowed, he spilled his father's blood!
> (*Oedipus*, p. 185)

After the prophet leaves and Oedipus has conferred with the elders, Creon meets with the king to try to defend himself against the charge of treason leveled at him by Oedipus. He begs his brother-in-law not to jump to conclusions, but to carefully consider the facts of the case. Oedipus responds that he cannot "relax his guard a moment" and announces that he does not want Creon merely banished, but dead (*Oedipus*, p. 194). The chorus begs Oedipus to reconsider, and Creon warns him that "sullen in yielding, brutal in your rage—you will go too far. It's perfect justice: natures like yours are hardest on themselves" (*Oedipus*, p. 198). At this point, Jocasta the queen, who has come to make peace between her brother Creon and her husband, Oedipus, insists on being told what has happened. Upon hearing that the source of the controversy was Tiresias's prophecy, Jocasta seeks to console her husband by relating to him a years-old prophecy that never came to pass. Apparently Laius had been told that he would suffer his death at the hands of his own son. Tortured by this prophecy, Laius and Jocasta gave their infant son to a servant, who tied his ankles and left him to die of exposure on the side of a mountain. And, Jocasta reminds Oedipus, Laius was actually killed years later, not by his son, but by

> ## RIDDLES AND THE SPHINX
>
> Stories, statues, and pictures of the Sphinx existed in ancient Greece, Egypt, Assyria, and Phoenicia. A mythological creature, its name stems from a Greek word for "monster" and its gender in Greek mythology seems to have been female. The Sphinx referred to in Sophocles' *Oedipus* was believed to have lived on a high rock outside Thebes. Greeks pictured the Sphinx as a winged creature with the body of a lion and the head of a woman. As was common in many versions of the myth of the Sphinx, she posed a particular danger to men, whom she carried off and devoured if they were not able to answer her riddle correctly. As Oedipus was passing the Sphinx on his way to Thebes, he was able to solve the riddle, thereby causing her to hurl herself off the rock in anger and plunge to her death. The Theban people rewarded Oedipus by making him their king, and offering him the hand of their queen, Jocasta, in marriage. Although not repeated verbatim in the play, legend has it that the Sphinx asked, What has one voice and walks with four feet in the morning, two feet in the afternoon, and three feet in the evening? The answer is "man, who crawls as a baby, walks erect as an adult, and needs a cane in his twilight years." Oedipus himself can actually be viewed as the subject of the riddle, since, according to some, he is a young man but must use a cane due to an injury he sustained as an infant on Mount Cicatheron (Segal, pp. 36-37).
>
> The Sphinx is not the only supernatural element that presents a challenge to Oedipus in the play. Much of the drama in the play is brought about by an oracle, a term that the ancient Greeks would use to refer to a shrine where people would come and pray to the gods for guidance. The gods were thought to communicate through select individuals known as priests, or prophets, who could reveal the gods' will and predict the future. Sophocles presents an interesting juxtaposition between the riddle of the Sphinx, which Oedipus can solve, and the riddles of the oracles, which are not as easy for him to decipher. When Oedipus questions the prophet Tiresias, the beleaguered King of Thebes complains that instead of answers, he's being given "riddles, murk and darkness" (*Oedipus*, p. 184). Tiresias taunts Oedipus, saying, "Ah, but aren't you the best man alive at solving riddles?" and at the end of his prophecy, challenges him to "go in and reflect on that, solve that" (*Oedipus*, pp. 184, 185). The irony is that Oedipus ultimately discovers the truth and solves the mystery of his identity, and that in so doing, he brings about his own downfall and destruction.

"strangers, thieves, at a place where three roads meet" (*Oedipus*, p. 201).

Oedipus, startled, questions his wife about the precise location and time of Laius's murder, also asking her for a physical description of the slain king. Hearing that there was one witness to the crime, a shepherd, Oedipus asks that he be sent for and pours out his fears to his wife. He recounts to her how he traveled to Delphi from his native Corinth in order to consult the oracle regarding his parentage after being called a bastard at a party. Instead of answering his question about his parents, the oracle informed Oedipus that he would one day kill his father and sleep with his mother. Assuming that his parents were the people who raised him, King Polybus and his wife Merope, Oedipus fled Corinth for Thebes to insure that this awful prophecy would never come to pass. On his way, he encountered a group of men traveling by wagon who haughtily tried to force him off the road, and in his anger, Oedipus killed all of them. Oedipus recalls that this occurred at Phocis, where the three roads meet, exactly where Laius was killed. As the audience has already been informed, after killing Laius, Oedipus proceeded to Thebes, stopping

Oedipus the King

Oedipus riddling with the Sphinx. Oil on canvas by Jean Auguste Dominique Ingres (1780–1867) titled *Oedipus and the Sphinx* (1808).

just outside the city to destroy the Sphinx, an awful creature who was terrorizing the Thebans. For this courageous act, they rewarded him with the hand in marriage of their newly widowed queen and the position of king.

Oedipus holds out one hope, however . . . according to the eyewitness, it was thieves who murdered the king, and since "one can't equal many" Oedipus cannot have been the killer (*Oedipus*, p. 208). He begs Jocasta to send for the

> ### OEDIPUS'S PUNISHMENT
>
> The messenger's description of Oedipus's self-blinding can aptly be described as gruesome:
>
> > He rips off her brooches, the long gold pins holding her robes—and lifting them high, looking straight up into the points, he digs them down the sockets of his eyes, crying, "You, you'll see no more the pain I suffered, all the pain I caused! Too long you looked on the ones you never should have seen, blind to the ones you longed to see, to know! Blind from this hour on! Blind in the darkness—blind!" His voice like a dirge, rising, over and over raising the pins, raking them down his eyes. And at each stroke blood spurts from the roots, splashing his beard, a swirl of it, nerves and clots—black hail of blood pulsing, gushing down.
> >
> > (*Oedipus*, p. 237)
>
> The vivid description features a punishment quite unparalleled in the Greek literary tradition. Moreover, an exploration of Athenian laws does not indicate that such punishments were the norm in Sophocles' time. In fact, the laws regarding homicide allow for the perpetrator to be exiled, or, if a surviving relative of the victim agreed, pardoned altogether.
>
> Previous versions of the Oedipus story had ended on a much different note. In Homer's ***Iliad***, for example, Oedipus dies on the battlefield, and in the ***Odyssey***, Oedipus continues his rule of Thebes (both also in *Literature and Its Times*). Even Aeschylus's version in *Seven Against Thebes*, which ends with Oedipus's self-blinding is quite different, in that the king is portrayed as one possessed by madness to torture and blind himself. Sophocles' Oedipus is fully conscious, sane, and aware of what he is doing. The theatrical blinding serves two purposes in Sophocles' play. First, it attests to Oedipus's free will and freedom of choice, a key issue for Sophocles. Second, it demonstrates a heroic element in Oedipus's character, his courage to gamely endure extraordinary pain and suffering.

shepherd immediately, to confirm that it was several men who killed Laius.

While they await the shepherd's arrival, a messenger arrives with the news that King Polybus is dead and that the people of Corinth want to make Oedipus their king. Oedipus is actually relieved to hear that the man he believed to be his father is dead, so tormented was he by the oracle's prediction that he would kill his own father. Jocasta is relieved too, and points out to Oedipus that the first part of the prophecy which he so feared turned out to be "nothing, worthless" (*Oedipus*, p. 214). Jocasta urges him to forget the second part as well, claiming that many men have dreamed of sharing their mother's bed, but that it means nothing. Oedipus, however, feels that as long as his erstwhile mother, Queen Merope lives, he still must live in fear of the second part of the prophecy coming to pass. The messenger, upon hearing this exchange and wishing to put his mind at ease once and for all, reveals to Oedipus that he was a foundling. The messenger turns out to be a shepherd, who found Oedipus as an infant and gave him to Polybus and his wife, a childless couple who were desperate for a baby of their own. When Oedipus asks the shepherd for more details about where and how he was found, the man replies that it was not he, but another shepherd who actually discovered the infant, with his ankles fastened, left to die on the side of Mount Cicatheron. Frantic, Oedipus asks if this second shepherd still lives, and where he can be found, and is told by his advisor that the man is already on his way to the palace. The second shepherd and the eyewitness to Laius's murder are one and the same.

Jocasta, coming to realize Oedipus's true identity, asks him not to pursue this any longer, telling him that an old man talking empty nonsense is not even worthy of his attention. Failing to convince him with this argument, she finally begs him to "stop—in the name of god, if you

Oedipus the King

love your own life, call off this search!" (*Oedipus*, p. 222). But Oedipus refuses to listen, insisting that he "must know it all, must see the truth at last" (*Oedipus*, p. 222). Jocasta, shrieking, yells at Oedipus that he is doomed and then runs from the palace. Upon the arrival of the second shepherd, Oedipus too discovers the awful truth about his identity. This shepherd admits that he disobeyed Laius, who gave orders to have the baby killed because of the awful prophecy he had received. Taking pity on the infant boy, the shepherd gave him away, hoping his new caretaker would take him far away from Thebes and give the baby another life. Oedipus did have the chance for a new life in Corinth, but in an ironic twist, for which Sophocles is famous, his consultation with the Oracle at Delphi as a young man actually brought him back to Thebes, which resulted in the oracle's prophecy coming to pass. Oedipus, crying out that he is "revealed at last" rushes through the doors. After the chorus sings a song about the cruel nature of fate, a messenger enters to relate the news of Jocasta's suicide and describes Oedipus's frenzied grief and guilt at the sight of her hanging in the noose. The messenger relays a graphic account of Oedipus's self-inflicted punishment, the gauging out of his own eyes with Jocasta's brooches.

Next we see Oedipus, a blind man being led by attendants, cursing himself and his fate, and begging Creon, the new Theban king, for banishment from the city. Creon reminds Oedipus that such decisions are now outside Oedipus's control. Sending a messenger to the Oracle at Delphi, Creon waits to discover what the gods wish him to do.

Creon, taking pity on Oedipus, sends for his two daughters, Antigone and Ismene. A tearful goodbye follows. After extracting a promise from Creon that he will look after Oedipus's sons, Oedipus is led away by the guards, presumably to live out the remainder of his life in exile. The play closes with the following song from the chorus:

> People of Thebes, my countrymen, look on Oedipus. He solved the famous riddle with his brilliance, he rose to power, a man beyond all power. Who could behold his greatness without envy? Now what a black sea of terror has overwhelmed him. Now as we keep our watch and wait the final day, count no man happy until he dies, free of pain at last.
>
> (*Oedipus*, p. 251)

Prophecy and the gods. The writings of the ancient historians, particularly Herodotus, demonstrate that oracles played a major role in Greek political and military affairs. Believed to be the means through which the gods make their will known to man, oracles were routinely consulted by statesmen and governments prior to any major policy decision, and individuals traveled to them with questions of a smaller scale as well.

At the time Sophocles gave prophecy its role in *Oedipus the King*, there was an intellectual revolution of sorts going on in Athens. The famous philosopher Socrates was engaging in a rationalist critique of many things, especially Athens's religious tradition. A band of so-called philosophers, known as sophists, prided themselves on being able to win any argument, or to successfully present any falsehood as truth, and they subjected conventional beliefs and practices to increased scrutiny. These intellectual forces, combined with the suspicion aroused by a growing number of peddlers who tried to pass themselves off as seers or prophets for hire, began to make the Athenians a bit more wary of even the most established of the ancient oracles. The questions surrounding the notion of prophecy, of whether or not the gods actually existed, of whether they were the creators and caretakers of an orderly cosmos, and of whether they made their will known through oracles, were very controversial ones in Sophocles' day. If the notion of divine knowledge and foreknowledge was discredited, the entire religious tradition was thrown into doubt. How could the gods exist, yet not know the future?

The question of what message Sophocles intended to convey in relation to this controversial religious issue is debatable. On the one hand, prophecies are "proven" true by the play. The prophecy that was revealed by the oracle did in fact come to pass, despite monumental efforts to thwart it. And in the end Oedipus, whose words can be understood to express a less-than-pious attitude when he makes statements such as "You pray to the gods? Let me grant your prayers. Come, listen to me"—is chastened (*Oedipus*, p. 172). As Oedipus and Jocasta question and challenge the veracity of the oracles, the chorus warns that "They are dying, the old oracles sent to Laius, now our masters strike them off the rolls. Nowhere Apollo's golden glory now—the gods, the gods go down" (*Oedipus*, p. 210). Yet ultimately the traditional religious view seems to prevail, as Oedipus discovers that the prophecies were true all along; man is ignorant, seems to be the message, and knowledge of the truth belongs to the gods alone.

THE ORACLE AT DELPHI

Delphi was a village located on Mount Parnassus on the northern side of the Gulf of Corinth. It owed its fame to the fact that it was home to the most renowned temple of Apollo. The Oracle at Delphi was the most respected of the ancient Greek oracles; people journeyed from far and wide to consult it, not only Greeks, but people from Egypt, Asia Minor, and Italy. Their donations to the city of Delphi contributed to the region's booming economy. The Greek city-states made such frequent and generous contributions that many of them (including Athens, Thebes, Syracuse, and Siphnos) established local offices or chapters of their treasury departments nearby. The ancients believed that the god Apollo spoke through the oracle, using a priestess named the Pythia as his mouthpiece. The priestess engaged in mysterious rituals (which included sacrifice, ceremonial bathing, and the inhalation of vapors) prior to answering a supplicant's question, and her predictions were often phrased in a very vague and general way. This not only made it possible to apply them to a variety of situations, but also left them subject to misinterpretation. The most famous example is that of Croesus, the king of Lydia who in 550 B.C.E. asked the oracle if he should attack Persia. The response came back that if Croesus crossed a river, he would indeed destroy a great empire. Confident in his prospective victory, he proceeded to go into battle, only to have all of his forces decimated. When he accused the oracle's prophecy of being false, the Pythia replied that her prediction had proven true. Croesus had, in fact, destroyed a great empire . . . his own.

The Pythia would enter a trancelike state before uttering a prophecy. Plutarch (c. 46-c. 120), a high priest of the temple, is one of several ancient sources who believed in the prophetic powers of the oracle and in the Pythia's being its mouthpiece. Most directly, he said, her trance was induced by vapors, or gases, which erupted from a chasm at the site and inspired her to be possessed by the gods. When subsequent archaeological investigations failed to find a chasm or any other geological feature that would produce vapors, the ancient sources were discredited, and alternative explanations sought for the Pythia's trance-like state. These included self-inducement via potassium cyanide (from laurel leaves which were chewed as part of the ritual) or an emotional, ecstatic trance arising from the power of suggestion. Recently, however, a four-year study proved that the ancients were quite right. A team of scientists, who have found fault lines at the site of the Oracle, confirm the presence of gases with narcotic/euphoric effects—such as ethane, methane, and ethylene—in the waters of a nearby spring. The emissions, produced by the bituminous limestone, would be very similar to the vapors described by Plutarch. They explain the Pythia's trance. "Our research," concluded the investigators, "has confirmed the validity of the ancient sources in virtually every detail" (Boer, p. 710).

Yet the audience is not left with the feeling that this traditional view is entirely satisfactory. Is the story of Oedipus's tragic downfall evidence that the gods created and maintain a just and well-ordered cosmos? Despite efforts by some scholars to uncover some awful flaw in Oedipus's character in an attempt to prove that he received his just desserts, most readers still find him an extremely sympathetic character who does not merit the suffering that befalls him. According to this view, even if the gods do exist, they are cruel and arbitrary and so leave no place in the world for meaningful human action. The other alternative, however, that there are no gods and no prophecies, and hence no design whatever to the universe, is equally unappealing. Before Jocasta realizes that the prophecy has come true, she is a proponent of the latter, chaotic view. She poses to Oedipus a rhetorical question: "What should a man fear? It's all chance, chance rules our lives. Not a man on earth can see a day ahead, groping through the dark. Better to live at random, best we can" (*Oedipus*, p. 215). Is this world view to be preferred to one of divine injustice, wherein the means and motives of the gods exist, but are inscrutable to man?

So where does Sophocles stand on the issue? Like most great works of literature, *Oedipus the King* does not settle the issue definitively, but rather presents us with "a kind of dialogue between the older and newer ways of looking at the world. Indeed, much of the creative energy in Periclean art derives from this transition between different conceptions of reality" (Segal, p. 11).

Predestination v. free will: A staple notion in Greek tragedy is the belief that all human actions are guided or determined by "fate." This unseen force may refer to the gods and their plans, or to some other unfathomable workings of the universe, but to refuse to submit to it was considered *hubris*, a sin of pride and arrogance. The issue of destiny was raised by all the Greek tragedians; Sophocles' own treatment of it presents an interesting contrast to that of some of his contemporaries.

Some scholars argue that in the plays of Aeschylus, for example, the characters seem impelled to act in certain ways as a result of the gods' power and influence. For example, when Aeschylus's Oedipus blinds himself, it is because a divine spirit or *daimon* drove him to it (Segal, pp. 54, 134). In Sophocles' drama, all the characters are portrayed as having the freedom to act. At each stage of *Oedipus the King*, the characters make choices. Yes, these choices have the effect of making the gods' prophecy come to pass; still they are, in Sophocles' view, to some degree a function of man's free will, of his own passions and desires. Oedipus, for example, lets his temper get the better of him at the crossroads and kills an entire wagonful of people, thus fulfilling the first part of the prophecy.

So too is Oedipus's tragic downfall from a heroic king to a blind and exiled beggar a function of his own action. Contrary to advice from Tiresias and Jocasta, who at several points urge caution, restraint, and the abandonment of his investigation into the past, Oedipus relentlessly forges ahead, a man of action fixated on solving this old mystery. Of course, Oedipus has noble motives; he begins his quest for the killer out of civic mindedness, to purge Thebes of its guilt and the resultant plague. Moreover, there is something admirable and heroic about his single-minded pursuit of the truth at any cost. Nonetheless, had Oedipus chosen to simply let the matter lie, his sins would never have been discovered, and his life could have continued undisturbed. After Oedipus has blinded himself and is lamenting his situation, he admits, "I've stripped myself, I gave the command myself" (*Oedipus*, p. 243).

Sources and literary context. The source for Sophocles' play was the storehouse of myths and legends that circulated among the ancient Greeks. The story of Oedipus, like that of other myths, was already very well known to the Athenians, and had been treated by other playwrights prior to Oedipus. So the audience was familiar with the characters and the basic plot. What the playwright offered was a new perspective and fresh presentation of the myth. Sophocles chose to have the dramatic action turn on Oedipus's moment of "discovery": the tension in the play builds as Oedipus investigates what's happened to Laius the King, and climaxes as he realizes the awful truth that he has, unknowingly, fulfilled the oracle's awful prophecy. Casting Oedipus in the role of investigator, and making him the engine of the discovery was an innovation of Sophocles: in several other versions of the myth, including Homer's, the truth is simply revealed to Oedipus via some sort of divine agency.

Sophocles' dramas, including *Oedipus the King*, were innovative for their time. Among his legacies to the world of drama are the various technical improvements Sophocles made to the theater, which were very well-received by the ancient Greeks. These included the enlargement of the chorus, and the addition of painted scenery. By far the most significant improvement, was the addition of a third actor to drama. This was a crucial development in the history of the theater, whose beginning has been traced to an Athenian named Thespis. Thespis added speech by an actor to the song and dance of the chorus. The introduction of a second actor, by Aeschylus, changed the narrative style into one that featured the dramatic relationship. Sophocles' addition of a third actor greatly enlarged the scope of dramatic possibilities.

Events in History at the Time the Play Was Written

Sexual license, a male prerogative; incest, a taboo. Sources agree that although attitudes to-

Statue of the Sphinx.

ward sexual practices were quite liberal in ancient Greece, this freedom existed only for the males. Married men were expected to keep their wives happy enough so that they would produce and rear as many healthy children as possible. As long as this was accomplished, the men were free to engage in sexual relations outside marriage. They might frequent male or female prostitutes known as courtesans or engage in relationships (often emotional as well as sexual) with young boys. Women had no such freedom. Fathers sought to have their daughters married at an early age in order to guard their chastity, and once married, women in ancient Greece did not have active social lives outside the home.

Liberal attitudes to men's sexual practices did not extend to incest. Sexual relationships between parents and their children, such as the one between Oedipus and his mother Jocasta, were strictly forbidden (although the ancient Greeks did not consider relations with more distant relatives incest; cousins could marry). Other Greek literature portrayed incestuous unions as resulting in the birth of hideous monsters, such as the sphinx (Hesiod's *Theogony*), or depicted incest as a deplorable practice accepted by barbarians or "non-Greeks" (Euripides's *Andromache*).

Plato's **Republic** (also in *Literature and Its Times*) provides additional insight into what the attitudes toward incest were. In his famous treatise on the most ideal organization of the state, Plato introduces the idea of communism of women and children. Private families will be abolished, as men and women will simply pair off according to lots that they draw for the sake of procreation. The state has much invested in the quality of its future citizens, so individuals will only be paired with mates who will produce the most desirable offspring and citizens. Once the couple is successful in reproducing, the union is abolished, the man and woman go their separate ways, and the offspring are taken away to be raised by the state in a public nursery. The goal is for members of these "families" not to even recognize each other, so that everyone will consider all fellow citizens as their parents, siblings, and so on. Once "individuals are beyond the age of procreation," according to Plato, they are "left to have intercourse with whomsoever they wish, except with a daughter, a mother, the children of their daughters, and the ancestors of their mother, a son, a father, the children of their sons" and so on (Plato, p. 140). But even for these older individuals, the one prohibition regarding sexual partners is against incest. Since family members will not be able to recognize each other, Plato devises a system whereby any two mates will consider every child born seven to ten months after their mating their son or their daughter. All children born in that time period will consider each other siblings. Finally other familial relationships, such as grandparents, will be designated in a similar manner.

Athenian theater in Sophocles' day. As opposed to the very secular nature of theatergoing for modern audiences, Sophocles' dramas and those of his contemporaries were performed at festivals for the god Dionysus. These festivals took place twice a year, in the spring and winter, and they lasted for several days. Plays began as simple religious rituals, wherein the chorus presented songs. In the year 534 the poet Thespis introduced an actor (*hypokrites*, meaning answerer or interpreter) who could deliver speeches of his own, as well as interact with the chorus. The festivals were state holidays, including religious rites such as prayer and the sacrifice of a goat or lamb; attendance was considered not an optional matter but an important civic responsibility.

While modern audiences subscribe to notions like separation of church and state, the ancient Athenians mixed religion and civic affairs. The state, in fact, subsidized performances by giving citizens the money to purchase their tickets, after obliging wealthy citizens to make contributions that would finance the performances. In addition to the important religious rites, there were political components to the festivals, such as the presentation of children orphaned by war and brought up at Athens's expense, or the display of silver tribute paid to Athens. Also the state answered various honors and distinctions to individuals during the festival. In keeping with the fact that Athens was a democratic regime, the state opened the festivals to all citizens (this would have excluded slaves, but not women, say some scholars; though not considered citizens of Athens women could attend). Even the incarcerated were granted bail in order to attend. Three playwrights presented their plays on three consecutive days, and won either first, second, or third prize. Athens's democratic structure was evident in the way in which the competition was organized. The citizenry at large selected ten judges to decide which plays would be awarded prizes, and the ten, it seems, took their cues from the reactions of the audience. The context of the theater in Sophocles' Athens is thus imbued with a political significance: "Drama was special to Athens as an intrinsic and key institution of the *democratic* city of the later fifth century.... Audiences sat through the day from first light on, expected to reflect and concentrate, as part of their role as citizens of Athens" (Beard, p. 88, italics Beard's). In the case of *Oedipus the King*, the performance might cause audiences to reflect on questions regarding the reliability of prophecy and its appropriate role in society, or the characteristics of an ideal ruler.

Oedipus the Tyrant. Other translations of the title "Oedipus the King" include Oedipus Tyrannus, or Oedipus the Tyrant. Although most scholars agree that the term *tyrant* did not have as pejorative a connotation in Sophocles' time as it would later acquire (starting in about the fourth century B.C.E.), the term did refer to one who did not have a legitimate basis for his power. Oedipus would be considered a tyrant in the strict sense of the term because he did not come to power via a natural succession to the throne, as a king would have. Other "illegitimate" rulers (Polycrates of Samos, Peisistratus of Athens) came to power by plotting or by force and, lacking constitutional or hereditary authority, were indeed ruthless in their attempts to hold on to their power.

The question of whether or not Oedipus is a tyrant has been a subject of seemingly endless debate by scholars and readers alike. There are those who argue that Oedipus epitomizes the Athenian ideal of the Golden Age. He is intelligent, confident, courageous, energetic, and proactive. These are all qualities referred to by

Pericles in a speech recounted in Thucydides's chronicle of the Peloponnesian War. Known as the Funeral Oration because its occasion is a memorial service for those men who died in the first year of battle, Pericles recounts these virtues as qualities that Athens and the Athenians posses in comparison to their enemy, Sparta. According to one view, Oedipus as portrayed by Sophocles is the fulfillment of Percile's idealized vision. Others disagree. They point to Oedipus's frequent outbursts of temper, his seeming inability to moderate his emotions, and his relentless suspicion of those around him (bordering on paranoia) as evidence that Sophocles intended to portray him as a tyrant. In fact, at one point the chorus, usually quite favorable towards Oedipus, chides him with a warning:

> Pride breeds the tyrant—violent pride, gorging, crammed to bursting with all that is overripe and rich with ruin—clawing up to the heights, headlong pride crashes down the abyss—sheer doom! No footing helps, all foothold lost and gone.
>
> (*Oedipus*, p. 209)

Even if we assume that, through Oedipus, Sophocles intended to warn others about the dangers of tyrannical rule, it is uncertain whom he might have regarded as the real-life tyrant. Pericles is a possibility, since many were critical of his use of power. Thucydides, for example, wrote that although Pericles's Athens was a democracy in name, it was in effect ruled by one man. Another possibility is that one can equate tyrant with the city of Athens itself, which at the height of its power ruled its "allies" quite ruthlessly, having to quash several revolts by other city-states who refused Athens its tribute or other support. Finally, the tyrant may represent the closed, militaristic, autocratic regime of Sparta, with which Athens was at war.

The Peloponnesian War. While some literary critics argue that Sophocles' plays focus more on the struggles of individual characters than on the political or social events of his day, Sophocles no doubt intended several of the issues raised in *Oedipus the King* to resonate in a particular way with his audience, in light of the events going on around them. Fifth-century B.C.E. Athenians had witnessed their city's ascension to a position of economic, military, intellectual, and social dominance in Greece under the leadership of the controversial but extraordinarily talented and effective statesman, Pericles. War broke out with Sparta in 432, a few years before the staging of *Oedipus the King*, and it would continue for two decades. Initially Athens was the most powerful of the city-states, but by the time *Oedipus* was first performed, the Peloponnesian War had begun to take a grim toll. Athenians had crowded together behind the walls of the city during an invasion by Sparta, and that, together with the overcrowding caused by war refugees pouring into Athens from outlying areas invaded by Sparta, such as Attica, resulted in the outbreak of an awful plague. Lasting for several years, the disease claimed a quarter of Athens's population, one of its most mourned victims being Pericles himself (who probably died about a year before the first performance of the play). How appropriate, then, that its first scene should consist of Oedipus's comforting citizens who have to come to him for relief from the terrible sickness that holds their city in its deathly grip!

> Our city—look around you, see with your own eyes—our ship pitches wildly, cannot lift her head from the depths, the red waves of death.... Thebes is dying. A blight on the fresh crops and the rich pastures, cattle sicken and die, and the women die in labor, children stillborn, and the plague, the fiery god of fever hurls down on the city, his lightning slashing through us ... plague in all its vengeance, devastating the house of Cadmus!
>
> (*Oedipus*, p. 160)

Thucydides, whose account chronicled his experience as a general during the war, described Athens's desperate suffering during the plague in terms very similar to those Sophocles uses in this first scene.

> Not many days after their [refugees] arrival in Attica the plague first began to show itself among the Athenians. It was said that it had broken out in many places previously ... but a pestilence of such extent and mortality was nowhere remembered. Neither were the physicians at first of any service, ignorant as they were of the proper way to treat it, but they died themselves the most thickly, as they visited the sick most often; nor did any human art succeed any better. Supplications in the temples, divinations, and so forth were found equally futile, till the overwhelming nature of the disaster at last put a stop to them altogether.
>
> (Thucydides, p. 94)

Oh my children, the new blood of ancient Thebes, why are you here? Huddling at my altar, praying before me, your branches wound in wool. Our city reeks with the smoke of burning incest, rings with cries for the Healer and the wailing for the dead.... Why here and kneeling, what preys upon you so? Some sudden fear? Some strong desire? You can trust me. I am ready to help, I'll do anything. I would be blind to misery not to pity my people kneeling at my feet.

(Oedipus, p. 159)

Another parallel between the experience of the Athenian audience and the citizens of Thebes in the play is the loss of an incredibly competent and revered leader. Just as Pericles had succeeded in raising Athens to the height of her glory, so had Thebes prospered and thrived under Oedipus, who had rescued it from the clutches of the malevolent Sphinx. Yet both cities tragically lost their beloved leaders due to events thought to be beyond human control, demonstrating the precariousness and uncertainty of existence.

Reception and impact. Sophocles' talent was lauded by audiences in his own day. Out of the 120 plays that he authored, 96 won prizes at festivals. While *Oedipus the King* only won second prize at the festival in which it figured, posterity has proven a more favorable judge. About a century after the debut of *Oedipus the King*, Aristotle's *Poetics* repeatedly referred to the play as a masterpiece of tragedy and cited it as a model for all playwrights to follow. The headmasters of Athens's leading institutions of learning, the Academy and the Lyceum, both agreed that the work of Sophocles surpassed that of his contemporaries Aeschylus and Euripides, and that *Oedipus the King* was the finest of Sophocles' plays.

During the Roman empire *Oedipus the King* made several appearances in versions written and/or produced by Julius Caesar, Nero, and Seneca. After that, the work of the tragedians seems to have faded from popularity until the sixteenth century, when the manuscripts of Greek tragedies began circulating again in Italy. Of these manuscripts, Sophocles' were the first to be reprinted.

The most famous modern reference to the play is its use as the cornerstone of psychoanalytic theory by Sigmund Freud in the early 1900s (see **On Dreams,** also in *Literature and Its Times*). According to Freud, childhood and family relationships are driven primarily by sexual urges of the children for their parents, particularly little boys for their mothers. Dubbed "the Oedipus complex," this theory has been discredited as a basis for psychoanalysis on an individual level and thus is no longer popular in psychoanalytic circles. Still, the theory's intellectual contribution cannot be minimized. In fact, some researchers argue that the Oedipus complex helps account for certain attitudes towards incest, when considered alongside other theories (of evolution and sociobiology). One scholar suggests Freud himself "might extract a certain intellectual excitement from the debate surrounding the Oedipus complex" and quotes the following passage from a letter Freud wrote:

> Mediocre spirits demand of science the kind of certainty which it cannot give, a sort of religious satisfaction. Only the real, rare, true scientific minds can endure doubt, which is attached to all our knowledge.
>
> (Freud in Bower, p. 116)

After reading *Oedipus the King*, one is left with the impression that Sophocles felt about drama the way Freud did about science. Perhaps that attitude is one of the reasons Sophocles' plays are so timeless and why audiences to this day remain attracted to the character of Oedipus.

—Despina Korovessis

For More Information

Baldry, H. C. *Ancient Greek Literature in its Living Context*. New York: McGraw-Hill, 1968.

Beard, Mary, and John Henderson. *Classics: A Very Short Introduction*. Oxford: Oxford University Press, 1995.

Boer, J. Z., J. R. Hale, and J. Chanton. "New Evidence for the Geological Origins of the Ancient Delphic Oracle (Greece)." *Geology* 28, no. 8 (August 2001): 707-10.

Bower, Bruce. *The Oedipus Complex: A Theory under Fire*. In *Readings on Sophocles*. Ed. Don Nardo. San Diego: Greenhaven Press, 1997.

Demand, Nancy. *Birth, Death, and Motherhood in Classical Greece*. Baltimore: Johns Hopkins University Press, 1994.

Grant, Michael. *A Guide to the Ancient World: A Dictionary of Classical Place Names*. New York: Barnes & Noble Books, 1986.

Plato. *The Republic of Plato*. Trans. Alan Bloom. New York: Basic Books, 1968.

Sealey, Raphael. *A History of the Greek City States, 700-338 B.C.* Berkley: University of California Press, 1976.

Segal, Charles. *Oedipus Tyrannus: Tragic Heroism and the Limits of Knowledge*. Oxford: Oxford University Press, 2001.

Sophocles. *The Three Theban Plays: Antigone, Oedipus the King, Oedipus at Colonus*. Trans. Robert Fagles. New York: Penguin Books, 1982.

Thucydides, *History of the Peloponnesian War*. Trans. Richard Crawley. London: Orion Publishing Group, 1993.

Woodard, Thomas, ed. *Sophocles: A Collection of Critical Essays*. New Jersey: Prentice-Hall, 1966.

On Dreams

by
Sigmund Freud

> **THE LITERARY WORK**
>
> A psychological study of the function, nature, and meaning of dreams; published in German (as *Über den Traum*) in 1901, in English in 1914.
>
> **SYNOPSIS**
>
> In *On Dreams*, Freud summarizes his earlier groundbreaking *The Interpretation of Dreams* (*Die Traumdeutung* [1900]). Against the prevailing scientific opinion of the day, this longer work argues that dreams have meaning and that every dream represents a wish of the dreamer.

A pioneer in exploring the hidden workings of the human mind, Sigmund Freud (1856-1939), the founder of psychoanalysis, has been called the most influential thinker of the twentieth century. Born into a Jewish family in Moravia (now part of the Czech Republic), Freud moved with his family to Vienna, Austria, where he lived from early boyhood until shortly before his death. After an education in which he studied the Greek and Latin classics as well as French and German literature, Freud turned to medicine and eventually to the infant science of psychology. By the late 1890s Freud had built on the insights of several coworkers to found the theory and practice of psychoanalysis. Among other revolutionary ideas, psychoanalysis proposes that much human behavior is governed by unconscious motives and that in adults many of these motives stem from sexual impulses shaped by long-forgotten childhood experiences. At the turn of the century, Freud published his first major work, *The Interpretation of Dreams*, which won him slow but growing recognition in the European medical community. Shortly afterward, he summarized his findings for a general readership in *On Dreams*. The volume foreshadows important concepts that Freud would elaborate in later books, such as *The Psychopathology of Everyday Life* (1901), *Three Essays on Sexuality* (1905), and *Civilization and Its Discontents* (1930). Despite his immense body of work, Freud always considered *The Interpretation of Dreams* his masterpiece, a view with which most observers have agreed. More than simply an inquiry into dreams, it, as well as *On Dreams*, lays out Freud's basic ideas of psychoanalytic theory.

Events in History at the Time of the Study

Vienna at the end of the nineteenth century. Freud's highly original thinking grew partly out of the unusual environment in which he lived and worked. Vienna in the last decades of the nineteenth century was a city of turbulent and intensely creative cultural turmoil. In the long run, Freudian psychoanalysis would be the most influential product of this ferment, but Viennese writers, artists, designers, architects, and musicians all made original and significant contribu-

On Dreams

Sigmund Freud

tions to European culture during this seminal period. Freud knew many of these avant-garde figures, and admired some though not all of them, for, unlike his psychological theories, Freud the man was socially quite conventional.

For example, Freud praised the psychological insight of the sophisticated novels of Arthur Schnitzler, who in the 1890s began to chronicle the sexual and other foibles of Viennese society.

From Arthur Schnitzler's "Lieutenant Gustl"

The girl in the [concert] box who was flirting with me before . . . . Where is she now? . . . Already gone. . . . Stupid of me—I left my opera glasses at home. . . . I wish the cute little one over there would turn around. . . . I wonder whether I ought to consider marriage seriously. . . . There's something to be said for always having a pretty little wife at home at your disposal.

(Schnitzler, p. 255)

Less to Freud's strongly classical taste in art (though later influenced by his ideas) were the works of modernist Viennese artists such as Gustav Klimt, Egon Schiele, and Oskar Kokoschka, who helped create the movement known as art nouveau, an attempt to create an innovative style characterized by a sinuous, organic asymmetrical type of line. Meanwhile, innovative composers such as Gustav Mahler, Alban Berg, and Arthur Schoenberg wrote music that reflected a similarly unconventional and iconoclastic spirit. The creative impulse that dominated 1890s Viennese artistic and intellectual culture aimed at overturning what its proponents saw as the stuffy and repressive values of traditional Austrian society. Not surprisingly, shocked establishment figures condemned the new styles and trends as morally degenerate, a charge they would also level against Freud as well.

Behind these cultural conflicts lay a political crisis that had its roots in the 1860s (the years of Freud's childhood) and came to a head around 1900, just as he was publishing *The Interpretation of Dreams* and *On Dreams*. During the early nineteenth century, Austria had been the leading nation in the slowly declining Habsburg Empire, a multiethnic entity that included today's Hungary, the Czech Republic, and Slovakia, as well as other lands. In 1867, after Hungary's unsuccessful attempt to secede from the empire, a political settlement called the *Ausgleich*, or Compromise, established the two largest parts of the former empire as separate states joined by a common monarch. The *Ausgleich* gave Hungary's ethnic majority, the Magyars, constitutional rights that allowed them to dominate in Hungary; in Austria the German ethnic majority preserved its rights to dominate this part of the so-called "dual monarchy." Appointing a liberal national government, Austria's emperor Franz Joseph undertook extensive building, education, and other municipal projects to modernize the capital city, Vienna. But the tenuous settlement could reverse neither the empire's decline, or the growing tendency in the Austrian half for the majority German population to blame minorities such as the Jews for the political problems.

As middle-class German-speaking Jews, the Freud family identified with the values of the liberal era, whose days were numbered. Its values were largely discredited after the fall of the liberal government in 1879 amid financial scandals and labor unrest. By the late 1890s, when Freud was recording the dreams he would analyze in *The Interpretation of Dreams*, Austrian society had grown increasingly polarized, as conservative governments sought to control dissatisfied workers and to placate rising nationalist movements within Austria's borders. The most aggressive movement, led by Czech nationalists, demanded for Czechs the same constitutional rights as Germans (such as elevating Czech to the status of official language, alongside German). Among the areas affected by such tensions were Bohemia and

Moravia (the Freuds' original home), where Czechs comprised local majorities and took the political offensive against ethnic Germans. In response to Czech pressures, the government decreed in 1897 that state employees in Bohemia and Moravia know both German and Czech. German nationalists in Vienna and other cities responded with violent rioting, and the conservative prime minister, Count Kasimir Felix von Badeni, was forced to resign.

Freud's dreams repeatedly touch on the bleak political situation of the 1890s. One dream, for example, "carried me back from the dreary present to the cheerful hopes of the 'Bürger' Ministry," by which Freud means the failed liberal government of his youth, which represented the interests of the middle-class, or bürgers (Freud, *The Interpretation of Dreams*, p. 193). Before analyzing another dream, Freud relates the real-life incident that triggered it: while waiting at the train station in Vienna, he caught sight of Count Thun, the reactionary aristocratic leader who replaced Count Badeni as prime minister. Freud reacted with barely suppressed hostility to the count's haughty manner, thinking "all sorts of insolent and revolutionary thoughts" (*The Interpretation of Dreams*, p. 209). Later that night, Freud dreamed of Count Thun contemptuously addressing a crowd of students.

Anti-Semitism. In interpreting the Count Thun dream, Freud explicitly associates the count's appearance in his dream with the most disturbing political development of the 1890s, Austria's rising anti-Semitism, reflected in fact and fiction such as this reference to a character named Kopetzy: "He's probably a Jew.... Supposed to be a lieutenant in the reserve as well! Well, he'd better not come to practice in our regiment! If they keep on commissioning so many Jews—then what's the point of all this anti-Semitism?" (Schnitzler, p. 253). In real life, Freud and other Viennese Jews saw the anti-Semitism manifest itself in the alarming growth in popularity of the Christian Social Party, whose virulently anti-Semitic leader, Karl Lueger, won election as Vienna's mayor in 1897 by portraying himself as the champion of the common people against wealthy Jewish capitalists. Anti-Semitism's victory in Vienna reflected another aspect of liberalism's collapse, for since the late eighteenth century, Austria's German liberals had worked to extend greater civil rights to the empire's Jewish minority. Middle-class Jews like Freud thus had more than one reason to identify with the defeated liberal tradition in Austria.

In the "*Bürger* Ministry" dream (described above), the "cheerful hopes" include Freud's youthful ambition to become a lawyer and go on to a political career. This ambition had been stirred by the appointment of several Jews as ministers in the liberal government of 1868, and Freud recalls his family's joy afterward. However, even during the liberal heyday, Austrian Jews remained largely excluded from politics. Medicine was one of the few professional fields open to Jews, but Freud's advancement was slowed because he was Jewish. Throughout his life, Freud experienced intense frustration with anti-Semitism, and his discussions of his dreams take as a given that anti-Semitism will close doors to Austrian Jews. Ultimately he interprets his "*Bürger* Ministry" dream as representing a wish that two Jewish friends with stalled medical careers be exposed as incompetent. Suggesting that they have been denied promotion for incompetence and not for their Jewishness, is a way Freud reasons, for his dreaming mind to make his own chances of promotion seem more favorable, when in fact he knows better.

SEX, DEATH, AND MADNESS IN VIENNA

The naturalized American psychologist Bruno Bettelheim (1903-90), himself born and educated in Vienna, suggests that Freud's interest in sex and death arose partly from a "morbid" preoccupation with these issues in late-nineteenth-century Viennese culture as a whole (Bettelheim, p. 10). In his essay "Freud's Vienna," Bettelheim offers the example of the 1889 suicide of the 30-year-old Crown Prince Rudolf. Heir to the imperial throne and married to a Belgian princess whom he did not love, Rudolf murdered his lover, Baroness Vetsera, after having sex with her. He then took his own life. The murder-suicide fascinated and astounded the Viennese public. "It was a shockingly vivid demonstration of the destructive tendencies inherent in man which Freud would investigate and describe later" (Bettelheim, p. 10). In his *The Interpretation of Dreams*, sex, death, and madness recur often in the dreams discussed—both Freud's and his patients'. In addition to society's focus on destructive tendencies, Bettelheim points to the mental instability of Rudolf's mother, the Empress Elizabeth, as a much discussed subject of the day. Elizabeth herself "extolled both death and madness in remarks such as 'The idea of death purifies' and 'Madness is truer than life'" (Bettelheim, p. 10).

On Dreams

The early development of psychoanalysis. As a medical student in the 1870s, Freud studied under leading teachers in biology and physiology, hoping for a career in medical research. However, by the early 1880s he had met a woman named Martha Bernays, whom he hoped to marry, and he knew that research would not pay him enough to raise a family. Soon after becoming engaged, Freud joined Vienna's General Hospital. There, for three years, he worked in one department after another: surgery, skin diseases, internal medicine, nervous diseases, psychiatry. Highly ambitious, he looked for a way to combine his research interests with a decent income and the prospect of advancement. Slowly, he began to focus on the mind, studying the ancient medical field of psychiatry (attempts to heal mental illness), then investigating the rapidly growing area of psychology (the study of the mind).

In 1885 Freud spent five months in Paris, where he studied under the well-known advocate of psychiatric hypnosis, Jean-Martin Charcot (whose hypnotic techniques hinted at the mind's hidden activity). Returning to Vienna, Freud married Martha Bernays, and the couple began raising a family. They would have six children, to whom scholars have traced many of the children's dreams cited in *The Interpretation of Dreams* and *On Dreams*. Also in the 1880s Freud established a partnership with physician Joseph Breuer, who had developed a method (the so-called "talking cure") in which a patient, a woman named Bertha Pappenheim, apparently eased some physical symptoms by simply talking about them. In 1880, while caring for her fatally ill father, Bertha Pappenheim had begun suffering a number of physical complaints: headaches, loss of appetite, weakness, coughing. The symptoms grew worse, until she was regularly reporting blackouts, rapid mood shifts, and hallucinations involving black snakes, skulls, and skeletons. After these symptoms eased, Bertha Pappenheim (whom Breuer called Anna O. to protect her privacy) went on to become a well-known champion of women's rights, but historians also consider her to have been the first patient of psychoanalysis.

In the 1890s, combining insights gained from the work of both Charcot and Breuer, as well as those from his friend Wilhem Fliess, Freud developed the ideas that would provide his approach, psychoanalysis, with a theoretical basis. (He first used the word *psychoanalysis* to describe his work in 1896.) Freud had opened a private medical practice before marrying, and as family life became more important to him, he moved his offices to rooms in the family home. The patients he saw there—many of them women—often reported problems similar to Bertha Pappenheim's. In cases where Freud found no physical cause, he began to feel more and more confident about concluding that somehow these medical problems originated in the mind. Doctors in the nineteenth century grouped such symptoms together under the general name "hysteria," and in 1895 Freud and Breuer published their work in a book called *Studies in Hysteria*. In the book they announced a technique called free association, in which they directed the patient to talk aimlessly, moving with apparent randomness from one topic to another. Free association, Freud believed, could give patients access to thoughts, feelings and memories hidden deep in the mind. Freud called this hidden part of the mind the "unconscious," a term that had already been used by other writers (e.g., by Thomas Car-

PSYCHOLOGY BEFORE FREUD

Doctors have long tried to help people whose mental processes have become disordered, even if psychiatric techniques before Freud's groundbreaking work would strike the modern observer as often cruel and barbaric. On the other hand, modern psychology emerged as a separate discipline only in the late nineteenth century. It grew largely out of the two disciplines of philosophy and physiology, and at first limited itself to questions that arose from one or the other of these two branches of inquiry. Such questions centered around issues having to do with the relationship of the mind to the body, the nature of consciousness, how we know things, and how we perceive the world through our senses. Wilhelm Wundt, for example, a German physiologist later known as the father of experimental psychology, explored sensory perception in the world's first psychological laboratory, which he established in Leipzig in 1879. Also during the 1870s, the American William James taught both psychology and philosophy at Harvard. Before focusing on philosophy exclusively, James pioneered studies in human consciousness, likening it to a purposeful stream in his book *The Principles of Psychology* (1890). One of Freud's revolutionary achievements was to help establish the field of clinical psychology, which attempts to apply psychological knowledge to help cure mental illness.

lyle in *On Heroes, Hero-Worship, and the Heroic in History* (1841): "Silent with closed lips . . . unconscious, that they were specially brave" [Carlyle in Simpson and Weiner, p. 923]).

Freud had noticed that his patients' free association often seemed to reveal childhood memories of a sexual nature, including being sexually molested. In mainstream nineteenth-century European culture, anything to do with sex was considered dirty and shameful. Strict rules governed conversation, especially between men and women, and sexual matters were considered unmentionable. Soon Freud was beginning to see sex—or rather, society's repressive attitudes toward sex—as more and more responsible for psychological problems like hysteria. The stress of holding back or repressing sexual memories, thoughts, or impulses, Freud began to believe, somehow created hysteria's symptoms. Freud's growing focus on the role of sex made Breuer highly uncomfortable, and after 1895 Breuer lost interest in further research. On his own now, based on the reports of his patients, Freud went on to develop what he believed was a revolutionary idea: that all neuroses (or mental imbalances) stemmed from repressed memories of childhood sexual abuse, usually by a father or male relative. How did the medical community respond? Leading authorities contemptuously rejected his so-called seduction theory, and in 1896 Freud himself had to admit that it was untenable. Many such memories, he now decided, represented fantasies rather than real events, though others undoubtedly reflected actual abuse.

Royal road to the unconscious. After a period of extreme disappointment at the failure of seduction theory, Freud collected himself. He still believed in an unconscious sexual origin for many neuroses, but now he began looking in a new direction for evidence. Even before abandoning seduction theory, Freud had begun to examine his own memories and feelings. For several years in the late 1890s, with growing rigor Freud analyzed himself through extensive free association. Among the childhood memories he unearthed were many of a sexual nature. Others seemed violent and aggressive, or combined sexuality with aggression. Freud also recorded and analyzed his dreams, for he had begun work on a book exploring his revolutionary conviction that dreams, if properly interpreted, could reveal important psychological truths. By 1898, as he wrote to his friend Wilhelm Fliess, he was "deep in the dream book" (Freud in Gay, p. 104). "The interpretation of dreams," he would write near the end of that book, "is the royal road to a knowledge of the unconscious activities of the mind" (*The Interpretation of Dreams*, p. 608).

The Study in Focus

The contents. In 13 brief chapters—some as short as a few pages—*On Dreams* outlines the major ideas that Freud presents in greater detail in *The Interpretation of Dreams*. Freud begins by distinguishing three main lines of previous thinking about dreams. The first comes from ancient beliefs, reflected in sources such as Greek mythology, that dreams are put in the dreamer's mind by divine or demonic powers. In modern times, poets, philosophers, and others have adapted this mythological explanation to reach related conclusions, attributing to dreams such spiritual functions as liberating an immaterial soul from the body. "In sharp contrast to this," Freud writes of the second line of previous thought, "the majority of medical writers adopt a view according to which dreams scarcely reach the level of psychic phenomena at all" (Freud, *On Dreams*, p. 6). These scientists maintain that dreams simply represent random, disordered activity in the sleeping brain. Popular opinion, the third main strand of thought, generally holds that "dreams have a meaning" that "relates to the prediction of the future and . . . can be discovered by some process of interpretation of a content which is often confused and puzzling" (Freud, *On Dreams*, p. 7).

Freud claims that the popular conception is closest to the truth. Dreams do have meaning, and that meaning can be interpreted. Furthermore this meaning is not supernatural but psychological. Dreams spring from the same unconscious impulses that, when unbalanced, result in mental illnesses such as phobias and obsessions. Psychoanalysis has been found useful in exposing those impulses, and so Freud proposes using its methods to interpret dreams. As in psychoanalysis, Freud warns that resistance from the conscious mind can hinder dream interpretation, for those methods rely on pursuing precisely the thoughts and associations "normally dismissed by our critical faculty as worthless rubbish" (*On Dreams*, p. 10).

Freud suggests that a dream acts "as a sort of *substitute* for the thought processes" and adds that it is much more compact than the thoughts for which it stands (*On Dreams*, p. 15; emphasis original). Having distinguished between a

On Dreams

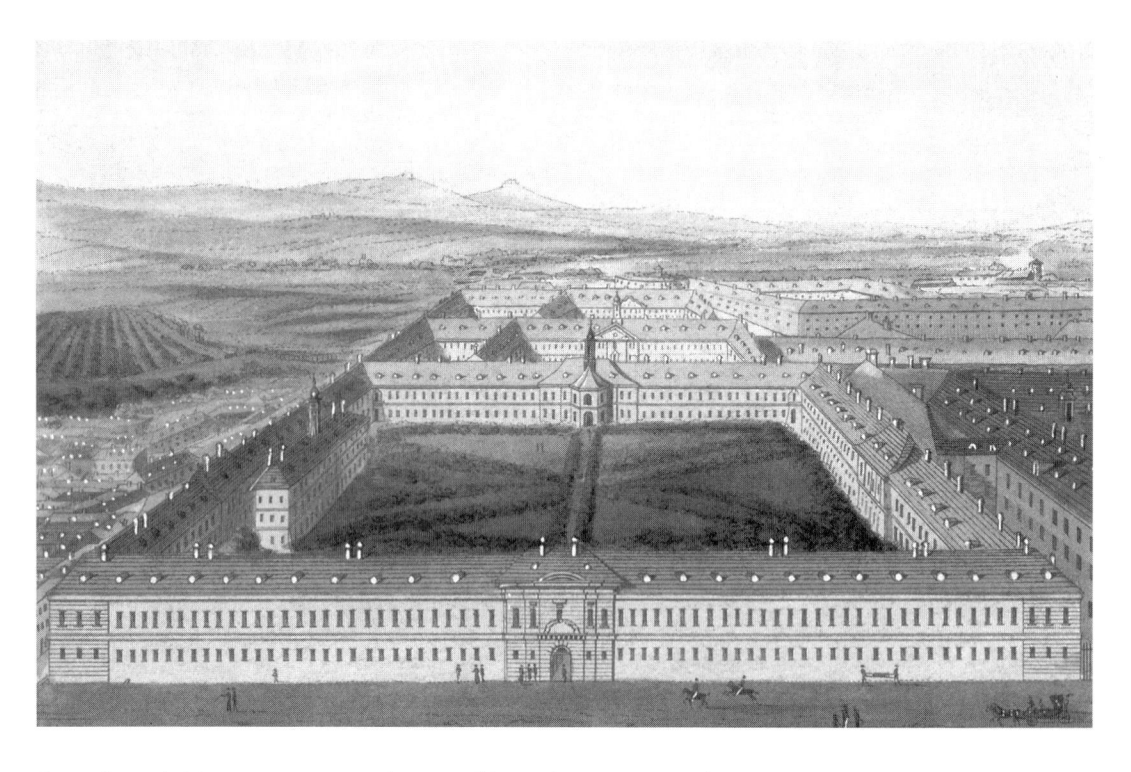

General Hospital in Vienna, Austria, where Freud began his career in medicine.

dream's surface details and the hidden thoughts the dream represents, Freud calls the details the dream's "manifest content" and the hidden thoughts its "latent content" or "dream thoughts." He further terms the transformation of latent content into manifest content the "dream work." The dreams themselves he divides into three categories: dreams that are coherent and easily understandable; dreams that are coherent yet whose meaning remains mysterious; and dreams that are fragmentary and also mysterious.

To illustrate the first category, he describes several children's dreams. In one, a little girl just under two years old was made ill by strawberries, which she nonetheless enjoyed eating. That night, she was heard in her sleep saying her name and adding, "*Stwawbewwies, wild stwawbewwies, omblet, pap!*" (*On Dreams*, p. 20; emphasis original). Freud suggests that she was dreaming of a favorite food that she believed she would no longer be allowed to eat, and characterizes this dream (and several others he cites) as "simple and undisguised *wish fulfillments* (*On Dreams*, p. 21; emphasis original). Adults, he writes, have similarly simple wish-fulfillment dreams.

In the other two more complex kinds of dream, the dream work proceeds through a process Freud calls "condensation," by which manifest content takes on several or even many latent meanings. He gives an example of a fragmentary dream he had of a group of people near a swimming pool. Analyzing the dream, he realized it combined images from two paintings he had seen with the memory of a similar scene from his childhood. The features of two or more people can be similarly combined in dreams, and the interpretation depends on what emotional associations the people who make up the composite have for the dreamer. For example, in the longer *Interpretation of Dreams*, Freud describes a dream he had in which a figure physically resembled his brother, but spoke like, behaved like, and bore the name of a doctor whom Freud knew. Along with condensation, the dream work proceeds through "dramatization," which transforms the dream thoughts into dynamic situations. Freud does not give an example of dramatization, but in *The Interpretation of Dreams* he explains that dramatization is what gives us the conviction that we *experience* a dream rather than merely *thinking* it.

Freud then introduces another concept that he calls "dream displacement," in which the central element of a dream's latent content is shifted or displaced into a peripheral role in the manifest content. In other words, the dream's main meaning is often to be found in a part of the dream that seems vague or unimportant in our recollections of the dream. Displacement reflects Freud's observation that dreams are triggered by trivial events, called "dream instigators," of the dreamer's recent past, most often the day before. Dreams can involve various degrees of displacement, but Freud suggests that the more trivial a dream appears to be, the more displacement is at work:

> Where the content of the dream treats of insignificant and uninteresting... material, analysis uncovers the numerous associative paths connecting these trivialities with things that are of the highest psychical importance in the dreamer's estimation. If what make their way into the content of dreams are impressions and material which are indifferent and trivial rather than justifiably stirring and interesting, that is only the effect of the process of displacement.
> (*On Dreams*, p. 36)

Our dreams are also difficult to understand because the dream thoughts "are represented symbolically by means of metaphors and similes, in images resembling those of poetic speech" (*On Dreams*, p. 39). Things or people that in the real world have a logical connection, for example, will be close to each other in time or space in the dream, the way a painter might depict famous poets from different periods of history as standing next to each other, in a single setting that has poetic associations. In another example, if someone appears in a ridiculous situation in our dreams, it is likely that we harbor feelings of contempt for that person. Our own feelings create all dream situations, Freud declares: "no dream is prompted by considerations other than egoistic ones" (*On Dreams*, p. 46).

In addition to condensation, displacement, and symbolism, Freud proposes a fourth and final technique by which the mind accomplishes the dream work. Called "revision," it works somewhat like waking thought and appears only in coherent dreams. Indeed, such dreams derive their coherence from revision, which amounts to a superficial attempt by the sleeping mind to interpret the dream content by arranging it into a story, which Freud suggests is always fragmentary in its original form. Revision allows us to awaken with the impression that a dream was well constructed and ordered.

Condensation and especially displacement are not peculiar to dreaming, Freud continues, but are psychological features of our normal waking lives. They give rise to such common phenomena as forgetting, slips of the tongue, and mistakes, all of which may appear random but in reality often conceal unconscious desires or motives. Displacement, which Freud calls "the heart of the problem," leads him to a discussion of such hidden motives (*On Dreams*, p. 56). By misdirecting the dreamer's attention, displacement hints at a dream's essential purpose: to conceal dream thoughts that are unacceptable or inadmissible to the dreamer's conscious mind. In psychoanalytical terms, the unconscious rejection or concealment of such thoughts is called "repression." Repression operates like a censor, monitoring the passage of thoughts from the unconscious to the conscious. During sleep, the censor relaxes just enough to let some repressed thoughts slip by in disguised form.

Just as simple dreams represent undisguised wish fulfillments, more complex dreams, whether fragmentary or coherent, usually represent disguised fulfillments of repressed wishes. In some cases, the disguise is insufficient or missing altogether, causing the dreamer to awaken

---

A DREAM INTERPRETATION FROM ON DREAMS

A young woman who nevertheless had been married for many years dreamed she was at the theater with her husband. In the dream, her husband mentioned that a friend of hers, Elise L., had also wanted to come with her fiancé. Since the engaged couple could only get three bad seats, the husband said, they had not come.

In analysis, Freud established the following associations in talking with the woman:

- The dream situation reminded her of an actual incident when she had rushed to the theater to buy tickets in advance, only to find plenty of seats left at curtain time. Her husband had teased her about being in such a needless hurry.
- The friend, Elise L., was three months younger than the woman (part of the significance of the number three).
- Shortly before the dream, in real life the young woman had learned from Elise L. that she was engaged (this incident was the dream instigator).

Based on these facts, Freud concluded that the dream signified the woman's repressed wish that she had not married as early as she had. Just as she rushed needlessly to the theater in real life, she had been in a needless hurry to find a husband and could have done better for herself if she had waited. The absurdity of the couple's obtaining three seats represents the absurdity she unconsciously attributes to her decision to marry so quickly.

with a sense of anxiety. Contrary to a popular view that dreams disturb sleep, Freud suggests that dreams generally act as "the guardians of sleep" (*On Dreams*, p. 65). This explains the common experience of incorporating sensory stimuli into a dream. A repeated knock, for example, may appear as some similar sound woven into the dream. The sensation of needing to urinate is also commonly woven into dreams in this way, allowing us to continue sleeping rather than acknowledge the intrusion. Protecting sleep is thus an important part of the function of dreams.

Having laid the theoretical groundwork, Freud in conclusion refines his earlier thesis that dreams represent disguised wish fulfillments: "most of the dreams of adults are traced back by analysis to *erotic wishes*" (*On Dreams*, p. 70; emphasis original). Openly sexual dreams are common, but even those dreams that seem wholly unerotic in content, Freud insists, can usually be traced to repressed erotic wishes. The reasons for this are cultural as well as psychological:

> No other group of instincts has been submitted to such far-reaching suppression by the demands of cultural education, while at the same time the sexual instincts are also the ones which, in most people, find it easiest to escape from the control of the highest mental agencies.
> (*On Dreams*, p. 71)

This helps to explain the psychological value of disguising erotic thoughts with dream symbolism, in which sexual objects such as the genitals can be represented by everyday items bearing a metaphorical resemblance to them. For example, "long and stiff objects, such as tree trunks and sticks, stand for the male genital, while cupboards, boxes, carriages or ovens may represent the uterus" (*On Dreams*, p. 72). Freud points out that such symbolism is found not only in dreams, but also in fairy tales, jokes, folklore, and literature.

Forbidden wishes. Freud argues that forbidden wishes lie at the heart of dream production. Curiously, forbidden wishes also lie at the heart of several crises in Freud's life as the theory took shape. In a seminal book on Viennese culture and politics at the end of the nineteenth century, *Fin-de-Siècle Vienna* (1980), historian Carl Schorske suggests that Freud's dream theories emerged from a three-fold crisis in his life—political, professional, and personal.

On the political level, Austria was undergoing problems that reflected those of Europe as a whole: "The Habsburg Empire was pulling apart at the seams internally as Europe was internationally" (Schorske, p. 185). Nationality had become a divisive issue—people were newly showing a fervent passion for their regional affiliation. Also the practice of identifying with one's social class became more common, as did divergent ways of looking at society and the place of humankind in it. It was a volatile time of social upheaval in both thought and deed. As a Jew, Freud had special reason for anxiety as the century drew to a close:

> The fall of Vienna to Karl Lueger's anti-Semites . . . was a stunning blow to the bearers of liberal culture, Jew and Gentile. The forces of racial prejudice and national hatred, which they had thought dispelled by the light of reason and rule of law, reemerged in terrifying force. . . . Sigmund Freud, by family background, conviction, and ethnic affiliation, belonged to the group most threatened by these new forces: Viennese liberal Jewry.
> (Schorkse, p. 185)

Meanwhile, Freud's professional and personal circumstances added an individual atmosphere out of which his dream theories emerged. On the professional level, Freud had experienced deep frustration due both to the failure of his seduction theory and to his slow advancement in the newly resurgent atmosphere of anti-Semitism. On a personal level, Freud's troubles were exacerbated by the death of his father in 1896.

Each of these three crises can be seen as reflecting hidden wishes comparable to those that Freud sees as driving dream production. In political terms, Austria's (and Europe's) liberal rulers had for a time suppressed, or made forbidden, the wishes of hatred and prejudice, which were violently forcing themselves to the surface just as Freud was writing. (Those same destructive wishes would soon play a great part in touching off two world wars—ending in a Holocaust that nearly annihilated European Jewry.) Turning to Freud's professional wishes, they were in several senses forbidden. Anti-Semitism thwarted his wishes for medical advancement just as it had thwarted his youthful dreams of a political career. On a deeper level, Freud himself "forbade" his own ambition, which at one point he calls "pathological" (*The Interpretation of Dreams*, p. 192). Feelings of guilt long kept him from engaging in the self-promotion ultimately required to secure the advancement he desired. Significantly, only after completing his dream books (which he viewed as his self-analysis) could Freud bring himself to call on powerful friends to put in a good word for him. Even then he felt deeply ambivalent about doing so. Finally, as *The Interpretation of Dreams* makes clear, Freud's relationship with his father hinged on forbidden wishes, including a repressed wish for his father's death. If Freud's theories suggest that dreams grow out of forbidden wishes, the theories themselves emerged from a historical and autobiographical context in which hidden wishes played an important role.

Sources and literary context. The dreams on which Freud based his theories came from four sources. First and most important were his own recorded dreams. Freud acknowledges many of the dreams he discusses as his own, and several times openly declines to give embarrassing or indiscrete details. Scholars have suggested that many of those dreams he attributes to other sources were in fact Freud's as well, leading to much speculation about the dreams' biographical meaning. Other dreams have been traced to family members. For example, the strawberry dream (see above) has been attributed to Freud's daughter Anna, later a famous psychoanalyst herself. In addition, Freud himself frequently attributes dreams he discusses to acquaintances (rarely to friends) and, finally, to patients. Nowhere does he identify the dreamer, except through fictitious names or initials.

Freud loved literature and read widely. He was inspired to go into medicine on hearing a poem, "Ode to Nature," by his favorite poet, the highly influential German author Johann Wolfgang von Goethe (1749-1832). Freud quotes Goethe frequently in *The Interpretation of Dreams*. Overall, like much late-nineteenth-century thought, Freud's thinking was shaped most profoundly by the revolutionary ideas of English naturalist Charles Darwin. By establishing the fact that living organisms evolve, and suggesting natural selection as the primary means by which evolution occurs, Darwin's book *The Origin of Species* (1859) founded modern biology. Freud repeatedly declared that his highest goal was to put psychology on a similarly sound scientific footing.

Reception and impact. Neither of Freud's two books on dreams sold well in the years immediately following their publication. *The Interpretation of Dreams*, for example, sold only 351 copies in its first six years. For decades, Freud and his strongest supporters (such as his disciple and first biographer, Ernest Jones) claimed that scholarly reviewers either ignored the books or dismissed them in a few brief unfavorable reviews.

The claims did much to reinforce what later observers have called the myth of Freud's early isolation, a heroic picture that Freud and his followers perhaps deliberately fostered. In fact, however, more recent scholars have uncovered close to 40 scholarly reviews of the two books within a few years of their publication, and most of these were strongly favorable. In 1899, for example, the very first reviewer of *The Interpretation of Dreams* called the book "epoch-making," while in 1901 a leading German psychologist, Paul Näcke, wrote that "the book is psychologically the most profound that dream psychology has produced so far" (Metzentin and Näcke in Sulloway, pp. 450-51).

By the 1910s both *The Interpretation of Dreams* and the shorter summary *On Dreams* had found a wide readership. In fact, by then Freud's work had begun to make an indelible impact not just on psychology but on modern Western culture as a whole. An early form of many ideas that would later pass into common usage can be found in Freud's discussions of dreams: examples include sibling rivalry and the Oedipal complex, in which a child feels sexual attraction towards a parent of the opposite sex and jealousy towards the other parent (see **Oedipus the King**, also in *Literature and Its Times*). Researchers today generally disagree with many details of Freud's dream theory, including his claim that all dreams represent wish fulfillments. Most, however, would agree with Freud's basic—and revolutionary—premise that dreams can tell us something significant about the hidden workings of the human mind.

—Colin Wells

For More Information

Bettelheim, Bruno. *Freud's Vienna and Other Essays*. New York: Alfred A. Knopf, 1990.
Freud, Sigmund. *The Interpretation of Dreams*. Trans. and ed. James Strachey. New York: Basic Books, 1955.
———. *On Dreams*. Trans. and ed. James Strachey. New York: Norton, 1951.
Gay, Peter. *Freud: A Life for Our Time*. New York: Norton, 1988.
Grinstein, Alexander. *On Sigmund Freud's Dreams*. Detroit: Wayne State University Press, 1968.
Hall, Calvin S. *A Primer of Freudian Psychology*. New York: Signet, 1954.
Porter, Laurence M. *The Interpretation of Dreams: Freud's Theories Revisited*. Boston: Twayne, 1987.
Robertson, Ritchie. Introduction and Notes to *The Interpretation of Dreams* by Sigmund Freud. Trans. Joyce Crick. Oxford: Oxford University Press, 1999.

Schnitzler, Arthur. "Lieutenant Gustl." In *Arthur Schnitzler: Plays and Stories*. Trans. Richard L. Simon. New York: Continuum, 1982.

Schorske, Carl. *Fin-de-Siècle Vienna: Politics and Culture*. New York: Vintage, 1981.

Simpson, J. A., and E. S. C. Weiner. *The Oxford English Dictionary*. Vol. 18. Oxford: Clarendon, 1989.

Sulloway, Frank J. *Freud, Biologist of the Mind: Beyond the Psychoanalytic Legend*. New York: Basic Books, 1979.

On the Origin of Species

by
Charles Darwin

The most influential scientific writer of the nineteenth century, Charles Robert Darwin (1809-82) sought a quiet life in rural Kent, where he was nonetheless plagued by gastrointestinal troubles, likely due to a tropical disease but undoubtedly exacerbated by worry. Charles was born to a wealthy Whig family, who had, after a couple of generations of vocal liberalism and Unitarian dissent, settled down into "Anglican respectability" (Desmond and Moore p. 19). Infinitely more interested in natural history than medicine (for which his family originally sent him to the University of Edinburgh) or divinity (for which he read at Cambridge University), Darwin put other pursuits on hold and accepted the post of naturalist and companion to Captain Fitzroy of the HMS *Beagle*. The voyage was decisive. Darwin spent five years on the *Beagle* (1831-36), exploring the world and gathering enough material to keep him busy for decades to come. Darwin's books enjoyed tremendous success. *The Descent of Man, and Selection in Relation to Sex* (1871), together with its predecessor *On the Origin of Species*, is considered the keystone of Darwin's work. Even his first book, which we now know as *The Voyage of the Beagle* (1839), was a dazzling success. But it took Darwin 20 years, after becoming convinced of the truth of its central ideas, to publish *On the Origin of Species*. He was fully sensitive to the potentially disturbing nature of his own work and to the social and familial upheavals it would ferment. Only the independent discovery of natural selection by another naturalist, Alfred Russel

> **THE LITERARY WORK**
> An essay on the question of how species develop; published in London in 1859.
>
> **SYNOPSIS**
> Positing a mechanism called "natural selection" for the evolution of new species from old, *On the Origin of Species* accounts for the presence of every species on earth through two simple principles: variation and selection.

Wallace, finally drove Darwin to publish "the book that shook the world" (Mayr, p. vii).

Events in History at the Time of the Essay

Economics and industry. Darwin observes in *On the Origin of Species* that "the struggle for existence" is "the doctrine of Malthus applied with manifold force to the whole animal and vegetable kingdom" (Darwin, *On the Origin of Species*, p. 63). He refers there to the sociological and economic principles put forth by Thomas Robert Malthus in his *Essay on Population* (1798), which Darwin read in 1838. Arguing that population, unchecked, always increases faster than its food supply, Malthus paints a grim picture of the miseries attendant on human overpopulation. These arguments take on particular poignancy in light

On the Origin of Species

Charles Darwin

of certain economic shifts of the mid-nineteenth century. In 1831, the year that Darwin sets off on the *Beagle*, the national census revealed 24 million people in Britain. This astonishing figure meant that the population had doubled in only 30 years. Meanwhile, the food supply began to look insufficient. Since 1815, the Corn Laws had protected agricultural interests in England by keeping up the price of domestic corn (a term that referred to grains such as wheat, barley, and oats rather than the American on-the-cob variety) and preventing the import of cheaper corn from abroad. Manufacturers, who wished to open up what came to be called "free trade" and to secure lower food prices for workers and higher profits for themselves, began to agitate for the repeal of the Corn Laws. In the end, however, what finally brought about their repeal was very bad weather. The year 1845 witnessed nearly incessant rains. Bad crops at home and potato famine in Ireland, which drove over a million Irish out of the country in search of food, painted an all-too-vivid picture of Malthusian scarcity. In 1846, parliament passed a three-year plan to lift the Corn Laws—a decision that may have had more symbolic than economic impact. The price of corn remained relatively unchanged, but the repeal of the Corn Laws made it clear that popular agitation could effectively bring about governmental change and that England was no longer the predominantly agrarian state it had once been.

Industry had come to stay, and the mid-nineteenth century was the era for many to enjoy it—in particular, the many who belonged to the burgeoning middle class. England thrived on its industrial progress, dominating the world's coal, cotton goods, and steel markets. With economic success abroad came considerable changes at home, including the migration of hundreds of thousands of workers into cities such as London and Manchester. The rapid increase in urban populations and industry strained resources of food and raw materials. Apparently abundance and scarcity went hand in hand.

Religion, reform, and natural theology. By the early nineteenth century, the Church of England (the Anglican Church) had dominated the religious and, in many ways, the political life of the country for centuries. Indeed, anyone attending Oxford or Cambridge had to swear to the "Thirty-nine Articles of the Anglican Faith." Dissenters, that is, protestants who did not belong to the Anglican Church, were thus barred from university education and from virtually all positions of power within England. But the period during which Darwin researched and wrote witnessed considerable change in the position of the Church and in official religious tolerance. In 1837, the year after Darwin returned from his voyage on the *Beagle*, the Registration Act lifted the Anglican monopoly on performing marriages, burials, and baptisms. The Catholic Emancipation Act of 1829 had made it possible for Catholics to hold office, and by 1862 even Oxford and Cambridge—the last bastions of Anglican-only higher education—were admitting Dissenters.

Meanwhile, there was considerable variety of opinion within the Church. By no means did all Anglicans subscribe to the literal truth of the Bible. Nor was all religious thought easily separable from scientific thought. During the first half of the nineteenth century, natural theology, based on the conviction that man could and should come to know God through reason and the senses, was at the height of its popularity in England. While still at Cambridge, Darwin read William Paley's *Natural Theology* (1802), in which Paley laid out his famous version of the "argument from design." Just as the workings of a watch imply a watchmaker, he argued, the complexity of creation attests to the presence of a creator. And if Paley's work was starting to look a bit dated towards mid-century, a series of eight works published in the 1830s, known as the "Bridgewater Treatises," reinvigorated the argument from design. Indeed, Darwin draws one of the epigraphs for *On the Origin of Species* from William Whewell's treatise: "But with regard to the material world, we can at least go so far as this—we can perceive that events are brought about not by insulated interpositions of Divine power, exerted in each particular case, but by the establishment of general laws" (Whewell in *Origin*, p. ii).

Dinosaurs, embryos, and women. In 1842, Sir Richard Owen coined the term "Dinosaria" in order to distinguish Megalosaurus, Iguanadon, and Hylaeosaurus from other ancient reptiles. Arguing that these were higher-order reptiles than the ones that succeeded them, Owen proposed the category in part to argue against the progressive implications of early evolutionary theory. His notion of the "archetype" proposed a "primal" pattern on which all vertebrates were based, a static pattern that could not change or evolve. Opposed to Owen's static view of species were many early evolutionists like Herbert Spencer and T. H. Huxley. Among the evolutionists was Ernst Haeckel, who is responsible for the phrase "ontogeny recapitulates phylogeny." His is the most famous articulation of the theory known as "parallelism," which connects the stages of development of the individual (ontogeny) with the stages of development of the species (phylogeny) or, for non-evolutionists, connects the stages of development of the individual with the hierarchical rungs of a static scale of being. Parallelism implied that as a person developed to adulthood, he or she went through all the lower stages of life, spending some time (usually as an embryo) in a fish stage, a reptile stage, and so on.

From the flip side, parallelism (or "recapitulation" as the theory is sometimes called) implied that the more youthful an individual seemed, the less evolved that individual was. Thus, recapitulation was often used to argue for hierarchical relations among humans. Not only children, but also non-whites and women (because, like children, they were smaller than men and lacked facial hair), were often taken to be less evolved than white men. In this way, evolutionary theory was used to reinforce social structures already in place. The first half of the nineteenth century witnessed a considerable constriction in the role of women, who were increasingly thought of as "angels in the home" for whom both public life and sex drives seemed inappropriate and incongruous. This view of women, as well as a confidence in women's good taste, is reflected in Darwin's theory of sexual selection (proposed in the *Origin*, but not explored at length until the *Descent*). Throughout the animal kingdom, vigorous and active males pursue relatively passive females, who nonetheless contribute to the strength and beauty of their species by choosing always the best and brightest among their suitors.

THE GREAT EXHIBITION AND THE CRYSTAL PALACE

In 1851, England seemed to be in a fine position indeed. It was wealthy and powerful, the center of a mighty empire. In fact, the world had not seen such an empire since the famous Roman one. Many took the opening of the Great Exhibition held in London's Hyde Park that year to be a sign of the might as well as the right of all things British. An international showcase of arts and manufactures, the Great Exhibition was the first world's fair in history. It opened on May 1 in the giant Crystal Palace, built of glass and iron and designed for the occasion by Joseph Paxton. The edifice itself inspired reverence and awe as well as a sense that industrial capitalism and progressive reform would lead to enduring national success. In essence, the dazzling spectacle secured an admiring nation's commitment to science. Six million people visited the Crystal Palace, witnessing its enormous engines, tropical plants, and artwork before it was disassembled in 1852 and taken to Sydenham in South London. Darwin enjoyed this new site rather more than he had enjoyed the original exhibition. Here the Palace was rebuilt with beautiful gardens and ornamental lakes, and here Richard Owen erected his life-size concrete dinosaurs, which still stand.

Wars abroad, unrest at home. Readers of *On the Origin of Species* will find it suffused with the language of war. Indeed, just one paragraph from the section on sexual selection yields a long list of war words: *shield, sword, spear, battle, weapons, courage* and *victory*. This may seem out of step for a country enjoying an extended domestic peace, but war could not be too far from the consciousness of the English at almost any time during the nineteenth century. Though the defeat of Napoleon in 1815 brought considerable relief, the war left Britain extremely sensitive to the possibility of revolution. The upper classes especially were anxious to avoid the kind of horrors that had taken place just over the channel in the French Revolution of 1789. A series of revolutions in Austria, Germany, Italy, and France in 1848 fueled the fear of class uprisings. Indeed, the Reform Bills of 1832, 1867, and 1884-85 can be understood as part of the attempt to rectify peacefully some of the class grievances settled so violently on the European continent. Designed to reapportion representation in Parliament in order to accommodate the growth of industrial cities in the north and designed also to extend the vote to a much larger number of people (male householders), these acts were revolutionary in that they allowed the middle classes to share power with the upper classes. Indeed, the acts can be said to mark the emergence of a new *species* of citizenry.

Though legislative reform kept life relatively peaceful at home, colonial interests led to trouble abroad. Fearful of Russian designs on India, Britain fought, along with France and Austria, in what was known as the Crimean War (1854-56); the goal was to keep Turkey out of Russian control. Though successful, the war was poorly run and evoked considerable public criticism. Moreover, the Indian Mutiny of 1857, though quickly suppressed, suggested that Indian nationalists would not always tolerate British rule and the westernization of Indian culture. Thus, the events of the 1850s would not only keep the fact of war before the eyes of the British, they would also begin to unsettle confidence in the dominance and permanence of the British empire. *On the Origin of Species* itself would reproduce the ambivalence of its culture, serving at once to foster and to assuage the anxieties attached to ideas of empire in Britain, even as that empire reached unprecedented heights.

The Essay in Focus

Contents summary. Though Darwin modestly terms its 500 pages and 14 chapters an "Abstract," the *Origin* is a rich piece of writing that reveals a mastery of a wide array of Victorian sciences, including botany, zoology, anatomy, paleontology, and geology. In London, Darwin was admitted to two clubs for pigeon fanciers, and a practical dimension infuses his writing. It displays a vast knowledge of the everyday experience of breeders and farmers, whose accounts furnish many of Darwin's examples throughout the *Origin*. These permeate the first chapter, "Variation under Domestication," in which Darwin eases his readership into an understanding of his radical view of nature through an extremely familiar, analogous case. If we wish to understand the variation and modification of species in nature, Darwin reasons, our knowledge of "variation under domestication" must be "the best and safest clue" (*Origin*, p. 4). He cites (to name a few) the Italian greyhound, the Spanish pointer, and the Blenheim spaniel; the Ribston-pippin apple and the Codlin apple; and a dazzling array of pigeons—the English carrier, the runt, the pouter, the barb, the short-faced tumbler, the Jacobin, the trumpeter, the laugher, and the fantail. Darwin thus paints a picture of the rich variety among domestic productions. But though the breeders who are his sources maintain almost indignantly that each domestic breed stems from a unique wild species, Darwin argues that even very distinct breeds descend from common wild ancestors. Indeed, it is from the very plasticity of form that breeders observe, from their capacity to select consciously or unconsciously for desired traits and to breed out undesirable ones, and from their ability to substantially alter a breed this way, that Darwin becomes convinced—and convinces his reader—of his two central ideas: first, individuals of a breed or species exhibit a range of differences or variations; and second, these individual differences, when selectively accumulated over the course of many generations, form the basis of larger differences, such as those that distinguish the prize Hereford from the wild longhorn. Thus, "nature gives successive variations; man adds them up in certain directions useful to him" (*Origin*, p. 30). In other words, nature provides variety; man selects and breeds for those variations that he deems desirable.

Darwin then reasons by analogy. What man can do, nature can do better. Of course, for selection to occur, there must be something to select; there must be variation. Thus, Darwin devotes his second chapter to "Variation under Nature." It is here that his concern with the individual distinguishes him from the "systematists" who precede him. The same differences that other works on natural history gloss over in order to present a coherent picture of a "type" become Darwin's central obsession. "These differences blend into each other in an insensible series; and a series impresses the mind with an actual passage" (*Origin*, p. 51). In this way, Darwin suggests that we can infer from the *variety* currently visible in nature, a series of *changes* that have taken place over time.

It remains for the next chapter, "Struggle for Existence" to posit a mechanism that can explain how species arise in nature. Here, Darwin elaborates a complex "economy of nature" in which both individuals and species compete for resources that, at some time or another, will be insufficiently abundant. The term "Struggle for Existence" often evokes a rather bloody picture—two carnivores fighting over the same piece of meat, or what Alfred, Lord Tennyson described as "Nature red in tooth and claw" in his poem *In Memoriam* (Tennyson, 56.15). But Darwin's chapter concerns something much larger and more metaphorical, "including dependence of one being on another, and including (which is more important) not only the life of the individual, but success in leaving progeny" (*Origin*, p. 62). It is here that Darwin first coins the term "natural selection," the subject of Chapter 4 and the keystone of Darwin's theory. "Natural selection"—a term intended to evoke the analogy to "man's power of selection"—is the process through which variations, however slight, that give an individual an advantage in the struggle for existence will accumulate (*Origin*, p. 61). Advantaged individuals will have more success in leaving offspring, who, in turn, may enjoy similar advantages and reproduce successfully, and so on, until small variations add up to large ones, individual differences yield new varieties, and varieties yield new species. Thus nature, like man, selects for profitable variations.

In Chapter 5, "Laws of Variation," Darwin connects the rich variety in nature established in earlier chapters to his theory of natural selection. It is here that he begins to address "the ordinary view of each species having been independently created," a view which he finds completely inadequate in explaining either the visible variations within species or the similarities between species (*Origin*, p. 155).

The chapters that follow address many of the difficulties associated with this theory. Chapters 6-8 take up a series of troubling questions; Chapters 9-12 consider the challenges (to and from natural selection) of geology, paleontology and geography; and Chapter 13 returns to the difficulties of classification, with a view to explaining these difficulties by the theory of descent with modification. Why, Darwin asks and answers, if species develop out of other species, don't we see more intermediate gradations that connect disparate but related forms through a complete spectrum of forms in between? Why do species appear so well defined? How can we believe that natural selection produces small and insignificant as well as vital and complex structures within a species? How does natural selection explain the development of complex instinctual behaviors—such as those that result in the elaborate social structures of certain ants or the exquisite architecture of the hive-bee's cell?

The first of these questions points to a recurring emphasis in these chapters: the close relation between natural selection and extinction. We don't see more intermediate forms in nature, Darwin argues in Chapter 4, precisely because the success of the species that we do observe implies their success *over* those species or varieties with whom they have competed in the struggle for existence. Species, he argues, are more likely to compete with, and therefore lead to the extinction of, species like themselves. Thus, competition leads to diversification in nature. So competition explains why species appear distinct in nature; however, it fails to explain why we do not see more transitional forms among *extinct* species. Darwin returns to this question—which is the challenge posed by geology and paleontology to the theory of natural selection—in chapters 9 and 10. With extreme care, he enumerates the multiple causes that have conjoined to make the fossil record extremely imperfect and full of gaps through which species have come and gone without leaving a trace.

Finally, following two chapters on geographical distribution, Darwin revisits the major points of *On the Origin of Species*. In this final chapter, he comes to consider the reasons why so many naturalists and geologists have clung to the view that species are immutable, even though variation within species is everywhere evident and clear distinctions cannot be drawn between species and well-marked varieties. In addressing this question, he addresses nothing less than the question of how science, indeed thought, works. Anticipating "the load of prejudice by which this subject is overwhelmed," Darwin—perhaps inadvertently—evokes the interpretive nature of what we call facts, which nevertheless take shape only in light of the theories through which we view them (*Origin*, p. 482). He leaves it predominantly to the future to embrace his theory, and predicts an impact almost as great as the one *On the Origin of Species* has turned out to have. Winding up the treatise, Darwin ends with a

On the Origin of Species

sense of awe inspired by the view of nature he has articulated. He finds in this view a grandeur all its own, that from the simple beginnings of a few or only one species "endless forms most beautiful and most wonderful have been, and are being, evolved" (*Origin*, p. 490).

Evolution and empire. A great deal of the fascination with *On the Origin of Species* comes from the fact that while producing a brilliant and influential work of science, Darwin reveals how much he is a man of his times. However much his *theories* may be separated from their social applications, his *language* speaks to an audience deeply concerned about the endurance of the empire.

There can be no doubt that when Darwin published *On the Origin of Species* in 1859, the British empire was strong and growing stronger. The essay—like much of the science that preceded it—carried the potential to shatter this confidence. In particular, the fear of extinction wrought by Victorian paleontology and inseparable (as Darwin emphasizes) from natural selection, suggested that species—even apparently powerful species like the dinosaurs—could and very likely would eventually die out. Since Victorians often confounded the concepts of species, race, and nation, the fear of extinction readily spilled over into a fear of racial or national decline. For the reader looking for reassurance that Great Britain did indeed rule the waves and would continue to do so, the essay provides plenty of material. Certainly, any sufficiently devout nationalist will find a source of pride in the assertion that "the whole body of English racehorses have come to surpass in fleetness and size the parent Arab stock" (*Origin*, p. 35). Within the struggle for existence, the practice of forcibly occupying another nation can look quite natural, "for in all countries, the natives have been so far conquered by naturalised productions [species who are not indigenous], that they have allowed foreigners to take firm possession of the land" (*Origin*, p. 83 sic). Also, in spite of the frightening facts of the fossil record, natural selection implies for Darwin that "forms of life which are now dominant tend to become still more dominant" (*Origin*, p. 59). In a way that seems to reinforce the rightness and even the inevitability of the imperial project (or class divisions, or gender disparity, according to the inclinations of the reader), Darwin develops a mechanism that explains how "the forms of life throughout the universe become divided into groups subordinate to groups" (*Origin*, p. 59).

Nonetheless, not all colonial practices were viewed equally within England. In the early part of the nineteenth century, the question of colonialism was hardly separable from the question of slavery. England officially ended its slave trade in 1807 (though this proved rather hard to enforce) and in 1834, Parliament put into effect a bill that would abolish slavery throughout the British empire. The abolitionist sentiment that effected these changes remained strong in England for the three succeeding decades during which slavery remained legal in the United States. In light of the prevailing sentiment, it is surprising that, at least on the face of things, *On the Origin of Species* seems to treat slavery as quite natural—instinctual, if only in ants. On closer inspection, however, Darwin's discussion of the slavemaking instinct reads like a cautionary tale. These remarkable ants have so developed this instinct, so thoroughly established the division of labor, that "The males and fertile females do no work. The workers or sterile females, though most energetic and courageous in capturing slaves, do no other work" (*Origin*, p. 219). They no longer can. The slavemaking ants live in a state of abject dependence on their slaves. Indeed, "so utterly helpless are the masters" that when shut up without a slave, "they could not even feed themselves and many perished of hunger" (*Origin*, p. 219). Thus though *On the Origin of Species* implicitly offers reassurances about the endurance of empire, it also portends evil for those who would carry such power too far. Its complex (sometimes seemingly contradictory) implications, moreover, anticipate the wide array of uses to which Darwin's theories would eventually be put under the very broad rubric of "Social Darwinism."

Sources and literary context. By the middle of the nineteenth century, evolutionary ideas suffused Victorian popular and scientific thought. No well-read and educated Victorian (including Darwin) could have been unfamiliar with the best-loved, most-read, and most-quoted work of mid-Victorian literature: Alfred, Lord Tennyson's *In Memoriam*, a consolatory poem written in memory of his friend Arthur Henry Hallam that articulated many of the broader fears and hopes of its moment. The poem raises, and in many ways resolves some of the anxieties wrought by the same sciences that influenced Darwin. Though Darwin was critical of Robert Chambers's *Vestiges of the Natural History of Creation* (published anonymously in 1844), Tennyson was fascinated by this same work. Chambers's book helped him reconcile his belief in God's love with his perception of nature's violence. In his poem he attempts to resolve the clash between evolutionary and Christian thought by developing a narrative of evolutionary progress that links the ape and tiger up through man to the divine itself. His poem indicates how thoroughly evolutionary ideas were already in the air while Darwin was writing (often in distressing ways, as in the perception of nature's violence mentioned above).

Moreover, Darwin was not the first scientist to develop a theory of evolution. His particular contribution was to posit a compelling mechanism—natural selection—to explain the process through which species could evolve. There were quite a few scientific theories of evolution in place before Darwin started writing. One of these was the work of Darwin's grandfather, Erasmus Darwin, a poet and physician, whose *Zoönomia* (1794) Darwin had read with enthusiasm as a teenager. Erasmus Darwin believed in the mutability of species, in the possibility of adaptation and variation in organisms, and in the importance of such changes for individual and species survival. Though influenced by these ideas, his grandson Charles did not embrace them or their implications wholesale. Yet Charles Darwin was no doubt disposed to be relatively sympathetic to some of the ideas of Lamarckian evolution when he encountered these first at Edinburgh. Jean-Baptiste de Lamarck, best known for his *Philosophie zoologique* (1809), posited a dynamic scale of nature in which organisms progressed up the scale of nature, becoming more and more complex because of the gradual accumulation of adaptations over many generations. Though Darwin would reject certain well-known Lamarckian ideas, such as spontaneous generation and the inheritance of characteristics acquired by an individual during its lifetime, *On the Origin of Species* would also adopt many important aspects of Lamarckian evolution, such as the possibility of transformation (or "transmutation") of species as well as the incredible long time scales required to make such changes. The controversy surrounding such works, moreover, may have influenced Darwin's decision whether and when to publish. Intrigued by such early evolutionary writings, he was nevertheless rather nervous lest his own ideas meet with similar rejection, and this nervousness accounts, in part, for his waiting so long to publish *On the Origin of Species*.

It was not, however, only the evolutionary sciences that influenced Darwin's thinking. In the 1830s, when Darwin was still very much a junior member of the scientific community, two schools of thought dominated and divided geological thinking. "Uniformitarians" contended that geological processes of the past were of the same kind and operated in the same degree as the processes now operating. "Catastrophists," on the other hand, depicted the earth's past as punctuated by violent and rapid upheavals, like volcanoes and floods, which would account for the changes in landscape and living forms indicated by the fossil record. Though Darwin's early training was steeped in catastrophism, he read Charles Lyell's *Principles of Geology* while on board the *Beagle*. Lyell's book was perhaps the foremost articulation of uniformitarian principles, and it not only shaped much of Darwin's geological thinking while on board the *Beagle*, but also laid the foundational premises necessary to develop the concepts he would eventually put forth in *On the Origin of Species*. In advocating the uniform nature of geological processes, Lyell emphasized a steady state view of the earth in which decay and formation are perpetually in process, a view that implied no particular progression or direction in terrestrial events, a view which would enable a scientist to explain the phenomena of the past by observing the events and causes of the present.

Reception and impact. The first edition of *On the Origin of Species* sold out the day it was published (November 24, 1859). A second edition, with very slight changes, was released just a month later (December 28). These changes, Darwin's first hurried response to some of the religious objections to the first edition, were clearly intended to make God more visible in his theory. In spite of such gestures to render *On the Origin of Species* compatible with religious thought, the most vehement resistance to Darwin's ideas came from religious thinkers—scientists among them. They objected on two counts. First, there were objections to the insufficient space left by natural selection for the intervention of God in the form of creation or miracles, and second, there were objections to the essay's failure to maintain a special place for humanity in the order of things. Though Darwin does attempt to address the first objection, he makes little mention of humankind (except as breeders) in the essay at all, saving that discussion for *The Descent of Man*. Actually, the disturbing closeness of humans to apes had already crept into British thought (indeed had been there for more than a century), and the essay's readers immediately picked up on its implications for the "monkey question." Perhaps the most famous clash over

On the Origin of Species

Illustration of the HMS *Beagle* in the Straits of Magellan. Darwin spent five years on the *Beagle*, an experience that would stimulate his future writings.

this question was the 1860 debate between the Bishop Samuel Wilberforce and Thomas Henry Huxley—an extremely vocal proponent of Darwinism, whose enthusiasm earned him the nickname "Darwin's bulldog."

The response to *On the Origin of Species*, however, was by no means limited to a simple clash between science and religion. Even religious opinion was divided. While some found the essay deeply offensive, other religious readers saw in it evidence of the richness and complexity of God's methods. Scientific readers were similarly divided. Undoubtedly, the essay marked a complete shift in the status of evolution in the scientific community. Earlier evolutionary theories were always on the fringes of biological thought; Darwin brought evolution to the center. Certainly by 1875, probably by 1865, virtually every British biologist was an evolutionist. Nonetheless, there remained considerable dissension regarding the *mechanism* of evolution, as evolutionists debated whether natural selection could do all that Darwin claimed. Even those who accepted that natural selection could accumulate small changes in visible ways debated whether these could ever be significant enough to yield new species. Outside of biology, perhaps the most vocal scientific opponents of Darwinism were the physicists, especially William Thomson, Lord Kelvin. The laws of thermodynamics, articulated and popularized at just about this time, put a limit on the age of the earth and sun that was far too short to accommodate the very long time scales required by evolutionary theory. Not until the discovery of radiation at the turn of the century did it look like the sun could endure long enough for evolution to make sense to physicists.

Darwin's ideas were also widely rejected and widely accepted by the general public. Needless to say, many Victorian readers objected to Darwinism for religious reasons. However, many found it quite satisfying to apply Darwinian principles to the social sphere. Such ideas, known collectively as "social Darwinism," could be used to argue for the rightness of extreme laissez-faire economics or for English imperialism, based on the notion that competition would ensure that the best—people, class, nation—would rise above the rest. Extrapolating from Darwin, people modified his line of thought; to some, it implied *progress* (rather than just *change*, which was Darwin's more modest focus). Herbert Spencer (1820-1903), who began to develop an evolutionary model of society even before the publication of *On the*

Origin of Species, was responsible for articulating many of the doctrines of social Darwinism. Indeed, it was Spencer who coined the term "survival of the fittest"—a term often associated with Darwin, who was eventually sufficiently influenced by Spencer's work to include this term in the fifth edition (1869) of *On the Origin of Species*. In spite of the fact that most of Darwin's twentieth-century fans would like to clear him of all charges of social Darwinism, he was rather divided on the subject himself, sometimes rejecting the notion that his ideas could be applied to social situations (as when he was accused of having proven that might makes right), sometimes worrying that modern social and medical practice (such as vaccination) were actually preserving the unfit. But whether accepted or rejected, Darwin's ideas found their way into virtually every area of Victorian thought, from race, empire, economics, politics, and religion to sexuality, childrearing, birth control, music, medicine and architecture. Certainly his ideas greatly affected the literature of the age, influencing works as varied as George Eliot's *Middlemarch* (1871-72), Robert Louis Stevenson's **The Strange Case of Dr. Jekyll and Mr. Hyde** (1886), H. G. Wells's **The Time Machine** (1895), and Virginia Woolf's *The Voyage Out* (1915) (Eliot's and Stevenson's works also in *WLAIT 4: British and Irish Literature and Its Times*).

—Barri Gold

For More Information

Beer, Gillian. "Introduction." *The Origin of Species*. 2d ed. New York: Oxford University Press, 1996.

———. *Darwin's Plots: Evolutionary Narrative in Darwin, George Eliot and Nineteenth-Century Fiction*. London: Ark, 1985.

Dale, Peter Allen. *In Pursuit of a Scientific Culture: Science, Art, and Society in the Victorian Age*. Madison: University of Wisconsin Press, 1989.

Darwin, Charles. *On the Origin of Species*. A facsimile of the first edition. Cambridge: Harvard University Press, 1998.

Desmond, Adrian, and James Moore. *Darwin: The Life of a Tormented Evolutionist*. New York: Norton, 1991.

Levine, George. *Darwin and the Novelists: Patterns of Science in Victorian Fiction*. Chicago: University of Chicago Press, 1988.

Lightman, Bernard, ed. *Victorian Science in Context*. Chicago: University of Chicago Press, 1997.

Mayr, Ernst. "Introduction." *On the Origin of Species*. Cambridge: Harvard University Press, 1998.

Ruse, Michael. *The Darwinian Revolution: Science Red in Tooth and Claw*. Chicago: University of Chicago Press, 1979.

Tennyson, Alfred. *In Memoriam*. Ed. Robert H. Ross. New York: Norton, 1973.

Passing

by
Nella Larsen

~

Nella Larsen (1891-1964) was born in Chicago of biracial parents, a white mother of Danish ancestry and a black father from the West Indies. Throughout her literary career she cultivated a sense of mystery about her past, so that many biographical details are uncertain. But her father seems to have died when she was two. Larsen was raised mostly in her mother's white middle-class social milieu. At age 16, however, she entered Fisk University's Normal Preparatory School, a high school in Nashville, Tennessee, associated with the well-known black university there. She stayed for only a year; scholars speculate that she may have felt uncomfortable in the unfamiliar black world she found at Fisk. Larsen later worked as a nurse and then as a librarian in New York City, giving up her job to write full time starting in 1926. In two years she published two successful novels, *Quicksand* (1928) and *Passing* (1929). *Quicksand* won the Harmon Foundation's Bronze Medal for Literature in 1928, and in 1930 Larsen became the first black woman to receive a fellowship in creative writing from the prestigious Guggenheim Foundation. However, she never completed her third novel and in fact did not publish again after receiving the fellowship. Critics have expressed bafflement and regret over this abrupt end to her literary career. Among other reasons, they cite the promise that *Passing* shows in its psychologically subtle portrayal of the complex problems that racially mixed men and especially women faced in the highly race-conscious America of the early twentieth century.

THE LITERARY WORK

A novel set in Chicago and New York in 1927; published in 1929.

SYNOPSIS

Tensions arise in the friendship between two black women, one of whom is "passing" as white.

Events in History at the Time of the Novel

America's color line. In the first quarter of the twentieth century the United States was a land sharply divided by color. In the South, where most blacks lived, the so-called Jim Crow laws fixed in place the separation of the races that had existed during the long centuries in which blacks had been enslaved. These laws mandated strict segregation under the various state, county, or municipal legal codes. Under the Jim Crow system, public facilities—from restaurants to restrooms, from shops to movie theaters, and from public schools to public transportation—either excluded blacks completely or shunted them into accommodations far inferior to those enjoyed by whites. In the North, where relatively few blacks lived before the early decades of the twentieth century, segregation was also found in many places but it usually existed on the unwritten level rather than in the law codes. Indeed, laws against segregation, dating from the post Civil

Passing

Nella Larsen

War Reconstruction era, were on the books in many parts of the North. By the early twentieth century, however, they were rarely enforced, and segregation prevailed in areas of most large northern cities. Blacks in the North generally lived in separate neighborhoods, attended separate schools, and were excluded from many public facilities.

Public segregation was only the most visible manifestation of the pervasive racial discrimination that saturated all areas of American society. Indeed, throughout Western civilization in the late nineteenth and early twentieth centuries, racism and racial thinking went largely unquestioned. It was an age in which white colonial empires, ruled by European states, controlled most of the world. These empires' racial aspects were famously exemplified in Rudyard Kipling's poem "The White Man's Burden" (1899), which glorifies the paternalistic brand of imperialism practiced by Great Britain. The "burden" of the title refers to the white man's obligation of conferring on other races what Britain's Kipling saw as the civilizing benefits of being conquered and ruled by whites, who in the process introduced their customs to the colonized. With its victory in the Spanish-American War (1898-1901), the United States took its first steps on the stage of world empire. Kipling's poem was in fact written to celebrate America's arrival as a colonial power (when it wrested the Philippines from Spanish control).

The racial assumptions of empire were underpinned by the accepted scientific theories of the day, which offered detailed and impressive-sounding explanations of whites' supposed superiority. While these racial theories have since been discredited, at the time they were almost universally accepted by the white-dominated societies of both North America and Europe. Even scientists who would later be seen as relatively enlightened espoused some racist views. For example, Franz Boas (1858-1942), the German-American researcher now viewed as the father of modern cultural anthropology, objected to ranking white European cultures above those of other peoples, and he rejected widespread attempts to demonstrate black mental inferiority. Yet Boas also thought, in the words of a recent historian, "that black Americans were genetically inferior to whites and that only through intermarriage and the subsequent modification of the black genetic inheritance would America solve its racial problems" (Wintz, p. 11). Others took more extreme positions. For example, Frederick Hoffman's *Race Traits and Tendencies of the American Negro* (1896) claimed that blacks' inferiority would cause their ultimate extinction. Charles Carroll's *The Negro, Beast or in the Image of God* (1900) blended religious theories with pseudo-science to repeat the common slavery-era assertion that blacks were subhuman and therefore lacked souls.

By the beginning of the twentieth century, the prevalence of racial thinking had contributed to a growing atmosphere of white hostility towards African Americans, whose position in American society had steadily worsened since the end of Reconstruction in the 1880s. In the North a small but unmistakable constellation of black elected public officials had largely vanished by 1900. In the South more than 2,500 lynchings (the torture and murder of black individuals by white mobs) occurred between 1885 and 1900. While the rate declined somewhat over the next two decades, the phenomenon spread during that period to areas such as the Midwest, so that more than 1,100 lynchings were perpetrated nationally between 1900 and the outbreak of World War I in 1917. Altogether nearly 3,500 lynchings have been documented for the period between 1882 and 1938, a conservative estimate since many lynchings escaped public notice. Lynching remained a very real and terrifying threat to blacks for decades. In *Passing*, Irene

Redfield, the novel's main character, beseeches her husband Brian not to mention it in front of their young children.

Equally threatening, if not more so, to African Americans' sense of safety were the violent and bloody race riots that broke out starting around the turn of the twentieth century. At first the most violent outbreaks occurred in the South, for example in Wilmington, North Carolina (1898), and in Atlanta, Georgia (1906). But angry white crowds also instigated random violence against blacks in New York City (1900), Springfield, Illinois (1904 and 1908), and Greensburg, Indiana (1906). World War I (1917-19), during which black soldiers met harsh discrimination in the military even as they were called upon to defend their country, exacerbated America's racial tensions. Violent confrontations between white and black soldiers left dozens killed in army bases across the country. Lynchings and race riots both rose in number sharply during the war, and racial violence took on a new edge when white and black troops returned afterward. Many young black men who had served in the war were no longer willing to tolerate racial abuse. They began fighting back more aggressively and more cohesively than before. In the tense summer of 1919, hundreds were killed as riots erupted in more than 25 northern and southern cities.

"Passing" over the color line. Racial thinking not only fostered disharmony. It also helped perpetuate the popular idea that any black blood in one's ancestry means that one is black, an assumption that has long been accorded an undisputed place in American attitudes toward race. Those of mixed white-and-black descent, known generally as mulattos, were included as a separate subcategory under "Negro" in the United States census numbers for blacks until 1910, at which time they comprised more than 20 percent of the total "Negro" population of some 10 million (Reuter, p. 118). After 1910 they were included without differentiation in the "Negro" population. *Passing* accurately reflects the popular perception that any black blood defined a person as black, in that Irene Redfield and her friend Clare Kendry are considered—and consider themselves—to be black, although both are of racially mixed descent.

On average, those mulattos with more white or light-skinned ancestors found it easier to "pass" in public for white (though as one of Irene's friends observes in the novel, the chances of inheritance will occasionally bring dark-skinned babies to two light-skinned parents). Early in the novel Irene recalls running into Clare in a high-class whites-only restaurant in Chicago; both women are light-skinned mulattos passing in the restaurant for white. However, Clare—blonde, blue-eyed, and fair-skinned—is passing permanently, as it were, while Irene is doing so only in order to be served in the luxurious establishment. Such short-term deceptions were common on the part of those whose light skin and other "white" features permitted them to pass, and it was rare for anyone thus passing to be publicly challenged.

It is not known how many tried passing on a long-term basis, the way the novel's Clare Kendry does, but a headline in the Pittsburgh *Courier* from May 1929 suggested a total of 20,000 passing at that time. Less than two decades later, the noted author and black leader Walter White (himself a light-skinned black) commented on passing in a widely read article called "Why I Choose to Remain a Negro":

> Every year approximately 12,000 white-skinned Negroes disappear—people whose absence cannot be explained by death or emigration. Nearly every one of the 14 million discernible Negroes in the United States knows at least one member of his race who is "passing"—the magic word which means that some Negroes can get by as whites, men and women who have decided that they will be happier and more successful if they flee from the proscription and humiliation which the American color line imposes on them.
>
> (White in Singh, p. 92)

The Great Migration and the founding of a black capital. The spread of segregation and racial violence in the North after the turn of the twentieth century reflects the hostile white reaction to a massive exodus of blacks from the rural South that quickened around that time. Called the Great Migration, this large-scale movement brought significant numbers of blacks to northern cities such as New York and Chicago for the first time. Though smaller numbers had begun moving north as early as the 1890s, in 1910 90 percent of American blacks still lived in the South. The most intense period of migration began around 1915 and persisted through the 1920s, as European immigration diminished and poor rural blacks were drawn north by a growing demand for unskilled labor. An estimated 1.3 million blacks flooded to the North's industrial cities between the end of World War I in 1918 and the beginning of the Great Depression in 1929. The largest number came to New York

Passing

City, the black population of which grew from just below 92,000 in 1910 to almost 330,000 in 1930, an increase of 250 percent. Meanwhile, black populations in other major cities—for example, Chicago, Detroit, and Cleveland—rose at an even higher rate, though their actual numbers were lower than New York's. Throughout this process, immigrants from the American South were joined by smaller numbers of blacks from the West Indies. Although the family history of the novel's Nella Larsen remains uncertain, her father may have been a West Indian mulatto of black and Danish descent who settled in Chicago sometime in the 1890s, in the very earliest stages of the Great Migration.

Whereas before the Great Migration New York's blacks had lived mostly in the squalid San Juan Hill and Tenderloin districts of Manhattan's East Side, the immigrants began establishing neighborhoods in the middle-class area known as Harlem, directly north of Central Park. By 1920 Harlem housed some 73,000 blacks, then two-thirds of Manhattan's black population; by 1930, its black population would rise to 164,000, or three-quarters of the island's blacks. They formed the majority population in the heart of this formerly white district, as they had since 1910. The rapid influx of newcomers reinforced and increased this majority, shaping it into a distinctive community not only in New York. Harlem was emerging as "the capital of black America" (Wintz, p. 20).

As black Harlem grew, it acquired an attractive mystique that made it not only a burgeoning population center but a vibrant cultural capital as well. Black intellectuals, writers, and artists from across America were drawn to it both as a place to live and as a symbol of a newfound sense of black identity. "In Harlem," wrote black intellectual Alain Locke (1886-1954), "Negro life is seizing upon its first chances for group expression and self-determination" (Locke in Singh, p. 9). A respected scholar and critic, Locke used the term "the New Negro" to describe this phenomenon, popularizing the phrase by using it as the title of a widely read anthology of black writing that he edited, *The New Negro* (1925). In his own influential reviews and essays, he publicized the work of younger black writers and artists, becoming "the liaison officer" of an upsurge of black culture that arose in the mid-1920s (Franklin, p. 416). This African American cultural movement has become known as the Harlem Renaissance.

The Harlem Renaissance. While the Harlem Renaissance is most commonly held to have lasted from the mid-1920s to the early 1930s, much of the groundwork for it had been laid by Alain Locke and other early proponents of black culture. James Weldon Johnson (1871-1938), a composer and diplomat as well as a writer and social reformer, played a major role in critiquing and promoting the work of younger black writers and artists. Another important founder of the Harlem Renaissance was Charles S. Johnson (1893-1956), editor of the National Urban League's magazine, *Opportunity*, which under his leadership surpassed W. E. B. Du Bois's *The Crisis* to become the leading black journal of the 1920s. Writers published in these and other Harlem periodicals included major voices of the Harlem Renaissance such as the poets Claude McKay (1890-1948), Langston Hughes (1902-67), and Countee Cullen (1903-46). Larsen knew Cullen well, and prefaces *Passing* with a brief quotation from one of his poems, "Heritage," which was published in his best known collection, *Color* (1925).

Although primarily a literary phenomenon, the Harlem Renaissance also influenced American culture in other ways, particularly in music.

THE BLACK MIDDLE CLASS

By 1900 a small black middle class had begun to emerge in America, mostly among the relatively few blacks who lived in the North. However, unlike in the white world, middle class status for blacks depended on education (often at a black institution such as Fisk Normal School, which Larsen attended) more than on income. Black society had a social structure unto itself: "Domestic servants, waiters, bellhops, barbers, and chauffeurs made up the black middle class; college teachers, lawyers, businessmen, and doctors formed the upper classes" (Singh, p. 71). One mark of having arrived in the upper classes was to employ black servants with darker skin than one's own, as Irene Redfield does in *Passing*. Some critics have understood such details to be humorous satire by Larsen on black social pretensions. One catchword for black middle-class self-improvement was "uplift," at which Irene's husband—a doctor, and thus a member of the upper classes—perhaps snobbishly pokes fun. "Uplifting the brother's no easy job," he jokes, as Irene busily helps to organize a charity ball for the "Negro Welfare League," a fictionalized black activist organization (Larsen, *Passing*, p. 83).

> ## HARLEM AND THE RISE OF BLACK NATIONALISM
>
> In 1909 the black scholar and political activist W. E. B. Du Bois (1868-1963) helped found the National Organization for the Advancement of Colored People (NAACP), the first nationwide organization to advocate the cause of African Americans. Significantly, although it was at first supported largely by progressive whites, the NAACP made its headquarters in Harlem. Du Bois himself moved to Harlem the following year, and from 1910 to 1934 he edited the NAACP's influential magazine *The Crisis*. Starting with his book *The Souls of Black Folk* (1903), Du Bois had long called for an educated black cultural elite to lead the struggle against racism and prejudice. His confrontational agenda conflicted with the more accommodating approach of the other major black leader of the time, Booker T. Washington (1856-1915), who argued not for a liberal arts educated elite, but for blacks to improve their situation in America through vocational training and hard work. A former slave, Washington had operated out of Tuskegee, Alabama, deep in the rural South, and his views evolved out of that environment. But as more blacks found themselves in a northern, urban milieu, they increasingly sought different answers. Du Bois and the NAACP offered one alternative, the Jamaican immigrant Marcus Garvey (1887-1940) offered another. Garvey settled in Harlem in 1916, where he recruited followers for his Universal Negro Improvement Association (UNIA). Proclaiming that black is strong and beautiful, not inferior as the American experience had conditioned its ex-slaves to believe, Garvey boomed his message to receptive ears. He took action as well, founding a steamship company, the Black Star Line, to promote commerce among blacks in America, Africa, and the West Indies, even trying to establish a colony in Africa as an alternative living space. On the streets of Harlem and in other cities, UNIA members participated in lively parades that featured uniformed marching troops in Garvey's Universal Africa Legion. Garvey attracted many enthusiastic followers (even critics estimated that his UNIA grew to at least 500,000 members). But middle-class reformers like Du Bois were skeptical of Garvey's exuberant, working-class radicalism, and the characters in *Passing* reflect their outlook rather than Garvey's. The novel's Irene Redfield, for example, helps organize a benefit dance in Harlem for the fictional "Negro Welfare League," which critics see as a conflation of the NAACP and the National Urban League, another important Harlem-based organization, founded in 1910 to promote the welfare of black city dwellers.

Harlem musicians Fletcher Henderson (1898-1952) and Duke Ellington (1899-1974) took jazz—an African American musical form that became a major contribution to world music—and adapted it for large, orchestra-style bands, turning them into so-called big bands. Such big bands soon became the norm on the American popular music scene. From 1927 to 1931, Ellington—a composer and band leader as well as a pianist—thrilled affluent white audiences at Harlem's glamorous and segregated night spot, the Cotton Club. The Cotton Club's celebrity in the white world suggests much about the fascination that Harlem and black culture began to exert on white society during the frenzied "Jazz Age" of the 1920s. Curious whites sought the thrill of partying uptown in what they perceived as Harlem's exotic environment, enjoying black entertainment but in exclusively white company.

This sudden penchant for black culture among affluent northern whites created a publishing market for many of the Harlem Renaissance's literary works. It was sparked by the popular white author Carl Van Vechten, whose controversial 1926 novel *Nigger Heaven* featured gritty depictions of daily life in Harlem and became a national bestseller. In the ensuing debate, some Harlem Renaissance personalities attacked

Passing

The upper-class of Harlem during the 1930s. Irene Redfield and Clare Kendry are members of Harlem's affluent circle.

the novel, while others defended it. Some became acquainted with the author himself. Van Vechten took a genuine interest in black culture and befriended a number of younger black writers, Nella Larsen among them. In *Passing*, the character of Hugh Wentworth is based on Van Vechten, and indeed the novel itself is dedicated to him, for Van Vechten had recommended the book for publication to Alfred Knopf, his own publisher. The white fascination for Harlem that Van Vechten initiated also plays a part in *Passing*. It gives the novel's Clare Kendry an excuse for spending time with her black friends in Harlem. Clare can masquerade as merely one of the "hundreds of white people" who attend events in Harlem "to see Negroes" and "to gaze on the great and the near-great while they gaze on the Negroes" (*Passing*, p. 104).

The Novel in Focus

The plot. *Passing* has a fairly straightforward plot line, although some complexity arises from the fact that the first third of the novel consists of an extended flashback. Entitled "Encounter," this flashback recounts Irene Redfield's and Clare Kendry's first meeting and its immediate aftermath, and makes up Part 1. Part 2, "Re-Encounter," describes their second meeting, while Part 3, "Finale," focuses on subsequent events. The narrative is in the third person, though it unfolds from Irene's point of view.

As the novel opens in October 1927, at Irene's home in Harlem, Irene has just received the letter from Clare that will lead to their second meeting as described in Part 2. The letter prompts Irene's extended reverie, the flashback through which the reader learns of their first chance meeting, two years earlier, in the summer at the whites-only Drayton Hotel in Chicago. At first, as both women sit alone in the Drayton's exclusive restaurant, they do not recognize each other. Irene fears that the attractive, blonde woman regarding her with such interest has realized that she, Irene, is a Negro, and is about to have her thrown out of the restaurant:

> They always took her for an Italian, a Spaniard, a Mexican, or a gipsy. Never . . . had they even remotely seemed to suspect that she was a Negro. . . . Nevertheless, Irene felt, in turn, anger, scorn, and fear slide over her. It wasn't that she was ashamed of being a Negro, or even of having it declared. It was the idea of being ejected from any place, even in the polite and tactful way that the Drayton would probably do it, that disturbed her.
>
> (*Passing*, pp. 16-17)

However, the woman turns out to be Clare Kendry, whom Irene knew as a child growing up in Chicago. Clare had disappeared from Irene's life after the death of Clare's father, an educated but alcoholic black man who worked as a janitor. As Irene now discovers, after her father's death Clare had moved away and was raised by her father's aunts. These grand-aunts, who were white, raised Clare as white. Their brother, Clare's grandfather, was said to have sown "a wild oat" with a young black girl, Clare's grandmother (*Passing*, p. 32). Clare's father was the result of that seduction. Wishing to keep their brother's seduction of a black girl a secret, her grand-aunts forbade Clare to reveal that she was black. It was as a young white girl that she met and married Jack Bellew, a wealthy white mining executive. Clare tells Irene that it's all been "worth the price," although Irene secretly finds Clare's passing "an abhorrent thing" (*Passing*, pp. 36, 37).

Both women are visiting Chicago, Irene to see her family and Clare with her husband on business. Clare invites Irene to tea in her hotel room the following Tuesday afternoon, along with another mulatto childhood friend, Gertrude Martin. Like Clare, Gertrude has married a white man, but Gertrude's husband Fred is aware that she is black. Gertrude has twin boys but has decided against having further children because she, not her husband, is afraid that their skin might be dark. Clare, who has a daughter, also cites that "hellish" prospect as a reason for having no more children. Irene, offended, embarrasses both women by asserting that her own husband and one of her boys have dark skin (*Passing*, p. 50).

Irene's discomfort is exacerbated by the arrival of Jack Bellew, Clare's husband, who quickly reveals himself to be a strident racist. Irene is shocked and surprised to hear him call Clare "Nig," since he does not know of her true racial status. Then Irene realizes that Bellew believes this to be merely an ironic reference to his wife's olive skin:

> "When we were first married, she was as white as—as—well as white as a lily. But I declare, she's getting darker and darker. I tell her if she don't look out, she'll wake up one of these days and find she's turned into a nigger." He roared with laughter. Clare's ringing bell-like laugh joined his.
>
> (*Passing*, pp. 54-55)

As Bellew continues to express his hatred of African Americans—"black scrimy devils," he calls them—Irene at first feels amused, then has difficulty concealing her rage and contempt (*Passing*, p. 57). The conversation moves on to other subjects before the party breaks up, but as the women bid each other goodbye, Irene decides firmly that she will have nothing further to do with Clare Kendry.

These are Irene's memories after receiving Clare's letter, which arrives at Irene's home in Harlem two years later. Part 2, "Re-Encounter," opens with Irene's pondering how to respond to the letter, in which Clare asks to see Irene again. She shows it to her husband Brian Redfield, a handsome and successful doctor, and they discuss it as their maid, "a small mahogany-colored creature" named Zulena, serves them breakfast (*Passing*, p. 79). Also weighing on Irene's mind is Brian's simmering "dislike and disgust for his profession and his country," which has persisted despite his success as a doctor (*Passing*, p. 84). His dissatisfaction shows itself in his long-held desire to move with his family to Brazil, which he imagines is free of racial discrimination. This fantasy alarms Irene, who views it as the greatest problem in their marriage.

Over the next several days, Irene puts off answering Clare's letter as she busies herself helping to organize a charity event, the annual benefit dance for the Negro Welfare League. However, when Clare turns up at her house in person, Irene finds herself newly charmed by the other woman's beauty. She warns Clare that visiting Harlem is dangerous for her, as it may lead to her husband's learning that she is black. Clare, lonely in her ongoing deception, does not seem to care about the risk of being discovered.

ESCAPE TO BRAZIL—MYTH AND REALITY

"The myth has persisted," about Brazil, says one historian "that there is no racial prejudice. The facts, alas contradict the boast," as do Brazilian novels (Burns, p. 322). Several decades before Larsen documented the anxieties and prejudices suffered by mulattos in the United States, a well-known Brazilian writer, Aluísio Azevedo, published a slice-of-life novel about this same issue. His *O Mulato* (1881, The Mulatto) concerns the love of a light-skinned, blue-eyed mulatto, Raimundo, for a white woman. The novel, which exposes the racism of the white women's family, leads ultimately to Raimundo's death, "a vengeance society wreaked upon him because he dared to be the equal of the 'white' Brazilians" (Burns, p. 205). His fate reflected prejudices in real-life Brazil in the late nineteenth and early twentieth centuries. Employers advertised for white-only workers, using not-so-subtle euphemisms: "good appearance," for example, meant that only light-skinned workers need apply. Branches of government discriminated too. The Brazilian Navy refused to hire blacks to posts demanding contact with foreigners. Still Irene's husband in *Passing* might be happier in Brazil, since he would be moving from a society in which he was a minority within a minority ethnic group to one in which he was part of the majority in a majority ethnic group. In 1890, out of 14.3 million Brazilians, mulattos and blacks together numbered 8 million (of which 6 million were mulatto). Also, though prejudice did exist in Brazil, there was less of it than in other multiracial societies of the day. By the 1920s, when Larsen's novel takes place, racial barriers had already begun to break down in Brazil. It was in the '20s that blacks were first hired to play on Rio de Janeiro soccer teams. By contrast, American baseball wouldn't hire its first black major league player (Jackie Robinson) until 1947.

During Clare's visit, Irene gets a phone call from Hugh Wentworth, a well-known white author, who is also helping with the charity dance. When she learns about the dance, Clare expresses her determination to attend, over Irene's protests. As she tells Irene, "You don't know, you can't realize how I want to see Negroes, to be with them again, to talk with them, to hear them laugh" (*Passing*, p. 108). Later, at the dance, Clare creates a sensation, dancing with many men (she dances several times with Brian Redfield). Clare also sparks the interest of Hugh Wentworth, who asks Irene about "the name, status, and race of the blonde beauty out of the fairy tale" whom he sees on the dance floor (*Passing*, p. 115). Turning their conversation to the subject of passing, Wentworth hints that he suspects Clare may be doing just that, and Irene does not contradict him. For Irene, the dance marks "the beginning of a new friendship with Clare Kendry," who now becomes a frequent visitor to the Redfield home (*Passing*, p. 120).

Part 3, "Finale," opens several months later. It is early December in Harlem, although as Irene admits to herself she feels little of the Christmas spirit. Brian is restless and distant, and Irene fears that the fantasy of moving to Brazil has renewed its grip on him. But when Brian criticizes Hugh Wentworth—who has not hidden his low opinion of Clare—to Irene and defends Clare, Irene is struck by the sudden intuition that her husband is having an affair with Clare. As Christmas comes and goes, her suspicion hardens to conviction, and Irene finds herself growing obsessed with a secret desire for Clare to leave, to be out of their lives.

When Clare, the Redfields, and others of their social set attend a large dinner party at the Harlem home of a black couple named Freeland, Irene finds it difficult to relax and enjoy herself. Suddenly the party is interrupted by the violent intrusion of Jack Bellew, who has tracked his wife to the Freelands. He confronts her next to the open window of their sixth-floor apartment: "So you're a nigger, a damned dirty nigger!" (*Passing*, p. 175). Irene runs to Clare, obsessed by the fear that if Clare is free of her husband, she might steal Brian away. Irene grabs Clare by the arm—and immediately afterward the group of partygoers, distracted by Bellew, is shocked to see that Clare has fallen from the open window. What exactly happened, the reader is told, "Irene Redfield never allowed herself to remember clearly" (*Passing*, p. 176). A white official soon arrives, and it is decided that Clare must have fainted.

Irene finds her knees giving out, and she herself faints. "Death by misadventure," Irene, through her dimmed consciousness, hears the white official conclude about Clare's apparent accident (*Passing*, p. 182).

Class, gender, and color. As Irene, Clare, and Gertrude Martin compare their experiences of motherhood in Part 1, Clare declares that she will have no more children: "I'm afraid. I nearly died of terror the whole nine months before Margery was born for fear that she might be dark" (*Passing*, p. 49). Gertrude, who like the other two women is light-skinned, agrees: "No more for me either. Not even a girl. It's awful the way it skips generations and then pops out. Why, he [Fred, Gertrude's white husband] actually said he didn't care what colour it turned out, if only I would stop worrying. But of course nobody wants a dark child" (*Passing*, p. 49). Like much else in *Passing* (and in Larsen's other novel, *Quicksand*), these comments reflect the ways class, gender, and color have often been intertwined in African American cultural attitudes. The relationship between class and color was long established in black society along the lines suggested above. Light skin was considered socially desirable, and the lighter the skin, the higher social status its wearer could claim. Indeed, the educated black middle class that emerged in the early twentieth century was largely a mulatto class. Thus, for example, the black leaders mentioned above were light-skinned blacks, as were many of the leading figures of the Harlem Renaissance. The mulattoes' privileged position resulted not just from white culture's color-consciousness, but from black culture's as well.

At the same time, as suggested by Gertrude's afterthought "not even a girl," differences existed in the ways that black women and black men were perceived. On one hand, black women frequently found it easier to support themselves (often through domestic work) than black men, and Gertrude's comment may be interpreted in this light. A girl might be preferable to her for this reason, among others. On the other hand, gender bias has permeated black society as well as white society. Black men have been accorded a greater degree of status and importance, and have been afforded more opportunities than women. Women, both black and white, were expected to conform to social roles of subservience, and black women had to contend with the added racial dimension. Hence, in deceiving her husband in the novel Clare commits a double offense: she violates the traditional obedience owed by a wife to her husband as well as the prohibition against transgressing the color line. As critic Cheryl Wall observes,

> In Larsen's novel, "passing" does not refer only to the sociological phenomenon of blacks crossing the color line. It represents additionally both the loss of racial identity and the denial of self required of women who conform to restrictive gender roles.... Irene and Clare... demonstrate the high price black women pay for their acquiescence and, ultimately, the high cost of rebellion.
>
> (Wall, p. 131)

Sources and literary context. Nella Larsen's sources for *Passing* include real-life models for the novel's characters, places, and events, as well as an established literary tradition of books about passing by both black and white American authors. Irene Redfield, according to Larsen's biographer Thadious Davis, "is modeled upon Larsen's girlhood friend Pearl Mayo, and also upon Irene McCoy, a prominent Chicagoan active in the YMCA" (Davis, p. 312). Hugh Wentworth and his wife Bianca are modeled on white author Carl van Vechten (as noted) and his wife Fania Marinoff, while the character of Brian Redfield is based on Larsen's own husband, the respected physicist Elmer Imes. The novel's Drayton Hotel, where Irene and Clare first meet in Chicago, is based on two well-known Chicago hotels, the Drake and the Morrison. While the novel's Negro Welfare League conflates the NAACP and the National Urban League, the charity ball that Irene helps organize is based on the real-life NAACP charity ball—an annual social event in Harlem.

The theme of passing had been treated tangentially in a number of novels about mulattoes starting in the 1870s, including Mark Twain's *The Tragedy of Pudd'nhead Wilson* (1894). The first novels to develop the subject fully were by black authors: Charles W. Chesnutt's *The House Behind the Cedars* (1900) and, most notably, James Weldon Johnson's pioneering work *The Autobiography of an Ex-Colored Man*, the first novel to feature a black narrator. With the advent of the Harlem Renaissance, passing became an especially popular theme, beginning with Walter White's *Flight* (1926). The prolific black female author Jessie Redmon Fauset, with whom Larsen is often compared, treated the subject in her novel *Plum Bun* (1928), which came out the same year as Larsen's *Quicksand*. *Flight*, *Plum Bun*, and *Passing* are often cited as the three classic Harlem Renaissance passing novels. In each, a middle-class mulatto woman gives in to the temptation to pass, marries a strongly racist white man, and finally expresses regret and a nostalgia for the warm company of black peers.

Reception. *Passing* was widely and favorably reviewed, garnering praise in both black publications, such as *The Crisis* and *Opportunity*, and mainstream white ones, such as the *Saturday Review of Literature*, the *New York Herald Tribune*, the *New York Times Book Review*, and the *Times* (of London) *Literary Supplement*. Reviewers, especially white ones, expressed fascination with the exoticism and intrigue of the subject matter, taking interest too in the elements of split personality inherent in it. The praise was qualified, however, by the pinpointing of a few "flaws." A number of critics found the ending contrived, complaining that the crowd staring at Clare could hardly have failed to notice Irene pushing her out the window, as the text strongly hints that she does. Some also found fault with the depiction of Clare Kendry, suggesting that her oft-described beauty rendered her one-dimensional. On the whole, the novel received a less enthusiastic reception than her previous work, *Quicksand*, had.

While some found Larsen's style lacking, others praised both her writing and the deftness with which she examines her characters' complex motivations. An anonymous critic in the *New York Times Book Review*, for example, applauded Larsen's "good, firm, tangible prose" and called the novel "an effective and convincing attempt to portray certain aspects of a vexatious problem" ("Beyond the Color Line," p. 14). "She has produced a work so fine, sensitive and distinguished" wrote W. B. Seabrook in *The Saturday Review of Literature*, "that it rises above race categories and becomes that rare object, a good novel" (Seabrook, p. 1,017).

—Colin Wells

For More Information

"Beyond the Color Line." *New York Times Book Review*, 28 April 1929, 14.

Burns, E. Bradford. *A History of Brazil*. New York: Columbia University Press, 1993.

Carby, Hazel. *Reconstructing Womanhood: The Emergence of the Afro-American Woman Novelist*. Oxford: Oxford University Press, 1987.

Christian, Barbara. *Black Woman Novelists: The Development of a Tradition*. Westport, Conn.: Greenwood Press, 1980.

Davis, Thadious M. *Nella Larsen: Novelist of the Harlem Renaissance*. Baton Rouge: Louisiana State University Press, 1994.

Franklin, John Hope, and Alfred A. Moss, Jr. *From Slavery to Freedom: A History of African Americans*. New York: Knopf, 2000.

Hutchinson, George. *The Harlem Renaissance in Black and White*. Cambridge, Mass.: Harvard University Press, 1995.

Larsen, Nella. *Passing*. New York: Modern Library, 2000.

McDowell, Deborah E. *The Changing Same: Black Women's Literature, Criticism, and Theory*. Bloomington: Indiana State University Press, 1995.

Reuter, Edward Byron. *The Mulatto in the United States*. New York: Negro Universities Press, 1918.

Seabrook, W. B. "Touch of the Tar-Brush," *The Saturday Review of Literature,* 18 May 1929, 1,017.

Singh, Amritjit. *The Novels of the Harlem Renaissance*. University Park, Pa.: Pennsylvania State University Press, 1976.

Wall, Cheryl A. *Women of the Harlem Renaissance*. Bloomington: Indiana State University Press, 1995.

Wintz, Cary D. *Black Culture and the Harlem Renaissance*. College Station, Tex.: Texas A & M University Press, 1996.

Plato's
Apology

by
Plato

> **THE LITERARY WORK**
>
> A dialogue set in the year 399 B.C.E.; although the exact date it was written is uncertain, some sources argue that it was written shortly after the year in which it is set.
>
> **SYNOPSIS**
>
> The *Apology* is a dramatization of the trial at which the philosopher Socrates was found guilty and condemned to death; its title comes from the Greek word *Apologia*, which means "defense."

Plato was born in 427 B.C.E. to an influential, politically active aristocratic family and received the fine education typical for a boy of his background in fifth-century Athens. His various interests included wrestling (he was a champion), politics (his aspirations included running for office), and writing. According to ancient tradition, Plato began his career as a writer anxious to become the next Sophocles, and started composing dramas that supposedly showed some promise. These he promptly sent home and burned upon hearing a lecture by a man destined to become not only Plato's, but the world's teacher: Socrates. Plato studied with Socrates for just under a decade, until the teacher was tried and condemned to death (399 B.C.E.). A young man of 28 at the time, Plato was so disillusioned by the death of Socrates that he left Athens and began to travel. He visited parts of Egypt, Sicily, and present-day Italy before returning to Athens at the age of 40 to found the philosophical school known as the Academy. Plato spent the majority of his time happily absorbed by his writing and teaching of students (among whom would be Aristotle). At the age of 60, Plato received an invitation to act as advisor to the government in Sicily. Plato had written the **Republic** (also in *Literature and Its Times*) by this time, and it was thought that under his guidance the new Sicilian ruler might become the philosopher-king depicted in that dialogue. Things did not go as planned, however; not only were Plato's proposals and ideas viewed as too radical, but Sicily's political situation was unstable to the point of being dangerous. The King, in an attempt to consolidate his power, began exiling and then assassinating several members of his court. Amidst this turmoil, the philosopher decided to return home to Athens, where he devoted himself to his Academy until his death at the age of 81. During Plato's lifetime Athens sank from a great empire to just one of the many Greek city-states jockeying for power. He bore witness to several of its brutal attacks on other city-states, which aggravated his already critical opinion of Athens because of Socrates' trial and execution. Plato's experiences in Sicily had confirmed that Athens was not unique in its less-than-scrupulous approach to public affairs. It should come as no surprise, then, that a great number of the 35 dialogues ascribed to him explore the relationship between morality, or virtue, and

Plato's *Apology*

Plato

politics. In his first dialogue, the *Apology*, Plato's portrayal of Socrates is that of a man committed to the truth at all costs, a man forced to stand trial in large part due to the misperceptions and wounded vanity of some of Athens's most preeminent citizens.

Events in History at the Time the Dialogue Takes Place

Socrates and his trial. The philosopher Socrates was born in 469 B.C.E. to a middle-class family. His mother was a midwife. His father, an artist/craftsman, earned enough to leave Socrates a small inheritance. By all accounts, this is what Socrates lived on until he was put to death by the city of Athens at the age of 70. Socrates had a wife, Xanthippe, and three children, but he never held a job or worked at a trade. All his time was spent practicing philosophy in Athens, and as he reminds us more than once in the *Apology*, he never received payment for his efforts. According to most sources, his family members came second to his philosophic mission; they received little financial or emotional support from him.

Socrates is sometimes spoken of as the first philosopher, but he actually built on the foundation of a group of early Greek thinkers known as the pre-Socratics. Individuals such as Thales, Parmenides, and Heraclitus grappled with questions that can aptly be described as "cosmological"—what is the nature and structure of the cosmos? what set of elements is the world composed of? Generally this first stage of Greek philosophers shared a focus on the external, material world. Sources tend to agree that Socrates developed a different focus; although he began his career as a natural philosopher, at some point he abandoned that inquiry and became a moral philosopher, more interested in man and his search for truth.

Although Socrates was a prolific philosopher, he left no treatises or writings. The only written records of Socrates and his thought are from other people. The majority of Socrates' ideas are handed down to us by Plato, a student of Socrates and one of his closest friends. Other accounts come to us by way of a contemporary of Socrates, Aristophanes, who was a poet and strident critic. Another of his students, Xenophon, wrote a version of Socrates' trial too, as well as accounts of his philosophic conversations.

We know for certain that Socrates was tried on the charges of corrupting the youth of Athens and not believing in the city's gods. Found guilty, he was put to death via ingestion of the poison hemlock. Precisely what transpired during the trial is a matter open to speculation and debate. To what extent the Socrates presented in Plato's *Apology* is the true, historic Socrates, and his speech a close rendition of what he actually said, is a controversial question.

The sophists. The pursuit of philosophy was considered a dangerous, unsavory practice in the Athens of Socrates' day. In part, this was due to the existence of sophists, men who became incredibly wealthy peddling their services as "teachers of wisdom." In reality, many of the sophists taught nothing more than the art of rhetoric. Athens was a very litigious society, and "the Sophists professed to teach the right way of winning these lawsuits," which, in other words, could easily mean "the art of teaching men how to make the unjust appear the just cause" (Copleston, p. 84).

The public at large probably found it hard to distinguish between Socrates and the sophists. It no doubt was difficult for them to differentiate the kind of arguments for which the sophists were famous from Socrates' questioning of Athenian citizens in pursuit of the truth. In fact, it is significant that the *Apology* opens with Socrates denying that he is a sophist, and with an attempt to demonstrate the difference between his teachings and theirs:

> How you, men of Athens, have been affected by my accusers, I do not know. For my part, even I nearly forgot myself because of them, so persuasively did they speak. And yet they have said, so to speak, nothing true. . . . They said you should beware that you are not deceived by me, since I am a clever speaker. They . . . will immediately be refuted by me in deed, as soon as it becomes apparent that I am not a clever speaker at all. . . . I am an orator—but not of their sort. So they, as I say, have said little or nothing true, while from me you will hear the whole truth.
>
> (Plato, *Apology*, pp. 63-64)

Another key distinction Socrates makes between himself and the sophists is to point out that he receives no payment for his discussions or arguments with young people. Socrates mentions by name well-known sophists such as Gorgias, Prodicus, and Hippias; and while they have earned a handsome living teaching young men from wealthy families the art of persuasive rhetoric, Socrates lives in abject poverty.

This association of Socrates with the sophists plagued him throughout his life and was difficult to overcome. They were held in very low regard by just about all segments of Athenian society, democrat and aristocrat alike. Perhaps that is one of the reasons that the most famous of the sophists appear so frequently as characters in Plato's dialogues; like most of Socrates' conversational partners, they are usually on the losing side of an argument, and Plato never misses an opportunity to poke fun at their flowery speeches, their tendency to focus on trivial and insignificant details during a debate, and their utter irreverence for the truth. One of Plato's dialogues, called *The Protagoras* after a well-known sophist, is quite telling in this respect. In this dialogue, Socrates concedes that Protagoras is superior in "speech-making," for he uses tactics that include making "a long speech in reply to every question, staving off objections and not giving answers, but spinning it out until most of the people listening forget what the question was" (Plato, *Protagoras*, p. 36). He himself cannot make such a speech, admits Socrates, but this skill is entirely different from genuine discussion and argument.

The conflict between poetry and philosophy. Ancient Greece was an extremely religious society. Belief in the gods played a major role in almost all aspects of daily life. In addition to the 12 major gods of Olympia, which all Greeks worshipped, each city-state had its own particular set of deities whose mythology often involved the founding of the city (for the Athenians, for example, this would include the goddess Athena). Citizens participated in all kinds of public religious rituals with their fellow citizens on a regular basis, and statesmen and military leaders frequently attempted to consult the gods to determine what their will was with regards to a specific decision or policy. Appeals were also made to the deities to determine what was right or just, a question to which the poets were thought to have particular insight. This was due partly to a belief that poets were inspired by muses, divine creatures who are privy to the ways of the gods. In fact, it was through epic and tragic poetry that the Greeks learned all about the gods, and came into intimate contact with their ways.

Socrates' generation showed high respect for its poets, regarding them as spokesmen for the gods and preservers of the society's religious

THE TEACHER OF TYRANTS?

An aspect of Socrates' career that aroused suspicion among Athenians (and which many believe helped prompt the prosecution to finally bring charges against him) were the political misadventures of his students. One former student, Alcibiades, was exiled several times for anti-democratic intrigue, which included the treacherous act of fleeing to Sparta and aiding it against Athens during the Peloponnesian War. Two other of Socrates' students, Critias and Charmides, were members of the Thirty Tyrants, an anti-democratic oligarchy that ruled Athens for a time. None of these instances could be brought up during Socrates' trial, because a general amnesty for political crimes was declared when Athens re-established democracy. It was thus impossible to charge Socrates with political crimes, but it has been argued that he nevertheless suffered guilt by association with these few students. It is presumably in reference to his students' participation in the oligarchy that Socrates says, "I have never been anyone's teacher; but if anyone, whether younger or older, desired to hear me speaking . . . I never begrudged it to him. . . . And whether any of them becomes an upright man or not, I would not justly be held responsible, since I have never promised or taught instruction to any of them" (*Apology*, p. 86).

Plato's *Apology*

traditions. On the other hand, his generation had little use for the notions of philosophers, which led to a rivalry that is apparent in the *Apology*. It has Socrates repeatedly mention and criticize a real-life comic poet of the day, Aristophanes, "the great reactionary who opposes with all the means at his disposal all the new-fangled things, be it the democracy, the Euripidean tragedy, or the pursuits of Socrates" (Strauss, p. 103).

Socrates used two insights to challenge the authority of the poets. Firstly, he observed a distinction between knowledge and opinion. In the *Apology*, Socrates describes his mission in life as a quest to discover the truth. What he finds is that all of the people he engages in dialogue have opinions about what is true, but these are often contradictory and illogical. These opinions do not seem to be the result of any kind of sustained analysis or even careful thought, and individual convictions are not strongly held. With very little effort, Socrates is able to persuade his dialogue partner to abandon his initial belief and proclaim another one true. Then Socrates examines yet another position, and the individual changes his mind again and adopts still another opinion as true. In this way, Socrates demonstrates that people's opinions on even the gravest matters are not based on fact, and have not been subject to careful scrutiny. Even some beliefs about the Greek gods are a matter of opinion rather than objective knowledge or truth.

Philosophers like Socrates made a second distinction that resulted in an attack on poets and the religious tradition—the distinction between nature and convention. There are things like trees and birds and the sun that exist in nature, no matter what men do. There are other things, like robes, temples, and chariots, that are conventional, or manmade. Is it not possible, ask the philosophers, that the existence of gods is conventional rather than natural? The gods might simply be a function of the poets' art, a fiction that is their creation. The creation, moreover, prevents men from asking questions about subjects such as the origin of man and the nature of the universe. The philosophers are not content with the so-called divine wisdom of the poets; they seek true knowledge rather than what they regard as religious myths about the nature of the cosmos. From the perspective of philosophy, the pronouncements of the poets do not provide definitive answers to the myriad questions of human existence. Meanwhile, the poets see the philosophers as dangerous in that they undermine piety, justice, and support of the city's laws and traditions. Poetry and philosophy are at such cross-purposes that it seems almost natural for some of Socrates' accusers to have been poets who bore him ill will. In fact, one interpretation of the *Apology* is that the dialogue is Plato's attempt to answer the charges of the poets against the pursuit of philosophy and to convince them that the questions, investigations, and criticisms that philosophy generates can be beneficial to the city.

The Dialogue in Focus

The plot. The *Apology*, thought to be one of Plato's earliest dialogues, is his portrayal of the trial and sentencing of his most esteemed teacher, Socrates. As the dialogue opens, Socrates seems to be preparing his audience, the jury, not to expect too much of him during his defense speech. First, he attempts to distinguish himself from the clever rhetoricians of his day by warning the jurors that unlike them, he will simply speak the truth "at random in the words that I happen upon," and not "in beautifully spoken speeches like theirs, adorned with phrases and words" (*Apology*, p. 64). Socrates, referring to his jurors as "the men of Athens," then entreats his fellow citizens to deal with him leniently, stating that although he is 70 years old, this is the first time he has ever appeared in court. A *xenos*, a stranger, or outsider to these proceedings, he asks for the court's sympathy.

After this introduction, Socrates lays out the charges against him. He divides them into two groups, emanating from what he calls the "old" and the "new" accusers. The new accusers are the men who brought the specific, "official" charges against him for which he is on trial. But Socrates says that the older accusers are far more dangerous; they are the ones who have been slandering him and turning public opinion against him for years. Since he views them as the larger threat, he deals with their charges first.

Socrates refers to some of the older poets as his first accusers, specifically Aristophanes, who parodied Socrates in his comedic satire the *Clouds*, a play performed in Athens 24 years before the trial began. According to Socrates, Aristophanes' play had made an informal "indictment" against him, accusing him of the following: "Socrates does injustice, and is meddlesome, by investigating things under the earth and the heavenly things, and by making the weaker speech the stronger, and by teaching others these same things" (*Apology*, p. 66).

> ### ARISTOPHANES' *CLOUDS*
>
> The poet Aristophanes dedicated an entire play to portraying Socrates and his philosophy as a dangerous influence on the city. The lead character is a "regular guy" named Strepsiades. He has made an imprudent marriage, has a bad relationship with his son, and is struggling with seemingly insurmountable debts due to the extravagance of his family. Strepsiades decides that he and his son will attend Socrates' school, the so-called "thinkery," to learn how to make the "weaker speech the stronger" and thus convince his creditors to forgive his debts. At the thinkery, a student of Socrates attempts to impress Strepsiades by recounting the "brilliant" investigations conducted by Socrates that very day. These include "how many of its own feet a flea could leap" when it jumped from person to person and whether "gnats hum through their mouth or through their behind" (Aristophanes, p. 122). As if these descriptions of Socrates were not sufficiently derogatory, the play says that while "investigating the courses and revolutions of the moon and gaping upwards," Socrates was "crapped on" by a lizard (Aristophanes, p. 122). Not only does the play portray Socratic investigations as ridiculous in the extreme; it also portrays the philosopher's preoccupation with metaphysical science as dangerous in that it distracts Socrates and his students from their own basic needs and city concerns. This is why when the play first introduces Socrates, he is hovering in the clouds, suspended from a basket, suggesting his detachment from ordinary citizens and their practical concerns.
>
> Aristophanes also portrays Socrates and his students as purveyors of the art of rhetoric associated with the sophists. S'tepsiades' son, Phidipides, is taught unjust speech at the thinkery, and is able to use it to his advantage with his father's creditors. But Strepsiades soon realizes the full ramifications of life in a society that throws off all its laws and traditions when his son returns from the thinkery proclaiming the uselessness of his father's old-fashioned ideas. Distraught, Strepsiades asks the god Hermes what to do and is told to burn down Socrates' thinkery; only then will society be rid of this disease known as unjust speech. Lawsuits and other civil remedies are not an option, because sophists can simply talk their way out of them by making "the weaker speech the stronger." Ironically *Clouds* closes with the death of Socrates, who some 20 years later refers to this very play in his self-defense speech. Athenian public opinion has been turned so heavily against him for so long by Aristophanes, says Socrates, that overcoming the jury's prejudice against him is hopeless. He has only an afternoon to defend himself, while Aristophanes has been slandering him for many years.

Socrates simply states that "none of these things is so" (*Apology*, p. 66). If anyone in the jury has ever heard him conversing about these topics, they should come forward. But, says Socrates, none of them can because he has never discussed the things Aristophanes accuses him of, and the same holds true for the rest of the rumors Aristophanes has spread about him. Socrates then admits that a member of the jury might well ask why he has been so slandered if he is innocent of all charges. His response is that the Athenians resent him because he possesses wisdom. In order to explain what kind of wisdom he has and why it is unique, he tells the jury how his quest for the truth began.

Socrates recounts how his friend Chaerephon paid a visit to the Oracle of Delphi and asked if there were any man alive wiser than Socrates. The oracle replied that Socrates was the wisest. Socrates recounts his reaction to the oracle's pronouncement for the jury:

Plato's *Apology*

> Whatever is the god saying, and what riddle is he posing? For I am conscious that I am not at all wise, either much or little. So what ever is he saying when he claims I am wisest? Surely he is not saying something false.... And for a long time I was at a loss about what ever he was saying, but then very reluctantly I turned to something like the following investigation of it.
>
> (*Apology*, p. 69)

Socrates' inquiry consisted of questioning the three most well-respected segments of society to prove that they were wiser. He questioned the politicians, the poets, and the craftsmen, always seeking out those reputed to be the wisest. Each time Socrates discovered that while the person knew quite a lot about their particular pursuit, the individual did not possess what could be called true human wisdom.

Socratic wisdom, it turns out, consists of being able to recognize and admit what he does not know, which distinguishes him from his fellow citizens: "As I went away, I reasoned ... 'I am wiser than this human being. For probably neither of us knows anything noble and good, but he supposes he knows something when he does not know, while I ... do not even suppose that I do'" (*Apology*, p. 70). Socrates then took on the mission of demonstrating to those who thought themselves wise that they really were not. This, according to Socrates, is the source of the slander against him. His line of questioning made him hateful, not only to the person questioned, but also "to many of those present" (*Apology*, p. 70). Was the person embarrassed or insulted by his line of questioning? If so, the person could easily fall back on the standard prejudices against philosophy, since there has been a long-standing suspicion of it in Athens.

Next Socrates turns to the specific charges against him by his new accusers, led by the poet Meletus. The charges of the official indictment are that Socrates corrupts the youth, and that he believes not in the gods of the city but in other *daimonia* (or spirits). Socrates brings Meletus to the stand in order to cross-examine him, and what follows is worthy of the most popular courtroom drama. As far as the first charge goes, Socrates, using his dialectic method, succeeds in getting Meletus to agree that: 1) one person alone cannot corrupt the youth—that would take an effort by many, and furthermore; 2) no one would deliberately corrupt the youth in his society, since it would be foolish to turn them into dangerous villains and then be forced to live among them.

> [Socrates] But tell us further, Meletus, before Zeus, whether it is better to dwell among upright citizens or villainous ones.... Do not the villainous do something bad to whoever are nearest to them, while the good do something good?
> [Meletus] Quite so.
> [Socrates] Is there anyone, then, who wishes to be harmed by those he associates with, rather than to be benefited?
> [Meletus] Of course not
> ...
> [Socrates] What then, Meletus? Are you so much wiser at your age than I at mine, that you have become cognizant that the bad always do something bad to those who are closest to them ... whereas I have come into so much ignorance that I am not even cognizant that if I ever do something wretched to any of my associates, I will risk getting back something bad from him?
>
> (*Apology*, p. 75)

Perhaps he has corrupted the youth involuntarily, admits Socrates, but in that case, the city should simply teach and admonish him, not punish him.

Socrates does a similarly brilliant job of disposing of the second charge against him. While the official charge is not believing in the gods of the city, Socrates gets Meletus to refine this charge while he is on the stand, and accuse Socrates of not believing in any gods at all. Socrates always claimed to hear a daimon, the voice of a spirit that warned him against or encouraged him toward a given action. Since such spirits were thought to be the children of gods, or nymphs, or some sort of divinity, Socrates was able to demonstrate that he did believe in gods after all, for "what human being would believe that there are children of gods, but not gods? It would be as strange as if someone believed in children of horses or asses—mules—but did not believe that there are horses and asses" (*Apology*, p. 78). Getting Meletus to change his accusation was a very clever move on Socrates' part, for it allowed him to avoid any discussion of the original charge, which is not believing in the city's gods, of whose traditional actions he was extremely critical.

Having dealt with the official charges against him, Socrates turns to one of the most poignant and powerful elements of his speech. He attempts to reconcile himself and his philosophy to the city of Athens. Socrates explains to the jury that his philosophizing, his relentless questioning and criticizing of fellow citizens is ultimately benefi-

Socrates drinking the poisonous hemlock.

cial for both individual citizens and the city as a whole:

> Best of men, you are an Athenian, from the city that is greatest and best reputed for wisdom and strength: are you not ashamed that you care for having as much money as possible, and reputation, and honor, but that you neither care for nor give thought to prudence, and truth, and how your soul will be the best possible? . . . So I, men of Athens, am now far from making a defense speech on my own behalf, as someone might suppose. I do it rather on your behalf, so that you do not do something wrong concerning the gift of the god to you by voting to condemn me. For if you kill me, you will not easily discover another of my sort . . . in fact, the god seems to me to have set me upon the city. . . . I awaken and persuade and reproach each one of you, and I do not stop settling down everywhere upon you the whole day.
> (*Apology*, p. 81)

In his argument, Socrates compares himself to a gadfly on the sluggish horse that is Athens, a vivid analogy that has endured over time. He admits that his relentless questioning of citizens is annoying, but maintains that it is also necessary, portraying himself not as the self-absorbed, materialistic sophist/scientist described by Aristophanes, but rather as an engaged social critic concerned for the well-being of his city. According to Socrates, Athens desperately needs him to remind citizens of the high and noble aspects of life that are more important than individual wealth, or beauty, or glory. He enlightens them as to what is just and virtuous, and encourages their development of these attributes. Socrates, then, is not only pursuing wisdom for its own sake or his own personal edification; he is pursuing wisdom so he can exhort citizens to virtue, which indicates there is an element of public spiritedness to his philosophy.

Socrates then attempts to garner sympathy from the jury, while simultaneously explaining his aloofness and detachment from ordinary obligations, which Aristophanes has criticized. The defendant tells the jury that he has neglected many aspects of his private life in order to fulfill his mission to the city of Athens. He lives in poverty and his own family has been "uncared for" all these years so that he might go to citizens privately, "as a father or an older brother," and persuade them to care for virtue (*Apology*, p. 82). (In fact, Socrates was known to spend all his time questioning fellow citizens or engaging in philosophical discussion with his followers.) So his philosophy, rather than consisting of abstract investigations of stars and gnats that are of little use to the city, actually focuses on the city and its affairs so much that Socrates neglects his own personal needs.

Plato's *Apology*

Next, Socrates attempts to account for his lack of involvement in public affairs, which would have been very damning in the eyes of the Athenians. Citizens were expected to participate in many facets of the democracy, and this included going to assemblies, holding public office, making speeches, and sitting on juries. Socrates admits that it might seem strange that he is "a busybody in private," while "in public I do not dare go up before your multitude to counsel the city" (*Apology*, p. 83). According to Socrates, his divine voice warned him not to enter politics, probably because if he had he would have been killed: "For there is no human being who will preserve his life if he genuinely opposed either you or any other multitude" (*Apology*, p. 83). If he had died young, he says, he would not have fulfilled his god-given purpose of goading his fellow Athenians to virtue.

All of Socrates' skillful argument comes to naught, for the jury finds him guilty. Then the sentencing phase of the trial begins. Meletus makes a speech requesting the death penalty, and Socrates is expected to make a counterproposal. Considering his various options, Socrates rejects exile, realizing that if his fellow citizens cast him out because of his philosophizing, so will every other city in the world. But what about, "being silent and keeping quiet" in exile? Socrates rejects this alternative, uttering the famous dictum that "the unexamined life is not worth living for a human being" (*Apology*, p. 92). Socrates makes an ironic counterproposal: he should be rewarded for his service to the city by being housed and fed at Athens' expense, like the victorious Olympic athletes. He concludes with a second counterproposal, a fine of 30 *minae*, quite a large sum of money. As shown, the options of exile and silence are unacceptable. Socrates is prepared rather to make the ultimate sacrifice for his pursuit of truth: his life.

Once the jury has deliberated and handed down the death sentence for Socrates, he addresses the jury again. Tellingly he now uses the word *judges* in his speech for the first time. (It was customary in those days to address the members of juries by the title of *judges* during court proceedings, but Socrates has not used that term until this point.) He says that he will call only the men who voted to acquit him judges, because they are the only "judges in truth" (*Apology*, p. 95). He says he is not worried about death, because his divine voice is silent. It has not warned him of impending evil or tried to stop him from anything he was going to say during his trial. Either, he surmises, death is like a quiet restful sleep, which is nothing to fear, or it is a journey to Hades, the underworld. But if there is a Hades, even death will not stop him in his pursuit of true knowledge:

> Certainly the greatest thing is that I would pass my time examining and searching out among those there—just as I do to those here—who among them is wise, and who supposes that he is, but is not. How much would one give, judges, to examine him who led the great army against Troy, or Odysseus, or Sisyphus, or the thousand others whom one might mention, both men and women? To converse and to associate with them and to examine them there would be inconceivable happiness.
> (*Apology*, p. 96)

Civil disobedience. Towards the end of his defense, Socrates decides to present the jurors with two examples of his political action. In this way he will offer proof of his commitment to virtue "not in speeches, but what *you* honor, deeds. (*Apology*, p. 83, emphasis Plato's).

The first example occurs during Socrates's tenure on the Athenian Council, which is the one political office he held during his lifetime. The citizenry of Athens were divided into administrative units called tribes, and every year men were chosen by lot to serve on an administrative council as *prytanes*, or board member for a portion of the year. In 406 B.C.E., Athens was in the midst of the Peloponnesian War with Sparta, a 27-year conflict which pitted democracy against oligarchy in a struggle for control of the Greek city-states. Socrates was serving as a *prytanes* when the ten generals who had commanded the Athenian naval fleet at the Battle of Arginusae were facing trial. Although the generals orchestrated a brilliant victory at Arginusae, which is an island in the Aegean Sea, they were forced to leave disabled ships and Athenian soldiers behind because of the confusion after battle and the arrival of a violent storm. Upon their return to Athens, the generals were brought up on charges of neglecting their duty, which included a charge of impiety because of their failure to insure that the dead soldiers received a decent burial with all the appropriate rites.

The board decided to try the generals together, which Socrates held was blatantly unfair; each commander had the right to be tried separately based on the merits of his own particular case. Socrates brought a motion challenging the decision, and according to legal procedure in fifth-century Athens, the trial should have been suspended until the motion was considered. But public indignation against the generals was so strong that the presiding officers brushed the motion aside and proceeded with the trial. All of the prytanes except Socrates succumbed to threats and other tactics of intimidation, and the trial culminated in the execution of the Athenian generals. Later, when cooler heads prevailed, the Athenians realized that they had committed an injustice. He alone, Socrates reminds his fellow citizens, refused to be a party to the "mob mentality" that had prevailed in Athens:

> I alone of the prytanes opposed your doing anything against the laws then, and I voted against it. And although the orators were ready to indict me and arrest me . . . I supposed that I should run the risk with the law and the just rather than side with you because of fear of prison or death when you were counseling unjust things.
> (*Apology*, p. 84)

The second instance of Socrates' involvement in the unjust proceedings of Athenian politics occurred not during the democracy, but during Athens' brief rule by an oligarchy. The Thirty Tyrants had been installed in Athens by the Spartans at the end of the Peloponnesian War, aided and abetted by Athenian citizens who had antidemocratic leanings. The regime enjoyed little popular support, and its brief tenure was maintained by the presence of a garrison of Spartan soldiers in Athens. In order to raise money to support this garrison, the Thirty Tyrants began to execute wealthy residents who were not Athenian citizens, and then liquidate their assets. When the Thirty Tyrants summoned Socrates, along with several other prominent citizens, and gave them the order to "arrest Leon the Salaminian and bring him from Salamis to die," Socrates refused (*Apology*, p. 84): "Perhaps I would have died because of this, if that government had not been quickly overthrown" (*Apology*, pp. 84-85).

With these two examples, Socrates demonstrates the difficulties of a public and political life. Communities do not always act justly, so there is often a conflict between true justice and the laws or will of the city. Socrates' primary commitment is to the pursuit of true justice, which has sometimes prompted his taking political action against the city-state. In retrospect, this pursuit of justice, without regard for its consequences, can be seen as heroic.

Sources and literary context. The source material for Plato's *Apology* was an actual event, the trial of Socrates. The only other account we have of the trial was the one written by Socrates' student Xenophon. Xenophon's *Apology* is sometimes described as corroborating evidence for Plato's account, since the two works are, in many respects, similar. However, others argue that Plato's *Apology* presents an idealized portrait of Socrates. This school of thought argues that Plato's and Xenophon's presentations of how Socrates conducted himself at the trial are indeed different, even contradictory, and that Plato's Socrates is nothing like the poet Aristophanes' portrayal of him either. These same scholars conclude that Plato, in attempting to respond to the various criticisms of his teacher, portrays a new Socrates in the *Apology*. This ideal Socrates is a teacher of civic virtue, interested in the concerns of the city. He has turned away from abstract philosophy as the lone pursuit of wisdom, and employs it to assist his fellow citizens in the attainment of true knowledge, which can be used in settling disagreements over what is good and just in Athens.

TWO PLATOS?

There is an ongoing debate among scholars as to the question of whether multiple authors are responsible for Plato's body of work. According to a few critics, there is a great disparity between Plato's earlier and later dialogues. A difference in tone, emphasis, perspective, and even conclusions has led some scholars to argue that certain dialogues were written by a student of Plato's. But it is equally possible in view of the fact that Plato's career spanned 40 years, that the mature Plato came to different conclusions than the young Plato, who was perhaps more susceptible to Socrates' teachings. In his later dialogues, Plato often relegates Socrates to a minor character, and no longer uses him as his mouthpiece.

Precisely how much of this account is Plato's simple transcription of Socrates' words, and how much is Plato's original thought is an ongoing debate that may never be settled definitively. Whatever the exact relationship between Socrates' words and Plato's writings, out of it was born a series of dialogues unparalleled in philosophic and literary achievement:

> It is to Plato's literary genius that Socrates owes his pre-eminent position as a secular saint of Western civilization. And it is Socrates who keeps Plato on the best-seller lists. Plato is the

Plato's *Apology*

only philosopher who turned metaphysics into drama. Without the enigmatic and engaging Socrates as the principal character of his dialogues, Plato would not be the only philosopher who continues to charm a wide audience in every generation.

(Stone, p. 4)

Events in History at the Time the Dialogue Was Written

Athenian imperialism. Athens dealt brutally with city-states that proved to be too independent for its taste, and Plato viewed these acts of the empire with "moral revulsion" (O'Hare, p. 2). In fact, some of the political realities of relationships between Athens and its allies were much harsher than one might assume. For example, a city-state was under strict instructions when initiated into the Delian League (an alliance of the various city-states originally formed for mutual protection against the common enemy of Persia, and ultimately dominated by Athens). The city-state had to adopt a constitution modelled on that of Athens, send offerings to the Athenian religious festivals, receive Athenian inspectors, adopt the Athenian systems of currency and weights and measurements, and require all of its own officials to take an oath of loyalty to Athens.

As Athens suffered increasing losses during the Peloponnesian War (432-404 B.C.E.), city-states that tried to assert their independence were appreciated even less. The examples of Melos and Mytilene are cases in point. When faced with the possible rebellion on the island of Mytilene, the Athenian assembly heard arguments for and against the total annihilation of its citizens. Although the arguments urging more moderate measures won the day, these consisted of bringing in thousands of Athenians to occupy the island as colonists, turning the inhabitants into serfs, and confiscating the island's fleet and fortifications. The massacre at Melos is an even more violent example of Athenian brutality. The Melians insisted on remaining neutral during the Peloponnesian War. Athens several times attempted to convince Melos to do otherwise, sending a large military contingent to the island to intimidate it, and one year later demanding tribute. When officials refused to comply, Athens sent a portion of its army to the island to convey in no uncertain terms that neutrality was no longer acceptable.

Melos was defeated after a long siege, whereupon the Athenian Assembly voted to execute all of Melos's male inhabitants, take its women and children as slaves, and send Athenians to occupy it. The orders were executed by the Athenian forces, with predictably gruesome results.

In view of such real-life incidents, Plato saw a great disparity between Athens' stated ideals of freedom and democracy and Athens' often ruthless practices towards its so-called allies. It is this type of incident that may have inspired him to argue that Athens was in dire need of a philosopher to instruct the Assembly on moral issues and to remind citizens of what virtue is.

Political and social change in Athens. As disappointing as the gulf between the theoretical and practical aspects of Athenian politics in the fifth century was for an idealist like Plato, the situation would worsen considerably in the fourth century. The Peloponnesian War seemed to have exhausted Athens both materially and spiritually. Philip II of Macedon found it easy to seize one part of Greece after another as he made his conquering way through the areas surrounding Macedonia. He placated Athens on the way, assuring the once great city that it had nothing to fear from him. A single individual, an orator by the name of Demosthenes, attempted to alert the Athenians to the danger Philip presented, pleading with them to send out forces against his approaching armies. But Athens was already in a desperate state militarily. No longer were its garrisons composed of citizens; the work of soldiers was doled out to paid mercenaries, a practice un-

---

> **TREASURES IN THE DIALOGUES**
>
> One of the contributions to Western thought for which Plato is famous is his choice of format. The strategy that Plato's Socrates uses is the dialectic method, whereby principles are examined and accepted or rejected via a dialogue consisting of questions and answers. In addition to the contributions that Plato's dialogues have made to philosophy, they are invaluable from a social and historical perspective. The dialogues are peppered with events and individuals that comprised Athenian intellectual life in the late fifth century B.C.E. We meet notorious politicians such as Alcibiades, famous playwrights such as Aristophanes, clever sophists, or teachers of wisdom, such as Gorgias and Protagoras, and numerous scholars, scientists, and other imminent personages. As one scholar has noted, "Plato is conveying not only ideas but a portrait of the society in which they were formed" (Segal, p. xii).

heard of in earlier days. Often as not, these mercenaries abandoned their post in the middle of a campaign to go off in search of a more lucrative war. This was a sad contrast to fifth-century Athens, when "Athenian forces were everywhere, the citizens ready for anything," and no one had to be reminded to defend the *polis* and their most vital interests (Kitto, p. 155-56). In the end, Philip conquered not only Athens, but all of Greece, which led to the eventual collapse of the *polis*, the political/social unit known as a city-state.

There is no question but that the political upheaval of his time had a profound impact on Plato and the ways in which he used Socrates's teachings in his writing. The decline of the Athenian empire, Athens' decades-long struggle between oligarchy and democracy, and the dissolution of the Greek political system based on the *polis* help explain Plato's concerns. They clarify why so much of his writing deals with questions of importance to political communities, such as what is the definition of virtue? the definition of justice? the organization of the best regime? the proper relationship between philosophy and politics? and the proper relationship between religion and politics?

Reception. Although Socrates was not successful in defending himself at trial, we know that he did convince a significant amount of the jurors, for it would only have taken 30 additional votes (out of a jury of 500) to acquit him. Socrates's students were devastated by their teacher's sentence, and a sequel to the *Apology* called the *Crito* tells of what lengths they were willing to go to save their teacher from what they saw as the height of injustice. In the *Crito*, a student visits a peaceful Socrates in his cell, offering to help him escape jail and the death sentence that awaits him the next day. Socrates refuses, arguing that even when laws or court verdicts are unjust, they must be respected and slowly challenged and changed, not blatantly disobeyed.

Aristotle, Plato's student, actually saw much in Plato's account of the trial that left something to be desired in terms of Socrates's performance.

Aristotle argues that Socrates neglected to follow the most basic rule in using persuasive rhetoric: do not anger those whom you are trying to persuade. In Aristotle's reading, Socrates seems to go out of his way to be antagonistic toward the jury, which is no way to get them to vote for him. Interestingly, what Aristotle saw as a defect, others through the ages have seen as inspiring. Socrates was a martyr for truth and knowledge. He refused to pander to the masses, choosing instead to stand and fight for the individual's right of free inquiry and free speech against the sometimes oppressive power of the state.

—Despina Korovessis

For More Information

Aristophanes. *Clouds*. In *Four Texts on Socrates: Plato's Euthyphro, Apology, and Crito and Aristophanes' Clouds*. Trans. Thomas G. West and Grace Starry West. Ithaca: Cornell University Press, 1984.

Copleston, Frederick, S. J. *Greece and Rome*. Vol. 1, *A History of Philosophy*. New York: Doubleday, 1993.

Finely, M. I. *Early Greece: The Bronze and Archaiac Ages*. New York: W. W. Norton, 1982.

Kitto, H. D. F. *The Greeks*. Middlesex: Penguin, 1952.

Nichols, Mary P. *Socrates and the Political Community: An Ancient Debate*. New York: SUNY Press, 1987.

O'Hare, R. M. *Plato*. Oxford: Oxford University Press, 1996.

Plato. *Apology*. In *Four Texts on Socrates: Plato's Euthyphro, Apology, and Crito and Aristophanes' Clouds*. Trans. Thomas G. West and Grace Starry West. Ithaca: Cornell University Press, 1984.

———. *Protagoras*. Trans. C. C. W. Taylor. Oxford: Oxford University Press, 1996.

Segal, Erich. Introduction to *The Dialogues of Plato*, by Plato. New York: Bantam, 1986.

Stone, I. F. *The Trial of Socrates*. New York: Random House, 1989.

Strauss, Leo. *The Rebirth of Classical Political Rationalism*. Chicago: University of Chicago Press, 1989.

Thucydides. *History of the Peloponnesian War*. Trans. Richard Crawley. London: Orion, 1993.

Richard III

by
William Shakespeare

> **THE LITERARY WORK**
>
> A historical play, set in England from 1483 to 1485; first performed in 1593, first published in 1598.
>
> **SYNOPSIS**
>
> An evil duke usurps the throne of England and eliminates all rival claimants, but is ultimately overthrown himself.

Born in 1564 in Stratford-on-Avon, England, William Shakespeare was the son of middle-class parents. Although not all the particulars of Shakespeare's education are known, it appears that he attended the local grammar school, where the curriculum apparently included rhetoric, Christian ethics, and classical literature. During the 1580s, after an early marriage to Anne Hathaway, who was eight years his senior, Shakespeare relocated to London. He moved there without her and began a career as an actor, then a playwright, for the theater company known as the Lord Chamberlain's Men. In the 1590s, Shakespeare wrote a series of historical plays dealing with England's past—specifically, the tumultuous struggle for the throne called the Wars of the Roses. *Richard III* is actually the last in a series of four plays. It is preceded by a trilogy about Henry VI—focusing on the bloody conflict between the royal houses of York and Lancaster. This last play in the series is notable for its title character; one of Shakespeare's greatest villains, he is a monstrous hunchback, whose wit, ambition, and audacity command the audience's attention.

Events in History at the Time the Play Takes Place

The Wars of the Roses—Richard comes to court. At issue in *Richard III* is a shift taking place in the seat of power in England. The medieval arrangement whereby feudal lords controlled certain domains had been changing to a more centralized system whereby a single king controlled the whole land and could deploy armies. Under Richard III, the final maneuvers to achieve this shift occurred. The subsequent king, Henry VII (Henry Tudor), married Elizabeth of York, and in so doing brought together two warring factions. No longer would there be a jockeying for power between factionalized descendants of two houses (York and Lancaster). The fateful marriage would instead give rise to a long line of Tudor monarchs who reigned over an increasingly united kingdom. *Richard III* occurs just prior to the marriage, near the end of the civil strife between York and Lancaster.

A longstanding conflict, the strife between York and Lancaster became known as the Wars of the Roses (1455-85) after the families' emblems. The white rose belonged to York; the red rose has been associated with the House of Lancaster.

Richard III

William Shakespeare

On the Side of the House of York
Richard, duke of York
Edward, earl of March, later Edward IV
Edmund, earl of Rutland
Richard, duke of Gloucester (later Richard III)
Elizabeth of York (future wife of Henry Tudor)

On the Side of the House of Lancaster
Henry VI
Queen Margaret of Anjou (married to Henry VI)
Prince Edward
Henry Tudor, earl of Richmond (Henry VII, of the new Tudor dynasty)

Those Who Switched Sides
Richard Neville, earl of Warwick (from York to Lancaster)
Lady Anne Neville (from York to Lancaster to York; married Richard of Gloucester)
Elizabeth Woodville (from Lancaster to York; married Edward IV)
George, duke of Clarence (from York to Lancaster to York)
Henry Stafford, duke of Buckingham (from York to Lancaster)
Robert Stanley, Lord Stanley (from York to Lancaster)

Although full-scale war did not erupt until the 1450s, the roots of the conflict date back to 1399, when King Richard II was deposed by his cousin Henry Bolingbroke, son of the duke of Lancaster. Bolingbroke ascended to the throne as Henry IV, while Richard II met a mysterious death in the Tower of London, a death that many believe was ordered by the new king (see *Henry IV, Part 1*, also in *Literature and Its Times*). Bolingbroke's son, Henry V, won famous victories and laid claim to the throne of France, England's greatest rival on the world scene. However, the early death of Henry V left England in the hands of his infant son, Henry VI, who proved to be a weak ruler, sickly and even prone to fits of madness. The royal court was dominated by Henry's queen, Margaret of Anjou, who was a generous friend to her adherents and an implacable foe to those she perceived as her enemies. The latter included Richard, duke of York (called York), who came to believe that his right to the throne was superior, because he was descended from the second son of Edward III, while Henry VI was descended from the third son.

Until the birth of a royal prince in 1453, York was recognized as heir to the throne after Henry VI. That same year, Henry VI suffered an episode of madness and York governed England as protector of the realm. After Henry recovered in 1454, York soon found himself excluded from the royal council, so he took up arms. Fighting broke out in 1455. Henry's side was defeated at the battle of St. Albans, but he remained king, with York serving as protector again. Conflict resumed in 1459, and the Yorkists were forced to flee the country. They returned in 1460, defeated the Lancastrians, imprisoned Henry VI, and forced him to name York and York's sons as his heirs. Queen Margaret of Anjou, whose own son was disinherited as a result, fled to Scotland and raised an army to continue the struggle. On December 30, 1460, the Lancastrians violated a Christmas truce by attacking the Yorkists outside Sandal Castle near Wakefield. York was killed. So were his second son, the earl of Rutland, and his ally, the earl of Salisbury. Their three heads, York's ornamented by a paper crown, were mounted over Micklegate Bar.

The Yorkist cause was swiftly taken up by York's eldest son, Edward, the earl of March, who defeated a Lancastrian army at Mortimer's Cross in 1461. Having won control over London, the Yorkists entered the city on March 4, 1461, and proclaimed their leader King Edward IV. They proceeded to crush the Lancastarian army at the battle of Towton, after which Henry VI, Queen Margaret, and their son fled to Scotland and then France. Once ensconced on the throne, Edward IV recalled his much younger brothers, George and Richard, from the French shores of Burgundy, where their mother, the duchess of York,

A Partial Genealogy of York and Lancaster Factions

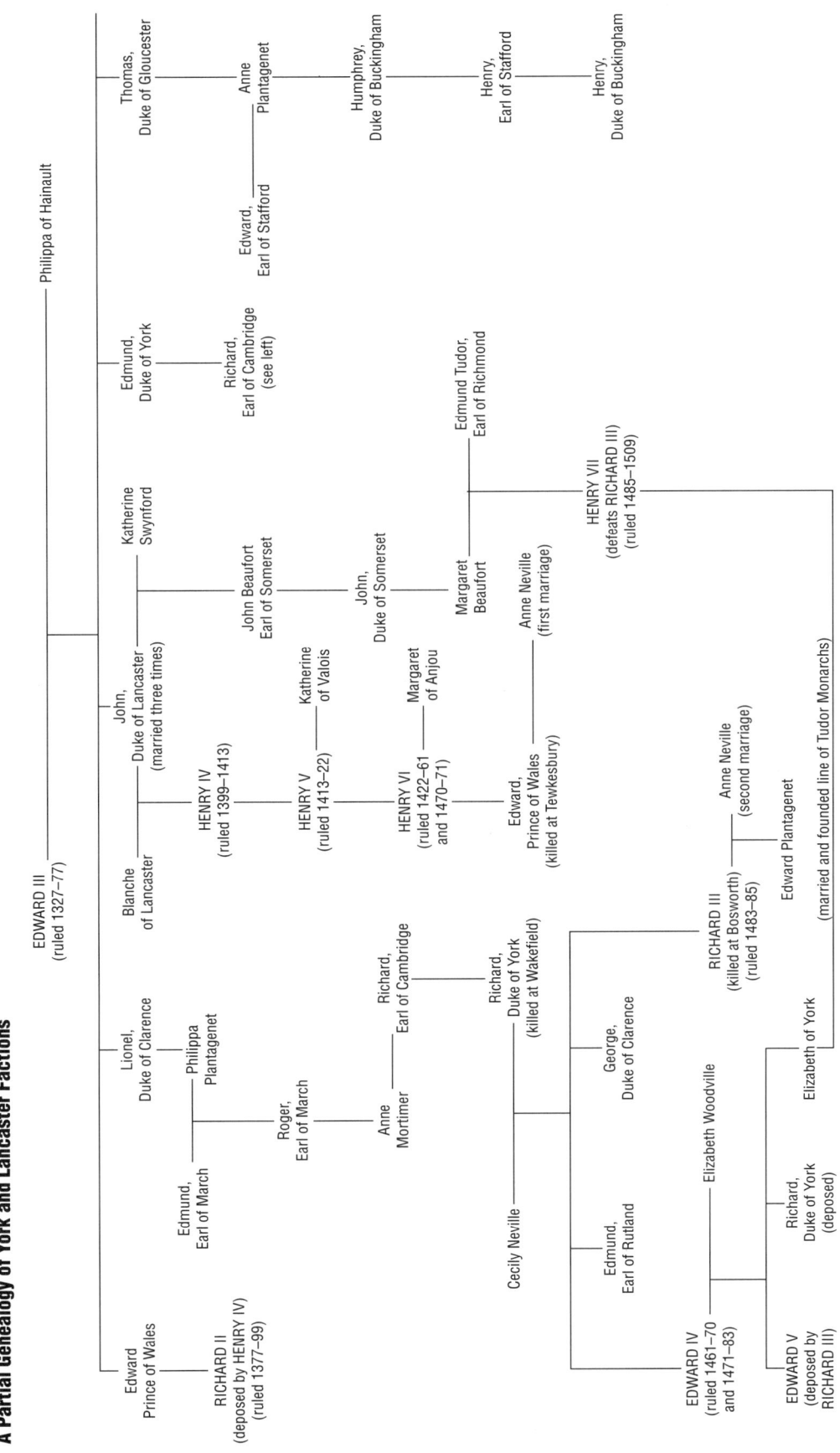

Richard III

EDWARD III (ruled 1327–77) — Philippa of Hainault

Children of Edward III:
- Edward, Prince of Wales
- Lionel, Duke of Clarence
- John, Duke of Lancaster (married three times) — Blanche of Lancaster; Katherine Swynford
- Edmund, Duke of York
- Thomas, Duke of Gloucester

Lancaster line (through John of Gaunt and Blanche):
- HENRY IV (ruled 1399–1413)
- HENRY V (ruled 1413–22) — Katherine of Valois
- HENRY VI (ruled 1422–61 and 1470–71) — Margaret of Anjou
- Edward, Prince of Wales (killed at Tewkesbury) — Anne Neville (first marriage)

Beaufort line (through John of Gaunt and Katherine Swynford):
- John Beaufort, Earl of Somerset
- John, Duke of Somerset
- Margaret Beaufort — Edmund Tudor, Earl of Richmond
- HENRY VII (defeats RICHARD III) (ruled 1485–1509) — Elizabeth of York (married and founded line of Tudor Monarchs)

York line (through Edmund, Duke of York):
- Richard, Earl of Cambridge (see left)

Through Lionel, Duke of Clarence:
- Philippa Plantagenet
- Roger, Earl of March
- Edmund, Earl of March
- Anne Mortimer — Richard, Earl of Cambridge
- Richard, Duke of York (killed at Wakefield) — Cecily Neville

Children of Richard, Duke of York and Cecily Neville:
- Edmund, Earl of Rutland
- EDWARD IV (ruled 1461–70 and 1471–83) — Elizabeth Woodville
- George, Duke of Clarence
- RICHARD III (killed at Bosworth) (ruled 1483–85) — Anne Neville (second marriage)

Children of Edward IV and Elizabeth Woodville:
- EDWARD V (deposed by RICHARD III)
- Richard, Duke of York (deposed)
- Elizabeth of York

Child of Richard III and Anne Neville:
- Edward Plantagenet

Through Thomas, Duke of Gloucester:
- Anne Plantagenet — Edmund, Earl of Stafford
- Humphrey, Duke of Buckingham
- Henry, Earl of Stafford
- Henry, Duke of Buckingham

RICHARD II (deposed by HENRY IV) (ruled 1377–99)

LITERATURE AND ITS TIMES ∾ SUPPLEMENT 1, PART 1

Richard III

had sent them for safety. George was created duke of Clarence; Richard, duke of Gloucester.

The Wars of the Roses—Richard enters the fray. Although the early years of the new king's reign seemed to promise peace and stability, a rift occurred in 1464 between Edward IV and the earl of Warwick, his chief ally. While Warwick had been negotiating an advantageous French marriage for the king, Edward had secretly wed Elizabeth Woodville Grey. Once Edward IV revealed his marriage, Warwick felt both humiliated and threatened by the queen's ambitious relatives, who dominated the court. Relations between Warwick and Edward deteriorated, and the earl attempted to win over to his side the king's brothers; he succeeded with George, duke of Clarence (known also as Clarence), but Richard, duke of Gloucester (known as Gloucester) remained loyal to the king.

Allying himself with the Lancasters, Warwick fled to France and returned in 1470 with an army. Clarence, now married to Warwick's elder daughter, sided with Warwick, going against his own brother, Edward. In response, Edward IV and his adherents, including Gloucester, fled to Burgundy, and Henry VI was restored to the throne. There was yet another turnaround, though. With help from his allies overseas, Edward returned to England and reclaimed the crown, defeating Lancastrian forces decisively at the battle of Barnet—where Warwick was killed—and the battle of Tewkesbury, where Henry VI's son, Prince Edward, was slain. Clarence, meanwhile, had deserted Warwick and returned to his brother's side, ever aiming to ally himself with the winner. Shortly after Edward IV's triumphant return to the throne, the captive Henry VI died mysteriously in the Tower of London. His queen, Margaret of Anjou, was exiled to France, where she died in 1482. With the elimination of the legitimate Lancastrian line, Edward IV enjoyed comparative peace for the rest of his reign. But the Wars of the Roses did not end here. Edward died in 1483, after which his brother Richard, duke of Gloucester usurped the throne. He confined his nephews in the Tower, then reigned as Richard III (1483-85) until the Wars of the Roses flared into a final episode, recounted in Shakespeare's play. In 1485 forces under Henry Tudor, earl of Richmond, who was related by marriage to the Lancastrians, defeated and killed Richard III. The York dynasty's bid for the throne had finally come to an end.

In Shakespeare's play, the bitter legacy of the Wars of the Roses casts a long shadow over all the characters. Continual references are made to atrocities committed by both sides. Old Queen Margaret slinks through King Edward's court, cursing her Yorkist enemies for the deaths of her husband and son, while the courtiers, led by Gloucester, revile her for her part in the deaths of the elder duke of York and earl of Rutland. The defeat of Richard III at Bosworth Field is presented by Shakespeare as the end of a terrible age and the beginning of a bright new era, heralded by the Tudors' accession to the throne.

Clarence and Gloucester. The relationship between Edward IV and his two younger brothers was complicated enough to inspire a play in its own right. Although Clarence and Edward had been reconciled during the latter's bid to reclaim the throne, it was not long before the brothers were again at odds. In 1477, after the death of his first wife in childbirth, Clarence made a matrimonial bid for the hand of Mary, daughter of the recently deceased duke of Burgundy and one of the greatest heiresses in Europe. Edward IV, however, refused to allow the marriage and instead suggested she marry his wife's brother, Earl Rivers, which incensed Clarence.

Thereafter, Clarence's behavior became increasingly erratic. He arrested and executed two of his late wife's servants, charging them with having poisoned her and her infant son. Later Clarence publicly accused the king of trying to destroy him, cast doubts on the validity of Edward's marriage to Elizabeth Woodville, and spread the story that Edward was the illegitimate offspring of an affair between the duchess of York and an unknown archer. Having gathered a handful of retainers and followers, Clarence ignited a small uprising, but it quickly flickered out.

In June 1477 Edward IV learned that Clarence had sought the hand of Mary of Burgundy for the main purpose of seizing the English throne. The king promptly had Clarence arrested on charges of treason and consigned to the Tower of London. On learning of Clarence's arrest, Gloucester attempted to intercede with Edward IV to spare their brother's life, but in early 1478 Clarence was tried by parliament on the charge of high treason, found guilty, and sentenced to death. The sentence was carried out on February 18, 1478; according to one current story, Clarence was drowned in a vat of his favorite malmsey wine.

By contrast, the relationship between Edward IV and his youngest brother, Richard, duke of Gloucester, was amicable, even close. Gloucester had remained loyal to the king throughout his brief exile and served as wing commander of Edward's army during the battles of Barnet and Tewkesbury. After Edward IV was restored to the throne, he bestowed still more honors on Gloucester; in addition to regaining his positions as Constable and Admiral of England, Gloucester was named Great Chamberlain and Steward of the Duchy of Lancaster beyond Trent. Finally, needing a capable military leader to deal with the frequent problems along the Scottish border, the king turned over to Gloucester all of Warwick's castles and estates that were located in the north country.

Before leaving for the North, Gloucester secured the king's permission to marry Anne Neville, Warwick's younger daughter and the widowed betrothed of Prince Edward, who had died at Tewkesbury. The couple, who had apparently known each other since childhood, married in 1472 and moved to Middleham Castle, the bride's former home in Yorkshire. Although occasionally summoned to King Edward's court in London, Gloucester spent most of the next decade in Yorkshire, where he acquired a reputation as a firm but fair provincial ruler. In 1482 Gloucester was given complete charge of a campaign against the Scots; he regained the forfeited city of Berwick-on-Tweed, and captured Edinburgh without the loss of a single man. The Scots subsequently sued for peace and Gloucester reaped further rewards for his success. The parliament made him permanent Warden of the West marches, as a result of which he acquired many lands and manors.

In Shakespeare's *Richard III*, little mention is made of either Clarence's treason or Gloucester's success in the North. Rather, in keeping with the historical and dramatic traditions of the Tudor dynasty, in power at the time Shakespeare wrote, he transforms Clarence into a gullible weakling and Gloucester into a scheming manipulator, whose loyalty to Edward IV is no more than a screen behind which his own ambition and lust for power are concealed.

Richard III takes the throne. In 1483 Edward IV, whose health had been deteriorating for some time, died at the early age of 40. Before his death, he appointed Gloucester as Protector and Defensor of the Realm, entrusting his brother with the care of his son and heir. At the time of his father's death, the future Edward V was 12 years old. As with Clarence, the relationship between Richard and the Woodvilles, the queen's family, was marked by mutual hostility and suspicion. Conflict arose within a week of the king's death. Apparently fearing that the Woodvilles intended to take over the government, Gloucester's allies urged him to secure the new king's custody and bring an armed escort with him to London.

Journeying south, Gloucester, along with his ally the Duke of Buckingham, planned to meet the king's party, led by Earl Rivers, at Northampton. On reaching Northampton, Gloucester learned from Rivers that the king had been sent on to Stony Stratford, 14 miles further along the road to London. The following morning, Rivers found himself surrounded by Gloucester's men while he himself was placed under arrest. Gloucester and Buckingham proceeded to Stony

Richard III

GLOUCESTER'S MARRIAGE

One of the most lurid scenes in Shakespeare's play is that of Gloucester seducing Lady Anne over the corpse of her dead father-in-law, Henry VI. While the actual story behind that marriage was not nearly as colorful, it contained its own moments of drama. Anne Neville and Richard of Gloucester were cousins who had known each other since childhood; Richard had been raised as a foster child by Anne's father, the earl of Warwick, at Middleham Castle in Yorkshire. There was a scheme to marry off Anne to Prince Edward, son of Queen Margaret, on the Lancaster side. But after the Lancastrians' defeats at Barnet and Tewkesbury, along with the deaths of Warwick and Prince Edward, Anne was brought to London and Gloucester secured King Edward's permission to marry her. Clarence, Anne's brother-in-law and guardian, refused to release her from his custody, however—mainly because he did not wish to share the forfeited Warwick estates with Gloucester. Anne herself mysteriously disappeared around this time. Gloucester found her, after several weeks of searching, working as a kitchen maid in the home of one of Clarence's retainers. Gloucester escorted her to the sanctuary of St. Martin le Grande, where she might be protected from Clarence or himself, if she so wished. Thereafter, Clarence and Gloucester wrangled for several months over the Warwick properties and Anne's guardianship; ultimately, Gloucester received Middleham and the Yorkshire estates, while Clarence kept the rest of the inheritance. With the dispute resolved, Anne Neville came out of sanctuary; she and Gloucester married quickly in spring 1472, without waiting for the papal dispensation usual in marriages between cousins, and returned to Middleham. Their only child, a son, was born the following year.

Stratford, met the king, and promptly arrested two more members of the Woodville faction, Sir Thomas Vaughn and Lord Richard Grey. Gloucester charged Vaughn and Grey with conspiring to remove him from the protectorship, thereby circumventing the late king's will. Having taken charge of his nephew, Gloucester and the king's party proceeded to London. Queen Elizabeth and her remaining children took sanctuary in Westminster Abbey.

After Gloucester's Protectorship was upheld by the royal council, the king's household was moved to the royal apartments in the Tower of London and the coronation day scheduled for June 24. A council delegation headed by the Archbishop of Canterbury persuaded Queen Elizabeth to release her second son, Richard, duke of York, into Gloucester's custody; the younger prince joined his brother in the Tower. Meanwhile, factions soon formed within the council itself. Resenting Buckingham's rising influences, several nobles conspired to end the Protectorship and restore the Woodvilles to power. Discovering the plot, Gloucester had the conspirators arrested and one of them, Lord Hastings, immediately executed. Shortly thereafter, Rivers, Grey, and Vaughn were also put to death.

The king's coronation was postponed, however, by startling news: the late Edward IV had secretly made a pre-contract of marriage between himself and Lady Eleanor Butler, daughter of the Earl of Shrewsbury. Lady Eleanor had died in 1468, but she was alive at the time of the king's marriage to Elizabeth Woodville. Since the pre-contract had not been set aside, it was considered binding. The Woodville marriage was therefore invalid in the eyes of the Church, and the children of the marriage were declared illegitimate; according to the law of the day, they could not inherit the throne.

After learning of the pre-contract, London's chief citizens held a meeting at Westminister on June 25 and drew up a petition asking Gloucester, as the only legitimate heir, to take the throne. Presented with the petition the following day, Gloucester accepted the crown and began his reign as King Richard III. The coronation of King Richard and Queen Anne was held at Westminster Abbey on July 6, 1483. An act known as the Titulus Regius (1484) disclosed the news of Edward IV's pre-contract and the illegitimacy of his children by Elizabeth Woodville. The deposed princes remained in the Tower; after a time, no further reference to them was made. Rumors circulated in England and abroad that King Richard had had his nephews put to death, but conclusive evidence was lacking and the princes' fate remains a mystery to this day.

Shakespeare's play adheres to the playwright's sixteenth-century sources, which ascribe the princes' deaths to Richard III. Shakespeare also reproduces another error from those sources. They identify Elizabeth Lucy—one of the late king's mistresses and the mother of two of his children—rather than Lady Eleanor Butler, as the woman with whom Edward IV had formed a pre-contract, an error that further complicated attempts to reconstruct the true sequence of events leading to the deposition of Edward V and the accession of Richard III.

The reign of Richard III. The manner in which Richard III acceded to the throne and the subsequent political turmoil overshadowed much of his actual reign, which lasted just over two years. In October 1483, three months after the coronation, the duke of Buckingham, formerly the king's strongest ally, revolted, involving himself in an uprising by the southern and southwestern counties. Originally, the rebellion was intended to restore Edward V and the Woodvilles to power; however, Buckingham and his new ally, Bishop John Morton of Ely, reportedly informed the rebels that the princes had been put to death, though the two claimed the manner of their deaths was unknown. The focus of the uprising then shifted to Henry Tudor, the earl of Richmond who was descended from the duke of Lancaster. Some historians speculate that Buckingham hoped to seize the throne for himself. Poor organization, reluctant troops, and a timely storm that washed out roads, bridges, and fields contributed to the failure of Buckingham's rebellion against Richard III, however. He was finally captured, turned over to agents of the king, and beheaded as a traitor. Henry Tudor, whose fleet was anchored off Plymouth, returned to France after learning of the duke's fate.

In January 1484 the first and only parliament of Richard's reign convened. The parliament regulated the activities of foreign merchants in England (exempting those engaged in the printing, binding, or selling of books) and initiated governmental reforms to protect the rights of ordinary citizens. A proclamation of the time, addressed to the people of Kent, stated, "The king's highness is fully determined to see due administration of justice throughout this his realm to be had and to reform, punish and subdue all extortions and oppressions in the same" (Anonymous in Potter, p. 52). While such legislative measures earned the king the increased support of the commons, the nobility and gentry were less pleased by this emphasis on reform.

The king's regional partiality also displeased the nobles, especially those from the South. Historian Jeremy Potter writes, "The rewards and favours bestowed on northerners by this king from the north were at the expense . . . of the southern nobility and gentry" (Potter, p. 48). Many disgruntled southern nobles participated in Buckingham's October rebellion, only to see their estates confiscated and bestowed upon northerners when the rebellion failed. The chasm between northern and southern interests widened, and the king was unable to heal the breach, a circumstance Potter sees as "the dire political failure of Richard's reign, and, more than any other, the reason for his downfall. . . . Those who joined Henry Tudor . . . wanted their estates back" (Potter, p. 48).

The king's personal life was no less complicated at this time. The deaths of the king's son and wife, barely a year apart, placed the succession in question again. After Queen Anne's death, possibly from tuberculosis, the rumor circulated that Richard had killed his wife in order to marry his niece, Elizabeth. The king publicly denied the rumor as the work of Henry Tudor's agents.

In 1485 Henry Tudor made another attempt against the throne, landing with his army at Milford Haven in South Wales. On learning of the invasion, Richard III gathered his own forces and marched toward Leicester. The two armies met on Redmore Plain outside the town of Market Bosworth. In the midst of the battle, a messenger on a hill pointed out to Richard the figure of Henry Tudor, mounted on his horse. The king and his forces charged toward Tudor but were ambushed by the troops of Lord Robert Stanley, one of Richard's vassals, who had abstained from the fighting until he knew which way the battle was going (the Stanleys had a reputation for switching allegiances suddenly). Nonetheless, King Richard fought fiercely, killing Tudor's standard-bearer before being himself slain by the Stanleys. According to legend, after the battle Sir William Stanley retrieved Richard's fallen crown from under a hawthorn bush and crowned Henry Tudor king of England. The late king's body was slung over a horse and carried to Leicester, where it was later buried in an unmarked grave.

Shakespeare's play essentially ignores the administrative details of Richard's reign, choosing instead to concentrate on his usurpation of the throne and the various murders he allegedly committed to keep the throne. The conflict between Richard and Henry Tudor is reimagined as a classic struggle between vice and virtue, with virtue—in the person of Henry Tudor—triumphant. Henry Tudor himself, not known historically as a great warrior, is depicted as slaying the king in single combat. No mention is made of the part the Stanleys played in determining the outcome of the final battle by switching sides at the last minute.

The Play in Focus

The plot. The play begins as King Edward IV's youngest brother, Richard, duke of Gloucester, muses about the peaceful conclusion to the recent wars, his own physical deformities, which render him an unattractive lover, and his plot to sow dissension between King Edward and their brother, George, duke of Clarence. Richard's scheme quickly bears fruit. After the king learns of a prophecy that his issue will be disinherited by someone whose name begins with the letter "G," George is arrested and sent to the Tower of London, frequently used as a prison. Richard, whom the play suggests was behind the prophecy, pretends to sympathize with the disconsolate George. Casting blame upon Edward's queen, Elizabeth, and her ambitious family, Richard promises to intercede for George's life. But inwardly he rejoices at his success and plans a romantic conquest of Lady Anne, the widow of Prince Edward, only son of the deposed and recently deceased King Henry VI. (The play makes Anne a widow, though historically she may have only been Edward's betrothed.) Entering with the coffin of her late father-in-law, Anne greets Richard's attempts to woo her with disgust and scorn, accusing him of having killed Henry VI and Prince Edward. Richard does not deny these charges but argues that his passionate love for Anne herself was the cause of his actions. Despite herself, Anne is moved by Richard's extravagant pleas, accepts a ring from him, and agrees to entertain his suit.

Members of the royal court, including Queen Elizabeth, gather to discuss the ill-health of King Edward. Informed of his brother's sickness, Richard arrives at court too. Richard and the Woodvilles—the queen's family—quarrel about the influence each wields over the king. The argument culminates with Richard's accusing the queen of poisoning Edward's mind against George. As the queen hotly denies this, Queen Margaret—the old, embittered widow of Henry VI—enters and curses the entire company with

Richard III

Richard III

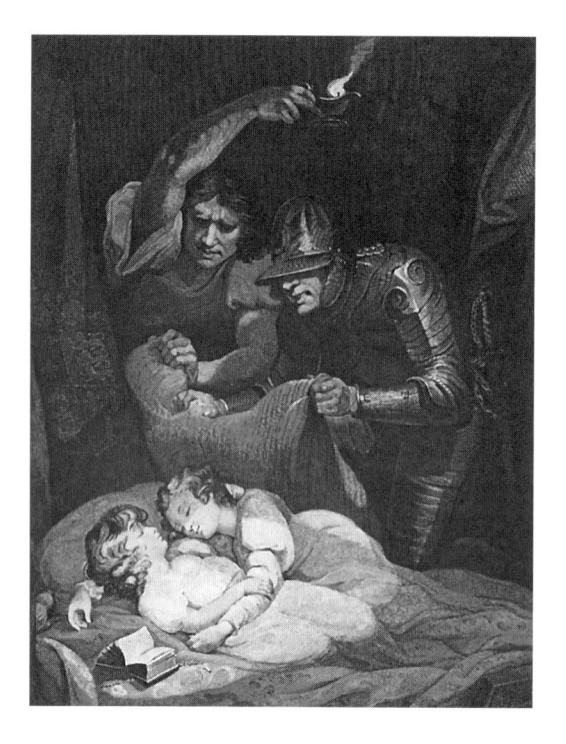

Sir James Tyrrel attempts to suffocate the young nephews of Richard III as they sleep.

misery and death. She directs most of her venom at Richard, whom she blames especially for the deaths of her husband and son. Those assembled remind Margaret of her own vindictive deeds during the war and dismiss her words as a madwoman's ravings. Meanwhile, Richard hires two murderers to kill Clarence in the Tower. The unfortunate brother pleads in vain for his life, learning at the last minute that Richard is responsible for his impending death.

Attempting to promote peace among his warring nobles, the ailing King Edward is distressed to learn from Richard of Clarence's death because the king had intended to spare him. Clarence's mother, the duchess of York, and his two young children are also grieved to hear of his death, but their lamentations are interrupted by Queen Elizabeth's report that King Edward too has died. Richard pretends to sympathize with the mourners and advises that the Prince of Wales—the future Edward V—be fetched from his castle in Ludlow to court. Once the people hear of the king's death, they express misgivings about England's welfare when governed by a child-ruler, especially in light of the continuing hostilities between the Woodville faction and the duke of Gloucester.

Awaiting the arrival of the crown prince, the queen and her younger son, the duke of York, are alarmed to hear that Richard and his ally, the Duke of Buckingham, have arrested and imprisoned Woodville adherents Lord Grey, Lord Rivers, and Lord Vaughn. The queen and her remaining children quickly take sanctuary with the archbishop of York. Richard, however, assumes the role of guardian to his brother's children and removes the duke of York from sanctuary. Claiming that the princes are under his protection, Richard has both Edward and his brother placed in the Tower of London, where they are to remain until Prince Edward's coronation.

With his nephews in his power, Richard consults with Buckingham and Sir William Catesby about which lords are likely to support his plans to seize the throne. Learning that Lord Hastings is staunchly loyal to the heirs of Edward IV, Richard successfully lures the gullible Hastings into a trap, accuses him of treason, and executes him immediately. The prisoners Grey, Rivers, and Vaughn are also killed on Richard's orders. Before their deaths, the condemned men reflect on how Margaret's curse has fallen upon each of them.

Having disposed of most of his enemies, Richard begins a campaign of innuendo and slander. At his behest, Buckingham circulates rumors that Edward IV and his children by the queen were illegitimate, owing to the late king's secret marriage to another woman. Shocked by these disclosures, London citizens, led by the lord mayor, approach Richard, who has arranged to be found in the company of priests, holding a prayer book. Impressed by his pious bearing, the citizens exhort Richard, as the only legitimate heir, to accept the crown. Richard pretends reluctance but finally agrees to become king, and coronation plans commence.

Queen Elizabeth, the Duchess of York, and Lady Anne attempt to visit the princes in the Tower, but are prevented from entering. The earl of Derby informs the horrified women that Richard has seized the throne and Anne must proceed to Westminster to be crowned as his queen. The three ladies lament their misfortunes and Richard's treachery, predicting doom and destruction for the country.

After his coronation, Richard decides the only way to secure his hold on the throne is to kill the princes. Buckingham balks at this plan, however, and thereby loses the king's favor. Meanwhile, the king hires Sir James Tyrrel to smother the princes in their sleep, and the murder is successfully carried out. Richard then rids himself of Queen Anne—whom he has secretly put to death after spreading rumors of her ill health—and Clarence's two children, imprisoning the son and forcing the daughter into a disadvantageous marriage. Still seeking to consolidate his position, Richard plans to marry his niece, Princess Elizabeth of York.

Queen Margaret pays a last gloating visit to the wretched Queen Elizabeth and duchess of York, now mourning the deaths of the young princes. Later, when Richard visits the queen and duchess, the two women bitterly revile him for his crimes. Unmoved, the king presses Queen Elizabeth to give him her daughter's hand in marriage, emphasizing the advantages such a match will bring to the girl and Elizabeth herself. To Richard's delight, the queen appears to capitulate.

In Brittany, Henry, earl of Richmond, amasses an army against Richard and invades England, landing at Milford. Disaffected nobles flock to his banner. His ally Buckingham is eventually captured and executed, but Henry's cause continues to attract followers.

The opposing armies of the king and Henry ride towards their inevitable confrontation. Henry promises to deliver England from Richard's tyranny; Henry's allies predict that the king's former friends will desert him now that they have seen his cruel, violent nature. On the eve of the battle at Bosworth Field, Richard is visited by the ghosts of his victims who predict his defeat and bid him to "despair and die" (Shakespeare, *Richard III*, 5.3.128). The same ghosts also wish success and good fortune to Henry. Waking in perturbation, Richard acknowledges his guilt and probable defeat, but determines to fight nonetheless. During the next day's battle, he fights furiously even after losing his horse and crying aloud for another. Henry kills the king in combat and ascends to the throne of England. The new king promises to wed Princess Elizabeth (eldest daughter of Edward IV and Queen Elizabeth), finally ending the long strife between the Houses of York and Lancaster by uniting them in marriage.

A royal enigma. Shakespeare's Richard III bristles with demonic energy, dominating the play from start to finish. The note of his unmitigated, zestful evil is sounded in the character's very first soliloquy when he declares, "I am determined to prove a villain" (*Richard III*, 1.1.30). Richard's blackened soul is reflected in his twisted body: he is hunchbacked and lame, with a withered arm. Several characters in the play revile him for his grotesque appearance. Before succumbing to his blandishments, Lady Anne addresses him as "thou lump of foul deformity" (*Richard III*, 1.2.57). Queen Margaret of Anjou condemns him even more venomously, calling him an "elvish-marked, abortive, rooting hog" and a "poisonous, bunch-backed toad" (*Richard III*, 1.3.228, 1.3.246). Far from being cowed by these insults, Richard takes a perverse pleasure in turning his opponents' words against them and gaining his own ends, remarking of his conquest of Anne, "Was ever woman in this humor wooed? / Was ever woman in this humor won?" (*Richard III*, 1.2.227-228). Beside Richard's rampant villainy, the virtuous characters in Shakespeare's play—even the earl of Richmond—tend to pale into hand-wringing insignificance.

Tudor historians upon whose accounts Shakespeare based his play readily cooperated in the creation of this monstrous figure. One historian, John Rous, who had praised Richard III in life as a prince who "all avarice set aside ruled his subjects in the realm full commendably," hastened to defame him after his death: "This King Richard, who was excessively cruel in his days, reigned for three years and a little more, in the way that Antichrist is to reign. And like the Antichrist to come, he was confounded at this moment of greatest pride" (Rous in Dockray, pp. 21-22). Rous also asserted that Richard was "retained within his mother's womb for two years and [emerged] with teeth and hair to his shoulders" (Rous in Dockray, p. 22). Polydore Vergil, who became the official historian of Henry VII, similarly wrote, "[Richard] was little of stature, deformed of body, the one shoulder being higher than the other, a short and sour countenance which seemed to savour of mischief, and utter evidently of craft and deceit" (Vergil in Dockroy, p. 23). Sir Thomas More, writing during the reign of Henry VIII, continued the process of mythmaking, calling Richard III "little of stature, ill-featured of limbs, crookbacked, his left shoulder much higher than his right, hard-favored of visage. . . . He was malicious, wrathful, envious" (More in Dockray, p. 24). While not everything written by Tudor historians can be automatically discounted, the more lurid accounts, such as those dealing with the king's birth and appearance, could probably be dismissed. What likenesses in the forms of portraits and sketches exist show little or no evidence of physical deformity. Indeed, a modern examination done on one famous portrait (c. 1520) revealed that the right shoulder had been crudely overpainted to suggest deformity.

The true character of Richard III likewise remains elusive. As duke of Gloucester, he appears to have been a loyal brother to Edward IV, following his king into exile and leading his armies

Richard III

to victory over the Lancastrians. Moreover, some of the crimes ascribed to Richard by Tudor historians and Shakespeare are contradicted by earlier sources, which, if not free of bias themselves, are nonetheless chronologically closer to the events described. The *Annals of Tewkesbury Abbey*, a collection of documents dating from 1327 to 1485, report that Prince Edward [son of Henry VI] was slain not by Richard's hand but on the battlefield at Tewkesbury. *John Warkworth's Chronicle*, which covers the first 13 years of the reign of Edward IV, makes a similar statement, "And there was slain in the field (at Tewkesbury) Prince Edward, who cried for succour to his brother-in-law the Duke of Clarence" (Warkworth in Dockray, p. 40). Reports of Richard's involvement in the death of Henry VI are also inconclusive. The Yorkist account, *Historie of the Arrivall of Edward IV*, claims that on hearing news of his son's death, Henry VI "took it to such great hatred, anger, and indignation that, of pure displeasure and melancholy, he died the 23rd of the month of May" (Anonymous in Dockray, p. 39). *John Warkworth's Chronicle* places Richard, along with several other lords, at the Tower on the night "King Harry [Henry VI] being inward in prison in the Tower of London, was put to death, the 21st of May, on a Tuesday night, between 11 and 12 of the clock" but refrains from open accusation (Warkworth in Dockray, p. 40). Indeed, modern historians speculate that, if Henry VI had been put to death, it was more likely to have been at the command of Edward IV, as the newly restored monarch. The death of the duke of Clarence is another act that contemporary historians ascribe to Edward IV rather than Richard, whose attempt to intercede for Clarence's life is recorded in the otherwise hostile writings of Italian historian Dominic Mancini and even mentioned later in Sir Thomas More's account.

The crime for which there is neither defense nor conclusive evidence of guilt remains the mysterious fate of Richard's deposed nephews. Contemporary rumors circulated throughout London and abroad, especially as the king's enemies fled overseas, that the princes had been put to death either by their uncle or one of his agents. Positive reports of the new king's character, however, circulated as well. Thomas Langton, Bishop of St. David's, wrote the following around August 1483:

> [The king] contents the people wherever he goes better than ever did any prince; for many a poor man that has suffered wrong many days has been relieved by him and his commands in his progress. And in many great cities and towns were great sums of money given to him which he has refused. On my faith I never liked the qualities of any prince as well as his; God has sent him to us for the welfare of us all.
> (Langton in Dockray, p. 87)

If not universally loved by his subjects, neither does Richard III appear to have been universally hated. In the north of England, where he had reigned for over a decade before his accession, the king was warmly praised and, on his death at Bosworth Field, deeply mourned. With surprising boldness, given the change in the royal regime, the city of York set down in its civic records on August 23, 1485 "that King Richard, late mercifully reigning over us, was, through great treason . . . piteously slain and murdered, to the great heaviness of this city" (*York Civic Records* in Potter, p. 94). That such different interpretations of the same ruler—as ruthless, child-killing usurper and merciful friend of the common people—could exist simultaneously serves as a testament to the subjective and contradictory nature of history itself.

Sources and literary context. Numerous historical sources were available to Shakespeare by the time he began writing *Richard III* around 1592. However much Tudor historians condemned and vilified the last king of the prior dynasty, there was no denying that they found him oddly fascinating. Indeed, Shakespeare had a wealth of material upon which to draw—Edward Hall's *The Union of Two Noble and Illustre Families of Lancaster and York* (1548), Raphael Holinshed's *The Chronicles of England, Scotland and Ireland* (1578), and Sir Thomas More's *History of King Richard III* (1557), which presented its subject as the very epitome of evil and corruption. Shakespeare was also familiar with the poem *A Mirror for Magistrates* (1559), which relates the tragedies of such historical figures as Clarence, Buckingham, and Hastings. He had early dramatic treatments of Richard III to draw on too, including *Ricardus Tertius* (1579), a three-part Senecan tragedy in Latin, by Thomas Legge, and the anonymous *True Tragedy of Richard III*, apparently performed a few years before its publication in 1594.

In writing his own play, Shakespeare took considerable liberties with historical events and their chronology, weaving back and forth in time as it suited his dramatic purpose. Therefore, the first act of the play deals with Clarence's arrest and death (1477-78), the onset of King Edward's final illness (1483), the death of Henry VI (1471),

> ### THE PRINCES IN THE TOWER—A DEADLY MYSTERY
>
> The fate of Edward IV's sons, the deposed princes, remains one of history's great unsolved mysteries. In 1674 the skeletons of two children, buried ten feet deep, were located during demolition of a staircase near the White Tower. Contemporaries immediately concluded the remains were those of the princes and had them interred in an urn in Westminster Abbey. However, there had been an earlier report of two similar skeletons in a walled-up chamber of the Tower; those, too, were thought to be the prince's bones. Modern examination of the remains at Westminster Abbey has determined that the skeletons were of pre-pubescent children in approximately the right age range to be the princes, but exact evidence as to the manner of death and, more importantly, to gender is still lacking. The Tower and its foundation contain many skeletons; the bones of an Iron Age youth were found as recently as 1977 during an excavation of the Inner Ward. Historian A. J. Pollard writes, "Essentially the bones are a red herring. They cannot settle the question of whether Richard III murdered the princes. It is not surprising, therefore, that in the light of the continuing uncertainty over the fate of the princes other culprits than those implicated in the contemporary sources have been advanced" (Pollard, p. 127). Those "other culprits" include the duke of Buckingham whose possible involvement is, in fact, suggested in contemporary sources; as a high-ranking noble and royal favorite, Buckingham may have known and had access to the princes' whereabouts. Still another case has been made for Henry VII who had at least as much to lose as his predecessor if the princes were alive at the time of his accession. After becoming king, Henry VII found reasons to imprison or execute potential Yorkist rivals for the throne, including the earl of Warwick, Clarence's son, barred from the succession by his father's treason. In 1502 Henry VII arrested a retainer of King Richard III's, a Sir James Tyrell, executing him on charges of treason, without a trial. After his death, it was announced that he had confessed to murdering the princes back in 1483. No actual confession by Tyrell has ever been found. But Tudor historians and Shakespeare had no hesitation about setting this revelation down as fact.

the courtship between Richard and Lady Anne (1472), and the appointment of Richard as Protector (1483). The most glaring anachronism in Shakespeare's play is its use of Queen Margaret of Anjou, who haunts the plot like a bitter ghost, heaping curses on the triumphant Yorkists; in fact, Queen Margaret had died in France in 1482.

Events in History at the Time the Play Was Written

England in the 1590s. The final decade of the reign of Queen Elizabeth I was a turbulent time, marked by religious conflicts between Protestants and Catholics, severe economic depression, and massive inflation. The childless, unmarried queen was in her 60s; many of the councilors who had advised and supported her in the earlier years of her reign were aging themselves or dead. Inevitably, the people's thoughts turned to the question of succession: who would be the next ruler of England? And would the transition proceed smoothly, or would the country again be plunged into bloody civil war over the person best suited to occupy the throne?

Despite these troubling issues, memories of recent English triumphs still fueled national pride. The defeat of the Spanish Armada by the English navy in 1588 brought about a resurgence of popularity for the queen and inspired a flood of historical plays, many of which celebrated England's past glories and might in battle. Shakespeare appears to have begun his own series of plays dealing with the Wars of the Roses around 1591-92. As in many of his historical plays, he focuses less on the accurate reconstruction of

Richard III

history than on themes relating to power, ambition, and the need for order. In his depiction of a war-torn England—descending to its lowest point with the usurpation of Richard III—and its eventual salvation by Henry Tudor, the founder of the Tudor line and Queen Elizabeth's grandfather, Shakespeare pays tribute to the past, acknowledges the difficulties of the present, and anticipates the future, hopefully but not complacently.

Reception. While no written record survives regarding the first performances of *Richard III*, apparently put on by Pembroke's Men in 1593, the play seems to have been quite popular with Shakespeare's audiences. Except for *Henry IV, Part I*, *Richard III* was the most frequently printed of all Shakespeare's plays before the earliest published collection of his them appeared in 1623.

WAS THE REAL RICHARD III HUNCHBACKED?

There is no evidence that the real Richard III was hunchbacked. Contemporary historians do not mention a severe deformity. A few descriptions suggest that one shoulder may have been more developed than another, the result perhaps of extensive arms training.

Aside from its subject matter, a reason for the play's success was its leading man: *Richard III* boasted no less than Richard Burbage, the foremost actor of Shakespeare's day, in the title role. Burbage was to be identified with the part for the remainder of his life.

As the seventeenth century progressed, historical dramas became less popular and *Richard III* was less frequently staged. Not until 1700, with the appearance of Colley Cibber's adaptation of the play, was *Richard III* widely performed. Cibber, mainly known as a comic actor, altered Shakespeare's text dramatically, omitting more than half the original lines and even cutting the number of characters to concentrate more on Richard, whom Cibber—of course—was playing. Critics were not kind; Aaron Hill, writing for *The Prompter*, compared Cibber's performance to "the distorted heavings of an unjointed caterpillar"

(Hill in Williamson and Person, p. 353). Two other actors soon eclipsed Cibber in the role of Richard: David Garrick and Edmund Kean, both of whom—like Burbage before them—were considered the foremost actors of their day. In a 1759 essay, Thomas Wilkes praised Garrick's depiction of the villainous king: "Shakespeare was always particularly careful in his characters, and in none more so than in Richard the Third, whom history has represented as the poet has drawn, deformed, wicked, perfidious, splenetic, and ambitious. All these marks of the character are spiritedly preserved by Garrick" (Wilkes in Williamson and Person, p. 363). Less than 60 years later, Edmund Kean received equally glowing reviews. The poet Lord Byron rhapsodized over Kean's performance, which many considered definitive, paying tribute to Shakespeare in the process: "By Jove! he is a soul! Life, nature, truth, without exaggeration or diminution. Richard is a man, and Kean is Richard" (Byron in Williamson and Person, p. 376).

—Pamela S. Loy

For More Information

Bloom, Harold, ed. *William Shakespeare Histories & Poems*. New York: Chelsea House, 1986.

———. *William Shakespeare's Richard III*. New York: Chelsea House, 1988.

Dockray, Keith. *Richard III: A Reader in History*. Brunswick Road: Alan Sutton, 1988.

Hanham, Alison. *Richard III and his Early Historians 1483-1535*. Oxford: Clarendon Press, 1975.

Kendall, Paul Murray. *Richard the Third*. New York: W. W. Norton, 1956.

Murph, Roxane C. *Richard III: The Making of a Legend*. Methuen: The Scarecrow Press, 1977.

Pollard, A. J. *Richard III and the Princes in the Tower*. New York: St. Martin's Press, 1991.

Potter, Jeremy. *Good King Richard? An Account of Richard III and his Reputation 1483-1983*. London: Constable, 1983.

Ross, Charles. *The Wars of the Roses*. New York: Thames and Hudson, 1976.

St. Aubyn, Giles. *The Year of Three Kings 1483*. New York: Atheneum, 1983.

Shakespeare, William. *Richard III*. London: Penguin, 2000.

Williamson, Sandra L., and James E. Person, Jr., eds. *Shakespearian Criticism*. Vol. 14. Detroit: Gale Research, 1991.

"Rothschild's Fiddle" and "The Lady with the Dog"

by
Anton Chekhov

Initially known in the West for plays such as *Three Sisters* (1901) and ***The Cherry Orchard*** (1904; also in *Literature and Its Times*), Anton Pavlovich Chekhov (1860-1904) has increasingly gained recognition in the region as a master of the short story, a status long accorded him by Russian readers. Trained as a doctor, Chekhov began writing while still a student. By the mid-1880s, he was supporting himself and his family by producing a steady output of short, humorous pieces for popular journals. In 1888, however, with his story "The Steppe," he embarked on a new phase, producing fewer but more profound stories. Often these tales lack much in the way of traditional plot, instead depicting in Chekhov's unique and gently ironic voice what might be termed everyday tragedies, both small and large. Over the next decade and a half, Chekhov published nearly 60 stories, many regarded as masterpieces, including "A Dreary Story" (1889), "Ward No. Six" (1892), "The Black Monk" (1894), and "Peasants" (1897). Modern critics rank "Rothschild's Fiddle" and "The Lady with the Dog" among his finest works, both in literary merit and in their realistic and careful observation of Russian life.

Events in History at the Time of the Short Stories

Russian writers and society in the 1890s. By the last decade of the nineteenth century, Russia had experienced a half-century of deep and often turbulent social change. In the 1830s and 1840s,

> **THE LITERARY WORKS**
> Two short stories set in Russia in the 1890s; published in Russian (as "Skripka Rotshilda" and "Dama s sobachkoy") in 1894 and 1899 respectively.
>
> **SYNOPSES**
> In "Rothschild's Fiddle" a dying old coffin maker in a provincial town gives his prized fiddle to a fellow-townsman, a Jew whom he has previously persecuted; in "The Lady with the Dog" two adulterous lovers decide to continue their relationship despite the painful complications it will inevitably bring to their lives.

liberal democratic influences from Western Europe had begun penetrating the shell of traditional absolutism within which the autocratic Russian emperors, or tsars, held in check both upper and lower classes alike. Then, from the 1850s to 1870s, these liberal voices found themselves oftentimes drowned out by a new generation of radicals. Whereas the liberals had advocated gradual reform of Russia's backward, feudal society, the radicals called for violent revolution. In 1881 a group of radicals assassinated Tsar Alexander II, initiating more than a decade of harsh government repression under his son and successor, Alexander III. Alexander III died in October 1894, about eight months after "Rothschild's Fiddle" was published; his son and

"Rothschild's Fiddle" and "The Lady with the Dog"

Anton Chekhov

successor Nicholas II, the last tsar, would pursue similarly repressive policies until he abdicated under the pressure of the Russian Revolution of 1917.

Before the 1880s, Russian writers—especially a number of remarkable novelists—occupied a central place in the nation's political and social ferment. From the late 1850s through the 1870s, the ideas of conservatives, liberals, and radicals had provided an ideological context for works whose majestic sweep would lead later critics to call that period the golden age of the Russian novel. Major examples include Ivan Turgenev's **Fathers and Sons** (1863) and Fyodor Dostoyevsky's **Crime and Punishment** (1866), artistic masterpieces that have endured yet focus on urgent political issues of their day (both also in Literature and Its Times). In contrast, Leo Tolstoy—often regarded as the greatest of Russian novelists—avoided topical political themes. To be sure, he drew on Russian history and society, but to create dramatic plots. These he infused with psychological insight to convey strongly moralistic views. For example, his **Anna Karenina** (1875-77; also in Literature and Its Times) depicts the slip of a nobleman's wife into madness and then suicide as a consequence of an adulterous love. In addition to such influential fictional works, there was a vigorous periodical press at the time. Critics conducted combative dialogues on social and political issues in widely read journals such as The Contemporary and The Russian Herald, which also published many of the best known novels in serial form.

By the early 1880s, however, this generation of writers was passing: Dostoyevsky died in 1881, and Turgenev in 1883. While Tolstoy remained active, after Anna Karenina he experienced a religious transformation that led him to nearly abandon complex, emotionally dramatic novels like Anna Karenina in favor of religious and moral tracts or, later, more didactic fiction. At the same time, the government of Alexander III was cracking down on liberals and radicals in a campaign that historians have seen as a significant step towards a totalitarian police state. Thus, Alexander III's oppressive reign began just as long dramatic novels with political and social content were becoming extinct on the Russian scene as a result of what one might call natural causes. In the face of government censorship, the voices of the social critics, too, were silenced or muted, and many of the leading journals were forced either to cease publication or to move away from political and social content.

The result by the mid-1880s was that Russian writers, formerly at the heart of cultural change, suddenly found themselves on the sidelines, and a pantheon of literary giants was replaced by a creative vacuum. Not until the 1890s would a major new talent emerge, and he would stand essentially alone. Anton Chekhov would dominate Russian fiction in the 1890s as no single figure had since the days of Alexander Pushkin in the 1820s and 1830s. Chekhov would take Russian literature in a new direction, away from the dramatic complexities of grand novels with momentous political or social messages, and into smaller, more intimate fictional worlds.

Contrasting attitudes of rural and city folk. Traditionally Russian society fell into three basic estates or classes: the ruling aristocracy, the priests, and the serfs and peasants. The grand social novels of the mid-nineteenth century had emerged as this age-old social system began to disintegrate. Although the government was pursuing rapid industrialization by the 1890s, rural peasants still made up about 80 percent of the population at the end of the century. They lived in small village communes or towns, whose people survived mostly by communal farming, lumbering, hunting, fishing or, like the coffin-maker Jacob Ivanov in "Rothschild's Fiddle," small-scale artisanship. Some historians question the long-accepted view that Russian peasants were generally falling into ever deeper poverty in the closing years of the nineteenth century. However, historians agree that Russians themselves felt this to be the case at the time, a perception reinforced by two major famines in 1891-92 and 1897-98.

Attitudes to poverty among nineteenth-century Russian peasants, however, differed sharply from those of their Western contemporaries. As Russian peasants struggled along at subsistence level, they did not generally aspire to the greater material prosperity that would have been the goal of a Western farmer, homesteader, or artisan. Instead, they viewed survival itself as a worthy ambition, and thought of superfluous wealth as morally suspect, since in their eyes it had to be gained at someone else's expense. An average Western laborer would see wealth as the fitting result of hard work and discipline, bringing well-deserved comfort and leisure. By contrast, a typical Russian peasant would see it as ill-gotten gain that brought only trouble, especially in the form of social censure. Society taught the peasant to strive not for earthly goods but for heavenly rewards, giving rise to Russian proverbs that reflect such values, such as "God smiles upon him who is satisfied with little" (Anonymous in Mironov, p. 481). In "Rothschild's Fiddle" the rural coffin-maker Jacob Ivanov, portrayed as obsessed with profit, represents a sharp divergence from this common attitude, which Russian readers would have recognized.

In contrast with the rural population of more than 120 million (including provincial towns), Russia in the 1890s counted only ten cities that each had more than 100,000 people, and only two large cities, St. Petersburg and Moscow, with populations of just over one million each. (London's population, by comparison, stood at over 6 million and New York City's at over 3 million.) Both Saint Petersburg and Moscow could boast significant industry by the turn of the twentieth century and a professional class of lawyers, doctors, and civil servants, who emerged here and in the smaller cities to challenge the traditional dominance of the aristocracy. In "The Lady with the Dog," Dmitry Gurov, the main character, works in a bank in Moscow and is very much the urban professional Muscovite. Gurov relishes the amenities of city life, enjoying "the lure of restaurants, clubs, dinner parties, anniversary celebrations; he was flattered to be visited by famous lawyers and actors, flattered to play cards with a professor at the Doctor's Club" (Chekhov, "The Lady with the Dog," p. 134).

The stimulation of life in Moscow or Saint Petersburg was often envied by middle- and upper-class residents of smaller provincial towns and cities, and such envy is a common theme in Russian literature. Anne von Diederitz, for example, the title character of "The Lady with the Dog," grew up in Saint Petersburg but lives in an unspecified town, where she is bored with her comfortable but provincial existence and her civil-servant husband, whom she describes as a good but spineless man. She and Gurov meet in the fashionable southern resort and spa town of Yalta, on the coast of the Black Sea, where he is on vacation and she has fled from boredom. Chekhov, who rose to professional status by virtue of his medical education, lived in Yalta during most of the last decade of his life and wrote "The Lady with the Dog" at his villa there. He had moved to Yalta in 1897 for its warm climate, to alleviate the symptoms of tuberculosis, from which he would die in 1904 at age 44.

CHEKHOV AND TOLSTOY'S *ANNA KARENINA*

Leo Tolstoy's influential masterpiece inspired a number of literary responses from Anton Chekhov, of which "The Lady with the Dog" is only the best-known example. Other stories include "The Duel" (1891) and "Anna on the Neck" (1898). In this last story, as in "The Lady with the Dog," the adulterous woman is named Anne, or Anna in Russian, but in other ways the stories diverge. Chekhov's fictional tone in relation to adultery, as illustrated by these two stories, ranges from satire ("Anna on the Neck") to pathos ("The Lady with the Dog"). His stories never, however, adopt Tolstoy's moral censure of the heroine's behavior.

Changing views of marriage and divorce. Despite their widely divergent settings, social milieux, and focus, "Rothschild's Fiddle" and "The Lady with the Dog" share an important subject, that of marriage. In the first story, Jacob's changed attitude to Rothschild, a Jew he has formerly persecuted, is precipitated by the death of Jacob's wife, Martha. Her death awakens Jacob to various parts of his life, including his marriage, in relation to which he reconsiders his own past behavior. In the second story, the two adulterous lovers Dmitry Gurov and Anne von

"Rothschild's Fiddle" and "The Lady with the Dog"

Diederitz despise their own spouses and come to love each other "like man and wife" ("Lady with the Dog," p. 140).

As both stories suggest, Russians' experiences of love and marriage were strongly determined by social class. For peasants like Jacob and Martha, marriage was often literally a matter of survival: subsisting might require more labor than one person could supply alone. It was not unusual for affection between the two spouses to play little or no role in such partnerships. While those (like Gurov and Anne) who were better off did not face the pressure of actual survival, for Russians of all classes marriage commonly involved little choice and was generally planned by a couple's parents, with an eye toward gaining financial or social advantage for the families. In "The Lady with the Dog," for example, Chekhov describes Gurov's marriage as having been "arranged early, in his second college year" ("Lady with the Dog," p. 128).

Russian society was strongly patriarchal. The law viewed both a wife and a couple's children as the husband's property, although married women were allowed, technically at least, to retain control of their dowries. The state considered marriage a religious matter, so for most Russians it fell under the authority of the Russian Orthodox Church. Traditionally, the church forbade divorce except in cases of "adultery, prolonged disappearance, sexual incapacity, and exile to Siberia after conviction for a felony" (Wagner, p. 67). Moreover, the church placed obstacles in the way of fulfilling even these stringent conditions, for example, requiring that several witnesses testify to an act of adultery before allowing it to be grounds for divorce. In accordance with the strongly paternal social outlook, adultery was considered a public matter, not a private one. Like other such issues of family authority (including insubordination against the husband or father) it was treated as both a crime (by the state) and a grave sin (by the church).

By the 1890s, however, an ideal of romantic marriage had begun filtering into the upper classes from Western Europe, and greater numbers of young people were resisting arranged marriages. The social stigma attached to divorce had started to lift as well. No longer was divorce quite so scandalous as when *Anna Karenina* had been published two decades earlier. While the Church would not grant significantly more divorces until after 1900, these social changes are reflected by a sharp rise in the number of petitions for formal separation, the legal equivalent of a Church divorce. Between 1889 and 1896 such requests nearly doubled, from under 2,000 to almost 3,500, and the numbers would continue to rise. At the end of "The Lady with the Dog" Chekhov hints that Dmitry Gurov and Anne von Diederitz might join that growing number, in seeking to "break these intolerable bonds" of their unhappy marriages ("Lady with the Dog," p. 141).

THE DAWN OF FEMINISM

Like Russian writers, Russian feminists suffered persecution during the oppressive regimes of the 1880s and 1890s. During the 1860s and 1870s, the feminists had made significant strides, especially in the area of education, with a number of women's colleges being established in this period. Chekhov's "The Lady with the Dog" describes Dmitry Gurov's wife as an earnest intellectual, which suggests that she might have studied at one of these new women's colleges. However, all but one were closed in the 1880s under Alexander III, and the nascent feminist movement was largely silenced. A revival of sorts began in the mid-1890s, aided by the growing proportion of women in the workforce (from 30 percent to 44 percent between 1885 and 1900). Educational opportunities for women also began to re-expand in the late 1890s: the first medical school for women opened in St. Petersburg in 1897.

The Short Stories in Focus

The plots—"Rothschild's Fiddle." Set in "a small town, more wretched than a village," the story opens with an ironic description of the town's "depressingly low death rate" that sets the tone for what follows ("Rothschild's Fiddle," p. 93). It also suggests the cynical point of view of the story's main character, the coffinmaker Jacob Ivanov. A bitter old man, Jacob is obsessed by what he sees as the opportunities for profit that life constantly and unfairly allows to evade him. The coffin maker, whose nickname is "Bronze," supplements his income from time to time by playing the fiddle with a band of Jewish musicians, performing at weddings in the town. The flutist for the band is a man to whom Jacob takes a violent disliking:

> A red-haired, emaciated Jew with a network of red and blue veins on his face. He was known as Rothschild after the noted millionaire. Now, this bloody little Jew even contrived to play the

"Rothschild's Fiddle" and "The Lady with the Dog"

RUSSIAN ANTI-SEMITISM

As in Western Europe, anti-Semitism had long been a feature of Russian society, but public and violent expressions of hostility towards Russian Jews surged during the 1880s to early 1900s. During this period, Russian mobs conducted anti-Jewish riots called pogroms, in which the rioters attacked Jewish neighborhoods in towns or cities, often with deadly results. The attacks gave expression to age-old hostility. Like other Europeans, many Russians viewed Jews as economically predatory, as relying on usury, for example, to make a profit at the expense of Christians, who, in theory at least, saw lending money at interest as morally objectionable. Living mostly in small towns, Russian Jews worked as peddlers, artisans, and traders in grain. A minority lived in the countryside, some of whom leased the right from landlords to sell liquor. This last trade prompted disparaging remarks from Russian officials, who accused Jews "of living at the expense of the peasantry and 'sucking their vital juices,' especially through control of the trade in distilled spirits" (Klier and Lambroza, p. 4). Periodic attempts were made to eject the Jews from the countryside and restrict them to the towns. The average official borrowed from Western Europe the false idea that Judaism taught followers to exploit the surrounding population, in this case, the Russian peasantry. By portraying his Christian main character in "Rothschild's Fiddle" as obsessed by profit, Chekhov may have intended to combat such misguided stereotypes. Chekhov's tale clearly wishes to create sympathy for the Jewish Rothschild, not an unusual goal for an author in this decade. Sympathetic literary treatments of Jews became common in the 1890s, as liberal writers reacted against their society's growing persecution of Jews. Subtle details in Chekhov's story bring to light not-so-subtle stereotypes of the era, which emerge most clearly in the Russian edition. Jacob complains about the flaky, scaly Rothschild, invoking a popular stereotype of Jews having a skin disease. Also the story ascribes the stifling smell of garlic to the Jewish band, invoking another pervasive stereotype of the day.

merriest tunes in lachrymose [tearful] style. For no obvious reason Jacob became more and more obsessed by hatred and contempt for Jews, and for Rothschild in particular.
("Rothschild's Fiddle," p. 93)

When Martha falls ill, Jacob takes her to the hospital, but the busy doctor has little time for her. She perceives that her days are numbered. Realizing that his wife of more than 50 years is dying, Jacob builds her a coffin. He reflects on the income he is losing by doing so for free, and she recalls their life 50 years earlier: "God gave us a little fair-haired baby, remember? We were always sitting by the river, you and I, singing songs under the willow tree" ("Rothschild's Fiddle," pp. 96-97). The little girl died, Martha continues with a bitter laugh, but Jacob can recall neither the child nor the singing under the willow. By the next morning, Martha has died.

The funeral goes smoothly, which pleases Jacob at first. Later, though, he is seized by regret, realizing "that never in his life had he been kind to Martha or shown her affection. . . . He had no more noticed her than a cat or a dog" ("Rothschild's Fiddle," p. 97). As Jacob returns home, Rothschild approaches and tells Jacob that Mister Moses, the band's leader, wants him to play with them. Jacob, who feels like crying, just wants to be left alone. But Rothschild persists, whereupon Jacob turns on him threateningly and chases him off. As Jacob slurs Rothschild (referring to him in the Russian original as a flaky, scaly Jew), several street urchins join in the chase, shouting *Yid* after the retreating Rothschild, the peasant word for "Jew."

Walking along the river, Jacob notices that he has come to the willow tree, and suddenly he remembers the baby Martha had recalled before

"Rothschild's Fiddle" and "The Lady with the Dog"

dying. Other memories overtake him, and with amazement he thinks about how he has ignored the river for 40 or 50 years. It could have profited him. All the ducks and geese—he could have bred and slaughtered the animals and sent them downriver to Moscow—the down feathers alone would have fetched ten rubles a year. Life seems to have flowed past without gain, "without enjoyment—gone aimlessly, with nothing to show for it" ("Rothschild's Fiddle," p. 99).

The next morning, feeling sick, he goes to the hospital. The same doctor gives him the same cursory treatment as usual, and Jacob returns home knowing that he is dying. On the way, he contemplates his approaching death, deciding:

> Death would be pure gain for him. He wouldn't have to eat, drink, pay taxes or offend folk. And since a man lies in his grave not just one but hundreds and thousands of years, the profit would be colossal. Man's life is debit, his death credit.
> ("Rothschild's Fiddle," p. 99)

At home he takes up his fiddle and begins to play, improvising a sad song that reflects "his wasted, profitless life" ("Rothschild's Fiddle," p. 100). Arriving to say that once again Mister Moses is calling on Jacob to play, Rothschild timidly approaches. He is afraid of being attacked again, but Jacob waves him in and Rothschild listens to him play as tears run down both their cheeks.

Jacob is sick all day, and that evening a priest hears his confession. When the priest asks him if he remembers any particular sin he has committed, Jacob thinks of Martha's unhappiness and of Rothschild, then says, "Give my fiddle to Rothschild" ("Rothschild's Fiddle," p. 100). Now everyone wonders how Rothschild got such a good fiddle, and when he plays Jacob's sad tune, everyone weeps. "So popular is this new tune," the story concludes, "that merchants and officials are always asking Rothschild over and making him play it a dozen times" ("Rothschild's Fiddle," p. 101).

"The Lady with the Dog." As the story opens, Dmitry Gurov, a professional man in his late thirties from Moscow, has just entered his third week of vacation at the Black Sea resort town of Yalta. Married with three young children, Gurov has for years been repeatedly unfaithful to his wife, a woman who considers herself as an "intellectual" and appears to be an unwomanly sort of woman ("Lady with the Dog," p. 127). He is now on vacation alone and hears of "a new arrival on the Esplanade: a lady with a dog" ("Lady with the Dog," p. 127).

Spotting the attractive young lady as she walks her white-haired dog on the promenade, he thinks to himself, "If she has no husband or friends here she might be worth picking up" ("Lady with the Dog," p. 127). One afternoon as he sits eating in an outdoor restaurant, she takes the table next to him and they strike up a conversation. A married woman named Anne von Diederitz, she has indeed come to Yalta alone and is already bored with the place. After leaving the restaurant, they stroll along the sea and chat before parting. Back in his hotel room, Gurov remembers "her slender, frail neck, her lovely grey eyes" and assumes that they will run into each other again before too long ("Lady with the Dog," p. 129).

It is a week later, and the two have indeed spent more time together. As they stand at the pier and watch a steamer come in, Gurov kisses the lady with the dog, and they go to her room. Gurov contrasts her hesitancy and inexperience with other women whom he has seduced, some lighthearted and cheerful, others harsh and overbearing. Afterwards, she is morose:

> She thought of it as her "downfall," it seemed, which was all very strange and inappropriate. Her features had sunk and faded, her long hair drooped sadly down each side of her face. She had struck a pensive, despondent pose....
> ("Lady with the Dog," pp. 130-31)

Bored by her remorse and naiveté, Gurov tries to cheer her up. They take a cab to the nearby port of Oreanda, where they sit on a bench by the sea until dawn and watch the beautiful sunrise. In coming days, however, she continues to be wracked by guilt and by the fear that he will no longer respect her. Then she gets a letter from her husband, who says he has eye trouble and asks her to return home soon. She tells Gurov that their affair is over and that they must never see each other again, and Gurov sees her off at the train station. Gurov, too, decides it is time to return home.

Back in Moscow, however, he finds he cannot forget her as easily as he thought. A month goes by and as the frigid Moscow winter sets in he thinks of her more and more. His life seems intensely boring to him, he is impatient with his friends and family, and he sleeps badly. He decides he must see her. Making up a story to his wife, he journeys by train to the town where Anne had told him she lives. After checking into a hotel, he sees an advertisement for the debut of a performance, just the sort of event she and her husband would likely attend. He himself

"Rothschild's Fiddle" and "The Lady with the Dog"

View of Moscow. Residents of small-town Russia often envied the big-city life, and this became a common theme in the literature of the time, including "Lady with a Dog."

goes and indeed spots her entering with a tall round-shouldered young man he assumes to be her husband. When she sees him approach, she turns pale; a moment later she walks out into the hallway and he follows. She tells him that she has thought of him constantly, too, but says he must leave. She promises to come see him in Moscow.

She begins visiting Moscow every two or three months, taking a room in a certain hotel. They spend time together in her room and manage to keep the affair secret. One morning he goes to see her and finds her emotionally wrought. She cannot stand the secrecy and feels that their lives are in ruins. Going to soothe her, he catches sight of himself in the mirror. His hair is turning gray. He marvels at how much he has aged in the last few years and how his looks have faded, feeling compassion for the lady with the dog.

> This life—still so warm and beautiful but probably just about to fade and wither like his own. Why did she love him so? Women had never seen him as he really was. What they loved was not his real self but a figment of their own imaginations—someone whom they dreamed of meeting all their lives. Then, when they realized their mistake, they had loved him all the same.
> ("Lady with the Dog," p. 140)

He realizes that he too—for the first time in his life—is in love, and that the love he shares with Anne has transformed them both. They discuss how they might end the secrecy and the deception, and reconfigure their lives to be together. As the story ends, Gurov feels that soon "the solution would be found and a wonderful new life would begin. But both could see that they still had a long, long way to travel—and that the most complicated and difficult part was only just beginning" ("Lady with the Dog," p. 141).

Chekhov's compassionate neutrality. Looking around him in 1892, Chekhov summed up his literary generation's sense of political and social disengagement:

> We truly lack a certain something: if you look up the skirts of our muse, all you see is a flat area. . . . We have neither immediate nor remote goals, and there is an emptiness in our souls. We have no politics. . . . I won't throw myself down a flight of stairs the way Garshin [a promising young writer who committed suicide in 1888] did, but neither will I flatter myself with thoughts of a better future.
> (Chekhov, *The Letters of Anton Chekhov*, p. 243)

Writing in the midst of this malaise, Chekhov rejected the grand dramatic canvases

"Rothschild's Fiddle" and "The Lady with the Dog"

and social messages of a Tolstoy or a Dostoyevsky. Instead, he used his natural affinity for the short story to comment subtly on political and social issues, and to probe the gray areas of the human heart within a more mundane context. Above all, Chekhov wished to explore the truth rather than to preach it, and accordingly he approached his characters with compassion rather than judgment.

Shaped by Chekhov's own inclinations as well as by the political environment of the 1890s, "Rothschild's Fiddle" and "The Lady with the Dog" both illustrate these concerns. The two stories do not so much ignore social issues as treat them in a determinedly undramatic way. "Rothschild's Fiddle," for example, touches on Russian society's long-standing anti-Semitism, but subordinates that issue to the moving but inconclusive interactions between Jacob, on the one hand, and Martha and Rothschild on the other. Similarly, Chekhov deliberately makes the adulterous lovers in "The Lady with the Dog" resemble those of *Anna Karenina*, but on a less ethically loaded, or judgmental, scale. In keeping with this less judgmental scale, events are left unresolved, as they frequently are in real life, rather than tied up in a neat package. In place of the gripping climax of Tolstoy's *Anna Karenina*, Chekhov withholds a dramatic denouement from the reader, instead ending optimistically but inconclusively, allowing for the possibility that the love affair might somehow just limp along without resolution one way or the other. Whereas the conclusion of Tolstoy's novel passes stern judgment on the immorality of its tragic adulteress, Anna, Chekhov downsizes his Anne to a "very ordinary little woman" in a story that does not condemn her for her adulterous behavior ("Lady with the Dog," p. 137).

Chekhov himself declared that the short story format did not give him room to tell his readers what to think, so he preferred to let them make up their own minds. But the artistic choice of striving for authorial neutrality can be ascribed only partly to the format. Innovative for its time, it was also a conscious reaction to Russian critics who demanded that literature deliver a clear social message, and to the novelists of a previous generation who had met and shaped those demands. Finally, it emerged as well from the oppressive political environment under Alexander III and Nicholas II. Their governments discouraged the expression of social and political opinions with unprecedented intensity, exerting pressures that happened to dovetail both with Chekhov's unique talents, and with the convenient passing of the earlier more strident literary generation.

Sources and literary context. Noting the diverse subject matter and striking originality of Chekhov's stories, critics have suggested that in general he relied more than most other writers on his imagination and broad observations, and less on specific models from either real life or literature. As the above discussion suggests, it may be that reaction played a stronger role than emulation in Chekhov's creative process; *Anna Karenina* is an example of the literature to which he reacted with "The Lady with the Dog." However, Chekhov certainly admired Tolstoy's writing, which was a major influence on Chekhov's early work, even if he had rejected the strain of puritanical didacticism in Tolstoy's fiction by the 1890s. Chekhov's preference for describing rather than judging his characters does have an immediate precursor in the technique of Ivan Turgenev, whose work Chekhov also admired greatly. While Chekhov was influenced by Turgenev's authorial objectivity, however, he did not follow the older writer in weaving stories around explicit political and ideological conflicts.

Some critics have seen the relatively positive attitude to love in "The Lady with the Dog" (which contrasts sharply with that found in earlier stories such as "Rothschild's Fiddle") as an echo of events in Chekhov's own life. Two years before writing the story, when Chekhov was still a bachelor with several unhappily concluded love affairs behind him, he met the actress Olga Knipper, who was starring in the Moscow production of his play *The Seagull*, and whom he would marry in 1901.

Reception. "Rothschild's Fiddle" was first published in the newspaper *The Russian Gazette* on February 6, 1894, and "The Lady with the Dog" was first published in the magazine *The Russian Idea* in December 1899. While "Rothschild's Fiddle" received less contemporary attention than some of Chekhov's other, longer stories, recent critics have acknowledged its combination of darkly ironic humor and emotional power. Thomas Winner, for example, has explored the story's juxtaposition of beauty (represented by music) and banality (represented by Jacob's cynicism).

"The Lady with the Dog," by contrast, made a deeper immediate impression on both readers and critics alike. It has been called Chekhov's best-known story. One early reaction came from a younger fellow writer, Maxim Gorky, who wrote enthusiastically to Chekhov in January 1900, the month after "The Lady with the Dog" appeared. Praising its simple delicacy, Gorky felt that the story had reached a pinnacle. Chekhov was bringing about the culmination of Russian realism, the name used for the diverse literary movement including the works of Turgenev, Dostoyevsky, and Tolstoy.

> Do you know what you're doing? You're killing Realism. And you'll succeed, too—for good, forever. It's a form that has outlived its time—really! No one can go further than you along its path, no one can write so simply about such simple things as you can. After the most inconsequential of your stories, everything else seems coarse, written with a log instead of a pen.
>
> (Gorky in Troyat, p. 239)

Later critics singled out "The Lady with the Dog" as superbly representative of a well-known innovation of Chekhov's, the so-called "zero ending." As the influential critic and author Vladimir Nabokov summarizes, "All the traditional rules of story-telling have been broken in this wonderful short story. . . . There is no problem, no regular climax, no point at the end. And it is one of the greatest stories ever written" (Nabokov, p. 32).

—Colin Wells

For More Information

Chekhov, Anton. "The Lady with the Dog." In *The Oxford Chekhov*. Vol. 7. Oxford: Oxford University Press, 1978.

———. *The Letters of Anton Chekhov*. Trans. Michael Heim. New York: Harper & Row, 1973.

———. "Rothschild's Fiddle." In *The Oxford Chekhov*. Vol. 9. Oxford: Oxford University Press, 1975.

Crankshaw, Edward. *In the Shadow of the Winter Palace: Russia's Drift Toward Revolution 1825-1917*. New York: Viking, 1976.

Edmondson, Linda Harriet. *Feminism in Russia, 1900-17*. Stanford: Stanford University Press, 1984.

Hingley, Ronald. *A New Life of Anton Chekhov*. New York: Knopf, 1976.

Klier, John D., and Shlomo Lambroza, eds. *Pogroms: Anti-Jewish Violence in Modern Russian History*. Cambridge: Cambridge University Press, 1992.

Mironov, Boris N., and Ben Eklof. *The Social History of Imperial Russia, 1700-1917*. Vol. 1. Boulder: Westview, 2000.

Nabokov, Valdimir. "Chekhov's Prose." In *Critical Essays on Anton Chekhov*. Ed. Thomas A. Eekman. Boston: G. K. Hall, 1989.

Troyat, Henri. *Chekhov*. New York: Dutton, 1986.

Wagner, William G. *Marriage, Property, and Law in Late Imperial Russia*. Oxford: Oxford University Press, 1994.

Winner, Thomas. *Chekhov and His Prose*. New York: Holt, Rhinehart & Winston, 1966.

The Secret Agent

by
Joseph Conrad

Joseph Conrad (1857-1924) was born Józef Teodor Konrad Korzeniowski in Berdichev, Poland, then part of the Russian empire. Conrad's father (a translator of Shakespeare into Polish) exposed him to Western European literature at an early age, including English authors such as Sir Walter Scott and Charles Dickens, among others. As a young man Conrad left Poland for a career as a sailor, and in 1886 he also became a British subject. He settled in Britain in 1894, anglicizing his name, devoting himself to writing, and in 1896 marrying an Englishwoman, Jessie George. The couple had two sons, Borys and John. Conrad began his first novel, *Almayer's Folly* (1895), while at sea, and his experiences as a sailor provided the basis for several of his best known tales, including the novels *The Nigger of the "Narcissus"* (1898) and *Lord Jim* (1900), as well as the novella *Heart of Darkness* (1902; also in *Literature and Its Times*). With *Nostromo* (1904), a story of revolution in a South American city, Conrad began a new phase in his career; in his next two novels, *The Secret Agent* and *Under Western Eyes* (1911), he retained the focus on political themes and urban settings begun with *Nostromo*. The third and less thematically unified phase of Conrad's career includes the novels *Chance* (1913) and *Victory* (1915), as well as collections of short stories. Conrad is considered one of the finest stylists of English prose, a remarkable achievement for a man who did not learn the language until his twenties. In *The Secret Agent* he uses the literary technique of irony to explore some of the political tensions that

> **THE LITERARY WORK**
>
> A novel set in London, England, in 1886; published in London in 1907.
>
> **SYNOPSIS**
>
> A terrorist acting under orders from the Russian Embassy hatches a plot to blow up London's Greenwich Observatory.

gripped Europe near the turn of the twentieth century.

Events in History at the Time of the Novel

An era of tense diplomacy. The four decades between the end of the Franco-Prussian War (1871) and the outbreak of World War I (1914) saw the last stage in the consolidation of Europe's global empires. Of the six European states known as the Great Powers—Britain, France, Russia, Italy, Germany, and Austria-Hungary—each except for the last one ruled over a global empire that was often in direct competition with the others. While peace existed in Europe between 1871 and 1914, it was increasingly strained by a complex and often shifting network of treaties and alliances among the Great Powers. This tangled web of diplomacy forms the general background to *The Secret Agent*, in which Adolf Verloc, the secret agent of the title, ultimately takes his

The Secret Agent

Joseph Conrad

orders from a high-level diplomat in the Russian Embassy in London.

Just as it drives the novel's plot, diplomatic intrigue (and for that matter, terrorism) would in real life spark the outbreak of World War I. While the war's outbreak lay seven years after the novel's publication, the period roughly between the novel's setting (1886) and publication (1907) saw the final formation of the alliances that would make up the two sides in the war. Throughout this period, at the core of Great Powers diplomacy lay two unchanging factors: first, a bitter enmity between France and Germany, the two countries that had fought the Franco-Prussian War; and second, Germany's equally strong alliance with Austria-Hungary. The wild cards in the diplomatic poker game of the era were Britain and Russia, the two countries that feature prominently in the novel.

In 1880, six years before the events in the novel occur, Russia formed a ten-year treaty alliance with Germany, so when the novel takes place, Russia is Germany's ally. In 1890, however, Russia's treaty with Germany expired, and four years later Russia concluded a military alliance with France, Germany's enemy. Meanwhile, Britain—earlier striving to remain aloof from such alliances, but suspicious of Germany's new and powerful navy—had been drifting towards an alliance with France that was formalized in 1904 (the so-called Entente Cordiale).

Finally, in 1907 Russia and Britain also signed an agreement, completing the Triple Entente, the three-way coalition that would face Germany and Austria-Hungary in war seven years later. Thus, during the period between the novel's setting and its publication, European diplomatic maneuvering had a monumental effect, one that would lead to a standoff between two opposing alliances—France, Britain, and Russia against Germany and Austria-Hungary. The standoff emerged when the two wild cards, Russia and Britain, sided with France, with Russia switching allegiances to do so and Britain finally committing itself to one side. Diplomacy, as most British readers would have known in 1907, had been responsible for transforming Britain's potential enemy—Russia—into its ostensible ally.

Terrorists and revolutionaries. The international scene was further complicated by the rise of revolutionary movements that often transcended the borders between countries. In Britain the greatest threat came from the Fenians, or Irish revolutionaries, part of the home-rule movement, which sought to end British rule in Ireland. Throughout the 1880s the Fenians attacked a number of well-known British institutions in London, including Parliament and the Tower of London, in a series of explosions commonly referred to in the British press as "dynamite outrages." Dynamite is also used in *The Secret Agent*. While the incident that directly inspired it occurred in the following decade, the tense and fearful atmosphere of 1880s London may have contributed to Conrad's decision to set the novel in 1886. Also Conrad had personal experience in the city that year. Having become an English subject in 1886, he spent much of the year in London. In the Author's Note to *The Secret Agent*, he tells of long, lonely walks through the city's gloomy streets as an unknown and friendless young man. On a more general level, the city suffered a severe depression from 1884 to 1887 and violent riots by dissatisfied London workers occurred in February 1886, causing panic in the city.

The most influential international revolutionary movements were anarchism and socialism, both of which had arisen earlier in the nineteenth century. While socialism called for collective control—usually by the government—of production and distribution, anarchism called for the elimination of government altogether. Labor unrest gave rise to these two movements in western European countries, including France, Germany, and Britain. But even more vigorous anarchist

ANARCHISM

The political philosophy of anarchism calls for the end of all forms of hierarchical authority, including governments, and the establishment of a society based on orderly relations between equals. The mix of men who founded the anarchist movement reflect its historically international character. The movement arose from ideas posed by the English philosopher William Godwin (1756-1836), though the first to call himself an anarchist was the French thinker Pierre Joseph Proudhon (1809-65), whose ideas were taken up by two Russians, Mikhail Bakunin (1814-76) and Prince Peter Kropotkin (1842-1921), both of whom lived parts of their lives as exiles in London. One scholar has described the period from 1880 to 1914 as "the heyday of the international anarchist movement" (Sonn, p. 11). In Paris, Rome, and other European cities a number of anarchist bombings occurred between 1890 and 1901, as anarchists adopted the radical terrorism they called "propaganda by the deed," which was meant to destroy society so that a new and more equitable world could arise (Sonn, p. 36). Anarchists were also active in America. An anarchist named Leon Czolgosz assassinated President William McKinley in 1901, for example.

In another, earlier American incident, in May 1886, a labor riot at Haymarket Square in Chicago was the scene of a violent explosion, killing eleven and leading to the arrest of eight anarchist leaders. Despite the fact that authorities could not identify the bomber, four of the arrested men were executed. One committed suicide in prison, and the three survivors were later pardoned. Perhaps coincidentally, the Haymarket Riot occurred at the same time as events in *The Secret Agent*, the spring of 1886. In the novel the most extreme anarchist beliefs are represented by a character known only as the Professor, who talks of using dynamite to make "a clean sweep and a clear start for a new conception of life" (Conrad, *The Secret Agent*, p. 71).

and socialist movements arose in Russia, becoming most threatening here, where autocratic rule had long stifled economic and social progress and thus engendered widespread poverty and political oppression. In 1881 a bomb-wielding anarchist assassinated the Russian tsar Alexander II, with the result that, on assuming power after his father's death, the new tsar, Alexander III, mounted a severe crackdown on such groups. Many revolutionaries and reformers fled Russia for western European cities such as Paris and London, where the Russian and other governments employed embassy personnel, police informers, and spies to keep tabs on them.

Prince Peter Kropotkin, a Russian who despite his noble title was the leading anarchist thinker in the late nineteenth century, offers an example of an anarchist's career. After a sensational escape from a Russian prison in 1876, Kropotkin had made his way to Switzerland, from which the Russian government, in its attack on anarchists, succeeded in getting him expelled after Alexander II's assassination. Kropotkin then moved to Paris, but again found himself in trouble, this time with the French government, which arrested him and imprisoned him for three years. After his release, he arrived in England in 1886—the year in which the novel takes place—and lived in London for the next 30 years (until the Russian Revolution of 1917 made him a hero and he returned to his homeland).

As Kropotkin's case illustrates, Russia was not the only government alarmed by anarchists and apt to persecute them. British newspaper reports in the mid-1890s claimed that a London jeweler named A. Coulon spied and informed on anarchists in London, quoting him as saying:

> I am in the service of the International Secret Police, which is subsidised by the Russian, German, and French Governments, and there is no movement of any of the members of the Anarchist party in London that is not duly communicated to these governments.
> (Coulon in Sherry, p. 318)

The Secret Agent

Whereas other governments actively persecuted anarchists, the British government and British police were generally content to monitor them without arresting or expelling them. Indeed, Coulon was reported to have informed on London's anarchists to the British police, independently of his activities for the "International Secret Police." Scholar Norman Sherry has suggested that newspaper reports about Coulon may have provided Conrad with inspiration for aspects of the novel's portrait of the secret agent, Verloc. One major difference is that whereas Coulon spied for the Russian, German, and French governments, the novel's Verloc spies just for the Russians. On the other hand, one of the major similarities is that, like Coulon, Verloc passes information to the British police without his other employers' knowledge.

THE GREENWICH BOMB OUTRAGE

On February 15, 1894, a mysterious explosion rocked London's Greenwich Park. A man was found kneeling on the ground, with one hand blown off and severe wounds to his body. Nearby were pieces of a shattered bottle. The man, thought to be a foreigner of about 30, died shortly afterward, and a card was found on his body with what newspaper accounts said was the word *Bourbon* on it.

BLOWN TO PIECES!
Victim an Anarchist (?)
Was he a member of a gang
who had fell designs on
London's safety?
(London *Morning Leader*, February 16, 1894, in Sherry, *Conrad's Western World*, p. 231)

Later investigation identified the man as Martial Bourdin, a French anarchist living in London, and concluded that he had perished in an attempt to blow up the Greenwich Observatory, a famous London landmark and scientific institution located in the park. Early reports suggested that Bourdin had stumbled over a root in the ground, prematurely detonating the bomb he was carrying, a theory investigators later discounted. This incident is the only known anarchist bombing to have occurred in London. Widely publicized as the Greenwich Bomb Outrage, it provided the direct inspiration for the central episode in *The Secret Agent*.

The Novel in Focus

Plot summary. The novel opens as Adolf Verloc leaves for the morning from the little London shop where he sells anarchist journals and pornographic literature. The shop occupies the front room of a small, grimy brick house in London's shabby Soho district, where Verloc lives with his family. Along with his wife, Winnie, the family includes her adoring brother Stevie, in a condition of mental retardation; and their unnamed mother, a stout working-class woman whose swollen ankles prevent her from getting around much. Despite Stevie's slowness, Verloc leaves him in charge of the store. Winnie is nearby, and anyway Verloc doesn't care much about the shop, which is actually just a front for what he tells Winnie is his "political" work (*Secret Agent*, p. 20). The stolid, plump Winnie—who married Verloc only because he is a good provider for herself, Stevie, and their mother—lacks any curiosity about Verloc's activities. As Verloc journeys through London's busy streets, the narrator ironically describes him as a protector of the city's wealthy, propertied class against working-class agitation. In reality Verloc is a fat and lazy man with an "air of moral nihilism" about him (*Secret Agent*, p. 25). (A popular philosophy of the day, nihilism held that there was no meaning or value in life and consequently no need to abide by any ethical principles.)

Verloc arrives at his destination, an embassy that the narrator does not name but suggests is that of Russia. There he meets with Mr. Vladimir, a high embassy official who has recently arrived to take over the embassy's "secret service" or spying operations in Britain (*Secret Agent*, p. 32). Verloc, Vladimir says, is supposed to be acting as an "agent provocateur"—that is, a double agent planted among a group of political activists to create incidents that will provoke hostility against them (*Secret Agent*, p. 34). For 11 years, first by the embassy in Paris and now by that in London, Verloc has been paid for undertaking such secret missions under the code name "agent Δ," the Greek letter delta (*Secret Agent*, p. 35). Vladimir now contemptuously declares that Verloc has done nothing, and demands that Verloc begin to earn his pay or be fired. Calling science "the sacrosanct fetish" of Victorian Britain, Vladimir suggests "a series of outrages" against scientific targets beginning with a bomb attack on the Greenwich Observatory (*Secret Agent*, p. 38). His strategy is to influence general British public opinion in favor of repressive action against the anarchists who live freely in London, and who ultimately represent a threat to his government. "A dynamite outrage must be provoked," Vladimir concludes: "I give you a month" (*Secret Agent*, p. 43).

Verloc's anarchist group includes four other men, who bicker constantly among themselves:

- Michaelis, a grossly obese ex-convict, paroled from a British prison after taking part in a holdup, now celebrated in London society for writing a memoir about his anarchistic activities
- Karl Yundt, a malevolent and toothless self-proclaimed terrorist who talks of destroying society but has actually "never in his life raised personally as much as his little finger against the social edifice" (*Secret Agent*, p. 51)
- Alexander Ossipon, a heavy-set former medical student who espouses socialistic doctrines and survives by sponging off naïve young women
- A fanatic known as the Professor, the only truly dangerous member of the group, a dynamite expert who always wears a bomb that he can detonate if threatened with arrest

It is from the Professor that Verloc obtains the dynamite needed to create the explosion at Greenwich Park.

The reader learns about the events around the explosion by piecing together information from the complex, sinuous narrative, which repeatedly switches perspectives and jumps forward and backward in time. In chronological order, the events occur as follows. After his conversation with Vladimir, Verloc meets with Michaelis, Yundt, and Ossipon at his house. About a week later Winnie's mother moves into an old-age home in London, believing that by removing herself from the household she improves the chances that Verloc will be willing to continue supporting Stevie. Winnie, also hoping to secure Verloc's affection for Stevie, keeps telling her husband how much her brother idolizes him and how Stevie would do anything for Verloc. Verloc realizes Stevie can be useful to him and begins taking Stevie out with him on his walks around London. After Stevie has been going around with Verloc for about a week, Verloc announces that he thinks it would be a good idea for Stevie to stay with Michaelis for a little while at Michaelis's house in the country, outside London. Again about a week goes by, and Verloc picks Stevie up from Michaelis's country house. At some unspecified time, he has also arranged for the Professor to give him the bomb. He takes Stevie to the park and passes the bomb over to him, along with detailed instructions, but Stevie stumbles over a root in the ground and the bomb explodes prematurely, blowing Stevie to pieces, killing him instantly.

> ### CONRAD'S IRONIC TECHNIQUE
>
> Critics have praised *The Secret Agent* as a masterpiece of sustained irony, the literary method by which the author intends his words to be understood in a way that goes against their surface meaning. For example, anarchism was well known for opposing the accumulation of private property (hence the famous dictum of the anarchist Pierre Joseph Poudhon, "property is theft"). Yet early in the novel Verloc is presented as a protector of society's wealthy, propertied class. This is how he fondly imagines himself. However, rather than being truly motivated by such lofty principles, Verloc is simply lazy and self-indulgent. Conrad hints at the true state of affairs by drawing attention to Verloc's approval of luxury and his aversion to physical effort:
>
>> He surveyed through the park railings the evidences of the town's opulence and luxury with an approving eye. All these people had to be protected. Protection is the first necessity of opulence and luxury. They had to be protected; the whole social order favourable to their hygienic idleness had to be protected against the shallow enviousness of unhygienic labour. It had to—and Mr. Verloc would have rubbed his hands with satisfaction had he not been constitutionally averse from every superfluous exertion.
>
> (*Secret Agent*, p. 24)

Among the scraps of Stevie's clothing is a label that Winnie has sewn into his coat giving their address. This label leads to the solution of the crime by the forces of law and order, who are, like the anarchists themselves, divided by conflicting interests and loyalties:

- Chief Inspector Heat of Scotland Yard's Special Crimes Division, whose career has benefited greatly over the years from information that his secret source, Verloc, has funneled to him about London's anarchist community; Inspector Heat regards his connection with Verloc as "private."
- The Assistant Commissioner of Police, Heat's unnamed superior, who upsets Heat by taking over the investigation and uncovering Verloc as the secret source of Heat's information (and his professional success).

The Secret Agent

Royal Greenwich Observatory in London, England.

- Sir Ethelred, Britain's Home Secretary, the Assistant Commissioner's immediate superior, an aristocratic politician who wants the anarchists kept under control but wishes to know nothing of the "details" involved.

Heat desires not to solve the crime, but merely to make a plausible arrest. He is unaware of Verloc's guilt, yet wants to protect Verloc to maintain him as a source of useful information. So Heat attempts to pin the crime on Michaelis, a known anarchist. The Assistant Commissioner, however, pressures Heat into revealing the address on the scrap of Stevie's clothing and rapidly pursues his own investigation, donning a disguise and interviewing both Winnie and then Verloc himself that same day. By the end of the day, he has uncovered the investigator, Vladimir, who moves among the highest social circles in London and enjoys diplomatic immunity from prosecution.

Also that same day Inspector Heat meets with Verloc, at Verloc's house. Overhearing their conversation, Winnie learns that Stevie has been killed and that her husband is responsible. After Heat leaves, she stabs Verloc with a carving knife, killing him, and in fleeing the house she meets Ossipon. Ossipon persuades her to give him all her cash (which Verloc had earlier withdrawn from the bank in preparation for fleeing). The plan, says Ossipon, is for her to escape with him to the Continent. They make reservations on a boat that will take them across the English Channel. However, Ossipon slips off the train as it pulls out of London to meet the boat, leaving Winnie destitute and alone.

The narrative then skips ahead ten days, to a meeting between Ossipon and the Professor at a London restaurant. Ossipon produces a newspaper article he has been carrying with the headline, "Suicide of Lady Passenger from a cross-Channel Boat" (*Secret Agent*, p. 249). He is haunted by the article's last words: *"An impenetrable mystery seems destined to hang for ever over this act of madness or despair"* (*Secret Agent*, p. 249; emphasis original). The novel ends as the two anarchists part company, Ossipon walking off with the newspaper's words ringing in his head, the Professor slipping into the city's busy streets like a deadly, invisible virus.

Ideological contrasts between England and Russia. In his conversation with Verloc, the Russian spymaster Vladimir shows contempt for British society, with its bourgeois or middle-class emphasis on freedom and the rule of law:

> This country is absurd with its sentimental regard for individual liberty. . . . The imbecile bourgeoisie of this country make themselves the accomplices of the very people whose aim is to drive them out of their houses to starve in ditches.
>
> (*Secret Agent*, p. 37)

Vladimir, who represents Russia's authoritarian political system, is not the only one to show disdain for Britain. The Professor too declares his enmity toward the British system, although he views it from the opposite end of the political spectrum, from the perspective of anarchism. But while the Professor also despises the ingrained respect for the rule of law in Britain, he at least recognizes such respect as a source of Britain's strength:

> To break up the superstition and worship of legality should be our aim. Nothing would please me more than to see Inspector Heat and his likes take to shooting us down in broad daylight with the approval of the public. Half our battle would be won then; the disintegration of the old morality would have set in its very temple.
>
> (*Secret Agent*, p. 71)

In the novel, the two political extremes of anarchism and Russian authoritarianism serve as foils for the British system, which lies between them on the political spectrum. Britain's open democracy ultimately comes across as strong and resilient, even with its many foibles (as humorously exemplified in the characters of Heat and Sir Ethelred).

As is well known, Conrad's father was a Polish patriot who had been imprisoned for anti-Russian activities when Conrad was a boy (Russia then ruled Poland). Critics have seen a link between Conrad's inherited hostility to Russian authoritarianism and his sincere though reserved embrace of British middle-class political values. Yet while certainly colored by his own background as a Pole, Conrad's attitude to Russia also reflects a suspicion shared by many in his adopted country. As Britain moved towards a military alliance with Tsarist Russia (which would come in 1907, the year the novel was published), such suspicions would have had a topical relevance to the novel's British readers. In the words of German novelist Thomas Mann, *The Secret Agent* "is an anti-Russian story, plainly enough, anti-Russian in a very British sense and spirit. Its background consists in politics on the large scale, in the whole conflict between the British and the Russian political ideology" (Mann in Watt, p. 102; see Mann's **Death in Venice**, also in *Literature and Its Times*).

Sources and literary context. As a general rule, Conrad relied heavily on real-life sources for both characters and plots in his works. Scholar Norman Sherry, who has specialized in tracing these sources, argues that *The Secret Agent* marks a departure for Conrad in method. Previously, explains Sherry, the writer used mainly his own life experiences (especially his life as a sailor) to shape his material; beginning with *Nostromo* and *The Secret Agent*, he would instead gather his ideas and information primarily from wide reading.

Conrad himself offers important information in his 1920 Author's Note to the novel. He relates how the idea for the book first came to him during a conversation about anarchists with a friend, whom he doesn't name but who was later revealed to be the influential novelist and critic Ford Madox Ford. They discussed "the already old story of the attempt to blow up the Greenwich Observatory," and the friend "remarked in his characteristically casual and omniscient manner, 'Oh, that fellow was half an idiot. His sister committed suicide afterwards'" (*The Secret Agent*, p. 9). Conrad voices his conviction that his friend had little if any actual experience of real anarchists, and that he himself "had seen even less of their kind than the omniscient friend who gave me the first suggestion for the novel" (*The Secret Agent*, p. 12). In a memoir of his friendship with Conrad, however, Ford disputes Conrad's account. Ford did indeed number anarchists among his friends and acquaintances, and he claims to have supplied Conrad with anarchist literature, including probably two publications from the 1890s that the novel mentions as journals sold in Verloc's shop: *The Gong* and *The Torch*.

Conrad also mentions reading the memoirs of an Assistant Commissioner of Police, Robert Anderson, who served during the 1890s and was thus in office during the Greenwich Bomb Outrage. (Anderson's book, *Sidelights on the Home Rule Movement*, was published in 1906, when Conrad had already written the first three chapters of the novel.) Sherry proposes Anderson as a partial model for the novel's unnamed Assistant Commissioner, suggesting that one of Anderson's predecessors, Howard Vincent, also provided some of the characteristics of the novel's Assistant Commissioner. Sir Ethelred, the novel's Home Secretary, is based largely on Sir William Harcourt, whom Conrad also mentions in the Author's Note. Harcourt was Home Secretary during the tenures of both Anderson in the 1890s and Vincent in the early 1880s, when Irish terrorists set off several explosions in London (see above).

HOW LIKELY A WAY TO DIE?

How common was suicide in late-nineteenth-century Britain? For females the rate dropped after 1870, then rose after 1886, the year in which *The Secret Agent* takes place. Statistics show that, like Winnie, the wife in the novel, a third of all female victims drowned themselves, the others generally resorting to poison, self-hanging, or cutting their own throats. In one sample city (Hull), the rate of female suicides climbed from 4.5 percent in the 1880s to 5.9 percent in the 1890s, a decade in which suicides for men peaked as well (Bailey, p. 129). For women in the prime of life, like Winnie, the most significant cause of suicide was the disintegration of personal relationships—the death of kin or neglect or abuse by a husband—along with a lack of viable alternatives for women in the society of the day. A plausible candidate for suicide, Winnie is unable to endure the loss of her brother; perhaps their relationship provided her with her only moral and emotional sustenance in a daily round of existence that likely included neglect by her husband.

The Secret Agent

Some Real-Life Models and Sources for The Secret Agent

Character	Real-life Models	Literary Source
Verloc	H. B. Samuels, a supposed anarchist but in reality a police informer, and the architect of the Greenwich Outrage (a plot that he, like the novel's Verloc, hatched to provoke an anti-anarchist backlash); A. Coulon, a secret agent and police informer planted among London's anarchists (Coulon was not connected with the Greenwich Outrage, but his activities were exposed by subsequent press investigations).	Newspaper accounts of the Greenwich Bomb Outrage; for Samuels, journalist David Nicoll's 1897 pamphlet *The Greenwich Mystery*; for Coulon, other writings by David Nicoll.
Stevie	Martial Bourdin, who carried the bomb in the Greenwich Outrage, was Samuel's brother-in-law; witnesses suggest that (like the novel's Stevie) he was unintelligent and idolized his brother-in-law. Bourdin and Samuels thus provided a source for the family relationship central to the novel.	Newspaper accounts of the Greenwich Bomb Outrage.
Chief Inspector Heat	Inspector Melville of Scotland Yard's Criminal Investigation Division (the real-life counterpart of the novel's Special Crimes Division). Melville relied on Coulon for secret information just as Heat relies on Verloc in the novel. Melville also investigated the Greenwich Outrage.	Newspaper accounts of Melville's investigations (including the Greenwich Outrage).
Michaelis	Michael Davitt, not an anarchist but a paroled Irish revolutionary who (like the novel's Michaelis) wrote memoirs that made him into a celebrity in the late 1880s. Responsible for "bomb outrages" in the early 1880s.	Davitt's 1885 book *Leaves from a Prison Diary*. For Michaelis's views, numerous works including Edward Bellamy's utopian novel *Looking Backward* (1888).
The Professor	Luke Dillon, an Irish terrorist nicknamed "Dynamite Dillon," who (like the novel's Professor) wore a bomb that he intended to detonate if captured.	Various articles and books about Dillon.

(Adapted from Sherry, *Conrad's Western World*, pp. 205-324)

In addition to the literary sources outlined above, Conrad used the writings of anarchists such as Peter Kropotkin, Mikhail Bakunin, and others to develop the views he attributes to the novel's anarchists. The major exception to Conrad's reliance on literary research to inspire characters, views, and events in the novel appears to be the wife Winnie, whom Sherry suggests was partly based on Conrad's own wife, Jessie.

Critics have noted that in their focus on urban squalor and grime, Conrad's descriptions of London in *The Secret Agent* owe much to similar descriptions in novels (such as *Bleak House* and *Our Mutual Friend*) by the British novelist Charles Dickens, one of Conrad's favorite writers. Dickens's influence has likewise been seen in Conrad's colorful, humorous, and idiosyncratic portraits of Mr. Vladimir, Inspector Heat, and Winnie's mother.

Conrad was among the earliest novelists to choose espionage and international intrigue as subjects. His letters reveal that with *The Secret Agent* he hoped to appeal to a broader audience than with his earlier books. His choice of subject may have been influenced by Erskine Childers' *The Riddle of the Sands* (1903), a highly popular work about the chance discovery of a German fleet preparing to invade England that is now considered to be the first modern espionage novel. As a recent Conrad biographer notes, both novels share a "sense that menace underlies seemingly normal life, and that this menace can indicate the activity of an enemy agent" (Batchelor, p. 157).

Reception. Though it did not in fact sell very well, *The Secret Agent* received generally favorable reviews in leading British journals, including *The Times Literary Supplement*, *The Spectator*, and *The Nation*, as well as some unfriendly (and uncomprehending) ones in lesser periodicals such as *Country Life* and the *Edinburgh Review*. An unsigned review in *The Times Literary Supplement* praised Conrad's "friendly irony" in depicting his characters, "and above all his delicate and perfectly tactful art, to make them human and incidentally to demonstrate how monotonous a life theirs can be" (Sherry, *Conrad: The Critical Heritage*, p. 185). Conrad's friend Edward Garnett, writing anonymously in *The Nation*, sounded two notes that would be picked up by many more recent critics. First, and more generally, Garnett celebrated Conrad's "astonishing mastery of our tongue," but he also singled out *The Secret Agent* as a major artistic departure for the author, emphasizing the novel's "ironical insight into the natural facts of life, into those permanent animal instincts which underlie our spiritual necessities and aspirations" (Garnett in Sherry, *Conrad: The Critical Heritage*, pp. 191, 192). Examples of these instincts might include Winnie's protectiveness toward Stevie, or Verloc's desperation when faced with the loss of his income. Garnett stressed the contrast between the novel's ironic depiction of basic human drives in a squalid urban setting, and the exotic tropical settings and mysterious, romantic atmospheres found in Conrad's earlier works.

Like Conrad's work in general, *The Secret Agent* was largely ignored by critics in the 1920s and 1930s. In 1948, however, in his book *The Great Tradition*, the influential critic F. R. Leavis restored both author and novel to a central place in scholarly criticism. Leavis named Conrad as one of the five greatest English novelists of all time, and declared *The Secret Agent* (along with *Nostromo*) to be "one of the two unquestionable classics of the first order that he added to the English novel" (Leavis in Page, p. 101).

—Colin Wells

For More Information

Bailey, Victor. *"This Rash Act": Suicide Across the Life Cycle in the Victorian City*. Stanford, Calif.: Stanford University Press, 1998.

Batchelor, John. *The Life of Joseph Conrad: A Critical Biography*. Oxford: Blackwell, 1994.

Conrad, Joseph. *The Secret Agent*. Garden City: Anchor, 1953.

Fleishman, Avrom. *Conrad's Politics: Community and Anarchy in the Fiction of Joseph Conrad*. Baltimore: Johns Hopkins, 1967.

Page, Norman. *A Conrad Companion*. New York: St. Martin's Press, 1986.

Sherry, Norman. *Conrad: The Critical Heritage*. London: Routledge, 1973.

———. *Conrad's Western World*. Cambridge: Cambridge University Press, 1971.

Sonn, Richard D. *Anarchism*. New York: Twayne, 1992.

Stedman Jones, Gareth. *Outcast London*. Oxford: Oxford University Press, 1971.

Watt, Ian, ed. *The Secret Agent: A Casebook*. London: Macmillan, 1973.

Sense and Sensibility

by
Jane Austen

> **THE LITERARY WORK**
>
> A novel set sometime between the 1790s and 1810s in the English countryside, in the counties of Sussex and Devonshire, and in London; published in 1811.
>
> **SYNOPSIS**
>
> Two genteel sisters, Elinor and Marianne Dashwood, born without fortunes, find suitable husbands.

Jane Austen was born on December 16, 1775, in Hampshire County; she was the seventh of eight children of George Austen, a clergyman of the Church of England. Austen family tradition holds that an early version of *Sense and Sensibility* (called "Elinor and Marianne") may have been written in 1795 when Austen was 20. At her own expense, Austen published the final, substantially revised *Sense and Sensibility* in London in 1811. The novel makes no reference to notable historical events but portrays social life in a period that seems contemporary with the end of the eighteenth and the beginning of the nineteenth centuries. *Sense and Sensibility* was the first of four novels—the others being *Pride and Prejudice* (1813), *Mansfield Park* (1814), and *Emma* (1816)—published in Austen's lifetime; *Northanger Abbey* and *Persuasion* were published posthumously in 1818, the year after Austen died. Austen herself never married, but, like the heroines of her novels and like many of her contemporaries, she was fascinated by marriage, especially by the kind of marriage prized by her contemporaries: marriage to a gentleman with a landed estate.

Events in History at the Time of the Novel

The gentry in early–eighteenth-century England. The dominant English political ideology between 1795 and 1811 taught that political power belonged to male landowners. These were the men thought to have the greatest stake in the welfare of the nation and to be capable of an educated and disinterested consideration of the nation's good. By the Qualifications Act of 1711, still in force in 1811, country Members of Parliament (MPs) were required to possess freehold land worth £600 a year, and MPs from the town boroughs were to possess land worth £300 a year. The standard calculation figured the capital value of an estate at 20 times its annual revenue, which meant a country MP was required to have a landed estate worth about £12,000. This ideology was challenged by radicals such as Thomas Paine, in his *The Rights of Man* (1791-92), and by members of the London Corresponding Society, organized in 1792 to facilitate communication among English groups agitating for extensions of the franchise and for increased civil liberties. But the successes of the radicals in the French Revolution—from the fall of the Bastille in 1789 to the spectacle of French aristocrats being guillotined—provoked reaction in

England against radical democratic ideas of power sharing. So power continued to rest with a gentleman in possession of a good estate. Someone of social consequence with economic security, such a gentleman was an attractive object on the marriage market.

The landed aristocracy shared power with the landed gentry and with a class that has usefully been described as the "pseudo-gentry"—that is, the group of gentlemen (and their families) who lacked sufficient land to be supported by income from it but who, nevertheless, tended to share the values and (to a lesser degree) the lifestyle of the gentry. This group included military officers or clergymen (like Austen's brothers and father) and barristers. Because family estates were generally inherited by the eldest son, younger brothers from the aristocracy and the "genuine" gentry, often lacking enough capital to support themselves in leisure, frequently entered these professions along with the pseudo-gentry. Whereas an aristocratic landowner might have an annual income of somewhere between £10,000 to £100,000 a year, a gentry income was more likely to be about £1,000 or £2,000 a year, and a Church of England clergyman might have to struggle along on a few hundred pounds or even less. Austen's novels, including *Sense and Sensibility*, are dominated by characters from the gentry and pseudo-gentry.

The right to vote was tied to the possession of an estate, albeit a much smaller one. Borough qualifications varied widely, but country electors had to possess freehold property worth 40 shillings a year; tenants with leases shorter than the terms of their lives did not qualify. Modern estimates place the proportion of adult males possessing the franchise in parliamentary elections at roughly 15 percent. Women neither stood as candidates for Parliament nor voted, which was one reason contemporaries thought allowing landed property to fall into female hands was a "waste." Nor were women generally thought to have the capacity to manage landed estates.

To be a gentleman who owned a substantial landed estate was to have not only what contemporaries considered the highest form of economic security; it also gave the landowner possible access to political power and patronage and significant local power. Specifically, the landowner could select tenants for his smaller farms or village houses. A good number of country gentlemen (possessed of at least £100 a year) also served unpaid stints as local Justices of the Peace (JPs), an office for which no formal legal training was required. JPs enjoyed summary jurisdiction over a wide array of misdemeanors, including drunkenness, bastardy suits, and poaching. In exercising this jurisdiction, they could have offenders whipped, fined, or incarcerated in a local house of correction.

One form of local power frequently attached to the ownership of land could be exercised by either a man or a woman, namely, the ability to nominate a clergyman as rector of the local parish church, a right called an "advowson." In *Sense and Sensibility* Colonel Brandon possesses an advowson, which he uses to facilitate Elinor's marriage. Of 11,600 positions for rector in Church of England parishes at the end of the eighteenth century, at least 5,500 were in the power of private landowners to bestow. Landowners understood the advowson to be a useful kind of patronage they might invoke to provide for younger brothers, other male relatives, dedicated tutors or secretaries, or dependents of political allies. Advowsons would sometimes be put up for sale or auction, though not everyone approved of the practice. In fact, Jane Austen's father was the incumbent of such a living, or post, which his uncle Frank had purchased in 1770 to bestow on him.

A rector with a Church of England living was himself a man with property rights and attendant powers, although his estate and his powers were smaller than those of his landed patron. While he held the living, he had a freehold estate in the church buildings and land. A major problem for clergymen like Jane Austen's father was that control of their estates ended with their lives, reverting to their patrons and leaving their widows and children without any inheritance (beyond what they were able to save). A rector was also entitled to tithes, that is, to one-tenth of the produce of the cultivated land in the parish. Since the Church of England was the state church, all residents of a parish were legally required to pay tithes and parish poor rates, even those residents who professed other religions (about 10 percent of the total population). Jane Austen's brother George, a Church of England clergyman with two livings, in one year earned about £300 from his lands and £600 from tithes. In *Sense and Sensibility*, Colonel Brandon gives a position of this sort as a gift to Edward Ferrars, enabling him to support the wife of his choice.

Inheritance laws and practices. In English common law, landed estates descended by primogeniture, that is, the eldest son inherited the whole estate; his younger brothers and his sisters inherited nothing and were thus dependent on his decency to make some provision for them. (Property other than land statutorily descended by a formula that treated all siblings equally; this distribution formula, along with primogeniture, operated unless individuals had altered the descent by wills or trusts, which they usually did in the upper classes, though the bulk of the estate would still be settled on the eldest son.) Primogeniture was clearly understood by contemporaries to be a way of ensuring that large estates remained large enough to support an upper-class person in an upper-class way of life. It also ensured that the division between the upper classes and the lower classes was maintained. If estates had been divided equally among all siblings, they would have become progressively smaller, and the aristocracy and the gentry would have risked becoming indistinguishable from small farmers.

Nevertheless, in this period the rigid application of common-law primogeniture was generally thought to be too harsh to younger sons and to daughters. In most upper-class families, couples married with prenuptial agreements drawn up by lawyers after negotiations between the fathers of the bride and groom. These agreements were called "marriage settlements." As indicated, they commonly preserved the bulk of the estate for the eldest son but also made provisions from the estate for others. Daughters and younger sons commonly received "portions" in land or money to be paid out of the estate, collectable upon marriage or upon reaching the age of majority. Newspaper marriage announcements often specified exactly how many pounds a fortunate bride possessed as her portion (as our own announcements now specify from what colleges and professional schools a bride has graduated, allowing a perhaps more discreet calculation of how much tuition money has been spent on her education). Austen knew very well that the size of a girl's portion strongly affected her attractiveness on the contemporary marriage market, and frequently specified in her novels exactly how many thousand pounds of portion the more fortunate young women possessed. Normally a marriage settlement also provided a woman with a jointure, that is, entitlement to a yearly income for her life should her husband die before her. The amount of a woman's jointure was normally related to the amount of the portion she brought to the marriage, the portion being used as a capital sum that could support the later jointure payments; contented and generous husbands might add to a wife's jointure during the marriage. Mrs. Jennings in *Sense and Sensibility* lives well on the income of her jointure.

Because marriage settlements were private contracts negotiated between families, their provisions were highly variable. No one, of course, could know in advance how many children would be born of a particular marriage or whether a husband would predecease his wife. Nor was it possible to predict exactly how much revenue a particular estate would be capable of generating 20 or 40 years into the future, some estate owners being both careful managers and lucky, others both spendthrift and unfortunate. Consequently, there was frequently tension between gentlemen who inherited an estate and the various other persons who had what amounted to legal liens on his estate in the form of portions, a jointure, or annuities that were supposed to be paid out of it. An heir might be short of cash through no fault of his own, or, as his dependents often suspected, too selfish or too self-indulgent to pay them what was due. Persons entitled to jointures or portions could sue for them, and there are ample records of such litigation. Yet there were practical impediments to poor people's litigating, and social and moral inhibitions about suing members of one's own family. Part of the heroines' problem in *Sense and Sensibility* is that they have a moral lien on their stepbrother's estate, derived from their relationship and from his promise to their dying father, rather than a legal lien.

Women and marriage. The higher in the social hierarchy a person was, the more limited the pool of suitable marriage partners. Royal marriages were still arranged for dynastic and political purposes, and economic considerations significantly affected aristocratic marriages as well. In the gentry and pseudo-gentry, a woman, possessed of her own reasonable portion, ideally married a gentleman possessed of a landed estate sufficient to allow the couple to live on its proceeds, or, at least, married a gentleman with a good income from his inheritance or profession. The Church, the law, and the military remained the respectable professions.

Again ideally, a young person of this class selected a marriage partner with the advice and consent of his or her parents. Young women, especially, were constantly instructed that they lacked the discernment to know whether a particular man would make a good husband; in practice, most sensibly relied on their parents

Sense and Sensibility

and other relatives to investigate the character and prospects of suitors. The Marriage Act of 1753 required the consent of parents or guardians to the marriage of anyone under the age of 21; elopement to Scotland was the only way to avoid the provisions of this act. Sometimes, parents themselves proposed candidates for a daughter's hand, but by this time, in these classes, it was generally thought to be an abuse of parental power to attempt to coerce a daughter to marry a man who, upon acquaintance, she disliked. In effect, both parents and children had something close to veto power. A daughter would normally not marry a man of whom her parents strongly disapproved, and parents would not normally try to force a daughter to marry a man she found distasteful. Similarly, since marriages were understood to be a union of two families, a responsible and well-behaved young woman would not normally attempt to marry into a family that found her unsuitable; Lucy's clandestine engagement in *Sense and Sensibility* exemplifies bad behavior for this reason. Family discussions over a girl's marriage often involved such tactics as parents warning daughters who might be lukewarm to a particular suitor that they were unlikely to have such a good chance again or daughters pleading with fond fathers to let them marry men with less than stellar prospects. Sometimes a marriage settlement secured a "portion" (amount) on a child without making it contingent on that child's good behavior. But, because of the way marriage settlements of this period were drafted, even if a child were entitled to a marriage portion, the settlement might give a parent the power to adjust the size of the settlement or even to withhold it altogether should the child attempt to make a marriage of which the parent did not approve. Parents also had the leverage over children that came from their right to deny them the inheritance of personal property by changing their wills and by threatening to withhold money and patronage from a disobedient child. (Almost no one would have totally disinherited an eldest son, especially one like Edward Ferrars in *Sense and Sensibility*; Mrs. Ferrars's indulgence in this peculiarly English parental privilege is clearly an abuse of parental power.) Although on rare occasions society was shocked by the elopement of a gentlewoman with a footman, for the most part gentlewomen themselves were not much tempted to desire marriages with men significantly socially or economically beneath them. As Amanda Vickery remarks, "wealth and rank had an intensely romantic, as well as mercenary appeal" (Vickery, p. 44). In practice, it was the rare gentry daughter who married against her parents' opposition.

The plight of portionless daughters. Lack of sufficient money for daughters' portions was more of a problem for the gentry and pseudo-gentry than headstrong romantic daughters eloping with unsuitable men. There were estates whose possessors were better at spending and mortgaging than at investing and saving, estates against which decision-makers had too optimistically charged larger portions and jointures than the assets could support, and estates where demographic roulette had produced numerous children or long-lived widows. All these led to genteel daughters who had small, negligible, or unpaid portions. Families with large numbers of children—Jane Austen was one of eight children—found it especially difficult to support all of them in genteel life. At the turn of the century, settlements often used some version of a formula for charging portions on the estate that gave one year's income from the estate as a portion for a single younger child, two years' income should there be two younger children, and up to three years' income should there be a necessity for dividing it between three or more younger children. Large families often hoped for assistance in providing for younger sons and for daughters from kin or other connections, like the assistance the Austens received when their childless distant cousins, the Knights, adopted the Austens' third son, Edward, as their heir. Edward, in turn, as it was hoped such a child would do, shared his good fortune with his widowed mother and his unmarried sisters, giving them a cottage at Chawton in which to live in 1808.

Well-off gentlemen sometimes pleased themselves by marrying attractive girls with tiny portions or no portions at all, but the absence of a portion was a significant obstacle to a good gentry marriage. Despite a few notable exceptions, the lot of an unmarried gentlewoman was usually unenviable. To be a married woman, mistress of one's own household, and the mother of children was what normally made a woman a respected adult. Among the gentry and pseudo-gentry, a single woman counted herself fortunate if she became the mistress of the home of some male relation who lacked a wife; she was likely to dread the day when she might be forced to lose status by going out as a governess or paid lady's companion, thus becoming a sort of upper-level domestic servant, or when she had to take up a post as a teacher in a boarding school.

Women's education. The few who thought seriously about the education of gentlewomen at the turn of the nineteenth century confronted the fact that gentlewomen were primarily being educated to be the wives and mothers of gentlemen. Early feminists, from Mary Astell (1666-1731) to Catherine Macaulay (1731-91) and Mary Wollstonecraft (1759-97), had argued vigorously that women naturally possessed as much reason as men and urged that gentlewomen be educated more like gentlemen, studying philosophy, theology, literature, science, and history (see *A Vindication of the Rights of Woman*, also in *Literature and Its Times*). These feminists lamented what they considered a superficial and "ornamental" ladies' education, which added dancing, music, drawing, and French to the basic instruction in housekeeping, morality, and Christianity that every mother was supposed to see that her daughter received. The problem, though, as these feminists acknowledged, was that, since no learned professions were open to women and women were denied roles in the governance of their country, it was hard to see what practical use educating women in classics or serious history would serve. While feminists lamented the failure to cultivate women's reason and urged that they would not be fully moral beings or adequate mothers without more rigorous education, most people probably agreed with political economist and philosopher Adam Smith that the typical ladies' education was sufficiently useful: "They are taught what their parents or guardians judge it necessary or useful for them to learn; and they are taught nothing else. Every part of their education tends evidently to some useful purpose; either to improve the natural attractions of their person, or to form their mind to reserve, to modesty, to chastity, and to economy; to render them both likely to become the mistresses of a family, and to behave properly when they have become such" (Smith, vol. 2, p. 302). The sporadic education Jane and her older sister, Cassandra, received was typical of their time and class: mostly educated at home by their mother, they were briefly sent to girls' boarding schools, once to a school run by a female family connection for a few months, and once to the Abbey School in Berkshire for less than a year. A watercolor artist was hired to instruct them at home. They could read as they liked in their father's library and benefit from the intellectual stimulation their better-educated brothers provided.

The Novel in Focus

Plot summary. *Sense and Sensibility* begins with a crisis over how inherited wealth will be distributed. Mr. and Mrs. Henry Dashwood and their three daughters have been living for ten years at Norland Park, a Sussex estate owned by Henry Dashwood's uncle. Unusually for a comedy, the novel begins with deaths: first the death of the uncle, and then, a year later, the death of Henry Dashwood himself. As was common in contemporary inheritance practices, the uncle had determined that Norland Park would be inherited in the male line, first by John Dashwood, Henry's son by his first marriage; then by John's son, Henry. At the uncle's death, Henry Dashwood, father of the heroines, inherits only the right to the income from the estate during his life. Because he enjoys the income from Norland for only one year—and because he has not saved much before coming into this inheritance—at his death he leaves his widow and his daughters only £7,000. To this, the uncle has added legacies of £1,000 each for the three daughters. The widow and the daughters thus have £10,000 between them. Conservatively invested, this would yield about £500 a year, enough for four gentlewomen to live modestly, but certainly not enough to support the more privileged life to which Norland has accustomed them. Nor is it enough to provide attractive "portions," the contemporary term for dowries, for three girls.

John Dashwood and his wife quickly move into the house he has inherited, reducing his stepmother and stepsisters to the undesirable condition of visitors in the house they had thought of as their home. Despite a promise made to his dying father to do everything in his power to make his stepmother and stepsisters comfortable, John rapidly allows his selfish wife to convince him that he cannot afford to make any additions to their capital.

Elinor at 19 and Marianne at 17 are of marriageable age; the obvious problem is how they are to marry without good portions. Three gentlemen are introduced in the first of the novel's three volumes, two of whom clearly qualify as potential husbands for the Dashwood girls: Edward Ferrars and John Willoughby, both in their twenties. The third gentleman, Colonel Brandon, in his late thirties, is less obviously a potential husband.

Sense and Sensibility

Kate Winslet (far left) as Marianne Dashwood and Emma Thompson (far right) as Elinor Dashwood star in this 1995 film production, directed by Ang Lee.

Edward Ferrars is Mrs. John Dashwood's brother, the elder son of a very rich and unpleasant mother. He is neither handsome, nor lively, nor conventionally ambitious. His mother wants him to go into politics, or at least the army, but "all his wishes centered in domestic comfort and the quiet of private life" (Austen, *Sense and Sensibility*, p. 49). Marianne finds Edward dull, but Elinor is attracted to his quiet manner, his intelligence, his "sentiments," and his goodness. He seems to like Elinor, but is so reserved and correct in his conduct that she is uncertain of his feelings.

Thanks to the kindness and charity of Sir John Middleton, a relative of Mrs. Dashwood's, Mrs. Dashwood and her daughters are able to settle into Barton Cottage, very near Barton Park, his estate. Sir John is a sociable country squire, fond of hunting; his wife, Lady Middleton, dotes on her children and can say nothing that is not insipid and commonplace. Her loquacious mother, Mrs. Jennings, also lives with the Middletons.

One day, running down a hill in a rainstorm with characteristic impetuosity, Marianne falls and twists her ankle. A handsome neighbor, Willoughby, rushes to her assistance, swoops her into his arms, and carries her back to Barton Cottage. Marianne quickly responds to his gallantry.

Sir John reports that Willoughby periodically stays in the neighborhood at Allenham Court, visiting the elderly Mrs. Smith, whose presumptive heir he is.

Edward's caution and correctness are contrasted to Willoughby's ardor and impulsiveness. Elinor suggests to Marianne that she would be wise to be more guarded in displaying her love for Willoughby, but Marianne insists that sincerity is preferable to reserve and that "the restraint of sentiments which were not in themselves illaudable . . . [would be] a disgraceful subjection of reason to commonplace and mistaken notions" (*Sense and Sensibility*, p. 84). Willoughby seeks chances to be alone with Marianne, becoming intimate enough to beg a lock of her hair as a keepsake. Although Willoughby has not introduced Marianne to Mrs. Smith, he drives her to Allenham to see the gardens and the house. When Elinor suggests that this excursion is improper, Marianne replies that she trusts her own feelings to tell her when she acts properly or not and that she feels no impropriety or wrong in what she has done.

A complication arrives in the person of Colonel Brandon, a respected friend of Sir John's, returned from service in India, who quickly grows fond of Marianne. Willoughby and Marianne amuse each other with witticisms at the absent colonel's expense. "Brandon," declares Willoughby, "is just the kind of man . . . whom everybody speaks well of, and nobody cares about; whom all are delighted to see, and nobody remembers to talk to" (*Sense and Sensibility*, p. 81). Later, just as the Middletons and the Dashwoods are to go on an excursion to the estate of Colonel Brandon's brother-in-law, the colonel receives a letter that forces him to cancel the excursion. He apologizes and departs immediately for London. Willoughby then departs with equal suddenness, pleading that Mrs. Smith is sending him to London to attend to her business. Edward, too, leaves after a constrained visit of only a week.

New visitors at Sir John's, Mr. and Mrs. Palmer, show the kind of ordinary but interesting pain Austen often discovers in marriages. Charlotte Palmer is a daughter of Mrs. Jennings. Her husband is an intelligent man whose temper has been soured by his marriage to a beautiful but foolish woman. Good-humored and even kind, Mrs. Palmer volubly persists in publicly interpreting her husband's coldness and rudeness to her as "droll" (*Sense and Sensibility*, p. 134).

Yet more relations of Mrs. Jennings visit, two sisters: Miss Steele, nearly 30, very plain, and Lucy Steele, about 22, pretty, and with "a smartness of air, which though it did not give actual elegance and grace, gave distinction to her person" (*Sense and Sensibility*, p. 142). Elinor pities Lucy, who has native intelligence without education, but is disgusted by her toadying to Lady Middleton. The first volume ends with a surprising revelation: Lucy confides to Elinor that she and Edward have been secretly engaged for four years. Edward proposed to her when he was a pupil studying with Lucy's uncle, Mr. Pratt. Elinor reluctantly accedes to Lucy's demand that she keep this engagement a secret.

In the second volume, neither Elinor nor Marianne having yet secured husbands, Mrs. Jennings volunteers to take them with her to London, confident that she can help them make good matches. Kind Mrs. Jennings is the widow of a man who has "traded with success in a less elegant part of town" (*Sense and Sensibility*, p. 170). As a retail tradesman, he ranked conspicuously below the gentry; nevertheless, he has provided well for his widow and for his two daughters. Mrs. Jennings is understandably, if indelicately, proud of the matches she has helped her daughters make, and determines to do as well for the Dashwood sisters.

Against Elinor's better judgment, Elinor and Marianne accept Mrs. Jennings's invitation to stay with her in London. Elinor recognizes Mrs. Jennings's basic decency, yet worries "that she is not a woman whose society can afford us pleasure, or whose protection will give us consequence" (*Sense and Sensibility*, p. 173). The role of introducing Elinor and Marianne to London society ought rightly to be played by Mr. and Mrs. John Dashwood, who ignore this obligation as they do so many others. Marianne is eager to be in London to discover what happened to Willoughby and to see him again. Given the degree of intimacy between Marianne and Willoughby and the fact that Marianne is apparently writing to him in London, Elinor suspects that they are secretly engaged. Meanwhile, Marianne, learning that Willoughby is indeed in London, anxiously but unavailingly expects him to visit her.

At a London party, Marianne accidentally discovers Willoughby with a fashionable young lady. He does his best to avoid her indiscreet advances; when she presses for an explanation, he replies coldly and withdraws. Distraught, Marianne retreats. Willoughby sends a letter announcing that he has "long been engaged elsewhere" and insisting that he never intended to convey anything beyond friendship and esteem to Marianne. Elinor finds this letter "impudently cruel"; Marianne is hysterical and grief-stricken (*Sense and Sensibility*, p. 196). Much to their surprise, Elinor and Mrs. Jennings learn that there never was an engagement between Marianne and Willoughby. Willoughby is to marry a Miss Grey, who has a portion of £50,000.

Colonel Brandon, calling on Elinor at Mrs. Jennings's London house, seeks to diminish Marianne's suffering by revealing to Elinor unhappy and embarrassing facts about his own history. When his first love, Eliza, was unwillingly married to his older brother, he retreated to India. Eliza's husband treated her badly and divorced her on grounds of adultery. She afterwards gave birth to an illegitimate child, Eliza Williams. Colonel Brandon rescued Eliza when her mother died, then placed the girl in the care of a respectable woman. At the age of 16, Eliza suddenly disappeared. We now learn that the mysterious letter calling Colonel Brandon away in the first volume contained news of little Eliza and led him to discover that she had been seduced by Willoughby, who then abandoned her and her baby. The colonel rescued them. When Elinor conveys these revelations to Marianne, they convince her that she was deluded about

Sense and Sensibility

Willoughby's character and cause her to begin to regard Colonel Brandon with more interest and sympathy.

After these revelations, mordant comedy is provided by Mrs. John Dashwood's London dinner party: Elinor watches Lucy Steele ingratiate herself with the proud and ill-natured Mrs. Ferrars. Although alert to the mind-numbing stupidity of the fashionable social world exemplified by this dinner party, Elinor nevertheless allows herself to be amused at the spectacle of the foolish Mrs. Ferrars and the foolish Mrs. John Dashwood behaving graciously to the obsequious Lucy—"whom of all others, had they known as much as she did [about Lucy's secret engagement to their relation], they would have been most anxious to mortify" (*Sense and Sensibility*, p. 239). Elinor has also been informed that Mrs. Ferrars would like to see Edward marry a Miss Morton, daughter of Lord Morton, who has a portion of £30,000, and that, as an inducement, she has offered Edward £1,000 a year to do so.

With some cruelty, Lucy calls on her rival Elinor to boast of her progress in Mrs. Ferrars's regard and of her confidence in Edward's affection for her. Faithful to her promise to keep Lucy's secret, Elinor has been suffering in silence. Edward himself then calls in the midst of this tête-à-tête, further trying Elinor's powers of self-control in an exceedingly awkward three-way conversation. The second volume ends with another triumph of Lucy over Elinor: John Dashwood finally sees that it is his duty to have Elinor and Marianne stay with the Dashwoods in London, but Mrs. Dashwood demurs; succumbing to Lucy's flattering attentions, she invites the Steele girls instead.

The third and final volume of *Sense and Sensibility* opens with a sudden reversal of Lucy Steele's fortunes: news of her engagement becomes public and the outraged Mrs. Ferrars and Mrs. John Dashwood turn her away. Edward refuses to marry Miss Morton and is disinherited by his mother. He has earlier expressed an interest in becoming a clergyman and is now reported to be seeking a Church living so that he can marry and support Lucy. Elinor is astonished when Colonel Brandon—not appreciating that Lucy's engagement to Edward pains Elinor—comes to her with a generous offer of a Church living worth about £200 a year for Edward. Duty requires Elinor to convey this ostensibly happy news to Edward, who receives it glumly. Edward's fashionable and foppish younger brother, Robert, who complacently enjoys his good fortune consequent on Edward's loss of their mother's favor, laments that Edward is reduced to anything so "ridiculous" as being a country clergyman. Robert furthermore reports that he considers Lucy "the merest awkward country girl, without style, or elegance, and almost without beauty" (*Sense and Sensibility*, p. 296). Meanwhile, Edward's independent fortune of £2,000 and this new £200 a year are far less than the opulence Lucy expected to enjoy with the elder son of Mrs. Ferrars.

Elinor and Marianne, now eager to go home to Barton Cottage, accept the Palmers' offer to return by way of the Palmer estate, Cleveland. There, Marianne indulges her love for wild nature by wandering about in the damp, and succumbs to a dangerous fever. The gravity of her illness arouses general fear that she might die.

Just as Marianne recovers enough to be out of danger, an amazed Elinor receives a visit from Willoughby, who calls on her at Cleveland in an attempt to palliate his guilt. He acknowledges that he courted Marianne despite his engagement to Miss Grey and his determination not to marry a poor woman, but declares that he did, involuntarily, become attached to Marianne. He sheds new light on his abrupt departure from Allenham when he confesses that, far from being sent to London on Mrs. Smith's business, Mrs. Smith was so appalled by his seduction and abandonment of Eliza Williams that she disinherited him and sent him away.

Elinor and Marianne return to Barton Cottage. Her illness has offered Marianne an occasion for serious reflection. She admits to Elinor that she behaved badly with Willoughby and declares that she now understands the importance of actively exerting control over one's feelings. The sisters walk out to the spot where Marianne first met Willoughby. There Marianne confesses that she has not only been imprudent, but that she has been "insolent and unjust" to those who have been kind to her, especially Elinor, for whose conduct and fortitude under similarly difficult circumstances she professes admiration (*Sense and Sensibility*, p. 337). Even Mrs. Dashwood, not notably reflective, now takes some responsibility for her own imprudence as Marianne's mother and recognizes that she has been blind to Elinor's suffering and remarkable virtues.

The novel concludes with a spate of marriages, some blissful, others uncomfortably realistic. The Dashwoods are at first distressed by what seems to be the news that Edward has married Lucy.

Sense and Sensibility

A wedding banquet c. 1812.

However, they soon learn—to their wonderment—that it is Robert Ferrars who has married Lucy. Edward and Elinor delight in the absurd letter Lucy has sent to inform him of this sudden transfer of her affections. Mrs. Ferrars's rage at Robert inspires her to bestow £10,000 on Edward, thus enabling Edward and Elinor to marry with a reasonable income (about £720 a year). Lucy's continued campaign of flattery directed at Mrs. Ferrars in time restores Robert and herself to favor, and subjects the Ferrars and the John Dashwoods to a life of jealous and quarrelsome intimacy with each other. Willoughby lives a very ordinary life, occupying himself with his hunting dogs and horses, living with a wife who is "not always out of humour" (*Sense and Sensibility,* p. 367). At 19, Marianne marries Colonel Brandon, learning to love him and make him deservedly happy.

Colonel Brandon, wealth, and the Indies. *Sense and Sensibility,* tells us that when Brandon was a young man his family had an estate that was much encumbered, that is, burdened with debt. His father was the legal guardian of the orphaned heiress Eliza, whom he married to Brandon's brother against her inclination, presumably in part to use her money to help pay up the debt on the estate. Brandon tells Elinor that when he lost Eliza to his brother, he withdrew from England to India by exchanging his commission in the regular army for one in the East India Company army. Returned from India, he now has the rank of colonel and is comfortably rich, in possession of a nice estate in Dorsetshire, able to support not only himself and Marianne, but also to make the generous gift of a living to Edward.

As is common in novels and plays of this period, distant parts of the British Empire like India are offstage presences, not directly represented, but referred to as places in which people die, from which people return, and—sometimes—where fortunes are made. Decades of parliamentary investigation into alleged corruption and crime by Englishmen seeking to enrich themselves in India, most famously in the impeachment trial of Warren Hastings, governor-general of India, contributed to a pervasive popular sense that there was something less than respectable, even shameful, about people who had been to India and about wealth from there. Willoughby takes advantage of this prejudice when he mocks Brandon as a man with "more money than he can spend" and as a man who knows all about "nabobs" (*Sense and Sensibility*, p. 82). "Nabob" was originally the English version of an Urdu word for the Mohammedan governors of the Mogul empire in India; it came to be used, often derisively, for English officials in

India who returned with large fortunes. Such people were ridiculed and feared, in part because they usually came from less-than-distinguished social positions, then used their fortunes to buy land, with its accompanying political and social power. For an English person to go to India in this period was a high-risk strategy not normally engaged in by the respectable or well-off because most English people who went to India died of disease or drowned before they could return home with any profits. To exchange a commission in the regular army for one in India would have seemed to many an act of desperation.

Jane Austen is characteristically coy about what Brandon did in India and what impact it had on his fortune. Some readers have assumed that he inherited his Delaford estate because his brother died, which is possible, but we are not told that his brother has died; the colonel may simply have purchased the Delaford estate, relying at least in part on money he has made in India—or he may have used money made in India to improve the condition of the family estate. Given his age when he went out to India and the expensiveness of commissions in the regular army (British army officers had to purchase their commissions), it seems likely that Brandon went to India at a rank considerably lower than colonel and rose in rank in India.

The English presence in India had officially begun in 1601 when the East India Company received its first royal charter giving it a trading monopoly there. After Robert Clive's success in 1757 at the Battle of Plassey in Bengal, Britain increasingly acquired sovereignty as well as wealth in India.

For the few fortunate men who survived long enough and had sufficient good fortune to rise to the rank of colonel in India, the financial rewards were considerable. A colonel's pay and allowances alone came to about £3,500 a year. But high-ranking officers in India also participated in the process of collecting taxes and shared in tax revenue. Officers in the British army in Europe rarely collected significant prize money after victories, but officers in the East India army regularly got not only prize money but also significant "presents" from grateful local Indian princes. Despite the efforts of the directors of the East India Company and of a "reforming" Parliament to reduce "private trading" by Englishmen in India, many military officers, like their civilian counterparts, also engaged in economically rewarding private enterprise. Thus, "a man who reached the rank of major in Bengal could expect with reasonable luck to make his fortune" (Marshall, *East Indian Fortunes,* p. 213). One Indian notable complained about what seemed to him to be the custom of the English in India—a custom "which every one of these emigrants holds to be a Divine obligation, I mean of grasping together as much money in this country as they can, and carrying it in immense sums to the kingdom of England" (Kahn in Marshall, *Oxford History,* p. 514).

India and the East India Company provided economic resources for the Austen family. Jane Austen's great-uncle Frank acted as agent for one of the company's surgeons in India, helping to repatriate the profits of his private trading. Philadelphia Austen, Jane's aunt, lacking a portion that would have made her attractive on the English marriage market, ventured out to India in 1752 to marry this rich surgeon, a man 20 years older than she, sight-unseen. (Spinsters so desperate that they traveled to India for husbands were a frequent object of contemporary ridicule.) Philadelphia's daughter, Eliza Hancock, was the goddaughter of Warren Hastings, the governor-general. Hastings, who was suspected of being Philadelphia's biological father, settled £10,000 on her. The family connection to India continued. In 1809-10 Jane's brother Frank, as captain of the British naval vessel *Saint Albans,* convoyed East India ships. Delivering 93 chests of gold and treasure to the Company in England, he gained over £3,000 in reward money and agent fees. *Sense and Sensibility* idealizes the quiet, rural English life that Elinor and Edward are to live, having "nothing to wish for, but . . . rather better pasturage for their cows" (*Sense and Sensibility*, p. 363). Yet, from her own experience, Austen knew that in many gentry and pseudo-gentry families, lives of such tranquil financial independence sometimes were made possible only by money earned in dangerous—and perhaps disreputable—adventures abroad.

Literary context. Most critics, from Austen's time to the present, have considered Austen more sympathetic to the conservative than to the radical side in the ideological wars of her day. Particularly in the 1790s, English writers frequently declared their political allegiances in no uncertain terms. Novelists such as Robert Bage, William Godwin, and Thomas Holcroft showed interest in and sympathy for the radical principles of the French Revolution and challenged the traditional political and social order of England. In Bage's *Hermsprong, or Man as He is Not* (1796),

> ## THE AGE OF SENSIBILITY
>
> Novelists and philosophers alike took ideologically fraught positions on "sensibility," a key term in Austen's title. Philosophically, sensibility was understood to be a faculty or capacity of sensation and emotion, as distinguished from reason (the capacity of cognition). Interest in sensibility began early in the eighteenth century. Philosophers like the third earl of Shaftesbury in *Characteristics of Man, Manners, Opinions, Times* (1711) turned away from the doctrine of original sin to postulate that human nature was benign and people had an innate power of sympathy for others and a natural capacity for virtue. At mid-century David Hume in *The Treatise of Human Nature* (1739-40) and Adam Smith in *A Theory of Moral Sentiments* (1759) carefully explored the psychological operations of the mind and the emotions, especially sympathy, seeking to offer secular foundations for morality. By the late eighteenth century, sensibility had become both fashionable and controversial. It became fashionable to present oneself as a person of exquisite sensibility, blessed with the capacity for acute feelings and an innate sense of virtue; heroes and heroines of sensibility quivered with feeling and shed frequent tears in novels and poems of sentiment and sensibility. At the same time, although most thinkers agreed that there was an important relation between sensibility and virtuous action, critics worried that the external marks of sensibility, increasingly conventionalized—the sigh, the quick responsiveness, the tear, speaking in praise of nature and poetry, the melancholy languishing look—could all too easily be imitated by an insensible person, bereft of a real moral sense or true sympathy (like the novel's Willoughby). Critics also worried that the pleasures of sensibility were becoming narcissistic, selfish pleasures, cultivated for their own sake and for the egoistic gratification of imagining oneself as a superior person, instead of producing—as originally theorized—a sympathy that bound an individual to others in the community and motivated active charity. Elinor's attentive nursing of her sick sister is a sign of true sensibility and Marianne's lovesick moping is a mark of sensibility run amuck. Austen and many other writers agreed that sensibility alone is not a sufficient ground of virtuous action, that reason and principle were also necessary, and that distinguishing between true and false sensibility could be challenging.

for instance, Lord Grondale has his daughter's suitor, the hero Hermsprong, tried for sedition because he has criticized the British constitution and read Thomas Paine's *The Rights of Man* (for which Paine was convicted of sedition). Such novelists were considered English radicals, or Jacobins, a terms that had initially been used for the members of a French political club established in 1789 to promote democracy and the equality of man.

Female novelists too, including Mary Hays in *The Memoirs of Emma Courtney* (1796) and *The Victim of Prejudice* (1799) and Mary Wollstonecraft in the posthumously published *Wrongs of Woman* (1798), showed sympathies for radical causes, and some vigorously attacked the conventional socialization of women, demanding new rights for women, and notoriously pursuing love outside the bounds of matrimony. Clearly, *Sense and Sensibility* is at a considerable remove from such bold critiques. Many critics have even supposed Jane Austen followed in the conservative footsteps of the so-called Antijacobins, like Jane West, the author of *Advantages of Education* (1793) and *A Tale of the Times* (1799), in which a supporter of the French Revolution proves to be a libertine seducer. Yet Austen did not admire the humourless didacticism of the writer Hannah More, whose *Coelebs in Search of a Wife* (1809) Austen refused to read. And, as critics have also noted, Austen does offer a scathing account of the ways in which patriarchy is unjust to women,

Sense and Sensibility

and a sharp dramatization of the kind of male narcissism and foolishness that patriarchal privilege can produce in men such as John Dashwood, Robert Ferrars, and John Willoughby.

Reception. The publication of *Sense and Sensibility* in 1811 attracted little notice, which is hardly surprising, given that it was the first published work of an author who at that point was without any literary reputation. Indeed, like all of Austen's novels, *Sense and Sensibility* was published without Austen's name on the title page. The title page indicated only that the work was "By a Lady." Moreover, the eighteenth-century idea that novels generally were only a kind of subliterature continued to dominate the reviews. Reviewers often expressed annoyance at having to read so many bad novels, condescended to the genre, and considered that one of their principal duties in reviewing a novel was to report whether it was likely to corrupt or to improve the morals of young readers, especially young female readers. Novels were blamed for encouraging young women to adopt foolish, even dangerous ideas, especially about men. In their review, critics vigorously attacked novels they thought inculcated unrealistic, even absurd, romantic standards of male behavior and female expectations.

Only the *Critical Review* and the *British Critic* noticed the publication of *Sense and Sensibility*, both finding it above the common level of novels and both pronouncing that it had a useful moral. *The Critical Review* thought the "chief merit" of the novel lay in its portrayal of Marianne and Willoughby:

> [That] furnishes a most excellent lesson to young ladies to curb that violent sensibility that too often leads to misery, and always to inconvenience and ridicule. To young men who make a point of playing with a young woman's affections, it will be no less useful, as it shows in strong colors the folly and criminality of sporting with the feelings of those whom their conduct tends to wound and render miserable.
> (Southam, p. 38)

The British Critic agreed that "our female friends . . . may peruse these volumes not only with satisfaction but with real benefits, for they may learn from them, if they please, many sober and salutary maxims for the Conduct of life, exemplified in a very pleasing and entertaining narrative" (Southam, p. 40)

—Susan Staves

For More Information

Austen, Jane. *Sense and Sensibility*. Harmondsworth, Middlesex: Penguin, 1969.

Butler, Marilyn. *Jane Austen and the War of Ideas*. Oxford: Clarendon, 1975.

Collins, Irene. *Jane Austen and the Clergy*. London: Hambledon, 1993.

Copeland, Edward, and Juliet McMaster. *The Cambridge Companion to Jane Austen*. Cambridge: Cambridge University Press, 1997.

Gilson, David. *A Bibliography of Jane Austen*. New Castle, Del.: Oak Knoll, 1997.

Johnson, Claudia L. *Jane Austen: Women, Politics and the Novel*. Chicago: University of Chicago Press, 1988.

Marshall, Peter, and Alaine Low, eds. *The Eighteenth Century*. Vol. 2 of *The Oxford History of the British Empire*. Oxford: Oxford University Press, 1998.

Marshall, P. J. *East Indian Fortunes: The British in Bengal in the Eighteenth Century*. Oxford: Clarendon Press, 1976.

Nokes, David. *Jane Austen: A Life*. New York: Farrar, Strauss, and Giroux, 1997.

Smith, Adam. *An Inquiry into the Nature and Causes of the Wealth of Nations*. Ed. Edwin Cannon. 2 vols. in 1. Chicago: University of Chicago Press, 1976.

Southam, B. C. *Jane Austen: The Critical Heritage*. London: Routledge & Kegan Paul, 1968.

Vickery, Amanda. *The Gentleman's Daughter: Women's Lives in Georgian England*. New Haven: Yale University Press, 1998.

"Shooting an Elephant"

by
George Orwell

George Orwell (1903-50) was born Eric Arthur Blair in Motihari, Bengal, where his father worked for the Opium Department of the Government of India. He had a relatively comfortable middle-class upbringing in England, first attending a private preparatory school and then winning a scholarship to Eton, an exclusive "public" secondary school (the name in England for a private school). On leaving Eton in 1921 he joined the Indian Imperial Police; he was posted to Burma in 1922. After five years of service, however, he resigned, unable any longer to stomach doing "the dirty work of Empire" and harboring an ambition to be a writer (Orwell, "Shooting an Elephant," p. 501). On his return to Europe, he spent a year and a half living in poverty in London and Paris, trying to share the life of the destitute and oppressed and doggedly teaching himself to write. In 1933, using the name George Orwell, he published his first book, based on these experiences, *Down and Out in Paris and London*. The next three years saw Orwell publish three novels, *Burmese Days* (1934), *A Clergyman's Daughter* (1935) and *Keep the Aspidistra Flying* (1936); he honed his skills as a reviewer and essayist during these years too. In 1936 the publisher Gollancz commissioned him to write a book on the economically depressed areas of northern England, which became *The Road to Wigan Pier* (1937). In the spring of that year Orwell was also asked to contribute something to *New Writing*, a new journal edited by John Lehmann. Orwell offered to write what he described as "a sketch . . . describing the shoot-

> **THE LITERARY WORK**
>
> An essay describing an incident from Orwell's time as a policeman in Burma in the 1920s; published in 1936.
>
> **SYNOPSIS**
>
> Orwell's responsibility for dealing with a rogue elephant becomes an occasion for reflection on the nature and effects of imperialism.

ing of an elephant," but only if Lehmann was likely to publish something of the sort ("Shooting an Elephant," p. 483). Lehmann replied that he would like to see it, and when he did, he liked what he saw. "His editorial acumen or 'instinct' . . . had led him straight to a masterpiece" (Stansky and Abrahams, p. 147): one that was about not simply the shooting of an elephant, but the tragedy, violence, and farce of imperialism.

Events in History at the Time of the Essay

The British empire in Burma. In the nineteenth century, the British, anxious to secure control of cotton, teak, and other natural resources, and of inland trade routes to western China, came increasingly into conflict with the Burmese kings. The British saw Burma as simply an extension of India, which they already ruled. So they

"Shooting an Elephant"

George Orwell

persistently tried "to bring the Burmese kings down to the level of Indian princes in a subservient relationship," while "the proud Burmese kings," for their part, "did everything possible to retain their sovereign status" (SarDesai, p. 111). The two nations went to war in 1824-26, and in 1851 the British occupied and annexed Lower Burma. Pressure from British trading interests for greater commercial opportunities in the region continued, and when in 1882 a new clique at the Burmese court insisted on a tougher line against the British, further conflict seemed inevitable. In 1885, the Burmese took legal action against a British company, the Bombay-Burmah Trading Corporation, for underpayment for timber. This legal action, along with fears that King Theebaw was considering an alliance with the French, precipitated Britain's declaration of war against Burma. After only 15 days, the British army took over Mandalay, the capital of Burma, and the royal family was sent unceremoniously into exile. On January 1, 1886, the British government announced the annexation of Upper Burma. The whole of Burma was now to be ruled directly by the British, as a province of India.

Under British rule, the economy and society of Burma were transformed. A growing rice export trade prompted vast areas of land in the Irrawaddy delta to be brought under cultivation, and the export of oil, minerals and timber also increased greatly. But these changes resulted in few benefits for the Burmese people: instead profits went to the South Indian moneylenders who provided cash to Burmese peasant farmers at interest rates of up to 50 per cent, and to the British companies involved in processing, shipping and exporting these goods. Along with the transport and financial networks that sustained this trade, the British established new administrative, judicial and education systems. These too had profound effects on Burma. Traditional rulers were bypassed, and the country was governed by British civil servants working with lower-level local leaders and with a new indigenous administrative class, the *a-so-ya-min*, who were chosen on the basis of training and merit rather than birth. Ironically people lost regard for traditional Buddhist education, which had led to levels of basic literacy in Burma in the mid-nineteenth century being far higher than those in Europe. A western education became the passport to a place in the new social hierarchy of British Burma, and gave rise to a new urban elite, whose "perspectives and occupational skills became very unlike those of their village-dwelling peasant compatriots" (Steinberg, p. 284).

Burmese resistance to British rule. The Burmese never accepted British rule. As soon as annexation was announced in 1886, armed uprisings began all over Burma. The British responded by burning down villages and executing those they saw as rebels *en masse*, but the uprisings continued until 1895 in some areas. Around the turn of the twentieth century, resistance began to take other forms. In towns and cities, the new urban elite established Buddhist groups with the aim of asserting a distinctive Burmese cultural identity, and in 1906, these groups united to form the Young Men's Buddhist Association (YMBA). Although ostensibly they were religious organizations, the real objective of the YMBA and its successor, the General Council of Burmese Associations (GCBA) was greater self-government for Burma. In 1921, the British responded to such nationalist demands by introducing a degree of political reform, providing for greater Burmese involvement in the central legislature and at the provincial level. However, this did not satisfy the nationalists; during the 1920s political activism spread throughout Burma. Activists established village-level nationalist organizations, which boycotted government officials and supported peasants who refused to pay taxes and rent. Younger Buddhist monks also became politically active, "attacking foreign rule, village headmen, the police and courts, tax collectors, and Indians" (Steinberg, p. 286). Tensions increased still further during the 1930s, as the worldwide depression hit Burmese rice growers hard, fueling resentment against the British government and moneylenders from India.

Orwell alludes to this atmosphere in "Shooting an Elephant," when he describes the strong anti-European feeling amongst the people of Moulmein, especially the young men, and the several thousand young Buddhist priests who seemed to have nothing to do "except stand on street corners and jeer at Europeans" ("Shooting an Elephant," p. 501). He treats the tensions between Burmese and Europeans at more length in *Burmese Days*, in which a British man is killed after helping to put down a peasant rebellion; the resulting tensions culminate in a riot.

The Indian Imperial Police in Burma. Political and economic tensions made policing the 13 million inhabitants of Burma in the 1920s and '30s a demanding task. Burma had the highest crime rate in the empire; violence against government officials was rising, and armed gangs of thieves, or "dacoits," roamed the countryside on the prowl for homes to rob. Most of the day-to-day policing was done by the 13,000 strong subordinate force of Burmese police; standing in reserve in case of emergency were British and Indian troops and the largely Indian military police. The 90 or so officers of the Indian Imperial Police—almost all British, despite an official policy in the 1920s of admitting more native-born officers—had a largely administrative role.

This role entailed considerable responsibility, however, especially given that many officers, including Orwell himself (under his given name—Blair), were very young. Orwell started as an assistant superintendent, responsible for such tasks as preparing cases for prosecution, compiling crime reports, and managing payroll and police supplies. In 1926, at the age of 23, Orwell became subdivisional officer—the senior police officer—at Moulmein in southern Burma, an important provincial center and commercial port. As subdivisional officer, his duties included supervising investigations, settling local quarrels, disciplining constables, observing interrogations of prisoners and testifying at important trials and inquests. This was the only time in his life, he later wrote, when he had been important enough to be "hated by large numbers of people" ("Shooting an Elephant," p. 501); it was here that the events he describes in Shooting an Elephant took place.

The Essay in Focus

The contents. "Shooting an Elephant" opens with a description of the anti-European feeling Orwell encountered while he was subdivisional police officer in Moulmein. This feeling was "aimless" and "petty," but "very bitter," and eventually the sneering and the insults "got badly on my nerves" ("Shooting an Elephant," p. 501). He writes that his experiences as a police officer had already turned him against the British empire and filled him with "an intolerable sense of guilt" ("Shooting an Elephant," p. 501). But his sympathy for the Burmese as victims of British oppression was complicated by a violent "rage against the evil-spirited little beasts [the Burmese with anti-European feelings] who tried to make my job impossible" ("Shooting an Elephant," pp. 501-02). This, he observes, is the kind of quandary that afflicts all British imperial officials. Orwell then recalls an experience that, in retrospect, casts light on the violence and futility of imperialism.

THE HSAYA SAN REBELLION

The most serious outbreak of anticolonial protest during the 1920s and '30s began in December 1930, in the Tharrawaddy District. It was led by Hsaya San, an organizer for the GCBA and a former Buddhist monk. The symbols of Hsaya San's leadership were traditional—including a white umbrella, formerly associated with the Burmese royalty. But the grievances that fuelled the revolt were contemporary ones: "taxation, crime, rice prices, land alienation, Indian immigration, and unemployment as well as the denigration of the Buddhist religion" (Steinberg, p. 288).

The rebellion spread quickly, and, after initially underestimating the threat, the British responded with force. The regular police, the military police, and the army were used against the rebels; 12,000 troops were mobilized, and aircraft was brought in. Before the authorities regained control, the rebels suffered 3,000 casualties; casualties on the government side numbered only 138 (Steinberg, p. 289).

Hsaya San was captured in late 1931, and was later tried and executed. The rebellion was not a complete failure, however. It demonstrated the government's indifference to peasant grievances, and "awakened public opinion, setting an example of sacrifice and anticolonial zeal that few could ignore" (Steinberg, p. 289).

"Shooting an Elephant"

"Shooting an Elephant"

MEMORIES OF ORWELL, NÉE BLAIR, THE POLICEMAN

Blair arrived in Burma at the age of 19, drawn there by his family connections with Burma, a taste for adventure, and the good salary attached to a posting in the Indian Imperial Police (Shelden, p. 86). There is some debate about the success of his police career. Bernard Crick argues that Blair was seen as a solitary eccentric, that he often did not get on with his superior officers, and that this led to his being given generally "poor and lonely postings" (Crick, p. 80). Blair clearly did not enjoy socializing with the other Europeans at their clubs—one fellow-officer, Roger Beadon, remembered him as "a very pleasant fellow to know," but also as an untidy-looking sort who preferred to keep to himself (Beadon in Coppard and Crick, p. 62). Michael Shelden argues, however, that Blair did his job well and made satisfactory progress in his career. He gave little or no sign to those around him that he was uncomfortable with his role as a servant of British imperialism, or that he wished to be a writer. Fellow-officer Beadon was astonished when *Burmese Days* appeared and he realized Blair was its author: "to find that George Orwell was Eric A. Blair . . . was rather like seeing a flying saucer arrive at your front door and wondering what it's going to do" (Beadon in Coppard and Crick, p. 65).

Another who encountered Blair the policeman was Maung Htin Aung, who later became Vice-Chancellor of the University of Rangoon. One day in November 1924, he was part of a group of students waiting at a railway station. As Blair, in civilian clothes, came down the station stairs, one of the group accidentally bumped into him, causing Blair to fall heavily. Furious, Blair raised his heavy cane to hit the boy on the head, but managed to control himself enough to hit him on the back instead. An argument ensued; when Blair got into a first-class train compartment, the students followed him and continued arguing until he got off the train. Htin Aung observes that Blair's attitude to students at this time seems to have been typical of his English contemporaries: Burmese students were generally viewed with suspicion or even hatred for their nationalist sympathies. But Bernard Crick suggests that there is something very "Orwell-like," and unlike the typical Englishman, in the fact that Blair did not call the police, but instead carried on arguing with the students in a train compartment until he reached his destination (Crick, p. 88).

Blair was troubled by his own behavior and by other acts of violence by Europeans against Burmese, and must have wondered what would have happened if he had not controlled himself. He would later use this incident as the basis for one in *Burmese Days*, where the Englishman Ellis strikes a Burmese boy and blinds him.

One day, one of his subordinate officers telephones him to say that an elephant has gone berserk in the bazaar, and will he please come and do something about it? On the way, Orwell discovers that the elephant is a tame elephant that has gone *must*—has slipped into a temporary frenzy. The elephant has already destroyed a hut, raided a fruit-stall, killed a cow, and vandalized the municipal rubbish-van; as he gets closer, he discovers it has also just killed a man, an Indian laborer, or *coolie*. He sends for an elephant rifle and pursues the elephant to a nearby paddy field, followed by a large crowd of locals. Having seen the gun, they think Orwell is going to shoot the elephant, and are keen for "a bit of fun"—and for the meat ("Shooting an Elephant," p. 503). Orwell, however, has no intention of shooting the elephant, and the instant he sees him he knows "with perfect certainty" that he ought not to do so ("Shooting an Elephant," p. 503). The elephant is now calmly eating grass; Orwell is sure that his must is passing, and that

A Burmese man directs an elephant to lift a tree trunk with its tusk.

he will simply wander around harmlessly until his *mahout*, or handler, comes to catch him.

But Orwell realizes that the watching crowd of more than 2,000 people confidently expects that he *will* shoot the elephant, and that if he does not, the crowd will laugh at him. This, he feels, would be intolerable. So, despite feeling that "it would be murder to shoot him," he takes aim and fires ("Shooting an Elephant," p. 504). But since he does not know exactly where to aim in order kill the elephant, Orwell has to shoot him three times before he falls. The essay describes the elephant "[sagging] flabbily to his knees," then rising again, and then trumpeting once before finally crashing to the ground ("Shooting an Elephant," p. 505). Orwell goes over to the elephant, only to discover that he is not dead. So Orwell fires two more shots at what he thinks must be the elephant's heart, but they have no apparent effect: the elephant is "dying, very slowly and in great agony, but in some world remote from me" ("Shooting an Elephant," p. 505). Orwell does not even have the power to put him out of his misery. He fires more shots from a smaller rifle but they too make no difference. Eventually Orwell cannot stand the animal's suffering any longer and leaves; he later hears that the elephant took half an hour to die, and that his body was stripped almost to the bones by the afternoon.

The owner of the elephant is furious that it has been killed, but cannot do anything about the matter as he is "only an Indian" ("Shooting an Elephant," p. 506). Legally Orwell was in the right because the elephant had killed a man, and the older Europeans support him, but the younger ones say, "it was a damn shame to shoot an elephant for killing a coolie, because an elephant"—valued at a hundred pounds or more—"was worth more than any damn Coringhee coolie" ("Shooting an Elephant," p. 506). Orwell admits that he was very glad the elephant *had* killed the coolie because it put him in the right—but wonders whether any of the other Europeans realized that he shot the elephant "solely to avoid looking a fool" ("Shooting an Elephant," p. 506).

"A sahib has got to act like a sahib." By analyzing why he killed the elephant when he did not want to and, what is more, knew he ought not to, Orwell explores the dynamics of imperialism. The incident, he writes, was tiny in itself, "but it gave me a better glimpse than I had had before of the real nature of imperialism—the real motives for which despotic governments act" ("Shooting an Elephant," p. 502). Standing in front of the crowd, he feels it willing him to kill the elephant, and at this moment he grasps the "hollowness" and "futility" of the empire ("Shooting an Elephant," p. 504). Armed with a gun in

"Shooting an Elephant"

front of an unarmed crowd, he would seem to be in control, but he is not. He is, instead:

> a sort of hollow, posing dummy, the conventionalized figure of a sahib. For it is the condition of [the white man's] rule that he shall spend his life in trying to impress the "natives," and so in every crisis he has got to do what the "natives" expect of him. He wears a mask, and his face grows to fit it. . . . A sahib has got to act like a sahib.
> ("Shooting an Elephant," p. 504)

To refuse to play the part—for example, to "trail feebly away," rifle in hand, instead of shooting the elephant— would look weak and indecisive, would add to the list of petty humiliations he suffers as an emblem of the empire: being tripped-up while playing football, for example, or being insulted, from a safe distance, on the street. "The crowd would laugh at me. And my whole life, every white man's life in the East, was one long struggle not to be laughed at" ("Shooting an Elephant," p. 504).

A "PUKKA SAHIB"

Sahib means "Englishman," or "European," and has also been used by peoples of India and Burma as a title of respect when addressing an Englishman or other European. A "pukka sahib" is a thorough sahib: an Englishman behaving as he was expected to by Indians and by other English people in India.

Of course, the other side of the coin was the constant stream of humiliations suffered by the Burmese under British rule. Orwell may have been tripped-up on the football field, but Burmese people suffered systematic, institutionalized discrimination. A Burmese student himself at the time, Maung Htin Aung recalls that his eldest brother U Tin Tut was asked in 1924 to play for the English regiment garrisoned in Rangoon in a rugby match against the European-only Gymkhana Club. U Tin Tut was a member of the Indian Civil Service and a British-trained lawyer. He had held a commission in the (British) Indian Army and captained the Cambridge University Rugby team, so he was a logical choice to bolster the strength of the regimental team. When the match ended, the players headed for the Gymkhana Club to shower and change. At this point, the club secretary ran out and told U Tin Tut that he could not enter the building, let alone use the showers because he was not a European. U Tin Tut later received personal apologies from individual players, but no official apology from the club. "Naturally," says Maung Htin Aung, "that was the last game of rugby that my brother ever played" (Aung, p. 26). The incident, concluded the Burma newspapers, was proof that the British considered the Burmese an inferior people,

Although Orwell recognizes that the chief evil of imperialism is that it destroys the freedom and dignity of its subject peoples, he addresses another evil in "Shooting an Elephant." His concern here is with the guilt and self-loathing that he feels results from taking on the role of imperialist "tyrant." As he sees it, imperialism destroys the freedom of not only the subject people but their rulers too ("Shooting an Elephant," p. 504). This is a view that he explores at greater length in *Burmese Days* and in *The Road to Wigan Pier*. The main character of *Burmese Days*, John Flory, shares Orwell's hatred of the empire and feels contempt for his fellow sahibs—and, inevitably, for himself. They are all the servants of an empire whose object is theft: a despotism in which, as Flory puts it, "the official holds the Burman down while the businessman goes through his pockets" (Orwell, *Complete Works* 2, p. 38). Such a view was, of course, unspeakable in European clubs, which were the social center of the sahibs' world. Only very occasionally could it be voiced aloud. In *The Road to Wigan Pier*, Orwell describes a night on a train in Burma when he and a man who worked in the Educational Service, whose name he never knew, cautiously sounded each other out and, each discovering that the other was "safe," talked for hours:

> we damned the British Empire—damned it from the inside, intelligently and intimately. It did us both good. But we had been speaking forbidden things, and in the haggard morning light when the train crawled into Mandalay, we parted as guiltily as any adulterous couple.
> (Orwell, *Complete Works* 5, p. 135)

Dissenters like Orwell and his companion felt their hatred of the empire had to be kept secret, and this secrecy was "corrupting" (*Complete Works* 2, p. 70). As the narrator of *Burmese Days* puts it, in a voice very close to Orwell's own:

> Your whole life is a life of lies. Year after year you sit . . . listening and eagerly agreeing while Colonel Bodger develops his theory that these bloody Nationalists should be boiled in oil. . . .

You see [English] louts fresh from school kicking grey-haired servants. The time comes when you burn with hatred of your own countrymen, when you long for a native rising to drown their Empire in blood. And in this there is nothing honourable, hardly even any sincerity. For, *au fond* [deep down], what do you care if the Indian Empire is a despotism, if Indians are bullied and exploited? You only care because the right of free speech is denied you. You are a creature of the despotism, a pukka sahib, tied tighter than a monk or a savage by an unbreakable system of taboos.
(Orwell, *Complete Works* 2, pp. 69-70)

In "Shooting an Elephant," Orwell contends that his feelings of guilt, hatred, and self-hatred are shared by all of the "Anglo-Indian" officials—the British people who worked in the various imperial services ("Shooting an Elephant," p. 502). He makes the same point even more strongly in *The Road to Wigan Pier*, asserting that "every Anglo-Indian is haunted by a sense of guilt," knowing that they really have no right "to invade a foreign country and hold the population down by force"; only those who are doing something "demonstrably useful," like forest officers, doctors, and engineers, seem to have an untroubled conscience (*Complete Works* 5, pp. 135-36). This may be overstating the case. But the experience of being complicit in "the dirty work of Empire" was certainly the beginning of the transformation of Eric Blair into George Orwell ("Shooting an Elephant," p. 501). Five years of working for an oppressive system left him feeling that "I had got to escape not merely from imperialism but from every form of man's dominion over man" (*Complete Works* 5, p. 138). It now struck him that the English working class "[played] the same part in England as the Burmese played in Burma," and he wanted "to be one of them and on their side against their tyrants" (*Complete Works* 5, p. 138). In the winter of 1927-28, keen to discover more about the lives of the poor, and vaguely hoping to rid himself of his sense of guilt, Orwell began to explore the slums and lodging houses of London's East End. After a few weeks, he went on the road as a tramp for the first time.

Sources and literary context. Although "Shooting an Elephant" is written in the first person and presents itself as an account of an actual incident from Orwell's time in Burma, it is not clear how close to the truth Orwell's narrative actually is. Orwell himself wrote that it was about an event that "came back to me very vividly the other day," and at least two men who worked in Burma at the same time recall his being called in to shoot a rogue elephant, a fairly common part of a policeman's work in Burma at that time (Orwell, *Complete Works* 10, p. 483). But apparently Orwell actually killed the elephant with a single shot, which means that the most memorable and harrowing part of the essay, the elephant's agonizing death and Orwell's powerlessness to hasten it, is an exaggeration. It is an exaggeration with a purpose, however. The needless and hideous killing of the elephant symbolizes "the evil, the dilemma, and the pathos of imperialism" (Stansky and Abrahams, p. 148). Orwell's "concern in the essay [is] to diminish the Empire, not to celebrate its ruthless efficiency" (Newsinger, p. 6).

The blurring of fiction and autobiography was not uncommon at the time Orwell was writing. When "Shooting an Elephant" was reprinted in *Penguin New Writing* (also edited by John Lehmann) in 1940, 12 of the 14 contributors "wrote in a similar, ambiguous, first-person descriptive vein" that was "truthful to experiences but not necessarily to fact" (Crick, p. 96). This mode of writing can be understood as part of a wider fashion in the 1930s for "eyewitness history," in which writers explored political and social issues through autobiography. Classics of this genre include Robert Byron's *The Road to Oxiana* and Christopher Isherwood's *Goodbye to Berlin*, as well as Orwell's own *The Road to Wigan Pier*. As Janet Montefiore observes, these texts "deploy a brilliant rhetoric of authenticity,

---

"POLITICS AND THE ENGLISH LANGUAGE"

In "Politics and the English Language," first published in 1946, Orwell famously argues that debased language leads to debased, corrupted thought—and vice versa. He proposes six basic rules to stop the "decay of language" and of political thought:

(i) Never use a metaphor, simile or other figure of speech which you are used to seeing in print.
(ii) Never use a long word where a short one will do.
(iii) If it is possible to cut a word out, always cut it out.
(iv) Never use the passive where you can use the active.
(v) Never use a foreign phrase, a scientific word or a jargon word if you can think of an everyday English equivalent.
(vi) Break any of these rules sooner than say anything [in an] outright barbarous [way].

(Orwell, *Complete Works* 17, p. 430)

"Shooting an Elephant"

which hindsight reveals to be the product of deliberate and skilful construction" (Montefiore, p. 11).

Reception. "Shooting an Elephant" was published in the second issue of *New Writing* in the autumn of 1936, and Lehmann liked it enough to reprint it as the opening piece in the first issue of his new journal, *Penguin New Writing*, in 1940. It has since been reprinted countless times in collections of Orwell's work and other anthologies, and on October 12, 1948 it was broadcast by the British Broadcasting Corporation. The essay has become an Orwell classic, praised for its "sharp visual memory" and its "acute" portrayal of guilt and authority, for its combination of "literary" and "moral" honesty and strength (Fyvel, Sykes, and Elliott in Meyers, pp. 306, 309, 340). Later critics have identified it as marking "the beginning of the major phase of Orwell's career," in which personal reminiscence and anecdote became the vehicle for a subtle exploration of political themes (Stansky and Abrahams, p. 147).

Since the 1950s, many American students have encountered "Shooting an Elephant" in composition courses, where it is among the most frequently used models of good prose. Orwell's famous "plain style"—the principles of which are outlined in another of his famous essays, "Politics and the English Language"—is often held up as a model to emulate.

Unfortunately, emulating Orwell is not as easy as it might seem: plain style, as Irving Howe observed sadly, is "that style which seems so easy to copy and is almost impossible to reach" (Howe in Meyers, p. 350). Orwell's command of it in "Shooting an Elephant" and his other mature essays, along with his skill in articulating "the complexity of seemingly simple experience" have led many critics to call him a master of the essay—in Howe's view, he was perhaps "the best English essayist . . . since Dr [Samuel] Johnson" (Stansky and Abrahams, p. 147; Howe in Meyers, p. 349).

—Ingrid Gunby

For More Information

Aung, Maung Htin. "George Orwell and Burma." In *The World of George Orwell*. Ed. Miriam Gross. London: Weidenfeld and Nicolson, 1971.

Coppard, Audrey, and Bernard Crick. *Orwell Remembered*. London: Ariel Books/BBC, 1984.

Crick, Bernard. *George Orwell: A Life*. London: Secker & Warburg, 1980.

Meyers, Jeffrey, ed. *George Orwell: The Critical Heritage*. London: Routledge & Kegan Paul, 1975.

Montefiore, Janet. *Men and Women Writers of the 1930s: The Dangerous Flood of History*. London: Routledge, 1996.

Newsinger, John. *Orwell's Politics*. New York: St. Martin's Press, 1999.

Orwell, George. *The Complete Works of George Orwell*. 20 vols. Ed. Peter Davison. London: Secker & Warburg, 1998.

———. "Shooting an Elephant." In *The Complete Works of George Orwell*. Vol. 10. Ed. Peter Davison. London: Secker & Warburg, 1998.

SarDesai, D. R. *Southeast Asia: Past & Present*. 4th ed. Boulder, Colo.: Westview Press, 1997.

Shelden, Michael. *Orwell: The Authorised Biography*. London: Heinemann, 1991.

Stansky, Peter, and William Abrahams. *Orwell: The Transformation*. London: Constable, 1979.

Steinberg, David Joel, ed. *In Search of Southeast Asia: A Modern History*. Honolulu: University of Hawaii Press, 1987.

Songs of Innocence and of Experience

by
William Blake

William Blake was born in 1757 in London, a place that would leave its mark on all his work. His father, a tradesman who sold hosiery, handed down to Blake a heritage of religious and political dissent. Disdainful of the restrictions of school, Blake was self-educated, until he began drawing lessons at the age of 10. After a seven-year apprenticeship as an engraver, Blake supported himself by engraving while he attended the Royal Academy. His study here, however, was short-lived because his iconoclasm conflicted with the academy's orthodoxy. In 1782 Blake married Catherine Boucher, forming an artistic partnership with her that would last a lifetime; two years later he opened his own printing business. Blake's distinctive style, the product of his visionary imagination and his varied artistic influences, was set with *Songs of Innocence,* the first of his books to interweave poetry and etchings. That only a few copies could be painstakingly produced was compensated for by the complete control that Blake exercised. In *Songs of Innocence and of Experience,* Blake describes society both as he sees it and as he believes it should be. He laments the alienation of the large city in "London," condemns child labor in two poems called "The Chimney Sweeper," and looks with sorrow on the subjection of Africans in "The Little Black Boy."

Events in History at the Time of the Poems

A revolutionary era. Revolutions—political, economic, and social—marked the second half

> **THE LITERARY WORK**
>
> A collection of engraved poems set mainly in England during the late eighteenth century, but also in timeless mythical places; *Songs of Innocence* was printed in 1789 and combined with *Songs of Experience* in 1794.
>
> **SYNOPSIS**
>
> Two complementary collections of lyric poems, *Songs of Innocence and of Experience* depict a state of joyous engagement with the world and a bitter detachment from the world.

of the eighteenth century. The French Revolution, which began with the storming of the Bastille in 1789, sent shock waves across the English Channel. At least initially, it inspired the liberal-minded because of its roots in Enlightenment thought, while frightening conservatives, who worried about the stability of English society and the rule of law. Rumblings of discontent had, in fact, been heard throughout the 1780s in England. William Blake was never an ideological follower, but as a young man in the 1780s he had associated with political radicals in London, who were critical of the British government. Two events in 1780 indicate the political turbulence of the times. During the Gordon Riots (named for Lord George Gordon, the leader), the volatile populace, ostensibly protesting the extension of property rights to Roman Catholics, went on a burning spree in London, attacking not only the

> ### THE POET AS REVOLUTIONARY: FROM BLAKE'S "PREFACE" TO HIS POEM *MILTON*
>
> And did those feet in ancient time,
> Walk upon Englands mountains green:
> And was the holy Lamb of god,
> On Englands pleasant pastures seen!
>
> And did the Countenance Divine,
> Shine forth upon our clouded hills?
> And was Jerusalem builded here,
> Among these dark Satanic Mills?
>
> Bring me my Bow of burning gold:
> Bring me my Arrows of desire:
> Bring me my Spear: O clouds unfold!
> Bring me my Chariot of fire!
>
> I will not cease from Mental fight,
> Nor shall my Sword sleep in my hand:
> Till we have built Jerusalem,
> In Englands green & pleasant Land.
>
> (Blake in Johnson and Grant, "Preface" to *Milton*, lines 1-16)

homes of supposed Catholic sympathizers but also symbols of authority such as the Bank of England. Blake himself was swept along by a mob and witnessed the burning of London's infamous prison, Newgate. The same year, Blake and two companions, out on a sketching expedition, were briefly taken prisoner by British soldiers who accused them of being spies for the French. Britain, intermittently at war with France throughout the eighteenth century, was in the midst of conflict with the French that ended temporarily with the Treaty of Paris in 1783. When the French Revolution began, Blake, like many of his class in London, was a republican sympathizer with pro-revolutionary sentiments. He began, though never finished or published, a lengthy epic poem entitled *The French Revolution*, in which monarchical France is depicted as sick and slumbering.

Revolution was not confined to politics, however. What we now call the "Industrial Revolution" steamed ahead in the second half of the eighteenth century, building on such inventions as Hargreaves's spinning jenny (1766), Arkwright's spinning frame (1768), and Cartwright's power loom (1785-90), all of which contributed to mechanizing the cotton industry; new technologies for making iron and steel also multi-plied. Increased profits and urbanization resulted as industries moved into factories, and people moved to the cities to work in them. Standards of living rose and England became a great exporter of goods, but alongside this increased wealth came increased crowding and pollution. Workers afraid of being displaced by technology protested, and sometimes destroyed, new equipment. Blake despised the mills; it is possible to see in Blake's own laborious method of printing a model of unalienated labor.

London. Eighteenth-century London seethed with energy. Crime and high culture coexisted as every class and occupation jostled together on the city's crowded streets. By the time Blake was born, the metropolis stretched far beyond the original Roman walls dating from the first century C.E. The fashionable moved to the rapidly developing West End; the poor lived in the East End; artisans continued to live in and adjacent to the old city. Blake himself was born above his parent's hosiery shop in Soho (the West End), a respectable neighborhood of craftsmen and merchants that would decline during his lifetime.

London was the United Kingdom's center of government, of commercial and colonial expansion, and of national mythology. As Samuel Johnson wrote in 1777, "When a man is tired of London, he is tired of life" (Johnson in Porter, p. 165). On its way to becoming the world's largest city, London dominated the nation: a tenth of the English and Welsh lived in London. It is no surprise that such a city was both celebrated and denounced. To Blake, London was Babylon and also Jerusalem—a place of confusion and conflict, but also of spiritual potential. The independent nature of its populace provided fruitful grounds for all types of political expression, from riots to reform. Blake's "London" in *Songs of Experience* focuses on the city's institutional power and the victims of that power: children forced to clean chimneys while even churches averted their gaze, soldiers assigned to control London's mobs or fight against revolutionary France, prostitutes (there were 50,000 in London) suffering under a society's hypocrisy.

Reform—the child chimney sweep. No one kept track of the number of London's destitute children. Arguably the worst off were those who, as young as four years old, cleaned the narrow chimneys that spat coal smoke into the London sky. These "climbing boys" crawled into flues measuring only seven inches square—flues that might contain still-burning soot. The master sweep who controlled them "encouraged" the boys to climb higher by pricking their feet, or lighting fires beneath them. Some were permitted the luxury of a wash once a year; some every five years. Sweeps often died from burns or suffocation; cancer and deformity shortened their unhappy lives.

Where did these children come from? Desperate parents apprenticed their children to master sweeps for 20 to 30 shillings. Parishes sold dependent orphaned children. Sympathy, when it existed, conflicted with self-interest. Londoners, with their narrow chimney flues, demanded the services of the tiny sweeps. Furthermore, there was no general sentiment against child labor at the time. Children were regarded as the possessions of their parents and as contributors to the family income.

Tireless reformers, however, pressed their cause. The most notable, Jonas Hanway, kept up a barrage of writing and committee forming. "These poor black urchins," he wrote, "have no protectors and are treated worse than a humane person would treat a dog" (Hanway in Cunningham, p. 53). Hanway's efforts culminated in the Act for the Better Regulation of Chimney Sweepers and their Apprentices, passed in 1788, the year before Blake's first published poem on the chimney sweep. Designed to combat some abuses by raising the minimum age for sweeps to eight years old and adding a primitive licensing system, Hanway's Act was often circumvented. Not until the latter part of the nineteenth century would regulations be properly enforced.

Reformers, appealing to the English belief in fairness and liberty, used the image of the black slave to forward their cause. Both sweeps and slaves were black, in bondage, and working in horrific conditions. The chimney sweepers, though, were slaves on English soil, their presence an everyday affront to the values of their country.

Slavery and the abolition movement. During the late eighteenth century, the largest slave trading country in the world was the United Kingdom. In the 1790s, the British trafficked in 45,000 slaves per year. The public had an insatiable appetite for the products of slave labor (especially sugar) from Britain's holdings in the West Indies and Caribbean. It also appreciated the wealth that accrued from slavery, both to English plantation owners and port cities, including London. Slave labor produced raw materials that could be refined in England and shipped to Britain's growing empire.

The Chimney Sweep, an 1863 painting by Jonathan Eastman Johnson, evokes Blake's tragic image of young boys forced to clean the chimneys of London.

During the decade of Blake's *Songs of Innocence and of Experience,* slavery and the slave trade were matters of constant debate. Religious forces combined to press the charge that England could not be a moral leader if it continued to traffic in human beings. Several prominent cases put the issue squarely in the public eye, the most sensational of which was that of the slave-carrying ship, the *Zong.* Fearing a shortage of water, and believing he would not collect insurance if slaves died on board, the shipmaster ordered 133 people thrown into the sea. The ship's owners then attempted to claim insurance for their lost property—each slave that had been murdered. The case galvanized and unified reformers. In 1787, Thomas Clarkson founded, in London, the Committee for Effecting the Abolition of the Slave Trade. This association turned the abolitionist movement into a national cause.

No doubt Blake would have been familiar with the situation of former slaves, 15,000 of whom made their home in London. One of them, Ottobah Cugoano, published his successful *Thoughts and Sentiments on the Evil and Wicked Traffic of Slavery* in 1787. Blake's knowledge dramatically increased, when, in the early 1790s, he worked on the engravings for John Stedman's *Narrative of Surinam,* which describes some of the horrors of slavery. Though Stedman's book ultimately

Songs of Innocence

supports the existence of the slave trade, Blake's plates display a frightening brutality. Several engravers worked on Stedman's book, but Blake's three engravings of tortured slaves, "A Negro Hung Alive by the Ribs to a Gallows," "Flagellation of a Female Samboe Slave," and "The Execution of Breaking on the Rack," are the most graphic and moving. Stedman's *Narrative* provided Blake with extraordinary images that fueled his conceptions of liberty and enslavement in such poems as *Visions of the Daughters of Albion* (1793) and *America: A Prophecy* (1793).

ENGLISH ABOLITION MOVEMENT: A CHRONOLOGY

1730 From this time until 1807, the United Kingdom is the world's largest slave trader
1772 *Mansfield* decision holds that slavery is not legal within England
1781 Murder of 133 slaves (thrown overboard) on the *Zong*
1783 Insurance claim for the *Zong* slaves
1783 First anti-slavery petition to Parliament
1787 Society for Effecting the Abolition of the Slave Trade founded by Quakers in London; publication of Ottobah Cugoano's *Thoughts and Sentiments on the Evil and Wicked Traffic of Slavery*
1788 Dolberi's Act limits number of slaves transported on ships
1792 Blake's first engravings for Stedman's *Narrative of Surinam*
1807 Slave trading abolished in British Empire
1833 Emancipation Act frees slaves (with conditions) in the West Indies
1838 Full freedom for slaves in the British Colonies
1840 First International Anti-Slavery Convention (London)

The Poems in Focus

Contents summary. *Songs of Innocence and of Experience* are "poem-pictures," engraved poems always meant to be read with their surrounding illustrations (Keynes, p. 10). When *Songs of Innocence* was first issued in 1789, it consisted of 23 engraved poems. *Songs of Experience*, which was issued together with *Songs of Innocence* in 1794, would eventually contain 26 engraved poems, including four ("The Little Girl Lost," "The Little Girl Found," "The School Boy," and "The Voice of the Ancient Bard") transferred there from *Songs of Innocence* because of their darker mood. Blake's poems portray and complicate the meanings of "innocence" and "experience," linking them not only to stages of life, but also to place and perspective.

The keynotes of *Songs of Innocence* are presented in the first poem, or "Introduction." The lyric speaker, "piping down the valleys wild," is implored by an angelic child to "pipe a song about a Lamb" (Blake, "Introduction," *Innocence*, lines 1,5). With its pastoral imagery, "valleys wild," and Pan-like speaker, this first poem also locates the ideal setting for innocence (Pan, the Greek god of flocks and shepherds, invented the musical reed pipe). Many of the poems in *Songs of Innocence* are pastoral, and take place among green hills and spring meadows in the company of lambs and shepherds. Those that are not set in the countryside often invoke it, so that little Tom in "The Chimney Sweeper" dreams of the country and the orphans of "Holy Thursday" are "flowers of London town" ("Holy Thursday," *Innocence*, line 5). In *Songs of Innocence* children are usually protected by caring adults, and God himself is incarnate and concerned. Just as a mother cannot "sit and hear / An infant groan, an infant fear," so God, who "becomes an infant small" mourns along with humans ("On Another's Sorrow," *Innocence*, lines 10-11, 26). The reigning image once again is of shepherd and sheep, and of God as both shepherd and lamb.

In the fallen world of *Songs of Experience*, even children have lost their innocence, and it is far less certain that the adult or even God is interested in the plight of the weak. Selfishness and cynicism have replaced concern and belief. Even virtue is questioned, as in the social critique of "The Human Abstract":

> Pity would be no more,
> If we did not make somebody Poor:
> And Mercy no more could be,
> If all were as happy as we;
> (Blake, "The Human Abstract," *Experience*, lines 1-4)

In the world of *Songs of Experience*, the idealized pastoral landscape appears far less often. The companion piece to *Songs of Innocence*'s "Holy Thursday," for example, tells us that for poor children, "their sun does never shine. / And their fields are bleak & bare" ("Holy Thursday," *Experience*, lines 9-10). When the setting is the countryside, as in *Experience*'s "Nurse's Song," corruption and jealousy have replaced laughter and joy.

Songs of Innocence and of Experience are linked by similar stylistic devices that initially may suggest that children are the poems' intended readers. Blake's use of a paratactic syntax, such as the "And" . . . "And" . . . "And" of his first poem, contributes to the seeming simplicity of his work. Blake often employs both repetition and trochaic meter (a stressed followed by an unstressed syllable), both of which are standard in children's verse. Alongside these techniques, however, Blake employs such sophisticated devices as paradox and irony, even within the "Introduction" to *Innocence*. "And I stain'd the water clear," states the speaker ("Introduction," *Innocence*, line 18). The writer dips his pen in ink, but he also uses his writing to make matters clear. Or, perhaps, he muddies the seeming clarity of the water, showing his readers the folly in what had only appeared true. Blake is a master of the paradoxical aphorism. "Without Contraries," he wrote in *The Marriage of Heaven and Hell*, "is no progression. Attraction and Repulsion, Reason and Energy, Love and Hate, are necessary to Human existence" (Blake in Johnson and Grant, *The Marriage of Heaven and Hell*, Plate 3). To these we might add "innocence" and "experience," what Blake calls in his subtitle, "the Two Contrary States of the Human Soul." His intended readers, therefore, are certainly not just children.

"London." The narrator of "London" (*Songs of Experience*) wanders through the streets of the city, telling us what he sees and hears. He encounters regulation, prohibition, suffering, and oppression. The streets and the river Thames he describes as "charter'd," a word that signifies the city's ancient liberties, codified in documents like the Magna Carta, as well as the restrictions imposed by city government and corporations, both of which are established by charter ("London," *Experience*, line 2). The denizens of the city feel only the restrictions. As he walks, the narrator passes other individuals who, like him, are alienated and sorrowful, marked, like so many wandering Cains, by "weakness" and "woe" ("London," *Experience*, line 4).

The speaker blames this condition on matters both internal and external that lead to people's imprisonment in "mind-forg'd manacles" ("London," *Experience*, line 8). The oppressors are institutions—the Church, the government, the legal institution of marriage. In each case, the voices of the victims become visible to the narrator: the chimney sweeper's cry changes the church, which implicitly condones child labor, from a refuge into a tomb; the sigh of the soldier turns to blood; the curse of the prostitute becomes the venereal disease that destroys marriages and blinds infants.

The narrator's terrifying vision presents us with a city far removed from the pastoral idylls found in *Songs of Innocence*. In this view of London, we are left with hypocrisy and a "hearse" ("London," *Experience*, line 16). The experienced speaker can generalize about social misery. Yet he is both horrified by and detached from a world that seems inescapable.

The top third of Blake's engraved poem "London" shows a young boy leading an old crippled man past a closed door. Further down the page, the young boy, alone, warms his hands at a fire.

> ### "AUTHOR & PRINTER"
>
> Blake signed his works "Author & Printer." Integral to the *Songs of Innocence and of Experience* is their medium, "illuminated printing." John Thomas Smith gave the following account in 1828 of Blake's mystical discovery of this labor-intensive method of engraving:
>
> > Blake, after deeply perplexing himself as to the mode of accomplishing the publication of his illustrated songs, without their being subject to the expense of letter-press, his brother Robert stood before him in one of his visionary imaginations, and so decidedly directed him in the way in which he ought to proceed, that he immediately followed his advice, by writing his poetry, and drawing his marginal subjects of embellishments in outline upon the copper-plate with an impervious liquid, and then eating the plain parts or lights away with aquafortis considerably below them, so that the outlines were left as a stereotype. The plates in this state were then printed in any tint that he wished, to enable him or Mrs. Blake to colour the marginal figures up by hand in an imitation of drawings.
>
> (Smith in Johnson and Grant, pp. 485-86)

These two homeless wanderers are shut out of indoor comfort and warmth. Perhaps, the old man, decrepit and helpless, incarnates London itself (Thompson in Wolfreys, p. 46).

"The Chimney Sweeper." Blake wrote two poems on the plight of the chimney sweeps; one for *Songs of Innocence*, the other for *Songs of Experience*. In both cases, he gives us the perspective of the child sweep. The little boy in *Songs of Innocence* is cheerful and resigned. He presents his

Songs of Innocence

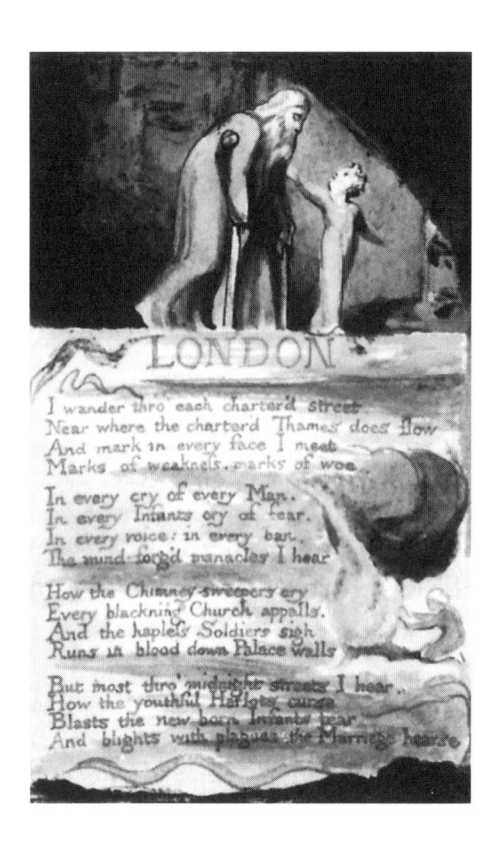

Illustration by Blake from "London," in *Songs of Experience*.

**POETIC COUNTERPARTS IN
SONGS OF INNOCENCE AND *OF EXPERIENCE***

The following *Songs* illuminate each other:

Innocence	Experience
"The Lamb"	"The Tyger"
"The Chimney Sweeper"	"The Chimney Sweeper"
"The Divine Image"	"The Human Abstract"
"Holy Thursday"	"Holy Thursday"
"Nurse's Song"	"Nurse's Song"
"Infant Joy"	"Infant Sorrow"

---

all the sweeps are released from their "coffins of black," the narrow death chutes of the chimneys, and find themselves in heaven ("The Chimney Sweeper," *Innocence,* line 12). In a pastoral landscape, they wash themselves and run naked. It is this part of the poem that forms Blake's accompanying illustration. We see Christ releasing a boy from his coffin to a green countryside full of naked playing children. Just before Tom wakes, an angel tells him that "if he'd be a good boy, / He'd have God for a father & never want joy" ("The Chimney Sweeper," *Innocence,* lines 19-20). Tom awakes in the dark and, sustained by his vision, returns to work. The poem ends with the speaker saying that "if all do their duty, they need not fear harm" ("The Chimney Sweeper," *Innocence,* line 24).

"The Chimney Sweeper" from *Songs of Experience* contains no comforting vision. The tone is not resignation but resentment. This little boy knows that he has been mistreated. Soliciting work on the Sabbath, the boy speaks with contempt of his guardians. The poem trades on the contrast between the boy's past and present life, his appearance and thoughts, and his life and that of his parents. Once he had been happy, but then his parents conscripted him to a life of woe. Outwardly he may still "dance & sing," but inwardly, he has been corrupted. While he works on Sunday, his parents sit in church. As in "London," this poem condemns a trinity of institutions, here "God & his Priest & King" ("The Chimney Sweeper," *Experience,* line 11), who encourage the downtrodden to wait for a better life in heaven. State and Church collude in the practice of child labor. The official message is similar to that in Tom Dacre's vision. But now the child sees the hypocrisy and understands that only some have to wait for their happiness.

Blake's illustration reinforces the contrasts found in the verse. The sweep is described as "a little black thing among the snow" ("The Chimney Sweeper," *Experience,* line 1). He used to take delight in the snow, but then was "clothed . . . in the clothes of death" ("The Chimney Sweeper," *Experience,* line 6). The engraving itself is almost no more than black and white. The dark sweep stands out, an incongruous being in the white snowstorm. His blackness marks him as a type of slave.

"The Little Black Boy." The black child who speaks in "The Little Black Boy" (*Songs of Innocence*) was born in "the southern wild" ("The Little Black Boy," *Innocence,* line 1). Addressing the

situation forthrightly. His mother is dead, and his father sold him to a master sweep while he was a tiny boy. He was so young that he could barely say "weep weep weep weep," a lisping version of the sweep's street call ("sweep sweep"), but also a touching indication of the sorrow within the labor ("The Chimney Sweeper," *Innocence,* line 3). (See verse on next page.)

The poem shifts from harsh reality to the dream vision of a fellow sweep. In Tom's dream,

English people, he declares that although he is black, "as if bereav'd of light," his "soul is white" ("The Little Black Boy," *Innocence*, lines 2, 4). His mother has taught him that his black body protects him from the strength of God's shining love, and that eventually souls are freed from their bodies to stand directly in God's presence. The little black boy then tells the little white boy that one day they both will play "round the tent of God like lambs" ("The Little Black Boy," *Innocence*, line 24). In fact, the black child offers to shade the white one until he too can bear the heat.

The text and the images link whiteness with souls, angels, and Christ himself. But these ideas coexist with the mother's positive reading of the black body—that it provides protection from the sun. Eventually, she says, bodies will not matter. In the boy's imagination, he becomes a teacher of the white child, repeating and expanding on his mother's lesson. Both will eventually part from their bodies—"I from black and he from white cloud free" ("The Little Black Boy," *Innocence*, line 23). When the two are alike, the English boy will love the black boy: "And then I'll stand and stroke his silver hair, / And be like him and he will then love me" ("The Little Black Boy," *Innocence*, lines 27-28).

In the pastoral heaven that Blake engraved with the poem, the white child stands in supplication before Christ, with the black child behind the white. The white boy and Christ look into each other's eyes, while the little black boy stands slightly to the side, as if he were a servant. Blake changed his coloring of this plate. Originally, the black child was depicted as white; later, he was colored black. Black or white, as David Bindman states, this child is removed from the loving pair of Christ and the white child (Bindman, p. 377).

Blake and the Romantic child. Blake's poetic children form part of a newly evolving Romantic discourse of the child as spiritually wise, and of childhood as a phase that should be protected, nurtured, and revered. In a 1799 letter, Blake proclaimed his belief in the wisdom of childhood:

> But I am Happy to find a Great Majority of Fellow Mortals who can Elucidate My Visions, & Particularly they have been Elucidated by Children, who have taken a greater delight in contemplating my Pictures than I even hoped. Neither Youth nor Childhood is Folly or Incapacity. Some Children are Fools & so are some Old Men. But There is a vast Majority on the side of Imagination or Spiritual Sensation. (Blake in Keynes, *The Letters of William Blake*, p. 30)

Prior to the seventeenth century, children were commonly seen as little adults, creatures

---

"THE CHIMNEY SWEEPER" (*SONGS OF INNOCENCE*)

When my mother died I was very young,
And my father sold me while yet my tongue
Could scarcely cry weep weep weep weep.
So your chimneys I sweep & in soot I sleep.

There's little Tom Dacre, who cried when his head
That curl'd like a lamb's back, was shav'd, so I said,
"Hush Tom never mind it, for when your head's bare,
You know that the soot cannot spoil your white hair."

And so he was quiet, & that very night,
As Tom was a sleeping he had such a sight,
That thousands of sweepers Dick, Joe, Ned & Jack
Were all of them lock'd up in coffins of black.

And by came an Angel who had a bright key,
And he open'd the coffins & set them all free.
Then down a green plain leaping laughing they run
And wash in a river and shine in the Sun.

Then naked & white, all their bags left behind,
They rise upon clouds, and sport in the wind.
And the Angel told Tom if he'd be a good boy,
He'd have God for his father & never want joy.

And so Tom awoke and we rose in the dark
And got with our bags & our brushes to work.
Tho' the morning was cold, Tom was happy & warm,
So if all do their duty, they need not fear harm.

"THE CHIMNEY SWEEPER" (*SONGS OF EXPERIENCE*)

A little black thing among the snow:
Crying weep, weep, in notes of woe!
"Where are thy father & mother" say
"They are both gone up to the church to pray.

"Because I was happy upon the heath,
And smil'd among the winter's snow:
They clothed me in the clothes of death,
And taught me to sing the notes of woe.

"And because I am happy, & dance & sing,
They think they have done me no injury:
And are gone to praise God & his Priest & King
Who make up a heaven of our misery."

Songs of Innocence

who needed to be civilized, weaned from their base instincts, and led to God. They were also expected to contribute to the family income. For poor children, little changed in the eighteenth century. Starting at the age of four or five, these children worked long hours on farms and in cottage industries and the new factories. If they ran afoul of the law and were older than seven, they could furthermore be charged as adults and hung or transported to a colony.

Life, in short, was difficult for the majority of children. But the eighteenth century saw efforts to contest child labor and to provide schooling for the poor. Criticism of child labor in cotton mills began in the 1780s, and, as mentioned above, a bill to regulate the employment of chimney sweeps passed in 1788. Charitable schools for the poor, many set up by the Society for the Propagation of Christian Knowledge (established in 1699), multiplied in the eighteenth century. Yet, despite these attempts, two-thirds of poor children received no schooling whatever. Those schools that did exist were intent on producing obedient workers, and so often combined education and employment. All the attempts at reform notwithstanding, it would be another 100 years before child labor was effectively controlled in England.

THE CRITICAL VOICE BEHIND "THE CHIMNEY SWEEPER"

"The Chimney Sweeper" relies on an adult reader, who feels the condemnation not of the boy, but of the poet. "*Your* chimneys I sweep & in soot I sleep," says the boy, implicating the reader in his fate. ("The Chimney Sweeper," *Innocence*, line 4, italics added). Little Tom Dacre's last name indicates that he was sold by the poorhouse (Lady Dacre Almshouse) that had taken him in (Ackroyd, p. 126). Not only the sweep but the reader should weep, and it is the reader who should feel the irony of the poem's moralism. The "angel" tells the child to obey authority; the speaker repeats pat phrases about "duty." Yet Tom, with his lamblike curls, signifies that children are as innocent as lambs, and created in God's image. The dereliction of duty on the part of adults has condemned these children to a painful and shortened existence.

Even in Blake's day, though, one could see the perception of the child beginning to change. From the seventeenth century onward, in the middle and upper classes, adults showed signs of an increased attention to children and how their minds worked. More mothers breastfed their babies instead of sending them to wet nurses. Children's toys and books multiplied. Especially for boys, childhood became a stage marked by schooling, and some parents took great interest in the emerging field of childhood development. One of the most popular texts in England was Jean-Jacques Rousseau's *Emile: or, On Education* (1762), which advocates that children be allowed to develop "naturally," through their contact with the natural world and in accord with their own instincts.

Blake's poems promote and extend these new attitudes to children. The frontispiece to *Songs of Innocence*, in which two children study at the lap of their nurse or mother and the title forms itself from the bending branches of a tree, suggests that the education of children should take place in nature. The proper activity of the child, *Songs of Innocence* shows, is outdoor play: "the little ones leaped & shouted & laugh'd / And all the hills ecchoed" ("Nurse's Song," *Innocence*, lines 15-16). Most importantly, innocence is by no means ignorance, but represents a natural responsiveness and sense of optimism. Children, moreover, Blake stresses, possess an instinctive spirituality.

> He [Christ] is meek & he is mild,
> He became a little child:
> I a child & thou a lamb,
> We are called by his name.
>   ("The Lamb," *Innocence*, lines 15-18)

The problem with the children in *Songs of Experience* is that they have grown up too soon. The babe of *Experience*, who struggles and sulks after being born into "the dangerous world" is already weary and petulant ("Infant Sorrow," *Experience*, line 2). The cynicism and despair of such children condemns the adult world, which has exploited rather than protected its young. The child chimney sweep is the most flagrant example, but also critiqued is the curbing of children's natural thoughts and desires, the imposition of orthodoxy. In "A Little Boy Lost," the child who speaks his mind and says that it is impossible to love anyone else more than the self, is martyred by the priest, "bound . . . in an iron chain," and "burn'd" ("A Little Boy Lost," *Experience*, lines 20, 21). In "The School-Boy," a young boy pleads to spend his time outdoors instead of in the prison of a schoolroom. The poem compares him to a bird born for joy but forced to sit in a cage. His incarceration, because it robs his childhood of pleasure, will stunt his adulthood. Through such charges Blake complicates the contemporary dialog on children.

Literary context. Blake's *Songs of Innocence and of Experience* revise the traditionally didactic songs for children that were popular in the eighteenth century, such as Isaac Watts's *Divine Songs for the Use of Children* (1715), John Newberry's *A Little Pretty Pocket-Book* (1744), and Anna Barbauld's *Hymns in Prose for Children* (1781). Watts's *Divine Songs,* which went through many editions, are overtly didactic. Alongside songs glorifying God are many that illustrate the consequences of bad behavior. Watts's famous "Against Idleness and Mischief," with its ever busy bee, counsels children not to waste time, "for Satan finds some mischief still / For idle hands to do" (Watts, "Against Idleness and Mischief," lines 11-12). Blake's poems, by contrast, extol the virtues of play.

Songs of Innocence and of Experience also holds a central place in the emerging Romantic literature. As with William Wordsworth's and Samuel Taylor Coleridge's **Lyrical Ballads** (1798; also in *Literature and Its Times*), Blake's *Songs* represent a democratization of poetry's subject matter. In his "Preface" to *Lyrical Ballads,* Wordsworth writes that he wants to represent "incidents of common life" in a language "near to the language of men" (Wordsworth in Mellor, pp. 574, 576). Like Blake, Wordsworth found in children an innate spirituality, best articulated in his "Ode" of 1807, when he declared that "Heaven lies about us in our infancy!" (Wordsworth in Mellor, "Ode," p. 604).

Reception. Because of Blake's labor-intensive method of printing, few copies of *Songs of Innocence and of Experience* were circulated during his lifetime. This illuminated book was his most successful, yet only 28 copies of the combined *Songs* exist. Blake's work was not completely unknown, however. "Holy Thursday" and "The Chimney Sweeper" from *Songs of Innocence* were anthologized while he lived. William Wordsworth, Samuel Taylor Coleridge, and Charles Lamb all appreciated the *Songs;* of the three, Lamb paid Blake the highest praise, referring to him in 1824 as one of the most extraordinary persons of his time. At his death in 1827, Blake was considered primarily an artist (and a mad artist at that), not a poet. Children especially appreciated his "visions," a development that delighted him.

Blake's reputation was resuscitated in the mid-nineteenth century by Alexander Gilchrist's biography (1863), by the Pre-Raphaelites, who were also painter-poets, and later by W. B. Yeats, who, like Blake, was a poet-mythmaker.

—Danielle E. Price

READING RACE IN "THE LITTLE BLACK BOY"

As with the *Songs of Innocence's* chimney sweep, the little black boy is a figure of innocence in part because he has imbibed conventional thought, in this case, European racism. The black boy's statement, therefore, that he is black "as if bereav'd of light" reflects the perceptions of the "civilizing" nations ("The Little Black Boy," *Innocence,* line 4). The boy's naïve desire for reconciliation also comments upon the intransigent racism of the English mind: the black boy cannot be loved as himself, but only when he resembles the white English boy. The black child has assumed a position of inferiority, even in his vision of heaven. Perhaps his "mind forg'd manacles" reflect missionary Christianity ("London," *Experience,* line 8). D. L. Macdonald claims that "a poem on such a subject, issued in such a year, must be interpreted in the light of the abolition movement" (Macdonald, p. 166). Blake implies that those "bereav'd of light" or reason are not the mother and child in the poem, but the proponents of slavery who continued to deny humanity to Africans.

For More Information

Ackroyd, Peter. *Blake: A Biography.* New York: Knopf, 1996.

Bindman, David. "Blake's Vision of Slavery Revisited." *Huntington Library Quarterly* 58, nos. 3 & 4 (1996): 373-382.

Blake, William. *Songs of Innocence and of Experience.* In *Blake's Poetry and Designs.* Ed. Mary Lynn Johnson and John E. Grant. New York: Norton, 1979.

Cunningham, Hugh. *The Children of the Poor: Representations of Childhood Since the Seventeenth Century.* Oxford: Basil Blackwell, 1991.

Johnson, Mary Lynn and John E. Grant, eds. *Blake's Poetry and Designs.* New York: Norton, 1979.

Keynes, Geoffrey, ed. "Introduction." *Songs of Innocence and of Experience,* by William Blake. London: Oxford University Press, 1977.

Songs of Innocence

———. *The Letters of William Blake.* Cambridge, Mass.: Harvard University Press, 1960.

Macdonald, D. L. "Pre-Romantic and Romantic Abolitionism: Cowper and Blake." *European Romantic Review* 4 (1994): 163-82.

Mellor, Anne K., and Richard E. Matlak. *British Literature 1780-1830.* Fort Worth, Tex.: Harcourt, 1996.

Porter, Roy. *London: A Social History.* Cambridge, Mass.: Harvard University Press, 1994.

Watts, Isaac. "Divine Songs for Children." In *The Poetical Works of Isaac Watts and Henry Kirke White.* Boston: Houghton Mifflin, 1910.

Wolfreys, Julian. *Writing London: The Trace of the Urban Text from Blake to Dickens.* London: Macmillan, 1998.

The Sound and the Fury

by
William Faulkner

> **THE LITERARY WORK**
>
> A novel set in rural Mississippi over three consecutive days in the spring of 1928, with an extended flashback to 1910; first published in 1929.
>
> **SYNOPSIS**
>
> Three brothers must cope with their sister's loss of virtue and the disintegration of their once-prominent Southern family.

William Cuthbert Falkner (he added the *u* to his last name in 1919) was born into a prominent Southern family on September 25, 1897. He spent his childhood in Oxford, Mississippi. He never attended college but read widely in classic and contemporary literature, relying on the guidance of friend and mentor Phil Stone, who was four years his senior. In 1918 Faulkner attempted to enlist in the U. S. Air Corps in order to fight in World War I. Rejected due to his small stature, he feigned his best British accent, went to Toronto, and enlisted in the Royal Air Force Training program. He never saw active duty, however, for an armistice was signed just before he completed his training. Faulkner spent the next few years traveling between Oxford, New York City, and New Orleans. His first (and only) volume of poetry, *The Marble Faun*, was published in 1924, and within the following three years he wrote and published his first two novels—*Soldier's Pay* (1926) and *Mosquitoes* (1927). It was not, however, until his third novel, *Flags in the Dust*, that Faulkner began to write about the South. Initially rejected for its length, *Flags in the Dust* was shortened, renamed *Sartoris*, and published early in 1929. By that time, Faulkner had already completed his next work, *The Sound and the Fury*. It too was rejected at first, but, unlike *Sartoris*, was published later that same year without extensive revision. On the heels of *The Sound and the Fury* came *As I Lay Dying* (1930) and *Sanctuary* (1931). Meanwhile, Faulkner began working as a Hollywood screenwriter, producing scripts for such films as *To Have and Have Not* (1945), an adaptation of Ernest Hemingway's novel, and *The Big Sleep* (1946), based upon the Raymond Chandler detective story, both of which starred Humphrey Bogart and Lauren Bacall. Ultimately Faulkner's prolific literary career spanned almost 40 years, during which he authored other distinguished novels, such as *Light in August* (1932) and *Absalom, Absalom!* (1936). He won both the Nobel Prize for Literature (1950) and the Pulitzer Prize for *A Fable* (1954) and *The Reivers* (1963). Perhaps Faulkner's best-known work, *The Sound and the Fury* is often regarded as his most important novel in light of its many literary innovations. In addition to employing a bold experimental style, it captures the pathos of a period of decline in Southern plantation history.

The Sound and the Fury

William Faulkner

Events in History at the Time of the Novel

Post-Civil War South. In an introduction to *The Sound and the Fury* that was not published until 1973, Faulkner claimed:

> "The South . . . is dead, killed by the Civil War. There is a thing known whimsically as the New South to be sure, but it is not the south. It is a land of Immigrants [sic] who are rebuilding the towns and cities into replicas of towns and cities in Kansas and Iowa and Illinois" (Faulkner, *The Sound and the Fury*, p. 229).

Perhaps in an attempt to preserve it for posterity, Faulkner devoted most of his career to articulating what he imagined as the true southerner experience. This South must have seemed alien and unfamiliar to those who had not experienced it themselves. Faulkner's is a lyrical and tragic vision of a region struggling with the legacy of slavery as well as the encroachment of industry and technology. Such developments would be difficult for the region to reconcile, given its traditions and genteel values.

Even before the Civil War, the South had considered itself to be fundamentally different from the rest of the United States. Unlike the "Wild West," the South prided itself on its sense of tradition and civilization, valuing decorum and gentility. Unlike the commercialized, industrialized North, which was littered with factories, it prized its agrarian heritage and the aristocratic character of plantation life. Above all else, the family and its values were the glue that held society together. Unlike the North and the West, which embraced urbanization and progress, Southerners tried as best they could to resist the pull of the city and its corrupting influences.

Much of the South, particularly the rural areas, had clung to the region's antebellum or pre-Civil War traditions despite the emancipation of the slaves and the changes introduced by the Reconstruction era of the 1860s and '70s. As they saw it, the fact that they could no longer keep slaves did not mean Southerners had to subscribe to the vulgar principles of capitalism. Many members of the older generations held fast to customary ways and resisted all change, a tendency captured, say some critics, by various character portrayals in Faulkner's fiction.

> The South which Faulkner had grown up in—particularly the rural South—was cut-off, inward-turning, backward-looking. It was a culture frozen in its virtues and vices, and even for the generation that grew up after World War I, that South offered an image of massive immobility in all ways, an image, if one was romantic, of the unchangeableness of the human condition, beautiful, sad, painful, tragic—sunlight slanting over a mellow autumn field, a field the more precious for the fact that the yield had been meagre.
> (Warren in Faulkner, *The Sound and the Fury*, p. 244)

In contrast to these older generations, the one that grew up after the Civil War seemed less wedded to traditional Southern values and adapted itself more easily to the changing social and economic orders of the day. Plantations began to be broken up and sold off to finance war debts, and the remaining land was divided into smaller farms because, without slave labor, large-scale farming was expensive and impractical. No longer able to count on inheriting the family plantation, many young Southern men began to migrate to the cities and enter into trade, manufacturing, or industry.

It is worth noting that many Southerners took great offense at Faulkner's depiction of the South, deeming the violence and degradation that informs some of his novels to be deliberate misrepresentations of their way of life. Other Southerners felt that Faulkner's version of the South, his Yoknapatawpha County, was its own

> ## STREAM OF CONSCIOUSNESS
>
> American psychologist William James first used this term in his *Principles of Psychology* (1890) to describe the unbroken flow of thoughts, perceptions, and feelings in the conscious mind. Since its initial applications in psychology, stream of consciousness has been adopted by writers and critics to describe a twentieth-century style of narration "that undertakes to reproduce without a narrator's intervention, the full spectrum and continuous flow of a character's mental process, in which sense perceptions mingle with conscious and half-conscious thoughts, memories, expectations, feelings and random associations" (Abrams, p. 299). In other words, instead of presenting an external description of the events, these events are always filtered through the perceptions of a character. Readers do not get an objective description of an action, only subjective descriptions. In *The Sound and the Fury*, when the retarded Benjy burns his hand on the stove and then sobs, his narration uses the underlined details to convey the event, since his slow-witted mind does not understand the concept of "burn."
>
>> I put my hand out to where the fire had been.
>> "Catch him," Dilsey said. "Catch him back."
>> My hand jerked back and I put it in my mouth and Dilsey caught me. I could still hear the clock between my voice. Dilsey reached back and hit Luster on the head. My voice was going louder every time.
>>
>> (*The Sound and the Fury*, p. 38)
>
> Ireland's James Joyce (*Ulysses* [1922]) and Britain's Virginia Woolf (*Mrs. Dalloway* [1925]) were celebrated for their innovations in stream of consciousness. With *The Sound and the Fury* (1929), Faulkner became the first American to apply such a complex narrative method.

invented microcosm: a self-contained, completely fabricated world that had no essential ties to reality, Southern or otherwise. Finally, a third group of Southerners, including writer and critic Robert Penn Warren, were drawn to Faulkner's work because they recognized "some truth about the South and their own Southernness that has been lying speechless in their experience" (Warner in Bassett, p. 1). Far from feeling insulted or alienated, they believed that Faulkner was able to illuminate some previously obscured aspect of their experience in a new and exciting way.

Southern Renascence. The period from 1920 to 1950 has been identified by many literary historians as the "Southern Renascence." During these decades, the South witnessed an extraordinary resurgence in literary creativity and criticism. In the 1920s, the region was home to the Fugitives, a group of poets located at Vanderbilt University in Nashville, Tennessee. The Fugitives, who greatly admired the work of T. S. Eliot (see ***The Waste Land***, also in *Literature and Its Times*), sought to combine Eliot's sense of literary tradition with Southern themes. Later, in the 1930s, many of these writers would reconfigure themselves into the Agrarians, adopting a more political stance towards problems facing the South. Thereafter, they would transform themselves into the New Critics, a group that had a profound influence on literary studies in the twentieth century. It has been suggested that the Southern literary reawakening was "the product of the creative tension between the Southern past and the pressures of the modern world" (Tate in Faulkner, *The Sound and the Fury*, p. 247). Robert Penn Warren reasoned that the First World War induced a kind of cultural shell shock in the South, bringing the region into "cultural collision with Europe and the North and the new order there" (Warren, p. 4). Such tensions presented the South with the opportunity "to create an art in order to objectify and grasp the nature of its own inner drama" (Warren, p. 4).

The Sound and the Fury

Whatever the explanation, there was remarkable literary experimentation, as well as confrontation with regional realities. Faulkner's experimentation and innovation in *The Sound and the Fury*—especially his use of stream-of-consciousness narrative technique—had a significant impact on the Southern literary landscape. Together with authors like Thomas Wolfe, Faulkner inspired a legion of poets and novelists to begin writing about the South and the Southern experience. These subjects became suddenly relevant and universal with the onset of the nation's Great Depression in 1929. The South had a unique perspective on the times because, unlike the rest of the country, it already knew failure, humiliation, and hardship; these were experiences it had known since Robert E. Lee's fateful surrender back in 1865. Moreover, the South was already in the midst of a regional agricultural depression when the Great Depression struck (see **Let Us Now Praise Famous Men,** also in *Literature and Its Times*). Given their unique experience, southern authors attempted with renewed confidence to write literature that not only acknowledged their separate regional character but also addressed more universal themes. They moved beyond meditations on the end of slavery and the Civil War to broader considerations of history and modernity. Their burst of creativity brought the South to the nation's attention, and later, when Faulkner won the Nobel Prize, their literary movement gained international prominence.

For whom the Belle tolls. The Southern Belle was a virtual institution in the pre-Civil War South, and her status was solidified in the twentieth century by Vivien Leigh in the film version of Margaret Mitchell's **Gone With the Wind** (also in *Literature and Its Times*). The Belle was feminine and flirtatious, but underneath her scintillating surface, she was pure and virtuous. She upheld the pillars of Southern society: the family and the church. Known as the "Angel of the Hearth," her worth was sometimes measured according to four cardinal virtues known as the attributes of "True Womanhood": piety, purity, submissiveness, and domesticity. Women were expected to uphold Christian values and set good examples, not only for children but also for men.

According to these tenets, piety not only enabled women to be good wives and mothers, but it also promised personal fulfillment and happiness. Sexual purity went hand-in-hand with piety, and its loss was one of the worst fates a woman could suffer. Inevitably men would try to seduce women, but women had to resist them at all costs. Chastity was the sole power and influence that a woman had over men; it was her greatest treasure and its bestowal to her husband on their wedding night was to be her most valuable gift. A "Fallen Woman" was considered by many of her contemporaries to be no woman at all—in fact, she was hardly human and often thought to be beset by disease or madness. Because of such a stigma, many women considered death preferable to the loss of their chastity. In *The Sound and the Fury*, Mrs. Compson holds such beliefs: when she discovers her 15-year-old daughter, Caddy, kissing a boy on the porch swing, she dons a black mourning veil and wears it for days.

Southern females were expected to be passive and obedient. Society regarded women as dependent on men and in need of their protection, much as children were. Incapable of independent thought and action, a woman, the belief was, needed a guardian—a father, an older brother, or a husband—to provide and care for her. Concerned only with the affairs of the household, she was expected to accept her duties with dignity and without question.

This set of precepts had a tenacious hold on society, but with the onset of the twentieth century, women's roles began to change significantly and so did their perceptions of themselves. As the South became less isolated and more cosmopolitan, Southern women began to feel increasingly constricted by the Southern Belle role. No longer content to be pious, pure, and domestic, women began to challenge these attitudes. Caddy Compson is a prime example of this phenomenon. She is not content with the docile female role that her family expects her to fill. Even as a young girl, when she and her brothers played together, her brother Quentin remembered, "she was never a queen or a fairy she was always a king or a giant or a general" (*The Sound and the Fury*, p. 198). Rejecting the typical female fantasies of beauty, she instead aligns herself with symbols of masculine authority and power.

Like Caddy, young women in the early twentieth century typically wanted to be more assertive and independent, to have a greater say in their own lives. They did not necessarily consider sex inherently sinful or dirty, and they longed to have a degree of control over whom they would marry. They began to seek employment outside the home, becoming secretaries, clerks, and telephone operators. In 1920, women won the vote, and as the decade wore on, Margaret Sanger waged a nationwide campaign for more accessible methods of birth control. These challenges, as in the novel, met with significant resistance not only from men, but also from older women, who wished to remain "safe" in the home.

Immigration. In 1865 the country was still largely a nation of farmers and small towns, but as the century wound to a close, this demographic underwent a drastic shift. By the turn of the twentieth century, most Americans lived in cities. Some of this change resulted from rural-to-urban migration, but to an even larger extent, it was due to waves of immigration from Central, Eastern, and Southern Europe. In contrast to the earlier, northern European immigrants, these newcomers, hailing primarily from Italy, Greece, and Russia, seemed less enthusiastic about assimilating into American culture, an attitude that prompted at least one anti-immigrant spokesperson to bemoan their presence:

"Unrestricted immigration . . . was slowly, insidiously eating away the very heart of the United States. What was being melted in the great Melting-Pot, losing all form and symmetry, all beauty and character, all nobility and usefulness, was the American nationality itself" (Fairchild in Curti, p. 782).

Many like-minded Americans perceived the new immigrants as a threat to their families and their own sense of national identity. As Quentin Compson joked, America was becoming "the land of the kike, the home of the wop," *kike* and *wop* being derogatory terms for "Jew" and "Italian" (*The Sound and the Fury*, p. 79). Quentin's joke—which distorts the lyrics of the "Star Spangled Banner" ("the land of the free, the home of the brave")—reflects a growing sense of anxiety and discomfort with "foreigners." A shopkeeper echoes this discomfort when he advises Quentin "to stay clear of them foreigners" (*The Sound and the Fury*, p. 81). Likewise, Jason Compson has little patience with immigrants, directing his abuse against the "dam eastern jews," whom he doesn't mind "as an individual . . . it's just the race . . . who produce nothing. They follow the pioneers into a new country and sell them clothes" (*The Sound and the Fury*, p. 120).

As a result of such tension and hostility, the early 1920s (1921 and 1924) witnessed the enactment of several national laws that imposed quotas on immigration, not only to restrict the number of immigrants entering the country but also to control their countries of origin and favor northern Europeans over immigrants from other regions. These laws, particularly the Johnson Act (1924), represented a turning point in the nation's history. Before this legislation, the United States, despite earlier restrictions on migrants from China (1882) and Japan (1908), was perceived as having an open-door policy to immigrants. This new law reduced the number of immigrants in any year to "two percent of the number of foreign-born individuals of any nationality resident in the continental United States as determined by the 1890 census, with a minimum quota of 100" (Curti, p. 781). The open door, it seems, had closed.

The big money. During the 1920s, after the First World War, the United Stated witnessed an unprecedented economic boom. Whereas in the pre-war era, during which many Americans regarded big business with suspicion, they started to change their minds after the war. Recognizing that industry and capitalism had proven essential to victory, Americans began to regard these forces as beneficial, as potentially bringing wealth and prosperity to all. Adopting this view, the federal government gave industry and the Wall Street financial houses free reign. The belief that anyone could make money if they invested in the stock market became widespread, prompting many Americans to do so. In 1923, sales on the New York Stock Exchange topped 235 million shares; by the end of 1928, sales had exceeded 1.1 billion shares.

Such investor confidence, however, was naïve and perhaps unfounded. Certain industries were not reaping the benefits of the new American prosperity. Agriculture, as suggested above, struggled mightily in the 1920s, and widespread calls for a federal subsidy fell on deaf ears. Choosing to believe that the good times were here to stay, many Americans kept pouring their money into the stock market and spending like there was no tomorrow. On October 7, 1929, Cape and Smith published *The Sound and the Fury*, Just three weeks later, on October 29, a date that would become known as "Black Tuesday," the New York stock market crashed, introducing global economic collapse and the Great Depression.

The Novel in Focus

The plot. The novel, set on the grounds of a rundown plantation that has seen better days, tells the story of the Compson family from 1898 through April 8, 1928. Jason and Caroline Compson have four children—Quentin, Caddy, Jason, and Benjy. In 1911, the family adopts

The Sound and the Fury

Caddy's daughter, named Quentin (after her uncle), because Caddy's husband had abandoned her. The novel is divided into four sections: "April Seventh, 1928"; "June Second, 1910"; "April Sixth, 1928"; and "April Eighth, 1928." The first three sections use stream-of-consciousness narration: each section is told from the perspective of one of the Compson boys. The final chapter is narrated by a third-person omniscient narrator whom many critics have identified as Faulkner himself. Caddy is the sole daughter in the Compson family. Her three brothers each experience a keen sense of loss when she grows sexually mature, and each of their narratives attempts to articulate what this loss means: for Benjy, it is a loss of love and innocence; for Quentin, it is the loss of honor and idealism; for Jason, the loss is financial. The sections are not in chronological order, but they follow a logical temporal sequence. The first section, "April Seventh," features many memories and flashbacks from as far back as 1898, and it recounts (in a fragmented way) most of the significant events of childhood in the Compson family. The next section, "June Second," by locating itself in 1910 (with flashbacks to 1909), follows the children into adolescence, while the final two sections are set almost exclusively in 1928 and detail the lives of the characters in adulthood. Together the four sections convey an overall impression of the family as a kaleidoscopic confusion of bitterness, tragedy, pathos, and pain.

April Seventh, 1928. April 7 is its narrator's Benjy Compson's thirty-third birthday, or in the words of another character, "he been three years old thirty years" (*The Sound and the Fury*, p. 11). Benjy, the youngest Compson child, is the novel's famous idiot narrator. He was born with severe mental deficiencies and is not capable of speech, only whimpers and wails. His narrative, what he would say if he could speak, alternates between sensory impressions and flashbacks. Benjy does not differentiate between the past and the present: memories are as real to him as things that happen today. Finally, since he has the mind of a child, he has no sense of consequence or reason; he understands only feeling and sensation. His narrative section, jumbled and fragmentary, is an attempt to articulate what it is to live in Benjy's world. As a child, he knew love and comfort in the form of his older sister Caddy. She took care of him, played with him, and nurtured him. She made sure that no harm came to him and comforted him when he was frightened. His love for her is childlike in its simplicity and might best be summed up in his association of her with the natural world: "Caddy smelled like trees" (*The Sound and the Fury*, p. 6).

This love is threatened, however, when Caddy starts to become interested in boys. On some level, Benjy perceives the danger that wearing perfume and kissing beaus on the porch swing represents for his world. They are indications that someday Caddy will leave him, and at such signs, he protests mightily by wailing and bellowing until she washes off the perfume. As long as she is chaste, he is safe and his childhood world remains intact. When Caddy loses her virginity, however, Benjy, in turn, loses her. Suddenly she no longer smells like trees, and unlike the perfume, this new scent cannot be washed off. Benjy's sense of loss pervades the first section of the novel, which finds him castrated and lonely, helping Luster, the young black teenager who is essentially his babysitter, look for a lost quarter. As they search the yard, they see men playing golf on the neighboring golf course. Benjy can see them "hitting":

> They were coming toward where the flag was and I went along the fence. Luster was hunting in the grass by the flower tree. Then they took the flag out, and they were hitting. Then they put the flag back and they went to the table, and he hit and the other hit. Then they went on . . .
> "Here caddie."
> (*The Sound and the Fury*, p. 3)

Since he has no understanding of the game, Benjy describes events as he sees them: instead of swinging golf clubs, the men are simply "hitting." Throughout the day, as shown here, Benjy is constantly reminded of his sister Caddy, though he cannot understand where she has gone or why he misses her so much.

June Second, 1910. The second section of the novel is an 18-year-old flashback to the spring of 1910. It is narrated by Benjy's older brother Quentin. Quentin's narrative, like his brother's, contains many flashbacks—some to childhood, some to adolescence. Like the first section of the novel, the narrative technique of "June Tenth" is disjointed and disorienting. Quentin's train of thought might appear haphazard and indiscriminant, but like Benjy's, all of Quentin's associations are somehow linked to his sister Caddy and her sexual maturity: her affair with a boy named Dalton Ames, her loss of virginity, her marriage to "that blackguard," Herbert Head (*The Sound and the Fury*, p. 77). Quentin cannot accept his sister's sexual maturity any more than Benjy can, but whereas Benjy's reaction consisted mainly of tears and wailings, Quentin's response was far more violent. First, he challenged Caddy's boyfriend, Dalton Ames, to a duel where Quentin then "passed out like a girl" (*The Sound and the Fury*, p. 103). To appease her brothers, Caddy breaks off her relationship with Ames, but begins to sleep with other boys, perhaps to punish herself for her disloyalty to her family. Quentin then proposes a double suicide for his sister and himself, but he is unable to follow through with it. In a desperate attempt to erase her intimacies with other men, he tries to convince their father that he and Caddy have committed incest (they have not), confessing "if i could tell you we did it would have been so and then the others wouldn't be so and then the world would roar away" (*The Sound and the Fury*, p. 112). Finally, when he learns of his sister's engagement (because she is pregnant), he asks her to run away with him and Benjy, but she refuses, and her marriage seals his fate. When Caddy weds Herbert Head, Quentin must accept the fact that their childhood bond is forever compromised. At the time that he tells his story, Quentin is almost finished with his freshman year at Harvard University in Cambridge, Massachusetts. Traumatized by all of the events in his past, he is emotionally unstable. He feels betrayed by Caddy's sexual promiscuity and guilty over his failure to preserve her honor. He has decided to commit suicide, and June Second is the day he has picked to die.

Quentin's final day is both extremely regimented and fraught with emotional torment. He dons his best suit, breaks his pocket watch (a graduation gift from his father), and cuts his classes. He packs his belongings and writes letters to his roommate and his family. He buys flat irons (to weigh himself down in the Charles River) and proceeds to go to the outskirts of Boston, where he encounters a scruffy little Italian girl who adopts him as a surrogate big brother. For his part, Quentin tries to help her get home but cannot find anyone to take care of her. Eventually, they come across her real brother, who accuses Quentin, in broken English, of kidnapping his sister. Coincidentally Quentin's friends happen upon him while he is being arrested and is arguing with the little girl's brother. They manage to extricate Quentin from the situation. As they leave the constable's office to resume their picnic, the sight of the little girl brings back all of Quentin's thoughts about sex, virginity, and Caddy's "fall from grace": "But still

The Sound and the Fury's fictional setting of Yoknapatawpha County is patterned after Oxford, Mississippi, where Faulkner resided. Pictured is Oxford's Confederate Monument.

I couldn't stop it and then I knew that if I tried too hard to stop it I'd be crying" (*The Sound and the Fury*, p. 93). The "it" refers to the memories Quentin has been trying to repress that day. Unable to block out thoughts of Caddy and her "disgrace," Quentin lashes out at a friend, Gerald Bland, and is assaulted not only by Bland but also by the memories. After his friends have stopped the fight, Quentin goes back to his dorm alone to clean himself up. As the section concludes, with his affairs now put in order, he brushes his teeth and hair before going to meet his death in the Charles River.

April Sixth, 1928. The novel's third section, "April Sixth, 1928," is narrated by 36-year-old Jason Compson, and it takes place on Good Friday (the Friday before Easter). If Benjy and Quentin can be said to represent childhood and adolescence respectively, Jason is an adult, the sort of adult who gives adulthood a bad name: he is corrosive anger and bitter resentment personified. He hates blacks, Jews, and even his own family. In addition, he suffers from a persecution complex, convinced that there is a vast conspir-

The Sound and the Fury

acy to make his life difficult. His brother, Quentin, had the chance to attend Harvard and in view of his suicide, wasted it, while Jason himself was not even allowed to attend the state university because by the time he was old enough there was no money left and he had to support the family. He especially hates his sister because her husband, who had promised Jason a job in his bank, abandoned her, taking Jason's employment prospects with him. Now Jason is saddled with the burden of taking care of Benjy and the rest of his family.

Jason vents his spleen on Caddy's daughter, Quentin (named after her deceased uncle), whom the family has adopted and raised after Caddy was abandoned by her husband. The novel does not reveal where Caddy is, only that she has been banned from the Compson house since 1911; no one is permitted even to speak her name. Still, she sends Jason a check for $200 each month to provide for her daughter. The source of her money remains undisclosed; it may be alimony from her ex-husband, or Caddy may have earned it in a less-reputable way, as Jason implies when he tells her "you'll get [child support money] the same way you got her" (*The Sound and the Fury*, p. 131). The section opens with one of his invectives: "Once a bitch, always a bitch, what I say" (*The Sound and the Fury*, p. 113). Taking after her mother, not only does Quentin wear too much make-up and dress immodestly, but she also cuts school and "runs around" town with men. After arguing with her, Jason drops Quentin off at school and proceeds to the hardware store where he ostensibly works. In reality, his day is spent doing just about everything but work: speculating on the cotton exchange, spying on his niece, and defrauding his family. He spends a good part of the day complaining about the "dam trifling niggers," the "dam eastern jews," and the red-necked, humpbacked farmers, all of whom he thinks have conspired to steal his money. As it turns out, the cotton trade, into which Jason has poured a significant amount of money, closed with a 40-point loss (a significant loss).

In addition to exchanging telegrams with his broker in New York, Jason spends his afternoon following his niece. He first sees Quentin in town (instead of school) with a man whose only distinguishing feature is a red bow tie. In the family car which he cannot drive without getting a splitting headache (from the gasoline fumes), Jason chases them out of town, and only returns to the store after they give him the slip by flattening one of his tires. Finally, he has constructed an elaborate ruse to cheat his sister, his niece, and his mother out of Quentin's child support. Jason has convinced his mother to burn Caddy's checks as a matter of pride and principle. Unbeknownst to Mrs. Compson, the checks she burns are not the ones Caddy has sent, but forgeries that Jason substitutes in their place; he then cashes Caddy's checks and keeps the money for himself.

April Eighth, 1928. The final section of the novel breaks out of the stream-of-consciousness style of narration and provides readers with their first objective perspective of the Compson family. Here, the physical characteristics of the characters and their surroundings are disclosed for the first time. Dilsey, the family servant, has an "indomitable skeleton . . . rising like a ruin or a landmark over somnolent and impervious guts" (*The Sound and the Fury*, p. 165). Benjy is a "big man" who moves "with a shambling gait like a trained bear" and has eyes that are the "pale sweet blue of cornflowers" (*The Sound and the Fury*, p. 171). Both Jason and Mrs. Compson are described as "cold"; Jason even has hair that curls "into stubborn hooks" (*The Sound and the Fury*, p. 174). Finally, the house, which might have been imagined as stately and grand, is revealed as "decaying," and "paintless with [a] rotting portico" (*The Sound and the Fury*, p. 85). By 1928, the Compson residence had apparently fallen into disrepair, resembling a run-down hovel more than an aristocratic estate.

This section takes place on Easter Sunday. Dilsey makes a fire and prepares breakfast for the family while trying to get ready to attend church. Jason appears and announces that he has been robbed—someone entered his bedroom, breaking the window, and then broke open his lock box, stealing the money he had kept hidden from his family. The family soon realizes that Miss Quentin is nowhere to be found. Her bedroom is empty. Mrs. Compson assumes that her granddaughter has, like her namesake uncle, committed suicide, but Jason thinks otherwise. He assumes that she has run away with her red-bow-tied boyfriend and sets off across the county in pursuit, imagining himself tearing through "the embattled legions of heaven and hell" (*The Sound and the Fury*, p. 190).

Meanwhile, Dilsey takes Benjy and her family to church. The sermon is delivered by a minister visiting from St. Louis, a Reverend Shegog, who works the congregation into a frenzy. Dilsey is especially moved by the message of Christ's suffering; she weeps openly and reflects: "I seed the beginning, en now I sees de endin" (*The Sound and the Fury*, p. 185). Her enigmatic pronouncement may apply to the Compson family line, which has reached its end: Quentin (the son) is dead; Benjy has been castrated; Jason is a confirmed bachelor whose "girlfriend" is a Memphis prostitute named Lorraine.

The section concludes with Benjy's weekly visit to the cemetery. Driving the horse and carriage, his caretaker, Luster, mistakenly goes to the wrong side of the statue in the town square. This minor alteration of Benjy's routine causes him to roar hysterically. Jason, who, having given up his search for his niece, happens to be in town, jumps aboard the carriage, belts Luster, and redirects the horse. Only this reassertion of order quiets Benjy. As soon as his routine is restored, the novel closes:

> At once Ben hushed . . . the broken flower drooped over Ben's fist and his eyes were empty and serene again as cornice and façade flowed smoothly once more from left to right, post and tree, window and doorway and signboard each in its ordered place.
> (*The Sound and the Fury*, p. 199)

A question of black and white. According to scholar Eric Sundquist, "Faulkner has, on the basis of his fiction and his public statements alike, been variously denounced as a racist and admired as a civil rights advocate" (Sundquist, p. ix). His treatment of race in *The Sound and the Fury* allows for both readings. The novel stresses differences between black and white, tending to favor the former over the latter. But it exposes a similarity too, portraying both races as being affected negatively by the passing of generations.

Two families are juxtaposed. The white Compsons, formerly aristocratic plantation owners, have fallen on hard times. The black Gibsons, a former slave family, lives with and takes care of the Compsons. The two families are as different in characteristics as they are in color, in a portrayal that is unusual for the early 1900s South. At one point Quentin observes that "niggers," as he calls them, "come into white people's lives . . . in sudden sharp black trickles that isolate white facts for an instant in unarguable truth like under a microscope" (*The Sound and the Fury*, p. 108). The implication is that the black characters bring the white characters into relief. With the possible exception of Caddy, the white characters emerge as obsessive, self-willed people, full of dark longing and bitter despair. By contrast, the black characters are compassionate and capable of fortitude.

Critics have measured Dilsey Gibson's character against Caroline Compson's. Both women are the matriarchs of their households. Dilsey, however, is far more adept at managing domestic affairs and mothering her children than Caroline Compson is. All talk, Mrs. Compson whines incessantly about her burdens and afflictions: Benjy's infirmity, Caddy's promiscuity, the untimely deaths of her husband and eldest son. She views all of these as evidence of divine punishment. Filling the maternal void left by Mrs. Compson, Dilsey does not complain. Instead, she acts: cooking, cleaning, taking care of the children, both the Compsons' and her own. Mrs. Compson protests to her son Jason that something must be done about Miss Quentin's wild ways, but she does nothing herself and even makes a vain effort to tell Jason not to lose his temper. Dilsey, on the other hand, not only talks back to Jason, but even steps in front of him to defend Miss Quentin.

By the novel's conclusion, Dilsey has become its moral center. The final section opens with a rather bleak description of a cold and dark Easter morning. Dilsey, despite her weathered appearance, stands tall and strong against the morning gloom. She has struggled to keep this family together and shield it from its inevitable decay. She has kept alive the belief that family and communal values can overcome the destructive forces of life. From her has come unconditional love. In contrast, the Compsons have repeatedly mistreated and exploited each other.

The final vision of Dilsey, however, is bittersweet. By the end of the novel, she is but a shadow of her former self, and there is a sense that attributes connected with her generation are passing away. Her descendants, Frony and Luster, seem to lack her patience, kindness, and determination. Both appear at least slightly touched by the same forces that have damned the Compson family: greed, self-interest, and vanity. Frony, for example, evinces worry on Easter Sunday about what the congregation must think of her, because her mother brings along Benjy: "I wish you wouldn't keep on bringin him to church, mammy. . . . Folks talkin" (*The Sound and the Fury*, p. 181). But Dilsey doesn't bat an eye at her fellow churchgoers' complaints about Benjy: "Tell um the good Lawd don't keer whether he bright or not. Don't nobody but white trash keer dat" (*The Sound and the Fury*, p. 103). She alone embodies hope for humanity in the

The Sound and the Fury

> **THE PARIS REVIEW—ONE OF THREE EXPLANATIONS**
>
> It began with a mental picture. I didn't realize at the time it was symbolical. The picture was of the muddy seat of a little girl's drawers in a pear tree where she could see through a window where her grandmother's funeral was taking place and report on what was happening to her brothers on the ground below. By the time I explained who they were and what they were doing and how her pants got muddy, I realized that it would be impossible to get it all into a short story and that it would have to be a book. And then I realized the symbolism of the soiled pants, and that image was replaced by the one of the fatherless and motherless girl climbing down the rainpipe to escape from the only home she had, where she had never been offered love or affection or understanding. I had already begun to tell it through the eyes of the idiot child since I felt that it would be more effective as told by someone who was capable of only knowing what happened, but not why. I saw that I had not told the story that time. I tried to tell it again, the same story through the eyes of another brother. That was still not it. I told it for the third time through the eyes of the third brother. That was still not it. I tried to gather the pieces together and fill in the gaps by making myself the spokesman. It was still not complete. . . . It's the book I feel tenderest towards. I couldn't leave it alone, and I never could tell it right, though I tried hard and would like to try again, though I'd probably fail again.
>
> (Faulkner, *Lion in the Garden*, p. 245)

novel. However, by April Sixth, 1928, Dilsey is old and frail. Her husband, Roskus, has died, and she herself moves with "painful and terrific slowness" (*The Sound and the Fury*, p. 167). Clearly, she is nearing the end of her days, and when she has passed away, the book suggests, an era will have passed with her.

Sources and literary context. Perhaps because he considered it his best work, Faulkner seems to have put almost as much thought into explaining the conception of *The Sound and the Fury* as he put into the novel itself. Various explanations exist. In 1933 he wrote an introduction for a new edition of the novel that contained one of these explanations. The introduction as a whole attempted to bridge the distance between *The Sound and the Fury* and Faulkner's earlier, more conventional works. It recounts the increasing difficulty he had with his publishers, who grew more reluctant as his writing grew more experimental. When he began *The Sound and the Fury*, he claims to have suddenly stopped caring about pleasing his publishers; he just wrote for himself:

> When I began, I had no plan at all. I wasn't even writing a book. I was thinking of books, publication, only in reverse, in saying to myself, I wont have to worry about publishers liking or not liking this at all. . . . Now I can write. . . . So I, who never had a sister and was fated to lose my daughter in infancy, set out to make myself a beautiful and tragic little girl.
>
> (Faulkner in Polk, p. 2)

Another version of the novel's beginnings surfaced in the *Paris Review*, after Faulkner won the Nobel Prize in 1950. This account credits the inspiration to a mental image of a girl's muddy drawers.

Lastly, Faulkner claimed that the novel had its inception as a short story about the Compson children that would have no plot. It would take as its subject "some children being sent away from the house during [their] grandmother's funeral. They were too young to be told what was going on and they saw things only incidentally to the games they were playing" (Faulkner, *Lion in the Garden*, p. 146).

Faulkner took the title of his novel from a famous speech found toward the end of Shakespeare's *Macbeth* (also in *Literature and Its Times*). The soliloquy is delivered by the doomed Macbeth upon learning of his wife's suicide:

> To-morrow, and to-morrow, and to-morrow,
> Creeps in this petty pace from day to day,

> To the last syllable of recorded time;
> And all our yesterdays have lighted fools
> The way to dusty death. Out, out, brief
>   candle!
> Life's but a walking shadow, a poor player
> That struts and frets his hour upon the stage,
> And then is heard no more. It is a tale
> Told by an idiot, full of sound and fury,
> Signifying nothing.
>   (Macbeth, 5.5.17-28)

While the most obvious connection to the novel is the mention of a "tale told by an idiot," namely Benjy Compson, there is more resonance between the two works. The Shakespeare passage serves not only to introduce Benjy; it also evokes the emotional tenor of the novel by suggesting the sense of futility and desolation that hangs over the House of Compson for most of the novel.

The town of Jefferson in Yoknapatawpha County, the setting of Faulkner's novel, shares much in common with Faulkner's own home town of Oxford. The fictional county is the setting of 13 separate volumes that Faulkner wrote between 1929 and 1962 plus several short stories. While there are definite similarities between Oxford, Mississippi, and its fictional counterpart, it should be remembered that the two locations are distinct. While part of Faulkner's project was to represent life in the South as he knew it, he also set out to re-imagine it in his fiction.

Finally, Faulkner shares something in common with later writers from Shakespeare's part of the world. Like early-twentieth-century British and Irish novelists, he experimented with the way to tell a story, using a stream-of-consciousness style that was groundbreaking for American literature. Faulkner was the first American author to employ such a technique. Even more striking than the technique, which was significant in its own right, was Faulkner's choice of narrative voices: a retarded man; a neurotic, angst-ridden adolescent; and a cold-hearted, despicable man, all three of whom are brothers.

Reception. The critical reception of *The Sound and the Fury* was mixed. Many reviewers responded to the novel with a blend of confusion and hostility. In a review for the *Nation* titled "Hardly Worth While," Clifton Fadiman asserted that Faulkner's themes and characters were too "trivial [and] unworthy of the enormous and complex craftsmanship expended upon them" (Fadiman in Bassett, p. 38). In the *Providence Sunday Journal*, Winfield Townley Scott found that the novel "tells us nothing" and proclaimed it "downright tiresome" (Scott in Bassett, p. 82). Ted Robinson claimed that the book gave him nightmares in the *Cleveland Plain Dealer*. Finally, Dudley Fitts, writing for *Hound and Horn* claimed that the novel "repels rather than invites," and that "the men and women of [the novel] are not real men and women at all, but dramatic clichés for all their individuality of vice and action" (Fitts in Bassett, p. 88). He even went so far as to recommend that Faulkner rearrange the sections of the narrative so that readers are not put off by Benjy's section of the novel. Fitts's review, however, was not entirely negative. Like many of the novel's other reviewers, he perceived similarities between Faulkner and James Joyce. Most such reviewers recognized that Faulkner was not simply parroting Joyce's technique but adapting Joyce's style to fit his own themes and subject matter.

Beyond favorable comparisons to Joyce, there were reviewers such as Evelyn Scott who found *The Sound and the Fury* to be "an important contribution to the permanent literature of fiction"

FAULKNER'S APPENDIX

Upon its republication in 1946, Faulkner added an appendix to *The Sound and the Fury*, claiming that it was "the key to the whole book" (*The Sound and the Fury*, p. 203). The Appendix contains character sketches of the entire Compson clan, not only the characters featured in the novel, but also their ancestors dating back to 1699 when the first Compsons arrived in the colonies from Scotland. In addition to the family history, the Appendix also supplies information that postdates the 1928 ending of the novel. We learn, for instance, that upon the death of Mrs. Compson, Jason committed his brother Benjy to a state asylum, as he had been threatening to do. In the 1920s, Caddy married and divorced a Hollywood moviemaker and, it is suggested, might have ended up with a German general in the 1940s. There are many inconsistencies between this Appendix and the text of the original novel, however. Apparently Faulkner did not have access to a copy of it when writing the Appendix all these years later, so he has, for example, Miss Quentin climbing down a rainpipe instead of the pear tree when she runs away. Such discrepancies, along with the addition of new information not in the novel, have occasioned reservations about the index and a feeling from critics that it ought to be approached with caution.

finding it "unique and distinguished" (Scott in Bassett, p. 77). Such critics acknowledged that Faulkner had created a poignant and moving depiction of the disintegration of the Compson family, even if they did not fully understand or appreciate it themselves. They seemed to realize that *The Sound and the Fury* represented a real breakthrough for American fiction.

At the same time, even the novel's fans acknowledged that this breakthrough would probably go unappreciated for quite some time. According to one critic, the novel was "too difficult in technique to become popular"; another speculated that general readers would either be "indifferent or contemptuous or openly hostile" (Wetherill and Crickmay in Bassett, p. 95, 91). It seems that such criticism was prophetic because the novel went out of print in the 1930s and was not reprinted until 1946, thanks to a burst of French interest in Faulkner. Translations by Jean-Paul Sartre and Albert Camus both were extremely influential and suggested that Americans should take another look at his work. The 1946 publication that followed—Malcolm Cowley's *The Portable Faulkner*—and Robert Penn Warren's review of this edition led, in turn, to the reissuing of Faulkner's early novels, a reappraisal of his writing, and ultimately to his winning the Nobel Prize in 1950. Most critics agree that the award was for his early fiction, especially *The Sound and the Fury*, which was republished in 1946 with an Appendix added by Faulkner himself.

—Erin Templeton

For More Information

Abrams, M. H. *A Glossary of Literary Terms*. 7th ed. Boston: Thomson Learning, 1999.

Bassett, John, ed. *William Faulkner: The Critical Heritage*. Boston: Routledge and Kegan Paul, 1975.

Blotner, Joseph. *Faulkner: A Biography*. New York: Random House, 1984.

Curti, Merle, Willard Thorpe, and Carlos Baker, eds. *American Issues: The Social Record*. Chicago: J. B. Lippincott, 1960.

Davis, Thadious M. *Faulkner's "Negro": Art and the Southern Context*. Baton Rouge: Louisiana State University Press, 1983.

Faulkner, William. *A Lion in the Garden: Interviews with William Faulkner, 1926-1962*. Ed. James B. Meriwether and Michael Millgate. New York: Random House, 1968.

———. *The Sound and the Fury*. Norton Critical Edition. Ed. David Minter. New York: W. W. Norton, 1994.

Inge, M. Thomas, ed. *William Faulkner: The Contemporary Reviews*. Cambridge: Cambridge University Press, 1995.

Millgate, Michael. *William Faulkner*. London: Oliver and Boyd, 1961.

Polk, Noel, ed. *New Essays on the Sound and the Fury*. Cambridge: Cambridge University Press, 1993.

Sundquist, Eric. *Faulkner: The House Divided*. Baltimore: Johns Hopkins University Press, 1983.

Warren, Robert Penn, ed. *Faulkner: A Collection of Critical Essays*. Englewood Cliffs, N.J.: Prentice-Hall, 1966.

"Spunk" and "Sweat"

by
Zora Neale Hurston

Zora Neale Hurston was born January 7, 1891, or 1901, in Eatonville, Florida, the first incorporated exclusively African American town in the United States. (The year of Hurston's birth, probably 1891, is in dispute). A voracious reader, Hurston learned to decipher words before kindergarten but obstacles in childhood, including the death of her mother when she was nine, prevented her from attending high school until her twenties. Hurston went on to attend Howard University, later earning a scholarship to Barnard College. At Barnard Hurston studied anthropology under the tutelage of famed social scientist Franz Boas before graduating in 1928. For several years she worked as an apprentice anthropologist, documenting the folklore of African Americans in the South, as well as Caribbean rituals and culture. Hurston had earlier won second prize in a magazine contest sponsored by the African American organization the Urban League (the so-called "Opportunity" contest). In 1935 she became the first African American to publish a detailed account of Southern folk traditions and the Southern black experience in *Mules and Men*. A decade earlier her first story, "Spunk," had incorporated Southern folk tales and colloquialisms. "Sweat" followed, incorporating colloquialisms too, but this time in a tale that showed her talent for depicting a slice of domestic life in a black southern town. Both stories signified her *entré* into the black cultural movement of the 1920s that would become known as the Harlem Renaissance.

THE LITERARY WORK
Two short stories, set in Eatonville, Florida, in the early 1900s; "Spunk" was first published in 1925, "Sweat" in 1926.

SYNOPSIS
In "Spunk," a small-town strongman steals another man's wife, kills her husband, and is ultimately avenged by what all perceive to be the dead man's spirit. "Sweat" centers on a hard-working washerwoman who triumphs over her scheming, adulterous husband.

Events in History at the Time of the Short Story

Separate but not equal. Although slavery was abolished in the United States in 1865, its legacy lay in the rampant discrimination against African Americans that remained an overt fact of life, especially in the southern states. Jim Crow or racial segregation laws kept African Americans from competing for jobs or mixing with Caucasians in schools and other public places in the South. The Supreme Court decision *Plessy v. Ferguson* (1896) validated segregation, sanctioning a "separate-but-equal" doctrine that would for half a century uphold discrimination on all fronts—education, business, housing, and politics. As black leader W. E. B. Du Bois saw it, "never before [had] a great and civilized folk threatened to adopt so cowardly a creed in the treatment of its fellow-

"Spunk" and "Sweat"

Zora Neale Hurston

citizens.... The new American creed says: fear to let black men even try to rise lest they become equals of the white" (Du Bois in Tomkins, p. 314). Decried by social activists, the color bar reflected serious cultural misunderstanding. Misguided "theories of blacks' innate intellectual inadequacy provided much of the rationale for slavery and for Jim Crow. They also accomplished something equally pernicious . . . they caused many blacks (if only subconsciously) to doubt their own abilities" (Cose in Von Dassanowsky, p. 33).

Eatonville's answer. Rather than continue to face discrimination by living under Jim Crow laws, some African Americans opted to form their own communities after Reconstruction. In 1886 Eatonville, Florida, became the first of many exclusively African American towns that spanned the South (Hurston's father, John, became its first mayor and wrote many of the town's bylaws). At least 60 black communities were formed between 1865 and 1915 in the South and in expanding western frontier territories. These were independent communities with their own schools, hospitals, city governments, and commercial centers. Though many labored outside their townships, traveling to nearby "white" cities to work during the day, they returned to their own community at night, and bought and sold goods in their own stores. "The black-town ideology . . . sought to combine economic self-help and moral uplift with an intense pride in race, while at the same time encouraging an active role in county and state politics" (Crockett, p. xiii). By creating a nurturing, safe environment in which to live and raise a family—as well as forging a firm economic and political base—the exclusively black towns gave African Americans what they were denied in other, white-dominated cities: power, pride, and self-determination. The successful black communities, such as Eatonville, furthermore defied the rationale behind discriminatory laws that insisted on black intellectual inferiority, proving that African Americans were perfectly capable of governing their own lives, shattering the racist myth that had been used to justify first slavery, then Jim Crow.

Besides challenging stereotypes, African American towns such as Eatonville benefited society in another major way: their exclusively black populations, outside what would later be called the "melting pot" of America, allowed them to preserve cultural traditions. Instead of being the "black backside of a white city," Eatonville was a kind of "Eden" where African Americans could feel completely at ease and cultural life could flourish (Hurston in Hemenway, p. 11). The center of social life in Eatonville was the corner store, and each night it was filled with music and storytelling. Drums, spirituals, and the blues accompanied elaborate "lying sessions" (Hurston in Hemenway, p. 12). Generations-old folk tales about the might of John Henry or B'rer Rabbit enraptured, educated, and entertained listeners. Children such as Hurston, growing up in this kind of nourishing environment, couldn't help but be charmed by their "folk" and emerge "drenched in light," with a stronger sense of self and of pride in their heritage (Hemenway, p. 11).

As shown in both "Spunk" and "Sweat," African American women were not entirely emancipated in the black towns. While the environment offered safety from the sexual aggression associated with both slavery and working in white households, many black women still held a precarious position at home. From slavery on, African American women had been forced into an impossible position. Their situation left them with formidable, often uncontrollable tasks—to keep their families together, to maintain their own sanity despite being treated like chattel, and to support their men who were denied key ingredients of their masculinity: command over their own lives and over what slave owners did with their wives and daughters. Hence, the role of women in relation to men in the black family was a byproduct of slavery and its aftermath. Once slavery ended, jobs that employed black men paid them so little that black women had to work to augment their spouses' meager income. In fact, it was not uncommon for black women, such as Delia Jones in "Sweat," to assume the bulk of responsibility for maintaining their households and to overlook many transgressions on the part of their husbands. At least 25 percent of married black women worked outside the home in 1900—eight times that of white women. Economically, as well as politically and socially, black women could not at this point afford to press for gender equality. It had to take a backseat to the more basic struggle for racial equality, or, more exactly, for the survival of all blacks. The women were too busy working to keep their families fed, clothed, and sheltered in the face of the major demon they were facing—racist society. Hurston, whose own mother had put up with a philandering husband, had something to say about the less basic but still pervasive issue of gender inequality, though. Her story "Sweat" portrays a community that does not sanction the husband's womanizing, and a wife who finally fights back at being exploited by him.

Race relations: North v. South. In 1900 two-thirds of the African American population lived in the rural South, working for scant wages as farm laborers, sharecroppers, tenant farmers, or domestics in the service of whites. Most lived in segregated towns, where they were relegated to the poorer sections and denied the right to vote or hold public office because of tactics such as literacy tests, poll taxes, or physical intimidation (lynchings, etc.). Those who dared to challenge the status quo, by claiming their constitutional rights or simply mixing with whites socially, risked being lynched by local mobs who took the law into their own hands. Lynchings, brutal murders generally committed in a public fashion, often entailed the hanging of the victim and sometimes dismemberment of the victim's body parts. Mostly a Southern practice committed against blacks, the practice claimed nearly 2,000 lives from 1880 to 1900, and continued somewhat less vigorously thereafter. There were 233 recorded lynchings in the 1920s, the decade in which Hurston's stories appeared.

By this time, terror, discrimination, and poverty had driven many African Americans north, where fewer Jim Crow laws and greater opportunity existed. Farmworkers in New York State earned double the salary of those in South Carolina ($26.13 compared to $10.79 per month [Tomkins, p. 314]), and factory jobs—created first by rapid industrialization, then by a labor shortage as a result of World War I—could be found. At first, the North seemed like the Promised Land. However, discrimination in both housing and employment existed there, too. Only in the North it was a de facto condition, one that existed in fact or practice rather than one prescribed by law. "Migration to northern cities resulted not in an end to Jim Crow segregation but rather in the establishment of new forms of de facto urban segregation in schools, swimming pools, restaurants, and theatres" (Tomkins, p. 271).

The Great Migration. The North may not have been the Promised Land, but it did offer more hope—and employment—than the South. From 1916 to 1919 about 500,000 African Americans migrated northward; many of the men filled jobs vacated by soldiers and enlisted in the military themselves. Encouraged by the National Association for the Advancement of Colored People, hundreds of thousands of African American men joined the U. S. Army and shipped out overseas to fight in World War I. More exactly, some 367,000 were called into service in segregated units. Exposure to artistic movements in Paris, London, and Berlin, where jazz was the rage, along with the Great Migration north, catalyzed what would become the New Negro movement. "For the black infantrymen who fought overseas, the war provided an opportunity to experience

---

"NEGRITUDE"

Rooted in the rejection of western, primarily Anglo Saxon domination of the social, cultural, and political world, Negritude was a movement that began in the Caribbean region in the late nineteenth century. It was essentially "a revalorization of Africa on the part of New World blacks, affirming an overwhelming pride in black heritage and culture, and asserting, in Marcus Garvey's words, that blacks are 'descendants of the greatest and proudest race who ever peopled the earth'" (Nesbitt, p. 1). The movement gained strength in Europe—primarily in London and Paris, where African and Caribbean arts and artists flourished. After being brought to the attention of African Americans in World War I, negritude became a predominant theme and catalyst of the Harlem Renaissance.

"Spunk" and "Sweat"

firsthand the rising importance of African cultures and to learn about the burgeoning popularity of negritude, a philosophy created by African and Caribbean poets that promoted the unity and beauty of peoples of African descent" (Campbell, p. 15). A sort of "spiritual emancipation" occurred when African American servicemen were exposed to this enlightened mentality. Once back in the States, they contributed to the birth of the "New Negro" (Locke in Campbell, p. 15).

The New Negro. The "New Negro" of the 1920s was an African American vehemently opposed to the status quo, politically active, and determined to change racist American policies through education, activism, and art. Unwilling to accept second-class citizenship, the New Negroes demanded that their votes be counted and their criticism be heard (Hemenway, p. 37). Recently created organizations, including the National Association for the Advancement of Colored People (established 1909-10), the Urban League (1910), and the Universal Negro Improvement Association (1914), championed various—and often opposing—causes of New Negroes. But primarily it was the artistic expression of African Americans, as exemplified in Alain Locke's *The New Negro* anthology, that gave the movement its direction.

Charles S. Johnson, editor of the Urban League's *Opportunity* magazine, believed that he could "redeem, through art, the standing of his people" (Johnson in Lewis, p. 90). His idea and Locke's anthology of African American prose, published in 1925, became the philosophy and manifesto of the movement, respectively. "The New Negro represented a 'spiritual coming of age,' a 'new soul' for black America, and its 'heralding sign' was the 'unusual burst of creative expression' in the works of younger artists like Zora Neale Hurston" (Hemenway, p. 39). Trailblazers, such as Locke and Johnson, believed that gifted African American artists could establish the cultural parity—or superiority—of African American society and thereby instill racial pride in African Americans and win cultural respect from other groups. This, they thought, would shatter racist stereotypes and lead to equality in other aspects of society.

Not everyone shared the same vision of how the artists should go about this, however. There was some controversy concerning the role that artists should play and the type of art they should produce. Many felt that given the racist climate in the United States, African Americans had a duty to promote only positive images of African American culture (there were nearly 5 million Ku Klux Klan members by 1925, who led a violent backlash against the growing diversity of American society). Fearful that depicting superstitious behavior or colloquial speech would reinforce negative stereotypes, Locke prefaced Hurston's short story "Spunk" (which he included in *The New Negro*) with a disclaimer, stating that all African Americans didn't speak and behave the way Hurston's characters did. Such disclaimers hint at restrictions, self- or otherwise-imposed, placed on the African American writer's freedom to create in Hurston's era. She herself resented such restrictions; in her mind, African American groups should be as free as any other group to create whatever inspired them. As the "race problem" heated up over the following decades, Hurston's liberated attitude would prove to be not only controversial but also destructive to her career.

The Harlem Renaissance. Despite the emergence of the New Negro, America remained, by and large, segregated and discriminatory. Blacks—especially women—continued to be relegated to menial jobs and while whites could come to black neighborhoods to socialize, blacks were barred entry to white establishments where they worked or entertained. In response, African Americans created their own city of refuge: Harlem. Alain Locke wrote enthusiastically, "In Harlem, Negro life is seizing upon its first chances for group expression and self-determination. . . . It is—or promises to be—a race capital" (Locke in Baker, p. 74). Indeed, by 1923

A WRITER AHEAD OF HER TIME

Zora Neale Hurston was a proud woman with enlightened beliefs for her era. Having grown up in a black town with a strong, nurturing mother, she had a fierce sense of self that she carried with her all her life—even in the face of racism and criticism by African Americans for pandering to whites.

> I have no race prejudice of any kind. My kinfolks, and my "skinfolks" are dearly loved. . . . But I see their same virtues and vices everywhere I look. So I give you all my right hand of fellowship and love, and hope for the same from you. In my eyesight, you lose nothing by not looking just like me. I will remember you all in my good thoughts, and I ask you kindly to do the same for me.
>
> (Hurston in Wall, p. 769)

approximately 300,000 African Americans lived in New York City—the vast majority in Harlem (Lewis, p. 26). It became the "Negro capital of the world," rich in enterprise and excitement—"a buzzing cultural capital of Afro-America" (Lewis, p. 27; Hemenway, p. 30). With the artists and activists of the New Negro movement converging on this burgeoning urban center, it won renown as the birthplace of the Harlem Renaissance—the creative outpouring of African Americans that energized the 1920s. Indeed the artists generated works portraying the black experience in ways that gave rise to growing self-confidence and racial pride.

Jazz resounded in the speakeasies as artists, writers, celebrities, and socialites of all races filled the streets, drawn to the rhythm and celebration of African American culture. Harlem was in vogue and going uptown was *the* thing to do on a Saturday night during the roaring 1920s. "In Harlem, it was like a foretaste of paradise," Arna Bontemps recalled. "A blue haze descended at night and with it strings of fairy lights on broad avenues" (Bontemps in Lewis, p. 103). African American artists of all genres thrived, leading to the publication of more of the country's African American writers from 1919 to 1930 than in any other decade prior to 1960. With Charles Johnson's support, Harlem produced its own counterparts to America's so-called "Lost Generation" writers (Ernest Hemingway, F. Scott Fitzgerald, John Dos Passos). The acclaimed African American literati included Jean Toomer, Claude McKay, Countee Cullen, Langston Hughes, Sterling A. Brown, Arna Bontemps, Marita Bonner, Jessie Redmon Fauset, Wallace Thurman, and Zora Neale Hurston, who playfully proclaimed herself "Queen of the Niggerati" (Hurston in Hemenway, p. 44).

Supporting the New Negro suddenly became the *cause célèbre* of liberal whites. White patrons, whom Hurston dubbed "Negrotarians" and who included genuine humanitarians as well as less noble curiosity-seekers, began not only frequenting Harlem but funding African American artists, schools, and associations (Lewis, p. 98). Hurston was personally supported by Mrs. Osgood Mason, a wealthy white philanthropist, in a mutual relationship that enabled Hurston to work as an anthropologist but also severely stifled her creative output. Other Harlem Renaissance artists and organizations were funded by white philanthropic entities (i. e., The Harmon and The Stokes Foundations). Mindful of this funding, many later criticized the results, accusing the artists of selling out or pandering to a white audience. The reality is that, regardless of the source of funding, African American artists "emerged for the first time in great numbers . . . driven by intense ethnic pride, political activism,

Dr. Franz Boas

THE RISE OF CULTURAL ANTHROPOLOGY

Though anthropology became a distinct science in the mid-1800s, it was not until 1899 that Franz Boas founded the first major department for its teaching at Columbia University in New York City. Boas promoted eyewitness studies of individual cultures and encouraged his students, such as Hurston, to go into the field. Under his guidance, Hurston compiled African American folklore of the South and Caribbean, which she published as *Mules and Men* and incorporated into her fiction. As Hurston's work helped illustrate, this type of research was groundbreaking in that it operated on the basis of parity between societies rather than on the previously held notion that some cultures were superior to others. Field research demonstrated that "the difference between the mentality of . . . peoples was one of degree and not of kind," a revolutionary finding that could be used to demolish racist arguments for the subjugation of any peoples (Radin, p. 9).

"Spunk" and "Sweat"

and a sense of unique cultural lineage which cut across geographic regionalism, inspiring Black artists to produce as they had never before dared" (Campbell, pp. 39, 14).

The Short Story in Focus

The plot. While "Spunk" serves as a homespun folktale, "Sweat" explores deep social and political issues. Both stories incorporate colloquialisms and vivid slice-of-life details of Eatonville in the early twentieth century, both celebrate African American culture, and both deal with the age-old subject of good versus evil.

"Spunk." "Lookah theah, folkses!" cried Elijah Mosley, slapping his leg gleefully. "Theah they go, big as life an' brassy as tacks" (Hurston, "Spunk," p. 1).

Hanging around the local store with the townsmen, Mosley peers out the window and passes the time prattling on and telling tales like they all do every evening after work. Today, at his instigation, they are talking about Spunk Banks, who has just walked by with Lena Kanty—another man's wife. Just as they comment on Spunk's imposing figure and renowned fearlessness, the "other man," Joe Kanty, walks into the store. Joe orders a soda and the townsmen all hush up. But not for long. Mosley can't stop himself and asks poor Joe, "How's yo' wife?" ("Spunk," p. 2).

Visibly disturbed and embarrassed, Joe begins to tremble and stare at the floor. The other townsmen chime in, going on about how Joe's wife passed the store clearly in the company of Spunk Banks. Realizing that the men all know his wife is keeping company with another man, Joe suffers from wounded pride. After some deliberation, he announces his intention to finally go after Spunk and draws a razor out of his pocket. The men all applaud him for "talkin' like a man" as he leaves the store and wanders into the woods ("Spunk," p. 2).

In truth, however, no one believes Joe will confront Spunk. First, Spunk's reputation as a tough guy is well known; secondly, Joe's "timid 'bout fightin'," and finally, they all know that Spunk packs a pistol ("Spunk," p. 3). The men agree that Lena has no respect for her husband and that Joe will just come back dejected, hanging his head because he has been unable to get back his wife.

The men are wrong, though; Joe never comes back. Instead, a pistol fires in the distance and a short while later Spunk saunters into the store. "Well," Spunk announces calmly, "Joe come out there wid a meat axe an' made me kill him" ("Spunk," p. 4).

The men all run to see Joe's dead body and then glare at Elijah Mosley for prodding the cuckolded husband to act so suicidally.

After a brief trial in which he claims self-defense, Spunk is acquitted. Life goes on in the town. Spunk and Lena move in together, planning to marry. Spunk continues riding the circle saw in the lumber mill that slices the enormous tree trunks, the most dangerous and rigorous job on the site. He has long done this job, for Spunk is a man who lives his life with no fear. Only now, out of the blue, a black bobcat appears and starts stalking him. One night, the bobcat is howling outside his house and he grabs his gun to shoot it but gets "so nervoused up he couldn't shoot" ("Spunk," p. 6).

The men gather at the store, chattering about how Spunk ought to be nervous after what he's done to Joe. According to them, Spunk thinks the bobcat is Joe, back from Hell for revenge! Laughing, they muse about how Joe was perhaps braver than Spunk and speculate about old Joe's coming back to get him.

The next evening the men gather again but this time there is no laughter. Spunk has been killed, cut to death falling into the circle saw. It was Joe, said a dying Spunk; he shoved me into it.

Spunk's body is laid out and the town gathers at his house for the wake. Life goes on, as the women eat and the men drink whiskey and wonder who will be Lena's next.

"Sweat." The story centers on Delia Jones, a hard-working washerwoman who has bought her own home and fed her husband by taking in the laundry of white folks. Once a "right pretty li'l trick," Delia is now worn and dried out like sugar cane that's been juiced (Hurston, "Sweat," p. 43). She is married to a philandering bully of a man who refuses to work.

As much as the townsfolk admire her—"Heah come Delia Jones.... Hot or col', rain or shine, jes'ez reg'lar ez de weeks roll roun'"—they look on her husband, Sykes, with disdain ("Sweat," p. 42). "He useter be so skeered uh losin' huh, she could make him do some parts of a husband's duty" one of the townsmen tells Lindsay ("Sweat," p. 43). "There oughter be a law about him," says Lindsay. "He ain't fit tuh carry guts tuh a bear" ("Sweat," p. 43).

For the better part of 15 years, Sykes has been carrying on, intimidating his wife with a bull whip and parading his mistresses in plain view. Now he has taken up with a fat woman, Bertha, whom he fattens further with sweets purchased with Delia's money. He and his sweetheart plan to get rid of Delia and take her house. But Delia, though scared of Sykes, has been pushed far enough.

Sykes gets hold of a rattlesnake, a creature he knows frightens Delia to death, and he lets it loose in the house. Delia returns home, finds the snake in her wash basket, and runs in alarm to the barn before it can bite her. She stays out there well into the night—long enough for Sykes to return home. Drunk, he stumbles through the house and fumbles for the light. The snake wakens and, before Sykes can locate the rattle, bites him. From outside, Delia hears his cries but knows that she cannot do anything to save him (since the nearest big hospital is in Orlando). Instead, she sidles over to the chinaberry tree in her yard, "where she waited in the growing heat while inside she knew the cold river [death] was creeping up and up to extinguish that eye which must know by now that she knew" ("Sweat," p. 53).

Folk art reclaimed. After Joe Kant confronts Spunk Banks and gets shot, one of the townsmen calls Joe the braver man:

> Lookit what he done; took a razor an' went out to fight a man he knowed toted a gun an' wuz a crack shot, too; 'nother thing Joe was skeered of Spunk, skeered plumb stiff! But he went jes' the same. It took him a long time to get his nerve up. Tain't nothin' for Spunk to fight when he ain't skeered of nothin'. Now, Joe's done come back to have it out wid the man that's got all he ever had.
>
> ("Spunk," p. 6)

Through this dialogue Hurston conveys the colloquial speech, the cadence, the "musicality" as Alice Walker terms it, of the way people really talked in 1920s Eatonville. Measured against standard English, the grammar is imperfect but Hurston cared little for such measurement. Her interest was in capturing the reality of the moment, the speech as spoken. For example, in "Sweat" Delia exclaims, "Dat niggah wouldn't fetch nothin' heah tuh save his rotten neck, but he kin run thew whut Ah brings quick enough," meaning he can use up her earnings in short order ("Sweat," p. 50). Delia's own words heighten the impact of her lament and add to the realism. By hearing her speech pattern, we get a more vivid picture of the strong, Southern woman Delia Jones is than would otherwise be the case.

Zora Neale Hurston, the anthropologist, is shown here beating a voodoo drum.

Hurston's stories—and later, her anthropological work—illustrate what Locke liked to call the "voice of the proletariat" (Locke in Hemenway, p. 40). Not only the variety of English spoken, but also, in Hurston's mind, the folktales, spirituals, the blues, and other oral traditions were triumphant creations of a culture that was forced by circumstance to turn inward. Hurston had her opponents, many of whom took vehement issue with her position. Because these arts were born of repression, such an opponent reviled the practice of them. In 1925, for example, there was a strike at Howard University; its students refused to sing spirituals. Charles Johnson articulated the attitude of these students in *The New Negro*, saying that folk art could serve for some as too painful a reminder of slavery or as an embarrassment due to the "incorrect" English and uncultured expression it incorporated.

But Hurston saw folklore as a celebration of African American culture and regarded this folklore as "art." Like Locke, Du Bois, and the proponents of Negritude, she viewed African American folklore as affirming the considerable creative powers of the black community. Against the grain of her time, she sought to reclaim this folklore in the voice of the African American to illustrate the beauty, dignity, and validity of her cultural traditions.

"Spunk" and "Sweat"

The thoughts conveyed in "Spunk" reveal the deep reflection that could occur during nightly "lying sessions" of a group of worldly wise black men. The seemingly superstitious plot twist of Joe's coming back as a black bobcat to avenge himself is an allegory of good conquering evil. This is no backward pagan community of which Hurston writes but a thinking, god-fearing people who know right from wrong.

At the same time, the story shows African Americans to be a people with universally shared traits, in keeping with her focus on people in general, rather than light- or dark-skinned peoples. Hurston saw human beings as individuals, not members of racial groups. Her story illustrates the same penchants for gossip, egging someone on, empathy, jealousy, and regret in her small town of Eatonville as one might find in any small town of the day.

Hurston's reclaiming of the folktale was years ahead of its time and often misunderstood. Others, including James Weldon Johnson (1871-1938), who published a compilation entitled *The Book of American Negro Spirituals* and Paul Robeson (1898-1976), who became famous for performing traditional African American musicals, also sought to record African American cultural history. Hurston set out on a different mission than these other artists, though; her interest was in capturing the storytelling nuances in ways that showed the African American experience to be as valid and culturally important as any in the world. "There is the sense of a long, ghostly procession behind Hurston: what might have existed if only more of the words and stories had been written down decades earlier, if only Phillis Wheatley (the first black American woman to publish an account of her experiences as a slave) had not tried to write like [the Englishman] Alexander Pope, if only literate slaves and their generations of children had not felt pressed to prove their claim to the sworn civilities" (Pierpont, pp. 152-53).

Sources and literary context. In setting "Spunk" in a carefully evoked southern context of the early 1900s, Hurston portrays a people through their own vernacular, documenting more than a folk story, recording history. Growing up in Eatonville, the first incorporated completely African American town, Hurston became immersed in the rich storytelling tradition of her people. The store in "Spunk" is clearly Joe Clarke's store of Eatonville, and the banter and superstitious beliefs are clearly those she heard so often as a child. Both Hurston and her groundbreaking story were adopted by leaders of the Harlem Renaissance, including Alain Locke and Charles S. Johnson, who recognized it and her as a "voice of the proletariat." Convinced that "writers like Zora Neale Hurston would help to prove the cultural parity of the races," they entered the story in the Urban League's *Opportunity* magazine contest and it won second prize (Johnson in Hemenway, p. 9).

Apart from reflecting a new emphasis on African American folklore as a genuine art form, "Spunk" represents a larger shift to the realist style in American literature of the 1920s. "Sweat" is even more fully representative of this style. Also rooted in her early childhood experience, "Sweat" foreshadowed the next major genre of African American writing: the protest novel. Though the story tackles gender, not racial politics, and Hurston was not seen as a political writer, contemporary re-evaluation of her writing insists that "Sweat" is, in fact, protest literature" (Glassman, p. 33).

Reception. "Spunk" received wide praise when published. Alain Locke selected it for inclusion in his definitive anthology, *The New Negro*, thereby establishing Hurston as a primary voice of the Harlem Renaissance. In the 1950s and 1960s African American writers and critics, including Sterling Brown and Richard Wright, accused Hurston of ignoring racial oppression and exploitation in the South and of pandering to racist stereotypes of blacks. In the decades of the civil rights movement Hurston's work, including "Spunk," did not get published because it did not deal with the race problem. Unable to get publishing contracts, she took menial jobs and died anonymously in a welfare-sponsored retirement home in Florida. Despite his criticism of her work, Brown agreed that "Spunk" "showed a command of folklore and idiom excelled by no earlier Negro novelist" (Brown in Jones, p. 211). But not until a decade after her death in 1960 did Hurston's story and work really receive their due. Robert Hemenway, who wrote her definitive biography in 1977, credited Hurston with having "liberated rural black folk from the prison of racial stereotypes and granted them dignity as cultural creators" (Hemenway in Jones, p. 222).

Alice Walker, who "discovered" Hurston in the 1970s and erected her tombstone posthumously, concludes with the quality she feels is most characteristic of Zora's work: racial health—a sense of black people as complete, complex, *undiminished* human beings, a sense that is lacking in so much black writing and literature"

(Walker in Hemenway, p. xii). "Sweat" was praised for its complexity and later for its power in asserting female rights. David Headon writes of the story's political as well as literary impact:

> In "Sweat" Zora Neale Hurston forcefully establishes an integral part of the political agenda of black literature of this century. She places at the foreground feminist questions concerning the exploitation, intimidation, and oppression inherent in so many relationships. It is not the civil rights of Du Bois and *Crisis*, but it is civil rights nonetheless.
>
> (Headon in Glassman, pp. 32-33)

—Diane Renée

For More Information

Baker, Houston A., Jr. *Modernism and the Harlem Renaissance*. Chicago: University of Chicago Press, 1987.

Crockett, Norman L. *The Black Towns*. Lawrence, Kans.: The Regents Press of Kansas, 1979.

Campbell, Mary Schmidt, ed. *Harlem Renaissance: Art of Black America*. Harlem: Harry Abrams, 1987.

Glassman, Steve, and Katherine Lee Siedel, eds. *Zora in Florida*. Orlando: University of Central Florida Press, 1991.

Hemenway, Robert E. *Zora Neale Hurston: A Literary Biography*. Chicago: University of Illinois Press, 1977.

Hurston, Zora Neale. "Spunk." In *Spunk: The Selected Short Stories of Zora Neale Hurston*. New York: Marlowe, 1985.

———. "Sweat." In *Spunk: The Selected Short Stories of Zora Neale Hurston*. New York: Marlowe, 1985.

Jones, Daniel, ed. *Contemporary Authors New Revision Series*. Vol. 61. Detroit: Gale, 1998.

Lewis, David Levering. *When Harlem Was in Vogue*. New York: Alfred A. Knopf, 1981.

Nesbitt, Nick. "Negritude." *African Writers Index: Origins of Negritude*. 2000. http://www.geocities.com/africanwriters/origins.html (9 Jan. 2002).

Pierpont, Claudia Roth. *Passionate Minds: Women Rewriting the World*. New York: Alfred A. Knopf, 2001.

Radin, Paul. *Social Anthropology*. New York: McGraw-Hill, 1933.

Tomkins, Vincent, ed. *American Decades*. Detroit: Gale, 1996.

Von Dassanowsky, Robert, ed. *Gale Encyclopedia of Multicultural America*. Vol. 1. Detroit: Gale, 2000.

Wall, Cheryl, ed. *Zora Neal Hurston: Folklore, Memoirs, and Other Writings*. New York: Library of America, 1995.

The Sun Also Rises

by
Ernest Hemingway

Born in Oak Park, Illinois (a suburb of Chicago), on July 21, 1899, Ernest Hemingway was the second of six children. His father, Clarence, a general practitioner of medicine, taught his son to hunt and fish, and, like his mother, was a strict disciplinarian. When Hemingway graduated from high school, he wanted to volunteer for the war effort, but his father arranged for him to work for the *Kansas City Star* as a reporter instead. In 1918, at the age of 18, Hemingway finally did join the war effort. He signed up with the Red Cross ambulance service and was assigned to the Italian Front as a Second Lieutenant. Hemingway served only a brief tour of duty before he was seriously wounded when an Austrian shell exploded just a few feet away from him. By the time he was well enough to return to the front, the fighting had stopped, so Hemingway returned to the United States and resumed his career as a reporter, by this time for *The Toronto Star Weekly*. Two years later, in October 1920, Hemingway went to Chicago where he met his future wife, Hadley Richardson, as well as Sherwood Anderson, who would have a profound effect on him. The newly wed Hemingways moved to Paris in late 1921 armed with letters of introduction to the Parisian literary scene written by Anderson. Thanks to these letters, Hemingway met James Joyce, Gertrude Stein, and Ezra Pound, all of whom would greatly influence the fledgling author. Shortly thereafter Hemingway embarked on a vigorous literary career. He published short stories and poetry, including *Three Stories and Ten*

> **THE LITERARY WORK**
>
> A novel set in Paris, France, and Pamplona, Spain, around 1925; first published in 1926.
>
> **SYNOPSIS**
>
> A group of disillusioned, post-World War I expatriates leave the bars and cafes of Paris's Left Bank for the Festival of San Fermin in Pamplona, Spain.

Poems (1923) and *In Our Time* (1925) as well as the satire *The Torrents of Spring* (1926) before releasing his first successful novel, *The Sun Also Rises*. Titled *Fiesta* in England when it first appeared, the novel captures the responses of expatriate characters to conditions in the period between two world wars.

Events in History at the Time the Novel Takes Place

Prohibition. The Eighteenth Amendment, one of the most controversial in United States history, took effect on January 17, 1920. Designed to frustrate the consumption of alcoholic beverages and eliminate the vice with which it was associated, this amendment forbid the manufacture, sale, and distribution of "intoxicating alcohol" in America (legally defined as any beverage with an alcoholic content greater than 0.5 percent, excluding sacramental or medicinal uses). Many Americans associated drinking alcohol with im-

The Sun Also Rises

Ernest Hemingway

morality. Even before it became illegal, several groups, such as the Women's Christian Temperance Union and the Anti-Saloon League, lobbied the government at the local, state, and national levels to make its sale unlawful. Temperance leaders felt disgusted by the way people acted while drinking and were concerned about the increasing numbers of saloons and bars springing up across America. Not only did these establishments promote intoxication; many of them also became known as dens of gambling and prostitution. If the law forced the saloons to close their doors, reasoned the reformers, and prohibited the consumption of alcohol, two goals would be achieved: people would stop drinking, and the vice connected with intoxication would disappear as well. According to one social worker of the day, outlawing the manufacture and sale of alcohol promised to "nearly wipe out prostitution and crime, improve labor, and 'substantially increase our national resources by setting free' vast amounts of human potential" derailed by the use of alcohol (Nash, p. 782). As it turned out, Prohibition (1920-33), the era in which the manufacture and sale of alcohol was in fact outlawed, did not stop Americans from drinking. One historian says it "just turned half the country into criminals who spent their money with bootleggers [traffickers in the illegal sale of alcohol] and in speakeasies [clubs that served bootlegged alcohol]" (Reynolds, p. 62). Indeed Prohibition was a dismal failure. "By the time the amendment was repealed in 1933, no one was certain which had cost the government more money—the ineffective enforcement of the law or the lost tax revenues from legitimate sales" (Reynolds, p. 62). Far from improving morality, the ban lent an air of intrigue and excitement to drinking. Critics could even argue that by glamorizing the speakeasy, Prohibition actually made alcohol more tantalizing to people, especially the younger generation, to which Hemingway and his crowd belonged.

Americans in Paris. In 1924 there were 32,000 permanent American residents in Paris, and an additional 12,000 tourists visited the so-called City of Light in July (Douglas, p. 108). The city boasted American jazz clubs and cinemas; Paris newspapers advertised American cigarettes; and major U.S. newspapers, such as the *New York Herald Tribune*, put out thriving Paris editions. Actually most of the Americans in France did not even speak French; so large was the English-speaking population that there seems to have been no need.

Some expatriates were attracted to the Continent by favorable currency exchange rates in postwar France. "From 1924-1926, the dollar value in francs made it possible for American writers to live quite well on their limited budgets" (Martin, p. 74). Other Americans went abroad because they felt that life in America was too provincial to provide an experience exciting enough for them. They were drawn instead to the glamorous images of life in Europe. Paris was, after all, one of the cultural capitals of the world in the 1920s. Not only was it home to a thriving literary community, but the other arts flourished there as well, and artists from around the world flocked to the City of Light. Igor Stravinsky (from Russia) and Erik Satie (France) led the way in music; Georges Braque (France), and Juan Gris and Pablo Picasso (from Spain) were pioneers in the visual arts; Sergey Palovich Diaghilev (from Russia) and Isadora Duncan (from the United States) broke new ground in the world of dance.

Such a burgeoning creative environment was not only conducive to artistic innovation; it also came with freedom from the moral restrictions of the United States (i.e., Prohibition). Some Americans lived abroad to circumvent Prohibition while others left home in protest not necessarily or only against Prohibition. The postwar political relations of the United States disturbed some of its citizens. Also, many resented the resistance to new forms of creative expression, a resistance they encountered even in progressive cities like New York, which often elevated a work's entertainment value and potential profit over its artistic innovation. Rejecting U.S. trends, whether they involved Prohibition, politics, or the conservative artistic environment, expatriates flocked to Europe to drink openly, create freely, and express their disdain not only for the American government but also for its, in their opinion, narrow-minded populace.

Nativism. By the early 1920s, "about half of the nation's population was first- or second-generation immigrant." (Douglas, p. 304). Consequently native-born, white Americans began to feel increasingly anxious about immigrant encroachment. Instead of welcoming immigrants as a never-ending supply of cheap labor, they started to feel threatened by the influx of uneducated foreigners who had no knowledge of the English language or American culture.

To fend off what it saw as the threat of foreign domination, the Ku Klux Klan (KKK) experienced a rebirth. A secret organization founded in the post-Civil War era, the Klan had then practiced violence against the newly freed black slaves. This time the KKK targeted not only blacks but also white, non-Nordic immigrants, Jews, and Roman Catholics. Its rebirth did not last long in New York or Boston—largely because of their large immigrant populations—but it flourished in smaller, less heterogeneous environments.

Although the Klan's methods were notorious, it was not alone in its practice of racial and immigrant hatred. Anti-Semitism and other forms of cultural intolerance riddled other sectors of society and the expatriate communities of Europe as well. At one point, automaker Henry Ford "tried to keep America vigilant against the threat Jews posed, not just to America but to Western civilization" by publishing "protocols of the Elders of Zion," a false document professing to be the Jewish "master plan" for gaining control of the free world (Reynolds, *Novel of the Twenties*, p. 52). *The Sun Also Rises* contains evidence of the same paranoia and anti-Semitism. That such sentiments are littered throughout Hemingway's novel is hardly surprising given the current of racism that coursed through parts of American society at the time. For example, in the first chapter Jake observes that Robert Cohn's nose was "certainly improved" by getting "permanently flattened" in a boxing match, ascribing to Cohn a stereotypical Jewish nose. Later the novel describes a "nigger drummer" as "all teeth and lips" (Hemingway, *The Sun Also Rises*, pp. 11, 69). In this regard, the novel is a product of values generally held by the society that gave rise to it, however offensive or unwarranted such values may be.

Portrait of a "lady." The main female character in *The Sun Also Rises*, Lady Brett Ashley, hails from Great Britain, the main male character, Jake Barnes, from America. In the post-World War I years, the status of both British and American women changed dramatically. Breaking away from the Victorian role of "angel of the hearth," women who had been solely responsible for the home and family entered new political, economic, and cultural arenas. The war had given a generation of women an education and the opportunity to test their abilities in the workforce. Also women won the vote in 1920. Newly enfranchised, they could now register their political views in the ballot box.

With this loosening of past restrictions, a new ideal came to dominate the decade—the image of the flapper. No longer confined to the house, the ideal "modern" woman could be found drinking, smoking, and dancing in public. She cut and bobbed her hair, shortened her skirts, tightened her sweaters, and maybe even threw off her stockings. And she mingled freely with men of her choice. Birth control and abortion were growing accessible, allowing for greater sexual freedom, and divorce was becoming a more viable option for the unhappy wife. Unlike women of the earlier Victorian era, the so-called "New Woman" no longer considered marriage a vital prerequisite for sexual satisfaction, social status, or financial stability. Such was the ideal, the image of feminism in the twenties.

In practice, the new freedom promised to women by the image proved elusive. Most states still outlawed the sale of any birth-control device, and their divorce laws nearly always gave men the advantage. While more women joined the work force, they commonly filled secretarial and other service posts, good training, it was thought, for housewives. In politics, women tended to vote as their husbands did, if they voted at all. Early in the 1920s they scored successes in getting congressmen to pass bills such as the Child Labor Amendment (1924). But then Congress began to rebuff female political suggestions, showing less concern for women's needs in the late 1920s. *The Sun Also Rises* appeared at the cusp of this about-face, when the image of the flapper boded well for women's rights advocates. Little did they know at this point that the image would "promise more freedom and equality for women than they actually achieved" (Nash, p. 774).

The Novel in Focus

The contents—epigraphs. Beginning the novel are two epigraphs. The first—"You are all a lost generation"— Hemingway attributed to Gertrude Stein in a conversation with her, though according to his notebooks, the words were not spoken by Stein herself to Hemingway and his generation, but rather were said to her by a French garage mechanic: "*c'est une generation perdue*" (*The Sun Also Rises*, p. vii). Apparently, the mechanic was trying to explain to Stein that younger mechanics were easier to train than those between the ages of 22 and 30, who had gone off to the war and wouldn't work anymore: "No one wants them. They are no good. They were spoiled" (Wagner-Martin, p. 6). The First World War left a generation of survivors disillusioned, demoralized, and disenchanted with government, religion, and conventional moral codes. The question raised by the novel is whether the members of this "lost generation" can ever be saved; whether they might be able somehow to find meaning, if not redemption, in the world around them. Hemingway's second epigraph, from which the title of the novel is taken, is excerpted from a famous passage in the book of *Ecclesiastes* in the King James Bible:

> One generation passeth away, and another generation cometh; but the earth abideth forever. . . . The sun also ariseth, and the sun goeth down, and hasteth to the place where he arose. . . . The wind goeth toward the south, and turneth about unto the north; it whirleth about continually, and the wind returneth again according to its circuits. . . . All the rivers run into the sea; yet the sea is not full; unto the place from whence the rivers come, thither they return again.
> (epigraph in *The Sun Also Rises*, p. vii)

This longer passage shifts attention away from Stein's "lost generation" to the abiding earth and to cycles of nature. Despite the hopelessness of the "lost generation," Earth survives and endures. Perhaps not everything is lost after all.

The contents—the plot. The novel is divided into three books, narrated retrospectively by Jake Barnes, an American newspaper correspondent living in Paris. It recounts a trip to Pamplona, Spain, that Jake and his friends took during the summer of 1924 or 1925. Accompanying Jake are his vacationing American friend, Bill Groton; his would-be lover, Lady Brett Ashley; her bankrupt and alcoholic fiancé, Mike Campbell; and the fifth-wheel, a Princeton Jew named Robert Cohn.

The first section of the novel takes place in Paris and centers on the lifestyle of the American expatriate: drinking in the many bars, clubs, and cafés of Paris's Latin Quarter. One particular evening receives more attention than the rest. On this occasion, out drinking with his friends, Jake encounters Brett Ashley. The two leave the bar together. Apparently Jake and Brett have known each other since the war. They love each other, but it is painful for them to be together because a war wound has left Jake impotent. Moreover, Brett, about to divorce, intends to marry yet another man when the paperwork is finalized. On this same night, Robert Cohn, disillusioned with his own overbearing mistress, also falls in love with Brett; he believes he can win her over with a romantic escape to San Sebastian, Spain, (a rich seaside resort, unlike Pamplona, an old inland city).

The second section of the novel centers on Jake's annual trip to Spain for the bullfights and

---

THE FESTIVAL OF SAN FERMIN

This festival is the occasion for Jake Barnes's pilgrimage to Spain. Dating back to 1591, the festival is an annual celebration that begins at noon on July 6 and lasts for seven days, concluding at midnight on July 14. The festival commences with the blast of a rocket and centers around festivities in honor of the Spanish saint San Fermin and the cultural phenomenon of bullfighting. Each morning, the bulls are brought into town, where crowds of people have the opportunity to participate in the now-famous (largely due to Hemingway's novel) running of the bulls. In Hemingway's time, after the animals were brought into the bullfighting ring, there were amateur bullfights. Hemingway apparently prided himself on his bravery and skill in these events. In 1924 the *Chicago Tribune* and *Toronto Daily Star* both reported on his escapades in the ring; both erroneously claimed he had been gored. (A friend of Hemingway's was injured in a fight, but neither man was gored.) In the 1920s, besides amateur fights, the festival featured some of Spain's most prominent bullfighters, *riau riau* (Basque) street dancing, and evenings of drinking and fireworks.

the festival of San Fermin. Jake and Bill travel together, and, on their way, they stop for a fishing expedition in rural Spain. Brett, her fiancé Mike, and the love-struck Robert Cohn meet them in Pamplona, where they stay at the Hotel Montoya. A long-time friend of Jake's by the name of Montoya is known for his *aficion*, or passion, for the bullfights and the authentic bullfighters (as opposed to those fighters who look good but possess no real skill). Of the group of expatriates, Jake alone shares this passion. During a week of carousing, however, Jake betrays this *aficion* (and his friend Montoya) by introducing a promising young bullfighter, 19 year-old Pedro Romero, to Brett, who is more interested in his tight green pants, which "he must use a shoe horn [to put on]," than his worth as a matador (*The Sun Also Rises*, p. 181). Unsurprisingly, Romero and Brett have an affair. Knowledge of it upsets Robert Cohn, a former boxing champion at Princeton. He calls Jake a "pimp" and knocks him out, then finds the couple and savagely beats Romero on the eve of his big fight. Despite his bruises, Romero fights with skill and courage, and after the festival ends, Brett leaves for Madrid with him, while the rest of the group disbands.

In the novel's third section, Jake, who has taken a detour to San Sebastian on his way back to France, receives a telegram from Brett, asking him to come to Madrid. Brett has decided not to be "one of those bitches that ruins children" and has left Pedro Romero (*The Sun Also Rises*, p. 247). Without him, however, she has no money to return to Paris and needs someone to come retrieve her. When Jake arrives, they have a long conversation about why the relationship with Romero would not have worked out: he wanted her to grow out her hair and be "more womanly," in other words, to settle down, something she was unwilling (or unable) to do (*The Sun Also Rises*, p. 246). The novel ends on a note of futility and frustration. Brett says, "Oh Jake . . . we could have had such a damned good time together," and Jake responds with the sardonic reply, "Yes . . . isn't it pretty to think so" (*The Sun Also Rises*, p. 251).

The aftermath of the Great War. According to one critic, "one of the most persistent themes of the twenties was the death of love in World War I . . . [and] Hemingway seems to have caught it whole and delivered it in lasting fictional form" (Spilka, p. 73). The war had been over for several years by the time Hemingway wrote *The Sun Also Rises*, yet it maintains a strong presence throughout the novel. This is not surprising, since "World War I was a mechanized horror unprecedented in human history, a war of 'futility' that exacted casualties hideous in the nature and number—and for no reason anyone could understand" (Spanier, p. 83). One would expect an event of such large-scale horror to leave lasting psychological and physical scars.

The result for a number of men in real life, as for Hemingway's Jake Barnes, "was a world without heroes. The heroes did not return from the trenches of World War I. . . . Those who remain alive are the walking wounded" (Reynolds, *Novel of the Twenties*, p. 22). The old systems of value, religion, honor, and sentiment were felt to be hollow after the experience of the trenches and the veteran hospitals. Who are the "walking wounded" of Hemingway's novel? Jake himself serves as the most obvious example. A pilot flying for the United States on the Italian front, he was shot down and left impotent. His injury is both physical and psychological. Physically, it has not lessened his ability to feel desire. So emotionally, it is a constant source of anguish for him, especially where Brett is concerned. Although they love each other, they can never consummate their relationship. They can, in other words, never completely connect, and so the novel suggests, they can never be truly happy together.

A Spanish matador averting a bull in Seville, Spain.

The Sun Also Rises

Jake and Brett had first met in Italy, where she worked as a nurse's aid in Milan's British hospital. Brett's life has also been turned upside-down by the war. Her first "true love" died of dysentery in an attempt to avoid the draft, and the man whom she married instead, Lord Ashley, was a sailor who suffered from the psychological disorder shell shock.

> When he came home, he wouldn't sleep in a bed. Always made Brett sleep on the floor. Finally, when he got really bad, he used to tell her he'd kill her. Always slept with a loaded service revolver. Brett used to take the shells out when he'd gone to sleep.
> (*The Sun Also Rises*, p. 207)

Given this description of Brett's "hell of a happy life with the British aristocracy," and given her futile love for Jake and the horrors she witnessed in the army hospitals, her promiscuity becomes more understandable (*The Sun Also Rises*, p. 207). Such conduct might be a way for her to block out thoughts of her past (and present) unhappiness.

Mike Campbell, Brett's alcoholic fiancé, is also a World War I veteran. He too tries to avoid thinking about the war by drinking and making light of the whole experience. For example, while in Pamplona, he recalls an invitation to a dinner with the Prince of Wales that required him to wear his medals. The requirement was a problem because Mike had never sent for the medals he had been awarded. In fact, he did not even know which ones he had received. To get medals for the occasion, he borrowed some from a tailor. Later on that evening, after the dinner had ended, he found them in his pocket and proceeded to give them out to random girls as if they were party favors or souvenirs with little regard for their real significance.

A number of the novel's minor characters have also been touched by the war (for example, Count Mippipopolous and the English fisherman Harris). A witness to the destruction and devastation of the Great War, each of these characters continue to suffer its effects. There is a clear difference between the characters in the novel who have been in the war, and those who have not. Those who have participated seem to comprise some sort of "in-crowd." They share similar values and perspectives, and they recognize each other right away. For example, when Brett introduces Count Mippipopolous to Jake, she tells him, "he's quite one of us" (*The Sun Also Rises*, p. 40). The count, we learn, has shared in similar experiences, having fought in seven wars and four revolutions; he has arrow wounds that run straight through to show for his troubles (*The Sun Also Rises*, pp. 66-67). Harris too shares a bond with Jake, telling him after the pre-fiesta fishing excursion in rural Spain, "You don't know what it means to me to have you chaps up here . . . I've not had much fun since the war" (*The Sun Also Rises*, p. 134).

Ultimately the war affected not only the lives of these characters, but also the way that they see the world around them. Jake imparts a heightened sense of his surroundings to his readers. He furthermore regards these surroundings as a soldier might, using a military frame of reference; the language of the battlefield infiltrates the fiesta. In Pamplona the festival "exploded," and the regular wicker chairs and tables of cafés were "replaced by cast-iron tables and severe folding chairs. The cafe was like a battleship stripped for action" (*The Sun Also Rises*, p. 157). Jake sees the everyday world through the perspective of his prior wartime experience.

Even Jake's style of narration might be a result of this experience. In the novel, the characters follow a rote, mechanical sequence of events: they get up in the morning, go to cafés, eat, drink, go home, and then finally sleep. This depiction might bear a striking resemblance to life in the trenches, where the soldiers rose, repaired, ate, dug, stood watch, then went to sleep. Such a rudimentary lifestyle, combined with the horrific events that seemed to continue nonstop, forced men to live entirely in the present moment, without regard for the *before* or the *after*. It is perhaps this attitude that explains the characters' lack of concern for consequences and Jake's lack of narrative introspection.

Sources and literary context. In Great Britain, novelists such as James Joyce and Virginia Woolf had begun to experiment with the form of the novel as early as 1913. It took American writers a bit longer than their British counterparts to produce a "modernist" novel. Such a novel would break with the literary traditions of the nineteenth century, that is, with a linear, largely chronological storyline, and coherent, realistic descriptions of characters and settings. Not until the mid-1920s did the United States catch up with their British counterparts through works such as F. Scott Fitzgerald's **The Great Gatsby** (also in *Literature and Its Times*) and Hemingway's *The Sun Also Rises*, which prepared the way for more radically experimental novels like William Faulkner's **The Sound and the Fury** (1929; also in *Literature and Its Times*). In fact, many critics thought of Hemingway's novel, with its ironic tone and stark, seemingly objective descriptions, as a sort of manifesto for the modern American novel.

The Sun Also Rises is noted for its misleadingly simple prose style and realistic dialogue. Aiming to represent experience directly, Hemingway's writing favored nouns, perhaps because they came the closest to communicating the person/place/thing itself, free of interpretation or inflection. Hemingway also avoided complex sentences, largely due to his training as a journalist and the influence of Gertrude Stein. His language and syntax are stripped down to their bare minimum, and his short, matter-of-fact sentence structure results in prose that withholds a sense of cause and effect. As a result, there is little awareness of consequence or emotional significance promoted by the novel. Readers are left to determine the significance of events on their own. These features make Hemingway's style stand out in sharp contrast to the rest of the fiction written by his contemporaries, both British and American.

Not only was the style of Hemingway's novel unusual for its time; his narrator, Jake Barnes, was remarkable as well. Unlike the traditional late-nineteenth century narrator who told readers exactly how to think and feel about the events of the novel, Jake merely relays events as they occur. His voice is characterized by its ironic understatement and flat, unemotional descriptions. Refusing introspection, Jake narrates his thoughts as they occur too, but he does not speculate on implications or consequences. Instead, he tells us only the facts, coldly and objectively, or so it seems.

The Sun Also Rises is a roman à clef, a fictionalized story based on real people and events. Hemingway himself explained:

> I believe that when you are writing stories about actual people . . . you should make them those people in everything except telephone addresses. [I] think that is the only justification for writing stories about actual people.
> (Hemingway in Reynolds, "Recovering Historical Context," p. 44)

The Hemingways made three trips to Spain for the bullfights in the early 1920s. The Sun Also Rises is based primarily on the events of their third trip in 1925. In fact, Jakes Barnes was even called "Hem" in the early drafts of manuscripts. Lady Brett Ashley is modeled after a woman named Duff Twysden, Mike Campbell on Pat Guthrie, Robert Cohn on Harold Loeb, and Pedro Romero on the actual bullfighter Nino de la Palma. Hemingway's wife, Hadley, was also on the trip, but strangely, although she has a role in early manuscripts of the text, she does not appear in the finished version of the novel. Her excision perhaps foreshadowed the Hemingways's divorce.

THE ICEBERG PRINCIPLE

One of the legendary doctrines that Hemingway claimed shaped his early fiction was known as the "iceberg principle":

> I always try to write on the principle of the iceberg. There is seven eighths of it under water for every part that shows. Anything you know you can eliminate and it only strengthens your iceberg.
> (Hemingway in Plimpton, p. 235)

According to these guidelines, anything that the author could assume the audience knew was omitted. The omission had little to do with how significant the information was. Details omitted from the text are at least as important as those details that are included.

Many events in the novel's plot have a solid basis in actual events. Twysden and Guthrie were engaged, and she had an affair with Harold Loeb while awaiting a divorce from her husband. Like his fictional counterpart Jake Barnes, Hemingway was jealous of their affair, but unlike Barnes, most critics agree, he and Twysden did not have a romantic relationship. This trip, in contrast to the Hemingways' two previous vacations, did not go as planned. For example, when the group arrived for their pre-fiesta fishing expedition in rural Spain, they found that loggers had polluted the stream. Then at the festival in Pamplona, the chemistry was off between Hemingway and his friends, and events occurred much the way Jake Barnes narrates them. The primary exception is the seduction of the bullfighter. In actuality, there was no connection between anyone in Hemingway's group and the Pedro Romero figure, Nino de la Palma.

Reception. The critical response to Hemingway's novel was overwhelming. Reviews largely fell into three main categories. In the first camp were those who felt disgusted with the novel, largely because of the lifestyle it portrayed: sex, drinking, and a lack of religious faith. The *Cincinnati Enquirer*, for example, called it "a most unpleasant book" (Stephens, p. 31). Such critics were disturbed that they could not locate an admirable hero in the novel and, more importantly, that there was no punishment for vice; Brett, for example, does not suffer on account of her promiscuous behavior. Such depictions of open sexuality, especially when combined with the novel's free-flowing alcohol and failure to mention religious beliefs, caused quite an uproar. The fear was that the book would corrupt young readers by encouraging immoral behavior.

Other reviewers criticized the novel for its lack of plot and shallow characters. The *Dial* complained:

> If to report correctly and endlessly the vapid talk and indolent thinking of Montparnasse café idlers is to write a novel, Mr. Hemingway has written a novel. His characters are as shallow as the saucers in which they stack their daily emotions, and instead of interpreting his material—or even challenging it—he has been content merely to make a carbon copy of a not particularly significant surface of life in Paris.
>
> (Stephens, p. 45)

In other words, said *The Dial*, Hemingway's characters lack emotional depth, and the novel is simply a transcription of the typical expatriate lifestyle of idleness and dissipation. Another critic writing for the *Chicago Daily Tribune* protested, "the book is [so] concerned with such utter trivialities that your sensitiveness objects violently to it" (Stephens, p. 39). In addition to the lack of plot and character development, reviewers objected to the novel's glamorization of this lifestyle. Even those who disliked the book praised Hemingway's formidable talent, in a regretful fashion. The *Chicago Tribune* critic remarked on "the wasting of a genuine gift" for writing (Stephens, p. 39). In short, the reviewers were frustrated with Hemingway for squandering his ability on what they regarded as meaningless drivel.

Other critics admired the novel. A reviewer for the *New York World* thought it contained "some of the finest and most restrained writing that this generation has produced" (Stephens, p. 38). There was praise too for Hemingway's realistic dialogue, which was "alive with the rhythms and idioms, the pauses and suspensions and innuendos and shorthands, of living speech" (Stephens, p. 34). Significantly, even those who praised the novel did not necessarily admire its story content or characters, as shown in this review from *The Boston Evening Transcript*:

> [The author] has lifted [his characters] out of the muck and mire in which they wallow with such desperate gusto, into the pages of his narrative, some of the mud and slime still clinging to their heels and clothing. To their woeful situation, he has managed to impart a poignant and aching beauty. The love affair between Brett and Jake has a sordid and futile loveliness unlike that in any recent novel.
>
> (Stephens, p. 37)

Hemingway, concluded this cadre of reviewers, had done an exceptional job of presenting the sentiments and disillusionment of a generation. The final picture may not have been a pretty one, but it was well drawn nevertheless.

—Erin E. Templeton

For More Information

Douglas, Ann. *Terrible Honesty: Mongrel Manhattan in the 1920's*. New York: Farrar, Strauss, and Giroux, 1995.

Hemingway, Ernest. *The Sun Also Rises*. New York: Simon and Schuster, 1926.

Martin, Wendy. "Brett Ashley as New Woman in *The Sun Also Rises*." In *New Essays on The Sun Also Rises*. New York: Cambridge University Press, 1987.

Mellow, James R. *Hemingway: A Life Without Consequences*. Boston: Houghton Mifflin, 1992.

Nash, Gary B., et al, eds. *The American People: Creating a Nation and a Society*. Vol. 2. New York: Harper & Row, 1990.

Plimpton, George, ed. *Writers at Work: The Paris Review Interviews*. Second series. New York: Viking Press, 1963.

Reynolds, Michael. "The *Sun* in Its Time: Recovering the Historical Context" in *New Essays on The Sun Also Rises*. New York: Cambridge University Press, 1987.

———. *The Sun Also Rises: A Novel of the Twenties*. Boston: Twayne, 1988.

Schwarz, Jeffrey A. "'The Saloon Must Go, and I Will Take It With Me': American Prohibition, Nationalism, and Expatriation in *The Sun Also Rises*." *Studies in the Novel* 33, no. 2 (summer 2001): 180-99.

Spanier, Sandra Whipple. "Hemingway's Unknown Soldier: Catherine Barkley, the Critics, and the Great War" in *New Essays on A Farewell to Arms*. New York: Cambridge University Press, 1990.

Spilka, Mark. "The Death of Love in *The Sun Also Rises*." In *The Merrill Studies in* The Sun Also Rises. Columbus, Ohio: Charles E. Merrill, 1969.

Stephens, Robert O., ed. *Ernest Hemingway: The Critical Reception*. New York: Burt Franklin and Co., 1977.

Wagner-Martin, Linda. "Introduction" in *New Essays on the Sun Also Rises*. New York: Cambridge University Press, 1987.

The Tale of Genji

by
Murasaki Shikibu

The Tale of Genji, considered the world's first great novel, describes the life of Japanese court society during the Heian period (794-1185) about 50 years before the lifetime of the author, Murasaki Shikibu (c. 973-1030). Murasaki Shikibu is a nickname (adopted from a character in the novel) of the court lady who composed the work while serving as companion to Shōshi, (988-1074), the daughter of the powerful regent Fujiwara no Michinaga (966-1027). During Murasaki Shikibu's lifetime, chapters of *The Tale of Genji* circulated independently; it was unusual to have a copy of all the chapters for consecutive reading. The earliest existing fragments of a complete manuscript appear in an early mid-twelfth-century scroll, the *Illustrated Genji Scroll*, which was transcribed 150 years after the death of the author. The final ten chapters of the novel present a style and atmosphere that is so markedly different from the rest of the novel that some scholars have suggested that these chapters were in fact authored by another person, perhaps Shōshi, whom Murasaki tutored. Convincing arguments can be made either way, but for most scholars Murasaki is the accepted author. Murasaki Shikibu was the daughter of Fujiwara no Tametoki (d. 1029), a scholar of Chinese who also served as governor in the province of Harima, Echizen, Japan. Their family was a distant lateral branch of the ruling Fujiwara clan that came to dominate Japanese court life during the Heian period. Although not politically powerful, the family was respected for its scholarly learning and connections. The writer's grandfa-

THE LITERARY WORK

A novel set in Japanese court society about 905-975; circulated in Japanese (as *Genji Monogatari*) in handwritten copies around 1010; first published in English in 1925-33.

SYNOPSIS

The novel follows the life of a handsome and charming courtier from his youthful amorous adventures to exile and renewed success; the death of his dearest companion, Murasaki; and betrayal by his son's close friend, Kashiwagi. In the full-length novel, after Genji's death, the focus shifts to his descendants.

ther had known Ki no Tsurayuki (c. 872-945), a poet, diarist and critic, who was the creative force behind the compilation of the Kokinshè, the great tenth-century collection of Japanese waka poetry. Tutored by her scholarly father, Murasaki Shikibu acquired some Chinese learning, unusual for a woman at the time. She married Fujiwara no Nobutaka (950-1001) and gave birth to a daughter in 999. Nobutaka died in the epidemic of 1001, and his widow, Murasaki, began writing *The Tale of Genji* around 1002. Three years later Fujiwara no Michinaga, the most powerful man at court, hired Murasaki Shikibu as a companion and tutor for his daughter, Shōshi. From Murasaki Shikibu's diary we learn that she had few specific duties and so had time to observe

The Tale of Genji

1889 woodblock print of Murasaki Shikibu composing *The Tale of Genji*.

court activities of the kind described in *The Tale of Genji*. When a chapter of the text was spirited out of her quarters by the Emperor, she worried about the unedited work's causing trouble among her friends at court. She writes:

> I was merely amusing myself with fictions, finding solace for my idleness in foolish words. Aware of my own insignificance, I had at least managed for the time being to avoid anything that might have been considered shameful or unbecoming; yet here I was, tasting the bitterness of life to the very full.
> (Murasaki Shikibu, The Diary of Lady Murasaki, p. 34)

Murasaki Shikibu's modest comments are a better indication of attitudes toward the art of fiction in her day than a realistic evaluation of her talent. Far more than a frivolity, her writing would prepare for posterity an enduring profile of Japanese court society that the world would not otherwise have.

Events in History at the Time the Novel Takes Place

Poetry in the palace. The culture of the tenth and early eleventh century was influenced by two major factors: first, cultural exchanges with China that had dominated preceding centuries abruptly came to an end in the ninth century due to political instability on the Chinese mainland, and secondly, the Fujiwara clan consolidated its power in Japan through "marriage politics." The family continued to marry Fujiwara daughters into the Emperor's line until, by the end of the tenth century, the family achieved complete political domination of the Heian court.

Beginning in the sixth century, the Japanese, having not developed a native writing system, quickly mastered the skills of Chinese writing and began to use this written language in government documents. In the ninth century Japan's Emperor Saga promoted Chinese poetry to such an extent that it completely dominated the cultural life of the court for centuries to come. All official documents were written in Chinese and educated courtiers were expected to compose poetry in Chinese as well. Young boys of noble birth were trained in Chinese poetic and historical classics. This emphasis on Chinese learning devalued Japanese poetry and prose, which had flourished before the ninth century. Still practiced in private life, though, particularly by women of the court, was a Japanese genre, the vernacular tradition of waka poetry. Waka poems are 31 syllables long and are divided into five lines of alternating length. The five-line poem follows a metrical pattern of 5-7-5-7-7 syllables per line.

During the ninth century the Japanese developed a syllabary, a set of written characters, each representing a syllable—based on Chinese characters so that the Japanese could transcribe their own vernacular verse. This syllabary, called kana writing, served other purposes too. Used to write casual social exchanges (invitations, notes of thanks or condolence) or to relate anecdotes, it provided women with a sorely needed means of written communication. Chinese learning was considered inappropriate for the education of young women, but syllabic kana writing was permissible. These realities led to the prominent position of waka poetry as the verse form used in the private lives of the women and their lovers. The great poet Ki no Tsurayuki elevates waka to the highest of arts, pointing out that though neglected, it survived in informal matters, in "the habitations of the amorous" (Ki no Tsurayuki in Konishi Jin'ichi, vol. 2, p. 217).

In the middle of the ninth century, waka poetry was experiencing a revival, partly due to a return to traditional values, but also because of the dynamics of marriage politics that allowed political power to be achieved through the female members of the family. The emperor's consorts (additional wives) and their companions living in the "rear palace" developed a salon culture that became a powerful cultural force during the ninth and tenth centuries. Murasaki Shikibu was a member of such an elite group of literary women. During this period poetry contests (called utaawase) were held frequently and the native waka verse began to replace the Chinese verse forms at banquets. The richness of this vernacular poetic tradition is preserved in *Kokinshū* (c. 905), a compilation of waka poetry ordered by Emperor Daigo and edited by Ki no Tsurayuki. The publication of this and other subsequent collections with imperial sponsorship elevated waka poetry as an important literary form. Murasaki Shikibu and her contemporaries used the *Kokinshū* as a model of poetic expression. Poetic exchanges in *The Tale of Genji* often cite or implicitly refer to poems from this collection that would be quite familiar to Murasaki's audience.

Economic and political conditions. The power of the Fujiwara clan reached its height during Murasaki Shikibu's lifetime, in part through the economic strength they gained by owning estates that were tax-exempt, a privilege enjoyed by the upper nobility and by religious institutions. Destitute land-owning peasants could avoid paying heavy taxes by "donating" their plots to these tax-exempt estates, then for low rent, could work the land in perpetuity. The estates of the Fujiwara swelled to accommodate those who sought such tax shelters, the economic power of the clan growing in the process. Meanwhile, the clan gained political power through "marriage politics," wedding their daughters to the emperor's family line, which allowed them to dominate affairs at court. Each young emperor had a Fujiwara mother whose father or brother or uncle would influence the boy's destiny. When the young emperor came to maturity he would marry a Fujiwara daughter. His Fujiwara father-in-law could continue to manipulate political appointments through his daughter. In the late ninth century the Fujiwara began a policy of putting a young boy on the throne and ruling Japan through the position of an older "Regent," who governed in the boy's stead.

In Murasaki Shikibu's day the regent and his officers carried on the actual business of governing while the emperor had little direct involvement in its practical details. The emperor's life was increasingly involved in a complex pattern of daily and seasonal rituals whose exact performance was believed to ensure the health and prosperity of the state. Care was taken not to commit a breach of decorum, since a serious breach was considered a threat to the health of the state. Such a breach might even be identified as an indirect cause of a natural disaster (for example, a flood, a famine, or some other pestilence). The more direct cause was often seen as the vengeful spirit of a high-ranking person whose reputation or political hopes the emperor had disappointed during the person's lifetime.

Murasaki Shikibu sets most of *The Tale of Genji*, however, in an earlier period, the first half of the tenth century, when emperors were directly involved in governing and in shaping cultural trends. During the early tenth century the power of the Fujiwara family had not yet solidified. The emperor still held political power. More exactly, the novel takes place during the reigns of Emperors Uda (ruled 887-897), his son, Daigo (ruled 897-930) and Murakami (ruled 946-967). Scholars have equated figures in *The Tale of Genji* with these particular emperors: the novel's Ichi no In with the historical Emperor Uda; the Kiritsubo Emperor (Genji's father) with the next historical leader, Emperor Daigo; and Genji's son by Fujitsubo, Emperor Reizei, with the historical Emperor Murakami.

Emperor Uda, who was not related to the Fujiwara family, was determined to control their growing influence over the court. After the death of the regent Mototsune, Emperor Uda refused to reappoint the position, and made a point of promoting men of other noble families, particularly those of learning and talent such as Sugawara no Michizane, considered to be one of the finest scholars and poets of the day. In 901 Daigo, Emperor Uda's son, ascended the throne and within a year he had instituted reforms. Daigo attempted to revive the Chinese legal and administrative system, strengthen central control, and limit the growth of tax-exempt private estates, which were starving the central government of important revenues. He took active interest in cultural matters too, compiling ritual manuals for festivals and ceremonies, and ordering compilations of history and poetic anthologies such as the *Kokinshū*. His reign was viewed by later periods as the flourishing of the "golden age" of government and culture.

Following in his predecessor's footsteps, Emperor Murakami, though closely related to the Fujiwara family, struck out on his own path too.

The Tale of Genji

His political decisions reveal an attempt to gain independence from his Fujiwara in-laws and further strengthen the power of the imperial house. Emperor Murakami did not appoint a successor after the death of the regent Tadahira (880-949) and there was no regent during the following 18 years of Murakami's reign (949-967).

Although the office was left vacant, competition between members of the Fujiwara to serve as regent was fierce, between the Morosuke branch (northern) and the Motokata branch (southern). Eventually, the Morosuke branch won, and its descendents went on to dominate Fujiwara politics for the next century. The powerful Michinaga (966-1027), regent during Murasaki Shikibu's lifetime, belonged to this branch of the family. Not trusting to the manipulation of marriage politics alone, the triumphant Morosuke branch attributed their success in part to their patronage of intellectually talented and powerful Buddhist priests whose rituals helped manipulate events in their favor.

Religious beliefs and practices in the Heian period. The belief that the emperor's family descended from Amaterasu, the sun goddess, was fundamental. From this basic belief arose others about the connection between the emperor and the health of the state. In time, these native beliefs became known as Shintō, or the "Way of the Gods." Shintō rituals included annual rites to promote the prosperity of the harvest and purification rituals to neutralize contact with polluting influences, such as death and blood. Some of these rituals became institutionalized in court ceremonies and were performed at imperial shrine centers such as Ise, which appears in *The Tale of Genji*. Shintō specialists performed other, similar rites at local shrines and at places thought to be sites of the sacred. An unusual rock, tree, or beautiful section of the coastline might be home to a powerful spirit and therefore a sacred site. According to local beliefs, such spirits, called kami, wielded great influence on the good and ill fortune of an area. Shintō specialists, male as well as female, conducted seasonal rituals, therefore, for the prosperity of the local harvest, or for the health of the community.

Buddhism, introduced from the Asian continent in the sixth century (552 C.E.), quickly harmonized with local beliefs in these sacred sites and spirits. Buddhism performed two important functions in Japanese religious life. First, it provided a philosophical framework within which Shintō beliefs about locally sacred sites could be accommodated. The local spirits were connected to Buddhist deities. A local kami residing in a mountain would, for example, promise to protect the Buddhist temple there as long as certain rites were performed at his sacred site. On occasion he would also serve as a local manifestation of a particular Buddhist deity. Second, Buddhism provided the Japanese with powerful means of dealing with contaminating and dangerous aspects of life, such as death and illness. Buddhism teaches that the world is impermanent and forever changing, but due to ignorance, human beings want to believe that they can achieve happiness by grasping at what they desire and avoiding what they dislike. Such grasping and avoiding causes suffering. Furthermore, the actions that one takes in life to acquire one's desires, or to avoid hateful circumstances, results in an accumulation of habits of mind and body, called karma, that shape future existences. A human who is cruel or greedy in this life will be reborn into a life of suffering, perhaps as a poor or ugly person, or worse, as an animal or dissatisfied spirit called a hungry ghost. Recognizing the futility of grasping at one's desires awakens one to the fundamental Buddhist truth of suffering and thereby cuts off or ends the cycle of birth, death, and rebirth. Ending the cycle is in fact the aim of Buddhist practice. To the medieval Japanese, however, the goal of desirelessness seemed beyond the capacity of ordinary people, so believers sought other means of achieving Buddhist spirituality. In the Heian period, one such alternative was belief in the saving power of Amida Buddha. Amida vowed that when he achieved enlightenment, he would create a Pure Land in which all beings would be at peace and could hear the Buddhist teachings, practice them, and easily attain awakening. All one needed to do to be reborn in Amida's Pure Land was to rely on Amida's saving grace and to recite the name of Amida, a practice employed in the novel.

Due to their understanding of the teachings of karma and rebirth, and their skills at chanting Buddhist scriptures, Buddhist priests in Heian culture gained a reputation as experts in dealing with the intermediate realms of the spirits of the dead. Because illness was believed to be caused by the vengeful anger of dissatisfied spirits, it could be alleviated through the intercession of Buddhist priests who chanted Buddhist scriptures and performed esoteric rituals. The words of these scriptures were believed to have great power in liberating such vengeful spirits from the angry emotions that bound them to living beings and caused them to inflict illness and harm on the living. In one part of the novel (the "Lavender" chapter), Genji, who is suffering from continual bouts of malaria, travels to a remote mountain hermitage. A Buddhist priest, who is believed to be an expert in rituals for dispelling illness, performs chanting services for Genji, insisting that he stay at the mountain hermitage for several days until the services are complete. On his return to the capital, Genji is questioned by the emperor, who plumbs him for details about the priest's skill in performing the rituals.

Having skilled Buddhist priests at their disposal was important to the emperor and his court. Through Buddhist scriptures and rituals, aristocrats could gain and hold onto power. In fact, aristocrats considered Buddhist rituals to be as important to maintaining power as administrating land and assets. Modern concepts such as the separation of church and state do not apply to the realities of court life during the Heian period. In fact, Buddhist scriptures such as the Lotus Sutra functioned in the political as well as the religious realm. A well-trained and intelligent priest would be a prime candidate for patronage, sponsored by aristocrats because his knowledge and skills were believed to produce effective rituals. Such a talented priest could bring about success for one's enemies, fulfill a patron's desires, and even assure forgiveness of his sins and salvation after death.

The career of the Tendai priest, Ryōgen (912-985) illustrates how firmly entwined religious and secular power became in the Heian period. Ryōgen was born to a family of little political influence, but he was intellectually talented. Ordained in the Tendai sect of Buddhism, Ryōgen was trained to debate points of doctrine in the *Lotus Sutra,* the fundamental Buddhist scripture of the sect. By winning several important public doctrinal debates early in his career, he attracted the attention of the Fujiwara regent, Tadahira, who in 939 contracted for Ryōgen to perform complex and lengthy rituals at his funeral for his salvation. After the death of Tadahira, Ryōgen gained the patronage of Morosuke of the Fujiwara northern branch. In exchange for support, Ryōgen performed rituals for the health and prosperity of the Morosuke Fujiwara family. Some of these rituals included guarding the health of pregnant Fujiwara women and changing the sexual identity of the fetus. In Ryōgen's time, men of talent could rise in the priestly hierarchy, just as they could in the political hierarchy. In the novel, Genji uses his talent and political tact to rise in the hierarchy, calling on priests as the occasion arises.

After Ryōgen's time rewards for intelligence, character, and seniority diminished, whether in the priestly or the political realm. Blood relationship began to take precedence: it was more important for a monk or priest to have a high-ranking family lineage than an intimate knowledge of the scriptures or a reputation for holiness or seniority. After Ryōgen's death the Fujiwara family appointed their own family members, usually second sons, as abbots of important temples. This parallels the increasing tendency in the eleventh and twelfth centuries to rely on birth rather than talent to fill positions of political authority.

FROM THE MOUTH OF THE BUDDHA

A sutra is a Buddhist scripture purported to be the word of the Buddha. Born in the sixth century B.C.E. in India, Buddha (563-483 B.C.E.) had a long preaching career during which he gave many sermons. About 500 years after his death, followers of the Buddhist doctrine began to write up what had been passed down in memory by his followers. Around the same time (about 100 B.C.E.-100 C.E.), a new kind of scripture emerged, which professed to be the "word of the Buddha" too because his teachings are universal, not bound by time or place. The Lotus Sutra belongs to this second set of scriptures, which are called Mahayana or "great vehicle" scriptures. Referred to several times in *The Tale of Genji*, the Lotus Sutra has had a great impact on East Asian Buddhist thought, art, and literature, including parables, stories and analogies that have influenced elite culture as well as popular literary and art traditions. The Lotus Sutra entered Japan from China in the early ninth century, becoming closely tied to nobles of the court, as shown in the novel. The sutra became especially revered in Japan, whose people would recite and transcribe it to protect the land, attain worldly benefits, or cleanse themselves of sins. The belief was that reciting or copying the Lotus Sutra brought merit to the person who reciter or copyist. Heartening in the text is a promise that "all shall attain the Buddha way;" over the years, interpreters would come to regard this sutra as enabling one to achieve enlightenment in this lifetime rather than over successive lifetimes.

Marriage and love in the Heian court. People today know of the amorous adventures of the Heian Court primarily through the diaries of women writers who act as a window into the

The Tale of Genji

cultural and social life of the upper classes. The life they describe is both elegant and tedious, punctuated by sexual adventures, but also so severely restricted by social rules as to be boring.

Heian society was polygamous. A man could marry more than one woman, though practically speaking, it was too expensive to have more than three wives. The primary rule of such polygamous marriages was that the first wife took precedence over all subsequent wives. At the time of his first marriage a man might be barely an adolescent, perhaps as young as 12 years old. The young wife, chosen from a family of suitably high social rank, would be about three or four years older; it was considered advantageous for the young man to be under the influence of a somewhat more mature woman. The dignity and position of the first wife had to be carefully preserved at all costs by her husband. A man risked becoming a social outcast if he treated a secondary wife with honors due the first wife, even if he felt more affection toward the later wife.

A marriage was official after the prospective husband had spent three nights with a woman. The first night was arranged through a go-between and conducted in "secret," though most of the household knew that the young woman was entertaining a man in her quarters. The man was expected to spend the whole night with her, parting from her at dawn with a show of great reluctance. As soon as he returned home, he had to send a letter containing a poem that referred to their evening together and expressed his longing to return to her side. A faithful servant delivered the letter and waited for a reply from the lady, an enviable errand, for he would be offered delicious treats and drinks while he waited. The young lady took great pains to compose a suitable reply; if she were young, the older women of the household would most likely compose the reply. Every aspect of the task—the choice of paper, the fragrance she gave it, and her calligraphy—indicated her breeding as much as the quality of the poem itself, reflecting on the refinement of the whole household.

The first and second night visits passed in much the same way, but on the third night, the young couple would be presented with a plate of "third night cakes," prepared by the household especially for the occasion. Accepting these cakes sealed the marriage. In the morning, the man remained in the woman's quarters, and the family welcomed him. A brief Shintō blessing and a feast would follow, making the marriage public and official. The new couple did not usually set up their own household; rather, the wife remained in her parents home until their death, practicing "matrilocal" marriage. If she became pregnant and delivered a child, the child stayed in her family's home until the age of maturity. Male courtiers often did not establish independent households until later in life.

Secondary marriages were conducted according to the same rules, although less formally. The second wife would remain in her family's home, or the man might install her in a wing of his own residence, though such an arrangement would expose her to the jealousy of other women of his household. He might wish to have his beloved near him, but open intimacy and favoritism would put her in a difficult position. In the polygamous society of Heian Japan, the worst behavior in a man was to abandon all sense of decorum by becoming too attached to the woman he loved. On the other hand, for women, the worst social sin was jealousy. The Heian Japanese ascribed great power to jealousy, believing it capable of destroying the happiness of others to the point of possessing the spirit of another woman and destroying her health. The twin themes of reckless male indulgence and female jealousy in male-female relations run throughout *The Tale of Genji*.

Society expected men to have affairs outside of marriage, and in these cases too the illicit lovers had to abide by certain rules. A man could have a number of nightly adventures, opportunities to prove his social and poetic skills as much as his virility. Married women were expected to be faithful to their husbands, but if discreet, an unmarried woman could enter into a number of simultaneous affairs without attracting criticism. Women lived a secluded life in semidarkness in their rooms. Two potential lovers would initially communicate with a barrier between them, a screen or curtain, with the man ogling to glimpse the woman's hair and form behind the screen. Female beauty was judged by the luxuriance of the cascade of long hair that often reached the floor, and by the woman's skill in choosing pleasing shades and color combinations of robes suitable to the season. Not considered beautiful, the naked human body was rarely seen. A sexual affair usually took place inside the woman's gloomy apartments, amidst a voluminous sea of robes in which she appeared to float. Social decorum required that the two realms of public and private life be kept strictly apart in Heian society. Overly intimate, obsessive, or exclusive domestic relationships were not the norm. To be sure, tendencies in these directions existed, but as shown in *The*

Tale of Genji, they could cause disorder in the smooth social relations of the court.

The Novel in Focus

The plot. Emperor Kiritsubo's deep love for one of his consorts, a beautiful and refined court lady, results in the birth of a beautiful baby boy, the future Genji. As the lady is of lower birth and has no powerful patrons at court, she is literally hounded to death by the jealousy of the other consorts. Fearing that these same forces of jealousy would be released on his young son the emperor hesitates to name the baby as a prince, and instead makes him a commoner, bestowing the name Genji on him. This name indicates to others that, although of royal blood, the boy is not a contender for the throne. He is therefore not a target of the jealous Kokiden, the emperor's primary consort, who hopes to place her own son on the throne. Although it is clear that the emperor favors the beautiful Genji, reducing him to commoner status means that he cannot be a prince. Thus at the outset of the novel, Genji is deprived of both his mother and his future as a prince.

The young child grows into a handsome youth, so accomplished in the refined arts of the court that everyone (except the jealous Kokiden) is charmed and delighted, awed by his other worldly perfection. The emperor has meanwhile discovered a lovely woman, Fujitsubo, who reminds him so powerfully of Genji's mother that he installs her in the palace and encourages young Genji to spend time in her apartments. When Genji becomes an adult, however, these privileges are suspended, but in the course of the novel he violates this stricture and becomes Fujitsubo's lover. Their union results in the birth of a son, Reizei, who will become emperor later in the novel. The current Emperor, unaware that the baby was fathered by Genji, accepts it as his own and raises the boy to be his successor.

While still a young man of 12, having just undergone the coming of age ceremony, Genji is married to the daughter of the powerful Minister of the Left. Lady Aoi, as she is called later in the novel, is beautiful, but her behavior to him is formal and cold. Genji feels frustrated and ill at ease in her presence. Satisfying himself elsewhere than at his wife's home, he has a number of nightly adventures. He pursues these escapades in league with his brother-in-law Tō no Chōjō, a willing companion. The two even have amorous relations with the same woman.

One night, Genji seduces a woman—her name is "Evening Faces" (Yūgao)—and brings her to a deserted mansion. Shy and retiring, the woman appears to be increasingly frightened by the mysterious mansion. Deep in the night, Genji perceives a figure by the bed. In the morning, the young woman is discovered to have died, perhaps haunted by the jealous spirit of one of Genji's other lovers, an older woman named Rōkujo. Yūgao leaves behind a daughter, not Genji's, but his brother-in-law's. The mother's death is ominous—it prefigures the death of Genji's wife, Aoi, who also dies possessed by the spirit of Rokujō.

Beset by malarial fevers, Genji visits the hermitage of a priestly healer in the mountains. There he discovers a charming little girl, less than ten years old, at a bishop's country temple. She lives with her grandmother, a nun who does not approve of Genji's attentions to the young girl. Although the child appears immature and unsophisticated, she reminds Genji strongly of Fujitsubo, for good reason, since she is Fujitsubo's niece. Unsuccessful at his first attempts to adopt the child, whom he dubs Murasaki (Lavender), Genji returns to court after his cure. He soon manages to abduct and adopt Murasaki, whose grandmother has died, leaving her with scant protection.

Genji secretly installs Murasaki near his own apartments, inviting other children to play with her, and filling her rooms with dolls and toys. He treats her tenderly, as if he were her own father, and she soon abandons her shyness, becoming open and affectionate with him. Meanwhile, news that Genji has brought a young woman to reside in his quarters reaches his wife, Lady Aoi. Not knowing of Genji's fatherly treatment of the girl, his wife assumes that Genji has taken this young girl as a lover, perhaps as a second wife.

Soon after this, Lady Aoi, pregnant with Genji's child, goes into labor and delivers a boy, Yogiri. The birth is very difficult, and priests are commissioned to chant scriptures for her baby's health. They begin to suspect possession by a vengeful spirit because all their efforts to exorcise the spirit from Aoi fail. In a gripping deathbed scene, Genji, torn with grief at his wife's bedside, has the shocking experience of hearing her speak in the refined voice of Lady Rokujō, clearly a sign of being possessed. The priests redouble their efforts, but Aoi finally breathes her last in Genji's arms. The distressed husband has finally discovered his wife's love for him. Deeply

The Tale of Genji

The Tale of Genji

Twelfth century painting depicting a scene from *The Tale of Genji*.

perturbed, Genji turns to Murasaki for comfort. At this point, his affection for her grows more than fatherly; he turns to her as a lover. Murasaki, though shocked by his demands, submits to him.

Genji's situation worsens when his father, the emperor, dies, and Kokiden's son, Suzaku, becomes the new emperor. Political power shifts from the Minister of the Left, Genji's father-in-law, to the Minister of the Right, Kokiden's father. Genji's fortunes become more tenuous, and Fujitsubo, the former emperor's consort, is also in a more precarious position. Although Genji can provide some shelter for her politically, Fujitsubo perceives that it is too dangerous for her to rely upon him, and she decides to retire from the court and become a nun.

For several months Genji had been conducting a secret but dangerous love affair with Oborozukiyo, Kokiden's sister and a consort of the new emperor as well. When this affair is exposed by her father, the Minister of the Right, Genji finds his situation politically and socially untenable and chooses a self-imposed exile from the capital to avoid Kokiden's anger. He leaves Murasaki in charge of his estates and business affairs in the capital.

At the relatively primitive coastal town of Suma, Genji meditates and performs rituals to purify himself of the sins he has committed in the capital city. He is surrounded by servants but far removed from the brilliant life of the court. Wild storms beat against the shore, threatening their lives, and Genji has prophetic and eerie dreams of the god of the sea and of his dead father. Meanwhile, news of Genji's presence spreads throughout the peninsula. A retired courtier, the resident priest at nearby Akashi, believes that Genji has been sent by the gods in answer to his prayers for a son-in-law. Hoping to entice Genji to visit his home, the priest arrives at Suma with his retinue just after Genji and his men have weathered a frightening and destructive storm. Genji takes the Akashi priest's arrival as a divine sign, and accepts his hospitality. At Akashi, the old priest and Genji spend hours talking and playing music. The priest speaks often of his daughter's prowess as a musician, hoping to incite Genji's interest. He encourages exchanges of letters between Genji and his daughter and finally arranges an evening liaison between them. Before Genji leaves Akashi, he has a new wife who is pregnant with his first daughter. This daughter will be the key to Genji's future political success; he will use her marriage to the crown prince to gain influence over future emperors.

During Genji's absence at court, the reigning emperor, Suzaku, has suffered an eye ailment and is concerned that his illness is caused by the vengeful spirit of the old emperor, Genji's father.

He summons Genji back to the capital and soon abdicates the throne. Now Reizei, the son of Fujitsubo and, thinks everyone, of Genji's father, becomes emperor. Genji, whom everyone believes to be his brother, is the natural person to look after Reizei's affairs. Reizei's true father (Genji) is still a secret that only the parents share. Genji's political fortunes now seem more secure, a development that emerges when he wins a court competition in the art of picture making. Afterward he will take steps to protect those close to him, manipulations that testify to his having matured emotionally and politically.

What the abridged version leaves out: Genji's decline. The abridged translation of *The Tale of Genji* ends at this triumphant moment for Genji. He has regained the respect and admiration of the court and has been promoted to the rank of minister. His political power is extensive. But the tale does not end here. The full version continues with a subsequent period of suffering and spiritual discovery connected to the sins of Genji's past.

Now quite powerful at court, Genji builds a large mansion for his retinue and for his women and children on lands bequeathed to him by Lady Rokujō. He installs a pleasure garden on the property and assembles all his ladies to live together in his mansion. Genji learns through a chance encounter that the daughter of a former lover, "Evening Faces," is in the capital. The daughter, Tamakazura, has been raised in the rural island of Kyūshū, and is naive and untutored in the arts of decorum and intrigue. She does not know that her father is Genji's one-time brother-in-law Tō no Chūjō, or that her mother died in Genji's arms during a night of lovemaking with him in an abandoned mansion in the capital. Genji installs the young Tamakazura in his household, at first treating her as his own daughter, but gradually developing romantic feelings for her. When the girl reacts with fear to his approaches, Genji resumes his fatherly role, seeking to make the best marriage match for her. Such matchmaking is complicated by Tamakazura's secret parentage, which blights her affection for To no Chojo's son, Kashiwagi.

Even as Genji's power nears its climax, there are signs that his world is beginning to crumble. Fujitsubo dies, and a priest who cared for her in illness reveals to Emperor Reizei the secret that Genji is his father, not his brother. An autumn storm destroys the carefully planned garden at Genji's mansion and in the chaos of it, Genji's acknowledged son, Yūgiri, catches a glimpse of Murasaki, and of Genji and Tamakazura in an intimate setting. Seeing his father's women opens Yūgiri's eyes, and suggests that Genji, unable to keep his women from being seen by his son, has lost a measure of control. Power is passing to the next generation.

Yūgiri marries Tō no Chūjō's daughter, bringing about an alliance between Genji's and Tō no Chūjō's families. Genji's daughter by the Akashi lady (during his time of exile) is presented at court. Now 40 years old, Genji has approached the height of his worldly power. He is honored by Reizei, the present emperor and Suzaku, the former emperor, who pay him a visit of state at his mansion.

The retired Emperor Suzaku persuades Genji to marry Suzaku's third daughter (Third Princess). This makes Murasaki jealous. She fears that Genji's attraction to the higher-ranking princess will supplant his affection for Murasaki. The Third Princess, however, is a careless immature young woman. One day Tō no Chūjō's son, Kashiwagi, catches sight of her when her cat displaces a blind. His passion inflamed, he plots to seduce her and succeeds, after which the princess foolishly allows Genji to discover a love note that Kashiwagi has written her. The discovery of her unfaithfulness enrages Genji. Knowing that he has been found out, Kashiwagi torments himself with fear and self-hatred. He dies after the Third Princess gives birth to his son, Kaoru. Suppressing his rage, Genji recognizes Kaoru as his own son. As everyone in this Buddhist society understands, the karmic seeds that were laid when Genji seduced his father's concubine, Fujitsubo, reached maturity when Kashiwagi seduced Genji's wife The Third Princess. Recognizing the recklessness of her behavior, she takes vows as a nun.

Murasaki, now seriously ill, declares her own intention to take Buddhist vows and leave behind the world of the court, but a distraught Genji refuses to let her leave him. Unable to retire as a nun, Murasaki orders a thousand copies of the Lotus Sutra, to be dedicated to the salvation of all living beings. The karmic rewards of this meritorious act, hopes Murasaki, will result in a better rebirth for her. At last she dies. Crushed by his loss of her, Genji retires from court life and die as well. The story continues with the fortunes of the younger generation: Kaoru, son of the Third Princess and Kashiwagi (whom Genji recognized as his own), and Niou, Genji's grandson (born to the daughter of the Akashi lady and the emperor). Kaoru and Niou,

The Tale of Genji

being nearly the same age, are thrown together as companions, much like Genji and Tō no Chūjō once were. But the younger men are less assured and more inclined to become entangled in unfulfilling situations.

Kaoru learns of the truth of his parentage on a trip to Uji, where he stays with an old prince who urges him to take care of the prince's two young daughters. The elder one, Oigimi, rejects a belated offer from Kaoru, and his sensitive nature prohibits him from forcefully possessing her sister, Nakanokimi in the face of the younger girl's tearful protest. The romance remains unconsummated. Instead, Kaoru convinces his friend, Niou, to marry the girl. In the end, however, Niou is unable to visit her often and both sisters feel neglected. Oigimi falls ill, and her will to live ebbs away. Her younger sister, Nakanokimi, leaves to live at the capital, where she gradually entrances Kaoru, who sees in her a resemblance to her older sister. He becomes deeply interested, but Nakanokimi, who is unhappy in the capital, discourages his affection, diverting his attention to her half-sister, Ukifune, whom, she says, bears an even stronger resemblance to Oigimi. When Kaoru meets Ukifune, the resemblance indeed strikes him, but before he can remove her to Uji, Niou tricks her into sleeping with him. Ukifune, attracted by both men, becomes emotionally unstable and tries to drown herself in the Uji River. She survives, thanks to a Buddhist prelate, who rescues her, gives her a home and servants and administers lay ordination. Karou learns of her miraculous survival, then courts her to be his wife. As the tale ends, Ukifune is debating whether to or not to marry him, and Kaoru is wondering how to win her affection.

Poetic exchanges in *The Tale of Genji*. In *The Tale of Genji* poetry is most commonly associated with love and sexual attraction. The novel equates the skilled poet to the ardent lover. In prose and speech, Japanese society called for honorific language. But poetry did not call for these formalities. It cast aside social conventions of language that created barriers between people, serving as a vehicle for intimacy between lovers and people of different social backgrounds.

About three-quarters of the poems in *The Tale of Genji* are sets of exchanges between intimates. A first poem sets the theme and the vocabulary of the exchange. The reply, using portions of this vocabulary, either adds nuance to the theme, or switches direction entirely. Poetic dialogues are used for all manner of emotional expressions, including humor and irritation. In the chapter "Heartvine," Genji's wife, Aoi, has fallen ill, and Genji is constantly by her side. He steals a moment to visit the Lady Rokujō, who is petulant at having been neglected. Genji passes a tense night with this lady friend, and when she sees him off in the morning, realizing that she is losing the battle for his heart, she sinks into sadness. Later that day a letter from Genji explains that his wife has taken a turn for the worse and that he cannot leave her side. Lady Rokujō's answer contains a poem:

> I go down the way of love and dampen my sleeves
> And go yet further, into the muddy fields.
> (Murasaki Shikibu, *The Tale of Genji*, p. 159)

She then comments, "A pity the well is so shallow" a reference to a poem from the collection *Kokin Rokujō*—"A pity the mountain well should be so shallow. / I seek to take water and only wet my sleeve." (Also called *Kokin Waka Rokujō*, this tenth-century collection is the oldest existing anthology of waka poetry arranged by topic.) The interchange illustrates the full command noble

---

THE KOTO

Heian courtiers were expected to be proficient in playing a number of different musical instruments. The *koto*, originally a term that referred to all stringed instruments, is the instrument most commonly mentioned in *The Tale of Genji*. Then, as now, there were 13-string kotos. About six feet long and made of two lengthy pieces of oak or paulownia wood, the koto had a main body with strings and movable bridges. Of equal tension, length, and thickness, the strings are stretched over the bridges. The tuning, of course, varies with the piece played, but there are always five tones. A koto sits on the floor, and the performer kneels to play it, moving its bridges up and down to achieve the different tunings. The sound is affected not only by the player and the tune, but also by how the instrument has been made—the way the wood has been cut from the tree and the patterns carved inside the koto to improve the music it makes. In the late twentieth century, when this translation of *The Tale of Genji* was published, a few households in Japan still had a koto, and playing one remained a sign of elite, cultured status

men and women of the period were expected to have over Japanese poetry. To engage in this type of love banter, they had to know classic verses well. Lady Rokujō can safely assume Genji will remember the poem referred to and will understand she is complaining of her lack of satisfaction from him. Through this reference to a traditional verse, her communiqué becomes a powerful, if oblique, criticism of his behavior toward her and her disappointment in it.

Genji receives the letter and first appreciates the beautiful handwriting, the best he has ever seen. He feels disappointed that of all the women he has known, there are none that he wants to give himself to completely; there is always some sense of dissatisfaction. His answer questions her reference to the old poem:

> You only wet your sleeves—what can this mean? That your feelings are not of the deepest, I should think. [Genji continues:]
> You only dip into the shallow waters,
> And I quite disappear into the slough?
> Do you think I would answer by letter and not in person if she were merely indisposed?
> (Tale of Genji, p. 159-60)

The interchange demonstrates how even less happy emotions of sexual frustration and pique were conveyed using subtle poetic references to deliver an impact greater than the direct expression of these trying emotions. Both characters lean on the older poem to express their dissatisfaction, extending its meaning to accommodate their real, present-day emotions. Their mutual frustration sparks and crackles in the poetic exchange. Neither has given an inch in the argument, and one gets the impression of the enormous emotional strength and power of Lady Rokujō. A worthy foil for Genji, she is unwilling to passively accept his excuses without revealing her own disappointment in him.

Sources and literary context. *The Tale of Genji* is a monogatari or "narrative fiction," a genre of prose writing that flourished from the ninth to the fourteenth centuries in Japan. The genre took various forms—long romances, short anecdotes, and historical accounts—but the method stayed constant. It entailed embedding a series of poems in a narrative form, after the precedent set by the Kokinshū, with each poem introduced by a short explanation of the circumstances of its composition. The individual poems were not meant to stand by themselves; context was provided by prose that linked one poem to others in the collection. Narrative prose tales such as *The Tale of Genji* arose from this practice of explaining the context of a poem. When Murasaki Shikibu wishes to advance the plot, she uses straightforward prose, but at important moments of emotional experience and realization, poetry dominates and time seems to stop as the characters express their deep feelings. The novel clearly regards poetry as the favored art and narrative fiction as secondary.

IN DEFENSE OF FICTION

In Murasaki's time the genre of narrative fiction was considered inferior to poetic composition. The very fact that we do not know Murasaki Shikibu's real name may be attributed to the genre's lack of prestige. She undoubtedly would have preferred to be thought of as a poetess, rather than as a novelist. Yet the novel itself defends the value of fiction. Finding Tamakazura surrounded by books of romance tales in her room one muggy rainy day, Genji laughs at her, scolding her gently for being so easily fooled by such fictions, exclaiming that there is not one word of truth in them. Tamakazura's response is that if one is accustomed to lying, then these tales must seem like lies, but to the honest person, they simply tell the truth. This comment seems to give Genji pause. He goes on to defend the fiction he has just criticized, arguing that histories such as the *Chronicles of Japan* only give one side of the picture. Fictional works, though they do not record the details of specific people, relate the author's experience of all things good and bad, evoking emotion (*mono no aware*) realistically and charitably, for the benefit of others. One is exposed to the pathos of life through stories, which is itself an expression of truth.

In the early development of narrative fiction, tales about poems were assembled into collections called *uta monogatari*. The earliest example is the *Ise monogatari*, written in the early tenth century. Around the same period, longer compositions with fully developed narratives also appeared. Among these longer compositions, known as *tsukuri monogatari* (courtly romances), are a few early tenth-century romances. Two of the best-known examples are Taketori monogatari (Tale of the Bamboo Cutter) and Utsubo monogatari (Tale of the Hollow Tree). *The Tale of Genji* is written in this tradition; with the writing of this romance, the development of this genre is believed to have peaked.

The Tale of Genji

Composition and reception. Even as it was being written, Murasaki Shikibu lost control of *The Tale of Genji*. It passed into the hands of others, and she worried that the unedited original would ruin her reputation. Since there was no printing at this time, all books were copied by hand, a task involving many people. The practice of hand-copying manuscripts was regarded as a means of improving one's skills in calligraphy. As a rule, highly regarded Waka poetry collections were copied faithfully, but copyists of monogatari would have felt less compunction about varying the content, since it was not considered to be serious literature. Readers often had separate chapters in their possession, but it was rare to have a single, complete copy of the book. The chapters circulated as Murasaki Shikibu wrote them; one person commonly read them to a crowd so that everyone could enjoy the story. The audience avidly consumed whatever section was available to read or hear. A passage in the *Sarashina Diaries* written about 50 years after Murasaki Shikibu's death shows the great value attached to *The Tale of Genji*. A young woman who longed to read it at last received a rare 50-volume set of the whole tale from her aunt. Her joy suggests how much she treasured the work: "Before I had been able to read only bits and pieces, and didn't really know how the story went. Now I had the whole Genji to read from the very first volume. When I lay down alone behind my screens and took it out to read, I would not have changed places even with the empress" (Bowring, p. 83).

By the twelfth century *The Tale of Genji* had attracted scholars. Fujiwara Shunzei (1114-1204) and his son Teika (1162-1241) worked to produce an authoritative text (the "Blue Covers" version). In 1255 a rival authority, Minamoto Mitsuyuki (1163-1244) produced his own text (the "Kawachi" version), which predominated for the next century and a half. It was not until the fifteenth century that Fujiwara Teika's version was recognized as superior, and most modern translations are based on it. The ongoing perception of fiction writing as an immoral occupation hindered universal applause, though. By the twelfth century, stories circulated that Murasaki Shikibu was suffering in hell for writing *The Tale of Genji*. The twelfth-century work *A Sutra for Genji* (1168) suggested that her novel misled the young. This work claimed that Murasaki appeared to someone in a dream to say that she had been cast into hell for creating such lies. She begged people to destroy their copies of *The Tale of Genji*, and instead make copies of the scriptures and offer them for her salvation. The suggestion was taken up in earnest. Services were held for Murasaki Shikibu's salvation in which writers copied out the 28 chapters of the Lotus Sutra, adding a chapter title from *The Tale of Genji* to each chapter heading from the scripture.

The critical mindset continued. In the thirteenth century, Murasaki Shikibu appears as a character in a type of Japanese play (the Noh play), begging people to write a poem in praise of Amida Buddha on each scroll of the novel so that she might be saved. But regard for the work as a great achievement continued as well. Like their twelfth-century predecessors, thirteenth-century scholars viewed *The Tale of Genji* as an important Japanese text. Some went so far as to call it a religious work, one that illustrated the Buddhist truths of impermanence and suffering for one's actions. As the centuries rolled on and fiction grew legitimate, the work sustained an avid readership. Today it is regarded as one of the world's earliest and foremost novels.

Both time specific and universal, *The Tale of Genji* continues to provide a window into court life in the Heian period in Japan and insight into the workings of human nature, especially that of the male gender. The novel's enduring appeal is evident in the enthusiasm for the translation by Edward Seidensticker, which has itself endured. Reviewers tended to compare Seidensticker's with another translation by Arthur Waley, the standard text for some 50 years. A critic for New York Review of Books found Seidensticker's translation pleasing in one way, wanting in another. "There are many amusing episodes in Seidensticker which are missing from Waley: on the other hand, one grasps the whole more easily from Waley's discursive page (V. S. Pritchett in Samudio and Mooney, p. 955). A second reviewer waxed enthusiastic for the newer translation:

> A comparison . . . shows Seidensticker to be more direct and colloquial. . . . Notes are minimal. . . . Shinto and Buddhist terms are more adequately handled. . . . This translation is unlikely to be matched for another century.
> (D. J. Pearce in Samudio and Mooney, p. 955)

—Diane Riggs

For More Information

Bargen, Doris G. *A Woman's Weapon: Spirit Possession in* The Tale of Genji. Honolulu: University of Hawaii, 1997.

Bowring, Richard. *The Tale of Genji*. ed. J. P. Stern. Cambridge: Cambridge University Press, 1988.

Field, Norma. *The Splendor of Longing* in The Tale of Genji. Princeton: Princeton University Press, 1987.

Konishi Jin'ichi. *A History of Japanese Literature*. Trans. Aileen Gatten and Mark Harbison. 3 vols. Princeton: Princeton University Press, 1991.

Malm, William P. *Japanese Music and Musical Instruments*. Rutland: Charles E. Tuttle, 2000.

Morris, Ivan. *The World of the Shining Prince*. New York: Kondansha, 1994.

Murasaki Shikibu. *Tale of Genji*. Trans. and abr. Edward G. Seidensticker, New York: Vintage, 1985.

———. *The Diary of Lady Murasaki*. Trans. Richard Bowring. London: Penguin, 1996.

Puette, William J. *The Tale of Genji: A Readers Guide*. Tokyo: Charles E. Tuttle, 1983.

Samudio, Josephine, and Martha T. Mooney, Eds. *Book Review Digest*. Vol. 73. New York: H. W. Wilson, 1978.

Shirane, Haruo. *The Bridge of Dreams: A Poetics of The Tale of Genji*. Stanford University Press, 1987.

Tanabe, George J. Jr., and Will Jane Tanabe, Eds. *Lotus Sutra in Japanese Culture*. Honolulu: University of Hawaii Press, 1989.

To the Lighthouse

by
Virginia Woolf

Virginia Woolf was born Adeline Virginia Stephen in 1882. Her family belonged to Victorian London's upper-middle-class intellectual elite; her father, Leslie Stephen, was an important biographer and first editor of the *Dictionary of National Biography* (1882-91). Woolf's education was informal but thorough. She read voraciously in her father's extensive library, and as a young woman eagerly participated in the intellectual and social world of her brother Thoby's university friends. This circle of friends formed the core of what would come to be known as the Bloomsbury Group, a cluster of artists and thinkers who were an important influence on British cultural and political life in the first decades of the twentieth century. Woolf herself was a critic, biographer, and essayist as well as a novelist. One of Woolf's several works was *To the Lighthouse*, her fifth novel and, in the eyes of many critics, her best. The most autobiographical of her novels, it explores Woolf's relationship with her family and memorializes her parents.

Events in History at the Time the Novel Takes Place

Post-Impressionism: revolution in the visual arts. After centuries devoted to realistic depictions of the world, the visual arts took a striking turn toward the conceptual at the end of the nineteenth century. Post-Impressionist painters like Georges Seurat (1859-91), Paul Cézanne (1839-1906), Paul Gauguin (1848-1903), and Vincent Van Gogh (1853-90) created art that

THE LITERARY WORK

A novel set in the western Scottish islands of the Hebrides on two days, separated by ten years, in the early twentieth century; published in 1927.

SYNOPSIS

A group of guests gather around the Ramsay family at their summer home. Ten years later, after the terrible events of World War I, many of the same guests return, and a long-promised journey to the lighthouse is finally completed.

turned its attention away from mirroring the exterior world and focused instead on interior experience. Their work paved the way for the abstract and expressionistic art that characterizes much of the twentieth century.

Impressionism, the movement in the visual arts committed to representing shifting patterns of color and light, was in many ways the culmination of the Realist tradition in art. The Post-Impressionism movement that followed was instead devoted to the exploration of intellectual concepts and emotional, rather than objective, perception. These shifts paralleled new thinking in other disciplines, including scientific research on optic phenomena (color and light) and an increasing focus in psychology on the uniqueness of each individual's experience. The works of Gauguin and Van Gogh clearly present this

To the Lighthouse

Virginia Woolf

emphasis on subjective experience. Van Gogh's *The Starry Night* (1889), one of western culture's most famous paintings, represents a vast landscape but also a deeply personal vision. Seurat's divisionist paintings (sometimes called pointillist), exemplified by the famous work *A Sunday Afternoon on the Island of La Grande Jatte* (1884-85), spring from an intellectual approach to painting; from afar, they appear to be cohesive images of subtle color variation, but viewed up close, the pictures break down into total abstraction. As the name pointillist suggests, the paintings are constructed of thousands of tiny points of primary colors.

Cézanne, considered the founder of modernist Cubism, focused many of his experiments on simplifications of form. Although his Post-Impressionist paintings clearly depict objects in the real world, they often do so with an emphasis on geometrical shape and blocks of color, on the "underlying structure" of a scene (Spalding, p. 39). Pears become ellipsoids; apples, cubes.

Although Post-Impressionist painting was a late nineteenth-century development in France, it did not arrive in Britain until 1910, when a close friend of Virginia Woolf's, Roger Fry (1866-1934), opened an exhibit called "Manet and the Post-Impressionists" at London's Grafton Galleries. Traditionalists—viewers and critics alike—were appalled. What had happened to Realism's techniques of perspective and coloration? But Fry argued passionately for this new approach to painting, writing in the catalog for his second Post-Impressionist exhibition (staged in 1912) that "These artists do not seek to give what can, after all, be but a pale reflex of actual appearance, but to arouse the conviction of a new and definite reality. They do not seek to imitate form, but to create form; not to imitate life, but to find an equivalent for life" (Fry in Spalding, p. 39).

These were radical ideas, and the exhibitions' effects on the London art scene were profound. Moreover, such ideas clearly found their way into Woolf's *To the Lighthouse*, which was itself an experiment in form, albeit literary. The artist Lily Briscoe, like Cezanne, attempts to grasp the underlying structure of what she sees. Her painting, described in terms of blocks of shape and color, confounds most of the Ramsays' guests. Her emphasis on painting as a way to record her vision—the world as she alone sees it—reflects the more emotional side of Post-Impressionism.

The Great War. The most monumental historical fact of the years spanned by *To the Lighthouse* was the conflict now called World War I (1914-18). At the time, it was known as the Great War, and some people hoped that it would be the war to end all wars.

Beginning in the 1880s, after the unification of Germany radically changed the balance of power in Europe, a number of military alliances were formed among the European powers, both major and minor. Germany, wishing to limit France's power, established alliances with Austria and, a bit later, Italy. France, in turn, established alliances with Russia and Great Britain. Although ostensibly designed to protect the countries involved from conflicts, this system of alliances actually created a situation in which all of the major powers would quickly become drawn into what might otherwise be a localized conflict. On June 28, 1914, the Archduke Francis Ferdinand, heir to the throne of Austria, was assassinated by a Serbian nationalist. Motivated by a number of internal concerns, the Austrian government issued an ultimatum to Serbia that was intended to provoke a small, local conflict. But Russia concluded that an Austrian takeover of Serbia was unacceptable and stepped in to defend Serbia. The alliance system then compelled one major power after another to enter the conflict. By August, troops all over Europe were marching off to war. Most believed the conflict would be over before Christmas.

They could not have been more wrong. The Great War was characterized by technology that had outpaced strategy, which led to the horrors of trench warfare. Soldiers spent weeks at a time living in fortified trenches dug into the earth, battling filth, vermin, and disease along with the enemy soldiers who would fire upon them from their fortified trenches a few hundred yards away. When the troops on either side did attempt a charge (a strategy held over from earlier forms of combat), they were mowed down by gunfire from the machine guns. A single "battle" could last for months, with casualties in the hundreds of thousands. By the end of the war, 12 million were dead and millions more had been injured or maimed.

Machine guns, tanks, submarines, fighter planes, and poison gas all became part of the military arsenal during the Great War, as did the concept of attacks on civilian cities from the air. Although the actual civilian casualties were relatively few, Germany did send Zeppelin raids to drop bombs on seaside towns in Britain. In a more old-fashioned approach, the Allies (France, Britain and Russia) starved Germany's population with an effective naval blockade that blocked incoming shipments of food and supplies. On both sides, government propaganda machines—also a new development—encouraged soldiers and civilians alike to do their part. For these reasons, World War I is often identified as the first "total" war.

In addition to the human casualties and economic disruptions created by the war, its psychological toll on Europe was enormous. A society that had conceived of itself as progressing steadily toward ever-higher forms of civilization found this confidence, in the phrasing of the time, blown to smithereens. Many Britons had enlisted to fight with the belief that they were setting out on a glorious adventure in the honorable defense of good against evil, but they often came home (if they came home at all) traumatized and disillusioned. Returning soldiers found that their experience of the war divided them from those who stayed home, and an entire literature of bitterness and alienation soon appeared. *To the Lighthouse*'s second section, "Time Passes," participates in this assessment of the war—which it never mentions by name—by describing its power to fragment and break: glass shatters, young men die, the contemplative life becomes impossible. It is an impersonal description, except for its bracketed remark about one of the Ramsay sons: "[A shell exploded. Twenty or thirty young men were blown up in France, among them Andrew Ramsay, whose death, mercifully, was instantaneous]" (*To the Lighthouse*, p. 133).

The Novel in Focus

The plot. *To the Lighthouse* consists largely of interior experience punctuated by exterior happenings. The first and longest section of the work, "The Window," occurs in one evening, a seemingly ordinary night in which the Ramsays and their guests engage in their own pursuits and then gather at the dinner table. The novel opens

---

"THE CHARGE OF THE LIGHT BRIGADE"

"Someone had blundered!" Mr. Ramsay bellows, quoting Alfred Tennyson's "The Charge of the Light Brigade" (1854) and thereby bringing into *To the Lighthouse* a variety of Victorian issues (*To the Lighthouse*, p. 25). Tennyson wrote the poem after reading a newspaper account of a tragically mishandled battle in the Crimean War (1854-56). Upon confused orders, a brigade of lightly armed British cavalry attempted to charge across open terrain that was defended by well-entrenched Russian heavy artillery. Only one quarter of the six hundred men survived. Tennyson's poem valorizes the heroism of the "Noble six hundred" who made the charge, asking rhetorically, "When can their glory fade?" ("The Charge of the Light Brigade," lines 55, 50). It also gives us the now well-worn phrase, "Theirs not to reason why / Theirs but to do and die" in a context that clearly praises their single-minded commitment to duty ("The Charge of the Light Brigade," lines 14-15).

Identifying with the poem, Mr. Ramsay sees himself as "the leader of a doomed expedition" in his quest to achieve the next stage of his intellectual achievement (*To the Lighthouse*, p. 36). The suggestion—made by both Mr. Ramsay himself and his friend Mr. Bankes—that his wife and family have held him back professionally betrays a tendency in Mr. Ramsay to look for external reasons for his defeat: someone (else) had blundered in his case, much as in Tennyson's poem.

The novel's allusion to this poem also reminds us of the Victorian idealization of honor and duty, values that would be questioned in the twentieth century, especially after World War I. In fact, in its grim specifics—virtually helpless men sent out to be mowed down by well-placed and well-armed opponents—the charge of the light brigade foreshadows some of the worst horrors of that coming war.

To the Lighthouse

with Mrs. Ramsay's assurance to her youngest child, James, that if the weather is fine the next day there will be a trip to the lighthouse. Her words create "an extraordinary joy" in James, but this is immediately crushed and turned to anger by Mr. Ramsay's statement that "it won't be fine" (Woolf, *To the Lighthouse*, pp. 3, 4). While thinking sympathetically about the way the lighthouse keeper lives, Mrs. Ramsay tries to stop James's spirits from falling, but one of the house's visitors, Charles Tansley, also discourages the boy. This leads Mrs. Ramsay to think about Charles Tansley, the poor graduate student mocked by her children. She recalls a trip into town the other day and her conversation with him along the way. At this juncture, the novel shifts perspective (a common device in Woolf's writing) to Charles Tansley's thoughts on the walk into town.

Still reassuring James, Mrs. Ramsay notices that her philosopher husband and Charles Tansley have stopped talking and that Mr. Ramsay is now loudly reciting poetry. Only Lily Briscoe, the visiting artist, has overheard him, Mrs. Ramsay concludes with relief, not wanting her husband to embarrass himself. At this point, she remembers she is supposed to keep still for the portrait that Lily is painting.

The novel now shifts to Lily's point of view, and her alarm at Mr. Ramsay's charging toward her. Lily generally dislikes it when people look at her painting. She makes an exception for William Bankes, an old friend of Mr. Ramsay's. Discomfitted by Mr. Ramsay glaring at them without seeming to see them, Lily and Mr. Bankes decide to walk down to view the bay. Mr. Bankes remembers the moment Mr. Ramsay's life diverged from his: walking down a road, Mr. Ramsay interrupted his intellectual solitude to comment on a pretty hen with a brood of chicks—and soon after he himself got married, which Mr. Bankes never did. He thinks about the Ramsay household and finances, the characteristics of the Ramsay children, what they give to their father, and what they have destroyed in and for him. Lily reminds him to consider Mr. Ramsay's work, and his thoughts circle back to Ramsay's early achievements in philosophy while Lily pictures in her mind the wooden kitchen table that functions as her visual image for Mr. Ramsay's abstract work on the nature of reality. Comparing the two men, Lily wonders how we determine liking and disliking for people. Suddenly she and Mr. Banks are interrupted by a flock of starlings, and Mr. Ramsay, still quoting poetry.

The novel returns to Mrs. Ramsay, who while using James to measure a stocking she is knitting for the lighthouse keeper's boy, sees William Bankes and Lily Briscoe together and decides that they should marry. Mr. Ramsay continues to insist to his wife that there is no chance of going to the lighthouse the following day and is enraged at his wife's attempts to blunt these remarks for their son. Soon embarrassed at his own anger, he takes a more conciliatory attitude toward his wife and strides off again, pondering his

---

"THE FISHERMAN AND HIS WIFE"

The fairy tale Mrs. Ramsay reads to James, "The Fisherman and His Wife," was first translated into English by Margaret Hunt in the 1884 collection *Grimm's Household Tales*. Woolf's quotations hold closely to this text and so are rooted firmly in Victorian literary culture. "The Fisherman and His Wife" is the story of a man who catches a magical flounder but then returns it to the sea when it tells him that it is actually an enchanted prince. The fisherman's wife, certain that the magical fish will grant a wish to the man who caught him and let him go, sends her husband back to the ocean to call the fish and wish for a nice cottage to replace their hovel. The fish does indeed grant the wish, and the fisherman believes they can now live very happily, but his wife is not satisfied. She sends the fisherman back to the flounder over and over again, wishing always for something better or grander: a castle instead of a cottage, to be king rather than a fisherman's wife, to be emperor rather than king, then to be the Pope, and finally to be Lord of the Universe. The flounder grants each wish until the last, when he returns the couple to their original status and lowly home.

While the obvious moral of this tale is that power and greed corrupt (a common message in folktales), there is also a decidedly subversive element in the wife's dissatisfaction with her level of wealth and power. The fact that she demands to be king rather than queen, and then eventually Pope (a position held by a man for which there is no female equivalent) is a radical demand for opportunity and status outside of the role of "wife." Thus, although Mrs. Ramsay is acting as the consummate wife and mother throughout these scenes in the novel, she is also voicing a contrary idea, that women might wish for more than this. The fact that in the story such wishes lead to disappointment is a reminder of the limited opportunities for nineteenth-century women.

achievements. Mr. Ramsay worries about his ability to proceed further intellectually and wonders if he will achieve long-lasting fame. He returns to his wife for sympathy, distracting her from the fairy tale she is reading to James.

Lily Briscoe and Mr. Bankes continue to discuss Mr. Ramsay's character. While they do, Lily realizes that being with the Ramsays changes her perception of life: "life, from being made up of little separate incidents which one lived one by one, became curled and whole like a wave which bore one up with it and threw one down it, there, with a dash on the beach" (*To the Lighthouse*, p. 47). Lily is overwhelmed by the love the Ramsays share and by Mr. Bankes's adoration of Mrs. Ramsay. When Lily turns to her painting, though, she is crushed by a sense of her own failure. She tries instead to understand Mrs. Ramsay's allure, which stems in part from her beauty but also from a secret wisdom. Mr. Bankes interrupts Lily's thoughts by asking what the purple triangle in her painting means. Lily tells him that it is Mrs. Ramsay and James, and that she is trying to capture them with shadow and light. Mr. Bankes's own favorite painting is a traditional landscape of trees by a river. As they end their discussion, Lily takes her canvas off the easel, while Cam, one of Mrs. Ramsay's daughters, runs by on the lawn.

Mrs. Ramsay sends Cam to inquire whether Minta Doyle and Paul Rayley have returned from a walk. Hoping that the two have become engaged, Mrs. Ramsay wonders if she has indirectly pressured Minta to marry. The story of "The Fisherman and His Wife" concluded, Mrs. Ramsay closes the book, and James is carried off to bed. Now Mrs. Ramsay, alone with her knitting, folds into herself: "All the being and the doing, expansive, glittering, vocal, evaporated; and one shrunk, with a sense of solemnity, to being oneself, a wedge-shaped core of darkness" (*To the Lighthouse*, p. 62). She watches the beams of the lighthouse until she becomes overfilled with delight. At that moment, Mr. Ramsay sees her and wants to interrupt her, but he waits for her to come to him. Mrs. Ramsay, sensing what her husband wishes, gets up and takes his arm.

Mr. and Mrs. Ramsay stroll and converse; it is about seven o'clock in the evening. They pass Lily Briscoe and Mr. Bankes, also out walking. For a moment, Mr. and Mrs. Ramsay appear to Lily as a symbol of marriage, while they stand still and watch their children, Prue and Jasper, play catch. Then the scene dissolves, Mr. Ramsay goes to his study, and Mrs. Ramsay asks her daughter Prue whether Nancy Ramsay accompanied Paul and Minta on their walk.

The point of view shifts to Nancy, who is indeed with Paul and Minta, as well as Andrew Ramsay, on a cliff walk. Paul and Minta are discovered in each other's arms—they have agreed to marry. But Minta loses her brooch on the beach and cries for her loss. After searching as much as they can, the four arrive just before the dinner of Beouf en Daube (beef stew). At the start of the meal, Mrs. Ramsay feels the burden of ensuring that her guests come together: "Nothing seemed to have merged. They all sat separate. And the whole of the effort of merging and flowing and creating rested on her" (*To the Lighthouse*, p. 83). Eventually, however, after the candles are lit, "some change at once went through them all . . . and they were all conscious of making a party together in a hollow, on an island" (*To the Lighthouse*, p. 97). Eventually, "everything felt just right" (*To the Lighthouse*, p. 104). When the dinner party concludes, Mrs. Ramsay feels satisfied:

> They [her guests] would, she thought, . . . however long they lived, come back to this night; this moon; this wind; this house: and to her too. It flattered her, where she was most susceptible of flattery, to think how, wound about in their hearts, however long they lived she would be woven.
> (*To the Lighthouse*, p. 113)

Mrs. Ramsay then goes to check on James and Cam, who should be sleeping. At almost 11:00 in the evening, the two children are squabbling over a pig skull on the wall. Cam is upset by its presence; James wants it in the room. Mrs. Ramsay softens the skull's presence for Cam by winding her own shawl around it, while she reassures James that the skull still remains. James asks his mother whether they will in fact go to the lighthouse the following day. Mrs. Ramsay tells him that the journey will not occur the next day, but on the first day the weather is good.

Mrs. Ramsay returns to knitting her stocking and reads poetry, in the same room where her husband leafs through Sir Walter Scott's *The Antiquary* (1816). Putting down her book, Mrs. Ramsay tells her husband that Paul and Minta are engaged. Mr. Ramsay, after informing his wife that she will not finish the stocking that evening, wants her to tell him that she loves him, but she cannot. Instead, she confirms his earlier statement: that they won't be able to go to the lighthouse. And in doing so, she lets him know she loves him.

The second section of the novel, "Time Passes," is the shortest part of the book, yet it covers a decade. The main characters here are time and nature, which wreak havoc on the Ramsays's summer house. Text in brackets reveals what happens over the course of many years to the people who gathered there: Mrs. Ramsay dies suddenly in her sleep; her daughter Prue Ramsay dies as a result of childbirth; her son Andrew Ramsay is killed in France during World War I. The house is about go to wrack and ruin, when two old charwomen are requested to put things in order once again. One September evening, Lily Briscoe returns to the house.

The final section of the novel, "The Lighthouse," takes place the morning after Lily Briscoe's return. Mr. Ramsay, James, and Cam, are finally going to take their trip to the lighthouse. Lily Briscoe will paint what she did not finish ten years before. As Lily stands before her easel, Mr. Ramsay approaches, desiring sympathy that Lily feels unable to give. Unable to say what Mr. Ramsay wants her to, Lily despairs, but she unwittingly strikes upon the perfect topic when she praises Mr. Ramsay's boots. The subject leads him to a brief sermon on boots and bootmakers, and he shows Lily how to tie the perfect knot. When he stoops over her shoe, Lily feels the sympathy she could not feel before. Mr. Ramsay then departs with Cam and James, who accompany their father sullenly across the lawn.

Lily Briscoe begins her painting, and as she does, she is assailed by the old doubt: that she cannot paint. She recalls Charles Tansley saying that "women can't paint, can't write" and then recalls a happier moment when she and Charles had skipped stones together, in Mrs. Ramsay's presence (*To the Lighthouse*, p. 159). Mrs. Ramsay, Lily thinks, gave Lily "this moment of friendship and liking," which has survived for all these years, "almost like a work of art" (*To the Lighthouse*, p. 160). Lily ponders the meaning of life, and then understands:

> The great revelation never did come. Instead there were little daily miracles, illuminations, matches struck unexpectedly in the dark: here was one. This, that, and the other; herself and Charles Tansley and the breaking wave; Mrs. Ramsay bringing them together; Mrs. Ramsay saying, "Life stand still here": Mrs. Ramsay making of the moment something permanent (as in another sphere Lily herself tried to make of the moment something permanent)—this was of the nature of a revelation. In the midst of chaos there was shape; this eternal passing and flowing (she looked at the clouds going and the leaves shaking) was struck into stability. Life stand still here, Mrs. Ramsay said. "Mrs. Ramsay! Mrs. Ramsay!" she repeated. She owed it all to her.
> (*To the Lighthouse*, p. 161)

Meanwhile, Mr. Ramsay, Cam, and James are sailing in a boat with a fisherman and his son. Cam and James, feeling united by their opposition to their father's tyranny, sit in silence, speaking only when they must.

On shore, Lily Briscoe considers what she has heard of Paul Rayley and Minta Doyle's failed marriage. Paul Rayley still appears to Lily as the exemplar of youth in love. Lily herself is glad she has never married, even though she loves William Bankes. Once more she thinks about Mrs. Ramsay, then cries, and calls her name aloud.

On the boat, halfway across the bay, Mr. Ramsay is reading a book. James imagines killing his father—so much does his father on occasion seem fierce and predatory. The boy vaguely remembers a long-ago scene, when his father announced that it would rain, and he would not be able to go to the lighthouse, when his mother's attention wandered from son to father. Cam creates an adventure story for herself and reflects on her father—deciding he is not so tyrannical after all. Mr. Ramsay finishes his book and parcels out lunch. He finally compliments James on his steering of the boat, giving James the praise he so desperately wants. Then Mr. Ramsay leaps from the boat to the lighthouse rock.

Lily Briscoe exclaims that Mr. Ramsay has landed. She turns to her canvas and paints her final line. The journey to the lighthouse is complete and the painting is finished.

Angel in the house vs. artist: women's roles in the early twentieth century. Mrs. Ramsay is the consummate matchmaker and supporter of the traditional wifely role. She encourages Paul Rayley and Minta Doyle to marry and envisions Lily Briscoe as William Bankes's wife. Her daughters find Mrs. Ramsay a formidable influence; only rarely can they "sport with infidel ideas which they had brewed for themselves of a life different from hers; in Paris, perhaps: a wilder life; not always taking care of some man or other" (*To the Lighthouse*, pp. 6-7). To Lily Briscoe, Mrs. Ramsay touts the married life as the only life worth having.

In her roles as wife and mother, Mrs. Ramsay is everything demanded by the Victorian ideal of the "angel in the house," the title of a well-known Victorian poem by Coventry Patmore. Mrs. Ramsay provides not only love and comfort to her husband, their eight children, and countless family friends, she is also responsible for the house-

Lighthouse on Hebrides Island, the setting of *To the Lighthouse*.

hold's harmony. She protects her children from too much knowledge (she hides the pig skull with her own shawl), her husband from money worries (she does not discuss the fifty pounds the greenhouse repairs will cost). The novel characterizes Mrs. Ramsay as a source of energy, but in providing energy to others, she depletes her own: "there was scarcely a shell of herself left for her to know herself by" (*To the Lighthouse*, p. 38). Thus, after Mrs. Ramsay has comforted her husband (a regular occurrence), she is worn out: "the whole fabric fell in exhaustion upon itself" (*To the Lighthouse*, p. 38).

Lily Briscoe, in choosing to paint Mrs. Ramsay with James, venerates mother and child. But Lily herself has chosen a different life, the solitary life of the artist, a life devoted to art rather than to a husband. And though Charles Tansley whispers that "Women can't paint, women can't write," Lily Briscoe perseveres, "clasp[ing] some miserable remnant of her vision to her breast, which a thousand forces did their best to pluck from her" (*To the Lighthouse*, pp. 48, 19).

The beginning of the twentieth century saw some women turn against the institution of marriage in favor of relationships without official sanction. A small minority praised free love and had children outside marriage; some had relationships with other women; some devoted themselves to work or causes. Writing at the end of the nineteenth century, the critic Walter Besant comments on the transformation in middle-class women's roles during the reign of Queen Victoria (1837-1901). Contemporary women, he states, have "invaded the professions"; furthermore, "necessity or no necessity they demand work, with independence and personal liberty. Whether they will take upon them the duties and responsibilities of marriage, they postpone for further consideration" (Besant, p. 1738-39). By 1911, a fifth of employers and managers were women, while they occupied a third of highly skilled white-collar jobs (e.g., teachers) and two-thirds of other professional positions (e.g., clerks).

By far, however, the greatest number of women were engaged in domestic service. The expanding middle class hired all sorts of servants, both in and out of the house, until, by 1911, there were more than 2 million servants (Perkins, p. 79). The solidly middle-class Ramsays employ at least a cook, a gardener, and a nursemaid. Passing mention is made of Mrs. McNab and Mrs. Bast, who, with their cleaning and scrubbing, rescue the summer house from certain ruin. Mostly this female labor, relatively inexpensive, remains unseen in the novel.

At the end of *To the Lighthouse*, Lily Briscoe remains happy that she has escaped Mrs. Ramsay's "mania . . . for marriage" (*To the Lighthouse*, p. 175). The marriage of Paul and Minta, which Mrs. Ramsay had set her heart on, became something of which Mrs. Ramsay would never have approved. Paul and Minta quarreled; Paul frequented coffee houses; Paul took up with another woman. Paul's infidelity, far from dooming this modern marriage, saved it, as the two reached an accommodation with each other and became "excellent friends" (*To the Lighthouse*, p. 174). The fate of Mrs. Ramsay herself illustrates some of the dangers for the Victorian woman. Unexpectedly, she dies midway through the novel. Why? We do not know. All we are told is that "[Mr. Ramsay, stumbling along a passage one dark morning, stretched his arms out, but Mrs. Ramsay having died rather suddenly the night before, his arms, though stretched out, remained empty]" (*To the Lighthouse*, p. 128). Mrs. Ramsay is no longer there to comfort her husband. Virginia Woolf's own mother, who provided the model for Mrs. Ramsay, also died unexpectedly, just shy of 50 years old. As Woolf's nephew writes of Julia Duckworth Stephen, "Everyone who wanted help turned to her knowing it would not be denied" (Bell, p. 38). Her greatest commitment was to her husband: "everyone needed her but he needed her most. With his temperament and his necessities this was too great a task for even the most heroic of wives" (Bell, p. 38). In the end, all the soothing and calming claimed her life.

In 1929, Virginia Woolf would write **A Room of One's Own** (also in *Literature and Its Times*), an essay that discusses the difficulty of being a female writer in a male-dominated world. Mrs. Ramsay, with her eight children and childlike husband, has neither the space, time, nor inclination to be an artist, though she does have an artist's delight in form and harmony. As she presides over the dinner table, she hopes no one will take a piece of fruit, and thus disturb the still-life perfection of the fruit bowl:

> Her eyes had been going in and out among the curves and shadows of the fruit, among the rich purples of the lowland grapes, then over the horny ridge of the shell, putting a yellow against a purple, a curved shape against a round shape, without knowing why she did it, or why, every time she did it, she felt more and more serene.
> (*To the Lighthouse*, pp. 108-09)

Lily Briscoe, though she has the time and the desire to paint, must constantly guard against her own feelings of inferiority, against voices from within and without that tell her she is a failure. Virginia Woolf, acclaimed writer that she was, reacted strongly to the criticism of others, and was intensely self-critical. Subject to bouts of mental illness throughout her life, she committed suicide in 1941 (during the darkest days of World War II), afraid of a Nazi German victory against Britain and of her own inability to withstand her illness and sustain her career as a writer.

Sources and literary context. *To the Lighthouse* is Virginia Woolf's most autobiographical novel. Her father, Leslie Stephen (1832-1904), was a Victorian intellectual, who, in 1882, the same year as Virginia Woolf's birth, took on the editorship of the *Dictionary of National Biography*. This compendium of significant national figures occupied Stephen for a decade, becoming a source of ill health for him and thus oppressing his family as well. In the ruminating Mr. Ramsay, Woolf attempts to capture her father's personality, using the letters of the dictionary to represent Mr. Ramsay's philosophical striving:

> It was a splendid mind. For if thought is like the keyboard of a piano, divided into so many notes, or like the alphabet is ranged in twenty-six letters all in order, then his splendid mind had no sort of difficulty in running over those letters one by one, firmly and accurately, until it had reached, say, the letter Q. . . . But after Q? What comes next? . . . if he could reach R it would be something.
> (*To the Lighthouse*, p. 34)

Virginia Woolf's mother, Julia Duckworth Stephen (1846-95), was the center of the family, and gave the character of Mrs. Ramsay her beauty and solicitude. Quentin Bell, in his biography of Virginia Woolf, claims that Woolf portrayed her mother as Mrs. Ramsay with more accuracy than even Leslie Stephen himself managed to do:

> Mrs. Ramsay in *To the Lighthouse*, although she is drawn only from a child's memories, seems to me more real and more convincing than Leslie's portrait. All the loveliness, the tenderness is there; but Mrs. Ramsay is not perfect . . . Mrs. Ramsay's relationship with her husband is capable of mockery. She is, as Leslie himself noticed, a matchmaker, but, as he did not notice, not always a wise one; there is a trace of self-assurance, a little blindness in her management of other people's affairs. In short Virginia's portrait of her mother is more human, more fallible, perhaps more likeable than that painted by Leslie.
> (Bell, p. 18)

The Stephen family spent summers at Talland House, in the southern English town of St. Ives, Cornwall. Undoubtedly, Woolf drew upon these vacations when writing *To the Lighthouse*. Talland House was always full of relatives and friends. A trip to the lighthouse occurred in 1892. All in all, Bell claims that the time spent at St. Ives was a touchstone for Woolf, a paradisal interlude to be visited in the imagination. In considering the place of *To the Lighthouse*, literary history is as significant as personal history. Virginia Woolf continued her experimentation with literary form in this novel, emphasizing the complexity of internal reality over external events. The movement of the mind in thoughts, emotions, and dreams, takes precedence over dramatic action. The technique for representing the currents of the mind, called "stream of consciousness," was also used by some of Woolf's most famous contemporaries, like James Joyce (1882-1941), as they worked to shape a fiction that would reflect the new verities of twentieth-century life.

Events in History at the Time the Novel Was Written

The Bloomsbury Group. This prominent group of artists and intellectuals influenced British society, publishing, and art. Centered in the heretofore unstylish Bloomsbury district of London, the origins of this clique may be dated to the year 1904, when Virginia Woolf (then Virginia Stephen) and her three siblings moved to the area. Around them clustered her brother Thoby's Cambridge friends, including future biographer Lytton Strachey (1880-1932), and Leonard Woolf (1880-1969), who married Virginia in 1912. Other luminaries who joined this circle were writer E. M. Forster (1879-1970), art critic Roger Fry (1866-1934), and painters Clive Bell (1881-1964) and Duncan Grant (1885-1978). (See Forster's ***Passage to India***, also in *Literature and Its Times*). Directly and indirectly they were influenced by G. E. Moore's *Principia Ethica* (1903), a philosophical text concluding that "personal affections and aesthetic enjoyments include *all* the greatest, and *by far* the greatest, goods that we can imagine" (Moore in Rosenbaum, p. 1). According to Leonard Woolf, Moore's "clarity, freshness, and common-sense," captivated the Bloomsbury members (L. Woolf in Rosenbaum, p. 104).

Bloomsbury was never an official group, so its list of members and even the dates of its existence are open to debate; arguably, though, Bloomsbury reached its peak of influence in the decade following World War I, when disaffection with contemporary society and its Victorian forerunner ran high. The tone was set by Lytton Strachey's two wry biographies: *Eminent Victorians* (1918) and *Queen Victoria* (1921). As Leonard Woolf explains, to understand Bloomsbury one must understand "the stuffy intellectual and moral suffocation which a young man felt weighing down upon him in Church and State, in the 'rules and conventions' of the last days of Victorian civilization" (L. Woolf in Rosenbaum, p. 107). The Bloomsbury Group scorned prudishness and authority, and valued irreverence and personal judgment and the ability to express one's opinions *well*. That two of its founding members were women—Virginia and Vanessa Stephen—attests to the way members were judged according as interesting individuals, rather than merely men or women.

The Bloomsbury Group was not just about talk, though conversation was very important. In 1917, Leonard and Virginia set up a small handpress in their dining room and founded Hogarth Press, which went on to publish not only Virginia Woolf's fiction but many other important modernist works, including T. S. Eliot's *Poems* (1919) and ***The Waste Land*** (1923; also in *Literature and Its Times*), Maxim Gorky's *Reminiscences of Tolstoy* (1920), and Freud's *Collected Papers* (1924), as well as short stories by E. M. Forster and Katherine Mansfield. Indeed, the Woolfs wanted to publish James Joyce's *Ulysses*, offered to them in 1918, but did not have the printing capacity to do so.

The artistic and philosophical output of the Bloomsbury Group was prodigious. Members produced paintings, biographies, essays, criticism, novels, and works on everything from psychology to economics. The last meeting of one of the group's incarnations, the Memoir Club, occurred in 1956. There is no doubt of the Bloomsbury Club's lasting effect on English intellectual life.

Reception. Virginia Woolf, as she was finishing *To the Lighthouse*, thought it was "easily the best of my books" (Woolf, *A Writer's Diary*, p. 101). Most critics have concurred, from her husband, who referred to it as a "psychological poem" and Virginia Woolf's "masterpiece," to Louis Kronenberger, writing for the *New York Times*, who praised the fuller vision and higher aims of Woolf's latest novel (Woolf, *A Writer's Diary*, p. 102; Kronenberger in Majumdar and McLaurin, p. 196). Critics usually hostile to Woolf's work demurred in this case. Even novelist Arnold Bennett (1867-1931), who disliked Virginia Woolf's writing as much as she disliked his, wrote that the novel "has stuff in it strong enough to withstand quite a lot of adverse criticism" (Arnold in Majumdar and McLaurin, p. 201).

Sensitive reviewers concurred on one point. As Rachel A. Taylor wrote, in *To the Lighthouse* "Nothing happens, and everything happens" (Taylor in Majumdar and McLaurin, p. 199). Or, as Conrad Aiken states, "The technical brilliance glows, melts, falls away; and there remains a poetic apprehension of life of extraordinary loveliness. Nothing happens, in this houseful of odd nice people, and yet all of life happens" (Aiken in Majumdar and McLaurin, p. 208). In *To the Lighthouse*, Virginia Woolf captured the psychological reality of a family and friends; she fulfilled her vision.

— Danielle E. Price and
Michelle N. McEvoy

For More Information

Arnason, H. H. *A History of Modern Art: Painting, Sculpture, Architecture, Photography*. New York: Harry N. Abrams, 1986.

Bell, Quentin. *Virginia Woolf: A Biography*. London: Triad/Paladin, 1987.

Besant, Walter. "The Queen's Reign." In *The Norton Anthology of English Literature: The Victorian Age*. Eds. M. H. Abrams and Stephen Greenblatt. New York: Norton, 2000.

Majumdar, Robin, and Allen McLaurin, eds. *Virginia Woolf: The Critical Heritage*. London: Routledge, 1975.

Perkin, Harold. *The Rise of Professional Society: England Since 1880*. London: Routledge, 1989.

Rosenbaum, S. P., Ed. *The Bloomsbury Group: A Collection of Memoirs, Commentary and Criticism*. London: Croom Helm, 1975.

Spalding, Frances. *British Art Since 1900*. London: Thames and Hudson, 1986.

Stokesbury, James L. *A Short History of World War I*. New York: William Morrow, 1981.

Tennyson, Alfred Lord. "The Charge of the Light Brigade." In *The Poems of Tennyson*. Vol. 2. Ed. Christopher Ricks. Berkeley: University of California Press, 1987.

Woolf, Virginia. *To the Lighthouse*. San Diego: Harvest, 1981.

———. *A Writer's Diary: Being Extracts from the Diary of Virginia Woolf*. Ed. Leonard Woolf. San Diego: Harvest, 1981.

The Trial

by
Franz Kafka

Franz Kafka (1883-1924) was born into a German-speaking Jewish family in Prague, capital of the province of Bohemia, which was located in the western part of the future Czechoslovakia. Bohemia was then part of the Austro-Hungarian empire. Educated in an upper-middle-class high school in which German was the principal language, Kafka obtained his law degree from Prague University in 1906. He found a job as legal advisor to a semi-public employee compensation agency, the Workers Accident Insurance Company for the Kingdom of Bohemia, where he had a successful career. Always interested in writing (much to the disappointment of his father, a practical-minded and dominating businessman), Kafka began to explore Czech and Yiddish as well as German literature. He became fascinated by the Jewish culture that his assimilated family had tended to ignore. In 1902 he befriended Max Brod, who would play an important role both in Kafka's life and in establishing his literary reputation. Declared medically unfit for military service in World War I, Kafka poured his energy into writing. He produced increasingly eccentric and ambitious narratives, including the novel-length *The Trial* and the long short stories "In the Penal Colony" and "The Transformation," usually called *Metamorphosis* in English. In 1922 Kafka started work on his novel *The Castle*, but his health, never robust, was deteriorating (he had been diagnosed with tuberculosis). He suffered frequent illnesses and nervous breakdowns. Though engaged to two different women, Kafka never married. He took

> **THE LITERARY WORK**
>
> A novel set in a unnamed city early in the twentieth century; published in German (as *Der Prozess*) in 1925, in English in 1937.
>
> **SYNOPSIS**
>
> Josef K., a young bank official, finds himself under investigation for an unknown crime by the police and judiciary. K. experiences strange and unpredictable meetings with neighbors, lawyers, and court officials before learning a distressing lesson about an individual's power in the face of the system.

increasing interest in the Zionist movement and the possibility of moving to Palestine. In Berlin in 1923 Kafka met Dora Dymant, a Jewish socialist 20 years younger than Kafka, and they planned to immigrate to Palestine together. This never happened, as Kafka became ill in April 1924 and died in Prague at the age of 40. After Kafka's death, Max Brod, disobeying his friend's final wishes, published the unfinished manuscripts of *The Trial* and *The Castle*. Kafka (in a handwritten note found among his papers) had instructed Brod to destroy the two works along with his other manuscripts. Gradually Franz Kafka's posthumous reputation increased. The dreamlike but psychologically accurate portrayal of the experiences of the hapless K., along with the portrayal of irresistible forces able to crush

The Trial

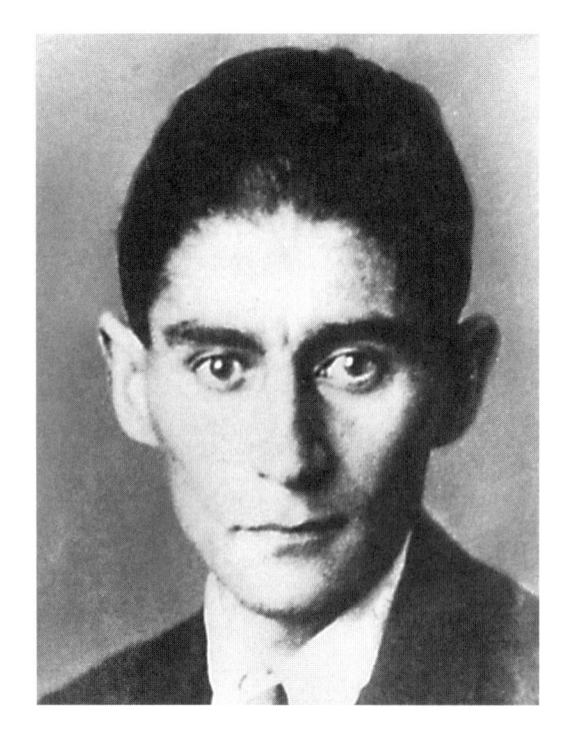

Franz Kafka

the individual human being, have made *The Trial* a classic of twentieth-century literature.

Events in History at the Time of the Novel

End of the patchwork empire. The world that Franz Kafka lived in for the first 30 years of his life offered the appearance of political stability. The Austro-Hungarian empire, ruled by the venerable Emperor Franz Josef (who had ascended the throne as an 18-year-old in 1848), was the largest political entity in Europe, not including tsarist Russia. It was a patchwork quilt of peoples, cultures, and territories stretching from the Italian Alps to the eastern Carpathian mountains in today's Ukraine. The Austrian royal family, the Habsburgs, had ruled it for 600 years. Despite the upheavals that had taken place since the middle of the nineteenth century, in particular the growth of nationalism and the rise of modern industrial society in the more advanced regions, Franz Josef was grudgingly recognized, and occasionally regarded with affection, by his Hungarian, Austrian, Polish, Czech, Slovak, Croat, and other subjects who lived within the empire's borders. From the royal seat in Vienna, the Austrian capital, the Habsburg monarchy, although deeply Catholic and Germanic in its character and traditions, governed in a pragmatic if inconsistent fashion over a large part of the population of central and eastern Europe, which included not only Roman Catholics but also Protestants, Jews, Eastern Orthodox, Moslems, and secular agnostics.

The appearance of stability was illusory, however. Half a century earlier, in 1848, there had been militant uprisings all over Europe, from Ireland to Hungary, and these had often been driven by a mixture of nationalist and social revolutionary desires. In particular, the world had been fascinated by the revolt of the Hungarian people against the ancient political structure in which they were second-class subjects, permanently under the thumb of the imperial administration in Vienna. The Hungarian uprising failed, but its leader, Lajos Kossuth, became a household name, even in the United States where he spent years in exile. The revolt led eventually, in 1867, to the creation of the Dual Monarchy, or the recognition of Hungary as a quasi-independent country under the constitutional protection of the Emperor—hence the term "Austro-Hungarian Empire."

Although many people in the latter half of the nineteenth century felt that the Habsburg Dual Monarchy was in practice one of the least authoritarian constitutional structures in Europe, this sentiment was not universal (a great number of Jews felt a complex loyalty to this asymmetric, multiethnic, multicultural entity). In Poland, Bohemia, Bosnia-Herzegovina, and elsewhere, a range of ethnically based national groups saw the empire as an oppressive system that had been imposed by the Congress of Vienna in 1815. At this Congress, the continent's various territorial sovereignties and borders had been established by the four major powers (Austria, Russia, Prussia, and Great Britain) after the wars and violent events of the previous 25 years, from the French Revolution to Napoleon Bonaparte's attempt to dominate Europe. As the historian Alan Palmer comments:

> Those who met at Vienna were acutely conscious of 'the [French] Revolution' and the Europe they conceived was conservative and repressive; they failed, however to see that another challenge . . . was developing within their own territories. For the subject nationalities 1815 had little significance, apart from confirming which particular monarchical institution was to deny them recognition.
>
> (Palmer, p. 28)

Ultimately nationalists across eastern Europe and the Balkans would challenge, again and again, the legitimacy of Austrian, Ottoman, and tsarist rule. These empires, the Habsburg Reich included, could have no future in the modern world, they said, which would be made up of independent nation-states.

The Prague Jews. The largest problem that nationalism in central and eastern Europe had to negotiate was the fact that almost no ethnic group lived alone in the area that it might reasonably claim as its national territory. Among the various ethnic groups present, there were not only multiple populations identified with specific regions (to take a major example, the mixture of Germans, Romanians, and Hungarians in Transylvania) but also peoples such as the Gypsies and the Jews. These last two groups were clearly identifiable nationalities in various parts of the region, but they did not have a geographically defined territory to which they could stake a claim. The case of Jews in the Duchy of Bohemia was especially curious.

With strong links to the Czech-speaking population since the Middle Ages, the Jewish community (concentrated in the city of Prague) had become increasingly more German in language and culture, due to the absorption of Bohemia into the Habsburg empire in the seventeenth century and the eventual removal of anti-Semitic laws throughout the Reich in the 1850s. The growth of Czech nationalism, however, had led during the second half of the nineteenth century to the revival and domination of Czech culture and language in large parts of Bohemia, including Prague.

The two exceptions to this development were the Sudetenland region in rural western Bohemia, which had a large German peasant-farmer population, and the German upper middle class of the Bohemian capital, Prague. By the turn of the century, a majority of the Prague Germans were Jews. The attitude of the Sudeten-Germans, which was to have grim consequences during and after World War II, was generally hostile to the Czechs: encouraged by the German government in Berlin, they treated the Czech people and Czech national aspirations with a mixture of fear and contempt, and they especially looked down upon the Prague Jews, whom they regarded as cosmopolitan aliens pretending to be German.

The Prague environment in which the young Kafka grew up was thus marked by three levels of isolation. First, Prague Jews were isolated nationally, as German speakers in a city that was becoming increasingly more Czech and that regarded German as the language and culture of both the disliked imperial authority in Vienna and the resentful Sudeten-German peasantry. Second, they were isolated culturally as Jews, even if they had abandoned much of the ritual and practice of their grandparents. And third, they were isolated politically because they were largely prosperous business and professional people who were cut off from other social classes.

PRAGUE

The place where the protagonist Josef K.'s fate unfolds, although not given a name in *The Trial*, is clearly Prague, the city on the Vltava River. A trading point as early as the tenth century, Prague came of age as the urban center of the Kingdom of Bohemia in the late Middle Ages. The fourteenth-century Hradcany Castle still dominates the city's skyline today. The collapse of Bohemia as an independent kingdom in the late 1520s led to Prague's decline as a political power in central Europe. Once a capital in an independent empire, it became just a city in the large Austrian and later Austro-Hungarian Empire. Not until there was a resurgence of Czech national culture during the nineteenth century would Prague begin to step back onto the European stage. Gradually it regained the aura of a prominent capital city, consolidating this image when it became the capital of a newly independent Czechoslovakia in 1918, shortly before *The Trial* was published.

The relationship to the non-Jewish Czech population was also a peculiar one for many Prague Jews of the upper middle class. Often they had Czech maids, cooks, and nannies in their childhood, but otherwise little or no connection with the majority population of the country in which they lived. This majority population, moreover, had become increasingly conscious of its own Bohemian culture and hostile to the Habsburg imperial project; in fact, after 1918, they would form an independent nation-state. Yet Prague Jews of the era lived in a peculiar "voluntary Ghetto, whose inhabitants had practically no connection with 'the street'" (Eisner, p. 26). Nevertheless, many of Prague's Jewish young boys had romantic memories of the Czech girls they had known as household servants during childhood, as reflected in the stories told by Kafka and others from this social background.

In July and August 1914 the major European alliances (France, Great Britain, and Russia on the one side; Germany and Austria-Hungary on the other side) became trapped in a series of military and foreign policy crises arising from the assassination, by a Bosnian Serb nationalist, of the Austrian Archduke Franz Ferdinand in the city of Sarajevo, in Bosnia-Herzegovina. War broke out across Europe, and over the four years of hostilities, the political map began to disintegrate. In 1917 Russian revolutionaries toppled the tsar and his government, transforming the most economically and politically primitive empire on the Eurasian land mass into the Soviet Union, the world's first communist state. Further west, the surrender of Germany and Austria-Hungary at the end of the war in 1918 was the final blow to the Habsburg Reich. The Czech leaders Tomas Masaryk and Edvard Bene had already won British, French, and American support for an independent Czechoslovakia (made up of Bohemia, Moravia, and Slovakia).

Although Franz Kafka lived through a period of vast social and political upheaval from 1914 on, there is little direct evidence of this in the shadowy, oblique vision of his fiction. In one way, the protagonist of *The Trial*, Joseph K., could be seen as a young Jewish bank official in Prague just before World War I, and his experiences an allegory for the psychological insecurity of the Jewish community in that city—people in the wrong place at the wrong time perhaps. The problem in *The Trial*, however, is not so much that one can be in the wrong place at the wrong time, but rather that everyday life seems to be the wrong place, and it always is the wrong time. Kafka's story may well be about the individual and the authorities, but it is also about the evil forces that play havoc with one's life.

The Novel in Focus

The plot. Josef K., a young but high-ranking official in a bank, is interrupted one morning by three police detectives who call at his apartment. The policemen inform him that "proceedings" have been opened against him. The three refuse to answer his questions about why he is being prosecuted and what he is supposed to have done, and they start eating the breakfast that K.'s landlady has prepared for him. They claim that they are only doing their job and have no particular explanation for what is happening. As the senior officer puts it,

> These gentlemen and I are merely marginal figures in your affair, and in fact know almost nothing about it. We could be wearing the most proper of uniforms and your case would not be a whit more serious. I can't report that you've been accused of anything, or more accurately, I don't know if you have.
> (Kafka, *The Trial*, p. 14)

The interview takes place in another apartment that the policemen have taken over, one belonging to his neighbor, a young woman called Fräulein Bürstner. Though she has already gone to work, K. is ill at ease being in her apartment with the officers.

Eventually K. is released from the questioning, and he too goes to work. Coming home that evening, he makes an attempt to talk to Fräulein Bürstner. He waits until she returns and meets her in the hallway; she invites him into her room and he begins to explain what happened. She misunderstands at first and accuses him of breaking into her apartment while she was out. When K. explains that it was an official action of some kind, Fräulein Bürstner calms down. There is clearly some kind of sexual attraction between K. and his neighbor, but their dialogue is interrupted suddenly by a banging on the adjoining door. The landlady's nephew is staying in the next room and Fräulein Bürstner is afraid that he will tell the landlady that she has been receiving male visitors in her room (something the landlady greatly disapproves of). K. promises to deal with any problems that may arise. As he leaves to go back to his own apartment, he kisses Fräulein Bürstner passionately for several minutes, which leaves her nervous and tired.

K. is summoned to an interview in a poor neighborhood of the city and has trouble finding the right office; he passes cramped apartments with half-dressed children and damp washing to get there. Not wanting to reveal why he has come, K. pretends that he is looking for a nonexistent carpenter named Lanz. This subterfuge does not stop him from being directed to the right office, a courtroom packed with spectators. The examining magistrate seems unclear as to who K. is and asks him if he is a house painter. K. replies that he is "the chief financial officer of a large bank," which provokes a burst of laughter from the onlookers (*The Trial*, p. 44). Disgruntled, K. makes a long speech about the unjustness of the prosecution, the chaos of the proceedings, and other grievances:

> [T]here can be no doubt that behind all the pronouncements of this court, and in my case, behind the arrest and today's inquiry, there exists an extensive organization. An organization that not only engages corrupt guards, inane inspec-

tors, and examining magistrates who are at best mediocre, but that supports as well a system of judges of all ranks, including the highest, with their inevitable innumerable entourage of assistants, scribes, gendarmes, and other aids, perhaps even hangmen, I won't shy away from the word.

(*The Trial*, p. 50)

K., curious as to why he has not received any further summons, visits the same location a week later. He discovers that the courtroom is actually an apartment that is occupied, when the court is not in session, by the court usher and his wife. K. has a strange conversation with the wife, who complains about being sexually harassed by the examining magistrate. Later, K. meets the court usher, who asserts that his wife is complicit in the affair. Moving through the complex of offices and apartments, K. meets various inhabitants of the neighborhood, including another man who is also being investigated by the court. K. feels sick and faint in the oppressive atmosphere and has to rush out of the building to get some fresh air.

A few days later, K. is passing a junk room in the bank building where he works and hears the sound of a beating. He pushes the door open and discovers to his amazement that two of the policemen who visited him that first morning are standing there half-naked, being flogged by a leather-garbed figure with a rod. They explain that they are being punished because K. criticized them before the examining magistrate (he mentioned their eating his breakfast, among other things). Plaintively, they appeal to him to intervene. The flogger is unimpressed and tells K. that they are just whiners who are only concerned with their own comfort. Although it is already evening, K. becomes worried that the screaming from the two officers will be heard all over the bank and tries to bribe the flogger so that he will stop. He claims that he cannot be bribed: his job is to flog, and that is what he is going to do. K. flees the corridor, trying not to feel guilty about what is taking place.

A short time later, K. receives a visit from his uncle Albert, who lives in the country. The uncle questions him about the prosecution. The uncle, who seems to think that K. is being too passive in the way he is dealing with the court authorities, brings him to see an old friend, an attorney called Huld. When they arrive, they discover from a young woman, Leni, that Huld is ill. Leni seems to be a housekeeper of some kind, but again there is a strong sexual element in the background of the action. Leni's relationship with the attorney is clearly more intimate than just that of a nurse-housemaid. Eventually they are admitted to Huld's bedroom and he listens to K.'s account of his case, commenting that his friend, the chief clerk of the court might be helpful. Surprised, K. and Uncle Albert are introduced to the other man, whom they had not observed sitting in the shadows of the gloomy bedroom.

A loud noise from outside the room distracts K., who goes to investigate. He discovers that Leni has thrown a plate against the wall to get his attention. K. is implicitly offered some kind of sexual favors by the young woman but feels awkward, as if he is not in charge of the situation. Nonetheless, he and Leni kiss and caress, and she gives him the key to the apartment. His uncle finds him eventually and they leave the house together, Albert attacking him for having wasted his time with a worthless girl while the lawyer Huld could have given him good advice.

Afterward, K. meets with Huld occasionally, and the attorney explains that he and his colleagues have a difficult job. They never know what the right thing to do is, since sometimes an action will work for one client, while the same action in the same circumstance will just make things worse for another client. Everything is really uncertain and nobody can predict from past events what the future will hold. The authorities have the whip hand, the dominating position, so it is unwise to irritate them. And, in any case, the whole system is in a kind of cosmic equilibrium, where a small change at one point will trigger a corresponding countereffect somewhere else. K. becomes confused and tired, not knowing whether the attorney is trying to encourage or depress him. Agonizing over the petition he is supposed to submit to the court, K. leaves it to the last possible moment. One of his clients at the bank tells K. about an artist named Titorelli, who also works for the court and who might have some influence over the judges. K. finds the painter Titorelli in the same kind of oppressive slum neighborhood in which the courtroom was located. Slatternly little girls proposition him as he climbs the stairs to the artist's apartment. Titorelli claims never to have heard of the man who had given K. his name and asks K. if he wants a portrait painted. K. sees that Titorelli is completing the portrait of a judge. In the picture is an image of Justice (with blindfold and scales) but with wings and wheels attached. "It's actually Justice and Victory in one," says the artist, "I'm commissioned to do it that way" (*The Trial*, p. 145). K. steers the conversation around to his legal

The Trial

Anthony Perkins as Josef K. in the 1963 film rendition of *The Trial*.

problems and Titorelli admits that he does in fact know the man who directed K. to him.

The artist explains that he knows the court well since he inherited the position of court painter from his father. There are, he says, three possible outcomes for K.—actual acquittal, apparent acquittal, and protraction. The first is due to innocence; the second is a measure that will grant acquittal but will, in fact, be followed by repeated arrests and re-openings of the case; and the last is a kind of permanent deferral of any bad consequences, a circumstance that obliges one to live with the trial forever. Actual acquittal is more a myth than a reality, however, for nobody has personal experience of any such acquittal's occurring.

At his next visit to Huld (having decided to dismiss the attorney from his case), K. discovers another client of the man, a merchant named Block. Block appears to have some sort of relationship with Leni as well, much to K.'s irritation. Block recounts the story of his judicial inquiry and relays that he has been fighting it with a number of lawyers for five years. He mentions the fact that there are shysters, petty lawyers, and great lawyers, although the last are more rumored than real:

> There's scarcely a single defendant who doesn't dream of them for a time after learning about them. Don't fall prey to that temptation. I don't know who the great lawyers are, and it's probably impossible to contact them.
> (*The Trial*, p. 179)

Eventually a major argument takes place among K., Block, and Huld, which Leni witnesses. Block attacks K. for wanting to dismiss Huld. In Block's view, K. is a beginner who has been under investigation for only a few weeks while Block has five years of experience. The lawyer interjects that neither Block nor K. have any real idea of the procedures of the law.

Some time later, K. is showing a business guest of the bank around the city and finds himself in the cathedral. Thinking that the church is empty, K. is surprised when a priest in the pulpit calls out his name. K. finds himself being questioned by the priest about how his case is going. The priest seems annoyed that K. doesn't grasp the true state of affairs. He tells K. the strange but suggestive story of a man from the country who wants to be admitted to the law. He is denied admittance by the doorman, who explains that he cannot allow the man to enter now. The man, who thinks that everyone should have access to the law, decides to wait. He waits for years and years, and eventually, just before his death, he asks why he is the only one who has ever come to request admittance. The doorman tells him that the door was meant for him only, and now he, the doorman, is going to close it.

On the night before K.'s thirty-first birthday, two men in dark overcoats call at his apartment. Holding him by his arms so he cannot escape, they take him out into the street. K. tries to engage them in conversation but they do not respond. At one point in their journey, a woman who might be his acquaintance from the next apartment, Fräulein Bürstner, comes across the street toward them, but K. is not sure if it is really she, and feels that appealing to her for help would be a pointless waste of energy. Crossing a bridge over a river in which there sits a small island on which K. remembers spending summer days relaxing, the three eventually leave the environs of the city, arriving at a small stone quarry that lies abandoned and desolate in the moonlight. The men remove K'.s jacket and shirt. One of them produces a long, sharp butcher's knife and offers it to K., apparently giving him the chance to commit suicide. K. has no strength left for this, and he is stabbed to death by the two men, who look on as he dies. His last thoughts are about the inaccessibility of justice and the shamefulness of his own end; "it seemed as though the shame was to outlive him" (*The Trial*, p. 231).

Women and misunderstanding—a personal parallel? A great deal of the dialogue in *The Trial* has a disconcerting effect because characters talk at cross-purposes. For example, when K. and Leni meet for the first time in the lawyer's house, he shows her a photo of Elsa, his fiancée. Leni thinks Elsa looks too big and muscular:

> "Big strong girls like that don't often know how to be anything but kind and gentle. But would she sacrifice herself for you?" "No," K. said, "she's neither kind and gentle, nor would she sacrifice herself for me. But so far I haven't demanded either of her. I've never even examined the picture as closely as you have." "So you don't care that much about her," said Leni, "she's not really your sweetheart." "Oh yes," said K., "I won't take back what I said."
> (*The Trial*, pp. 107-108)

K.'s remark seems to be peculiarly coldhearted about Elsa, or else he misses some subtleties of meaning in the conversation. It is almost as if Leni and K. are speaking a language in which one of them is not totally fluent. In *Franz Kafka and Prague*, Pavel Eisner comments that the children of German Jews in Prague began their conscious lives surrounded by Czech women:

> From the domestics the children learned the Czech language, but imperfectly and with the most primitive vocabulary; but even this they forgot in their later years.... One spoke Czech, in German Jewish circles, only with domestics and other people of inferior status; it was beyond their capacity to write down a few Czech words with approximately correct spelling and grammar, and indeed it was beyond their needs. On the other hand, the young German Jew received his first erotic initiation usually from Czech women.
> (Eisner, pp. 23-24)

STATE TERROR?

Often *The Trial* is read as a narrative about totalitarian state terror. In one way, *The Trial* could well be a very subjective, almost fable-like premonition of what the experience of such a totalitarian state might be like. At the same time, however, it is obviously not the organized terror of the Soviet occupation or of a Czech entity that serves as the model for the authoritarian presence in Kafka's novel. First, the Soviet experience happened after he wrote the novel; second, the new Czechoslovakia was a democracy without a secret police.

Nonetheless, the action of *The Trial* clearly involves a kind of uncontrolled and ramshackle mechanism that is concerned only with its own bureaucratic procedures and has no interest in the individual. This could be either the legal system itself (rather than the law as a metaphor for something else again), or the creaking, anachronistic Austro-Hungarian imperial administration. In any case, the events in the story are presented in such an exaggerated, dreamlike style that it is difficult to draw a precise dividing line between reality and fantasy. The fact that the novel seems to speak to the later experience of totalitarian regimes in the twentieth century only confirms the power of Kafka's vision.

Eisner argues that it is no coincidence that Kafka often selects names for his females that could be both German and Czech, like "Leni," which brings to mind his own German-speaking milieu and the more exotic Prague of the native Czechs. Moreover, the women who people Kafka's pages usually belong to a lower social class; they are in some way being "kept" by the men with whom they are involved. This reflects the kind of relationship with Czech girls that someone like Kafka, a relatively well-off bank official and son of a businessman, would have had (or could have had) (Eisner, pp. 56-58).

The Trial

In *The Trial* the unpredictability of the sexual moves of which K. is sometimes active initiator and at other times passive recipient suggests that something is not quite in balance. His sudden lunge at Fräulein Bürstner and the sexual advances made to him by the court usher's wife are part and parcel of a specter of misunderstanding that seems to overshadow all such adventures. K. is portrayed as obviously neurotic (a condition made worse by the court proceedings hanging over him, of course), and, as his relationships with women show, the source of his neurosis may be more social than private. Or, to put it another way, his inability to connect his private desires and feelings with the normal social intercourse in his environment can be seen as leading to his confused and obsessive behavior. K. is caught, in his romantic life, between the chilly strength of Elsa, his respectable fiancée, and the warm sensuality of Leni, the housekeeper of dubious virtue. The dilemma seems to echo his creator's own. His protagonist seems caught between the respectable marriage that Kafka himself kept planning and then rejecting and the brief liaisons with the Czech girls who had fascinated him since boyhood.

Sources and literary context. Although Kafka's work is highly original, there are three very different authors from his part of the world whose works appeared during the same period and shared with Kafka some ideas and approaches. Kafka was a reluctant admirer of the Austrian writer Sigmund Freud, whose psychoanalytic theories provoked some hostility on Kafka's part but whose work he regarded as important and suggestive. In particular, a prominent motif in *The Trial* may have been influenced by a 1914 essay by Freud, "The Moses of Michelangelo" (Pasley, pp. 144-47). In this essay Freud discusses peculiar aspects of the sculpture in Rome that shows Moses, from the biblical Book of Exodus, at the moment of casting down the Tablets of the Law when he returns to discover the Israelites worshipping the golden calf. Freud points out that the figure seems rather to be controlling his angry impulse, with the effect that Moses appears to be caught forever in a moment of both psychic stability and nervous physical movement. The threat of his wrath is frozen in time, and the judgment will never be delivered. This corresponds, curiously enough, to the way in which the painting of the judge that K. sees in attorney Huld's house is described, "as if he were about to spring up at any moment in a violent and perhaps wrathful outburst" (*The Trial*, p. 105). As in Freud's reading of Michelangelo's statue, K. is both afraid of the wrath of the law *and* afraid that his moment of judgment will never come.

Gustav Meyrinck was a popular Austrian writer who scored a major success with *The Golem* (1916), his gothic reworking of the legend of the monster of clay created by a Prague rabbi to aid the Jewish community at a time of crisis. The golem is a dangerous being, capable of great evil, although summoned to do good. Set in the old Prague ghetto (which was demolished in the 1890s), Meyrinck's story is marked by an atmosphere of dark, narrow streets, gloomy houses, and a sense of being haunted by the past. Meyrinck was not Jewish himself, but his book showed a feel for Jewish folklore and legends, and there are moments in *The Trial* when K's unnamed city seems as eerie as old Prague in *The Golem*.

The last of the three writers whose work shows a connection to Kafka's—although his style is radically different—is Jaroslav Hasek, author of the satirical anti-military novel *The Good Soldier Schweik* (1921), probably the most popular novel ever written by a Czech author. As one critic has observed, "Both Kafka and his contemporary Jaroslav Hasek . . . were such critics of the Habsburg bureaucracy that preservation of the individual against organizations characterizes nearly all their work" (Karl, p. 140). Hasek's comic account of the apparently simple-minded Corporal Schweik, who carries out the orders of his superiors with such faithful precision that he reduces the military operations of the Austrian army to total chaos, seems far away from the anguished uncertainties of K., but both these writers had a sense of the individual being at war with the demands of organizations. Their experience as citizens and subjects of the Austro-Hungarian Empire led both Hasek and Kafka to very different types of literary expression, but also to what was in many ways a common theme.

Publication and reception. Franz Kafka published only a very small number of his longer stories during his lifetime (*Metamorphosis* appeared in 1915). His three novels, *The Trial*, *The Castle*, and *Amerika* (the latter sometimes known as *The Man Who Disappeared*), were all published posthumously. As mentioned at the outset, Max Brod disobeyed Kafka's final instructions to destroy his unpublished manuscripts. Brod justified himself as follows:

> My decision [rests] simply and solely on the fact that Kafka's unpublished work contains the most wonderful treasures, and measured

against his own work, the best things he has written.

(Brod in "Publisher's Note," *The Trial*, p. viii)

Brod campaigned for recognition of his friend's unique talent and lobbied publishers throughout Europe to bring out Kafka's work. *The Trial* was first published in Berlin in 1925, a year after Kafka's death; *The Castle* and *Amerika* were published in Munich in 1926 and 1927, respectively, to positive critical response.

The novelist Herman Hesse (author of *Steppenwolf* and *The Glass Bead Game*, et al.) described *The Trial* in the *Berliner Tageblatt* on September 9, 1925 as "a web composed of the finest strands of dreams . . . with a technique of such purity and a vision of such intense power that an eerie pseudo-reality appears, at first like a nightmare, oppressive and intimidating, until the secret of this text dawns on the reader" (Hesse in Born, p. 92; trans. M. Griffin). In an issue of his influential magazine *Die Weltbühne* of March 9, 1926, writer and editor Kurt Tucholsky called it "the strangest and most powerful book of the last few years" (Tucholsky in Born, p. 106; trans. M. Griffin).

In Britain the poet Edwin Muir and his wife Willa translated *The Castle* into English in 1930, and their translation of *The Trial* followed in 1935. As in Germany and Austria, the critical response was exceptional even when there was confusion about how to interpret the novel, as shown by a review in *The New Yorker*:

> The story is like a nightmare without the relieving touch of fantasy. . . . It may be a study in persecution mania. It may be—I think it is—a religious legend.
>
> (Fadiman, p. 69)

In a similar vein, the poet Stephen Spender described Kafka's stories as "penetrating reality in order to discover a system of truth," and K. as the outsider who "has the stranger's fresh view of life and the reality beyond life" (Spender, p. 347).

Whatever might be said about the ambiguities of *The Trial*, however, a new and more pressing problem was now on the horizon. The Nazi takeover of Germany in 1933 brought punitive sanctions against Jewish publishers and publications. The small Schocken firm, founded in Berlin in 1931, was permitted to publish books of Jewish interest but to sell them to Jews only. This company offered Kafka's work its first real breakthrough, publishing all his novels, and selections from his short stories and aphorisms as well. Thereafter, his work not only received positive reviews but also became commercially successful. When Nazi officials noticed that the books were selling well to both Jews and non-Jews, however, they placed both Kafka and Brod on the list of banned authors.

The Nazi threat to European Jewry (Kafka's three sisters would eventually perish in the Holocaust) and the outbreak of World War II soon intervened, and over the next few years Schocken had to move its publishing business from Berlin, to Prague, to Palestine, and finally to New York. In 1946 Schocken reissued the old Muir translations, which this time met with substantial commercial success. Franz Kafka was soon recognized as one of the major writers of the twentieth century.

THE TRANSLATOR'S "TRIAL"

The Trial has been haunted by a host of vexing problems for translators who have rendered the novel into English. The difficulties begin with the title. The original title in German is *Der Prozess*. "Prozess" does not mean "the trial" so much as the entire proceedings from investigation to completion of the judicial "process." In German, "die Gerichtsverhandlung" comes closer to our sense of what a trial is—the actual courtroom event when the prosecution presents its case, the defense counters, and the jury makes its findings. It is obvious that no real "trial" in our sense of the word takes place in Kafka's *The Trial*. The next difficulty is posed by the very first sentence of the novel. In German it reads: "Jemand musste Josef. K. verleumdet haben, denn ohne dass er etwas Böses getan hätte, wurde er eines Morgens verhaftet." The Muir translation (as revised in 1968) runs: "Someone must have been telling lies about Josef K., for without having done anything wrong he was arrested one fine morning" (Muir, p. 7). Breon Mitchell's version (the one used for this entry) makes a different impression: "Someone must have slandered Josef. K., for one morning, without having done anything truly wrong, he was arrested." "Slander" is technically correct, but Mitchell inserts "truly" before wrong, thus giving the impression that K. might have done something mildly wrong. The German casts the sentence in the subjunctive mood (with the verb getan hätte), which, curiously, raises a doubt about K.'s innocence at the same time as it asserts it. So Mitchell's version is, on the one hand, tighter, and on the other he also risks a looser translation in order to capture the note of uncertainty in the German original.

Kafka's reputation in his native Czechoslovakia, however, had some strange twists and turns. Despite considerable effort after World War II to maintain a neutral East-West position, Czechoslovakia had fallen under the domination of its large Communist Party and become a Soviet Bloc country. The Czech communists had no time for the gloomy, oblique fantasies of Kafka's fiction. Under their direction, his grave in the Prague-Strasnice cemetery was overgrown and abandoned for many years. It was only in the 1980s that the communist government realized that "Kafka and Prague" was a selling point for tourists. Gradually they permitted Kafka-related events and information to appear. It is one of the ironies that Kafka might have expected: that he had become a world-famous author, but that his own country (and his home city Prague) would almost deny his existence for many years.

—Martin Griffin

For More Information

Born, Jürgen, ed. *Franz Kafka: Kritik und Rezeption 1924-1938*. Frankfurt, Germany: S. Fischer, 1983.

Eisner, Pavel. *Franz Kafka and Prague*. Trans. Lowry Nelson and René Wellek. New York: Golden Griffin, 1950.

Fadiman, Clifton. Review of *The Trial,* by Franz Kafka. *The New Yorker*, 23 October 1937, 68-69.

Kafka, Franz. *The Trial*. Trans. Breon Mitchell. New York: Schocken, 1998.

Karl, Frederick R. *Franz Kafka: Representative Man*. New York, Ticknor and Fields, 1991.

Muir, Willa, and Edwin Muir, trans. *The Trial*, by Franz Kafka. London: Minerva, 1992.

Palmer, Alan. *The Lands Between: A History of East-Central Europe since the Congress of Vienna*. London: Weidenfeld and Nicolson, 1970.

Pasley, Malcolm. "Two Literary Sources of Kafka's *Der Prozess.*" *Forum for Modern Language Studies* 3, no. 2 (April 1967): 142-47.

Spender, Stephen. "Franz Kafka." Review of *The Trial*. *The New Republic*, 27 October 1937, 347-48.

Twelfth Night, Or, What You Will

by
William Shakespeare

Born in Stratford-upon-Avon, England in 1564, William Shakespeare was a glove maker's son who later became the most famous of British playwrights and poets. Educated at the free local grammar school in Stratford and married young to Anne Hathaway, by whom he had three children, Shakespeare appears to have journeyed to London sometime in the 1580s. Players' records from 1594 verify his presence as a cast member for the acting troupe known as the Lord Chamberlain's Men. During the 1590s, Shakespeare began his career as a playwright; between 1594 and 1598, he composed most of his historical plays, along with comedies such as *Two Gentlemen of Verona* and **A Midsummer Night's Dream**, and tragedies such as *Titus Andronicus* and **Romeo and Juliet** (also in *Literature and Its Times*). *Twelfth Night* appears to have been written between 1598 and 1601, along with such major works as *Much Ado about Nothing, As You Like It*, and **Hamlet** (also in *Literature and Its Times*). Like many of Shakespeare's comedies, *Twelfth Night* is not set at a specific historical period; rather, its frame of reference corresponds to Shakespeare's own time, touching on festive occasions, religious tensions, and the prevailing social order.

Events in History at the Time of the Play

Twelfth Night. The play's primary title alludes to a Christian holiday, the Feast of the Epiphany, which marks the culmination of the 12 days of Christmas on January 6th. (Its secondary title,

> **THE LITERARY WORK**
>
> A comedy set in Illyria (known later as Albania and Yugoslavia), at an unspecified historical time; first performed c. 1600-1602; first printed in 1623.
>
> **SYNOPSIS**
>
> Separated from her twin brother after a shipwreck, a young woman disguises herself as a young man to serve a duke, but unwittingly captures the heart of the countess whom the duke is courting; further romantic complications ensue when the twin brother arrives, but all is happily resolved.

What You Will, has been construed, alternately, as a throwaway like *As You Like It* or *Much Ado about Nothing*, or as a pun on Shakespeare's first name.) Epiphany celebrates the coming of the Magi or Three Wise Men, who recognize Jesus as savior, the baptism of Jesus, and, later, the miracle at Cana (John 2:1-12), when Jesus transformed water into wine at a wedding celebration. By Shakespeare's time, however, Epiphany, or Twelfth Night (held on January 5th), was being celebrated in England more as a secular holiday, with dancing, feasting, and revelry. The following entry for January 6, 1594, appeared in the memoirs of Anthony Bacon, a gentleman at court: "Twelfth Night was celebrated at Court by dancing which continued till 1 o'clock after midnight, the Queen being seated in a high throne, and

Twelfth Night, Or, What You Will

William Shakespeare

next to her chair the Earl of Essex with whom she often devised in sweet and favourable manner" (Bacon in Harrison, vol. 1, p. 221).

The exact significance of Twelfth Night to Shakespeare's comedy has fueled much speculation by historians and literary scholars. Some have proposed that the play was first performed or meant to be performed on Twelfth Night; others have attempted—not altogether successfully—to find references or allusions to Epiphany within the text of the play itself. Yet there is no evidence to suggest that the events of *Twelfth Night* take place during that eponymous holiday. Another theory—perhaps more plausible—suggests that Shakespeare wanted to evoke the spirit of revelry and mirth by his choice of title. Proponents of this theory point out that the Feast of the Epiphany was also the Feast of Fools, a mock-religious celebration popular in medieval Europe from about the twelfth to the fifteenth century. Originally the Feast of Fools, in which clergy and laity participated, took place within the confines of a cathedral or church; in a reversal of roles, the sub deacons—the lowest-ranking members of the clergy—assumed the privileges and powers of their ecclesiastical superiors for a few hours.

By the fourteenth and fifteenth centuries, however, the Feast of Fools had moved out of the church and into the town square, as ordinary citizens took part. Processions, music, and verse were added to the celebration, which became more riotous and secular as a result. At that point, the Feast of Fools was presented as a wild pageant, over which a Lord of Misrule—or Festus—presided. Displeased by the increased vulgarity and rowdiness, church authorities attempted to abolish or restrict the festivities but the public thwarted their efforts. Although the popularity of the Feast of Fools had dwindled by Shakespeare's time, its influence may be detected in several of his comedies, including *Twelfth Night*. The drunken reveler, Sir Toby Belch, embodies the spirit of a Lord of Misrule, while Olivia's witty, observant fool, who offers pungent insights on most of the other characters, is named Feste. The play's plot, with its various ruses, reversals of fortunes, and instances of mistaken identity between twins Viola and Sebastian, is also in keeping with the general atmosphere of the Feast of Fools.

Puritanism. Although *Twelfth Night* concerns itself mainly with secular romance and merriment, Shakespeare makes several revealing allusions to contemporary religious tensions. Internal conflicts within the Protestant Church of England had arisen soon after Elizabeth I took the throne in 1558. Elizabeth's father, Henry VIII had divided the country along religious lines by breaking with the Roman Catholic Church and establishing the Protestant Church of England with himself as head. Mary Tudor, Henry's elder daughter wished England to return to the Catholic faith. During her reign, English Protestants were compelled either to convert to the queen's Catholic faith on pain of death or go into exile abroad. Many who fled to the Continent experienced forms of worship that they considered "purer"—strongly influenced by the teachings of John Calvin and free of Catholicism—than those prescribed in England's 1552 Prayer Book. These Puritans—as they came to be called—believed that Roman Catholics had perverted Christianity from true doctrine and worship, and desired, above all else, that the Church of England be "purified" and restored to its original condition as described in Scripture. Unlike most Protestants in the religious mainstream, Puritans held that God had "elected" or predestined certain persons for salvation, and that man could not hope to attain heaven through performing good works but only by the grace of God. The strictest Puritans also believed that true Christians should adopt a more austere lifestyle, which entailed dressing simply, behaving more soberly, and shunning worldly entertainments.

> ## ILLYRIA, ITALY, OR ENGLAND?
>
> In Shakespeare's time, the real-world Illyria corresponded to a region located on the western coast of the Balkan peninsula, consisting of today's Albania and the former Yugoslavia. In the third century B.C.E. Illyria first became a political power. During the centuries that followed, wars raged throughout the region; Illyria was conquered and ruled, in turn, by the Macedonians, the Romans, the Byzantine Empire, and finally the Ottoman Empire, which controlled the area at the time of *Twelfth Night*'s composition. However, few details beyond Shakespeare's use of the name locate his play in the historical Illyria. Viola's initial plan to disguise herself as a eunuch to serve the duke Orsino might suggest an Ottoman (Turkish) setting, but the play never refers to that possibility again. Similarly the real Illyria's past history of seafaring and piracy—Rome's conquest of Illyria had been provoked by the latter's attacks on Roman trading vessels—is only sketchily explored, mainly to provide a plausible reason for arresting a character in the play (Antonio). Shakespeare's Illyria is closer in atmosphere to the romantic, illusory realms of myths and fairy tales, like the Greece of his *A Midsummer Night's Dream*. As in earlier comedy, *Twelfth Night* combines language, names, and customs from different cultures in a manner that transcends history and geography, while creating a play that remains accessible to its audience. The country's name is Illyria, but its denizens have either Italianate names (Orsino, Olivia, Malvolio, Curio) or English names (Sir Toby Belch, Sir Andrew Aguecheek). The structure of Illyrian society as portrayed in the play reflects that of Elizabethan England, and the humor, complete with puns, topic allusions, and comic songs, is English too.

On returning to England at the beginning of Queen Elizabeth's reign, Puritans hoped to persuade her to adopt the Calvinist conception of the Church; under the leadership of Thomas Cartwright, they advocated the abolition of bishops, elimination of almost all rituals and ceremonies, and stricter enforcement of church discipline. But, while Elizabeth I was a Protestant monarch, she did not favor the Puritans, whose aims she considered too radical. Instead, she favored a more mainstream Protestantism, which retained several "impure" ceremonial rituals and practices, such as the celebration of semi-religious holidays (including Twelfth Night) and the observances of certain saints' days. Frustrated by the queen's opposition, some Puritans—known as Separatists—set up their own congregations, claiming that the Church of England threatened their salvation by not being a "true" church. The Separatist movement had little impact on the Church of England, but the Puritans' frustrations continued to mount over the years. Between 1607 and 1609 a new group of Separatists fled England and settled in Leiden, Holland. In 1620 a portion of this group— known as the Pilgrims—emigrated to America, founding the Plymouth colony.

The Puritans' sternness and austerity, along with their frequent disapproval of secular entertainments such as music and plays, made them an easy target for ridicule. In *Twelfth Night*, Shakespeare portrays Puritanism, as personified by the censorious Malvolio, as inimical to the festival spirit of his play. During a heated confrontation, Sir Toby snaps at the steward, "Dost thou think because thou art virtuous, there shall be no more cakes and ale?" (*Twelfth Night*, 2.3.114-115). Maria, another character in the household, however, maintains that Malvolio is actually worse than a Puritan because his assumption of virtue is a pose, "The devil a Puritan that he is, or anything constantly, but a time-pleaser, an affectioned ass, that cons state without book, and utters it by great swarths" (*Twelfth Night*, 2.3.146-149). Her harsh criticism turns out to be justified; alone in the garden, the steward fantasizes about such earthly pleasures as marrying the lady of the house, Olivia, wearing jewels and a "branched velvet gown," while Sir Toby bows and scrapes before Count Malvolio (*Twelfth Night*, 2.4.47-48).

The professional fool. Since antiquity, in many cultures, it had been the frequent practice of royal and noble households to include a fool, specifically a professional clown whose purpose was to provide entertainment for his master. This entertainment could take many forms, including singing, storytelling, juggling, tumbling, or simple jesting and horseplay. Similarly, fools themselves came in all forms and temperaments. Some—like dwarves—were physically atypical or even deformed; others were considered simple-minded but enjoyed a privileged status as "innocents," who were not to be harmed.

Most professional fools, however, had full possession of their mental faculties and sufficient wit to gain their masters' favor, trust, and confidence. Depending on the generosity of those masters, some fools were richly rewarded for their entertainment skills with gifts of money, fine clothes, or even property. Queen Mary Tudor provided well for her own fool, an "innocent" by the name of Jane, even summoning healers to treat Jane during several bouts of illness. Successful fools could—and often did—exert a subtle influence over an employer, either for their own or someone else's benefit. For example, Will Somers, the highly regarded fool of Henry VIII of England, persuaded the often-tyrannical king to pardon Somers's former master, Richard Farmor, who had been stripped of his possessions for showing kindness to a priest who was out of royal favor. Bending to the "will of Will," the King restored some of Farmor's properties.

Fools were generally supposed to possess more liberties than most courtiers, because, theoretically, they could utter unpalatable truths or outrageous remarks without suffering reprisals. The Italian scholar Erasmus wrote of the fools of his own time: "They can speak truth, and even open insults, and be heard with positive pleasure; indeed, the words that would cost a wise man his life are surprisingly enjoyable when uttered by a clown. For truth has a genuine power to please if it manages not to give offence, but this is something the gods have granted only to fools" (Erasmus in Southworth, p. 9). However, the bond between master and fool could be precarious, the latter being dependent on the former not only for his livelihood but also for his very identity. Moreover, in some cases, even a fool could cross the line and lose his master's favor. Master Sexton, an elderly "innocent" who served Henry VIII before Will Somers's time, was banished from court because he had praised Queen Catherine of Aragon—whom the king was trying to divorce—and spoken unflatteringly of Anne Boleyn, whom the king was intending to marry. Sexton's ultimate fate remains unknown.

Like her father and sister before her, Queen Elizabeth employed a fool, or rather, a succession of fools during her reign. She bestowed particular favor on Richard Tarlton, a comedian who was also a leading actor in the Queen's Players and the author of several ballads and plays. Tarlton thus kept a foot in two worlds—that of the court and that of the popular stage, which gave him greater autonomy than the fools who had previously served Tudor monarchs. Significantly, several performers with talents similar to those of Tarlton turned increasingly to the popular stage as a means of earning their livelihoods. Fools were gradually transforming themselves into players.

In *Twelfth Night*, Feste seems to exemplify this more independent, autonomous breed of fool, wandering freely between Olivia's household—from which he is often mysteriously absent—and Orsino's court, receiving largesse from both. Moreover, Feste is prepared at any time to provide entertainment, satiric commentary, or simple home truths to any likely audience—singing love songs for the duke, mocking Orsino's self-induced melancholy, and criticizing Olivia's excessive display of mourning for her brother. His success at his calling does not go unnoticed; after an exchange of banter with Feste, Viola remarks, "This fellow is wise enough to play the fool, / And to do that well, craves a kind of wit: / He must observe their mood on whom he jests, / The quality of persons, and the time, / And like the haggard, check at every feather / That comes before his eye. This is a practice / As full of labour as a wise man's art" (*Twelfth Night*, 3.1.61-67).

Gentlemen, servants, and the social order. Although Elizabeth I ruled over her subjects as an absolute monarch, control of her government and society still resided mainly in the hands of those who were considered "gentlemen." In his treatise on English society, *De Republica Anglorum* (ca. 1600), Sir Thomas Smith, defined the term "gentlemen" within its specific Elizabethan context: "Who can live idly and without manual labor and will bear the port, charge, and countenance of a gentleman, he shall be called 'master,' for that is the title which men give to esquires and other gentlemen, and shall be taken for a gentleman" (Smith in Singman, p. 12).

THE ELIZABETHAN STEWARD

Within the domestic hierarchy of the Elizabethan household, the steward often reigned supreme. In addition to keeping and organizing the household accounts, which required mathematical ability and a strong sense of economy, the steward was responsible for all aspects of the house, gardens, and lands. He might also be a good huntsman and archer. Many stewards were highly trained and educated for their positions; the entire household might be judged on how well the steward performed his duties. Thus, Malvolio, in *Twelfth Night*, occupies a position of considerable power in Olivia's household; a high-ranking countess, Olivia nevertheless consults his opinion on various matters, domestic and personal, which suggests that Malvolio is at least a competent steward. Even Malvolio's secret ambition to attain a higher social position—hopefully by marrying Olivia—is not wholly outlandish, though his conviction that Olivia loves him is based less on evidence than on vanity. Social mobility was indeed possible during the Elizabethan period—though frowned on by established aristocrats, such as the play's Sir Toby Belch. Marriage to someone of superior rank provided one of the surest ways to achieve a higher status. Encouraging such a development, a noblewoman, widowed or holding the title in her own right, could marry men considered their social inferiors. In real life, for example, Lettice, the widowed countess of Leicester, married the much younger and less exalted Sir Christopher Blount in 1589. In the play, Malvolio cites a dramatic precedent of a noblewoman wedding her servant: "The Lady of the Strachy married the yeoman of the wardrobe," referring to a match that may have been Shakespeare's own invention (*Twelfth Night*, 2.5.39-40).

Freedom from manual labor generally implied that gentlemen possessed sufficient land to live off the rents paid by their tenants. Therefore, the landed, titled nobility—dukes, marquises, earls, viscounts, and barons, in descending order—occupied the topmost position of the hierarchy that subdivided the gentlemanly class. Knights—who had received their titles as an accolade from the monarch—ranked below the nobility, but above esquires (squires) and simple gentlemen. According to seventeenth-century estimates, nobles, knights, and esquires made up less than 1 percent of the population, simple gentleman about 1 percent (Singman, pp. 12-13). Not all gentlemen were landowners, however; officers in the queen's army and navy were considered gentlemen, as were government officials, clergymen, physicians, lawyers, scholars, and indeed anyone who possessed a university education.

Significantly, gentle birth did not prevent a high percentage of men and women from entering the service of another family. Historian Jeffrey L. Singman writes, "Between the ages of 20 and 24, some 80% of men and 50% of women went away from home in service from just before puberty until marriage, or a period of about 10 years" (Singman, p. 16). This phenomenon did not represent a decrease in social status. On the contrary, young people—even those belonging to the aristocracy—might accumulate money, acquire social polish, and make useful acquaintances and contacts while working in upper-class households. Gently-born servants—employed as pages, gentlemen-ushers, and ladies-in-waiting—lived with the family they were serving and ranked above household workers like cooks, grooms, and even stewards; they were also in better positions to improve their stations in life through education and patronage.

In *Twelfth Night,* Shakespeare portrays the dynamics of the relationship between master and servant, both in Duke Orsino's court and Olivia's household, according to the Elizabethan model. A circle of well-born gentlemen, to which the disguised Viola is soon admitted, surrounds the duke. Similarly, the waiting-gentlewoman Maria attends upon Olivia. Servants of lesser rank in the countess's household include Feste the fool—

Twelfth Night, Or, What You Will

whose exact position tends to fluctuate according to his mistress's favor—and Malvolio, the steward. Malvolio secretly cherishes ambitions above his station, thirsting to marry Olivia and become the next count.

The Play in Focus

The plot. The play begins as Orsino, the noble duke of Illyria, sighs over his unrequited love for the Countess Olivia. Recently bereft of her brother, Olivia has vowed to mourn his death for seven years in deep seclusion.

Elsewhere in Illyria, a shipwreck has cast several people ashore. One of the survivors, Viola, mourns the loss of her twin brother, Sebastian, in the wreck but dares to hope he might have been rescued too. Recognizing their location, the ship's captain tells Viola about Orsino and the duke's hopeless passion for Countess Olivia. Hearing that Olivia also mourns a brother, Viola wishes she could serve the countess, but learns that Olivia will not receive anyone. Viola then enlists the captain's help to disguise herself as a boy and take service with Orsino instead.

The plan is successful: the disguised Viola, now called "Cesario" rises quickly in Orsino's esteem, becoming the duke's favorite companion. Orsino delegates Cesario to woo Olivia on his behalf; Cesario agrees, but wistfully, because she secretly loves the duke herself.

Meanwhile, Olivia's household experiences several disruptions, including the continued presence of her drunken kinsman Sir Toby Belch who has brought one of his boon-companions, Sir Andrew Aguecheek, to the estate to woo the countess; Feste, the family's fool, has also returned, after a lengthy and unexplained absence. Maria, Olivia's waiting-gentlewoman, tries to keep order, as does Malvolio, Olivia's steward, though the latter's arrogance and haughtiness offend Sir Toby, Feste, and several others in the household. Hostilities run especially deep between Malvolio and Feste.

Arriving in the midst of a typical domestic dispute, Cesario manages to gain an audience with Olivia. She refuses to entertain Orsino's suit but finds herself captivated by the young messenger's wit and beauty. After Cesario leaves, Olivia sends Malvolio after the supposed youth with a ring, which the countess claims was left behind. Receiving the ring, Viola (alias Cesario) is dismayed to realize that Olivia has fallen in love with her disguise and believes she is a man in truth. Not knowing what to do, Viola resolves to let time unravel the problem.

Meanwhile, Sebastian, Viola's brother, turns out to be alive: Antonio, a former pirate, rescued him from the shipwreck and the two men have since become close friends. Sebastian reveals his true identity and the history of his lost twin sister to Antonio, and expresses his wish to seek his fortune at Orsino's court. Although Antonio has enemies in Illyria, he resolves to accompany his friend.

Back in Illyria, tensions between Malvolio and other members of Olivia's household culminate in a heated nighttime confrontation during which the steward furiously chastises Sir Toby, Sir Andrew, and Feste for drunken revelry. Enraged by Malvolio's overbearing ways, the revelers resolve to revenge themselves on him. Maria, who has been in love with Sir Toby for years, decides to throw in her lot with the conspirators and hatches a plan to humiliate the steward. Playing upon Malvolio's vanity, Maria forges an anonymous letter in Olivia's handwriting and leaves it for the steward to find in the garden. Malvolio reads the letter, which seems to corroborate his secret conviction that Olivia loves him and instructs him to affect a haughty demeanor with others and to wear yellow stockings with crossgarters as proof of his having received the letter. The conspirators watch from their hiding places and gleefully anticipate Malvolio's downfall.

Back at Orsino's court, the duke continues to pine for Olivia. Viola, still in disguise as Cesario, attempts to persuade Orsino that his passion is unlikely to be reciprocated and lets her own mask slip enough to relate a sad story about her "sister" who was deeply in love with a man but never told him of her love. Although affected by Cesario's tale, Orsino remains adamant about wooing Olivia and again sends Cesario to the countess. Olivia receives Cesario cordially, apologizes for her previous subterfuge with the ring, but ends by confessing her own burgeoning love for the messenger. Cesario reiterates her loyalty to her master, expresses her inability to love any woman, and pleads in vain for Olivia to transfer her affections to Orsino instead. Further confusion is imminent, for, unbeknownst to Cesario, Sebastian and Antonio reach Illyria. The two friends separate so Sebastian can explore the city—which Antonio, given his past misdeeds cannot do in safety. The former pirate loans Sebastian his purse in case he needs to purchase something beyond his means.

In Olivia's house, the conspirators' prank comes to a climax as Malvolio presents himself to his mistress as instructed by the letter: yellow-

Twelfth Night, Or, What You Will

Engraving of Olivia, Maria and Malvolio in Act 3, Scene 4 of Shakespeare's *Twelfth Night*.

stockinged, cross-gartered, and smiling. Startled by the sudden changes in her usually sober steward, Olivia believes that Malvolio has gone mad and instructs Maria to have him confined somewhere for his own safety. Sir Toby and Maria have the steward bound and locked up in a dark room.

With Malvolio currently removed, Sir Toby and his friend Sir Andrew decide to get rid of Cesario next, so Sir Andrew can woo Olivia without rivals. Sir Toby persuades his cowardly companion to challenge Cesario to a duel. When Cesario again calls on behalf of Orsino, Sir Toby waylays the messenger and imparts the news of Sir Andrew's challenge; an alarmed Cesario tries to extricate herself from the quarrel but to no avail. In a spirit of mischief, Sir Toby lets each participant believe his rival is a deadly duelist. Quaking, Cesario and Sir Andrew prepare to duel, but a passing Antonio, seeing a youth he believes to be Sebastian in trouble, intervenes to save his friend. Officers of the duke arrive on the scene at this point and, recognizing Antonio as a pirate, arrest him. Addressing Cesario as "Sebastian," Antonio asks for the return of his purse to extricate himself from this situation, but Cesario does not understand to what he is referring. Accusing "Sebastian" of ingratitude, Antonio leaves with the officers. Bewildered by the possibility of Sebastian's being alive, Cesario wanders off in a daze. Sir Toby and Sir Andrew, now believing Cesario to be a coward, decide to follow and beat the messenger.

Instead of Cesario, however, Sir Toby and Sir Andrew find Sebastian. Already vexed by Antonio's absence and the strange behavior of some Illyrians who act as if they already know him, Sebastian defends himself when the two knights attack him. Olivia enters and puts an end to the fight, ordering her kinsman away in disgust. Like everyone else, the countess mistakes Sebastian for Cesario and invites him into her house; the young man complies.

Back on Olivia's estate, Malvolio continues to languish in his prison. Feste taunts his nemesis in both an assumed guise, as Sir Thopas the parson, and in his own form, but, on hearing from Sir Toby about how the jest has soured and should be ended, the fool agrees to carry a message from Malvolio to Olivia. Unaware of this situation, Olivia busies herself fetching a priest, who marries her to the confused but willing Sebastian.

The various complications build to a climax as Orsino finally decides to pay court to Olivia himself and calls upon her with his retinue, which includes Cesario. Outside the countess's house, the duke encounters his officers and his old enemy Antonio. Bitter words pass between the two erstwhile enemies, and Antonio once

Twelfth Night, Or, What You Will

again accuses Cesario, the duke's servant, of ingratitude. Orsino dismisses Antonio's words as a madman's ravings, saying that Cesario has served in his court the whole time he was supposedly with Antonio. Olivia then enters and Orsino renews his suit; the countess once again rejects his advances and, sensing her partiality for Cesario, the duke threatens to avenge his thwarted love on the youth. Olivia then claims Cesario as her husband, summoning the priest as a witness. Outraged by this betrayal—which Cesario denies—Orsino orders his favorite from his company.

EXPLORATION AND PIRACY

Although the action of *Twelfth Night* is mainly based on land, the sea is a continual presence in the play, a possible homage by Shakespeare to England's growing dominance as a seafaring nation. Between the 1560s and 1590s, English privateers—armed private ships commissioned to combat warships or commercial vessels belonging to the enemy—had conducted raids on Spanish merchant ships, heightening the rivalry between the two nations. Meanwhile, English and Dutch piracy was mounting in the Mediterranean Sea. In 1588 England's victory over the Spanish Armada broke Spain's monopoly in the New World, opening it up for trade with and colonization by the English. By 1601-02, the period when *Twelfth Night* was written, England was continuing to expand its territorial holdings throughout the world. The nation's forays into piracy and empire-building are both referenced in Shakespeare's play—the former in the character of Antonio, a former pirate and enemy of Orsino's, the latter in Maria's mocking description of how Malvolio "does smile his face into more lines than is in the new map with the augmentation of the Indies," a literal allusion to just such a map printed in 1599 (*Twelfth Night*, 3.3.75-77).

Just then an injured Sir Toby and Sir Andrew enter, complaining about how Cesario attacked them both. Cesario denies these charges too, but the mystery is finally solved by the appearance of Sebastian, who explains to Olivia that he was only defending himself and offers his apologies. Seeing Antonio, Sebastian greets his friend with relief, then reacts, like the others, with amazement at the sight of his double, Cesario. Confirming each other's identities, Viola and Sebastian joyfully reunite. Olivia realizes she was infatuated with a woman but has married a man, and greets Viola as a sister, while Orsino recognizes the true nature of Cesario's love for him and claims her hand in marriage.

Viola's revelation that Malvolio has had her ally, the sea captain, imprisoned on some charge brings the steward back to mind. At this point, Olivia receives Malvolio's message accusing her of having misled him and quickly frees him. On seeing the letter that brought about Malvolio's humiliation, Olivia recognizes the handwriting as Maria's. Another servant, Fabian—also part of the conspiracy—confesses the nature of the jest practiced on Malvolio and further reveals that Sir Toby has married Maria to protect her from possible reprisals; Malvolio exits, swearing revenge on everybody, but Orsino commands that the matter be settled peacefully. The play concludes as the two betrothed couples enter Olivia's house in peace and harmony, while Feste sings a song about the ages of man. The song has a melancholy refrain—"For the rain it raineth every day"—reminding us that, with the twelfth night of Christmas, festivities end, and sober everyday reality begins once again (*Twelfth Night*, 5.1.391).

Gender roles. Much has been made of the cross-dressing element in Shakespeare's comedies. Julia in *Two Gentlemen of Verona*, Portia in *The Merchant of Venice*, Rosalind in *As You Like It*, and Viola in *Twelfth Night* all adopt a masculine disguise, for various reasons. Julia wants to be near her true love, Portia means to save her husband's closest friend from a moneylender's grasp, Rosalind hopes to avoid thieves and attackers during her travels to the Forest of Arden, and Viola intends to enter Duke Orsino's service and, at the same time, preserve the memory of her presumed-dead twin brother, on whom she models her new disguise.

Shakespeare's reliance on the cross-dressing female in his works is partly attributable to her presence in the original tales and the Italian Renaissance plays from which he borrowed his plots. Moreover, the device was a comedic staple, guaranteed to amuse Elizabethan audiences, if for no other reason than that all women's parts at the time were performed by boys. The comic irony of a boy playing a girl playing a boy did not escape those who saw Shakespeare's works onstage.

On another level, however, such masquerades as Viola's in *Twelfth Night* might have a deeper import. Although Viola, in particular, finds herself in several difficult situations because of her disguise—having to court Olivia while secretly loving Orsino, and being forced to fight a duel with Sir Andrew Aguecheek—she nonetheless gains the companionship and favor of the duke, becoming his trusted friend within days of their acquaintance. She, along with the other cross-dressing women of Shakespeare's plays, comes to enjoy the same autonomy as men: to speak, act, and think freely. Such privileges were not to be taken lightly, especially given the strict gender roles of the time.

Although England was ruled by a strong-willed queen who often referred to herself as a "prince," women in general were second-class citizens. As children, daughters fell under their father's control, and upon marriage, women became subordinate to their husbands in every way. A widow, however, might assume control over her husband's household or business after his death, thus receiving legal recognition as an independent individual. Significantly, in England, wives were given more freedom than most of their counterparts on the Continent. Van Meteren, a contemporary Dutch historian, observed,

> Wives in England are entirely in the power of their husbands, their lives only excepted . . . yet they are not kept so strictly as they are in Spain or elsewhere. Nor are they shut up but they have the free management of the house or housekeeping, after the fashion of those of the Netherlands, and others [of] their neighbours. They go to market to buy what they like best to eat. They are well-dressed, fond of taking it easy, and commonly leave the care of household matters and drudgery to their servants. . . . This is why England is called the paradise of married women.
> (Van Meteren in Pritchard, p. 29)

Despite their more extensive privileges, English wives still did not enjoy the full legal rights, economic opportunities, and social status experienced by their husbands. Professions such as law and medicine were closed to them, as were the universities. They were still expected to confine their energies and abilities to keeping house and raising families, "and not to meddle with matters abroad, nor to bear office in a city or commonwealth no more than children or infants" (Smith in Singman, p. 18). Perhaps more than one woman of Shakespeare's era took a vicarious pleasure in the adventures of Viola, Rosalind, and Portia when she saw them portrayed onstage.

Sources and literary context. In most of his plays, Shakespeare follows an established practice of reusing and revising plots and subplots from various sources; *Twelfth Night* is no exception. The basic plot of disguised siblings and confused love comes from the Italian play *Gl'Ingannati* (*The Deceived Ones*, 1531). It is unclear whether Shakespeare actually read *Gl'Ingannati*; however, he seems to have found a similar plot in the tale of "Apolonius and Silla," by Barnabe Riche, which was published in *Riche His Farewell to Militarie Profession* (1581). *Twelfth Night* uses several elements from Riche's version—the shipwreck that separates the look-alike siblings, the brother's arrival on the scene and his amorous reception by the lady being courted by the Duke, and the lady's claiming the disguised sister as her husband.

Shakespeare also emulates familiar classical models, specifically the Roman comic playwright Plautus, known for his fast-paced comedies, which employed themes of lost siblings and disguises. Plautus's comedy *Menaechmi*, the source of Shakespeare's earlier play *The Comedy of Errors*, may have been reused during the composition of *Twelfth Night*. The play's bittersweet exploration of love, love's excesses, and marital choices appears to be Shakespeare's own inspiration. So too does the character of Feste, who was probably written for Robert Armin, who succeeded Will Kempe as the primary player of fools in the Lord Chamberlain's Men. While Kempe's specialty was playing rustic clowns and buffoons, Armin, who possessed a fine singing voice, was better suited to play polished, courtly fools whose "fooling" was largely assumed for their profession.

Generally considered the last of Shakespeare's true comedies, *Twelfth Night* anticipates such problem plays as *All's Well that Ends Well* and *Measure for Measure,* in which love and marriage are not so happily or harmoniously achieved. The romantic resolution of the situation between the primary couples, however, links *Twelfth Night* more closely with the sunny earlier comedies, such as *As You Like It* and *Much Ado about Nothing*.

Reception. The exact date of *Twelfth Night's* premiere is not known. Some contend that the play was meant to be performed on Twelfth Night, 1601, when Queen Elizabeth's court was entertaining a distinguished Italian guest, Don Virginio Orsino, duke of Bracciano—hence, the name "Orsino" for Shakespeare's duke. However, the first written allusion to a performance of *Twelfth Night*—on February 2, 1602—appears in the diary of John Manningham, a student at the Middle Temple in London, one of the Inns of Court where young men went to study law.

Twelfth Night, Or, What You Will

At the Middle Temple Feast this night they had a play called *Twelfth Night* or *What you Will*, much like the *Comedy of Errors*, or *Menechmi* in Plautus, but most like and near to that in Italian called *Inganni*. A good practice in it to make the Steward believe his lady widow was in love with him by counterfeiting a letter as from his lady in general terms, telling him what she liked best in him, and prescribing his gesture in smiling, his apparel, etc.; and then when he came to practise making him believe they took him to be mad.

(Manningham in Harrison, p. 320)

Like Manningham, early audiences particularly enjoyed the gulling of Malvolio. In fact, in 1623 *Twelfth Night* seems to have been performed under the title *Malvolio*. Leonard Digges (1588-1635)—in a poem in praise of Shakespeare—specifically mentions Malvolio as an audience pleaser: "To heare Malvolio that crosse-garter'd Gull. / Briefe, there is nothing in his wit fraught Booke, / Whose sound we would not heare" (Digges in Harris and Scott, p. 539). Several reviewers likewise chose to focus upon the character of Olivia's haughty steward in their commentary. Noted critic Richard Steele observed in the *Spectator*, "[Malvolio] has Wit, Learning, and discernment, but temper'd with an Allay of Envy, Self-Love, and Detraction" (Steele in Harris and Scott, p. 540).

Other elements of *Twelfth Night* also garnered praise. Charles Gildon, the first critic to write an extended commentary on Shakespeare's plays, enjoyed the romantic subplot, declaring that "Olivia's Declaration of Love to Viola is very fine and pathetick" (Gildon in Harris and Scott, p. 540). During the eighteenth century, *Twelfth Night* took an occasional beating from reviewers who preferred works based on classical models and found the play's plot contrivances foolish, unbelievable, or indecorous. The critic Samuel Johnson conceded its merits, calling *Twelfth Night* "elegant and easy, and in some of the lighter scenes exquisitely humorous" but concluded that "the marriage of Olivia and the succeeding perplexity, though well enough contrived to divert on stage, wants credibility, and fails to produce the proper instruction required in the drama, as it exhibits no just picture of life" (Johnson in Harris and Scott, p. 542).

Despite its detractors, *Twelfth Night* remained popular with audiences. From its Drury Lane debut in 1741, it was continually revived, and a later generation of critics—more tolerant of Shakespeare's dramatic devices—expressed warm appreciation for the play's exploration of love and imagination. German Romantic critic August Wilhelm Schlegel wrote, "The Twelfth Night, or What you Will [*sic*], unites the entertainment of an intrigue, contrived with great ingenuity, to a rich fund of comic characters and situations, and the beauteous colours of an ethereal poetry" (Schlegel in Harris and Scott, p. 544). Finally, William Hazlitt, the leading Shakespearean critic of the Romantic era, summed up the play's enduring appeal:

> [*Twelfth Night*] is justly considered as one of the most delightful of Shakespeare's comedies. It is full of sweetness and pleasantry. It is perhaps too good-natured for comedy. It has little satire, and no spleen. It aims at the ludicrous rather than the ridiculous. It makes us laugh at the follies of mankind, not despise them, and still less bear any ill-will towards them.
>
> (Hazlitt in Harris and Scott, p. 544)

—Pamela S. Loy

For More Information

Arlidge, Anthony. *Shakespeare and the Prince of Love*. London: Giles de la Mare, 2000.

Barber, C. L. *Shakespeare's Festive Comedy*. Princeton: Princeton University Press, 1959.

Billington, Michael, ed. *RSC Directors' Shakespeare: Twelfth Night*. London: Nick Hern, 1990.

Brimacombe, Peter. *All the Queen's Men*. New York: St. Martin's Press, 2000.

Harris, Laurie Lanzen, and Mark W. Scott, eds. *Shakespearean Criticism*. Vol. 1. Detroit: Gale Research, 1984.

Harrison, G. B. *The Elizabethan Journals*. 2 vols. Garden City: Anchor, 1965.

Notkoff, Tania, ed. *Readings on Twelfth Night*. San Diego: Greenhaven Press, 2001.

Pritchard, R. E. *Shakespeare's England: Life in Elizabethan & Jacobean Times*. Phoenix Mill: Sutton, 1999.

Shakespeare, William. *Twelfth Night*. London: Routledge, 1975.

Singman, Jeffrey L. *Daily Life in Elizabethan England*. Westport: Greenwood Press, 1995.

Southworth, John. *Fools and Jesters at the English Court*. Phoenix Mill: Sutton, 1998.

Williams, Neville. *The Sea Dogs: Privateers, Plunder and Piracy in the Elizabethan Age*. New York: Macmillan, 1975.

Wide Sargasso Sea

by
Jean Rhys

> **THE LITERARY WORK**
>
> A novel set in the British West Indies—especially Jamaica and the Windward Islands—and England during the mid-nineteenth century; published in 1966.
>
> **SYNOPSIS**
>
> A young Creole woman marries an English gentleman but racial prejudices and his infidelity take their toll on her sanity.

Born in 1890 in Roseau, Dominica, the West Indies, Jean Rhys was of mixed parentage. Her father, Dr. William Rhys, was a Welshman, and her mother, Minna Williams, was a Creole. In 1907, Rhys left Dominica to attend the Perse School in Cambridge, England, but spent only one term there; the following year, she entered the Academy of Dramatic Art to study acting, but left to join a chorus line. In 1919, after a sporadic theatrical career and several failed relationships, Rhys left England to marry Jean Lenglet, a French-Dutch songwriter and journalist; the pair lived on the European Continent. In 1923, however, Lenglet was arrested on a charge of illegal entry into France and extradited to Holland. Rhys returned to England alone, where she began a career as a writer, publishing her first book, *The Left Bank and Other Stories* (1927). More works followed: the semi-autobiographical *Postures* (called *Quartet* in the United States; 1928); *After Leaving Mr. Mackenzie* (1930); *Voyage in the Dark* (1934); and *Good Morning, Midnight* (1939). Divorced from Lenglet in 1932, Rhys married two more times: first to Leslie Tilden Smith, a publisher's reader, who died in 1945, then to Max Hamer, a retired naval officer, who died in 1964. With Hamer, Rhys lived a retired life in Europe, Cornwall, and, finally, Devon. Returning to the literary scene in 1966, she garnered critical acclaim with *Wide Sargasso Sea*, which tells the story of a minor character in Charlotte Brontë's classic novel *Jane Eyre* (also in *Literature and Its Times*). This minor character is the insane first wife of the classic's main male figure, Edward Rochester. *Wide Sargasso Sea* was especially praised for its portrayal of a doomed interracial romance between a Creole woman and a white Englishman. In giving it and the marginalized woman the leading role, Rhys's novel shows a faithfulness to preoccupations of her own volatile times.

Events in History at the Time the Novel Takes Place

The British West Indies—an overview. At the time of *Wide Sargasso Sea*, Jamaica and the Windward Islands (Dominica, St. Lucia, St. Vincent, Grenada, and the Grenadines) were governed by the British. Spain had been first among the European nations to gain a foothold in the New World in the late fifteenth century. Many of the Caribbean islands, including Jamaica, Trinidad,

Wide Sargasso Sea

Jean Rhys

and Hispaniola, were settled by the Spanish in the wake of Christopher Columbus's voyages of exploration. However, Spain's dominance as a world power waned in the sixteenth and seventeenth centuries, allowing other nations—England, France, and the Netherlands—to acquire territories in the Americas and the Caribbean. The British settled Barbados in 1625, then seized Jamaica from the Spanish in 1655. Initially regarded as an inferior acquisition—a poor consolation for Britain's failure to capture Hispaniola or Cuba—Jamaica became the most important of Britain's Caribbean colonies by 1750.

Jamaica's rise to prominence was mainly attributable to two factors: the establishment of sugar plantations and the importation of African slaves to work those plantations. Originally, British colonists in the Caribbean had cultivated tobacco—a popular New World crop. Caribbean tobacco, however, could not compete in quality or quantity with that produced elsewhere, necessitating the introduction of sugar cane. During the 1700s, the British colonies in the Caribbean gave themselves over to the production of sugar, which became virtually the only crop. Large plantations requiring vast tracts of land and amounts of capital replaced the small farms that had produced cotton and tobacco. Jamaica, which possessed abundant land and an ideal climate, had become the greatest sugar producer in the British Empire by 1750, a distinction it retained until the 1830s, when the Emancipation Act of 1833 freed the slaves.

As an inevitable result of the thriving sugar industry, the transatlantic slave trade increased. Between 1700 and 1810 the number of slaves brought to the New World more than tripled, and between 1811 and 1830, about 32,000 slaves per year were imported. An estimated 17 percent of 10 million Africans brought to the Americas were sent to the British Caribbean (Meditz and Hanratty, p. 18). While the whites held a superior social position and all the real power on the islands, the population of the British West Indies became predominantly black. The earliest white colonists had aspired to recreate British society in the West Indies by bringing their law, political institutions, and religion to the tropics, but the dream of making the West Indies a culturally British part of the world never materialized. Instead the sugar industry established a plantation society, in which a white minority presided over a nonwhite majority: "In the early nineteenth century, whites constituted less than 5 percent of the total population of Jamaica, Grenada, Nevis, St. Vincent, and Tabago and less than 10 percent of the population of Angulla, Montserrat, St. Kitts, St. Lucia, and the Virgin Islands" (Meditz and Hanratty, p. 18).

Not surprisingly, British Caribbean society was divided along lines of class, caste, and color. The three main divisions consisted of free white persons, free nonwhite persons, and slaves. Subdivisions existed even within those categories—successful, upper-class whites who owned thriving plantations and numerous slaves were considered superior to white servants, day laborers, and even independent farmers. Socially, free nonwhites—a group that originated from miscegenation between European masters and African slaves—ranked below even the poor whites, but many, especially those who had been free for generations, had made places for themselves as artisans, merchants, and even planters and slave owners. The degree of success and acceptance that free nonwhites found, however, often depended to a large degree on skin color; nonwhites with fairer complexions usually had an advantage over those with darker complexions. Though more numerous than any other group, slaves occupied the lowest position in Caribbean society. In 1834 the racial breakdown in Jamaica alone was 20,000 whites, 46,000 free nonwhites, and 310,000 slaves out of an estimated 376,000 people (Rogozinski, p. 114). The inequities of a plantation society with such a lop-

West Indies slaves rejoice at the news of their emancipation.

sided population come to the fore in *Wide Sargasso Sea*. Continually explored in the novel are the ongoing tensions between whites, non-whites, and slaves, especially after the emancipation of the slaves, when the fortunes of the Cosway family decline.

Emancipation of slaves in the British colonies. During the 1780s movements to abolish slavery began to take shape in Britain. An increasing number of Europeans, led by intellectuals and evangelists, came to believe that slavery was unjust, immoral, and evil. Some of them became activists, forming groups like the Society for the Abolition of the Slave Trade (1787), which pressed the British government, submitting petitions against the slave trade. William Wilberforce, a wealthy and influential politician, became a prominent spokesperson for the abolitionists. He initiated a series of parliamentary inquiries that exposed the horrors and inhumanities of the slave trade, including the use of shackles, thumbscrews, and branding irons on the flesh of the human cargo carried by slave ships.

Despite strong resistance from several quarters, the anti-slavery movement gained momentum during the early nineteenth century. In 1807 Parliament abolished the slave trade, effective as of March 1, 1808. Abolitionists continued to push for the end of slavery in the colonies altogether. Bolstering their efforts was a series of slave revolts, which erupted on all the British islands, including Barbados and Jamaica. The Jamaican uprising, which took place in December 1831, was especially violent: more than 60,000 slaves participated in the revolt, which covered an area of some 750 square miles. By the time British troops and militia suppressed the rebellion at the end of January 1832, 540 slaves and 14 whites had died, and over 200 sugar plantations had been burned and pillaged. The resulting outrage—over the revolt and its suppression—was a contributing factor to the passage of the Abolition Act of 1833, which ended slavery in the British Empire as of August 1834. To ease the transition, Parliament introduced a system by which farm laborers had to work as "apprentices" for their former masters until 1840. But the system proved too unwieldy to implement, so Parliament ended it two years early. On August 1, 1838, full emancipation took place, freeing an estimated 750,000 slaves in the British colonies.

Unprepared for emancipation, planters in the British Caribbean suffered an immediate reversal of fortune. One historian speaks of an unfortunate confluence of circumstances:

> Emancipation sharply increased a planter's costs precisely as his income from the harvest was dropping. When prices fell by half—as they did between 1840 and 1848—planters had to double their output merely to stay even. But cane

Wide Sargasso Sea

production fell after emancipation—by 50 percent on Jamaica—as the former slaves fled from the harsh routines of field labor. Many plantations operated at a loss, and government revenues plummeted.

(Rogozinksi, p. 185)

In *Wide Sargasso Sea*, the Cosway family is caught in the middle of this economic and racial maelstrom. The death of Mr. Cosway and the emancipation of the slaves in 1838 have led to the ruin of the family plantation. The local blacks, now free, jeer at the widowed Mrs. Cosway as she becomes increasingly poor and shabby; her daughter, Antoinette, is similarly mocked and called a "white cockroach" by black children (Rhys, *Wide Sargasso Sea*, p. 23). Antoinette's sometime playmate, Tia, tells her, "Old time white people nothing but white nigger now, and black nigger better than white nigger" (*Wide Sargasso Sea*, p. 24).

THE CREOLES: RACE OR CULTURE?

The term "Creole" has taken on various meanings over the years. Coming into widespread use around the sixteenth century, in the West Indies it first referred to descendants of French, Spanish, or Portuguese settlers, then came to refer to the descendants of all kinds of Europeans living in the West Indies and of Africans too. The term came to imply some degree of mixed-race ancestry. Rhys's novel uses "Creole" this way, to imply mixed blood ancestry—with all the tensions such a designation might evoke among the nineteenth-century British. Like other Europeans, the British harbored fears of becoming "creolized" by living in the colonies, that is, of acquiring the characteristics, even the appearance, of colored peoples by physical immersion in their culture. These fears are manifest in the character of the sheltered white Englishman, Rochester, in *Wide Sargasso Sea*. To Rochester, his bride, Antoinette Cosway, is a Creole first and a woman second. He distrusts her beauty, even as he is drawn to it, most obviously because it is different from the purely European beauty he has been brought up to admire, and more subtly because his attraction to her threatens to "taint" him.

Marriage and property rights. During the first half of the nineteenth century, women living within the British Empire had few property rights, especially after marriage. However wealthy or well situated a woman might be as a spinster, her entire situation changed once she became a wife. The law recognized only one person in the marriage: the husband. Married women had no independent legal existence; everything they owned, earned, or inherited belonged to their husbands. Wives did not even have the right to sign contracts, make wills, or spend their own income. Even the children born of marriage were considered the property of the fathers, who could control and educate them as they saw fit.

Some brides' families tried to arrange safeguards before the marriages took place. Well-to-do fathers and guardians often insisted on a marriage settlement, a type of prenuptial agreement that protected the interests of their daughters and wards. Before the wedding, a bridegroom would have to sign a deed of settlement, a contract that set aside a sum of money for his wife as her personal property. Marriage settlements ensured that wives would have some independent income, especially if their husbands died or went bankrupt; a husband could not appropriate his wife's settlement money to pay his debts. Settlements were distinct from dowries, the money or property brought by the bride from her family into the marriage. Although some families made legal arrangements to protect the bride's dowry, an unscrupulous husband could seize control and spend it for his own purposes.

In *Wide Sargasso Sea*, Antoinette finds herself at the mercy of her new husband, not least because of her lack of property rights. Her stepbrother, Richard Mason, who arranges her marriage to Edward Rochester, fails to provide for her future security. No settlements are made on her behalf and Antoinette's large dowry passes into Rochester's hands the moment they are married. The unhappy bride explains to her old nurse, Christophine, "And you must understand I am not rich now. I have no money of my own at all, everything I had belongs to him. . . . That is English law" (*Wide Sargasso Sea*, p. 110).

The Novel in Focus

The plot. *Wide Sargasso Sea* is divided into three parts. The first is the childhood narrative of Antoinette Cosway, a young Creole girl living on the impoverished Jamaican estate of Coulibri, with her widowed mother, Annette, and her mentally and physically enfeebled brother, Pierre. Annette, who originally came from Martinique, is rejected alike by local whites and by the recently freed black slaves. Lacking a male protector, the Cosways lead an increasingly poor and shabby existence; Annette devotes most of her energies to caring for the sickly Pierre, while Antoinette is left to the care of her devoted black nurse, Christophine. Rejected by other children, Antoinette runs wild in the Jamaican rainforest, deriving some comfort from her untamed surroundings. With Christophine's help, she makes friends with a little black girl named Tia, though the friendship is not unmarked by feelings of jealousy and rivalry. One day, after a quarrel, Tia switches clothes with Antoinette, taking the latter's newly laundered dress and leaving her own shabbier one behind. Forced to don Tia's dress, Antoinette returns home to find her mother entertaining several wealthy white guests, who laugh at the child's tattered appearance. That night, Antoinette dreams she is walking in the forest with someone who hates her and wakes in distress, feeling as though her world is changing irrevocably.

Some time later, Annette captivates and marries Mr. Mason, a wealthy English planter with properties in Trinidad. Antoinette, serving as bridesmaid, hears unkind whispers about her family from the wedding guests and fears for her mother's happiness. At first, matters seem to improve at Coulibri, at least materially. Mason repairs the estate, buys new furniture, and hires more servants, but fails to perceive how the family's new prosperity angers the natives. Annette vainly pleads with Mason to sell Coulibri and let them settle elsewhere.

Finally, the local blacks form a mob that attacks and burns the estate, killing Pierre and driving Annette into madness. Antoinette does not escape unharmed. Her former friend Tia throws a stone at her, delivering a blow to her head. On recovering several weeks later, Antoinette learns that Pierre has died and her mother has been sent away to the country. Antoinette recalls her mother's screams and her threats to kill Mr. Mason but keeps the memories to herself. Later Antoinette visits her mother at her new abode, only to be rejected by her when she does not see Pierre there too.

Antoinette is sent to live in a convent school in the part of Jamaica known as Spanish Town. Walking to the convent, she is taunted by two native children but defended by her mixed-blood cousin, Alexander Cosway, for whom she forms a lasting affection. At the convent, Antoinette finds a refuge and begins to make friends. She sees little of her stepfather during this period; after she turns 17, however, Mason visits to tell her he wishes to arrange a secure future for her. Disturbed by the sense of impending change, Antoinette again has the nightmare of walking with someone who hates her, but this time she sees that her companion in the dream is a man who brings her to an enclosed garden and seems to want to shut her away behind stone walls. As before, she awakes distraught. One of the nuns tries to console her with a cup of hot chocolate, but the drink reminds Antoinette of her mother's funeral the previous year, saddening her further. Still unsettled, she returns to her bed in the dormitory.

THE YOUNGER SON'S PORTION

The ancient system known as primogeniture ensured that, among landed upper-class British families, the bulk of the property was left—by the father—to the eldest son. Unless the father made provision for them, younger sons usually had to shift for themselves. Most tried to enter a respectable profession, such as the church, the army, the navy, or the law. Others sought wealthy wives, supposing prospective brides were willing to ally themselves with younger sons who could only inherit if their elder brothers died. As a youngest son with few prospects, Rochester grudgingly consents to marriage with a Creole heiress who has a dowry of 30,000 pounds, equivalent to $600,000 or more in the United States today. However, after the deaths of his father and elder brother, Rochester inherits the family money and property, by which time his mad wife has become an embarrassment to him.

The novel's second part, which begins some time later, is narrated by Edward Rochester, Antoinette's new husband, who is also the younger son of a prominent English family.

Rochester's father and elder brother, along with Mr. Mason's son Richard, have arranged his marriage to Antoinette, now a considerable heiress, thanks to the dowry settled on by her stepfather, Mr. Mason. The young couple are honeymooning on one of the Windward Islands at Granbois, a small estate formerly belonging to Antoinette's mother. Recently recovered from fever, Rochester chafes at his situation, though he feels a reluctant attraction to his bride. Thinking back to the days before the wedding, Rochester remembers that Antoinette had also expressed doubts about going through with the ceremony; not wanting to return home as a jilted suitor, Rochester had persuaded her with kisses and reassurances of "peace, happiness, safety" (*Wide Sargasso Sea*, p. 79). Now Rochester's resentments and misgivings resurface; he finds himself overwhelmed by the vividness and mystery of the West Indies, especially as personified in his bride. For her part, Antoinette, already in love with her husband, tries to bridge the cultural and emotional gap, revealing memories of her childhood to him. Rochester partly responds to her need for intimacy, and they share a night of happiness.

The chasm soon reopens, however; Rochester complains about Antoinette's familiarity with the native servants at Granbois, especially her old nurse, Christophine. Antoinette is bewildered and amused by her husband's peevishness. For a time, the newlyweds continue to find harmony in the marriage bed, though Rochester denies to himself that he feels anything more than lust for his wife. But matters deteriorate when Rochester starts receiving letters from a local mulatto who calls himself Daniel Cosway and claims to be Antoinette's half-brother, by her slaveowner father. Daniel also claims that there is "bad blood" in Antoinette's family, that her mother was a madwoman, and Antoinette is destined to become one too. Infected by Daniel's malice, Rochester becomes further estranged from his wife and stops sleeping with her. Wandering through the rainforest in distress over what he has learned, Rochester becomes lost and needs the help of a manservant to get back to Granbois safely.

Meanwhile, Antoinette feels increasingly isolated by the coldness of her husband, the malice of her mulatto maid Amelie, and even the defection of Christophine, who leaves Granbois rather than become a bone of contention between the couple. Unaware of Daniel's letters and their effect on her husband, Antoinette visits Christophine in the latter's own home, confides in her about her marital woes, and asks how she might regain her husband's love. Rochester, says Antoinette, does not even call her by her given name anymore. Instead he addresses her as Bertha to separate her from her mother and her mother's heritage. Christophine advises her to leave Rochester, arguing "When man don't love you, more you try, more he hate you, man like that. If you love them they treat you bad, if you don't love them they after you night and day bothering your soul case out" (*Wide Sargasso Sea*, p. 109). Antoinette refuses to abandon her husband, instead pleading for a love potion that will win back his affections. Although Christophine has some reputation as a practitioner of obeah, she is reluctant to comply. Christophine warns Antoinette that Rochester may hate her even more afterwards. She also suggests that Antoinette tell Rochester the truth about the insanity in her family before anyone can poison his mind against her. Ultimately, Christophine gives Antoinette the potion, not for payment but for the latter's promise to speak to her husband.

Rochester's narrative resumes as he receives a second letter from Daniel, containing more of the same accusations against Antoinette's family. At Amelie's suggestion, Rochester decides to visit Daniel at his home in the lower village; the embittered mulatto insists that everything in his letters is true, recounting how he visited Coulibri when Mr. Cosway was alive and how the old man denied paternity and drove Daniel off his property. Although Daniel received some monetary compensation from Cosway, he considered it meager compared to what Cosway gave his acknowledged son, Alexander, and Alexander's son, Sandi (Antoinette's cousin and protector on her first day at the convent-school). Besides reiterating his story about Antoinette's "bad blood," Daniel insinuates that she and Sandi were lovers. Rochester listens to these stories with mounting disgust, then storms from the house when Daniel demands 500 pounds for his silence.

Back at Granbois, hearing at last of Daniel's letters, Antoinette dismisses them as lies, rejects Daniel's claim to kinship, and tells Rochester her side of the story. She speaks of her family's poverty, her mother's remarriage, and the fire at Coulibri that killed her brother and caused her mother's insanity. Although Rochester has privately decided to believe Daniel's story, he is stirred by Antoinette's distress and by the aphrodisiac she has secretly placed in the wine. Still insisting on calling her Bertha, Rochester takes her to bed.

On awakening the next morning, Rochester feels ill and soon discovers that Antoinette has drugged him. As Christophine predicted, his revulsion towards his wife revives and he revenges himself on her by having sex with the maid Amelie just outside the bedroom he shares with Antoinette. Afterwards, Rochester finds Amelie less attractive than before, and Amelie herself now pities her mistress and wishes only to leave Granbois; she takes Rochester's money and departs. Antoinette discovers Rochester's infidelity; heartbroken, she drowns her sorrows in drink, then lashes out at her husband, claiming to hate him for his insult to her and for the way he has polluted Granbois, one of the few places she loved. Christophine arrives to console her distraught mistress; later, Rochester and Christophine themselves face off, the native woman berating the Englishman for his crimes against his wife:

> Everybody know that you marry her for her money and you take it all. And then you want to break her up, because you jealous of her. She is more better than you, she have better blood in her and she don't care for money—it's nothing for her. . . . You fool the girl. You make her think you can't see the sun for looking at her.
> (*Wide Sargasso Sea*, p. 152)

Christophine's accusations do not impress Rochester; nor does he listen to what she has to say about Daniel's being a liar or Antoinette's still loving him and needing his love to survive. Instead, Rochester orders Christophine from the house, threatening to have her arrested for giving Antoinette the drugs used on him. Already imprisoned once for practicing obeah, Christophine departs, though not without denouncing Rochester one last time as unworthy of Antoinette.

Bitter, disillusioned, and vengeful, Rochester resolves to make Antoinette pay for all his disappointments in the marriage. He plans to take her away from Granbois and back to Jamaica. On the morning of their departure, he is tempted to ask Antoinette's forgiveness and attempt to make a fresh start with her, but her enduring hatred strengthens his own and they remain coldly estranged.

The third part of *Wide Sargasso Sea* takes place some years later as Grace Poole, a servant at Thornfield Hall in England, relates how Rochester inherited the family property after the deaths of his father and brother. On Rochester's orders, Antoinette was locked up in an attic of the house, tended only by Grace Poole and another servant. Grace notices how the West Indian woman seems to live in her own world; nonetheless, the servant does not dare to turn her back on her charge.

Antoinette then takes up the narrative; she cannot remember where she is, how long she has been in the attic, nor why she has been brought there, but she is always cold and hoping for the chance to escape. She notices that Grace drinks heavily. One morning, Antoinette wakes up feeling stiff and sore; Grace informs her that her stepbrother, Richard Mason, visited the night before and Antoinette attacked him with a knife. On being reminded of the encounter, Antoinette can only recall that Richard did not recognize her. Memories of the West Indies, including an affectionate parting from her cousin Sandi, haunt her; she asks Grace for the red dress she used to wear in the islands. Holding the dress up to herself, Antoinette imagines fire spreading across the room.

That night, Antoinette has the dream that has plagued her twice before, but now she knows how it ends. In her dream, she sees herself taking the keys from the sleeping Grace, slipping out of the attic to wander through Thornfield Hall, which she sets afire by knocking over some candles. Running up to the roof to escape the heat of the blaze, Antoinette sees her life in Jamaica flashing before her. She hears a man calling for "Bertha" but looking down from the battlements, she sees the pool at Coulibri and Tia beckoning to her. Antoinette jumps down to join her friend, and wakes up in the attic again. Grace also awakens but Antoinette feigns sleep until the servant is snoring again. Knowing now what she must do, Antoinette steals Grace's keys and escapes from the attic in earnest. The novel ends as she slips down the passage with a candle, planning to turn her dreams into reality.

OBEAH—FORBIDDEN MAGIC

Several references are made in *Wide Sargasso Sea* to obeah, the shamanic folk religion practice by African slaves in Jamaica. Conjurers or "obeah men" and "obeah women" were hired to curse or do harm to enemies (including whites), although they might also be called upon to heal and work charms of protection or love. Obeah practitioners were said to use such materials as blood (human or animal), broken bottles, eggshells, grave dirt, and rum in their spells. While white slave owners usually dismissed obeah as idle superstition, some accused obeah men of cursing and poisoning whites. Outlawed in Jamaica in 1760, obeah continued to be practiced in secret. In the novel, Christophine, Antoinette's old nurse, is an obeah woman, though she takes care not to be caught practicing her craft, especially after having been jailed for it before. She tries to dissuade Antoinette from using obeah to win back Rochester's love, warning her former charge that the Englishman will hate her if he discovers the spell cast on him. Sadly, her prediction proves all too accurate; obeah becomes yet another contributing factor to the widening gap of cultural misunderstanding between Antoinette and Rochester.

Wide Sargasso Sea

Anatomy of a madwoman. Throughout *Wide Sargasso Sea*, the threat of madness hovers over Antoinette and her family like a storm cloud, undermining whatever security or happiness they try to achieve. Pierre, Antoinette's brother, is born with apparent physical and mental handicaps; Annette, her mother, suffers a permanent breakdown after Pierre's death; and Antoinette ends her own days as a madwoman confined in the attic of her estranged husband's ancestral home.

Rhys, however, allows for ambiguity in her depiction of madness within the Cosway family. Two supporting characters—one malevolent, one benign—present differing viewpoints on the cause of the Cosways' insanity. Daniel, the jealous mulatto who claims to be Antoinette's half-brother, informs Rochester that old Cosway "die raving like his father before him" and that Annette succumbed to "that madness that is in her, and in all these white Creoles" (*Wide Sargasso Sea*, p. 96). Daniel predicts that Antoinette will end up as both her parents did because of "the bad blood she have from both sides" (*Wide Sargasso Sea*, p. 97). By contrast, Christophine, Antoinette's nurse, offers a more sympathetic explanation for what happened to Annette: "They drive her to it. When she lose her son she lose herself for a while and they shut her away. They tell her she is mad, they act like she is mad. . . . In the end—mad I don't know—she give up, she care for nothing" (*Wide Sargasso Sea*, p. 157). Christophine then accuses Rochester of trying to do the same thing to Antoinette that Mr. Mason had done to Antoinette's mother: "You want her money but you don't want her. It is in your mind to pretend she is mad. I know it. The doctors say what you want them to say" (*Wide Sargasso Sea*, p. 160). To the end, Rhys seems to leave it up to the reader to decide whether Antoinette's ultimate withdrawal into her own world is the result of hereditary insanity, exacerbated by drink and passion, or is her only defense against her husband's cruelty and betrayal.

The uncertainty surrounding Antoinette's condition reflects the complex attitudes towards mental illness during the period in which *Wide Sargasso Sea* takes place. Nineteenth-century Britain witnessed significant changes in the care of the insane. Early in the century, doctors treated the mentally ill (who were often confined in madhouses) with purges, blisters, and bleedings. The belief was that such methods rendered their patients docile and easier to manage. Later, however, with the establishment of private asylums, which offered improved living conditions, inmates received less violent and more humane treatment from the doctors in charge. Patients were often permitted outdoor exercise in pleasant surroundings instead of being confined to cells or chained to walls.

Methods of treating the mentally ill continued in a state of flux, owing to the ongoing debate over what factors caused insanity. Early nineteenth-century writers on the subject tended to believe that madness resulted from some moral cause, such as the patient's lack of moderation or overindulgence in certain appetites. If the patient's will and conscience were appealed to, reasoned the writers, recovery from insanity was possible: "Habit, perseverance, the will and character may each constitute such a counteracting force" (Skultans, p. 2). Later writers, however, concentrated on other possible factors, including heredity, character, and gender. In 1828 George Man Burrows declared unequivocally, "Hereditary predisposition, therefore, is a prominent cause of mental derangement," adding:

> Sometimes, in a large family, we find all the forms and relations of insanity developed in a remarkable manner. Mania, melancholia, hypochondriasis, apoplexy, paralysis, epilepsy, convulsions, chorea, hysteria, &c., or high nervous irritability are often found to pervade one or the other of the same progeny [offspring].
> (Burrows in Skultans, p. 204)

Women were considered especially vulnerable to hereditary insanity, possibly because of the multiple physical changes—puberty, menstruation, childbirth, and menopause—they would undergo during their sexual development. The nineteenth-century view of women as physically and emotionally fragile creatures also contributed to the belief that they were more susceptible to madness. Thomas Laycock wrote in 1840, "It is widely acknowledged that the affectability of the female sex has its counterpart in that of children, mental emotions and movements are excited in both with equal facility" (Laycock in Skultans, p. 4). The transmission of insanity between generations of women was therefore only to be expected. Writing in 1875, Andrew Wynter declared,

> It is agreed by all alienist physicians, that girls are far more likely to inherit insanity from their mothers than from the other parent. . . . If the daughter of an insane mother very much resembles her in feature and in temperament, the chances are that she is more likely to inherit the disease than other daughters who are not so like.
> (Wynter in Skultans, p. 235)

In *Wide Sargasso Sea*, Rhys continually emphasizes the resemblance between the doomed Antoinette and her equally star-crossed mother. "Tied to a lunatic for life," says Rochester, "a drunken lying lunatic—gone her mother's way" (*Wide Sargasso Sea*, p. 164). The emphasis seems to reveal an awareness of these prevailing nineteenth-century theories, however little scientific merit they hold today.

Sources and literary context. Charlotte Brontë's famous novel *Jane Eyre* was the primary source of inspiration for *Wide Sargasso Sea*. Indeed Rhys had long been fascinated with the enigmatic figure of the first Mrs. Rochester, as stated in an interview done for the *Guardian*:

> The mad wife in *Jane Eyre* always interested me. I was convinced that Charlotte Brontë must have had something against the West Indies, and I was angry about it. Otherwise, why did she take a West Indian for that horrible lunatic, for that really dreadful creature? I hadn't really formulated the idea of vindicating the mad woman in a novel but when I was rediscovered I was encouraged to do so.
>
> (Rhys in Nebeker, p. 126)

Although *Wide Sargasso Sea* uses a historical rather than a contemporary setting, Rhys probably drew upon some of her personal experiences: her love of the West Indies, her sense of being caught between British and Caribbean cultures, her ambivalence toward West Indian blacks, and her various failed relationships and troubled marriages.

Like *Jane Eyre*, *Wide Sargasso Sea* might be best described as a Gothic romance, a type of prose fiction characterized by a gloomy, brooding atmosphere; an exotic, often medieval, setting; melodramatic or macabre events; and often a touch of the supernatural. The West Indian flavor of Rhys's novel has prompted at least one reviewer, Walter Allen, to describe it as a "Caribbean Gothic" (Allen in Wolfe, p. 158). More recently, critics and literary scholars have cited *Wide Sargasso Sea* as an example of postcolonial literature because of its exploration of such themes as imperialism, racism, and the problematic relationship between colonized and colonizer.

Events in History at the Time the Novel was Written

Racial diversity in postcolonial Britain. The publication of *Wide Sargasso Sea* in 1966 coincided with a particularly turbulent period in British history. In the years following the Second World War, Great Britain began to divest itself of its various colonies throughout the world. The process of decolonization, which took several decades, was to have major consequences upon the ethnic composition of Britain proper. In 1948 the British Nationality Act ascribed British citizenship to all subjects in the United Kingdom, its existing colonies, and even newly independent Commonwealth countries. That same year 492 Jamaicans arrived in Britain on the S.S. *Empire Windrush*, marking the start of large-scale immigration by blacks to Britain. About 66,000 West Indians immigrated to the United Kingdom during the period from 1948 to 1961.

TWO PERSPECTIVES ON THE LEADING MAN

In her novel, *Jane Eyre*, Charlotte Brontë paints a very different picture of Rochester's youthful marriage and first wife. Accused of attempted bigamy on his wedding day to Jane, Rochester admits the charge but furiously defends his actions:

> Bigamy is an ugly word!—I meant, however, to be a bigamist; but fate has out-manoeuvred me, or Providence has checked me,—perhaps the last. I am little better than a devil at this moment; and, as my pastor there would tell me, deserve no doubt the sternest judgments of God, even to the quenchless fire and deathless worm. Gentlemen, my plan is broken up:—what this lawyer and his client say is true: I have been married, and the woman to whom I was married lives! You say you never heard of a Mrs. Rochester at the house up yonder, Wood; but I daresay you have many a time inclined your ear to gossip about the mysterious lunatic kept there under watch and ward. Some have whispered to you that she is my bastard half-sister: some, my cast-off mistress. I now inform you that she is my wife, whom I married fifteen years ago,—Bertha Mason by name . . . Bertha Mason is mad; and she came of a mad family; idiots and maniacs through three generations? Her mother, the Creole, was both a madwoman and a drunkard!—as I found out after I had wed the daughter: for they were silent on family secrets before. Bertha, like a dutiful child, copied her parent in both points. I had a charming partner—pure, wise, modest: you can fancy I was a happy man. I went through rich scenes! . . . I invite you all to come up to the house and visit Mrs. Poole's patient, and my wife! You shall see what sort of a being I was cheated into espousing, and judge whether or not I had a right to break the compact, and seek sympathy with something at least human.
>
> (Brontë, p. 256)

Wide Sargasso Sea

Between 1958 and 1968 an estimated one million immigrants—mostly from former colonies—entered England, bringing with them a variety of languages, cultures, and religions that were to change the ethnic makeup of the nation forever. Many British whites resented and feared these newcomers, harboring racist views of Asian and African immigrants. In 1958 race riots broke out in Nottingham and London. During the 1960s and 1970s the British government began to take a role in counteracting racial prejudice. In 1965 the Race Relations Act prohibited racial discrimination in public places, outlawed the promotion of racial hatred, and established a Race Relations Board to hear and mediate complaints.

Although *Wide Sargasso Sea* takes place in the nineteenth century, the racial tensions and prejudices that exist between characters in the novel may have heightened its relevance to modern readers. Rochester, as a white Englishman, seems especially prejudiced, distrusting the beauty of his Creole bride Antoinette because it is not an English or European beauty and objecting to her embracing and kissing her black West Indian nurse, Christophine: "I wouldn't hug and kiss them . . . I couldn't" (*Wide Sargasso Sea*, p. 91). The morning after Rochester sleeps with Amelie, Antoinette's maid, he notices that "her skin was darker, her lips thicker than I had thought" (*Wide Sargasso Sea*, p. 140).

Reviews. After Rhys's absence from the writing world, *Wide Sargasso Sea* was eagerly anticipated and warmly praised. British critics were positive on the whole. The reviewer for *The Spectator* called *Wide Sargasso Sea* "a magnificent comeback," while the *Times Literary Supplement* devoted a long essay to the novel, contending that it represents the culmination of the author's art.

American critics were similarly enthusiastic when *Wide Sargasso Sea* appeared in the United States the following summer. Walter Allen, writing for the *New York Times Book Review*, expressed some reservations as to whether *Wide Sargasso Sea* could stand alone, without reference to *Jane Eyre*, but nonetheless called the novel "a considerable tour de force by any standards" and "a triumph of atmosphere" (Allen in Samudio, p. 1092). Similarly, Francis Hope wrote in the *New Statesman* that *Wide Sargasso Sea* is "a work of some power, and some poetry" (Hope in Samudio, p. 1092). Finally, Elizabeth Frazier, reviewer for *Library Journal*, declared that "Miss Rhys has brilliantly and imaginatively constructed the girlhood and the marriage of . . . the mysterious madwoman in *Jane Eyre*" and predicted that the number of Jean Rhys aficionados would be "considerably increased by this excellent tour de force" (Frazier in Samudio, p. 1092).

—Pamela S. Loy

For More Information

Booker, M. Keith, and Dubravka Juraga. *The Caribbean Novel in English*. Portsmouth, N.H.: Heinemann, 2001.

Brontë, Charlotte. *Jane Eyre*. New York: W. W. Norton, 1971.

Jones, Kathleen. *Lunacy, Law, and Conscience 1744-1845*. London: Routledge & Kegan Paul, 1955.

Meditz, Sandra W., and Dennis M. Hanratty, eds. *Islands of the Commonwealth Caribbean: A Regional Study*. Washington, D.C.: Federal Research Division, 1989.

Nebeker, Helen. *Jean Rhys, Woman in Passage: A Critical Study of the Novels of Jean Rhys*. Montréal: Eden Press Women's Publications: 1981.

Rhys, Jean. *Smile Please*. New York: Harper & Row, 1979.

———. *Wide Sargasso Sea*. New York: W. W. Norton, 1966.

Rogozinski, Jan. *A Brief History of the Caribbean*. New York: Facts on File, 1992.

Samudio, Josephine, ed. *Book Review Digest*. New York: H. W. Wilson, 1968.

Skultans, Vieda. *Madness and Morals: Ideas on Insanity in the Nineteenth Century*. London: Routledge & Kegan Paul, 1975.

Wolfe, Peter. *Jean Rhys*. Boston: Twayne, 1980.

Index

Note: Bold print indicates the volume number. For example, **4**:145, 148 indicates Volume 4, pages 145 and 148. **S1.1** represents *Supplement 1, Part 1*. **S1.2** represents *Supplement 1, Part 2*.

A

Aaron, Hank   **4**:145, 148
Abbey, Edward, *Desert Solitaire*   **S1.2**:95–103
Abernathy, Ralph   **5**:89 (*illus.*)
Abolitionists, Abolition of slavery
   John Brown's raid on Harper's Ferry   **2**:188–94
   changing little for freed slaves   **5**:19–20
   controversy and disagreement with, in North   **2**:9, 315, 404
   as core political issue by mid-19th century   **2**:88, 242
   early efforts   **2**:22–4
   emancipation in British colonies, planters' ruin   **S1.1**:495–6
   Emancipation Proclamation (1862)   **2**:59, 60 (*sidebar*), 135, 308, 309
   English abolition movement chronology   **S1.1**:410 (*sidebar*)
   land for freed slaves, proposals for   **2**:41
   Liberia   **2**:404
   murder of antislavery newspaper editor   **S1.2**:231
   Underground Railroad   **2**:16, 60, 62, 189, 238, 406–7
   women decrying sexual overtones of slave abuse   **S1.2**:229
   women's role in   **2**:23–4
   (*See also* African Americans; Jim Crow laws; Reconstruction)
Abortion   **5**:51, 136
Abraham Lincoln: The Prairie Years, Sandburg, Carl   **2**:1–7
"Absurd," concept of   **4**:400, **S1.2**:406, 444 (*sidebar*), 476

Achebe, Chinua
   Anthills of the Savannah   **S1.2**:39–49, 203
   political activism   **S1.2**:48
   Things Fall Apart   **2**:360–5, **S1.2**:203
Acheson, Dean   **5**:101
Achilles   **1**:169–70, 171 (*illus.*)
Across Five Aprils, Hunt, Irene   **2**:8–14
Adam and Eve   **1**:301–2, **S1.1**:145 (*sidebar*)
Adams, John   **1**:29, 72, 94
Adams, John Quincy   **1**:209
Adams, Richard, *Watership Down*   **5**:346–51
Addison, Joseph   **1**:307
Adoption of children, by African Americans   **4**:33
Adultery, infidelity   **5**:273, 287
   in *Anna Karenina*   **2**:34–40, **S1.1**:368
   in *Ethan Frome*   **2**:125–9
   in *Madame Bovary*   **2**:209–15
   in *Medea*   **1**:238–41
   in *Scarlet Letter, The,*   **1**:351–7
   (*See also,* Love and marriage; Sexual dimension of life)
Adventures of Don Quixote, The, Cervantes Saavedra, Miguel de   **1**:1–7, **S1.1**:189
Adventures of Huckleberry Finn, The, Twain, Mark   **2**:15–21
Adventures of Sherlock Holmes, The, Doyle, Arthur Conan   **S1.1**:279
Advertising
   fostering consumer culture   **3**:26
   targeting teenagers   **4**:392
   WWII-related ads excluding minorities   **4**:197
Advise and Consent   **5**:4
Aegean Sea   **1**:60 (*map*)
Aeneas. *See Aeneid, The*
Aeneid, The, Virgil   **1**:8–13
   parallels to *Beowulf*   **1**:49

Index

Aeneid, The, Virgil (*continued*)
   parallels to Shakespeare's *The Tempest*   1:383
Aeschylus   S1.1:308
Aesthetic Movement and "art for art's sake"   S1.1:64, 179, 182, 202
Affirmative action   5:181, 183–4, 342, S1.2:256, 375
AFL (American Federation of Labor)   3:44
Africa and Africans
   in 16th-century England   1:299
   Algeria   3:212
   apartheid in South Africa   1:63, 3:86
   Belgian Congo   2:145–6, 150–1
   Ethiopia   4:67
   Gambia   5:298
   Ghana   4:314
   impact of WWI   3:292–3
   independence movements   4:314
   ivory trade   2:147
   Kenya   3:290–6
   Liberia   2:404
   Maasai   3:295
   Medea as Egyptian "woman of color"   1:240 (*sidebar*)
   Moors   1:297, 299
   natives as "squatters"   3:293–4
   Nigeria   2:360–2, 364–5, 3:84, 4:314, S1.2:39–48
   oral tradition and griots   5:298–300, 301–2
   Organization of African Unity (OAU)   S1.2:43
   post-WWI economic problems   3:293
   racism of colonial powers   2:360–5, 3:291
   Rhodesia   4:165–6
   Tanzania   3:290
   (*See also* Colonialism, imperialism, and interventionism; Slave trade; South Africa)
African American men
   "humiliations, emasculation" faced by   4:53–4, 5:146, 328–9, S1.1:430, 431
   physicians in Georgia   3:154–5, 156–7
   relationship of class, race, and manhood   4:313–14
   as soldiers in Vietnam War   5:102–3
African Americans in 19th century
   churches as cornerstones of community   5:189
   exodus from South to West   3:249–50
   gospel songs and black spirituals   2:398, 402, 407, 4:258
   mixed race offspring and color prejudice   5:21
   "Negritude" movement   S1.1:431 (*sidebar*), 432
   (*See also* Civil War; Jim Crow laws; Segregation; Slavery in America; Slaves)
African Americans in 20th century
   adopting white society's values   4:52
   adoption of children   4:33
   in black ghettos. *See* Ghettos
   black-white wealth disparity, un- and under-employment   S1.2:422–3
   class, social stratification among   4:2–3, 30
   communism and   1:398–9, 3:164, 238–9
   community, kinship, and closeness   2:341–2, 3:383–4, 394, 4:52
   crime, some turning to   4:145
   crime, victims of   4:31, 5:340–1
   divisive "blacker than thou" attitudes   S1.2:231
   during Great Depression   3:154, 236–7
   education   4:3, 5:342
   employment opportunities and limitations   4:311, 5:341 (*sidebar*)
   family life   3:80, 84–6, 353–5, 375, 422–3, 4:33, 5:68, 145–6, 329–30
   gains for few, tensions for many   S1.2:427–9
   ghettoization inspiring protest movements, offering safety from racism   S1.2:423
   Harlem Renaissance   3:159–65, 256, 321, 384–5, 421, 4:204 (*sidebar*), 207, 247–8, 5:67–8, S1.1:336–8, 337 (*sidebar*), 432–4
   Hollywood's stereotypical images of   2:142, 4:50, 369
   interest in genealogy   S1.2:228, 389,
   in *Loving v. Virginia*, anti-miscegenation statutes declared unconstitutional   S1.2:232
   middle class   3:252, 255, 387–8, 4:2, 51, S1.1:336 (*sidebar*), 340, S1.2:427–8
   mixed race offspring and color prejudice   2:49, 3:17–18, 81, 83, 387–8, 4:3, 50, 51–2, 5:130, S1.1:340
   names issue, rejection of slave names and label of "negro"   S1.2:429
   need for engagement with past, roots, and inherited history   S1.2:228, 384, 385–6, 393–4, 426–7
   "Negritude" movement   S1.1:431 (*sidebar*), 432
   "New Negro" of 1920s   S1.1:336, 432
   oral tradition   5:298–300, 301–2
   poverty of many   3:37, 4:5 (*sidebar*), 145, 5:329
   race colonies   3:383
   religion's importance to   3:372
   riot following assassination of Martin Luther King, Jr. (1968)   5:112 (*sidebar*)
   riots in central Los Angeles (1992)   5:340, S1.2:353 (*sidebar*), 354
   riots in major cities (Watts, Harlem, Detroit)   5:340, S1.2:424, 428, 429
   in South after WWII   S1.2:249–51
   widest recorded unemployment gap in 1980s   S1.2:429
   (*See also* Civil rights movement; Great Migration; Jim Crow laws; Segregation)
African Americans, literary works concerning
   Adventures of Huckleberry Finn, The   2:15–21
   "Ain't I a Woman?"   2:22–7
   "Almos' a Man"   4:1–6
   Autobiography of Malcolm X, The   5:11–18
   "Bear, The"   2:47–53
   Beloved   2:59–65
   Benito Cereno   1:37–43
   Betsey Brown   4:28–34
   Black Boy   3:36–43
   Bluest Eye, The   4:49–57

Color Purple, The 3:80–7
Confessions of Nat Turner, The 2:93–8
Cry, the Beloved Country 4:94–100
Fences 4:144–50
Fire Next Time, The 5:107–14
for colored girls who have considered suicide / when the rainbow is enuf 5:115–21
Gathering of Old Men, A 5:129–34
Gone with the Wind 2:137–44
Hero Ain't Nothin' but a Sandwich, A 5:143–8
His Own Where 5:149–55
Home to Harlem 3:159–65
"I Have a Dream" 5:185–93, S1.2:269
I Know Why the Caged Bird Sings 4:201–8
Incidents in the Life of a Slave Girl 2:168–73
Invisible Man 4:209–15
John Brown's Final Speech 2:188–94
Leaves of Grass 2:197
"Letter from Birmingham Jail," Martin Luther King, Jr. S1.2:269–77
Manchild in the Promised Land 4:247–53
Member of the Wedding, The 4:254–9
Narrative of the Life of Frederick Douglass 2:236–41, S1.2:229, 231
Native Son 3:236–42
Not without Laughter 3:249–56
Passing, Larsen, Nella S1.1:333–42
Piano Lesson, The S1.2:379–86
Praisesong for the Widow S1.2:387–95
Raisin in the Sun, A 4:309–15
Roots 5:298–305, S1.2:228, 236, 427
Song of Solomon S1.2:421–30
Souls of Black Folk, The 2:340–6
Sounder 3:370–6
"Spunk" and "Sweat" S1.1:429–37, S1.2:266
Sweet Whispers, Brother Rush 5:328–32
Their Eyes Were Watching God 3:383–9, S1.2:266
Tituba of Salem Village 1:393–9
Uncle Remus 2:397–402
Uncle Tom's Cabin 2:403–9
Understand This 5:339–45
Up From Slavery 2:410–15
"Worn Path, The" 3:418–24
African American women
   accused of black male-bashing 3:87, 5:121
   African-style clothing and hairdos 4:56, 5:145, 300
   black feminism 2:64, 3:86–7, 354–5, 4:56, 5:92–3, 117, S1.2:394 (sidebar)
   caught at intersection of racial and sexual politics S1.2:235
   cosmetics for 4:50, 56
   devaluation of 3:80–2, 4:54, 5:115–16
   differences with white women in civil rights and feminist movements 3:354–5, 5:92–3, 117
   as domestic workers S1.2:422–3
   employment in South 3:418–19
   as heads of families 3:355, 375, 423
   as "mammies" 3:392
   race- and gender-based limitations upon 5:115–16, S1.1:340–1
   severe hardships S1.1:430–1
   sexual abuse of 2:49, 60, 169, 406, 4:54, 5:117, S1.2:236
   as single heads of households 2:65, 3:80, 423, 4:2, 5:68, 117, 328–9, S1.2:256
African Methodist Episcopal Church 3:83
Afrikaans language S1.2:118, 122–3
Afrikaners (Boers) S1.2:115, 116, 122–3
Agee, James
   Death in the Family, A 3:100–5
   Let Us Now Praise Famous Men S1.2:259–68
Age of Innocence, The, Wharton, Edith S1.1:1–9
Age of Reason 1:268–9, 272
Agnosticism 3:265
Agriculture, farming
   Bracero Program 3:34, 4:44, S1.2:369 (sidebar)
   by Cherokee 5:29
   in California 3:269–71, 275, 334–5, S1.2:368
   chemicalization of, in 1950s 4:203
   in Chile 5:163–4, 165
   Corn Laws S1.1:324
   diverse peoples as migrant laborers S1.2:163
   Dust Bowl of 1930s 3:34, 46, 138–40, 4:297
   in England 2:353–4, 358, 3:2, 5–6, S1.1:209–10, 324
   families displaced by large corporations 3:92, 269
   hard times in 1920s 3:25, 94–5
   Homestead Act (1870) 2:322–3, 3:244, 257, S1.1:281–4
   Irish potato famines S1.1:324
   Louisiana sugar plantations S1.2:250–1, 252 (sidebar)
   mechanization of, in 1930s and 1940s 4:203 (sidebar)
   in Mexico's *ejidos* system 3:282
   in Mexico's hacienda system 3:29, 278, 282, S1.2:87, 432, 502
   migrant workers and discrimination 3:29–30, 49, 140–2, 269–71, 275, 335, 337, 4:297 (sidebar)
   in New England 1:102, 217, 2:125
   nurture versus exploitation debate 3:262
   pesticides ("biocides") 4:337–42
   racism against Japanese farmers 4:331
   skyrocketing production and surpluses of 1960s 4:338
   social stratification of owners versus workers 3:336
   in South Africa 4:94
   Soviet Five-Year Plans 4:132
   Spanish and Mexican land grant system in West S1.2:340–1
   Spreckels sugar interests 3:269, 270 (sidebar), 319
   tenant farming in 10th-century Japan S1.1:451
   tenant farming in 20th-century Japan S1.2:410, 411 (sidebar)

Index

Agriculture, farming (*continued*)
   tenant farming and sharecropping   2:42, 411, 3:80, 249, 370–1, S1.2:259–60, 262
   in Texas of 1900s   3:244
   training in, of, and by blacks in "Movable School"   3:380
   unions for farm workers   3:34, 49–50, 141, 275, 4:175–6
   United Farm Workers   4:175, 300–2, 409, 5:171, S1.2:368–9
   water control in New Mexico   S1.2:341–3
   working conditions, long hours   3:244 (*sidebar*)
   (*See also* Cattle ranching; Cotton)
AIDS (Acquired Immune Deficiency Syndrome)   5:9
Aiken, Conrad   3:414
AIM (American Indian Movement)   2:79 (*sidebar*), 5:246–7, S1.2:165
"Ain't I a Woman?," Truth, Sojourner   2:22–7
Air pollution   4:9
Alaska   3:52–6, 261 (*sidebar*)
Albania   2:101
Albee, Edward, *Zoo Story*   4:397–402
Alcatraz Island, seizure by American Indians   2:79 (*sidebar*), S1.2:165
Alchemy   1:384, 385 (*sidebar*)
Alcibiades   S1.1:345 (*sidebar*)
Alcohol and alcoholism
   among American Indians   1:220, 4:83, 189 (*sidebar*), 5:361, S1.2:33, 291, 294–5
   among Irish   3:220, 398, 400
   among Russians   S1.1:59
   among war wives   4:317
   among Welsh   3:65–6
   Anti-Saloon League and temperance movements   2:25 (*sidebar*), 85–6, 3:69, 75, 147, 401
   Prohibition (Eighteenth Amendment)   3:22–3, S1.1:439–40
   saloons as social halls   3:219, 398, 400
   as women's issue   2:25 (*sidebar*), 3:219
   (*See also* Prohibition)
Alcott, Louisa May, *Little Women*   2:202–8
Aldrin, Edwin E. ("Buzz") Jr.   5:82, 292, 295 (*illus.*)
Aleichem, Sholom   3:123
Alemán Valdés, Miguel   S1.2:88
Alexander the Great (4th century B.C. conqueror)   1:169 (*sidebar*)
Alexander I, Czar of Russia   S1.1:52
Alexander II, Czar of Russia   3:57, 120, S1.1:53, 58, 101, 118, 367, 379
Alexander III, Czar of Russia   3:120, S1.1:58, 119, 367, 368, 379
Alexie, Sherman, *The Lone Ranger and Tonto Fistfight in Heaven*   S1.2:287–96
Alfonso II, duke of Ferrara   S1.1:292–3, 298 (*illus.*)
Alger, Horatio, *Ragged Dick*   2:301–7
Algeria   3:211–13, S1.2:441–3
Alianza, La   4:175–6, 321
Alice's Adventures in Wonderland, Carroll, Lewis   2:28–33

Alice's Restaurant   S1.2:109 (*sidebar*)
Ali Khan, Liaquat   S1.2:330, 331
Ali, Muhammad   5:70 (*sidebar*), 72 (*illus.*), 307–8
All Creatures Great and Small, Herriott, James   3:1–7
Allegories
   Animal Farm   4:14–20
   Blindness   S1.2:63–71
   and fable   4:16 (*sidebar*), 19
Allen, Chesney   S1.2:469–70
Allende, Isabel, *House of the Spirits, The*   5:163–70
Allende, Salvador   5:164–5, 166 (*illus.*), 168–9
Allen, Ethan   3:98 (*sidebar*)
All My Sons, Miller, Arthur   S1.2:1–8
All the Pretty Horses, McCarthy, Cormac   S1.2:9–17
All Quiet on the Western Front, Remarque, Erich Maria   3:8–14
Almanacs, *Poor Richard's Almanac*, Franklin, Benjamin   1:309–15
Almásy, Lázló   S1.2:125–6
"Almos' a Man," Wright, Richard   4:1–6
Alvarez, Julia, *In the Time of the Butterflies*   S1.2:205–15
Amadis of Gaul   1:6
Amazons   1:58–9, 61–2, 258, 259–60
American Childhood, An, Dillard, Annie   4:7–13
American Communist Party
   popularity of, during Great Depression   3:45
   standing against racism   3:40
   (*See also* Communism)
American Dream
   achievement as impossible for black men   4:313
   achieving social status through wealth   S1.1:2
   achieving through hard work and frugality   2:302, 305, 4:111
   achieving through salesmanship in 1950s   4:111
   Ben Franklin as embodiment of   1:26–7, 309
   in colonial times   1:97
   Dreiser's preoccupation with   2:331–2
   merit rather than rank determining success   1:72
American Indian Movement (AIM)   2:79 (*sidebar*), 5:246–7, S1.2:165
American Indians in 16th century, decimated by smallpox   5:214
American Indians in 17th century
   displayed in Renaissance Europe   1:383
   glass beads from French   S1.2:30 (*sidebar*)
American Indians in 18th century
   as allies of British in Revolutionary War   1:108
   as allies of French in French and Indian War   1:204–5
   arrival of whites and decimation of natives   S1.2:161–3, 163 (*sidebar*)
   decimated by smallpox   1:220, 352, S1.1:132, 132 (*sidebar*)
   enslaved   1:103, 2:175

Index

French and Indian War (Seven Years' War) 1:93, 123, 204–6
land, natural resources as considered by 1:220, 2:78, 178
legends and folklore 1:332
Paxton Boys massacre 1:220–1
pressure of westward expansion of American colonists 1:108, 204, 220–1
Puritans' view of 1:102, 422
Uncas 1:207 (sidebar), 208
"walking purchase" of land from 1:220 (sidebar)
white fur traders S1.1:131
American Indians in 19th century
art 2:348–9, 351–2
at boarding schools S1.2:32, 478
Battle of Wounded Knee 2:69, 78
BIA (Bureau of Indian Affairs) 5:246
Black Hills War (1876) 2:67–8, 77
buffalo, Great Plains tribes' dependency on 2:66–7, 75
buffalo as staff of life S1.1:130 (sidebar), 131 (illus.)
consensus-based power structure S1.1:136
Crazy Horse 2:348 (illus.)
Dawes Act (1887) 2:68, 179, 4:186, S1.2:31
decimated by smallpox 2:347, S1.1:132, 132 (sidebar)
defended by Bret Harte 2:287
family and family life 2:347
forced farming and Christian education S1.2:288
Ghost Dance 2:69, 77–8, S1.2:31
goldminers, whiskey traders, missionaries, settlers, and soldiers S1.1:132
holy men 2:71–2
horse culture of Plains tribes 5:364 (sidebar)
killing of white trappers S1.1:131
Kiowa tribal calendars S1.2:482, 483–4, 483 (sidebar), 484 (illus.)
massacre on the Marias S1.1:132–3
missions, missionaries and 2:161–2, 392 (sidebar)
national guilt felt by whites 2:79
Ongpatonga 1:209 (illus.)
parallels to Anglo-Saxons after Norman Conquest 1:257
peyote religion 4:188
post Civil War policy S1.2:30–3
religion of 2:71–2, 78
Removal Act (1830) 1:208–10, 2:316, 317 (sidebar)
reservations policies of U.S. Government 1:224, 2:67, 68, 73, 76, 79, 179, 316, 317 (sidebar), 351, 4:186–7
Sand Creek Massacre 2:77
"second parents" among Sioux 2:347
spirituality of 2:72, 161, 5:246
Sun Dance 2:349 (sidebar), 4:187–8, S1.2:480–2

"Trail of Tears" 5:29–30
treaties and U.S. Government's failure to enforce 2:75–6, 162
Wright's Boneyard and slaughter of Indians' horses S1.2:289–90
American Indians in 20th century
activism and Native American Renaissance S1.1:137–8, S1.2:164–5
alcoholism 1:220, 4:83, 189 (sidebar), 5:361, S1.2:33, 291, 294–5
basketball and sports S1.2:292, 292 (sidebar), 293–4
BIA (Bureau of Indian Affairs) 5:246
Bloody Island Massacre S1.2:164 (sidebar)
Catholic Church 5:244, 361–2
citizenship status 4:80
Civil Rights Act of 1964 affecting 2:351 (sidebar)
cultural mixture of American Southwest 4:320–1
humor, Trickster figures, and Coyote S1.2:290–1, 290 (sidebar)
Indian identity and cultural introspection S1.2:477–8
Indian Reorganization Act 2:73, 4:186, S1.2:478
matrilineal cultures 4:82 (sidebar)
military service 4:80, 185–7, 5:362–3
mission school of Anglican Church 5:195
National Congress of American Indians (NCAI) S1.2:164–5
Navajo Night Chant 4:188
notable athletes S1.2:293 (sidebar)
Pomos S1.2:163–5, 163 (sidebar), 165 (sidebar), 167–8
poverty of 5:360–1
prestige factor of Indian ancestry 5:30
questioning anthropologists' representations of Indians S1.2:478–9
Red Power, AIM, and rights movements 2:79 (sidebar), 179, 351, 5:246–7, S1.2:165, 477–8, 479 (illus.)
relocation program 4:186–7
reservations and "termination" laws S1.2:163–5
reservation system S1.2:287–9
seizure of Alcatraz Island 2:79 (sidebar), S1.2:165
seizure of Wounded Knee village 2:79 (sidebar)
self-determination policies 2:351, 4:190–1
storytelling, powers of 4:83 (sidebar), 85, 188, 189, 192
tribal rights 2:73
U.S. Government attempts to stop all native religious practices S1.2:481
American Indians by tribe
Arawak (Taino) 5:214
Blackfeet S1.1:129–30
Carib S1.2:19, 20, 387

Index

American Indians by tribe (*continued*)
    Cherokee   **5**:29–30
    Cheyenne   **2**:75, 79
    Chippewa   **5**:243–50
    Chiricahua Apache   **2**:74–5
    Coastal Miwoks   **S1.2**:162
    Cree   **5**:361 (sidebar), 362 (illus.), 364 (sidebar)
    Delaware (Lenape)   **1**:206, 219–20
    Iroquois   **1**:108, 110, 205–6
    Jemez Pueblo   **4**:187, 189–90, 191
    Kiowa   **4**:186, 187–8, **S1.2**:480–5, 480 (sidebar)
    Kwakiutl (Canada)   **5**:194–200
    Laguna Pueblo   **4**:79–86
    Métis   **5**:244
    Modoc   **2**:79
    Mohegan   **1**:352
    Narragansett   **1**:352
    Navajo   **2**:79, **4**:80, 186, 188, **5**:360, **S1.2**:99
    Nez Percé   **2**:75, 79, 160–7
    Ojibwe   **S1.2**:29–34
    Pequot   **1**:352
    Pomo   **S1.2**:161–2, 163 (sidebar)
    Pueblo   **4**:47
    Shoshoni   **S1.1**:130
    Sioux   **2**:66–7, 347–50, **5**:360
    Spokane   **S1.2**:289
    Ute   **2**:79
    Yahi   **2**:174, 175, 177
    Yakima   **S1.2**:290
    Yaqui (Mexico)   **S1.2**:87–8
    Zuni Pueblo   **4**:186
American Indians, literary works concerning
    Antelope Wife, The (Ojibwe)   **S1.2**:29–37
    "Bear, The" (Chickasaw)   **2**:47–53
    Black Elk Speaks (Oglala Sioux)   **2**:66–73
    Bury My Heart at Wounded Knee (Western tribes)   **2**:74–80
    Ceremony (Laguna Pueblo)   **4**:79–86
    Drums Along the Mohawk (Iroquois)   **1**:108
    Fools Crow (Blackfeet)   **S1.1**:129–38, **S1.2**:168
    Grand Avenue (Pomo)   **S1.2**:161–9
    House Made of Dawn (Navajo, Jemez Pueblo, and WWII veterans)   **4**:185–92, **S1.1**:137
    I Heard the Owl Call My Name (Kwakiutl)   **5**:194–200
    Ishi, Last of His Tribe (Yahi)   **2**:174–80
    "I Will Fight No More Forever" (Nez Percé)   **2**:160–7
    Last of the Mohicans, The (Delaware and Iroquois)   **1**:204–10
    Leaves of Grass (America's Indian heritage)   **2**:195–201
    Light in the Forest, The (Delaware)   **1**:219–24
    Lone Ranger and Tonto Fistfight in Heaven, The (Spokane)   **S1.2**:287–96
    Love Medicine (Chippewa)   **5**:243–50
    Story Catcher, The (Oglala Sioux)   **2**:347–52
    Tempest, The (Europeans' explorations of New World)   **1**:383
    The Way to Rainy Mountain (Kiowa)   **S1.2**:477–86
    Yellow Raft in Blue Water, A (Cree)   **5**:360–6
American Revolution
    in *April Morning*   **S1.1**:11–20
    Continental Congress   **1**:125
    Declaration of Independence   **1**:93–100
    in *Drums Along the Mohawk*   **1**:107–14
    influence of *Common Sense*   **1**:71–7, 94
    influence of "Give Me Liberty or Give Me Death" speech   **1**:122–8
America. *See* Colonial America; United States
Amistad mutiny   **1**:43
Anarchism   **S1.1**:62, 378–80, 379 (sidebar)
Anaya, Rudolfo A.
    Bless Me, Ultima   **4**:42–8
    Heart of Aztlán   **4**:171–6
"Ancient Mariner, Rime of the," Coleridge, Samuel Taylor   **S1.1**:208, 210–11, 213, 216
Anderson, Robert, *I Never Sang for My Father*   **5**:201–7
Anderson, Sherwood, on *Babbitt*   **3**:27
André, Major John   **1**:213 (sidebar)
"Angel of the Hearth"   **S1.1**:420
Angelou, Maya, *I Know Why the Caged Bird Sings*   **4**:201–8
Angels in America, Kushner, Tony   **5**:1–10
"Angels in the house," women as queens of domestic sphere   **S1.1**:141, 293, 294, 294 (sidebar), 325, 468–70
Anglican Church (Church of England)
    degrees of difference from Catholicism   **1**:233 (sidebar)
    Dissenters   **1**:129, 338, 342, 407, 411, **3**:265
    formation by Henry VIII   **1**:232
    landowners' right to nominate rectors   **S1.1**:388
    loosening of restrictions on Catholics   **S1.1**:324
    Puritans wanting to "purify," distraught over "corruption"   **1**:78, 351, 393
    return of, to status as national religion   **1**:129
    tensions with Catholics in Charles I's time   **1**:305–6
    Test Acts   **S1.1**:209
    (*See also* Puritanism)
Anglo-Saxon England   **1**:44–5, 153, 181
    Norman Conquest of   **1**:181, 250–1, 290
Animal Farm, Orwell, George   **4**:14–20
    politically motivated rejection by publishers   **5**:252–3
Animals, stories concerning
    All Creatures Great and Small   **3**:1–7
    Bless the Beasts and Children   **5**:34–8
    Call of the Wild, The   **3**:51–6
    Day No Pigs Would Die, A   **3**:94–9
    Red Pony, The   **3**:334–7
    Sounder   **3**:370–6
    Watership Down   **5**:346–51
Anna Karenina, Tolstoy, Leo   **2**:34–40, **S1.1**:368
Anne, Queen of England   **1**:130–1, 342
Anne, Queen of France   **1**:389

Index

Annesley, Brian   **1**:201
Annie John, Kincaid, Jamaica   **S1.2**:19–27
Anonymous, *Beowulf*   **1**:44–50, **S1.2**:171, 176 (sidebar)
Antelope Wife, The, Erdrich, Louise   **S1.2**:29–37
Anthills of the Savannah, Achebe, Chinua   **S1.2**:39–49, 203
Anthony, Susan B.   **S1.1**:8
Anthropology
   American Indians questioning representations of Indians   **S1.2**:478–9
   comparative   **5**:42
   cultural   **S1.1**:433 (sidebar), **S1.2**:266
   interest in Polynesian peoples' origins   **4**:221–7
   researchers' interest in American Indians   **2**:72, 179
   social, Wharton's novels as   **S1.1**:7
Antigone, Sophocles   **1**:14–21, **S1.2**:7
Antinomians   **1**:352, 357
Anti-Semitism
   in accusations of fix of 1919 World Series   **4**:261
   of African Americans   **4**:376–7
   among American expatriots in Europe   **S1.1**:441
   of Argentina's "dirty war"   **5**:210
   Beilis case in Russia   **S1.1**:120
   in Brooklyn   **3**:402
   of Charles Lindbergh   **4**:373
   collapse of liberalism in late 1800s Austria   **S1.1**:315, 320
   condemnation of, by some Russian intellectuals   **S1.1**:120
   contributing to generation gap   **5**:203
   diminishing in 1950s and 1960s   **5**:203
   Dreyfus affair   **1**:91–2, 364 (sidebar), **S1.1**:121
   during controversy over Palestine   **S1.2**:474
   in England   **1**:182–3, **2**:264–5
   of Father Charles Coughlin   **4**:373
   in *The Fixer* (Bernard Malamud)   **S1.1**:117–28
   of *The Foundations of the Nineteenth Century*   **S1.2**:305
   in Germany   **1**:370, **4**:157–9
   Henry Ford   **S1.1**:441
   holocaust denial   **4**:40
   in Italy   **1**:243–4, 246
   Kristallnacht   **4**:159, 162–3
   moneylending   **1**:182–3, **2**:264
   nationalism   **1**:364
   origins of "ghetto"   **1**:244, 249
   Pale of Settlement   **3**:119–20, 121
   pogroms and persecution   **1**:364, **3**:119–21, **S1.1**:117–21, 120 (sidebar)
   in Poland   **1**:364
   "Protocols of the Elders of Zion"   **S1.1**:120 (sidebar), 441
   in Russia or Soviet Union   **1**:364, **3**:119–21, 124–5, **5**:122, **S1.1**:127–8, 371 (sidebar)
   in United States of 1940s   **4**:236–7, 373
   in U.S. military   **4**:36–7
   in Wharton's works   **3**:170
   (*See also* Holocaust)
Antiwar literature
   All Quiet on the Western Front   **3**:8–14
   Catch-22   **4**:66–72
   Fallen Angels   **5**:101–6
   Farewell to Arms, A   **3**:112–18
   Red Badge of Courage, The   **2**:308–13
   Slaughterhouse Five   **4**:343–8
   Things They Carried, The   **S1.2**:451–8
   Waste Land, The   **3**:411–17, **S1.1**:259
Apartheid. *See* South Africa
Appalachian Trail   **5**:278–9
Apprentice system   **S1.1**:150
April Morning, Fast, Howard   **S1.1**:11–20
Arabs, anti-Zionism   **4**:107
Arbor Day   **S1.1**:284 (sidebar)
Archery   **1**:253
Argentina   **5**:208–11, 212–13
Aristide, Jean-Bertrand   **S1.2**:247
Aristophanes   **S1.1**:344, 346, 347 (sidebar)
Aristotle
   commenting upon *Republic*   **1**:328
   influence in 16th century   **1**:233
   influence on Jefferson   **1**:100
   teacher of Plato   **S1.1**:343
   woodcut of   **1**:326 (*illus.*)
Armenia   **3**:338–43, **4**:199
Arms control   **4**:71, **5**:126, 225, 239, 252 (sidebar)
Armstrong, Neil A.   **5**:82, 292
Armstrong, William H., *Sounder*   **3**:370–6
Army. *See* Military
Arnold, Benedict   **1**:213 (sidebar)
Arnold, Thomas   **2**:373–4
Art, artists, and intellectuals
   aesthetes, decadents, and dandies   **S1.1**:179, 182
   Aesthetic movement and "art for art's sake"   **S1.1**:64, 179, 182, 202
   African   **4**:56
   art as barrier against chaos and loss of faith   **3**:117
   artist as heroic individual   **S1.1**:64
   art nouveau   **S1.1**:314
   art and patronage   **S1.1**:293 (sidebar)
   art as propaganda in Colombia   **S1.2**:463
   avant-garde   **S1.2**:76
   balking at bourgeois conservatism   **S1.1**:63
   basketmaking and survival   **S1.2**:167–8
   benefitting from New Deal's Federal Writers' Project   **3**:237, **S1.2**:267 (sidebar)
   benefitting from New Deal's Works Progress Administration   **3**:391, 424
   Black arts movement   **4**:207, **S1.2**:231
   Bloomsbury Group   **3**:356, 358–9, **S1.1**:463, 471–2
   bourgeoisie versus bohemianism   **S1.1**:162
   Caravaggio and "tenebrism"   **S1.2**:128 (sidebar)
   caricaturist John Leech   **S1.1**:38 (sidebar)
   Carnegie Institute of Pittsburgh   **4**:9
   Chicano   **S1.2**:369

Art, artists, and intellectuals (*continued*)
    Cubism   S1.1:464
    first International Exhibition for   4:8 (*sidebar*)
    French atelier system of teaching   3:266
    German cultural nationalism   S1.1:63
    Impressionist   S1.1:463
    Jewish American authors   S1.1:127
    liberalizing influence on Russian army officers   S1.1:100
    Modernism   3:411, 5:42, S1.1:444
    moved to interpret and preserve American pioneer epoch   S1.1:287
    muralists of Mexico   S1.2:88
    as nonconforming, restless, alienated   S1.1:6, 205
    in Paris of 1920s   S1.1:440–1
    Paris as western capital of   3:265–6
    patrons for   1:88, S1.1:293 (*sidebar*)
    photojournalism   S1.2:262–3
    picaresque, appeal of   S1.1:193 (*sidebar*)
    Post-Impressionist   S1.1:463–4
    prejudice against women as   2:186, 203, 212, 424–5, 5:282 (*sidebar*)
    pre-Raphaelite brotherhood   S1.1:139, 146–7
    Primitivism   3:385 (*sidebar*)
    pseudonyms   S1.2:283 (*sidebar*)
    responsibility to society   S1.2:77, 80
    rise of "new aristocracy"   S1.2:406–7
    South's Fugitives, Agrarians, and New Critics   S1.1:419–20
    suffering from mental and emotional disabilities
        T. S. Eliot's wife   3:412–13
        Gilman   2:427
        Plath   4:21–6
        Woolf   3:358
    surrealism   S1.2:76
    Victorian prejudice against women as writers   1:415 (*sidebar*), 2:56, 186, 203, 212, 424–5
    women as writers of children's stories   S1.1:146
    women as writers of science fiction   5:239
    writers of sensibility   S1.1:213–14
    (*See also* Harlem Renaissance; Literary experimentation and categories; Music)
Arthur, King of Celtic England   1:288, 290
    in *Once and Future King, The*   1:288–94, S1.2:174
Art nouveau   S1.1:314
Asimov, Isaac, *Foundation*   5:122–8
Astrology   1:346, 350
Astrophil and Stella   S1.1:156
Athena   1:282, 283
Athens. *See under* Greece in ancient times
Atom bomb
    creating "atomic anxiety"   4:255, 5:126, S1.2:310–11
    decision to use   4:178–9
    Hiroshima and Nagasaki as targets   4:179–82, 180 (*illus.*), 181 (*sidebar*), S1.2:131, 219 (*sidebar*), 220, 311
    Manhattan Project   4:71, 81–2, 316, 5:123
    Soviets' capability   4:183, 5:96, 126
    test site at Bikini atoll   5:124 (*illus.*)
    UN attempts to regulate   5:96
    (*See also* Nuclear weapons)
Atomic energy. *See* Nuclear energy
Atwood, Margaret, *Handmaid's Tale, The*   5:135–42
"Augustan" neoclassicism   S1.1:207–8
Augustus Caesar   S1.1:171–2
Aunt Julia and the Scriptwriter, Vargas Llosa, Mario   S1.2:51–61
Austen, Jane
    Emma   S1.1:89–97
    Pride and Prejudice   2:295–300
    Sense and Sensibility   S1.1:387–98
Australia   S1.1:151
Austro-Hungarian empire   3:11 (*sidebar*), S1.1:314, 474–5, 476
Autobiography of Benjamin Franklin, The, Franklin, Benjamin   1:22–9
Autobiography of Malcolm X, The, X, Malcolm and Alex Haley   5:11–18
Autobiography of Miss Jane Pittman, The (novel), Gaines, Ernest J.   5:19–26
Autobiography. *See* Biography and autobiography
Automobiles   2:128 (*sidebar*), 3:23, 77, 88–9, 94, 101, 5:40 (*illus.*), S1.2:281
Aviation
    breaking sound barrier   5:293–4
    early airplanes   S1.2:494 (*sidebar*)
    golden age of   3:211–12
    Lindbergh and   3:367
    Right Stuff, The   5:291–7
    UFOs (unidentified flying objects)   4:347–8, 5:59 (*illus.*)
    Wright brothers   S1.2:489–90
    (*See also* Space Age; Transportation; War weaponry)
Awakening, The, Chopin, Kate   3:15–20
Azerbaijan   3:343
Aztlán   4:173, 174–5, 176

B

Ba'al Shem Tov   4:87
Babbitt, Lewis, Sinclair   3:21–7, S1.1:289
Babe Ruth   4:262, 265
Babeuf, Gracchus   S1.1:45
Babi Yar massacre   4:120
Baby boom   1:224, 2:325–6, 4:38, 74, 240, S1.2:107
Backswording   2:375
Baer, Dov   4:89
Bakke, Allan   5:181
Bakunin, Mikhail   S1.1:101 (*sidebar*), 102, 379 (*sidebar*)
Balaguer, Joaquin   S1.2:213
Baldwin, James, *Fire Next Time, The*   5:107–14
Ballad stanza   S1.1:212 (*sidebar*)
Baptists   5:19, 188

Baraka, Amiri (Leroi Jones)   **4**:207
Barbed wire   **3**:113, 260
"Barn Burning," Faulkner, William   **2**:41–6
Barrett Browning, Elizabeth, *Sonnets from the Portuguese*   **S1.1**:291, 297, 297 (*sidebar*)
Barrio Boy, Galarza, Ernesto   **3**:28–35
Baseball
    Aaron, Hank   **4**:145, 148
    changing strategies of play   **4**:261–2
    creation of two-league system   **4**:261
    growing popularity leading to scouts   **3**:284
    history of scandals   **4**:260–1, 265
    Jackie Robinson   **4**:146, **S1.2**:251 (*sidebar*)
    minor leagues and decrease in college-educated players   **4**:261
    Negro League   **4**:145, 148
    Pittsburgh Pirates   **4**:10
    Babe Ruth   **4**:262, 265
    segregation in   **4**:146, 147
    White ("Black") Sox fix of 1919 World Series   **3**:149–50, **4**:260–1
    (*See also Shoeless Joe*)
Baudelaire, Charles   **S1.1**:182, 202
Bay of Pigs fiasco   **5**:226
Bean Trees, The, Kingsolver, Barbara   **5**:27–33
Bearden, Romare   **S1.2**:384, 385 (*sidebar*)
"Bear, The,", Faulkner, William   **2**:47–53
Beat movement   **4**:75
    (*See also* Counterculture)
Beauty: A Retelling of the Story of Beauty and the Beast, McKinley, Robin   **1**:30–6
Becker, Charles   **3**:149
Becket, Thomas   **1**:146
Beckett, Samuel, *Waiting for Godot*   **S1.2**:467–76
Begin, Menachem   **4**:103, 105, 107
Behaviorism   **5**:45
Behavior modification and conditioning   **5**:156–7
Behn, Aphra   **3**:361–2
Beilis case (anti-Semitism in Russia)   **S1.1**:120
Belaúnde, Fernando   **5**:334
Belgium   **2**:146–7, 150–1, **3**:9, **4**:254, 357, 359
Bellamy, Edward   **2**:423
Bell, Clive   **3**:356
Belle of Amherst, The, Luce, William   **2**:54–8
Bellecourt, Clyde   **5**:247 (*illus.*)
Belleforest, François de   **1**:139, 141 (*sidebar*)
Belle Glade, Florida   **3**:383–4
Bell Jar, The, Plath, Sylvia   **4**:21–7
Belmont, August   **S1.1**:6
Beloved, Morrison, Toni   **2**:59–65
Benito Cereno, Melville, Herman   **1**:37–43
Bentham, Jeremy   **S1.1**:33 (*sidebar*), 295
Beowulf, Anonymous   **1**:44–50, **S1.2**:171, 176 (*sidebar*)
    influence upon Tolkien   **1**:153
Bergson, Henri   **3**:213
Betsey Brown, Shange, Ntozake   **4**:28–34
Bettelheim, Bruno   **S1.1**:315 (*sidebar*)
Bible, as source for Milton's *Paradise Lost*   **1**:301
Biblical scholarship and "higher criticism"   **S1.1**:295

Bierce, Ambrose
    as character in *The Old Gringo*   **3**:279, 280, 281
    "Occurrence at Owl Creek Bridge, An"   **2**:255–60
Biko, Stephen   **S1.2**:116–17, 119
Bildungsroman (coming-of-age novel)   **3**:264, 311, **4**:47, **S1.2**:19–27
Bilingual education   **4**:45, **5**:172, 179–81, 183, 217, **S1.2**:375–6
Billy Budd, Melville, Herman   **1**:51–6
Biloxi Blues, Simon, Neil   **4**:35–41
Biography and autobiography
    Abraham Lincoln: The Prairie Years, Sandburg, Carl   **2**:1–7
    American Childhood, An, Dillard, Annie   **4**:7–13
    Autobiography of Benjamin Franklin, The   **1**:22–9
    Autobiography of Malcolm X, The, Malcolm X as told to Alex Haley   **5**:11–18
    Barrio Boy, Galarza, Ernesto   **3**:28–35
    Belle of Amherst, The (Emily Dickinson), Luce, William   **2**:54–8
    Black Boy, Wright, Richard   **3**:36–43
    Black Elk Speaks, Neihardt, John G.   **2**:66–73
    Bound for Glory, Guthrie, Woody   **3**:44–50
    Diary of a Young Girl, The, Frank, Anne   **4**:116–23
    Endless Steppe, The: Growing Up in Siberia, Hautzig, Esther   **4**:131–6
    Farewell to Manzanar, Houston, Jeanne W. and James D. Houston   **4**:137–43
    Hiroshima Diary, Hachiya, Michihiko   **4**:177–84
    Hunger of Memory, A: An Autobiography, Rodriquez, Richard   **5**:178–84, **S1.2**:370
    I Know Why the Caged Bird Sings, Angelou, Maya   **4**:201–8
    Incidents in the Life of a Slave Girl, Jacobs, Harriet   **2**:168–73
    Incidents in the Life of a Slave Girl, The, Jacobs, Harriet   **2**:168–73
    Manchild in the Promised Land, Brown, Claude   **4**:247–53
    Narrative of the Life of Frederick Douglass, Douglass, Frederick   **2**:16, 236–41, **S1.2**:229, 231
    Out of Africa, Dinesen, Isak   **3**:290–6
    So Far from the Bamboo Grove, Watkins, Yoko K.   **4**:349–55
    Up From Slavery, Washington, Booker T.   **2**:410–15
    Way to Rainy Mountain, The, Momaday, N. Scott   **S1.2**:477–86
    West with the Night, Markham, Beryl   **S1.2**:487–97
    Woman Warrior, The, Kingston, Maxine Hong   **5**:352–9
Birmingham, Alabama   **S1.2**:272–4, 277, 423
Black arts movement   **4**:207, **S1.2**:231
Black Boy, Wright, Richard   **3**:36–43

Index

Black Consciousness Movement (BCM) S1.2:116–17, 122
Black Death (bubonic plague) 1:159, 160, 344, 345, 350, S1.2:135
Black Elk Speaks, Neihardt, John G. 2:66–73
Black feminism 2:64, 3:86–7, 354–5, 4:56, 5:92–3, 117, S1.2:394 (*sidebar*)
"Black is Beautiful" slogan 4:54, 56, S1.1:337 (*sidebar*), S1.2:428, 429
Black Muslims and Nation of Islam 3:238, 325, 4:56, 248–50, 5:12–13, 69, 110–11, 302, S1.2:276
Black Panther Party 4:54, 56, 207, S1.2:429
Black Power movement 2:97–8, 3:43, 325, 4:56, 207, 5:143–4, S1.2:232
Blacks. *See* African Americans
Black, Tom Campbell S1.2:489, 490 (*sidebar*), 492, 494
Blair, Eric Arthur. *See* Orwell, George
Blake, William 1:410 (*sidebar*), 416, 2:92
  Songs of Innocence and of Experience S1.1:407–16
Blavatsky, Helena Petrova S1.1:82
Bleriot, Louis S1.2:490
Bless the Beasts and Children, Swarthout, Glendon 5:34 8
Bless Me, Ultima, Anaya, Rudolfo A. 4:42–8
Bleuler, Eugen S1.1:200
Bligh, Cap't. William 1:273–4, 276–7, 4:64 5
Blindness, Saramago, José S1.2:63–71
Blindness. *See* Disabled persons
Blitz ("blitzkrieg") bombing of England's cities S1.2:130 (*sidebar*), 300 (*sidebar*)
Blixen, Baron Bror von S1.2:489, 493
Blixen, Karen. *See* Dinesen, Isak
Blood Wedding, Lorca, Federico García S1.2:73–82
Bloody Island Massacre S1.2:164 (*sidebar*)
Bloomsbury Group 3:356, 358–9, S1.1:463, 471–2
Blue Ridge Mountains 5:278
Blues, the 3:254 (*sidebar*), 4:258
Bluest Eye, The, Morrison, Toni 4:49–57
Blum, Léon S1.2:443
Boas, Franz S1.1:7, 334, 429, 433 (*illus.*), S1.2:266
Boethius 1:344, 345–6, 350
Bohemia
  Czech Republic S1.1:283 (*sidebar*)
  Prague S1.1:475 (*sidebar*)
  Sudetenland S1.1:475
Bohemianism S1.1:162
Boleyn, Anne 1:149, 150, 231
Bolt, Robert, *Man for All Seasons, A* 1:231–7
Bomb squads of WWII S1.2:130 (*sidebar*)
Books, personal libraries as symbol of nonconformity S1.1:6
Booth, John Wilkes 2:191
Bosch, Juan S1.2:213
Bosnia 2:37–9
Boston, Massachusetts 3:43, S1.1:201
Bound for Glory, Guthrie, Woody 3:44 50

Bouquet, Col. Henry 1:221
Bourgeoisie S1.1:46
Bowling 1:335 (*sidebar*)
Boxer Rebellion in China (1900) 3:205, 5:354
Boxing 5:68–9, S1.2:251 (*sidebar*)
Bracero Program 3:34, 4:44, S1.2:369 (*sidebar*)
Bradbury, Ray
  Dandelion Wine 3:88–93, S1.2:309
  Fahrenheit 451 5:95–100, S1.2:309
  Martian Chronicles, The S1.2:309–15
10224 Braddock, Gen'l. Edward 1:205
Bradford, Richard, *Red Sky at Morning* 4:316–22
Brahmans 1:365, 367 (*sidebar*)
Brain food (milk and prunes) S1.2:187 (*sidebar*)
Brave New World, Huxley, Aldous 5:39–45, 141, 157, 252
Brazil S1.1:339 (*sidebar*)
Brighton, England S1.1:90
Brink, André, *Dry White Season, A* S1.2:115–24
Britain. *See* England
Brock, Alice S1.2:109 (*sidebar*)
Brontë, Charlotte, *Jane Eyre* 1:415 (*sidebar*), 419, 2:181–7, S1.1:493, S1.2:24 5
Brontë, Emily, *Wuthering Heights* 1:413–19
Bronze Age of ancient Greece 1:14, 258, 280, 283 (*sidebar*)
Brooke, Arthur 1:347, 349 (*sidebar*)
Brook Farm (utopian community) 1:357, 2:418
Brooklyn, New York 3:397–8, 4:88, 5:149–51
Brotherhood of Sleeping Car Porters 3:42
Brown, Claude, *Manchild in the Promised Land* 4:247–53
Brown, Clifford 4:376
Brown, Dee, *Bury My Heart at Wounded Knee* 2:74 80
Browning, Robert, "My Last Duchess" and Other Poems S1.1:291–9
Brown, John 2:89 (*sidebar*), 172
  Final Speech 2:188–94
Brown v. Board of Education 3:375, 4:29–30, 314, 5:90, 108, 180, 181, S1.1:19, S1.2:231, 256, 270
Brutus (Marcus Junius Brutus) 1:190, 191, 192–3
10224 Bubonic plague (Black Death) 1:159, 160, 344, 345, 350, S1.2:135
Buckingham, Duke of (George Villiers) 1:388, 389
Buck, Pearl S., *Good Earth, The* 3:131–7
Buddhism 1:365–9, 3:186–7, 5:48, S1.1:452, S1.2:414
Buffalo Bill (William F. Cody) 2:68, 177
Buffalo (bison) 2:66, 67, 75, 5:34 5, S1.1:130 (*sidebar*), 131 (*illus.*)
Bullfighting S1.1:442 (*sidebar*), 443 (*illus.*)
Bull from the Sea, The, Renault, Mary 1:57–63
Bunche, Ralph 4:255, 5:54
Burial customs
  among Canadian Kwakiutl 5:197
  in ancient Greece 1:18–19
  catacombs in Sicily 2:82
  mourning traditions in Victorian England 1:414 15

Index

Burke, Edmund   1:52–3, 359, 362, 373 (*sidebar*), 408
Burns, Olive Ann, *Cold Sassy Tree*   3:75–9
Bury My Heart at Wounded Knee, Brown, Dee   2:74 80
Butler, Octavia, *Kindred*   S1.2:227–37
Byng, Admiral   S1.1:25, 25 (*sidebar*)
Byron, George Gordon Noel, Baron (Lord Byron)   1:115, 116, 119, 120, 2:110, S1.1:86

C

Caen, Herb   3:226
Caesar, Julius   1:12, 136, S1.1:170
Cailleach (Celtic goddess)   S1.1:232–3
Caine, Hall   S1.1:80
Caine Mutiny, The, Wouk, Herman   4:58–65
Cajuns   4:365, 5:21, 130, S1.2:253 (*sidebar*)
California
    Central and San Joaquin Valleys   S1.2:375, 385
    Clear Lake   4:340–1
    farming and migrant workers   3:29–30, 49, 140–2, 269–71, 275, 335, 337, 4:297 (*sidebar*)
    Mexican immigrants and Native Americans   S1.2:162
    Sacramento   3:30
    Salinas Valley   3:334 5
    South Central Los Angeles   5:339–42
    Spanish mission system   2:392, 394, 395
    timeline: colonization to independence   2:392 (*sidebar*)
    Watts   S1.2:423
    (*See also* San Francisco)
Caligula   S1.1:172
Calles, Plutarco Elías   S1.2:86 (*sidebar*), 87
Call of the Wild, The, London, Jack   3:51–6
Calvin, John, and Calvinism   2:54, 55, 3:377–8, 4:10, 304
Camus, Albert   S1.2:470
    Stranger, The   S1.2:441–9
Canada, Kwakiutl of British Columbia   5:194 200
Canals
    Panama   3:231–2, 270
    Suez   3:184, 4:107, S1.2:131
    U.S. system of   2:230
Candide, Voltaire, François Marie Arouet de   S1.1:21–30
Canterbury Tales, The, Chaucer, Geoffrey   1:64 70
    Shakespeare influenced by   1:262
Capitalism
    in America's Gilded Age   2:20, 306, 328
    ethics and regulation, lack of   4:9
    failures of, enhancing appeal of communism   3:208, 210
    Hellman's attack on excesses of   3:207, 210
    laissez-faire   S1.1:42
    in Latin America   S1.2:52–3
    origin of term   S1.1:43 (*sidebar*)
    Steinbeck's warning about   3:144
    theory of role of unemployment   S1.1:220
    versus socialism and Marxism   3:321, 4:18–19
    (*See also* Industrial Revolution, industrialization)
Capital punishment   4:379–80, 5:131, S1.2:257
Capone, Alphonse   3:366
Capote, Truman
    as basis for character in *To Kill a Mockingbird*   3:395
    "Christmas Memory, A"   3:68–74
Cárdenas, Lázaro   S1.2:87
Caribbean islands
    Antigua   S1.2:19–26
    Cuba. *See* Cuba
    Dominican Republic. *See* Dominican Republic
    Grenada   S1.2:387–90, 391 (*illus.*)
    Grenadines   S1.2:388
    Haiti (formerly Saint-Domingue)   5:116–17, S1.2:239–47
    Puerto Rico   3:277, 4:385–6, 388–9, 401, 5:214 21
    slavery   1:39, S1.1:494 6, S1.2:20, 240, 393 (*sidebar*)
    Trinidad   S1.2:183–4
    West Indies   2:183–4, S1.1:493–6
Carlyle, Thomas   1:375, 2:92
Carmichael, Stokely   2:98, 3:325, 4:55 (*illus.*), 56, 5:145 (*illus.*), S1.2:424, 428, 429
Carnegie, Andrew   2:306, 4:8, 9
Carranza, Venustiano   3:279, S1.2:85, 86, 503
Carrie, King, Stephen   5:46–52
Carroll, Lewis, *Alice's Adventures in Wonderland*   2:28–33
Carson, Rachel, *Silent Spring*   4:337–42, 5:35, S1.2:103
Carter, Jimmy   S1.2:247
Carthage   1:10, 12
Carver, George Washington   3:418
"Cask of Amontillado, The," Poe, Edgar Allan   2:81–6
Cassady, Neal   S1.2:357, 362 (*sidebar*), 363 (*illus.*)
Castles (stately homes) of England   S1.2:137 (*sidebar*)
Castro, Fidel   2:273, 4:279, 5:225, S1.2:53, 58–9
"Catastrophists"   S1.1:329
Catch-22, Heller, Joseph   4:66–72, 5:318 (*sidebar*)
Catcher in the Rye, Salinger, J. D.   4:73–8, 5:318 (*sidebar*)
Catesby, Robert   1:229 (*sidebar*)
Cather, Willa
    My Ántonia   S1.1:281–90
    O Pioneers!   3:257–63, S1.1:281
Catholic Church
    Mexico's attempts to break power of   S1.2:84, 86, 502
    public opposition to Dominican Republic's Trujillo   S1.2:209
    syncretistic accommodation of native beliefs and practices   S1.2:499–501
    Virgin of Guadalupe and conversion of Mexican Indians   S1.2:499–501, 500 (*illus.*), 507, 508

Index

Catholicism and Catholic Church
    among American Indians   **5**:244, 361–2, 365–6
    anti-Semitism of   **2**:264
    archbishop and English king in conflict   **S1.1**:259–62
    Catholic emancipation in Great Britain and Ireland   **S1.1**:239–40
    celibacy for priests   **S1.1**:260–1
    clerical accountability to church law versus royal courts of law   **S1.1**:261
    comparison to Anglican Church   **1**:233 (*sidebar*)
    conflict with English Protestants   **1**:131, 132, 229, 305–6
    control of education in France   **2**:210
    criticisms by
        Cervantes   **1**:6–7
        Chaucer   **1**:65
        Dante   **1**:174 5, **3**:111
        Joyce   **3**:111
    Crusades   **1**:182, 291
    cult of Our Lady of Fatima   **5**:365–6
    decline in Scotland   **4**:304 5
    equivocation doctrine   **1**:230
    Gregorian Reforms   **S1.1**:260–1
    Inquisition   **1**:2, 3, **S1.1**:23, 190–1
    investiture controversy   **S1.1**:261
    in Ireland   **1**:269, **3**:107–8, 109–10, 305–7
    Jesuits   **3**:307–8, **S1.1**:23, 24
    loosening of restrictions on Catholics in universities or political office   **S1.1**:324
    in medieval England and Europe   **1**:49–50, 65
    Merton, Thomas   **5**:280–1
    monasticism   **3**:186–7, **5**:280
    opposition to contraception   **4**:304 (*sidebar*)
    parochial schools   **5**:62–3
    Penitentes   **4**:318 (*sidebar*)
    perpetuation of machismo sentiment   **5**:173
    pilgrimages   **1**:64 70, 145–6
    popes   **1**:174, 176, 296, 344, 345
    Protestant Reformation against abuses   **1**:231, **2**:113, **S1.1**:108
    question of tolerance or support for Nazis   **S1.1**:267–8
    simony   **S1.1**:260
    Test Acts, anti-Catholic laws and resentment   **S1.1**:209
    Trappist monks   **5**:280
    (*See also* Protestantism)
Cattle ranching
    in American West   **S1.2**:98–9
    cowboys and horses   **S1.2**:10 (*sidebar*)
    grazing rights and U.S. Forest Service   **S1.2**:341 (*sidebar*)
    on Great Plains   **2**:321–2
    leather trade on California missions   **2**:392
    on reservations   **4**:79
    Spanish and Mexican land grant system in West   **S1.2**:340–1
    (*See also* Agriculture, farming)
Caudillos and caudillismo   **S1.2**:83

Cedras, Raoul   **S1.2**:247
Celts
    Britons (Gauls)   **1**:196–7
    Scotland   **1**:187
Censorship and banning of literary works
    in 14th- and 15th-century Europe   **1**:349
    Adventures of Don Quixote, The   **1**:4
    blacklisting by McCarthyites or HUAC   **1**:84, 398, **3**:178, 208, 209 (*illus.*), **4**:71, 72, 110, 398, **5**:2, 3 (*illus.*), 96, 97, 127, **S1.1**:11, **S1.2**:280, 310, 364
    Brave New World   **5**:45
    by Colombia's Rojas Pinilla   **S1.2**:461, 463
    by czars   **S1.1**:368
    by Nazis   **3**:13, **5**:99, **S1.1**:481
    by Smith Act (1940)   **5**:97
    by Soviet dictatorship   **4**:286, **5**:96
    Candide   **S1.1**:29
    Catcher in the Rye   **4**:78, **5**:62
    in Communist China   **5**:98
    Flowers for Algernon   **4**:156
    Hero Ain't Nothin' but a Sandwich, A   **5**:148
    His Own Where   **5**:154
    Mexico   **S1.2**:91 (*sidebar*)
    motion picture industry and Hollywood's production code   **S1.2**:143
    One Day in the Life of Ivan Denisovich   **4**:285
    in Peru   **S1.2**:54
Central America
    Guatemala and refugees   **5**:27–9
    Panama Canal   **3**:231–2, 270
    (*See also* Mexico)
Central Intelligence Agency (CIA)   **4**:293
Ceremonies and celebrations
    ancient Roman religious holidays   **1**:191–2
    Arbor Day   **S1.1**:284 (*sidebar*)
    Carriacouan's "Big Drums"   **S1.2**:389
    Chinese New Year   **5**:75, 76 (*illus.*)
    Christmas
        A Doll's House   **2**:111–17
        "Child's Christmas in Wales, A"   **3**:63–7
        "Christmas Memory, A"   **3**:68–74
        "Worn Path, The"   **3**:418–24
    Feast of the Epiphany, Feast of Fools, and Twelfth Night   **S1.1**:483–4
    Indian healing ceremonies   **4**:82–3, **5**:249
    Kwakiutl tribe
        Candlefish   **5**:196 (*sidebar*)
        hamatsa (Cannibal Dance)   **5**:196–7
        potlatch   **5**:198 (*illus.*), 199
    (*See also* Burial customs)
Ceremony, Silko, Leslie Marmon   **4**:79–86
Cervantes Saavedra, Miguel de
    Adventures of Don Quixote, The   **1**:1–7
    in Battle of Lepanto   **1**:296 (*sidebar*)
    Little Gipsy Girl, The   **S1.1**:189–98
Cézanne, Paul   **S1.1**:464
Chagall, Marc   **3**:123
Chamberlain, Neville   **4**:357, 359, **S1.2**:300–1
Chambers, Whittaker   **5**:96, **S1.2**:280

Index

Chaplin, Charlie **3**:101
Charcot, Jean Martin **S1.1**:82
Charity, philanthropy
   sponsored by tycoons of industry **S1.1**:226
   in Victorian Age **S1.1**:154 (*sidebar*)
Charles I of England **1**:299, 303, 304 (*illus.*), 305, 306
Charles II of England **1**:129, 130, 306, 337, 338
Charles X of France **1**:391
Chartism **S1.1**:31–2, 43, 325–6
Chateaubriand, François René de **1**:165
Chaucer, Geoffrey, *Canterbury Tales, The* **1**:64 70
Chávez, César **3**:33 (*illus.*), 34, **4**:47, 175, 300–2, 409, **S1.2**:368, 372 (*illus.*)
Chekhov, Anton **S1.1**:367–75
   Cherry Orchard, The **3**:57–62
   "Rothschild's Fiddle" and "The Lady with the Dog" **S1.1**:367–75
Chennault, Claire **3**:190
Chernobyl disaster **5**:286, 287 (*illus.*)
Chernyshevsky, Nikolai **S1.1**:102, 103 (*illus.*), 105, 106
Cherry Orchard, The, Chekhov, Anton **3**:57–62
Chesapeake Bay **4**:216–17, 219
Chiang Kai-shek **3**:189, 190 (*illus.*)
Chicago
   in 1920s **3**:89–90
   barrios of **5**:174
   black activism **3**:238
   ethnic makeup **3**:176
   Martin Luther King, Jr.'s northern civil rights campaign **5**:174
   in late 19th century **2**:327–8, 330 (*illus.*)
   meat-packing industry **2**:328 (*sidebar*)
   South Side and Black Belt **3**:237–8, **4**:309–11
   streetcars **2**:328
   suburbs of **5**:261–2
Chicanos
   affirmative action programs **5**:181, 183–4, 342, **S1.2**:256, 375
   César Chávez **3**:33 (*illus.*), 34, **4**:47, 175, 300–2, 409
   discrimination **5**:178
      zoot suit riots of 1940s **4**:295–7, 403–10
   education dropout rates and reform efforts **5**:179
   family life **4**:45
   folk healing (*curanderos*) **4**:45
   Hispanos of New Mexico **S1.2**:343
   immigration to United States from Mexico **3**:282, **4**:44 8
   life in New Mexico **4**:45
   literary Renaissance of 1960s and 1970s **5**:172–3
   Luna (land) and Marez (sea) **4**:47
   mestizo (mixed-race) heritage **5**:172
   myth of Aztlán **4**:174
   origin of term **5**:171
   pachuco zoot-suit culture of 1950s **4**:173, 295–7, 403

   post-WWII community **5**:178–9
   rights movement **4**:47–8, 300–2, **5**:171–2, 179
      Brown Berets **4**:176, **S1.2**:367–9
      Chicanas **3**:202, **5**:174, **S1.2**:505
      Community Service Organization (CSO) **4**:300
      El Teatro Campesino **4**:409, **5**:172
      G.I. Forum **4**:300
      impact of military service on **4**:44
      internal dissention **S1.2**:504
      La Alianza **4**:175–6, 321
      La Raza Unida **4**:176
      League of United Latin American Citizens (LULAC) **4**:300
      Mexican American Legal Defense and Education Fund (MALDEF) **5**:179
      table grape boycott **4**:175, 301 (*illus.*), 409
      United Farm Workers **4**:175, 300–2, 409, **5**:171, **S1.2**:368–9
   Richard Rodriguez's autobiography **5**:178–84
   Rubén Salazar **4**:410
   Vietnam War protesters **4**:409–10
   WWII military service **4**:44
   (*See also* Latinos)
Child abuse
   Fetal Alcohol Syndrome **5**:361
   relationship to poverty **5**:329 (*sidebar*)
   suicide **5**:288, 289–90
Childbearing
   abortion **5**:51, 136
   by unwed couples **5**:267
   midwifery **4**:218
   in vitro **5**:42–3
   (*See also* Family and family life)
Childhood's End, Clarke, Arthur **5**:53–60
Child labor **2**:103–4, 335 (*sidebar*), **3**:76 (*sidebar*), 77 (*illus.*), 285, **S1.1**:32–3, 42, 408–9, 414, 414 (*sidebar*)
Childress, Alice, *Hero Ain't Nothin' but a Sandwich, A* **5**:143–8
"Child's Christmas in Wales, A," Thomas, Dylan **3**:63–7
Chile **5**:163–70
Chimney sweeps **S1.1**:408–9, 409 (*illus.*), 414, 414 (*sidebar*)
China
   chronology
      Opium Wars (1839–42 and 1856–60) **5**:354
      Taiping Rebellion (1851–64) **5**:354
      Hong Kong conceded to Great Britain **5**:354
      Boxer Rebellion (1900) **3**:205, **5**:354
      civil strife (1911–49) **3**:189–90, **5**:229, 254
      Republican era (1912–49) **5**:229–30, 354
      Japanese invasion (1930s 40s) **3**:189–90, **4**:59, **5**:229–30
      communist victory in civil war (1949) **5**:254, 354 5

Index

China (*continued*)
    Sino-Indian War (1962) **S1.2**:151–2
    Nixon's historic visit (1972) **5**:358
    Confucius **3**:193 (*sidebar*)
    divorce in **2**:370, 371, **3**:132, 193, **5**:230
    dynasties and alien invaders **3**:189
    footbinding of girls **3**:135, **5**:230 (*sidebar*)
    Guomindang **4**:126 (*sidebar*), **5**:230, 254
    marriages as business deals **3**:192–3
    missionaries **3**:133
    opium addiction **3**:134 (*sidebar*)
    peasant farmers **3**:131–2
    prostitution in **3**:135
    superstition and syncretism **3**:133, 190–1
    Taiwan **3**:190, **5**:254
    women in **2**:366–7, 368 (*sidebar*), 370–1, **3**:132–3, 134 5, **5**:352, 355
Chinese and Chinese Americans
    assimilation of second generation **5**:231–2, 234 5
    Chinese New Year festival **5**:75, 76 (*illus.*)
    defended by Bret Harte **2**:287
    immigration in 19th century **2**:367–8, 370 (*sidebar*), 371, **4**:124 7
    immigration in 20th century **2**:368, **4**:125, 127, 129
    as miners in Old West **2**:367–8, 369 (*illus.*)
    as "model minority" **3**:194
    in New York's Chinatown **4**:126
    racism and prejudice against **2**:175, 287, 367–8, 370 (*sidebar*), 371, **3**:30, **4**:124 7, 194, 330, **5**:230–1
    in San Francisco's Chinatown **3**:226, **5**:74 5, 77–9
    tongs **4**:129
Chinese and Chinese Americans, literary works concerning
    Donald Duk **5**:74 80
    Eat a Bowl of Tea **4**:124 30
    Joy Luck Club, The **5**:229–35
    Kitchen God's Wife, The **3**:189–95
    Thousand Pieces of Gold, McCunn, Ruthanne Lum **2**:366–71
    Woman Warrior, The **5**:352–9
Chin, Frank, *Donald Duk* **5**:74 80
Chisholm, Shirley **S1.2**:429
Chivalry **1**:2, 66, 291
Chocolate War, The, Cormier, Robert **5**:61–6
Cholera **2**:103, **S1.1**:67 (*sidebar*)
Chopin, Kate, *Awakening, The* **3**:15–20
Chorus in Greek drama **1**:10
Chosen, The, Potok, Chaim **4**:87–93
Christian, Fletcher **1**:273, 274
Christianity
    among pioneers of midwest **3**:259
    Baldwin on "racist hypocrisy" of **5**:112
    challenged by theory of evolution **S1.1**:246–7
    clergymen extolling WWI **3**:10
    missionaries **2**:118–19, 147, 161–2, 361–2, **3**:133, 280, **5**:195
    Russian Orthodox **S1.1**:54
    Salvation Army **S1.1**:220–1
    suicide as sin **4**:22
    Sunday Observance Bill **S1.1**:36 (*sidebar*)
    Syrian Christians of India **S1.2**:158
    Victorian revival of Christmas traditions **S1.1**:34 6
    (*See also* Catholicism and Catholic Church; Protestantism; Puritanism)
Christmas Carol, A, Dickens, Charles **S1.1**:31–9
"Christmas Memory, A," Capote, Truman **3**:68–74
Chu, Luis, *Eat a Bowl of Tea* **4**:124 30
Churchill, Winston **1**:237, **5**:53, 95
    Speech on the Evacuation at Dunkirk **4**:356–63
CIA (Central Intelligence Agency)
    experiments with drugs **4**:293–4
    role in Cuba's Bay of Pigs "invasion" **5**:226
Cicero **1**:327
Cicotte, Eddie **3**:149, **4**:260
Ciénaga massacre (Colombia) **2**:270
Cinema. *See* Motion picture industry
CIO (Congress of Industrial Organizations) **3**:44
Cisneros, Sandra
    House on Mango Street, The **5**:171–7, **S1.2**:374
    Woman Hollering Creek **S1.2**:499–509
Citizenship
    in ancient Athens **1**:241
    for Chinese immigrants **5**:231
    for Puerto Ricans **5**:215
City-states
    of ancient Greece **1**:286, 327–8
    of Italy **1**:379–80
Civil disobedience, Socrates on **S1.1**:350–1
Civil Disobedience, Thoreau, Henry David **2**:87–92, **S1.2**:271 (*sidebar*)
Civil rights movement
    activism for FEPC (Fair Employment Practices Commission) **3**:42
    affirmative action **5**:181, 183–4, 342, **S1.2**:256, 375
    American Indians **4**:190–1, **5**:246–7
    anti-integrationist **5**:15
    assassinations of leaders **4**:54, **5**:112 (*sidebar*)
    autobiographies as genre **4**:205, **5**:304
    backlash, fear and misunderstanding **S1.2**:429
    BCM (Black Consciousness Movement) **S1.2**:116–17, 122
    Birmingham, Alabama, events in **S1.2**:272–4, 277, 423
    Black arts movement **4**:207
    black feminism **2**:64, **3**:86–7, 354 5, **4**:56, **5**:92–3, 117, **S1.2**:394 (*sidebar*)
    "Black is Beautiful" slogan **4**:54, 56, **S1.1**:337 (*sidebar*), **S1.2**:428, 429
    Black Muslims and Nation of Islam **3**:238, 325, **4**:56, 248–50, **5**:12–13, 69, 110–11, 302, **S1.2**:276
    black nationalism, separatism, and Pan-Africanism **3**:160, 238, 325, **4**:56, 211, 311–12
    Black Panther Party **4**:54, 56, 207, **S1.2**:429

Black Power movement   2:97–8, 3:43, 325, 4:56, 207, 5:143–4, S1.2:232
Black Power and Stokely Carmichael   2:98, 3:325, 4:55 (*illus.*), 56, 5:145 (*illus.*), S1.2:424, 428, 429
Chicano. *See* Chicanos
Civil Rights Acts of 1957, 1964, and 1965   2:97, 3:354, 375, 4:148, 5:91
CORE (Congress of Racial Equality)   3:42, 4:376, S1.2:270
disillusionment, backlash, tokenism of 1970s   S1.2:427
educated blacks and schools in central role   S1.2:255, 256–7
efforts of 1940s and 1950s   4:28–9, 255
efforts of 1960s   S1.1:127
emphasizing African heritage   5:300–2
exclusive African American towns   S1.1:430
FBI & J. Edgar Hoover's theory of communist inspiration of   1:399
focus on South, then North   2:13, 5:25
fostered by Harlem Renaissance   3:163–4, 256, S1.1:337 (*sidebar*)
fostering literary efforts
  autobiographies   4:205, 5:304
  ethnic and cultural explorations   4:92–3, 207, 5:15, 62, 145, 217, 300–2
  women's studies programs   5:117
Freedom Rides   5:88–90, S1.1:127, S1.2:272, 423
gay rights movement   4:241
judicial opposition in 1980s to   5:1–2
King's approach   S1.2:275–6
King's approach, compared to Malcolm X's   4:250, 5:13, 15, 111, S1.2:276, 423
in Louisiana   5:25
March on Washington (1963)   5:110, 186–8
Mexican American activism and Brown Berets   4:176, S1.2:367–9
militancy and Malcolm X   2:98, 3:324 5, 4:54, 249–50, 5:69–70, 110, 111, S1.2:276, 423
in Missouri   4:28–9
NAACP   2:342, 415, 3:250, 320, 396, 4:195, 255, 310, 5:88, 120 (*sidebar*), S1.1:432, S1.2:270
Niagara Movement (1905)   3:250, 320
OAAU (Organization of Afro-American Unity)   5:16–17
origins and growth of   2:97, 3:42–3, 4:28–9, 155–6, 255, 314 15, 5:185, 192, 300, S1.1:127
  Alabama as testing ground   2:220–1, 3:73, 395–6, 4:314 15, 5:11, 88–90, 185–6
pacifist versus outspoken, sometimes violent protest   4:205, 207
passive resistance and nonviolence   5:11–12, 108, 189, 192, S1.2:271 (*sidebar*)
phase 1, nonviolent protest achieving legislation   S1.2:423–4
phase 2, publicly combative, urban-focused Black Power Movement   S1.2:424, 428–9

race riots in "long hot summer" of 1966   2:97–8, 4:207, S1.2:424
Red Power, AIM, and rights movements   2:79 (*sidebar*), 179, 351, 5:246–7, S1.2:165, 477–8, 479 (*illus.*)
SCLC (Southern Christian Leadership Conference)   5:189, S1.2:271
seeking African roots   3:86, 5:145
self-empowerment philosophies   3:325
sit-ins at all-white lunch counters   S1.1:19, S1.2:271, 423
SNCC (Student Nonviolent Coordinating Committee)   4:56, 5:300, S1.2:271
in South Africa   S1.2:319–20
southern and northern blacks joining   S1.2:423
students' free speech movement   5:311
timeline of important events   S1.2:230 (*sidebar*)
TV's role in creating public support for   5:108
UNIA (United Negro Improvement Association)   3:160, 4:211, S1.1:337 (*sidebar*), 432
urban blacks' involvement in   5:143
women's equality advocates   S1.2:234 5
women's involvement in   5:92–3
WPC (Women's Political Council)   5:88
Civil War
  blockade runners   2:138–9
  causes of   2:130–1
  Chancellorsville   2:309
  demise of plantations and wilderness   2:49, 53
  desertion from armies   2:10–11, 312
  draft of mostly poor and lower classes   2:256, 309
  Emancipation Proclamation (1862)   2:59, 60 (*sidebar*), 135, 308, 309
  families torn by conflicting loyalties   2:10
  in Georgia   2:139, 140 (*illus.*)
  Gettysburg   2:131–2
  glorification vs. reality of battle   2:257, 258, 308, 309 (*sidebar*), 312, 313
  industrialization of meat-packing   3:175
  John Brown's raid at Harper's Ferry contributing to   2:190
  major battles of   2:131 (*sidebar*)
  Northerners' point of view   2:11, 22
  overview of   2:308–10
  railroads' importance   2:255, 256 (*illus.*)
  Shiloh   2:257
  Southerners' point of view   2:11, 22
  in southern Illinois   2:9–10
  spies   2:255–6
  Union Army leadership troubles and poor morale   2:308–10
  Vicksburg   2:217
  western migration and Mexican War contributing to   2:88, 89, 395, 405
  Walt Whitman, impact on   2:195–6
  (*See also* Reconstruction)
Clairvoyance   5:239
Clarke, Arthur, *Childhood's End*   5:53–60

Index

Clark, Walter Van Tilburg, *Ox-Bow Incident, The* 2:288–94
Class divisions and social stratification
   achieving high social status and wealth as American Dream   S1.1:2
   African American men, class, race, and manhood   4:313–14
   African Americans in 20th century   4:2–3, 30
   Algerian colons, French-educated Muslims, and indigenous Muslims   S1.2:442 (*sidebar*)
   American Civil War draft of mostly poor and lower classes   2:256, 309
   America's upper class "old money" and nouveaux riches   S1.1:1–4
   Asians as "model minority"   S1.2:351–2
   blacks, whites, Cajuns and Creoles   S1.2:253 (*sidebar*)
   Boston's "first families"   S1.1:201
   Brahmin and untouchables in India   S1.2:152–3, 158
   British Caribbean society   S1.1:494
   Burmese urban elite and peasant villagers   S1.1:400
   Chicanos versus newly arrived immigrants   S1.2:374
   Colombian upper versus lower classes   S1.2:461–2
   Colonial America   1:97, 102, 108
   colonizers versus colonized   S1.2:448
   continuing after loss of empire and influx of immigrants   S1.2:192 (*sidebar*)
   England, class mobility and changing social order   S1.1:91, 141, 240
   England, evolution theory reinforcing social structures   S1.1:325
   England's class consciousness   1:338, 342, 376, 413–14, 2:152–3, 157, 277–8, 296–7, 3:312, 315–16, 326–7, 5:347–8
   England's Elizabethan Age, marriage and social mobility   S1.1:487 (*sidebar*)
   England's Elizabethan gentlemen and stewards   S1.1:486–8, 487 (*sidebar*)
   England's Gypsies   S1.1:243 (*sidebar*)
   England's influx of commonwealth citizens   S1.2:192 (*sidebar*)
   England's new industrial elite   S1.1:150
   England's Victorian Age   2:152–3, 157, 358
   English hierarchy of blood, birth, land, and leisure   S1.1:150
   forced acculturation, assimilation of American Indians   S1.2:30–4, 34 (*illus.*)
   France's class hatreds   1:358–60, 361, 371–2, 2:224
   full-blood versus half-blood Indians   S1.2:31
   Maoist communism emphasizing Indian caste divisions   S1.2:153
   Marx and Engels on class struggle between bourgeoisie and proletariat   S1.1:45–9
   Mexican Americans' alienation from mainstream culture   S1.2:504 5
   Norway in 1800s   S1.1:161
   Peruvian   S1.2:53–4, 57
   resistance to change in American South   S1.2:260
   rise of "new (English) aristocracy"   S1.2:406–7
   Roman patricians versus plebians   S1.1:170
   Russian nobles, priests, peasants and serfs   S1.1:51–4, 99–103, 100 (*sidebar*), 368–9
   Spain's Gypsies   S1.1:191–2, 195–7, 197 (*sidebar*)
   Spain's nobility and questionable blood purity   S1.1:192–3
   suburban "American" versus inner-city ethnic   S1.2:358–9
   in Trinidad   S1.2:184 5, 186, 187, 191
   upper- versus lower-class African Americans   S1.2:428
   urban American Indians   S1.2:33
   "white" Americans versus Mexican Americans   S1.2:504
   (*See also* Middle class)
Clay, Cassius. *See* Ali, Muhammad
Clemens, Samuel. *See* Twain, Mark
Cleopatra   1:190, S1.1:171
Clinton, Bill   S1.2:247
Clipper ships   2:391
Clothing
   for slaves   2:237
   (*See also* Fashions)
Coal mining   3:63, 64
Cody, William F. (Buffalo Bill)   2:68, 177
Cohn, Roy   5:2–4
Cold Sassy Tree, Burns, Olive Ann   3:75–9
Cold War
   anticommunism fever   S1.2:280
   arms race   5:252 (*sidebar*), S1.2:311
   Berlin Blockade   S1.2:363
   Berlin Wall   5:238, 293
   Churchill's "iron curtain" speech   S1.2:4
   Cuban missile crisis and Bay of Pigs   4:135, 5:225, 226, 238–9, 293, S1.2:180
   dashing hopes for socialist Europe   S1.2:474
   division of Germany into East and West   S1.2:309–10
   "domino" theory   2:13–14, S1.2:452 (*sidebar*)
   end with collapse of communist regimes   S1.1:49
   FBI investigations   4:129, 5:127
   fear of Communist China and Chinese immigrants   4:129
   fear of nuclear war   4:12, 13 (*illus.*), 5:53, 59, 225
   fear of "radicalism"   1:399, 4:236
   fear of "socialized" medicine   4:12
   fear of Soviet strength   4:110, 5:225, 292
   fostering American interventions in third world   1:223
   as indirect, hostile competition of ideologies   5:225, 254, 292
   iron curtain for Eastern Europe   5:95–6, S1.2:4

Kennedy's olive branch with militancy   5:224 6
McCarthyism and HUAC   1:84, 398, 3:178, 208, 209 (illus.), 4:71, 72, 110, 398, 5:2, 3 (illus.), 96, 97, 127, S1.1:11, S1.2:280, 310, 364
Marshall Plan's advantages   5:123–4, 224, 292, S1.2:310
NATO (North Atlantic Treaty Organization)   5:124, 224, 292, S1.2:310
"Red Scare"   1:84 6, 3:105, 4:71–2, 5:2, 127
reflected in *Grendel*   S1.2:179–80
reflected in United Nations   5:254
space race   5:53, 81, 321–2, S1.2:181, 311–12
trade as weapon in   5:126
Truman Doctrine (1947–49)   4:110, 5:123–4, S1.2:310
Truman's loyalty program for federal employees   4:72, 236
United States as postwar ally   S1.2:474
U.S.-Soviet competition for global influence   5:95–6, S1.2:4
U.S.-Soviet competition in space   5:53
United States support for oppressive Latin American military dictatorships   5:27–8
(*See also* Communism)
Coleridge, Samuel Taylor   1:116, 416
 Lyrical Ballads   S1.1:207–17
 opium addiction   S1.1:215
Collett, Camilla   S1.1:160, 161 (*sidebar*)
Colombia   2:268–70, 272–3, S1.2:459–65
Colonial America
 American Revolution   1:122–7
 Boston Tea Party   1:125
 class and economic stratification   1:97, 102, 108
 democracy and revolutionary fervor   1:71–2, 74, 76–7, 93–4, 96–7, 108
 Dutch in New Netherland (New York)   1:211, 212, 330–2, 333 (*illus.*), 335 (*sidebar*), 336
 French and Indian War (Seven Years' War)   1:93, 123, 204 6, S1.1:14
 indentured servants   1:394
 materialism   1:102, 105, 311
 militias and Continental Army   1:110 (*sidebar*)
 money, credit, and inflation   1:103–4
 neocolonialism as economic dominance   S1.2:131
 New England area   1:78–80
 New York area   1:107–8, 110, 112 (*illus.*)
 Pilgrims founding Plymouth colony   S1.1:485
 population and economic growth   1:310
 reactions to Stamp, Tea, Townshend, Intolerable, Molasses Acts   1:93, 94 (*sidebar*), 102, 123–5
 regional conflicts   1:211–12
 rhetoric in   1:123
 smuggling   1:102–3
 towns and cities   1:102
 westward expansion   1:102, 103, 107, 204
 Yankee stereotype   1:217
 (*See also* American Indians; American Revolution; Slavery in America; United States)

Colonialism, imperialism, and interventionism
 American
  bolstered by social Darwinism   3:234 5
  Chile   5:164 5
  Cuba   3:231, 278, 4:135, 5:225, 226, 238–9, 293
  Dominican Republic   5:220, S1.2:206, 213
  El Salvador   3:282
  Grenada   S1.2:388
  Guam   3:277
  Guatemala   5:27–8
  Haiti   S1.2:242 (*sidebar*)
  Latin America   3:231, 277–8, 280–1
  Liberia   2:404
  Monroe Doctrine (1823) and "big stick" corollary (1904)   3:277
  Nicaragua   3:282
  Panama Canal   3:231–2
  Philippines   3:101, 278
  Puerto Rico   3:277, 4:385–6, 5:215
  Spanish-American War (1898)   3:101, 278
  support for Latin American dictators   S1.2:208
 Athenian   S1.1:352
 Belgian   2:145–6, 150–1
 British
  in America. *See* Colonial America
  Antigua   S1.2:20–1, 24, 25–6
  bolstered by overseas commerce   1:337
  Burma   S1.1:399–406
  criticized by H. G. Wells   3:406, 410
  decolonization of late 1940s   4:165, S1.1:501–2
  earned wealth as suspect   S1.1:395–6
  East Africa (Kenya)   3:290–1, S1.2:487–9
  empire covering one fourth of globe   S1.1:79
  end of   5:107
  fostering sense of superiority   2:154
  Grenada   S1.2:387
  India. *See* India
  Ireland. *See* Ireland and the Irish
  Nigeria and Igbo people   2:360–2, 364 5, 3:84, 4:314, S1.2:39–48
  Orwell on despotism and futility of empire   S1.1:403–5
  Palestine   4:102–5
  racism, greed, Christianizing mission, as uneasy legacy   S1.1:151–2
  rapid expansion in Elizabethan Age   S1.2:399
  rapid expansion in Victorian Age   S1.1:151–2
  Rhodesia   4:165–6
  South Africa   S1.2:317–18
  South African War (Boer War)   S1.2:116, 123
  Tasmania   3:406
  Trinidad   S1.2:183–8, 190–1
  viewed as "bettering" and "civilizing" "savage" native peoples   1:118, 2:118–19, 146, 3:84

British (*continued*)
    Wales   1:149
    West Indies   2:183–4, S1.1:493–6, 501–2
    xenophobia   S1.1:140
in China   3:205
Dutch   1:338, S1.2:317
European   S1.1:62, 377–8
exploration as enterprise of empire   S1.2:125
French
    Algeria   3:211–13, S1.2:441–3
    Grenada   S1.2:387
    Indochina (Vietnam)   5:101, 306, S1.2:452
    Saint-Domingue (Haiti)   5:116–17
German   3:290
Imperial Roman   S1.1:170
Italian   4:67
Japanese   4:58–9, 92, 177–8, 349–54
missionaries   2:118–19, 147, 161–2, 183, 361–2, 3:133, 280
racial assumptions   1:118, 2:118–19, 146, 3:84, 234 5, S1.1:151–2, 334
relationship to slavery   S1.1:328
segregation of rulers and ruled   3:182
Spanish
    Colombia   2:268
    Mexico   5:172
    Puerto Rico   5:214 15
Colonias   S1.2:92 (sidebar)
Colorado River   S1.2:97 (sidebar)
Color Purple, The, Walker, Alice   3:80–7
Comedy
    Dickens's skill in   S1.1:157 (sidebar)
    music hall and variety acts   S1.2:469–70
    stoic comedians   S1.2:475 (sidebar)
Comiskey, Charles   3:149, 5:314, 316
Common Sense, Paine, Thomas   1:71–7
    effectiveness of   1:94
Communal movements
    Communards and Paris Commune   1:363
    Shakerism   3:95, 99
    Twin Oaks colony   5:279
Communism
    anti-Bolshevik reactions of 1920s   3:21–2, 44
    appeal of, to blacks   3:164, 238–9
    birth in Industrial Revolution   S1.1:45
    in China   3:136, 194
    collapse   S1.1:49
    communists as targets of Holocaust   4:160, 267
    comparison to socialism and Marxism   S1.1:45 (sidebar)
    contrast with capitalism   4:166
    in Dominican Republic   S1.2:210 (sidebar)
    global disillusion with, following revelations of Stalin's purges   4:166
    Great Depression enhancing appeal of   3:39–40, 45, 129, 208–10
    influence on Jack London   3:52
    labor organizers accused of   3:144
    landowners as "capitalist" enemies of   4:282

in Latin America   S1.2:52–3
Maoism emphasizing Indian caste divisions   S1.2:153
Marxism   3:59, 179, 321, 4:18–19
opposition to racism and prejudice   3:40, 4:211
origin of term   S1.1:45
as theory   4:166
use of folksongs   3:47, 50
(*See also* Cold War; Soviet Union)
Communist Manifesto, The, Marx, Karl and Friedrich Engels   1:376, S1.1:41–9
Competition, role of, in Darwin's theory of evolution   S1.1:327
Computers   5:97, 127
Comstock Lode (Nevada silver mines)   2:288–9, 290 (sidebar)
Comte, Auguste   3:213
Confessions of Nat Turner, The, Styron, William   2:93–8
Confucius   3:193 (sidebar)
Congregationalists   1:357, 424 5
Connell, Richard, "Most Dangerous Game, The"   3:231–5
Conquest and colonization, Mexico's northern territories by United States   S1.2:83
Conrad, Joseph
    Heart of Darkness   2:145–51
    Secret Agent, The   S1.1:377–85
Conroy, Pat, *Prince of Tides, The*   5:285–90
Conservatism
    fundamentalism and New, Religious Right   5:137–9
    pro-business policies of Reagan presidency   5:1
Contender, The, Lipsyte, Robert   5:67–73
Cookbooks   S1.2:107–8, 109 (sidebar)
Copernicus, Nicolaus   1:24, 94, 305, S1.1:107, 113
Corcoran, Thomas "Tommy the Cork" Gardiner   3:402
CORE (Congress of Racial Equality)   3:42, 4:376, S1.2:270
Corey, Giles   1:83 (sidebar), 395
Corinth   1:238, 241
Cormier, Robert, *Chocolate War, The*   5:61–6
Corn Laws   S1.1:324
Cortés, Hernán   S1.2:93, 499
Cosmology   S1.1:344
Cossacks   3:233
Cotton
    causing soil exhaustion   3:390
    crop failures from boll weevil   4:2
    as "King" Cotton   2:15, 22, 44 (*illus.*), 168, 403
    North-South contention over trade in   3:203–4
    plummeting of profits in 1920s and 1930s   3:153, 390, 391, S1.2:381
    for typhus prevention, advantages of clothing and bedding of   1:115
Cotton Club of Harlem   S1.1:337
Cotton, John   1:352

Coughlin, Father Charles **4**:373
Coulon, A **S1.1**:379–80
Counterculture (beatniks, hippies, and protesters)
    in 1950s **4**:75, 289, 293, 399–400
    in 1960s **5**:37, 64 (*sidebar*), 83, 158, 237, 272, 279, 308–10, 323–5, **S1.2**:108–9
Count of Monte-Cristo, The, Dumas, Alexandre **2**:99–104
Courtship, marriage plotting **S1.1**:94
Coxey, Jacob S. and Coxey's Army **3**:51–2
Crane, Stephen, *Red Badge of Courage, The* **2**:308–13
Craven, Margaret, *I Heard the Owl Call My Name* **5**:194 200
Creationism **2**:30
"Credibility gap" **S1.2**:457–8
Creoles **3**:15–18, **4**:365, **5**:21, 130, **S1.1**:494 5, 496 (*sidebar*), **S1.2**:253 (*sidebar*)
Creon **1**:15, 17, 18, 19
Crime
    blacks and Latinos as victims of **4**:31, **5**:340–1
    blacks turning to **4**:145
    by Chinese American tongs **4**:129
    creation of police detectives **2**:153–4
    depicted in *Crime and Punishment* **S1.1**:51–60, 368
    depicted in *Felicia's Journey* **S1.2**:133–40
    depicted in *House Gun, The* **S1.2**:195–204
    depicted in *The Stranger* **S1.2**:441–9
    depicted in *The Trial* **S1.1**:473–82
    drug-related **4**:250–1
    during Reconstruction, violence and unequal justice for freed slaves **5**:20–1
    early police forces **S1.1**:272, 274, 278 (*sidebar*)
    by gangs, juvenile delinquents **4**:251, 386, 387–9
    gangsters (*tsotsi*) of South Africa **4**:97
    gang truce in Los Angeles **5**:341
    outlaws on American western frontier **1**:256–7
    outlaws in medieval England **1**:252–3
    Pinkerton's National Detective Agency **3**:225–6
    Prohibition fostering corruption, bootlegging, and gangsterism **3**:69, 147–8, 366–7, 401
    public perception, flamboyant news reporting **S1.1**:272
    Scotland Yard **S1.1**:272, 272 (*sidebar*)
    serial murders **S1.2**:136
    in slums, ghettos **5**:13, 67–8, 112, 146, 150, 339–42
    Sûreté **S1.1**:278 (*sidebar*)
    switchblades **S1.2**:235 (*sidebar*)
    by teenagers **S1.2**:284 5
    in Victorian Age **S1.1**:151
    (*See also* Law enforcement; Law and legal systems; Lynching)
Crimean War **S1.1**:326, 456
Crime and Punishment, Dostoyevsky, Fyodor **S1.1**:51–60, 368, **S1.2**:200

Cristero rebellion (1926–29) **S1.2**:86
Cromwell, Oliver **1**:299, 306, **S1.1**:35
Crucible, The, Miller, Arthur **1**:78–86
Crusades **1**:182, 291
Cry, the Beloved Country, Paton, Alan **4**:94 100
Cryptography **S1.1**:275 (*sidebar*), 277
Crystal Palace and Great Exhibition of 1851 **S1.1**:325 (*sidebar*)
Cuba
    admiration in Latin America for Revolution **S1.2**:83, 94
    American interventions of 1898 and 1901 **3**:231, 278
    Bay of Pigs and missile crisis **4**:135, **5**:225, 226, 238–9, 293
    Castro **2**:273, **4**:279, **5**:225, **S1.2**:53, 58–9
    personalismo **4**:275
    religion **4**:274 5
    Revolution of 1950s **2**:273
    role of luck **4**:275–6
Cubism **S1.1**:464
Cultural anthropology **S1.1**:433 (*sidebar*), **S1.2**:266
Cuvier, Georges **S1.1**:274
Cyprus **1**:296
Cyrano de Bergerac, Rostand, Edmond **1**:87–92
Cyrano de Bergerac, Savinien de **1**:87, 88 (*sidebar*), 89–90
Czech Republic **S1.1**:283 (*sidebar*)

D

Daisy Miller, James, Henry **2**:105–10
Daly, Carroll John **3**:227
Dam construction **S1.2**:97 (*sidebar*), 342–3
Damnation. *See* Sin and damnation
Dana, Richard Henry, Jr., *Two Years before the Mast* **2**:391–6
Dance **4**:387
Dandelion Wine, Bradbury, Ray **3**:88–93, **S1.2**:309
Dante Alighieri
    Divine Comedy **1**:175 (*sidebar*), 178
    Inferno **1**:174 80
    influence on Joyce **3**:111
Danticat, Edwidge, *Krik? Krak!* **S1.2**:239–48
Daoism (also Taoism) **5**:237
D.A.R. (Daughters of the American Revolution) **S1.2**:144 (*sidebar*)
"Dark Ages" **S1.2**:171–2
D'Artagnan (Charles-Ogier de Batz de Castelmore) **1**:387
Darwin, Charles **2**:29, 119, **S1.1**:246–7, 321
    On the Origin of Species **S1.1**:80, 139–40, 246, 274, 323–31, **S1.2**:299
Darwin, Erasmus **1**:116, **S1.1**:329
Darwinism. *See* Evolution
Daughters of the American Revolution (D.A.R.) **S1.2**:144 (*sidebar*)
Dawes Act (1887) **2**:68, 179, **4**:186, **S1.2**:31
Dawn, Wiesel, Elie **4**:101–8

Index

Day No Pigs Would Die, A, Peck, Robert Newton   3:94 9
DDT   4:338–9
Deafness. *See* Disabled persons
Dean, James   4:392, 400
Dean, John   5:159 (*illus.*)
Dearborn, Henry   S1.2:208
Death of Artemio Cruz, The, Carlos Fuentes   S1.2:83–94
Death in the Family, A, Agee, James   3:100–5
Death of Ivan Ilyich, The, Tolstoy, Leo   S1.1:71–8
Death of a Salesman, Miller, Arthur   4:109–15
Death in Venice, Mann, Thomas   S1.1:61–9
De Beauvoir, Simone   4:167
Debs, Eugene V.   3:54, 175
Decadent movement   S1.1:182
Decembrist Revolt   S1.1:52, 101
Declaration of Independence, The, Jefferson, Thomas   1:93–100
   comparison to language in *Common Sense*   1:76
   evoked in King's "I Have Dream" speech   5:191
   evoked in Lincoln's Gettysburg Address   2:134 5
Declaration of the Rights of Man (French Revolution)   1:372
Declaration of Sentiments (for women's rights)   2:24, 55, 204, 3:16
Dee, John   1:385 (*sidebar*)
Defoe, Daniel   1:131, 268, 342
   Robinson Crusoe   1:337–43
De Gaulle, Charles   3:214
De Klerk, F. W.   S1.2:196
Delamere, Hugh Cholmondeley, Baron   3:295
Delaware (Lenape) Indians   1:206, 219–20
Delphi   S1.1:307 (*sidebar*)
Democracy
   in 19th-century America   2:87–8, 89–91
   in ancient Greece   1:18, 321, 322, S1.1:310
   at King Arthur's round table   1:292
   before and after publication of *Common Sense*   1:74
   coming to Japan   S1.2:014
   coming to South Africa   S1.2:196
   individualism and egalitarianism contributing to   2:302
   influence of Declaration of Independence upon   1:100
   Kennedy's call for defense of freedom   5:226–7
   rise of common people as political force in France   1:164, 165
   role of printing press in promoting   1:162 (*sidebar*)
   Whitman as poet of   2:196
   (*See also* Suffrage)
Demosthenes   S1.1:352
Denmark   1:136–8, 141
Depression, The. *See* Great Depression, The (1930s)
Desert Solitaire: A Season in the Wilderness, Abbey, Edward   S1.2:95–103

Dessalines, Jean Jacques   S1.2:242 (*sidebar*)
Detective fiction. *See* Mystery and detective stories
De Tocqueville, Alexis   2:106
Developmental disabilities. *See* Disabled persons
Devil (Satan)
   comparative conceptions of   5:57 (*sidebar*)
   in Dante's *Inferno*   1:177, 179 (*illus.*)
   Lucifer in Milton's *Paradise Lost*   1:301–3, 305
   Mephistopheles in Goethe's *Faust*   S1.1:112
   Puritans' belief in   1:79–81, 102, 393, 394
"Devil and Tom Walker, The," Irving, Washington   1:101–6
DeWitt, John   4:138
Dialectical materialism   S1.1:47 (*sidebar*)
Dialectic method   S1.1:352
Dialogues, Plato's *Apology*, Plato   S1.1:343–53
Diary of a Young Girl, The, Frank, Anne   4:116–23
Diaspora   4:101
Díaz, Porfirio   3:28–30, 197, 278, S1.2:83, 431, 432, 501–2
Dickens, Charles   2:92, 375, S1.1:384
   Christmas Carol, A   S1.1:31–9
   Great Expectations   S1.1:149–58
   Oliver Twist   2:261–7
   Tale of Two Cities, A   1:371–8
Dickinson, Emily   2:54 8
Dictaphone   S1.2:147 (*sidebar*)
Dictatorships
   African tendency toward   S1.2:42–3
   Argentina's military rulers   5:208–11, 212–13
   Athens' Thirty Tyrants   1:322, 324, 325 (*sidebar*), S1.1:345 (*sidebar*)
   caudillos and caudillismo   S1.2:83
   Chile's military junta   5:169
   Colombia's Rojas Pinilla   S1.2:461, 461 (*sidebar*)
   Communist China   5:254–5
   Cuba's Castro   2:273, 4:279, 5:225, S1.2:53, 58–9
   Dominican Republic's Trujillo   S1.2:205–9, 207 (*illus.*), 212, 213, 241 (*sidebar*)
   England and "divine right" of Charles I   1:303
   Haiti's Duvaliers   S1.2:241–2, 242 (*sidebar*)
   insisting on national loyalty over religious faith and individual conscience   S1.1:266
   Italy's Mussolini   2:293–4, 4:66–7, 305 (*illus.*), S1.1:177, S1.2:299
   Japan's prewar military   4:178, 183
   Mexico's Díaz   3:28–30, 197, 278, S1.2:83, 431, 432, 501–2
   Oedipus as tyrant   S1.1:310–11
   opposition to, in *Twenty-Thousand Leagues under the Sea*   2:387
   Orwell's attacks upon   5:254 (*sidebar*)
   Peru's military junta   5:333–4
   Peru's Odría   S1.2:52, 55
   Portugal's Salazar   S1.2:64
   rise in 1930s   S1.2:299
   Russian czars   S1.1:52
   Spain's Primo de Rivera   S1.2:74

warnings against   1:18
(*See also* Fascism; Hitler, Adolf; Napoleon Bonaparte; Soviet Union; Stalin, Josef)
Diem, Ngo Dinh   5:102, S1.2:452
Diet, nutrition
   of concentration camp inmates   4:268
   foods and convenience in 1950s America   S1.2:107–9
   of poor farmers   3:371
   of Siberian work camp inmates   4:283–4
   of slaves   2:237
Dillard, Annie
   American Childhood, An   4:7–13
   Pilgrim at Tinker Creek   5:278–84
Dinesen, Isak, *Out of Africa*   3:290–6
Dinner at the Homesick Restaurant, Tyler, Anne   S1.2:105–13
Disabled persons
   in almshouses in 18th-century America   2:216, 219 (*sidebar*)
   attitudes toward   S1.2:145 (*sidebar*)
   clubfooted   3:264
   education for   2:216–17, 221–2
   Independent Living movement   2:123
   overcoming pity   2:218–19
   views of, in 1970s   2:123
   views of, in Victorian Age   2:119–20
   (*See also* Mental and emotional disabilities)
Discrimination. *See* Racism and prejudice
Diseases
   AIDS   5:9
   atomic radiation sickness   4:181
   bronchitis   2:335
   bubonic plague (Black Death)   1:159, 160, 344, 345, 350
   cancer   2:335, 4:340
   cholera   2:103, S1.1:67 (*sidebar*)
   disabilities   S1.2:145 (*sidebar*)
   epidemics among mission Indians   S1.2:162
   "fainting"   3:420
   Fetal Alcohol Syndrome   S1.2:294
   "hysteria"   2:425
   leprosy   2:362
   leukemia   S1.2:435 (*sidebar*)
   measles   1:220
   "nerves" (stress, depression)   2:278–9
   neurofibromatosis   2:122
   pellagra   S1.2:263
   plague   S1.1:311
   pluerosis   S1.2:145 (*sidebar*)
   polio   4:9–10
   postcombat syndrome   4:80 (*sidebar*)
   postpartum depression   2:425
   Post-Traumatic Stress Disorder (P.T.S.D.)   S1.2:455 (*sidebar*)
   Proteus syndrome   2:122
   puerperal fever   3:285
   rabies   3:387, 406
   radioactive poisoning   4:85
   respiratory   2:335, 3:2, 76, 219, 223
   resulting from depression   5:273
   scarlet fever   2:206 (*sidebar*)
   sickle cell anemia   2:362 (*sidebar*)
   smallpox   1:220, 352, 2:347, 5:214
   "trench fever"   S1.2:299
   trench foot and trench fever   3:9, 115 (*sidebar*)
   tuberculosis   2:335, 3:2, 219, 223, S1.1:35 (*sidebar*)
   typhoid, typhus   2:185 (*sidebar*), 3:2
   venereal   4:37
   venereal, in Victorian Age   S1.1:141–2
   (*See also* Alcohol and alcoholism; Drug, substance abuse; Health issues; Medicine; Mental and emotional disabilities)
Dissenters. *See* Anglican Church
District Governor's Daughters, The, Collett, Camilla   S1.1:160
Divine Comedy. *See* Inferno
Divorce
   in 1800s   2:126, 127, 158, 212, 355–6
   in America, 19th-century upper classes   S1.1:8
   on American Western frontier   S1.1:284
   among Issei couples   4:332
   in China   2:370, 371, 3:132, 193, 5:230
   in czarist Russia   2:37, 39, S1.1:370
   Doyle's support for reform   2:158
   in early 20th-century America   3:167–8, 272, 368
   in England of 1800s   S1.1:92
   in Imperial Rome   S1.1:172–3
   in Japan   S1.2:414
   for Jews   3:427, 429 (*sidebar*)
   legalization spurred by Protestantism   2:113
   remarriage   4:242
   soaring rate of, in late 20th century   2:65, 4:241–2, 5:36, 138, 267, 273, 286–8
Dix, Dorothy   3:17
Dobrolyubov, Nikolai   S1.1:102, 105
Doctorow, E. L., *Ragtime*   3:319–25
Doctors. *See* Diseases; Medicine
Documents
   Declaration of Independence (American Revolution)   1:93–100
   Declaration of the Rights of Man (French Revolution)   1:372
   Declaration of Sentiments (for women's rights in America)   2:24, 55, 204, 3:16
   (*See also* Essays; Narratives; Speeches)
Dodgson, Charles Lutwidge. *See* Carroll, Lewis
Doerr, Harriet, *Stones For Ibarra*   S1.2:431–9
Doll's House, A, Ibsen, Henrik   2:111–17
Dominican Republic
   Balaguer elected president   S1.2:213
   Bosch presidency   S1.2:213
   communist movement   S1.2:210 (*sidebar*)
   control by Haiti   S1.2:205
   invasion of Haiti   S1.2:241 (*sidebar*)
   population mostly mulattos   S1.2:205–6
   public opposition of Catholic Church   S1.2:209

Dominican Republic (*continued*)
    resistance and human rights abuses   S1.2:207–9
    as Spanish colony   S1.2:205
    Trujillo dictatorship   S1.2:205–9, 207 (illus.), 212, 213, 241 (sidebar)
    United States' interventions   5:220, S1.2:206, 213
Donald Duk, Chin, Frank   5:74 80
Don Quixote. *See Adventures of Don Quixote, The*
Doolittle, James "Jimmy"   4:68
Dorris, Michael, *Yellow Raft in Blue Water, A*   5:360–6
Dostoyevsky, Fyodor, *Crime and Punishment*   S1.1:51–60, 368, S1.2:200
Douglass, Frederick
    influence upon Toni Morrison   2:63
    Narrative of the Life of Frederick Douglass   2:16, 236–41, S1.2:229, 231
    on *Uncle Tom's Cabin*   2:409
Douglas, Stephen A.   2:2, 242
Doyle, Arthur Conan, *Hound of the Baskervilles*   2:152-9
Dracula, Stoker, Bram   S1.1:79–87, 140, 146
Draft. *See* Military draft
Drama. *See* Plays; Theater
Dramatic monologues   S1.1:204
Dreams
    as "dream messages" from ancestors   S1.2:393
    Freud's theory of   S1.1:317
    visions of Blackfeet   S1.1:136
Dreiser, Theodore, *Sister Carrie*   2:327–33
Dreyfus, Alfred   1:91–2, 364 (sidebar), S1.1:121
Drug, substance abuse
    among African Americans   4:250–1
    among American Indians   4:83
    attitudes of 1950s   5:99 (sidebar)
    among beatniks   4:75
    dealers' self-concept as respectable and superior   5:341–2
    drug traffic and "narco-terrorism" by United States   S1.2:17
    experiments by CIA   4:293–4
    fines and prison required by Boggs Act (1951)   5:99 (sidebar)
    LSD   4:288, 289, 292, 293–4, 5:82–3, 324 5
    marijuana   S1.2:359
    morphine addiction   3:218–19, 223
    Narcotics Control Act (1956)   4:250
    opium addiction   S1.1:215
    opium addiction in China   3:134 (sidebar)
    opium products   3:379
    in prep schools   4:74
    by Puerto Ricans   5:217
    psychedelic   5:82–3
    risk of AIDS   5:342
    suspicions of conspiracy by white officials to allow in ghettos   5:144
    unequal, unjust penalties for dealing   5:342
    Vietnam soldiers   S1.2:454
    among youth of 1950s   4:173
    (*See also* Alcohol and alcoholism)

Drums Along the Mohawk, Edmonds, Walter D.   1:107–14
Drury, Allen   5:4
Dry White Season, A, André Brink   S1.2:115–24
Dubliners, Joyce, James   3:106–11
Du Bois, W. E. B.
    advocating education for "talented tenth"   3:250, 385
    advocating no toleration of segregation or inequality   3:320
    aggressive, confrontational agenda   S1.1:337 (sidebar), S1.2:428
    co-founder of NAACP   S1.2:270
    compared to Booker T. Washington   2:345 (sidebar), 3:250, 320, 385, S1.1:337 (sidebar)
    criticism of *Up from Slavery*   2:415
    Niagara Movement   S1.2:428
    Souls of Black Folk, The   2:340–6, 3:162–3
Dueling   1:389 (sidebar)
Dumas, Alexandre
    Count of Monte-Cristo, The   2:99–104
    Three Musketeers, The   1:386–92
Du Maurier, Daphne, *Rebecca*   3:326–33
Duncan, King of Scotland   1:225
Dune, Herbert, Frank   5:81-7
Dunkirk evacuation   4:356, 358 (illus.), 359–63
Dust Bowl, The   3:34, 46, 138–40, 4:297
Dutch in New Netherland (New York)   1:211, 212, 330-2, 333 (illus.), 335 (sidebar), 336
Dutch Reformed Church   1:331, 425
Duvalier, François "Papa Doc"   S1.2:241
Duvalier, Jean Claude "Baby Doc"   S1.2:241-2
Dyer, Brigadier-General R. E. H.   S1.2:328
Dystopian literature
    Blindness as   S1.2:69
    Brave New World as   5:141, 252
    described   5:100, 141, 252
    Handmaid's Tale, The as   5:141
    Nineteen Eighty-Four as   5:100, 141
    The Martian Chronicles   S1.2:309–15

E

Earhart, Amelia   S1.2:491, 495
Earth Day   5:279 (sidebar), S1.2:102, 180-1
Earthquakes, in Chile   5:168 (sidebar)
East Germany   S1.2:309–10
Eat a Bowl of Tea, Chu, Luis   4:124 30
Eatonville, Florida   3:383, S1.1:430
Edmonds, Walter D., *Drums Along the Mohawk*   1:107–14
Education
    in 19th-century America   2:42–3, 204 5
    for African Americans
        in blacks-only schools   2:413, 3:371, 375, S1.2:256
        Brown v. Board of Education   3:375, 4:29–30, 314, 5:90, 108, 180, 181, S1.1:19, S1.2:231, 256, 270
        demand for more control by   5:144

dropout rates of **5**:342
forbidden use of libraries **3**:40, 371
freed slaves **2**:411–12, 413, 414
improvements in **3**:375, 420
integrated **3**:43, 396, **4**:29–30, 31 (*illus.*), 314, **5**:116, 131–2, 181
in "Movable School" **3**:380
negative effects of segregation on **4**:33
Afrikaans language required in South Africa **S1.2**:118
of American Indian children **5**:244, 246, 361–2, **S1.2**:32, 478
at prep schools **4**:74
bilingual **4**:45, **5**:172, 179–81, 183, 217, **S1.2**:375–6
of black South Africans **4**:97
boarding schools **S1.2**:32, 478
of British colonial subjects **S1.2**:21, 24
Burmese **S1.1**:400
creating generation gap **5**:182, 198, 244, 246
creating social barriers between family members and generations **S1.2**:186
criticality for Jews **3**:425
for disabled persons **2**:216–17, 221–2, **4**:151–2
free secondary schooling in Britain **S1.2**:474
GI Bill **S1.2**:358
by governesses in Victorian Age **2**:182, 183 (*sidebar*), 378–80
increases in school attendance during Depression **3**:153–4
in Japan **S1.2**:219
in Japanese schools in 1930s California **4**:333
Lau v. Nichols **5**:180
as means to social mobility **S1.1**:150
Mexican Americans and anti-intellectualism **S1.2**:370
in Mexico **S1.2**:84
of migrant farm workers' children **3**:144 (*sidebar*)
minority studies programs
    African American history **5**:147–8
    in Black English or Ebonics **5**:145, 154, 342
    black studies programs **5**:147–8, **S1.2**:236, 429
    Chicano **S1.2**:369
    increasing college enrollments **5**:217
    Puerto Rican history and culture **5**:217
    women's studies **5**:117
promoted by G.I.. Bill **3**:92, **4**:73
school desegregation by forced busing **S1.2**:429
schools handling contentious issues **5**:311–12
in small communities **4**:217
as source of anxiety for parents on American Western frontier **S1.1**:284
in Southern mill towns **3**:78, **4**:256
in Southern rural towns during Depression **3**:352
textbook content reviewed by Religious Right **5**:138

through Americorps program **5**:340
in Trinidad **S1.2**:185–6
University of California v. Bakke **5**:181
Education, of men
    apprenticeship system **2**:262, **S1.1**:150
    in boarding schools **4**:240
    boys' street gangs **3**:400–1
    in colonial America **1**:23, 123
    in czarist Russia **3**:58
    English schools **2**:372–7, **3**:346
    fagging **2**:375
    G.I.. Bill (1944) **3**:92, **4**:73
    hunting as rite of passage **2**:48
    importance for achieving middle-class status **2**:303
    in New Netherland **1**:212–13
    in private, prep schools **4**:325–7, **5**:62–3
    "ragged schools" in England **S1.1**:32, 242 (*sidebar*)
    reforms in 19th-century England **3**:265, **S1.1**:242 (*sidebar*)
    scientific, in France **2**:386
    in skills of knighthood **1**:182 (*sidebar*), 290–1
    in traditional Jewish communities of Eastern Europe **3**:425–6
    Wollstonecraft on **1**:410
Education, of women
    in 17th-century England (Tudor era) **1**:232–3, 236
    in 17th-century France **1**:30
    in 18th-century France **1**:32
    in 18th-century New Netherland **1**:212–13
    in 19th-century America vs. Europe **2**:106
    in 19th-century England **1**:412, **2**:30, 181–2, 297, 422–3, **S1.1**:95, 391
    in 19th-century France **1**:408, **2**:210, 245
    in 19th-century New England **2**:55, 56 (*sidebar*), 203
    in 19th-century South **2**:42
    in 20th-century America **1**:35
    in 20th-century Scotland **4**:303–4
    Ben Franklin on **1**:24 (*sidebar*)
    blacks on athletic scholarships **4**:149
    college and increased opportunities for **5**:174
    Jewish **3**:427, 430
    skepticism for **1**:236
    in Victorian Age **1**:412, **2**:30, 181–2, 422–3
    Wollstonecraft on **1**:409–10, **2**:297
Edward I of England **1**:244, 291
Edward IV of England **S1.1**:356, 358–9, 360
Edward V of England **S1.1**:359
Egypt
    after WWII **S1.2**:131
    Six-Day War with Israel **4**:107
Eichmann, Adolf **4**:107 (*sidebar*), 269, 270, 272, 273, **5**:210
Eisenhower, Dwight D. **4**:398, **5**:53, 91
Eleanor of Aquitaine **1**:250
Electroshock therapy **S1.2**:149 (*sidebar*)
Elephant Man, The, Pomerance, Bernard **2**:118–24

Index

Eliezer, Israel Ben   **4**:87
Eliot, George (Marian Evans), *Mill on the Floss, The*   **S1.1**:239–48
Eliot, T.S.   **5**:42
   Love Song of J. Alfred Prufrock, The   **S1.1**:199–206, 259
   Murder in the Cathedral   **S1.1**:259–70
   Waste Land, The   **3**:411–17, **S1.1**:259
Elizabethan Age
   belief in supernatural   **1**:4, 141, 142 (*sidebar*), 194 5, 227–8, 262, 346, 350
   bubonic plague   **1**:344, 350
   concepts of sin and damnation   **1**:143
   education of women in Tudor era   **1**:232–3, 236
   family life and obligations   **1**:203
   foreign influence, corruption   **1**:150
   growth of American colonies   **1**:149
   imported words from science, literature, and exploration   **S1.2**:399–400
   kinship ties   **1**:141, 145
   maritime exploration, empire building, privateers, and piracy   **S1.1**:490 (*sidebar*)
   popularity of history plays   **1**:150
   popularity of revenge tragedies   **1**:142
   popularity of satire and puns   **1**:349
   religious conflicts and economic depression, inflation   **S1.1**:365
   struggle for succession   **S1.2**:400
   theater as controversial   **S1.2**:399
   treatment of insane   **1**:203
   wars with Spain   **1**:1–2
Elizabeth I of England
   bolstering national pride   **1**:349
   Catholic faction's opposition to   **1**:149, 349
   conspiracy of Earl of Essex   **1**:194, 349
   courtiers   **1**:263
   favoring mainstream Protestantism   **S1.1**:485
   proving effectiveness of female monarch   **1**:233, 236
   rivalry with, execution of Mary, Queen of Scots   **1**:141, 149, 150, 349
   succession of crown to James of Scotland   **1**:201
   unification and commercial strengthening of England   **1**:150, 201, 263
   as virgin queen   **1**:201, 261, 262–3, 350
Elizabeth II of England   **S1.2**:406–7
Elliott-Lynn, Sophie, Lady Heath   **S1.2**:495
Ellison, Ralph, *Invisible Man*   **4**:209–15
Emancipation
   Emancipation Proclamation (1862)   **2**:59, 60 (*sidebar*), 135, 308, 309
   life little changed for freed slaves   **5**:19–20
   (*See also* Abolitionists, Abolition of slavery)
Embrey, Sue Kunitomi   **4**:143
Emerson, Ralph Waldo
   influence on Dickinson   **2**:57
   on John Brown   **2**:193
   as model for Prof. Bhaer in *Little Women*   **2**:207
   opposition to war with Mexico   **2**:89

Self-Reliance   **2**:314 20
   support for abolition   **2**:315, 316
   support for American Indians   **2**:316, 317
   support for Thoreau   **2**:417
   as transcendentalist   **1**:356, **2**:92, 314
   on *Two Years before the Mast*   **2**:396
Emma, Austen, Jane   **S1.1**:89–97
Employment issues for women. *See under* Victorian women; Women in 20th century
Endless Steppe, The: Growing Up in Siberia, Hautzig, Esther   **4**:131–6
Engels, Friedrich, *Communist Manifesto, The*   **1**:376, **S1.1**:41–9
England in Roman times
   evidence of gladiator arenas   **S1.1**:232
   Hadrian's and Antonine Walls   **S1.1**:230 (*sidebar*), 231
   Picts in northern regions (Scotland)   **S1.1**:229–30
England in medieval times
   Anglo-Saxons   **1**:44 5, 153, 181, **S1.2**:172
   Black Death, vagrant laborers, poverty, and workhouses   **S1.2**:135
   Celts, Britons, and Arthurian legends   **1**:196–7, 288, 289 (*illus.*), 290
   expulsion of Jews   **1**:244, 246, 248
   feudalism   **1**:65–6, 153
   king versus church, Henry II versus Thomas Becket   **S1.1**:259–62
   Magna Carta   **1**:255
   Norman Conquest   **1**:181, 251–3
   relations with Scotland   **1**:145, 149–50
   Romans   **1**:288
   royal forests   **1**:251–2
   Saxon invaders and Wales   **1**:288
   Vikings   **1**:49, 138, 226, **S1.2**:172
   wars with France   **1**:159, 160
England in 15th century, Wars of the Roses   **S1.1**:355–65
England in 16th century
   Henry VIII   **1**:149, 150, 231, 232, 234 (*illus.*)
   (*See also* Elizabeth; Elizabethan Age)
England in 17th century
   civil war, execution of King Charles I, and Restoration   **1**:129, 303, 305–6
   class consciousness   **1**:338
   foreign influences upon   **1**:150
   Glorious Revolution and William of Orange   **1**:130, 338–9, 342–3
   growth of tolerance   **1**:299–300
   Gunpowder Plot   **1**:229
   slave trading by   **1**:337–8, **2**:361
   wars with France   **1**:130–1, 305
   wars with Spain   **1**:87, 201
England in 18th century
   anti-Catholic Gordon Riots   **S1.1**:407–8
   British Royal Navy   **1**:273–9
   class consciousness   **1**:342
   Dissenters and Test Act   **1**:129, 338, 342, 407, 411

economic anxiety and social mobility
S1.1:149–50
enclosures of commons (a community's common fields)   S1.1:91, 209–10
French and Indian War   1:93, 123, S1.1:14
historic rivalry with France   1:391–2
inflation and hard times   S1.1:210, 213 (sidebar)
landowning male gentry   S1.1:387–9
London vs. country living   2:296–7
London as world's largest city   S1.1:408
as power in foreign trade   1:400, 401
publishing industry's growth   1:342
reactions to French Revolution   1:359–60, 372–3, 373 (sidebar), 376, 408, S1.1:89–90, 387–8, 407
Tories vs. Whigs   1:129–31, 305–6, 311, 337, 342
wars with France   1:51–2, 93, 123, 204 6, 220–1
wars with Spain   1:130–1
(See also American Revolution)
England in 19th century
apprenticeship system   2:262
British Royal Navy   1:51–6, 404 5
Catholic emancipation   S1.1:239–40
changes in agriculture and industry   S1.1:240
Chartist demonstrations and fear of revolution   S1.1:325–6
Crimean War with Russia   S1.1:326, 465
democracy and respect for law   S1.1:382–3
failure of new Poor Law   S1.1:32–3
leading industrialization   S1.1:41, 42
monarchs, morals, and manners of Regency   S1.1:90–2
nouveaux riches   3:327
rapid expansion of empire   S1.1:151–2
repeal of Corn Laws and victory for free trade   S1.1:324
socialism and Fabian Society   S1.1:219, 221
suffrage Reform Bills   S1.1:326
War of 1812   1:53
(See also Victorian Age; Victorian women)
England in 20th century
arms manufacturing and dealing   S1.1:221–2, 221 (sidebar)
birthrate, population decline   3:347, 5:348
British Library   3:360
British Royal Navy   4:229
classes, and fading of social hierarchies   3:312, 315–16, 326–7, 5:347–8
consumerism, materialism, conspicuous consumption   1:237, 3:344 5, 348
as cultural superpower in 1950s   4:307 (sidebar)
despair, decay, and decline   2:275–6, 3:344 5, 348, 5:39–40
fascism in 1930s   4:304
General Strike of 1926   5:40
homeless and "rough sleeping"   S1.2:135
immigration from Commonwealth   S1.1:237–8
Labour government, "welfare state," and postwar hopefulness (1945–51)   S1.2:473–4
Labour Party   S1.1:221
London "season"   3:312
nationalism and socialism   4:231
post-WWII decline and recovery   3:66, 4:229, 231, 5:256–7
poverty and workhouses   S1.1:219–21
Scotland   4:305
Wales   3:63–4, 66
in WWI   3:9, 11 (sidebar)
Yorkshire   3:1–3
English Patient, The, Ondaatje, Michael   S1.2:125–32
Enlightenment, The (Age of Reason)
American   2:416
American "moral sense"   1:94, 96
backlash as Romantic movement   1:106
as belief in reason, science, and "progress": perfectibility of humankind and its institutions   1:24 5, 268, 2:416, S1.1:29
decline of religious influence and increase of materialism   1:102, 311
early scientific discoveries fostering   1:24 5, 94, 96
failures of, fostering fierce satires   1:272
Franklin's common sense approach to experimentation   1:25–6
influence on Patrick Henry   1:123
Jewish (*Haskalah*)   3:120, 426, 4:88, S1.1:122 (sidebar)
"natural rights" theories of John Locke   1:100
questioning, observation, experimentation, and exploration   S1.2:404 5
treatment of disabled persons   2:119–20
Entailment   2:296 (sidebar)
Entertainment
automobile trips   S1.2:281–2, 358
ballroom dancing   S1.2:320 (sidebar)
carnival season of Italy and France   2:81–2
circuses and freak shows   2:33, 120, 329
dancing   3:23
drive-in restaurants of 1950s   4:392 (sidebar)
illicit wartime amusements   4:37, 38
as industry   2:329
jazz clubs   3:161, S1.1:337
jesters, fools, and clowns   S1.1:486
lotteries   4:235–6
minstrel shows   2:16–17, 21, 398
music halls and variety theater   S1.2:469
ouija board   5:56
practical jokes   1:212
pubs in England   3:3
radio   3:154, 364 5, 4:386, 391, S1.2:54 5, 59, 143
standardization of, in 1920s   3:101
stoic comedians   S1.2:475 (sidebar)
tale-telling and storytelling   1:49, 66–8, 70, 2:397, 3:421, 4:83 (sidebar), 85, S1.2:425 (sidebar), 426

Entertainment (*continued*)
    taverns   1:331, 3:219, 398, 400
    theaters and concert halls   2:329
    travel, tourism, cruises   S1.2:388
    for troops of WWII   4:38, 68–9
    visits to stately homes of England   S1.2:137 (*sidebar*)
    of working and middle classes   2:303–4
    (*See also* Games and sports; Motion picture industry; Television)
Environment, environmental movement
    Abbey in forefront of emerging movement   S1.2:95
    air pollution   4:9
    Chernobyl disaster   5:286, 287 (*illus.*)
    Colorado River   S1.2:97 (*sidebar*)
    Colorado River dams controversy   S1.2:1–2, 98, 101
    concerns reflected in *Dune*   5:85–6
    conservation of buffalo   5:34 5
    dam construction and "conservancy districts"   S1.2:342–3
    destruction of wilderness   2:49, 53
    first Earth Day (April 22, 1970)   5:279 (*sidebar*), S1.2:102, 180–1
    national park system   S1.2:95–103
    nuclear waste disposal   5:286
    pesticides ("biocides") and DDT   4:337–42, 5:347, 351
    rabbit population in England   5:347
    reflected in *Grendel*   S1.2:180–1
    rise of   S1.2:98
    Santa Barbara oil spill disaster   S1.2:180
    Sierra Club   S1.2:98 (*sidebar*)
    Tolkien as precursor   S1.2:299 (*sidebar*)
    Walden movement and Twin Oaks colony   5:279
Epic poems   1:49, 153, 172, 173, 282 (*sidebar*), 285
    (*See also* Poetry)
Epigrams   S1.1:184 (*sidebar*)
"Equality" in America
    Emancipation Proclamation (1862)   2:59, 60 (*sidebar*), 135, 308, 309
    on eve of Revolution   1:99
    individualism and egalitarian ideals of late 19th century   2:302
    (*See also* Civil rights movement; Segregation; Women's rights movement)
Equal Rights Amendment (ERA)   3:79, 5:51, 136, 358–9
Equivocation doctrine   1:230
Erasmus, Desiderius   1:2, 6, S1.1:486
Erdrich, Louise
    Antelope Wife, The   S1.2:29–37
    Love Medicine   5:243–50
Escapism
    fantasies of African American youths   4:4 (*sidebar*)
    as response to despair   5:40

    Thurber's Walter Mitty   3:364, 369
Espionage
    Civil War spies   2:255–6
    Cold War spies   4:71–2
    Rosenbergs executed for   4:72, 380, 381 (*illus.*), 5:2, 127
Esquivel, Laura, *Like Water for Chocolate*   3:196–202
Essays
    Civil Disobedience, Thoreau, Henry David   2:87–92, S1.2:271 (*sidebar*)
    Common Sense, Paine, Thomas   1:71–7, 94
    Communist Manifesto, The, Marx, Karl and Friedrich Engels   1:376, S1.1:41–9
    Desert Solitaire: A Season in the Wilderness, Abbey, Edward   S1.2:95–103
    Fire Next Time, The, Baldwin, James   5:107–14
    "Letter from Birmingham Jail," King, Dr. Martin Luther, Jr.   S1.2:269–77
    Let Us Now Praise Famous Men, Agee, James   S1.2:259–68
    Modest Proposal, A, Swift, Jonathan   1:266–72
    On Dreams, Freud, Sigmund   S1.1:200, 312, 313–22
    On the Origin of Species, Darwin, Charles   S1.1:80, 139–40, 246, 274, 323–31, S1.2:299
    Pilgrim at Tinker Creek, Dillard, Annie   5:278–84
    Prince, The, Machiavelli, Niccolò   1:316–20
    Republic, Plato   1:321–9
    Room of One's Own, A, Woolf, Virginia   3:356–63, S1.1:470
    Self-Reliance, Emerson, Ralph Waldo   2:314 20
    Shooting an Elephant, Orwell, George   S1.1:399–406
    Silent Spring, Carson, Rachel   4:337–42, S1.2:103
    Souls of Black Folk, The, Du Bois, W. E. B.   2:340–6
    Vindication of the Rights of Woman, A, Wollstonecraft, Mary   1:406–12, S1.1:391
    Walden, Thoreau, Henry David   2:416–21, S1.2:98, 102
Essex (Robert Devereaux, Earl of Essex)   1:194, 248, 349
Ethan Frome, Wharton, Edith   2:125–9, S1.1:9
Ethiopia   4:67
Ethnicities. *See* African Americans; American Indians; Chinese and Chinese Americans; Japanese and Japanese Americans; Jews; Latinos; Puerto Rico and Puerto Ricans
Ethnic and cultural conflicts. *See* Anti-Semitism; Racism and prejudice
Ethnology   2:232–3
Etiquette
    as concern of 18th-century American society   S1.1:4
    forms of address   S1.1:93 (*sidebar*)
    social calls and calling cards   S1.1:4
Eugenics   3:272, 4:152, 5:41–2, S1.2:306

Euripides, *Medea*   1:238–41
Europe
   appeal of, to American expatriot artists, intellectuals   S1.1:440–1
   appeal of, to American upper class   2:105–6
   Austro-Hungarian empire   S1.1:314, 474 5
   Bohemia, Czechs and Germans in Sudetenland, Czech Republic   S1.1:283 (sidebar), 475–6, 475 (sidebar), 482
   Congress of Vienna (1815)   S1.1:474
   consolidation, competition, and alliances in late 1800s, early 1900s   S1.1:377–8
   Hungarian uprising of 1848   S1.1:474
   late 1800s as golden age of middle class   S1.1:61–2
   medieval "Dark Ages"   S1.2:171–2
   opposing alliances of Entente Cordial and Triple Entente   S1.1:378
Europe, James Reese   3:162 (sidebar), 163 (illus.)
"Everything That Rises Must Converge," O'Connor, Flannery   5:88–94
Evolution, theory of
   as challenge to comfort of belief in permanent natural order   S1.1:140
   as challenge to religious orthodoxy   S1.1:246–7
   as cultural evolutionism   S1.1:7
   as Darwin's theory of (Darwinism)   1:293, 2:29, 121
   expounded in Darwin's *On the Origin of Species*   S1.1:80, 139–40, 246, 274, 323–31, S1.2:299
   far-reaching impact on society   S1.1:330–1
   and fear of degeneration   S1.1:85–6
   fostering belief in progress and man's capacity to reform   2:195, 3:378
   fostering doubt of man's divine nature   3:378
   fostering notion of "progress"   S1.1:330
   fostering religious skepticism   S1.1:80
   fostering social Darwinism   S1.1:85–6, 328, 330–1
   interest of H. G. Wells in   3:404 5
   opposed by religious-minded   3:102, 404, 5:138
   Scopes Trial   3:102 (sidebar)
   as social Darwinism ("survival of the fittest")
      competition implying progress   S1.1:85–6, 330–1
      contributing to racism   2:341
      extraordinary (superior) man theory   S1.1:54, 58
      impact on views of poor and disabled   2:217, 306, 312, 3:207, 410
      implying hierarchy of cultures, species, or races   S1.1:140, 328, 334, S1.2:134
      H. G. Wells' criticism of   3:410
      white superiority, Manifest Destiny, and "white man's burden"   2:119, 147, 341, 3:170, 172, 182 (sidebar)
   and theory of natural selection, extinction, and competition   S1.1:140, 327, 329
   Victorians' fear of extinction and racial or national decline   S1.1:328
Exiles
   American expatriots in Paris   S1.1:440–1
   Thomas Mann and Nazi Germany   S1.1:63 (sidebar)
Existentialism   S1.2:405–6, 443–5, 470–1
Extinction, role of, in Darwin's theory of evolution   S1.1:327
Extrasensory perception (ESP)   5:47, 239

F

Fabian Society   S1.1:219, 221
Fabre, Jean Henri Casimer   5:282
Fahrenheit 451, Bradbury, Ray   5:95–100, S1.2:309
Fairfield, John   2:189
Fallen Angels, Myers, Walter Dean   5:101–6
Falwell, Jerry   5:137–8, 140 (illus.)
Family and family life
   in 19th-century England   S1.1:240–1
   in 19th-century New England   2:54, 126–7
   in 20th-century England   3:347
   of African Americans   3:80, 84 6, 353–5, 375, 422–3, 4:33, 5:68, 145–6, 329–30, S1.1:340, S1.2:382, 389, 393, 426
   on American Western frontier   S1.1:284
   ancestors and descendants, connecting with   S1.2:393
   assumptions and practices undergoing change   S1.1:76
   brother-sister bond in Victorian Age   S1.1:245–6
   in Celtic society   1:197
   changing roles within   5:139
   Chicano   4:45
   in China   3:131–2, 192–3
   in colonial America   1:207–8, 217, 221, 334
   in colonial New England   S1.1:15
   discrepancy between "ideal" and fact   S1.2:104 9
   in Dylan Thomas's work   3:65
   (*See also* Divorce; Love and marriage)
   in Elizabethan, Jacobean England   1:141, 150, 203
   of gang members, and gangs as substitutes for   5:266–7
   intergenerational conflicts
      among African Americans   3:255, 4:252
      among American Indians   5:244, 246
      among Canadian Kwakiutl   5:198
      among Chicanos   5:182
      among Chinese Americans   5:358
      over marriage to person of differing ethnicity   5:203–4, 232
      over WWII   4:327
   Japanese mothers   S1.2:415–17
   Mexican American   4:172–3, S1.2:369–70, 374
   negative effects of machismo   3:201, 4:278–9, 299, 5:167, 173–4, 337, S1.2:370

Index

Family and family life (*continued*)
  parenting styles in colonial New England
    S1.1:18–19
  pro-family movement of religious right
    5:138–9
  role of black female servants in 4:257–8
  in sharecropper families 3:370–1, 373, 375
  single-female heads of households 2:65, 3:80,
    423, 4:2, 5:68, 117, 136, 138, 267, 328–9,
    S1.2:256
  in slave families 2:60, 169, 237–8, 405, 406,
    410, 4:204 5
  in South 3:78, 80
  in stepfamilies 5:36
  for Truman Capote 3:72
Family and family life: literary works depicting
  Annie John S1.2:19–27
  Antelope Wife, The S1.2:29–37
  Beloved 2:59–65
  Betsey Brown 4:28–34
  Bless Me, Ultima 4:42–8
  Bluest Eye, The 4:49–57
  Cold Sassy Tree 3:75–9
  Color Purple, The 3:80–7
  Dandelion Wine 3:88–93, S1.2:309
  Death in the Family, A 3:100–5
  Death of a Salesman 4:109–15
  Dinner at the Homesick Restaurant S1.2:105–13
  Doll's House, A 2:111–17
  Ethan Frome 2:125–9
  Fathers and Sons S1.1:99–106, 368
  Fences 4:144 50
  Fiddler on the Roof 3:119–24
  Glass Menagerie, The S1.2:141–50
  God of Small Things, The S1.2:151–60
  Gone with the Wind 2:137–44
  Good Earth, The 3:131–7
  Grand Avenue S1.2:161–9
  Hamlet 1:136–43
  Heart of Aztlán 4:171–6
  Hedda Gabler S1.1:159–68, S1.2:7
  Hero Ain't Nothin' but a Sandwich, A 5:143–8
  His Own Where 5:149–55
  House for Mr. Biswas, A S1.2:21, 183–93
  Human Comedy, The 4:193–200
  I Never Sang for My Father 5:201–7
  In Nueva York 5:214 21
  Jacob Have I Loved 4:216–20
  King Lear 1:196–203
  Like Water for Chocolate 3:196–202
  Little Foxes, The 3:203–10
  Little Women 2:202–8
  Long Day's Journey into Night 3:218–24
  Love Medicine 5:243–50
  Man without a Face, The 4:240–6
  Member of the Wedding, The 4:254 9
  Mill on the Floss, The S1.1:239–48
  Not without Laughter 3:249–56
  Ordinary People 5:259–64
  Parrot in the Oven S1.2:367–77
  Piano Lesson, The S1.2:379–86
  Pocho 4:295–302
  Prince of Tides, The 5:285–90
  Raisin in the Sun, A 4:309–15
  Red Sky at Morning 4:316–22
  Roll of Thunder, Hear My Cry 3:350–5
  Runner, The 5:306–13
  Sense and Sensibility S1.1:387–98
  "Seventeen Syllables" 4:330–6
  Shizuko's Daughter S1.2:409–19
  Song of Solomon S1.2:421–30
  Sons and Lovers 2:334 9
  Sounder 3:370–6
  Sound and the Fury, The S1.1:417–28
  Sweet Whispers, Brother Rush 5:328–32
  To the Lighthouse S1.1:463–72
  Tree Grows in Brooklyn, A 3:397–403
  Yellow Raft in Blue Water, A 5:360–6
  (See also Autobiography)
Fantasy
  Alice's Adventures in Wonderland 2:28–33
  *Beauty: A Retelling of the Story of Beauty and the
    Beast* 1:30–6
  "Devil and Tom Walker, The" 1:101–6
  Grendel S1.2:171–81
  Handmaid's Tale, The 5:135–42
  Hobbit, The 1:152–8, S1.2:301
  Lord of the Rings, The S1.2:178, 297–307
  "Rip Van Winkle" 1:330–6
  "Secret Life of Walter Mitty, The" 3:364 9
  (See also Folklore and fairy tales; Science fiction)
Farce S1.1:182
Fard, W. D. 5:12–13, 110
Farewell to Arms, A, Hemingway, Ernest 3:112–18
Farewell to Manzanar, Houston, Jeanne W. and
  James D. Houston 4:137–43
Farley, James Aloysius 3:402
Farman, Henri S1.2:490
Farming. See Agriculture, farming
Fascism
  characteristics of 4:304, 306–7
  depression of 1930s enhancing appeal of
    3:129
  described 1:293–4
  Nazism S1.2:116, 123
  neo-fascists 4:40
  origins in Italy 4:66
  origin of term S1.1:177
  Ox-Bow Incident 2:293
  (See also Nazis)
Fashions
  African-style clothing and hairdos 4:56, 5:145,
    300
  American Indian style 5:247
  cosmetics for African American women 4:50,
    56
  global popularity of American 1:223
  as symbols of generational conflict 5:271–2
  women's
    daring styles of 1920s 3:23

Index

"New Look" of 1940s and 1950s   **4**:22
　restrictiveness in Victorian era   **3**:420
　as status symbol   **2**:246, 247 (*sidebar*)
　in youth culture of 1950s   **4**:172, 392
　"zoot suits"   **4**:173, 403, 404 5, 408–9
　(*See also* Clothing)
Fast, Howard, *April Morning*   **S1.1**:11–20
Fate
　in ancient Greece   **1**:169
　in Middle Ages   **1**:160
　portents in Elizabethan era   **1**:194 5
Fathers and Sons, Turgenev, Ivan   **S1.1**:99–106, 368
Faulkner, William
　"Barn Burning"   **2**:41–6
　"Bear, The"   **2**:47–53
　Sound and the Fury, The   **S1.1**:417–28
Fauset, Jessie Redmon   **S1.1**:341
Faust, Goethe, Johann Wolfgang von   **S1.1**:107–16
FDR. *See* Roosevelt, Franklin Delano
Feast of the Epiphany, Feast of Fools, and Twelfth Night   **S1.1**:483–4
Felicia's Journey, Trevor, William   **S1.2**:133–40
Felsch, Oscar "Happy"   **3**:149
Feltre, Fra Bernardino de   **1**:244
Feminine Mystique, The, and Betty Friedan   **1**:62, **2**:58, **3**:430, **4**:11 (*sidebar*), 167, 241, 394, **5**:51 (*illus.*), 136, **S1.2**:285–6
Feminism. *See* Women's rights movement (and feminism)
Fences, Wilson, August   **4**:144 50
Fencing   **1**:141
Fenians (Irish revolutionaries)   **S1.1**:378
FEPC (Fair Employment Practices Commission)   **3**:42
Fetal Alcohol Syndrome   **S1.2**:294
Feudalism   **1**:65–6, 159–61, 187, 290, **S1.1**:355
Fiddler on the Roof, Stein, Joseph   **3**:119–24
Film. *See* Motion picture industry
Finch-Hatton, Denys   **S1.2**:489, 492
Fire Next Time, The, Baldwin, James   **5**:107–14
First Inaugural Address, Roosevelt, Franklin D.   **3**:125–30
Fischer, Bram   **S1.2**:122
Fishing
　aquaculture   **5**:285–6
　crabs and oysters   **4**:216–17, 219
　game fish   **4**:274, 275 (*sidebar*), 279 (*sidebar*)
　by Kwakiutl of British Columbia   **5**:195
　shrimping   **5**:285–6
Fitzgerald, F. Scott, *Great Gatsby, The*   **3**:146–52
Fixer, The, Malamud, Bernard   **S1.1**:117–28
Flannagan, Bud   **S1.2**:469–70
Flappers and the "New Woman"   **S1.1**:80–1, 181–2, 441–2, **S1.2**:105
Flaubert, Gustave, *Madame Bovary*   **2**:209–15
Fleming, Alexander   **3**:365–6
Florence, Italy   **1**:174 6, 316–18
Florida
　Belle Glade   **3**:383–4

Eatonville   **3**:383, **S1.1**:430
Flowers for Algernon, Keyes, Daniel   **4**:151–6
Folklore and fairy tales
　adapted to American themes   **1**:335
　African   **2**:63, 64
　American Indian   **1**:332
　of American South   **2**:48–9
　Beauty: A Retelling of the Story of Beauty and the Beast,
　McKinley, Robin   **1**:30–6
　Caribbean   **S1.2**:20
　Dutch   **1**:332
　efforts to collect in late 19th century   **2**:397
　Germanic   **1**:105, 106
　Hurston's interest in   **S1.1**:435–6, **S1.2**:266
　impact of Disney fairy tales on socialization of girls   **1**:36
　Merry Adventures of Robin Hood, The, Pyle, Howard   **1**:250–7
　mixed with Judeo-Christian beliefs   **1**:50, 138
　origins of *Beowulf* in   **1**:49
　Pre-Columbian beliefs   **S1.2**:436 (*sidebar*)
　preserved in exclusive African American towns   **S1.1**:430
　as social commentary and criticism   **1**:31–2, 36
　spirits of dead tied to land   **S1.2**:425 (*sidebar*)
　"The Fisherman and His Wife"   **S1.1**:466 (*sidebar*)
　Uncle Remus, Harris, Joel Chandler   **2**:397–402
　in Yorkshire, England   **1**:418–19
　(*See also* Myth)
Food. *See* Diet, nutrition
Fools Crow, Welch, James   **S1.1**:129–38, **S1.2**:168
Football   **4**:145–6, 147, **5**:63
for colored girls who have considered suicide / when the rainbow is enuf, Shange, Ntozake   **5**:115–21
Ford Foundation   **S1.1**:226
Ford, Henry and Ford Motor Company   **3**:23, 77, 88, 101, **5**:43 (*illus.*), 44 5, **S1.1**:441
Fordism   **5**:46
Forster, E. M.   **3**:356
　Passage to India, A   **3**:297–304
Fortune magazine   **S1.2**:262
Fort William Henry Massacre   **1**:205
Foundation, Asimov, Isaac   **5**:122–8
Fourier, Charles   **S1.1**:44
France in 15th century   **1**:159–61
France in 16th century, invasion of Italy   **1**:317
France in 17th century
　dueling   **1**:389 (*sidebar*)
　Gascons   **1**:386, 391
　musketeers   **1**:386, 387
　wars and civil turmoil   **1**:87–9, 305, 386–9
　women's position in   **1**:30
France in 18th century
　class hatred   **1**:358–60, 361, 371–2
　love and marriage   **1**:31
　wars with England   **1**:51–2, 93, 123, 130–1, 204 6, 220–1, 360
　women's position in   **1**:408, 409

France in 18th century: French Revolution
    American Revolution's contributions to   2:223–4
    echoes in *Frankenstein*   1:116
    emigrés fleeing   1:360–1, 372
    English reactions to   1:359–60, 372–3, 373 (*sidebar*), 376, 408, S1.1:89–90, 387–8, 407
    guillotine   1:360 (*sidebar*), 373, 373 (*illus.*)
    Jacobins   1:372
    origins of   1:51, 358–60, 371–2, 372 (*illus.*), 2:223–4, 295
    Paris Commune and Communards   1:363
    Reign of Terror   1:372, 2:102, 224, S1.1:208
    storming of Bastille   1:358, 362 (*illus.*), 372, 2:224
    ushering in modern age   S1.1:114
    women ignored in proposals for education reform   1:408
France in 19th century
    bourgeoisie   2:209–10
    censorship in   2:383
    class hatred   2:224
    Dreyfus affair   1:91–2, 364 (*sidebar*), S1.1:121
    historic rivalry with England   1:391–2
    Industrial Age in   2:103–4
    landmark historical dates   1:160 (*sidebar*)
    Louis Napoleon and end of republic (1848)   2:228–9
    Napoleonic era and wars   2:99–100, 224, 227 (*sidebar*), 245, 295–6, S1.1:114, 208
    Paris as capital of Western art   3:265–6
    Republican government of 1870s   1:91
    Restoration of monarchy after Napoleon (1816)   2:100–1, 224
    Revolution of July 1830   1:163–5, 391, 2:100, S1.1:45
    Revolution of 1832   2:224 5
    wars with England   1:123, 130–1, 159, 160, 204 6, 220–1, 305, 360
    White Terror (1815)   2:102
    women, education and rights   1:32, 2:210, 245
France in 20th century
    African colonies   3:211–13
    as nonracist haven for Richard Wright   4:4
    in WWI   3:9, 11 (*sidebar*)
    WWII underground and *maquis*   S1.2:467–9, 469 (*sidebar*)
Franchise (voting rights). *See* Suffrage (right to vote)
Franco, Francisco   4:67
Frank, Anne, *Diary of a Young Girl, The*   4:116–23
Frankenstein, Shelley, Mary   1:115–21
Franklin, Benjamin
    Autobiography of Benjamin Franklin, The   1:22–9
    as embodiment of American Dream   1:26–7, 309
    Poor Richard's Almanac   1:309–15
Freedom Rides   5:88–90, S1.1:127, S1.2:272, 423
Freemasons (Masons)   2:82
Free will   S1.1:308
French and Indian War (Seven Years' War)   1:93, 123, 204 6, 220–1, S1.1:14

French Revolution. *See* France in 18th century: French Revolution
Freud, Sigmund   2:336, 5:260, 261
    "The Moses of Michelangelo"   S1.1:480
    On Dreams   S1.1:200, 312, 313–22
    psychoanalysis   4:168 (*sidebar*), 5:42, 260–1, 263
Frick, Henry Clay   4:8
Friedan, Betty, *The Feminine Mystique*   1:62, 2:58, 3:430, 4:11 (*sidebar*), 167, 241, 394, 5:51 (*illus.*), 136, S1.2:285–6
Friedrich, Richter, Hans Peter   4:157–64
Fry, Roger   S1.1:464
Fuchs, Klaus   4:72
Fuentes, Carlos
    The Death of Artemio Cruz   S1.2:83–94
    Old Gringo, The   3:277–83
Fugard, Athol, *"MASTER HAROLD" and the boys*   S1.2:317–25
Fugitive Slave Acts (1793 and 1850)   1:42, 2:16, 62, 170, 189, 410
Fujimori, Alberto   5:334
Fuller, Edward   3:149
Fuller, Margaret   1:356, 357
Fundamentalism and New, Religious Right   5:137–9

G

Gaddafi, Muammar   S1.2:131
Gaelic League   3:109, 308–9
Gaines, Ernest J.
    Autobiography of Miss Jane Pittman, The   5:19–26
    Gathering of Old Men, A   5:129–34
    Lesson Before Dying, A   S1.2:249–58
Galarza, Ernesto, *Barrio Boy*   3:28–35
Galileo   1:305
Galíndez, Jesús   S1.2:212
Games and sports
    archery and quarterstaff fencing   1:253
    backswording   2:375
    basketball and American Indians   S1.2:292, 292 (*sidebar*), 293–4
    bowling   1:335 (*sidebar*)
    boxing   5:68–9
    boxing and Joe Louis   S1.2:251 (*sidebar*)
    bullfighting   S1.1:442 (*sidebar*), 443 (*illus.*)
    "chicken"   4:172
    cryptography   S1.1:275 (*sidebar*), 277
    fencing   1:141
    first African American accomplishments   S1.2:251 (*sidebar*)
    football   4:145–6, 147, 5:63
    frog-jumping contests   2:251–2
    gambling in mining camps   2:250, 282–3
    gladiators   S1.1:231–2, 232 (*sidebar*), 235–6
    hero-worship of players   4:262
    horse racing in England   3:345–6
    hunting   2:47–8, 3:232

hurling 3:109, 309
involving animals 1:212
jingling matches 2:375
mahjong 5:232 (sidebar)
racism continuing into 1980s 4:149
river-running, rafting S1.2:102
rodeo 5:362, 364 (sidebar)
rugby in England 2:374 5
running feats of Jemez Pueblo 4:191
tournaments of knights' skills 1:291
values inculcated in students 5:63
(See also Baseball; Entertainment)
Gandhi, (Mahatma) Mohandas Karamchand 2:92, 3:298–300, :299 (illus.), 302, 5:192, S1.2:271 (sidebar), 328, 329, 368
Gandil, Arnold "Chick" 3:149, 4:260, 5:314, 315
García Lorca, Federico. See Lorca, Federico García
García Márquez, Gabriel
  One Hundred Years of Solitude 2:268–74
  "One of These Days" S1.2:459–66
  "Tuesday Siesta" S1.2:459–66
Garden of Eden 1:301–2, S1.1:145 (sidebar)
Gardner, John, *Grendel* S1.2:171–81
Garnet, Father Henry 1:230
Garrison, William Lloyd 2:23, 89 (sidebar), 242, S1.2:229
Garvey, Marcus 3:160, 163, 4:211, 312, S1.1:337 (sidebar), S1.2:428
Gaskell, Elizabeth S1.1:246
Gathering of Old Men, A, Gaines, Ernest J. 5:129–34
Gay rights movement 4:241
Geller, Uri 5:48
Gematriya 4:89
Gender roles in Shakespeare's comedies S1.1:490–1
Genealogy S1.2:228, 389, 427
Geoffrey of Monmouth 1:290
George I of England 1:131, 266, 342
George II of England 1:130, 269, 270 (illus.)
George III of England 1:93, 95 (illus.), 97
Germany
  Berlin Wall 5:238, 293
  early 20th century 1:370
  education in post-WWII period ignoring Third Reich 4:163
  fascism in 1:293–4
  national culture and political unification S1.1:62–3
  relations with Italy S1.1:65 (sidebar)
  Thomas Mann's lifelong exile from S1.1:63 (sidebar)
  Tripartite Pact (Japan, Germany, Italy; 1940) 4:59
  WWI 1:277–8, 3:8, 11 (sidebar)
  (See also Hitler; Nazis)
Gettysburg Address, Lincoln, Abraham 2:130–6
  influence on white South Africans of 20th century 4:99
Ghana 4:314

Ghettos
  black 4:30–1, 5:71–2, 143, 149–51, S1.2:421–3, 426–7
    Bedford-Stuyvesant 5:149–51
    crime in 5:13, 67–8, 112, 146, 150, 339–42
    drugs, suspicions of conspiracy by white officials to allow 5:144
    South Central Los Angeles 5:339–42
  Brooklyn 3:397–8, 4:88
  hospitals in, as overcrowded 5:150
  Jewish 1:244, 249, 4:118
  schools in, as overcrowded and inadequate 5:151–2
Ghibellines 1:174, 175, 345
Ghost Dance 2:69, 77–8, S1.2:31
Ghosts. See Supernatural
Ghost stories S1.1:37
GI Bill 3:92, 4:73, S1.2:358
Gibson, William, *Miracle Worker, The* 2:216–22
Gilded Age (late 19th-century America) 2:20, 199, 306, 312, 328, 331, S1.1:2
Gilman, Charlotte Perkins 3:168–9
  "Yellow Wallpaper, The" 2:422–8
Gilroy, Beryl S1.2:25
Ginsberg, Allen 4:75, 5:83, 84 (illus.), 324, S1.2:359, 363
"Give Me Liberty or Give Me Death," Henry, Patrick 1:122–8
Giwa, Dele S1.2:42 (sidebar)
Gladiators S1.1:231–2, 232 (sidebar), 235–6
Glass Menagerie, The, Williams, Tennessee S1.2:141–50
Glenn, John 5:292, 296
Gloucester, duke of (later, Richard III of England) S1.1:358–9, 359 (sidebar)
Glover, Goodwife (Goody) 1:79
"Goblin Market, The," Rossetti, Christina S1.1:139–47
Goddard, Robert 5:54
God of Small Things, The, Roy, Arundhati S1.2:151–60
Godwin, William 1:115, 119, 407, 411–12, 411 (illus.), S1.1:379 (sidebar)
Goethe, Johann Wolfgang von
  Faust S1.1:107–16
  influence on young Russians S1.1:100
Gogol, Nikolai S1.1:101 (sidebar)
Golden Notebook, The, Lessing, Doris 4:165–70
Golding, William, *Lord of the Flies* 4:228–34
Goldman, Emma 3:321
Gold rushes and silver strikes
  in Black Hills of Dakota 2:67–8
  boom towns 2:289
  in California 2:174 5, 195, 249–50, 281–4
  on Cherokee land in Oklahoma 5:29
  Chinese immigration for 4:124, 5:74, 352
  Klondike 3:52–6, 261 (sidebar)
  miners subject to robbers 1:256
  in Nevada 2:288–9, 290 (sidebar)

Index

Gold rushes and silver strikes (*continued*)
    in Nez Percé territory   2:162
    (*See also* Mining and mining industry)
Golem, legend of   **S1.1**:480
Gómez, Laureano   **S1.2**:461, 461 (*sidebar*)
Gone with the Wind, Mitchell, Margaret   2:137–44, **S1.1**:420
González, Henry B.   **S1.2**:504
Good Earth, The, Buck, Pearl S.   3:131–7
Good, Sarah   1:79, 395, 396
The Good Soldier Schweik   **S1.1**:480
Good versus evil. *See* Sin and damnation
Gorbachev, Mikhail   5:8
Gordimer, Nadine, *House Gun, The*   **S1.2**:195–204
Gothic horror stories and romances   2:81, 85, 185, 3:338
    Jane Eyre   1:415 (*sidebar*), 419, 2:181–7, **S1.1**:493, **S1.2**:24 5
    Rebecca   3:326–33
    Wide Sargasso Sea   **S1.1**:493–502, **S1.2**:178
Gouzenko, Igor   4:72
Governesses in Victorian Age   2:182, 183 (*sidebar*), 378–80
Gowrie Conspiracy   1:229
Grady, Henry   2:399
Graetz, Heinrich   4:89
Grand Avenue, Sarris, Greg   **S1.2**:161–9
Grant, Duncan   3:356
Grant, Ulysses S.   2:217
Grapes of Wrath, The, Steinbeck, John   3:138–45, **S1.2**:267, 347
Graves, Robert, *I, Claudius*   **S1.1**:169–78
"Graying" of America   5:202–4
Great Awakenings
    in American colonies   1:73, 106, 122
    in early 19th-century America   1:424 5
Great Britain. *See* England
"Great Chain of Being"   1:201, 203, **S1.1**:208
Great Depression, The (1930s)
    in agriculture   3:32, 34, 138–40, 153, 247, 350–1, **S1.2**:261
    causes of   3:125, 138
    communism's appeal enhanced   3:39–40, 45, 129, 208–10, **S1.2**:261
    comparisons to hard times of Reconstruction   2:143–4
    Coxey's Army   3:51–2
    "depression within the Depression"   **S1.2**:142
    Dust Bowl   3:34, 46, 138–40, 4:297
    in England   5:39–40
    growth of large-scale farming syndicates   2:45
    hobo tradition   3:46, 270
    homelessness   3:126, 140, 142
    impact on African Americans   3:154, 236–7
    impact in Algeria   **S1.2**:442–3
    impact on husbands and fathers, wives and mothers   **S1.2**:106
    impact on South   3:68–9, **S1.2**:260–2
    investing sprees, good times, and Black Tuesday   **S1.1**:421
    labor unrest and strengthening of unions   **S1.2**:144
    New Deal programs
        Agricultural Adjustment Act (AAA)   3:247, **S1.2**:142, 262
        Civilian Conservation Corps (CCC)   **S1.2**:142, 262
        Fair Labor Standards Act (FLSA)   3:49
        Farm Security Administration (FSA)   3:142, **S1.2**:262
        Federal Emergency Relief Administration (FERA)   1:113
        Federal Theater Project   **S1.2**:261
        Federal Writers' Project   3:237, **S1.2**:261–2, 267 (*sidebar*)
        National Labor Relations Act (NLRA)   3:128, **S1.2**:144
        National Recovery Act (NRA)   3:390–1, **S1.2**:142
        purposes of   3:45, 142, **S1.2**:261, 262
        questionable effectiveness   3:69, 128, **S1.2**:1
        Social Security System   3:49, 128, **S1.2**:262
        Tennessee Valley Authority (TVA)   **S1.2**:142, 262
        Works Progress Administration (WPA)   3:128, 391, 423–4, 4:44, **S1.2**:142, 261
    Okies   3:140
    plight of sharecroppers and tenant farmers   3:105, 350–1, **S1.2**:259–60, 262
    rural Southern education   3:352
    slowing northward migration of blacks   **S1.2**:380
    soup kitchens   3:45 (*illus.*)
    stock market crash and bank failures   3:125–6, 208, **S1.2**:260–1
    teamwork, as preoccupation of Steinbeck   3:337
    welfare state's beginnings in   **S1.2**:261
    widespread unemployment and poverty   3:68, 126, 350, **S1.2**:141–2
    WWII helping to end   2:45, 3:424, **S1.2**:142
Great Exhibition of 1851   **S1.1**:325 (*sidebar*)
Great Expectations, Dickens, Charles   **S1.1**:149–58
Great Gatsby, The, Fitzgerald, F. Scott   3:146–52
Great Goddess (ancient Greece)   1:59, 61–2
Great Migration (1915–1960)
    affecting Harlem Renaissance   3:159–65, 256, 321, 384, 421
    blacks and issue of union membership   3:39, 4:210
    causing increase of single female-headed families   3:80, 423, 4:2
    demand for unskilled labor in North   **S1.1**:335
    estimates of numbers of   4:2, 50, 203, **S1.1**:335, 431
    exacerbating racial tensions in Northern cities   2:6
    housing discrimination in North   3:39, 159, 4:30–1
    increasing with WWI   3:236, 384, **S1.2**:379
    increasing with WWII   4:51

making race a national question 4:209–10
network of information sources S1.2:380, 381
northern "promised land" as slum ghetto S1.2:421–3, 426–7
offering hope, then disillusion 3:39, 80, 159, 236, 4:50–1
to Pittsburgh's steel and coal industries 4:144
railroads S1.2:381–2, 382 (sidebar)
reasons for 4:202–3
reverse migration in 1970s to 1990s S1.2:385
sharecroppers fleeing economic and racial oppression 3:351
shift from rural to urban S1.2:380
targeting Chicago and New York City 4:309, S1.1:335–6
transforming African Americans' sense of identity 4:210
two phases of 4:309
Great Powers (European) S1.1:377–8
Great War, The. I
Great War, The. *See* World War
Greece, invasion of Turkey (1920) 3:340
Greece in ancient times
  Athens
    citizenship law 1:241
    declining fortunes S1.1:343, 352–3
    Parthenon 1:240
    Pericles 1:17, 18, 240, 241, 322
    Plato 1:321–2, 328, S1.1:343
    Socrates 1:240, 322, 323 (illus.), 324, 327, S1.1:343
    Sophists 1:19, 240, S1.1:306, 344 5, 347 (sidebar)
    Theseus 1:57, 61 (sidebar), 258, 259
    Thirty Tyrants 1:322, 324, 325 (sidebar), S1.1:345 (sidebar)
  Bronze Age 1:14, 258, 280, 283 (sidebar)
  burial rites 1:18–19
  civic, human laws versus divine 1:17, 20
  concept of barbarians 1:173
  Corinth 1:238, 241
  "Dark Ages" 1:167, 172, 283 (sidebar), 286
  Delphi S1.1:307 (sidebar)
  Mycenaean Age 1:57–9, 167, 258, 281–2, 283 (sidebar)
  Peloponnesian War 1:241, 324, 328, S1.1:311–12, 352
  position of women in 1:17, 20, 58–9, 230–40, 259
  ritual sacrifice 1:283
  Sparta 1:324 5, 328
  suicide as honorable 4:22
  Thebes 1:14, S1.1:301–2
  Trojan War 1:8, 14, 166–9, 281, 283 (sidebar)
Greek myths
  basis of *Aeneid* in 1:9
  basis of *Antigone* in 1:14
  basis of *Medea* in 1:238
  basis of *Midsummer Night's Dream* in 1:259 (sidebar)

Great Goddess and Amazons 1:58–9, 61–2, 258, 259–60
  Ovid's *Metamorphoses* as source of 1:262
  as sources of ideas for humanists 1:380
  as sources for Milton's *Paradise Lost* 1:301
  Zeus 1:9, 59, 61, 170, 282, 283, 301
Greene, Bette, *Summer of My German Soldier* 4:371–7
Green Mountain Boys 3:98 (sidebar)
Grendel, Gardner, John S1.2:171–81
Griffes 3:18
Grissom, Gus 5:296
Guatemala 5:27–9
Guelphs 1:174, 175, 345
Guest, Judith, *Ordinary People* 5:259–64
Guillotine, Dr. Joseph Ignace 1:360
Guillotine, the 1:360 (sidebar), 373, 373 (illus.)
Gulliver's Travels
  Swift, Jonathan 1:129–35, S1.1:29
  War of the Worlds compared to 3:410
Gunpowder Plot 1:229
Guthrie, Woody
  Bound for Glory 3:44 50
  on songs of New Deal era 3:128 (sidebar)
Gutiérrez, José Angel S1.2:504
Gypsies
  in England 3:3
  in Spain S1.1:191–2, 195–7, 195 (illus.), 197 (sidebar)
  as victims of holocaust 4:119, 160, 267

H

Hachiya, Michihiko, *Hiroshima Diary* 4:177–84
Hacienda system, hacendados, and debt peonage 3:29, 278, 282, S1.2:87, 432, 502
Hades 1:283, 285
Haeckel, Ernst S1.1:325
Haiti (formerly Saint-Domingue)
  depicted in *Krik? Krak!* S1.2:239–48
  Duvaliers' regime S1.2:241–2, 242 (sidebar)
  emigration to New York S1.2:247
  history of political instability S1.2:242 (sidebar)
  massacre by army of Dominican Republic S1.2:241 (sidebar)
  oral storytelling tradition S1.2:246
  refugee "boat people" S1.2:242–3, 247
  religion S1.2:240 (sidebar)
  struggle for independence S1.2:239–41, 242 (sidebar)
  Toussaint L'Ouverture 5:116–17, S1.2:240
  women in Haitian society S1.2:243–4
Haley, Alex
  Autobiography of Malcolm X, The (with Malcolm X) 5:11–18
  Roots 5:298–305, S1.2:228, 236, 427
Hall, James Norman, *Mutiny on the Bounty* 1:273–9
Hamer, Fanny Lou 3:354

Index

Hamilton, Charles V.   S1.2:428
Hamilton, Virginia, *Sweet Whispers, Brother Rush*   5:328–32
Hamlet, Shakespeare, William   1:136–43, S1.2:398
Hammett, Dashiell
  influence upon Hellman   3:210
  Maltese Falcon, The   3:225–30
Handmaid's Tale, The, Atwood, Margaret   5:135–42
Hansberry, Lorraine, *Raisin in the Sun, A*   4:309–15
Harding, Warren G.   3:22 (illus.)
Hardy, Thomas, *Tess of the D'Urbervilles*   2:353–9
Harlem, New York   4:247–8, 5:67–8
Harlem Renaissance   3:159–65, 256, 321, 384 5, 421, 4:204 (sidebar), 207, 247–8, 5:67–8, S1.1:336–8, 337 (sidebar), 432–4
Harrington, Michael   5:266 (sidebar)
Harris, Joel Chandler, *Uncle Remus*   2:397–402
Harte, Bret, "Outcasts of Poker Flat, The"   2:281–7
Hart, Leo   3:144 (sidebar)
Harwood, Richard   4:40
Hasek, Jaroslav   S1.1:480
Hasidim   3:425, 426, 4:87–90, 5:283 (sidebar)
Haskalah (Jewish Enlightenment)   3:120, 426, 4:88, S1.1:122 (sidebar)
Hate groups
  Knights of the White Camellia   5:21 (sidebar)
  (*See also* Anti-Semitism; Ku Klux Klan)
Hathorne, John   1:83 (sidebar), 396, 420, 422, 424 (sidebar), 425 (sidebar)
Hathorne, William   1:420, 424 (sidebar)
Hautzig, Esther, *Endless Steppe, The: Growing Up in Siberia*   4:131–6
Hawthorne, Nathaniel
  Scarlet Letter, The   1:351–7
  "Young Goodman Brown"   1:420–6
Haya de la Torre, Raul   5:333, 334
Hays, Mary   1:412
Hazlitt, William   S1.1:217
Health issues
  Medicaid   5:68
  overcrowding of hospitals in ghettos   5:150
  scientific improvements in Victorian Age   1:115, 2:119
  (*See also* Disabled persons; Diseases; Drug, substance abuse; Mental and emotional disabilities)
Heart of Aztlán, Anaya, Rudolfo A.   4:171–6
Heart of Darkness, Conrad, Joseph   2:145–51, S1.2:458
Heart Is a Lonely Hunter, The, McCullers, Carson   3:153–8
Hebrides   1:226
Hector   1:170
Hedda Gabler, Ibsen, Henrik   S1.1:159–68, S1.2:7
Hegel, Wilhelm Friedrich   S1.1:47 (sidebar), 48, 52 (sidebar), 100
Heinlein, Robert A., *Stranger in a Strange Land*   5:321–7

Heinz, Henry   4:8
Heisenberg, Werner   5:283
Helen of Troy   1:8, 166, 168 (illus.), 281
Heller, Joseph, *Catch-22*   4:66–72
Hellman, Lillian, *Little Foxes, The*   3:203–10
Hell's Angels   S1.2:365
Hell. *See* Devil (Satan); *Inferno*; *Paradise Lost*; Sin and damnation
Hemingway, Ernest
  Farewell to Arms, A   3:112–18
  Old Man and the Sea, The   4:274 80
  Sun Also Rises, The   S1.1:439–47
Henry II of England   1:250, 251, 254 5, S1.1:259, 262
Henry IV of England   1:144, S1.1:356
Henry IV, Part I, Shakespeare, William   1:144 51, S1.2:400
Henry, Patrick
  as "American, not Virginian"   1:96–7
  "Give Me Liberty or Give Me Death" speech   1:122–8
Henry V of England   1:146, S1.1:356
Henry VI of England   S1.1:356
Henry VII of England (Henry Tudor)   S1.1:355, 360, 361, 365 (sidebar)
Henry VIII of England   1:149, 150, 231, 232, 234 (illus.), S1.1:484, 486
Herbert, Frank, *Dune*   5:81–7
Hero Ain't Nothin' but a Sandwich, A, Childress, Alice   5:143–8
Herodotus   1:286, S1.2:127 (sidebar)
Herriott, James, *All Creatures Great and Small*   3:1–7
Herzen, Aleksandr   S1.1:101 (sidebar)
Herzl, Theodore   4:102
Hesse, Hermann, *Siddhartha*   1:365–70
Heyerdahl, Thor, *Kon-Tiki*   4:221–7
Hidalgos   1:2–3
"Higher criticism" by Biblical scholars   S1.1:295
Highlanders of Scotland   1:187
Highway System, America's Interstate   3:73, S1.2:97, 281, 358
Hinduism   3:300, 302
Hine, Lewis   3:285
Hinton, S. E., *Outsiders, The*   5:265–70
Hippies. *See* Counterculture
Hippolyta and Amazons   1:58–9, 61–2, 258, 259–60
Hirohito, Emperor of Japan   4:178, 183
Hiroshima Diary, Hachiya, Michihiko   4:177–84
Hiroshima and Nagasaki as targets of first atom bombs   4:179–82, 180 (illus.), 181 (sidebar), S1.2:131, 219 (sidebar), 220, 311
Hirsch, Samson Raphael   4:90 (sidebar)
His Own Where, Jordan, June   5:149–55
Hispanics. *See* Chicanos; Latinos
Hispanos of New Mexico   S1.2:339–44, 346–7
Hiss, Alger   4:110, 5:96, S1.2:280, 363, 364
Historical fiction   S1.1:19
Historical linguistics   S1.2:305

Histories
   Bury My Heart at Wounded Knee, Brown, Dee   **2**:74 80
   Two Years before the Mast, Dana, Richard Henry, Jr.   **2**:391–6
Hitler, Adolf   **1**:113–14, 294, **3**:210, **4**:157–8, 305 (*illus.*), 356–7, **5**:122–3, **S1.2**:64 5, 299–301
Hobbit, The, Tolkien, J.R.R.   **1**:152–8, **S1.2**:301
Holinshed, Raphael   **1**:148, 227
Holland   **4**:116–19
Holland, Isabelle, *Man without a Face, The*   **4**:240–6
Hollywood. *See* Motion picture industry
Holocaust
   adding to urgency of Zionist appeal   **4**:102
   beginnings within Germany (1933–38)   **3**:401–3, **4**:267
   collusion of some Jews in   **4**:269–70, 272–3
   concentration camps   **4**:160–1, 194, 267–73
   as cultural sickness resting in conception of Jew as satanic enemy of Christ   **S1.1**:126
   delayed United States acceptance of proof   **3**:403
   denial by anti-Semites and neo-fascists   **4**:40
   described   **4**:119–20, **S1.2**:65–6
   estimates of number of victims   **4**:194
   as experienced by Samuel Beckett   **S1.2**:468, 471
   extension outside German borders (1939)   **3**:403, **4**:267
   as "final solution"   **4**:267
   Israel exacting justice for atrocities   **4**:107 (*sidebar*)
   Jews in Siberia "spared"   **4**:134
   Kristallnacht   **4**:159, 162–3
   liberation of Buchenwald   **4**:269, 272
   made easier by Nazis' deceptions and some Jews' willingness to be deceived   **4**:272, 273
   Nazi "scapegoating" of Jews (1933–39)   **4**:159–60
   in occupied Holland   **4**:117–18
   reactions of Germans to   **4**:194
   righteous heroes saving lives   **S1.2**:66, 69
   subsequent pressure upon Jewish women to bear children   **3**:430
   Vrba-Wetzler report and warnings to Hungarian Jews   **4**:269, 272
   war crimes trials   **4**:272–3
   (*See also Diary of a Young Girl, The*; *Friedrich*; *Night*)
Holy Grail legends   **4**:264 5
Holy League   **1**:296
Holy Roman Empire   **1**:87, 174, 176, 344, 345
Homelessness
   of deinstitutionalized mental patients   **4**:289
   during The Great Depression of 1930s   **3**:126, 140, 142
   "rough sleeping" in England   **S1.2**:135
   in South Africa   **4**:97
   of Vietnam veterans   **5**:106

Homer
   Iliad   **1**:166–73
   Odyssey   **1**:280–7
Home to Harlem, McKay, Claude   **3**:159–65
Homosexuality
   in *Angels in America*   **5**:1–10
   in *Biloxi Blues*   **4**:38
   in *Catcher in the Rye*   **4**:74
   in *Death in Venice*   **S1.1**:68
   in *Dracula* and Stoker's life   **S1.1**:86 (*sidebar*)
   growth of gay subculture   **4**:241, 245–6
   lesbianism   **3**:327–8, 357, 362
   lesbianism in Victorian Age   **S1.1**:142
   Lorca   **S1.2**:75
   male prostitution   **S1.1**:185
   in *Man without a Face, The*   **4**:244
   in military   **4**:38, 39–40
   Mormonism   **5**:4 5
   as reported by Kinsey   **4**:398 (*sidebar*), **5**:324
   seen as pathological deviance   **4**:77
   targeted by Nazis in Holocaust   **4**:119, 160
   targeted by New, Religious Right   **5**:136, 137–8
   in Victorian Age   **S1.1**:180, 185
   Wilde   **S1.1**:86 (*sidebar*), 180
Hood, Robin   **1**:188, 255 (*sidebar*)
   (*See also Merry Adventures of Robin Hood, The*)
Hoover, Herbert   **3**:126–7, **S1.2**:261
Hoover, J. Edgar   **1**:84 (*sidebar*), 399
Horror fiction
   Carrie   **5**:46–52
   Frankenstein   **1**:115–21
   Psycho   **5**:46–7
Hound of the Baskervilles, The, Doyle, Arthur Conan   **2**:152–9
House Gun, The, Gordimer, Nadine   **S1.2**:195–204
House Made of Dawn, Momaday, N. Scott   **4**:185–92, **S1.1**:137
House of Mirth, The, Wharton, Edith   **3**:166–73
House for Mr. Biswas, A, Naipaul, V. S.   **S1.2**:21, 183–93
House of Stairs, Sleator, William   **5**:156–62
House of the Spirits, The, Allende, Isabel   **5**:163–70
House on Mango Street, The, Cisneros, Sandra   **5**:171–7, **S1.2**:374
Housing
   adobes   **4**:318
   in barrios   **5**:174
   in black ghettos. *See* Ghettos
   discrimination against African Americans   **2**:13, **3**:39, 237, **4**:30–1, 310, **5**:13
   Levittowns   **S1.2**:281
   postwar prosperity, GI Bill, and home ownership   **4**:73
   racial violence   **4**:310 (*sidebar*)
   racist restrictions ruled illegal   **4**:201
   rent control ordinances   **4**:384, 400
   rent supplements   **5**:68
   shacks of sharecropper families   **3**:371
   slums of Saint Petersburg, Russia   **S1.1**:53 (*sidebar*)

Housing (*continued*)
   in slum tenements of New York **3**:397–8, **4**:384 5, 401, **5**:67–8, 149–50
   sod houses **S1.1**:283
   in South Africa **4**:95, 96–7
   South African shortages **S1.2**:118
   streetcars' impact on **4**:366
   suburbia **4**:73, 384, 385, **5**:261–2, **S1.2**:358–9, 364, 422
   tenements in slums of New York **S1.1**:3 (*sidebar*)
Houston, Jeanne W. and James D. Houston, *Farewell to Manzanar* **4**:137–43
Howe, Samuel Gridley **2**:217
"Howl," Ginsberg, Allen **S1.2**:359, 363
Hsaya San Rebellion, Burma **S1.1**:401 (*sidebar*)
HUAC (House Unamerican Activities Committee) and McCarthyism **1**:84, 398, **3**:178, 208, 209 (*illus.*), **4**:71, 72, 110, 398, **5**:2, 3 (*illus.*), 96, 97, 127, **S1.1**:11, **S1.2**:280, 310, 364
Hubris **S1.1**:308
Huerta, Dolores **4**:47
Huerta, Victoriano **3**:278–9, **S1.2**:14 (*sidebar*), 85, 503
Hughes, Langston **3**:164
   Not without Laughter **3**:249–56
Hughes, Thomas, *Tom Brown's Schooldays* **2**:372–7
Hugo, Victor
   Hunchback of Notre Dame, The **1**:159–65
   on John Brown **2**:193
   Les Misérables **2**:223–9
Human Comedy, The, Saroyan, William **4**:193–200
Humanism **1**:2, 142, 233, 380, 381, **5**:138, **S1.1**:107, 114 (*sidebar*), **S1.2**:223, 224 5
Hume, David **S1.1**:397 (*sidebar*)
Hunchback of Notre Dame, The, Hugo, Victor **1**:159–65
Hundred Years' War **1**:159, 160
Hungary **4**:166, **S1.1**:474
Hunger of Memory, A: An Autobiography, Rodriguez, Richard **5**:178–84, **S1.2**:370
Hunt, Irene, *Across Five Aprils* **2**:8–14
Hurston, Zora Neale **S1.2**:389
   "Spunk" and "Sweat" **S1.1**:429–37, **S1.2**:266
   Their Eyes Were Watching God **3**:383–9, **S1.2**:266
Hutchinson, Anne **1**:352–3, 352 (*sidebar*)
Huxley, Aldous, *Brave New World* **5**:39–45
Huxley, Thomas Henry **3**:265, 404, **5**:324 5, **S1.1**:330
Hydrogen bomb **4**:183

I

Ibsen, Henrik
   challenging sexual double standard **3**:406, **S1.1**:163 (*sidebar*)
   Doll's House, A **2**:111–17
   Hedda Gabler **S1.1**:159–68, **S1.2**:7
   influence on Arthur Miller **S1.2**:7

I, Claudius, Graves, Robert **S1.1**:169–78
Idaho **2**:367
Igbo of Africa **2**:360–2, **S1.2**:40
"I Have a Dream," King, Dr. Martin Luther, Jr. **5**:185–93, **S1.2**:269
I Heard the Owl Call My Name, Craven, Margaret **5**:194 200
I Know Why the Caged Bird Sings, Angelou, Maya **4**:201–8
Iliad, Homer **1**:9, 166–73
Illinois. *See* Chicago
Imagining Argentina, Thornton, Laurence **5**:208–13
Imagism **3**:413–14, **S1.1**:205
Imlay, Gilbert **1**:410
Immigration in 19th century
   Britons' fears of reverse colonization **S1.1**:140
   Chinese **2**:367–8, 370 (*sidebar*), 371, **4**:124 7, **5**:74
   Chinese Exclusion Acts (1882 and 1902) **2**:368, **4**:125, **5**:74, 231
   Czech **S1.1**:282 (*sidebar*)
   Geary Act (1892) **2**:368, **4**:125
   Irish **3**:107, 398–9
   Jewish **3**:121
   spurring America's westward expanion **S1.1**:271
   Swedish **3**:243–4, 259–60
   swelling demand for basic housing **S1.1**:3 (*sidebar*)
   to steel mills **4**:8
   to Western homesteads **3**:258–61, **S1.1**:281–4
   urbanization with **2**:302, 327, **3**:166
Immigration in 20th century
   America as "salad bowl" rather than melting pot **5**:176
   anti-immigrant bigotry and fears **3**:233, 402, **4**:330–1, **5**:180, **S1.1**:421
   Armenian **4**:199
   California Alien Land Act (1913) **4**:331
   Chinese **2**:368, **4**:125, 127, 129, **5**:229, 352–4
   Chinese Exclusion Act and Geary Acts (1904, 1922, 1924) **2**:368, **5**:231
   Commonwealth citizens to U.K. **S1.1**:237–8, **S1.2**:192 (*sidebar*)
   Czech **S1.1**:282 (*sidebar*)
   feelings of shame and inferiority among children of immigrants **5**:78–9
   generational conflicts between children and parents **4**:385, **5**:78–9, 182, 358
   Guatemalan political refugees **5**:28–9
   Haitian refugee "boat people" **S1.2**:242–3, 247
   illegal from Mexico **S1.2**:375
   immigration acts (1924, 1965, 1980) **4**:331, **5**:28, 75 (*sidebar*)
   Irish **3**:401–2, **S1.2**:133–5
   Japanese **3**:30, **4**:137, 143, 330–1
   Japanese "picture brides" **4**:331–2
   Jewish **3**:121, **4**:92, 102–3, 104 (*illus.*), 106
   Korean **S1.2**:349–52, 351 (*sidebar*), 353–4
   Literacy Test (1917) **3**:233
   Mexican **3**:29–30, **4**:44 8, **S1.2**:432

myth of "model minority"   S1.2:351–2
National Origins Act (1924)   3:233
nativism   S1.1:441
"open door" closing with Johnson Act (1924)   S1.1:421
porous U.S.-Mexican border   S1.2:11
Puerto Rican   4:385, 5:215–16, S1.2:504
relaxation, then tightening of quotas   S1.2:279–80, 349
restrictions of 1920s enhancing opportunity for blacks   4:203
Russian   3:233
Sanctuary Movement   5:29
to Toronto, Canada   S1.2:131 (*sidebar*)
urbanization with   3:101, 102
violence and racism   S1.2:474
War Brides Act (1945)   4:124, 127, 5:231
West Indian to U.K.   S1.1:501–2
Imperialism. *See* Colonialism, imperialism, and interventionism
Importance of Being Earnest, The, Wilde, Oscar   S1.1:179–87
Impressionism   S1.1:463
Impressment of sailors by Royal Navy   1:52
Inaugural Addresses
    Kennedy, John F.   5:222–8
    Roosevelt, Franklin D.   3:125–30
Incest   4:52
Incidents in the Life of a Slave Girl, Jacobs, Harriet   2:168–73
    influence upon Toni Morrison   2:63
India
    Buddhism   1:365–9, 3:186–7, 5:48
    caste and communism in Kerala   S1.2:152–3, 158
    caste system   1:366, 3:182, 184, S1.2:157–8
    chronology
        500s to 300s B.C.   1:365
        British East India Company (1639–1773)   3:297–8
        British rule (1773–1947)   2:182–4, 276–7, 3:181–2, 297–8
        emigration to Trinidad (1838–1917)   S1.2:183–4
        Sepoy Rebellion, Indian Mutiny, civilian unrest, repression, atrocities (1857)   S1.1:157, 326
        Victoria crowned Empress of India (1877)   S1.1:157
        Amritsar massacre (1919)   3:298
        Jallianwala Bagh massacre (1919)   S1.2:328–9
        national strike (1919)   S1.2:328
        wartime denial of basic civil rights and due process (1919)   S1.2:328
        Gandhi's "non-violent non-cooperation" program (1920)   S1.2:329 (*sidebar*)
        Hindu-Muslim division, unity, resistance to British rule (1920–1947)   S1.2:329
        nationalism (1920s)   3:298–300
        riots in Calcutta begin "civil war of secession" (1946)   S1.2:329 (*sidebar*)
        independence, partition, and communal violence (1947)   S1.2:132, 331, 331 (*illus.*)
        Gandhi assassinated (1948)   S1.2:329 (*sidebar*)
        Indira assassinated, sons in politics (1984)   S1.2:332 (*sidebar*)
        war with China over Himalayan border (1962)   S1.2:151–2, 329 (*sidebar*)
        Naxalbari uprising (1967)   S1.2:153–4
        neocolonial nepotism, corruption, bureaucracy (1970s and 1980s)   S1.2:332–3
        Bangladesh (Indo-Pak) War and independence (1971)   S1.2:329 (*sidebar*), 331–2
        Indira Gandhi, state of emergency, forced sterilizations, slum clearance, election fraud (1975)   S1.2:329 (*sidebar*), 331–2, 333
        Rajiv Gandhi assassinated (1991)   S1.2:332 (*sidebar*)
    civil service   3:185
    emigration to Trinidad (1838–1917)   S1.2:183–4
    infrastructure   3:184 5
    map   3:183 (*illus.*)
    religions   1:366, 3:300–1, 302
Indians (Native Americans). *See* American Indians
Individualism
    capitalism versus collectivism and communalism   S1.2:346
    classical liberalism   3:268
    criticism of "cult" of   5:2 (*sidebar*)
    decline in, during 1950s era of conformity   4:382, 5:323–4
    egalitarian ideals in 19th-century America   2:302
    machine age as debasing   5:41, 46
    Teddy Roosevelt popularizing "Old West" myth of   5:206
    of Thoreau   2:88–9
Industrial Revolution, industrialization
    allowing growth of middle class   2:118, 153
    and birth of communism   S1.1:45
    burgeoning middle class   S1.1:324
    child labor   2:103–4, 335 (*sidebar*), 3:76 (*sidebar*), 77 (*illus.*), 285, S1.1:32–3, 42, 408–9, 414, 414 (*sidebar*)
    class, commerce, and dangerous imports   S1.1:140–1
    in Colombia   S1.2:460
    creating serious social problems   S1.1:42
    democracy and capitalism, shift toward   2:334 5
    early socialist movements in response   S1.1:44 5
    in England and Europe   S1.1:41–4, 62, 91
    factory system at heart of   S1.1:42, 43 (*sidebar*)
    in France   2:103–4, 245–6
    from "home made" to "factory made"   S1.1:43 (*sidebar*)

Index

Industrial Revolution, industrialization (*continued*)
    impact of steam engine   S1.1:209
    in Japan   S1.2:218
    leading to European large-scale commercial farming, decline of small family farm   S1.1:283
    leading to Romantic movement   1:106, 115–16
    leading to worker-owner class distinctions   2:303
    profits and unemployment   S1.1:149–50
    profits and urbanization versus pollution and overcrowding   S1.1:408
    reaction of Luddites   1:119–20, 120 (*illus.*), S1.1:91
    social and economic improvement and upheaval   1:106, 2:417
    stimulants of   1:115, 336, 417
    women's increasing opportunities for jobs   2:423
    working conditions and attempts to improve   3:174 5, 178–9
    working conditions and worker's revolts   1:363, 2:328, 329, 404
    (*See also* Capitalism; Labor movements and unions; Urbanization)
I Never Sang for My Father, Anderson, Robert   5:201–7
Inferno, Dante Alighieri   1:174 80
Inheritance
    by American Indians   S1.2:32
    by entailment   2:296 (*sidebar*)
    English landed estates   S1.1:388–9
    India's inequitable laws   S1.2:158 (*sidebar*)
    marriage settlements, portions, and jointures   S1.1:389, 390, 496
    primogeniture   S1.1:91, 388–9, 497 (*sidebar*)
In medias res   2:62
In Memoriam, Tennyson, Alfred, Lord   S1.1:328–9
In Nueva York, Mohr, Nicholasa   5:214 21
Inquisition   1:2, 3, S1.1:23, 190–1
Integration
    Baldwin on moral standards of   5:113
    Brown v. Board of Education   3:375, 4:29–30, 314, 5:90, 108, 180, 181, S1.1:19, S1.2:231, 256, 270
    opposition of Malcolm X to   5:15, S1.2:276
    of schools   3:43, 396, 4:29–30, 31 (*illus.*), 314, 5:116, 131–2, 181
    slow pace of   4:33–4
    of University of Mississippi   5:19
Internment of Japanese Americans (1942–44)   4:138–43, 195, 335–6
Interstate Highway System   3:73, S1.2:97, 281, 358
Interventionism. *See* Colonialism, imperialism, and interventionism
In the Time of the Butterflies
    Julia Alvarez   S1.2:205–15
    Mirabal sisters of Dominican Republic   S1.2:205–15, 213 (*sidebar*), 214 (*illus.*)
Invisible Man, Ellison, Ralph   4:209–15

Ionesco, Eugène   4:400, S1.2:476
Ireland and the Irish
    Absentees   1:266, 269, 269 (*sidebar*)
    Catholic emancipation   S1.1:239–40
    Catholicism in   1:269, 3:107–8, 109–10, 305–7
    concessions by James I   1:131
    cultural revival   3:108–9, 308–9
    emigration to Britain   S1.2:133–5
    English subjugation of   1:131–2, 267, 3:106–7, 305–6, S1.1:236, S1.2:134
    famine and emigration in mid-19th century   2:302
    Fenian revolutionaries   S1.1:378
    Home Rule movement   3:109, 307
    Irishmen in British Army   S1.2:136 (*sidebar*)
    Irishness as depicted in *Kim*   3:187
    Irish Republican Army (IRA) attacks on British outposts   S1.1:237
    misgovernment and economic decline in 18th century   1:266–9
    North versus South, Ireland versus British rule   S1.1:237
    Parnell, Charles   3:109–10
    Potato Famine ("The Great Hunger," "Hungry 40s")   3:107, S1.1:324
    Protestants and Patriots   1:267
    (*See also* England)
Irish Americans
    growing acceptance of   3:401–2
    sense of community   3:400–1
    stereotypes of heavy drinking   3:220, 398, 400
Irony as literary technique   S1.1:381 (*sidebar*)
Irving, Washington
    "Devil and Tom Walker, The"   1:101–6
    "Legend of Sleepy Hollow, The"   1:211–18
    "Rip Van Winkle"   1:330–6
    The Sketch Book   1:335–6
    on slavery   1:103
Ishi, Last of His Tribe, Kroeber, Theodora   2:174 80
Islam   1:296, 3:300
    Nation of Islam   3:238, 325, 4:56, 248–50, 5:12–13, 69, 110–11, 302, S1.2:276
Israel
    Biblical history of   4:101
    as British mandate of Palestine   4:102–3, 105
    conflicts with Arabs   4:106–8
    Hasidic opposition to   4:88
    immigration to
        denied by Soviet government   3:124
        from Europe of 1880s   3:121
    Six-Day War (1967)   4:93
    War of Independence (1948–49)   4:106
    Women's Equal Rights Law (1951)   3:430
Italy
    in 16th century   1:316
    in ancient times   1:9
    as exotic destination for northern Europeans   S1.1:65 (*sidebar*)
    fascism in   1:293–4

540   LITERATURE AND ITS TIMES ～ SUPPLEMENT 1, PART 1

Florence 1:174 6, 316–18
    Jews in 1:246, 248–9
    map of 1:345 (*illus.*)
    Milan 1:379–80
    Mussolini, Benito 2:293–4, 4:66–7, 305 (*illus.*), S1.1:177, S1.2:299
    Venice 1:242–6, 295–7
    Verona 1:344 5
    WWI, during and after 3:11 (*sidebar*), 113–14, 4:66–7, S1.2:126–7
Ithaca 1:281
Ivanhoe, Scott, Sir Walter 1:181–8, S1.1:246
"I Will Fight No More Forever," Chief Joseph 2:160–7

J

Jackson, Andrew 1:209–10
Jackson, Shirley, "Lottery, The" 4:235–9
Jackson, "Shoeless" Joe 3:149, 4:265, 5:314, 316
Jacob Have I Loved, Paterson, Katherine 4:216–20
Jacobs, Harriet, *Incidents in the Life of a Slave Girl* 2:168–73
James, Henry
    Daisy Miller 2:105–10
    on *The Strange Case of Dr. Jekyll and Mr. Hyde* 3:382
    Turn of the Screw, The 2:378–83
James I of England (James IV of Scotland)
    belief in supernatural and witchcraft 1:228, 384, 385
    concessions to Irish 1:131
    daughter's marriage subject to her own approval 1:385
    increase of political and religious factions 1:299
    parallels to life of Hamlet 1:141
    subject of regicidal conspiracies 1:229, 230
    succession to throne of England 1:141, 149, 150, 201
    support for theater and arts 1:299
James II of England 1:130
Jamestown, Virginia 1:379, 384, 394
Jane Eyre, Brontë, Charlotte 1:415 (*sidebar*), 419, 2:181–7, S1.1:493, S1.2:24 5
Japan
    in 19th century 4:177
    after Meiji Restoration and Emperor Mutsuhito S1.2:217–20, 411, 415
    changing attitudes and generational gap S1.2:414 15
    conformism, group identity and membership S1.2:410–12, 414
    consumer revolution S1.2:221, 221 (*sidebar*)
    court society of 10th century S1.1:449–61
    dictatorship of prewar military 4:178, 183
    Emperor Hirohito 4:178, 183
    Emperor system and Emperor's divinity S1.2:218 (*sidebar*), 220, 411
    feudalism, samurai code, loyalty S1.2:410

frosty relations with Korea 4:353–4
    Fujiwara clan S1.1:451–2
    furor over textbooks' coverage of WWII 4:354
    haragei S1.2:411
    idealizing racial purity, ethnic homogeneity, and cultural conformity S1.2:224
    imperialism of
        Asian territorial conquests 4:58–9, S1.2:219
        countries conquered during WWII 5:123 (*sidebar*)
        invasion of China 3:189–90, 5:229–30
        invasion and occupation of Korea 4:59, 177, 349–54
    Japanese culture and outside world S1.2:223–4
    Korean laborers in 4:353
    Nagasaki and Hiroshima as targets of atom bombs 4:179–82, 180 (*illus.*), 181 (*sidebar*), S1.2:131, 220, 311
    "Peach Constitution" S1.2:410
    postwar rise to affluence S1.2:220–1
    post-WWII Allied occupation S1.2:409–10
    rapprochement with South Korea 4:354
    Russo-Japanese War 4:59
    Self-Defense Force controversy S1.2:220
    suicide S1.2:414
    Tokugawa dynasty, daimyo, samurai, and isolationism S1.2:218, 411
    WWII 4:58–61
    "Yamato spirit" S1.2:224
    zaibatsu and *keiretsu* S1.2:218, 220, 410
Japan, the Ambiguous, and Myself, Oe, Kenzaburo S1.2:217–25
Japanese and Japanese Americans
    as farm workers 3:30
    immigration 3:30, 4:137, 143, 330–1
    Issei and Nisei 4:137
Japanese and Japanese Americans, works concerning
    Farewell to Manzanar 4:137–43
    Hiroshima Diary 4:177–84
    Japan, the Ambiguous, and Myself S1.2:217–25
    "Seventeen Syllables" 4:330–6
    Shizuko's Daughter S1.2:409–19
    So Far from the Bamboo Grove 4:349–55
    Tale of the Genji, The S1.1:449–61, S1.2:222
Jara, Victor 5:164, 168
Jason 1:238–9
Jazz 3:162 (*sidebar*), 4:258, S1.1:337, S1.2:359
Jefferson, Thomas
    Declaration of Independence, The 1:93–100
    on Patrick Henry 1:127
Jerusalem 1:182
Jesuits 3:307–8, S1.1:23, 24
Jews
    in America 3:430
    assimilation, threat of 3:120, 123, 430, 4:88, 90 (*sidebar*), 91
    in Austria of late 1800s S1.1:314 15
    British offer of homeland in Africa 3:291
    criticality of education for 3:425

Jews (*continued*)
   Diaspora   4:101
   divorce   3:427, 429 (sidebar)
   education of women   3:427, 430
   in England   1:182–3, 185, 2:264 5
   expulsion or conversion to Christianity   1:244, 246, 2:264, S1.1:189
   flourishing Jewish American authors   S1.1:127
   Gematriya   4:89
   in ghettos   1:244, 249, 4:118
   Golem, legend of   S1.1:480
   Hasidim   3:425, 426, 4:87–90, 5:283 (sidebar)
   immigrating to America and Israel   3:121
   immigration in 20th century   3:121, 4:92, 102–4, 106
   in Italy   1:243, 246, 248–9
   Jewish Enlightenment (*Haskalah*)   3:120, 426, 4:88, S1.1:122 (sidebar)
   Levantines   1:248
   Marranos   1:248, 249
   marriage-bed custom   3:428 (sidebar)
   Mitnagdim   3:426
   as "model minority"   S1.2:351
   moneylending   1:182–3, 2:264
   Orthodox   4:93
   of Poland   4:131–2
   in Prague's "voluntary ghetto"   S1.1:475–6
   revival of American   4:91–2, 93
   role and rights of women   3:427–30
   in Russia   S1.1:117–21, 120 (sidebar), 127–8
   suicide and   3:428, 4:22
   traditional marriage   3:119
   under Caligula   S1.1:172
   Zionism   3:121, 4:88, 101–2
   (*See also* Anti-Semitism; Holocaust)
Jews, literary works concerning
   Biloxi Blues   4:35–41
   Chosen, The   4:87–93
   Dawn   4:101–8
   Diary of a Young Girl, The   4:116–23
   Endless Steppe, The: Growing Up in Siberia   4:131–6
   Fiddler on the Roof   3:119–24
   Fixer, The, Malamud, Bernard   S1.1:117–28
   Friedrich   4:157–64
   Night   4:267–73
   Summer of My German Soldier   4:371–7
   A Tree Grows in Brooklyn   3:402
   "Yentl the Yeshiva Boy"   3:425–31
Jim Crow laws
   African American responses to   2:413
   based in misguided theories of race   S1.1:429–30
   challenges to, by black soldiers of WWI   3:252
   challenges to, by black soldiers of WWII   S1.2:249–50
   coming under fire in 1930s and 1940s   2:53
   described   3:81, 351, 5:90, S1.1:333–5, S1.2:250, 255, 255 (*illus.*), 256
   federal authorities ignoring   4:1
   origins of term   2:21, 341, 3:351
   unwritten rules of racial deference   S1.2:254 5
   upheld by *Plessy v. Ferguson*   2:21, 341, 399–400, 413, 3:351, 375, 419, 4:1, 5:90, 107–8, S1.1:429, S1.2:256, 269–70
Jinnah, Muhammad Ali   S1.2:328, 329
Johannesburg, South Africa   S1.2:117
John Brown's Final Speech, Brown, John   2:188–94
John I of England   1:251
Johnson, Amy   S1.2:491, 495
Johnson, Charles S.   S1.1:336
Johnson, James Weldon   S1.1:336, 341, 436
Johnson, Lyndon Baines   3:324, 4:347, 375, 5:68, 102, S1.2:453, 457
Johnson, Samuel   1:307
Jolly Roger (pirates' flag)   1:401
Jones, Leroi (Amiri Baraka)   4:207
Jonson, Ben   1:150, 300
Jordan, June, *His Own Where*   5:149–55
Joseph, Chief of Wallowa Nez Percé, "I Will Fight No More Forever"   2:160–7
Joyce, James   5:42
   Dubliners   3:106–11
   Portrait of the Artist as a Young Man, A   3:305–11
Joy Luck Club, The, Tan, Amy   5:229–35
Juárez, Benito   S1.2:83
Julius Caesar   1:169 (sidebar), 189–91
Julius Caesar, Shakespeare, William   1:189–95
Jung, Carl Gustav   3:329, S1.1:200
Jungle, The, Sinclair, Upton   3:174 80
Jupiter   1:191

K

Kafka, Franz, *Trial, The*   S1.1:473–82
Kalenjin people of Kenya   S1.2:488–9
Kansas-Nebraska Act (1854)   1:42, 2:5 (sidebar), 172, 193
Karma   1:367, S1.1:452
Kashmir   S1.2:331
Kasztner, Rezso   4:269–70, 272–3
Katherine of Aragon   1:231
Keats, John   1:406
Keegan, John   S1.2:2
Keller, Helen   2:220 (*illus.*)
   (*See also Miracle Worker, The*)
Kelly, Charles T. and Kelly's Army   3:51–2
Kennedy, John F.
   appeal to, by King for civil rights   5:186
   Bay of Pigs and Cuban Missile Crisis   4:135, 5:225, 226, 238–9, 293, S1.2:180
   challenges of "New Frontier"   S1.1:19
   environmental concerns   4:338, 341 (sidebar)
   expanding United States role in Vietnam   4:375
   Inaugural Address   5:222–8, S1.1:19–20
   intervention on behalf of civil rights protesters in Alabama   5:12

moon walk goal launching space race 5:81, 292, 293 (*sidebar*), 321–2
opposing Nixon for president 5:321–2
Peace Corps S1.1:20
President's Panel on Mental Retardation 4:152
sending "advisors" to Vietnam 5:158, 307
Kennedy, Joseph P. 3:402
Kennedy, Robert 5:90
Kentucky
in Civil War 2:60 (*sidebar*)
slavery in 2:59–60
Kenya 3:290–6, S1.2:487–9
Kerensky, Alexander 3:232
Kerouac, Jack 4:75, S1.2:281
On the Road S1.2:357–66
Kesey, Ken, *One Flew over the Cuckoo's Nest* 4:288–94
Keyes, Daniel, *Flowers for Algernon* 4:151–6
Keynes, John Maynard 3:356
Kherdian, David, *Road from Home, The* 3:338–43
Khrushchev, Nikita 4:135, 166, 286, 398, 399 (*illus.*), 5:225, S1.1:128
Kim, Kipling, Rudyard 3:181–8
Kim, Jay S1.2:354 (*sidebar*)
Kincaid, Jamaica, *Annie John* S1.2:19–27
Kindred, Butler, Octavia S1.2:227–37
King, Dr. Martin Luther, Jr. 5:14 (*illus.*), 89 (*illus.*), 109 (*illus.*)
appeal to Kennedy for help in civil rights movement 5:12, 186
assassination of 4:54, 5:112 (*sidebar*)
criticism of, by Malcolm X 4:250, 5:13, 15, 111, S1.2:276
education and pastorate 5:108
influenced by Ghandi and passive resistance 2:92, 5:108, 189, 192
influenced by Thoreau 2:92
"Letter from Birmingham Jail" S1.2:269–77
organization of Montgomery bus boycott 5:11, 88, 108
protesting residential segregation 2:12 (*illus.*), 13, 97
speech: "I Have a Dream" 5:185–93, S1.2:269
King Lear, Shakespeare, William 1:196–203
King, Rodney 5:340, S1.2:354
Kingsolver, Barbara, *Bean Trees, The* 5:27–33
King, Stephen, *Carrie* 5:46–52
Kingston, Maxine Hong, *Woman Warrior, The* 5:352–9
Kinsella, W. P., *Shoeless Joe* 5:314 20
Kinsey, Alfred Charles and Kinsey Report 4:75, 241, 398–9 (*sidebar*), 5:324
Kipling, Rudyard, *Kim* 3:181–8
Kipsigis people S1.2:489
Kitchen God's Wife, The, Tan, Amy 3:189–95
Klondike 3:52–6, 261 (*sidebar*)
Knights and knighthood 1:182 (*sidebar*), 290–1
Knights of the White Camellia 5:21 (*sidebar*)
Knowles, John, *Separate Peace, A* 4:323–9
Knox, John 4:304

Kolbe, Saint Maximilian S1.1:268 (*sidebar*)
Kon-Tiki, Heyerdahl, Thor 4:221–7
Korea
emigration to America S1.2:349–50
frosty relations with Japan 4:353–4
invasion by Japan 4:59, 177
occupation by Japan 4:349–50
reprisals against fleeing Japanese 4:350, 352 (*sidebar*)
Korean Americans, in *Native Speaker* S1.2:349–55
Korean War 1:223, 3:73, 4:92
Krik? Krak!, Danticat, Edwidge S1.2:239–48
Kristallnacht 4:159, 162–3
Kroeber, Theodora, *Ishi, Last of His Tribe* 2:174 80
Kropotkin, Prince Peter S1.1:379, 379 (*sidebar*)
Krupp, Friedrich Alfred S1.1:221
Krutch, Joseph Wood S1.2:102
Ku Klux Klan
backlash against diversity of society S1.1:432
birth of, in 1865–66 2:141 (*sidebar*), 412, 3:102, 5:21
law enforcement officers enlisting in 4:4, 202
lynchings and violence against blacks 2:141 (*sidebar*), 143 (*sidebar*), 412, 3:419, 5:25, 130, S1.2:250
re-emergence during
1920s xenophobic, anti-Bolshevik era 2:143 (*sidebar*), 3:22, 4:201–2
1940s 4:201–2
1960s civil rights era 5:21 (*sidebar*), 25, S1.2:423
Kushner, Tony, *Angels in America* 5:1–10

L

Labor movements and unions
accused of being "red" (communist or socialist) 3:144
AFL (American Federation of Labor) 3:44
African Americans excluded, then included 2:341, 3:250, 4:210–11
Agricultural Labor Relations Act (1975) 4:48
anti-labor and anti-Bolshevik reactions of 1920s 3:21–2
attempts to limit power of, Taft-Hartley Act (1947) 4:172, 173 (*sidebar*)
Brotherhood of Sleeping Car Porters 3:42, S1.2:381
Carnegie Steel and Homestead Strike (1892) 3:321
CIO (Congress of Industrial Organizations) 3:44
"closed" and "union" shops 4:173 (*sidebar*)
conflicts with management 2:328, 336 (*sidebar*)
Debs, Eugene V. 3:54
discontented industrialized workers in wave of European revolutions S1.1:43, 44 (*sidebar*)
in Europe of 1800s S1.1:52

Index

Labor movements and unions (*continued*)
   for farm workers   3:34, 49–50, 141, 275
   forbidden in early years of Industrial Revolution   S1.1:42
   growth of   2:328, 336 (sidebar), 341, 3:176 (sidebar)
   leaders cooperating with business owners   4:172
   leaders' corruption   4:145
   Mexican Americans   4:172, 175–6, S1.2:368
   in Mexico   S1.2:91 (sidebar)
   National Labor Relations Act (1933)   3:128
   opposition from big business   S1.2:144
   opposition to   3:44, 141, 155 (sidebar), 208
   Pinkerton's detectives hired to thwart   3:225
   STFU (Southern Tenant Farmers' Union)   3:208
   strikes and violence   3:176 (sidebar), 179, 4:109
   strikes, violence, and strengthening of unions in Great Depression, The (1930s)   S1.2:144
   table grape boycott   4:175, S1.2:368
   in Trinidad   S1.2:188
   UAW (United Auto Workers)   S1.2:144
   UFW (United Farm Workers)   4:175, 300–2, 409, 5:171, S1.2:368–9
   Wagner Act and NRLA   S1.2:144
"Lady with the Dog, The," Chekhov, Anton   S1.1:367–75
Laissez-faire capitalism   S1.1:42
La Llorona   S1.2:507 (sidebar)
Lamarck, Jean-Baptiste de   S1.1:275, 329
Language. *See* Linguistic considerations
Laroche, Raymonde de   S1.2:495
Larsen, Nella, *Passing*   S1.1:333–42
Lasch, Christopher   4:111
Last of the Mohicans, The, Cooper, James Fenimore   1:204 10
Latin America
   Argentina   5:208–11, 212–13
   Chile   5:163–70
   Colombia   2:268–70, 272–3, S1.2:459–65
   Guatemala   5:27–9
   Peru   4:221, 222, 5:333–8, S1.2:51–2, 53–5, 59
   (*See also* Mexico)
Latinos
   Chicanos. *See* Chicanos
   concepts of *machismo* and *marianismo*   3:201, 4:278–9, 299, 5:167, 173–4, 337, S1.2:370
   curanderos   3:199, 4:45
   decline of paternal authority   4:172–3
   enlisting in military for WWII   4:44
   help to Dust Bowl migrants   4:297 (sidebar)
   as Hispanics, Chicanos, or Boricuas   S1.2:373
   life in barrios   4:172 (sidebar)
   men admired for adultery   5:337
   mestizo or mixed-race heritage   5:172, 334
   Puerto Rico and Puerto Ricans   3:277, 4:385–6, 388–9, 401, 5:214 21
   the Virgin de Guadalupe and La Malinche   5:173, S1.2:501, 507–8
   women's roles   4:299, 5:167–8, 173–4, S1.2:507–8
   in WWII   4:295, 406
   (*See also* Cuba; Mexico)
Latinos, literary works concerning
   Barrio Boy   3:28–35
   Bless Me, Ultima   4:42–8
   Heart of Aztlán   4:171–6
   House of the Spirits, The   5:163–70
   House on Mango Street, The   5:171–7
   Hunger of Memory, A: An Autobiography   5:178–84, S1.2:370
   Imagining Argentina   5:208–13
   In Nueva York   5:214 21
   Like Water for Chocolate   3:196–202
   Milagro Beanfield War, The   S1.2:339–47
   Old Gringo, The   3:277–83
   Old Man and the Sea, The   4:274 80
   One Hundred Years of Solitude   2:268–74
   Parrot in the Oven   S1.2:367–77
   Pocho   4:295–302
   Time of the Hero, The   5:333–8
   Woman Hollering Creek and Other Stories   S1.2:499–509
Laudanum   3:379
Laurents, Arthur, *et al.*, *West Side Story*   4:384 90
Law enforcement
   absence on American frontier   2:323
   absence on rural California farms   3:274
   at Democratic National Convention of 1968   5:271
   attacking civil rights protesters   5:23 (illus.)
   Indian Imperial Police in Burma   S1.1:401
   officers enlisting in Ku Klux Klan   4:4, 202
   prisons   3:371, 374 (illus.)
   secret forces of dictators   S1.2:43
   slave patrols   2:190 (sidebar)
   in South, enforcing white supremacy   S1.2:251–2, 255
   in South, prisoners hired out as "slave" labor   S1.2:252
   (*See also* Crime; Vigilantism)
Law and legal systems
   American jury system   4:378–9
   anti-miscegenation statutes   S1.2:232
   Beilis case (anti-Semitism in Russia)   S1.1:120
   capital punishment   4:379–80, 5:131
   capital punishment and race   S1.2:257
   child molestation laws   S1.2:280–1, 284
   class discrimination of Victorian Age   S1.1:151
   conviction, then successful appeal in Sleepy Lagoon murder case   4:405
   Dreyfus Affair   1:91–2, 364 (sidebar), S1.1:121
   English justices of the peace   S1.1:388
   in French Algeria   S1.2:446 (sidebar)
   inequities in Hispanos' water rights   S1.2:340–4, 346–7
   judicial opposition in 1980s to civil rights legislation   5:1–2
   jury system   4:379, S1.1:262

"law of the cutlass" in Trinidad S1.2:186 (*sidebar*)
lawyers' apprenticeships and circuit riding 2:1–2
legal challenges to internment of Japanese 4:140–1
legal challenges to restrictive housing covenants 4:310
as legislation. *See under individual topics, e. g.* Civil rights movement; Great Depression; labor movements and unions; Segregation
medieval "trial by ordeal" S1.1:261
prisons S1.1:262
race and criminal justice system S1.2:251–2, 255
race and wrongful convictions S1.2:257
Scotland Yard S1.1:272, 272 (*sidebar*)
South Africa's constitution S1.2:197, 198 (*sidebar*)
trial of Socrates S1.1:345
weakness of Prohibition as legislation 3:22–3, 69
Lawrence, D. H.
"Rocking-Horse Winner, The" 3:344 9
Sons and Lovers 2:334 9
Law, Ruth S1.2:495
Leary, Timothy 5:82–3, 324
Leaves of Grass, Whitman, Walt 2:195–201
Le Chambon, France S1.2:471
Lee, Ann 3:95
Lee, Chang-rae, *Native Speaker* S1.2:349–55
Leech, John S1.1:38 (*sidebar*)
Lee, Harper, *To Kill a Mockingbird* 3:390–6
Le Fanu, J. Sheridan S1.1:86, 278
Left Hand of Darkness, The, LeGuin, Ursula 5:236–42
Legal systems. *See* Law and legal systems
"Legend of Sleepy Hollow, The," Irving, Washington 1:211–18
Legends. *See* Myth
Legislation. *See under individual topics, e. g.* Civil rights movement; Great Depression; labor movements and unions; Segregation
LeGuin, Ursula, *Left Hand of Darkness, The* 5:236–42
Leibniz, Gottfried Wilhelm Von S1.1:22, 23 (*sidebar*)
Lenape (Delaware) Indians 1:206, 219–20
Lenin, Vladimir 4:14, 15 (*illus.*)
Leopold, King of Belgium 2:146–7, 150–1
Lepanto, Battle of 1:296
Lermontov, Mikhail S1.1:101 (*sidebar*)
Lesbianism. *See under* Homosexuality
Lessing, Doris, *Golden Notebook, The* 4:165–70
Lesson Before Dying, A, Gaines, Ernest J. S1.2:249–58
"Letter from Birmingham Jail," King, Dr. Martin Luther, Jr. S1.2:269–77
Let Us Now Praise Famous Men, Agee, James S1.2:259–68

Leuchter, Fred. A. 4:40
Levantine Jews 1:248
Levellers 1:359
Levittowns S1.2:281
Lewis, C. S. 1:158
Lewis, John L. 3:155 (*sidebar*)
Lewis, Oscar 5:266
Lewis, Sinclair, *Babbitt* 3:21–7, S1.1:289
Liberalism, classical
collapse of, in late 1800s Austria S1.1:315, 320
complacency of S1.2:202
individualism 3:268
targeted by New Right 5:136
versus radicals in Russian intergenerational conflict S1.1:99–103, 367
Liberia 2:404
Libya S1.2:131
Libyan Desert S1.2:125
Liddell, Alice 2:29 (*illus.*)
Light in the Forest, The, Richter, Conrad 1:219–24
Like Water for Chocolate, Esquivel, Laura 3:196–202
Lincoln, Abraham
biography of 2:1–7
Emancipation Proclamation (1862) 2:59, 60 (*sidebar*), 135, 308, 309
Gettysburg Address 2:130–6
influence on white South Africans of 20th century 4:99
quote from *Declaration of Independence* 1:99
on race 2:3, 5
Walt Whitman on 2:196 (*sidebar*)
Lindbergh, Anne Morrow S1.2:496
Lindbergh, Charles 3:367, 4:373
Lindner, Robert 4:77–8
"Lines Composed a Few Miles Above Tintern Abbey," Wordsworth, William S1.1:211–12, 213, 215, 215 (*sidebar*)
Linguistic considerations
Afrikaans S1.2:118, 122–3
alliteration 5:223
American Indian writers' use of English, oppressor's language S1.1:138
bilingual creation of *A Dry White Season* S1.2:122
Black English, or Ebonics 5:145, 154, 342
Churchill's rhetoric 4:361–2
colloquial prose of Lardner 4:262 (*sidebar*)
Dutch place-names in New York 1:331 (*sidebar*)
Elizabethan Age's imported words from science, literature, and exploration S1.2:399–400
English accents 3:4 5, 313–14
English imposed on slaves and colonial subjects S1.2:21
English and Irish expressions S1.2:139 (*sidebar*)
English as melding of French and Old English 1:183 (*sidebar*)

Index

Linguistic considerations (*continued*)
    ethnic idioms, street slang, and group identification   **4**:249 (*sidebar*), 386
    ethnic, racist slurs   **4**:32, 386
    fading, loss of native or immigrants' languages   **4**:85, 142
    first modern language grammar (Castilian Spanish)   **S1.1**:189–90
    Gaelic League   **3**:109, 308–9
    ghetto street slang   **5**:17
    Japanese name formats   **S1.2**:217
    Kennedy's rhetoric   **5**:186
    King's rhetoric   **5**:223–4
    metaphor   **5**:186
    Mycenaean alphabet   **1**:172 (*sidebar*)
    "naming," power of   **5**:176
    non-Greek-speakers as barbarians   **1**:173 (*sidebar*)
    oratory, rhetoric of speeches   **5**:186, 223
    Orwell on debasement of language and thought   **S1.1**:405 (*sidebar*)
    Phoenician alphabet   **1**:286–7
    plain, simple language of common men   **1**:72–3, 76, 163, 342
    problematic translation of *The Trial*   **S1.1**:481 (*sidebar*)
    pronouns, inclusive   **5**:186
    puns and phrases in Shakespeare   **1**:348–9, **S1.2**:399
    puns in Victorian Age   **2**:30
    repetition   **5**:186
    rhyme   **5**:223
    rhythm   **5**:223
    Roman names   **1**:190
    Roosevelt's (Franklin Delano) rhetoric   **3**:127
    South African colloquialisms   **S1.2**:322 (*sidebar*)
    Southern dialect
        in *Cold Sassy Tree*   **3**:79
        in *Color Purple, The*   **3**:87
        in *Gathering of Old Men, A*   **5**:133
        in *Huckleberry Finn*   **2**:17
        in "Spunk" and "Sweat,"   **S1.1**:432
        in *Uncle Remus*   **2**:397, 398–9
    Southwestern dialects   **4**:321 (*sidebar*)
    suppression of native languages by colonialists   **4**:350
    Western dialect in "Notorious Jumping Frog"   **2**:252
    Yiddish   **3**:120
Lipsyte, Robert, *Contender, The*   **5**:67–73
Literary experimentation and categories
    for adolescents and young adults, as genre   **5**:61–2, 265–6, 268–70, 331
    Aesthetic movement   **S1.1**:202
    allegory and fable   **4**:16 (*sidebar*), 19, **S1.2**:70
    almanacs (*Poor Richard's Almanac*)   **1**:309–15
    Arundhati Roy's nonchronological narrative technique   **S1.2**:154 (*sidebar*)
    autobiography as "eyewitness history"   **S1.1**:405
    bildungsroman   **3**:264, 311, **4**:47, **S1.2**:19–27
    Blake's illuminated printing   **S1.1**:411 (*sidebar*)
    calendarios de las señoritas (Mexican magazines for women)   **3**:196–7
    Chekhov's compassionate neutrality   **S1.1**:373–4
    Chekhov's small, intimate fictional worlds   **S1.1**:368
    Chekhov's "zero endings"   **S1.1**:375
    contes philosophiques   **S1.1**:29
    courtship, marriage plotting   **S1.1**:94
    crime stories and "Newgate Novels"   **2**:83, 267
    detective fiction   **2**:325, **3**:226–7, **S1.1**:267 (*sidebar*), 271
    development in 17th-century French salons   **1**:88
    dramatic monologue   **S1.1**:204, 298
    dystopian   **5**:100, 141, 252, **S1.2**:69
    of Enlightenment   **2**:211 (*sidebar*)
    espionage novel   **S1.1**:385
    for ethnic groups, minorities   **5**:62
    fantasy mixed with real world   **S1.2**:63
    future history   **5**:127
    German works   **S1.1**:114 (*sidebar*)
    ghost stories   **S1.1**:37
    Gothic horror stories and romances   **2**:81, 85, 185, **3**:338, **S1.1**:278, 501
    Hemingway's iceberg principle   **S1.1**:445 (*sidebar*), **S1.2**:375
    Hemingway's simple prose style   **S1.1**:445
    historical fiction   **S1.1**:19
    horror fiction   **5**:46–7
    Imagism   **3**:413–14
    irony   **S1.1**:381 (*sidebar*)
    Japanese symbolic kana writing   **S1.1**:450
    Kerouac's nonstop prose   **S1.2**:362
    Kincaid's rhythmic repetition   **S1.2**:26
    Latin American   **2**:273
    "magical" realism   **2**:271, 273, **3**:196, 202, **4**:48, **5**:169, 213, 330
    Martinez's figurative language   **S1.2**:375
    metafiction or metanarrative   **S1.2**:179
    modernism and symbolism   **S1.1**:202, 205, 444, **S1.2**:203
    neoclassicism   **S1.1**:113, 207–8
    paradoxical aphorisms   **S1.1**:411
    "picong" satire   **S1.2**:186–7
    pornographic   **3**:381
    postcolonial literature   **S1.1**:501
    printing and publishing, impact of advances in   **1**:160, 162 (*sidebar*), **2**:234, 306, 419
    protest novel   **S1.1**:126, 436
    pulp magazines   **2**:325, **3**:226–7
    realism and psychological realism   **S1.1**:157
    realism. *See* Realism
    repetition as literary device   **4**:70
    roman à clef   **S1.1**:445
    romances   **2**:210
    of Romantic era. *See* Romantic movement
    Russian Realism   **S1.1**:101 (*sidebar*)
    satirical. *See* Satire

science fiction. *See* Science fiction
serial characters, stories, novels **S1.1**:156 (*sidebar*)
"Sestiger" movement **S1.2**:115, 123
slave narratives. *See* Slave narratives
as social anthropology **S1.1**:6, 7–8
Southern Renascence in **3**:421, **S1.1**:419–20
stream of consciousness technique **3**:111, 358, **S1.1**:419 (*sidebar*), 420, 427, 471
Sturm und Drang (storm and stress) movement **S1.1**:113
sympathetic treatment of Jews **S1.1**:371 (*sidebar*)
thrillers, psychological **3**:328–9
utopian **5**:251–2
vampire fiction **S1.1**:146
westerns **2**:321, 325
Wilder's view of importance of **3**:288
(*See also* Biography and autobiography; Censorship and banning of literary works; Documents; Essays; Narratives; Novels; Plays; Short stories; Speeches)
Little Foxes, The, Hellman, Lillian **3**:203–10
Little Gipsy Girl, The, Cervantes, Miguel de **S1.1**:189–98
Little Prince, The, Saint-Exupéry, Antoine de **3**:210–17
Little Women, Alcott, Louisa May **2**:202–8
Livia Drusilla **S1.1**:171 (*sidebar*)
Lobotomy **4**:290, **S1.2**:148, 149 (*sidebar*)
Locke, Alain **3**:256, 389
Locke, John **1**:100, **S1.1**:216
Locke, Richard Adams **S1.1**:273 (*sidebar*)
Lolita, Nabokov, Vladimir **S1.2**:279–86
London
 Blitz ("blitzkrieg") **S1.2**:130 (*sidebar*), 300 (*sidebar*)
 Crystal Palace and Great Exhibition of 1851 **S1.1**:325 (*sidebar*)
 and the "London Season" **S1.1**:180–1
 rapid industrialization and urbanization **S1.1**:324
 rise of "new aristocracy" **S1.2**:406–7
 as trendsetter in Victorian Age **1**:417
London, Jack, *Call of the Wild, The* **3**:51–6
Lone Ranger and Tonto Fistfight in Heaven, The, Alexie, Sherman **S1.2**:287–96
Long Day's Journey into Night, O'Neill, Eugene **3**:218–24
López, Dr. Roderigo **1**:248
López Pumarejo, Alfonso **S1.2**:460, 461, 461 (*sidebar*)
Lorca, Federico García, *Blood Wedding* **S1.2**:73–82
Lord of the Flies, Golding, William **4**:228–34, **S1.2**:69
Lord of the Rings, The, Tolkien, J.R.R. **S1.2**:178, 297–307
"Lost generation" (post-WWI) **3**:13, 112, 116–17, **S1.1**:442
Lotteries **4**:235–6

"Lottery, The," Jackson, Shirley **4**:235–9
Louisiana **3**:15–18, **4**:365–6, **5**:21, 22, 25, 130, 131–2
Louis, Joe **S1.2**:251 (*sidebar*)
Louis Napoleon **2**:228–9
Louis Phillippe of France **1**:164
Louis XI of France **1**:160
Louis XIII of France **1**:386, 387, 388
Louis XIV of France **1**:31, 87, 88, 130, 386, 387, **3**:212
Louis XVI of France **1**:51, 358, 359, 372
Louis XVIII of France **1**:391
L'Ouverture, Toussaint **5**:116–17
Love and marriage
 in 18th-century France **1**:31
 in 19th-century England **S1.1**:92, 94 5, 180–1, 241, 293–4, 389–91
 in 19th-century New York **S1.1**:3–4
 according to Thurber **3**:367–8
 adultery, infidelity **5**:273, 287
 among Norwegian upper classes **S1.1**:161–2
 in ancient Greece **1**:285
 children of immigrants marrying Caucasians **5**:232
 in China and Chinese culture **3**:132, 192–3, 194, **4**:128
 in colonial America **1**:24
 courtship and social class **S1.1**:180–2
 in czarist Russia **S1.1**:369–70
 debutantes' "coming out" **3**:326–7
 destructiveness and power as portrayed by Dickens **S1.1**:156–7
 in early 17th-century England **1**:263–4, 385
 for England's landed gentry **1**:414, **2**:296, 354 5, **3**:326–7
 happiness versus duty in **3**:271–2
 idealized by Victorians **S1.1**:296–7
 ideal of romantic versus arranged marriage **S1.1**:370
 in Imperial Rome **S1.1**:172–3
 interracial **S1.1**:340, **S1.2**:232
 Japanese "picture brides" **4**:331–2
 in Japan's 10th century Heian court **S1.1**:453–5
 limited options for English gentlewomen **S1.1**:389–91
 marriage settlements, portions, and jointures **S1.1**:389, 390, 496
 of new money to old titles **S1.1**:181
 in Peru **S1.2**:57
 polygamy **5**:4
 problems of adjustment to retirement **5**:203, 273
 sexual dimension of, in 19th century **2**:212, 423
 or spinsterhood **2**:297
 for traditional Jews **3**:119, 123
 for underage teens **5**:151
 in Victorian Age **2**:116, 336, **S1.1**:141–2
 War Brides Act (1945) **4**:124, 127, **5**:231
 Wollstonecraft on **1**:410–11

Index

Love and marriage (*continued*)
   for women of 1970s   **2**:58
   (*See also* Adultery, infidelity; Divorce; Family and family life)
Love and marriage, works emphasizing
   Age of Innocence, The   **S1.1**:1–9
   All the Pretty Horses, McCarthy, Cormac   **S1.2**:9–17
   Anna Karenina   **2**:34 40, **S1.1**:368
   Beauty: A Retelling   **1**:30–6
   Blood Wedding   **S1.2**:73–82
   Color Purple, The   **3**:80–7
   Daisy Miller   **2**:105–10
   Doll's House, A   **2**:111–17
   Emma   **S1.1**:89–97
   Ethan Frome   **2**:125–9
   Farewell to Arms, A   **3**:112–18
   Gone with the Wind   **2**:137–44
   Handmaid's Tale, The   **5**:135–42
   His Own Where   **5**:149–55
   House of Mirth, The   **3**:166–73
   Jane Eyre   **1**:415 (*sidebar*), 419, **2**:181–7, **S1.1**:493, **S1.2**:24 5
   Kitchen God's Wife, The   **3**:189–95
   Like Water for Chocolate   **3**:196–202
   Love Medicine   **5**:243–50
   Madame Bovary   **2**:209–15
   Merchant of Venice, The   **1**:247
   Midsummer Night's Dream, A   **1**:258–65
   Misanthrope, The, Molière, Jean-Baptiste Poquelin de   **S1.1**:249–57
   "My Last Duchess" and Other Poems   **S1.1**:291–9
   Othello   **1**:297
   Passing   **S1.1**:333–42
   Pride and Prejudice   **2**:295–300
   Romeo and Juliet   **1**:346
   Scarlet Letter   **1**:351–7
   Sense and Sensibility, Austen, Jane   **S1.1**:387–98
   "Seventeen Syllables"   **4**:330–6
   Sons and Lovers   **2**:334 9
   Tess of the D'Urbervilles   **2**:353–9
   Twelfth Night, Or, What You Will, Shakespeare, William   **S1.1**:483–92
   Wide Sargasso Sea   **S1.1**:493–502, **S1.2**:178
   Wuthering Heights   **1**:413–19
Love Medicine, Erdrich, Louise   **5**:243–50
"Love Song of J. Alfred Prufrock, The," Eliot, T. S.   **S1.1**:199–206, 259
Lower classes   **1**:363, 366, 366 (*sidebar*)
LSD (lysergic acid diethylamide)   **4**:288, 289, 292, 293–4, **5**:82–3, 324 5
Luce, Henry R.   **S1.2**:262
Luce, William, *Belle of Amherst, The*   **2**:54 8
Lucifer. *See* Devil (Satan)
Luddite movement   **1**:119–20, 120 (*illus.*), **S1.1**:91
Lugh (Celtic god)   **S1.1**:232–3
Luther, Martin   **1**:231–2, 232 (*illus.*), **2**:113, **S1.1**:108
Luxembourg   **4**:254 5

Lyell, Sir Charles   **S1.1**:274, 329
Lynching
   advocation of, by racist propaganda   **2**:400
   anti-lynching crusader Ida B. Wells-Barnett   **3**:83, 238
   ASWPL (Association of Southern Women for the Prevention of Lynching)   **3**:391–2, **5**:133
   of black soldiers during WWII   **4**:197
   by Ku Klux Klan   **2**:141 (*sidebar*), 143 (*sidebar*), 412, **3**:419, **5**:130–1, **S1.2**:250
   "defense of white womanhood" excuse   **5**:133
   Dyer Antilynching Bill   **3**:392
   economic aspect of excuses for   **3**:83, 391
   estimates of deaths from   **2**:341, **3**:37, 83, 238, 419, **4**:202, **5**:131, **S1.1**:334 5, 431
   FDR's reason for refusal to sign Dyer Antilynching Bill   **3**:154, 392, **4**:202
   horrific cruelties   **S1.1**:431
   horrific cruelties of   **2**:412, **3**:274, 391
   increasing with desperation of Great Depression (1930s)   **3**:45
   in Northern states   **3**:238
   perpetrators generally escaping punishment   **3**:274
   police joining mobs   **4**:4, 202
   sexual aspect of excuses for   **3**:83, 238, 273
   as Southern phenomenon   **3**:238, **S1.2**:257
   to prevent exercise of voting rights   **2**:412, **3**:419
   of whites   **3**:273–4
Lyrical Ballads, Wordsworth, William and Samuel Taylor Coleridge   **S1.1**:207–17

M

MacArthur, Douglas   **4**:80–1, 350, **S1.2**:410
Macaulay, Thomas Babington   **S1.1**:44, 48
Macbeth, Shakespeare, William   **1**:225–30
McCarthy, Cormac, *All the Pretty Horses*   **S1.2**:9–17
McCarthy, Joseph and McCarthyism and HUAC   **1**:84, 398, **3**:178, 208, 209 (*illus.*), **4**:71, 72, 110, 398, **5**:2, 3 (*illus.*), 96, 97, 127, **S1.1**:11, **S1.2**:280, 310, 364
McCullers, Carson
   Heart Is a Lonely Hunter, The   **3**:153–8
   Member of the Wedding, The   **4**:254 9
McCunn, Ruthanne Lum, *Thousand Pieces of Gold*   **2**:366–71
Machiavelli, Niccolò, *Prince, The*   **1**:316–20
Machismo   **3**:201, **4**:278–9, 299, **5**:167, 173–4, 337, **S1.2**:370
McKay, Claude, *Home to Harlem*   **3**:159–65
McKay, Mabel   **S1.2**:161, 168
McKinley, Robin, *Beauty: A Retelling of the Story of Beauty and the Beast*   **1**:30–6
McMullin, Fred   **3**:149
Madame Bovary, Flaubert, Gustave   **2**:209–15
Madero, Francisco   **3**:29, 197, 278, **S1.2**:14 (*sidebar*), 85, 502

"Magical" realism   **2**:271, 273, **3**:196, 202, **4**:48, **5**:169, 213, 330
Magna Carta   **1**:255
Mahler, Gustav   **S1.1**:68
Maimon, Solomon   **4**:88
Major Barbara, Shaw, George Bernard   **S1.1**:219–27
Malamud, Bernard
    Fixer, The   **S1.1**:117–28
    Natural, The   **4**:260–6
Malcolm II of Scotland   **1**:225
Malcolm III of Scotland   **1**:226
La Malinche and malinchista   **S1.2**:93, 507, 507 (*sidebar*), 508
Mallory, Thomas   **1**:290, 293
Maltese Falcon, The, Hammett, Dashiell   **3**:225–30
Malthus, Thomas Robert   **S1.1**:32, 323
Man for All Seasons, A, Bolt, Robert   **1**:231–7
Manchester, England   **S1.1**:42, 43, 324
Manchild in the Promised Land, Brown, Claude   **4**:247–53
Manchuria   **4**:59, 178, 350, **5**:230
Mandela, Nelson   **S1.2**:196, 320, 324
Manhattan Project   **4**:71, 81–2, 316
Manicheanism   **S1.1**:28
Manifest Destiny   **2**:76 (*sidebar*), **3**:234, **S1.1**:136
Mann, Thomas, *Death in Venice*   **S1.1**:61–9
Manorial system   **1**:251
Man without a Face, The, Holland, Isabelle   **4**:240–6
Mao Zedong   **3**:136, 189, **5**:254
"Maquis"   **S1.2**:467–9, 469 (*sidebar*)
Mark Antony   **1**:13, 189, 191, **S1.1**:171
Markham, Beryl, *West with the Night*   **S1.2**:487–97
Mark of the Horse Lord, The, Sutcliff, Rosemary   **S1.1**:229–38
Marooning   **1**:401–2
Marranos   **1**:248, 249
Marriage, of East Indians in Trinidad   **S1.2**:185
Marshall, Paule, *Praisesong for the Widow*   **S1.2**:387–95
Marshall Plan   **5**:123–4, 224, 292, **S1.2**:310
Marsh, Ngaio   **3**:329
Martian Chronicles, The, Bradbury, Ray   **S1.2**:309–15
Martí, José
    influence on other revolutionaries   **S1.2**:211 (*sidebar*)
    role in Cuban War of Independence   **S1.2**:211 (*sidebar*)
Martinez, Victor, *Parrot in the Oven*   **S1.2**:367–77
Martinez, Vilma   **5**:179
Marxism
    comparison to communism and socialism   **S1.1**:45 (*sidebar*)
    concept of capitalists versus proletariat   **3**:321
    concepts of "wage slavery" and "estranged labor"   **3**:179, **4**:18–19
    in Czarist Russia   **3**:59
    (*See also* Communism)
Marx, Karl   **1**:376, **3**:232
    Communist Manifesto, The   **S1.1**:41–9

Mary (Stuart), Queen of Scots   **1**:141, 149–50, 349
Mary (Tudor), Queen of England ("Bloody Mary")   **S1.1**:484
Masons (Freemasons)   **2**:82
"MASTER HAROLD" and the boys, Fugard, Athol   **S1.2**:317–25
Mather, Cotton
    associated with Puritan excess   **1**:213
    comparison to J. Edgar Hoover   **1**:84 (*sidebar*)
    excerpt from *Bonifacius*   **1**:28
    impact of *Memorable Providences*   **1**:79, 80, 396
    impact of *The Wonders of the Invisible World*   **1**:80, 80 (*illus.*), 422, 424
Mather, Increase   **1**:424
Matlovich, Leonard Jr.   **4**:39
Maugham, W. Somerset, *Of Human Bondage*   **3**:264 8
Maupassant, Guy de, "Necklace, The"   **2**:244 8
Meat-packing industry   **3**:175
Medea, Euripides   **1**:238–41
Media
    black press airing grievances of black soldiers in WWII   **4**:195
    broadcasting in Peru   **S1.2**:54 5
    contributing to anti-Japanese hysteria of WWII   **4**:138, 140, 141, 194
    creating crime-ridden image of Central Park   **4**:401
    decrying racial violence   **4**:310 (*sidebar*)
    fanning 1940s hysteria over zoot suiters and "Mexican goon squads"   **4**:296, 404, 405
    FDR's popularity with and concealment of disability   **3**:127
    Fortune magazine   **S1.2**:262
    misrepresentation of "black power"   **4**:56
    misrepresentation of Malcolm X   **5**:16
    muckraking journalists   **3**:176, 320
    "New Journalism"   **5**:293
    newspapers   **1**:268, **3**:279, **S1.2**:91 (*sidebar*)
    overlooking violence against minorities and homeless   **4**:401
    patriotic emphasis during WWII   **4**:371
    photojournalism   **S1.2**:262–3
    role in consolidation of Japanese culture in California   **4**:332
    Time magazine   **S1.2**:262
    use of, for propaganda   **4**:66–7
    "yellow journalism"   **3**:279
    (*See also* Radio; Television)
Medici, House of   **1**:316, 317, 318
Medici, Marie de'   **1**:387
Medicine
    ambulances of WWI   **3**:114
    Chinese   **3**:194 (*sidebar*)
    Chippewa "love medicine"   **5**:249
    homeopathy   **3**:68–9
    Indian remedies   **3**:68–9, **5**:249, **S1.2**:294
    Latino *curanderos*   **3**:199, **4**:45
    as male dominated   **4**:218

Medicine (*continued*)
    midwifery   **4**:218
    Navajo Night Chant   **4**:188
    opium products   **3**:379
    penicillin   **3**:366
    polio vaccines   **4**:10
    "socialized," 1950s fear of   **4**:12
    (*See also* Diseases)
Medicine bundles   **S1.1**:133 (*sidebar*), **S1.2**:294
Mediterranean
    Albania   **2**:101
    in ancient times   **1**:9
    Egypt   **4**:107, **S1.2**:131
    Ethiopia   **4**:67
    Libya   **S1.2**:131
    Palestine   **4**:102–3, 105, **5**:54
    Peloponnesian War   **1**:241, 324, 328, **S1.1**:311–12, 352
    Sicily   **4**:67
    Suez Canal   **3**:184, **4**:107, **S1.2**:131
    (*See also* Greece in ancient times; Israel; Italy; Turkey)
"Meeting at Night" and "Parting at Morning," Browning, Robert   **S1.1**:291–9
Melanesia   **4**:222
Melville, Herman   **2**:92
    Benito Cereno   **1**:37–43
    Billy Budd   **1**:51–6
    Moby Dick   **2**:230–5
    praise for "Young Goodman Brown"   **1**:425
Member of the Wedding, The, McCullers, Carson   **4**:254 9
Memoirs. *See* Biography and autobiography; Essays
Mencken, H. L.
    on *Babbitt*   **3**:25, 27
    influence on Sinclair Lewis   **3**:26–7
    on Scopes Trial   **3**:102 (*sidebar*)
    on Southern culture   **3**:40 (*sidebar*)
Mendel, Gregor   **2**:217
Mendelssohn, Moses   **4**:88
Menelaus   **1**:281
Mental and emotional disabilities
    association with pressure to conform   **4**:74
    asylums, institutions
        abuses in   **3**:244 5
        deinstitutionalization   **4**:289
        as fashionable "resorts"   **3**:413
        hospitalization in   **3**:272, **4**:77
    changing attitudes in 1950s and 1960s   **4**:151–6
    connectedness of mental health and human relationships   **4**:153
    developments in psychology   **3**:329, 378, **4**:77
    education for children   **4**:151–2
    effects of childhood abuse   **5**:289–90
    eugenic sterilization of retarded   **3**:272, **4**:152, **5**:41, 42
    Fetal Alcohol Syndrome   **5**:361
    "frontier madness"   **3**:259
    history of   **4**:288–9
    madness in *Hamlet*   **1**:136–43, **S1.2**:398
    madness in *Wide Sargasso Sea*   **S1.1**:493–502, **S1.2**:178
    National Association for Retarded Children (NARC)   **4**:151
    schizophrenia, paranoid delusions   **S1.2**:148
    in Shakespeare's time   **1**:139 (*sidebar*), 203
    stigma of   **5**:262–3
    targeted by Nazis in Holocaust   **4**:119
    treatments for
        electroconvulsive therapy (ECT)   **4**:24 (*sidebar*), 289–90
        electroshock therapy   **S1.2**:149 (*sidebar*)
        lobotomy   **4**:290, **S1.2**:148, 149 (*sidebar*)
        methods of 19th century   **S1.1**:500
        methods of 1940s and 1950s   **4**:289–90
        pyschosurgery   **4**:290
        "rest cure"   **2**:425–6
        tranquilizing drugs   **4**:289
    in Victorian Age   **2**:119–20, 184, 185–6, 278–9, **S1.1**:500–1
    women as vulnerable and emotionally fragile   **S1.1**:500–1
    of WWII veterans   **4**:80 (*sidebar*), 325
Merchant of Venice, Shakespeare, William   **1**:242–9
    parallels to *Ivanhoe*   **1**:187
Meredith, James   **5**:19, **S1.2**:256
Merry Adventures of Robin Hood, The, Pyle, Howard   **1**:250–7
Merton, Thomas   **5**:280–1
Metamorphoses, Ovid   **1**:262
Methodism   **2**:357–8, **S1.1**:208–9
Metropolitan Opera House   **S1.1**:2, 3
Mexican Americans
    ambivalent cultural identity   **S1.2**:503–4
    racism of "white" Americans   **S1.2**:504
    remaking of self-image   **S1.2**:504 5
    in United States   **S1.2**:501
    versus vendidos   **S1.2**:504 5
    women breaking with tradition   **S1.2**:505
    (*See also* Chicanos; Latinos)
Mexican War   **2**:88, 89, 242, **5**:172, **S1.2**:340, 367, 431
Mexico
    ambivalence, close ties to United States   **3**:282, **S1.2**:16
    chronology
        Cortés' conquest (1520s)   **S1.2**:93, 499
        Malinche and Cortés   **S1.2**:93, 507, 507 (*sidebar*), 508
        Catholicism and Virgin of Guadalupe (1531)   **S1.2**:499–501, 500 (*illus.*), 507, 508
        War of Independence (1810–21)   **S1.2**:83
        Santa Anna dictatorship (1833-55)   **S1.2**:83
        loss of northern territories to United States (1848)   **S1.2**:83, 501
        attempts at land reform (1857)   **S1.2**:84
        attempts to break power of Catholic Church (1857)   **S1.2**:84, 86, 502
        War of the French Intervention and Emperor Maximilian (1862–66)   **S1.2**:83, 501

Díaz dictatorship ("Porfiriato") (1876–1911) 3:28–30, 197, 278, **S1.2**:83, 431, 432, 501–2
   land grabs by land companies, hacendados, and caciques (1883–94) **S1.2**:502
   labor unrest at Cananea mines **S1.2**:432, 433 (*sidebar*)
   Carranza's role in Revolution **S1.2**:85, 86, 503
   dual legacy of reform plus dictatorship (1910) **S1.2**:83–5
   Madero presidency (1910) **S1.2**:85, 502
   Obregón's role in Revolution **S1.2**:85, 86–7, 86 (*sidebar*)
   Revolution and caudillos (1910–24) 3:29, 278–9, 4:295, 296 (*sidebar*), **S1.2**:84 (*illus.*), 85–8, 86 (*sidebar*), 432–3
   Zapata's role in revolution **S1.2**:84 (*illus.*), 85, 86, 501–3, 501 (*sidebar*), 502 (*illus.*), 504 (*sidebar*)
   Huerta coup and presidency (1912–14) **S1.2**:85, 503
   civil strife (1920s and 1930s) **S1.2**:86–7
   Calles presidency (1924 28) **S1.2**:86 (*sidebar*), 87
   Cristero rebellion (1926–29) **S1.2**:86
   Yaqui Indian revolt and suppression (1926–27) **S1.2**:87–8
   electoral showdown and assassinations (1928) **S1.2**:86 (*sidebar*)
   land reform and oil industry nationalizations (1930s) **S1.2**:87
   Cárdenas presidency (1934 40) **S1.2**:87
   betrayal of the Revolution, (1940s 50s) **S1.2**:87–8
   Bracero Program (1942–1964) 3:34, 4:44, **S1.2**:369 (*sidebar*)
   Alemán presidency (1946-52) **S1.2**:88
   "Mexican miracle" (1945–1965) **S1.2**:433
   widened industrial base at mid-century **S1.2**:11
   newspapers' self-censorship (1959) **S1.2**:91 (*sidebar*)
   political and economic turbulence (1960s and 1970s) **S1.2**:438
   Tlatelolco massacre and national tragedy **S1.2**:438
   urbanization, industrial growth, and search for national identity (mid-1900s) **S1.2**:92–3
  ejidos system 3:282
  hacienda system 3:29, 278, 282, **S1.2**:87, 432, 502
  immigration to United States from 3:282, 4:44 8, **S1.2**:369
  mining industry 3:28
  oil discovery and production **S1.2**:16
  PRI and one-party democracy 3:282
  upper-class flight to suburban colonias **S1.2**:92 (*sidebar*)
  women in 3:197–8, 200–2
Meyrinck, Gustav **S1.1**:480
Micronesia 4:222
Middle Ages
  as depicted in *Beowulf* 1:44 50
  as depicted in Chaucer 1:64 70
  importance of kings and kinship 1:153
Middle class
  African Americans in 20th century 3:252, 255, 387–8, 4:2, 51, **S1.2**:389, 427
  in American East 2:303, 306
  bourgeoisie of France 2:209–10, 245–6
  bourgeoisie of Norway **S1.1**:162
  education as means to social mobility **S1.1**:150
  in England 1:66, 72, 338, 342, 371, 2:118, 153, 354, 3:312, **S1.1**:240
  importance of proper manners 2:297
  industrialization allowing growth of 2:118, 153
  mid-1900s America **S1.2**:106
  moving to suburbs 4:73, 384, 385, 5:261–2, **S1.2**:358–9, 364, 422
  professionals **S1.1**:150
  replacing aristocracy of Old South 4:364 5
  Russian **S1.1**:99
Midnight's Children, Rushdie, Salman **S1.2**:327–37
Midsummer Night's Dream, A, Shakespeare, William 1:258–65
Midwifery 4:218
Migrant farm workers 3:29–30, 34, 49, 140–2, 143 (*sidebar*), 269–71, 275, 335, 337, 4:297 (*sidebar*)
  braceros 3:34, 4:44, **S1.2**:369 (*sidebar*)
Milagro Beanfield War, The, Nichols, John **S1.2**:339–47
Milan, Italy 1:379–80
Military
  African Americans in 3:160, 424
  American Indians in 4:80, 185–7, 5:362–3
  anti-Semitism in 4:36–7
  Army training camps 4:36
  authority and mutiny 4:63–4
  British "batmen" 3:348
  Claire Chennault and American Volunteer Group 3:190
  desertion during Civil War 2:10–11, 312
  desertion in Vietnam 2:13 (*sidebar*)
  "Flying Tigers" 3:190
  homosexuals in 4:38, 39–40
  illicit wartime amusements 4:37, 38
  Latinos in 4:44
  racial discrimination in 3:41–2, 4:195, 197, 212
  reservists and regulars 4:63 (*sidebar*)
  United Service Organizations (USO) 4:38
  (*See also* War)
Military draft
  of American Indians for WWII 4:80
  of blacks for Vietnam 5:102–3, **S1.2**:453 (*sidebar*)
  of Chicanos for Vietnam 4:176

Military draft (*continued*)
   of Chinese Americans for WWII   **4**:127
   of disadvantaged for Vietnam (Project 100,000)
      5:102–3, 158, 307
   dodging and avoiding   **2**:256, 309, **4**:324, 327
   first American peacetime draft (1940)   **4**:35, 324 5
   induction process   **4**:35–6
   of mostly poor and lower classes for Civil War   **2**:256, 309
   of Nisei for WWII   **4**:140 (*sidebar*)
   of poor, lower classes for Civil War   **2**:256, 309
   of Puerto Ricans for WWI   **5**:215
   as target of blacks' protest   **4**:213
   for WWII in 1940   **4**:35, 324 5
Miller, Arthur
   All My Sons   **S1.2**:1–8
   Crucible, The   **1**:78–86
   Death of a Salesman   **4**:109–15
   importance in American theater   **1**:85
Mill on the Floss, The, Eliot, George (Marian Evans)   **S1.1**:239–48
Mill, John Stuart   **2**:182 (*sidebar*), **S1.1**:33 (*sidebar*), 54, 102, 247
Mills, C. Wright   **4**:74
Milton, John, *Paradise Lost*   **1**:301–8
Minh, Ho Chi   **5**:101
Mining and mining industry
   accidents and disease   **2**:335
   child labor   **2**:335 (*sidebar*)
   in Chile   **5**:163, 164
   Chinese in   **2**:367, **5**:352
   coal   **3**:63, 64, **4**:9, **5**:39–40
   in Mexico   **3**:28, **S1.2**:92, 432, 434 (*illus.*)
   uranium   **S1.2**:99
   (*See also* Gold rushes and silver strikes; *Thousand Pieces of Gold*)
Minneapolis, Minnesota   **S1.2**:33
Minotaur   **1**:259
Minstrel shows   **2**:16–17, 21
Minutemen   **S1.1**:12, 13 (*sidebar*)
Mirabal sisters of Dominican Republic, *In the Time of the Butterflies*   **S1.2**:205–15, 213 (*sidebar*), 214 (*illus.*)
Miracle Worker, The, Gibson, William   **2**:216–22
Misanthrope, The, Molière, Jean-Baptiste Poquelin de   **S1.1**:249–57
Les Misérables, Hugo, Victor   **2**:223–9
Missionaries   **2**:118–19, 147, 161–2, 361–2, **3**:133, 280, **5**:195
Mississippi   **S1.2**:381
Mississippi River   **2**:16, 17
Missouri Compromise (1820)   **2**:5 (*sidebar*), 15–16, 22
Mitchell, Margaret, *Gone with the Wind*   **2**:137–44
Mithras (Roman god)   **S1.1**:233
Mitnagdim   **3**:426
Moby Dick, Melville, Herman   **2**:230–5
Modernism   **3**:411, **5**:42, **S1.1**:202, 205, 444, **S1.2**:203

Modest Proposal, A, Swift, Jonathan   **1**:266–72
Mohammed, Sufi Abdul   **4**:211
Mohr, Nicholasa, *In Nueva York*   **5**:214 21
Molière, Jean-Baptiste Poquelin de, *Misanthrope, The*   **S1.1**:249–57
Momaday, N. Scott
   on *Bury My Heart at Wounded Knee*   **2**:79
   House Made of Dawn   **4**:185–92, **S1.1**:137
   Way to Rainy Mountain, The   **S1.2**:477–86
Monasticism   **3**:186–7
   Trappist monks   **5**:280
Money
   in colonial America   **1**:103–4, 310
   "Wood's Coins" in Ireland   **1**:268
Moneylending (usury)   **1**:103–4, 182–3, 243, 243 (*sidebar*), 247
Monologues   **S1.1**:204
Monroe, James   **1**:209
Monro, Lt. Col. George   **1**:205
Moors   **1**:297, 299, **3**:212, 213, **S1.1**:190
More, Sir Thomas   **1**:232, 233, 237
Mori, Koyoko, *Shizuko's Daughter*   **S1.2**:409–19
Mormonism   **5**:4
Morrison, Toni   **S1.2**:389
   Beloved   **2**:59–65
   Bluest Eye, The   **4**:49–57
   Song of Solomon   **S1.2**:421–30
Mortimer family   **1**:144, 145, 145 (*illus.*)
"The Moses of Michelangelo"   **S1.1**:480
"Most Dangerous Game, The," Connell, Richard   **3**:231–5
Motion picture industry
   "blacklist"   **S1.2**:280
   Caucasian ideal of beauty reinforced by   **4**:50
   development   **3**:3, 89, 101, **S1.2**:475 (*sidebar*)
   early farces, slapsticks, and stoic comedians   **S1.2**:475 (*sidebar*)
   end of golden age of (1920s 45)   **4**:75–6
   escapism and golden age of Hollywood   **S1.2**:143–4
   ethnic stereotypes used by   **2**:142, **4**:50, 369
   female as sex object   **4**:393
   Hollywood's production code and censorship   **S1.2**:143
   Indian popular cinema of 1960s   **S1.2**:155 (*sidebar*)
   influence on Samuel Beckett   **S1.2**:475 (*sidebar*)
   late 1940s attempts to address real issues   **4**:75–6
   patriotic films for WWII   **4**:325
   reflecting and influencing teenagers and generation gap   **4**:392, 394, **S1.2**:285
   "road movies"   **S1.2**:281
   as target of witch hunts for "Reds"   **4**:236
   "thrillers" as new genre   **3**:329
   (*See also* Television)
Mott, Lucretia Coffin   **2**:24, 55, **3**:16
Mountbatten, Louis   **S1.2**:330
Moynihan, Daniel
   Moynihan Report (1965)   **3**:355, 375

on Project 100,000   **5**:103
Muhammad, Elijah   **3**:239 (*illus.*), **4**:249, **5**:13, 69, 110–11
Mulattos   **3**:18, **S1.1**:335, **S1.2**:205–6
Multiculturalism
   America as "salad bowl" rather than melting pot   **5**:176
   encouraging autobiographies   **3**:32, 34
   ethnic studies programs
      in Black English, or Ebonics   **5**:145, 154, 342
      black studies programs   **5**:147–8, **S1.2**:236, 429
      increasing college enrollments   **5**:217
      Puerto Rican history and culture   **5**:217
   women's studies   **5**:117
   (*See also* African Americans; American Indians; Chinese and Chinese Americans; Japanese and Japanese Americans; Jews; Latinos; Puerto Rico and Puerto Ricans)
Muralists of Mexico   **S1.2**:88
Murasaki Shikibu, *Tale of the Genji, The*   **S1.1**:449–61, **S1.2**:222
Murder in the Cathedral, Eliot, T. S.   **S1.1**:259–70
Murder mysteries. *See* Mystery and detective stories
"Murders in the Rue Morgue, The," Poe, Edgar Allan   **S1.1**:271–9
Murphy, Charles F.   **3**:148, 399
Murphy, Gerald   **S1.2**:212
Music
   The Beatles   **S1.2**:4 7
   blues   **3**:254 (*sidebar*), **4**:258
   Chinese opera   **5**:75
   dance   **4**:387
   effectiveness in theatrical productions   **4**:258
   folksongs of 1930s and 1940s   **3**:47, 128
   gospel songs and black spirituals   **2**:398, 402, 407, **4**:258
   importance to slaves   **2**:398
   Japanese   **S1.1**:458 (*sidebar*)
   jazz   **3**:162 (*sidebar*), **4**:258, **S1.1**:337, **S1.2**:359
   Metropolitan Opera House   **S1.1**:2, 3
   New Chilean Song   **5**:164
   ragtime   **3**:321 (*sidebar*)
   reflecting generation gap   **4**:386, **S1.2**:285
   rock 'n' roll   **4**:172, 386, 391–2
   Smith, Bessie   **3**:253 (*illus.*)
   spirituals   **S1.1**:435
   Welsh regard for   **3**:65
Musicals
   for colored girls , Shange, Ntozake   **5**:115–21
   golden age on Broadway   **4**:387
   West Side Story, Laurents, Arthur, *et al.*   **4**:384 90
Musketeers   **1**:386, 387
Muslim Turks   **1**:296
Mussolini, Benito   **2**:293–4, **4**:66–7, 305 (*illus.*), **S1.1**:177, **S1.2**:299
Mutiny
   aboard *Amistad*   **1**:43

aboard HMS *Bounty*   **1**:273–9, 276 (*illus.*)
aboard USS *Somers*   **1**:56
at Spithead and Nore   **1**:53
in *Benito Cereno*   **1**:37–43
in *Billy Budd*   **1**:51–6
in *Caine Mutiny, The*   **4**:58–65
Mutiny on the Bounty, Nordhoff, Charles and James Norman Hall   **1**:273–9
My Antonía, Cather, Willa   **S1.1**:281–90
Mycenaean Age of ancient Greece   **1**:57–9, 167, 258, 281–2, 283 (*sidebar*)
Myers, Walter Dean, *Fallen Angels*   **5**:101–6
"My Last Duchess" and Other Poems, Browning, Robert   **S1.1**:291–9
Myrdal, Gunnar   **S1.2**:252
Mystery and detective stories
   Hound of the Baskervilles   **2**:152–9
   Jane Eyre   **1**:415 (*sidebar*), 419, **2**:181–7, **S1.1**:493, **S1.2**:24 5
   Maltese Falcon, The   **3**:225–30
   "Murders in the Rue Morgue, The," Poe, Edgar Allan   **S1.1**:271–9
   rise of   **2**:325, **3**:226–7, **S1.1**:273 (*sidebar*)
   Strange Case of Dr. Jekyll and Mr. Hyde, The   **3**:377–82, **S1.1**:185
Mysticism   **1**:416
   Hasidic Jews   **3**:425, 426
Myth
   ancient Greek   **S1.1**:301, 308
   Arthurian   **1**:288, 290
   Chinese   **5**:77 (*sidebar*), 358
   comparative anthropology   **5**:42
   creation of   **1**:152
   disguising contemporary social criticism   **1**:15, 63
   founding of Rome   **1**:10 (*sidebar*)
   Holy Grail legends   **4**:264 5
   Irish   **3**:109
   Mexican and Aztlán   **4**:173, 174 5, 176
   Norse   **1**:50, 152, 153, 156, **S1.1**:166
   of the Western cowboy   **S1.2**:10
   (*See also* Folklore and fairy tales; Greek myth)

N

NAACP (National Association for the Advancement of Colored People)   **2**:342, 415, **3**:250, 320, 396, **4**:195, 255, 310, **5**:88, 120 (*sidebar*), **S1.1**:432, **S1.2**:270
Nabokov, Vladimir, *Lolita*   **S1.2**:279–86
Nagasaki and Hiroshima as targets of first atom bombs   **4**:179–82, 180 (*illus.*), 181 (*sidebar*), **S1.2**:131, 220, 311
Naipaul, V. S., *House for Mr. Biswas, A*   **S1.2**:21, 183–93
Nairobi, Kenya   **3**:293, **S1.2**:488
Namboodiripad, E. M. S.   **S1.2**:159, 159 (*sidebar*)
"Naming," power of   **5**:176, **S1.2**:47, 390 (*sidebar*)
Nandi people   **S1.2**:489

Index

Napoleon Bonaparte
    admiration of Goethe   S1.1:114
    as archtype of superman and hero of Romantic movement   S1.1:52 (sidebar), 58 (illus.)
    as controversial among Frenchmen   2:225 (sidebar)
    dissolution of Holy Roman Empire   S1.1:114
    retaking Haiti   S1.2:240
    rise and fall   2:99–100, 224, 295–6
    self-coronation in Notre Dame Cathedral   1:163
Napoleonic code   4:365
Narrative of the Life of Frederick Douglass, Douglass, Frederick   2:16, 236–41, S1.2:229, 231
    inspiring resistance on part of slaves   2:16
Narratives
    Black Elk Speaks, Neihardt, John G.   2:66–73
    Bury My Heart at Wounded Knee, Brown, Dee   2:74 80
    Kon-Tiki, Heyerdahl, Thor   4:221–7
    Two Years before the Mast, Dana, Richard Henry, Jr.   2:391–6
    (*See also* Slave narratives)
NASA (National Aeronautics and Space Administration)   5:81, 291
Nasser, Gamal Abdel   S1.2:131
Nationalism and search for national identity
    Afrikaner   S1.2:115, 116, 122–3
    anti-Semitism   1:364
    as aspect of fascism   4:304
    of Black Muslims and Nation of Islam   3:238, 325, 4:56, 248–50, 5:12–13, 69, 110–11, 302, S1.2:276
    of black separatists   3:160
    caused by economic hardship   1:113
    challenging European empires   S1.1:474 5
    criticized in *The English Patient*   S1.2:130
    ethnic movements   1:363–4
    in Europe of 1800s   S1.1:52
    extremes of   1:292, 293–4
    in *Hound of the Baskervilles*   2:157
    in India   S1.2:328–30, 332–3
    in Trinidad   S1.2:188
    under Young Turks   3:339
National Labor Relations Act (1933)   3:128
National Organization of Women (NOW)   1:62, 4:22, 394, 5:136, 237
Nation of Islam   3:238, 325, 4:56, 248–50, 5:12–13, 69, 110–11, 302, S1.2:276
Native Americans. *See* American Indians
Native Son, Wright, Richard   3:236–42
Native Speaker, Lee, Chang-rae   S1.2:349–55
Nativism   S1.1:441
NATO (North Atlantic Treaty Organization)   5:124, 224, 292, S1.2:310
Natsume, Soseki   S1.2:222
Naturalism   1:293
Natural selection, theory of   S1.1:140, 327, 329
Natural, The, Malamud, Bernard   4:260–6, S1.1:117

Natural theology   S1.1:324 5
Nature
    celebration of   1:413, 416
    and the supernatural, to Romantics   S1.1:213–14
    (*See also* Romantic movement)
Nazis
    abuses ignored by organized religion   S1.1:267–8
    achieving dictatorship   4:158
    anti-Semitism fostering emigration of Jews   4:102
    brutality   S1.2:64
    condemnation of *All Quiet on the Western Front*   3:13
    countries conquered by   5:123 (sidebar)
    escaping to Argentina   5:210
    execution of Remarque's sister   3:14
    as fascists   S1.2:116, 123
    Great Depression enhancing appeal of facism   3:129
    Hitler Youth Movement   S1.1:268
    nationalism of   1:294
    neo-nazis   4:163–4
    plans for extermination of Jews and "undesirables"   3:124
    rabid racism and belief in Aryan superiority   4:158, 193, 5:42
    remilitarization of Germany   4:356–7
    rise of and consolidation of power   4:157, 158, 356–7
    (*See also* Holocaust; World War II)
Nebraska   3:257–8, 260, S1.1:282–3, 288–9
"Necklace, The," Maupassant, Guy de   2:244 8
Nehru "Dynasty"   S1.2:332 (sidebar), 333
Nehru, Jawaharlal   S1.2:132, 151, 152, 329
Nehru, Motilal   S1.2:329
Neihardt, John G., *Black Elk Speaks*   2:66–73
Neoclassicism   S1.1:113, 207–8
Neocolonialism   S1.2:131
Neruda, Pablo   5:164, 168
New Deal *See under* Great Depression, The
New England
    agricultural decline   2:125–6
    Boston   3:43
    Boston Tea Party   1:125
    Massachusetts   1:78–80, 355, 395–7
"New Journalism"   5:293
Newman, John Henry, Cardinal   S1.1:295
New Mexico
    Chicano life in   4:45, 171
    Gallup   4:83
    Hispanos   S1.2:339–44, 346–7
    Laguna Pueblo   4:79–80, 85
    Los Alamos   4:81, 316–17
    Manhattan Project   4:71, 81–2, 316–17
    Sagrado   4:318
    Tierra Amarilla   4:174
    Trinity Site detonation of atom bomb   4:81–2
    Walatowa (Jemez Pueblo)   4:187

WWII village life 4:318–21
"New Negro" S1.1:336, 432
New Netherland (New York) 1:211, 212
New Orleans 3:15
Newspapers
    Mexican, self-censorship S1.2:91 (*sidebar*)
    origins of 1:268
    "yellow journalism" 3:279
Newton, Huey P. 4:54
Newton, Sir Isaac 1:24, 94
"New Woman" S1.1:80–1, 181–2, 441–2, S1.2:105
New York
    beats S1.2:364 5
    Brooklyn 3:397–8, 4:88, 5:149–51
    Chinatown 4:126
    Dutch in (New Netherland) 1:211, 212, 330–2, 333 (*illus.*), 335 (*sidebar*), 336
    Hudson Valley 1:330–2, 333 (*illus.*), 334 5, 336
    in late 18th century 1:107–8, 110
    Mohawk Valley 1:108, 110, 112 (*illus.*)
    New York City 2:301–7, 313, 3:146–7
        Central Park 4:401
        "garbage riots" (1969) 5:220 (*sidebar*)
        Haitians S1.2:247
        Harlem and Harlem Renaissance 3:159–65, 256, 321, 384 5, 421, 4:204 (*sidebar*), 207, 247–8, 5:67–8, S1.1:336–8, 337 (*sidebar*), 432–4
        Harlem's Cotton Club S1.1:337
        Manhattan's West Side 4:384 9, 400–1
        Puerto Ricans 4:385–6, 388–9, 401, 5:214 21
        Spanish Harlem (*El Barrio*) 5:214, 216–17
        tenements in slums S1.1:3 (*sidebar*)
        Tweed Ring 2:306–7
        Tammany Hall 3:148–9, 398–9
Niagara Movement (1905) 3:250, 320
Nicholas I, Czar of Russia S1.1:52, 100–1
Nicholas II, Czar of Russia 3:121, 232, S1.1:119, 368
Nichols, John, *Milagro Beanfield War, The* S1.2:339–47
Nietzsche, Friedrich 3:54, S1.1:52 (*sidebar*), 68
Nigeria 2:360–2, 364 5, 3:84, 4:314, S1.2:39–48
Night, Wiesel, Elie 4:267–73
Nihilism S1.1:54, 105 (*sidebar*), 380, S1.2:179, 445, 470
Nineteen Eighty-Four, Orwell, George 5:251–8
    as dystopian 5:100
Nirvana 1:366, 367
Nixon, Richard
    "kitchen debate" with Khrushchev 4:398, 399 (*illus.*), 5:321–2
    loss to Kennedy attributed to poor appearance on TV 5:223
    re-election signifying anti-black backlash S1.2:429
    use of anti-communism for campaign 5:96

visit to Communist China 5:358
    Watergate scandal 3:99, 5:158–9, 263, 317
Nobel, Alfred S1.1:226–7
"Noon Wine," Porter, Katherine Anne 3:243–8
Nordhoff, Charles, *Mutiny on the Bounty* 1:273–9
Norman Conquest of Anglo-Saxon England 1:181, 250–1, 290
Norse myths 1:50, 152, 153, 156, S1.1:166
North Carolina 2:168
North Dakota 5:244
Norway 1:137–8, 2:111–13, S1.1:159 62
"Notorious Jumping Frog of Calaveras County, The," Twain, Mark 2:249–54
Notre Dame cathedral 1:161, 162 (*illus.*), 163, 164 (*sidebar*)
Not without Laughter, Hughes, Langston 3:249–56
Novellas
    Awakening, The, Chopin, Kate 3:15–20
    Daisy Miller, James, Henry 2:105–10
    Heart of Darkness, The, Conrad, Joseph 2:145–51
    Little Gipsy Girl, The, Cervantes Saavedra, Miguel de S1.1:189–98
    Of Mice and Men, Steinbeck, John 3:269–76
    Turn of the Screw, The, James, Henry 2:378–83
Novels
    Across Five Aprils, Hunt, Irene 2:8–14
    Adventures of Don Quixote, The, Cervantes Saavedra, Miguel de 1:1–7
    Adventures of Huckleberry Finn, The, Twain, Mark 2:15–21
    Age of Innocence, The S1.1:1–9
    Alice's Adventures in Wonderland, Carroll, Lewis 2:28–33
    All Creatures Great and Small, Herriott, James 3:1–7
    All the Pretty Horses, McCarthy, Cormac S1.2:9–17
    All Quiet on the Western Front, Remarque, Erich Maria 3:8–14
    Animal Farm, Orwell, George 4:14 20
    Anna Karenina, Tolstoy, Leo 2:34 40, S1.1:368
    Annie John, Kincaid, Jamaica S1.2:19–27
    Antelope Wife, The, Erdrich, Louise S1.2:29–37
    Anthills of the Savannah, Achebe, Chinua S1.2:39–49, 203
    April Morning, Fast, Howard S1.1:11–20
    Aunt Julia and the Scriptwriter, Vargas Llosa, Mario S1.2:51–61
    Autobiography of Miss Jane Pittman, The, Gaines, Ernest J. 5:19–26
    Babbitt, Lewis, Sinclair 3:21–7, S1.1:289
    Bean Trees, The, Kingsolver, Barbara 5:27–33
    Beauty: A Retelling of the Story of Beauty and the Beast,
    McKinley, Robin 1:30–6
    Bell Jar, The, Plath, Sylvia 4:21–7
    Beloved, Morrison, Toni 2:59–65
    Benito Cereno, Melville, Herman 1:37–43
    Betsey Brown, Shange, Ntozake 4:28–34

Index

Novels (*continued*)
- *Billy Budd*, Melville, Herman **1**:51–6
- *Bless the Beasts and Children*, Swarthout, Glendon **5**:34 8
- *Bless Me, Ultima*, Anaya, Rudolfo A. **4**:42–8
- *Blindness*, Saramago, José **S1.2**:63–71
- *Bluest Eye, The*, Morrison, Toni **4**:49–57
- *Brave New World*, Huxley, Aldous **5**:39–45
- *Bull from the Sea, The*, Renault, Mary **1**:57–63
- *Caine Mutiny, The*, Wouk, Herman **4**:58–65
- *Call of the Wild, The*, London, Jack **3**:51–6
- *Candide*, Voltaire, François Marie Arouet de **S1.1**:21–30
- *Carrie*, King, Stephen **5**:46–52
- *Catch-22*, Heller, Joseph **4**:66–72
- *Catcher in the Rye*, Salinger, J. D. **4**:73–8
- *Ceremony*, Silko, Leslie Marmon **4**:79–86
- *Childhood's End*, Clarke, Arthur **5**:53–60
- *Chocolate War, The*, Cormier, Robert **5**:61–6
- *Chosen, The*, Potok, Chaim **4**:87–93
- *Cold Sassy Tree*, Burns, Olive Ann **3**:75–9
- *Color Purple, The*, Walker, Alice **3**:80–7
- *Confessions of Nat Turner, The*, Styron, William **2**:93–8
- *Contender, The*, Lipsyte, Robert **5**:67–73
- *Count of Monte-Cristo, The*, Dumas, Alexandre **2**:99–104
- *Crime and Punishment*, Dostoyevsky, Fyodor **S1.1**:51–60, 368, **S1.2**:200
- *Cry, the Beloved Country*, Paton, Alan **4**:94 100
- *Dandelion Wine*, Bradbury, Ray **3**:88–93, **S1.2**:309
- *Dawn*, Wiesel, Elie **4**:101–8
- *Day No Pigs Would Die, A*, Peck, Robert Newton **3**:94 9
- *The Death of Artemio Cruz*, Carlos Fuentes **S1.2**:83–94
- *Death in the Family, A*, Agee, James **3**:100–5
- *Death of Ivan Ilyich, The*, Tolstoy, Leo **S1.1**:71–8
- *Dinner at the Homesick Restaurant*, Tyler, Anne **S1.2**:105–13
- *Donald Duk*, Chin, Frank **5**:74 80
- *Dracula*, Stoker, Bram **S1.1**:79–87, 140, 146
- *Drums Along the Mohawk*, Edmonds, Walter D. **1**:107–14
- *Dry White Season, A*, André Brink **S1.2**:115–24
- *Dune*, Herbert, Frank **5**:81–7
- *Eat a Bowl of Tea*, Chu, Luis **4**:124 30
- *Emma*, Austen, Jane **S1.1**:89–97
- *English Patient, The*, Ondaatje, Michael **S1.2**:125–32
- *Ethan Frome*, Wharton, Edith **2**:125–9
- *Fahrenheit 451*, Bradbury, Ray **5**:95–100, **S1.2**:309
- *Fallen Angels*, Myers, Walter Dean **5**:101–6
- *Farewell to Arms, A*, Hemingway, Ernest **3**:112–18
- *Fathers and Sons*, Turgenev, Ivan **S1.1**:99–106, 368
- *Felicia's Journey*, Trevor, William **S1.2**:133–40
- *Fixer, The*, Malamud, Bernard **S1.1**:117–28
- *Flowers for Algernon*, Keyes, Daniel **4**:151–6
- *Fools Crow*, Welch, James **S1.1**:129–38, **S1.2**:168
- *Foundation*, Asimov, Isaac **5**:122–8
- *Frankenstein*, Shelley, Mary **1**:115–21
- *Friedrich*, Richter, Hans Peter **4**:157–64
- *Gathering of Old Men, A*, Gaines, Ernest J. **5**:129–34
- *God of Small Things, The*, Roy, Arundhati **S1.2**:151–60
- *Golden Notebook, The*, Lessing, Doris **4**:165–70
- *Gone with the Wind*, Mitchell, Margaret **2**:137–44
- *Good Earth, The*, Buck, Pearl S. **3**:131–7
- *Grand Avenue*, Sarris, Greg **S1.2**:161–9
- *Grapes of Wrath, The*, Steinbeck, John **3**:138–45, **S1.2**:267, 347
- *Great Expectations*, Dickens, Charles **S1.1**:149–58
- *Great Gatsby, The*, Fitzgerald, F. Scott **3**:146–52
- *Grendel*, Gardner, John **S1.2**:171–81
- *Gulliver's Travels*, Swift, Jonathan **1**:129–35, **S1.1**:29
- *Handmaid's Tale, The*, Atwood, Margaret **5**:135–42
- *Heart of Aztlán*, Anaya, Rudolfo A. **4**:171–6
- *Heart Is a Lonely Hunter, The*, McCullers, Carson **3**:153–8
- *Hero Ain't Nothin' but a Sandwich, A*, Childress, Alice **5**:143–8
- *His Own Where*, Jordan, June **5**:149–55
- *Hobbit, The*, Tolkien, J.R.R. **1**:152–8, **S1.2**:301
- *Home to Harlem*, McKay, Claude **3**:159–65
- *Hound of the Baskervilles*, Doyle, Arthur Conan **2**:152–9
- *House Gun, The*, Gordimer, Nadine **S1.2**:195–204
- *House Made of Dawn*, Momaday, N. Scott **4**:185–92, **S1.1**:137
- *House of Mirth, The*, Wharton, Edith **3**:166–73
- *House for Mr. Biswas, A*, Naipaul, V. S. **S1.2**:21, 183–93
- *House of Stairs*, Sleator, William **5**:156–62
- *House of the Spirits, The*, Allende, Isabel **5**:163–70
- *House on Mango Street, The*, Cisneros, Sandra **5**:171–7, **S1.2**:374
- *Human Comedy, The*, Saroyan, William **4**:193–200
- *Hunchback of Notre Dame, The*, Hugo, Victor **1**:159–65
- *I, Claudius*, Graves, Robert **S1.1**:169–78
- *I Heard the Owl Call My Name*, Craven, Margaret **5**:194 200
- *Imagining Argentina*, Thornton, Laurence **5**:208–13
- *In Nueva York*, Mohr, Nicholasa **5**:214 21
- *In the Time of the Butterflies*, Julia Alvarez **S1.2**:205–15

Invisible Man, Ellison, Ralph   4:209–15
Ishi, Last of His Tribe, Kroeber, Theodora   2:174 80
Ivanhoe, Scott, Sir Walter   1:181–8
Jacob Have I Loved, Paterson, Katherine   4:216–20
Jane Eyre, Brontë, Charlotte   1:415 (*sidebar*), 419, 2:181–7, S1.1:493, S1.2:24 5
Joy Luck Club, The, Tan, Amy   5:229–35
Jungle, The, Sinclair, Upton   3:174 80
Kim, Kipling, Rudyard   3:181–8
Kindred, Butler, Octavia   S1.2:227–37
Kitchen God's Wife, The, Tan, Amy   3:189–95
Last of the Mohicans, The, Cooper, James Fenimore   1:204 10
Left Hand of Darkness, The, LeGuin, Ursula   5:236–42
Lesson Before Dying, A, Gaines, Ernest J.   S1.2:249–58
Light in the Forest, The, Richter, Conrad   1:219–24
Like Water for Chocolate, Esquivel, Laura   3:196–202
Little Prince, The, Saint-Exupéry, Antoine de   3:210–17
Little Women, Alcott, Louisa May   2:202–8
Lolita, Nabokov, Vladimir   S1.2:279–86
Lord of the Flies, Golding, William   4:228–34
Lord of the Rings, The, Tolkien, J.R.R.   S1.2:178, 297–307
Love Medicine, Erdrich, Louise   5:243–50
Madame Bovary, Flaubert, Gustave   2:209–15
Maltese Falcon, The, Hammett, Dashiell   3:225–30
Man without a Face, The, Holland, Isabelle   4:240–6
Mark of the Horse Lord, The, Sutcliff, Rosemary   S1.1:229–38
Merry Adventures of Robin Hood, The, Pyle, Howard   1:250–7
Midnight's Children, Rushdie, Salman   S1.2:327–37
Milagro Beanfield War, The, Nichols, John   S1.2:339–47
Mill on the Floss, The, Eliot, George (Marian Evans)   S1.1:239–48
Les Misérables, Hugo, Victor   2:223–9
Moby Dick, Melville, Herman   2:230–5
Mutiny on the Bounty, Nordhoff, Charles and James Norman Hall   1:273–9
My Antonía, Cather, Willa   S1.1:281–90
Native Son, Wright, Richard   3:236–42
Native Speaker, Lee, Chang-rae   S1.2:349–55
Natural, The, Malamud, Bernard   4:260–6
Night, Wiesel, Elie   4:267–73
Nineteen Eighty-Four, Orwell, George   5:251–8
Not without Laughter, Hughes, Langston   3:249–56
Of Human Bondage, Maugham, W. Somerset   3:264 8

Old Gringo, The, Fuentes, Carlos   3:277–83
Old Man and the Sea, The, Hemingway, Ernest   4:274 80
Oliver Twist, Dickens, Charles   2:261–7
One Day in the Life of Ivan Denisovich, Solzhenitsyn, Alexander   4:281–7
One Flew over the Cuckoo's Nest, Kesey, Ken   4:288–94
One Hundred Years of Solitude, García Márquez, Gabriel   2:268–74
On the Road, Kerouac, Jack   4:75, S1.2:281, 357–66
O Pioneers!, Cather, Willa   3:257–63, S1.1:281
Ordinary People, Guest, Judith   5:259–64
Outsiders, The, Hinton, S. E.   5:265–70
Ox-Bow Incident, The, Clark, Walter Van Tilburg   2:288–94
Parrot in the Oven, Martinez, Victor   S1.2:367–77
Passage to India, A, Forster, E.M.   3:297–304
Passing, Larsen, Nella   S1.1:333–42
Pigman, The, Zindel, Paul   5:271–7
Pocho, Villarreal, José Antonio   4:295–302
Portrait of the Artist as a Young Man, A, Joyce, James   3:305–11
Praisesong for the Widow, Marshall, Paule   S1.2:387–95
Pride and Prejudice, Austen, Jane   2:295–300
Prime of Miss Jean Brodie, The, Spark, Muriel   4:303–8
Prince of Tides, The, Conroy, Pat   5:285–90
Ragged Dick, Alger, Horatio   2:301–7
Ragtime, Doctorow, E. L.   3:319–25
Rebecca, du Maurier, Daphne   3:326–33
Red Badge of Courage, The, Crane, Stephen   2:308–13
Red Pony, The, Steinbeck, John   3:334 7
Red Sky at Morning, Bradford, Richard   4:316–22
Road from Home, The, Kherdian, David   3:338–43
Robinson Crusoe, Defoe, Daniel   1:337–43
Roll of Thunder, Hear My Cry, Taylor, Mildred   3:350–5
Roots, Haley, Alex   5:298–305, S1.2:228, 236, 427
Runner, The, Voigt, Cynthia   5:306–13
Scarlet Letter, The, Hawthorne, Nathaniel   1:351–7
Scarlet Pimpernel, The, Orczy, Baroness Emmuska   1:358–64
Secret Agent, The, Conrad, Joseph   S1.1:377–85
Sense and Sensibility, Austen, Jane   S1.1:387–98
Separate Peace, A, Knowles, John   4:323–9
Shane, Schaefer, Jack   2:321–6
Shizuko's Daughter, Mori, Koyoko   S1.2:409–19
Shoeless Joe, Kinsella, W. P.   5:314 20
Siddhartha, Hesse, Hermann   1:365–70
Sister Carrie, Dreiser, Theodore   2:327–33
Slaughterhouse Five, Vonnegut, Kurt, Jr.   4:343–8

Novels (*continued*)
   Song of Solomon, Morrison, Toni   **S1.2**:421–30
   Sons and Lovers, Lawrence, D. H.   **2**:334 9
   Sounder, Armstrong, William H.   **3**:370–6
   Sound and the Fury, The, Faulkner, William   **S1.1**:417–28
   Stones For Ibarra, Doerr, Harriet   **S1.2**:431–9
   Story Catcher, The, Sandoz, Mari   **2**:347–52
   Strange Case of Dr. Jekyll and Mr. Hyde, The, Stevenson, Robert Louis   **3**:377–82, **S1.1**:185
   Stranger in a Strange Land, Heinlein, Robert A.   **5**:321–7
   Stranger, The, Camus, Albert   **S1.2**:441–9
   Summer of My German Soldier, Greene, Bette   **4**:371–7
   Sun Also Rises, The, Hemingway, Ernest   **S1.1**:439–47
   Sweet Whispers, Brother Rush, Hamilton, Virginia   **5**:328–32
   Tale of the Genji, The, Murasaki Shikibu   **S1.1**:449–61, **S1.2**:222
   Tale of Two Cities, A, Dickens, Charles   **1**:371–8
   Tess of the D'Urbervilles, Hardy, Thomas   **2**:353–9
   Their Eyes Were Watching God, Hurston, Zora Neale   **3**:383–9, **S1.2**:266
   Things Fall Apart, Achebe, Chinua   **2**:360–5, **S1.2**:203
   Things They Carried, The, O'Brien, Tim   **S1.2**:451–8
   Thousand Pieces of Gold, McCunn, Ruthanne Lum   **2**:366–71
   Three Musketeers, The, Dumas, Alexandre   **1**:386–92
   Time of the Hero, The, Vargas Llosa, Mario   **5**:333–8
   Tituba of Salem Village, Petry, Ann   **1**:393–9
   To Kill a Mockingbird, Lee, Harper   **3**:390–6
   To the Lighthouse, Woolf, Virginia   **S1.1**:463–72
   Tom Brown's Schooldays, Hughes, Thomas   **2**:372–7
   Treasure Island, Stevenson, Robert Louis   **1**:400–5
   Tree Grows in Brooklyn, A, Smith, Betty   **3**:397–403
   Trial, The, Kafka, Franz   **S1.1**:473–82
   Twenty-Thousand Leagues under the Sea, Verne, Jules   **2**:384 90
   Uncle Tom's Cabin, Stowe, Harriet Beecher   **2**:403–9
   Understand This, Tervalon, Jervey   **5**:339–45
   War of the Worlds, The, Wells, H.G.   **3**:404 10, **S1.1**:140, **S1.2**:314
   Watership Down, Adams, Richard   **5**:346–51
   Wide Sargasso Sea, Rhys, Jean   **S1.1**:493–502, **S1.2**:178
   Wuthering Heights, Brontë, Emily   **1**:413–19
   Yellow Raft in Blue Water, A, Dorris, Michael   **5**:360–6
Novels, types and innovations
   birth of   **1**:341–2
   Cather's framing device, inconsistent chronology, and plotting   **S1.1**:289
   crime stories and "Newgate Novels"   **2**:83, 267
   detective fiction   **2**:325, **3**:226–7, **S1.1**:267 (sidebar), 271
   "dime" novels with romance, adventure, and violence   **2**:306, **3**:226–7
   espionage novels   **S1.1**:385
   as fanciful, insufficiently instructivee   **S1.1**:95 (sidebar)
   as frivolous subliterature   **S1.1**:398
   Gothic horror stories and romances   **2**:81, 85, 185, **3**:338, **S1.1**:278, 501
   horror fiction   **5**:46–7
   Japanese defense of fiction   **S1.1**:459 (sidebar)
   pastoral novels   **1**:6
   protest novels   **S1.1**:126, 436
   Regency romances   **S1.1**:97
   romances   **5**:331, **S1.1**:95–6
   "stream of consciousness" writing   **3**:111, 358, **S1.1**:419 (sidebar), 420, 427, 471
   Tale of the Genji, The as world's first   **S1.1**:449–61, **S1.2**:222
   westerns   **2**:321, 325
NOW (National Organization of Women)   **1**:62, **4**:22, 394, **5**:136, 237
Nuclear energy   **5**:124, 127, 286
   Chernobyl disaster   **5**:286, 287 (illus.)
Nuclear weapons
   arms control   **4**:71, **5**:126, 225, 239, 252 (sidebar)
   arms race   **5**:252 (sidebar), **S1.2**:311
   hydrogen bomb   **4**:183
   (*See also* Atom bomb)

O

OAS (Organization of the American States)   **S1.2**:209
Oates, Joyce Carol, "Where Are You Going, Where Have You Been?"   **4**:391–6
Obeah (Caribbean shamanic folk religion)   **S1.1**:499 (sidebar), **S1.2**:21 (sidebar)
Oberth, Hermann   **S1.2**:311 (sidebar)
Obregón, Ivaro   **S1.2**:85, 86–7, 86 (sidebar)
O'Brien, Tim, *Things They Carried, The*   **S1.2**:451–8
Occultism   **S1.1**:81–2
"Occurrence at Owl Creek Bridge, An," Bierce, Ambrose   **2**:255–60, **3**:281
O'Connor, Flannery, "Everything That Rises Must Converge"   **5**:88–94
Octavian (Octavius Caesar)   **1**:12 (sidebar), 13
Octoroons   **3**:18
Odria, Manuel   **5**:333–4
Odyssey, Homer   **1**:280–7
   Odysseus in underworld   **1**:284 (illus.)
   parallels to *Ivanhoe*   **1**:187
Oedipus complex (Freud)   **2**:336–7, **S1.1**:321

Oedipus the King, Sophocles   **S1.1**:301–12
Oe, Kenzaburo, *Japan, the Ambiguous, and Myself*   **S1.2**:217–25
Of Human Bondage, Maugham, W. Somerset   **3**:264 8
Of Mice and Men, Steinbeck, John   **3**:269–76
Ohio River, Underground Railroad   **2**:16, 60
Oil booms of 1920s   **3**:45–6
Oil industry   **S1.2**:87
"Okies"   **3**:46, 47, 49
Oklahoma   **5**:29, 269
Old age. *See* Senior citizens
Old Gringo, The, Fuentes, Carlos   **3**:277–83
Old Man and the Sea, The, Hemingway, Ernest   **4**:274 80
"Old money" versus *nouveaux riches*   **3**:327, **S1.1**:1–3, 8
Oliver Twist, Dickens, Charles   **2**:261–7
Olympians   **1**:301
Once and Future King, The, White, T.H.   **1**:288–94, **S1.2**:174
Ondaatje, Michael, *English Patient, The*   **S1.2**:125–32
On Dreams, Freud, Sigmund   **S1.1**:200, 312, 313–22
One Day in the Life of Ivan Denisovich, Solzhenitsyn, Alexander   **4**:281–7
One Flew over the Cuckoo's Nest, Kesey, Ken   **4**:288–94, **5**:318 (*sidebar*)
One Hundred Years of Solitude, García Márquez, Gabriel   **2**:268–74
O'Neill, Eugene, *Long Day's Journey into Night*   **3**:218–24
"One of These Days," García Márquez, Gabriel   **S1.2**:459–66
Ongpatonga   **1**:209 (*illus.*)
On the Origin of Species, Darwin, Charles   **S1.1**:80, 139–40, 246, 274, 323–31, **S1.2**:299
On the Road, Kerouac, Jack   **4**:75, **S1.2**:281, 357–66
"Open Window, The," Saki   **2**:275–80
O Pioneers!, Cather, Willa   **3**:257–63
Opium addiction   **S1.1**:215
Oppenheimer, Robert   **4**:316
Oracles and Sphinx   **S1.1**:303 (*sidebar*), 304 (*illus.*), 306–8, 309 (*illus.*)
Oral storytelling
  African Americans' oral tradition   **5**:298–300, 301–2
  Haitian   **5**:298–300, 301–2
  as key element of African societies   **S1.2**:425 (*sidebar*), 426
  oral tradition and griots   **5**:298–300, 301–2
  revival of Kiowa oral tradition   **S1.2**:484 5
Orczy, Baroness Emmuska, *Scarlet Pimpernel, The*   **1**:358–64
Ordinary People, Guest, Judith   **5**:259–64
Oregon Trail   **S1.1**:131
"Organic connectedness"   **S1.2**:179
Organization of African Unity (OAU)   **S1.2**:43

Organization of the American States (OAS)   **S1.2**:209
Orozco, José Clemente   **S1.2**:88
Orwell, George
  Animal Farm   **4**:14 20
  "Lion and the Unicorn, The"   **S1.2**:473
  Nineteen Eighty-Four   **5**:251–8
  Shooting an Elephant   **S1.1**:399–406
Osborne, Sarah   **1**:79, 395, 396
Ospina Pérez, Mariano   **S1.2**:460, 461, 461 (*sidebar*)
Othello, Shakespeare, William   **1**:295–300
Ottoman Turks   **1**:295–6, **3**:338–40
Our Town, Wilder, Thornton   **3**:284 9
Out of Africa, Dinesen, Isak   **3**:290–6
"Outcasts of Poker Flat, The," Harte, Bret   **2**:281–7
Outsiders, The, Hinton, S. E.   **5**:265–70
Ovid, *Metamorphoses*   **1**:262
Owen, Robert   **S1.1**:44
Owen, Sir Richard   **S1.1**:325
Ox-Bow Incident, The, Clark, Walter Van Tilburg   **2**:288–94

P

Pabel, Reinhold   **4**:373 (*sidebar*)
Pacificism   **1**:23 (*sidebar*), 142, 365, 369, 370
Padilla, Heberto   **S1.2**:59
Paine, Thomas
  Common Sense   **1**:71–7, 94
  opposition to slavery   **1**:72 (*sidebar*)
  The Rights of Man   **1**:52, **S1.1**:387
Pakistan   **3**:300, 301
  conflicts with India   **S1.2**:329 (*sidebar*), 330–2
Paláez, Manuel   **S1.2**:87
Palestine   **4**:102–3, 105, **5**:54
  (*See also* Israel)
Paley, William   **S1.1**:324 5
Pamphlets
  by Swift   **1**:132
  Common Sense, Paine, Thomas   **1**:71–7
  Modest Proposal, A, Swift, Jonathan   **1**:266–72
  popularity in England   **1**:268
  popularity and limitations in colonies   **1**:72–3, 122
Panama Canal   **3**:231–2, 270
Pankhurst, Emmeline   **2**:335–6, **3**:359
Pappenheim, Bertha   **S1.1**:316
Paradise Lost, Milton, John   **1**:301–8
  influence on Herman Melville   **1**:54
  popularity in America   **1**:307
"Parallelism"   **S1.1**:325
Paranormal phenomena   **2**:383 (*sidebar*), **5**:47–8, 56, 239
Paredes, Américo   **5**:172
Paris, France
  as capital of western art   **3**:265–6
  Notre Dame cathedral   **1**:161, 162 (*illus.*), 163, 164 (*sidebar*)

Index

Paris (Trojan prince)   1:8, 166, 281
Parks
   Navajo Tribal   S1.2:99
   U. S. National   S1.2:95–8, 96 (sidebar), 99–102
Parks, Rosa   3:73, 5:11, 88, 185, S1.2:270–1
Parnell, Charles   3:109–10
Parody   1:4
Parole   S1.1:158
Parris, Rev. Samuel   1:79, 83 (sidebar), 394, 395, 421
Parrot in the Oven, Martinez, Victor   S1.2:367–77
Parthenon   1:240
"Parting at Morning," Browning, Robert   S1.1:291–9
Passage to India, A, Forster, E.M.   3:297–304
Passing, Larsen, Nella   S1.1:333–42
Pastoral novels   1:6
Paterson, Katherine, *Jacob Have I Loved*   4:216–20
Paton, Alan, *Cry, the Beloved Country*   4:94 100
Paxton Boys massacre   1:220–1, 221 (illus.)
Paz, Octavio
   on limits of Mexicans' faith   S1.2:501
   on Mexicans and exploitation   S1.2:93
Peace Corps   S1.1:20
Peck, Robert Newton, *Day No Pigs Would Die, A*   3:94 9
Peloponnesian War   1:241, 324, 328, S1.1:311–12, 352
Pennsylvania   1:22, 71–2, 310
   Pittsburgh   4:7–9, 144, 149
Percy family   1:144 5, 149
Pericles of ancient Athens   1:17, 18, 240, 241, 322
Periodicals, rise of   S1.1:273 (sidebar), 274
Perón, Juan and Eva   5:208–9, 210
Persephone   1:283
Peru   4:221, 222, 5:333–8
Pesticides ("biocides")   4:337–42, 5:347, 351
Peter the Great, Czar   S1.1:71–2
Petrarch   1:345, 348
Petry, Ann, *Tituba of Salem Village*   1:393–9
Philadelphia, Pennsylvania   1:71–2, 310
Philanthropy. *See* Charity, philanthropy
Philip II of Macedon   S1.1:352, 353
Philippines   3:101
   Bataan Death March   4:81
Phillips, Wendell   2:89 (sidebar)
Philosophy
   Biblical scholarship and "higher criticism"   S1.1:295
   concept of "the absurd"   4:400, S1.2:406, 444 (sidebar), 476
   conflict with poetry   S1.1:345–6
   cosmology   S1.1:344
   dialectical materialism   S1.1:47 (sidebar)
   dialectic method   S1.1:352
   existentialism   S1.2:405–6, 443–5, 470–1
   historical materialism   S1.1:48
   humanism   1:2, 142, 233, 380, 381, 5:138, S1.1:107, 114 (sidebar), S1.2:223, 224 5
   individualism and capitalism versus collectivism and communalism   S1.2:346
   Leibnizian optimism   S1.1:21–2, 23 (sidebar)
   limits of   S1.1:28–9
   Manicheanism   S1.1:28
   materialistic view of universe   S1.2:179
   nihilism   S1.1:54, 105 (sidebar), 380, S1.2:179, 445, 470
   occultism   S1.1:81–2
   phrenology   S1.1:82 (sidebar)
   pre-Socratics   S1.1:344
   prophecy and gods   S1.1:306–8
   rationalism   S1.1:81
   Sartre and existentialism versus Whitehead and "organic connectedness"   S1.2:179, 405–6, 443–5, 470–1
   sensibility versus reason   S1.1:397 (sidebar)
   Socrates' vision of social critic   S1.1:349
   sophists   1:19, 240, S1.1:306, 344 5, 347 (sidebar)
   Theosophical Society   S1.1:82
   uses of dissatisfaction, endeavor, and error   S1.1:112–13
   utilitarianism   S1.1:32, 33 (sidebar), 295
Phoenician alphabet   1:286–7
Phonograph   S1.1:80
Photography   S1.1:287
Photojournalism   S1.2:262–3
Phrenology   2:211, S1.1:82 (sidebar)
Piano Lesson, The, Wilson, August   S1.2:379–86
"Picong" satire   S1.2:186–7
Picts   S1.1:229–30
Pigman, The, Zindel, Paul   5:271–7
Pilgrimages   1:64 70, 145–6, 182
Pilgrim at Tinker Creek, Dillard, Annie   5:278–84
Pilgrims   S1.1:485
Pinkerton's National Detective Agency   3:225–6
Pinochet, August   5:169 (illus.)
Piracy   1:400–2, 405
Pisarev, Dmitri   S1.1:54, 102
Pittsburgh, Pennsylvania   4:7–9, S1.2:380, 381, 381 (sidebar)
Plath, Sylvia, *Bell Jar, The*   4:21–7
Plato
   Academy   1:328
   complaining of Homer   1:285, 286 (sidebar)
   Plato's *Apology*   S1.1:343–53
   Republic   1:321–9, S1.1:309–10
Plato's *Apology*, Plato   S1.1:343–53
Playboy of the Western World, Synge, John Millington   S1.2:476
Plays
   All My Sons, Miller, Arthur   S1.2:1–8
   Angels in America, Kushner, Tony   5:1–10
   Antigone, Sophocles   1:14 21
   Belle of Amherst, The, Luce, William   2:54 8
   Biloxi Blues, Simon, Neil   4:35–41
   Blood Wedding, Lorca, Federico García   S1.2:73–82
   Cherry Orchard, The, Chekhov, Anton   3:57–62

Crucible, The, Miller, Arthur   1:78–86
Cyrano de Bergerac, Rostand, Edmond   1:87–92
Death of a Salesman, Miller, Arthur   4:109–15
Doll's House, A, Ibsen, Henrik   2:111–17
Elephant Man, The, Pomerance, Bernard   2:118–24
Faust, Goethe, Johann Wolfgang von   S1.1:107–16
Fences, Wilson, August   4:144 50
Fiddler on the Roof, Stein, Joseph   3:119–24
for colored girls who have considered suicide / when the rainbow is enuf, Shange, Ntozake   5:115–21
Glass Menagerie, The, Williams, Tennessee   S1.2:141–50
Hamlet, Shakespeare, William   1:136–43, S1.2:398
Hedda Gabler, Ibsen, Henrik   S1.1:159–68, S1.2:7
Henry IV, Part I, Shakespeare, William   1:144 51
Importance of Being Earnest, The, Wilde, Oscar   S1.1:179–87
I Never Sang for My Father, Anderson, Robert   5:201–7
Julius Caesar, Shakespeare, William   1:189–95
King Lear, Shakespeare, William   1:196–203
Little Foxes, The, Hellman, Lillian   3:203–10
Long Day's Journey into Night, O'Neill, Eugene   3:218–24
Macbeth, Shakespeare, William   1:225–30
Major Barbara, Shaw, George Bernard   S1.1:219–27
Man for All Seasons, A, Bolt, Robert   1:231–7
"MASTER HAROLD" and the boys, Fugard, Athol   S1.2:317–25
Medea, Euripides   1:238–41
Member of the Wedding, The, McCullers, Carson   4:254 9
Merchant of Venice, The Shakespeare, William   1:242–9
Midsummer Night's Dream, A, Shakespeare, William   1:258–65
Miracle Worker, The, Gibson, William   2:216–22
Misanthrope, The, Molière, Jean-Baptiste Poquelin de   S1.1:249–57
Murder in the Cathedral, Eliot, T.S.   S1.1:259–70
Oedipus the King, Sophocles   S1.1:301–12
Othello, Shakespeare, William   1:295–300
Our Town, Wilder, Thornton   3:284 9
Piano Lesson, The, Wilson, August   S1.2:379–86
Plato's Apology, Plato   S1.1:343–53
Playboy of the Western World, Synge, John Millington   S1.2:476
Pygmalion, Shaw, George Bernard   3:312–18
Raisin in the Sun, A, Hansberry, Lorraine   4:309–15
Richard III, Shakespeare, William   S1.1:355–66
Romeo and Juliet, Shakespeare, William   1:344 50
Rosencrantz and Guildenstern Are Dead, Stoppard, Tom   S1.2:178, 397–407
Streetcar Named Desire, A, Williams, Tennessee   4:364 70, S1.2:141
Tempest, The, Shakespeare, William   1:379–85
Twelfth Night, Or, What You Will, Shakespeare, William   S1.1:483–92
Twelve Angry Men, Rose, Reginald (screenplay)   4:378–83
Waiting for Godot, Beckett, Samuel   S1.2:467–76
West Side Story, Laurents, Arthur, et al.   4:384 90
Zoo Story, Albee, Edward   4:397–402
Zoot Suit, Valdez, Luis   4:403–10
Plays, types and innovations
   actors   S1.1:310
   by Sophocles   S1.1:308, 310
   choreopoems   5:115, 117–18, 120–1
   dramatic renaissance in Elizabethan Age   S1.2:399
   evolution from simple religious rituals   S1.1:310
   gender roles in Shakespeare's comedies   S1.1:490–1
   histories   1:150
   marriage of modern language and classical allusion   S1.1:259
   modern drama in verse   S1.1:259
   morality plays   1:148
   music halls and variety acts   S1.2:469
   revenge tragedies   1:142
   second English dramatic renaissance   S1.2:406
   Stoppard's settings without visible character   S1.2:397–8
   theater of "the absurd"   4:400, S1.2:406, 444 (sidebar), 476
Plessy v. Ferguson (Supreme Court ruling allowing segregation)   2:21, 341, 399–400, 413, 3:351, 375, 419, 4:1, 5:90, 107–8, S1.1:429, S1.2:256, 269–70
Plutarch   1:193–4, S1.1:307 (sidebar)
Pocho, Villarreal, José Antonio   4:295–302
Poe, Edgar Allan
   "Cask of Amontillado, The"   2:81–6
   "Murders in the Rue Morgue, The"   S1.1:271–9
Poetry
   Aeneid, The, Virgil   1:8–13
   Beowulf, Anonymous   1:44 50, S1.2:171, 176 (sidebar)
   Canterbury Tales, The, Chaucer, Geoffrey   1:64 70
   "Goblin Market, The," Rossetti, Christina   S1.1:139–47
   Iliad, Homer   1:166–73
   Inferno, Dante Alighieri   1:174 80
   In Memoriam, Tennyson, Alfred, Lord   S1.1:328–9

Poetry (*continued*)
   Leaves of Grass, Whitman, Walt   **2**:195–201
   Love Song of J. Alfred Prufrock, The, Eliot, T.S.   **S1.1**:199–206, 259
   Lyrical Ballads, Wordsworth, William, and Samuel Taylor Coleridge   **S1.1**:207–17
   "Meeting at Night" and "Parting at Morning," Browning, Robert   **S1.1**:291–9
   "My Last Duchess," Browning, Robert   **S1.1**:291–9
   Odyssey, Homer   **1**:280–7
   Paradise Lost, Milton, John   **1**:301–8
   "Prospice," Browning, Robert   **S1.1**:291–9
   Songs of Innocence and of Experience, Blake, William   **S1.1**:407–16
   Waste Land, The, Eliot, T.S.   **3**:411–259

Poetry, types and innovations
   Anglo-Saxon poetry   **S1.2**:178 (*sidebar*)
   ballad stanza   **S1.1**:212 (*sidebar*)
   blank verse   **1**:303 (*sidebar*)
   choreopoems   **5**:117–18
   conflict with philosophy   **S1.1**:345–6
   epic poems   **1**:49, 153, 172, 173, 282 (*sidebar*), 285
   haiku   **4**:333, 334
   Imagism   **S1.1**:205
   jazz-influenced approach   **S1.2**:363
   Lyrical Ballads as literary milestone   **S1.1**:212 (*sidebar*), 216 (*sidebar*)
   Romantic movement   **S1.1**:207–8
   waka poetry (Japanese)   **S1.1**:450
   Welsh regard for   **3**:64

Pogroms
   against Armenians   **3**:342
   against Jews. *See* Anti-Semitism

Poland
   of 1800s   **2**:384 5
   "capitalists" deported from, by Soviets   **4**:131–2
   Nazi invasion of   **3**:214, **4**:193
   Stalin-Hitler partition agreement   **4**:17, 131

"Polis" or Greek city-state   **1**:286, 327–8

Political parties in America
   American Communist Party   **3**:40
   Democratic, as party of Irish Americans   **3**:401–2
   Democratic South becoming Republican   **3**:79
   Republicans of Progressive era   **3**:286
   Socialist Labor Party   **3**:174 5
   ward bosses   **3**:398
   Whigs, Democrats, and Republicans   **2**:2, 87

Politics, political movements
   activism and Native American Renaissance   **S1.2**:164 5
   anarchism   **S1.1**:62, 378–80, 379 (*sidebar*)
   babouvistes   **S1.1**:45
   Burmese   **S1.1**:400–1
   campaigning in mid-19th century   **2**:2
   chartism   **S1.1**:31–2, 43
   Chinese American influence on   **4**:126–7
   during Reconstruction, African Americans in   **2**:412
   enactment of income tax   **3**:285, 320
   enactment of referenda provisions   **3**:285
   first recall act   **3**:319
   involvement versus liberal complacency   **S1.2**:202
   Irish American neighborhoods   **3**:398–9
   Korean American activism   **S1.2**:354 (*sidebar*)
   Mexican students in Tlatelolco massacre   **S1.2**:438
   New York's Tammany Hall   **3**:148–9, 398–9
   nihilism   **S1.1**:105 (*sidebar*), 380
   politicians' invocation of Lincoln   **2**:7
   Russian radicals versus conservatives   **S1.1**:53–4
   "superfluous man" concept   **S1.1**:105 (*sidebar*)
   Teapot Dome scandal   **3**:25
   televised debates costing Nixon 1960 presidential election   **5**:223
   terrorists and revolutionaries of late 1800s   **S1.1**:378–80
   (*See also* Civil rights movement; Terrorism)

Polygamy, in 10th-century Japan   **S1.1**:454
Polynesia   **4**:222
Pomerance, Bernard, *Elephant Man, The*   **2**:118–24
Pomo Indians   **S1.2**:161–2, 163–5, 163 (*sidebar*), 165 (*sidebar*), 167–8
Poorhouses, almshouses in 18th-century America   **2**:216, 219 (*sidebar*)
Poor Richard's Almanac, Franklin, Benjamin   **1**:309–15
Pope, Alexander   **1**:343, **S1.1**:23 (*sidebar*)

Popes
   Boniface VIII   **1**:176, 177
   competing for control of Tuscany   **1**:174
   conflicts with Holy Roman Emperors   **1**:174, 176, 344, 345
   fathering children   **1**:296

Pornography
   Lolita as tragedy   **S1.2**:285 (*sidebar*)
   prevalence in Victorian Age   **3**:381

Porter, Katherine Anne, "Noon Wine"   **3**:243–8
Portrait of the Artist as a Young Man, A, Joyce, James   **3**:305–11
   as example of bildungsroman   **3**:264, 311
Portugal, Lisbon earthquake (1755)   **S1.1**:22–4, 26 (*illus.*)
"Positivism"   **3**:213
Postcolonial literature   **S1.1**:501
Post-Impressionism   **S1.1**:463–4
Post-traumatic stress disorder   **5**:106, **S1.1**:455 (*sidebar*)
Potato famines in Ireland   **S1.1**:324
Potlatch ceremony of Kwakiutl   **5**:198 (*illus.*), 199
Potok, Chaim, *Chosen, The*   **4**:87–93
Pound, Ezra   **3**:413–14, 416, **5**:42
Poynings Law   **1**:267
Prague   **S1.1**:475 (*sidebar*)
Prairie Years, The. *See* Abraham Lincoln: The Prairie Years

Praisesong for the Widow, Marshall, Paule   S1.2:387–95
Predestination   4:304, S1.1:308
Prejudice. *See* Racism and prejudice
Premarital sex   5:324
Pre-Raphaelite brotherhood   S1.1:139, 146–7
Presbyterianism   4:10, 304
Presley, Elvis   4:172, 386
Pre-Socratics   S1.1:344
Pride and Prejudice, Austen, Jane   2:295–300
Prime of Miss Jean Brodie, The, Spark, Muriel   4:303–8
Primitivism   3:385 (*sidebar*)
Primogeniture   S1.1:91, 388–9, 497 (*sidebar*)
Prince, The, Machiavelli, Niccolò   1:316–20
    influence in early 16th century   1:233
    influence upon Shakespeare   1:200, 380
Prince of Tides, The, Conroy, Pat   5:285–90
Printing and publishing
    advances in   1:160, 162 (*sidebar*), 2:234, 306, 419
    Candide   S1.1:29
    chapbooks (pamphlets)   S1.1:108
    Dickens's revolution in   S1.1:156 (*sidebar*)
    first penny paper (*New York Sun*)   S1.1:273 (*sidebar*)
    muckraking magazines   3:176
    paperback books   2:325
    pulp magazines   2:325, 3:226–7
    rise of periodicals   S1.1:273 (*sidebar*), 274
    short stories in magazines   S1.1:278
Prisons   3:371, 374 (*illus.*)
Privateers   1:400
Proctor, John   1:81 (*sidebar*), 83 (*sidebar*)
Progress, belief in
    destroyed by WWI   3:412
    fostered by Enlightenment (Age of Reason)   1:24 5, 268, 2:416
    Goethe's objections to   S1.1:115
    H. G. Wells's objections to   3:409
    implying hierarchy of species or races   S1.1:140, 328, 334, S1.2:134
    reality belying   3:217, 227
    science and technology ("positivism") as 19th century's evidence for   2:416, 3:213
    Second Great Awakening contributing to   2:417–18
    Stephen Crane's objections to   2:313
    tempered by Victorians' doubt   3:314
    utopian philosophies of 19th century   2:195
    widely accepted except by Darwin   S1.1:330–1
    (*See also* Evolution; Science and technology)
Prohibition
    disillusionment with   3:69, 227, 401
    as Eighteenth Amendment   S1.1:439
    fostering corruption, bootlegging, and gangsterism   3:69, 147–8, 366–7, 401, S1.1:439–40
    restrictions retained in South   4:207 (*sidebar*)
    in San Francisco   3:226

    support by Anti-Saloon League and temperance movements   2:25 (*sidebar*), 85–6, 3:69, 75, 147, 401
    support from rural, anti-urban areas   3:69–70
    Volstead Act   3:147, 151, 401
    weaknesses of, as legislation   3:22–3, 69
    (*See also* Alcohol and alcoholism)
Project 100,000, draft of disadvantaged for Vietnam   5:102–3, 158, 307
Proletariat   S1.1:46
Propaganda
    as aspect of fascism   4:304, 5:253
    pro-war, from Hollywood   4:325
    use by British   5:252, 257
    use by Soviets   5:252
    use of media for   4:66–7
Prophecy and gods   S1.1:306–8
"Prospice," Browning, Robert   S1.1:291–9
Prosser, Gabriel   1:39, 42, 2:94
Prostitution
    in China   3:135
    in England in early 20th century   S1.1:226
    of female Chinese immigrants   2:366–7
    male   S1.1:185
    near military installations   4:37
    serving gold miners of California   2:283–4
    in Victorian Age   S1.1:141–2, 247
    women driven to, by lack of work
        America of 1880s   2:328–9
        France of 1800s   2:228
        Victorian England   2:264, 355
    women kept as, for repayment of debts (Victorian London)   2:264
Protestantism
    African Methodist Episcopal Church   3:83
    all-black churches   3:250, 252
    Anglican Church (Church of England)   1:78, 123, 129, 232, 233 (*sidebar*), 306, 351, 393
    anti-Catholic prejudice and policies   1:74, 132, 230, 269
    Baptists   5:19, 188
    Christian Socialist movement   2:377
    clergymen denouncing women's rights activists   2:25
    creationism   2:30
    decline of influence in late 18th century   1:102
    decline of influence in late 19th century   2:329
    Dutch Reformed Church   1:331, 425
    establishment of distinct denominations in colonial America   1:106
    evangelism in England   S1.1:90
    fundamentalists and New, Religious Right   5:137–9
    Great Awakening in American colonies   1:73, 106, 122, 424 5
    in Ireland   1:267, 269
    Methodism   2:357–8, S1.1:208–9
    Presbyterianism   4:10, 304
    as protest against abuses of Catholic Church   1:231

Protestantism (*continued*)
　Quakerism   1:23, 2:22, 25, 88–9
　as Reformation of Catholic Church   1:231, 2:113, S1.1:108
　revival meetings   1:425, 2:315–16
　Second Great Awakening in America   1:424 5, 2:23, 315–16, 404, 417–18
　segregation of churches   5:189
　Shakerism   3:95–9
　spread of, spurring legalization of divorce   2:113
　television evangelists   5:31–2
　Unitarianism   2:54, 315
　(*See also* Puritanism)
Protest movements. *See* Civil rights movement; Counterculture
Protest novels   S1.1:126, 436
"Protocols of the Elders of Zion"   S1.1:120 (*sidebar*), 441
Proudhon, Pierre Joseph   S1.1:45
Psychology
　before Freud   S1.1:316 (*sidebar*)
　behavior modification and conditioning   5:156–7
　changing views of mental illness   4:289
　conceptions of intelligence   4:152–3
　conflicting theories of nature of mankind   4:233–4
　connectedness of mental health and human relationships   4:153
　development of   3:329, 378, 4:77
　dreams and the unconscious   S1.1:67–8
　early study of human behavior and consciousness   S1.1:200
　ethical considerations of experimentation   4:153
　insistence on domesticity and dependence for women   4:167
　as means of rehabilitation of nonconformists   4:399
　paranormal phenomena   2:383 (*sidebar*), 5:47–8, 56, 239
　psychiatry   4:289 (*sidebar*)
　psychoanalysis   4:168 (*sidebar*), 5:42, 260–1, 262, S1.1:313, 316–21
　PTSD (post-traumatic stress disorder)   5:106
　schizophrenia and "split personalities"   S1.1:200
　theories of absent father   4:244 5
　theories of community collusion in evil   4:238
　twins and struggle for identity   4:219
　(*See also* Mental and emotional disabilities; Suicide)
Ptolemy   1:305
Puerto Rico, emigration to United States (1940–50s)   S1.2:504
Puerto Rico and Puerto Ricans   3:277, 4:385–6, 388–9, 401, 5:214–21
Pullman, George   S1.2:381
Punishments
　in 19th-century America   2:17
　in 19th-century France   2:225, 228
　aboard ships of Royal Navy   1:273–4, 275 (*illus.*)
　branding   1:420
　by Spanish Inquisition (garrocha, toca, and potro)   S1.1:190–1
　capital   4:379–80, 5:131, S1.1:151
　collective, in British colonies   2:362
　death penalty becomes rare   S1.1:158
　of drug users, racial inequality of   4:250
　dueling   1:389 (*sidebar*)
　in Elizabethan England   1:198 (*sidebar*)
　of English schoolboys   2:373–4
　exile, banishment from ancient Athens   S1.1:305 (*sidebar*), 306
　feuds   2:17 (*sidebar*)
　flogging   2:394, 395
　guillotining   1:373
　hazing on ship   2:394
　for homosexuality   S1.1:185, 186 (*sidebar*)
　inequality of, for blacks   5:16
　marooning   1:401–2
　Oedipus's self-blinding   S1.1:305 (*sidebar*)
　parole   S1.1:158
　poison   S1.1:344
　in Portugal in Salazar's prisons   S1.2:64 5
　prisons   3:371, 374 (*illus.*)
　prison terms   S1.1:151
　public hanging   1:374
　quartering   1:373–4
　of seamen   2:394, 395
　Siberian labor camps   S1.1:53
　in Southern prisons and road, chain gangs   3:371, 374 (*illus.*)
　in Soviet Union, Siberian exile and forced labor   4:132, 282
　tarring and feathering   2:17 (*sidebar*)
　transportation   S1.1:151
Puns
　in Shakespeare   1:348–9
　in Victorian Age   2:30
Puritanism
　Antinomians   1:352, 357
　austerity and discipline   1:78, 101, 393–4
　belief in witchcraft and Satan   1:79–81, 394, 395–6, 421–3
　Calvinism   2:54, 55, 3:377–8, 4:304
　closing down of playhouses   S1.2:399
　concept of conversion   2:55 (*sidebar*)
　Congregationalists   1:357, 424 5
　Defoe influenced by   1:338
　doctrines of   1:23, 101–2, 352, 393–4
　Franklin influenced by   1:311
　good works and redemption   1:23, 101–2, 352
　Half-Way Covenant   1:421
　hardships faced by colonists in New England   1:351
　immigration to New England   1:421
　intolerance   1:102, 394
　Milton influenced by   1:307

parenting styles in colonial New England
S1.1:18–19
Pilgrims   S1.1:485
as "purifier" of Church of England   1:299, 420,
S1.1:484 6
Separatist movement   S1.1:485
suppression of medieval Christmas traditions
S1.1:35
Pushkin, Aleksandr   S1.1:101 (sidebar)
Putnam, Ann   1:79, 83 (sidebar), 396
Pygmalion, Shaw, George Bernard   3:312–18
Pyle, Ernie   S1.2:3 (sidebar)
Pyle, Howard, *Merry Adventures of Robin Hood, The*
1:250–7
Pyramus and Thisbe   1:259 (sidebar)

Q

Quadroons   3:17–18
Quakerism   1:23, 2:22, 25, 88–9
Qualchan (Yakima warrior)   S1.2:290
Quarterstaff fencing   1:253
Quimby, Harriet   S1.2:495
Quixote. *See Adventures of Don Quixote, The*

R

Rabbits   5:336–7, 348 (*illus.*)
Racism and prejudice
American Communist Party's stand against
3:40, 4:211
in American jury system before 1969   4:379
(sidebar)
of Aryans, neo-Nazis, and neo-fascists   4:40,
50, 5:42
in concept of "white man's burden"   2:147,
3:170, 172, 182 (sidebar)
Cuban communism's attempts to overcome
S1.2:53
eliminating through claiming of identity   5:176
of eugenics movement   5:42
FEPC (Fair Employment Practices Commission)
to investigate   3:42
social Darwinism and theory of hierarchy of races
contributing to   2:341, S1.1:334, S1.2:305
(*See also* Holocaust; South Africa)
Racism and prejudice, against
African Americans
among immigrants   4:52
antiblack propaganda   2:400
Baldwin's condemnation of   5:111, 113
"black" accents and diction   S1.2:231–2
capital punishment and race   S1.2:257
in Caucasian standards of beauty   4:49–50
combated by DuBois   2:343–6
covert   4:314
creating self-hatred   4:53–4, 5:116
de facto segregation in North   S1.1:431
economic   4:30–1, 33
educated blacks targeted   S1.2:255
exacerbated by economic competition   2:43
Faulkner's evenhandedness   S1.1:425–6
housing discrimination   2:13, 3:39, 237,
4:30–1
Kerouac's naivete   S1.2:361–2
in legal and prison systems   3:371
by labor unions   2:341
Lincoln on   2:3, 5
in minstrel shows   2:16–17, 21, 398
mulattos passing as white   S1.1:335
in New South   2:399–400, 3:36–7, 41, 203,
320
in professional sports   4:149
race riots of early 20th century   2:6, 404,
3:160, 252, 321, 4:310, S1.1:335
race riots of 1940s   4:197, 201, 213, 247,
248 (*illus.*)
race and wrongful convictions   S1.2:257
"science" of ethnology contributing to
2:232–3
Scottsboro case   3:39, 239
sexual taboos   3:391
social Darwinism and theory of hierarchy of
races contributing to   2:341, S1.1:334
soldiers in WWII   4:212–13
stereotyping justifying slavery   1:39, 41, 42,
394, 2:403, 404
unwritten rules of racial deference
S1.2:254 5
as viewed by Styron   2:97
by white supremacists   3:352
(*See also* Ku Klux Klan; Lynching;
Segregation; Slavery)
African blacks   1:63, 2:360–5, 3:291, 4:94 100
Africans and other non-whites   S1.1:415
(sidebar)
American Indians. *See* American Indians
Anglos   4:320
Armenians   4:200
blacks of Brazil   S1.1:339 (sidebar)
Caribbean natives and creoles   S1.1:494 5, 496
(sidebar), 502
Chinese and Chinese Americans   2:175, 287,
367–8, 370 (sidebar), 371, 3:30, 4:124 7, 194,
330, 5:230–1
colonial subjects   S1.1:334
East Indians   S1.2:330
Germans during WWII   4:375
immigrants from Commonwealth to Britain
S1.1:238, 501–2
immigrants in general   4:194, S1.1:441
Irish   3:220, 221 (sidebar), S1.2:134 5
Japanese   3:30, 4:137, 138–43, 194, 195, 330–1
Jews. *See* Anti-Semitism
Korean Americans   S1.2:353–4, 353 (sidebar)
Latinos
deportations of braceros in 1930s   3:34, 4:44
mestizos or *criollos*   5:334 6
in Southwest   4:320
zoot suit riots of 1940s   4:295–7, 403–10

Racism and prejudice, against (*continued*)
    lower castes in India   **1**:366, **2**:183, **3**:182, 184, 300, **S1.2**:152–3
    migrant farm workers   **3**:29–30, 34, 49, 140–2, 143 (*sidebar*), 269–71, 275, 335, 337, **4**:297 (*sidebar*), **S1.2**:373
    Moors   **1**:297, 299, 300
    nonwhite immigrants   **S1.2**:474
    nonwhites of Trinidad   **S1.2**:184 6, 187–8, 190–1
    Poles   **4**:369
    in post-WWII South   **S1.2**:24 5
    "primitives" with justifications of social Darwinism   **S1.1**:85–6, 328, 330–1
    Spain's Gypsies   **S1.1**:191–2, 195–7, 197 (*sidebar*)
    users of sign language   **2**:217
Radio
    in 1920s America   **S1.2**:143
    Amos 'n' Andy show   **3**:364 5
    Dylan Thomas's broadcasts   **3**:66–7
    FDR taking advantage of   **3**:127, **S1.2**:143
    Lux Radio Theater   **3**:365
    new teenage audience of 1950s   **4**:386, 391
    Orson Welles' *War of the Worlds* broadcast   **3**:154, 365, 408 (*sidebar*), **S1.2**:143
    in Peru   **S1.2**:54
    popularity of   **3**:3, 45, 154, **S1.2**:143
    "thrillers" produced on   **3**:329
Ragged Dick, Alger, Horatio   **2**:301–7
"Ragged schools" in England   **S1.1**:32, 242 (*sidebar*)
Ragtime, Doctorow, E. L.   **3**:319–25
Raiche, Bessica   **S1.2**:495
Railroads
    in East Africa, "Lunatic Express"   **S1.2**:488
    in England   **2**:353, 354, 358
    in France   **2**:209–10
    in India   **3**:184 5
Railroads in the United States
    California population boom and   **2**:175, 195
    Chinese workers on   **4**:124, 125, **5**:75–7, 78 (*illus.*)
    contributing to western migration   **2**:327, **S1.1**:281, 282
    federal and state funding for expansion of   **2**:230
    hobo tradition of 1930s   **3**:46
    importance in Civil War   **2**:255, 256 (*illus.*)
    importance to travelers   **2**:175
    luxury travel in Pullman cars   **2**:306
    raising farm incomes   **2**:417
    refrigerated cars for transport of perishables   **2**:328, **3**:175
    Thoreau's disapproval of   **2**:416
Raisin in the Sun, A, Hansberry, Lorraine   **4**:309–15
Ranching. *See* Cattle ranching
Randolph, A. Philip   **3**:42, 159–60, **4**:255, **5**:186, 188

Ray, Satyajit   **S1.2**:155 (*sidebar*)
Reagan, Ronald   **S1.2**:310
Realism
    Bierce on   **2**:259–60
    of Crane   **2**:312
    described   **2**:259, **S1.1**:157
    of Dreiser   **2**:327, 331
    of Hurston   **S1.1**:436
    of Joyce, as "slice of life"   **3**:111
    levels of   **1**:4, 6 (*sidebar*)
    in literature for young adults   **5**:265–6, 276
    "magical"   **2**:271, 273, **3**:196, 202, **4**:48, **5**:169, 213, 330
    of *Les Misérables*   **2**:229
    versus stereotypes   **1**:42
    Whitman's impact on   **2**:200
Rebecca, du Maurier, Daphne   **3**:326–33
"Recapitulation"   **S1.1**:325
Reconnaissance planes   **5**:96
Reconstruction
    African Americans in politics   **2**:412
    Black Codes   **2**:412, **5**:21
    carpetbaggers and scalawags   **2**:141
    civil rights granted, then ignored   **2**:21, 340–1, 412
    demise of plantations and wilderness   **2**:49, 53
    economy of South   **2**:41–2
    education of freed slaves   **2**:411–12, 413, 414
    end of   **2**:412–13
    Force Acts (1871 and 1872)   **2**:412
    Freedman's Bureau   **2**:411
    in Georgia   **2**:139–40
    Ku Klux Klan   **2**:141 (*sidebar*), 143 (*sidebar*), 412
    lack of training or means of survival for freed slaves   **2**:59, 411
    sharecropping and tenant farming   **2**:42, 411
    violence and unequal justice for freed slaves   **5**:20–1
    white backlash following   **2**:340–1, 412–13
    (*See also* Jim Crow laws; Segregation)
Red Badge of Courage, The, Crane, Stephen   **2**:308–13
Red Pony, The, Steinbeck, John   **3**:334 7
Red Power movement   **2**:79 (*sidebar*)
"Red Scare"   **1**:84 6, **3**:105, **4**:71–2, **5**:2, 127 (*See also* Cold War)
Red Sky at Morning, Bradford, Richard   **4**:316–22
Reformation, Protestant   **1**:231, **2**:113, **S1.1**:108
Reform movements of 19th century
    child labor laws   **2**:103–4
    encouraged by belief in progress   **2**:195, 196
    multifaceted nature of   **2**:23
    as response to rapid change of Industrial Revolution   **2**:417
    settlement houses   **3**:397–8
    strengthened by Romantic movement   **2**:316
    temperance movement   **2**:25 (*sidebar*), 85, **3**:147
    utopian societies of 1840s   **2**:418
    women's involvement in   **2**:423

Reform movements of 20th century
    against child labor   3:76 (*sidebar*), 77 (*illus.*)
    during Progressive Era   3:75–6
    Independent Living Movement   2:123
    Pure Food and Drug Act (1906)   3:179
    temperance movement   3:69, 75, 147
    (*See also* Civil rights movement; Prohibition)
Refugees   5:28–9
Reincarnation   3:300
Reisman, David   4:75, 111, 382
Religion
    acceptance and resistance to Darwin's ideas
        S1.1:329, 330
    agnosticism   3:265
    of American Indians
        Black Elk as holy man, U.S. Government
            forbidding Sun Dance   2:71–2
        Chippewa *manitou*   5:246, 249 (*sidebar*)
        dreams and visions   S1.1:136, S1.2:30
        Ghost Dance   2:69, 77–8, S1.2:31
        healing ceremonies for returning war veterans
            5:363
        medicine bundles   S1.1:133 (*sidebar*)
        Navajo Night Chant   4:188
        Nez Percé   2:161
        Ojibwe   S1.2:30
        peyote of Kiowa   4:188
        Pueblo Indians   4:79
        Sun Dance   2:72, 349 (*sidebar*), 4:187–8,
            S1.1:133, 134 (*sidebar*), S1.2:480–2
        Yahi   2:178
    in ancient Greece   1:15–16, 169, S1.1:345
    ancient sacrificial rites   4:238
    Buddhism   1:365–9, 3:186–7, 5:48, S1.1:452,
        S1.2:414
    in China   3:133, 190, 193
    comparative conceptions of   5:57 (*sidebar*)
    conflicts with Darwinists   3:102, 404
    conflicts with non-believers in 20th century
        3:102
    cults   5:83–4
    Daoism (also Taoism)   5:237
    doubt and skepticism of late Victorian Age
        S1.1:80
    Eastern, in America   5:237
    freedom of, in America   1:73–4
    "Great Chain of Being"   1:201, 203, S1.1:208
    Haitian   S1.2:240 (*sidebar*)
    Hinduism   3:300, 302
    in India   1:366, 3:300–1
    Islam   1:296, 3:300
    Japanese Shinto   S1.1:452, S1.2:414
    miracles and paranormal phenomena   5:48
    monasticism   3:186–7
    moral sense directed toward political issues
        1:96
    Mormonism   5:4, S1.2:98
    Nation of Islam   3:238, 325, 4:56, 248–50,
        5:12–13, 69, 110–11, 302, S1.2:276
    natural theology   S1.1:324 5

    Obeah (Caribbean shamanic folk religion)
        S1.1:499 (*sidebar*), S1.2:21 (*sidebar*)
    occultism   S1.1:81–2
    People's Temple and Jim Jones   5:84
    pilgrimages   1:64
    rationalistic versus mystical, emotional   1:425,
        3:426
    reincarnation   3:300
    of Roman Britain   S1.1:232–3
    of Roman soldiers (Mithras)   S1.1:233
    versus science in Victorian Age   2:29–30, 121–2
    sutras (Buddhist scriptures)   S1.1:453 (*sidebar*)
    syncretism   3:190–1, 4:44 (*sidebar*)
    tolerance in colonial America   S1.1:15 (*sidebar*)
    transcendentalism   1:356–7, 2:54, 92, 314,
        316–19, 416, 418–19
    Unification Church   5:83
    Unitarianism   S1.1:209
    Zen Buddhism   4:334
    (*See also* Christianity; Greek myth; Jews; Sin and damnation)
Remarque, Erich Maria, *All Quiet on the Western Front*   3:8–14
Renaissance   1:2, 380, S1.1:107
Renan, Ernest   3:213
Renault, Mary, *Bull from the Sea, The*   1:57–63
Republican Party of 1830s   2:2
Republic, Plato   1:321–9, S1.1:309–10
Requiem, Akhmatova, Anna
Resistance movements, French during WWII
    S1.2:467–9, 469 (*sidebar*)
"Resurrection men"   1:120–1
Retirement, problems of adjustment to   5:203, 273
Reuther, Walter   S1.2:144
Revival meetings   1:425
Revolution, French. *See* France in 18th century: French Revolution
Revolutions of 1848   1:376
Rhetoric
    of Churchill's speeches   4:361–2
    in colonial America   1:123
    of Kennedy's speeches   5:223
    of King's oratory   5:186
Rhodesia   4:165–6
Rhys, Jean, *Wide Sargasso Sea*   S1.1:493–502,
    S1.2:178
Ricardo, David   S1.1:48
Richard I of England (the Lion-Hearted)   1:181–2,
    184 (*illus.*), 188, 251
Richard II of England   1:144
Richard III, Shakespeare, William   S1.1:355–66,
    S1.2:400
Richard III of England (previously duke of
    Gloucester)   S1.1:358–61, 359 (*sidebar*), 363–4,
    366 (*sidebar*)
Richelieu, Cardinal Duc de   1:387–9
Richter, Conrad, *Light in the Forest, The*   1:219–24
Richter, Hans Peter, *Friedrich*   4:157–64
Riegner, Gerhardt,   3:403
Right Stuff, The, Wolfe, Tom   5:291–7

Index

Riis, Jacob   3:169 (*sidebar*), 285, 320
"Rime of the Ancient Mariner, The," Coleridge, Samuel Taylor   S1.1:208, 210–11, 213, 216
"Rip Van Winkle," Irving, Washington   1:330–6
Risberg, Charles "Swede"   3:149
Rivera, Diego   S1.2:88, 89 (*illus.*)
Road from Home, The, Kherdian, David   3:338–43
Roberts, Oral   5:31–2
Robeson, Paul   1:389–90, S1.1:436
Robespierre, Maximilien   1:359 (*illus.*), 372
Robinson Crusoe, Defoe, Daniel   1:337–43
Robinson, Jackie   4:146, S1.2:251 (*sidebar*)
Rockefeller, John D.   2:306
"Rocking-Horse Winner, The," Lawrence, D.H.   3:344 9
Rock 'n' roll   4:172, 386, 391–2
Rodeo   5:362, 364 (*sidebar*)
Rodriguez, Richard, *Hunger of Memory, A: An Autobiography*   5:178–84, S1.2:370
Roe, Alliot Verdun   S1.2:490
Rojas Pinilla, Gustavo   S1.2:461, 461 (*sidebar*)
Roll of Thunder, Hear My Cry, Taylor, Mildred   3:350–5
Romantic movement
   appreciation for nature and supernatural   S1.1:213–14
   children as spiritually wise   S1.1:413–15
   Darwin's influence on   1:116
   disapproval of Industrial Revolution   1:115–16, 120
   emphasizing emotion, imagination, mystery, individuality, and nationalism   1:106, 115, 118–19, 217, 406
   favoring plain speech of common people   1:163
   imagination versus reason   S1.1:96
   influence on Dumas   2:104
   influence on Emerson   2:316–17, 319
   influence of French Revolution   1:116
   influence on Hermann Hesse   1:365, 370
   interest in medieval romance   1:413
   interest in past   2:104
   link to political and revolutionary fervor   S1.1:208
   opposed to bourgeois conventions   S1.1:63
   as reaction against Neoclassicism and rationality of Enlightenment   1:106, 217, 406, S1.1:208
   reflections in Emily Brontë's works   1:413
   reflections in Goethe   S1.1:113
   reflections in Jane Austen's works   2:300
   transcendentalism   1:356–7, 2:54, 92, 314, 316–19, 416, 418–19
Rome (imperial Roman capital)
   chaos in last century B.C.   1:12, 89–90
   civil war, republic, and dictatorship   1:190, S1.1:169–72
   conquest of Britain   S1.1:230–1
   deification of mortals   S1.1:173
   as early Etruscan village   1:9
   gladiators   S1.1:231–2, 232 (*sidebar*), 235–6
   marriage and divorce in   S1.1:172–3

   mythical founding of   1:10 (*sidebar*)
   religious holidays   1:191–2
Romeo and Juliet, Shakespeare, William   1:344 50
   as model for *West Side Story*   4:384
Room of One's Own, A, Woolf, Virginia   3:356–63, S1.1:146 (*sidebar*), 470
Roosevelt, Eleanor   3:154, 392, 395, 424, 4:297
Roosevelt, Franklin Delano
   authorizing internment of Japanese Americans   4:138
   First Inaugural Address   3:125–30
   invocation of Lincoln   2:7
   New Deal   1:113, 3:45, 69, 128, 141
   political appointments of Irish Americans   3:401–2
   political support from Sandburg   2:7
   reason for refusal to sign Dyer Antilynching Bill   3:154, 392
   support for equal rights   4:255
Roosevelt, Theodore
   as big game hunter   3:232 (*sidebar*)
   "big stick" corollary to Monroe Doctrine   3:277
   coining term "muckrakers"   3:176
   expansionism of   3:101, 231
   popularizing "Old West" myth of individualism   5:206
   as Progressive reformer   3:284 5
   support for preservation of buffalo   5:34
   support for trade union movement   3:420
   as trust buster   3:167
Roots, Haley, Alex   5:298–305, S1.2:228, 236, 427
Rosenberg, Julius and Ethel   4:72, 380, 381 (*illus.*), 5:2, 127, S1.2:280, 363–4
Rosencrantz and Guildenstern Are Dead, Stoppard, Tom   S1.2:178, 397–407
Rose, Reginald, *Twelve Angry Men* (screenplay)   4:378–83
Rossetti, Christina, "Goblin Market, The"   S1.1:139–47
Rostand, Edmond, *Cyrano de Bergerac*   1:87–92
Rotarians   5:202
"Rothschild's Fiddle" and "The Lady with the Dog," Chekhov, Anton   S1.1:367–75
Rothstein, Arnold   3:149–50, 4:261, 5:315, 316 (*illus.*)
Rousseau, Jean-Jacques   1:409 (*sidebar*), S1.1:414
Roy, Arundhati, *God of Small Things, The*   S1.2:151–60
Rudolf, Crown Prince of Habsburg   S1.1:315 (*sidebar*)
Runner, The, Voigt, Cynthia   5:306–13
Rush, Benjamin   4:289
Rushdie, Salman, *Midnight's Children*   S1.2:327–37
Ruskin, John   S1.1:294
Russia, czarist
   anti-Semitism and pogroms   1:364, 3:119–21, S1.1:117–21, 120 (*sidebar*)
   Bolshevik Revolution   4:14, 16
   Bolsheviks and Mensheviks   4:14
   bureaucracy and reforms   S1.1:71–3, 126

Cossacks 3:233
Crimean War with Britain S1.1:326, 465
Decembrist Revolt S1.1:52, 101
decline of nobility 2:35–6, 3:57
education reform 3:58
emancipation of serfs 2:34
industrialization 4:14
land ownership 3:57–8, 60
liberals versus radicals in intergenerational conflict S1.1:99–103, 367
local government 2:35
marriage and divorce 2:37, 39, S1.2:369–70
oppression of Poland 2:384 5
"Pale of (Jewish) Settlement" S1.1:118
peasants and *intelligentsia* 3:58, 4:14, S1.1:54
reform and reaction in 19th century, Westernizers versus Slavophiles S1.1:51–4
reforms of 1860s in ministry of justice S1.1:72–3
revolution of 1905 1:363, 3:59, 232
Russo-Japanese War (1904 05) 4:59
Russo-Turkish war 2:37–9
society of 1890s S1.1:367–70
as threat to British-controlled Punjab 3:184, 185
women's rights movement 2:37, 39
WWI 3:8, 11 (*sidebar*)
(*See also* Soviet Union)
Russian Orthodox Church S1.1:54
Rustin, Bayard 5:188
Rymer, James Malcolm S1.1:86
Ryogen (Tendai priest) S1.1:453

S

Sacatras 3:18
Sackville-West, Vita 3:361–2
Sailboats 2:395
Saint-Domingue (Haiti) 5:116–17
Saint-Exupéry, Antoine de, *Little Prince, The* 3:210–17, S1.2:496
Saint Petersburg, Russia S1.1:53 (*sidebar*)
Saint-Simon, Henri de S1.1:44
Saki, "Open Window, The" 2:275–80
Salazar, Rubén 4:47, 410
Salem, Massachusetts 1:78–80, 355, 395–7
Salinas Valley, California 3:334 5
Salinger, J. D.
  Catcher in the Rye 4:73–8
  as reclusive 5:319
Salk, Jonas Edward 4:10
Salvation Army S1.1:220–1
Sandburg, Carl
  Abraham Lincoln: The Prairie Years 2:1–7
  on *Call of the Wild* 3:56
Sand, George (Amantine-Aurore-Lucile Dupin) 2:212, 3:406
Sandoz, Mari, *Story Catcher, The* 2:347–52
San Francisco
  in 1920s 3:226
  beats S1.2:364
  Chinatown 3:226, 5:74 5, 77–9

prejudice against Chinese 2:367–8
vigilantes 2:286–7
Santa Anna, Antonio Lopez S1.2:83
Santa Barbara oil spill disaster S1.2:180
Santos, Eduardo S1.2:460, 461 (*sidebar*)
Saramago, José, *Blindness* S1.2:63–71
Saroyan, William, *Human Comedy, The* 4:193–200
Sarris, Greg, *Grand Avenue* S1.2:161–9
Sartre, Jean-Paul S1.2:179, 443, 444, 445, 470, 471
Satan. *See* Devil (Satan)
Satire
  Adventures of Don Quixote, The 1:4, 6–7
  Candide S1.1:21–30
  "Devil and Tom Walker, The" 1:101–6
  Gulliver's Travels 1:129–35, S1.1:29
  Importance of Being Earnest, The S1.1:179–87
  Modest Proposal, A 1:266–72
  use in Shakespeare's time 1:349
Saxo Grammaticus 1:136, 139, 141 (*sidebar*)
Scarlet Letter, The, Hawthorne, Nathaniel 1:351–7
Scarlet Pimpernel, The, Orczy, Baroness Emmuska 1:358–64
Schaefer, Jack, *Shane* 2:321–6
Schiller, Friedrich S1.1:100
Schizophrenia and "split personalities" S1.1:200
Schlafly, Phyllis 5:136–7, 138 (*illus.*)
Schooners 1:401
Schopenhauer, Arthur S1.2:471
Schumacher, Raoul S1.2:496, 496 (*sidebar*)
Science fiction 2:388–9, 4:347, 5:54 6, 126 (*sidebar*)
  Brave New World 5:39–45
  Childhood's End 5:53–60
  Dune 5:81–7
  episodes in *Slaughterhouse Five* 4:347
  Fahrenheit 451 5:95–100, S1.2:309
  Foundation 5:122–8
  House of Stairs 5:156–62
  Kindred S1.2:227–37
  Left Hand of Darkness, The 5:236–42
  Martian Chronicles, The, Bradbury, Ray S1.2:309–15
  Nineteen Eighty-Four 5:251–8
  purported UFOs 4:347–8, 5:59 (*illus.*)
  as "speculative fiction" 5:141
  Stranger in a Strange Land 5:321–7
  Them! S1.2:312
  Jules Verne as father of 2:388–9
  War of the Worlds, The 3:404 10, S1.1:140, S1.2:314
  H. G. Wells as father of 2:389
  women writers of 5:239
  (*See also* Fantasy)
Science and technology
  American Enlightenment 2:416
  anthropology 2:72, 179, 4:221–7, 5:42, S1.1:7–8
  assembly line production and mass production 3:89, 100–1, 102

Index

Science and technology (*continued*)
    automobile   2:128 (*sidebar*), 3:23, 77, 88–9, 94, 101, 5:40 (*illus.*)
    aviation   3:211–12, 367, 5:96, 293–4, S1.2:489–90
    behaviorism   5:45
    Bradbury's ambivalence about technology   S1.2:313–14
    civilian applications of war technology   4:236
    computers   5:97, 127
    contraceptives   2:211, 5:272, 324
    cotton gin   2:403
    cultural anthropology   S1.1:433 (*sidebar*), S1.2:266
    dam construction and "conservancy districts"   S1.2:342–3
    dictaphone   S1.2:147 (*sidebar*)
    discoveries creating secular, nonreligious outlook   S1.1:80
    drugs and pharmaceuticals   3:379
    electricity   3:89
    in Elizabethan Age   1:142 (*sidebar*), 200
    in Enlightenment   1:24 6, 268–9, 272
    "ethnology"   2:232–3
    eugenics   3:272, 4:152, 5:41–2, S1.2:306
    explorations   1:118 (*sidebar*)
    explosives   5:76
    extrasensory perception (ESP)   5:47, 239
    factory system   S1.1:42
    on farms   3:5–6
    film, motion pictures   S1.2:475 (*sidebar*)
    in Franklin's day   1:24 6
    Galileo, Copernicus, and Newton   1:24, 94, 305, S1.1:107, 113
    historical linguistics   S1.2:305
    indoor plumbing   3:77
    Industrial Revolution   1:115, 336, 2:119
    influence on H. G. Wells   3:404 5
    inoculations against disease   3:378, 406
    jet engine   4:71
    knowledge appearing in new detective stories   S1.1:274 5
    mechanism   S1.1:22
    motion pictures   3:3, 89, 101
    nuclear energy   5:124, 127, 286
    optics, color and light   S1.1:463
    "parallelism," or "recapitulation"   S1.1:325
    Pasteur's discoveries   3:285, 406
    penicillin   3:366
    pesticides ("biocides") and DDT   4:337–42
    phonograph   S1.1:80
    photography   S1.1:287
    "phrenology"   2:211
    physics and principle of indeterminacy   5:283
    population growth theories   S1.1:323–4
    printing and publishing   1:160, 162 (*sidebar*), 2:234, 306, 419
    professionalization and specialization of   2:119
    providing potential for nuclear annihilation   S1.2:474
    psychiatry   4:289 (*sidebar*)
    psychoanalysis   4:168 (*sidebar*), 5:42, 260–1, 263, S1.1:316–17
    psychokinesis and telekinesis   5:47–8
    radio   3:3, 45, 89
    rationalism and order in Victorian Age   S1.1:81
    religion and   2:29–30, 121–2
    "resurrection men"   1:120–1
    in Romantic period   1:116
    satellites in space   5:54
    space exploration   5:53, 54, 81–2, S1.2:181
    steam power   S1.1:43 (*sidebar*)
    steamships   2:391, 394 5
    steam threshing machine   2:354
    submarines   2:385–6
    telecommunications   5:54
    telegraph   S1.1:80
    telephone   2:128 (*sidebar*), 3:77
    thermodynamics   S1.1:330
    tractors   3:6, 92
    typewriter   S1.1:80–1
    "Uniformitarians" versus "Catastrophists"   S1.1:329
    (*See also* Evolution; Industrial Revolution, industrialization; Progress, belief in; Psychology; Railroads; Television; War weaponry)
SCLC (Southern Christian Leadership Conference)   5:189, S1.2:271
Scopes Trial   3:102 (*sidebar*)
Scotland
    Calvinism in   3:377, 4:304
    Celtic inhabitants   S1.1:229–30
    education of women in 1930s   4:303–4
    Gowrie Conspiracy   1:229
    Hebrides   1:226
    Highlanders   1:187
    as Presbyterians   4:10, 304
    status of women in 11th century   1:226
    in time of *Macbeth* (11th century)   1:225–6
    troubled relations with England   1:145, 150, 181, 187, 201
Scotland Yard   S1.1:272, 272 (*sidebar*)
Scottsboro case   3:39, 239
Scott, Sir Walter
    emulated by Cooper   1:208
    friend of Washington Irving   1:105
    influencing George Eliot   S1.1:246
    influencing Hugo   1:165
    Ivanhoe   1:181–8
Seale, Bobby   4:54
Second Great Awakening   1:424 5, 2:23, 404, 417–18
Secret Agent, The, Conrad, Joseph   S1.1:377–85
"Secret Life of Walter Mitty, The," Thurber, James   3:364 9
Secular humanism   5:138
Segregation
    acceptance for time being by Booker T. Washington   2:341, 342, 343, 344, 345, 410, 413, 414, 3:162, 250, 320, 385

of churches 5:189
documentation of negative effects 4:32–3
in New Orleans 3:17–18, 5:22
in North S1.1:333–4, 431, S1.2:422–3
protest by (multiracial) high school football team 4:29
in public facilities 3:38 (illus.), 42 (illus.), 4:29 (illus.)
in public transportation 5:88–90, 185–6
in schools for disabled 2:221 (sidebar)
in South 1:399, 2:97, 3:419, 4:28–9, 373–4, 5:22, S1.1:333–5
in Southern jails S1.2:252
in Supreme Court rulings
  overturned for residential housing, interstate bus travel 4:201
  overturned for schools in *Brown v. Board of Education* 3:375, 4:29–30, 314, 5:90, 108, 180, 181, S1.1:19, S1.2:231, 256, 270
  sanctioned by *Plessy v. Ferguson* 2:21, 341, 399–400, 413, 3:351, 375, 419, 4:1, 5:90, 107–8, S1.1:429, S1.2:256, 269–70
of U.S. military during WWII 3:41–2, 4:195, 197, 374 (sidebar)
(*See also* Civil rights movement; Integration; Jim Crow laws)
Self-Reliance, Emerson, Ralph Waldo 2:314 20
Senior citizens
  loneliness, depression, serious illness, and suicide 5:273, 275 (illus.)
  problems of adjustment to retirement 5:203, 273
Sense and Sensibility, Austen, Jane S1.1:387–98
Separate Peace, A, Knowles, John 4:323–9
Serbia 3:8, 11 (sidebar)
Serial characters, stories, novels S1.1:156 (sidebar)
Serling, Rod 4:379, 383 (illus.)
"Sestiger" movement S1.2:115, 123
Seurat, Georges S1.1:464
"Seventeen Syllables," Yamamoto, Hisaye 4:330–6
Sex education
  for mentally handicapped 4:152
  programs of 1960s 5:153 (sidebar)
  social purity movement of late 19th century 2:423
Sexual dimension of life
  in 19th century 2:212, 423, S1.1:161 (sidebar)
  abuse of African American women 4:54
  abuse of female slaves 2:49, 60, 169, 406, S1.2:229
  adultery, infidelity 5:273, 287
  AIDS 5:9
  Catholic and Presbyterian views on 4:304 (sidebar)
  changing mores 5:272–3
  child molestation laws S1.2:280–1, 284
  conception, contraception, and artificial insemination S1.1:142
  contraceptives 2:211, 5:272, 324
  dangerous desire and seduction of innocents S1.1:143–5

effects of childhood abuse 5:289–90
"free love" movement of 1960s 5:272
in Freudian psychoanalytic theory S1.1:317, 320
Freud's arguments against repression 3:23
for German Jews in Prague S1.1:479–80
harassment of women in workplace 1:35
hypocrisy of public attitudes 4:75
impotence 4:128
incest 4:52, S1.1:309–10
interracial taboos, miscegenation 3:391, S1.2:232
Japan in 10th century S1.1:454
Kinsey Report 4:75, 241, 398–9 (sidebar), 5:324
licentiousness as male prerogative in ancient Greece S1.1:308–10
in *Lolita* S1.2:279–86
promiscuity of "lost generation" S1.1:444, 447
rape 4:395, 5:117, 136, 141
sexual revolution of 1960s and 1970s 5:151
treatment in literature as shocking 4:74
Victorian marriage, prostitution, infidelity, and disease S1.1:141–2, 184 5
Victorians' repression of 2:334, 336, 338–9, 355, 3:18, 380–1
(*See also* Homosexuality; Love and marriage; Prostitution)
Shakerism 3:95–9
Shakespeare, William
  Hamlet 1:136–43, S1.2:398
  Henry IV, Part I 1:144 51
  importance in Elizabethan Age S1.2:399
  Julius Caesar 1:189–95
  King Lear 1:196–203
  Macbeth 1:225–30
  Merchant of Venice, The 1:242–9
  Midsummer Night's Dream, A 1:258–65
  Othello 1:295–300
  Richard III S1.1:355–66
  Romeo and Juliet 1:344 50
  Tempest, The 1:379–85
  Twelfth Night, Or, What You Will S1.1:483–92
Shane, Schaefer, Jack 2:321–6
Shange, Ntozake
  Betsey Brown 4:28–34
  for colored girls who have considered suicide / when the rainbow is enuf 5:115–21
Sharecropping and tenant farming 2:42, 411, 3:80, 104, 105, 249, 350–1, 370–1, 418, 4:2, S1.2:259–60, 262
  STFU (Southern Tenant Farmers' Union) 3:208
Shaw, George Bernard
  on *Hedda Gabler* S1.1:165
  Major Barbara S1.1:219–27
  Pygmalion 3:312–18
Shelley, Mary
  daughter of Mary Wollstonecraft 1:115, 116, 407
  Frankenstein 1:115–21

Index

Shelley, Percy Bysshe   1:115, 116, 119
Shepard, Alan   5:292, 296
Sherman, William Tecumseh   2:139, 140 (*illus.*), 165 (*sidebar*)
Shinto religion   S1.1:452, S1.2:414
Shipping industry
   of early 19th century   2:391–2, 393, 394–5
   longshoremen   3:161 (*sidebar*)
Ships
   privateers   1:400
   sailboats   2:395
   schooners   1:401
   steam-powered   1:404 (*sidebar*), 2:394 5
Shizuko's Daughter, Mori, Koyoko   S1.2:409–19
Shoeless Joe, Kinsella, W. P.   5:314 20
"Shooting an Elephant," Orwell, George   S1.1:399–406
Short stories
   "Almos' a Man," Wright, Richard   4:1–6
   "Barn Burning," Faulkner, William   2:41–6
   "Bear, The,", Faulkner, William   2:47–53
   "Cask of Amontillado, The," Poe, Edgar Allan   2:81–6
   "Child's Christmas in Wales, A," Thomas, Dylan   3:63–7
   Christmas Carol, A, Dickens, Charles   S1.1:31–9
   "Christmas Memory, A," Capote, Truman   3:68–74
   "Devil and Tom Walker, The," Irving, Washington   1:101–6
   Dubliners, Joyce, James   3:106–11
   "Everything That Rises Must Converge," O'Connor, Flannery   5:88–94
   Grand Avenue, Sarris, Greg   S1.2:161–9
   Krik? Krak!, Danticat, Edwidge   S1.2:239–48
   "Legend of Sleepy Hollow, The," Irving, Washington   1:211–18
   Lone Ranger and Tonto Fistfight in Heaven, The, Alexie, Sherman   S1.2:287–96
   "Lottery, The," Jackson, Shirley   4:235–9
   Martian Chronicles, The, Bradbury, Ray   S1.2:309–15
   "Most Dangerous Game, The," Connell, Richard   3:231–5
   "Murders in the Rue Morgue, The," Poe, Edgar Allan   S1.1:271–9
   "Necklace, The," Maupassant, Guy de   2:244 8
   "Noon Wine," Porter, Katherine Anne   3:243–8
   "Notorious Jumping Frog of Calaveras County, The," Twain, Mark   2:249–54
   "Occurrence at Owl Creek Bridge, An," Bierce, Ambrose   2:255–60
   "One of These Days," García Márquez, Gabriel   S1.2:459–66
   "Open Window, The," Saki   2:275–80
   origin of genre   S1.1:274
   "Outcasts of Poker Flat, The," Harte, Bret   2:281–7
   "Rip Van Winkle," Irving, Washington   1:330–6
   "Rocking-Horse Winner, The," Lawrence, D.H.   3:344 9
   "Rothschild's Fiddle" and "The Lady with the Dog," Chekhov, Anton   S1.1:367–75
   "Secret Life of Walter Mitty, The," Thurber, James   3:364 9
   "Seventeen Syllables," Yamamoto, Hisaye   4:330–6
   "Spunk" and "Sweat," Hurston, Zora Neale   S1.1:429–37, S1.2:266
   "Tuesday Siesta," García Márquez, Gabriel   S1.2:459–66
   "Where Are You Going, Where Have You Been?," Oates, Joyce Carol   4:391–6
   Woman Hollering Creek and Other Stories, Sandra Cisneros   S1.2:499–509
   "Worn Path, The," Welty, Eudora   3:418–24
   "Yellow Wallpaper, The," Gilman, Charlotte Perkins   2:422–8
   "Yentl the Yeshiva Boy," Singer, Isaac Bashevis   3:425–31
   "Young Goodman Brown," Hawthorne, Nathaniel   1:420–6
Siberia   4:133–5
Sicily   4:67
Siddartha Gautama   1:365–8
Siddhartha, Hesse, Hermann   1:365–70
Sierra Club   S1.2:98 (*sidebar*)
Silent Spring, Carson, Rachel   4:337–42, 5:35, S1.2:103
Silko, Leslie Marmon, *Ceremony*   4:79–86
Silver. *See* Gold rushes and silver strikes
Simon, Neil, *Biloxi Blues*   4:35–41
Sinclair, Upton
   in *Faust*   S1.1:108, 112
   Jungle, The   3:174–80, 320
Sin and damnation
   beliefs of Calvinists   3:377, 4:304
   beliefs of Puritans   1:23, 393, 421
   beliefs in Shakespeare's time   1:143
   crime, guilt, and responsibility   S1.2:202
   depictions in morality plays   1:148
   forbidden fruit as sexual temptation   S1.1:145 (*sidebar*)
   guilt in *The Scarlet Letter*   1:351, 355–6
   in *Paradise Lost*   1:301, 306
   predestination versus free will   4:304, S1.1:308
   in "Young Goodman Brown"   1:420–6
Singer, Isaac Bashevis, "Yentl the Yeshiva Boy"   3:425–31
Sister Carrie, Dreiser, Theodore   2:327–33
Sit-ins at all-white lunch counters   S1.1:19, S1.2:271, 423
Skinner, B. F.   5:156, 279
Slaughterhouse Five, Vonnegut, Kurt, Jr.   4:343–8
Slave narratives
   described   2:171, 4:205
   Douglass, Frederick (*Narrative of the Life of Frederick Douglass*)   2:236–41, S1.2:229, 231
   emergence in antebellum period   S1.2:231

Jacobs, Harriet (*Incidents in the Life of a Slave Girl*)
    2:168–73
  by Northrup, Solomon   2:410
  Roots as   5:298–305, S1.2:228, 236
Slavery, in Trinidad   S1.2:183–4
Slavery in America
  of American Indians by forced indenture   2:175
  of American Indians by Spanish missionaries
    S1.2:162
  bans on interracial marriage (anti-miscegenation
    laws)   S1.2:232
  causing rift between North and South   2:88,
    172, 188, 403–4
  of Chinese prostitutes   2:366–7
  in colonial America   1:394, 2:93, 175
  Compromise of 1850   2:404 5
  extent of, in Old South   2:188, 405, 410
  Fugitive Slave Acts (1793 and 1850)   1:42,
    2:16, 62, 170, 189, 404 5, 410
  Kansas-Nebraska Act (1854)   1:42, 2:5
    (*sidebar*), 172, 193
  in Kentucky   2:59–60
  Kongo kingdom and   2:145
  legacy of, in late 20th century   2:65
  in Maryland   2:236–7
  Missouri Compromise (1820)   2:5 (*sidebar*),
    15–16, 22
  Nat Turner's Rebellion   2:169–70, S1.2:229
  in North Carolina   2:168
  opposition of
    Patrick Henry   1:126 (*sidebar*)
    Thomas Paine   1:72 (*sidebar*)
    Henry David Thoreau   1:88, 89 (*sidebar*)
  racist justifications of   1:39, 41, 42, 394,
    2:403, 404
  references to, deleted from Declaration of
    Independence   1:98
  reliance upon, for harvesting of cotton   2:15,
    22, 44 (*illus.*), 59, 168, 403
  slave codes and patrollers   1:103, 2:189, 190
    (*sidebar*), S1.2:233, 235 (*sidebar*)
  as soul-corrupting for whites   2:52, 408
  Southern states avoiding mention in state
    constitutions   1:99 (*sidebar*)
  teaching reading as forbidden   S1.2:231
  Underground Railroad   2:16, 60, 62, 189, 238,
    406–7
  whites' feelings of guilt at   2:52, 53
  (*See also* Abolitionists, Abolition of slavery;
    African Americans)
Slavery in North America
  among Canadian Kwakiutl   5:194 5
  brought by Spaniards to Puerto Rico   5:214
  Caribbean   S1.1:494 6, S1.2:20
  revolts   S1.1:495, S1.2:240
  in Trinidad   S1.2:183–4
Slaves
  Amistad mutiny   1:43
  arson by   2:189
  cimaroons   1:401–2

communities and culture   2:407
  escapes, rebellions, and resistance   1:39, 43,
    401–2, 2:60, 93, 94 5, 169–70, 188–9, 406–7,
    S1.2:240
  family life   2:60, 169, 237–8, 405, 406, 410,
    3:423, 4:204 5
  female, sexual abuse of   2:49, 60, 169, 406
  food and clothing   2:237
  freed before Emancipation Proclamation
    2:93–4, 168–9, 238
  ill-prepared for freedom   2:411
  literacy   2:16, 24 5, S1.2:231
  living and working conditions   2:189 (*sidebar*),
    237, 405, 410
  loyalty of some to white masters during Civil
    War   2:410–11
  music   2:398, 407
  punishment   2:240–2, 405, 410
  religion   2:407, 3:83
  Russian serfs as   S1.1:51–2, 99
  social distinctions between   3:387
  use of cunning and manipulative behavior   2:401
Slave trade
  auction block   1:40 (*illus.*)
  Caribbean sugar industry   S1.1:494
  diagram of slave ship   1:38 (*illus.*)
  English involvement in, prohibition of   1:274
    5, 299, 337–8, 2:361, S1.1:409–10, 410 (*sidebar*)
  impelled by need for labor   1:103
  "middle passage"   S1.2:393 (*sidebar*)
  missionaries' attempts to atone for   2:361–2
  overview   1:37, 103
  to plantations on Grenada   S1.2:387
  traders despised   1:103
  Zong slave ship   S1.1:409
Sleator, William, *House of Stairs*   5:156–62
Smith, Adam   S1.1:48, 391, 397 (*sidebar*)
Smith, Bessie   3:253 (*illus.*)
Smith, Betty, *Tree Grows in Brooklyn, A*   3:397–403
Smith, Henry Nash   3:226
Smith, Joseph Jr.   5:4
Smoking. *See* Tobacco
SNCC (Student Nonviolent Coordinating
  Committee)   4:56, 5:300, S1.2:228, 271
Social calls and calling cards   S1.1:4
Social Darwinism. *See under* Evolution
Socialism
  American, birth of   3:174 5
  comparison to communism and Marxism
    S1.1:45 (*sidebar*)
  European and Russian   S1.1:378–9
  Fabian Society   S1.1:219, 221
  labor unions accused of   3:144
  opposed by fascism   4:66
  origin of term   S1.1:44
  popular among European immigrants   3:321
  utopian   5:251–2, S1.1:52
Social Security System   3:128
Social stratification. *See* Class divisions and social
  stratification

Socrates   1:240, 322–4, 327, **S1.1**:306, 343
So Far from the Bamboo Grove, Watkins, Yoko K.   **4**:349–55
Soldaderas and soldadas   **S1.2**:90 (*sidebar*)
Solzhenitsyn, Alexander, *One Day in the Life of Ivan Denisovich*   **4**:281–7
Songs of Innocence and of Experience, Blake, William   **S1.1**:407–16
Song of Solomon, Morrison, Toni   **S1.2**:421–30
Sons and Lovers, Lawrence, D. H.   **2**:334 9
   as example of bildungsroman   **3**:264
Sophists   **1**:19, 240, **S1.1**:306, 344 5, 347 (*sidebar*)
Sophocles
   Antigone   **1**:14 21, **S1.2**:7
   Oedipus the King   **S1.1**:301–12
Soto, Gary   **S1.2**:374
Souls of Black Folk, The, Du Bois, W. E. B.   **2**:340–6, **3**:320
Sounder, Armstrong, William H.   **3**:370–6
Sound and the Fury, The, Faulkner, William   **S1.1**:417–28
The Sound of Music   **S1.2**:155 (*sidebar*)
Sousa Mendes, Aristides de   **S1.2**:66
South, The
   of 1980s   **3**:78–9
   anti-Yankee bias   **3**:76
   Christmas traditions   **3**:69
   fading glory   **S1.2**:147–8
   Faulkner's lyrical, tragic vision   **S1.1**:418
   folklore in   **2**:48–9
   homeopathy and Indian remedies   **3**:68–9
   hunting in   **2**:47–8
   Illinois' ties to   **2**:8–9
   industrialization, decline of agriculture and aristocracy   **3**:76, 203, **4**:364 5, 368, **5**:91, 129–30
   "King" Cotton   **2**:15, 22, 44 (*illus.*), 168, 403
   lack of industrial development, infrastructure after Civil War   **S1.2**:262
   mixed race offspring   **2**:49, **3**:17–18, 81, 83
   "New"   **3**:72–3, 203
   plantation life   **2**:137–8
   pride in agrarian heritage and aristocratic plantation life   **S1.1**:418
   pride in tradition, decorum, gentility   **S1.1**:418
   religious influences   **3**:76–7
   resistance to change   **S1.1**:418
   segregation in   **1**:399, **2**:97, **3**:419, **4**:28–9, 373–4, **5**:22, **S1.1**:333–5
   social stratification in rural areas and small towns   **3**:393
   Southern belle as institution   **S1.1**:419–20
   Southern belle as passive and obedient   **S1.1**:420
   Southern Renascence   **S1.1**:419–20
   storytelling tradition   **3**:421
   tenant farming and sharecropping   **2**:42, 411, **3**:80, 249, 370–1, **S1.2**:259–60, 262
   textile mills and mill towns   **3**:76, 153, 203–4, **4**:256
   womanhood, ideal of   **3**:19, 392–3, **4**:366–7, **S1.1**:420
   women rejecting docility   **S1.1**:420–1
   (*See also* Civil War; Jim Crow laws; Reconstruction)
South Africa
   Afrikaner National Party voted into power   **S1.2**:116, 123
   apartheid and racism   **1**:63, **3**:86, **4**:94 100, **S1.2**:115–16, 195–7, 197 (*sidebar*), 203 (*sidebar*), 319–20, 322–4
   Black Consciousness Movement's hostility to white activists   **S1.2**:122
   constitution   **S1.2**:197, 198 (*sidebar*)
   end of apartheid   **S1.2**:324
   ethnic population   **S1.2**:116 (*sidebar*)
   guns, violence, and crime   **S1.2**:197–8
   immigration of Dutch, becoming "Afrikaners"   **S1.2**:115, 122–3
   nationhood and beginning of racial separation   **S1.2**:317–19
   police torture of detainees   **S1.2**:119
   police violence in Soweto (1976-77)   **S1.2**:117–19, 118 (*illus.*), 123
   South African War (Boer War) (1899-1902)   **S1.2**:116, 123
   torture by police/security forces   **S1.2**:119
   Truth and Reconciliation Commission   **S1.2**:203 (*sidebar*)
   Union of South Africa (1910)   **S1.2**:123
   World War II's impact on voters   **S1.2**:116
South Carolina   **5**:285–6
Southey, Robert   **1**:121, **S1.1**:216
South Pacific
   climate   **4**:231 (*sidebar*)
   island fighting and major sea battles (1942–45)   **4**:60–1
   island peoples' origins   **4**:221–2
   Japanese conquests in WWII   **4**:178
   Philippines   **3**:101, **4**:81
Soviet Union
   anti-Semitism   **3**:124 5, **5**:122, **S1.1**:127–8
   anti-Zionism   **4**:107–8
   atomic bomb capability   **4**:183, **5**:96, 126
   centralized planning and control of means of production   **5**:124
   de-Stalinization   **4**:285–6
   European conquests and sphere of influence   **5**:123 (*sidebar*), 224, 253–4
   Five-Year Plans and forced labor   **4**:16, 132
   forced collectivization of agriculture   **4**:281–5
   Gorbachev and "perestroika"   **5**:8
   gulag system of labor camp prisons   **4**:282–5, **5**:239 (*sidebar*)
   invasion of Armenia   **3**:340
   invasion of Poland   **3**:340, **4**:131
   propaganda   **5**:252
   reprisals against Japanese in Korea and Manchuria   **4**:350
   seen as "controlling" international communism   **4**:166

Siberia **4**:133–5
Sputniks and space program **5**:81, 291, 292, 293, 294, 321
Stalin-Hitler non-aggression pact (1939) **3**:210, 214, **4**:17
Stalin's reign of terror and purges **4**:16–17, 166
suppression of Hungarian uprising (1956) **4**:166
suppression of religion **S1.1**:269 (*sidebar*)
totalitarianism **4**:16
Ukraine, Babi Yar massacre **4**:120
(*See also* Russia)
Soweto (SOuthWEstern TOwnships), South Africa **S1.2**:117–19, 118 (*illus.*), 123
Space Age
Dillard's musings **5**:279–80, 281 (*sidebar*)
manned space flight highlights **5**:294 (*sidebar*)
moon landing **5**:81–2
NASA (National Aeronautics and Space Administration) **5**:81, 291
Right Stuff, The **5**:291–7
satellites for communications **5**:54
treaty prohibiting military use of space **5**:239
U.S.-Soviet competition in space race **5**:53, 81, 321–2, **S1.2**:311–12
(*See also* Aviation; War weaponry)
Space race **5**:53, 81, 321–2, **S1.2**:181, 311–12
Spain
Civil War and Franco (1936–39) **4**:67, **S1.1**:177, **S1.2**:74, 87, 142–3, 300
Cortés' conquest of Mexico (1520s) **S1.2**:93, 499
decline of empire **1**:1–3
defeat and humiliation by United States, conflict between "two Spains" **S1.2**:73–5, 75 (*sidebar*), 80
expulsion of Jews **S1.1**:189
fascism in **1**:293–4, **4**:67, **S1.1**:177
Golden Age **S1.1**:189–91, 192–3
Gypsies **S1.1**:191–2, 192 (*sidebar*), 195 (*illus.*)
Inquisition **1**:2–3, **S1.1**:190–1, 192 (*sidebar*)
invasion of Italy **1**:317
Moriscos and Conversos **S1.1**:190, 193
role of honor in society **S1.2**:79 (*sidebar*)
Second Republic **S1.2**:74
union of kingdoms **S1.1**:189–90
wars with England and France **1**:1–2, 87, 88, 130–1, 201, 305
Spanish-American War (1898) **3**:101, 278, **S1.2**:73
Spark, Muriel, *Prime of Miss Jean Brodie, The* **4**:303–8
Sparta **1**:324 5, 328
Speeches
"Ain't I a Woman?," Truth, Sojourner **2**:22–7
"John Brown's Final Speech," Brown, John **2**:188–94
"First Inaugural Address," Roosevelt, Franklin D. **3**:125–30

"Gettysburg Address, The," Lincoln, Abraham **2**:130–6
"Give Me Liberty or Give Me Death," Henry, Patrick **1**:122–8
"I Have a Dream," King, Dr. Martin Luther, Jr. **5**:185–93, **S1.2**:269
"Inaugural Address," Kennedy, John F. **5**:222–8
"I Will Fight No More Forever," Joseph, Chief **2**:160–7
Japan, the Ambiguous, and Myself, Oe, Kenzaburo **S1.2**:217–25
"On the Evacuation at Dunkirk," Churchill, Winston **4**:356–63
Spencer, Herbert **2**:341, **S1.1**:330–1
Sphinx and oracles **S1.1**:303 (*sidebar*), 304 (*illus.*), 306–8, 309 (*illus.*)
Spinoza, Benedict (Baruch) **S1.1**:123 (*sidebar*)
Spock, Benjamin **4**:21–2
Sports. *See* Entertainment; Games and sports
Spreckels, Claus and sugar interests **3**:269, 270 (*sidebar*), 319
"Spunk" and "Sweat," Hurston, Zora Neale **S1.1**:429–37, **S1.2**:266
Sputnik **5**:81, 291, 292, 293, 294, 321
Stalin, Josef
banning books depicting life in West **5**:96
British outrage at **4**:17
Five-Year Plans for economic development **4**:16, 282
forced collectivization of agriculture **4**:281–2, **5**:122
as Marxist Party member **4**:14, 15 (*illus.*)
non-aggression pact with Hitler **3**:210, 213–14, **4**:17
oppression or extermination of Jews **3**:123–4
political prisoners exiled to Siberian gulags **4**:282–5, **5**:239 (*sidebar*)
purges of opponents **4**:16–17, **5**:122, 254
(*See also* Soviet Union)
Stanley, Henry Morton **2**:146
Stanton, Elizabeth Cady **2**:24, 55, **3**:16, **S1.1**:8
Stately homes of England **S1.2**:137 (*sidebar*)
Steam engine **S1.1**:209
Steamships **1**:404 (*sidebar*), **2**:391, 394 5
Steinbeck, John
Grapes of Wrath, The **3**:138–45, **S1.2**:267, 347
Of Mice and Men **3**:269–76
Red Pony, The **3**:334 7
Stein, Joseph, *Fiddler on the Roof* **3**:119–24
Stein, Saint Edith **S1.1**:268 (*sidebar*)
Stevenson, Robert Louis
on *Pride and Prejudice* **2**:300
Strange Case of Dr. Jekyll and Mr. Hyde, The **3**:377–82, **S1.1**:185
on *Tess of the D'Urbervilles* **2**:359
Treasure Island **1**:400–5
STFU (Southern Tenant Farmers' Union) **3**:208
Stock market
1929 crash and bank failures **3**:125–6, 208
speculation fever of 1920s **3**:146

Index

Stock market (*continued*)
    speculations in trusts and railroads of 1900   3:167 (sidebar)
    (See also Great Depression)
"Stoic" comedians   S1.2:475 (sidebar)
Stoicism   1:192–3
Stoker, Bram, *Dracula*   S1.1:79–87, 140, 146
Stoneham, C. A.   3:149
Stones For Ibarra, Doerr, Harriet   S1.2:431–9
Stoppard, Tom, *Rosencrantz and Guildenstern Are Dead*   S1.2:178, 397–407
Story Catcher, The, Sandoz, Mari   2:347–52
Storytelling. *See* Oral storytelling
Stowe, Harriet Beecher
    relationship with Harriet Jacobs   2:172
    Uncle Tom's Cabin   2:403–9
Strachey, Lytton   3:356
Strange Case of Dr. Jekyll and Mr. Hyde, The, Stevenson, Robert Louis   3:377–82, S1.1:185
Stranger in a Strange Land, Heinlein, Robert A.   5:321–7
Stranger, The, Camus, Albert   S1.2:441–9
"Stream of consciousness" writing   3:111, 358, S1.1:419 (sidebar), 420, 427, 471
Streetcar Named Desire, A, Williams, Tennessee   4:364 70, S1.2:141
Streetcars   2:328, 3:25, 4:366
Sturm und Drang (storm and stress) movement   S1.1:113
Stuyvesant, Peter   1:331
Styron, William, *Confessions of Nat Turner, The*   2:93–8
Submarines   2:385–6
Suburbia   4:73, 384, 385, 5:261–2, S1.2:358–9, 364, 422
Sudetenland   S1.1:475
Suez Canal   3:184, 4:107, S1.2:131
Suffrage (right to vote)
    for African Americans   4:148
        granted by 14th and 15th Amendments   5:21
        Jim Crow laws restricting   3:37, 352, 419, 4:1, 5:22, S1.2:250, 271
        Mississippi Plan (1890) preventing   5:22
        protected by Civil Rights and Voting Rights Acts (1957 and 1965)   5:22, 186
    for American Indians   4:80
    denial through vote fraud   S1.2:250
    for English and Irish Catholics   S1.1:239–40
    expansion by elimination of property qualifications   2:302
    hindered for freed blacks   2:341
    with land ownership   S1.1:387, 388
    to middle-class men in 1832   S1.1:43
    Nationality Act (1940)   4:80
    Reform Bills enfranchising middle class   S1.1:326
    for women. *See* Women's suffrage
    women's suffrage movement   S1.1:81, 155

Sugihara, Chiune   S1.2:66
Suicide, by
    American Indians   4:83, S1.2:33
    ancient Greeks   4:22
    depressed individuals   5:259–60
    elderly   5:273, 275 (illus.)
    in *for colored girls who have considered suicide / when the rainbow is enuf*   5:115–21
    interned Japanese Americans   4:140
    Japanese   S1.2:414
    Japanese girls in Korea (1944 45)   4:350, 353
    Jews   3:428, 4:22
    Jim Jones and 911 members of People's Temple   5:84
    kamikazi pilots   4:61 (sidebar), 62 (illus.)
    Madame Bovary   2:211–12
    men   4:23, 114 (sidebar)
    prep school students   4:74
    Shange, attempts   5:120
    Sylvia Plath   4:22–6
    teenagers   5:259–60, 261
    victims of childhood abuse   5:288, 289–90
    Vietnam War veterans   5:106
    white males   5:273
    women   4:22–6, S1.1:383 (sidebar)
Sullivan, Joseph   3:149
Summer of My German Soldier, Greene, Bette   4:371–7
Sumner, William   3:207
Sun Also Rises, The, Hemingway, Ernest   S1.1:439–47
Sun Dance   2:349 (sidebar), 4:187–8, S1.1:133, 134 (sidebar), S1.2:480–2
Sun Yat-Sen, Dr.   4:126, 5:229
Supernatural
    alchemy   1:384, 385 (sidebar)
    astrology   1:346, 350
    belief in, by American Indians   4:83
    belief in *curanderismo*   4:45
    belief in, in China   3:133
    belief in, in Elizabethan-Jacobean era   1:194 5, 227–8, 262, 346, 350
    belief in, in Victorian England   1:418–19, 2:185, 383
    in *Beloved*   2:63
    in *Beowulf*   1:46–8, 49
    brujas (witches)   4:46
    dreams related to   1:424
    as element in Native American fiction   S1.1:138
    ghost stories   S1.1:37
    in Haitian religion   S1.2:240 (sidebar)
    in *Hamlet*   1:138, 141, 142 (sidebar)
    in *The Hobbit*   1:152–8, S1.2:301
    in *Julius Caesar*   1:195
    in "Legend of Sleepy Hollow, The"   1:213, 215, 217
    in *Lyrical Ballads*   S1.1:213
    "mysteriousness" of African and African American culture   5:330
    mysticism   1:416

paranormal phenomena 2:383 (*sidebar*),
  5:47–8, 56, 239
 in *Piano Lesson, The* S1.2:379–86
 in *Romeo and Juliet* 1:346, 350
 Sphinx and oracles S1.1:303 (*sidebar*), 304
  (*illus.*), 306–8, 309 (*illus.*)
 superstitions associated with Chinese New Year
  5:75, 76 (*illus.*)
 in *Tempest, The* 1:381, 383
 in *Turn of the Screw, The* 2:381
 (*See also* Witchcraft)
Sûreté S1.1:278 (*sidebar*)
"Survival of the fittest" S1.1:330–1
Sutcliff, Rosemary, *Mark of the Horse Lord, The*
  S1.1:229–38
Swarthout, Glendon, *Bless the Beasts and Children*
  5:34 8
Sweden, immigration to United States 3:243–4,
  259–60
Sweet Whispers, Brother Rush, Hamilton, Virginia
  5:328–32
Swift, Jonathan
 criticism of *Robinson Crusoe* 1:343
 Gulliver's Travels 1:129–35, S1.1:29
 Modest Proposal, A 1:266–72
Sydney, Sir Philip S1.1:156
Symbolism S1.1:202, 205
Syncretism 3:190–1, 4:44 (*sidebar*)
Synge, John Millington, *Playboy of the Western World*
  S1.2:476

T

Tahiti, 1:274, 278, 392
Taine, Hippolyte 3:213
Taiwan 3:190, 5:254
Tale of the Genji, The, Murasaki Shikibu
  S1.1:449–61, S1.2:222
Tale of Two Cities, A, Dickens, Charles 1:371–8
Tammany Hall, New York 3:148–9, 398–9
Tan, Amy
 Joy Luck Club, The 5:229–35
 Kitchen God's Wife, The 3:189–95
Tasmania 3:406
Taverns 1:331
Taylor, Harriet S1.1:247
Taylor, Mildred, *Roll of Thunder, Hear My Cry*
  3:350–5
Teapot Dome scandal 3:25
Technology. *See* Science and technology
Teilhard de Chardin, Pierre 5:93
Telecommunications 5:54
Telegraph S1.1:80
Telekinesis 5:47–8
Telenovelas S1.2:59–60, 506
Telepathy 5:239
Television
 as babysitter 5:36–7
 Bonanza creating sense of family security
  5:203 (*sidebar*)

 debates costing Nixon 1960 presidential election
  5:223
 development 3:92, 5:96–7, S1.2:149
 golden age of TV drama 4:379
 impact on conduct of Vietnam War and antiwar
  sentiment 5:37
 impact on public support for civil rights
  protesters 5:108
 interconnectedness versus loneliness of viewers
  4:398
 role in arousing disgust at Southern bigotry
  S1.2:273 (*sidebar*)
 spreading conformity 4:236
 telenovelas S1.2:59–60, 506
 violent content of programming 5:62
 westerns 5:201–2
 (*See also* Media)
Television evangelists 5:31–2, 137–8, 140 (*illus.*)
Temperance movement 2:25 (*sidebar*), 85–6,
  3:69, 75, 147
Tempest, The, Shakespeare, William 1:379–85
Templars 1:182, 185 (*sidebar*)
Tenant farming. *See* Sharecropping and tenant
 farming
"Tenebrism" S1.2:128 (*sidebar*)
Tennyson, Alfred, Lord
 In Memoriam S1.1:328–9
 "The Charge of the Light Brigade" S1.1:465
  (*sidebar*)
Terrorism
 anarchism of late 1800s, early 1900s S1.1:62,
  378–80, 379 (*sidebar*)
 Arab against Israel 4:106
 by Argentine military junta 5:209–10, 212–13
 by Chilean military junta 5:169
 Greenwich Bomb Outrage S1.1:380 (*sidebar*)
 by Guatemalan military 5:28
 Haymarket Riot S1.1:379 (*sidebar*)
 of Herut Party in Israel 4:107
 of Irgun in British Mandatory Palestine 4:103
 (*See also* Ku Klux Klan)
Tervalon, Jervey, *Understand This* 5:339–45
Tess of the D'Urbervilles, Hardy, Thomas 2:353–9
Test Acts S1.1:209
Texas S1.2:9–10
Theater
 Chinese opera 5:75
 in early 1900s in America 3:220–1
 Elizabethan 1:261–2, 263, S1.2:399
 El Teatro Campesino 4:409, 5:172
 golden age of television drama 3:92, 4:236,
  379
 importance in ancient Greece 1:19–20, 240
 innovations of Wilder 3:287–8
 musicals 4:387
 in postmodern era 2:123
 realism in 1:92
 supported by James I 1:299
 Teatro Rodante Puertorriqueño 5:216
 (*See also* Plays)

Index

Theater of the absurd **4**:400, **S1.2**:406, 444 (*sidebar*), 476
Thebes **1**:14, **S1.1**:301–2
"The Charge of the Light Brigade" **S1.1**:465 (*sidebar*)
"The Fisherman and His Wife" **S1.1**:466 (*sidebar*)
Their Eyes Were Watching God, Hurston, Zora Neale **3**:383–9, **S1.2**:266
Theosophical Society **S1.1**:82
Thermodynamics **S1.1**:330
Theseus **1**:57, 61 (*sidebar*), 258, 259
Thespis **S1.1**:308, 310
"The Woman Question" **S1.1**:155
Things Fall Apart, Achebe, Chinua **2**:360–5, **S1.2**:203
Things They Carried, The, O'Brien, Tim **S1.2**:451–8
Thirty Years War **1**:87, 88, 388, 388 (*sidebar*)
Thisbe **1**:259 (*sidebar*)
Thomas, Dylan, "Child's Christmas in Wales, A" **3**:63–7
Thomson, James **S1.1**:213–14
Thoreau, Henry David
    Civil Disobedience **2**:87–92, **S1.2**:271 (*sidebar*)
    influence on Dickinson **2**:57
    influence on King **5**:192, **S1.2**:271 (*sidebar*)
    on John Brown **2**:193
    as transcendentalist **1**:356, **2**:92, 416
    Walden **2**:416–21, **S1.2**:98, 102
Thornton, Laurence, *Imagining Argentina* **5**:208–13
Thousand Pieces of Gold, McCunn, Ruthanne Lum **2**:366–71
Three Musketeers, The, Dumas, Alexandre **1**:386–92
Thucydides **1**:14, **S1.1**:311
Thurber, James, "Secret Life of Walter Mitty, The" **3**:364–9
Tiberius **S1.1**:172
Tibet **S1.2**:151–2
Tijerina, Lopez Reies **4**:175, 176, 321, **S1.2**:343, 343 (*sidebar*)
Time of the Hero, The, Vargas Llosa, Mario **5**:333–8
Time magazine **S1.2**:262
"Tintern Abbey," Wordsworth, William **S1.1**:211–12, 213, 215, 215 (*sidebar*)
Titans **1**:301
Tituba (in real life) **1**:79, 83 (*sidebar*), 394–6, 422–3
Tituba of Salem Village, Petry, Ann **1**:393–9
Tobacco
    cigars **3**:65
    rise during 1920s in popularity of smoking **3**:89
    snuff **3**:71 (*sidebar*)
    for women **3**:19, 23, 167, 168 (*illus.*)
To Kill a Mockingbird, Lee, Harper **3**:390–6
To the Lighthouse, Woolf, Virginia **S1.1**:463–72
Tolkien, J.R.R.
    Hobbit, The **1**:152–8, **S1.2**:301
    Lord of the Rings, The **S1.2**:178, 297–307

Tolstoy, Leo
    Anna Karenina **2**:34–40, **S1.1**:368
    Death of Ivan Ilyich, The **S1.1**:71–8
    on *Uncle Tom's Cabin* **2**:409
Tom Brown's Schooldays, Hughes, Thomas **2**:372–7
Tonantzín **S1.2**:499, 501
Toronto, Canada **S1.2**:131 (*sidebar*)
Torture by police/security forces **S1.2**:119
Totalitarianism. *See* Dictatorship
Tournaments **1**:291
Towns and cities, growth of. *See* Urbanization
Transcendentalism **1**:356–7, **2**:54, 92, 314, 316–19, 416, 418–19
Transportation
    Appalachian Trail **5**:278–9
    automobiles **2**:128 (*sidebar*), **3**:23, 77, 88–9, 94, 101, **5**:40 (*illus.*), **S1.2**:281
    aviation **3**:211–12
    canals **2**:230, **3**:184, 231–2, 270, **4**:107
    public
        elevated trams in New York City **S1.1**:3 (*sidebar*)
        segregation of **5**:88–90, 185–6
    roads and highways **3**:77, 91
        Blue Ridge Parkway **5**:278
        Burma Shave roadside signs **S1.2**:281 (*sidebar*)
        creating suburbs **5**:262
        Interstate Highway System **3**:73, **S1.2**:97, 281, 358
        Route 66 **3**:140, **S1.2**:358
    Santa Fe Trail **S1.2**:339–40
    sled dogs **3**:52–6
    steamships **1**:404 (*sidebar*), **2**:391, 394–5
    streetcars **2**:328, **3**:25, **4**:366
    (*See also* Aviation; Railroads in United States)
Transportation (forced resettlement in colonies) as punishment **S1.1**:151, 158
Traveling salesmen **S1.2**:107 (*sidebar*)
Treasure Island, Stevenson, Robert Louis **1**:400–5
Treatments for **4**:290, **S1.2**:148, 149 (*sidebar*)
Tree Grows in Brooklyn, A, Smith, Betty **3**:397–403
Trevor, William, *Felicia's Journey* **S1.2**:133–40
Trial, The, Kafka, Franz **S1.1**:473–82
Trojan War **1**:8, 14, 166–9, 281, 283 (*sidebar*)
Trotsky, Leon **4**:16, **5**:254
Trujillo Molina, Rafael Leonidas **S1.2**:205–9, 207 (*illus.*), 212, 213, 241 (*sidebar*)
Truman Doctrine **4**:110, **5**:123–4, **S1.2**:310
Truman, Harry S **4**:72, 173 (*sidebar*), **5**:96, 123, **S1.2**:2, 363
Truth, Sojourner, "Ain't I a Woman?" **2**:22–7
Tuberculosis **2**:335, **3**:2, 219, 223, **S1.1**:35 (*sidebar*)
Tubman, Harriet **2**:189
Tudor, Henry (later Henry VII of England) **S1.1**:355, 360, 361, 365 (*sidebar*)
"Tuesday Siesta," García Márquez, Gabriel **S1.2**:459–66

Turgenev, Ivan, *Fathers and Sons*   S1.1:99–106, 368
Turkey
   Ali Pasha   2:101
   genocide of Armenians   3:338–43, 4:199
   "guest" workers from, in Europe   4:163–4
   under Ottoman Turks   1:295–6, 3:338–40
   WWI and British occupation of former holdings   4:102
   Young Turks   3:339, 340, 342
Turner, Nat   2:93–4, 95, 169–70, 188, S1.2:229
   (*See also Confessions of Nat Turner, The*)
Turn of the Screw, The, James, Henry   2:378–83
Tuskegee Institute   2:413, 414
Twain, Mark
   Adventures of Huckleberry Finn, The   2:15–21
   "Notorious Jumping Frog of Calaveras County, The"   2:249–54
Twelfth Night, Or, What You Will, Shakespeare, William   S1.1:483–92
Twelve Angry Men, Rose, Reginald (screenplay)   4:378–83
Twenty-Thousand Leagues under the Sea, Verne, Jules   2:384 90
Twinship   4:219
Two Years before the Mast, Dana, Richard Henry, Jr.   2:391–6
Tyler, Anne, *Dinner at the Homesick Restaurant*   S1.2:105–13
Tyler, Wat (Peasant's Revolt of 1381)   1:65
Typewriter   S1.1:80–1

U

UAW (United Auto Workers)   S1.2:144
UFOs (unidentified flying objects)   4:347–8, 5:59 (*illus.*)
Ukraine, Babi Yar massacre   4:120
Uncas   1:207 (*sidebar*), 208
Uncle Remus, Harris, Joel Chandler   2:397–402
Uncle Tom's Cabin, Stowe, Harriet Beecher   2:403–9
   aggravating North-South rift over slavery   2:172
Underground Railroad   2:16, 60, 62, 189, 238, 406–7
Understand This, Tervalon, Jervey   5:339–45
UNIA (United Negro Improvement Association)   3:160, 4:211, S1.1:337 (*sidebar*), 432
"Uniformitarians"   S1.1:329
Unions. *See* Labor movements and unions
Unitarianism   2:54, 315, S1.1:209
United Auto Workers (UAW)   S1.2:144
United Nations   4:103, 107–8
   birth of   5:53–4
   Cold War reflected in   5:254
   "Convention Relating to Status of Refugees"   5:28–9
   Declaration of Women's Rights (1967)   5:174
United Service Organizations (USO)   4:38

United States in 19th century
   American Enlightenment   2:416
   American literature, birth of   1:210, 211, 217, 218, 335–6, 2:419
   American literature, maturation of   2:109, 234 5
   appeal of European travel to middle- to upper-class Americans   2:105–6
   belief in progress   2:195, 196, 313, 416
   canal system   2:230
   conquest of Mexico's northern territories (1848)   S1.2:83, 501
   conservatism and commerce   2:199, 306, 312, 328, 331
   democracy, growth of   2:87–8, 89–91
   depressions in later years   3:51, 169
   dissent, protest, and civil disobedience   2:87, 89, 90, 312
   economic growth   2:195, 230, 416
   Gilded Age   2:20, 199, 306, 312, 328, 331, S1.1:2
   Hispanos in New Mexico   S1.2:339–44, 346–7
   immigration, hard times, labor unrest, and urban riots   S1.1:272, 282
   Jackson administration   2:314 15
   Mexican War   2:88, 89, 242, 5:172, S1.2:340, 367, 431
   rural New England   2:125–6
   War of 1812   1:53, 2:416
   whaling industry   2:230, 232–4
   (*See also* Civil War; Railroads in United States; Reconstruction; Slavery in America; West, The; Western migration)
United States in 20th century: Progressive Era (1900–1919)
   as era of reform   3:75–6, 284 5
   labor unions, support for   3:420
   muckraking journalists   3:176, 320
   multifaceted agenda of   3:285, 319–20
   postwar return to (probusiness) normalcy   3:21
   reformers as elitist   3:319
   reforming zeal carried to other countries   3:280
   trust busters and Teddy Roosevelt   3:167
   women's roles changing   3:271–2, 280 (*sidebar*)
   Woodrow Wilson   3:279–80, 319
   World War I (1917–18). *See* World War I
United States in 20th century: Roaring Twenties (1920–1929)
   agricultural depression   3:94 5, 138–40, S1.1:421
   assembly line/mass production   3:89, 100–1, 102
   boomtowns   3:25
   buying on credit   3:89
   car culture   3:23
   consumer/mass culture, advertising   3:26, 89, 100–1, 102
   fear of immigration from Central, Eastern, and Southern Europe   S1.1:421

United States in 20th century: Roaring Twenties (1920–1929) (*continued*)
   gangsters and St. Valentine's Day Massacre   **3**:366–7
   machine age as degrading individualism and culture   **5**:41
   modern morals and changing status of women   **3**:23, 228–9
   postwar economic boom   **3**:146
   Prohibition. *See* Prohibition
   race riots (1919)   **2**:6, 404, **3**:160, 252, 321, **4**:310
   San Francisco's corruption   **3**:226
   stock market speculation fever   **3**:146
   Teapot Dome scandal   **3**:25
   United Fruit Company in South America   **2**:269–70

United States in 20th century: Thirties (1930–1940). *See* Great Depression, The

United States in 20th century: World War II (1941–45). *See* World War II

United States in 20th century: 1946–1959
   age of big government   **4**:110
   baby boom   **1**:224, **2**:325–6, **4**:38, 74, 240, **S1.2**:107
   beats and beatniks, counterculture, hippies, and protesters   **4**:75, 289, 293, 399–400, **S1.2**:364 5, 364 (*sidebar*)
   beats' yearning for otherness and authenticity of African Americans   **S1.2**:361–2
   Cold War. *See* Cold War
   consumerism, credit buying, and conformity, alienation   **3**:2, 91, **4**:73–4, 110–11, 236, 328, 397–401, **5**:322–3, **S1.2**:359, 364
   cultural underground   **S1.2**:364
   disillusion, dehumanization, and dystopian literature   **5**:252
   divide between norm (safe) and deviant (unsafe)   **S1.2**:359
   divorce rate increase   **4**:38
   environmental movement and national park system   **S1.2**:95–103
   global commercial and cultural influence   **1**:223, **3**:92
   "heroes" as powerful and nonconformist   **4**:262, 292, 381–2
   inflation and anxiety   **4**:109–10
   mass culture and influence of television   **4**:111, 379, 398
   paranoia and timidity   **S1.2**:363–4
   postwar boom, prosperity, growth of suburbs   **4**:73, 109–10, 328, 384, 385, **5**:261–2, **S1.2**:358–9, 364, 422
   teenage culture   **4**:172, 391–3, 394 5
   teenagers and juvenile crime   **S1.2**:284 5
   War Brides Act   **4**:124, 127, **5**:231
   white male economic dominance   **4**:397
   women and cult of domesticity   **4**:237, 240–1
   women as sex objects   **4**:393

United States in 20th century: 1960s
   activists, rights movements   **S1.1**:19
   appeal of Eastern religions   **5**:237, 281
   Chicano activism   **S1.2**:342–3, 367–9, 504 5
   civil rights protests. *See* Civil rights movement
   counterculture, hippies, and protesters   **5**:37, 64 (*sidebar*), 83, 158, 237, 272, 279, 308–10, 323–5, **S1.2**:108–9, 178
   cults, iconoclasm, rebels as heros   **5**:83–4, 318 (*sidebar*), 323–4
   decade of tumult   **5**:309 (*sidebar*)
   environment, concern for   **4**:337–42, **5**:85–6, 279, **S1.2**:180–1
   feminism. *See* Women's rights movement (and feminism)
   "free love" movement   **5**:272
   "graying" of America   **5**:202–4
   Johnson's Great Society and War on Poverty   **3**:324, **5**:68, 150, 266
   Kennedy and idealistic youth   **S1.1**:19–20
   riots   **2**:97–8, **3**:324, **4**:207, **5**:112 (*sidebar*), 340, **S1.2**:424
   self-fulfillment and human potential movement   **5**:204, 287–8
   teens as subculture   **S1.1**:19
   (*See also* Vietnam War)

United States in 20th century: 1970s 1980s
   antibusing incidents   **3**:324
   disillusion with government after Nixon and Watergate   **3**:99, **5**:158–9, 263, 317
   environment, concern for   **5**:279 (*sidebar*)
   feminism. *See* Women's rights movement (and feminism)
   Hispanic boom   **S1.2**:375–6
   judicial opposition to civil rights legislation   **5**:1–2
   "me" generation and self-help movements   **5**:263, 287–8
   official apology and monetary compensation to Japanese Americans for WWII internment   **4**:143, 195
   probusiness conservatism (Reagan presidency)   **5**:1
   recession, unemployment, and welfare cuts   **5**:1, 329
   rise of New Right and religious fundamentalists   **5**:136–9
   sexual revolution   **5**:151, **S1.2**:230 (*sidebar*), 505
   (*See also* Vietnam War)

United States in 20th century: 1990s
   reactionary measures against Chicanos   **S1.2**:375–6
   riots   **S1.2**:354

United States Military. *See* Military

Up From Slavery, Washington, Booker T.   **2**:410–15

Urbanization
   in 19th-century America   **2**:125, 195, 301–4
   in 19th-century England   **1**:106, 217, 417, **2**:118, 353, 354, 358
   in 19th-century France   **2**:103–4, 209

in 20th-century America   3:25, 73, 88–9,
    4:171–2
in 20th-century South   5:91
in 20th-century South Africa   4:95
on American East Coast   S1.1:271
by American Indians in 20th century   4:186,
    S1.2:154
in Chile   5:164
cities viewed as hotbeds of sin   3:69
of colonial America   1:102
czarist Russia   S1.1:369
department stores made possible by   2:303
with immigration   2:302, 327, 3:101, 102, 166
in Japan   S1.2:218, 221
London   S1.1:324
Mexican Americans   4:171
in mill towns   S1.1:209
Minneapolis Ojibwe   S1.2:33
promoting individualism   2:302
replacing rural, agrarian society   2:312, 327,
    5:91
rise of crime and police detectives   2:153–4
(*See also* Ghettos; Housing)
U.S. Army. *See* Military
U.S.S.R. *See* Soviet Union
USS *Somers*   1:56
Usury (moneylending)   1:103–4, 182–3, 243, 247
Utilitarianism   S1.1:32, 33 (*sidebar*), 295
Utopian socialism   5:251–2, S1.1:52
Utopian societies
    depicted in literature   5:251–2
    in novel *Looking Backward* (1888)   2:423
    of 1840s   2:418
    Shakers   3:95–9
    Twin Oaks colony   5:279
    Walden movement   5:279

V

Valdez, Luis   5:172
    Zoot Suit   4:403–10
Vampire fiction   S1.1:146
Vampire legends   S1.1:84 (*sidebar*)
Vanderbilt, Alva   S1.1:2
Vanderbilt, Cornelius   S1.1:2
Vanderbilt, William H.   S1.1:2
Van Dine, S. S.   3:227
Van Gogh, Vincent   S1.1:463–4
Vargas Llosa, Mario   5:211 (*sidebar*)
    Aunt Julia and the Scriptwriter   S1.2:51–61
        political activism   S1.2:59, 59 (*sidebar*)
    Time of the Hero, The   5:333–8
Veblen, Thorstein   3:169
Vechten, Carl Van   S1.1:337–8
Vendidos   S1.2:504 5
Venice, Italy   1:242–6, 295–7
Verne, Jules
    Twenty-Thousand Leagues under the Sea   2:384 90
    H. G. Wells compared to   3:410
Verona, Italy   1:344 5

Verrall, Richard   4:40
Vesey, Denmark   2:94 5
Veterinarians   3:1
Victor Emmanuel III, King of Italy   4:66, 67
Victorian Age (1837–1901)
    anxiety toward "otherness," fear of differences
        S1.1:140
    charity   2:264
    circuses and freak shows   2:33, 120, 329
    class divisions and social stratification   1:376,
        413–14, 2:152–3, 157, 277–8, 296–7, 358,
        S1.1:240
    conformity, respectability, versus uncertainty,
        repression, hypocrisy   S1.1:184 6
    crime   2:262–4, S1.1:151, 272
    debt, bankruptcy, and poorhouses   2:211–12,
        261–2, 266
    divorce   2:158, 355–6
    earnestness, sobriety, religiosity versus hedonism,
        frivolity   S1.1:179–80
    economic and agricultural depression, foreign
        competition   2:152, 353
    economic depression in "Hungry '40s," despair,
        and disenfranchisement   S1.1:31–2, 44
        (*sidebar*)
    education, progress in   1:412, 2:334
    empire, arrogance, and deep anxiety
        S1.1:79–80
    England as world's leading economic power
        2:334
    humor and puns   2:30
    hypocrisy of   3:381
    idealization of honor and duty   S1.1:465
        (*sidebar*)
    imperialism   2:118–19
    landed gentry's decline   2:354 5
    London as center of   1:417, 2:20, 196
    love and marriage in. *See under* Love and
        marriage
    marriage, prostitution, and disease   S1.1:141–2
    medievalism   S1.1:291–2
    men's roles in   2:107–8, 336
    mining industry   2:335
    mourning traditions   1:414 15
    nuclearization and changing family dynamics
        S1.1:240–1
    philanthropy   S1.1:154 (*sidebar*)
    police, reorganization of   2:153–4
    pride plus anxiety   3:405–6, 408–9
    public school system   2:372–7
    rationalism and order   S1.1:81
    science, evolution, fear of degeneration or
        extinction, and crisis of faith   S1.1:85–6, 295,
        327, 328, 329
    science, society, and idea of progress   S1.1:330
    science vs. religion   2:29–30, 3:404
    sexual repression   2:334, 336, 338–9, 355,
        3:18, 380–1
    urbanization with industrialization   1:417,
        2:118, 353, 354, 358

Victorian Age (1837–1901) (*continued*)
    work ethic and circumscribed codes of behavior/decorum   2:20, 108, 196, 378–9, 3:381
    Yorkshire   1:417–18
    (*See also* Colonialism, imperialism, and interventionism)
Victorian women
    American stereotype of   2:107
    as "angels in the house" and queen of domestic sphere   S1.1:141, 293, 294, 294 (*sidebar*), 325, 468–70
    divorce   2:158, 355–6
    as domestic, passive   S1.1:470
    dowries for   2:246
    education of   1:412, 2:30, 181–2, 422–3
    emancipation of, opponents and proponents   1:356, 3:167
    employment
        denial of meaningful work   2:426, 427
        as domestic servants   S1.1:470
        as governesses   2:182, 183 (*sidebar*), 378–80
        limited opportunities for   2:203, 355, S1.1:141
        need to supplement husband's income   3:168–9
        in prostitution   2:228, 264, 328–9, 355, S1.1:141
    evolution and the "Woman Question"   2:423–4
    fashionable clothing as restricting   3:420
    fashion and home furnishings for status   2:246, 247 (*sidebar*), 3:420
    as "feminine"   2:204, 206–7
    as "helpless"   3:19
    as "hysterical"   2:425
    ignorant preferred to educated, by men   2:380
    inequities of sexual double standard   S1.1:142
    as innocent and chaste   2:422–5
    lack of rights   2:356
    marriage and domestic roles for   2:106–7, 108, 116, 202, 303, 336, 3:167, S1.1:241, 245
    as "maternal"   2:212, 404
    "New Woman"   S1.1:80–1, 181–2
    as organizers of philanthropies   S1.1:154 (*sidebar*)
    prejudice against as writers   1:415 (*sidebar*), 2:56, 186, 203, 212, 424–5
    shopping and department stores   2:303
    social calls   3:321–3
    as spinsters in England   2:297
    supposed moral superiority of   2:106, 3:16, 18, 167, 228
    "The Woman Question"   S1.1:154 (*sidebar*), 155
    view of themselves as "interesting"   2:106
    (*See also* Love and marriage)
Victoria, Queen of England   2:28, 335
Vidocq, Eugène François   3:226, S1.1:278 (*sidebar*)
Vienna, Austria   S1.1:313–15, 315 (*sidebar*)

Vietnam War
    American Indian soldiers in   5:362–3
    arising from Cold War's "domino theory"   2:13–14, 4:347, 375, 5:101–2, 158, S1.2:452 (*sidebar*)
    arising from French hopes to recolonize Indochina   5:306–7
    atrocities, compared to those inflicted upon American Indians   2:79
    black soldiers in   5:102–3
    combat against jungle guerillas   5:103
    in context of Cold War   S1.2:451–3
    depicted in *The Things They Carried*   S1.2:451–8
    Diem regime   S1.2:452
    draft of Chicanos   4:176
    draft of disadvantaged for (Project 100,000)   5:102–3, 158, 307
    drafted African Americans in disproportionately high numbers   S1.2:453 (*sidebar*)
    drug abuse by soldiers   S1.2:454
    fall of South Vietnam to communist North   5:307
    government credibility gap and antiwar movement   S1.2:457–8
    hostility of populace differing from previous U.S. wars   S1.2:453–4
    impact on American culture   S1.2:454 5
    Johnson's escalation of involvement   5:158, 307
    Kennedy's sending of "advisors"   5:158, 307
    MyLai Massacre   S1.2:454 (*sidebar*)
    protested by
        anti-Vietnam war movements   2:13–14, 3:98, 324, 4:347, 5:105–6, 158, 307–8, S1.1:19, S1.2:178
        blacks   4:207, 5:103 (*sidebar*)
        Chicanos   4:409–10
        students at Kent State University   5:158
        women and mothers   5:308
        young men subject to draft   5:307–8
        young people   5:271
    reflected in *Grendel*   S1.2:179–80
    return of POWs   4:376
    seen as West's failure to contain communism   4:135
    soldiers' experience   S1.2:453–4
    soldiers and Post-Traumatic Stress Disorder (P.T.S.D.)   S1.2:455 (*sidebar*)
    Tonkin Gulf Resolution and Johnson's policy of escalation   S1.2:453, 457
    U.S. forces withdrawn from   4:375–6
    U.S. soldiers questioning purposes of   5:104 5
    U.S. soldiers' reasons for enlisting   5:307 (*sidebar*)
    veterans' postwar experience   5:105–6, S1.2:454 5
    Vietnam Memorial   5:105 (*illus.*), 106, 312
    as world's first "television" war   5:3–7, 37
Vigilantism
    in frontier West   1:256–7, 2:323–4
    in rural California   3:273–4
    in San Francisco of 1850s   2:286–7

tarring and feathering by mobs 2:17 (sidebar)
(*See also* Ku Klux Klan; Lynching)
Vikings 1:49, 138, 226, S1.2:172
Villa, Francisco "Pancho" (Doroteo Arango) 3:197, 279, S1.2:84 (*illus.*), 86
Villarreal, José Antonio 5:172
Pocho 4:295–302
Vindication of the Rights of Woman, A, Wollstonecraft, Mary 1:406–12, 2:297, S1.1:241, 391
Viracocha people 4:221, 222
Virgil
Aeneid, The 1:8–13
as character in Dante's *Inferno* 1:176–7, 178–9
Virginia 1:379, 384, 394, 5:278–84
Virgin Mary
contrasted with La Malinche as image of womanhood S1.2:507–8
as Virgin of Guadalupe (Mexico) S1.2:499–501, 500 (*illus.*), 507, 508
Voigt, Cynthia, *Runner, The* 5:306–13
Voltaire, François Marie Arouet de, *Candide* S1.1:21–30
Von Blixen, Bror S1.2:489, 493
Von Braun, Werner S1.2:311
Vonnegut, Kurt, Jr., *Slaughterhouse Five* 4:343–8
Vorster, B. J. S1.2:119
Voting rights. *See* Suffrage (right to vote)

W

Waiting for Godot, Beckett, Samuel S1.2:406, 467–76
Waka poetry (Japanese) S1.1:450
Walden, Thoreau, Henry David 2:416–21, S1.2:98, 102
Wales 1:288, 3:63–4, 66
Walker, Alice, *Color Purple, The* 3:80–7, S1.2:389
Wallace, Alfred Russell S1.1:323
Wallenberg, Raoul S1.2:66
Walpole, Robert 1:266, 269
War
antiwar sentiment. *See* Antiwar literature
Arab-Israeli Six-Day War (1967) 4:93
Cold War 1:84, 223, 388–9
England's civil war 1:303, 305–6
England's wars with France 1:51–2, 93, 123, 130–1, 159, 160, 204 6, 220–1, 305
England's wars with Spain 1:1–2, 87, 88, 130–1, 201, 306
French and Indian War (Seven Years' War) 1:93, 123, 204 6, 220–1, S1.1:14, 24 5
glorification vs. reality of battle 2:257, 258, 308, 309 (*sidebar*), 312, 313, 3:9–11, 12–13, 4:69–70
Korean 1:223, 3:73, 4:92
Mexican 2:88, 89, 242, 5:172, S1.2:340, 367, 431
Mexican Revolution S1.2:85–6
Napoleonic 2:99–100, 295–6, S1.1:100, 114
Peloponnesian 1:241, 324, 328, S1.1:311–12, 352

Revolutions of 1848 (Europe) 1:376, S1.1:44 (*sidebar*), 102
Russo-Turkish 2:37–9
Sino-Indian (1962) S1.2:151–2
Spanish-American (1898) 3:101, 278, S1.2:73
Thirty Years 1:87, 88, 388, 388 (*sidebar*)
Trojan 1:8, 14, 166–9, 281, 281 (*illus.*), 283 (*sidebar*)
Vietnam. *See* Vietnam War
War of 1812 1:53, 2:416
Wars of the Roses S1.1:355–65
(*See also* American Revolution; Antiwar literature; Civil War; France in 18th century: French Revolution; Military; Vietnam War; World War I; World War II)
War on Poverty 3:324, 5:68, 150, 266
Warren, Mary 1:81 (*sidebar*), 83 (*sidebar*)
War weaponry
aircraft
bombers 4:67–8
dive-bombers 4:359
fighter bombers 4:67
fighters 4:361, S1.1:465
helicopters 4:71
jets 4:71
reconnaissance in WWI S1.2:490
aircraft carriers 4:59
arms manufacturing and dealing S1.1:221–2, 221 (*sidebar*), S1.2:2
atomic/nuclear 4:71
arms control proposals 4:71, 5:126, 225, 239, 252 (*sidebar*)
hydrogen bomb 4:183, 5:126
Manhattan Project 4:71, 81–2, 316
missiles 5:124
(*See also* Atom bomb)
barbed wire used as 3:113
in *Beowulf* 1:46 (*illus.*)
field artillery 3:113
incendiary bombs 4:179
Indians' horses and guns S1.1:130, 135 (*illus.*)
landing craft 4:60
machine gun 3:9, 113, S1.1:465
minesweepers 4:61
poison gas S1.1:465
rockets 5:54, 96, S1.2:311–12, 311 (*sidebar*)
submarines 1:277–8, S1.1:465
tanks S1.1:465
technological enhancements during WWI 3:113, S1.1:465
technology causing anxiety 3:406, 4:255
War of the Worlds, The, Wells, H.G. 3:404 10, S1.1:140, S1.2:314
Orson Welles' October 1938 broadcast of 3:154, 365, 408 (*sidebar*), S1.2:143
Washington, Booker T.
advocating (temporary) acceptance of segregation 2:341, 342, 343, 344, 345, 410, 413, 414, 3:162, 250, 320, 385

Index

Washington, Booker T. (*continued*)
  advocating vocational training and hard work   S1.1:337 (sidebar), S1.2:428
  autobiography: *Up From Slavery*   2:410–15
  compared to Du Bois   2:345 (sidebar), 3:162, 250, 320, 385, S1.1:337 (sidebar), S1.2:428
Waste Land, The, Eliot, T.S.   3:357, 411–17, S1.1:259
Watergate scandal   3:99, 5:158–9, 263, 317
Watership Down, Adams, Richard   5:346–51
Watkins, Yoko K., *So Far from the Bamboo Grove*   4:349–55
Watson, John Boradus   5:45
Watt, James   S1.1:209
Way to Rainy Mountain, The, Momaday, N. Scott   S1.2:477–86
Weaver, George "Buck"   3:149
Webb, Beatrice   S1.1:222 (sidebar)
Webb, Stanley   S1.1:222 (sidebar)
Weizmann, Chaim   4:102, 103
Welch, James, *Fools Crow*   S1.1:129–38, S1.2:168
Weld, Theodore D.   2:242
"Welfare state"   S1.2:474
Welles, Orson   3:365, 408
Wells-Barnett, Ida B.   3:83, 420
Wells Fargo   2:293
Wells, H. G.
  influenced by science and Darwinism   3:404 5
  on *Portrait of the Artist as a Young Man*   3:309 (sidebar), 311
  rejection of Christianity   3:404
  War of the Worlds, The   3:404 10, S1.1:140, S1.2:314
Welty, Eudora, "Worn Path, The"   3:418–24
Wesley, John   S1.1:208
West, The
  California gold rush   2:174 5, 195, 249–50, 281–4
  Chinese prostitutes   2:366–7
  disappearance of the frontier   S1.1:288–9
  gunfighters   2:323–4
  homesteaders   2:127 (sidebar), 128, 322–3, 3:244, 257, 259, 260–1, S1.1:281–4
  humor, practical jokes, and tall tales   2:250–1
  Nebraska   3:257–8, 260, S1.1:282–3, 288–9
  racism against Chinese   2:175, 287, 367–8, 370 (sidebar), 371
  ranching and cattle barons on Great Plains   2:321–2
  Teddy Roosevelt popularizing "Old West" myth of individualism   5:206
  settling and demise of frontier   2:312
  Wells Fargo   2:293
  women on frontier   2:323
Western migration
  beginning in colonial times   1:102, 103, 107
  California gold rush   2:174 5, 195, 249–50
  Donner Party   2:282 (sidebar)
  encouraged by Homestead Act (1870)   2:322–3, 3:244, 257, S1.1:281–4
  encouraged by U.S. Government   2:314
  end of western frontier   2:68
  hardship and survivalism   3:259–60
  increasing job opportunities for women in East   2:423
  land speculators   3:258
  Manifest Destiny   2:76 (sidebar), 3:234, S1.1:136
  Mexican War   2:88, 89, 242, 395, 5:172, S1.2:340
  Nevada silver strikes   2:288–9, 290 (sidebar)
  Oregon Trail   S1.1:131
  pressures upon American Indians   2:67, 74
  railroads   2:175, 195
  single women absent from   2:56, 250
  to Nebraska   3:257–8, S1.1:282
  (*See also* Gold rushes and silver strikes)
West Germany   S1.2:309–10
West Indies   2:183–4, S1.1:493–6
West with the Night, Markham, Beryl   S1.2:487–97
Weston, Jessie L.   3:415
West Side Story, Laurents, Arthur, et al.   4:384 90
Wet-nurses   2:211
Whaling industry   2:230, 232–4
Wharton, Edith
  Age of Innocence, The   S1.1:1–9
  Ethan Frome   2:125–9, S1.1:9
  House of Mirth, The   3:166–73
Wheatley, Phillis   S1.1:436, S1.2:389
"Where Are You Going, Where Have You Been?," Oates, Joyce Carol   4:391–6
Whewell, William   S1.1:325
Whitehead, Alfred North   S1.2:179
"White man's burden" and white supremacy   2:119, 147, 341, 3:170, 172, 182 (sidebar)
Whitman, Walt
  on imperialism   3:300 (sidebar)
  Leaves of Grass   2:195–201
Whyte, William   4:75, 382
Wide Sargasso Sea, Rhys, Jean   S1.1:493–502, S1.2:178
Wiesel, Elie
  Dawn   4:101–8
  Night   4:267–73
Wiesenthal, Simon   4:273
Wight, James Alfred. *See* Herriott, James
Wilberforce, Bishop Samuel   S1.1:330
Wilberforce, William   S1.1:495
Wilde, Oscar   S1.1:82
  Importance of Being Earnest, The   S1.1:179–87
Wilder, Thornton, *Our Town*   3:284 9
Wilhelm II, Kaiser (Germany)   3:8
Wilkins, Roy   5:186, 188
William the Conqueror   1:250, 290
William of Orange   1:130
Williams, Claude "Lefty"   3:149, 4:260, 261, 5:316
Williams, Eric   S1.2:184, 188
Williamson, Joel   3:387
Williams, Paulette Linda. *See* Shange, Ntozake

Williams, Tennessee
 Glass Menagerie, The   **S1.2**:141–50
 Streetcar Named Desire, A   **4**:364 70, **S1.2**:141
Wilson, August
 Fences   **4**:144 50
 Piano Lesson, The   **S1.2**:379–86
Wilson, Edmund
 praise for *Animal Farm*   **4**:19–20
 praise for *The Waste Land*   **3**:417
Wilson, Woodrow   **3**:279–80, 319
Winthrop, Gov. John   **1**:78, 352 (*sidebar*)
Witchcraft
 belief in, by Latinos (*brujas*)   **4**:46
 belief in, by Puritans   **1**:79–81, 102, 393, 394
 belief in, in medieval Scotland   **1**:227–8
 in *The Crucible*   **1**:78–86
 in "The Devil and Tom Walker"   **1**:101–6
 interest of James I in   **1**:228
 in *Macbeth*   **1**:227–8
 spectral evidence of   **1**:421–2
 in *Tituba of Salem Village*   **1**:394 7
 witches' sabbath   **1**:423 (*illus.*)
 witch trials   **1**:79, 83, 85 (*illus.*), 355, 395–6, 397 (*illus.*)
 in "Young Goodman Brown"   **1**:420–6
 (*See also* Supernatural)
Wolfe, Tom, *Right Stuff, The*   **5**:291–7
Wollstonecraft, Mary
 as first English feminist   **3**:359, **S1.1**:241
 mother of Mary Shelley   **1**:115, 116, 407
 similarities to, in Elizabeth Bennet   **2**:297
 tribute by William Blake   **1**:410 (*sidebar*)
 Vindication of the Rights of Woman, A   **1**:406–12, **S1.1**:391
Woman Hollering Creek and Other Stories, Cisneros, Sandra   **S1.2**:499–509
Woman Warrior, The, Kingston, Maxine Hong   **5**:352–9
Women, (*See also* African American women; Education of women; Love and marriage; Victorian women)
Women in ancient times
 as "Great Goddesses" and Amazons   **1**:58–9, 61–2, 258, 259–60
 in Greece   **1**:17, 20, 58–9, 259, 327, **S1.1**:309
 Imperial Rome   **S1.1**:172–3
 Japanese salon culture of emperor's consorts   **S1.1**:451
 names in Rome   **1**:190 (*sidebar*)
 Plato on leadership roles for   **1**:325, 327
 as rulers in Celtic England   **1**:197
 as spoils of war   **1**:8, 169, 170–1
Women in medieval times
 as depicted by Chaucer   **1**:69
 Japanese women subject to sexual double standard   **S1.1**:454
 in Scotland   **1**:226
Women in 15th century, in salons of Paris   **1**:31, 88–9
Women in 16th century
 prejudice against, as leaders   **1**:236
 in Tudor and Elizabethan England   **1**:232–3, 236, 263–4, **S1.1**:491
 (*See also* Elizabeth I of England)
Women in 17th century, targeted in witchhunts   **1**:80
Women in 18th century
 on colonial farms   **1**:334
 defiance of convention   **1**:406, 407, 409
 urging education and rights for   **1**:406, 408–11
 as wet-nurses   **2**:211
Women in 19th century
 American or British
  as arbiters of upper class society   **S1.1**:3–4
  expectation of probably loveless marriage   **S1.1**:160 (*sidebar*)
  hardship and isolation of farms and homesteads   **2**:127 (*sidebar*), 128, **3**:259, 260–1, **S1.1**:284
  involvement in abolition of slavery   **2**:23–4
  involvement in reform movements   **2**:423
  marriage and loss of property rights   **S1.1**:496
  in prostitution   **2**:228, 264, 283–4, 328–9, 355, **4**:37
  Southern ideal of, 3.19, 392–3, **2**:138
  subordination to husband   **S1.1**:8, 496
  by suicide   **S1.1**:383 (*sidebar*)
  teaching freed slaves   **2**:411–12
  as wet-nurses   **2**:211
  (*See also* Victorian women)
 Chinese   **2**:366–7, 368 (*sidebar*), 370–1
 French   **2**:212, 244, 247
 Japanese   **S1.2**:219
 Russian   **S1.1**:76, 370
Women in 20th century
 activism
  participation in Progressive Era's reform movements   **3**:75, 76
  protesting Vietnam War   **5**:308
 African   **S1.2**:47
 Chicanas   **S1.2**:505
 Chinese   **3**:132–3, 134 5, 191–3, **4**:128
 dangers of childbirth   **3**:285–6
 daughters, relationship with   **S1.2**:23–4
 emancipation of
  flappers and the "New Woman"   **S1.1**:80–1, 181–2, 441–2, **S1.2**:105
  Japanese   **S1.2**:415
  negative portrayals in detective fiction of 1920s   **3**:228–9
  new freedoms of 1920s   **3**:147
  opponents and proponents   **3**:167
  single mothers of 1950s as "irrational"   **4**:169 (*sidebar*)
 employment for   **2**:326, **3**:271, **5**:138
  in aviation   **S1.2**:494 5
  as chorus girls   **2**:329
  in domestic service   **S1.1**:470
  during Great Depression   **S1.2**:147 (*sidebar*)
  as midwives   **4**:218

Index

Women in 20th century (*continued*)
 employment for (*continued*)
  as repugnant to Religious Right **5**:137
  in Salvation Army in high-ranking positions **S1.1**:220
  as threat to traditional male power **S1.2**:235–6
  as typists **S1.1**:80–1
  in wartime and afterwards **4**:21–2, 74, 166–7, 196 (*illus.*), 197–8, **S1.2**:2, 106–7
 fashions for. *See* Fashions
 Haitian **S1.2**:243–4
 image issues
  as domestic, passive, and "feminine" **1**:33–4, 35–6, **2**:326, **4**:22, 74, 167, 237, 240–1
  self-sacrifice, self-abnegation **S1.2**:93
  women rejecting docility **S1.1**:420–1
 importance of marriage **3**:168
 Japanese **S1.2**:219, 409–19, 418 (*sidebar*)
 Jewish **3**:427–30
 in Maoist thought **3**:136
 Mexican **3**:197–8, 200–2, **S1.2**:15
 Mexican soldaderas and soldadas **S1.2**:90 (*sidebar*), 503
 rural life
  isolation of **3**:271
  for sharecropper families **3**:370–1
  on Texas frontier **3**:246
 sexual issues
  as "repository of honor" **S1.2**:15
  as sexual goddesses, sex objects **4**:74, 393
  subject to sexual double standard **4**:38, 74, 395, **S1.1**:420–1
  victims of male sexual aggression **S1.2**:236
  violence and gender **S1.1**:154 6
 as single heads of households **2**:65, **3**:80, 423, **4**:2, **5**:68, 117, 136, 138, 267, 328–9, **S1.2**:107, 256
 suicide **4**:22–6
 (*See also* African American women)
Women's rights movement (and feminism)
 in 19th-century Norway **S1.1**:166
 abortion and *Roe v. Wade* **5**:51, 136
 advocating self-determination **5**:138–9
 antifeminist backlash **5**:136
 association with Civil rights movement **S1.2**:234 5
 authors active in
  Gilman **2**:424
  Le Guin's take on **5**:237–8
  Morrison **2**:64
  Renault's sympathy with **1**:62
  Woolf **3**:330–2
 battered wives shelters **5**:136
 black feminism **2**:64, **3**:86–7, 354 5, **4**:56, **5**:92–3, 117, **S1.2**:394 (*sidebar*)
 in Britain **3**:359, **S1.1**:92
 Chicana women's movement **3**:202
 combating anxiety over women in public sphere **S1.1**:144
 in czarist Russia **2**:37, 39
 educated women at core of **5**:135
 elusive freedoms of 1920s **S1.1**:441–2
 hiatus between 1918 and 1960s **5**:135–6
 impact of Friedan's *The Feminine Mystique* **1**:62, **2**:58, **3**:430, **4**:11 (*sidebar*), 167, 241, 394, **5**:51 (*illus.*), 136, **S1.2**:285–6
 landmark legislation of 1880s **S1.1**:155
 legislation affecting
  Civil Rights Act (1964), Title VII **1**:35, **5**:136
  Equal Pay Act (1963) **1**:35, **5**:237
  Equal Rights Amendment (ERA) **3**:79, **5**:51, 136, 358–9, **S1.2**:230 (*sidebar*)
  Higher Education Act (1972), Title IX, **5**:136
 in Mexico **3**:201–2
 National Organization of Women (NOW) **1**:62, **4**:22, 394, **5**:136, 237
 in Norway **2**:112–13
 origins in
  19th century **2**:22, 24, 25, 27, 55, 204, 423, **3**:16, **S1.1**:8
  abolitionist movement **2**:24, 204
  civil rights movement of 20th century **1**:35, **2**:58, **S1.2**:230 (*sidebar*)
  discontent of women in 1950s **4**:167–70, **5**:136
  EEOC's refusal to enforce Title VII **5**:237
  Friedan's *Feminine Mystique* **1**:62, **2**:58, **3**:430, **4**:11 (*sidebar*), 167, 241, 394, **5**:51 (*illus.*), 136, **S1.2**:285–6
  gender discrimination in workplace **1**:35, **5**:136
  myths of women's selfless inclination to serve and nurture **5**:136, 288
  objections to sexual double standard **4**:38, 74, 395, **S1.1**:142, 163 (*sidebar*)
  oppression and discrimination **2**:23–4, 355–6, 380, 422, 423–6
  sexual harassment in workplace **1**:35
  women's subordination to men **4**:169, 170
 rape crisis centers **5**:136
 role of women's clubs **2**:336, **3**:16–17, 287 (*sidebar*)
 Russian feminism, dawn of **S1.1**:370 (*sidebar*)
 in Victorian England **2**:335, **S1.1**:247
 "women's liberation" **S1.2**:286
 women's studies programs resulting **5**:117
Women's rights and roles, discussion pertaining to
 Annie John **S1.2**:22–4
 Antigone **1**:14 21
 Canterbury Tales, The **1**:68–9
 Ethan Frome **2**:126–7, 128–9
 "Goblin Market, The" **S1.1**:141–2, 143–5
 Left Hand of Darkness, The **5**:237–8, 239–40, 242
 "Lottery, The" **4**:237
 Macbeth **1**:226
 Maltese Falcon, The **3**:228–9
 Midsummer Night's Dream, A **1**:259–60, 261–4

Mill on the Floss, The S1.1:241
"Noon Wine" 3:246–7
Odyssey 1:282, 285
Of Mice and Men 3:271–2
Passage to India, A 3:301–2
Sweet Whispers, Brother Rush 5:329
To the Lighthouse S1.1:463–72
Turn of the Screw, The 2:379–80, 381–2
Woman Hollering Creek and Other Stories S1.2:503–5, 507
"Worn Path, The" 3:420–1
Women's rights and roles, literary works emphasizing
"Ain't I a Woman?" 2:22–7
Anna Karenina 2:34 40, S1.1:368
Annie John S1.2:19–27
Awakening, The 3:15–20
Beauty: A Retelling of the Story of Beauty and the Beast 1:30–6
Belle of Amherst, The 2:54 8
Bell Jar, The 4:21–7
Beloved 2:59–65
Bluest Eye, The 4:49–57
Carrie 5:46–52
Color Purple, The 3:80–7
Daisy Miller 2:105–10
Dinner at the Homesick Restaurant, Tyler, Anne S1.2:105–13
Doll's House, A 2:111–17
Emma S1.1:89–97
Felicia's Journey S1.2:133–40
for colored girls who have considered suicide / when the rainbow is enuf 5:115–21
Glass Menagerie, The S1.2:141–50
Golden Notebook, The 4:165–70
Gone with the Wind 2:137–44
Handmaid's Tale, The 5:135–42
House of Mirth, The 3:166–73
House of the Spirits, The 5:163–70
House on Mango Street, The 5:171–7
I Know Why the Caged Bird Sings 4:201–8
Incidents in the Life of a Slave Girl 2:168–73
In the Time of the Butterflies S1.2:205–15, 213 (sidebar), 214 (illus.)
Jacob Have I Loved 4:216–20
Jane Eyre 1:415, 415 (sidebar), 419, 2:181–7, S1.1:493, S1.2:24 5
Joy Luck Club, The 5:229–35
Kitchen God's Wife, The 3:189–95
Like Water for Chocolate 3:196–202
Little Women 2:202–8
Madame Bovary 2:209–15
Medea 1:238–41
Member of the Wedding, The 4:254 9
O Pioneers! 3:257–63, S1.1:281
Out of Africa 3:290–6
Passing S1.1:333–42
Playboy of the Western World S1.2:476
Pride and Prejudice 2:295–300
Prime of Miss Jean Brodie, The 4:303–8
Pygmalion 3:312–18
Rebecca 3:326–33
Room of One's Own, A 3:356–63, S1.1:470
Scarlet Letter, The 1:351–7
Sense and Sensibility S1.1:387–98
"Seventeen Syllables" 4:330–6
Shizuko's Daughter, Mori, Koyoko S1.2:409–19
Sister Carrie 2:327–33
"Spunk" and "Sweat" S1.1:429–37, S1.2:266
Streetcar Named Desire, A 4:364 70, S1.2:141
Sweet Whispers, Brother Rush (portions of) 5:329
Tess of the D'Urbervilles 2:353–9
Their Eyes Were Watching God 3:383–9, S1.2:266
Thousand Pieces of Gold 2:366–71
Turn of the Screw, The 2:378–83
Vindication of the Rights of Woman, A 1:406–12, 2:297, S1.1:391
West with the Night S1.2:487–97
"Where Are You Going, Where Have You Been?" 4:391–6
Wide Sargasso Sea S1.1:493–502, S1.2:178
Woman Warrior, The 5:352–9
Wuthering Heights 1:413–19
Yellow Raft in Blue Water, A 5:360–6
"Yellow Wallpaper, The" 2:422–8
"Yentl the Yeshiva Boy" 3:425–31
Women's suffrage
in 19th-century Norway S1.1:166
agitation for change 2:335–6, 3:16
in Britain in 1919 and 1930 3:359
in California in 1911 3:271
in Chile in 1952 5:167
defeated in many states of United States 3:286–7
denounced in Victorian Age 2:335
expanding by 1890 2:424
in Kansas (1861), although limited 2:424
ratification denied in Alabama 3:392
in United States in 1920 3:76, 287
in Wyoming in 1869 2:323
Woodstock Music and Art Fair (1969) 5:65 (illus.), 324
Woolf, Virginia 5:42, S1.1:146 (sidebar)
Room of One's Own, A 3:356–63, S1.1:470
To the Lighthouse S1.1:463–72
Wordsworth, William 1:416, S1.1:245
Lyrical Ballads S1.1:207–17
Workhouses for poor S1.2:135
World War I
Africa, impact on 3:292–3
ambulance service 3:114
arms manufacturing and dealing S1.1:221–2, 221 (sidebar)
Austro-Hungarian empire breakup S1.1:476
Battle of the Somme S1.2:298
British occupation of former Ottoman Empire 4:102
casualties 3:11 (sidebar), S1.1:465, S1.2:298

Index

World War I (*continued*)
 causes and outbreak **1**:157–8, **3**:8–9, 112–13, 411, **S1.1**:377–8, 464, 476, **S1.2**:297–8
 international arms buildup **S1.1**:222
 Italy's role in **3**:113–14
 lack of concern for consequences **S1.1**:444
 losses, destruction **1**:157–8, **3**:11 (*sidebar*), 411–12
 "lost generation" **3**:13, 112, 116–17, **S1.1**:442
 navies' roles in **1**:277–8
 "No Man's Land" **S1.2**:298–9
 older generations supporting **3**:9–11, 12–13
 Ottoman slaughter of Armenians **3**:339–40
 postwar issues
  disillusionment, death of love, and despair **3**:227, 412, **S1.1**:443–4, 465
  German reparations, inflation, and unemployment **4**:157
  global expansion **1**:223, **3**:21, 88
 propaganda machines involving civilians in first "total war" **S1.1**:465
 proving H. G. Wells's fiction as prophetic **3**:406
 racial issues
  African Americans as employees and soldiers **3**:160, 252, **4**:144, 145, 212–13
  African American veterans no longer tolerating abuse **S1.1**:335, 431–2
  segregation of U.S. military **4**:212–13
  violent riots on army bases **S1.1**:335
 reasons for joining **1**:278
 Russian defeats, civil war, revolution (1917) **3**:232–3
 sacrifices on German home front **3**:11
 technological enhancements of weaponry **3**:113
 Treaty of Berlin (1921) **3**:88
 trench warfare **3**:9, 113, 115 (*sidebar*), **S1.1**:465, **S1.2**:298, 299

World War II
 on American home front
  America as arsenal for democracy, unprecedented economic growth **S1.2**:1–2
  American mobilization for **2**:45, **3**:424, **4**:325
  for American South, industrialization and economic recovery from the Great Depression **2**:53, **3**:72–3
  anti-German fervor **S1.2**:149
  black women at work **S1.2**:249–50
  cynicism and opportunism **4**:371
  families of servicemen **4**:317–18
  German prisoners of war **4**:371–3
  intergenerational conflict **4**:327, **S1.2**:6–7
  media's patriotic emphasis on war issues **4**:371
  persecution and internment of Japanese Americans (1942–44) **4**:137–43, 194 5, 335–6
  rationing and inflation **3**:424, **5**:256–7
  Truman Committee investigations of production scandals **S1.2**:2 (*sidebar*)
  women at work **4**:21–2, 74, 166–7, 196 (*illus.*), 197–8, **S1.2**:2
 America's prewar isolationism **4**:323, 362, **S1.2**:1, 6, 149
 aviation
  bomber crews **4**:68–70
  Lindbergh's contributions to **3**:367
 causes **1**:113–14, **4**:157, 356–7, **S1.2**:130, 299, 443
 chronology
  annexations by dictators, appeasement by Chamberlain (1935–39) **5**:123 (*sidebar*), 224, 253–4, **S1.2**:300–1
  Nazi precursor conquests in Europe (1935–36) **1**:113–14, **3**:213, 214, **4**:357
  Japanese precursor conquests in Asia (1937–45) **1**:113–14, **3**:213, 214, **4**:357, **S1.2**:219
  British "appeasements" of Hitler (1936–39) **4**:356, 357, 362, **S1.2**:300–1
  Rome-Berlin Axis (1936) **4**:67
  Nazi persecutions leading to immigration to America **S1.2**:279–80
  Stalin-Hitler nonaggression pact (1939) **3**:210, 214, **4**:357, **S1.2**:301
  Poland partitioned by Germany and Soviet Union (1939) **4**:131
  France and England declare war on Germany (1939) **3**:214
  French unpreparedness (1939) **3**:213–14
  Tripartite Pact (Japan, Germany, Italy; 1940) **4**:59
  standoff at Maginot Line **4**:357
  "blitzkrieg"; Germany invades Belgium, Luxembourg, and France **4**:254 5, 357, 359
  first American peacetime draft (1940) **4**:35, 324 5
  Blitz ("blitzkrieg") bombing of England's cities **S1.2**:130 (*sidebar*), 300 (*sidebar*)
  Italy helps Nazis (1940) **4**:67
  German occupation of Holland (1940) **4**:116–19
  Dunkirk, evacuation of (May 1940) **4**:356, 358 (*illus.*), 359–63
  German invasion of Russia, (1941) **3**:124, **4**:131
  Pearl Harbor (1941) **4**:59, 178, 323
  Lend-Lease (1941–45) **4**:228–9, 363
  Pacific theater (1942–45) **4**:60–1, 80–1, 178
  Philippines' Bataan Death March **4**:81
  Aleutian islands, battles for (1942–43) **4**:254
  Allies establish North African base (1942–44) **3**:214
  North Africa, Operation Salaam, and Almásy's mission (1942) **S1.2**:126–7
  emergence of De Gaulle (1943) **3**:214
  Allied invasion of Sicily (1943) **4**:67
  Italy declares war on Germany (1943) **4**:67

Allies' Italian campaign (1943–1945)
  S1.2:126-7
 kamikazi missions (1944) 4:61 (*sidebar*),
  62 (*illus.*)
 liberation of France (1944) 3:214
 Battle of the Bulge (Dec. 1944) 4:343
 Yalta Conference (Feb. 1945) 4:344
 Dresden, firebombing by Allies (Feb. 1945)
  4:343-4
 victory finalized at Potsdam Conference (May
  1945) S1.2:309-10
 founding of United Nations 5:54
 atomic bombing of Japan (Aug. 1945)
  4:178-82, 180 (*illus.*), 181 (*sidebar*), S1.2:220
 Nuremberg war crimes trials of former Nazis
  4:272-3
Churchill's rhetoric and determination
  4:361-2
French underground and *maquis* S1.2:467-9,
  469 (*sidebar*)
Nazi and Japanese atrocities, and American and
  British internment of aliens S1.2:468
Palestine 4:102-5
postwar issues
 American prosperity, European and Japanese
  devastation S1.2:3-4, 281-2, 358
 baby boom 1:224, 2:325-6, 4:38, 74, 240,
  S1.2:107
 Britain 4:229, 231, 5:256-7
 consumer society S1.2:314
 emphasis on home and materialism
  2:325-6, S1.2:3 (*sidebar*)
 GI Bill S1.2:358
 Japan's devastation by bombing S1.2:409-10
 Marshall Plan 5:123-4, 224, 292, S1.2:310
 relatedness and larger human responsibility
  S1.2:6
 world facing moral, ethical, and scientific
  questions S1.2:405
 (*See also* Cold War)
racial issues
 African Americans as employees and soldiers
  3:424
 American Indians in 4:80-1
 black soldiers 4:212-13, S1.2:249-50
 Chicano rights movement watershed 4:44
 Latinos in 4:295, 406
 race riots of 1940s 4:197, 201, 213, 247,
  248 (*illus.*), 295-7, 403-10
 racism 4:199, 200
 segregation of U.S. military 3:41-2, 4:195,
  197, 374 (*sidebar*)
 (*See also* Holocaust)
soldiers
 aimlessness and materialism upon return to
  civilian life S1.2:3 (*sidebar*)
 combat experience, psychological casualties,
  and postcombat syndrome 4:80 (*sidebar*),
  325, S1.2:3
 reservists and regulars 4:63 (*sidebar*)

 South Africa, impact on S1.2:318-19
 (*See also* Holocaust; Nazis)
"Worn Path, The," Welty, Eudora 3:418-24
Wouk, Herman, *Caine Mutiny, The* 4:58-65
WPA (Works Progress Administration) 3:128,
  391, 423-4, 4:44
Wright, Richard
 "Almos' a Man" 4:1-6
 on anti-Semitism of his youth 4:376
 Black Boy 3:36-43
 as critic of Hurston 3:385, 389
 Native Son 3:236-42
 on *The Heart Is a Lonely Hunter* 3:157
Wright, Wilbur and Orville S1.2:489-90
Writers. *See* Art, artists, and intellectuals
Wuthering Heights, Brontë, Emily 1:413-19
Wyoming, women's suffrage in 1869 2:323

X

Xenophon S1.1:344, 351
X, Malcolm 2:98, 3:324 5, 4:54, 249-50,
  5:69-70, 111, S1.2:276, 423
 with Alex Haley, *Autobiography of Malcolm X, The*
  5:11-18

Y

Yamamoto, Hisaye, "Seventeen Syllables" 4:330-6
Yankees 1:217, 332, 334, 335, 2:8-9, 137
Yaqui Indians of Mexico S1.2:87-8
Yeager, Chuck 5:293
Yellow Raft in Blue Water, A, Dorris, Michael
  5:360-6
"Yellow Wallpaper, The," Gilman, Charlotte Perkins
  2:422-8
"Yentl the Yeshiva Boy," Singer, Isaac Bashevis
  3:425-31
Yorkshire, England 1:417-18, 3:1-3, 5-6
"Young Goodman Brown," Hawthorne, Nathaniel
  1:420-6
Young Turks 3:339, 340, 342
Youth
 adolescence in hiding from Holocaust 4:121-2
 advertising targeting teenagers 4:392
 antiestablishment rebellion 5:272
 crime by teenagers S1.2:284 5
 dance 4:387
 distinctive *pachuco* culture of 1950s 4:173,
  296
 distinctive teenage culture of 1950s 4:172,
  391-3, 394 5
 facing conflict and violence 5:268-9
 gang membership 4:251, 386, 387-9, 5:216
 gang truce in Los Angeles 5:341
 generation gap 4:386, 394, 5:198, S1.2:285
 juvenile delinquency 4:251, 386, 387-9, 5:37
 literature for adolescents, as genre 5:61-2,
  265-6, 268-70
 moral laxity of war years 4:37

Youth (*continued*)
    motion picture industry influencing teenagers   **4**:392, 394, **S1.2**:285
    peer pressure and negativity   **5**:65–6, 71–2, 217
    protesting against Vietnam War   **5**:271
    psychotherapy for   **5**:260–1
    radio's teenage audience of 1950s   **4**:386, 391
    students' free speech movement   **5**:311
    suicide by teenagers   **5**:259–60, 261
    television as babysitter   **5**:36–7
    television as too violent   **5**:62
Yukon territory and Klondike River   **3**:52–6, 261 (*sidebar*)

Z

Zapata, Emiliano   **3**:197, 198 (*illus.*), **S1.2**:14 (*sidebar*), 84 (*illus.*), 85, 86, 501–3, 501 (*sidebar*), 502 (*illus.*), 504 (*sidebar*)
Zen Buddhism   **4**:334
Zeus   **1**:9, 59, 61, 170, 282, 283, 301
Zindel, Paul, *Pigman, The*   **5**:271–7
Zionism   **3**:121, **4**:88, 101–2
    Arabic anti-Zionism   **4**:107
    Soviet anti-Zionism   **4**:107–8
Zoo Story, Albee, Edward   **4**:397–402
Zoot Suit, Valdez, Luis   **4**:403–10
Zundel, Ernst   **4**:40

MAGNIFICAT HIGH SCHOOL
RESOURCE CENTER
ROCKY RIVER, OH 44116-3397

FOR REFERENCE

Do Not Take From This Room